America's Top-Rated Cities: A Statistical Handbook

Volume 1

2021
Twenty-Eighth Edition

America's Top-Rated Cities: A Statistical Handbook

Volume 1: Southern Region

A UNIVERSAL REFERENCE BOOK

Grey House Publishing

Cover image: Dallas, Texas

PRESIDENT: Richard Gottlieb
PUBLISHER: Leslie Mackenzie
EDITORIAL DIRECTOR: Laura Mars
SENIOR EDITOR: David Garoogian

RESEARCHER & WRITER: Jael Bridgemahon
PRODUCTION MANAGER: Kristen Hayes
MARKETING DIRECTOR: Jessica Moody

A Universal Reference Book
Grey House Publishing, Inc.
4919 Route 22
Amenia, NY 12501
518.789.8700 • Fax 845.373.6390
www.greyhouse.com
books@greyhouse.com

While every effort has been made to ensure the reliability of the information presented in this publication, Grey House Publishing neither guarantees the accuracy of the data contained herein nor assumes any responsibility for errors, omissions or discrepancies. Grey House accepts no payment for listing; inclusion in the publication of any organization, agency, institution, publication, service or individual does not imply endorsement of the editors or publisher.

Errors brought to the attention of the publisher and verified to the satisfaction of the publisher will be corrected in future editions.

Except by express prior written permission of the Copyright Proprietor no part of this work may be copied by any means of publication or communication now known or developed hereafter including, but not limited to, use in any directory or compilation or other print publication, in any information storage and retrieval system, in any other electronic device, or in any visual or audio-visual device or product.

This publication is an original and creative work, copyrighted by Grey House Publishing, Inc. and is fully protected by all applicable copyright laws, as well as by laws covering misappropriation, trade secrets and unfair competition.

Grey House has added value to the underlying factual material through one or more of the following efforts: unique and original selection; expression; arrangement; coordination; and classification.

Grey House Publishing, Inc. will defend its rights in this publication.

Copyright © 2021 Grey House Publishing, Inc.
All rights reserved

Twenty-eighth Edition
Printed in the USA

Publisher's Cataloging-in-Publication Data
(Prepared by The Donohue Group, Inc.)

America's top-rated cities. Vol. 1, Southern region : a statistical handbook. — 1992-

   v. : ill. ; cm.
   Annual, 1995-
   Irregular, 1992-1993
   ISSN: 1082-7102

1. Cities and towns--Ratings--Southern States--Statistics--Periodicals. 2. Cities and towns--Southern States--Statistics--Periodicals. 3. Social indicators--Southern States--Periodicals. 4. Quality of life--Southern States-- Statistics--Periodicals. 5. Southern States--Social conditions--Statistics--Periodicals. I. Title: America's top rated cities. II. Title: Southern region

HT123.5.S6 A44
307.76/0973/05   95644648

4-Volume Set	ISBN: 978-1-64265-821-7
Volume 1	**ISBN: 978-1-64265-823-1**
Volume 2	ISBN: 978-1-64265-824-8
Volume 3	ISBN: 978-1-64265-825-5
Volume 4	ISBN: 978-1-64265-826-2

Athens, Georgia

Background	1
Rankings	2
Business Environment	3
Demographics	3
Economy	4
Income	5
City Finances	6
Employment	7
Taxes	8
Transportation	9
Businesses	10
Living Environment	11
Cost of Living	11
Housing	11
Health	13
Education	15
Employers	16
Public Safety	16
Politics	17
Sports	17
Climate	17
Hazardous Waste	17
Air Quality	17

Atlanta, Georgia

Background	19
Rankings	20
Business Environment	24
Demographics	24
Economy	25
Income	26
City Finances	27
Employment	28
Taxes	29
Transportation	30
Businesses	31
Living Environment	33
Cost of Living	33
Housing	33
Health	35
Education	37
Employers	38
Public Safety	39
Politics	40
Sports	40
Climate	40
Hazardous Waste	40
Air Quality	40

Austin, Texas

Background	43
Rankings	44
Business Environment	48
Demographics	48
Economy	49
Income	50
City Finances	51
Employment	52
Taxes	53
Transportation	54
Businesses	55
Living Environment	57
Cost of Living	57
Housing	57
Health	59
Education	61
Employers	62
Public Safety	63
Politics	63
Sports	63
Climate	63
Hazardous Waste	64
Air Quality	64

Baton Rouge, Louisiana

Background	67
Rankings	68
Business Environment	71
Demographics	71
Economy	72
Income	73
City Finances	74
Employment	75
Taxes	76
Transportation	77
Businesses	78
Living Environment	79
Cost of Living	79
Housing	79
Health	81
Education	83
Employers	84
Public Safety	84
Politics	84
Sports	85
Climate	85
Hazardous Waste	85
Air Quality	85

Cape Coral, Florida

Background	87
Rankings	88
Business Environment	90
Demographics	90
Economy	91
Income	92
City Finances	93
Employment	94
Taxes	95
Transportation	96
Businesses	97
Living Environment	98
Cost of Living	98
Housing	98
Health	100
Education	102
Employers	103
Public Safety	103
Politics	103
Sports	104
Climate	104
Hazardous Waste	104
Air Quality	104

Charleston, South Carolina

Background	107
Rankings	108
Business Environment	111
Demographics	111
Economy	112
Income	113
City Finances	114
Employment	115
Taxes	116
Transportation	117
Businesses	118
Living Environment	119
Cost of Living	119
Housing	119
Health	121
Education	123
Employers	124
Public Safety	124
Politics	124
Sports	125
Climate	125
Hazardous Waste	125
Air Quality	125

Clarksville, Tennessee

Background	127
Rankings	128
Business Environment	129
Demographics	129
Economy	130
Income	131
City Finances	132
Employment	133
Taxes	134
Transportation	135
Businesses	136
Living Environment	137
Cost of Living	137
Housing	137
Health	139
Education	141
Employers	142
Public Safety	142
Politics	142
Sports	143
Climate	143
Hazardous Waste	143
Air Quality	143

College Station, Texas

Background	145
Rankings	146
Business Environment	147
Demographics	147
Economy	148
Income	149
City Finances	150
Employment	151
Taxes	152
Transportation	153
Businesses	154
Living Environment	155
Cost of Living	155
Housing	155
Health	157
Education	159
Employers	160
Public Safety	160
Politics	160
Sports	161
Climate	161
Hazardous Waste	161
Air Quality	161

Columbia, South Carolina

Background.................................. 163
Rankings..................................... 164
Business Environment................. 167
   Demographics............................ 167
   Economy................................... 168
   Income..................................... 169
   City Finances............................ 170
   Employment............................. 171
   Taxes.. 172
   Transportation......................... 173
   Businesses................................ 174
Living Environment..................... 175
   Cost of Living........................... 175
   Housing.................................... 175
   Health....................................... 177
   Education................................. 179
   Employers................................ 180
   Public Safety............................ 180
   Politics..................................... 181
   Sports....................................... 181
   Climate.................................... 181
   Hazardous Waste..................... 181
   Air Quality............................... 182

Dallas, Texas

Background.................................. 185
Rankings..................................... 186
Business Environment................. 190
   Demographics............................ 190
   Economy................................... 191
   Income..................................... 192
   City Finances............................ 193
   Employment............................. 194
   Taxes.. 195
   Transportation......................... 196
   Businesses................................ 197
Living Environment..................... 199
   Cost of Living........................... 199
   Housing.................................... 199
   Health....................................... 201
   Education................................. 203
   Employers................................ 204
   Public Safety............................ 205
   Politics..................................... 206
   Sports....................................... 206
   Climate.................................... 206
   Hazardous Waste..................... 207
   Air Quality............................... 207

El Paso, Texas

Background.................................. 209
Rankings..................................... 210
Business Environment................. 213
   Demographics............................ 213
   Economy................................... 214
   Income..................................... 215
   City Finances............................ 216
   Employment............................. 217
   Taxes.. 218
   Transportation......................... 219
   Businesses................................ 220
Living Environment..................... 221
   Cost of Living........................... 221
   Housing.................................... 221
   Health....................................... 223
   Education................................. 225
   Employers................................ 226
   Public Safety............................ 226
   Politics..................................... 226
   Sports....................................... 227
   Climate.................................... 227
   Hazardous Waste..................... 227
   Air Quality............................... 227

Fort Worth, Texas

Background.................................. 229
Rankings..................................... 230
Business Environment................. 233
   Demographics............................ 233
   Economy................................... 234
   Income..................................... 235
   City Finances............................ 236
   Employment............................. 237
   Taxes.. 238
   Transportation......................... 239
   Businesses................................ 240
Living Environment..................... 241
   Cost of Living........................... 241
   Housing.................................... 241
   Health....................................... 243
   Education................................. 245
   Employers................................ 246
   Public Safety............................ 246
   Politics..................................... 247
   Sports....................................... 247
   Climate.................................... 247
   Hazardous Waste..................... 247
   Air Quality............................... 248

Houston, Texas

Background.................................. 251
Rankings.................................... 252
Business Environment....................... 256
   Demographics............................. 256
   Economy................................. 257
   Income.................................. 258
   City Finances........................... 259
   Employment.............................. 260
   Taxes................................... 261
   Transportation.......................... 262
   Businesses.............................. 263
Living Environment......................... 265
   Cost of Living.......................... 265
   Housing................................. 265
   Health.................................. 267
   Education............................... 269
   Employers............................... 271
   Public Safety........................... 271
   Politics................................ 272
   Sports.................................. 272
   Climate................................. 272
   Hazardous Waste......................... 272
   Air Quality............................. 273

Huntsville, Alabama

Background.................................. 275
Rankings.................................... 276
Business Environment....................... 278
   Demographics............................ 278
   Economy................................. 279
   Income.................................. 280
   City Finances........................... 281
   Employment.............................. 282
   Taxes................................... 283
   Transportation.......................... 284
   Businesses.............................. 285
Living Environment......................... 286
   Cost of Living.......................... 286
   Housing................................. 286
   Health.................................. 288
   Education............................... 290
   Employers............................... 291
   Public Safety........................... 291
   Politics................................ 291
   Sports.................................. 292
   Climate................................. 292
   Hazardous Waste......................... 292
   Air Quality............................. 292

Jacksonville, Florida

Background.................................. 295
Rankings.................................... 296
Business Environment....................... 299
   Demographics............................ 299
   Economy................................. 300
   Income.................................. 301
   City Finances........................... 302
   Employment.............................. 303
   Taxes................................... 304
   Transportation.......................... 305
   Businesses.............................. 306
Living Environment......................... 307
   Cost of Living.......................... 307
   Housing................................. 307
   Health.................................. 309
   Education............................... 311
   Employers............................... 312
   Public Safety........................... 312
   Politics................................ 313
   Sports.................................. 313
   Climate................................. 313
   Hazardous Waste......................... 313
   Air Quality............................. 313

Lafayette, Louisiana

Background.................................. 315
Rankings.................................... 316
Business Environment....................... 317
   Demographics............................ 317
   Economy................................. 318
   Income.................................. 319
   City Finances........................... 320
   Employment.............................. 321
   Taxes................................... 322
   Transportation.......................... 323
   Businesses.............................. 324
Living Environment......................... 325
   Cost of Living.......................... 325
   Housing................................. 325
   Health.................................. 327
   Education............................... 329
   Employers............................... 330
   Public Safety........................... 330
   Politics................................ 331
   Sports.................................. 331
   Climate................................. 331
   Hazardous Waste......................... 331
   Air Quality............................. 331

Lakeland, Florida

Background... 333
Rankings.. 334
Business Environment........................ 336
   Demographics.................................... 336
   Economy.. 337
   Income... 338
   City Finances................................... 339
   Employment..................................... 340
   Taxes... 341
   Transportation.................................. 342
   Businesses....................................... 343
Living Environment............................ 344
   Cost of Living................................... 344
   Housing.. 344
   Health.. 346
   Education... 348
   Employers.. 349
   Public Safety.................................... 349
   Politics... 350
   Sports.. 350
   Climate.. 350
   Hazardous Waste............................. 350
   Air Quality....................................... 350

Memphis, Tennessee

Background... 353
Rankings.. 354
Business Environment........................ 358
   Demographics.................................... 358
   Economy.. 359
   Income... 360
   City Finances................................... 361
   Employment..................................... 362
   Taxes... 363
   Transportation.................................. 364
   Businesses....................................... 365
Living Environment............................ 366
   Cost of Living................................... 366
   Housing.. 366
   Health.. 368
   Education... 370
   Employers.. 371
   Public Safety.................................... 371
   Politics... 372
   Sports.. 372
   Climate.. 372
   Hazardous Waste............................. 372
   Air Quality....................................... 373

Miami, Florida

Background... 375
Rankings.. 376
Business Environment........................ 379
   Demographics.................................... 379
   Economy.. 380
   Income... 381
   City Finances................................... 382
   Employment..................................... 383
   Taxes... 384
   Transportation.................................. 385
   Businesses....................................... 386
Living Environment............................ 388
   Cost of Living................................... 388
   Housing.. 388
   Health.. 390
   Education... 392
   Employers.. 393
   Public Safety.................................... 394
   Politics... 394
   Sports.. 394
   Climate.. 394
   Hazardous Waste............................. 395
   Air Quality....................................... 395

Midland, Texas

Background... 397
Rankings.. 398
Business Environment........................ 399
   Demographics.................................... 399
   Economy.. 400
   Income... 401
   City Finances................................... 402
   Employment..................................... 403
   Taxes... 404
   Transportation.................................. 405
   Businesses....................................... 406
Living Environment............................ 407
   Cost of Living................................... 407
   Housing.. 407
   Health.. 409
   Education... 411
   Employers.. 412
   Public Safety.................................... 412
   Politics... 413
   Sports.. 413
   Climate.. 413
   Hazardous Waste............................. 413
   Air Quality....................................... 413

Nashville, Tennessee

Background	415
Rankings	416
Business Environment	420
Demographics	420
Economy	421
Income	422
City Finances	423
Employment	424
Taxes	425
Transportation	426
Businesses	427
Living Environment	428
Cost of Living	428
Housing	428
Health	430
Education	432
Employers	433
Public Safety	434
Politics	435
Sports	435
Climate	435
Hazardous Waste	435
Air Quality	435

New Orleans, Louisiana

Background	437
Rankings	438
Business Environment	442
Demographics	442
Economy	443
Income	444
City Finances	445
Employment	446
Taxes	447
Transportation	448
Businesses	449
Living Environment	450
Cost of Living	450
Housing	450
Health	452
Education	454
Employers	455
Public Safety	455
Politics	456
Sports	456
Climate	456
Hazardous Waste	457
Air Quality	457

Orlando, Florida

Background	459
Rankings	460
Business Environment	464
Demographics	464
Economy	465
Income	466
City Finances	467
Employment	468
Taxes	469
Transportation	470
Businesses	471
Living Environment	472
Cost of Living	472
Housing	472
Health	474
Education	476
Employers	477
Public Safety	477
Politics	478
Sports	478
Climate	478
Hazardous Waste	478
Air Quality	479

San Antonio, Texas

Background	481
Rankings	482
Business Environment	486
Demographics	486
Economy	487
Income	488
City Finances	489
Employment	490
Taxes	491
Transportation	492
Businesses	493
Living Environment	494
Cost of Living	494
Housing	494
Health	496
Education	498
Employers	499
Public Safety	499
Politics	500
Sports	500
Climate	500
Hazardous Waste	501
Air Quality	501

Savannah, Georgia

Background	503
Rankings	504
Business Environment	506
Demographics	506
Economy	507
Income	508
City Finances	509
Employment	510
Taxes	511
Transportation	512
Businesses	513
Living Environment	514
Cost of Living	514
Housing	514
Health	516
Education	518
Employers	519
Public Safety	519
Politics	520
Sports	520
Climate	520
Hazardous Waste	520
Air Quality	520

Tallahassee, Florida

Background	523
Rankings	524
Business Environment	526
Demographics	526
Economy	527
Income	528
City Finances	529
Employment	530
Taxes	531
Transportation	532
Businesses	533
Living Environment	534
Cost of Living	534
Housing	534
Health	536
Education	538
Employers	539
Public Safety	539
Politics	540
Sports	540
Climate	540
Hazardous Waste	540
Air Quality	540

Tampa, Florida

Background	543
Rankings	544
Business Environment	548
Demographics	548
Economy	549
Income	550
City Finances	551
Employment	552
Taxes	553
Transportation	554
Businesses	555
Living Environment	557
Cost of Living	557
Housing	557
Health	559
Education	561
Employers	562
Public Safety	562
Politics	563
Sports	563
Climate	563
Hazardous Waste	563
Air Quality	564

Tuscaloosa, Alabama

Background	567
Rankings	568
Business Environment	569
Demographics	569
Economy	570
Income	571
City Finances	572
Employment	573
Taxes	574
Transportation	575
Businesses	576
Living Environment	577
Cost of Living	577
Housing	577
Health	579
Education	581
Employers	582
Public Safety	582
Politics	582
Sports	583
Climate	583
Hazardous Waste	583
Air Quality	583

Appendixes

Appendix A: Comparative Statistics A-3
Appendix B: Metropolitan Area Definitions A-171
Appendix C: Government Type & Primary County .. A-175
Appendix D: Chambers of Commerce............. A-177
Appendix E: State Departments of Labor A-183

Introduction

This twenty-eighth edition of *America's Top-Rated Cities* is a concise, statistical, 4-volume work identifying America's top-rated cities with estimated populations of approximately 100,000 or more. It profiles 100 cities that have received high marks for business and living from prominent sources such as *Forbes, Fortune, U.S. News & World Report, The Brookings Institution, U.S. Conference of Mayors, The Wall Street Journal,* and *CNNMoney.*

Each volume covers a different region of the country—Southern, Western, Central, Eastern—and includes a detailed Table of Contents, City Chapters, Appendices, and Maps. Each city chapter incorporates information from hundreds of resources to create the following major sections:
- **Background**—lively narrative of significant, up-to-date news for both businesses and residents. These combine historical facts with current developments, "known-for" annual events, and climate data.
- **Rankings**—fun-to-read, bulleted survey results from over 230 books, magazines, and online articles, ranging from general (Great Places to Live), to specific (Friendliest Cities), and everything in between.
- **Statistical Tables**—87 tables and detailed topics that offer an unparalleled view of each city's Business and Living Environments. They are carefully organized with data that is easy to read and understand.
- **Appendices**—five in all, appearing at the end of each volume. These range from listings of Metropolitan Statistical Areas to Comparative Statistics for all 100 cities.

This new edition of *America's Top-Rated Cities* includes cities that not only surveyed well, but ranked highest using our unique weighting system. We looked at violent crime, property crime, population growth, median household income, housing affordability, poverty, educational attainment, and unemployment. You'll find that we have included several American cities despite less-than-stellar numbers. New York, Los Angeles, and Miami remain world-class cities despite challenges faced by many large urban centers. Part of the criteria, in most cases, is that it be the "primary" city in a given metropolitan area. For example, if the metro area is Raleigh-Cary, NC, we would consider Raleigh, not Cary. This allows for a more equitable core city comparison. In general, the core city of a metro area is defined as having substantial influence on neighboring cities. A final consideration is location—we strive to include as many states in the country as possible.

New to this edition are:
Volume 1 - Memphis, TN
Volume 2 - Riverside, CA
Volume 4 - Cincnnati, OH

Praise for previous editions:

> "...[ATRC] has...proven its worth to a wide audience...from businesspeople and corporations planning to launch, relocate, or expand their operations to market researchers, real estate professionals, urban planners, job-seekers, students...interested in...reliable, attractively presented statistical information about larger U.S. cities."
> —ARBA

> "...For individuals or businesses looking to relocate, this resource conveniently reports rankings from more than 300 sources for the top 100 US cities. Recommended..."
> —Choice

> "...While patrons are becoming increasingly comfortable locating statistical data online, there is still something to be said for the ease associated with such a compendium of otherwise scattered data. A well-organized and appropriate update...
> —Library Journal

BACKGROUND
Each city begins with an informative Background that combines history with current events. These narratives often reflect changes that have occurred during the past year, and touch on the city's environment, politics, employment, cultural offerings, and climate, and include interesting trivia. For example: Peregrine Falcons were rehabilitated and released into the wild from Boise City's World Center for Birds of Prey; Grand Rapids was the first city to introduce fluoride into its drinking water in 1945; and Thomas Alva Edison discovered the phonograph and the light bulb in the city whose name was changed in 1954 from Raritan Township to Edison in his honor. This year, many backgrounds incluce an interesting fact about how the city is reacting to the COVID-19 pandemic.

RANKINGS

This section has rankings from a possible 233 books, articles, and reports. For easy reference, these Rankings are categorized into 16 topics including Business/Finance, Dating/Romance, and Health/Fitness.

The Rankings are presented in an easy-to-read, bulleted format and include results from both annual surveys and one-shot studies. **Fastest-Growing Economies** ... **Best Drivers** ... **Most Well-Read** ... **Most Wired** ... **Healthiest for Women** ... **Best for Minority Entrepreneurs** ... **Safest** ... **Best to Retire** ... **Most Polite** ... **Best for Moviemakers** ... **Most Frugal** ... **Best for Bikes** ... **Most Cultured** ... **Least Stressful** ... **Best for Families** ... **Most Romantic** ... **Most Charitable** ... **Best for Telecommuters** ... **Best for Singles** ... **Nerdiest** ... **Fittest** ... **Best for Dogs** ... **Most Tattooed** ... **Best for Wheelchair Users**, and more. A number of these relate specifically to COVID-19.

Sources for these Rankings include both well-known magazines and other media, including *Forbes, Fortune, USA Today, Condé Nast Traveler, Gallup, Kiplinger's Personal Finance, Men's Journal,* and *Travel + Leisure,* as well as *Asthma & Allergy Foundation of America, American Lung Association, League of American Bicyclists, The Advocate, National Civic League, National Alliance to End Homelessness, MovieMaker Magazine, National Insurance Crime Bureau, Center for Digital Government, National Association of Home Builders,* and the *Milken Institute.*

Rankings cover a variety of geographic areas; see Appendix B for full geographic definitions.

STATISTICAL TABLES

Each city chapter includes a possible 87 tables and detailed topics—44 in Business and 43 in Living. Over 90% of statistical data has been updated.

Business Environment includes hard facts and figures on 8 major categories, including Demographics, Income, Economy, Employment, and Taxes. *Living Environment* includes 11 major categories, such as Cost of Living, Housing, Health, Education, Safety, and Climate.

To compile the Statistical Tables, editors have again turned to a wide range of sources, some well known, such as the *U.S. Census Bureau, U.S. Environmental Protection Agency, Bureau of Labor Statistics, Centers for Disease Control and Prevention,* and the *Federal Bureau of Investigation,* plus others like *The Council for Community and Economic Research, Texas A&M Transportation Institute,* and *Federation of Tax Administrators.*

APPENDICES: Data for all cities appear in all volumes.
- **Appendix A**—*Comparative Statistics*
- **Appendix B**—*Metropolitan Area Definitions*
- **Appendix C**—*Government Type and County*
- **Appendix D**—*Chambers of Commerce and Economic Development Organizations*
- **Appendix E**—*State Departments of Labor and Employment*

Material provided by public and private agencies and organizations was supplemented by original research, numerous library sources and Internet sites. *America's Top-Rated Cities, 2021,* is designed for a wide range of readers: private individuals considering relocating a residence or business; professionals considering expanding their businesses or changing careers; corporations considering relocating, opening up additional offices or creating new divisions; government agencies; general and market researchers; real estate consultants; human resource personnel; urban planners; investors; and urban government students.

Customers who purchase the four-volume set receive free online access to *America's Top-Rated Cities* allowing them to download city reports and sort and rank by 50-plus data points.

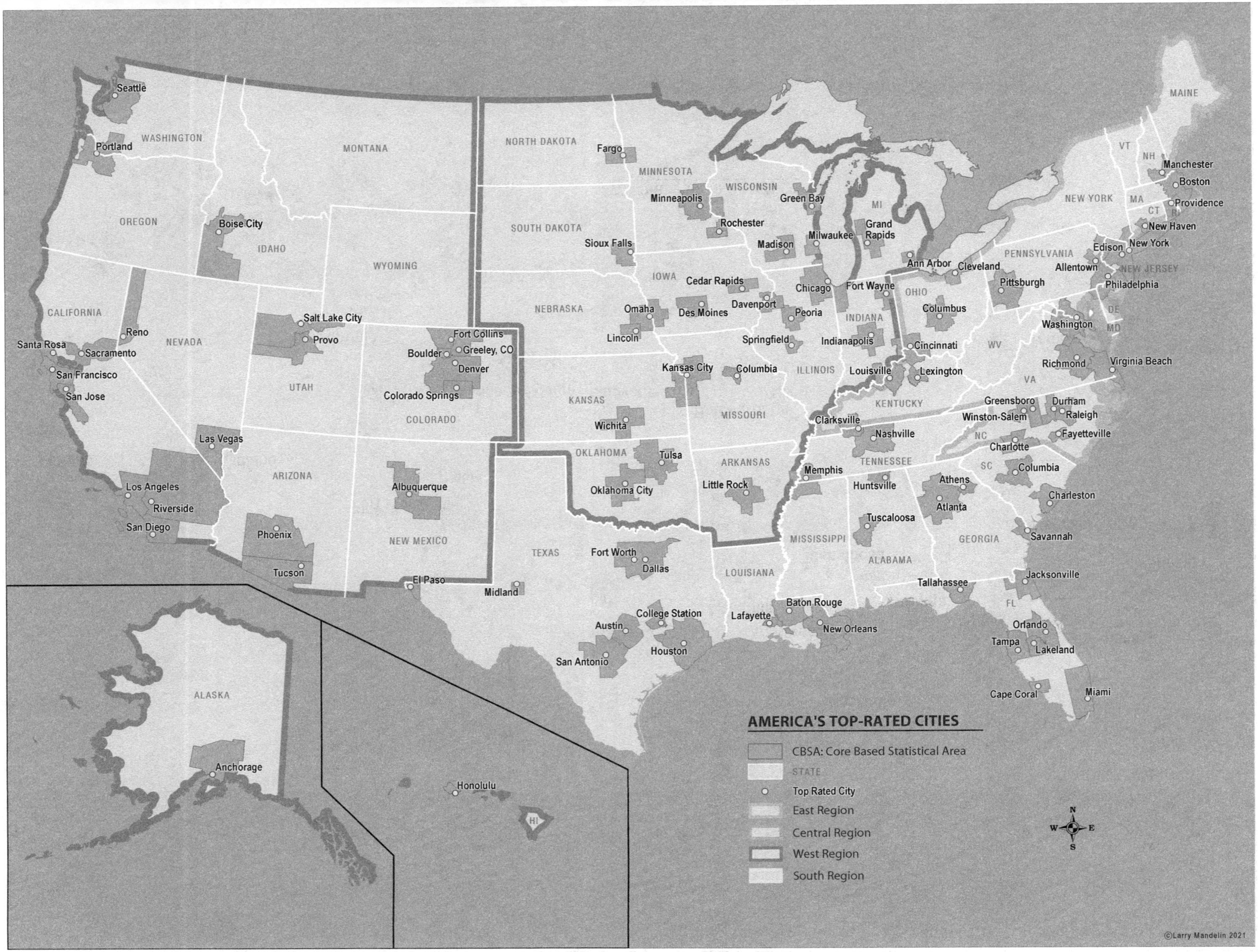
AMERICA'S TOP-RATED CITIES
CBSA: Core Based Statistical Area
STATE
Top Rated City
East Region
Central Region
West Region
South Region
N
W
E
S
WASHINGTON
OREGON
CALIFORNIA
NEVADA
IDAHO
MONTANA
WYOMING
UTAH
ARIZONA
COLORADO
NEW MEXICO
NORTH DAKOTA
SOUTH DAKOTA
NEBRASKA
KANSAS
OKLAHOMA
TEXAS
MINNESOTA
IOWA
MISSOURI
ARKANSAS
LOUISIANA
WISCONSIN
ILLINOIS
MI
INDIANA
OHIO
KENTUCKY
TENNESSEE
MISSISSIPPI
ALABAMA
GEORGIA
FL
SC
NC
VA
WV
PENNSYLVANIA
NEW YORK
NEW JERSEY
DE
MD
VT
NH
MA
CT
RI
MAINE
ALASKA
HI
Seattle
Portland
Boise City
Santa Rosa
Sacramento
Reno
San Francisco
San Jose
Salt Lake City
Provo
Fort Collins
Greeley, CO
Boulder
Denver
Colorado Springs
Las Vegas
Los Angeles
Riverside
San Diego
Phoenix
Tucson
Albuquerque
El Paso
Midland
Fargo
Minneapolis
Rochester
Sioux Falls
Omaha
Lincoln
Des Moines
Cedar Rapids
Davenport
Kansas City
Wichita
Tulsa
Oklahoma City
Fort Worth
Dallas
Austin
College Station
San Antonio
Houston
Green Bay
Madison
Milwaukee
Grand Rapids
Chicago
Peoria
Springfield
Columbia
Little Rock
Memphis
Lafayette
Baton Rouge
New Orleans
Ann Arbor
Fort Wayne
Indianapolis
Louisville
Cincinnati
Lexington
Columbus
Cleveland
Clarksville
Nashville
Huntsville
Tuscaloosa
Athens
Atlanta
Tallahassee
Pittsburgh
Allentown
Philadelphia
Edison
New York
New Haven
Providence
Boston
Manchester
Washington
Richmond
Virginia Beach
Greensboro
Winston-Salem
Durham
Raleigh
Fayetteville
Charlotte
Columbia
Charleston
Savannah
Jacksonville
Orlando
Tampa
Lakeland
Cape Coral
Miami
Anchorage
Honolulu
©Larry Mandelin 2021

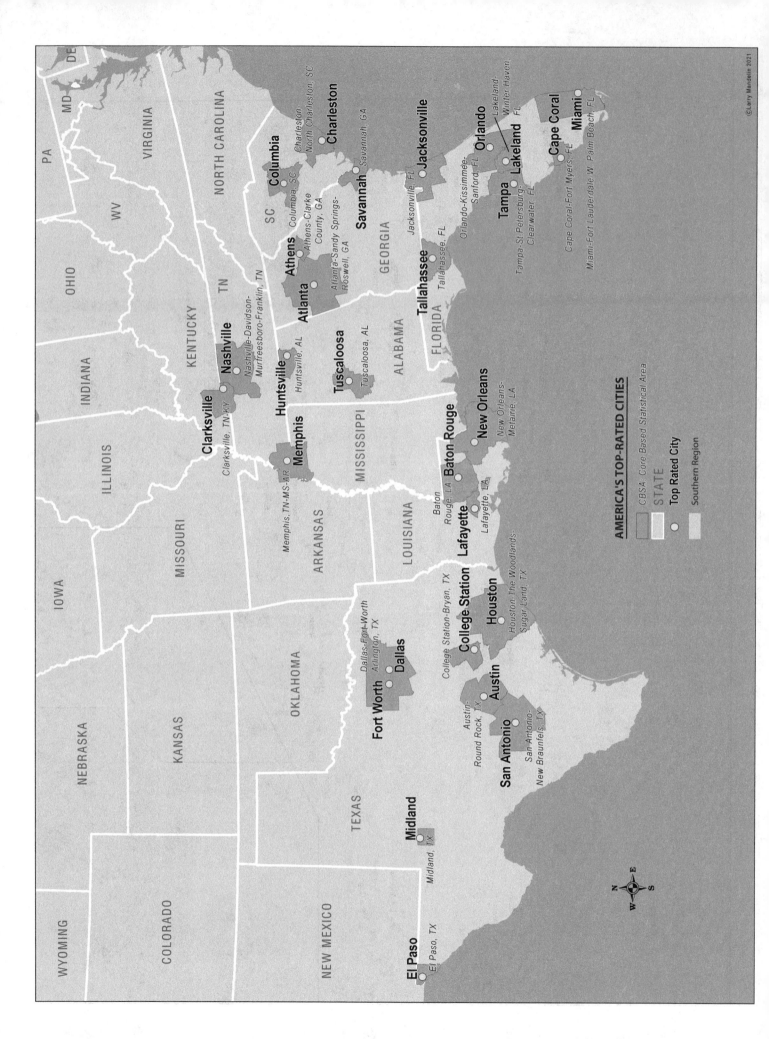

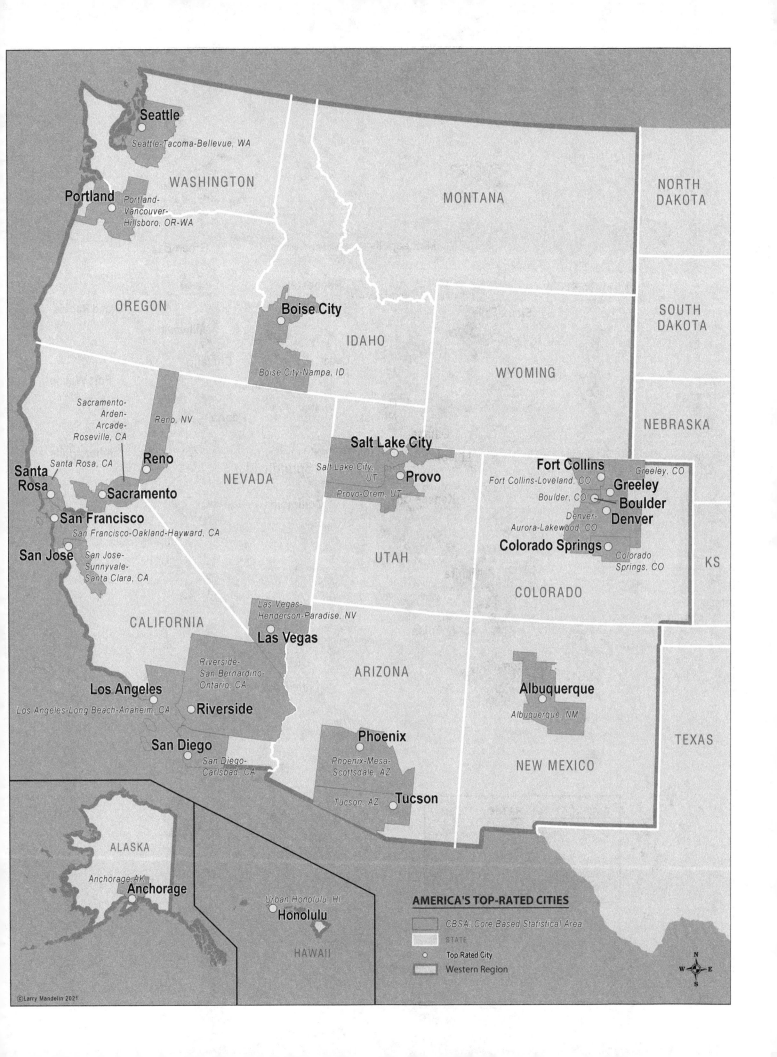

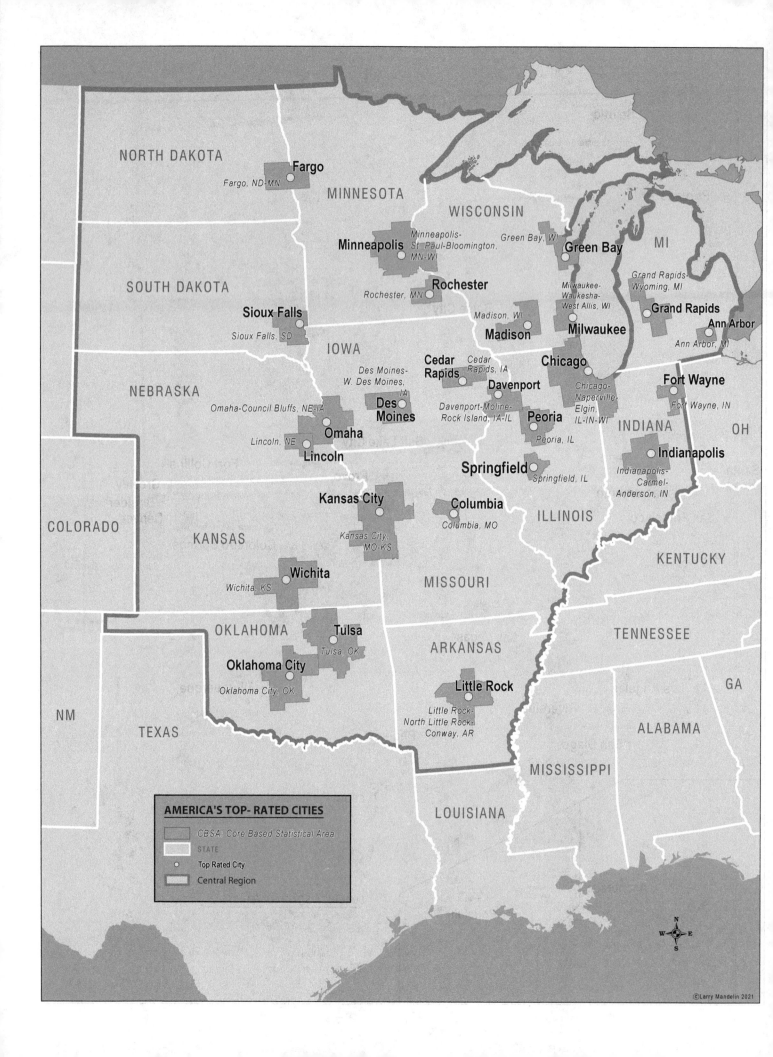

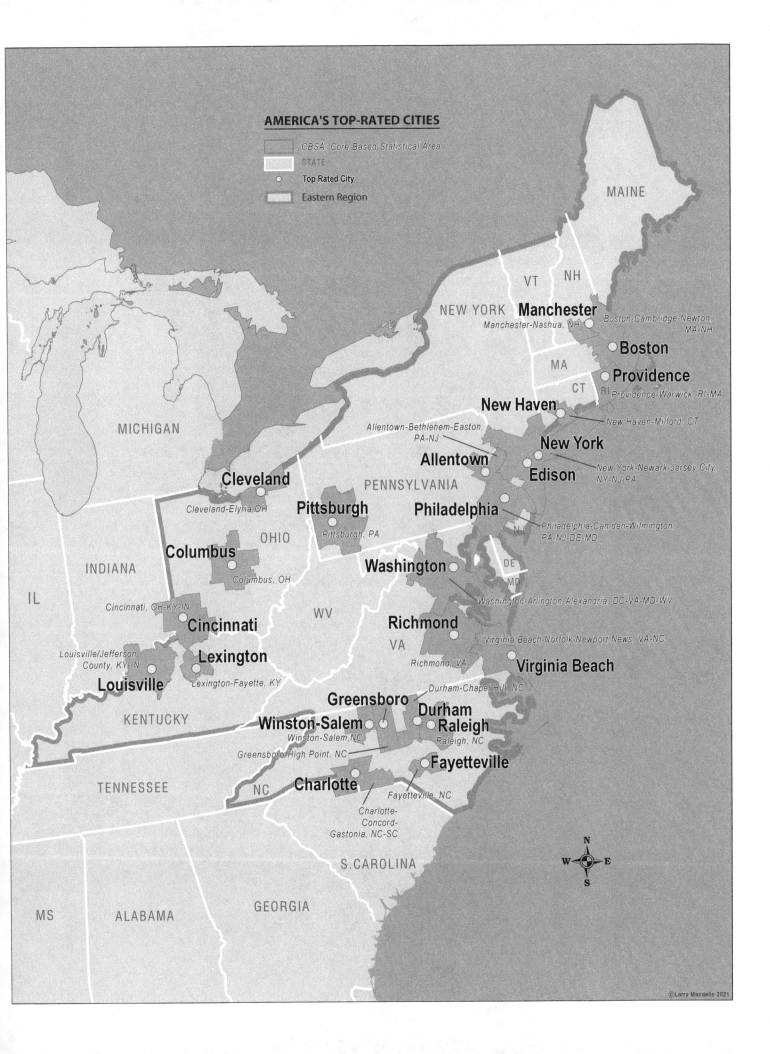

Athens, Georgia

Background

Athens, home to the University of Georgia, retains its old charms while cultivating new ideas. Antebellum homes that grace the city still stand because Gen. William Tecumseh Sherman's March to the Sea took a route that left this northeast Georgia town intact (while burning Atlanta, about 60 miles to the southwest). The Athens Music History Walking Tour, available through the local convention and visitors' bureau, stops at Weaver D's soul food restaurant with the slogan, "Automatic for the People," that went national as the name of locally-grown REM's 1992 album. In 2020, the city launched the Athens Music Walk of Fame.

Present-day Athens started as a small settlement where an old Cherokee trail crossed the Oconee River. In 1785 the state's General Assembly chartered the university, which established a campus here in 1801. Three years later, the school held its first graduation ceremony. The city was named for the ancient Greece's center of learning.

Undoubtedly the major influence in the city and surrounding Clarke County, the University of Georgia is also the area's largest employer. The comprehensive land grant and sea-grant institution offers all levels of degree programs in numerous disciplines. Other educational institutions in Athens are the Navy Supply School, Athens Technical College, and branches of Piedmont College and Old Dominion University.

Other major employers are focused on health care, government, and manufacturing. They include Athens Regional Medical Center and St. Mary's Health Care System, which have enlarged their facilities and specialized in areas including oncology, pediatrics and heart disease. Manufacturing is a major employment sector.

The city's official government merged with its home county in 1991, creating the Unified Government of Athens-Clark County.

With its shops, boutiques and restaurants, Athens offers plenty to do. The Georgia State Museum of Art, Museum of Natural History, and the State Botanical Garden here are affiliated with the university. The restored 1910 Morton Theater once hosted Cab Calloway, Duke Ellington, and Louis Armstrong, and now hosts dramatic and musical performances. Undoubtedly the strong presence of young people in Athens has contributed to its burgeoning artistic scene. The city center is home to bars, galleries, cafes, and music venues that cater to the city's creative climate. The annual AthFest in June, hosts 120 bands to support local education. The city's charms, attractive to all ages, have not gone unnoticed by the media. Athens has been named one of the best places for small business, the best college town for retirees, and the best place to recapture your youth. The city also has a lively bicycle culture, and hosts several annual bicycle races.

> Athens Ciné was among the first cinemas to adapt to a "virtual ticketing system" when COVID-19 threatened business.

The climate is mild, with average temperatures about 20 degrees warmer than the U.S. average. Snowfall is next to nothing, but precipitation is at its highest from January-March. Spring is lovely, with three to four inches of rain, sunshine up to 70 percent of the time starting in April, and temperatures averaging in the 70s.

Rankings

General Rankings

- In their seventh annual survey, Livability.com looked at data for more than 1,000 small to mid-sized U.S. cities to determine the rankings for Livability's "Top 100 Best Places to Live" in 2020. Athens ranked #32. Criteria: housing and affordable living; vibrant economy; social and civic engagement; education; demographics; health care options; transportation & infrastructure; and abundant lifestyle amenities. *Livability.com, "Top 100 Best Places to Live 2020" October 2020*

Business/Finance Rankings

- The Athens metro area appeared on the Milken Institute "2021 Best Performing Cities" list. Rank: #78 out of 201 small metro areas (population over 60,000). Criteria: job growth; wage and salary growth; high-tech output growth; housing affordability; household broadband access. *Milken Institute, "Best-Performing Cities 2021," February 16, 2021*

- *Forbes* ranked 203 smaller metro areas (population under 268,000) to determine the nation's "Best Small Places for Business and Careers." The Athens metro area was ranked #6. Criteria: costs (business and living); job growth (past and projected); income growth; quality of life; educational attainment (college and high school); projected economic growth; cultural and leisure opportunities; workplace tolerance laws; net migration patterns. *Forbes, "The Best Small Places for Business and Careers 2019," October 30, 2019*

Safety Rankings

- The National Insurance Crime Bureau ranked 384 metro areas in the U.S. in terms of per capita rates of vehicle theft. The Athens metro area ranked #231 (#1 = highest rate). Criteria: number of vehicle theft offenses per 100,000 inhabitants in 2019. *National Insurance Crime Bureau, "Hot Spots 2019," July 21, 2020*

Seniors/Retirement Rankings

- From its Best Cities for Successful Aging indexes, the Milken Institute generated rankings for metropolitan areas, weighing data in nine categories—health care, wellness, living arrangements, transportation and convenience, financial characteristics, education, employment, community engagement, and overall livability. The Athens metro area was ranked #62 overall in the small metro area category. *Milken Institute, "Best Cities for Successful Aging, 2017" March 14, 2017*

- Athens was identified as #16 of 20 most popular places to retire in the Southeast region by *Topretirements.com*. The site separated its annual "Best Places to Retire" list by major U.S. regions for 2019. The list reflects the 20 cities that visitors to the website are most interested in for retirement, based on the number of times a city's review was viewed on the website. *Topretirements.com, "20 Most Popular Places to Retire in the Southeast: 2019," October 16, 2019*

Business Environment

DEMOGRAPHICS

Population Growth

Area	1990 Census	2000 Census	2010 Census	2019* Estimate	Population Growth (%) 1990-2019	Population Growth (%) 2010-2019
City	86,561	100,266	115,452	124,719	44.1	8.0
MSA[1]	136,025	166,079	192,541	208,457	53.2	8.3
U.S.	248,709,873	281,421,906	308,745,538	324,697,795	30.6	5.2

Note: (1) Figures cover the Athens-Clarke County, GA Metropolitan Statistical Area; (*) 2015-2019 5-year estimated population
Source: U.S. Census Bureau, 1990 Census, Census 2000, Census 2010, 2015-2019 American Community Survey 5-Year Estimates

Household Size

Area	One	Two	Three	Four	Five	Six	Seven or More	Average Household Size
City	33.4	35.2	14.6	11.2	3.6	1.5	0.4	2.40
MSA[1]	28.9	35.4	15.2	13.1	4.9	1.7	0.9	2.50
U.S.	27.9	33.9	15.6	12.9	6.0	2.3	1.4	2.60

Note: (1) Figures cover the Athens-Clarke County, GA Metropolitan Statistical Area
Source: U.S. Census Bureau, 2015-2019 American Community Survey 5-Year Estimates

Race

Area	White Alone[2] (%)	Black Alone[2] (%)	Asian Alone[2] (%)	AIAN[3] Alone[2] (%)	NHOPI[4] Alone[2] (%)	Other Race Alone[2] (%)	Two or More Races (%)
City	63.2	28.0	3.9	0.1	0.1	2.1	2.6
MSA[1]	72.0	20.6	3.1	0.1	0.1	1.8	2.3
U.S.	72.5	12.7	5.5	0.8	0.2	4.9	3.3

Note: (1) Figures cover the Athens-Clarke County, GA Metropolitan Statistical Area; (2) Alone is defined as not being in combination with one or more other races; (3) American Indian and Alaska Native; (4) Native Hawaiian and Other Pacific Islander
Source: U.S. Census Bureau, 2015-2019 American Community Survey 5-Year Estimates

Hispanic or Latino Origin

Area	Total (%)	Mexican (%)	Puerto Rican (%)	Cuban (%)	Other (%)
City	10.9	6.7	0.7	0.4	3.1
MSA[1]	8.6	5.0	0.7	0.3	2.6
U.S.	18.0	11.2	1.7	0.7	4.3

Note: Persons of Hispanic or Latino origin can be of any race; (1) Figures cover the Athens-Clarke County, GA Metropolitan Statistical Area
Source: U.S. Census Bureau, 2015-2019 American Community Survey 5-Year Estimates

Ancestry

Area	German	Irish	English	American	Italian	Polish	French[2]	Scottish	Dutch
City	8.4	8.2	8.0	4.3	3.0	1.6	1.7	2.7	1.0
MSA[1]	8.6	9.4	9.1	7.9	2.8	1.2	1.6	2.8	0.9
U.S.	13.3	9.7	7.2	6.2	5.1	2.8	2.3	1.7	1.2

Note: Figures are the percentage of the total population reporting a particular ancestry. The nine most commonly reported ancestries in the U.S. are shown. Figures include multiple ancestries (e.g. if a person reported being Irish and Italian, they were included in both columns); (1) Figures cover the Athens-Clarke County, GA Metropolitan Statistical Area; (2) Excludes Basque
Source: U.S. Census Bureau, 2015-2019 American Community Survey 5-Year Estimates

Foreign-born Population

Area	Any Foreign Country	Asia	Mexico	Europe	Caribbean	Central America[2]	South America	Africa	Canada
City	10.1	2.9	3.0	0.9	0.4	1.0	1.0	0.7	0.2
MSA[1]	7.8	2.3	2.1	0.8	0.3	0.9	0.7	0.5	0.1
U.S.	13.6	4.2	3.5	1.5	1.3	1.1	1.0	0.7	0.2

Note: (1) Figures cover the Athens-Clarke County, GA Metropolitan Statistical Area; (2) Excludes Mexico.
Source: U.S. Census Bureau, 2015-2019 American Community Survey 5-Year Estimates

Athens, Georgia

Marital Status

Area	Never Married	Now Married[2]	Separated	Widowed	Divorced
City	54.4	32.2	1.6	3.5	8.2
MSA[1]	42.7	41.9	1.6	4.7	9.1
U.S.	33.4	48.1	1.9	5.8	10.9

Note: Figures are percentages and cover the population 15 years of age and older; (1) Figures cover the Athens-Clarke County, GA Metropolitan Statistical Area; (2) Excludes separated
Source: U.S. Census Bureau, 2015-2019 American Community Survey 5-Year Estimates

Disability by Age

Area	All Ages	Under 18 Years Old	18 to 64 Years Old	65 Years and Over
City	11.5	6.6	9.4	35.1
MSA[1]	12.5	6.0	10.1	35.8
U.S.	12.6	4.2	10.3	34.5

Note: Figures show percent of the civilian noninstitutionalized population that reported having a disability. Disability status is determined from six types of difficulty: vision, hearing, cognitive, ambulatory, self-care, and independent living. For children under 5 years old, hearing and vision difficulty are used to determine disability status. For children between the ages of 5 and 14, disability status is determined from hearing, vision, cognitive, ambulatory, and self-care difficulties. For people aged 15 years and older, they are considered to have a disability if they have difficulty with any one of the six difficulty types; Note: (1) Figures cover the Athens-Clarke County, GA Metropolitan Statistical Area
Source: U.S. Census Bureau, 2015-2019 American Community Survey 5-Year Estimates

Age

Area	Under Age 5	Age 5–19	Age 20–34	Age 35–44	Age 45–54	Age 55–64	Age 65–74	Age 75–84	Age 85+	Median Age
City	5.3	20.8	34.5	11.2	8.8	8.8	6.3	3.2	1.0	28.0
MSA[1]	5.4	21.1	27.1	12.0	11.0	10.7	7.8	3.8	1.2	32.2
U.S.	6.1	19.1	20.7	12.6	13.0	12.9	9.1	4.6	1.9	38.1

Note: (1) Figures cover the Athens-Clarke County, GA Metropolitan Statistical Area
Source: U.S. Census Bureau, 2015-2019 American Community Survey 5-Year Estimates

Gender

Area	Males	Females	Males per 100 Females
City	59,357	65,362	90.8
MSA[1]	100,687	107,770	93.4
U.S.	159,886,919	164,810,876	97.0

Note: (1) Figures cover the Athens-Clarke County, GA Metropolitan Statistical Area
Source: U.S. Census Bureau, 2015-2019 American Community Survey 5-Year Estimates

Religious Groups by Family

Area	Catholic	Baptist	Non-Den.	Methodist[2]	Lutheran	LDS[3]	Pentecostal	Presbyterian[4]	Muslim[5]	Judaism
MSA[1]	4.4	16.3	2.3	8.4	0.4	0.8	2.8	2.0	0.4	0.2
U.S.	19.1	9.3	4.0	4.0	2.3	2.0	1.9	1.6	0.8	0.7

Note: Figures are the number of adherents as a percentage of the total population; (1) Figures cover the Athens-Clarke County, GA Metropolitan Statistical Area; (2) Methodist/Pietist; (3) Latter Day Saints; (4) Reformed; (5) Figures are estimates
Source: Association of Statisticians of American Religious Bodies, 2010 U.S. Religion Census: Religious Congregations & Membership Study

Religious Groups by Tradition

Area	Catholic	Evangelical Protestant	Mainline Protestant	Other Tradition	Black Protestant	Orthodox
MSA[1]	4.4	21.1	9.8	1.7	2.5	0.1
U.S.	19.1	16.2	7.3	4.3	1.6	0.3

Note: Figures are the number of adherents as a percentage of the total population; (1) Figures cover the Athens-Clarke County, GA Metropolitan Statistical Area
Source: Association of Statisticians of American Religious Bodies, 2010 U.S. Religion Census: Religious Congregations & Membership Study

ECONOMY

Gross Metropolitan Product

Area	2017	2018	2019	2020	Rank[2]
MSA[1]	10.1	10.5	10.8	11.2	205

Note: Figures are in billions of dollars; (1) Figures cover the Athens-Clarke County, GA Metropolitan Statistical Area; (2) Rank is based on 2018 data and ranges from 1 to 381
Source: U.S. Conference of Mayors, U.S. Metro Economies: GMP & Employment 2018-2020, September 2019

Economic Growth

Area	2015-17 (%)	2018 (%)	2019 (%)	2020 (%)	Rank[2]
MSA[1]	6.8	1.5	1.3	1.4	6
U.S.	1.9	2.9	2.3	2.1	—

Note: Figures are real gross metropolitan product (GMP) growth rates and represent average annual percent change; (1) Figures cover the Athens-Clarke County, GA Metropolitan Statistical Area; (2) Rank is based on 2017 2-year average annual percent change and ranges from 1 to 381
Source: U.S. Conference of Mayors, U.S. Metro Economies: GMP & Employment 2018-2020, September 2019

Metropolitan Area Exports

Area	2014	2015	2016	2017	2018	2019	Rank[2]
MSA[1]	320.8	327.4	332.1	297.7	378.2	442.1	219

Note: Figures are in millions of dollars; (1) Figures cover the Athens-Clarke County, GA Metropolitan Statistical Area; (2) Rank is based on 2019 data and ranges from 1 to 386
Source: U.S. Department of Commerce, International Trade Administration, Office of Trade and Economic Analysis, Industry and Analysis, Exports by Metropolitan Area, data extracted March 24, 2021

Building Permits

Area	Single-Family 2018	Single-Family 2019	Pct. Chg.	Multi-Family 2018	Multi-Family 2019	Pct. Chg.	Total 2018	Total 2019	Pct. Chg.
City	345	517	49.9	261	766	193.5	606	1,283	111.7
MSA[1]	729	821	12.6	340	770	126.5	1,069	1,591	48.8
U.S.	855,300	862,100	0.7	473,500	523,900	10.6	1,328,800	1,386,000	4.3

Note: (1) Figures cover the Athens-Clarke County, GA Metropolitan Statistical Area; Figures represent new, privately-owned housing units authorized (unadjusted data); All permit data are based on estimates with imputation
Source: U.S. Census Bureau, Manufacturing, Mining, and Construction Statistics, Building Permits, 2018, 2019

Bankruptcy Filings

Area	Business Filings 2019	Business Filings 2020	% Chg.	Nonbusiness Filings 2019	Nonbusiness Filings 2020	% Chg.
Clarke County	0	5	n/a	338	228	-32.5
U.S.	22,780	21,655	-4.9	752,160	522,808	-30.5

Note: Business filings include Chapter 7, Chapter 9, Chapter 11, Chapter 12, Chapter 13, Chapter 15, and Section 304; Nonbusiness filings include Chapter 7, Chapter 11, and Chapter 13
Source: Administrative Office of the U.S. Courts, Business and Nonbusiness Bankruptcy, County Cases Commenced by Chapter of the Bankruptcy Code, During the 12-Month Period Ending December 31, 2019 and Business and Nonbusiness Bankruptcy, County Cases Commenced by Chapter of the Bankruptcy Code, During the 12-Month Period Ending December 31, 2020

Housing Vacancy Rates

Area	Gross Vacancy Rate[2] (%) 2018	2019	2020	Year-Round Vacancy Rate[3] (%) 2018	2019	2020	Rental Vacancy Rate[4] (%) 2018	2019	2020	Homeowner Vacancy Rate[5] (%) 2018	2019	2020
MSA[1]	n/a	n/a	n/a	n/a	n/a	n/a	n/a	n/a	n/a	n/a	n/a	n/a
U.S.	12.3	12.0	10.6	9.7	9.5	8.2	6.9	6.7	6.3	1.5	1.4	1.0

Note: (1) Figures cover the Athens-Clarke County, GA Metropolitan Statistical Area; (2) The percentage of the total housing inventory that is vacant; (3) The percentage of the housing inventory (excluding seasonal units) that is year-round vacant; (4) The percentage of rental inventory that is vacant for rent; (5) The percentage of homeowner inventory that is vacant for sale; n/a not available
Source: U.S. Census Bureau, Housing Vacancies and Homeownership Annual Statistics: 2018, 2019, 2020

INCOME

Income

Area	Per Capita ($)	Median Household ($)	Average Household ($)
City	23,726	38,311	59,118
MSA[1]	27,653	47,214	70,940
U.S.	34,103	62,843	88,607

Note: (1) Figures cover the Athens-Clarke County, GA Metropolitan Statistical Area
Source: U.S. Census Bureau, 2015-2019 American Community Survey 5-Year Estimates

Household Income Distribution

Area	Under $15,000	$15,000 -$24,999	$25,000 -$34,999	$35,000 -$49,999	$50,000 -$74,999	$75,000 -$99,999	$100,000 -$149,999	$150,000 and up
City	21.0	14.6	11.3	13.3	14.1	8.7	9.9	7.2
MSA[1]	16.4	12.1	10.3	13.5	15.2	10.2	12.6	9.6
U.S.	10.3	8.9	8.9	12.3	17.2	12.7	15.1	14.5

Note: (1) Figures cover the Athens-Clarke County, GA Metropolitan Statistical Area
Source: U.S. Census Bureau, 2015-2019 American Community Survey 5-Year Estimates

Athens, Georgia

Poverty Rate

Area	All Ages	Under 18 Years Old	18 to 64 Years Old	65 Years and Over
City	29.9	33.7	32.2	9.4
MSA[1]	22.0	25.1	23.8	8.1
U.S.	13.4	18.5	12.6	9.3

Note: Figures are percentage of people whose income during the past 12 months was below the poverty level;
(1) Figures cover the Athens-Clarke County, GA Metropolitan Statistical Area
Source: U.S. Census Bureau, 2015-2019 American Community Survey 5-Year Estimates

CITY FINANCES

City Government Finances

Component	2017 ($000)	2017 ($ per capita)
Total Revenues	280,298	2,262
Total Expenditures	251,655	2,031
Debt Outstanding	263,978	2,130
Cash and Securities[1]	445,378	3,594

Note: (1) Cash and security holdings of a government at the close of its fiscal year, including those of its dependent agencies, utilities, and liquor stores.
Source: U.S. Census Bureau, State & Local Government Finances 2017

City Government Revenue by Source

Source	2017 ($000)	2017 ($ per capita)	2017 (%)
General Revenue			
From Federal Government	6,742	54	2.4
From State Government	2,865	23	1.0
From Local Governments	51,598	416	18.4
Taxes			
Property	53,763	434	19.2
Sales and Gross Receipts	21,322	172	7.6
Personal Income	0	0	0.0
Corporate Income	0	0	0.0
Motor Vehicle License	0	0	0.0
Other Taxes	5,256	42	1.9
Current Charges	78,983	637	28.2
Liquor Store	0	0	0.0
Utility	19,833	160	7.1
Employee Retirement	32,871	265	11.7

Source: U.S. Census Bureau, State & Local Government Finances 2017

City Government Expenditures by Function

Function	2017 ($000)	2017 ($ per capita)	2017 (%)
General Direct Expenditures			
Air Transportation	2,191	17	0.9
Corrections	19,258	155	7.7
Education	0	0	0.0
Employment Security Administration	0	0	0.0
Financial Administration	8,853	71	3.5
Fire Protection	13,267	107	5.3
General Public Buildings	6,738	54	2.7
Governmental Administration, Other	10,848	87	4.3
Health	1,860	15	0.7
Highways	12,712	102	5.1
Hospitals	0	0	0.0
Housing and Community Development	0	0	0.0
Interest on General Debt	16,430	132	6.5
Judicial and Legal	14,136	114	5.6
Libraries	2,009	16	0.8
Parking	0	0	0.0
Parks and Recreation	11,785	95	4.7
Police Protection	31,323	252	12.4
Public Welfare	737	5	0.3
Sewerage	14,813	119	5.9
Solid Waste Management	7,645	61	3.0
Veterans' Services	0	0	0.0
Liquor Store	0	0	0.0
Utility	22,891	184	9.1
Employee Retirement	12,644	102	5.0

Source: U.S. Census Bureau, State & Local Government Finances 2017

EMPLOYMENT

Labor Force and Employment

Area	Civilian Labor Force Dec. 2019	Civilian Labor Force Dec. 2020	% Chg.	Workers Employed Dec. 2019	Workers Employed Dec. 2020	% Chg.
City	59,225	58,747	-0.8	57,596	55,706	-3.3
MSA[1]	99,032	97,723	-1.3	96,483	93,287	-3.3
U.S.	164,007,000	160,017,000	-2.4	158,504,000	149,613,000	-5.6

Note: Data is not seasonally adjusted and covers workers 16 years of age and older; (1) Figures cover the Athens-Clarke County, GA Metropolitan Statistical Area
Source: Bureau of Labor Statistics, Local Area Unemployment Statistics

Unemployment Rate

Area	Jan.	Feb.	Mar.	Apr.	May	Jun.	Jul.	Aug.	Sep.	Oct.	Nov.	Dec.
City	3.5	3.5	4.7	12.2	9.0	7.7	7.9	5.8	5.9	4.3	5.1	5.2
MSA[1]	3.2	3.3	4.3	11.1	8.0	6.7	6.7	4.9	4.9	3.7	4.4	4.5
U.S.	4.0	3.8	4.5	14.4	13.0	11.2	10.5	8.5	7.7	6.6	6.4	6.5

Note: Data is not seasonally adjusted and covers workers 16 years of age and older; (1) Figures cover the Athens-Clarke County, GA Metropolitan Statistical Area
Source: Bureau of Labor Statistics, Local Area Unemployment Statistics

Average Wages

Occupation	$/Hr.	Occupation	$/Hr.
Accountants and Auditors	31.70	Maintenance and Repair Workers	17.30
Automotive Mechanics	20.50	Marketing Managers	61.60
Bookkeepers	17.40	Network and Computer Systems Admin.	32.20
Carpenters	19.10	Nurses, Licensed Practical	21.50
Cashiers	10.70	Nurses, Registered	34.10
Computer Programmers	32.80	Nursing Assistants	13.20
Computer Systems Analysts	43.70	Office Clerks, General	16.00
Computer User Support Specialists	21.30	Physical Therapists	38.70
Construction Laborers	14.80	Physicians	95.70
Cooks, Restaurant	12.70	Plumbers, Pipefitters and Steamfitters	n/a
Customer Service Representatives	15.80	Police and Sheriff's Patrol Officers	21.10
Dentists	n/a	Postal Service Mail Carriers	24.90
Electricians	26.30	Real Estate Sales Agents	27.20
Engineers, Electrical	51.50	Retail Salespersons	12.20
Fast Food and Counter Workers	9.80	Sales Representatives, Technical/Scientific	22.10
Financial Managers	52.40	Secretaries, Exc. Legal/Medical/Executive	15.70
First-Line Supervisors of Office Workers	24.60	Security Guards	15.60
General and Operations Managers	45.40	Surgeons	121.10
Hairdressers/Cosmetologists	10.30	Teacher Assistants, Exc. Postsecondary*	9.90
Home Health and Personal Care Aides	12.00	Teachers, Secondary School, Exc. Sp. Ed.*	28.30
Janitors and Cleaners	12.50	Telemarketers	n/a
Landscaping/Groundskeeping Workers	16.10	Truck Drivers, Heavy/Tractor-Trailer	24.10
Lawyers	37.80	Truck Drivers, Light/Delivery Services	22.30
Maids and Housekeeping Cleaners	10.10	Waiters and Waitresses	11.10

Note: Wage data covers the Athens-Clarke County, GA Metropolitan Statistical Area; (*) Hourly wages were calculated from annual wage data based on a 40 hour work week; n/a not available.
Source: Bureau of Labor Statistics, Metro Area Occupational Employment & Wage Estimates, May 2020

Employment by Industry

Sector	MSA[1] Number of Employees	MSA[1] Percent of Total	U.S. Percent of Total
Construction, Mining, and Logging	n/a	n/a	5.5
Education and Health Services	n/a	n/a	16.3
Financial Activities	n/a	n/a	6.1
Government	27,800	29.8	15.2
Information	n/a	n/a	1.9
Leisure and Hospitality	9,600	10.3	9.0
Manufacturing	n/a	n/a	8.5
Other Services	n/a	n/a	3.8
Professional and Business Services	8,500	9.1	14.4
Retail Trade	10,600	11.3	10.9
Transportation, Warehousing, and Utilities	n/a	n/a	4.6
Wholesale Trade	n/a	n/a	3.9

Note: Figures are non-farm employment as of December 2020. Figures are not seasonally adjusted and include workers 16 years of age and older; (1) Figures cover the Athens-Clarke County, GA Metropolitan Statistical Area; n/a not available
Source: Bureau of Labor Statistics, Current Employment Statistics, Employment, Hours, and Earnings

Employment by Occupation

Occupation Classification	City (%)	MSA[1] (%)	U.S. (%)
Management, Business, Science, and Arts	40.6	41.3	38.5
Natural Resources, Construction, and Maintenance	5.8	7.2	8.9
Production, Transportation, and Material Moving	13.7	14.1	13.2
Sales and Office	19.0	19.3	21.6
Service	21.0	18.2	17.8

Note: Figures cover employed civilians 16 years of age and older; (1) Figures cover the Athens-Clarke County, GA Metropolitan Statistical Area
Source: U.S. Census Bureau, 2015-2019 American Community Survey 5-Year Estimates

Occupations with Greatest Projected Employment Growth: 2020 – 2022

Occupation[1]	2020 Employment	2022 Projected Employment	Numeric Employment Change	Percent Employment Change
Laborers and Freight, Stock, and Material Movers, Hand	126,370	132,960	6,590	5.2
Fast Food and Counter Workers	134,770	139,200	4,430	3.3
Software Developers and Software Quality Assurance Analysts and Testers	44,810	47,890	3,080	6.9
Home Health and Personal Care Aides	47,800	50,800	3,000	6.3
General and Operations Managers	84,320	87,250	2,930	3.5
Maids and Housekeeping Cleaners	26,600	29,080	2,480	9.3
Cooks, Restaurant	38,680	41,070	2,390	6.2
Maintenance and Repair Workers, General	44,140	46,510	2,370	5.4
Registered Nurses	81,380	83,690	2,310	2.8
Customer Service Representatives	111,220	113,240	2,020	1.8

Note: Projections cover Georgia; (1) Sorted by numeric employment change
Source: www.projectionscentral.com, State Occupational Projections, 2020–2022 Short-Term Projections

Fastest-Growing Occupations: 2020 – 2022

Occupation[1]	2020 Employment	2022 Projected Employment	Numeric Employment Change	Percent Employment Change
Nurse Practitioners	8,440	9,520	1,080	12.8
Hotel, Motel, and Resort Desk Clerks	8,960	10,030	1,070	11.9
Occupational Therapy Assistants	1,220	1,350	130	10.7
Film and Video Editors	1,670	1,840	170	10.2
Lighting Technicians and Media and Communication Equipment Workers, All Other	1,010	1,110	100	9.9
Baggage Porters and Bellhops	1,020	1,120	100	9.8
Animal Trainers	1,250	1,370	120	9.6
Physical Therapist Assistants	2,790	3,050	260	9.3
Maids and Housekeeping Cleaners	26,600	29,080	2,480	9.3
Information Security Analysts (SOC 2018)	3,910	4,250	340	8.7

Note: Projections cover Georgia; (1) Sorted by percent employment change and excludes occupations with numeric employment change less than 50
Source: www.projectionscentral.com, State Occupational Projections, 2020–2022 Short-Term Projections

TAXES

State Corporate Income Tax Rates

State	Tax Rate (%)	Income Brackets ($)	Num. of Brackets	Financial Institution Tax Rate (%)[a]	Federal Income Tax Ded.
Georgia	5.75	Flat rate	1	5.75	No

Note: Tax rates as of January 1, 2021; (a) Rates listed are the corporate income tax rate applied to financial institutions or excise taxes based on income. Some states have other taxes based upon the value of deposits or shares.
Source: Federation of Tax Administrators, State Corporate Income Tax Rates, January 1, 2021

State Individual Income Tax Rates

State	Tax Rate (%)	Income Brackets ($)	Personal Exemptions ($) Single	Married	Depend.	Standard Ded. ($) Single	Married
Georgia	1.0 - 5.75	750 - 7,001 (i)	2,700	7,400	3,000	4,600	6,000

Note: Tax rates as of January 1, 2021; Local- and county-level taxes are not included; Federal income tax is not deductible on state income tax returns; (i) The Georgia income brackets reported are for single individuals. For married couples filing jointly, the same tax rates apply to income brackets ranging from $1,000, to $10,000.
Source: Federation of Tax Administrators, State Individual Income Tax Rates, January 1, 2021

Various State Sales and Excise Tax Rates

State	State Sales Tax (%)	Gasoline[1] (¢/gal.)	Cigarette[2] ($/pack)	Spirits[3] ($/gal.)	Wine[4] ($/gal.)	Beer[5] ($/gal.)	Recreational Marijuana (%)
Georgia	4	33.96	0.37	3.79	1.51	0.48	Not legal

Note: All tax rates as of January 1, 2021; (1) The American Petroleum Institute has developed a methodology for determining the average tax rate on a gallon of fuel. Rates may include any of the following: excise taxes, environmental fees, storage tank fees, other fees or taxes, general sales tax, and local taxes; (2) The federal excise tax of $1.0066 per pack and local taxes are not included; (3) Rates are those applicable to off-premise sales of 40% alcohol by volume (a.b.v.) distilled spirits in 750ml containers. Local excise taxes are excluded; (4) Rates are those applicable to off-premise sales of 11% a.b.v. non-carbonated wine in 750ml containers; (5) Rates are those applicable to off-premise sales of 4.7% a.b.v. beer in 12 ounce containers.
Source: Tax Foundation, 2021 Facts & Figures: How Does Your State Compare?

State Business Tax Climate Index Rankings

State	Overall Rank	Corporate Tax Rank	Individual Income Tax Rank	Sales Tax Rank	Property Tax Rank	Unemployment Insurance Tax Rank
Georgia	31	7	36	27	24	39

Note: The index is a measure of how each state's tax laws affect economic performance. The lower the rank, the more favorable a state's tax system is for business. States without a given tax are given a ranking of 1. The scores/rankings for the District of Columbia do not affect other states. The 2021 index represents the tax climate as of July 1, 2020.
Source: Tax Foundation, State Business Tax Climate Index 2021

TRANSPORTATION

Means of Transportation to Work

Area	Drove Alone	Car-pooled	Bus	Subway	Railroad	Bicycle	Walked	Other Means	Worked at Home
City	72.5	10.0	4.6	0.0	0.0	1.4	4.4	1.5	5.6
MSA[1]	76.3	10.3	2.8	0.0	0.0	0.9	2.9	1.2	5.6
U.S.	76.3	9.0	2.4	1.9	0.6	0.5	2.7	1.4	5.2

Note: Figures are percentages and cover workers 16 years of age and older; (1) Figures cover the Athens-Clarke County, GA Metropolitan Statistical Area
Source: U.S. Census Bureau, 2015-2019 American Community Survey 5-Year Estimates

Travel Time to Work

Area	Less Than 10 Minutes	10 to 19 Minutes	20 to 29 Minutes	30 to 44 Minutes	45 to 59 Minutes	60 to 89 Minutes	90 Minutes or More
City	17.4	48.3	16.9	8.8	3.6	3.0	2.0
MSA[1]	14.1	41.1	21.4	12.9	4.7	3.5	2.2
U.S.	12.2	28.4	20.8	20.8	8.3	6.4	2.9

Note: Note: Figures are percentages and include workers 16 years old and over; (1) Figures cover the Athens-Clarke County, GA Metropolitan Statistical Area
Source: U.S. Census Bureau, 2015-2019 American Community Survey 5-Year Estimates

Key Congestion Measures

Measure	1982	1992	2002	2012	2017
Annual Hours of Delay, Total (000)	n/a	n/a	n/a	n/a	3,800
Annual Hours of Delay, Per Auto Commuter	n/a	n/a	n/a	n/a	27
Annual Congestion Cost, Total (million $)	n/a	n/a	n/a	n/a	77
Annual Congestion Cost, Per Auto Commuter ($)	n/a	n/a	n/a	n/a	548

Note: n/a not available
Source: Texas A&M Transportation Institute, 2019 Urban Mobility Report

Freeway Travel Time Index

Measure	1982	1987	1992	1997	2002	2007	2012	2017
Urban Area Index[1]	n/a	n/a	n/a	n/a	n/a	n/a	n/a	1.11
Urban Area Rank[1,2]	n/a	n/a	n/a	n/a	n/a	n/a	n/a	n/a

Note: Freeway Travel Time Index—the ratio of travel time in the peak period to the travel time at free-flow conditions. For example, a value of 1.30 indicates a 20-minute free-flow trip takes 26 minutes in the peak (20 minutes x 1.30 = 26 minutes); (1) Covers the Athens-Clarke County GA urban area; (2) Rank is based on 101 larger urban areas (#1 = highest travel time index); n/a not available
Source: Texas A&M Transportation Institute, 2019 Urban Mobility Report

Public Transportation

Agency Name / Mode of Transportation	Vehicles Operated in Maximum Service[1]	Annual Unlinked Passenger Trips[2] (in thous.)	Annual Passenger Miles[3] (in thous.)
Athens Transit System			
Bus (directly operated)	21	1,273.0	4,618.9
Demand Response (directly operated)	3	7.3	37.6

Note: (1) Number of revenue vehicles operated by the given mode and type of service to meet the annual maximum service requirement. This is the revenue vehicle count during the peak season of the year; on the week and day that maximum service is provided. Vehicles operated in maximum service (VOMS) exclude atypical days and one-time special events; (2) Number of passengers who boarded public transportation vehicles. Passengers are counted each time they board a vehicle no matter how many vehicles they use to travel from their origin to their destination. (3) Sum of the distances ridden by all passengers during the entire fiscal year.
Source: Federal Transit Administration, National Transit Database, 2019

Air Transportation

Airport Name and Code / Type of Service	Passenger Airlines[1]	Passenger Enplanements	Freight Carriers[2]	Freight (lbs)
Athens Municipal (AHN)				
Domestic service (U.S. carriers - 2020)	7	1,267	2	37,098
International service (U.S. carriers - 2019)	0	0	0	0

Note: (1) Includes all U.S.-based major, minor and commuter airlines that carried at least one passenger during the year; (2) Includes all U.S.-based airlines and freight carriers that transported at least one pound of freight during the year.
Source: Bureau of Transportation Statistics, The Intermodal Transportation Database, Air Carriers: T-100 Domestic Market (U.S. Carriers), 2020; Bureau of Transportation Statistics, The Intermodal Transportation Database, Air Carriers: T-100 International Market (U.S. Carriers), 2019

BUSINESSES

Major Business Headquarters

Company Name	Industry	Rankings Fortune[1]	Forbes[2]
No companies listed	-	-	-

Note: (1) Companies that produce a 10-K are ranked 1 to 500 based on 2019 revenue; (2) All private companies with at least $2 billion in annual revenue through the end of their most current fiscal year are ranked 1 to 219; companies listed are headquartered in the city; dashes indicate no ranking
Source: Fortune, "Fortune 500," June/July 2020; Forbes, "America's Largest Private Companies," 2020

Living Environment

COST OF LIVING

Cost of Living Index

Composite Index	Groceries	Housing	Utilities	Transportation	Health Care	Misc. Goods/Services
n/a	n/a	n/a	n/a	n/a	n/a	n/a

Note: The Cost of Living Index measures regional differences in the cost of consumer goods and services, excluding taxes and non-consumer expenditures, for professional and managerial households in the top income quintile. It is based on more than 50,000 prices covering almost 60 different items for which prices are collected three times a year by chambers of commerce, economic development organizations or university applied economic centers in each participating urban area. The numbers shown should be read as a percentage above or below the national average of 100. For example, a value of 115.4 in the groceries column indicates that grocery prices are 15.4% higher than the national average. Small differences in the index numbers should not be interpreted as significant; n/a not available.
Source: The Council for Community and Economic Research, Cost of Living Index, 2020

Grocery Prices

Area[1]	T-Bone Steak ($/pound)	Frying Chicken ($/pound)	Whole Milk ($/half gal.)	Eggs ($/dozen)	Orange Juice ($/64 oz.)	Coffee ($/11.5 oz.)
City[2]	n/a	n/a	n/a	n/a	n/a	n/a
Avg.	11.78	1.39	2.05	1.47	3.57	4.34
Min.	8.03	0.94	1.03	0.74	2.94	3.02
Max.	15.86	2.65	4.31	3.77	5.44	8.69

*Note: (1) Values for the local area are compared with the average, minimum and maximum values for all 284 areas in the Cost of Living Index; (2) Figures cover the Athens GA urban area; n/a not available; **T-Bone Steak** (price per pound); **Frying Chicken** (price per pound, whole fryer); **Whole Milk** (half gallon carton); **Eggs** (price per dozen, Grade A, large); **Orange Juice** (64 oz. Tropicana or Florida Natural); **Coffee** (11.5 oz. can, vacuum-packed, Maxwell House, Hills Bros, or Folgers).*
Source: The Council for Community and Economic Research, Cost of Living Index, 2020

Housing and Utility Costs

Area[1]	New Home Price ($)	Apartment Rent ($/month)	All Electric ($/month)	Part Electric ($/month)	Other Energy ($/month)	Telephone ($/month)
City[2]	n/a	n/a	n/a	n/a	n/a	n/a
Avg.	368,594	1,168	170.86	100.47	65.28	184.30
Min.	190,567	502	91.58	31.42	26.08	169.60
Max.	2,227,806	4,738	470.38	280.31	280.06	206.50

*Note: (1) Values for the local area are compared with the average, minimum and maximum values for all 284 areas in the Cost of Living Index; (2) Figures cover the Athens GA urban area; n/a not available; **New Home Price** (2,400 sf living area, 8,000 sf lot, in urban area with full utilities); **Apartment Rent** (950 sf 2 bedroom/1.5 or 2 bath, unfurnished, excluding all utilities except water); **All Electric** (average monthly cost for an all-electric home); **Part Electric** (average monthly cost for a part-electric home); **Other Energy** (average monthly cost for natural gas, fuel oil, coal, wood, and any other forms of energy except electricity); **Telephone** (price includes the base monthly rate plus taxes and fees for three lines of mobile phone service).*
Source: The Council for Community and Economic Research, Cost of Living Index, 2020

Health Care, Transportation, and Other Costs

Area[1]	Doctor ($/visit)	Dentist ($/visit)	Optometrist ($/visit)	Gasoline ($/gallon)	Beauty Salon ($/visit)	Men's Shirt ($)
City[2]	n/a	n/a	n/a	n/a	n/a	n/a
Avg.	115.44	99.32	108.10	2.21	39.27	31.37
Min.	36.68	59.00	51.36	1.71	19.00	11.00
Max.	219.00	153.10	250.97	3.46	82.05	58.33

*Note: (1) Values for the local area are compared with the average, minimum and maximum values for all 284 areas in the Cost of Living Index; (2) Figures cover the Athens GA urban area; n/a not available; **Doctor** (general practitioners routine exam of an established patient); **Dentist** (adult teeth cleaning and periodic oral examination); **Optometrist** (full vision eye exam for established adult patient); **Gasoline** (one gallon regular unleaded, national brand, including all taxes, cash price at self-service pump if available); **Beauty Salon** (woman's shampoo, trim, and blow-dry); **Men's Shirt** (cotton/polyester dress shirt, pinpoint weave, long sleeves).*
Source: The Council for Community and Economic Research, Cost of Living Index, 2020

HOUSING

Homeownership Rate

Area	2012 (%)	2013 (%)	2014 (%)	2015 (%)	2016 (%)	2017 (%)	2018 (%)	2019 (%)	2020 (%)
MSA[1]	n/a	n/a	n/a	n/a	n/a	n/a	n/a	n/a	n/a
U.S.	65.4	65.1	64.5	63.7	63.4	63.9	64.4	64.6	66.6

Note: (1) Figures cover the Athens-Clarke County, GA Metropolitan Statistical Area; n/a not available
Source: U.S. Census Bureau, Housing Vacancies and Homeownership Annual Statistics: 2012-2020

House Price Index (HPI)

Area	National Ranking[2]	Quarterly Change (%)	One-Year Change (%)	Five-Year Change (%)	Since 1991Q1 (%)
MSA[1]	66	1.41	7.40	43.79	181.78
U.S.[3]	–	3.81	10.77	38.99	205.12

Note: The HPI is a weighted repeat sales index. It measures average price changes in repeat sales or refinancings on the same properties. This information is obtained by reviewing repeat mortgage transactions on single-family properties whose mortgages have been purchased or securitized by Fannie Mae or Freddie Mac since January 1975; (1) Figures cover the Athens-Clarke County, GA Metropolitan Statistical Area; (2) Rankings are based on annual percentage change for all metro areas containing at least 15,000 transactions over the last 10 years and ranges from 1 to 253; (3) figures based on a weighted average of Census Division estimates using a seasonally adjusted, purchase-only index; all figures are for the period ending December 31, 2020
Source: Federal Housing Finance Agency, Change in Metropolitan Area House Price Indexes, April 7, 2021

Median Single-Family Home Prices

Area	2018	2019	2020p	Percent Change 2019 to 2020
MSA[1]	n/a	n/a	n/a	n/a
U.S. Average	261.6	274.6	299.9	9.2

Note: Figures are median sales prices of existing single-family homes in thousands of dollars; (p) preliminary; n/a not available; (1) Figures cover the Athens-Clarke County, GA Metropolitan Statistical Area
Source: National Association of Realtors, Median Sales Price of Existing Single-Family Homes for Metropolitan Areas, 4th Quarter 2020

Qualifying Income Based on Median Sales Price of Existing Single-Family Homes

Area	With 5% Down ($)	With 10% Down ($)	With 20% Down ($)
MSA[1]	n/a	n/a	n/a
U.S. Average	59,266	56,147	49,908

Note: Figures are preliminary; Qualifying income is based on a mortgage rate of 2.81%. Monthly principal and interest payment is limited to 25% of income; n/a not available; (1) Figures cover the Athens-Clarke County, GA Metropolitan Statistical Area
Source: National Association of Realtors, Qualifying Income Based on Median Sales Price of Existing Single-Family Homes for Metropolitan Areas, 4th Quarter 2020

Home Value Distribution

Area	Under $50,000	$50,000 -$99,999	$100,000 -$149,999	$150,000 -$199,999	$200,000 -$299,999	$300,000 -$499,999	$500,000 -$999,999	$1,000,000 or more
City	6.3	12.9	19.9	21.9	20.3	12.7	5.4	0.7
MSA[1]	8.8	12.2	17.4	17.3	21.0	16.1	6.2	1.0
U.S.	6.9	12.0	13.3	14.0	19.6	19.3	11.4	3.4

Note: Figures are percentages and cover owner-occupied housing units; (1) Figures cover the Athens-Clarke County, GA Metropolitan Statistical Area
Source: U.S. Census Bureau, 2015-2019 American Community Survey 5-Year Estimates

Year Housing Structure Built

Area	2010 or Later	2000 -2009	1990 -1999	1980 -1989	1970 -1979	1960 -1969	1950 -1959	1940 -1949	Before 1940	Median Year
City	3.8	17.7	20.3	15.6	16.5	12.2	6.6	2.4	4.8	1985
MSA[1]	5.0	18.1	21.7	17.4	15.3	10.1	5.5	2.0	5.0	1987
U.S.	5.2	14.0	13.9	13.4	15.2	10.6	10.3	4.9	12.6	1978

Note: Figures are percentages except for Median Year; Note: (1) Figures cover the Athens-Clarke County, GA Metropolitan Statistical Area
Source: U.S. Census Bureau, 2015-2019 American Community Survey 5-Year Estimates

Gross Monthly Rent

Area	Under $500	$500 -$999	$1,000 -$1,499	$1,500 -$1,999	$2,000 -$2,499	$2,500 -$2,999	$3,000 and up	Median ($)
City	7.9	59.5	24.2	6.6	1.4	0.2	0.1	856
MSA[1]	8.4	59.5	23.6	6.2	1.5	0.5	0.2	853
U.S.	9.4	36.2	30.0	14.0	5.6	2.4	2.4	1,062

Note: Figures are percentages except for Median; Gross rent is the contract rent plus the estimated average monthly cost of utilities (electricity, gas, and water and sewer) and fuels (oil, coal, kerosene, wood, etc.) if these are paid by the renter (or paid for the renter by someone else); (1) Figures cover the Athens-Clarke County, GA Metropolitan Statistical Area
Source: U.S. Census Bureau, 2015-2019 American Community Survey 5-Year Estimates

HEALTH

Health Risk Factors

Category	MSA[1] (%)	U.S. (%)
Adults aged 18–64 who have any kind of health care coverage	n/a	87.3
Adults who reported being in good or better health	n/a	82.4
Adults who have been told they have high blood cholesterol	n/a	33.0
Adults who have been told they have high blood pressure	n/a	32.3
Adults who are current smokers	n/a	17.1
Adults who currently use E-cigarettes	n/a	4.6
Adults who currently use chewing tobacco, snuff, or snus	n/a	4.0
Adults who are heavy drinkers[2]	n/a	6.3
Adults who are binge drinkers[3]	n/a	17.4
Adults who are overweight (BMI 25.0 - 29.9)	n/a	35.3
Adults who are obese (BMI 30.0 - 99.8)	n/a	31.3
Adults who participated in any physical activities in the past month	n/a	74.4
Adults who always or nearly always wears a seat belt	n/a	94.3

Note: n/a not available; (1) Figures cover the Athens-Clarke County, GA Metropolitan Statistical Area; (2) Heavy drinkers are classified as adult men having more than 14 drinks per week and adult women having more than 7 drinks per week; (3) Binge drinkers are classified as males having five or more drinks on one occasion or females having four or more drinks on one occasion
Source: Centers for Disease Control and Prevention, Behaviorial Risk Factor Surveillance System, SMART: Selected Metropolitan Area Risk Trends, 2017

Acute and Chronic Health Conditions

Category	MSA[1] (%)	U.S. (%)
Adults who have ever been told they had a heart attack	n/a	4.2
Adults who have ever been told they have angina or coronary heart disease	n/a	3.9
Adults who have ever been told they had a stroke	n/a	3.0
Adults who have ever been told they have asthma	n/a	14.2
Adults who have ever been told they have arthritis	n/a	24.9
Adults who have ever been told they have diabetes[2]	n/a	10.5
Adults who have ever been told they had skin cancer	n/a	6.2
Adults who have ever been told they had any other types of cancer	n/a	7.1
Adults who have ever been told they have COPD	n/a	6.5
Adults who have ever been told they have kidney disease	n/a	3.0
Adults who have ever been told they have a form of depression	n/a	20.5

Note: n/a not available; (1) Figures cover the Athens-Clarke County, GA Metropolitan Statistical Area; (2) Figures do not include pregnancy-related, borderline, or pre-diabetes
Source: Centers for Disease Control and Prevention, Behaviorial Risk Factor Surveillance System, SMART: Selected Metropolitan Area Risk Trends, 2017

Health Screening and Vaccination Rates

Category	MSA[1] (%)	U.S. (%)
Adults aged 65+ who have had flu shot within the past year	n/a	60.7
Adults aged 65+ who have ever had a pneumonia vaccination	n/a	75.4
Adults who have ever been tested for HIV	n/a	36.1
Adults who have ever had the shingles or zoster vaccine?	n/a	28.9
Adults who have had their blood cholesterol checked within the last five years	n/a	85.9

Note: n/a not available; (1) Figures cover the Athens-Clarke County, GA Metropolitan Statistical Area.
Source: Centers for Disease Control and Prevention, Behaviorial Risk Factor Surveillance System, SMART: Selected Metropolitan Area Risk Trends, 2017

Disability Status

Category	MSA[1] (%)	U.S. (%)
Adults who reported being deaf	n/a	6.7
Are you blind or have serious difficulty seeing, even when wearing glasses?	n/a	4.5
Are you limited in any way in any of your usual activities due of arthritis?	n/a	12.9
Do you have difficulty doing errands alone?	n/a	6.8
Do you have difficulty dressing or bathing?	n/a	3.6
Do you have serious difficulty concentrating/remembering/making decisions?	n/a	10.7
Do you have serious difficulty walking or climbing stairs?	n/a	13.6

Note: n/a not available; (1) Figures cover the Athens-Clarke County, GA Metropolitan Statistical Area.
Source: Centers for Disease Control and Prevention, Behaviorial Risk Factor Surveillance System, SMART: Selected Metropolitan Area Risk Trends, 2017

Mortality Rates for the Top 10 Causes of Death in the U.S.

ICD-10[a] Sub-Chapter	ICD-10[a] Code	County[2]	U.S.
		Age-Adjusted Mortality Rate[1] per 100,000 population	
Malignant neoplasms	C00-C97	138.6	149.2
Ischaemic heart diseases	I20-I25	56.1	90.5
Other forms of heart disease	I30-I51	95.3	52.2
Chronic lower respiratory diseases	J40-J47	33.1	39.6
Other degenerative diseases of the nervous system	G30-G31	63.9	37.6
Cerebrovascular diseases	I60-I69	50.5	37.2
Other external causes of accidental injury	W00-X59	20.1	36.1
Organic, including symptomatic, mental disorders	F01-F09	20.3	29.4
Hypertensive diseases	I10-I15	26.8	24.1
Diabetes mellitus	E10-E14	14.7	21.5

Note: (a) ICD-10 = International Classification of Diseases 10th Revision; (1) Mortality rates are a three-year average covering 2017-2019; (2) Figures cover Clarke County.
Source: Centers for Disease Control and Prevention, National Center for Health Statistics. Underlying Cause of Death 1999-2019 on CDC WONDER Online Database

Mortality Rates for Selected Causes of Death

ICD-10[a] Sub-Chapter	ICD-10[a] Code	County[2]	U.S.
		Age-Adjusted Mortality Rate[1] per 100,000 population	
Assault	X85-Y09	6.6	6.0
Diseases of the liver	K70-K76	15.3	14.4
Human immunodeficiency virus (HIV) disease	B20-B24	Suppressed	1.5
Influenza and pneumonia	J09-J18	7.8	13.8
Intentional self-harm	X60-X84	15.7	14.1
Malnutrition	E40-E46	Unreliable	2.3
Obesity and other hyperalimentation	E65-E68	Suppressed	2.1
Renal failure	N17-N19	20.9	12.6
Transport accidents	V01-V99	9.4	12.3
Viral hepatitis	B15-B19	Suppressed	1.2

Note: (a) ICD-10 = International Classification of Diseases 10th Revision; (1) Mortality rates are a three-year average covering 2017-2019; (2) Figures cover Clarke County; Data are suppressed when the data meet the criteria for confidentiality constraints; Mortality rates are flagged as unreliable when the rate would be calculated with a numerator of 20 or less.
Source: Centers for Disease Control and Prevention, National Center for Health Statistics. Underlying Cause of Death 1999-2019 on CDC WONDER Online Database

Health Insurance Coverage

Area	With Health Insurance	With Private Health Insurance	With Public Health Insurance	Without Health Insurance	Population Under Age 19 Without Health Insurance
City	86.5	68.5	26.9	13.5	7.3
MSA[1]	87.6	69.5	28.5	12.4	6.7
U.S.	91.2	67.9	35.1	8.8	5.1

Note: Figures are percentages that cover the civilian noninstitutionalized population; (1) Figures cover the Athens-Clarke County, GA Metropolitan Statistical Area
Source: U.S. Census Bureau, 2015-2019 American Community Survey 5-Year Estimates

Number of Medical Professionals

Area	MDs[3]	DOs[3,4]	Dentists	Podiatrists	Chiropractors	Optometrists
County[1] (number)	399	19	69	6	27	21
County[1] (rate[2])	313.5	14.9	53.8	4.7	21.0	16.4
U.S. (rate[2])	282.9	22.7	71.2	6.2	28.1	16.9

13059
Note: Data as of 2019 unless noted; (1) Data covers Clarke County; (2) Rate per 100,000 population; (3) Data as of 2018 and includes all active, non-federal physicians; (4) Doctor of Osteopathic Medicine
Source: U.S. Department of Health and Human Services, Health Resources and Services Administration, Bureau of Health Professions, Area Resource File (ARF) 2019-2020

EDUCATION

Public School District Statistics

District Name	Schls	Pupils	Pupil/Teacher Ratio	Minority Pupils[1] (%)	Free Lunch Eligible[2] (%)	IEP[3] (%)
Clarke County	21	13,512	11.7	79.1	92.0	14.3

Note: Table includes school districts with 2,000 or more students; (1) Percentage of students that are not non-Hispanic white; (2) Percentage of students that are eligible for the free lunch program; (3) Percentage of students that have an Individualized Education Program.
Source: U.S. Department of Education, National Center for Education Statistics, Common Core of Data, Local Education Agency (School District) Universe Survey: School Year 2018-2019; U.S. Department of Education, National Center for Education Statistics, Common Core of Data, Public Elementary/Secondary School Universe Survey: School Year 2018-2019

Highest Level of Education

Area	Less than H.S.	H.S. Diploma	Some College, No Deg.	Associate Degree	Bachelor's Degree	Master's Degree	Prof. School Degree	Doctorate Degree
City	12.1	19.8	17.1	6.9	22.1	13.4	3.0	5.6
MSA[1]	12.2	24.5	16.8	7.1	19.9	11.8	3.1	4.5
U.S.	12.0	27.0	20.4	8.5	19.8	8.8	2.1	1.4

Note: Figures cover persons age 25 and over; (1) Figures cover the Athens-Clarke County, GA Metropolitan Statistical Area
Source: U.S. Census Bureau, 2015-2019 American Community Survey 5-Year Estimates

Educational Attainment by Race

Area	High School Graduate or Higher (%) Total	White	Black	Asian	Hisp.[2]	Bachelor's Degree or Higher (%) Total	White	Black	Asian	Hisp.[2]
City	87.9	90.9	81.5	94.5	57.0	44.0	54.8	18.6	73.2	19.8
MSA[1]	87.8	90.1	80.3	91.0	60.0	39.4	44.5	17.6	69.9	22.2
U.S.	88.0	89.9	86.0	87.1	68.7	32.1	33.5	21.6	54.3	16.4

Note: Figures shown cover persons 25 years old and over; (1) Figures cover the Athens-Clarke County, GA Metropolitan Statistical Area; (2) People of Hispanic origin can be of any race
Source: U.S. Census Bureau, 2015-2019 American Community Survey 5-Year Estimates

School Enrollment by Grade and Control

Area	Preschool (%) Public	Private	Kindergarten (%) Public	Private	Grades 1 - 4 (%) Public	Private	Grades 5 - 8 (%) Public	Private	Grades 9 - 12 (%) Public	Private
City	67.9	32.1	92.6	7.4	91.9	8.1	88.8	11.2	88.5	11.5
MSA[1]	67.9	32.1	90.9	9.1	90.1	9.9	86.0	14.0	86.7	13.3
U.S.	59.1	40.9	87.6	12.4	89.5	10.5	89.4	10.6	90.1	9.9

Note: Figures shown cover persons 3 years old and over; (1) Figures cover the Athens-Clarke County, GA Metropolitan Statistical Area
Source: U.S. Census Bureau, 2015-2019 American Community Survey 5-Year Estimates

Higher Education

Four-Year Colleges Public	Private Non-profit	Private For-profit	Two-Year Colleges Public	Private Non-profit	Private For-profit	Medical Schools[1]	Law Schools[2]	Voc/Tech[3]
1	0	0	1	0	0	0	1	1

Note: Figures cover institutions located within the city limits and include main campuses only; (1) includes schools accredited by the Liaison Committee on Medical Education and the American Osteopathic Association's Commission on Osteopathic College Accreditation; (2) includes ABA-accredited schools, schools with provisional ABA accreditation, and state accredited schools; (3) includes all schools with programs that are less than 2 years.
Source: National Center for Education Statistics, Integrated Postsecondary Education System (IPEDS), 2019-20; Wikipedia, List of Medical Schools in the United States, accessed April 2, 2021; Wikipedia, List of Law Schools in the United States, accessed April 2, 2021

According to *U.S. News & World Report*, the Athens-Clarke County, GA metro area is home to one of the top 200 national universities in the U.S.: **University of Georgia** (#47 tie). The indicators used to capture academic quality fall into a number of categories: assessment by administrators at peer institutions; retention of students; faculty resources; student selectivity; financial resources; alumni giving; high school counselor ratings of colleges; and graduation rate. *U.S. News & World Report, "America's Best Colleges 2021"*

According to *U.S. News & World Report*, the Athens-Clarke County, GA metro area is home to one of the top 100 law schools in the U.S.: **University of Georgia** (#27 tie). The rankings are based on a weighted average of 12 measures of quality: peer assessment score; assessment score by lawyers/judges; median LSAT scores; median undergrad GPA; acceptance rate; employment rates for graduates; placement success; bar passage rate; faculty resources; expenditures per student; student/faculty ratio; and library resources. *U.S. News & World Report, "America's Best Graduate Schools, Law, 2022"*

Athens, Georgia

According to *U.S. News & World Report,* the Athens-Clarke County, GA metro area is home to one of the top 75 business schools in the U.S.: **University of Georgia (Terry)** (#39 tie). The rankings are based on a weighted average of the following nine measures: quality assessment; peer assessment; recruiter assessment; placement success; mean starting salary and bonus; student selectivity; mean GMAT and GRE scores; mean undergraduate GPA; and acceptance rate. *U.S. News & World Report,* "America's Best Graduate Schools, Business, 2022"

EMPLOYERS

Major Employers

Company Name	Industry
Athens Regional Health Care	Healthcare
Athens-Clarke County	Government
Baldor	Industrial motors
Burton+Burton	Balloons & gifts
Carrier Transicold	Truck refrigeration units
Caterpillar	Excavators
Certainteed	Fiberglass insulation
Clarke County School District	Education
DialAmerica	Telemarketing
McCann	Aerospace products
Merial	Animal health products
Noramco	Medical grade products
Pilgrim's	Food processing
Power Partners	Transformers, chillers, solar panels
Skaps	Non-woven plastics
St. Mary's Healthcare	Healthcare
University of Georgia	Higher education

Note: Companies shown are located within the Athens-Clarke County, GA Metropolitan Statistical Area.
Source: Hoovers.com; Wikipedia

PUBLIC SAFETY

Crime Rate

Area	All Crimes	Violent Crimes				Property Crimes		
		Murder	Rape[3]	Robbery	Aggrav. Assault	Burglary	Larceny-Theft	Motor Vehicle Theft
City	3,562.0	4.8	45.6	98.5	266.6	546.8	2,415.5	184.1
Suburbs[1]	1,855.9	1.2	18.1	14.5	111.2	289.0	1,349.3	72.5
Metro[2]	2,882.3	3.4	34.7	65.0	204.7	444.1	1,990.8	139.7
U.S.	2,757.7	5.3	41.7	98.6	249.2	429.7	1,695.5	237.7

Note: Figures are crimes per 100,000 population; (1) All areas within the metro area that are located outside the city limits; (2) Figures cover the Athens-Clarke County, GA Metropolitan Statistical Area; (3) All figures shown were reported using the revised Uniform Crime Reporting (UCR) definition of rape.
Source: FBI Uniform Crime Reports, 2017 (data for 2019 was not available)

Hate Crimes

Area	Number of Quarters Reported	Number of Incidents per Bias Motivation					
		Race/Ethnicity/Ancestry	Religion	Sexual Orientation	Disability	Gender	Gender Identity
City	n/a	n/a	n/a	n/a	n/a	n/a	n/a
U.S.	4	3,963	1,521	1,195	157	69	198

Note: n/a not available.
Source: Federal Bureau of Investigation, Hate Crime Statistics 2019

Identity Theft Consumer Reports

Area	Reports	Reports per 100,000 Population	Rank[2]
MSA[1]	635	297	124
U.S.	1,387,615	423	-

Note: (1) Figures cover the Athens-Clarke County, GA Metropolitan Statistical Area; (2) Rank ranges from 1 to 391 where 1 indicates greatest number of identity theft reports per 100,000 population
Source: Federal Trade Commission, Consumer Sentinel Network Data Book 2020

Fraud and Other Consumer Reports

Area	Reports	Reports per 100,000 Population	Rank[2]
MSA[1]	1,190	557	330
U.S.	3,385,133	1,031	-

Note: (1) Figures cover the Athens-Clarke County, GA Metropolitan Statistical Area; (2) Rank ranges from 1 to 391 where 1 indicates greatest number of fraud and other consumer reports per 100,000 population
Source: Federal Trade Commission, Consumer Sentinel Network Data Book 2020

POLITICS

2020 Presidential Election Results

Area	Biden	Trump	Jorgensen	Hawkins	Other
Clarke County	70.1	28.1	1.6	0.1	0.1
U.S.	51.3	46.8	1.2	0.3	0.5

Note: Results are percentages and may not add to 100% due to rounding
Source: Dave Leip's Atlas of U.S. Presidential Elections

SPORTS

Professional Sports Teams

Team Name	League	Year Established

No teams are located in the metro area
Source: Wikipedia, Major Professional Sports Teams of the United States and Canada, April 6, 2021

CLIMATE

Average and Extreme Temperatures

Temperature	Jan	Feb	Mar	Apr	May	Jun	Jul	Aug	Sep	Oct	Nov	Dec	Yr.
Extreme High (°F)	79	80	85	93	95	101	105	102	98	95	84	77	105
Average High (°F)	52	56	64	73	80	86	88	88	82	73	63	54	72
Average Temp. (°F)	43	46	53	62	70	77	79	79	73	63	53	45	62
Average Low (°F)	33	36	42	51	59	66	70	69	64	52	42	35	52
Extreme Low (°F)	-8	5	10	26	37	46	53	55	36	28	3	0	-8

Note: Figures cover the years 1945-1990
Source: National Climatic Data Center, International Station Meteorological Climate Summary, 9/96

Average Precipitation/Snowfall/Humidity

Precip./Humidity	Jan	Feb	Mar	Apr	May	Jun	Jul	Aug	Sep	Oct	Nov	Dec	Yr.
Avg. Precip. (in.)	4.7	4.6	5.7	4.3	4.0	3.5	5.1	3.6	3.4	2.8	3.8	4.2	49.8
Avg. Snowfall (in.)	1	1	Tr	Tr	0	0	0	0	0	Tr	Tr	Tr	2
Avg. Rel. Hum. 7am (%)	79	77	78	78	82	83	88	89	88	84	81	79	82
Avg. Rel. Hum. 4pm (%)	56	50	48	45	49	52	57	56	56	51	52	55	52

Note: Figures cover the years 1945-1990; Tr = Trace amounts (<0.05 in. of rain; <0.5 in. of snow)
Source: National Climatic Data Center, International Station Meteorological Climate Summary, 9/96

Weather Conditions

Temperature			Daytime Sky			Precipitation		
10°F & below	32°F & below	90°F & above	Clear	Partly cloudy	Cloudy	0.01 inch or more precip.	0.1 inch or more snow/ice	Thunderstorms
1	49	38	98	147	120	116	3	48

Note: Figures are average number of days per year and cover the years 1945-1990
Source: National Climatic Data Center, International Station Meteorological Climate Summary, 9/96

HAZARDOUS WASTE

Superfund Sites

The Athens-Clarke County, GA metro area has no sites on the EPA's Superfund Final National Priorities List. There are a total of 1,375 Superfund sites with a status of proposed or final on the list in the U.S. *U.S. Environmental Protection Agency, National Priorities List, April 7, 2021*

AIR QUALITY

Air Quality Trends: Ozone

	1990	1995	2000	2005	2010	2015	2016	2017	2018	2019
MSA[1]	n/a	n/a	n/a	n/a	n/a	n/a	n/a	n/a	n/a	n/a
U.S.	0.088	0.089	0.082	0.080	0.073	0.068	0.069	0.068	0.069	0.065

Note: (1) Data covers the Athens-Clarke County, GA Metropolitan Statistical Area; n/a not available. The values shown are the composite ozone concentration averages among trend sites based on the highest fourth daily maximum 8-hour concentration in parts per million. These trends are based on sites having an adequate record of monitoring data during the trend period. Data from exceptional events are included.
Source: U.S. Environmental Protection Agency, Air Quality Monitoring Information, "Air Quality Trends by City, 1990-2019"

Air Quality Index

Area	Percent of Days when Air Quality was...[2]					AQI Statistics[2]	
	Good	Moderate	Unhealthy for Sensitive Groups	Unhealthy	Very Unhealthy	Maximum	Median
MSA[1]	67.1	32.9	0.0	0.0	0.0	87	44

Note: (1) Data covers the Athens-Clarke County, GA Metropolitan Statistical Area; (2) Based on 365 days with AQI data in 2019. Air Quality Index (AQI) is an index for reporting daily air quality. EPA calculates the AQI for five major air pollutants regulated by the Clean Air Act: ground-level ozone, particle pollution (aka particulate matter), carbon monoxide, sulfur dioxide, and nitrogen dioxide. The AQI runs from 0 to 500. The higher the AQI value, the greater the level of air pollution and the greater the health concern. There are six AQI categories: "Good" AQI is between 0 and 50. Air quality is considered satisfactory; "Moderate" AQI is between 51 and 100. Air quality is acceptable; "Unhealthy for Sensitive Groups" When AQI values are between 101 and 150, members of sensitive groups may experience health effects; "Unhealthy" When AQI values are between 151 and 200 everyone may begin to experience health effects; "Very Unhealthy" AQI values between 201 and 300 trigger a health alert; "Hazardous" AQI values over 300 trigger warnings of emergency conditions (not shown).
Source: U.S. Environmental Protection Agency, Air Quality Index Report, 2019

Air Quality Index Pollutants

Area	Percent of Days when AQI Pollutant was...[2]					
	Carbon Monoxide	Nitrogen Dioxide	Ozone	Sulfur Dioxide	Particulate Matter 2.5	Particulate Matter 10
MSA[1]	0.0	0.0	37.3	0.0	62.7	0.0

Note: (1) Data covers the Athens-Clarke County, GA Metropolitan Statistical Area; (2) Based on 365 days with AQI data in 2019. The Air Quality Index (AQI) is an index for reporting daily air quality. EPA calculates the AQI for five major air pollutants regulated by the Clean Air Act: ground-level ozone, particle pollution (also known as particulate matter), carbon monoxide, sulfur dioxide, and nitrogen dioxide. The AQI runs from 0 to 500. The higher the AQI value, the greater the level of air pollution and the greater the health concern.
Source: U.S. Environmental Protection Agency, Air Quality Index Report, 2019

Maximum Air Pollutant Concentrations: Particulate Matter, Ozone, CO and Lead

	Particulate Matter 10 (ug/m^3)	Particulate Matter 2.5 Wtd AM (ug/m^3)	Particulate Matter 2.5 24-Hr (ug/m^3)	Ozone (ppm)	Carbon Monoxide (ppm)	Lead (ug/m^3)
MSA[1] Level	n/a	9.8	21	0.063	n/a	n/a
NAAQS[2]	150	15	35	0.075	9	0.15
Met NAAQS[2]	n/a	Yes	Yes	Yes	n/a	n/a

Note: (1) Data covers the Athens-Clarke County, GA Metropolitan Statistical Area; Data from exceptional events are included; (2) National Ambient Air Quality Standards; ppm = parts per million; ug/m^3 = micrograms per cubic meter; n/a not available.
Concentrations: Particulate Matter 10 (coarse particulate)—highest second maximum 24-hour concentration; Particulate Matter 2.5 Wtd AM (fine particulate)—highest weighted annual mean concentration; Particulate Matter 2.5 24-Hour (fine particulate)—highest 98th percentile 24-hour concentration; Ozone—highest fourth daily maximum 8-hour concentration; Carbon Monoxide—highest second maximum non-overlapping 8-hour concentration; Lead—maximum running 3-month average
Source: U.S. Environmental Protection Agency, Air Quality Monitoring Information, "Air Quality Statistics by City, 2019"

Maximum Air Pollutant Concentrations: Nitrogen Dioxide and Sulfur Dioxide

	Nitrogen Dioxide AM (ppb)	Nitrogen Dioxide 1-Hr (ppb)	Sulfur Dioxide AM (ppb)	Sulfur Dioxide 1-Hr (ppb)	Sulfur Dioxide 24-Hr (ppb)
MSA[1] Level	n/a	n/a	n/a	n/a	n/a
NAAQS[2]	53	100	30	75	140
Met NAAQS[2]	n/a	n/a	n/a	n/a	n/a

Note: (1) Data covers the Athens-Clarke County, GA Metropolitan Statistical Area; Data from exceptional events are included; (2) National Ambient Air Quality Standards; ppm = parts per million; ug/m^3 = micrograms per cubic meter; n/a not available.
Concentrations: Nitrogen Dioxide AM—highest arithmetic mean concentration; Nitrogen Dioxide 1-Hr—highest 98th percentile 1-hour daily maximum concentration; Sulfur Dioxide AM—highest annual mean concentration; Sulfur Dioxide 1-Hr—highest 99th percentile 1-hour daily maximum concentration; Sulfur Dioxide 24-Hr—highest second maximum 24-hour concentration
Source: U.S. Environmental Protection Agency, Air Quality Monitoring Information, "Air Quality Statistics by City, 2019"

Atlanta, Georgia

Background

Atlanta was born of a rough-and-tumble past, first as a natural outgrowth of a thriving railroad network in the 1840s, and second as a resilient go-getter that proudly rose again above the rubble of the Civil War.

Blanketed over the rolling hills of the Piedmont Plateau, at the foot of the Blue Ridge Mountains, Georgia's capital stands 1,000 feet above sea level. Atlanta is located in the northwest corner of Georgia where the terrain is rolling to hilly, and slopes downward to the east, west, and south.

Atlanta proper begins at the "terminus," or zero mile mark, of the now defunct Western and Atlantic Railroad Line. However its metropolitan area comprises 28 counties that include Fulton, DeKalb, Clayton and Gwinnet, among others. Population-wise, Atlanta is the largest city in the southeast United States, and has been growing at a steady rate for the last decade. Within the city itself, Atlanta's has a diversified economy that allows for employment in a variety of sectors such as manufacturing, retail, and government.

The city hosts many of the nation's Fortune 500 company headquarters, including CNN, as well as the nation's Centers for Disease Control and Prevention (CDC). The city boasts an involved city government that seeks to work closely with its business community, due in part to a change in the city charter in 1974, when greater administrative powers were vested in the mayoral office, and the city inaugurated its first black mayor.

While schools in the city remain predominantly black and schools in its suburbs predominantly white, Atlanta boasts a racially progressive climate. The Martin Luther King, Jr. Historic Site and Preservation District is located in the Sweet Auburn neighborhood, which includes King's birth home and the Ebenezer Baptist Church, where both he and his father preached. The city's consortium of black colleges that includes Morehouse College and the Interdenominational Theological Center testifies to the city's appreciation for a people who have always been one-third of Atlanta's population. Atlanta continues to be a major regional center for film and television production, with Tyler Perry Studios, Turner Studios and EVE/ScreenGems Studio in the city.

> Governor Kemp sued Atlanta Mayor Keisha Lance Bottoms to block the city from enforcing its mandate to wear a mask in public and other rules related to the COVID-19 pandemic.

Indeed, King is one of Atlanta's two Nobel Peace Prize winners. The second, former President Jimmy Carter, famously of Plains, Georgia, also brings his name to Atlanta via the Carter Center. Devoted to human rights, the center is operated with neighboring Emory University, and sits adjacent to the Jimmy Carter Library and Museum on a hill overlooking the city. Habitat for Humanity, also founded by Carter, is headquartered in Atlanta. The city's largest city park, Westside Park at Bellwood Quarry is scheduled for completion in the 2020s.

Hartsfield-Jackson Atlanta International Airport, the world's busiest passenger airport, underwent significant expansion in recent years. MARTA, the city's public transport system, is the nation's 9th largest and transports on average 500,000 passengers daily on a 48-mile, 38-station rapid rail system with connections to hundreds of bus routes.

The Appalachian chain of mountains, the Gulf of Mexico, and the Atlantic Ocean influence Atlanta's climate. Temperatures are moderate to hot throughout the year, but extended periods of heat are unusual and the city rarely reaches 100-degrees. Atlanta winters are mild with a few, short-lived cold spells. Summers can be humid.

Rankings

General Rankings

- The Atlanta metro area was identified as one of America's fastest-growing areas in terms of population and business growth by *MagnifyMoney*. The area ranked #32 out of 35. The 100 most populous metro areas in the U.S. were evaluated on their change from 2011-2016 in the following categories: people and housing; workforce and employment opportunities; growing industry. *www.businessinsider.com, "The 35 Cities in the US with the Biggest Influx of People, the Most Work Opportunities, and the Hottest Business Growth," August 12, 2018*

- Atlanta was selected as one of the best places to live in America by *Outside Magazine*. Criteria included population, park acreage, neighborhood and resident diversity, new and upcoming things of interest, and opportunities for outdoor adventure. *Outside Magazine, "The 12 Best Places to Live in 2019," July 11, 2019*

- The human resources consulting firm Mercer ranked 231 major cities worldwide in terms of overall quality of life. Atlanta ranked #64. Criteria: political, social, economic, and socio-cultural factors; medical and health considerations; schools and education; public services and transportation; recreation; consumer goods; housing; and natural environment. *Mercer, "Mercer 2019 Quality of Living Survey," March 13, 2019*

Business/Finance Rankings

- The Brookings Institution ranked the nation's largest cities based on income inequality. Atlanta was ranked #1 (#1 = greatest inequality). Criteria: the "95/20 ratio," a figure representing the income at which a household earns more than 95 percent of all other households, divided by the income at which a household earns more than only 20 percent of all other households. *Brookings Institution, "Household Income Inequality, Largest Cities of 97 Large U.S. Metro Areas, 2014-2016," February 5, 2018*

- The Brookings Institution ranked the 100 largest metro areas in the U.S. based on income inequality. Atlanta was ranked #26 (#1 = greatest inequality). Criteria: the "95/20 ratio," a figure representing the income at which a household earns more than 95 percent of all other households, divided by the income at which a household earns more than only 20 percent of all other households. *Brookings Institution, "Household Income Inequality, 100 Largest U.S. Metro Areas, 2014-2016," February 5, 2018*

- *Forbes* ranked the 100 largest metro areas in the U.S. in terms of the "Best Cities for Young Professionals." The Atlanta metro area ranked #21 out of 25. Criteria: median rent of a two-bedroom apartment; job growth and unemployment rate; median salary of college graduates with 5 or less years of work experience; networking opportunities; social outlook; percentage of population 25 years of age and older with college degrees. *Forbes.com, "America's 25 Best Cities for Young Professionals in 2017," May 22, 2017*

- Payscale.com ranked the 32 largest metro areas in terms of wage growth. The Atlanta metro area ranked #21. Criteria: private-sector and education professional wage growth between the 4th quarter of 2019 and the 4th quarter of 2020. *PayScale, "Wage Trends by Metro Area-4th Quarter," January 11, 2021*

- The Atlanta metro area was identified as one of the most debt-ridden places in America by the finance site Credit.com. The metro area was ranked #7. Criteria: residents' average credit card debt as well as median income. *Credit.com, "25 Cities With the Most Credit Card Debt," February 28, 2018*

- Atlanta was identified as one of America's most frugal metro areas by *Coupons.com*. The city ranked #8 out of 25. Criteria: digital coupon usage. *Coupons.com, "America's Most Frugal Cities of 2017," March 22, 2018*

- Atlanta was cited as one of America's top metros for new and expanded facility projects in 2020. The area ranked #4 in the large metro area category (population over 1 million). *Site Selection, "Top Metros of 2020," March 2021*

- Atlanta was identified as one of the happiest cities to work in by CareerBliss.com, an online community for career advancement. The city ranked #3 out of 10. Criteria: an employee's relationship with his or her boss and co-workers; daily tasks; general work environment; compensation; opportunities for advancement; company culture and job reputation; and resources. *Businesswire.com, "CareerBliss Happiest Cities to Work 2019," February 12, 2019*

- The Atlanta metro area appeared on the Milken Institute "2021 Best Performing Cities" list. Rank: #21 out of 200 large metro areas (population over 250,000). Criteria: job growth; wage and salary growth; high-tech output growth; housing affordability; household broadband access. *Milken Institute, "Best-Performing Cities 2021," February 16, 2021*

- *Forbes* ranked the 200 most populous metro areas to determine the nation's "Best Places for Business and Careers." The Atlanta metro area was ranked #13. Criteria: costs (business and living); job growth (past and projected); income growth; quality of life; educational attainment (college and high school); projected economic growth; cultural and leisure opportunities; workplace tolerance laws; net migration patterns. *Forbes, "The Best Places for Business and Careers 2019: Seattle Still On Top," October 30, 2019*
- Mercer Human Resources Consulting ranked 209 cities worldwide in terms of cost-of-living. Atlanta ranked #60 (the lower the ranking, the higher the cost-of-living). The survey measured the comparative cost of over 200 items (such as housing, food, clothing, household goods, transportation, and entertainment) in each location. *Mercer, "2020 Cost of Living Survey," June 9, 2020*

Children/Family Rankings

- Atlanta was selected as one of the most playful cities in the U.S. by KaBOOM! The organization's Playful City USA initiative honors cities and towns across the nation that have made their communities more playable. Criteria: pledging to integrate play as a solution to challenges in their communities; making it easy for children to get active and balanced play; creating more family-friendly and innovative communities as a result. *KaBOOM! National Campaign for Play, "2017 Playful City USA Communities"*

Culture/Performing Arts Rankings

- Atlanta was selected as one of the 25 best cities for moviemakers in North America. COVID-19 has spurred a quest for great film cities that offer more creative space, lower costs, and more great outdoors. NYC & LA were intentionally excluded. Criteria: longstanding reputations as film-friendly communities; efforts to deal with pandemic-specific challenges; and establish appropriate COVID-19 guidelines. The city was ranked #2. *MovieMaker Magazine, "Best Places to Live and Work as a Moviemaker, 2021," January 26, 2021*

Dating/Romance Rankings

- Atlanta was selected as one of the nation's most romantic cities with 100,000 or more residents by Amazon.com. The city ranked #9 of 20. Criteria: per capita sales of romance novels, relationship books, romantic comedy movies, romantic music, and sexual wellness products. *Amazon.com, "Top 20 Most Romantic Cities in the U.S.," February 1, 2017*

Education Rankings

- Personal finance website *WalletHub* analyzed the 150 largest U.S. metropolitan statistical areas to determine where the most educated Americans are putting their degrees to work. Criteria: education levels; percentage of workers with degrees; education quality and attainment gap; public school quality rankings; quality and enrollment of each metro area's universities. Atlanta was ranked #28 (#1 = most educated city). *www.WalletHub.com, "Most and Least Educated Cities in America," July 20, 2020*
- Atlanta was selected as one of America's most literate cities. The city ranked #6 out of the 84 largest U.S. cities. Criteria: number of booksellers; library resources; Internet resources; educational attainment; periodical publishing resources; newspaper circulation. *Central Connecticut State University, "America's Most Literate Cities, 2018," February 2019*

Environmental Rankings

- The U.S. Environmental Protection Agency (EPA) released a list of U.S. metropolitan areas with the most ENERGY STAR certified buildings in 2019. The Atlanta metro area was ranked #5 out of 25. *U.S. Environmental Protection Agency, "2020 Energy Star Top Cities," March 2020*
- Atlanta was highlighted as one of the 25 metro areas most polluted by year-round particle pollution (Annual PM 2.5) in the U.S. during 2016 through 2018. The area ranked #23. *American Lung Association, "State of the Air 2020," April 21, 2020*

Health/Fitness Rankings

- For each of the 100 largest cities in the United States, the American Fitness Index®, published by the American College of Sports Medicine and the Anthem Foundation, evaluated community infrastructure and 33 health behaviors including preventive health, levels of chronic disease conditions, pedestrian safety, air quality, and community resources that support physical activity. Atlanta ranked #18 for "community fitness." *americanfitnessindex.org, "2020 ACSM American Fitness Index Summary Report," July 14, 2020*

- The Atlanta metro area was identified as one of the worst cities for bed bugs in America by pest control company Orkin. The area ranked #13 out of 50 based on the number of bed bug treatments Orkin performed from December 2019 to November 2020. *Orkin, "New Year, New Top City on Orkin's 2021 Bed Bug Cities List: Chicago," February 1, 2021*

- Atlanta was identified as a "2021 Spring Allergy Capital." The area ranked #42 out of 100. Three groups of factors were used to identify the most challenging cities for people with allergies during the spring season: annual spring pollen levels; over the counter medicine use; number of board-certified allergy specialists. *Asthma and Allergy Foundation of America, "Spring Allergy Capitals 2021," February 23, 2021*

- Atlanta was identified as a "2021 Fall Allergy Capital." The area ranked #61 out of 100. Three groups of factors were used to identify the most challenging cities for people with allergies during the fall season: annual fall pollen levels; over the counter medicine use; number of board-certified allergy specialists. *Asthma and Allergy Foundation of America, "Fall Allergy Capitals 2021," February 23, 2021*

- Atlanta was identified as a "2019 Asthma Capital." The area ranked #68 out of the nation's 100 largest metropolitan areas. Criteria: estimated asthma prevalence; crude death rate from asthma; and ER visits due to asthma. Risk factors analyzed but not factored in the rankings: annual pollen score; annual air quality; public smoking laws; number of board-certified asthma specialists; rescue medication use; controller medication use; uninsured rate; poverty rate. *Asthma and Allergy Foundation of America, "Asthma Capitals 2019: The Most Challenging Places to Live With Asthma," May 7, 2019*

Pet Rankings

- Atlanta appeared on *The Dogington Post* site as one of the top cities for dog lovers, ranking #18 out of 20. The real estate brokerage, Redfin and Rover, the largest pet sitter and dog walker network, compiled a list from over 14,000 U.S. cities to come up with a "Rover Rank." Criteria: highest count of dog walks, the city's Walk Score®, for-sale home listings that mention "dog," number of dog walkers and pet sitters and the hours spent and distance logged. *www.dogingtonpost.com, "The 20 Most Dog-Friendly Cities of 2019," April 4, 2019*

Real Estate Rankings

- FitSmallBusiness looked at 50 of the largest metropolitan areas in the U.S. to determine which metro was the best to start a real estate business. Data was compiled from such sources as: Zillow, Trulia, U.S. Census Bureau, and the Bureau of Labor Statistics. Criteria: location; inventory; annual wages; median sales price of homes; days on the market; median price cut percentage; and other factors that would influence real estate professional growth. The Atlanta metro area ranked #23. *fitsmallbusiness.com, "The Best Cities to Become a Real Estate Agent in 2018," January 30, 2018*

- *WalletHub* compared the most populated U.S. cities to determine which had the best markets for real estate agents. Atlanta ranked #22 where demand was high and pay was the best. Criteria: sales per agent; annual median wage for real-estate agents; monthly average starting salary for real estate agents; real estate job density and competition; unemployment rate; home turnover rate; housing-market health index; and other relevant metrics. *www.WalletHub.com, "2019's Best Places to Be a Real Estate Agent," April 24, 2019*

- According to Penske Truck Rental, the Atlanta metro area was named the #2 moving destination in 2019, based on one-way consumer truck rental reservations made through Penske's website, rental locations, and reservations call center. *gopenske.com/blog, "Penske Truck Rental's 2019 Top Moving Destinations," January 22, 2020*

- Atlanta was ranked #126 out of 268 metro areas in terms of housing affordability in 2020 by the National Association of Home Builders (#1 = most affordable). Criteria: the share of homes sold in that area affordable to a family earning the local median income, based on standard mortgage underwriting criteria. *National Association of Home Builders®, NAHB-Wells Fargo Housing Opportunity Index, 4th Quarter 2020*

Safety Rankings

- Allstate ranked the 200 largest cities in America in terms of driver safety. Atlanta ranked #178. Criteria: internal property damage claims over a two-year period from January 2016 to December 2017. The report helps increase the importance of safety and awareness behind the wheel. *Allstate, "Allstate America's Best Drivers Report, 2019" June 24, 2019*

- The National Insurance Crime Bureau ranked 384 metro areas in the U.S. in terms of per capita rates of vehicle theft. The Atlanta metro area ranked #74 (#1 = highest rate). Criteria: number of vehicle theft offenses per 100,000 inhabitants in 2019. *National Insurance Crime Bureau, "Hot Spots 2019," July 21, 2020*

Seniors/Retirement Rankings

- From its Best Cities for Successful Aging indexes, the Milken Institute generated rankings for metropolitan areas, weighing data in nine categories—health care, wellness, living arrangements, transportation and convenience, financial characteristics, education, employment, community engagement, and overall livability. The Atlanta metro area was ranked #62 overall in the large metro area category. *Milken Institute, "Best Cities for Successful Aging, 2017" March 14, 2017*

Sports/Recreation Rankings

- Atlanta was chosen as one of America's best cities for bicycling. The city ranked #42 out of 50. Criteria: cycling infrastructure that is safe and friendly for all ages; energy and bike culture. The editors evaluated cities with populations of 100,000 or more. *Bicycling, "The 50 Best Bike Cities in America," October 10, 2018*

Transportation Rankings

- Atlanta was identified as one of the most congested metro areas in the U.S. The area ranked #8 out of 10. Criteria: yearly delay per auto commuter in hours. *Texas A&M Transportation Institute, "2019 Urban Mobility Report," December 2019*

- According to the INRIX "2019 Global Traffic Scorecard," Atlanta was identified as one of the most congested metro areas in the U.S. The area ranked #10 out of 10. Criteria: average annual time spent in traffic and average cost of congestion per motorist. *Inrix.com, "Congestion Costs Each American Nearly 100 hours, $1,400 A Year," March 9, 2020*

Women/Minorities Rankings

- *Travel + Leisure* listed the best cities in and around the US for a memorable and fun girls' trip, even on a budget. Whether it is for a special occasion or just to get away, Atlanta is sure to have something for all the ladies in your tribe. *Travel + Leisure, "25 Girls' Weekend Getaways That Won't Break the Bank," June 8, 2020*

- Atlanta was selected as one of the gayest cities in America by *The Advocate*. The city ranked #6 out of 25. Criteria, among many: Trans Pride parades/festivals; gay rugby teams; lesbian bars; LGBT centers; theater screenings of "Moonlight"; LGBT-inclusive nondiscrimination ordinances; and gay bowling teams. *The Advocate, "Queerest Cities in America 2017" January 12, 2017*

- Personal finance website *WalletHub* compared more than 180 U.S. cities across two key dimensions, "Hispanic Business-Friendliness" and "Hispanic Purchasing Power," to arrive at the most favorable conditions for Hispanic entrepreneurs. Atlanta was ranked #24 out of 182. Criteria includes: share of Hispanic-Owned Businesses; Hispanic entrepreneurship rate to median annual income of Hispanics; Small Business-Friendliness score; cost of living; and number of Hispanics with at least a bachelor's degree. *WalletHub.com, "2019's Best Cities for Hispanic Entrepreneurs," May 1, 2019*

Miscellaneous Rankings

- *MoveHub* ranked 446 hipster cities across 20 countries, using its *alternative* Hipster Index and Atlanta came out as #14 among the top 50. Criteria: population over 150,000; number of vintage boutiques; density of tattoo parlors; vegan places to eat; coffee shops; and density of vinyl record stores. *www.movehub.com, "The Hipster Index: Brighton Pips Portland to Global Top Spot," February 20, 2020*

- In its roundup of St. Patrick's Day parades "Gayot" listed the best festivals and parades of all things Irish. The festivities in Atlanta as among the best. *www.gayot.com, "Best St. Patrick's Day Parades," March 2020*

- The watchdog site, Charity Navigator, conducted a study of charities in major markets both to analyze statistical differences in their financial, accountability, and transparency practices and to track year-to-year variations in individual philanthropic communities. The Atlanta metro area was ranked #18 among the 30 metro markets in the rating category of Overall Score. *www.charitynavigator.org, "2017 Metro Market Study," May 1, 2017*

- *WalletHub* compared the 150 most populated U.S. cities to determine their operating efficiency. A "Quality of City Services" score was constructed for each city and then divided by the total budget per capita to reveal which were managed the best. Atlanta ranked #132. Criteria: financial stability; economy; education; safety; health; infrastructure and pollution. *www.WalletHub.com, "2020's Best- & Worst-Run Cities in America," June 29, 2020*

- The National Alliance to End Homelessness listed the 25 most populous metro areas with the highest rate of homelessness. The Atlanta metro area had a high rate of homelessness. Criteria: number of homeless people per 10,000 population in 2016. *National Alliance to End Homelessness, "Homelessness in the 25 Most Populous U.S. Metro Areas," September 1, 2017*

Business Environment

DEMOGRAPHICS

Population Growth

Area	1990 Census	2000 Census	2010 Census	2019* Estimate	Population Growth (%) 1990-2019	Population Growth (%) 2010-2019
City	394,092	416,474	420,003	488,800	24.0	16.4
MSA[1]	3,069,411	4,247,981	5,268,860	5,862,424	91.0	11.3
U.S.	248,709,873	281,421,906	308,745,538	324,697,795	30.6	5.2

Note: (1) Figures cover the Atlanta-Sandy Springs-Roswell, GA Metropolitan Statistical Area; (*) 2015-2019 5-year estimated population
Source: U.S. Census Bureau, 1990 Census, Census 2000, Census 2010, 2015-2019 American Community Survey 5-Year Estimates

Household Size

Area	One	Two	Three	Four	Five	Six	Seven or More	Average Household Size
City	46.8	30.7	10.6	7.2	3.0	1.1	0.7	2.20
MSA[1]	26.8	31.6	17.0	14.3	6.4	2.5	1.4	2.70
U.S.	27.9	33.9	15.6	12.9	6.0	2.3	1.4	2.60

Note: (1) Figures cover the Atlanta-Sandy Springs-Roswell, GA Metropolitan Statistical Area
Source: U.S. Census Bureau, 2015-2019 American Community Survey 5-Year Estimates

Race

Area	White Alone[2] (%)	Black Alone[2] (%)	Asian Alone[2] (%)	AIAN[3] Alone[2] (%)	NHOPI[4] Alone[2] (%)	Other Race Alone[2] (%)	Two or More Races (%)
City	40.9	51.0	4.4	0.3	0.0	1.0	2.4
MSA[1]	53.4	34.2	5.9	0.4	0.0	3.4	2.7
U.S.	72.5	12.7	5.5	0.8	0.2	4.9	3.3

Note: (1) Figures cover the Atlanta-Sandy Springs-Roswell, GA Metropolitan Statistical Area; (2) Alone is defined as not being in combination with one or more other races; (3) American Indian and Alaska Native; (4) Native Hawaiian and Other Pacific Islander
Source: U.S. Census Bureau, 2015-2019 American Community Survey 5-Year Estimates

Hispanic or Latino Origin

Area	Total (%)	Mexican (%)	Puerto Rican (%)	Cuban (%)	Other (%)
City	4.3	2.0	0.6	0.3	1.4
MSA[1]	10.7	5.6	1.0	0.4	3.6
U.S.	18.0	11.2	1.7	0.7	4.3

Note: Persons of Hispanic or Latino origin can be of any race; (1) Figures cover the Atlanta-Sandy Springs-Roswell, GA Metropolitan Statistical Area
Source: U.S. Census Bureau, 2015-2019 American Community Survey 5-Year Estimates

Ancestry

Area	German	Irish	English	American	Italian	Polish	French[2]	Scottish	Dutch
City	6.1	5.6	7.2	5.4	2.6	1.4	1.7	1.8	0.6
MSA[1]	6.6	6.6	7.2	9.2	2.5	1.2	1.4	1.7	0.6
U.S.	13.3	9.7	7.2	6.2	5.1	2.8	2.3	1.7	1.2

Note: Figures are the percentage of the total population reporting a particular ancestry. The nine most commonly reported ancestries in the U.S. are shown. Figures include multiple ancestries (e.g. if a person reported being Irish and Italian, they were included in both columns); (1) Figures cover the Atlanta-Sandy Springs-Roswell, GA Metropolitan Statistical Area; (2) Excludes Basque
Source: U.S. Census Bureau, 2015-2019 American Community Survey 5-Year Estimates

Foreign-born Population

Area	Any Foreign Country	Asia	Mexico	Europe	Caribbean	Central America[2]	South America	Africa	Canada
City	7.6	3.2	0.7	1.3	0.6	0.1	0.6	0.7	0.3
MSA[1]	13.8	4.6	2.6	1.2	1.4	1.1	1.1	1.6	0.2
U.S.	13.6	4.2	3.5	1.5	1.3	1.1	1.0	0.7	0.2

Note: (1) Figures cover the Atlanta-Sandy Springs-Roswell, GA Metropolitan Statistical Area; (2) Excludes Mexico.
Source: U.S. Census Bureau, 2015-2019 American Community Survey 5-Year Estimates

Marital Status

Area	Never Married	Now Married[2]	Separated	Widowed	Divorced
City	55.2	27.3	1.9	5.1	10.5
MSA[1]	35.3	47.4	1.9	4.6	10.8
U.S.	33.4	48.1	1.9	5.8	10.9

Note: Figures are percentages and cover the population 15 years of age and older; (1) Figures cover the Atlanta-Sandy Springs-Roswell, GA Metropolitan Statistical Area; (2) Excludes separated
Source: U.S. Census Bureau, 2015-2019 American Community Survey 5-Year Estimates

Disability by Age

Area	All Ages	Under 18 Years Old	18 to 64 Years Old	65 Years and Over
City	11.9	4.7	9.7	36.8
MSA[1]	10.0	3.5	8.4	32.5
U.S.	12.6	4.2	10.3	34.5

Note: Figures show percent of the civilian noninstitutionalized population that reported having a disability. Disability status is determined from six types of difficulty: vision, hearing, cognitive, ambulatory, self-care, and independent living. For children under 5 years old, hearing and vision difficulty are used to determine disability status. For children between the ages of 5 and 14, disability status is determined from hearing, vision, cognitive, ambulatory, and self-care difficulties. For people aged 15 years and older, they are considered to have a disability if they have difficulty with any one of the six difficulty types; Note: (1) Figures cover the Atlanta-Sandy Springs-Roswell, GA Metropolitan Statistical Area
Source: U.S. Census Bureau, 2015-2019 American Community Survey 5-Year Estimates

Age

Area	Under Age 5	Age 5–19	Age 20–34	Age 35–44	Age 45–54	Age 55–64	Age 65–74	Age 75–84	Age 85+	Median Age
City	5.4	16.9	30.7	13.8	11.8	9.8	6.8	3.4	1.4	33.3
MSA[1]	6.4	21.0	20.6	14.0	14.3	11.8	7.5	3.2	1.1	36.4
U.S.	6.1	19.1	20.7	12.6	13.0	12.9	9.1	4.6	1.9	38.1

Note: (1) Figures cover the Atlanta-Sandy Springs-Roswell, GA Metropolitan Statistical Area
Source: U.S. Census Bureau, 2015-2019 American Community Survey 5-Year Estimates

Gender

Area	Males	Females	Males per 100 Females
City	237,192	251,608	94.3
MSA[1]	2,834,134	3,028,290	93.6
U.S.	159,886,919	164,810,876	97.0

Note: (1) Figures cover the Atlanta-Sandy Springs-Roswell, GA Metropolitan Statistical Area
Source: U.S. Census Bureau, 2015-2019 American Community Survey 5-Year Estimates

Religious Groups by Family

Area	Catholic	Baptist	Non-Den.	Methodist[2]	Lutheran	LDS[3]	Pentecostal	Presbyterian[4]	Muslim[5]	Judaism
MSA[1]	7.5	17.5	6.9	7.9	0.5	0.8	2.6	1.8	0.8	0.6
U.S.	19.1	9.3	4.0	4.0	2.3	2.0	1.9	1.6	0.8	0.7

Note: Figures are the number of adherents as a percentage of the total population; (1) Figures cover the Atlanta-Sandy Springs-Roswell, GA Metropolitan Statistical Area; (2) Methodist/Pietist; (3) Latter Day Saints; (4) Reformed; (5) Figures are estimates
Source: Association of Statisticians of American Religious Bodies, 2010 U.S. Religion Census: Religious Congregations & Membership Study

Religious Groups by Tradition

Area	Catholic	Evangelical Protestant	Mainline Protestant	Other Tradition	Black Protestant	Orthodox
MSA[1]	7.5	26.1	9.8	2.9	3.2	0.3
U.S.	19.1	16.2	7.3	4.3	1.6	0.3

Note: Figures are the number of adherents as a percentage of the total population; (1) Figures cover the Atlanta-Sandy Springs-Roswell, GA Metropolitan Statistical Area
Source: Association of Statisticians of American Religious Bodies, 2010 U.S. Religion Census: Religious Congregations & Membership Study

ECONOMY

Gross Metropolitan Product

Area	2017	2018	2019	2020	Rank[2]
MSA[1]	391.0	409.9	431.6	452.0	10

Note: Figures are in billions of dollars; (1) Figures cover the Atlanta-Sandy Springs-Roswell, GA Metropolitan Statistical Area; (2) Rank is based on 2018 data and ranges from 1 to 381
Source: U.S. Conference of Mayors, U.S. Metro Economies: GMP & Employment 2018-2020, September 2019

Economic Growth

Area	2015-17 (%)	2018 (%)	2019 (%)	2020 (%)	Rank[2]
MSA[1]	3.7	2.8	3.6	2.6	47
U.S.	1.9	2.9	2.3	2.1	—

Note: Figures are real gross metropolitan product (GMP) growth rates and represent average annual percent change; (1) Figures cover the Atlanta-Sandy Springs-Roswell, GA Metropolitan Statistical Area; (2) Rank is based on 2017 2-year average annual percent change and ranges from 1 to 381
Source: U.S. Conference of Mayors, U.S. Metro Economies: GMP & Employment 2018-2020, September 2019

Metropolitan Area Exports

Area	2014	2015	2016	2017	2018	2019	Rank[2]
MSA[1]	19,870.3	19,163.9	20,480.1	21,748.0	24,091.6	25,800.8	14

Note: Figures are in millions of dollars; (1) Figures cover the Atlanta-Sandy Springs-Roswell, GA Metropolitan Statistical Area; (2) Rank is based on 2019 data and ranges from 1 to 386
Source: U.S. Department of Commerce, International Trade Administration, Office of Trade and Economic Analysis, Industry and Analysis, Exports by Metropolitan Area, data extracted March 24, 2021

Building Permits

Area	Single-Family 2018	Single-Family 2019	Pct. Chg.	Multi-Family 2018	Multi-Family 2019	Pct. Chg.	Total 2018	Total 2019	Pct. Chg.
City	1,184	728	-38.5	5,312	2,555	-51.9	6,496	3,283	-49.5
MSA[1]	26,506	26,261	-0.9	12,935	6,575	-49.2	39,441	32,836	-16.7
U.S.	855,300	862,100	0.7	473,500	523,900	10.6	1,328,800	1,386,000	4.3

Note: (1) Figures cover the Atlanta-Sandy Springs-Roswell, GA Metropolitan Statistical Area; Figures represent new, privately-owned housing units authorized (unadjusted data); All permit data are based on estimates with imputation
Source: U.S. Census Bureau, Manufacturing, Mining, and Construction Statistics, Building Permits, 2018, 2019

Bankruptcy Filings

Area	Business Filings 2019	Business Filings 2020	% Chg.	Nonbusiness Filings 2019	Nonbusiness Filings 2020	% Chg.
Fulton County	173	152	-12.1	4,013	2,591	-35.4
U.S.	22,780	21,655	-4.9	752,160	522,808	-30.5

Note: Business filings include Chapter 7, Chapter 9, Chapter 11, Chapter 12, Chapter 13, Chapter 15, and Section 304; Nonbusiness filings include Chapter 7, Chapter 11, and Chapter 13
Source: Administrative Office of the U.S. Courts, Business and Nonbusiness Bankruptcy, County Cases Commenced by Chapter of the Bankruptcy Code, During the 12-Month Period Ending December 31, 2019 and Business and Nonbusiness Bankruptcy, County Cases Commenced by Chapter of the Bankruptcy Code, During the 12-Month Period Ending December 31, 2020

Housing Vacancy Rates

Area	Gross Vacancy Rate[2] (%) 2018	2019	2020	Year-Round Vacancy Rate[3] (%) 2018	2019	2020	Rental Vacancy Rate[4] (%) 2018	2019	2020	Homeowner Vacancy Rate[5] (%) 2018	2019	2020
MSA[1]	7.8	7.6	5.8	7.4	7.3	5.4	6.6	7.0	6.4	1.1	1.3	0.8
U.S.	12.3	12.0	10.6	9.7	9.5	8.2	6.9	6.7	6.3	1.5	1.4	1.0

Note: (1) Figures cover the Atlanta-Sandy Springs-Roswell, GA Metropolitan Statistical Area; (2) The percentage of the total housing inventory that is vacant; (3) The percentage of the housing inventory (excluding seasonal units) that is year-round vacant; (4) The percentage of rental inventory that is vacant for rent; (5) The percentage of homeowner inventory that is vacant for sale
Source: U.S. Census Bureau, Housing Vacancies and Homeownership Annual Statistics: 2018, 2019, 2020

INCOME

Income

Area	Per Capita ($)	Median Household ($)	Average Household ($)
City	47,424	59,948	106,300
MSA[1]	35,296	68,316	94,723
U.S.	34,103	62,843	88,607

Note: (1) Figures cover the Atlanta-Sandy Springs-Roswell, GA Metropolitan Statistical Area
Source: U.S. Census Bureau, 2015-2019 American Community Survey 5-Year Estimates

Household Income Distribution

Area	Under $15,000	$15,000 -$24,999	$25,000 -$34,999	$35,000 -$49,999	$50,000 -$74,999	$75,000 -$99,999	$100,000 -$149,999	$150,000 and up
City	15.4	9.6	8.0	10.6	14.8	10.3	12.8	18.5
MSA[1]	8.4	7.6	8.3	12.1	17.8	13.3	16.2	16.1
U.S.	10.3	8.9	8.9	12.3	17.2	12.7	15.1	14.5

Note: (1) Figures cover the Atlanta-Sandy Springs-Roswell, GA Metropolitan Statistical Area
Source: U.S. Census Bureau, 2015-2019 American Community Survey 5-Year Estimates

Poverty Rate

Area	All Ages	Under 18 Years Old	18 to 64 Years Old	65 Years and Over
City	20.8	33.5	18.1	16.1
MSA[1]	12.1	17.4	10.7	8.6
U.S.	13.4	18.5	12.6	9.3

Note: Figures are percentage of people whose income during the past 12 months was below the poverty level;
(1) Figures cover the Atlanta-Sandy Springs-Roswell, GA Metropolitan Statistical Area
Source: U.S. Census Bureau, 2015-2019 American Community Survey 5-Year Estimates

CITY FINANCES

City Government Finances

Component	2017 ($000)	2017 ($ per capita)
Total Revenues	2,499,195	5,388
Total Expenditures	2,287,500	4,931
Debt Outstanding	7,204,186	15,530
Cash and Securities[1]	5,462,299	11,775

Note: (1) Cash and security holdings of a government at the close of its fiscal year, including those of its dependent agencies, utilities, and liquor stores.
Source: U.S. Census Bureau, State & Local Government Finances 2017

City Government Revenue by Source

Source	2017 ($000)	2017 ($ per capita)	2017 (%)
General Revenue			
From Federal Government	54,964	118	2.2
From State Government	14,690	32	0.6
From Local Governments	252,442	544	10.1
Taxes			
Property	357,879	771	14.3
Sales and Gross Receipts	162,924	351	6.5
Personal Income	0	0	0.0
Corporate Income	0	0	0.0
Motor Vehicle License	0	0	0.0
Other Taxes	118,524	256	4.7
Current Charges	841,487	1,814	33.7
Liquor Store	0	0	0.0
Utility	279,605	603	11.2
Employee Retirement	345,169	744	13.8

Source: U.S. Census Bureau, State & Local Government Finances 2017

City Government Expenditures by Function

Function	2017 ($000)	2017 ($ per capita)	2017 (%)
General Direct Expenditures			
Air Transportation	675,730	1,456	29.5
Corrections	33,439	72	1.5
Education	0	0	0.0
Employment Security Administration	0	0	0.0
Financial Administration	24,737	53	1.1
Fire Protection	79,639	171	3.5
General Public Buildings	19,160	41	0.8
Governmental Administration, Other	36,082	77	1.6
Health	1,038	2	0.0
Highways	100,985	217	4.4
Hospitals	0	0	0.0
Housing and Community Development	7,788	16	0.3
Interest on General Debt	174,887	377	7.6
Judicial and Legal	31,863	68	1.4
Libraries	0	0	0.0
Parking	0	0	0.0
Parks and Recreation	54,051	116	2.4
Police Protection	191,304	412	8.4
Public Welfare	19,620	42	0.9
Sewerage	14,261	30	0.6
Solid Waste Management	40,706	87	1.8
Veterans' Services	0	0	0.0
Liquor Store	0	0	0.0
Utility	447,999	965	19.6
Employee Retirement	231,503	499	10.1

Source: U.S. Census Bureau, State & Local Government Finances 2017

Atlanta, Georgia

EMPLOYMENT

Labor Force and Employment

Area	Civilian Labor Force Dec. 2019	Civilian Labor Force Dec. 2020	% Chg.	Workers Employed Dec. 2019	Workers Employed Dec. 2020	% Chg.
City	264,779	266,767	0.8	256,964	248,040	-3.5
MSA[1]	3,128,881	3,107,968	-0.7	3,045,413	2,939,513	-3.5
U.S.	164,007,000	160,017,000	-2.4	158,504,000	149,613,000	-5.6

Note: Data is not seasonally adjusted and covers workers 16 years of age and older; (1) Figures cover the Atlanta-Sandy Springs-Roswell, GA Metropolitan Statistical Area
Source: Bureau of Labor Statistics, Local Area Unemployment Statistics

Unemployment Rate

Area	Jan.	Feb.	Mar.	Apr.	May	Jun.	Jul.	Aug.	Sep.	Oct.	Nov.	Dec.
City	3.6	3.7	5.4	13.4	11.9	11.0	10.6	8.6	8.4	6.1	7.4	7.0
MSA[1]	3.2	3.3	4.4	12.7	9.9	8.6	8.6	6.4	6.6	4.6	5.6	5.4
U.S.	4.0	3.8	4.5	14.4	13.0	11.2	10.5	8.5	7.7	6.6	6.4	6.5

Note: Data is not seasonally adjusted and covers workers 16 years of age and older; (1) Figures cover the Atlanta-Sandy Springs-Roswell, GA Metropolitan Statistical Area
Source: Bureau of Labor Statistics, Local Area Unemployment Statistics

Average Wages

Occupation	$/Hr.	Occupation	$/Hr.
Accountants and Auditors	42.20	Maintenance and Repair Workers	20.20
Automotive Mechanics	23.10	Marketing Managers	70.00
Bookkeepers	21.80	Network and Computer Systems Admin.	43.80
Carpenters	20.60	Nurses, Licensed Practical	23.20
Cashiers	11.10	Nurses, Registered	36.50
Computer Programmers	44.50	Nursing Assistants	16.60
Computer Systems Analysts	45.30	Office Clerks, General	17.80
Computer User Support Specialists	28.20	Physical Therapists	42.80
Construction Laborers	16.50	Physicians	127.00
Cooks, Restaurant	13.40	Plumbers, Pipefitters and Steamfitters	26.50
Customer Service Representatives	17.70	Police and Sheriff's Patrol Officers	24.70
Dentists	77.10	Postal Service Mail Carriers	25.40
Electricians	27.80	Real Estate Sales Agents	35.10
Engineers, Electrical	47.60	Retail Salespersons	13.90
Fast Food and Counter Workers	10.00	Sales Representatives, Technical/Scientific	41.80
Financial Managers	72.80	Secretaries, Exc. Legal/Medical/Executive	17.70
First-Line Supervisors of Office Workers	28.90	Security Guards	13.90
General and Operations Managers	60.00	Surgeons	120.80
Hairdressers/Cosmetologists	18.30	Teacher Assistants, Exc. Postsecondary*	12.00
Home Health and Personal Care Aides	12.90	Teachers, Secondary School, Exc. Sp. Ed.*	30.60
Janitors and Cleaners	12.70	Telemarketers	13.90
Landscaping/Groundskeeping Workers	15.30	Truck Drivers, Heavy/Tractor-Trailer	24.00
Lawyers	71.80	Truck Drivers, Light/Delivery Services	19.20
Maids and Housekeeping Cleaners	10.70	Waiters and Waitresses	11.10

Note: Wage data covers the Atlanta-Sandy Springs-Roswell, GA Metropolitan Statistical Area; (*) Hourly wages were calculated from annual wage data based on a 40 hour work week; n/a not available.
Source: Bureau of Labor Statistics, Metro Area Occupational Employment & Wage Estimates, May 2020

Employment by Industry

Sector	MSA[1] Number of Employees	MSA[1] Percent of Total	U.S. Percent of Total
Construction	128,100	4.7	5.1
Education and Health Services	359,300	13.1	16.3
Financial Activities	181,800	6.6	6.1
Government	329,700	12.0	15.2
Information	97,900	3.6	1.9
Leisure and Hospitality	243,700	8.9	9.0
Manufacturing	165,400	6.0	8.5
Mining and Logging	1,700	0.1	0.4
Other Services	91,900	3.4	3.8
Professional and Business Services	535,600	19.5	14.4
Retail Trade	290,200	10.6	10.9
Transportation, Warehousing, and Utilities	169,100	6.2	4.6
Wholesale Trade	147,200	5.4	3.9

Note: Figures are non-farm employment as of December 2020. Figures are not seasonally adjusted and include workers 16 years of age and older; (1) Figures cover the Atlanta-Sandy Springs-Roswell, GA Metropolitan Statistical Area
Source: Bureau of Labor Statistics, Current Employment Statistics, Employment, Hours, and Earnings

Employment by Occupation

Occupation Classification	City (%)	MSA[1] (%)	U.S. (%)
Management, Business, Science, and Arts	53.9	41.7	38.5
Natural Resources, Construction, and Maintenance	2.7	7.8	8.9
Production, Transportation, and Material Moving	8.6	12.7	13.2
Sales and Office	20.2	22.6	21.6
Service	14.6	15.2	17.8

Note: Figures cover employed civilians 16 years of age and older; (1) Figures cover the Atlanta-Sandy Springs-Roswell, GA Metropolitan Statistical Area
Source: U.S. Census Bureau, 2015-2019 American Community Survey 5-Year Estimates

Occupations with Greatest Projected Employment Growth: 2020 – 2022

Occupation[1]	2020 Employment	2022 Projected Employment	Numeric Employment Change	Percent Employment Change
Laborers and Freight, Stock, and Material Movers, Hand	126,370	132,960	6,590	5.2
Fast Food and Counter Workers	134,770	139,200	4,430	3.3
Software Developers and Software Quality Assurance Analysts and Testers	44,810	47,890	3,080	6.9
Home Health and Personal Care Aides	47,800	50,800	3,000	6.3
General and Operations Managers	84,320	87,250	2,930	3.5
Maids and Housekeeping Cleaners	26,600	29,080	2,480	9.3
Cooks, Restaurant	38,680	41,070	2,390	6.2
Maintenance and Repair Workers, General	44,140	46,510	2,370	5.4
Registered Nurses	81,380	83,690	2,310	2.8
Customer Service Representatives	111,220	113,240	2,020	1.8

Note: Projections cover Georgia; (1) Sorted by numeric employment change
Source: www.projectionscentral.com, State Occupational Projections, 2020–2022 Short-Term Projections

Fastest-Growing Occupations: 2020 – 2022

Occupation[1]	2020 Employment	2022 Projected Employment	Numeric Employment Change	Percent Employment Change
Nurse Practitioners	8,440	9,520	1,080	12.8
Hotel, Motel, and Resort Desk Clerks	8,960	10,030	1,070	11.9
Occupational Therapy Assistants	1,220	1,350	130	10.7
Film and Video Editors	1,670	1,840	170	10.2
Lighting Technicians and Media and Communication Equipment Workers, All Other	1,010	1,110	100	9.9
Baggage Porters and Bellhops	1,020	1,120	100	9.8
Animal Trainers	1,250	1,370	120	9.6
Physical Therapist Assistants	2,790	3,050	260	9.3
Maids and Housekeeping Cleaners	26,600	29,080	2,480	9.3
Information Security Analysts (SOC 2018)	3,910	4,250	340	8.7

Note: Projections cover Georgia; (1) Sorted by percent employment change and excludes occupations with numeric employment change less than 50
Source: www.projectionscentral.com, State Occupational Projections, 2020–2022 Short-Term Projections

TAXES

State Corporate Income Tax Rates

State	Tax Rate (%)	Income Brackets ($)	Num. of Brackets	Financial Institution Tax Rate (%)[a]	Federal Income Tax Ded.
Georgia	5.75	Flat rate	1	5.75	No

Note: Tax rates as of January 1, 2021; (a) Rates listed are the corporate income tax rate applied to financial institutions or excise taxes based on income. Some states have other taxes based upon the value of deposits or shares.
Source: Federation of Tax Administrators, State Corporate Income Tax Rates, January 1, 2021

State Individual Income Tax Rates

State	Tax Rate (%)	Income Brackets ($)	Personal Exemptions ($) Single	Married	Depend.	Standard Ded. ($) Single	Married
Georgia	1.0 - 5.75	750 - 7,001 (i)	2,700	7,400	3,000	4,600	6,000

Note: Tax rates as of January 1, 2021; Local- and county-level taxes are not included; Federal income tax is not deductible on state income tax returns; (i) The Georgia income brackets reported are for single individuals. For married couples filing jointly, the same tax rates apply to income brackets ranging from $1,000, to $10,000.
Source: Federation of Tax Administrators, State Individual Income Tax Rates, January 1, 2021

Various State Sales and Excise Tax Rates

State	State Sales Tax (%)	Gasoline[1] (¢/gal.)	Cigarette[2] ($/pack)	Spirits[3] ($/gal.)	Wine[4] ($/gal.)	Beer[5] ($/gal.)	Recreational Marijuana (%)
Georgia	4	33.96	0.37	3.79	1.51	0.48	Not legal

Note: All tax rates as of January 1, 2021; (1) The American Petroleum Institute has developed a methodology for determining the average tax rate on a gallon of fuel. Rates may include any of the following: excise taxes, environmental fees, storage tank fees, other fees or taxes, general sales tax, and local taxes; (2) The federal excise tax of $1.0066 per pack and local taxes are not included; (3) Rates are those applicable to off-premise sales of 40% alcohol by volume (a.b.v.) distilled spirits in 750ml containers. Local excise taxes are excluded; (4) Rates are those applicable to off-premise sales of 11% a.b.v. non-carbonated wine in 750ml containers; (5) Rates are those applicable to off-premise sales of 4.7% a.b.v. beer in 12 ounce containers.
Source: Tax Foundation, 2021 Facts & Figures: How Does Your State Compare?

State Business Tax Climate Index Rankings

State	Overall Rank	Corporate Tax Rank	Individual Income Tax Rank	Sales Tax Rank	Property Tax Rank	Unemployment Insurance Tax Rank
Georgia	31	7	36	27	24	39

Note: The index is a measure of how each state's tax laws affect economic performance. The lower the rank, the more favorable a state's tax system is for business. States without a given tax are given a ranking of 1. The scores/rankings for the District of Columbia do not affect other states. The 2021 index represents the tax climate as of July 1, 2020.
Source: Tax Foundation, State Business Tax Climate Index 2021

TRANSPORTATION

Means of Transportation to Work

Area	Car/Truck/Van Drove Alone	Car/Truck/Van Carpooled	Bus	Subway	Railroad	Bicycle	Walked	Other Means	Worked at Home
City	67.1	6.3	6.6	3.4	0.2	1.1	5.0	2.2	8.1
MSA[1]	77.3	9.2	2.0	0.8	0.1	0.2	1.3	1.6	7.4
U.S.	76.3	9.0	2.4	1.9	0.6	0.5	2.7	1.4	5.2

Note: Figures are percentages and cover workers 16 years of age and older; (1) Figures cover the Atlanta-Sandy Springs-Roswell, GA Metropolitan Statistical Area
Source: U.S. Census Bureau, 2015-2019 American Community Survey 5-Year Estimates

Travel Time to Work

Area	Less Than 10 Minutes	10 to 19 Minutes	20 to 29 Minutes	30 to 44 Minutes	45 to 59 Minutes	60 to 89 Minutes	90 Minutes or More
City	6.8	28.7	26.4	22.2	7.6	5.2	3.1
MSA[1]	7.0	22.1	19.6	24.9	12.3	10.4	3.8
U.S.	12.2	28.4	20.8	20.8	8.3	6.4	2.9

Note: Note: Figures are percentages and include workers 16 years old and over; (1) Figures cover the Atlanta-Sandy Springs-Roswell, GA Metropolitan Statistical Area
Source: U.S. Census Bureau, 2015-2019 American Community Survey 5-Year Estimates

Key Congestion Measures

Measure	1982	1992	2002	2012	2017
Annual Hours of Delay, Total (000)	32,678	85,177	175,407	215,539	237,405
Annual Hours of Delay, Per Auto Commuter	22	39	55	64	77
Annual Congestion Cost, Total (million $)	242	888	2,341	3,800	4,337
Annual Congestion Cost, Per Auto Commuter ($)	510	913	1,466	1,411	1,508

Note: Covers the Atlanta GA urban area
Source: Texas A&M Transportation Institute, 2019 Urban Mobility Report

Freeway Travel Time Index

Measure	1982	1987	1992	1997	2002	2007	2012	2017
Urban Area Index[1]	1.10	1.13	1.18	1.23	1.25	1.26	1.24	1.30
Urban Area Rank[1,2]	19	21	18	15	19	24	26	19

Note: Freeway Travel Time Index—the ratio of travel time in the peak period to the travel time at free-flow conditions. For example, a value of 1.30 indicates a 20-minute free-flow trip takes 26 minutes in the peak (20 minutes x 1.30 = 26 minutes); (1) Covers the Atlanta GA urban area; (2) Rank is based on 101 larger urban areas (#1 = highest travel time index)
Source: Texas A&M Transportation Institute, 2019 Urban Mobility Report

Public Transportation

Agency Name / Mode of Transportation	Vehicles Operated in Maximum Service[1]	Annual Unlinked Passenger Trips[2] (in thous.)	Annual Passenger Miles[3] (in thous.)
Metropolitan Atlanta Rapid Transit Authority (MARTA)			
Bus (directly operated)	448	51,447.8	243,578.3
Demand Response (purchased transportation)	169	808.9	10,374.0
Heavy Rail (directly operated)	212	65,217.3	450,023.1
Streetcar Rail (directly operated)	2	285.1	214.1

Note: (1) Number of revenue vehicles operated by the given mode and type of service to meet the annual maximum service requirement. This is the revenue vehicle count during the peak season of the year; on the week and day that maximum service is provided. Vehicles operated in maximum service (VOMS) exclude atypical days and one-time special events; (2) Number of passengers who boarded public transportation vehicles. Passengers are counted each time they board a vehicle no matter how many vehicles they use to travel from their origin to their destination. (3) Sum of the distances ridden by all passengers during the entire fiscal year.
Source: Federal Transit Administration, National Transit Database, 2019

Air Transportation

Airport Name and Code / Type of Service	Passenger Airlines[1]	Passenger Enplanements	Freight Carriers[2]	Freight (lbs)
Hartsfield-Jackson Atlanta International Airport (ATL)				
Domestic service (U.S. carriers - 2020)	29	18,881,518	22	353,816,127
International service (U.S. carriers - 2019)	9	5,108,495	7	82,299,120

Note: (1) Includes all U.S.-based major, minor and commuter airlines that carried at least one passenger during the year; (2) Includes all U.S.-based airlines and freight carriers that transported at least one pound of freight during the year.
Source: Bureau of Transportation Statistics, The Intermodal Transportation Database, Air Carriers: T-100 Domestic Market (U.S. Carriers), 2020; Bureau of Transportation Statistics, The Intermodal Transportation Database, Air Carriers: T-100 International Market (U.S. Carriers), 2019

BUSINESSES

Major Business Headquarters

Company Name	Industry	Fortune[1]	Forbes[2]
Coca-Cola	Beverages	88	-
Cox Enterprises	Media	-	14
Delta Air Lines	Airlines	68	-
Genuine Parts	Wholesalers, Diversified	171	-
Graphic Packaging Holding	Packaging, Containers	477	-
HD Supply Holdings	Wholesalers, Diversified	478	-
Holder Construction	Construction	-	101
Home Depot	Specialty Retailers, Other	26	-
Intercontinental Exchange	Securities	459	-
Newell Brands	Home Equipment, Furnishings	316	-
PulteGroup	Homebuilders	309	-
RaceTrac Petroleum	Convenience Stores & Gas Stations	-	25
Southern Company	Electric and Gas Utilities	153	-
UPS	Delivery	43	-
Veritiv	Wholesalers, Diversified	412	-

Note: (1) Companies that produce a 10-K are ranked 1 to 500 based on 2019 revenue; (2) All private companies with at least $2 billion in annual revenue through the end of their most current fiscal year are ranked 1 to 219; companies listed are headquartered in the city; dashes indicate no ranking
Source: Fortune, "Fortune 500," June/July 2020; Forbes, "America's Largest Private Companies," 2020

Fastest-Growing Businesses

According to *Inc.*, Atlanta is home to nine of America's 500 fastest-growing private companies: **OneTrust** (#1); **LeaseQuery** (#29); **Goods & Services** (#31); **Rented** (#61); **Propellant Media** (#78); **adtechnacity** (#106); **GROUNDFLOOR** (#402); **BMarko Structures** (#470); **Florence Healthcare** (#494). Criteria: must be an independent, privately-held, for-profit, U.S. corporation, proprietorship or partnership as of December 31, 2019; revenues must be at least $100,000 in 2016 and $2 million in 2019; must have four-year operating/sales history. *Inc., "America's 500 Fastest-Growing Private Companies," 2020*

According to *Fortune*, Atlanta is home to one of the 100 fastest-growing companies in the world: **Floor & Decor Holdings** (#48). Companies were ranked by their revenue growth rate; their EPS growth rate; and their three-year annualized total return to investors for the period ending June 30, 2020. Criteria for inclusion: a company, foreign or domestic, must trade on a major U.S. stock exchange; must file quarterly reports with the SEC; must have a minimum market capitalization of $250 million; must have a stock price of at least $5 on June 30, 2020; must have been trading continuously since June 30, 2017; must have revenue and net income for the four quarters ended on or before April 30, 2020, of at least $50 million and $10 million, respectively; and must have posted a compound annual growth in revenue and earnings per share of at least 15% annually over the three years ending on or before April 30, 2020. Real estate investment trusts, limited-liability companies, limited parterships, business development companies, closed-end investment firms, companies about to be acquired, and companies that lost money in the quarter ending April 30, 2020 were excluded. *Fortune, "100 Fastest-Growing Companies," 2020*

According to Deloitte, Atlanta is home to 19 of North America's 500 fastest-growing high-technology companies: **OneTrust** (#4); **CharterUP** (#8); **FIXD** (#11); **LeaseQuery** (#26); **Calendly** (#97); **GROUNDFLOOR** (#102); **FullStory** (#106); **GreenPrint** (#228); **Terminus** (#229); **SalesLoft** (#274); **MacStadium** (#286); **AODocs** (#368); **CallRail** (#370); **Springbot, Inc.** (#371); **QGenda** (#373); **Wahoo Fitness** (#405); **Azalea Health** (#408); **Mobilewalla** (#497); **ShootProof LLC** (#498). Companies are ranked by percentage growth in revenue over a four-year period. Criteria for inclusion: company must be headquartered within North America; must own proprietary intellectual property or technology that is sold to customers in products that contributes to a significant portion of the company's operating revenue; must have been in business for a minumum of four years with 2016 operating revenues of at least $50,000 USD/CD and 2019 operating revenues of at least $5 million USD/CD. *Deloitte, 2020 Technology Fast 500™*

Minority Business Opportunity

Atlanta is home to four companies which are on the *Black Enterprise* Industrial/Service list (100 largest companies based on gross sales): **H. J. Russell & Co.** (#25); **Jackmont Hospitality** (#27); **B & S Electric Supply Co.** (#72); **Sudu Logistics** (#98). Criteria: operational in previous calendar year; at least 51% black-owned and manufactures/owns the product it sells or provides industrial or consumer services. Brokerages, real estate firms and firms that provide professional services are not eligible. *Black Enterprise, B.E. 100s, 2019*

Atlanta is home to one company which is on the *Black Enterprise* Auto Dealer list (45 largest dealers based on gross sales): **The Baran Co.** (#15). Criteria: company must be operational in previous calendar year and be at least 51% black-owned. *Black Enterprise, B.E. 100s, 2019*

Atlanta is home to one company which is on the *Black Enterprise* Bank list (15 largest banks based on total assets, capital, deposits and loans, including mortgage-backed securities for the calendar year): **Citizens Bancshares Corp. (Citzens Trust Bank)** (#5). Only commercial banks or savings and loans that are classified by the Federal Reserve as black institutions and have been fully operational for the previous calendar year were considered. *Black Enterprise, B.E. 100s, 2019*

Living Environment

COST OF LIVING

Cost of Living Index

Composite Index	Groceries	Housing	Utilities	Transportation	Health Care	Misc. Goods/Services
101.3	105.0	103.3	84.6	102.1	102.2	102.4

Note: The Cost of Living Index measures regional differences in the cost of consumer goods and services, excluding taxes and non-consumer expenditures, for professional and managerial households in the top income quintile. It is based on more than 50,000 prices covering almost 60 different items for which prices are collected three times a year by chambers of commerce, economic development organizations or university applied economic centers in each participating urban area. The numbers shown should be read as a percentage above or below the national average of 100. For example, a value of 115.4 in the groceries column indicates that grocery prices are 15.4% higher than the national average. Small differences in the index numbers should not be interpreted as significant; Figures cover the Atlanta GA urban area.
Source: The Council for Community and Economic Research, Cost of Living Index, 2020

Grocery Prices

Area[1]	T-Bone Steak ($/pound)	Frying Chicken ($/pound)	Whole Milk ($/half gal.)	Eggs ($/dozen)	Orange Juice ($/64 oz.)	Coffee ($/11.5 oz.)
City[2]	14.32	1.30	1.99	1.25	3.76	4.92
Avg.	11.78	1.39	2.05	1.47	3.57	4.34
Min.	8.03	0.94	1.03	0.74	2.94	3.02
Max.	15.86	2.65	4.31	3.77	5.44	8.69

Note: (1) Values for the local area are compared with the average, minimum and maximum values for all 284 areas in the Cost of Living Index; (2) Figures cover the Atlanta GA urban area; **T-Bone Steak** (price per pound); **Frying Chicken** (price per pound, whole fryer); **Whole Milk** (half gallon carton); **Eggs** (price per dozen, Grade A, large); **Orange Juice** (64 oz. Tropicana or Florida Natural); **Coffee** (11.5 oz. can, vacuum-packed, Maxwell House, Hills Bros, or Folgers).
Source: The Council for Community and Economic Research, Cost of Living Index, 2020

Housing and Utility Costs

Area[1]	New Home Price ($)	Apartment Rent ($/month)	All Electric ($/month)	Part Electric ($/month)	Other Energy ($/month)	Telephone ($/month)
City[2]	380,418	1,245	-	87.42	33.41	185.10
Avg.	368,594	1,168	170.86	100.47	65.28	184.30
Min.	190,567	502	91.58	31.42	26.08	169.60
Max.	2,227,806	4,738	470.38	280.31	280.06	206.50

Note: (1) Values for the local area are compared with the average, minimum and maximum values for all 284 areas in the Cost of Living Index; (2) Figures cover the Atlanta GA urban area; **New Home Price** (2,400 sf living area, 8,000 sf lot, in urban area with full utilities); **Apartment Rent** (950 sf 2 bedroom/1.5 or 2 bath, unfurnished, excluding all utilities except water); **All Electric** (average monthly cost for an all-electric home); **Part Electric** (average monthly cost for a part-electric home); **Other Energy** (average monthly cost for natural gas, fuel oil, coal, wood, and any other forms of energy except electricity); **Telephone** (price includes the base monthly rate plus taxes and fees for three lines of mobile phone service).
Source: The Council for Community and Economic Research, Cost of Living Index, 2020

Health Care, Transportation, and Other Costs

Area[1]	Doctor ($/visit)	Dentist ($/visit)	Optometrist ($/visit)	Gasoline ($/gallon)	Beauty Salon ($/visit)	Men's Shirt ($)
City[2]	119.80	105.78	110.27	2.23	47.13	27.27
Avg.	115.44	99.32	108.10	2.21	39.27	31.37
Min.	36.68	59.00	51.36	1.71	19.00	11.00
Max.	219.00	153.10	250.97	3.46	82.05	58.33

Note: (1) Values for the local area are compared with the average, minimum and maximum values for all 284 areas in the Cost of Living Index; (2) Figures cover the Atlanta GA urban area; **Doctor** (general practitioners routine exam of an established patient); **Dentist** (adult teeth cleaning and periodic oral examination); **Optometrist** (full vision eye exam for established adult patient); **Gasoline** (one gallon regular unleaded, national brand, including all taxes, cash price at self-service pump if available); **Beauty Salon** (woman's shampoo, trim, and blow-dry); **Men's Shirt** (cotton/polyester dress shirt, pinpoint weave, long sleeves).
Source: The Council for Community and Economic Research, Cost of Living Index, 2020

HOUSING

Homeownership Rate

Area	2012 (%)	2013 (%)	2014 (%)	2015 (%)	2016 (%)	2017 (%)	2018 (%)	2019 (%)	2020 (%)
MSA[1]	62.1	61.6	61.6	61.7	61.5	62.4	64.0	64.2	66.4
U.S.	65.4	65.1	64.5	63.7	63.4	63.9	64.4	64.6	66.6

Note: (1) Figures cover the Atlanta-Sandy Springs-Roswell, GA Metropolitan Statistical Area
Source: U.S. Census Bureau, Housing Vacancies and Homeownership Annual Statistics: 2012-2020

House Price Index (HPI)

Area	National Ranking[2]	Quarterly Change (%)	One-Year Change (%)	Five-Year Change (%)	Since 1991Q1 (%)
MSA[1]	110	1.95	6.57	40.75	164.55
U.S.[3]	—	3.81	10.77	38.99	205.12

Note: The HPI is a weighted repeat sales index. It measures average price changes in repeat sales or refinancings on the same properties. This information is obtained by reviewing repeat mortgage transactions on single-family properties whose mortgages have been purchased or securitized by Fannie Mae or Freddie Mac since January 1975; (1) Figures cover the Atlanta-Sandy Springs-Roswell, GA Metropolitan Statistical Area; (2) Rankings are based on annual percentage change for all metro areas containing at least 15,000 transactions over the last 10 years and ranges from 1 to 253; (3) figures based on a weighted average of Census Division estimates using a seasonally adjusted, purchase-only index; all figures are for the period ending December 31, 2020
Source: Federal Housing Finance Agency, Change in Metropolitan Area House Price Indexes, April 7, 2021

Median Single-Family Home Prices

Area	2018	2019	2020p	Percent Change 2019 to 2020
MSA[1]	219.9	233.2	260.8	11.8
U.S. Average	261.6	274.6	299.9	9.2

Note: Figures are median sales prices of existing single-family homes in thousands of dollars; (p) preliminary; (1) Figures cover the Atlanta-Sandy Springs-Roswell, GA Metropolitan Statistical Area
Source: National Association of Realtors, Median Sales Price of Existing Single-Family Homes for Metropolitan Areas, 4th Quarter 2020

Qualifying Income Based on Median Sales Price of Existing Single-Family Homes

Area	With 5% Down ($)	With 10% Down ($)	With 20% Down ($)
MSA[1]	52,052	49,312	43,833
U.S. Average	59,266	56,147	49,908

Note: Figures are preliminary; Qualifying income is based on a mortgage rate of 2.81%. Monthly principal and interest payment is limited to 25% of income; (1) Figures cover the Atlanta-Sandy Springs-Roswell, GA Metropolitan Statistical Area
Source: National Association of Realtors, Qualifying Income Based on Median Sales Price of Existing Single-Family Homes for Metropolitan Areas, 4th Quarter 2020

Home Value Distribution

Area	Under $50,000	$50,000 -$99,999	$100,000 -$149,999	$150,000 -$199,999	$200,000 -$299,999	$300,000 -$499,999	$500,000 -$999,999	$1,000,000 or more
City	4.5	10.1	9.6	10.6	16.6	19.7	20.2	8.8
MSA[1]	3.7	9.2	14.8	18.0	22.5	20.7	9.3	1.8
U.S.	6.9	12.0	13.3	14.0	19.6	19.3	11.4	3.4

Note: Figures are percentages and cover owner-occupied housing units; (1) Figures cover the Atlanta-Sandy Springs-Roswell, GA Metropolitan Statistical Area
Source: U.S. Census Bureau, 2015-2019 American Community Survey 5-Year Estimates

Year Housing Structure Built

Area	2010 or Later	2000 -2009	1990 -1999	1980 -1989	1970 -1979	1960 -1969	1950 -1959	1940 -1949	Before 1940	Median Year
City	8.1	22.3	10.6	7.9	8.4	12.6	11.7	6.1	12.3	1979
MSA[1]	6.2	24.3	21.5	17.7	13.0	7.6	4.8	1.9	2.9	1991
U.S.	5.2	14.0	13.9	13.4	15.2	10.6	10.3	4.9	12.6	1978

Note: Figures are percentages except for Median Year; Note: (1) Figures cover the Atlanta-Sandy Springs-Roswell, GA Metropolitan Statistical Area
Source: U.S. Census Bureau, 2015-2019 American Community Survey 5-Year Estimates

Gross Monthly Rent

Area	Under $500	$500 -$999	$1,000 -$1,499	$1,500 -$1,999	$2,000 -$2,499	$2,500 -$2,999	$3,000 and up	Median ($)
City	11.3	27.5	33.6	18.8	5.6	1.7	1.5	1,153
MSA[1]	4.8	28.9	45.0	16.1	3.4	0.9	0.8	1,156
U.S.	9.4	36.2	30.0	14.0	5.6	2.4	2.4	1,062

Note: Figures are percentages except for Median; Gross rent is the contract rent plus the estimated average monthly cost of utilities (electricity, gas, and water and sewer) and fuels (oil, coal, kerosene, wood, etc.) if these are paid by the renter (or paid for the renter by someone else); (1) Figures cover the Atlanta-Sandy Springs-Roswell, GA Metropolitan Statistical Area
Source: U.S. Census Bureau, 2015-2019 American Community Survey 5-Year Estimates

HEALTH

Health Risk Factors

Category	MSA[1] (%)	U.S. (%)
Adults aged 18–64 who have any kind of health care coverage	80.9	87.3
Adults who reported being in good or better health	84.0	82.4
Adults who have been told they have high blood cholesterol	29.2	33.0
Adults who have been told they have high blood pressure	30.8	32.3
Adults who are current smokers	14.9	17.1
Adults who currently use E-cigarettes	4.5	4.6
Adults who currently use chewing tobacco, snuff, or snus	3.7	4.0
Adults who are heavy drinkers[2]	5.3	6.3
Adults who are binge drinkers[3]	13.6	17.4
Adults who are overweight (BMI 25.0 - 29.9)	33.6	35.3
Adults who are obese (BMI 30.0 - 99.8)	29.9	31.3
Adults who participated in any physical activities in the past month	72.3	74.4
Adults who always or nearly always wears a seat belt	96.0	94.3

Note: (1) Figures cover the Atlanta-Sandy Springs-Roswell, GA Metropolitan Statistical Area; (2) Heavy drinkers are classified as adult men having more than 14 drinks per week and adult women having more than 7 drinks per week; (3) Binge drinkers are classified as males having five or more drinks on one occasion or females having four or more drinks on one occasion
Source: Centers for Disease Control and Prevention, Behaviorial Risk Factor Surveillance System, SMART: Selected Metropolitan Area Risk Trends, 2017

Acute and Chronic Health Conditions

Category	MSA[1] (%)	U.S. (%)
Adults who have ever been told they had a heart attack	3.0	4.2
Adults who have ever been told they have angina or coronary heart disease	2.8	3.9
Adults who have ever been told they had a stroke	3.2	3.0
Adults who have ever been told they have asthma	12.3	14.2
Adults who have ever been told they have arthritis	19.2	24.9
Adults who have ever been told they have diabetes[2]	10.4	10.5
Adults who have ever been told they had skin cancer	4.7	6.2
Adults who have ever been told they had any other types of cancer	5.4	7.1
Adults who have ever been told they have COPD	5.2	6.5
Adults who have ever been told they have kidney disease	2.5	3.0
Adults who have ever been told they have a form of depression	15.5	20.5

Note: (1) Figures cover the Atlanta-Sandy Springs-Roswell, GA Metropolitan Statistical Area; (2) Figures do not include pregnancy-related, borderline, or pre-diabetes
Source: Centers for Disease Control and Prevention, Behaviorial Risk Factor Surveillance System, SMART: Selected Metropolitan Area Risk Trends, 2017

Health Screening and Vaccination Rates

Category	MSA[1] (%)	U.S. (%)
Adults aged 65+ who have had flu shot within the past year	63.3	60.7
Adults aged 65+ who have ever had a pneumonia vaccination	72.8	75.4
Adults who have ever been tested for HIV	48.8	36.1
Adults who have ever had the shingles or zoster vaccine?	26.0	28.9
Adults who have had their blood cholesterol checked within the last five years	90.3	85.9

Note: n/a not available; (1) Figures cover the Atlanta-Sandy Springs-Roswell, GA Metropolitan Statistical Area.
Source: Centers for Disease Control and Prevention, Behaviorial Risk Factor Surveillance System, SMART: Selected Metropolitan Area Risk Trends, 2017

Disability Status

Category	MSA[1] (%)	U.S. (%)
Adults who reported being deaf	5.4	6.7
Are you blind or have serious difficulty seeing, even when wearing glasses?	4.4	4.5
Are you limited in any way in any of your usual activities due of arthritis?	9.6	12.9
Do you have difficulty doing errands alone?	5.2	6.8
Do you have difficulty dressing or bathing?	2.7	3.6
Do you have serious difficulty concentrating/remembering/making decisions?	10.3	10.7
Do you have serious difficulty walking or climbing stairs?	12.0	13.6

Note: (1) Figures cover the Atlanta-Sandy Springs-Roswell, GA Metropolitan Statistical Area.
Source: Centers for Disease Control and Prevention, Behaviorial Risk Factor Surveillance System, SMART: Selected Metropolitan Area Risk Trends, 2017

Mortality Rates for the Top 10 Causes of Death in the U.S.

ICD-10[a] Sub-Chapter	ICD-10[a] Code	Age-Adjusted Mortality Rate[1] per 100,000 population County[2]	U.S.
Malignant neoplasms	C00-C97	142.1	149.2
Ischaemic heart diseases	I20-I25	48.8	90.5
Other forms of heart disease	I30-I51	57.4	52.2
Chronic lower respiratory diseases	J40-J47	25.0	39.6
Other degenerative diseases of the nervous system	G30-G31	52.5	37.6
Cerebrovascular diseases	I60-I69	42.1	37.2
Other external causes of accidental injury	W00-X59	27.1	36.1
Organic, including symptomatic, mental disorders	F01-F09	19.6	29.4
Hypertensive diseases	I10-I15	41.9	24.1
Diabetes mellitus	E10-E14	19.8	21.5

Note: (a) ICD-10 = International Classification of Diseases 10th Revision; (1) Mortality rates are a three-year average covering 2017-2019; (2) Figures cover Fulton County.
Source: Centers for Disease Control and Prevention, National Center for Health Statistics. Underlying Cause of Death 1999-2019 on CDC WONDER Online Database

Mortality Rates for Selected Causes of Death

ICD-10[a] Sub-Chapter	ICD-10[a] Code	Age-Adjusted Mortality Rate[1] per 100,000 population County[2]	U.S.
Assault	X85-Y09	11.6	6.0
Diseases of the liver	K70-K76	10.6	14.4
Human immunodeficiency virus (HIV) disease	B20-B24	5.5	1.5
Influenza and pneumonia	J09-J18	9.7	13.8
Intentional self-harm	X60-X84	11.3	14.1
Malnutrition	E40-E46	4.8	2.3
Obesity and other hyperalimentation	E65-E68	1.9	2.1
Renal failure	N17-N19	16.7	12.6
Transport accidents	V01-V99	10.8	12.3
Viral hepatitis	B15-B19	1.1	1.2

Note: (a) ICD-10 = International Classification of Diseases 10th Revision; (1) Mortality rates are a three-year average covering 2017-2019; (2) Figures cover Fulton County; Data are suppressed when the data meet the criteria for confidentiality constraints; Mortality rates are flagged as unreliable when the rate would be calculated with a numerator of 20 or less.
Source: Centers for Disease Control and Prevention, National Center for Health Statistics. Underlying Cause of Death 1999-2019 on CDC WONDER Online Database

Health Insurance Coverage

Area	With Health Insurance	With Private Health Insurance	With Public Health Insurance	Without Health Insurance	Population Under Age 19 Without Health Insurance
City	89.7	69.2	28.3	10.3	4.9
MSA[1]	87.2	69.3	26.8	12.8	7.5
U.S.	91.2	67.9	35.1	8.8	5.1

Note: Figures are percentages that cover the civilian noninstitutionalized population; (1) Figures cover the Atlanta-Sandy Springs-Roswell, GA Metropolitan Statistical Area
Source: U.S. Census Bureau, 2015-2019 American Community Survey 5-Year Estimates

Number of Medical Professionals

Area	MDs[3]	DOs[3,4]	Dentists	Podiatrists	Chiropractors	Optometrists
County[1] (number)	5,365	134	756	56	586	183
County[1] (rate[2])	510.9	12.8	71.1	5.3	55.1	17.2
U.S. (rate[2])	282.9	22.7	71.2	6.2	28.1	16.9

13121

Note: Data as of 2019 unless noted; (1) Data covers Fulton County; (2) Rate per 100,000 population; (3) Data as of 2018 and includes all active, non-federal physicians; (4) Doctor of Osteopathic Medicine
Source: U.S. Department of Health and Human Services, Health Resources and Services Administration, Bureau of Health Professions, Area Resource File (ARF) 2019-2020

Best Hospitals

According to *U.S. News,* the Atlanta-Sandy Springs-Roswell, GA metro area is home to five of the best hospitals in the U.S.: **Emory St. Joseph's Hospital** (1 adult specialty); **Emory University Hospital Midtown** (1 adult specialty); **Emory University Hospital at Wesley Woods** (8 adult specialties); **Northside Hospital-Atlanta** (1 adult specialty); **Shepherd Center** (1 adult specialty). The hospitals listed were nationally ranked in at least one of 16 adult or 10 pediatric specialties. Only 134 hospitals nationwide were nationally ranked in one or more adult or pediatric specialty; this number increases to 178 counting specialized centers within hospitals. Twenty hospitals in the U.S. made the Honor Roll. The Best Hospitals Honor Roll takes both the national rankings and the procedure and condition ratings into account. Hospitals received points if they were nationally ranked in one of the

16 adult specialties—the higher they ranked, the more points they got—and how many ratings of "high performing" they earned in the 10 procedures and conditions. *U.S. News Online, "America's Best Hospitals 2020-21"*

According to *U.S. News*, the Atlanta-Sandy Springs-Roswell, GA metro area is home to one of the best children's hospitals in the U.S.: **Children's Healthcare of Atlanta** (10 pediatric specialties). The hospital listed was highly ranked in at least one of 10 pediatric specialties. Eighty-eight children's hospitals in the U.S. were nationally ranked in at least one specialty. Hospitals received points for being ranked in a specialty, and the 10 hospitals with the most points across the 10 specialties make up the Honor Roll. *U.S. News Online, "America's Best Children's Hospitals 2020-21"*

EDUCATION

Public School District Statistics

District Name	Schls	Pupils	Pupil/Teacher Ratio	Minority Pupils[1] (%)	Free Lunch Eligible[2] (%)	IEP[3] (%)
Atlanta Public Schools	89	52,377	13.1	84.1	73.6	11.1
Fulton County	107	94,491	14.8	72.0	41.0	10.2
State Charter Schls-GA Cyber Acad.	1	11,173	28.4	55.3	35.4	13.6

Note: Table includes school districts with 2,000 or more students; (1) Percentage of students that are not non-Hispanic white; (2) Percentage of students that are eligible for the free lunch program; (3) Percentage of students that have an Individualized Education Program.
Source: U.S. Department of Education, National Center for Education Statistics, Common Core of Data, Local Education Agency (School District) Universe Survey: School Year 2018-2019; U.S. Department of Education, National Center for Education Statistics, Common Core of Data, Public Elementary/Secondary School Universe Survey: School Year 2018-2019

Highest Level of Education

Area	Less than H.S.	H.S. Diploma	Some College, No Deg.	Associate Degree	Bachelor's Degree	Master's Degree	Prof. School Degree	Doctorate Degree
City	9.1	18.9	15.3	4.9	28.9	15.1	5.3	2.5
MSA[1]	10.4	23.9	19.5	7.6	24.0	10.6	2.5	1.5
U.S.	12.0	27.0	20.4	8.5	19.8	8.8	2.1	1.4

Note: Figures cover persons age 25 and over; (1) Figures cover the Atlanta-Sandy Springs-Roswell, GA Metropolitan Statistical Area
Source: U.S. Census Bureau, 2015-2019 American Community Survey 5-Year Estimates

Educational Attainment by Race

Area	High School Graduate or Higher (%) Total	White	Black	Asian	Hisp.[2]	Bachelor's Degree or Higher (%) Total	White	Black	Asian	Hisp.[2]
City	90.9	97.7	84.4	96.1	82.5	51.8	78.0	25.7	84.6	46.0
MSA[1]	89.6	91.0	90.5	87.5	64.9	38.6	42.6	30.2	58.1	20.6
U.S.	88.0	89.9	86.0	87.1	68.7	32.1	33.5	21.6	54.3	16.4

Note: Figures shown cover persons 25 years old and over; (1) Figures cover the Atlanta-Sandy Springs-Roswell, GA Metropolitan Statistical Area; (2) People of Hispanic origin can be of any race
Source: U.S. Census Bureau, 2015-2019 American Community Survey 5-Year Estimates

School Enrollment by Grade and Control

Area	Preschool (%) Public	Private	Kindergarten (%) Public	Private	Grades 1 - 4 (%) Public	Private	Grades 5 - 8 (%) Public	Private	Grades 9 - 12 (%) Public	Private
City	54.3	45.7	84.5	15.5	87.8	12.2	79.5	20.5	80.1	19.9
MSA[1]	56.0	44.0	86.9	13.1	91.0	9.0	89.2	10.8	89.9	10.1
U.S.	59.1	40.9	87.6	12.4	89.5	10.5	89.4	10.6	90.1	9.9

Note: Figures shown cover persons 3 years old and over; (1) Figures cover the Atlanta-Sandy Springs-Roswell, GA Metropolitan Statistical Area
Source: U.S. Census Bureau, 2015-2019 American Community Survey 5-Year Estimates

Higher Education

Four-Year Colleges Public	Private Non-profit	Private For-profit	Two-Year Colleges Public	Private Non-profit	Private For-profit	Medical Schools[1]	Law Schools[2]	Voc/Tech[3]
3	9	6	3	0	4	2	3	8

Note: Figures cover institutions located within the city limits and include main campuses only; (1) includes schools accredited by the Liaison Committee on Medical Education and the American Osteopathic Association's Commission on Osteopathic College Accreditation; (2) includes ABA-accredited schools, schools with provisional ABA accreditation, and state accredited schools; (3) includes all schools with programs that are less than 2 years.
Source: National Center for Education Statistics, Integrated Postsecondary Education System (IPEDS), 2019-20; Wikipedia, List of Medical Schools in the United States, accessed April 2, 2021; Wikipedia, List of Law Schools in the United States, accessed April 2, 2021

According to *U.S. News & World Report,* the Atlanta-Sandy Springs-Roswell, GA metro area is home to two of the top 200 national universities in the U.S.: **Emory University** (#21); **Georgia Institute of Technology** (#35 tie). The indicators used to capture academic quality fall into a number of categories: assessment by administrators at peer institutions; retention of students; faculty resources; student selectivity; financial resources; alumni giving; high school counselor ratings of colleges; and graduation rate. *U.S. News & World Report,* "*America's Best Colleges 2021*"

According to *U.S. News & World Report,* the Atlanta-Sandy Springs-Roswell, GA metro area is home to two of the top 100 liberal arts colleges in the U.S.: **Spelman College** (#54 tie); **Agnes Scott College** (#61 tie). The indicators used to capture academic quality fall into a number of categories: assessment by administrators at peer institutions; retention of students; faculty resources; student selectivity; financial resources; alumni giving; high school counselor ratings of colleges; and graduation rate. *U.S. News & World Report,* "*America's Best Colleges 2021*"

According to *U.S. News & World Report,* the Atlanta-Sandy Springs-Roswell, GA metro area is home to two of the top 100 law schools in the U.S.: **Emory University** (#29 tie); **Georgia State University** (#78 tie). The rankings are based on a weighted average of 12 measures of quality: peer assessment score; assessment score by lawyers/judges; median LSAT scores; median undergrad GPA; acceptance rate; employment rates for graduates; placement success; bar passage rate; faculty resources; expenditures per student; student/faculty ratio; and library resources. *U.S. News & World Report,* "*America's Best Graduate Schools, Law, 2022*"

According to *U.S. News & World Report,* the Atlanta-Sandy Springs-Roswell, GA metro area is home to one of the top 75 medical schools for research in the U.S.: **Emory University** (#22 tie). The rankings are based on a weighted average of 11 measures of quality: quality assessment; peer assessment score; assessment score by residency directors; research activity; total research activity; average research activity per faculty member; student selectivity; median MCAT total score; median undergraduate GPA; acceptance rate; and faculty resources. *U.S. News & World Report,* "*America's Best Graduate Schools, Medical, 2022*"

According to *U.S. News & World Report,* the Atlanta-Sandy Springs-Roswell, GA metro area is home to two of the top 75 business schools in the U.S.: **Emory University (Goizueta)** (#26 tie); **Georgia Institute of Technology (Scheller)** (#28 tie). The rankings are based on a weighted average of the following nine measures: quality assessment; peer assessment; recruiter assessment; placement success; mean starting salary and bonus; student selectivity; mean GMAT and GRE scores; mean undergraduate GPA; and acceptance rate. *U.S. News & World Report,* "*America's Best Graduate Schools, Business, 2022*"

EMPLOYERS

Major Employers

Company Name	Industry
Apartments.com	Apartment locating service
Aquilex Holdings	Facilities support services
AT&T	Engineering services
Children's Healthcare of Atlanta	Healthcare
Clayton County Board of Education	Public elementary & secondary schools
County of Gwinnett	County government
Delta Air Lines	Air transportation, scheduled
Georgia Department of Behavioral Health	Administration of public health programs
Georgia Department of Human Resoures	Administration of public health programs
Georgia Department of Transportation	Regulation, administration of transportation
IBM	Engineering services
Internal Revenue Service	Taxation department, government
Lockheed Martin Aeronautical Company	Aircraft
NCR Corporation	Calculating and accounting equipment
Northide Hospital	Healthcare
Progressive Logistics Services	Labor organizations
Robert Half International	Employment agencies
Saint Joseph's Hospital	Healthcare
The Coca-Cola Company	Bottled and canned soft drinks
The Fulton-Dekalb Hospital Authority	General medical & surgical hospitals
The Home Depot	Hardware stores
U.S. Army	U.S. military
WellStar Kennestone Hospital	General medical & surgical hospitals
World Travel Partners Group	Travel agencies

Note: Companies shown are located within the Atlanta-Sandy Springs-Roswell, GA Metropolitan Statistical Area.
Source: Hoovers.com; Wikipedia

Best Companies to Work For

Alston & Bird; Delta Air Lines, headquartered in Atlanta, are among "The 100 Best Companies to Work For." To pick the best companies, *Fortune* partnered with the Great Place to Work Institute. Two-thirds of a company's score is based on the results of the Institute's Trust Index survey, which is sent to a random sample of employees from each company. The questions related to attitudes about management's credibility, job satisfaction, and camaraderie. The other third of the scoring is based on the company's responses to the Institute's Culture Audit, which includes detailed questions about pay and benefit programs, and a series of open-ended questions about hiring practices, internal communication, training, recognition programs, and diversity efforts. Any company that is at least five years old with more than 1,000 U.S. employees is eligible. *Fortune, "The 100 Best Companies to Work For," 2020*

Children's Healthcare of Atlanta, headquartered in Atlanta, is among the "100 Best Companies for Working Mothers." Criteria: paid time off and leaves; workforce profile; benefits; women's issues and advancement; flexible work; company culture and work life programs. *Working Mother, "100 Best Companies for Working Mothers," 2020*

Children's Healthcare of Atlanta; Southern Co, headquartered in Atlanta, are among the "100 Best Places to Work in IT." To qualify, companies had to be U.S.-based organizations or be non-U.S.-based employers that met the following criteria: have a minimum of 300 total employees at a U.S. headquarters and a minimum of 30 IT employees in the U.S., with at least 50% of their IT employees based in the U.S. The best places to work were selected based on compensation, benefits, work/life balance, employee morale, and satisfaction with training and development programs. In addition, *InsiderPro* and *Computerworld* looked at retention efforts, programs for recognizing and rewarding outstanding performances, and benefits such as flextime, elder care and child care, and reimbursement for college tuition and the cost of pursuing technology certifications. *InsiderPro and Computerworld, "100 Best Places to Work in IT," 2020*

Childrens Healthcare of Atlanta, headquartered in Atlanta, is among the "Top Companies for Executive Women." This list is determined by organizations filling out an in-depth survey that measures female demographics at every level, but with an emphasis on women in senior corporate roles, with profit & loss (P&L) responsibility, and those earning in the top 20 percent of the organization. *Working Mother* defines P&L as having responsibility that involves monitoring the net income after expenses for a department or entire organization, with direct influence on how company resources are allocated. *Working Mother, "Top Companies for Executive Women," 2020+*

Children's Healthcare of Atlanta, headquartered in Atlanta, is among the "Best Companies for Dads." *Working Mother's* newest list recognizes the growing importance companies place on giving dads time off and support for their families. Rankings are determined by measuring gender-neutral or paternity leave offered, as well as actual time taken, phase-back policies, child- and dependent-care benefits, and corporate support groups for men and dads. *Working Mother, "Best Companies for Dads," 2020*

PUBLIC SAFETY

Crime Rate

Area	All Crimes	Violent Crimes				Property Crimes		
		Murder	Rape[3]	Robbery	Aggrav. Assault	Burglary	Larceny-Theft	Motor Vehicle Theft
City	5,423.2	17.7	49.4	221.5	480.1	621.2	3,366.4	666.8
Suburbs[1]	2,666.3	4.6	24.0	82.5	168.8	373.2	1,770.4	242.7
Metro[2]	2,895.7	5.7	26.1	94.1	194.7	393.9	1,903.2	278.0
U.S.	2,593.1	5.0	44.0	86.1	248.2	378.0	1,601.6	230.2

Note: Figures are crimes per 100,000 population; (1) All areas within the metro area that are located outside the city limits; (2) Figures cover the Atlanta-Sandy Springs-Roswell, GA Metropolitan Statistical Area; (3) All figures shown were reported using the revised Uniform Crime Reporting (UCR) definition of rape.
Source: FBI Uniform Crime Reports, 2018 (data for 2019 was not available)

Hate Crimes

Area	Number of Quarters Reported	Number of Incidents per Bias Motivation					
		Race/Ethnicity/ Ancestry	Religion	Sexual Orientation	Disability	Gender	Gender Identity
City	3	0	1	0	0	0	0
U.S.	4	3,963	1,521	1,195	157	69	198

Source: Federal Bureau of Investigation, Hate Crime Statistics 2019

Identity Theft Consumer Reports

Area	Reports	Reports per 100,000 Population	Rank[2]
MSA[1]	53,964	896	14
U.S.	1,387,615	423	-

Note: (1) Figures cover the Atlanta-Sandy Springs-Roswell, GA Metropolitan Statistical Area; (2) Rank ranges from 1 to 391 where 1 indicates greatest number of identity theft reports per 100,000 population
Source: Federal Trade Commission, Consumer Sentinel Network Data Book 2020

Fraud and Other Consumer Reports

Area	Reports	Reports per 100,000 Population	Rank[2]
MSA[1]	73,880	1,227	7
U.S.	3,385,133	1,031	-

Note: (1) Figures cover the Atlanta-Sandy Springs-Roswell, GA Metropolitan Statistical Area; (2) Rank ranges from 1 to 391 where 1 indicates greatest number of fraud and other consumer reports per 100,000 population
Source: Federal Trade Commission, Consumer Sentinel Network Data Book 2020

POLITICS

2020 Presidential Election Results

Area	Biden	Trump	Jorgensen	Hawkins	Other
Fulton County	72.6	26.2	1.2	0.0	0.0
U.S.	51.3	46.8	1.2	0.3	0.5

Note: Results are percentages and may not add to 100% due to rounding
Source: Dave Leip's Atlas of U.S. Presidential Elections

SPORTS

Professional Sports Teams

Team Name	League	Year Established
Atlanta Braves	Major League Baseball (MLB)	1966
Atlanta Falcons	National Football League (NFL)	1966
Atlanta Hawks	National Basketball Association (NBA)	1968
Atlanta United FC	Major League Soccer (MLS)	2017

Note: Includes teams located in the Atlanta-Sandy Springs-Roswell, GA Metropolitan Statistical Area.
Source: Wikipedia, Major Professional Sports Teams of the United States and Canada, April 6, 2021

CLIMATE

Average and Extreme Temperatures

Temperature	Jan	Feb	Mar	Apr	May	Jun	Jul	Aug	Sep	Oct	Nov	Dec	Yr.
Extreme High (°F)	79	80	85	93	95	101	105	102	98	95	84	77	105
Average High (°F)	52	56	64	73	80	86	88	88	82	73	63	54	72
Average Temp. (°F)	43	46	53	62	70	77	79	79	73	63	53	45	62
Average Low (°F)	33	36	42	51	59	66	70	69	64	52	42	35	52
Extreme Low (°F)	-8	5	10	26	37	46	53	55	36	28	3	0	-8

Note: Figures cover the years 1945-1990
Source: National Climatic Data Center, International Station Meteorological Climate Summary, 9/96

Average Precipitation/Snowfall/Humidity

Precip./Humidity	Jan	Feb	Mar	Apr	May	Jun	Jul	Aug	Sep	Oct	Nov	Dec	Yr.
Avg. Precip. (in.)	4.7	4.6	5.7	4.3	4.0	3.5	5.1	3.6	3.4	2.8	3.8	4.2	49.8
Avg. Snowfall (in.)	1	1	Tr	Tr	0	0	0	0	0	0	Tr	Tr	2
Avg. Rel. Hum. 7am (%)	79	77	78	78	82	83	88	89	88	84	81	79	82
Avg. Rel. Hum. 4pm (%)	56	50	48	45	49	52	57	56	56	51	52	55	52

Note: Figures cover the years 1945-1990; Tr = Trace amounts (<0.05 in. of rain; <0.5 in. of snow)
Source: National Climatic Data Center, International Station Meteorological Climate Summary, 9/96

Weather Conditions

Temperature			Daytime Sky			Precipitation		
10°F & below	32°F & below	90°F & above	Clear	Partly cloudy	Cloudy	0.01 inch or more precip.	0.1 inch or more snow/ice	Thunder-storms
1	49	38	98	147	120	116	3	48

Note: Figures are average number of days per year and cover the years 1945-1990
Source: National Climatic Data Center, International Station Meteorological Climate Summary, 9/96

HAZARDOUS WASTE

Superfund Sites

The Atlanta-Sandy Springs-Roswell, GA metro area has no sites on the EPA's Superfund Final National Priorities List. There are a total of 1,375 Superfund sites with a status of proposed or final on the list in the U.S. *U.S. Environmental Protection Agency, National Priorities List, April 7, 2021*

AIR QUALITY

Air Quality Trends: Ozone

	1990	1995	2000	2005	2010	2015	2016	2017	2018	2019
MSA[1]	0.104	0.103	0.101	0.087	0.076	0.070	0.073	0.068	0.068	0.071
U.S.	0.088	0.089	0.082	0.080	0.073	0.068	0.069	0.068	0.069	0.065

Note: (1) Data covers the Atlanta-Sandy Springs-Roswell, GA Metropolitan Statistical Area. The values shown are the composite ozone concentration averages among trend sites based on the highest fourth daily maximum 8-hour concentration in parts per million. These trends are based on sites having an adequate record of monitoring data during the trend period. Data from exceptional events are included.
Source: U.S. Environmental Protection Agency, Air Quality Monitoring Information, "Air Quality Trends by City, 1990-2019"

Air Quality Index

Area	Percent of Days when Air Quality was...[2]					AQI Statistics[2]	
	Good	Moderate	Unhealthy for Sensitive Groups	Unhealthy	Very Unhealthy	Maximum	Median
MSA[1]	44.4	50.4	4.9	0.3	0.0	172	52

Note: (1) Data covers the Atlanta-Sandy Springs-Roswell, GA Metropolitan Statistical Area; (2) Based on 365 days with AQI data in 2019. Air Quality Index (AQI) is an index for reporting daily air quality. EPA calculates the AQI for five major air pollutants regulated by the Clean Air Act: ground-level ozone, particle pollution (aka particulate matter), carbon monoxide, sulfur dioxide, and nitrogen dioxide. The AQI runs from 0 to 500. The higher the AQI value, the greater the level of air pollution and the greater the health concern. There are six AQI categories: "Good" AQI is between 0 and 50. Air quality is considered satisfactory; "Moderate" AQI is between 51 and 100. Air quality is acceptable; "Unhealthy for Sensitive Groups" When AQI values are between 101 and 150, members of sensitive groups may experience health effects; "Unhealthy" When AQI values are between 151 and 200 everyone may begin to experience health effects; "Very Unhealthy" AQI values between 201 and 300 trigger a health alert; "Hazardous" AQI values over 300 trigger warnings of emergency conditions (not shown).
Source: U.S. Environmental Protection Agency, Air Quality Index Report, 2019

Air Quality Index Pollutants

Area	Percent of Days when AQI Pollutant was...[2]					
	Carbon Monoxide	Nitrogen Dioxide	Ozone	Sulfur Dioxide	Particulate Matter 2.5	Particulate Matter 10
MSA[1]	0.0	2.5	46.8	0.0	50.7	0.0

Note: (1) Data covers the Atlanta-Sandy Springs-Roswell, GA Metropolitan Statistical Area; (2) Based on 365 days with AQI data in 2019. The Air Quality Index (AQI) is an index for reporting daily air quality. EPA calculates the AQI for five major air pollutants regulated by the Clean Air Act: ground-level ozone, particle pollution (also known as particulate matter), carbon monoxide, sulfur dioxide, and nitrogen dioxide. The AQI runs from 0 to 500. The higher the AQI value, the greater the level of air pollution and the greater the health concern.
Source: U.S. Environmental Protection Agency, Air Quality Index Report, 2019

Maximum Air Pollutant Concentrations: Particulate Matter, Ozone, CO and Lead

	Particulate Matter 10 (ug/m^3)	Particulate Matter 2.5 Wtd AM (ug/m^3)	Particulate Matter 2.5 24-Hr (ug/m^3)	Ozone (ppm)	Carbon Monoxide (ppm)	Lead (ug/m^3)
MSA[1] Level	40	10.8	24	0.075	2	n/a
NAAQS[2]	150	15	35	0.075	9	0.15
Met NAAQS[2]	Yes	Yes	Yes	Yes	Yes	n/a

Note: (1) Data covers the Atlanta-Sandy Springs-Roswell, GA Metropolitan Statistical Area; Data from exceptional events are included; (2) National Ambient Air Quality Standards; ppm = parts per million; ug/m^3 = micrograms per cubic meter; n/a not available.
Concentrations: Particulate Matter 10 (coarse particulate)—highest second maximum 24-hour concentration; Particulate Matter 2.5 Wtd AM (fine particulate)—highest weighted annual mean concentration; Particulate Matter 2.5 24-Hour (fine particulate)—highest 98th percentile 24-hour concentration; Ozone—highest fourth daily maximum 8-hour concentration; Carbon Monoxide—highest second maximum non-overlapping 8-hour concentration; Lead—maximum running 3-month average
Source: U.S. Environmental Protection Agency, Air Quality Monitoring Information, "Air Quality Statistics by City, 2019"

Maximum Air Pollutant Concentrations: Nitrogen Dioxide and Sulfur Dioxide

	Nitrogen Dioxide AM (ppb)	Nitrogen Dioxide 1-Hr (ppb)	Sulfur Dioxide AM (ppb)	Sulfur Dioxide 1-Hr (ppb)	Sulfur Dioxide 24-Hr (ppb)
MSA[1] Level	16	50	n/a	5	n/a
NAAQS[2]	53	100	30	75	140
Met NAAQS[2]	Yes	Yes	n/a	Yes	n/a

Note: (1) Data covers the Atlanta-Sandy Springs-Roswell, GA Metropolitan Statistical Area; Data from exceptional events are included; (2) National Ambient Air Quality Standards; ppm = parts per million; ug/m^3 = micrograms per cubic meter; n/a not available.
Concentrations: Nitrogen Dioxide AM—highest arithmetic mean concentration; Nitrogen Dioxide 1-Hr—highest 98th percentile 1-hour daily maximum concentration; Sulfur Dioxide AM—highest annual mean concentration; Sulfur Dioxide 1-Hr—highest 99th percentile 1-hour daily maximum concentration; Sulfur Dioxide 24-Hr—highest second maximum 24-hour concentration
Source: U.S. Environmental Protection Agency, Air Quality Monitoring Information, "Air Quality Statistics by City, 2019"

Austin, Texas

Background

Starting out in 1730 as a peaceful Spanish mission on the north bank of the Colorado River in south-central Texas, Austin soon engaged in an imbroglio of territorial wars, beginning when the "Father of Texas," Stephen F. Austin, annexed the territory from Mexico in 1833 as his own. Later, the Republic of Texas named the territory Austin in honor of the colonizer, and conferred upon it state capital status. Challenges to this decision ensued, ranging from an invasion by the Mexican government to reclaim its land, to Sam Houston's call that the capital ought to move from Austin to Houston.

During peaceful times, however, Austin has been called the "City of the Violet Crown." Coined by the short story writer, William Sydney Porter, or O. Henry, the name refers to the purple mist that circles the surrounding hills of the Colorado River Valley.

This city of technological innovation is home to a strong computer and electronics industry. Austin offers hundreds of free wireless spots, including its city parks, and its technology focus has traditionally drawn numerous high-tech companies. A major Samsung Electronics computer chip plant was built in Austin in the late 1990s with expansions and a new, huge facility, since. Along with this technology growth came increased traffic, especially on Interstate 35, the main highway linking the U.S. and Mexico. An 89-mile bypass has helped to relieve some of the traffic difficulties long associated with I-35, after which Facebook opened a sales and operations facility in the city.

In addition to its traditional business community, Austin is home to the main campus of the University of Texas. The university provides Austin with diverse lifestyles; today there is a solid mix of white-collar workers, students, professors, blue-collar workers, musicians and artists, and members of the booming tech industry who all call themselves Austinites.

The influx of young people centered on university life has contributed to the city's growth as a thriving live music scene. It is so important to the city that its local government maintains the Austin Music Commission to promote the local music industry.

A notable industry conference takes place here each spring. The South by Southwest Conference (SXSW) showcases more than 2,000 performers at 90+ venues throughout the city. The growing film and interactive industries have been added to the conference in recent years.

> South by Southwest Festival (SXSW) went digital this year, with keynotes, networking, Music Festival showcases, and Film Festival screenings.

The civic-minded city operates from a new city hall, which is also home to a public plaza facing Town Lake. One of the town's cultural hubs, the Long Center for the Performing Arts, underwent a major renovation in the last decade. And the city finally has its first major-league professional sports team—Austin FC—part of the Major League Soccer League and scheduled to play in 2021.

It is most likely Austinites' pride in their creative and independent culture that has spawned a movement to keep the city from too much corporate development. The slogan "Keep Austin Weird" was adopted by the Austin Independent Business Alliance as a way to promote local and alternative business.

Austin's skyline is no longer dominated by the Texas State Capitol and the University of Texas. Many new high-rise towers have been constructed in recent years, including The Austonian, with more high-rise projects under construction in Austin's downtown.

Austin consistently gets high marks in best city surveys. The city sits at a desirable location along the Colorado River, and many recreational activities center on the water. For instance, Austin boasts three spring-fed swimming pools enjoyed by its residents, as well as the Lance Armstrong Crosstown Bikeway. The city has more than 100 miles of bike paths.

The climate of Austin is subtropical with hot summers. Winters are mild, with below-freezing temperatures occurring on an average of 25 days a year. Cold spells are short, seldom lasting more than two days. Daytime temperatures in summer are hot, while summer nights are usually pleasant. In February 2021, a series of severe winter storms caused record low temperatures in Austin, falling below Anchorage, Alaska, and causing a massive electricity generation failure in the state.

Rankings

General Rankings

- *US News & World Report* conducted a survey of more than 3,000 people and analyzed the 150 largest metropolitan areas to determine what matters most when selecting the next place to live. Austin ranked #3 out of the top 25 as having the best combination of desirable factors. Criteria: cost of living; quality of life; net migration; job market; desirability; and other factors. *realestate.usnews.com, "The 25 Best Places to Live in the U.S. in 2020-21," October 13, 2020*

- The Austin metro area was identified as one of America's fastest-growing areas in terms of population and business growth by *MagnifyMoney*. The area ranked #1 out of 35. The 100 most populous metro areas in the U.S. were evaluated on their change from 2011-2016 in the following categories: people and housing; workforce and employment opportunities; growing industry. *www.businessinsider.com, "The 35 Cities in the US with the Biggest Influx of People, the Most Work Opportunities, and the Hottest Business Growth," August 12, 2018*

- The Austin metro area was identified as one of America's fastest-growing areas in terms of population and economy by *Forbes*. The area ranked #8 out of 25. The 100 most populous metro areas in the U.S. were evaluated on the following criteria: estimated population growth; employment; economic output; wages; home values. *Forbes, "America's Fastest-Growing Cities 2018," February 28, 2018*

- Austin appeared on *Travel + Leisure's* list of the 15 best cities in the United States. The city was ranked #10. Criteria: sights/landmarks; culture; food; friendliness; shopping; and overall value. *Travel + Leisure, "The World's Best Awards 2020" July 8, 2020*

Business/Finance Rankings

- According to *Business Insider*, the Austin metro area is a prime place to run a startup or move an existing business to. The area ranked #9. Nearly 190 metro areas were analyzed on overall economic health and investments. Data was based on the 2019 U.S. Census Bureau American Community Survey, the marketing company PitchBook, Bureau of Labor Statistics employment report, and Zillow. Criteria: percentage of change in typical home values and employment rates; quarterly venture capital investment activity; and median household income. *www.businessinsider.com, "The 25 Best Cities to Start a Business-Or Move Your Current One," January 12, 2021*

- 24/7 Wall Street used metro data from the Bureau of Labor Statistics' Occupational Employment database to identify the cities with the highest percentage of those employed in jobs requiring knowledge in the science, technology, engineering, and math (STEM) fields as well as average wages for STEM jobs. The Austin metro area was #9. *247wallst.com, "15 Cities with the Most High-Tech Jobs," January 11, 2020*

- Based on metro area social media reviews, the employment opinion group Glassdoor surveyed 50 of the most populous U.S. metro areas and equally weighed cost of living, hiring opportunity, and job satisfaction to compose a list of "25 Best Cities for Jobs." Median pay and home value, and number of active job openings were also factored in. The Austin metro area was ranked #24 in overall job satisfaction. *www.glassdoor.com, "Best Cities for Jobs," February 25, 2020*

- The Brookings Institution ranked the nation's largest cities based on income inequality. Austin was ranked #47 (#1 = greatest inequality). Criteria: the "95/20 ratio," a figure representing the income at which a household earns more than 95 percent of all other households, divided by the income at which a household earns more than only 20 percent of all other households. *Brookings Institution, "Household Income Inequality, Largest Cities of 97 Large U.S. Metro Areas, 2014-2016," February 5, 2018*

- The Brookings Institution ranked the 100 largest metro areas in the U.S. based on income inequality. Austin was ranked #37 (#1 = greatest inequality). Criteria: the "95/20 ratio," a figure representing the income at which a household earns more than 95 percent of all other households, divided by the income at which a household earns more than only 20 percent of all other households. *Brookings Institution, "Household Income Inequality, 100 Largest U.S. Metro Areas, 2014-2016," February 5, 2018*

- *Forbes* ranked the 100 largest metro areas in the U.S. in terms of the "Best Cities for Young Professionals." The Austin metro area ranked #2 out of 25. Criteria: median rent of a two-bedroom apartment; job growth and unemployment rate; median salary of college graduates with 5 or less years of work experience; networking opportunities; social outlook; percentage of population 25 years of age and older with college degrees. *Forbes.com, "America's 25 Best Cities for Young Professionals in 2017," May 22, 2017*

- Payscale.com ranked the 32 largest metro areas in terms of wage growth. The Austin metro area ranked #15. Criteria: private-sector and education professional wage growth between the 4th quarter of 2019 and the 4th quarter of 2020. *PayScale, "Wage Trends by Metro Area-4th Quarter," January 11, 2021*

- Austin was cited as one of America's top metros for new and expanded facility projects in 2020. The area ranked #6 in the large metro area category (population over 1 million). *Site Selection, "Top Metros of 2020," March 2021*

- Austin was identified as one of the happiest cities to work in by CareerBliss.com, an online community for career advancement. The city ranked #10 out of 10. Criteria: an employee's relationship with his or her boss and co-workers; daily tasks; general work environment; compensation; opportunities for advancement; company culture and job reputation; and resources. *Businesswire.com, "CareerBliss Happiest Cities to Work 2019," February 12, 2019*

- The Austin metro area appeared on the Milken Institute "2021 Best Performing Cities" list. Rank: #3 out of 200 large metro areas (population over 250,000). Criteria: job growth; wage and salary growth; high-tech output growth; housing affordability; household broadband access. *Milken Institute, "Best-Performing Cities 2021," February 16, 2021*

- *Forbes* ranked the 200 most populous metro areas to determine the nation's "Best Places for Business and Careers." The Austin metro area was ranked #8. Criteria: costs (business and living); job growth (past and projected); income growth; quality of life; educational attainment (college and high school); projected economic growth; cultural and leisure opportunities; workplace tolerance laws; net migration patterns. *Forbes, "The Best Places for Business and Careers 2019: Seattle Still On Top," October 30, 2019*

Culture/Performing Arts Rankings

- Austin was selected as one of the 25 best cities for moviemakers in North America. COVID-19 has spurred a quest for great film cities that offer more creative space, lower costs, and more great outdoors. NYC & LA were intentionally excluded. Criteria: longstanding reputations as film-friendly communities; efforts to deal with pandemic-specific challenges; and establish appropriate COVID-19 guidelines. The city was ranked #3. *MovieMaker Magazine, "Best Places to Live and Work as a Moviemaker, 2021," January 26, 2021*

Dating/Romance Rankings

- Austin was selected as one of the best cities for post grads by *Rent.com*. The city ranked among the top 10. Criteria: jobs per capita; unemployment rate; mean annual income; cost of living; rental inventory. *Rent.com, "Best Cities for College Grads," December 11, 2018*

Education Rankings

- Personal finance website *WalletHub* analyzed the 150 largest U.S. metropolitan statistical areas to determine where the most educated Americans are putting their degrees to work. Criteria: education levels; percentage of workers with degrees; education quality and attainment gap; public school quality rankings; quality and enrollment of each metro area's universities. Austin was ranked #9 (#1 = most educated city). *www.WalletHub.com, "Most and Least Educated Cities in America," July 20, 2020*

- Austin was selected as one of America's most literate cities. The city ranked #15 out of the 84 largest U.S. cities. Criteria: number of booksellers; library resources; Internet resources; educational attainment; periodical publishing resources; newspaper circulation. *Central Connecticut State University, "America's Most Literate Cities, 2018," February 2019*

Environmental Rankings

- Sperling's BestPlaces assessed the 50 largest metropolitan areas of the United States for the likelihood of dangerously extreme weather events or earthquakes. In general the Southeast and South-Central regions have the highest risk of weather extremes and earthquakes, while the Pacific Northwest enjoys the lowest risk. Of the most risky metropolitan areas, the Austin metro area was ranked #2. *www.bestplaces.net, "Avoid Natural Disasters: BestPlaces Reveals The Top 10 Safest Places to Live," October 25, 2017*

- The U.S. Environmental Protection Agency (EPA) released a list of U.S. metropolitan areas with the most ENERGY STAR certified buildings in 2019. The Austin metro area was ranked #17 out of 25. *U.S. Environmental Protection Agency, "2020 Energy Star Top Cities," March 2020*

Food/Drink Rankings

- The U.S. Chamber of Commerce Foundation conducted an in-depth study on local food truck regulations, surveyed 288 food truck owners, and ranked 20 major American cities based on how friendly they are for operating a food truck. The compiled index assessed the following: procedures for obtaining permits and licenses; complying with restrictions; and financial obligations associated with operating a food truck. Austin ranked #7 overall (1 being the best). *www.foodtrucknation.us, "Food Truck Nation," March 20, 2018*

Health/Fitness Rankings

- For each of the 100 largest cities in the United States, the American Fitness Index®, published by the American College of Sports Medicine and the Anthem Foundation, evaluated community infrastructure and 33 health behaviors including preventive health, levels of chronic disease conditions, pedestrian safety, air quality, and community resources that support physical activity. Austin ranked #31 for "community fitness." *americanfitnessindex.org, "2020 ACSM American Fitness Index Summary Report," July 14, 2020*

- Austin was identified as a "2021 Spring Allergy Capital." The area ranked #66 out of 100. Three groups of factors were used to identify the most challenging cities for people with allergies during the spring season: annual spring pollen levels; over the counter medicine use; number of board-certified allergy specialists. *Asthma and Allergy Foundation of America, "Spring Allergy Capitals 2021," February 23, 2021*

- Austin was identified as a "2021 Fall Allergy Capital." The area ranked #50 out of 100. Three groups of factors were used to identify the most challenging cities for people with allergies during the fall season: annual fall pollen levels; over the counter medicine use; number of board-certified allergy specialists. *Asthma and Allergy Foundation of America, "Fall Allergy Capitals 2021," February 23, 2021*

- Austin was identified as a "2019 Asthma Capital." The area ranked #77 out of the nation's 100 largest metropolitan areas. Criteria: estimated asthma prevalence; crude death rate from asthma; and ER visits due to asthma. Risk factors analyzed but not factored in the rankings: annual pollen score; annual air quality; public smoking laws; number of board-certified asthma specialists; rescue medication use; controller medication use; uninsured rate; poverty rate. *Asthma and Allergy Foundation of America, "Asthma Capitals 2019: The Most Challenging Places to Live With Asthma," May 7, 2019*

Pet Rankings

- Austin appeared on *The Dogington Post* site as one of the top cities for dog lovers, ranking #13 out of 20. The real estate brokerage, Redfin and Rover, the largest pet sitter and dog walker network, compiled a list from over 14,000 U.S. cities to come up with a "Rover Rank." Criteria: highest count of dog walks, the city's Walk Score®, for-sale home listings that mention "dog," number of dog walkers and pet sitters and the hours spent and distance logged. *www.dogingtonpost.com, "The 20 Most Dog-Friendly Cities of 2019," April 4, 2019*

Real Estate Rankings

- FitSmallBusiness looked at 50 of the largest metropolitan areas in the U.S. to determine which metro was the best to start a real estate business. Data was compiled from such sources as: Zillow, Trulia, U.S. Census Bureau, and the Bureau of Labor Statistics. Criteria: location; inventory; annual wages; median sales price of homes; days on the market; median price cut percentage; and other factors that would influence real estate professional growth. The Austin metro area ranked #13. *fitsmallbusiness.com, "The Best Cities to Become a Real Estate Agent in 2018," January 30, 2018*

- *WalletHub* compared the most populated U.S. cities to determine which had the best markets for real estate agents. Austin ranked #42 where demand was high and pay was the best. Criteria: sales per agent; annual median wage for real-estate agents; monthly average starting salary for real estate agents; real estate job density and competition; unemployment rate; home turnover rate; housing-market health index; and other relevant metrics. *www.WalletHub.com, "2019's Best Places to Be a Real Estate Agent," April 24, 2019*

- According to Penske Truck Rental, the Austin metro area was named the #10 moving destination in 2019, based on one-way consumer truck rental reservations made through Penske's website, rental locations, and reservations call center. *gopenske.com/blog, "Penske Truck Rental's 2019 Top Moving Destinations," January 22, 2020*

- Austin was ranked #13 in the top 20 out of the 100 largest metro areas in terms of house price appreciation in 2020 (#1 = highest rate). *Federal Housing Finance Agency, House Price Index, 4th Quarter 2020*

- Austin was ranked #161 out of 268 metro areas in terms of housing affordability in 2020 by the National Association of Home Builders (#1 = most affordable). Criteria: the share of homes sold in that area affordable to a family earning the local median income, based on standard mortgage underwriting criteria. *National Association of Home Builders®, NAHB-Wells Fargo Housing Opportunity Index, 4th Quarter 2020*

Safety Rankings

- Allstate ranked the 200 largest cities in America in terms of driver safety. Austin ranked #160. Criteria: internal property damage claims over a two-year period from January 2016 to December 2017. The report helps increase the importance of safety and awareness behind the wheel. *Allstate, "Allstate America's Best Drivers Report, 2019" June 24, 2019*

- The National Insurance Crime Bureau ranked 384 metro areas in the U.S. in terms of per capita rates of vehicle theft. The Austin metro area ranked #138 (#1 = highest rate). Criteria: number of vehicle theft offenses per 100,000 inhabitants in 2019. *National Insurance Crime Bureau, "Hot Spots 2019," July 21, 2020*

Seniors/Retirement Rankings

- From its Best Cities for Successful Aging indexes, the Milken Institute generated rankings for metropolitan areas, weighing data in nine categories—health care, wellness, living arrangements, transportation and convenience, financial characteristics, education, employment, community engagement, and overall livability. The Austin metro area was ranked #6 overall in the large metro area category. *Milken Institute, "Best Cities for Successful Aging, 2017" March 14, 2017*

- Austin was identified as #15 of 20 most popular places to retire in the Southwest region by *Topretirements.com*. The site separated its annual "Best Places to Retire" list by major U.S. regions for 2019. The list reflects the 20 cities that visitors to the website are most interested in for retirement, based on the number of times a city's review was viewed on the website. *Topretirements.com, "20 Most Popular Places to Retire in the Southwest for 2019," October 2, 2019*

Sports/Recreation Rankings

- Austin was chosen as one of America's best cities for bicycling. The city ranked #13 out of 50. Criteria: cycling infrastructure that is safe and friendly for all ages; energy and bike culture. The editors evaluated cities with populations of 100,000 or more. *Bicycling, "The 50 Best Bike Cities in America," October 10, 2018*

Women/Minorities Rankings

- *Travel + Leisure* listed the best cities in and around the US for a memorable and fun girls' trip, even on a budget. Whether it is for a special occasion or just to get away, Austin is sure to have something for all the ladies in your tribe. *Travel + Leisure, "25 Girls' Weekend Getaways That Won't Break the Bank," June 8, 2020*

- The *Houston Chronicle* listed the Austin metro area as #2 in top places for young Latinos to live in the U.S. Research was largely based on housing and occupational data from the largest metropolitan areas performed by *Forbes* and NBC Universo. Criteria: percentage of 18-34 year-olds; Latino college grad rates; and diversity. *blog.chron.com, "The 15 Best Big Cities for Latino Millenials," January 26, 2016*

- *Women's Health*, together with the site Yelp, identified the 15 "Wellthiest" spots in the U.S. Austin appeared among the top for happiest, healthiest, outdoorsiest and Zen-iest. *Women's Health, "The 15 Wellthiest Cities in the U.S." July 5, 2017*

- Personal finance website *WalletHub* compared more than 180 U.S. cities across two key dimensions, "Hispanic Business-Friendliness" and "Hispanic Purchasing Power," to arrive at the most favorable conditions for Hispanic entrepreneurs. Austin was ranked #17 out of 182. Criteria includes: share of Hispanic-Owned Businesses; Hispanic entrepreneurship rate to median annual income of Hispanics; Small Business-Friendliness score; cost of living; and number of Hispanics with at least a bachelor's degree. *WalletHub.com, "2019's Best Cities for Hispanic Entrepreneurs," May 1, 2019*

Miscellaneous Rankings

- While the majority of travel ground to a halt in 2020, plugged-in travel influencers and experts were able to rediscover their local regions. Austin appeared on a *Forbes* list of 15 U.S. cities that provided solace as well as local inspiration. Whether it be quirky things to see and do, delicious take out, outdoor exploring and daytrips, these places are must-see destinations. *Forbes, "Bucket List Travel: The 15 Best U.S. Destinations For 2021," January 1, 2021*

- *WalletHub* compared the 150 most populated U.S. cities to determine their operating efficiency. A "Quality of City Services" score was constructed for each city and then divided by the total budget per capita to reveal which were managed the best. Austin ranked #78. Criteria: financial stability; economy; education; safety; health; infrastructure and pollution. *www.WalletHub.com, "2020's Best- & Worst-Run Cities in America," June 29, 2020*

Business Environment

DEMOGRAPHICS

Population Growth

Area	1990 Census	2000 Census	2010 Census	2019* Estimate	Population Growth (%) 1990-2019	Population Growth (%) 2010-2019
City	499,053	656,562	790,390	950,807	90.5	20.3
MSA[1]	846,217	1,249,763	1,716,289	2,114,441	149.9	23.2
U.S.	248,709,873	281,421,906	308,745,538	324,697,795	30.6	5.2

Note: (1) Figures cover the Austin-Round Rock, TX Metropolitan Statistical Area; (*) 2015-2019 5-year estimated population
Source: U.S. Census Bureau, 1990 Census, Census 2000, Census 2010, 2015-2019 American Community Survey 5-Year Estimates

Household Size

Area	One	Two	Three	Four	Five	Six	Seven or More	Average Household Size
City	34.5	32.8	14.3	11.4	4.5	1.5	1.0	2.40
MSA[1]	27.9	33.1	15.6	13.9	6.1	2.1	1.2	2.70
U.S.	27.9	33.9	15.6	12.9	6.0	2.3	1.4	2.60

Note: (1) Figures cover the Austin-Round Rock, TX Metropolitan Statistical Area
Source: U.S. Census Bureau, 2015-2019 American Community Survey 5-Year Estimates

Race

Area	White Alone[2] (%)	Black Alone[2] (%)	Asian Alone[2] (%)	AIAN[3] Alone[2] (%)	NHOPI[4] Alone[2] (%)	Other Race Alone[2] (%)	Two or More Races (%)
City	72.6	7.8	7.6	0.7	0.1	7.8	3.5
MSA[1]	76.0	7.3	5.9	0.5	0.1	6.7	3.6
U.S.	72.5	12.7	5.5	0.8	0.2	4.9	3.3

Note: (1) Figures cover the Austin-Round Rock, TX Metropolitan Statistical Area; (2) Alone is defined as not being in combination with one or more other races; (3) American Indian and Alaska Native; (4) Native Hawaiian and Other Pacific Islander
Source: U.S. Census Bureau, 2015-2019 American Community Survey 5-Year Estimates

Hispanic or Latino Origin

Area	Total (%)	Mexican (%)	Puerto Rican (%)	Cuban (%)	Other (%)
City	33.9	27.2	0.9	0.7	5.2
MSA[1]	32.4	26.8	0.9	0.5	4.3
U.S.	18.0	11.2	1.7	0.7	4.3

Note: Persons of Hispanic or Latino origin can be of any race; (1) Figures cover the Austin-Round Rock, TX Metropolitan Statistical Area
Source: U.S. Census Bureau, 2015-2019 American Community Survey 5-Year Estimates

Ancestry

Area	German	Irish	English	American	Italian	Polish	French[2]	Scottish	Dutch
City	10.4	7.4	7.4	3.1	3.0	1.7	2.3	2.0	0.8
MSA[1]	12.3	7.7	7.9	3.8	2.7	1.6	2.4	2.0	0.8
U.S.	13.3	9.7	7.2	6.2	5.1	2.8	2.3	1.7	1.2

Note: Figures are the percentage of the total population reporting a particular ancestry. The nine most commonly reported ancestries in the U.S. are shown. Figures include multiple ancestries (e.g. if a person reported being Irish and Italian, they were included in both columns); (1) Figures cover the Austin-Round Rock, TX Metropolitan Statistical Area; (2) Excludes Basque
Source: U.S. Census Bureau, 2015-2019 American Community Survey 5-Year Estimates

Foreign-born Population

Area	Any Foreign Country	Asia	Mexico	Europe	Caribbean	Central America[2]	South America	Africa	Canada
City	18.8	6.0	7.4	1.3	0.6	1.7	0.6	0.8	0.3
MSA[1]	15.2	4.5	6.4	1.1	0.4	1.2	0.6	0.7	0.3
U.S.	13.6	4.2	3.5	1.5	1.3	1.1	1.0	0.7	0.2

Note: (1) Figures cover the Austin-Round Rock, TX Metropolitan Statistical Area; (2) Excludes Mexico.
Source: U.S. Census Bureau, 2015-2019 American Community Survey 5-Year Estimates

Marital Status

Area	Never Married	Now Married[2]	Separated	Widowed	Divorced
City	43.2	40.9	1.7	3.1	11.0
MSA[1]	36.4	47.4	1.7	3.7	10.8
U.S.	33.4	48.1	1.9	5.8	10.9

Note: Figures are percentages and cover the population 15 years of age and older; (1) Figures cover the Austin-Round Rock, TX Metropolitan Statistical Area; (2) Excludes separated
Source: U.S. Census Bureau, 2015-2019 American Community Survey 5-Year Estimates

Disability by Age

Area	All Ages	Under 18 Years Old	18 to 64 Years Old	65 Years and Over
City	8.4	3.9	6.9	30.7
MSA[1]	9.2	3.7	7.6	31.4
U.S.	12.6	4.2	10.3	34.5

Note: Figures show percent of the civilian noninstitutionalized population that reported having a disability. Disability status is determined from six types of difficulty: vision, hearing, cognitive, ambulatory, self-care, and independent living. For children under 5 years old, hearing and vision difficulty are used to determine disability status. For children between the ages of 5 and 14, disability status is determined from hearing, vision, cognitive, ambulatory, and self-care difficulties. For people aged 15 years and older, they are considered to have a disability if they have difficulty with any one of the six difficulty types; Note: (1) Figures cover the Austin-Round Rock, TX Metropolitan Statistical Area
Source: U.S. Census Bureau, 2015-2019 American Community Survey 5-Year Estimates

Age

Area	Under Age 5	Age 5–19	Age 20–34	Age 35–44	Age 45–54	Age 55–64	Age 65–74	Age 75–84	Age 85+	Median Age
City	6.4	16.7	30.2	16.0	11.9	9.8	5.6	2.3	1.0	33.3
MSA[1]	6.4	19.7	24.3	15.5	12.9	10.6	6.7	2.7	1.1	34.7
U.S.	6.1	19.1	20.7	12.6	13.0	12.9	9.1	4.6	1.9	38.1

Note: (1) Figures cover the Austin-Round Rock, TX Metropolitan Statistical Area
Source: U.S. Census Bureau, 2015-2019 American Community Survey 5-Year Estimates

Gender

Area	Males	Females	Males per 100 Females
City	482,605	468,202	103.1
MSA[1]	1,059,553	1,054,888	100.4
U.S.	159,886,919	164,810,876	97.0

Note: (1) Figures cover the Austin-Round Rock, TX Metropolitan Statistical Area
Source: U.S. Census Bureau, 2015-2019 American Community Survey 5-Year Estimates

Religious Groups by Family

Area	Catholic	Baptist	Non-Den.	Methodist[2]	Lutheran	LDS[3]	Pentecostal	Presbyterian[4]	Muslim[5]	Judaism
MSA[1]	16.0	10.3	4.5	3.6	2.0	1.2	0.8	1.1	1.2	0.3
U.S.	19.1	9.3	4.0	4.0	2.3	2.0	1.9	1.6	0.8	0.7

Note: Figures are the number of adherents as a percentage of the total population; (1) Figures cover the Austin-Round Rock, TX Metropolitan Statistical Area; (2) Methodist/Pietist; (3) Latter Day Saints; (4) Reformed; (5) Figures are estimates
Source: Association of Statisticians of American Religious Bodies, 2010 U.S. Religion Census: Religious Congregations & Membership Study

Religious Groups by Tradition

Area	Catholic	Evangelical Protestant	Mainline Protestant	Other Tradition	Black Protestant	Orthodox
MSA[1]	16.0	16.1	6.3	3.9	1.4	0.1
U.S.	19.1	16.2	7.3	4.3	1.6	0.3

Note: Figures are the number of adherents as a percentage of the total population; (1) Figures cover the Austin-Round Rock, TX Metropolitan Statistical Area
Source: Association of Statisticians of American Religious Bodies, 2010 U.S. Religion Census: Religious Congregations & Membership Study

ECONOMY

Gross Metropolitan Product

Area	2017	2018	2019	2020	Rank[2]
MSA[1]	145.1	156.6	164.6	174.0	25

Note: Figures are in billions of dollars; (1) Figures cover the Austin-Round Rock, TX Metropolitan Statistical Area; (2) Rank is based on 2018 data and ranges from 1 to 381
Source: U.S. Conference of Mayors, U.S. Metro Economies: GMP & Employment 2018-2020, September 2019

Economic Growth

Area	2015-17 (%)	2018 (%)	2019 (%)	2020 (%)	Rank[2]
MSA[1]	6.3	4.4	3.5	2.6	9
U.S.	1.9	2.9	2.3	2.1	—

Note: Figures are real gross metropolitan product (GMP) growth rates and represent average annual percent change; (1) Figures cover the Austin-Round Rock, TX Metropolitan Statistical Area; (2) Rank is based on 2017 2-year average annual percent change and ranges from 1 to 381
Source: U.S. Conference of Mayors, U.S. Metro Economies: GMP & Employment 2018-2020, September 2019

Metropolitan Area Exports

Area	2014	2015	2016	2017	2018	2019	Rank[2]
MSA[1]	9,400.0	10,094.5	10,682.7	12,451.5	12,929.9	12,509.0	30

Note: Figures are in millions of dollars; (1) Figures cover the Austin-Round Rock, TX Metropolitan Statistical Area; (2) Rank is based on 2019 data and ranges from 1 to 386
Source: U.S. Department of Commerce, International Trade Administration, Office of Trade and Economic Analysis, Industry and Analysis, Exports by Metropolitan Area, data extracted March 24, 2021

Building Permits

Area	Single-Family 2018	Single-Family 2019	Pct. Chg.	Multi-Family 2018	Multi-Family 2019	Pct. Chg.	Total 2018	Total 2019	Pct. Chg.
City	4,433	4,568	3.0	8,850	10,141	14.6	13,283	14,709	10.7
MSA[1]	17,030	18,426	8.2	13,005	13,611	4.7	30,035	32,037	6.7
U.S.	855,300	862,100	0.7	473,500	523,900	10.6	1,328,800	1,386,000	4.3

Note: (1) Figures cover the Austin-Round Rock, TX Metropolitan Statistical Area; Figures represent new, privately-owned housing units authorized (unadjusted data); All permit data are based on estimates with imputation
Source: U.S. Census Bureau, Manufacturing, Mining, and Construction Statistics, Building Permits, 2018, 2019

Bankruptcy Filings

Area	Business Filings 2019	Business Filings 2020	% Chg.	Nonbusiness Filings 2019	Nonbusiness Filings 2020	% Chg.
Travis County	118	175	48.3	737	529	-28.2
U.S.	22,780	21,655	-4.9	752,160	522,808	-30.5

Note: Business filings include Chapter 7, Chapter 9, Chapter 11, Chapter 12, Chapter 13, Chapter 15, and Section 304; Nonbusiness filings include Chapter 7, Chapter 11, and Chapter 13
Source: Administrative Office of the U.S. Courts, Business and Nonbusiness Bankruptcy, County Cases Commenced by Chapter of the Bankruptcy Code, During the 12-Month Period Ending December 31, 2019 and Business and Nonbusiness Bankruptcy, County Cases Commenced by Chapter of the Bankruptcy Code, During the 12-Month Period Ending December 31, 2020

Housing Vacancy Rates

Area	Gross Vacancy Rate[2] (%) 2018	2019	2020	Year-Round Vacancy Rate[3] (%) 2018	2019	2020	Rental Vacancy Rate[4] (%) 2018	2019	2020	Homeowner Vacancy Rate[5] (%) 2018	2019	2020
MSA[1]	9.7	10.7	7.0	8.7	10.3	6.8	7.0	8.2	6.6	1.2	1.8	2.0
U.S.	12.3	12.0	10.6	9.7	9.5	8.2	6.9	6.7	6.3	1.5	1.4	1.0

Note: (1) Figures cover the Austin-Round Rock, TX Metropolitan Statistical Area; (2) The percentage of the total housing inventory that is vacant; (3) The percentage of the housing inventory (excluding seasonal units) that is year-round vacant; (4) The percentage of rental inventory that is vacant for rent; (5) The percentage of homeowner inventory that is vacant for sale
Source: U.S. Census Bureau, Housing Vacancies and Homeownership Annual Statistics: 2018, 2019, 2020

INCOME

Income

Area	Per Capita ($)	Median Household ($)	Average Household ($)
City	43,043	71,576	102,876
MSA[1]	39,827	76,844	104,847
U.S.	34,103	62,843	88,607

Note: (1) Figures cover the Austin-Round Rock, TX Metropolitan Statistical Area
Source: U.S. Census Bureau, 2015-2019 American Community Survey 5-Year Estimates

Household Income Distribution

Area	Under $15,000	$15,000 -$24,999	$25,000 -$34,999	$35,000 -$49,999	$50,000 -$74,999	$75,000 -$99,999	$100,000 -$149,999	$150,000 and up
City	8.6	6.5	7.9	11.6	17.5	12.3	16.6	19.0
MSA[1]	7.3	6.0	7.3	11.1	17.3	13.3	18.1	19.8
U.S.	10.3	8.9	8.9	12.3	17.2	12.7	15.1	14.5

Note: (1) Figures cover the Austin-Round Rock, TX Metropolitan Statistical Area
Source: U.S. Census Bureau, 2015-2019 American Community Survey 5-Year Estimates

Poverty Rate

Area	All Ages	Under 18 Years Old	18 to 64 Years Old	65 Years and Over
City	13.2	18.0	12.3	9.4
MSA[1]	10.8	13.3	10.5	7.2
U.S.	13.4	18.5	12.6	9.3

Note: Figures are percentage of people whose income during the past 12 months was below the poverty level;
(1) Figures cover the Austin-Round Rock, TX Metropolitan Statistical Area
Source: U.S. Census Bureau, 2015-2019 American Community Survey 5-Year Estimates

CITY FINANCES

City Government Finances

Component	2017 ($000)	2017 ($ per capita)
Total Revenues	4,015,745	4,310
Total Expenditures	3,849,840	4,131
Debt Outstanding	5,394,498	5,789
Cash and Securities[1]	6,209,821	6,664

Note: (1) Cash and security holdings of a government at the close of its fiscal year, including those of its dependent agencies, utilities, and liquor stores.
Source: U.S. Census Bureau, State & Local Government Finances 2017

City Government Revenue by Source

Source	2017 ($000)	2017 ($ per capita)	2017 (%)
General Revenue			
From Federal Government	60,258	65	1.5
From State Government	21,781	23	0.5
From Local Governments	14,313	15	0.4
Taxes			
Property	497,941	534	12.4
Sales and Gross Receipts	351,445	377	8.8
Personal Income	0	0	0.0
Corporate Income	0	0	0.0
Motor Vehicle License	0	0	0.0
Other Taxes	41,751	45	1.0
Current Charges	792,031	850	19.7
Liquor Store	0	0	0.0
Utility	1,674,853	1,797	41.7
Employee Retirement	391,179	420	9.7

Source: U.S. Census Bureau, State & Local Government Finances 2017

City Government Expenditures by Function

Function	2017 ($000)	2017 ($ per capita)	2017 (%)
General Direct Expenditures			
Air Transportation	144,256	154	3.7
Corrections	0	0	0.0
Education	0	0	0.0
Employment Security Administration	0	0	0.0
Financial Administration	39,913	42	1.0
Fire Protection	167,989	180	4.4
General Public Buildings	0	0	0.0
Governmental Administration, Other	51,064	54	1.3
Health	151,137	162	3.9
Highways	171,289	183	4.4
Hospitals	0	0	0.0
Housing and Community Development	68,638	73	1.8
Interest on General Debt	89,763	96	2.3
Judicial and Legal	37,956	40	1.0
Libraries	74,050	79	1.9
Parking	236	<1	<0.1
Parks and Recreation	172,325	184	4.5
Police Protection	347,610	373	9.0
Public Welfare	0	0	0.0
Sewerage	161,367	173	4.2
Solid Waste Management	111,076	119	2.9
Veterans' Services	0	0	0.0
Liquor Store	0	0	0.0
Utility	1,573,387	1,688	40.9
Employee Retirement	266,068	285	6.9

Source: U.S. Census Bureau, State & Local Government Finances 2017

EMPLOYMENT

Labor Force and Employment

Area	Civilian Labor Force Dec. 2019	Dec. 2020	% Chg.	Workers Employed Dec. 2019	Dec. 2020	% Chg.
City	601,055	606,519	0.9	587,607	576,501	-1.9
MSA[1]	1,255,200	1,267,150	1.0	1,224,993	1,202,103	-1.9
U.S.	164,007,000	160,017,000	-2.4	158,504,000	149,613,000	-5.6

Note: Data is not seasonally adjusted and covers workers 16 years of age and older; (1) Figures cover the Austin-Round Rock, TX Metropolitan Statistical Area
Source: Bureau of Labor Statistics, Local Area Unemployment Statistics

Unemployment Rate

Area	Jan.	Feb.	Mar.	Apr.	May	Jun.	Jul.	Aug.	Sep.	Oct.	Nov.	Dec.
City	2.6	2.5	3.6	12.5	11.6	7.4	6.9	5.6	6.4	4.9	5.7	4.9
MSA[1]	2.8	2.6	3.8	12.2	11.4	7.3	6.8	5.5	6.3	5.0	5.9	5.1
U.S.	4.0	3.8	4.5	14.4	13.0	11.2	10.5	8.5	7.7	6.6	6.4	6.5

Note: Data is not seasonally adjusted and covers workers 16 years of age and older; (1) Figures cover the Austin-Round Rock, TX Metropolitan Statistical Area
Source: Bureau of Labor Statistics, Local Area Unemployment Statistics

Average Wages

Occupation	$/Hr.	Occupation	$/Hr.
Accountants and Auditors	37.30	Maintenance and Repair Workers	18.10
Automotive Mechanics	26.40	Marketing Managers	74.00
Bookkeepers	21.00	Network and Computer Systems Admin.	41.10
Carpenters	19.30	Nurses, Licensed Practical	23.80
Cashiers	12.30	Nurses, Registered	35.20
Computer Programmers	42.40	Nursing Assistants	14.70
Computer Systems Analysts	41.20	Office Clerks, General	19.60
Computer User Support Specialists	25.90	Physical Therapists	41.50
Construction Laborers	15.90	Physicians	107.00
Cooks, Restaurant	13.20	Plumbers, Pipefitters and Steamfitters	25.20
Customer Service Representatives	17.30	Police and Sheriff's Patrol Officers	36.90
Dentists	77.50	Postal Service Mail Carriers	25.90
Electricians	25.90	Real Estate Sales Agents	32.50
Engineers, Electrical	52.10	Retail Salespersons	13.90
Fast Food and Counter Workers	11.30	Sales Representatives, Technical/Scientific	51.10
Financial Managers	73.00	Secretaries, Exc. Legal/Medical/Executive	18.80
First-Line Supervisors of Office Workers	31.40	Security Guards	16.10
General and Operations Managers	57.30	Surgeons	123.60
Hairdressers/Cosmetologists	15.90	Teacher Assistants, Exc. Postsecondary*	12.60
Home Health and Personal Care Aides	11.10	Teachers, Secondary School, Exc. Sp. Ed.*	28.50
Janitors and Cleaners	14.50	Telemarketers	16.80
Landscaping/Groundskeeping Workers	15.60	Truck Drivers, Heavy/Tractor-Trailer	21.40
Lawyers	69.40	Truck Drivers, Light/Delivery Services	23.40
Maids and Housekeeping Cleaners	11.30	Waiters and Waitresses	11.40

Note: Wage data covers the Austin-Round Rock, TX Metropolitan Statistical Area; (*) Hourly wages were calculated from annual wage data based on a 40 hour work week; n/a not available.
Source: Bureau of Labor Statistics, Metro Area Occupational Employment & Wage Estimates, May 2020

Employment by Industry

Sector	MSA[1] Number of Employees	Percent of Total	U.S. Percent of Total
Construction, Mining, and Logging	71,200	6.4	5.5
Education and Health Services	124,900	11.2	16.3
Financial Activities	69,700	6.3	6.1
Government	188,300	16.9	15.2
Information	40,500	3.6	1.9
Leisure and Hospitality	106,400	9.6	9.0
Manufacturing	65,000	5.9	8.5
Other Services	42,300	3.8	3.8
Professional and Business Services	207,400	18.7	14.4
Retail Trade	111,900	10.1	10.9
Transportation, Warehousing, and Utilities	29,000	2.6	4.6
Wholesale Trade	54,400	4.9	3.9

Note: Figures are non-farm employment as of December 2020. Figures are not seasonally adjusted and include workers 16 years of age and older; (1) Figures cover the Austin-Round Rock, TX Metropolitan Statistical Area
Source: Bureau of Labor Statistics, Current Employment Statistics, Employment, Hours, and Earnings

Employment by Occupation

Occupation Classification	City (%)	MSA[1] (%)	U.S. (%)
Management, Business, Science, and Arts	50.3	46.8	38.5
Natural Resources, Construction, and Maintenance	7.4	8.3	8.9
Production, Transportation, and Material Moving	6.9	8.2	13.2
Sales and Office	20.3	21.5	21.6
Service	15.2	15.2	17.8

Note: Figures cover employed civilians 16 years of age and older; (1) Figures cover the Austin-Round Rock, TX Metropolitan Statistical Area
Source: U.S. Census Bureau, 2015-2019 American Community Survey 5-Year Estimates

Occupations with Greatest Projected Employment Growth: 2020 – 2022

Occupation[1]	2020 Employment	2022 Projected Employment	Numeric Employment Change	Percent Employment Change
Fast Food and Counter Workers	336,530	411,690	75,160	22.3
Waiters and Waitresses	165,570	206,920	41,350	25.0
Home Health and Personal Care Aides	303,520	344,240	40,720	13.4
Retail Salespersons	315,590	349,820	34,230	10.8
Heavy and Tractor-Trailer Truck Drivers	199,460	228,650	29,190	14.6
Laborers and Freight, Stock, and Material Movers, Hand	193,000	219,670	26,670	13.8
Cooks, Restaurant	88,540	114,250	25,710	29.0
Customer Service Representatives	276,080	295,790	19,710	7.1
General and Operations Managers	197,410	216,580	19,170	9.7
Office Clerks, General	310,080	327,500	17,420	5.6

Note: Projections cover Texas; (1) Sorted by numeric employment change
Source: www.projectionscentral.com, State Occupational Projections, 2020–2022 Short-Term Projections

Fastest-Growing Occupations: 2020 – 2022

Occupation[1]	2020 Employment	2022 Projected Employment	Numeric Employment Change	Percent Employment Change
Motion Picture Projectionists	150	300	150	100.0
Ushers, Lobby Attendants, and Ticket Takers	5,740	8,920	3,180	55.4
Locker Room, Coatroom, and Dressing Room Attendants	340	510	170	50.0
Athletes and Sports Competitors	270	400	130	48.1
Amusement and Recreation Attendants	13,130	19,400	6,270	47.8
Hotel, Motel, and Resort Desk Clerks	16,140	23,160	7,020	43.5
Sound Engineering Technicians	330	460	130	39.4
Gaming Dealers	220	300	80	36.4
Baggage Porters and Bellhops	1,250	1,670	420	33.6
Lodging Managers	3,300	4,330	1,030	31.2

Note: Projections cover Texas; (1) Sorted by percent employment change and excludes occupations with numeric employment change less than 50
Source: www.projectionscentral.com, State Occupational Projections, 2020–2022 Short-Term Projections

TAXES

State Corporate Income Tax Rates

State	Tax Rate (%)	Income Brackets ($)	Num. of Brackets	Financial Institution Tax Rate (%)[a]	Federal Income Tax Ded.
Texas	(w)	–	–	(w)	No

Note: Tax rates as of January 1, 2021; (a) Rates listed are the corporate income tax rate applied to financial institutions or excise taxes based on income. Some states have other taxes based upon the value of deposits or shares; (w) Texas imposes a Franchise Tax, otherwise known as margin tax, imposed on entities with more than $1,130,000 total revenues at rate of 0.75%, or 0.375% for entities primarily engaged in retail or wholesale trade, on lesser of 70% of total revenues or 100% of gross receipts after deductions for either compensation or cost of goods sold.
Source: Federation of Tax Administrators, State Corporate Income Tax Rates, January 1, 2021

State Individual Income Tax Rates

State	Tax Rate (%)	Income Brackets ($)	Personal Exemptions ($) Single	Married	Depend.	Standard Ded. ($) Single	Married
Texas				– No state income tax –			

Note: Tax rates as of January 1, 2021; Local- and county-level taxes are not included
Source: Federation of Tax Administrators, State Individual Income Tax Rates, January 1, 2021

Various State Sales and Excise Tax Rates

State	State Sales Tax (%)	Gasoline[1] (¢/gal.)	Cigarette[2] ($/pack)	Spirits[3] ($/gal.)	Wine[4] ($/gal.)	Beer[5] ($/gal.)	Recreational Marijuana (%)
Texas	6.25	20	1.41	2.4	0.2	0.2	Not legal

Note: All tax rates as of January 1, 2021; (1) The American Petroleum Institute has developed a methodology for determining the average tax rate on a gallon of fuel. Rates may include any of the following: excise taxes, environmental fees, storage tank fees, other fees or taxes, general sales tax, and local taxes; (2) The federal excise tax of $1.0066 per pack and local taxes are not included; (3) Rates are those applicable to off-premise sales of 40% alcohol by volume (a.b.v.) distilled spirits in 750ml containers. Local excise taxes are excluded; (4) Rates are those applicable to off-premise sales of 11% a.b.v. non-carbonated wine in 750ml containers; (5) Rates are those applicable to off-premise sales of 4.7% a.b.v. beer in 12 ounce containers.
Source: Tax Foundation, 2021 Facts & Figures: How Does Your State Compare?

State Business Tax Climate Index Rankings

State	Overall Rank	Corporate Tax Rank	Individual Income Tax Rank	Sales Tax Rank	Property Tax Rank	Unemployment Insurance Tax Rank
Texas	11	47	6	35	36	16

Note: The index is a measure of how each state's tax laws affect economic performance. The lower the rank, the more favorable a state's tax system is for business. States without a given tax are given a ranking of 1. The scores/rankings for the District of Columbia do not affect other states. The 2021 index represents the tax climate as of July 1, 2020.
Source: Tax Foundation, State Business Tax Climate Index 2021

TRANSPORTATION

Means of Transportation to Work

Area	Drove Alone	Car-pooled	Bus	Subway	Railroad	Bicycle	Walked	Other Means	Worked at Home
City	73.7	9.1	3.2	0.1	0.1	1.3	2.4	1.3	8.7
MSA[1]	76.3	9.2	1.8	0.1	0.1	0.8	1.8	1.2	8.8
U.S.	76.3	9.0	2.4	1.9	0.6	0.5	2.7	1.4	5.2

Note: Figures are percentages and cover workers 16 years of age and older; (1) Figures cover the Austin-Round Rock, TX Metropolitan Statistical Area
Source: U.S. Census Bureau, 2015-2019 American Community Survey 5-Year Estimates

Travel Time to Work

Area	Less Than 10 Minutes	10 to 19 Minutes	20 to 29 Minutes	30 to 44 Minutes	45 to 59 Minutes	60 to 89 Minutes	90 Minutes or More
City	9.5	31.8	24.3	22.1	7.1	3.8	1.4
MSA[1]	9.6	27.1	22.3	23.1	10.0	6.1	1.8
U.S.	12.2	28.4	20.8	20.8	8.3	6.4	2.9

Note: Note: Figures are percentages and include workers 16 years old and over; (1) Figures cover the Austin-Round Rock, TX Metropolitan Statistical Area
Source: U.S. Census Bureau, 2015-2019 American Community Survey 5-Year Estimates

Key Congestion Measures

Measure	1982	1992	2002	2012	2017
Annual Hours of Delay, Total (000)	4,500	11,088	30,035	54,518	68,187
Annual Hours of Delay, Per Auto Commuter	16	26	45	55	66
Annual Congestion Cost, Total (million $)	34	116	403	966	1,248
Annual Congestion Cost, Per Auto Commuter ($)	205	349	736	1,047	1,269

Note: Covers the Austin TX urban area
Source: Texas A&M Transportation Institute, 2019 Urban Mobility Report

Freeway Travel Time Index

Measure	1982	1987	1992	1997	2002	2007	2012	2017
Urban Area Index[1]	1.10	1.14	1.16	1.23	1.28	1.32	1.31	1.34
Urban Area Rank[1,2]	19	19	23	15	13	9	13	11

Note: Freeway Travel Time Index—the ratio of travel time in the peak period to the travel time at free-flow conditions. For example, a value of 1.30 indicates a 20-minute free-flow trip takes 26 minutes in the peak (20 minutes x 1.30 = 26 minutes); (1) Covers the Austin TX urban area; (2) Rank is based on 101 larger urban areas (#1 = highest travel time index)
Source: Texas A&M Transportation Institute, 2019 Urban Mobility Report

Public Transportation

Agency Name / Mode of Transportation	Vehicles Operated in Maximum Service[1]	Annual Unlinked Passenger Trips[2] (in thous.)	Annual Passenger Miles[3] (in thous.)
Capital Metropolitan Transportation Authority (CMTA)			
Bus (purchased transportation)	315	28,313.3	115,922.3
Commuter Bus (purchased transportation)	38	779.9	14,695.7
Demand Response (purchased transportation)	163	706.9	6,003.7
Hybrid Rail (purchased transportation)	12	729.5	11,187.6
Vanpool (purchased transportation)	255	548.9	20,766.9

Note: (1) Number of revenue vehicles operated by the given mode and type of service to meet the annual maximum service requirement. This is the revenue vehicle count during the peak season of the year; on the week and day that maximum service is provided. Vehicles operated in maximum service (VOMS) exclude atypical days and one-time special events; (2) Number of passengers who boarded public transportation vehicles. Passengers are counted each time they board a vehicle no matter how many vehicles they use to travel from their origin to their destination. (3) Sum of the distances ridden by all passengers during the entire fiscal year.
Source: Federal Transit Administration, National Transit Database, 2019

Air Transportation

Airport Name and Code / Type of Service	Passenger Airlines[1]	Passenger Enplanements	Freight Carriers[2]	Freight (lbs)
Austin-Bergstrom International (AUS)				
Domestic service (U.S. carriers - 2020)	25	3,105,157	13	82,386,798
International service (U.S. carriers - 2019)	5	36,226	5	9,100,322

Note: (1) Includes all U.S.-based major, minor and commuter airlines that carried at least one passenger during the year; (2) Includes all U.S.-based airlines and freight carriers that transported at least one pound of freight during the year.
Source: Bureau of Transportation Statistics, The Intermodal Transportation Database, Air Carriers: T-100 Domestic Market (U.S. Carriers), 2020; Bureau of Transportation Statistics, The Intermodal Transportation Database, Air Carriers: T-100 International Market (U.S. Carriers), 2019

BUSINESSES

Major Business Headquarters

Company Name	Industry	Rankings Fortune[1]	Forbes[2]
No companies listed	-	-	-

Note: (1) Companies that produce a 10-K are ranked 1 to 500 based on 2019 revenue; (2) All private companies with at least $2 billion in annual revenue through the end of their most current fiscal year are ranked 1 to 219; companies listed are headquartered in the city; dashes indicate no ranking
Source: Fortune, "Fortune 500," June/July 2020; Forbes, "America's Largest Private Companies," 2020

Fastest-Growing Businesses

According to *Inc.*, Austin is home to eight of America's 500 fastest-growing private companies: **Quality Innovation** (#60); **Kinect Solar** (#130); **Sedera** (#193); **Wursta** (#232); **Basemakers** (#386); **Iris Telehealth** (#397); **Pathway Vet Alliance** (#431); **Digital Thrive** (#473). Criteria: must be an independent, privately-held, for-profit, U.S. corporation, proprietorship or partnership as of December 31, 2019; revenues must be at least $100,000 in 2016 and $2 million in 2019; must have four-year operating/sales history. *Inc., "America's 500 Fastest-Growing Private Companies," 2020*

According to *Initiative for a Competitive Inner City (ICIC)*, Austin is home to one of America's 100 fastest-growing "inner city" companies: **High Five Events** (#35). Criteria for inclusion: company must be headquartered in or have 51 percent or more of its physical operations in an economically distressed urban area; must be an independent, for-profit corporation, partnership or proprietorship; must have 10 or more employees and have a five-year sales history that includes sales of at least $200,000 in the base year and at least $1 million in the current year with no decrease in sales over the two most recent years. Companies were ranked overall by revenue growth over the five-year period between 2015 and 2019. *Initiative for a Competitive Inner City (ICIC), "Inner City 100 Companies," 2020*

According to Deloitte, Austin is home to eight of North America's 500 fastest-growing high-technology companies: **OJO Labs** (#29); **Blue Prism** (#127); **DISCO** (#181); **Eagle Eye Networks** (#187); **Digital Turbine, Inc.** (#296); **ClearDATA** (#382); **Upland Software, Inc.** (#458); **ActivTrak** (#480). Companies are ranked by percentage growth in revenue over a four-year period. Criteria for inclusion: company must be headquartered within North America; must own proprietary intellectual property or technology that is sold to customers in products that contributes to a significant portion of the company's operating revenue; must have been in business for a minumum of four years with 2016 operating revenues of at least $50,000 USD/CD and 2019 operating revenues of at least $5 million USD/CD. *Deloitte, 2020 Technology Fast 500™*

Minority Business Opportunity

Austin is home to two companies which are on the *Black Enterprise* Auto Dealer list (45 largest dealers based on gross sales): **Barnett Auto Group** (#22); **JMC Auto Group** (#25). Criteria: company must be operational in previous calendar year and be at least 51% black-owned. *Black Enterprise, B.E. 100s, 2019*

Austin is home to one company which is on the *Black Enterprise* Private Equity list (10 largest private equity firms based on capital under management): **Vista Equity Partners** (#1). Criteria: company must be operational in previous calendar year and be at least 51% black-owned. *Black Enterprise, B.E. 100s, 2019*

Living Environment

COST OF LIVING

Cost of Living Index

Composite Index	Groceries	Housing	Utilities	Transportation	Health Care	Misc. Goods/Services
101.9	92.2	110.3	94.9	89.7	108.8	103.3

Note: The Cost of Living Index measures regional differences in the cost of consumer goods and services, excluding taxes and non-consumer expenditures, for professional and managerial households in the top income quintile. It is based on more than 50,000 prices covering almost 60 different items for which prices are collected three times a year by chambers of commerce, economic development organizations or university applied economic centers in each participating urban area. The numbers shown should be read as a percentage above or below the national average of 100. For example, a value of 115.4 in the groceries column indicates that grocery prices are 15.4% higher than the national average. Small differences in the index numbers should not be interpreted as significant; Figures cover the Austin TX urban area.
Source: The Council for Community and Economic Research, Cost of Living Index, 2020

Grocery Prices

Area[1]	T-Bone Steak ($/pound)	Frying Chicken ($/pound)	Whole Milk ($/half gal.)	Eggs ($/dozen)	Orange Juice ($/64 oz.)	Coffee ($/11.5 oz.)
City[2]	9.67	1.02	1.84	1.39	3.22	4.23
Avg.	11.78	1.39	2.05	1.47	3.57	4.34
Min.	8.03	0.94	1.03	0.74	2.94	3.02
Max.	15.86	2.65	4.31	3.77	5.44	8.69

Note: (1) Values for the local area are compared with the average, minimum and maximum values for all 284 areas in the Cost of Living Index; (2) Figures cover the Austin TX urban area; **T-Bone Steak** (price per pound); **Frying Chicken** (price per pound, whole fryer); **Whole Milk** (half gallon carton); **Eggs** (price per dozen, Grade A, large); **Orange Juice** (64 oz. Tropicana or Florida Natural); **Coffee** (11.5 oz. can, vacuum-packed, Maxwell House, Hills Bros, or Folgers).
Source: The Council for Community and Economic Research, Cost of Living Index, 2020

Housing and Utility Costs

Area[1]	New Home Price ($)	Apartment Rent ($/month)	All Electric ($/month)	Part Electric ($/month)	Other Energy ($/month)	Telephone ($/month)
City[2]	370,234	1,530	-	105.65	45.12	185.50
Avg.	368,594	1,168	170.86	100.47	65.28	184.30
Min.	190,567	502	91.58	31.42	26.08	169.60
Max.	2,227,806	4,738	470.38	280.31	280.06	206.50

Note: (1) Values for the local area are compared with the average, minimum and maximum values for all 284 areas in the Cost of Living Index; (2) Figures cover the Austin TX urban area; **New Home Price** (2,400 sf living area, 8,000 sf lot, in urban area with full utilities); **Apartment Rent** (950 sf 2 bedroom/1.5 or 2 bath, unfurnished, excluding all utilities except water); **All Electric** (average monthly cost for an all-electric home); **Part Electric** (average monthly cost for a part-electric home); **Other Energy** (average monthly cost for natural gas, fuel oil, coal, wood, and any other forms of energy except electricity); **Telephone** (price includes the base monthly rate plus taxes and fees for three lines of mobile phone service).
Source: The Council for Community and Economic Research, Cost of Living Index, 2020

Health Care, Transportation, and Other Costs

Area[1]	Doctor ($/visit)	Dentist ($/visit)	Optometrist ($/visit)	Gasoline ($/gallon)	Beauty Salon ($/visit)	Men's Shirt ($)
City[2]	117.55	121.27	114.00	2.00	50.41	32.54
Avg.	115.44	99.32	108.10	2.21	39.27	31.37
Min.	36.68	59.00	51.36	1.71	19.00	11.00
Max.	219.00	153.10	250.97	3.46	82.05	58.33

Note: (1) Values for the local area are compared with the average, minimum and maximum values for all 284 areas in the Cost of Living Index; (2) Figures cover the Austin TX urban area; **Doctor** (general practitioners routine exam of an established patient); **Dentist** (adult teeth cleaning and periodic oral examination); **Optometrist** (full vision eye exam for established adult patient); **Gasoline** (one gallon regular unleaded, national brand, including all taxes, cash price at self-service pump if available); **Beauty Salon** (woman's shampoo, trim, and blow-dry); **Men's Shirt** (cotton/polyester dress shirt, pinpoint weave, long sleeves).
Source: The Council for Community and Economic Research, Cost of Living Index, 2020

HOUSING

Homeownership Rate

Area	2012 (%)	2013 (%)	2014 (%)	2015 (%)	2016 (%)	2017 (%)	2018 (%)	2019 (%)	2020 (%)
MSA[1]	60.1	59.6	61.1	57.5	56.5	55.6	56.1	59.0	65.4
U.S.	65.4	65.1	64.5	63.7	63.4	63.9	64.4	64.6	66.6

Note: (1) Figures cover the Austin-Round Rock, TX Metropolitan Statistical Area
Source: U.S. Census Bureau, Housing Vacancies and Homeownership Annual Statistics: 2012-2020

House Price Index (HPI)

Area	National Ranking[2]	Quarterly Change (%)	One-Year Change (%)	Five-Year Change (%)	Since 1991Q1 (%)
MSA[1]	30	3.27	8.26	41.08	401.86
U.S.[3]	–	3.81	10.77	38.99	205.12

Note: The HPI is a weighted repeat sales index. It measures average price changes in repeat sales or refinancings on the same properties. This information is obtained by reviewing repeat mortgage transactions on single-family properties whose mortgages have been purchased or securitized by Fannie Mae or Freddie Mac since January 1975; (1) Figures cover the Austin-Round Rock, TX Metropolitan Statistical Area; (2) Rankings are based on annual percentage change for all metro areas containing at least 15,000 transactions over the last 10 years and ranges from 1 to 253; (3) figures based on a weighted average of Census Division estimates using a seasonally adjusted, purchase-only index; all figures are for the period ending December 31, 2020
Source: Federal Housing Finance Agency, Change in Metropolitan Area House Price Indexes, April 7, 2021

Median Single-Family Home Prices

Area	2018	2019	2020p	Percent Change 2019 to 2020
MSA[1]	315.9	329.2	367.1	11.5
U.S. Average	261.6	274.6	299.9	9.2

Note: Figures are median sales prices of existing single-family homes in thousands of dollars; (p) preliminary; (1) Figures cover the Austin-Round Rock, TX Metropolitan Statistical Area
Source: National Association of Realtors, Median Sales Price of Existing Single-Family Homes for Metropolitan Areas, 4th Quarter 2020

Qualifying Income Based on Median Sales Price of Existing Single-Family Homes

Area	With 5% Down ($)	With 10% Down ($)	With 20% Down ($)
MSA[1]	73,009	69,166	61,481
U.S. Average	59,266	56,147	49,908

Note: Figures are preliminary; Qualifying income is based on a mortgage rate of 2.81%. Monthly principal and interest payment is limited to 25% of income; (1) Figures cover the Austin-Round Rock, TX Metropolitan Statistical Area
Source: National Association of Realtors, Qualifying Income Based on Median Sales Price of Existing Single-Family Homes for Metropolitan Areas, 4th Quarter 2020

Home Value Distribution

Area	Under $50,000	$50,000 -$99,999	$100,000 -$149,999	$150,000 -$199,999	$200,000 -$299,999	$300,000 -$499,999	$500,000 -$999,999	$1,000,000 or more
City	2.2	2.2	4.8	9.1	24.3	33.0	20.1	4.3
MSA[1]	3.3	3.9	6.9	12.7	27.8	28.3	13.9	3.2
U.S.	6.9	12.0	13.3	14.0	19.6	19.3	11.4	3.4

Note: Figures are percentages and cover owner-occupied housing units; (1) Figures cover the Austin-Round Rock, TX Metropolitan Statistical Area
Source: U.S. Census Bureau, 2015-2019 American Community Survey 5-Year Estimates

Year Housing Structure Built

Area	2010 or Later	2000 -2009	1990 -1999	1980 -1989	1970 -1979	1960 -1969	1950 -1959	1940 -1949	Before 1940	Median Year
City	12.8	18.1	15.7	19.6	15.9	7.6	4.9	2.6	2.8	1988
MSA[1]	16.4	25.1	18.1	16.4	11.6	4.9	3.3	1.8	2.3	1995
U.S.	5.2	14.0	13.9	13.4	15.2	10.6	10.3	4.9	12.6	1978

Note: Figures are percentages except for Median Year; Note: (1) Figures cover the Austin-Round Rock, TX Metropolitan Statistical Area
Source: U.S. Census Bureau, 2015-2019 American Community Survey 5-Year Estimates

Gross Monthly Rent

Area	Under $500	$500 -$999	$1,000 -$1,499	$1,500 -$1,999	$2,000 -$2,499	$2,500 -$2,999	$3,000 and up	Median ($)
City	3.1	18.1	45.2	22.4	7.1	2.3	1.8	1,280
MSA[1]	3.1	19.4	44.5	22.7	6.7	2.1	1.6	1,273
U.S.	9.4	36.2	30.0	14.0	5.6	2.4	2.4	1,062

Note: Figures are percentages except for Median; Gross rent is the contract rent plus the estimated average monthly cost of utilities (electricity, gas, and water and sewer) and fuels (oil, coal, kerosene, wood, etc.) if these are paid by the renter (or paid for the renter by someone else); (1) Figures cover the Austin-Round Rock, TX Metropolitan Statistical Area
Source: U.S. Census Bureau, 2015-2019 American Community Survey 5-Year Estimates

HEALTH

Health Risk Factors

Category	MSA[1] (%)	U.S. (%)
Adults aged 18–64 who have any kind of health care coverage	78.4	87.3
Adults who reported being in good or better health	85.0	82.4
Adults who have been told they have high blood cholesterol	32.2	33.0
Adults who have been told they have high blood pressure	26.5	32.3
Adults who are current smokers	12.5	17.1
Adults who currently use E-cigarettes	4.8	4.6
Adults who currently use chewing tobacco, snuff, or snus	4.2	4.0
Adults who are heavy drinkers[2]	8.4	6.3
Adults who are binge drinkers[3]	22.9	17.4
Adults who are overweight (BMI 25.0 - 29.9)	32.8	35.3
Adults who are obese (BMI 30.0 - 99.8)	29.3	31.3
Adults who participated in any physical activities in the past month	75.2	74.4
Adults who always or nearly always wears a seat belt	98.3	94.3

Note: (1) Figures cover the Austin-Round Rock, TX Metropolitan Statistical Area; (2) Heavy drinkers are classified as adult men having more than 14 drinks per week and adult women having more than 7 drinks per week; (3) Binge drinkers are classified as males having five or more drinks on one occasion or females having four or more drinks on one occasion
Source: Centers for Disease Control and Prevention, Behavioral Risk Factor Surveillance System, SMART: Selected Metropolitan Area Risk Trends, 2017

Acute and Chronic Health Conditions

Category	MSA[1] (%)	U.S. (%)
Adults who have ever been told they had a heart attack	2.0	4.2
Adults who have ever been told they have angina or coronary heart disease	2.5	3.9
Adults who have ever been told they had a stroke	2.6	3.0
Adults who have ever been told they have asthma	11.3	14.2
Adults who have ever been told they have arthritis	17.4	24.9
Adults who have ever been told they have diabetes[2]	9.6	10.5
Adults who have ever been told they had skin cancer	4.8	6.2
Adults who have ever been told they had any other types of cancer	5.6	7.1
Adults who have ever been told they have COPD	3.1	6.5
Adults who have ever been told they have kidney disease	2.4	3.0
Adults who have ever been told they have a form of depression	16.7	20.5

Note: (1) Figures cover the Austin-Round Rock, TX Metropolitan Statistical Area; (2) Figures do not include pregnancy-related, borderline, or pre-diabetes
Source: Centers for Disease Control and Prevention, Behavioral Risk Factor Surveillance System, SMART: Selected Metropolitan Area Risk Trends, 2017

Health Screening and Vaccination Rates

Category	MSA[1] (%)	U.S. (%)
Adults aged 65+ who have had flu shot within the past year	63.4	60.7
Adults aged 65+ who have ever had a pneumonia vaccination	74.2	75.4
Adults who have ever been tested for HIV	46.3	36.1
Adults who have ever had the shingles or zoster vaccine?	29.3	28.9
Adults who have had their blood cholesterol checked within the last five years	86.9	85.9

Note: n/a not available; (1) Figures cover the Austin-Round Rock, TX Metropolitan Statistical Area.
Source: Centers for Disease Control and Prevention, Behavioral Risk Factor Surveillance System, SMART: Selected Metropolitan Area Risk Trends, 2017

Disability Status

Category	MSA[1] (%)	U.S. (%)
Adults who reported being deaf	5.2	6.7
Are you blind or have serious difficulty seeing, even when wearing glasses?	3.6	4.5
Are you limited in any way in any of your usual activities due of arthritis?	10.1	12.9
Do you have difficulty doing errands alone?	5.3	6.8
Do you have difficulty dressing or bathing?	2.4	3.6
Do you have serious difficulty concentrating/remembering/making decisions?	9.8	10.7
Do you have serious difficulty walking or climbing stairs?	9.5	13.6

Note: (1) Figures cover the Austin-Round Rock, TX Metropolitan Statistical Area.
Source: Centers for Disease Control and Prevention, Behavioral Risk Factor Surveillance System, SMART: Selected Metropolitan Area Risk Trends, 2017

Mortality Rates for the Top 10 Causes of Death in the U.S.

ICD-10[a] Sub-Chapter	ICD-10[a] Code	Age-Adjusted Mortality Rate[1] per 100,000 population County[2]	U.S.
Malignant neoplasms	C00-C97	120.3	149.2
Ischaemic heart diseases	I20-I25	64.1	90.5
Other forms of heart disease	I30-I51	33.1	52.2
Chronic lower respiratory diseases	J40-J47	26.7	39.6
Other degenerative diseases of the nervous system	G30-G31	51.3	37.6
Cerebrovascular diseases	I60-I69	34.3	37.2
Other external causes of accidental injury	W00-X59	33.9	36.1
Organic, including symptomatic, mental disorders	F01-F09	33.8	29.4
Hypertensive diseases	I10-I15	20.8	24.1
Diabetes mellitus	E10-E14	14.9	21.5

Note: (a) ICD-10 = International Classification of Diseases 10th Revision; (1) Mortality rates are a three-year average covering 2017-2019; (2) Figures cover Travis County.
Source: Centers for Disease Control and Prevention, National Center for Health Statistics. Underlying Cause of Death 1999-2019 on CDC WONDER Online Database

Mortality Rates for Selected Causes of Death

ICD-10[a] Sub-Chapter	ICD-10[a] Code	Age-Adjusted Mortality Rate[1] per 100,000 population County[2]	U.S.
Assault	X85-Y09	3.1	6.0
Diseases of the liver	K70-K76	13.7	14.4
Human immunodeficiency virus (HIV) disease	B20-B24	1.3	1.5
Influenza and pneumonia	J09-J18	9.1	13.8
Intentional self-harm	X60-X84	12.8	14.1
Malnutrition	E40-E46	2.0	2.3
Obesity and other hyperalimentation	E65-E68	1.7	2.1
Renal failure	N17-N19	9.7	12.6
Transport accidents	V01-V99	9.8	12.3
Viral hepatitis	B15-B19	1.4	1.2

Note: (a) ICD-10 = International Classification of Diseases 10th Revision; (1) Mortality rates are a three-year average covering 2017-2019; (2) Figures cover Travis County; Data are suppressed when the data meet the criteria for confidentiality constraints; Mortality rates are flagged as unreliable when the rate would be calculated with a numerator of 20 or less.
Source: Centers for Disease Control and Prevention, National Center for Health Statistics. Underlying Cause of Death 1999-2019 on CDC WONDER Online Database

Health Insurance Coverage

Area	With Health Insurance	With Private Health Insurance	With Public Health Insurance	Without Health Insurance	Population Under Age 19 Without Health Insurance
City	86.4	73.3	20.2	13.6	8.9
MSA[1]	87.5	74.5	21.7	12.5	8.1
U.S.	91.2	67.9	35.1	8.8	5.1

Note: Figures are percentages that cover the civilian noninstitutionalized population; (1) Figures cover the Austin-Round Rock, TX Metropolitan Statistical Area
Source: U.S. Census Bureau, 2015-2019 American Community Survey 5-Year Estimates

Number of Medical Professionals

Area	MDs[3]	DOs[3,4]	Dentists	Podiatrists	Chiropractors	Optometrists
County[1] (number)	3,993	239	920	53	433	208
County[1] (rate[2])	320.3	19.2	72.2	4.2	34.0	16.3
U.S. (rate[2])	282.9	22.7	71.2	6.2	28.1	16.9

48453
Note: Data as of 2019 unless noted; (1) Data covers Travis County; (2) Rate per 100,000 population; (3) Data as of 2018 and includes all active, non-federal physicians; (4) Doctor of Osteopathic Medicine
Source: U.S. Department of Health and Human Services, Health Resources and Services Administration, Bureau of Health Professions, Area Resource File (ARF) 2019-2020

EDUCATION

Public School District Statistics

District Name	Schls	Pupils	Pupil/Teacher Ratio	Minority Pupils[1] (%)	Free Lunch Eligible[2] (%)	IEP[3] (%)
Austin ISD	130	80,032	14.5	70.4	49.4	12.1
Eanes ISD	11	8,132	13.6	31.6	3.2	8.6
Harmony Science Academy (Austin)	7	4,025	15.2	85.5	64.3	7.3
Lake Travis ISD	9	10,738	17.8	32.9	11.4	8.2
Wayside Schools	4	2,095	13.3	84.5	50.0	7.4

Note: Table includes school districts with 2,000 or more students; (1) Percentage of students that are not non-Hispanic white; (2) Percentage of students that are eligible for the free lunch program; (3) Percentage of students that have an Individualized Education Program.
Source: U.S. Department of Education, National Center for Education Statistics, Common Core of Data, Local Education Agency (School District) Universe Survey: School Year 2018-2019; U.S. Department of Education, National Center for Education Statistics, Common Core of Data, Public Elementary/Secondary School Universe Survey: School Year 2018-2019

Best High Schools

According to *U.S. News,* Austin is home to six of the top 500 high schools in the U.S.: **Liberal Arts and Science Academy (LASA)** (#34); **Richards School for Young Women Leaders** (#135); **Chaparral Star Academy** (#260); **Westlake High School** (#298); **KIPP Austin Collegiate** (#354); **Westwood High School** (#398). Nearly 18,000 public, magnet and charter schools were ranked based on their performance on state assessments and how well they prepare students for college. *U.S. News & World Report, "Best High Schools 2020"*

Highest Level of Education

Area	Less than H.S.	H.S. Diploma	Some College, No Deg.	Associate Degree	Bachelor's Degree	Master's Degree	Prof. School Degree	Doctorate Degree
City	10.6	15.6	16.7	5.4	32.3	13.6	3.3	2.5
MSA[1]	10.1	19.1	19.6	6.5	28.8	11.6	2.5	1.9
U.S.	12.0	27.0	20.4	8.5	19.8	8.8	2.1	1.4

Note: Figures cover persons age 25 and over; (1) Figures cover the Austin-Round Rock, TX Metropolitan Statistical Area
Source: U.S. Census Bureau, 2015-2019 American Community Survey 5-Year Estimates

Educational Attainment by Race

Area	High School Graduate or Higher (%) Total	White	Black	Asian	Hisp.[2]	Bachelor's Degree or Higher (%) Total	White	Black	Asian	Hisp.[2]
City	89.4	91.2	89.6	93.9	72.3	51.7	55.1	28.8	77.0	25.8
MSA[1]	89.9	91.4	91.0	92.5	74.0	44.8	46.7	29.1	71.8	23.0
U.S.	88.0	89.9	86.0	87.1	68.7	32.1	33.5	21.6	54.3	16.4

Note: Figures shown cover persons 25 years old and over; (1) Figures cover the Austin-Round Rock, TX Metropolitan Statistical Area; (2) People of Hispanic origin can be of any race
Source: U.S. Census Bureau, 2015-2019 American Community Survey 5-Year Estimates

School Enrollment by Grade and Control

Area	Preschool (%) Public	Private	Kindergarten (%) Public	Private	Grades 1 - 4 (%) Public	Private	Grades 5 - 8 (%) Public	Private	Grades 9 - 12 (%) Public	Private
City	51.0	49.0	86.9	13.1	89.3	10.7	88.9	11.1	91.0	9.0
MSA[1]	51.5	48.5	88.1	11.9	90.7	9.3	90.7	9.3	92.4	7.6
U.S.	59.1	40.9	87.6	12.4	89.5	10.5	89.4	10.6	90.1	9.9

Note: Figures shown cover persons 3 years old and over; (1) Figures cover the Austin-Round Rock, TX Metropolitan Statistical Area
Source: U.S. Census Bureau, 2015-2019 American Community Survey 5-Year Estimates

Higher Education

Four-Year Colleges Public	Private Non-profit	Private For-profit	Two-Year Colleges Public	Private Non-profit	Private For-profit	Medical Schools[1]	Law Schools[2]	Voc/Tech[3]
2	6	5	0	0	3	1	1	8

Note: Figures cover institutions located within the city limits and include main campuses only; (1) includes schools accredited by the Liaison Committee on Medical Education and the American Osteopathic Association's Commission on Osteopathic College Accreditation; (2) includes ABA-accredited schools, schools with provisional ABA accreditation, and state accredited schools; (3) includes all schools with programs that are less than 2 years.
Source: National Center for Education Statistics, Integrated Postsecondary Education System (IPEDS), 2019-20; Wikipedia, List of Medical Schools in the United States, accessed April 2, 2021; Wikipedia, List of Law Schools in the United States, accessed April 2, 2021

According to *U.S. News & World Report*, the Austin-Round Rock, TX metro area is home to one of the top 200 national universities in the U.S.: **University of Texas at Austin** (#42 tie). The indicators used to capture academic quality fall into a number of categories: assessment by administrators at peer institutions; retention of students; faculty resources; student selectivity; financial resources; alumni giving; high school counselor ratings of colleges; and graduation rate. *U.S. News & World Report, "America's Best Colleges 2021"*

According to *U.S. News & World Report*, the Austin-Round Rock, TX metro area is home to one of the top 100 law schools in the U.S.: **University of Texas—Austin** (#16 tie). The rankings are based on a weighted average of 12 measures of quality: peer assessment score; assessment score by lawyers/judges; median LSAT scores; median undergrad GPA; acceptance rate; employment rates for graduates; placement success; bar passage rate; faculty resources; expenditures per student; student/faculty ratio; and library resources. *U.S. News & World Report, "America's Best Graduate Schools, Law, 2022"*

According to *U.S. News & World Report*, the Austin-Round Rock, TX metro area is home to one of the top 75 business schools in the U.S.: **University of Texas—Austin (McCombs)** (#18 tie). The rankings are based on a weighted average of the following nine measures: quality assessment; peer assessment; recruiter assessment; placement success; mean starting salary and bonus; student selectivity; mean GMAT and GRE scores; mean undergraduate GPA; and acceptance rate. *U.S. News & World Report, "America's Best Graduate Schools, Business, 2022"*

EMPLOYERS

Major Employers

Company Name	Industry
Accenture	Management consulting & software development center
Apple	Computer maker's tech & admin support center
Applied Materials	Semiconductor manufacturing equip, mfg
AT&T	Telecommunications
Austin Community College	Higher education, public
Austin School Independent District	Public education
City of Austin	Municipal government
Dell	Computer technology solutions & equipment mfg./sales
Federal Government	Government
Flextronics	Contract electronics mfg. & integrated supply chain svcs
Hays Consolidated ISD	Public education
IBM	Computer systems, hardware, software, & chip R&D
Keller Williams Realty	Residential real estate
Leander Independent School District	Public education
National Instruments	Virtual instrumentation software & hardware mfg
NXP Semiconductors	Semiconductor chip design & mfg.
Pflugerville Independent School District	Public education
Round Rock Independent School District	Public education
Samsung Austin Semiconductor	Semiconductor chip mfg., R&D
Seton Healthcare Family	Healthcare
St. David's Healthcare Partnership	Healthcare
State of Texas	State government
Texas State University-San Marcos	Higher education, public
Travis County	Government
U.S. Internal Revenue Service	Government, regional call & processing center
University of Texas at Austin	Higher education, public
Whole Foods Market	Grocery stores

Note: Companies shown are located within the Austin-Round Rock, TX Metropolitan Statistical Area.
Source: Hoovers.com; Wikipedia

Best Companies to Work For

Tokyo Electron U.S. Holdings, headquartered in Austin, is among the "100 Best Places to Work in IT." To qualify, companies had to be U.S.-based organizations or be non-U.S.-based employers that met the following criteria: have a minimum of 300 total employees at a U.S. headquarters and a minimum of 30 IT employees in the U.S., with at least 50% of their IT employees based in the U.S. The best places to work were selected based on compensation, benefits, work/life balance, employee morale, and satisfaction with training and development programs. In addition, *InsiderPro* and *Computerworld* looked at retention efforts, programs for recognizing and rewarding outstanding performances, and benefits such as flextime, elder care and child care, and reimbursement for college tuition and the cost of pursuing technology certifications. *InsiderPro and Computerworld, "100 Best Places to Work in IT," 2020*

Kendra Scott, headquartered in Austin, is among the "Top Companies for Executive Women." This list is determined by organizations filling out an in-depth survey that measures female demographics at every level, but with an emphasis on women in senior corporate roles, with profit & loss (P&L) responsibility, and those earning in the top 20 percent of the organization. *Working Mother* defines P&L as having responsibility that involves monitoring the net income after expenses for a department or entire organization, with direct influence on how company resources are allocated. *Working Mother, "Top Companies for Executive Women," 2020+*

PUBLIC SAFETY

Crime Rate

Area	All Crimes	Violent Crimes				Property Crimes		
		Murder	Rape[3]	Robbery	Aggrav. Assault	Burglary	Larceny-Theft	Motor Vehicle Theft
City	4,111.4	3.2	54.2	98.5	245.0	440.5	2,962.9	307.1
Suburbs[1]	1,564.4	1.9	43.6	23.6	126.5	212.3	1,059.4	97.1
Metro[2]	2,697.1	2.5	48.3	56.9	179.2	313.8	1,905.9	190.5
U.S.	2,489.3	5.0	42.6	81.6	250.2	340.5	1,549.5	219.9

Note: Figures are crimes per 100,000 population; (1) All areas within the metro area that are located outside the city limits; (2) Figures cover the Austin-Round Rock, TX Metropolitan Statistical Area; (3) All figures shown were reported using the revised Uniform Crime Reporting (UCR) definition of rape.
Source: FBI Uniform Crime Reports, 2019

Hate Crimes

Area	Number of Quarters Reported	Race/Ethnicity/Ancestry	Religion	Sexual Orientation	Disability	Gender	Gender Identity
City	4	5	2	3	0	0	0
U.S.	4	3,963	1,521	1,195	157	69	198

Source: Federal Bureau of Investigation, Hate Crime Statistics 2019

Identity Theft Consumer Reports

Area	Reports	Reports per 100,000 Population	Rank[2]
MSA[1]	7,028	316	111
U.S.	1,387,615	423	-

Note: (1) Figures cover the Austin-Round Rock, TX Metropolitan Statistical Area; (2) Rank ranges from 1 to 391 where 1 indicates greatest number of identity theft reports per 100,000 population
Source: Federal Trade Commission, Consumer Sentinel Network Data Book 2020

Fraud and Other Consumer Reports

Area	Reports	Reports per 100,000 Population	Rank[2]
MSA[1]	20,065	901	47
U.S.	3,385,133	1,031	-

Note: (1) Figures cover the Austin-Round Rock, TX Metropolitan Statistical Area; (2) Rank ranges from 1 to 391 where 1 indicates greatest number of fraud and other consumer reports per 100,000 population
Source: Federal Trade Commission, Consumer Sentinel Network Data Book 2020

POLITICS

2020 Presidential Election Results

Area	Biden	Trump	Jorgensen	Hawkins	Other
Travis County	71.4	26.4	1.5	0.3	0.4
U.S.	51.3	46.8	1.2	0.3	0.5

Note: Results are percentages and may not add to 100% due to rounding
Source: Dave Leip's Atlas of U.S. Presidential Elections

SPORTS

Professional Sports Teams

Team Name	League	Year Established
Austin FC	Major League Soccer (MLS)	2021

Note: Includes teams located in the Austin-Round Rock, TX Metropolitan Statistical Area.
Source: Wikipedia, Major Professional Sports Teams of the United States and Canada, April 6, 2021

CLIMATE

Average and Extreme Temperatures

Temperature	Jan	Feb	Mar	Apr	May	Jun	Jul	Aug	Sep	Oct	Nov	Dec	Yr.
Extreme High (°F)	90	97	98	98	100	105	109	106	104	98	91	90	109
Average High (°F)	60	64	72	79	85	91	95	96	90	81	70	63	79
Average Temp. (°F)	50	53	61	69	75	82	85	85	80	70	60	52	69
Average Low (°F)	39	43	50	58	65	72	74	74	69	59	49	41	58
Extreme Low (°F)	-2	7	18	35	43	53	64	61	47	32	20	4	-2

Note: Figures cover the years 1948-1990
Source: National Climatic Data Center, International Station Meteorological Climate Summary, 9/96

Austin, Texas

Average Precipitation/Snowfall/Humidity

Precip./Humidity	Jan	Feb	Mar	Apr	May	Jun	Jul	Aug	Sep	Oct	Nov	Dec	Yr.
Avg. Precip. (in.)	1.6	2.3	1.8	2.9	4.3	3.5	1.9	1.9	3.3	3.5	2.1	1.9	31.1
Avg. Snowfall (in.)	1	Tr	Tr	0	0	0	0	0	0	0	Tr	Tr	1
Avg. Rel. Hum. 6am (%)	79	80	79	83	88	89	88	87	86	84	81	79	84
Avg. Rel. Hum. 3pm (%)	53	51	47	50	53	49	43	42	47	47	49	51	48

Note: Figures cover the years 1948-1990; Tr = Trace amounts (<0.05 in. of rain; <0.5 in. of snow)
Source: National Climatic Data Center, International Station Meteorological Climate Summary, 9/96

Weather Conditions

Temperature			Daytime Sky			Precipitation			
10°F & below	32°F & below	90°F & above	Clear	Partly cloudy	Cloudy	0.01 inch or more precip.	0.1 inch or more snow/ice	Thunder-storms
<1	20	111	105	148	112	83	1	41

Note: Figures are average number of days per year and cover the years 1948-1990
Source: National Climatic Data Center, International Station Meteorological Climate Summary, 9/96

HAZARDOUS WASTE

Superfund Sites

The Austin-Round Rock, TX metro area has no sites on the EPA's Superfund Final National Priorities List. There are a total of 1,375 Superfund sites with a status of proposed or final on the list in the U.S.
U.S. Environmental Protection Agency, National Priorities List, April 7, 2021

AIR QUALITY

Air Quality Trends: Ozone

	1990	1995	2000	2005	2010	2015	2016	2017	2018	2019
MSA[1]	0.088	0.089	0.088	0.082	0.074	0.073	0.064	0.070	0.072	0.065
U.S.	0.088	0.089	0.082	0.073	0.068	0.069	0.068	0.069	0.069	0.065

Note: (1) Data covers the Austin-Round Rock, TX Metropolitan Statistical Area. The values shown are the composite ozone concentration averages among trend sites based on the highest fourth daily maximum 8-hour concentration in parts per million. These trends are based on sites having an adequate record of monitoring data during the trend period. Data from exceptional events are included.
Source: U.S. Environmental Protection Agency, Air Quality Monitoring Information, "Air Quality Trends by City, 1990-2019"

Air Quality Index

Area	Percent of Days when Air Quality was...[2]					AQI Statistics[2]	
	Good	Moderate	Unhealthy for Sensitive Groups	Unhealthy	Very Unhealthy	Maximum	Median
MSA[1]	68.2	31.2	0.5	0.0	0.0	115	44

Note: (1) Data covers the Austin-Round Rock, TX Metropolitan Statistical Area; (2) Based on 365 days with AQI data in 2019. Air Quality Index (AQI) is an index for reporting daily air quality. EPA calculates the AQI for five major air pollutants regulated by the Clean Air Act: ground-level ozone, particle pollution (aka particulate matter), carbon monoxide, sulfur dioxide, and nitrogen dioxide. The AQI runs from 0 to 500. The higher the AQI value, the greater the level of air pollution and the greater the health concern. There are six AQI categories: "Good" AQI is between 0 and 50. Air quality is considered satisfactory; "Moderate" AQI is between 51 and 100. Air quality is acceptable; "Unhealthy for Sensitive Groups" When AQI values are between 101 and 150, members of sensitive groups may experience health effects; "Unhealthy" When AQI values are between 151 and 200 everyone may begin to experience health effects; "Very Unhealthy" AQI values between 201 and 300 trigger a health alert; "Hazardous" AQI values over 300 trigger warnings of emergency conditions (not shown).
Source: U.S. Environmental Protection Agency, Air Quality Index Report, 2019

Air Quality Index Pollutants

Area	Percent of Days when AQI Pollutant was...[2]					
	Carbon Monoxide	Nitrogen Dioxide	Ozone	Sulfur Dioxide	Particulate Matter 2.5	Particulate Matter 10
MSA[1]	0.0	1.9	48.8	0.0	49.3	0.0

Note: (1) Data covers the Austin-Round Rock, TX Metropolitan Statistical Area; (2) Based on 365 days with AQI data in 2019. The Air Quality Index (AQI) is an index for reporting daily air quality. EPA calculates the AQI for five major air pollutants regulated by the Clean Air Act: ground-level ozone, particle pollution (also known as particulate matter), carbon monoxide, sulfur dioxide, and nitrogen dioxide. The AQI runs from 0 to 500. The higher the AQI value, the greater the level of air pollution and the greater the health concern.
Source: U.S. Environmental Protection Agency, Air Quality Index Report, 2019

Maximum Air Pollutant Concentrations: Particulate Matter, Ozone, CO and Lead

	Particulate Matter 10 (ug/m^3)	Particulate Matter 2.5 Wtd AM (ug/m^3)	Particulate Matter 2.5 24-Hr (ug/m^3)	Ozone (ppm)	Carbon Monoxide (ppm)	Lead (ug/m^3)
MSA[1] Level	38	9.5	21	0.065	2	n/a
NAAQS[2]	150	15	35	0.075	9	0.15
Met NAAQS[2]	Yes	Yes	Yes	Yes	Yes	n/a

Note: (1) Data covers the Austin-Round Rock, TX Metropolitan Statistical Area; Data from exceptional events are included; (2) National Ambient Air Quality Standards; ppm = parts per million; ug/m^3 = micrograms per cubic meter; n/a not available.
Concentrations: Particulate Matter 10 (coarse particulate)—highest second maximum 24-hour concentration; Particulate Matter 2.5 Wtd AM (fine particulate)—highest weighted annual mean concentration; Particulate Matter 2.5 24-Hour (fine particulate)—highest 98th percentile 24-hour concentration; Ozone—highest fourth daily maximum 8-hour concentration; Carbon Monoxide—highest second maximum non-overlapping 8-hour concentration; Lead—maximum running 3-month average
Source: U.S. Environmental Protection Agency, Air Quality Monitoring Information, "Air Quality Statistics by City, 2019"

Maximum Air Pollutant Concentrations: Nitrogen Dioxide and Sulfur Dioxide

	Nitrogen Dioxide AM (ppb)	Nitrogen Dioxide 1-Hr (ppb)	Sulfur Dioxide AM (ppb)	Sulfur Dioxide 1-Hr (ppb)	Sulfur Dioxide 24-Hr (ppb)
MSA[1] Level	12	32	n/a	2	n/a
NAAQS[2]	53	100	30	75	140
Met NAAQS[2]	Yes	Yes	n/a	Yes	n/a

Note: (1) Data covers the Austin-Round Rock, TX Metropolitan Statistical Area; Data from exceptional events are included; (2) National Ambient Air Quality Standards; ppm = parts per million; ug/m^3 = micrograms per cubic meter; n/a not available.
Concentrations: Nitrogen Dioxide AM—highest arithmetic mean concentration; Nitrogen Dioxide 1-Hr—highest 98th percentile 1-hour daily maximum concentration; Sulfur Dioxide AM—highest annual mean concentration; Sulfur Dioxide 1-Hr—highest 99th percentile 1-hour daily maximum concentration; Sulfur Dioxide 24-Hr—highest second maximum 24-hour concentration
Source: U.S. Environmental Protection Agency, Air Quality Monitoring Information, "Air Quality Statistics by City, 2019"

Baton Rouge, Louisiana

Background

Baton Rouge, the capital of Louisiana, stretches along the Istrouma Bluff on the east bank of the Mississippi River, and is the key industrial city in the area, at the center of an immense industrial and shipping complex. The seat of government for East Baton Rouge Parish, the city's greater metropolitan area, includes Baton Rouge itself, Baker, and Zachary. The metropolitan area is the second-largest in the state, next to New Orleans.

Originally the site of an Indian village, and an important trade center since 1699 when a French expedition first explored the area, Baton Rouge was incorporated in 1817 and made the state capital in 1882.

Baton Rouge, or "Red Stick," is so-named because of a distinctive boundary marker between the Oumas and Bayagoula tribes. The pole was used in earlier times as a point of reference by the many missionaries, traders, and settlers who traveled this way on the Mississippi River.

The historical complexity of Baton Rouge is hinted at by the various elements that appear on the official city flag, which is laid out on a field of crimson, and features, of course, the red, white, and blue of the United States. The flag also displays the fleur-de-lis of France, the Castile of Spain, and the union jack of Great Britain. This portrait, though, only begins to do justice to Baton Rouge's rich history. The city has lived under seven distinct governments in its 300-year development from trading post to modern metropolis: French, English, Spanish, West Floridian, Louisiana, Confederate, and American.

The state capitol building in Baton Rouge is one of America's most notable buildings. Completed in 1932, the 34-story building is located on the old campus of Louisiana State University, and surrounded by 27 acres of landscaped grounds. Ten miles of walks and drives are bordered by a collection of trees, flowering shrubs, bulbs, and flower beds, which are tended to yield maximal color in every season. From the capitol's observation tower, one can see for 30 miles in every direction. Louisiana's legendary Governor and Senator Huey P. Long, under whose administration the building was constructed, was assassinated in a corridor here in 1935 and is buried in the front grounds. A 12-foot bronze statue by Charles Keck memorializes The Kingfish, as Long was nicknamed.

Although the effects of the 2005 Katrina and Rita hurricanes were obviously felt in Baton Rouge, the city was not damaged as profoundly as was New Orleans. One of the most substantial effects was that Baton Rouge became, overnight, the largest city in Louisiana, as population temporarily surged by more than 200,000 as it accepted persons displaced by the hurricanes. In the wake of Katrina, much of the economic activity once centered in New Orleans transferred to Baton Rouge. As the city continued to meet the challenges presented by the unprecedented storms, a more prosperous Baton Rouge emerged.

As many cities in the country have enlarged their convention centers, so has Baton Rouge. The city's Riverside Centroplex Convention Center underwent major expansion, adding 100,000 square feet of convention space, 20,000 square feet of state-of-the-art meeting space and a ballroom. Although the center was used as an emergency resource in the post-Katrina period, it is now operating for its original purpose.

The film industry in Louisiana had increased dramatically in the last decade. The Baton Rouge Film Commission reported that the industry brings into the local economy more than $90 million annually. The city's increasing visual arts scene includes the Shaw Center for the Arts, the Louisiana Arts and Science Museum and the Baton Rouge Gallery. In addition to the city's strong performing arts and music scenes, the annual Mardi Gras festivals are among the city's most popular events.

Louisiana State University, a traditional leader among the nation's institutions, is located here, as are Southern University and A&M College, the largest predominantly African-American institution in the nation. In 2017, the city's youth writing organization Forward Arts won the international poetry slam Brave New Voices.

Baton Rouge has a humid, subtropical climate with mild winters and humid summers, moderate to heavy rainfall and the possibility of damaging winds and tornadoes yearlong. The city was affected by the August 2016 Louisiana floods.

Rankings

General Rankings

- The U.S. Conference of Mayors and Waste Management, Inc. sponsor the City Livability Awards Program, which recognize mayors for exemplary leadership in developing and implementing specific programs that improve the quality of life in America's cities. Baton Rouge received an Outstanding Achievement Award in the large cities category. *U.S. Conference of Mayors, "2019 City Livability Awards"*

Business/Finance Rankings

- Baton Rouge was the #20-ranked city for savers, according to a study by the finance site GOBankingRates, which considered the prospects for people trying to save money. Criteria: average monthly cost of grocery items; median home listing price; median rent; median income; transportation costs; gas prices; and the cost of eating out for an inexpensive and mid-range meal in 100 U.S. cities. *www.gobankingrates.com, "The 20 Best (and Worst) Places to Live If You're Trying to Save Money," August 27, 2019*

- Baton Rouge was ranked #20 among 100 U.S. cities for most difficult conditions for savers, according to a study by the finance site GOBankingRates. Criteria: average monthly cost of grocery items; median home listing price; median rent; median income; transportation costs; gas prices; and the cost of eating out for an inexpensive and mid-range meal. *www.gobankingrates.com, "The 20 Best (and Worst) Places to Live If You're Trying to Save Money," August 27, 2019*

- The Brookings Institution ranked the nation's largest cities based on income inequality. Baton Rouge was ranked #9 (#1 = greatest inequality). Criteria: the "95/20 ratio," a figure representing the income at which a household earns more than 95 percent of all other households, divided by the income at which a household earns more than only 20 percent of all other households. *Brookings Institution, "Household Income Inequality, Largest Cities of 97 Large U.S. Metro Areas, 2014-2016," February 5, 2018*

- The Brookings Institution ranked the 100 largest metro areas in the U.S. based on income inequality. Baton Rouge was ranked #13 (#1 = greatest inequality). Criteria: the "95/20 ratio," a figure representing the income at which a household earns more than 95 percent of all other households, divided by the income at which a household earns more than only 20 percent of all other households. *Brookings Institution, "Household Income Inequality, 100 Largest U.S. Metro Areas, 2014-2016," February 5, 2018*

- Baton Rouge was cited as one of America's top metros for new and expanded facility projects in 2020. The area ranked #3 in the mid-sized metro area category (population 200,000 to 1 million). *Site Selection, "Top Metros of 2020," March 2021*

- The Baton Rouge metro area appeared on the Milken Institute "2021 Best Performing Cities" list. Rank: #157 out of 200 large metro areas (population over 250,000). Criteria: job growth; wage and salary growth; high-tech output growth; housing affordability; household broadband access. *Milken Institute, "Best-Performing Cities 2021," February 16, 2021*

- *Forbes* ranked the 200 most populous metro areas to determine the nation's "Best Places for Business and Careers." The Baton Rouge metro area was ranked #148. Criteria: costs (business and living); job growth (past and projected); income growth; quality of life; educational attainment (college and high school); projected economic growth; cultural and leisure opportunities; workplace tolerance laws; net migration patterns. *Forbes, "The Best Places for Business and Careers 2019: Seattle Still On Top," October 30, 2019*

Children/Family Rankings

- Baton Rouge was selected as one of the most playful cities in the U.S. by KaBOOM! The organization's Playful City USA initiative honors cities and towns across the nation that have made their communities more playable. Criteria: pledging to integrate play as a solution to challenges in their communities; making it easy for children to get active and balanced play; creating more family-friendly and innovative communities as a result. *KaBOOM! National Campaign for Play, "2017 Playful City USA Communities"*

Dating/Romance Rankings

- Baton Rouge was ranked #1 out of 25 cities that stood out for inspiring romance and attracting diners on the website OpenTable.com. Criteria: percentage of people who dined out on Valentine's Day in 2018; percentage of romantic restaurants as rated by OpenTable diner reviews; and percentage of tables seated for two. *OpenTable, "25 Most Romantic Cities in America for 2019," February 7, 2019*

Education Rankings

- Personal finance website *WalletHub* analyzed the 150 largest U.S. metropolitan statistical areas to determine where the most educated Americans are putting their degrees to work. Criteria: education levels; percentage of workers with degrees; education quality and attainment gap; public school quality rankings; quality and enrollment of each metro area's universities. Baton Rouge was ranked #112 (#1 = most educated city). *www.WalletHub.com, "Most and Least Educated Cities in America," July 20, 2020*

Health/Fitness Rankings

- For each of the 100 largest cities in the United States, the American Fitness Index®, published by the American College of Sports Medicine and the Anthem Foundation, evaluated community infrastructure and 33 health behaviors including preventive health, levels of chronic disease conditions, pedestrian safety, air quality, and community resources that support physical activity. Baton Rouge ranked #78 for "community fitness." *americanfitnessindex.org, "2020 ACSM American Fitness Index Summary Report," July 14, 2020*

- Baton Rouge was identified as a "2021 Spring Allergy Capital." The area ranked #48 out of 100. Three groups of factors were used to identify the most challenging cities for people with allergies during the spring season: annual spring pollen levels; over the counter medicine use; number of board-certified allergy specialists. *Asthma and Allergy Foundation of America, "Spring Allergy Capitals 2021," February 23, 2021*

- Baton Rouge was identified as a "2021 Fall Allergy Capital." The area ranked #39 out of 100. Three groups of factors were used to identify the most challenging cities for people with allergies during the fall season: annual fall pollen levels; over the counter medicine use; number of board-certified allergy specialists. *Asthma and Allergy Foundation of America, "Fall Allergy Capitals 2021," February 23, 2021*

- Baton Rouge was identified as a "2019 Asthma Capital." The area ranked #84 out of the nation's 100 largest metropolitan areas. Criteria: estimated asthma prevalence; crude death rate from asthma; and ER visits due to asthma. Risk factors analyzed but not factored in the rankings: annual pollen score; annual air quality; public smoking laws; number of board-certified asthma specialists; rescue medication use; controller medication use; uninsured rate; poverty rate. *Asthma and Allergy Foundation of America, "Asthma Capitals 2019: The Most Challenging Places to Live With Asthma," May 7, 2019*

Real Estate Rankings

- *WalletHub* compared the most populated U.S. cities to determine which had the best markets for real estate agents. Baton Rouge ranked #155 where demand was high and pay was the best. Criteria: sales per agent; annual median wage for real-estate agents; monthly average starting salary for real estate agents; real estate job density and competition; unemployment rate; home turnover rate; housing-market health index; and other relevant metrics. *www.WalletHub.com, "2019's Best Places to Be a Real Estate Agent," April 24, 2019*

- Baton Rouge was ranked #46 out of 268 metro areas in terms of housing affordability in 2020 by the National Association of Home Builders (#1 = most affordable). Criteria: the share of homes sold in that area affordable to a family earning the local median income, based on standard mortgage underwriting criteria. *National Association of Home Builders®, NAHB-Wells Fargo Housing Opportunity Index, 4th Quarter 2020*

Safety Rankings

- To identify the most dangerous cities in America, 24/7 Wall Street focused on violent crime categories—murder, non-negligent manslaughter, rape, robbery, and aggravated assault—and property crime as reported in the FBI's 2019 annual Uniform Crime Report. Criteria also included median income from American Community Survey and unemployment figures from Bureau of Labor Statistics. For cities with populations over 100,000, Baton Rouge was ranked #34. *247wallst.com, "America's 50 Most Dangerous Cities" November 16, 2020*

- Allstate ranked the 200 largest cities in America in terms of driver safety. Baton Rouge ranked #188. Criteria: internal property damage claims over a two-year period from January 2016 to December 2017. The report helps increase the importance of safety and awareness behind the wheel. *Allstate, "Allstate America's Best Drivers Report, 2019" June 24, 2019*

- Baton Rouge was identified as one of the most dangerous cities in America by NeighborhoodScout. The city ranked #71 out of 100 (#1 = most dangerous). Criteria: number of violent crimes per 1,000 residents. The editors evaluated cities with 25,000 or more residents. *NeighborhoodScout.com, "2021 Top 100 Most Dangerous Cities in the U.S.," January 2, 2021*

- The National Insurance Crime Bureau ranked 384 metro areas in the U.S. in terms of per capita rates of vehicle theft. The Baton Rouge metro area ranked #137 (#1 = highest rate). Criteria: number of vehicle theft offenses per 100,000 inhabitants in 2019. *National Insurance Crime Bureau, "Hot Spots 2019," July 21, 2020*

Seniors/Retirement Rankings

- From its Best Cities for Successful Aging indexes, the Milken Institute generated rankings for metropolitan areas, weighing data in nine categories—health care, wellness, living arrangements, transportation and convenience, financial characteristics, education, employment, community engagement, and overall livability. The Baton Rouge metro area was ranked #66 overall in the large metro area category. *Milken Institute, "Best Cities for Successful Aging, 2017" March 14, 2017*

Women/Minorities Rankings

- Personal finance website *WalletHub* compared more than 180 U.S. cities across two key dimensions, "Hispanic Business-Friendliness" and "Hispanic Purchasing Power," to arrive at the most favorable conditions for Hispanic entrepreneurs. Baton Rouge was ranked #83 out of 182. Criteria includes: share of Hispanic-Owned Businesses; Hispanic entrepreneurship rate to median annual income of Hispanics; Small Business-Friendliness score; cost of living; and number of Hispanics with at least a bachelor's degree. *WalletHub.com, "2019's Best Cities for Hispanic Entrepreneurs," May 1, 2019*

Miscellaneous Rankings

- Baton Rouge was selected as a 2020 Digital Cities Survey winner. The city ranked #3 in the mid-sized city (125,000 to 249,999 population) category. The survey examined and assessed how city governments are utilizing technology to improve transparency, enhance cybersecurity, and respond to the pandemic. Survey questions focused on ten initiatives: cybersecurity, citizen experience, disaster recovery, business intelligence, IT personnel, data governance, collaboration, infrastructure modernization, cloud computing, and mobile applications. *Center for Digital Government, "2020 Digital Cities Survey," November 10, 2020*

- *WalletHub* compared the 150 most populated U.S. cities to determine their operating efficiency. A "Quality of City Services" score was constructed for each city and then divided by the total budget per capita to reveal which were managed the best. Baton Rouge ranked #61. Criteria: financial stability; economy; education; safety; health; infrastructure and pollution. *www.WalletHub.com, "2020's Best- & Worst-Run Cities in America," June 29, 2020*

Business Environment

DEMOGRAPHICS

Population Growth

Area	1990 Census	2000 Census	2010 Census	2019* Estimate	Population Growth (%) 1990-2019	Population Growth (%) 2010-2019
City	223,299	227,818	229,493	224,149	0.4	-2.3
MSA[1]	623,853	705,973	802,484	854,318	36.9	6.5
U.S.	248,709,873	281,421,906	308,745,538	324,697,795	30.6	5.2

Note: (1) Figures cover the Baton Rouge, LA Metropolitan Statistical Area; (*) 2015-2019 5-year estimated population
Source: U.S. Census Bureau, 1990 Census, Census 2000, Census 2010, 2015-2019 American Community Survey 5-Year Estimates

Household Size

Area	One	Two	Three	Four	Five	Six	Seven or More	Average Household Size
City	36.2	32.4	15.6	9.0	4.1	1.7	0.9	2.60
MSA[1]	28.7	33.8	16.7	12.3	5.6	1.9	0.9	2.70
U.S.	27.9	33.9	15.6	12.9	6.0	2.3	1.4	2.60

Note: (1) Figures cover the Baton Rouge, LA Metropolitan Statistical Area
Source: U.S. Census Bureau, 2015-2019 American Community Survey 5-Year Estimates

Race

Area	White Alone[2] (%)	Black Alone[2] (%)	Asian Alone[2] (%)	AIAN[3] Alone[2] (%)	NHOPI[4] Alone[2] (%)	Other Race Alone[2] (%)	Two or More Races (%)
City	38.7	54.7	3.5	0.3	0.1	1.5	1.3
MSA[1]	59.2	35.3	1.9	0.2	0.0	1.4	1.9
U.S.	72.5	12.7	5.5	0.8	0.2	4.9	3.3

Note: (1) Figures cover the Baton Rouge, LA Metropolitan Statistical Area; (2) Alone is defined as not being in combination with one or more other races; (3) American Indian and Alaska Native; (4) Native Hawaiian and Other Pacific Islander
Source: U.S. Census Bureau, 2015-2019 American Community Survey 5-Year Estimates

Hispanic or Latino Origin

Area	Total (%)	Mexican (%)	Puerto Rican (%)	Cuban (%)	Other (%)
City	3.7	1.1	0.3	0.2	2.1
MSA[1]	4.0	1.5	0.3	0.2	2.0
U.S.	18.0	11.2	1.7	0.7	4.3

Note: Persons of Hispanic or Latino origin can be of any race; (1) Figures cover the Baton Rouge, LA Metropolitan Statistical Area
Source: U.S. Census Bureau, 2015-2019 American Community Survey 5-Year Estimates

Ancestry

Area	German	Irish	English	American	Italian	Polish	French[2]	Scottish	Dutch
City	5.2	5.0	4.5	5.5	3.3	0.4	6.9	1.3	0.3
MSA[1]	6.8	6.6	5.0	7.8	4.7	0.5	12.3	1.1	0.3
U.S.	13.3	9.7	7.2	6.2	5.1	2.8	2.3	1.7	1.2

Note: Figures are the percentage of the total population reporting a particular ancestry. The nine most commonly reported ancestries in the U.S. are shown. Figures include multiple ancestries (e.g. if a person reported being Irish and Italian, they were included in both columns); (1) Figures cover the Baton Rouge, LA Metropolitan Statistical Area; (2) Excludes Basque
Source: U.S. Census Bureau, 2015-2019 American Community Survey 5-Year Estimates

Foreign-born Population

Area	Any Foreign Country	Asia	Mexico	Europe	Caribbean	Central America[2]	South America	Africa	Canada
City	5.5	2.8	0.4	0.5	0.2	1.0	0.2	0.3	0.0
MSA[1]	4.0	1.5	0.7	0.3	0.2	0.9	0.2	0.2	0.1
U.S.	13.6	4.2	3.5	1.5	1.3	1.1	1.0	0.7	0.2

Note: (1) Figures cover the Baton Rouge, LA Metropolitan Statistical Area; (2) Excludes Mexico.
Source: U.S. Census Bureau, 2015-2019 American Community Survey 5-Year Estimates

Marital Status

Area	Never Married	Now Married[2]	Separated	Widowed	Divorced
City	50.2	30.4	2.0	6.4	11.0
MSA[1]	37.2	43.2	2.1	6.1	11.4
U.S.	33.4	48.1	1.9	5.8	10.9

Note: Figures are percentages and cover the population 15 years of age and older; (1) Figures cover the Baton Rouge, LA Metropolitan Statistical Area; (2) Excludes separated
Source: U.S. Census Bureau, 2015-2019 American Community Survey 5-Year Estimates

Disability by Age

Area	All Ages	Under 18 Years Old	18 to 64 Years Old	65 Years and Over
City	16.8	8.5	14.6	40.3
MSA[1]	14.8	6.2	13.0	38.1
U.S.	12.6	4.2	10.3	34.5

Note: Figures show percent of the civilian noninstitutionalized population that reported having a disability. Disability status is determined from six types of difficulty: vision, hearing, cognitive, ambulatory, self-care, and independent living. For children under 5 years old, hearing and vision difficulty are used to determine disability status. For children between the ages of 5 and 14, disability status is determined from hearing, vision, cognitive, ambulatory, and self-care difficulties. For people aged 15 years and older, they are considered to have a disability if they have difficulty with any one of the six difficulty types; Note: (1) Figures cover the Baton Rouge, LA Metropolitan Statistical Area
Source: U.S. Census Bureau, 2015-2019 American Community Survey 5-Year Estimates

Age

Area	Under Age 5	Age 5–19	Age 20–34	Age 35–44	Age 45–54	Age 55–64	Age 65–74	Age 75–84	Age 85+	Median Age
City	6.7	19.6	28.3	10.5	10.1	11.1	8.0	3.9	1.9	31.5
MSA[1]	6.5	20.1	22.7	12.7	12.2	12.2	8.4	3.9	1.4	35.6
U.S.	6.1	19.1	20.7	12.6	13.0	12.9	9.1	4.6	1.9	38.1

Note: (1) Figures cover the Baton Rouge, LA Metropolitan Statistical Area
Source: U.S. Census Bureau, 2015-2019 American Community Survey 5-Year Estimates

Gender

Area	Males	Females	Males per 100 Females
City	107,345	116,804	91.9
MSA[1]	417,717	436,601	95.7
U.S.	159,886,919	164,810,876	97.0

Note: (1) Figures cover the Baton Rouge, LA Metropolitan Statistical Area
Source: U.S. Census Bureau, 2015-2019 American Community Survey 5-Year Estimates

Religious Groups by Family

Area	Catholic	Baptist	Non-Den.	Methodist[2]	Lutheran	LDS[3]	Pentecostal	Presbyterian[4]	Muslim[5]	Judaism
MSA[1]	22.6	18.2	9.6	4.6	0.3	0.8	1.1	0.6	0.2	0.1
U.S.	19.1	9.3	4.0	4.0	2.3	2.0	1.9	1.6	0.8	0.7

Note: Figures are the number of adherents as a percentage of the total population; (1) Figures cover the Baton Rouge, LA Metropolitan Statistical Area; (2) Methodist/Pietist; (3) Latter Day Saints; (4) Reformed; (5) Figures are estimates
Source: Association of Statisticians of American Religious Bodies, 2010 U.S. Religion Census: Religious Congregations & Membership Study

Religious Groups by Tradition

Area	Catholic	Evangelical Protestant	Mainline Protestant	Other Tradition	Black Protestant	Orthodox
MSA[1]	22.6	24.9	5.7	1.6	5.2	0.1
U.S.	19.1	16.2	7.3	4.3	1.6	0.3

Note: Figures are the number of adherents as a percentage of the total population; (1) Figures cover the Baton Rouge, LA Metropolitan Statistical Area
Source: Association of Statisticians of American Religious Bodies, 2010 U.S. Religion Census: Religious Congregations & Membership Study

ECONOMY

Gross Metropolitan Product

Area	2017	2018	2019	2020	Rank[2]
MSA[1]	53.2	56.3	58.3	61.0	59

Note: Figures are in billions of dollars; (1) Figures cover the Baton Rouge, LA Metropolitan Statistical Area; (2) Rank is based on 2018 data and ranges from 1 to 381
Source: U.S. Conference of Mayors, U.S. Metro Economies: GMP & Employment 2018-2020, September 2019

Economic Growth

Area	2015-17 (%)	2018 (%)	2019 (%)	2020 (%)	Rank[2]
MSA[1]	1.6	0.8	1.2	2.4	170
U.S.	1.9	2.9	2.3	2.1	—

Note: Figures are real gross metropolitan product (GMP) growth rates and represent average annual percent change; (1) Figures cover the Baton Rouge, LA Metropolitan Statistical Area; (2) Rank is based on 2017 2-year average annual percent change and ranges from 1 to 381
Source: U.S. Conference of Mayors, U.S. Metro Economies: GMP & Employment 2018-2020, September 2019

Metropolitan Area Exports

Area	2014	2015	2016	2017	2018	2019	Rank[2]
MSA[1]	7,528.3	6,505.4	6,580.5	8,830.3	10,506.1	8,981.2	40

Note: Figures are in millions of dollars; (1) Figures cover the Baton Rouge, LA Metropolitan Statistical Area; (2) Rank is based on 2019 data and ranges from 1 to 386
Source: U.S. Department of Commerce, International Trade Administration, Office of Trade and Economic Analysis, Industry and Analysis, Exports by Metropolitan Area, data extracted March 24, 2021

Building Permits

Area	Single-Family 2018	Single-Family 2019	Pct. Chg.	Multi-Family 2018	Multi-Family 2019	Pct. Chg.	Total 2018	Total 2019	Pct. Chg.
City	282	354	25.5	58	0	-100.0	340	354	4.1
MSA[1]	3,509	3,612	2.9	413	10	-97.6	3,922	3,622	-7.6
U.S.	855,300	862,100	0.7	473,500	523,900	10.6	1,328,800	1,386,000	4.3

Note: (1) Figures cover the Baton Rouge, LA Metropolitan Statistical Area; Figures represent new, privately-owned housing units authorized (unadjusted data); All permit data are based on estimates with imputation
Source: U.S. Census Bureau, Manufacturing, Mining, and Construction Statistics, Building Permits, 2018, 2019

Bankruptcy Filings

Area	Business Filings 2019	Business Filings 2020	% Chg.	Nonbusiness Filings 2019	Nonbusiness Filings 2020	% Chg.
East Baton Rouge Parish	37	49	32.4	771	435	-43.6
U.S.	22,780	21,655	-4.9	752,160	522,808	-30.5

Note: Business filings include Chapter 7, Chapter 9, Chapter 11, Chapter 12, Chapter 13, Chapter 15, and Section 304; Nonbusiness filings include Chapter 7, Chapter 11, and Chapter 13
Source: Administrative Office of the U.S. Courts, Business and Nonbusiness Bankruptcy, County Cases Commenced by Chapter of the Bankruptcy Code, During the 12-Month Period Ending December 31, 2019 and Business and Nonbusiness Bankruptcy, County Cases Commenced by Chapter of the Bankruptcy Code, During the 12-Month Period Ending December 31, 2020

Housing Vacancy Rates

Area	Gross Vacancy Rate[2] (%) 2018	2019	2020	Year-Round Vacancy Rate[3] (%) 2018	2019	2020	Rental Vacancy Rate[4] (%) 2018	2019	2020	Homeowner Vacancy Rate[5] (%) 2018	2019	2020
MSA[1]	13.0	13.9	12.6	11.8	13.0	11.8	7.6	10.2	7.4	1.4	1.9	1.7
U.S.	12.3	12.0	10.6	9.7	9.5	8.2	6.9	6.7	6.3	1.5	1.4	1.0

Note: (1) Figures cover the Baton Rouge, LA Metropolitan Statistical Area; (2) The percentage of the total housing inventory that is vacant; (3) The percentage of the housing inventory (excluding seasonal units) that is year-round vacant; (4) The percentage of rental inventory that is vacant for rent; (5) The percentage of homeowner inventory that is vacant for sale
Source: U.S. Census Bureau, Housing Vacancies and Homeownership Annual Statistics: 2018, 2019, 2020

INCOME

Income

Area	Per Capita ($)	Median Household ($)	Average Household ($)
City	28,491	44,470	70,902
MSA[1]	31,082	58,912	81,614
U.S.	34,103	62,843	88,607

Note: (1) Figures cover the Baton Rouge, LA Metropolitan Statistical Area
Source: U.S. Census Bureau, 2015-2019 American Community Survey 5-Year Estimates

Household Income Distribution

Area	Under $15,000	$15,000-$24,999	$25,000-$34,999	$35,000-$49,999	$50,000-$74,999	$75,000-$99,999	$100,000-$149,999	$150,000 and up
City	18.2	13.1	11.0	12.0	15.5	9.1	11.4	9.7
MSA[1]	12.6	9.8	9.4	11.5	16.4	11.9	15.5	12.9
U.S.	10.3	8.9	8.9	12.3	17.2	12.7	15.1	14.5

Note: (1) Figures cover the Baton Rouge, LA Metropolitan Statistical Area
Source: U.S. Census Bureau, 2015-2019 American Community Survey 5-Year Estimates

Poverty Rate

Area	All Ages	Under 18 Years Old	18 to 64 Years Old	65 Years and Over
City	24.8	35.7	23.9	11.5
MSA[1]	15.9	21.8	14.9	10.0
U.S.	13.4	18.5	12.6	9.3

Note: Figures are percentage of people whose income during the past 12 months was below the poverty level;
(1) Figures cover the Baton Rouge, LA Metropolitan Statistical Area
Source: U.S. Census Bureau, 2015-2019 American Community Survey 5-Year Estimates

CITY FINANCES

City Government Finances

Component	2017 ($000)	2017 ($ per capita)
Total Revenues	1,099,707	4,811
Total Expenditures	1,253,703	5,485
Debt Outstanding	1,319,370	5,772
Cash and Securities[1]	2,841,120	12,429

Note: (1) Cash and security holdings of a government at the close of its fiscal year, including those of its dependent agencies, utilities, and liquor stores.
Source: U.S. Census Bureau, State & Local Government Finances 2017

City Government Revenue by Source

Source	2017 ($000)	2017 ($ per capita)	2017 (%)
General Revenue			
From Federal Government	65,055	285	5.9
From State Government	48,756	213	4.4
From Local Governments	0	0	0.0
Taxes			
Property	206,331	903	18.8
Sales and Gross Receipts	338,615	1,481	30.8
Personal Income	0	0	0.0
Corporate Income	0	0	0.0
Motor Vehicle License	0	0	0.0
Other Taxes	5,094	22	0.5
Current Charges	306,952	1,343	27.9
Liquor Store	0	0	0.0
Utility	5,007	22	0.5
Employee Retirement	103,042	451	9.4

Source: U.S. Census Bureau, State & Local Government Finances 2017

City Government Expenditures by Function

Function	2017 ($000)	2017 ($ per capita)	2017 (%)
General Direct Expenditures			
Air Transportation	23,935	104	1.9
Corrections	60,293	263	4.8
Education	11,897	52	0.9
Employment Security Administration	0	0	0.0
Financial Administration	28,276	123	2.3
Fire Protection	89,638	392	7.1
General Public Buildings	10,632	46	0.8
Governmental Administration, Other	18,721	81	1.5
Health	49,454	216	3.9
Highways	44,090	192	3.5
Hospitals	96,131	420	7.7
Housing and Community Development	66,834	292	5.3
Interest on General Debt	78,588	343	6.3
Judicial and Legal	47,660	208	3.8
Libraries	41,927	183	3.3
Parking	694	3	0.1
Parks and Recreation	13,922	60	1.1
Police Protection	155,471	680	12.4
Public Welfare	5,684	24	0.5
Sewerage	182,051	796	14.5
Solid Waste Management	40,836	178	3.3
Veterans' Services	0	0	0.0
Liquor Store	0	0	0.0
Utility	34,597	151	2.8
Employee Retirement	80,869	353	6.5

Source: U.S. Census Bureau, State & Local Government Finances 2017

EMPLOYMENT

Labor Force and Employment

Area	Civilian Labor Force Dec. 2019	Dec. 2020	% Chg.	Workers Employed Dec. 2019	Dec. 2020	% Chg.
City	111,969	112,989	0.9	106,514	104,304	-2.1
MSA[1]	417,880	416,461	-0.3	399,191	391,186	-2.0
U.S.	164,007,000	160,017,000	-2.4	158,504,000	149,613,000	-5.6

Note: Data is not seasonally adjusted and covers workers 16 years of age and older; (1) Figures cover the Baton Rouge, LA Metropolitan Statistical Area
Source: Bureau of Labor Statistics, Local Area Unemployment Statistics

Unemployment Rate

Area	Jan.	Feb.	Mar.	Apr.	May	Jun.	Jul.	Aug.	Sep.	Oct.	Nov.	Dec.
City	5.7	4.1	6.2	14.7	15.0	11.6	11.3	9.1	8.8	10.1	9.2	7.7
MSA[1]	5.1	3.8	5.6	13.0	12.6	9.6	9.2	7.2	7.0	8.0	7.2	6.1
U.S.	4.0	3.8	4.5	14.4	13.0	11.2	10.5	8.5	7.7	6.6	6.4	6.5

Note: Data is not seasonally adjusted and covers workers 16 years of age and older; (1) Figures cover the Baton Rouge, LA Metropolitan Statistical Area
Source: Bureau of Labor Statistics, Local Area Unemployment Statistics

Average Wages

Occupation	$/Hr.	Occupation	$/Hr.
Accountants and Auditors	31.10	Maintenance and Repair Workers	21.10
Automotive Mechanics	22.30	Marketing Managers	50.40
Bookkeepers	20.00	Network and Computer Systems Admin.	37.90
Carpenters	24.70	Nurses, Licensed Practical	20.40
Cashiers	10.10	Nurses, Registered	31.30
Computer Programmers	40.40	Nursing Assistants	12.30
Computer Systems Analysts	39.70	Office Clerks, General	13.90
Computer User Support Specialists	24.20	Physical Therapists	43.10
Construction Laborers	17.90	Physicians	104.40
Cooks, Restaurant	12.00	Plumbers, Pipefitters and Steamfitters	29.40
Customer Service Representatives	16.40	Police and Sheriff's Patrol Officers	21.20
Dentists	91.40	Postal Service Mail Carriers	25.30
Electricians	26.20	Real Estate Sales Agents	20.10
Engineers, Electrical	53.10	Retail Salespersons	12.80
Fast Food and Counter Workers	9.50	Sales Representatives, Technical/Scientific	38.40
Financial Managers	53.60	Secretaries, Exc. Legal/Medical/Executive	17.00
First-Line Supervisors of Office Workers	24.60	Security Guards	15.20
General and Operations Managers	56.40	Surgeons	140.20
Hairdressers/Cosmetologists	14.00	Teacher Assistants, Exc. Postsecondary*	10.60
Home Health and Personal Care Aides	9.70	Teachers, Secondary School, Exc. Sp. Ed.*	25.90
Janitors and Cleaners	11.00	Telemarketers	13.70
Landscaping/Groundskeeping Workers	15.10	Truck Drivers, Heavy/Tractor-Trailer	20.20
Lawyers	54.50	Truck Drivers, Light/Delivery Services	16.70
Maids and Housekeeping Cleaners	10.60	Waiters and Waitresses	9.80

Note: Wage data covers the Baton Rouge, LA Metropolitan Statistical Area; (*) Hourly wages were calculated from annual wage data based on a 40 hour work week; n/a not available.
Source: Bureau of Labor Statistics, Metro Area Occupational Employment & Wage Estimates, May 2020

Employment by Industry

Sector	MSA[1] Number of Employees	Percent of Total	U.S. Percent of Total
Construction	41,000	10.5	5.1
Education and Health Services	52,500	13.5	16.3
Financial Activities	16,700	4.3	6.1
Government	77,800	20.0	15.2
Information	4,400	1.1	1.9
Leisure and Hospitality	34,300	8.8	9.0
Manufacturing	29,300	7.5	8.5
Mining and Logging	700	0.2	0.4
Other Services	14,900	3.8	3.8
Professional and Business Services	47,900	12.3	14.4
Retail Trade	41,200	10.6	10.9
Transportation, Warehousing, and Utilities	15,300	3.9	4.6
Wholesale Trade	13,000	3.3	3.9

Note: Figures are non-farm employment as of December 2020. Figures are not seasonally adjusted and include workers 16 years of age and older; (1) Figures cover the Baton Rouge, LA Metropolitan Statistical Area
Source: Bureau of Labor Statistics, Current Employment Statistics, Employment, Hours, and Earnings

Employment by Occupation

Occupation Classification	City (%)	MSA[1] (%)	U.S. (%)
Management, Business, Science, and Arts	36.5	36.1	38.5
Natural Resources, Construction, and Maintenance	8.3	10.6	8.9
Production, Transportation, and Material Moving	12.8	13.2	13.2
Sales and Office	22.0	22.5	21.6
Service	20.4	17.5	17.8

Note: Figures cover employed civilians 16 years of age and older; (1) Figures cover the Baton Rouge, LA Metropolitan Statistical Area
Source: U.S. Census Bureau, 2015-2019 American Community Survey 5-Year Estimates

Occupations with Greatest Projected Employment Growth: 2020 – 2022

Occupation[1]	2020 Employment	2022 Projected Employment	Numeric Employment Change	Percent Employment Change
Fast Food and Counter Workers	21,880	22,580	700	3.2
Home Health and Personal Care Aides	35,530	36,200	670	1.9
Registered Nurses	40,540	41,050	510	1.3
Cooks, Restaurant	11,020	11,530	510	4.6
Stockers and Order Fillers	20,590	21,030	440	2.1
Medical Assistants	8,110	8,440	330	4.1
Nurse Practitioners	3,080	3,390	310	10.1
Medical and Health Services Managers	4,970	5,230	260	5.2
Licensed Practical and Licensed Vocational Nurses	18,340	18,580	240	1.3
Waiters and Waitresses	24,100	24,340	240	1.0

Note: Projections cover Louisiana; (1) Sorted by numeric employment change
Source: www.projectionscentral.com, State Occupational Projections, 2020–2022 Short-Term Projections

Fastest-Growing Occupations: 2020 – 2022

Occupation[1]	2020 Employment	2022 Projected Employment	Numeric Employment Change	Percent Employment Change
Nurse Practitioners	3,080	3,390	310	10.1
Occupational Therapy Assistants	670	730	60	9.0
Physician Assistants	1,130	1,210	80	7.1
Physical Therapist Assistants	1,410	1,510	100	7.1
Speech-Language Pathologists	1,240	1,310	70	5.6
Medical and Health Services Managers	4,970	5,230	260	5.2
Cooks, Restaurant	11,020	11,530	510	4.6
Respiratory Therapists	2,480	2,590	110	4.4
Physical Therapist Aides	1,630	1,700	70	4.3
Medical Assistants	8,110	8,440	330	4.1

Note: Projections cover Louisiana; (1) Sorted by percent employment change and excludes occupations with numeric employment change less than 50
Source: www.projectionscentral.com, State Occupational Projections, 2020–2022 Short-Term Projections

TAXES

State Corporate Income Tax Rates

State	Tax Rate (%)	Income Brackets ($)	Num. of Brackets	Financial Institution Tax Rate (%)[a]	Federal Income Tax Ded.
Louisiana	4.0 - 8.0	25,000 - 200,001	5	4.0 - 8.0	Yes

Note: Tax rates as of January 1, 2021; (a) Rates listed are the corporate income tax rate applied to financial institutions or excise taxes based on income. Some states have other taxes based upon the value of deposits or shares.
Source: Federation of Tax Administrators, State Corporate Income Tax Rates, January 1, 2021

State Individual Income Tax Rates

State	Tax Rate (%)	Income Brackets ($)	Personal Exemptions ($) Single	Personal Exemptions ($) Married	Personal Exemptions ($) Depend.	Standard Ded. ($) Single	Standard Ded. ($) Married
Louisiana	2.0 - 6.0	12,500 - 50,001 (b)	4,500	9,000 (k)	1,000	(k)	(k)

Note: Tax rates as of January 1, 2021; Local- and county-level taxes are not included; Federal income tax is deductible on state income tax returns; (b) For joint returns, taxes are twice the tax on half the couple's income; (k) The amounts reported for Louisiana are a combined personal exemption-standard deduction.
Source: Federation of Tax Administrators, State Individual Income Tax Rates, January 1, 2021

Various State Sales and Excise Tax Rates

State	State Sales Tax (%)	Gasoline[1] (¢/gal.)	Cigarette[2] ($/pack)	Spirits[3] ($/gal.)	Wine[4] ($/gal.)	Beer[5] ($/gal.)	Recreational Marijuana (%)
Louisiana	4.45	20.01	1.08	3.03	0.76	0.4	Not legal

Note: All tax rates as of January 1, 2021; (1) The American Petroleum Institute has developed a methodology for determining the average tax rate on a gallon of fuel. Rates may include any of the following: excise taxes, environmental fees, storage tank fees, other fees or taxes, general sales tax, and local taxes; (2) The federal excise tax of $1.0066 per pack and local taxes are not included; (3) Rates are those applicable to off-premise sales of 40% alcohol by volume (a.b.v.) distilled spirits in 750ml containers. Local excise taxes are excluded; (4) Rates are those applicable to off-premise sales of 11% a.b.v. non-carbonated wine in 750ml containers; (5) Rates are those applicable to off-premise sales of 4.7% a.b.v. beer in 12 ounce containers.
Source: Tax Foundation, 2021 Facts & Figures: How Does Your State Compare?

State Business Tax Climate Index Rankings

State	Overall Rank	Corporate Tax Rank	Individual Income Tax Rank	Sales Tax Rank	Property Tax Rank	Unemployment Insurance Tax Rank
Louisiana	42	35	32	49	23	4

Note: The index is a measure of how each state's tax laws affect economic performance. The lower the rank, the more favorable a state's tax system is for business. States without a given tax are given a ranking of 1. The scores/rankings for the District of Columbia do not affect other states. The 2021 index represents the tax climate as of July 1, 2020.
Source: Tax Foundation, State Business Tax Climate Index 2021

TRANSPORTATION

Means of Transportation to Work

Area	Car/Truck/Van Drove Alone	Car/Truck/Van Carpooled	Public Transportation Bus	Public Transportation Subway	Public Transportation Railroad	Bicycle	Walked	Other Means	Worked at Home
City	80.3	9.8	2.4	0.0	0.0	0.6	3.4	0.6	2.9
MSA[1]	84.8	8.7	0.8	0.0	0.0	0.3	1.5	0.9	3.1
U.S.	76.3	9.0	2.4	1.9	0.6	0.5	2.7	1.4	5.2

Note: Figures are percentages and cover workers 16 years of age and older; (1) Figures cover the Baton Rouge, LA Metropolitan Statistical Area
Source: U.S. Census Bureau, 2015-2019 American Community Survey 5-Year Estimates

Travel Time to Work

Area	Less Than 10 Minutes	10 to 19 Minutes	20 to 29 Minutes	30 to 44 Minutes	45 to 59 Minutes	60 to 89 Minutes	90 Minutes or More
City	11.9	39.3	25.5	15.1	3.6	2.8	1.9
MSA[1]	9.8	27.7	22.0	22.5	9.2	6.5	2.3
U.S.	12.2	28.4	20.8	20.8	8.3	6.4	2.9

Note: Note: Figures are percentages and include workers 16 years old and over; (1) Figures cover the Baton Rouge, LA Metropolitan Statistical Area
Source: U.S. Census Bureau, 2015-2019 American Community Survey 5-Year Estimates

Key Congestion Measures

Measure	1982	1992	2002	2012	2017
Annual Hours of Delay, Total (000)	2,849	5,924	11,445	22,891	28,362
Annual Hours of Delay, Per Auto Commuter	12	22	31	48	58
Annual Congestion Cost, Total (million $)	22	63	155	414	525
Annual Congestion Cost, Per Auto Commuter ($)	249	357	536	841	1,011

Note: Covers the Baton Rouge LA urban area
Source: Texas A&M Transportation Institute, 2019 Urban Mobility Report

Freeway Travel Time Index

Measure	1982	1987	1992	1997	2002	2007	2012	2017
Urban Area Index[1]	1.06	1.09	1.11	1.14	1.16	1.20	1.21	1.23
Urban Area Rank[1,2]	43	40	49	47	54	38	34	30

Note: Freeway Travel Time Index—the ratio of travel time in the peak period to the travel time at free-flow conditions. For example, a value of 1.30 indicates a 20-minute free-flow trip takes 26 minutes in the peak (20 minutes x 1.30 = 26 minutes); (1) Covers the Baton Rouge LA urban area; (2) Rank is based on 101 larger urban areas (#1 = highest travel time index)
Source: Texas A&M Transportation Institute, 2019 Urban Mobility Report

Public Transportation

Agency Name / Mode of Transportation	Vehicles Operated in Maximum Service[1]	Annual Unlinked Passenger Trips[2] (in thous.)	Annual Passenger Miles[3] (in thous.)
Capital Area Transit System (CATS)			
Bus (directly operated)	63	3,709.0	13,350.4
Demand Response (purchased transportation)	19	94.8	1,094.4

Note: (1) Number of revenue vehicles operated by the given mode and type of service to meet the annual maximum service requirement. This is the revenue vehicle count during the peak season of the year; on the week and day that maximum service is provided. Vehicles operated in maximum service (VOMS) exclude atypical days and one-time special events; (2) Number of passengers who boarded public transportation vehicles. Passengers are counted each time they board a vehicle no matter how many vehicles they use to travel from their origin to their destination. (3) Sum of the distances ridden by all passengers during the entire fiscal year.
Source: Federal Transit Administration, National Transit Database, 2019

Air Transportation

Airport Name and Code / Type of Service	Passenger Airlines[1]	Passenger Enplanements	Freight Carriers[2]	Freight (lbs)
Baton Rouge Metropolitan (BTR)				
Domestic service (U.S. carriers - 2020)	18	176,069	2	1,240
International service (U.S. carriers - 2019)	1	51	0	0

Note: (1) Includes all U.S.-based major, minor and commuter airlines that carried at least one passenger during the year; (2) Includes all U.S.-based airlines and freight carriers that transported at least one pound of freight during the year.
Source: Bureau of Transportation Statistics, The Intermodal Transportation Database, Air Carriers: T-100 Domestic Market (U.S. Carriers), 2020; Bureau of Transportation Statistics, The Intermodal Transportation Database, Air Carriers: T-100 International Market (U.S. Carriers), 2019

BUSINESSES

Major Business Headquarters

Company Name	Industry	Rankings Fortune[1]	Rankings Forbes[2]
Turner Industries Group	Construction	-	150

Note: (1) Companies that produce a 10-K are ranked 1 to 500 based on 2019 revenue; (2) All private companies with at least $2 billion in annual revenue through the end of their most current fiscal year are ranked 1 to 219; companies listed are headquartered in the city; dashes indicate no ranking
Source: Fortune, "Fortune 500," June/July 2020; Forbes, "America's Largest Private Companies," 2020

Living Environment

COST OF LIVING

Cost of Living Index

Composite Index	Groceries	Housing	Utilities	Transportation	Health Care	Misc. Goods/Services
97.0	97.6	93.2	76.8	94.4	103.2	105.0

Note: The Cost of Living Index measures regional differences in the cost of consumer goods and services, excluding taxes and non-consumer expenditures, for professional and managerial households in the top income quintile. It is based on more than 50,000 prices covering almost 60 different items for which prices are collected three times a year by chambers of commerce, economic development organizations or university applied economic centers in each participating urban area. The numbers shown should be read as a percentage above or below the national average of 100. For example, a value of 115.4 in the groceries column indicates that grocery prices are 15.4% higher than the national average. Small differences in the index numbers should not be interpreted as significant; Figures cover the Baton Rouge LA urban area.
Source: The Council for Community and Economic Research, Cost of Living Index, 2020

Grocery Prices

Area[1]	T-Bone Steak ($/pound)	Frying Chicken ($/pound)	Whole Milk ($/half gal.)	Eggs ($/dozen)	Orange Juice ($/64 oz.)	Coffee ($/11.5 oz.)
City[2]	11.70	1.42	2.65	1.53	3.69	4.26
Avg.	11.78	1.39	2.05	1.47	3.57	4.34
Min.	8.03	0.94	1.03	0.74	2.94	3.02
Max.	15.86	2.65	4.31	3.77	5.44	8.69

Note: (1) Values for the local area are compared with the average, minimum and maximum values for all 284 areas in the Cost of Living Index; (2) Figures cover the Baton Rouge LA urban area; **T-Bone Steak** (price per pound); **Frying Chicken** (price per pound, whole fryer); **Whole Milk** (half gallon carton); **Eggs** (price per dozen, Grade A, large); **Orange Juice** (64 oz. Tropicana or Florida Natural); **Coffee** (11.5 oz. can, vacuum-packed, Maxwell House, Hills Bros, or Folgers).
Source: The Council for Community and Economic Research, Cost of Living Index, 2020

Housing and Utility Costs

Area[1]	New Home Price ($)	Apartment Rent ($/month)	All Electric ($/month)	Part Electric ($/month)	Other Energy ($/month)	Telephone ($/month)
City[2]	333,881	1,144	101.95	-	-	179.00
Avg.	368,594	1,168	170.86	100.47	65.28	184.30
Min.	190,567	502	91.58	31.42	26.08	169.60
Max.	2,227,806	4,738	470.38	280.31	280.06	206.50

Note: (1) Values for the local area are compared with the average, minimum and maximum values for all 284 areas in the Cost of Living Index; (2) Figures cover the Baton Rouge LA urban area; **New Home Price** (2,400 sf living area, 8,000 sf lot, in urban area with full utilities); **Apartment Rent** (950 sf 2 bedroom/1.5 or 2 bath, unfurnished, excluding all utilities except water); **All Electric** (average monthly cost for an all-electric home); **Part Electric** (average monthly cost for a part-electric home); **Other Energy** (average monthly cost for natural gas, fuel oil, coal, wood, and any other forms of energy except electricity); **Telephone** (price includes the base monthly rate plus taxes and fees for three lines of mobile phone service).
Source: The Council for Community and Economic Research, Cost of Living Index, 2020

Health Care, Transportation, and Other Costs

Area[1]	Doctor ($/visit)	Dentist ($/visit)	Optometrist ($/visit)	Gasoline ($/gallon)	Beauty Salon ($/visit)	Men's Shirt ($)
City[2]	114.78	104.33	127.76	1.89	50.62	40.67
Avg.	115.44	99.32	108.10	2.21	39.27	31.37
Min.	36.68	59.00	51.36	1.71	19.00	11.00
Max.	219.00	153.10	250.97	3.46	82.05	58.33

Note: (1) Values for the local area are compared with the average, minimum and maximum values for all 284 areas in the Cost of Living Index; (2) Figures cover the Baton Rouge LA urban area; **Doctor** (general practitioners routine exam of an established patient); **Dentist** (adult teeth cleaning and periodic oral examination); **Optometrist** (full vision eye exam for established adult patient); **Gasoline** (one gallon regular unleaded, national brand, including all taxes, cash price at self-service pump if available); **Beauty Salon** (woman's shampoo, trim, and blow-dry); **Men's Shirt** (cotton/polyester dress shirt, pinpoint weave, long sleeves).
Source: The Council for Community and Economic Research, Cost of Living Index, 2020

HOUSING

Homeownership Rate

Area	2012 (%)	2013 (%)	2014 (%)	2015 (%)	2016 (%)	2017 (%)	2018 (%)	2019 (%)	2020 (%)
MSA[1]	71.4	66.6	64.8	64.2	64.8	66.9	66.6	66.2	72.1
U.S.	65.4	65.1	64.5	63.7	63.4	63.9	64.4	64.6	66.6

Note: (1) Figures cover the Baton Rouge, LA Metropolitan Statistical Area
Source: U.S. Census Bureau, Housing Vacancies and Homeownership Annual Statistics: 2012-2020

House Price Index (HPI)

Area	National Ranking[2]	Quarterly Change (%)	One-Year Change (%)	Five-Year Change (%)	Since 1991Q1 (%)
MSA[1]	230	1.37	3.54	17.61	188.52
U.S.[3]	–	3.81	10.77	38.99	205.12

Note: The HPI is a weighted repeat sales index. It measures average price changes in repeat sales or refinancings on the same properties. This information is obtained by reviewing repeat mortgage transactions on single-family properties whose mortgages have been purchased or securitized by Fannie Mae or Freddie Mac since January 1975; (1) Figures cover the Baton Rouge, LA Metropolitan Statistical Area; (2) Rankings are based on annual percentage change for all metro areas containing at least 15,000 transactions over the last 10 years and ranges from 1 to 253; (3) figures based on a weighted average of Census Division estimates using a seasonally adjusted, purchase-only index; all figures are for the period ending December 31, 2020
Source: Federal Housing Finance Agency, Change in Metropolitan Area House Price Indexes, April 7, 2021

Median Single-Family Home Prices

Area	2018	2019	2020p	Percent Change 2019 to 2020
MSA[1]	210.6	216.4	229.7	6.1
U.S. Average	261.6	274.6	299.9	9.2

Note: Figures are median sales prices of existing single-family homes in thousands of dollars; (p) preliminary; (1) Figures cover the Baton Rouge, LA Metropolitan Statistical Area
Source: National Association of Realtors, Median Sales Price of Existing Single-Family Homes for Metropolitan Areas, 4th Quarter 2020

Qualifying Income Based on Median Sales Price of Existing Single-Family Homes

Area	With 5% Down ($)	With 10% Down ($)	With 20% Down ($)
MSA[1]	44,883	42,521	37,797
U.S. Average	59,266	56,147	49,908

Note: Figures are preliminary; Qualifying income is based on a mortgage rate of 2.81%. Monthly principal and interest payment is limited to 25% of income; (1) Figures cover the Baton Rouge, LA Metropolitan Statistical Area
Source: National Association of Realtors, Qualifying Income Based on Median Sales Price of Existing Single-Family Homes for Metropolitan Areas, 4th Quarter 2020

Home Value Distribution

Area	Under $50,000	$50,000 -$99,999	$100,000 -$149,999	$150,000 -$199,999	$200,000 -$299,999	$300,000 -$499,999	$500,000 -$999,999	$1,000,000 or more
City	5.6	17.7	15.6	19.4	21.4	12.9	5.8	1.6
MSA[1]	8.7	12.3	15.0	20.4	24.0	14.3	4.3	1.0
U.S.	6.9	12.0	13.3	14.0	19.6	19.3	11.4	3.4

Note: Figures are percentages and cover owner-occupied housing units; (1) Figures cover the Baton Rouge, LA Metropolitan Statistical Area
Source: U.S. Census Bureau, 2015-2019 American Community Survey 5-Year Estimates

Year Housing Structure Built

Area	2010 or Later	2000 -2009	1990 -1999	1980 -1989	1970 -1979	1960 -1969	1950 -1959	1940 -1949	Before 1940	Median Year
City	5.9	9.9	8.7	12.9	22.4	17.3	11.7	5.9	5.3	1974
MSA[1]	9.4	19.8	14.6	15.0	17.4	10.2	6.9	2.9	3.9	1986
U.S.	5.2	14.0	13.9	13.4	15.2	10.6	10.3	4.9	12.6	1978

Note: Figures are percentages except for Median Year; Note: (1) Figures cover the Baton Rouge, LA Metropolitan Statistical Area
Source: U.S. Census Bureau, 2015-2019 American Community Survey 5-Year Estimates

Gross Monthly Rent

Area	Under $500	$500 -$999	$1,000 -$1,499	$1,500 -$1,999	$2,000 -$2,499	$2,500 -$2,999	$3,000 and up	Median ($)
City	10.1	54.4	25.7	5.9	3.2	0.5	0.3	879
MSA[1]	8.9	50.9	29.0	7.6	2.9	0.4	0.3	922
U.S.	9.4	36.2	30.0	14.0	5.6	2.4	2.4	1,062

Note: Figures are percentages except for Median; Gross rent is the contract rent plus the estimated average monthly cost of utilities (electricity, gas, and water and sewer) and fuels (oil, coal, kerosene, wood, etc.) if these are paid by the renter (or paid for the renter by someone else); (1) Figures cover the Baton Rouge, LA Metropolitan Statistical Area
Source: U.S. Census Bureau, 2015-2019 American Community Survey 5-Year Estimates

HEALTH

Health Risk Factors

Category	MSA[1] (%)	U.S. (%)
Adults aged 18–64 who have any kind of health care coverage	86.7	87.3
Adults who reported being in good or better health	80.3	82.4
Adults who have been told they have high blood cholesterol	36.4	33.0
Adults who have been told they have high blood pressure	36.6	32.3
Adults who are current smokers	21.7	17.1
Adults who currently use E-cigarettes	4.2	4.6
Adults who currently use chewing tobacco, snuff, or snus	5.9	4.0
Adults who are heavy drinkers[2]	7.0	6.3
Adults who are binge drinkers[3]	20.5	17.4
Adults who are overweight (BMI 25.0 - 29.9)	34.5	35.3
Adults who are obese (BMI 30.0 - 99.8)	33.0	31.3
Adults who participated in any physical activities in the past month	67.7	74.4
Adults who always or nearly always wears a seat belt	94.6	94.3

Note: (1) Figures cover the Baton Rouge, LA Metropolitan Statistical Area; (2) Heavy drinkers are classified as adult men having more than 14 drinks per week and adult women having more than 7 drinks per week; (3) Binge drinkers are classified as males having five or more drinks on one occasion or females having four or more drinks on one occasion
Source: Centers for Disease Control and Prevention, Behaviorial Risk Factor Surveillance System, SMART: Selected Metropolitan Area Risk Trends, 2017

Acute and Chronic Health Conditions

Category	MSA[1] (%)	U.S. (%)
Adults who have ever been told they had a heart attack	4.8	4.2
Adults who have ever been told they have angina or coronary heart disease	4.6	3.9
Adults who have ever been told they had a stroke	4.6	3.0
Adults who have ever been told they have asthma	16.1	14.2
Adults who have ever been told they have arthritis	24.2	24.9
Adults who have ever been told they have diabetes[2]	11.2	10.5
Adults who have ever been told they had skin cancer	3.8	6.2
Adults who have ever been told they had any other types of cancer	6.9	7.1
Adults who have ever been told they have COPD	7.1	6.5
Adults who have ever been told they have kidney disease	2.6	3.0
Adults who have ever been told they have a form of depression	19.4	20.5

Note: (1) Figures cover the Baton Rouge, LA Metropolitan Statistical Area; (2) Figures do not include pregnancy-related, borderline, or pre-diabetes
Source: Centers for Disease Control and Prevention, Behaviorial Risk Factor Surveillance System, SMART: Selected Metropolitan Area Risk Trends, 2017

Health Screening and Vaccination Rates

Category	MSA[1] (%)	U.S. (%)
Adults aged 65+ who have had flu shot within the past year	58.3	60.7
Adults aged 65+ who have ever had a pneumonia vaccination	81.4	75.4
Adults who have ever been tested for HIV	42.6	36.1
Adults who have ever had the shingles or zoster vaccine?	23.2	28.9
Adults who have had their blood cholesterol checked within the last five years	86.7	85.9

Note: n/a not available; (1) Figures cover the Baton Rouge, LA Metropolitan Statistical Area.
Source: Centers for Disease Control and Prevention, Behaviorial Risk Factor Surveillance System, SMART: Selected Metropolitan Area Risk Trends, 2017

Disability Status

Category	MSA[1] (%)	U.S. (%)
Adults who reported being deaf	6.1	6.7
Are you blind or have serious difficulty seeing, even when wearing glasses?	7.3	4.5
Are you limited in any way in any of your usual activities due of arthritis?	13.2	12.9
Do you have difficulty doing errands alone?	7.2	6.8
Do you have difficulty dressing or bathing?	4.8	3.6
Do you have serious difficulty concentrating/remembering/making decisions?	11.2	10.7
Do you have serious difficulty walking or climbing stairs?	15.1	13.6

Note: (1) Figures cover the Baton Rouge, LA Metropolitan Statistical Area.
Source: Centers for Disease Control and Prevention, Behaviorial Risk Factor Surveillance System, SMART: Selected Metropolitan Area Risk Trends, 2017

Mortality Rates for the Top 10 Causes of Death in the U.S.

ICD-10[a] Sub-Chapter	ICD-10[a] Code	County[2]	U.S.
Malignant neoplasms	C00-C97	156.4	149.2
Ischaemic heart diseases	I20-I25	100.3	90.5
Other forms of heart disease	I30-I51	96.6	52.2
Chronic lower respiratory diseases	J40-J47	31.0	39.6
Other degenerative diseases of the nervous system	G30-G31	60.1	37.6
Cerebrovascular diseases	I60-I69	48.9	37.2
Other external causes of accidental injury	W00-X59	45.9	36.1
Organic, including symptomatic, mental disorders	F01-F09	22.7	29.4
Hypertensive diseases	I10-I15	3.7	24.1
Diabetes mellitus	E10-E14	5.3	21.5

Age-Adjusted Mortality Rate[1] per 100,000 population

Note: (a) ICD-10 = International Classification of Diseases 10th Revision; (1) Mortality rates are a three-year average covering 2017-2019; (2) Figures cover East Baton Rouge Parish.
Source: Centers for Disease Control and Prevention, National Center for Health Statistics. Underlying Cause of Death 1999-2019 on CDC WONDER Online Database

Mortality Rates for Selected Causes of Death

ICD-10[a] Sub-Chapter	ICD-10[a] Code	County[2]	U.S.
Assault	X85-Y09	23.3	6.0
Diseases of the liver	K70-K76	13.3	14.4
Human immunodeficiency virus (HIV) disease	B20-B24	7.4	1.5
Influenza and pneumonia	J09-J18	14.1	13.8
Intentional self-harm	X60-X84	13.2	14.1
Malnutrition	E40-E46	6.0	2.3
Obesity and other hyperalimentation	E65-E68	Suppressed	2.1
Renal failure	N17-N19	27.9	12.6
Transport accidents	V01-V99	17.4	12.3
Viral hepatitis	B15-B19	1.9	1.2

Note: (a) ICD-10 = International Classification of Diseases 10th Revision; (1) Mortality rates are a three-year average covering 2017-2019; (2) Figures cover East Baton Rouge Parish; Data are suppressed when the data meet the criteria for confidentiality constraints; Mortality rates are flagged as unreliable when the rate would be calculated with a numerator of 20 or less.
Source: Centers for Disease Control and Prevention, National Center for Health Statistics. Underlying Cause of Death 1999-2019 on CDC WONDER Online Database

Health Insurance Coverage

Area	With Health Insurance	With Private Health Insurance	With Public Health Insurance	Without Health Insurance	Population Under Age 19 Without Health Insurance
City	90.3	59.2	41.1	9.7	3.5
MSA[1]	91.7	66.4	35.5	8.3	3.3
U.S.	91.2	67.9	35.1	8.8	5.1

Note: Figures are percentages that cover the civilian noninstitutionalized population; (1) Figures cover the Baton Rouge, LA Metropolitan Statistical Area
Source: U.S. Census Bureau, 2015-2019 American Community Survey 5-Year Estimates

Number of Medical Professionals

Area	MDs[3]	DOs[3,4]	Dentists	Podiatrists	Chiropractors	Optometrists
Parish[1] (number)	1,717	32	334	20	55	61
Parish[1] (rate[2])	388.4	7.2	75.9	4.5	12.5	13.9
U.S. (rate[2])	282.9	22.7	71.2	6.2	28.1	16.9

22033
Note: Data as of 2019 unless noted; (1) Data covers East Baton Rouge Parish; (2) Rate per 100,000 population; (3) Data as of 2018 and includes all active, non-federal physicians; (4) Doctor of Osteopathic Medicine
Source: U.S. Department of Health and Human Services, Health Resources and Services Administration, Bureau of Health Professions, Area Resource File (ARF) 2019-2020

EDUCATION

Public School District Statistics

District Name	Schls	Pupils	Pupil/ Teacher Ratio	Minority Pupils[1] (%)	Free Lunch Eligible[2] (%)	IEP[3] (%)
East Baton Rouge Parish	85	40,668	17.9	88.7	50.5	10.0
University View Academy Inc.	1	3,019	22.7	38.5	52.2	9.9

Note: Table includes school districts with 2,000 or more students; (1) Percentage of students that are not non-Hispanic white; (2) Percentage of students that are eligible for the free lunch program; (3) Percentage of students that have an Individualized Education Program.
Source: U.S. Department of Education, National Center for Education Statistics, Common Core of Data, Local Education Agency (School District) Universe Survey: School Year 2018-2019; U.S. Department of Education, National Center for Education Statistics, Common Core of Data, Public Elementary/Secondary School Universe Survey: School Year 2018-2019

Best High Schools

According to *U.S. News,* Baton Rouge is home to one of the top 500 high schools in the U.S.: **Baton Rouge Magnet High School** (#255). Nearly 18,000 public, magnet and charter schools were ranked based on their performance on state assessments and how well they prepare students for college. *U.S. News & World Report, "Best High Schools 2020"*

Highest Level of Education

Area	Less than H.S.	H.S. Diploma	Some College, No Deg.	Associate Degree	Bachelor's Degree	Master's Degree	Prof. School Degree	Doctorate Degree
City	12.0	27.8	22.5	4.5	19.3	8.8	2.6	2.5
MSA[1]	12.6	32.2	21.4	6.2	18.0	6.6	1.7	1.3
U.S.	12.0	27.0	20.4	8.5	19.8	8.8	2.1	1.4

Note: Figures cover persons age 25 and over; (1) Figures cover the Baton Rouge, LA Metropolitan Statistical Area
Source: U.S. Census Bureau, 2015-2019 American Community Survey 5-Year Estimates

Educational Attainment by Race

Area	High School Graduate or Higher (%) Total	White	Black	Asian	Hisp.[2]	Bachelor's Degree or Higher (%) Total	White	Black	Asian	Hisp.[2]
City	88.0	96.2	82.2	84.1	73.9	33.2	53.4	15.9	54.7	21.7
MSA[1]	87.4	90.5	82.8	86.1	67.5	27.6	31.9	18.5	53.2	16.4
U.S.	88.0	89.9	86.0	87.1	68.7	32.1	33.5	21.6	54.3	16.4

Note: Figures shown cover persons 25 years old and over; (1) Figures cover the Baton Rouge, LA Metropolitan Statistical Area; (2) People of Hispanic origin can be of any race
Source: U.S. Census Bureau, 2015-2019 American Community Survey 5-Year Estimates

School Enrollment by Grade and Control

Area	Preschool (%) Public	Private	Kindergarten (%) Public	Private	Grades 1 - 4 (%) Public	Private	Grades 5 - 8 (%) Public	Private	Grades 9 - 12 (%) Public	Private
City	66.8	33.2	75.3	24.7	80.3	19.7	79.5	20.5	80.8	19.2
MSA[1]	57.1	42.9	76.9	23.1	81.4	18.6	81.7	18.3	81.4	18.6
U.S.	59.1	40.9	87.6	12.4	89.5	10.5	89.4	10.6	90.1	9.9

Note: Figures shown cover persons 3 years old and over; (1) Figures cover the Baton Rouge, LA Metropolitan Statistical Area
Source: U.S. Census Bureau, 2015-2019 American Community Survey 5-Year Estimates

Higher Education

Four-Year Colleges Public	Private Non-profit	Private For-profit	Two-Year Colleges Public	Private Non-profit	Private For-profit	Medical Schools[1]	Law Schools[2]	Voc/ Tech[3]
3	1	1	1	2	5	0	2	9

Note: Figures cover institutions located within the city limits and include main campuses only; (1) includes schools accredited by the Liaison Committee on Medical Education and the American Osteopathic Association's Commission on Osteopathic College Accreditation; (2) includes ABA-accredited schools, schools with provisional ABA accreditation, and state accredited schools; (3) includes all schools with programs that are less than 2 years.
Source: National Center for Education Statistics, Integrated Postsecondary Education System (IPEDS), 2019-20; Wikipedia, List of Medical Schools in the United States, accessed April 2, 2021; Wikipedia, List of Law Schools in the United States, accessed April 2, 2021

According to *U.S. News & World Report,* the Baton Rouge, LA metro area is home to one of the top 200 national universities in the U.S.: **Louisiana State University—Baton Rouge** (#153 tie). The indicators used to capture academic quality fall into a number of categories: assessment by administrators at peer institutions; retention of students; faculty resources; student selectivity; financial resources; alumni giving; high school counselor ratings of colleges; and graduation rate. *U.S. News & World Report, "America's Best Colleges 2021"*

According to *U.S. News & World Report*, the Baton Rouge, LA metro area is home to one of the top 75 business schools in the U.S.: **Louisiana State University—Baton Rouge (Ourso)** (#68 tie). The rankings are based on a weighted average of the following nine measures: quality assessment; peer assessment; recruiter assessment; placement success; mean starting salary and bonus; student selectivity; mean GMAT and GRE scores; mean undergraduate GPA; and acceptance rate. *U.S. News & World Report*, "America's Best Graduate Schools, Business, 2022"

EMPLOYERS

Major Employers

Company Name	Industry
Baton Rouge General Medical Center	General medical & surgical hospitals
CB&I	Engineering, procurement and construction
City of Baton Rouge-E Baton Rouge Parish	City/county government
East Baton Rouge Parish Public Schools	Public elementary & secondary schools
ExxonMobil Chemical-Baton Rouge Refinery	Petroleum refining
Louisiana State University	Public coeducational university
Our Lady of the Lake Regional Medical Ctr	General medical & surgical hospitals
Performance Contractors	Industrial construction and pipe fabrication
State of Louisiana	State government
Turner Industries	Heavy industrial construction and maintenance

Note: Companies shown are located within the Baton Rouge, LA Metropolitan Statistical Area.
Source: Hoovers.com; Wikipedia

PUBLIC SAFETY

Crime Rate

Area	All Crimes	Murder	Rape[3]	Robbery	Aggrav. Assault	Burglary	Larceny -Theft	Motor Vehicle Theft
City	6,226.7	31.7	23.6	292.3	588.7	1,023.3	3,904.9	362.1
Suburbs[1]	3,048.0	7.9	29.9	42.8	339.8	380.5	2,107.7	139.3
Metro[2]	3,871.0	14.1	28.3	107.4	404.3	547.0	2,573.0	197.0
U.S.	2,489.3	5.0	42.6	81.6	250.2	340.5	1,549.5	219.9

Note: Figures are crimes per 100,000 population; (1) All areas within the metro area that are located outside the city limits; (2) Figures cover the Baton Rouge, LA Metropolitan Statistical Area; (3) All figures shown were reported using the revised Uniform Crime Reporting (UCR) definition of rape.
Source: FBI Uniform Crime Reports, 2019

Hate Crimes

Area	Number of Quarters Reported	Race/Ethnicity/Ancestry	Religion	Sexual Orientation	Disability	Gender	Gender Identity
City	4	0	0	1	0	0	0
U.S.	4	3,963	1,521	1,195	157	69	198

Source: Federal Bureau of Investigation, Hate Crime Statistics 2019

Identity Theft Consumer Reports

Area	Reports	Reports per 100,000 Population	Rank[2]
MSA[1]	4,506	527	48
U.S.	1,387,615	423	-

Note: (1) Figures cover the Baton Rouge, LA Metropolitan Statistical Area; (2) Rank ranges from 1 to 391 where 1 indicates greatest number of identity theft reports per 100,000 population
Source: Federal Trade Commission, Consumer Sentinel Network Data Book 2020

Fraud and Other Consumer Reports

Area	Reports	Reports per 100,000 Population	Rank[2]
MSA[1]	7,097	830	86
U.S.	3,385,133	1,031	-

Note: (1) Figures cover the Baton Rouge, LA Metropolitan Statistical Area; (2) Rank ranges from 1 to 391 where 1 indicates greatest number of fraud and other consumer reports per 100,000 population
Source: Federal Trade Commission, Consumer Sentinel Network Data Book 2020

POLITICS

2020 Presidential Election Results

Area	Biden	Trump	Jorgensen	Hawkins	Other
East Baton Rouge Parish	55.5	42.5	1.2	0.0	0.8
U.S.	51.3	46.8	1.2	0.3	0.5

Note: Results are percentages and may not add to 100% due to rounding
Source: Dave Leip's Atlas of U.S. Presidential Elections

SPORTS

Professional Sports Teams

Team Name	League	Year Established
No teams are located in the metro area		

Source: Wikipedia, Major Professional Sports Teams of the United States and Canada, April 6, 2021

CLIMATE

Average and Extreme Temperatures

Temperature	Jan	Feb	Mar	Apr	May	Jun	Jul	Aug	Sep	Oct	Nov	Dec	Yr.
Extreme High (°F)	82	85	91	92	98	103	101	102	99	94	87	85	103
Average High (°F)	61	65	71	79	85	90	91	91	87	80	70	64	78
Average Temp. (°F)	51	54	61	68	75	81	82	82	78	69	59	53	68
Average Low (°F)	41	44	50	57	64	70	73	72	68	57	48	43	57
Extreme Low (°F)	9	13	20	32	44	53	58	59	43	30	21	8	8

Note: Figures cover the years 1948-1995
Source: National Climatic Data Center, International Station Meteorological Climate Summary, 9/96

Average Precipitation/Snowfall/Humidity

Precip./Humidity	Jan	Feb	Mar	Apr	May	Jun	Jul	Aug	Sep	Oct	Nov	Dec	Yr.
Avg. Precip. (in.)	4.9	5.1	4.8	5.5	5.0	4.4	6.6	5.4	4.1	3.1	4.2	5.3	58.5
Avg. Snowfall (in.)	Tr	Tr	Tr	0	0	0	0	0	0	0	Tr	Tr	Tr
Avg. Rel. Hum. 6am (%)	85	85	86	89	91	91	92	93	91	89	88	86	89
Avg. Rel. Hum. 3pm (%)	59	55	52	52	54	57	62	61	59	51	53	57	56

Note: Figures cover the years 1948-1995; Tr = Trace amounts (<0.05 in. of rain; <0.5 in. of snow)
Source: National Climatic Data Center, International Station Meteorological Climate Summary, 9/96

Weather Conditions

Temperature			Daytime Sky			Precipitation		
10°F & below	32°F & below	90°F & above	Clear	Partly cloudy	Cloudy	0.01 inch or more precip.	0.1 inch or more snow/ice	Thunder-storms
< 1	21	86	99	150	116	113	< 1	73

Note: Figures are average number of days per year and cover the years 1948-1995
Source: National Climatic Data Center, International Station Meteorological Climate Summary, 9/96

HAZARDOUS WASTE

Superfund Sites

The Baton Rouge, LA metro area is home to three sites on the EPA's Superfund National Priorities List: **Combustion, Inc.** (final); **Devil's Swamp Lake** (proposed); **Petro-Processors of Louisiana, Inc.** (final). There are a total of 1,375 Superfund sites with a status of proposed or final on the list in the U.S. *U.S. Environmental Protection Agency, National Priorities List, April 7, 2021*

AIR QUALITY

Air Quality Trends: Ozone

	1990	1995	2000	2005	2010	2015	2016	2017	2018	2019
MSA[1]	0.105	0.091	0.090	0.090	0.075	0.069	0.066	0.069	0.069	0.066
U.S.	0.088	0.089	0.082	0.080	0.073	0.068	0.069	0.068	0.069	0.065

Note: (1) Data covers the Baton Rouge, LA Metropolitan Statistical Area. The values shown are the composite ozone concentration averages among trend sites based on the highest fourth daily maximum 8-hour concentration in parts per million. These trends are based on sites having an adequate record of monitoring data during the trend period. Data from exceptional events are included.
Source: U.S. Environmental Protection Agency, Air Quality Monitoring Information, "Air Quality Trends by City, 1990-2019"

Air Quality Index

Area	Percent of Days when Air Quality was...[2]					AQI Statistics[2]	
	Good	Moderate	Unhealthy for Sensitive Groups	Unhealthy	Very Unhealthy	Maximum	Median
MSA[1]	61.4	36.2	2.5	0.0	0.0	119	45

Note: (1) Data covers the Baton Rouge, LA Metropolitan Statistical Area; (2) Based on 365 days with AQI data in 2019. Air Quality Index (AQI) is an index for reporting daily air quality. EPA calculates the AQI for five major air pollutants regulated by the Clean Air Act: ground-level ozone, particle pollution (aka particulate matter), carbon monoxide, sulfur dioxide, and nitrogen dioxide. The AQI runs from 0 to 500. The higher the AQI value, the greater the level of air pollution and the greater the health concern. There are six AQI categories: "Good" AQI is between 0 and 50. Air quality is considered satisfactory; "Moderate" AQI is between 51 and 100. Air quality is acceptable; "Unhealthy for Sensitive Groups" When AQI values are between 101 and 150, members of sensitive groups may experience health effects; "Unhealthy" When AQI values are between 151 and 200 everyone may begin to experience health effects; "Very Unhealthy" AQI values between 201 and 300 trigger a health alert; "Hazardous" AQI values over 300 trigger warnings of emergency conditions (not shown).
Source: U.S. Environmental Protection Agency, Air Quality Index Report, 2019

Air Quality Index Pollutants

Area	Percent of Days when AQI Pollutant was...[2]					
	Carbon Monoxide	Nitrogen Dioxide	Ozone	Sulfur Dioxide	Particulate Matter 2.5	Particulate Matter 10
MSA[1]	0.0	1.6	47.9	0.3	50.1	0.0

Note: (1) Data covers the Baton Rouge, LA Metropolitan Statistical Area; (2) Based on 365 days with AQI data in 2019. The Air Quality Index (AQI) is an index for reporting daily air quality. EPA calculates the AQI for five major air pollutants regulated by the Clean Air Act: ground-level ozone, particle pollution (also known as particulate matter), carbon monoxide, sulfur dioxide, and nitrogen dioxide. The AQI runs from 0 to 500. The higher the AQI value, the greater the level of air pollution and the greater the health concern.
Source: U.S. Environmental Protection Agency, Air Quality Index Report, 2019

Maximum Air Pollutant Concentrations: Particulate Matter, Ozone, CO and Lead

	Particulate Matter 10 (ug/m^3)	Particulate Matter 2.5 Wtd AM (ug/m^3)	Particulate Matter 2.5 24-Hr (ug/m^3)	Ozone (ppm)	Carbon Monoxide (ppm)	Lead (ug/m^3)
MSA[1] Level	51	9.2	23	0.070	1	0
NAAQS[2]	150	15	35	0.075	9	0.15
Met NAAQS[2]	Yes	Yes	Yes	Yes	Yes	Yes

Note: (1) Data covers the Baton Rouge, LA Metropolitan Statistical Area; Data from exceptional events are included; (2) National Ambient Air Quality Standards; ppm = parts per million; ug/m^3 = micrograms per cubic meter; n/a not available.
Concentrations: Particulate Matter 10 (coarse particulate)—highest second maximum 24-hour concentration; Particulate Matter 2.5 Wtd AM (fine particulate)—highest weighted annual mean concentration; Particulate Matter 2.5 24-Hour (fine particulate)—highest 98th percentile 24-hour concentration; Ozone—highest fourth daily maximum 8-hour concentration; Carbon Monoxide—highest second maximum non-overlapping 8-hour concentration; Lead—maximum running 3-month average
Source: U.S. Environmental Protection Agency, Air Quality Monitoring Information, "Air Quality Statistics by City, 2019"

Maximum Air Pollutant Concentrations: Nitrogen Dioxide and Sulfur Dioxide

	Nitrogen Dioxide AM (ppb)	Nitrogen Dioxide 1-Hr (ppb)	Sulfur Dioxide AM (ppb)	Sulfur Dioxide 1-Hr (ppb)	Sulfur Dioxide 24-Hr (ppb)
MSA[1] Level	10	45	n/a	16	n/a
NAAQS[2]	53	100	30	75	140
Met NAAQS[2]	Yes	Yes	n/a	Yes	n/a

Note: (1) Data covers the Baton Rouge, LA Metropolitan Statistical Area; Data from exceptional events are included; (2) National Ambient Air Quality Standards; ppm = parts per million; ug/m^3 = micrograms per cubic meter; n/a not available.
Concentrations: Nitrogen Dioxide AM—highest arithmetic mean concentration; Nitrogen Dioxide 1-Hr—highest 98th percentile 1-hour daily maximum concentration; Sulfur Dioxide AM—highest annual mean concentration; Sulfur Dioxide 1-Hr—highest 99th percentile 1-hour daily maximum concentration; Sulfur Dioxide 24-Hr—highest second maximum 24-hour concentration
Source: U.S. Environmental Protection Agency, Air Quality Monitoring Information, "Air Quality Statistics by City, 2019"

Cape Coral, Florida

Background

Tucked along Florida's Gulf Coast 71 miles south of Sarasota, Cape Coral is a mid-twentieth century community grown from a development launched in 1957. Today, at 115 square miles, it is Florida's third-largest city by land mass and the most populous city between Tampa and Miami. To the east across the Caloosahatchee River lies Fort Myers, and to the west across Pine Island and Pine Island sound lie the fabled barrier islands of Captiva and Sanibel.

Baltimore brothers Leonard and Jack Rosen purchased the former Redfish Point for $678,000 in 1957 and renamed the property Cape Coral. By June of the following year "the Cape," as it is known, was receiving its first residents. The city incorporated in 1970 when its population reached 11,470.

Despite the city's relative youth, this self-named "Waterfront Wonderland" has developed an interest in its roots. It fosters a Cape Coral Historical Museum that is housed in the original snack bar from the local country club, and one of its oldest historical documents is the Cape's 1961 phone book.

Four hundred precious miles of salt water and fresh water canals slice through the city, providing water access to abundant recreational boaters and numerous opportunities for waterfront living.

Following the economic downturn in 2008, Cape Coral has rebounded, named a "most improved" housing market in a National Association of Builders report. The Army Reserve purchased a 15-acre Cape Coral site for use as an Army Reserve Training Center for local reservists.

Industry-wise, Cape Coral has Foreign Trade Zones in two of its three industrial parks, the 92.5 acre North Cape Industrial Park—home to light manufacturers, service industry and warehouses—and the Mid Cape Commerce Park which, at 143.37 acres, is comprised of service industries and warehouses.

A VA Clinic was recently built by the U.S. Dept. of Veteran's Affairs at the Hancock Creek Commerce Park and Indian Oaks Trade Centre. It provides a full range of services ranging from mental health and diagnostic radiology to urology and a full complement of imaging services such as CT scans and nuclear medicine. It is the centerpiece of a Veterans Investment Zone initiative designed to draw office, medical parks, assisted living facilities and the like.

Today the U.S. Bureau of Labor Statistics tracks Cape Coral's success in conjunction with that of nearby Fort Myers, and the region boasts trade, transportation and utilities as its largest economic sector. Essentially, this is a retirement and tourism destination.

> After drummer Willie Miller was tested positive for COVID-19, he raised awareness and helped his community through benefit concerts supporting struggling local food banks.

Significant recreational opportunities are available in the area, and include the Four Mile Cove Ecological Preserve with its nature trail, picnic area, and warm weather kayak rentals. The Cape Coral Yacht Club, located where the city first began, includes a fishing pier, beach, and community pool. The 18-hole public Coral Oaks Golf Course (replete with pro shop and pub), the Northwest Softball Complex, the William Bill Austen Youth Center Eagle Skate Park, the Strausser BMX Sports Complex, and even the Pelican Sport Soccer Complex show the city's diverse recreational opportunities.

To the east of Cape Coral—on the other side of Fort Myers—is both the Florida Gulf Coast University and Southwest Florida International Airport.

Cape Coral's climate borders on perfect, with an average 335 days per year of sunshine (albeit hot and humid ones in summer time). Annual rainfall is 53.37 inches, with the most rain coming in summer. The city dries out from October into May.

Rankings

General Rankings

- The Cape Coral metro area was identified as one of America's fastest-growing areas in terms of population and economy by *Forbes*. The area ranked #9 out of 25. The 100 most populous metro areas in the U.S. were evaluated on the following criteria: estimated population growth; employment; economic output; wages; home values. *Forbes, "America's Fastest-Growing Cities 2018," February 28, 2018*

Business/Finance Rankings

- The Brookings Institution ranked the nation's largest cities based on income inequality. Cape Coral was ranked #93 (#1 = greatest inequality). Criteria: the "95/20 ratio," a figure representing the income at which a household earns more than 95 percent of all other households, divided by the income at which a household earns more than only 20 percent of all other households. *Brookings Institution, "Household Income Inequality, Largest Cities of 97 Large U.S. Metro Areas, 2014-2016," February 5, 2018*

- The Brookings Institution ranked the 100 largest metro areas in the U.S. based on income inequality. Cape Coral was ranked #73 (#1 = greatest inequality). Criteria: the "95/20 ratio," a figure representing the income at which a household earns more than 95 percent of all other households, divided by the income at which a household earns more than only 20 percent of all other households. *Brookings Institution, "Household Income Inequality, 100 Largest U.S. Metro Areas, 2014-2016," February 5, 2018*

- The Cape Coral metro area appeared on the Milken Institute "2021 Best Performing Cities" list. Rank: #23 out of 200 large metro areas (population over 250,000). Criteria: job growth; wage and salary growth; high-tech output growth; housing affordability; household broadband access. *Milken Institute, "Best-Performing Cities 2021," February 16, 2021*

- *Forbes* ranked the 200 most populous metro areas to determine the nation's "Best Places for Business and Careers." The Cape Coral metro area was ranked #63. Criteria: costs (business and living); job growth (past and projected); income growth; quality of life; educational attainment (college and high school); projected economic growth; cultural and leisure opportunities; workplace tolerance laws; net migration patterns. *Forbes, "The Best Places for Business and Careers 2019: Seattle Still On Top," October 30, 2019*

Education Rankings

- Personal finance website *WalletHub* analyzed the 150 largest U.S. metropolitan statistical areas to determine where the most educated Americans are putting their degrees to work. Criteria: education levels; percentage of workers with degrees; education quality and attainment gap; public school quality rankings; quality and enrollment of each metro area's universities. Cape Coral was ranked #107 (#1 = most educated city). *www.WalletHub.com, "Most and Least Educated Cities in America," July 20, 2020*

Health/Fitness Rankings

- Cape Coral was identified as a "2021 Spring Allergy Capital." The area ranked #33 out of 100. Three groups of factors were used to identify the most challenging cities for people with allergies during the spring season: annual spring pollen levels; over the counter medicine use; number of board-certified allergy specialists. *Asthma and Allergy Foundation of America, "Spring Allergy Capitals 2021," February 23, 2021*

- Cape Coral was identified as a "2021 Fall Allergy Capital." The area ranked #35 out of 100. Three groups of factors were used to identify the most challenging cities for people with allergies during the fall season: annual fall pollen levels; over the counter medicine use; number of board-certified allergy specialists. *Asthma and Allergy Foundation of America, "Fall Allergy Capitals 2021," February 23, 2021*

- Cape Coral was identified as a "2019 Asthma Capital." The area ranked #100 out of the nation's 100 largest metropolitan areas. Criteria: estimated asthma prevalence; crude death rate from asthma; and ER visits due to asthma. Risk factors analyzed but not factored in the rankings: annual pollen score; annual air quality; public smoking laws; number of board-certified asthma specialists; rescue medication use; controller medication use; uninsured rate; poverty rate. *Asthma and Allergy Foundation of America, "Asthma Capitals 2019: The Most Challenging Places to Live With Asthma," May 7, 2019*

Real Estate Rankings

- *WalletHub* compared the most populated U.S. cities to determine which had the best markets for real estate agents. Cape Coral ranked #27 where demand was high and pay was the best. Criteria: sales per agent; annual median wage for real-estate agents; monthly average starting salary for real estate agents; real estate job density and competition; unemployment rate; home turnover rate; housing-market health index; and other relevant metrics. *www.WalletHub.com, "2019's Best Places to Be a Real Estate Agent," April 24, 2019*

- Cape Coral was ranked #189 out of 268 metro areas in terms of housing affordability in 2020 by the National Association of Home Builders (#1 = most affordable). Criteria: the share of homes sold in that area affordable to a family earning the local median income, based on standard mortgage underwriting criteria. *National Association of Home Builders®, NAHB-Wells Fargo Housing Opportunity Index, 4th Quarter 2020*

Safety Rankings

- To identify the safest cities in America, 24/7 Wall Street focused on violent crime categories—murder, non-negligent manslaughter, rape, robbery, and aggravated assault—and property crime as reported in the FBI's 2018 annual Uniform Crime Report. Criteria also included median income from American Community Survey and unemployment figures from Bureau of Labor Statistics. For cities with populations over 100,000, Cape Coral was ranked #28. *247wallst.com, "America's Safest Cities" January 15, 2020*

- Allstate ranked the 200 largest cities in America in terms of driver safety. Cape Coral ranked #10. Criteria: internal property damage claims over a two-year period from January 2016 to December 2017. The report helps increase the importance of safety and awareness behind the wheel. *Allstate, "Allstate America's Best Drivers Report, 2019" June 24, 2019*

- The National Insurance Crime Bureau ranked 384 metro areas in the U.S. in terms of per capita rates of vehicle theft. The Cape Coral metro area ranked #275 (#1 = highest rate). Criteria: number of vehicle theft offenses per 100,000 inhabitants in 2019. *National Insurance Crime Bureau, "Hot Spots 2019," July 21, 2020*

Seniors/Retirement Rankings

- From its Best Cities for Successful Aging indexes, the Milken Institute generated rankings for metropolitan areas, weighing data in nine categories—health care, wellness, living arrangements, transportation and convenience, financial characteristics, education, employment, community engagement, and overall livability. The Cape Coral metro area was ranked #93 overall in the large metro area category. *Milken Institute, "Best Cities for Successful Aging, 2017" March 14, 2017*

Women/Minorities Rankings

- Personal finance website *WalletHub* compared more than 180 U.S. cities across two key dimensions, "Hispanic Business-Friendliness" and "Hispanic Purchasing Power," to arrive at the most favorable conditions for Hispanic entrepreneurs. Cape Coral was ranked #53 out of 182. Criteria includes: share of Hispanic-Owned Businesses; Hispanic entrepreneurship rate to median annual income of Hispanics; Small Business-Friendliness score; cost of living; and number of Hispanics with at least a bachelor's degree. *WalletHub.com, "2019's Best Cities for Hispanic Entrepreneurs," May 1, 2019*

Miscellaneous Rankings

- Cape Coral was selected as a 2020 Digital Cities Survey winner. The city ranked #2 in the mid-sized city (125,000 to 249,999 population) category. The survey examined and assessed how city governments are utilizing technology to improve transparency, enhance cybersecurity, and respond to the pandemic. Survey questions focused on ten initiatives: cybersecurity, citizen experience, disaster recovery, business intelligence, IT personnel, data governance, collaboration, infrastructure modernization, cloud computing, and mobile applications. *Center for Digital Government, "2020 Digital Cities Survey," November 10, 2020*

Business Environment

DEMOGRAPHICS

Population Growth

Area	1990 Census	2000 Census	2010 Census	2019* Estimate	Population Growth (%) 1990-2019	Population Growth (%) 2010-2019
City	75,507	102,286	154,305	183,942	143.6	19.2
MSA[1]	335,113	440,888	618,754	737,468	120.1	19.2
U.S.	248,709,873	281,421,906	308,745,538	324,697,795	30.6	5.2

Note: (1) Figures cover the Cape Coral-Fort Myers, FL Metropolitan Statistical Area; (*) 2015-2019 5-year estimated population
Source: U.S. Census Bureau, 1990 Census, Census 2000, Census 2010, 2015-2019 American Community Survey 5-Year Estimates

Household Size

Area	One	Two	Three	Four	Five	Six	Seven or More	Average Household Size
City	23.8	43.1	14.2	12.4	4.4	1.6	0.6	2.80
MSA[1]	28.0	44.7	11.6	9.0	4.1	1.6	0.9	2.60
U.S.	27.9	33.9	15.6	12.9	6.0	2.3	1.4	2.60

Note: (1) Figures cover the Cape Coral-Fort Myers, FL Metropolitan Statistical Area
Source: U.S. Census Bureau, 2015-2019 American Community Survey 5-Year Estimates

Race

Area	White Alone[2] (%)	Black Alone[2] (%)	Asian Alone[2] (%)	AIAN[3] Alone[2] (%)	NHOPI[4] Alone[2] (%)	Other Race Alone[2] (%)	Two or More Races (%)
City	89.5	5.2	1.8	0.2	0.0	1.8	1.6
MSA[1]	84.4	8.6	1.6	0.2	0.1	3.4	1.8
U.S.	72.5	12.7	5.5	0.8	0.2	4.9	3.3

Note: (1) Figures cover the Cape Coral-Fort Myers, FL Metropolitan Statistical Area; (2) Alone is defined as not being in combination with one or more other races; (3) American Indian and Alaska Native; (4) Native Hawaiian and Other Pacific Islander
Source: U.S. Census Bureau, 2015-2019 American Community Survey 5-Year Estimates

Hispanic or Latino Origin

Area	Total (%)	Mexican (%)	Puerto Rican (%)	Cuban (%)	Other (%)
City	20.9	2.0	5.0	7.8	6.1
MSA[1]	21.4	6.0	4.3	4.9	6.2
U.S.	18.0	11.2	1.7	0.7	4.3

Note: Persons of Hispanic or Latino origin can be of any race; (1) Figures cover the Cape Coral-Fort Myers, FL Metropolitan Statistical Area
Source: U.S. Census Bureau, 2015-2019 American Community Survey 5-Year Estimates

Ancestry

Area	German	Irish	English	American	Italian	Polish	French[2]	Scottish	Dutch
City	14.1	11.5	7.3	15.3	10.4	3.5	2.2	1.6	1.2
MSA[1]	13.5	11.0	8.1	14.3	7.7	3.3	2.3	1.8	1.3
U.S.	13.3	9.7	7.2	6.2	5.1	2.8	2.3	1.7	1.2

Note: Figures are the percentage of the total population reporting a particular ancestry. The nine most commonly reported ancestries in the U.S. are shown. Figures include multiple ancestries (e.g. if a person reported being Irish and Italian, they were included in both columns); (1) Figures cover the Cape Coral-Fort Myers, FL Metropolitan Statistical Area; (2) Excludes Basque
Source: U.S. Census Bureau, 2015-2019 American Community Survey 5-Year Estimates

Foreign-born Population

Area	Any Foreign Country	Asia	Mexico	Europe	Caribbean	Central America[2]	South America	Africa	Canada
City	15.2	1.4	0.7	2.1	6.8	0.7	2.8	0.1	0.6
MSA[1]	16.7	1.3	2.5	2.0	5.9	1.8	2.0	0.1	1.1
U.S.	13.6	4.2	3.5	1.5	1.3	1.1	1.0	0.7	0.2

Note: (1) Figures cover the Cape Coral-Fort Myers, FL Metropolitan Statistical Area; (2) Excludes Mexico.
Source: U.S. Census Bureau, 2015-2019 American Community Survey 5-Year Estimates

Marital Status

Area	Never Married	Now Married[2]	Separated	Widowed	Divorced
City	25.5	52.0	1.5	7.3	13.7
MSA[1]	26.2	50.8	1.6	8.2	13.2
U.S.	33.4	48.1	1.9	5.8	10.9

Note: Figures are percentages and cover the population 15 years of age and older; (1) Figures cover the Cape Coral-Fort Myers, FL Metropolitan Statistical Area; (2) Excludes separated
Source: U.S. Census Bureau, 2015-2019 American Community Survey 5-Year Estimates

Disability by Age

Area	All Ages	Under 18 Years Old	18 to 64 Years Old	65 Years and Over
City	12.9	3.4	9.3	29.9
MSA[1]	13.9	3.8	9.9	28.2
U.S.	12.6	4.2	10.3	34.5

Note: Figures show percent of the civilian noninstitutionalized population that reported having a disability. Disability status is determined from six types of difficulty: vision, hearing, cognitive, ambulatory, self-care, and independent living. For children under 5 years old, hearing and vision difficulty are used to determine disability status. For children between the ages of 5 and 14, disability status is determined from hearing, vision, cognitive, ambulatory, and self-care difficulties. For people aged 15 years and older, they are considered to have a disability if they have difficulty with any one of the six difficulty types; Note: (1) Figures cover the Cape Coral-Fort Myers, FL Metropolitan Statistical Area
Source: U.S. Census Bureau, 2015-2019 American Community Survey 5-Year Estimates

Age

Area	Under Age 5	Age 5–19	Age 20–34	Age 35–44	Age 45–54	Age 55–64	Age 65–74	Age 75–84	Age 85+	Median Age
City	4.4	15.9	15.7	11.4	14.2	15.7	13.2	6.7	2.8	46.7
MSA[1]	4.7	15.2	15.8	10.3	11.9	14.1	15.5	9.3	3.3	48.5
U.S.	6.1	19.1	20.7	12.6	13.0	12.9	9.1	4.6	1.9	38.1

Note: (1) Figures cover the Cape Coral-Fort Myers, FL Metropolitan Statistical Area
Source: U.S. Census Bureau, 2015-2019 American Community Survey 5-Year Estimates

Gender

Area	Males	Females	Males per 100 Females
City	91,158	92,784	98.2
MSA[1]	361,232	376,236	96.0
U.S.	159,886,919	164,810,876	97.0

Note: (1) Figures cover the Cape Coral-Fort Myers, FL Metropolitan Statistical Area
Source: U.S. Census Bureau, 2015-2019 American Community Survey 5-Year Estimates

Religious Groups by Family

Area	Catholic	Baptist	Non-Den.	Methodist[2]	Lutheran	LDS[3]	Pentecostal	Presbyterian[4]	Muslim[5]	Judaism
MSA[1]	16.2	5.0	3.0	2.5	1.2	0.5	4.4	1.4	0.9	0.2
U.S.	19.1	9.3	4.0	4.0	2.3	2.0	1.9	1.6	0.8	0.7

Note: Figures are the number of adherents as a percentage of the total population; (1) Figures cover the Cape Coral-Fort Myers, FL Metropolitan Statistical Area; (2) Methodist/Pietist; (3) Latter Day Saints; (4) Reformed; (5) Figures are estimates
Source: Association of Statisticians of American Religious Bodies, 2010 U.S. Religion Census: Religious Congregations & Membership Study

Religious Groups by Tradition

Area	Catholic	Evangelical Protestant	Mainline Protestant	Other Tradition	Black Protestant	Orthodox
MSA[1]	16.2	14.3	4.6	2.0	0.3	0.2
U.S.	19.1	16.2	7.3	4.3	1.6	0.3

Note: Figures are the number of adherents as a percentage of the total population; (1) Figures cover the Cape Coral-Fort Myers, FL Metropolitan Statistical Area
Source: Association of Statisticians of American Religious Bodies, 2010 U.S. Religion Census: Religious Congregations & Membership Study

ECONOMY

Gross Metropolitan Product

Area	2017	2018	2019	2020	Rank[2]
MSA[1]	28.3	30.0	31.8	33.4	93

Note: Figures are in billions of dollars; (1) Figures cover the Cape Coral-Fort Myers, FL Metropolitan Statistical Area; (2) Rank is based on 2018 data and ranges from 1 to 381
Source: U.S. Conference of Mayors, U.S. Metro Economies: GMP & Employment 2018-2020, September 2019

Economic Growth

Area	2015-17 (%)	2018 (%)	2019 (%)	2020 (%)	Rank[2]
MSA[1]	2.7	3.7	3.7	3.0	83
U.S.	1.9	2.9	2.3	2.1	—

Note: Figures are real gross metropolitan product (GMP) growth rates and represent average annual percent change; (1) Figures cover the Cape Coral-Fort Myers, FL Metropolitan Statistical Area; (2) Rank is based on 2017 2-year average annual percent change and ranges from 1 to 381
Source: U.S. Conference of Mayors, U.S. Metro Economies: GMP & Employment 2018-2020, September 2019

Metropolitan Area Exports

Area	2014	2015	2016	2017	2018	2019	Rank[2]
MSA[1]	496.6	487.3	540.3	592.3	668.0	694.9	190

Note: Figures are in millions of dollars; (1) Figures cover the Cape Coral-Fort Myers, FL Metropolitan Statistical Area; (2) Rank is based on 2019 data and ranges from 1 to 386
Source: U.S. Department of Commerce, International Trade Administration, Office of Trade and Economic Analysis, Industry and Analysis, Exports by Metropolitan Area, data extracted March 24, 2021

Building Permits

Area	Single-Family 2018	Single-Family 2019	Pct. Chg.	Multi-Family 2018	Multi-Family 2019	Pct. Chg.	Total 2018	Total 2019	Pct. Chg.
City	2,245	1,878	-16.3	356	810	127.5	2,601	2,688	3.3
MSA[1]	5,803	5,633	-2.9	3,918	3,472	-11.4	9,721	9,105	-6.3
U.S.	855,300	862,100	0.7	473,500	523,900	10.6	1,328,800	1,386,000	4.3

Note: (1) Figures cover the Cape Coral-Fort Myers, FL Metropolitan Statistical Area; Figures represent new, privately-owned housing units authorized (unadjusted data); All permit data are based on estimates with imputation
Source: U.S. Census Bureau, Manufacturing, Mining, and Construction Statistics, Building Permits, 2018, 2019

Bankruptcy Filings

Area	Business Filings 2019	Business Filings 2020	% Chg.	Nonbusiness Filings 2019	Nonbusiness Filings 2020	% Chg.
Lee County	57	79	38.6	1,254	1,112	-11.3
U.S.	22,780	21,655	-4.9	752,160	522,808	-30.5

Note: Business filings include Chapter 7, Chapter 9, Chapter 11, Chapter 12, Chapter 13, Chapter 15, and Section 304; Nonbusiness filings include Chapter 7, Chapter 11, and Chapter 13
Source: Administrative Office of the U.S. Courts, Business and Nonbusiness Bankruptcy, County Cases Commenced by Chapter of the Bankruptcy Code, During the 12-Month Period Ending December 31, 2019 and Business and Nonbusiness Bankruptcy, County Cases Commenced by Chapter of the Bankruptcy Code, During the 12-Month Period Ending December 31, 2020

Housing Vacancy Rates

Area	Gross Vacancy Rate[2] (%) 2018	2019	2020	Year-Round Vacancy Rate[3] (%) 2018	2019	2020	Rental Vacancy Rate[4] (%) 2018	2019	2020	Homeowner Vacancy Rate[5] (%) 2018	2019	2020
MSA[1]	41.5	40.0	35.1	16.6	17.9	15.8	5.8	8.5	15.5	3.0	2.3	1.9
U.S.	12.3	12.0	10.6	9.7	9.5	8.2	6.9	6.7	6.3	1.5	1.4	1.0

Note: (1) Figures cover the Cape Coral-Fort Myers, FL Metropolitan Statistical Area; (2) The percentage of the total housing inventory that is vacant; (3) The percentage of the housing inventory (excluding seasonal units) that is year-round vacant; (4) The percentage of rental inventory that is vacant for rent; (5) The percentage of homeowner inventory that is vacant for sale
Source: U.S. Census Bureau, Housing Vacancies and Homeownership Annual Statistics: 2018, 2019, 2020

INCOME

Income

Area	Per Capita ($)	Median Household ($)	Average Household ($)
City	29,970	61,599	76,925
MSA[1]	33,543	57,832	82,544
U.S.	34,103	62,843	88,607

Note: (1) Figures cover the Cape Coral-Fort Myers, FL Metropolitan Statistical Area
Source: U.S. Census Bureau, 2015-2019 American Community Survey 5-Year Estimates

Household Income Distribution

Area	Under $15,000	$15,000 -$24,999	$25,000 -$34,999	$35,000 -$49,999	$50,000 -$74,999	$75,000 -$99,999	$100,000 -$149,999	$150,000 and up
City	8.7	7.8	9.1	13.7	20.5	15.8	15.3	9.1
MSA[1]	9.4	9.1	10.3	13.9	19.6	13.2	13.3	11.3
U.S.	10.3	8.9	8.9	12.3	17.2	12.7	15.1	14.5

Note: (1) Figures cover the Cape Coral-Fort Myers, FL Metropolitan Statistical Area
Source: U.S. Census Bureau, 2015-2019 American Community Survey 5-Year Estimates

Poverty Rate

Area	All Ages	Under 18 Years Old	18 to 64 Years Old	65 Years and Over
City	10.4	13.1	10.3	8.6
MSA[1]	13.1	22.1	12.8	7.9
U.S.	13.4	18.5	12.6	9.3

Note: Figures are percentage of people whose income during the past 12 months was below the poverty level;
(1) Figures cover the Cape Coral-Fort Myers, FL Metropolitan Statistical Area
Source: U.S. Census Bureau, 2015-2019 American Community Survey 5-Year Estimates

CITY FINANCES

City Government Finances

Component	2017 ($000)	2017 ($ per capita)
Total Revenues	369,796	2,110
Total Expenditures	375,700	2,144
Debt Outstanding	820,362	4,682
Cash and Securities[1]	739,296	4,219

Note: (1) Cash and security holdings of a government at the close of its fiscal year, including those of its dependent agencies, utilities, and liquor stores.
Source: U.S. Census Bureau, State & Local Government Finances 2017

City Government Revenue by Source

Source	2017 ($000)	2017 ($ per capita)	2017 (%)
General Revenue			
From Federal Government	3,542	20	1.0
From State Government	45,939	262	12.4
From Local Governments	653	4	0.2
Taxes			
Property	76,333	436	20.6
Sales and Gross Receipts	22,659	129	6.1
Personal Income	0	0	0.0
Corporate Income	0	0	0.0
Motor Vehicle License	0	0	0.0
Other Taxes	13,596	78	3.7
Current Charges	53,835	307	14.6
Liquor Store	0	0	0.0
Utility	28,803	164	7.8
Employee Retirement	45,311	259	12.3

Source: U.S. Census Bureau, State & Local Government Finances 2017

City Government Expenditures by Function

Function	2017 ($000)	2017 ($ per capita)	2017 (%)
General Direct Expenditures			
Air Transportation	0	0	0.0
Corrections	0	0	0.0
Education	22,982	131	6.1
Employment Security Administration	0	0	0.0
Financial Administration	25,118	143	6.7
Fire Protection	27,105	154	7.2
General Public Buildings	0	0	0.0
Governmental Administration, Other	3,674	21	1.0
Health	0	0	0.0
Highways	24,788	141	6.6
Hospitals	0	0	0.0
Housing and Community Development	1,673	9	0.4
Interest on General Debt	9,723	55	2.6
Judicial and Legal	1,199	6	0.3
Libraries	0	0	0.0
Parking	18	<1	<0.1
Parks and Recreation	20,389	116	5.4
Police Protection	34,991	199	9.3
Public Welfare	0	0	0.0
Sewerage	25,053	143	6.7
Solid Waste Management	0	0	0.0
Veterans' Services	0	0	0.0
Liquor Store	0	0	0.0
Utility	66,473	379	17.7
Employee Retirement	22,684	129	6.0

Source: U.S. Census Bureau, State & Local Government Finances 2017

EMPLOYMENT

Labor Force and Employment

Area	Civilian Labor Force Dec. 2019	Civilian Labor Force Dec. 2020	% Chg.	Workers Employed Dec. 2019	Workers Employed Dec. 2020	% Chg.
City	93,172	90,468	-2.9	90,578	86,083	-5.0
MSA[1]	353,248	344,421	-2.5	344,074	327,001	-5.0
U.S.	164,007,000	160,017,000	-2.4	158,504,000	149,613,000	-5.6

Note: Data is not seasonally adjusted and covers workers 16 years of age and older; (1) Figures cover the Cape Coral-Fort Myers, FL Metropolitan Statistical Area
Source: Bureau of Labor Statistics, Local Area Unemployment Statistics

Unemployment Rate

Area	Jan.	Feb.	Mar.	Apr.	May	Jun.	Jul.	Aug.	Sep.	Oct.	Nov.	Dec.
City	3.2	3.0	4.4	16.2	14.0	10.0	11.0	7.2	6.0	5.2	5.2	4.8
MSA[1]	3.1	3.0	4.3	14.6	13.0	9.6	10.7	7.1	5.9	5.4	5.4	5.1
U.S.	4.0	3.8	4.5	14.4	13.0	11.2	10.5	8.5	7.7	6.6	6.4	6.5

Note: Data is not seasonally adjusted and covers workers 16 years of age and older; (1) Figures cover the Cape Coral-Fort Myers, FL Metropolitan Statistical Area
Source: Bureau of Labor Statistics, Local Area Unemployment Statistics

Average Wages

Occupation	$/Hr.	Occupation	$/Hr.
Accountants and Auditors	31.30	Maintenance and Repair Workers	19.00
Automotive Mechanics	21.30	Marketing Managers	54.40
Bookkeepers	20.50	Network and Computer Systems Admin.	35.40
Carpenters	20.00	Nurses, Licensed Practical	21.40
Cashiers	12.00	Nurses, Registered	34.10
Computer Programmers	43.00	Nursing Assistants	15.30
Computer Systems Analysts	37.50	Office Clerks, General	17.10
Computer User Support Specialists	23.30	Physical Therapists	41.30
Construction Laborers	16.80	Physicians	126.00
Cooks, Restaurant	15.40	Plumbers, Pipefitters and Steamfitters	21.60
Customer Service Representatives	16.50	Police and Sheriff's Patrol Officers	26.00
Dentists	83.50	Postal Service Mail Carriers	25.50
Electricians	21.90	Real Estate Sales Agents	25.90
Engineers, Electrical	53.80	Retail Salespersons	13.40
Fast Food and Counter Workers	10.90	Sales Representatives, Technical/Scientific	35.10
Financial Managers	54.90	Secretaries, Exc. Legal/Medical/Executive	18.30
First-Line Supervisors of Office Workers	27.10	Security Guards	13.10
General and Operations Managers	47.50	Surgeons	117.60
Hairdressers/Cosmetologists	15.60	Teacher Assistants, Exc. Postsecondary*	15.00
Home Health and Personal Care Aides	12.70	Teachers, Secondary School, Exc. Sp. Ed.*	31.80
Janitors and Cleaners	14.40	Telemarketers	13.60
Landscaping/Groundskeeping Workers	14.80	Truck Drivers, Heavy/Tractor-Trailer	21.10
Lawyers	n/a	Truck Drivers, Light/Delivery Services	18.20
Maids and Housekeeping Cleaners	11.50	Waiters and Waitresses	12.60

Note: Wage data covers the Cape Coral-Fort Myers, FL Metropolitan Statistical Area; (*) Hourly wages were calculated from annual wage data based on a 40 hour work week; n/a not available.
Source: Bureau of Labor Statistics, Metro Area Occupational Employment & Wage Estimates, May 2020

Employment by Industry

Sector	MSA[1] Number of Employees	MSA[1] Percent of Total	U.S. Percent of Total
Construction, Mining, and Logging	34,200	12.6	5.5
Education and Health Services	31,100	11.5	16.3
Financial Activities	13,300	4.9	6.1
Government	43,100	15.9	15.2
Information	2,600	1.0	1.9
Leisure and Hospitality	36,600	13.5	9.0
Manufacturing	6,600	2.4	8.5
Other Services	10,900	4.0	3.8
Professional and Business Services	38,000	14.0	14.4
Retail Trade	40,400	14.9	10.9
Transportation, Warehousing, and Utilities	6,600	2.4	4.6
Wholesale Trade	7,800	2.9	3.9

Note: Figures are non-farm employment as of December 2020. Figures are not seasonally adjusted and include workers 16 years of age and older; (1) Figures cover the Cape Coral-Fort Myers, FL Metropolitan Statistical Area
Source: Bureau of Labor Statistics, Current Employment Statistics, Employment, Hours, and Earnings

Employment by Occupation

Occupation Classification	City (%)	MSA[1] (%)	U.S. (%)
Management, Business, Science, and Arts	30.8	31.2	38.5
Natural Resources, Construction, and Maintenance	12.2	12.3	8.9
Production, Transportation, and Material Moving	9.9	10.0	13.2
Sales and Office	28.0	25.9	21.6
Service	19.1	20.5	17.8

Note: Figures cover employed civilians 16 years of age and older; (1) Figures cover the Cape Coral-Fort Myers, FL Metropolitan Statistical Area
Source: U.S. Census Bureau, 2015-2019 American Community Survey 5-Year Estimates

Occupations with Greatest Projected Employment Growth: 2020 – 2022

Occupation[1]	2020 Employment	2022 Projected Employment	Numeric Employment Change	Percent Employment Change
Fast Food and Counter Workers	172,590	214,590	42,000	24.3
Waiters and Waitresses	141,990	180,530	38,540	27.1
Retail Salespersons	264,490	292,340	27,850	10.5
Cooks, Restaurant	79,150	103,770	24,620	31.1
Maids and Housekeeping Cleaners	63,280	81,030	17,750	28.0
Cashiers	204,540	221,530	16,990	8.3
Registered Nurses	189,240	202,880	13,640	7.2
Laborers and Freight, Stock, and Material Movers, Hand	147,740	160,650	12,910	8.7
First-Line Supervisors of Food Preparation and Serving Workers	51,820	64,080	12,260	23.7
Stockers and Order Fillers	130,980	142,780	11,800	9.0

Note: Projections cover Florida; (1) Sorted by numeric employment change
Source: www.projectionscentral.com, State Occupational Projections, 2020–2022 Short-Term Projections

Fastest-Growing Occupations: 2020 – 2022

Occupation[1]	2020 Employment	2022 Projected Employment	Numeric Employment Change	Percent Employment Change
Hotel, Motel, and Resort Desk Clerks	11,930	18,100	6,170	51.7
Locker Room, Coatroom, and Dressing Room Attendants	930	1,360	430	46.2
Lodging Managers	3,190	4,420	1,230	38.6
Manicurists and Pedicurists	2,640	3,580	940	35.6
Bartenders	31,430	42,540	11,110	35.3
Gaming Cage Workers	320	430	110	34.4
Parking Lot Attendants	11,200	15,040	3,840	34.3
Gaming Dealers	2,660	3,560	900	33.8
Baggage Porters and Bellhops	3,520	4,670	1,150	32.7
Cooks, Restaurant	79,150	103,770	24,620	31.1

Note: Projections cover Florida; (1) Sorted by percent employment change and excludes occupations with numeric employment change less than 50
Source: www.projectionscentral.com, State Occupational Projections, 2020–2022 Short-Term Projections

TAXES

State Corporate Income Tax Rates

State	Tax Rate (%)	Income Brackets ($)	Num. of Brackets	Financial Institution Tax Rate (%)[a]	Federal Income Tax Ded.
Florida	4.458 (e)	Flat rate	1	4.458 (e)	No

Note: Tax rates as of January 1, 2021; (a) Rates listed are the corporate income tax rate applied to financial institutions or excise taxes based on income. Some states have other taxes based upon the value of deposits or shares; (e) The Florida tax rate may be adjusted downward if certain revenue targets are met.
Source: Federation of Tax Administrators, State Corporate Income Tax Rates, January 1, 2021

State Individual Income Tax Rates

State	Tax Rate (%)	Income Brackets ($)	Personal Exemptions ($) Single	Married	Depend.	Standard Ded. ($) Single	Married
Florida				– No state income tax –			

Note: Tax rates as of January 1, 2021; Local- and county-level taxes are not included
Source: Federation of Tax Administrators, State Individual Income Tax Rates, January 1, 2021

Various State Sales and Excise Tax Rates

State	State Sales Tax (%)	Gasoline[1] (¢/gal.)	Cigarette[2] ($/pack)	Spirits[3] ($/gal.)	Wine[4] ($/gal.)	Beer[5] ($/gal.)	Recreational Marijuana (%)
Florida	6	42.46	1.339	6.5	2.25	0.48	Not legal

Note: All tax rates as of January 1, 2021; (1) The American Petroleum Institute has developed a methodology for determining the average tax rate on a gallon of fuel. Rates may include any of the following: excise taxes, environmental fees, storage tank fees, other fees or taxes, general sales tax, and local taxes; (2) The federal excise tax of $1.0066 per pack and local taxes are not included; (3) Rates are those applicable to off-premise sales of 40% alcohol by volume (a.b.v.) distilled spirits in 750ml containers. Local excise taxes are excluded; (4) Rates are those applicable to off-premise sales of 11% a.b.v. non-carbonated wine in 750ml containers; (5) Rates are those applicable to off-premise sales of 4.7% a.b.v. beer in 12 ounce containers.
Source: Tax Foundation, 2021 Facts & Figures: How Does Your State Compare?

State Business Tax Climate Index Rankings

State	Overall Rank	Corporate Tax Rank	Individual Income Tax Rank	Sales Tax Rank	Property Tax Rank	Unemployment Insurance Tax Rank
Florida	4	6	1	21	13	2

Note: The index is a measure of how each state's tax laws affect economic performance. The lower the rank, the more favorable a state's tax system is for business. States without a given tax are given a ranking of 1. The scores/rankings for the District of Columbia do not affect other states. The 2021 index represents the tax climate as of July 1, 2020.
Source: Tax Foundation, State Business Tax Climate Index 2021

TRANSPORTATION

Means of Transportation to Work

Area	Car/Truck/Van Drove Alone	Car/Truck/Van Car-pooled	Public Transportation Bus	Public Transportation Subway	Public Transportation Railroad	Bicycle	Walked	Other Means	Worked at Home
City	81.7	9.0	0.1	0.0	0.0	0.2	0.8	1.2	7.0
MSA[1]	79.0	10.2	0.6	0.0	0.0	0.6	1.2	2.0	6.3
U.S.	76.3	9.0	2.4	1.9	0.6	0.5	2.7	1.4	5.2

Note: Figures are percentages and cover workers 16 years of age and older; (1) Figures cover the Cape Coral-Fort Myers, FL Metropolitan Statistical Area
Source: U.S. Census Bureau, 2015-2019 American Community Survey 5-Year Estimates

Travel Time to Work

Area	Less Than 10 Minutes	10 to 19 Minutes	20 to 29 Minutes	30 to 44 Minutes	45 to 59 Minutes	60 to 89 Minutes	90 Minutes or More
City	7.9	23.9	23.5	26.5	10.4	5.8	2.0
MSA[1]	8.7	25.3	23.1	25.6	10.2	5.1	2.0
U.S.	12.2	28.4	20.8	20.8	8.3	6.4	2.9

Note: Note: Figures are percentages and include workers 16 years old and over; (1) Figures cover the Cape Coral-Fort Myers, FL Metropolitan Statistical Area
Source: U.S. Census Bureau, 2015-2019 American Community Survey 5-Year Estimates

Key Congestion Measures

Measure	1982	1992	2002	2012	2017
Annual Hours of Delay, Total (000)	1,180	3,107	7,442	13,449	15,733
Annual Hours of Delay, Per Auto Commuter	10	19	31	36	37
Annual Congestion Cost, Total (million $)	9	33	100	240	289
Annual Congestion Cost, Per Auto Commuter ($)	123	224	418	592	672

Note: Covers the Cape Coral FL urban area
Source: Texas A&M Transportation Institute, 2019 Urban Mobility Report

Freeway Travel Time Index

Measure	1982	1987	1992	1997	2002	2007	2012	2017
Urban Area Index[1]	1.06	1.08	1.11	1.14	1.17	1.21	1.18	1.17
Urban Area Rank[1,2]	43	44	49	47	41	36	40	49

Note: Freeway Travel Time Index—the ratio of travel time in the peak period to the travel time at free-flow conditions. For example, a value of 1.30 indicates a 20-minute free-flow trip takes 26 minutes in the peak (20 minutes x 1.30 = 26 minutes); (1) Covers the Cape Coral FL urban area; (2) Rank is based on 101 larger urban areas (#1 = highest travel time index)
Source: Texas A&M Transportation Institute, 2019 Urban Mobility Report

Public Transportation

Agency Name / Mode of Transportation	Vehicles Operated in Maximum Service[1]	Annual Unlinked Passenger Trips[2] (in thous.)	Annual Passenger Miles[3] (in thous.)
Lee County Transit (LeeTran)			
Bus (directly operated)	48	2,971.7	15,690.8
Demand Response (directly operated)	40	140.6	1,761.0
Vanpool (purchased transportation)	16	68.6	2,629.3

Note: (1) Number of revenue vehicles operated by the given mode and type of service to meet the annual maximum service requirement. This is the revenue vehicle count during the peak season of the year; on the week and day that maximum service is provided. Vehicles operated in maximum service (VOMS) exclude atypical days and one-time special events; (2) Number of passengers who boarded public transportation vehicles. Passengers are counted each time they board a vehicle no matter how many vehicles they use to travel from their origin to their destination. (3) Sum of the distances ridden by all passengers during the entire fiscal year.
Source: Federal Transit Administration, National Transit Database, 2019

Air Transportation

Airport Name and Code / Type of Service	Passenger Airlines[1]	Passenger Enplanements	Freight Carriers[2]	Freight (lbs)
Southwest Florida International Airport (RSW)				
Domestic service (U.S. carriers - 2020)	19	2,874,895	10	12,883,723
International service (U.S. carriers - 2019)	3	926	0	0

Note: (1) Includes all U.S.-based major, minor and commuter airlines that carried at least one passenger during the year; (2) Includes all U.S.-based airlines and freight carriers that transported at least one pound of freight during the year.
Source: Bureau of Transportation Statistics, The Intermodal Transportation Database, Air Carriers: T-100 Domestic Market (U.S. Carriers), 2020; Bureau of Transportation Statistics, The Intermodal Transportation Database, Air Carriers: T-100 International Market (U.S. Carriers), 2019

BUSINESSES

Major Business Headquarters

Company Name	Industry	Rankings Fortune[1]	Forbes[2]
No companies listed	-	-	-

Note: (1) Companies that produce a 10-K are ranked 1 to 500 based on 2019 revenue; (2) All private companies with at least $2 billion in annual revenue through the end of their most current fiscal year are ranked 1 to 219; companies listed are headquartered in the city; dashes indicate no ranking
Source: Fortune, "Fortune 500," June/July 2020; Forbes, "America's Largest Private Companies," 2020

Living Environment

COST OF LIVING

Cost of Living Index

Composite Index	Groceries	Housing	Utilities	Transportation	Health Care	Misc. Goods/Services
100.9	100.2	90.6	98.1	111.9	106.7	106.6

Note: The Cost of Living Index measures regional differences in the cost of consumer goods and services, excluding taxes and non-consumer expenditures, for professional and managerial households in the top income quintile. It is based on more than 50,000 prices covering almost 60 different items for which prices are collected three times a year by chambers of commerce, economic development organizations or university applied economic centers in each participating urban area. The numbers shown should be read as a percentage above or below the national average of 100. For example, a value of 115.4 in the groceries column indicates that grocery prices are 15.4% higher than the national average. Small differences in the index numbers should not be interpreted as significant; Figures cover the Cape Coral-Fort Myers FL urban area.
Source: The Council for Community and Economic Research, Cost of Living Index, 2020

Grocery Prices

Area[1]	T-Bone Steak ($/pound)	Frying Chicken ($/pound)	Whole Milk ($/half gal.)	Eggs ($/dozen)	Orange Juice ($/64 oz.)	Coffee ($/11.5 oz.)
City[2]	11.21	1.92	2.40	1.51	3.36	3.34
Avg.	11.78	1.39	2.05	1.47	3.57	4.34
Min.	8.03	0.94	1.03	0.74	2.94	3.02
Max.	15.86	2.65	4.31	3.77	5.44	8.69

Note: (1) Values for the local area are compared with the average, minimum and maximum values for all 284 areas in the Cost of Living Index; (2) Figures cover the Cape Coral-Fort Myers FL urban area; **T-Bone Steak** (price per pound); **Frying Chicken** (price per pound, whole fryer); **Whole Milk** (half gallon carton); **Eggs** (price per dozen, Grade A, large); **Orange Juice** (64 oz. Tropicana or Florida Natural); **Coffee** (11.5 oz. can, vacuum-packed, Maxwell House, Hills Bros, or Folgers).
Source: The Council for Community and Economic Research, Cost of Living Index, 2020

Housing and Utility Costs

Area[1]	New Home Price ($)	Apartment Rent ($/month)	All Electric ($/month)	Part Electric ($/month)	Other Energy ($/month)	Telephone ($/month)
City[2]	328,513	1,061	158.56	-	-	187.80
Avg.	368,594	1,168	170.86	100.47	65.28	184.30
Min.	190,567	502	91.58	31.42	26.08	169.60
Max.	2,227,806	4,738	470.38	280.31	280.06	206.50

Note: (1) Values for the local area are compared with the average, minimum and maximum values for all 284 areas in the Cost of Living Index; (2) Figures cover the Cape Coral-Fort Myers FL urban area; **New Home Price** (2,400 sf living area, 8,000 sf lot, in urban area with full utilities); **Apartment Rent** (950 sf 2 bedroom/1.5 or 2 bath, unfurnished, excluding all utilities except water); **All Electric** (average monthly cost for an all-electric home); **Part Electric** (average monthly cost for a part-electric home); **Other Energy** (average monthly cost for natural gas, fuel oil, coal, wood, and any other forms of energy except electricity); **Telephone** (price includes the base monthly rate plus taxes and fees for three lines of mobile phone service).
Source: The Council for Community and Economic Research, Cost of Living Index, 2020

Health Care, Transportation, and Other Costs

Area[1]	Doctor ($/visit)	Dentist ($/visit)	Optometrist ($/visit)	Gasoline ($/gallon)	Beauty Salon ($/visit)	Men's Shirt ($)
City[2]	123.46	110.14	85.53	2.45	33.41	25.30
Avg.	115.44	99.32	108.10	2.21	39.27	31.37
Min.	36.68	59.00	51.36	1.71	19.00	11.00
Max.	219.00	153.10	250.97	3.46	82.05	58.33

Note: (1) Values for the local area are compared with the average, minimum and maximum values for all 284 areas in the Cost of Living Index; (2) Figures cover the Cape Coral-Fort Myers FL urban area; **Doctor** (general practitioners routine exam of an established patient); **Dentist** (adult teeth cleaning and periodic oral examination); **Optometrist** (full vision eye exam for established adult patient); **Gasoline** (one gallon regular unleaded, national brand, including all taxes, cash price at self-service pump if available); **Beauty Salon** (woman's shampoo, trim, and blow-dry); **Men's Shirt** (cotton/polyester dress shirt, pinpoint weave, long sleeves).
Source: The Council for Community and Economic Research, Cost of Living Index, 2020

HOUSING

Homeownership Rate

Area	2012 (%)	2013 (%)	2014 (%)	2015 (%)	2016 (%)	2017 (%)	2018 (%)	2019 (%)	2020 (%)
MSA[1]	n/a	n/a	n/a	62.9	66.5	65.5	75.1	72.0	77.4
U.S.	65.4	65.1	64.5	63.7	63.4	63.9	64.4	64.6	66.6

Note: (1) Figures cover the Cape Coral-Fort Myers, FL Metropolitan Statistical Area
Source: U.S. Census Bureau, Housing Vacancies and Homeownership Annual Statistics: 2012-2020

House Price Index (HPI)

Area	National Ranking[2]	Quarterly Change (%)	One-Year Change (%)	Five-Year Change (%)	Since 1991Q1 (%)
MSA[1]	84	3.11	7.07	33.53	188.18
U.S.[3]	—	3.81	10.77	38.99	205.12

Note: The HPI is a weighted repeat sales index. It measures average price changes in repeat sales or refinancings on the same properties. This information is obtained by reviewing repeat mortgage transactions on single-family properties whose mortgages have been purchased or securitized by Fannie Mae or Freddie Mac since January 1975; (1) Figures cover the Cape Coral-Fort Myers, FL Metropolitan Statistical Area; (2) Rankings are based on annual percentage change for all metro areas containing at least 15,000 transactions over the last 10 years and ranges from 1 to 253; (3) figures based on a weighted average of Census Division estimates using a seasonally adjusted, purchase-only index; all figures are for the period ending December 31, 2020
Source: Federal Housing Finance Agency, Change in Metropolitan Area House Price Indexes, April 7, 2021

Median Single-Family Home Prices

Area	2018	2019	2020p	Percent Change 2019 to 2020
MSA[1]	251.0	258.7	289.0	11.7
U.S. Average	261.6	274.6	299.9	9.2

Note: Figures are median sales prices of existing single-family homes in thousands of dollars; (p) preliminary; (1) Figures cover the Cape Coral-Fort Myers, FL Metropolitan Statistical Area
Source: National Association of Realtors, Median Sales Price of Existing Single-Family Homes for Metropolitan Areas, 4th Quarter 2020

Qualifying Income Based on Median Sales Price of Existing Single-Family Homes

Area	With 5% Down ($)	With 10% Down ($)	With 20% Down ($)
MSA[1]	59,012	55,906	49,695
U.S. Average	59,266	56,147	49,908

Note: Figures are preliminary; Qualifying income is based on a mortgage rate of 2.81%. Monthly principal and interest payment is limited to 25% of income; (1) Figures cover the Cape Coral-Fort Myers, FL Metropolitan Statistical Area
Source: National Association of Realtors, Qualifying Income Based on Median Sales Price of Existing Single-Family Homes for Metropolitan Areas, 4th Quarter 2020

Home Value Distribution

Area	Under $50,000	$50,000 -$99,999	$100,000 -$149,999	$150,000 -$199,999	$200,000 -$299,999	$300,000 -$499,999	$500,000 -$999,999	$1,000,000 or more
City	1.6	3.1	11.1	22.6	34.1	20.2	6.5	0.9
MSA[1]	6.2	8.9	11.8	16.4	24.5	20.2	9.2	2.8
U.S.	6.9	12.0	13.3	14.0	19.6	19.3	11.4	3.4

Note: Figures are percentages and cover owner-occupied housing units; (1) Figures cover the Cape Coral-Fort Myers, FL Metropolitan Statistical Area
Source: U.S. Census Bureau, 2015-2019 American Community Survey 5-Year Estimates

Year Housing Structure Built

Area	2010 or Later	2000 -2009	1990 -1999	1980 -1989	1970 -1979	1960 -1969	1950 -1959	1940 -1949	Before 1940	Median Year
City	3.8	37.8	17.8	22.9	11.9	4.7	0.8	0.2	0.1	1995
MSA[1]	5.6	31.3	17.7	21.4	14.8	5.5	2.5	0.5	0.7	1993
U.S.	5.2	14.0	13.9	13.4	15.2	10.6	10.3	4.9	12.6	1978

Note: Figures are percentages except for Median Year; Note: (1) Figures cover the Cape Coral-Fort Myers, FL Metropolitan Statistical Area
Source: U.S. Census Bureau, 2015-2019 American Community Survey 5-Year Estimates

Gross Monthly Rent

Area	Under $500	$500 -$999	$1,000 -$1,499	$1,500 -$1,999	$2,000 -$2,499	$2,500 -$2,999	$3,000 and up	Median ($)
City	0.9	22.4	46.8	22.5	5.0	1.0	1.4	1,244
MSA[1]	4.2	29.8	43.3	14.3	4.8	1.6	2.0	1,154
U.S.	9.4	36.2	30.0	14.0	5.6	2.4	2.4	1,062

Note: Figures are percentages except for Median; Gross rent is the contract rent plus the estimated average monthly cost of utilities (electricity, gas, and water and sewer) and fuels (oil, coal, kerosene, wood, etc.) if these are paid by the renter (or paid for the renter by someone else); (1) Figures cover the Cape Coral-Fort Myers, FL Metropolitan Statistical Area
Source: U.S. Census Bureau, 2015-2019 American Community Survey 5-Year Estimates

HEALTH

Health Risk Factors

Category	MSA[1] (%)	U.S. (%)
Adults aged 18–64 who have any kind of health care coverage	n/a	87.3
Adults who reported being in good or better health	n/a	82.4
Adults who have been told they have high blood cholesterol	n/a	33.0
Adults who have been told they have high blood pressure	n/a	32.3
Adults who are current smokers	n/a	17.1
Adults who currently use E-cigarettes	n/a	4.6
Adults who currently use chewing tobacco, snuff, or snus	n/a	4.0
Adults who are heavy drinkers[2]	n/a	6.3
Adults who are binge drinkers[3]	n/a	17.4
Adults who are overweight (BMI 25.0 - 29.9)	n/a	35.3
Adults who are obese (BMI 30.0 - 99.8)	n/a	31.3
Adults who participated in any physical activities in the past month	n/a	74.4
Adults who always or nearly always wears a seat belt	n/a	94.3

Note: n/a not available; (1) Figures cover the Cape Coral-Fort Myers, FL Metropolitan Statistical Area; (2) Heavy drinkers are classified as adult men having more than 14 drinks per week and adult women having more than 7 drinks per week; (3) Binge drinkers are classified as males having five or more drinks on one occasion or females having four or more drinks on one occasion
Source: Centers for Disease Control and Prevention, Behavioral Risk Factor Surveillance System, SMART: Selected Metropolitan Area Risk Trends, 2017

Acute and Chronic Health Conditions

Category	MSA[1] (%)	U.S. (%)
Adults who have ever been told they had a heart attack	n/a	4.2
Adults who have ever been told they have angina or coronary heart disease	n/a	3.9
Adults who have ever been told they had a stroke	n/a	3.0
Adults who have ever been told they have asthma	n/a	14.2
Adults who have ever been told they have arthritis	n/a	24.9
Adults who have ever been told they have diabetes[2]	n/a	10.5
Adults who have ever been told they had skin cancer	n/a	6.2
Adults who have ever been told they had any other types of cancer	n/a	7.1
Adults who have ever been told they have COPD	n/a	6.5
Adults who have ever been told they have kidney disease	n/a	3.0
Adults who have ever been told they have a form of depression	n/a	20.5

Note: n/a not available; (1) Figures cover the Cape Coral-Fort Myers, FL Metropolitan Statistical Area; (2) Figures do not include pregnancy-related, borderline, or pre-diabetes
Source: Centers for Disease Control and Prevention, Behaviorial Risk Factor Surveillance System, SMART: Selected Metropolitan Area Risk Trends, 2017

Health Screening and Vaccination Rates

Category	MSA[1] (%)	U.S. (%)
Adults aged 65+ who have had flu shot within the past year	n/a	60.7
Adults aged 65+ who have ever had a pneumonia vaccination	n/a	75.4
Adults who have ever been tested for HIV	n/a	36.1
Adults who have ever had the shingles or zoster vaccine?	n/a	28.9
Adults who have had their blood cholesterol checked within the last five years	n/a	85.9

Note: n/a not available; (1) Figures cover the Cape Coral-Fort Myers, FL Metropolitan Statistical Area.
Source: Centers for Disease Control and Prevention, Behaviorial Risk Factor Surveillance System, SMART: Selected Metropolitan Area Risk Trends, 2017

Disability Status

Category	MSA[1] (%)	U.S. (%)
Adults who reported being deaf	n/a	6.7
Are you blind or have serious difficulty seeing, even when wearing glasses?	n/a	4.5
Are you limited in any way in any of your usual activities due of arthritis?	n/a	12.9
Do you have difficulty doing errands alone?	n/a	6.8
Do you have difficulty dressing or bathing?	n/a	3.6
Do you have serious difficulty concentrating/remembering/making decisions?	n/a	10.7
Do you have serious difficulty walking or climbing stairs?	n/a	13.6

Note: n/a not available; (1) Figures cover the Cape Coral-Fort Myers, FL Metropolitan Statistical Area.
Source: Centers for Disease Control and Prevention, Behaviorial Risk Factor Surveillance System, SMART: Selected Metropolitan Area Risk Trends, 2017

Mortality Rates for the Top 10 Causes of Death in the U.S.

ICD-10[a] Sub-Chapter	ICD-10[a] Code	Age-Adjusted Mortality Rate[1] per 100,000 population County[2]	U.S.
Malignant neoplasms	C00-C97	125.1	149.2
Ischaemic heart diseases	I20-I25	73.9	90.5
Other forms of heart disease	I30-I51	20.1	52.2
Chronic lower respiratory diseases	J40-J47	28.9	39.6
Other degenerative diseases of the nervous system	G30-G31	40.1	37.6
Cerebrovascular diseases	I60-I69	26.6	37.2
Other external causes of accidental injury	W00-X59	52.2	36.1
Organic, including symptomatic, mental disorders	F01-F09	5.1	29.4
Hypertensive diseases	I10-I15	22.3	24.1
Diabetes mellitus	E10-E14	16.6	21.5

Note: (a) ICD-10 = International Classification of Diseases 10th Revision; (1) Mortality rates are a three-year average covering 2017-2019; (2) Figures cover Lee County.
Source: Centers for Disease Control and Prevention, National Center for Health Statistics. Underlying Cause of Death 1999-2019 on CDC WONDER Online Database

Mortality Rates for Selected Causes of Death

ICD-10[a] Sub-Chapter	ICD-10[a] Code	Age-Adjusted Mortality Rate[1] per 100,000 population County[2]	U.S.
Assault	X85-Y09	5.8	6.0
Diseases of the liver	K70-K76	14.8	14.4
Human immunodeficiency virus (HIV) disease	B20-B24	1.5	1.5
Influenza and pneumonia	J09-J18	6.1	13.8
Intentional self-harm	X60-X84	14.6	14.1
Malnutrition	E40-E46	0.6	2.3
Obesity and other hyperalimentation	E65-E68	1.8	2.1
Renal failure	N17-N19	4.0	12.6
Transport accidents	V01-V99	17.3	12.3
Viral hepatitis	B15-B19	1.1	1.2

Note: (a) ICD-10 = International Classification of Diseases 10th Revision; (1) Mortality rates are a three-year average covering 2017-2019; (2) Figures cover Lee County; Data are suppressed when the data meet the criteria for confidentiality constraints; Mortality rates are flagged as unreliable when the rate would be calculated with a numerator of 20 or less.
Source: Centers for Disease Control and Prevention, National Center for Health Statistics. Underlying Cause of Death 1999-2019 on CDC WONDER Online Database

Health Insurance Coverage

Area	With Health Insurance	With Private Health Insurance	With Public Health Insurance	Without Health Insurance	Population Under Age 19 Without Health Insurance
City	87.4	65.9	36.8	12.6	8.6
MSA[1]	86.7	62.4	43.6	13.3	9.3
U.S.	91.2	67.9	35.1	8.8	5.1

Note: Figures are percentages that cover the civilian noninstitutionalized population; (1) Figures cover the Cape Coral-Fort Myers, FL Metropolitan Statistical Area
Source: U.S. Census Bureau, 2015-2019 American Community Survey 5-Year Estimates

Number of Medical Professionals

Area	MDs[3]	DOs[3,4]	Dentists	Podiatrists	Chiropractors	Optometrists
County[1] (number)	1,439	225	384	64	211	97
County[1] (rate[2])	190.7	29.8	49.8	8.3	27.4	12.6
U.S. (rate[2])	282.9	22.7	71.2	6.2	28.1	16.9

12071
Note: Data as of 2019 unless noted; (1) Data covers Lee County; (2) Rate per 100,000 population; (3) Data as of 2018 and includes all active, non-federal physicians; (4) Doctor of Osteopathic Medicine
Source: U.S. Department of Health and Human Services, Health Resources and Services Administration, Bureau of Health Professions, Area Resource File (ARF) 2019-2020

EDUCATION

Public School District Statistics

District Name	Schls	Pupils	Pupil/Teacher Ratio	Minority Pupils[1] (%)	Free Lunch Eligible[2] (%)	IEP[3] (%)
Lee	121	94,410	17.9	61.5	45.1	12.2

Note: Table includes school districts with 2,000 or more students; (1) Percentage of students that are not non-Hispanic white; (2) Percentage of students that are eligible for the free lunch program; (3) Percentage of students that have an Individualized Education Program.
Source: U.S. Department of Education, National Center for Education Statistics, Common Core of Data, Local Education Agency (School District) Universe Survey: School Year 2018-2019; U.S. Department of Education, National Center for Education Statistics, Common Core of Data, Public Elementary/Secondary School Universe Survey: School Year 2018-2019

Highest Level of Education

Area	Less than H.S.	H.S. Diploma	Some College, No Deg.	Associate Degree	Bachelor's Degree	Master's Degree	Prof. School Degree	Doctorate Degree
City	8.2	37.3	21.0	10.1	15.8	5.3	1.3	0.9
MSA[1]	11.6	31.0	20.3	8.9	17.6	7.2	2.2	1.2
U.S.	12.0	27.0	20.4	8.5	19.8	8.8	2.1	1.4

Note: Figures cover persons age 25 and over; (1) Figures cover the Cape Coral-Fort Myers, FL Metropolitan Statistical Area
Source: U.S. Census Bureau, 2015-2019 American Community Survey 5-Year Estimates

Educational Attainment by Race

Area	High School Graduate or Higher (%)					Bachelor's Degree or Higher (%)				
	Total	White	Black	Asian	Hisp.[2]	Total	White	Black	Asian	Hisp.[2]
City	91.8	92.3	89.3	88.5	86.9	23.3	23.7	19.8	24.7	18.7
MSA[1]	88.4	90.0	79.5	88.6	71.0	28.2	29.4	15.9	45.3	14.8
U.S.	88.0	89.9	86.0	87.1	68.7	32.1	33.5	21.6	54.3	16.4

Note: Figures shown cover persons 25 years old and over; (1) Figures cover the Cape Coral-Fort Myers, FL Metropolitan Statistical Area; (2) People of Hispanic origin can be of any race
Source: U.S. Census Bureau, 2015-2019 American Community Survey 5-Year Estimates

School Enrollment by Grade and Control

Area	Preschool (%)		Kindergarten (%)		Grades 1 - 4 (%)		Grades 5 - 8 (%)		Grades 9 - 12 (%)	
	Public	Private	Public	Private	Public	Private	Public	Private	Public	Private
City	84.8	15.2	94.8	5.2	92.0	8.0	93.0	7.0	91.8	8.2
MSA[1]	65.5	34.5	89.7	10.3	92.6	7.4	91.5	8.5	90.8	9.2
U.S.	59.1	40.9	87.6	12.4	89.5	10.5	89.4	10.6	90.1	9.9

Note: Figures shown cover persons 3 years old and over; (1) Figures cover the Cape Coral-Fort Myers, FL Metropolitan Statistical Area
Source: U.S. Census Bureau, 2015-2019 American Community Survey 5-Year Estimates

Higher Education

Four-Year Colleges			Two-Year Colleges			Medical Schools[1]	Law Schools[2]	Voc/Tech[3]
Public	Private Non-profit	Private For-profit	Public	Private Non-profit	Private For-profit			
0	0	0	0	0	0	0	0	1

Note: Figures cover institutions located within the city limits and include main campuses only; (1) includes schools accredited by the Liaison Committee on Medical Education and the American Osteopathic Association's Commission on Osteopathic College Accreditation; (2) includes ABA-accredited schools, schools with provisional ABA accreditation, and state accredited schools; (3) includes all schools with programs that are less than 2 years.
Source: National Center for Education Statistics, Integrated Postsecondary Education System (IPEDS), 2019-20; Wikipedia, List of Medical Schools in the United States, accessed April 2, 2021; Wikipedia, List of Law Schools in the United States, accessed April 2, 2021

EMPLOYERS

Major Employers

Company Name	Industry
Arthrex	Medical device manufacturer
Charlotte County School District	Education
Charlotte Regional Medical Center	Healthcare
Chico's Fas	Retail
City of Cape Coral	Municipal government
Collier County Administration	Government
Collier County Public Schools	Education
Florida Gulf Coast University	Education
Home Depot	Retail
Lee County School District	Education
Lee County Sherriff's Office	Government
Lee Memorial Health System	Healthcare
NCH Naples Hospitals	Healthcare
Palm Automotive	Auto sales
Publix Supermarkets	Retail grocery
St. Joseph Preferred Healthcare Inc	Healthcare
U.S. Sugar	Manufacturing
United States Postal Service	U.S. postal service
Wal-Mart Stores	Retail
Winn-Dixie	Grocery stores

Note: Companies shown are located within the Cape Coral-Fort Myers, FL Metropolitan Statistical Area.
Source: Hoovers.com; Wikipedia

PUBLIC SAFETY

Crime Rate

Area	All Crimes	Murder	Rape[3]	Robbery	Aggrav. Assault	Burglary	Larceny -Theft	Motor Vehicle Theft
City	1,237.0	2.6	8.2	18.5	87.0	141.1	895.5	83.9
Suburbs[1]	1,476.1	3.1	40.1	61.0	201.4	186.4	880.9	103.2
Metro[2]	1,415.7	3.0	32.0	50.3	172.4	174.9	884.6	98.3
U.S.	2,489.3	5.0	42.6	81.6	250.2	340.5	1,549.5	219.9

Note: Figures are crimes per 100,000 population; (1) All areas within the metro area that are located outside the city limits; (2) Figures cover the Cape Coral-Fort Myers, FL Metropolitan Statistical Area; (3) All figures shown were reported using the revised Uniform Crime Reporting (UCR) definition of rape.
Source: FBI Uniform Crime Reports, 2019

Hate Crimes

Area	Number of Quarters Reported	Race/Ethnicity/ Ancestry	Religion	Sexual Orientation	Disability	Gender	Gender Identity
City	4	1	0	1	0	0	0
U.S.	4	3,963	1,521	1,195	157	69	198

Source: Federal Bureau of Investigation, Hate Crime Statistics 2019

Identity Theft Consumer Reports

Area	Reports	Reports per 100,000 Population	Rank[2]
MSA[1]	1,923	250	160
U.S.	1,387,615	423	-

Note: (1) Figures cover the Cape Coral-Fort Myers, FL Metropolitan Statistical Area; (2) Rank ranges from 1 to 391 where 1 indicates greatest number of identity theft reports per 100,000 population
Source: Federal Trade Commission, Consumer Sentinel Network Data Book 2020

Fraud and Other Consumer Reports

Area	Reports	Reports per 100,000 Population	Rank[2]
MSA[1]	6,715	871	59
U.S.	3,385,133	1,031	-

Note: (1) Figures cover the Cape Coral-Fort Myers, FL Metropolitan Statistical Area; (2) Rank ranges from 1 to 391 where 1 indicates greatest number of fraud and other consumer reports per 100,000 population
Source: Federal Trade Commission, Consumer Sentinel Network Data Book 2020

POLITICS

2020 Presidential Election Results

Area	Biden	Trump	Jorgensen	Hawkins	Other
Lee County	39.9	59.1	0.5	0.1	0.3
U.S.	51.3	46.8	1.2	0.3	0.5

Note: Results are percentages and may not add to 100% due to rounding
Source: Dave Leip's Atlas of U.S. Presidential Elections

SPORTS

Professional Sports Teams

Team Name	League	Year Established
No teams are located in the metro area		

Source: Wikipedia, Major Professional Sports Teams of the United States and Canada, April 6, 2021

CLIMATE

Average and Extreme Temperatures

Temperature	Jan	Feb	Mar	Apr	May	Jun	Jul	Aug	Sep	Oct	Nov	Dec	Yr.
Extreme High (°F)	88	91	93	96	99	103	98	98	96	95	95	90	103
Average High (°F)	75	76	80	85	89	91	91	92	90	86	80	76	84
Average Temp. (°F)	65	65	70	74	79	82	83	83	82	77	71	66	75
Average Low (°F)	54	54	59	62	68	73	74	75	74	68	61	55	65
Extreme Low (°F)	28	32	33	39	52	60	66	67	64	48	34	26	26

Note: Figures cover the years 1948-1995
Source: National Climatic Data Center, International Station Meteorological Climate Summary, 9/96

Average Precipitation/Snowfall/Humidity

Precip./Humidity	Jan	Feb	Mar	Apr	May	Jun	Jul	Aug	Sep	Oct	Nov	Dec	Yr.
Avg. Precip. (in.)	2.0	2.2	2.6	1.7	3.6	9.3	8.9	8.9	8.2	3.5	1.4	1.5	53.9
Avg. Snowfall (in.)	0	0	0	0	0	0	0	0	0	0	0	0	0
Avg. Rel. Hum. 7am (%)	90	89	89	88	87	89	90	91	92	90	90	90	90
Avg. Rel. Hum. 4pm (%)	56	54	52	50	53	64	68	67	66	59	58	57	59

Note: Figures cover the years 1948-1995; Tr = Trace amounts (<0.05 in. of rain; <0.5 in. of snow)
Source: National Climatic Data Center, International Station Meteorological Climate Summary, 9/96

Weather Conditions

Temperature			Daytime Sky			Precipitation		
32°F & below	45°F & below	90°F & above	Clear	Partly cloudy	Cloudy	0.01 inch or more precip.	0.1 inch or more snow/ice	Thunder-storms
1	18	115	93	220	52	110	0	92

Note: Figures are average number of days per year and cover the years 1948-1995
Source: National Climatic Data Center, International Station Meteorological Climate Summary, 9/96

HAZARDOUS WASTE

Superfund Sites

The Cape Coral-Fort Myers, FL metro area has no sites on the EPA's Superfund Final National Priorities List. There are a total of 1,375 Superfund sites with a status of proposed or final on the list in the U.S. *U.S. Environmental Protection Agency, National Priorities List, April 7, 2021*

AIR QUALITY

Air Quality Trends: Ozone

	1990	1995	2000	2005	2010	2015	2016	2017	2018	2019
MSA[1]	n/a	n/a	n/a	n/a	n/a	n/a	n/a	n/a	n/a	n/a
U.S.	0.088	0.089	0.082	0.080	0.073	0.068	0.069	0.068	0.069	0.065

Note: (1) Data covers the Cape Coral-Fort Myers, FL Metropolitan Statistical Area; n/a not available. The values shown are the composite ozone concentration averages among trend sites based on the highest fourth daily maximum 8-hour concentration in parts per million. These trends are based on sites having an adequate record of monitoring data during the trend period. Data from exceptional events are included.
Source: U.S. Environmental Protection Agency, Air Quality Monitoring Information, "Air Quality Trends by City, 1990-2019"

Air Quality Index

Area	Percent of Days when Air Quality was...[2]					AQI Statistics[2]	
	Good	Moderate	Unhealthy for Sensitive Groups	Unhealthy	Very Unhealthy	Maximum	Median
MSA[1]	89.9	9.9	0.3	0.0	0.0	108	36

Note: (1) Data covers the Cape Coral-Fort Myers, FL Metropolitan Statistical Area; (2) Based on 365 days with AQI data in 2019. Air Quality Index (AQI) is an index for reporting daily air quality. EPA calculates the AQI for five major air pollutants regulated by the Clean Air Act: ground-level ozone, particle pollution (aka particulate matter), carbon monoxide, sulfur dioxide, and nitrogen dioxide. The AQI runs from 0 to 500. The higher the AQI value, the greater the level of air pollution and the greater the health concern. There are six AQI categories: "Good" AQI is between 0 and 50. Air quality is considered satisfactory; "Moderate" AQI is between 51 and 100. Air quality is acceptable; "Unhealthy for Sensitive Groups" When AQI values are between 101 and 150, members of sensitive groups may experience health effects; "Unhealthy" When AQI values are between 151 and 200 everyone may begin to experience health effects; "Very Unhealthy" AQI values between 201 and 300 trigger a health alert; "Hazardous" AQI values over 300 trigger warnings of emergency conditions (not shown).
Source: U.S. Environmental Protection Agency, Air Quality Index Report, 2019

Air Quality Index Pollutants

Area	Carbon Monoxide	Nitrogen Dioxide	Ozone	Sulfur Dioxide	Particulate Matter 2.5	Particulate Matter 10
MSA[1]	0.0	0.0	68.8	0.0	30.1	1.1

Percent of Days when AQI Pollutant was...[2]

Note: (1) Data covers the Cape Coral-Fort Myers, FL Metropolitan Statistical Area; (2) Based on 365 days with AQI data in 2019. The Air Quality Index (AQI) is an index for reporting daily air quality. EPA calculates the AQI for five major air pollutants regulated by the Clean Air Act: ground-level ozone, particle pollution (also known as particulate matter), carbon monoxide, sulfur dioxide, and nitrogen dioxide. The AQI runs from 0 to 500. The higher the AQI value, the greater the level of air pollution and the greater the health concern.
Source: U.S. Environmental Protection Agency, Air Quality Index Report, 2019

Maximum Air Pollutant Concentrations: Particulate Matter, Ozone, CO and Lead

	Particulate Matter 10 (ug/m^3)	Particulate Matter 2.5 Wtd AM (ug/m^3)	Particulate Matter 2.5 24-Hr (ug/m^3)	Ozone (ppm)	Carbon Monoxide (ppm)	Lead (ug/m^3)
MSA[1] Level	51	7.4	14	0.062	n/a	n/a
NAAQS[2]	150	15	35	0.075	9	0.15
Met NAAQS[2]	Yes	Yes	Yes	Yes	n/a	n/a

Note: (1) Data covers the Cape Coral-Fort Myers, FL Metropolitan Statistical Area; Data from exceptional events are included; (2) National Ambient Air Quality Standards; ppm = parts per million; ug/m^3 = micrograms per cubic meter; n/a not available.
Concentrations: Particulate Matter 10 (coarse particulate)—highest second maximum 24-hour concentration; Particulate Matter 2.5 Wtd AM (fine particulate)—highest weighted annual mean concentration; Particulate Matter 2.5 24-Hour (fine particulate)—highest 98th percentile 24-hour concentration; Ozone—highest fourth daily maximum 8-hour concentration; Carbon Monoxide—highest second maximum non-overlapping 8-hour concentration; Lead—maximum running 3-month average
Source: U.S. Environmental Protection Agency, Air Quality Monitoring Information, "Air Quality Statistics by City, 2019"

Maximum Air Pollutant Concentrations: Nitrogen Dioxide and Sulfur Dioxide

	Nitrogen Dioxide AM (ppb)	Nitrogen Dioxide 1-Hr (ppb)	Sulfur Dioxide AM (ppb)	Sulfur Dioxide 1-Hr (ppb)	Sulfur Dioxide 24-Hr (ppb)
MSA[1] Level	n/a	n/a	n/a	n/a	n/a
NAAQS[2]	53	100	30	75	140
Met NAAQS[2]	n/a	n/a	n/a	n/a	n/a

Note: (1) Data covers the Cape Coral-Fort Myers, FL Metropolitan Statistical Area; Data from exceptional events are included; (2) National Ambient Air Quality Standards; ppm = parts per million; ug/m^3 = micrograms per cubic meter; n/a not available.
Concentrations: Nitrogen Dioxide AM—highest arithmetic mean concentration; Nitrogen Dioxide 1-Hr—highest 98th percentile 1-hour daily maximum concentration; Sulfur Dioxide AM—highest annual mean concentration; Sulfur Dioxide 1-Hr—highest 99th percentile 1-hour daily maximum concentration; Sulfur Dioxide 24-Hr—highest second maximum 24-hour concentration
Source: U.S. Environmental Protection Agency, Air Quality Monitoring Information, "Air Quality Statistics by City, 2019"

Charleston, South Carolina

Background

Charleston is located on the state's Atlantic coastline, 110 miles southeast of Columbia and 100 miles north of Savannah, Georgia. The city, named for King Charles II of England, is the county seat of Charleston County. Charleston is located on a bay at the end of a peninsula between the Ashley and Cooper rivers. The terrain is low-lying and coastal with nearby islands and inlets.

In 1670, English colonists established a nearby settlement, and subsequently moved to Charleston's present site. Charleston became an early trading center for rice, indigo, cotton and other goods. As the plantation economy grew, Charleston became a slave-trading center. In 1861, the Confederacy fired the cannon shot that launched the Civil War from the city's Battery, aimed at the Union's Fort Sumter in Charleston Harbor. Charleston was under siege during the Civil War, and experienced many difficulties during Reconstruction. Manufacturing industries including textiles and ironwork became important in the nineteenth century.

Charleston is part of a commercial and cultural center and southern transportation hub whose port is among the nation's busiest shipping facilities. Charleston's other economic sectors include manufacturing, health care, business and professional services, defense activity, retail and wholesale trade, tourism, education and construction.

Charleston is a popular tourist area, based on its scenery, history and recreation. The city's center is well known for its historic neighborhoods with distinctive early southern architecture and ambiance. As one of the first American cities in the early twentieth century to actively encourage historic restoration and preservation, Charleston has undertaken numerous revitalization initiatives, including the Charleston Place Hotel and retail complex, and Waterfront Park.

In 2000, the Confederate submarine the *HL Hunley*, which sank in 1864, was raised, and brought to a conservation laboratory at the old Charleston Naval Base. Author Patricia Cornwell has been involved in the creation of a museum to house the submarine.

Charleston is a center for health care and medical research. SPAWAR (US Navy Space and Naval Warfare Systems Command) is the area's largest single employer followed by the Medical University of South Carolina. Other area educational institutions include The College of Charleston, The Citadel Military College, Trident Technical College, Charleston Southern University, and a campus of Johnson and Wales University.

> The lowest number of passengers in a decade flew in and out of Charleston International Airport in 2020 after the coronavirus devastated the air travel industry.

The Charleston area has numerous parks, including one with a skateboard center, and public waterfront areas. Coastal recreation activities such as boating, swimming, fishing and beaches are popular, as are golf and other land sports.

The Charleston Museum is the nation's oldest, founded in 1773. There are also several former plantations in the area. Other attractions include the South Carolina Aquarium, the American Military Museum, the Drayton Hall Plantation Museum, the Gibbes Museum of Art, the Karpeles Manuscript Museum and the North Charleston Convention Center and Performing Arts Center. Cultural organizations include the Spoleto Festival and the annual Charleston International Film Festival, CIFF.

In 2015, 21-year-old Dylann Roof entered Charleston's historic Emanuel African Methodist Episcopal Church and opened fire, killing nine people. The attack garnered national attention, and sparked a debate on racism, Confederate symbolism in Southern states, and gun violence. A month after the attack, the Confederate battle flag was removed from the South Carolina State House.

In 2020, the city formally apologized for its role in the American slave trade.

The nearby Atlantic Ocean moderates the climate, especially in winter, and keeps summer a bit cooler than expected. Expect Indian summers in fall, and a possible hurricane, while spring sharply turns from the cold winds of March to lovely May. Severe storms are possible.

Rankings

General Rankings

- For its "Best for Vets: Places to Live 2019" rankings, *Military Times* evaluated 599 cities (83 large, 234 medium, 282 small) and compared the locations across three broad categories: veteran and military culture/services; economic indicators; and livability factors such as health, crime, traffic, and school quality. Charleston ranked #24 out of the top 50, in the medium-sized city category (population of 100,000-249,999). Data points more specific to veterans and the military weighed more heavily than others. rebootcamp.militarytimes.com, "Military Times Best Places to Live 2019," September 10, 2018

- The Charleston metro area was identified as one of America's fastest-growing areas in terms of population and business growth by *MagnifyMoney*. The area ranked #4 out of 35. The 100 most populous metro areas in the U.S. were evaluated on their change from 2011-2016 in the following categories: people and housing; workforce and employment opportunities; growing industry. www.businessinsider.com, "The 35 Cities in the US with the Biggest Influx of People, the Most Work Opportunities, and the Hottest Business Growth," August 12, 2018

- Charleston was selected as one of the best places to live in America by *Outside Magazine*. Criteria included population, park acreage, neighborhood and resident diversity, new and upcoming things of interest, and opportunities for outdoor adventure. *Outside Magazine*, "The 12 Best Places to Live in 2019," July 11, 2019

- Charleston appeared on *Travel + Leisure's* list of the 15 best cities in the United States. The city was ranked #1. Criteria: sights/landmarks; culture; food; friendliness; shopping; and overall value. *Travel + Leisure*, "The World's Best Awards 2020" July 8, 2020

- For its 33rd annual "Readers' Choice Awards" survey, *Condé Nast Traveler* ranked its readers' favorite cities in the U.S. These places brought feelings of comfort in a time of limited travel. The list was broken into large cities and cities under 250,000. Charleston ranked #1 in the small city category. *Condé Nast Traveler*, Readers' Choice Awards 2020, "Best Small Cities in the U.S." October 6, 2020

- In their seventh annual survey, Livability.com looked at data for more than 1,000 small to mid-sized U.S. cities to determine the rankings for Livability's "Top 100 Best Places to Live" in 2020. Charleston ranked #48. Criteria: housing and affordable living; vibrant economy; social and civic engagement; education; demographics; health care options; transportation & infrastructure; and abundant lifestyle amenities. *Livability.com*, "Top 100 Best Places to Live 2020" October 2020

Business/Finance Rankings

- The Brookings Institution ranked the nation's largest cities based on income inequality. Charleston was ranked #11 (#1 = greatest inequality). Criteria: the "95/20 ratio," a figure representing the income at which a household earns more than 95 percent of all other households, divided by the income at which a household earns more than only 20 percent of all other households. *Brookings Institution*, "Household Income Inequality, Largest Cities of 97 Large U.S. Metro Areas, 2014-2016," February 5, 2018

- The Brookings Institution ranked the 100 largest metro areas in the U.S. based on income inequality. Charleston was ranked #27 (#1 = greatest inequality). Criteria: the "95/20 ratio," a figure representing the income at which a household earns more than 95 percent of all other households, divided by the income at which a household earns more than only 20 percent of all other households. *Brookings Institution*, "Household Income Inequality, 100 Largest U.S. Metro Areas, 2014-2016," February 5, 2018

- The Charleston metro area appeared on the Milken Institute "2021 Best Performing Cities" list. Rank: #29 out of 200 large metro areas (population over 250,000). Criteria: job growth; wage and salary growth; high-tech output growth; housing affordability; household broadband access. *Milken Institute*, "Best-Performing Cities 2021," February 16, 2021

- *Forbes* ranked the 200 most populous metro areas to determine the nation's "Best Places for Business and Careers." The Charleston metro area was ranked #24. Criteria: costs (business and living); job growth (past and projected); income growth; quality of life; educational attainment (college and high school); projected economic growth; cultural and leisure opportunities; workplace tolerance laws; net migration patterns. *Forbes*, "The Best Places for Business and Careers 2019: Seattle Still On Top," October 30, 2019

Culture/Performing Arts Rankings

- Charleston was selected as one of "America's Favorite Cities." The city ranked #5 in the "Architecture" category. Respondents to an online survey were asked to rate their favorite place (population over 100,000) in over 65 categories. *Travelandleisure.com*, "America's Favorite Cities for Architecture 2016," March 2, 2017

Education Rankings

- Personal finance website *WalletHub* analyzed the 150 largest U.S. metropolitan statistical areas to determine where the most educated Americans are putting their degrees to work. Criteria: education levels; percentage of workers with degrees; education quality and attainment gap; public school quality rankings; quality and enrollment of each metro area's universities. Charleston was ranked #52 (#1 = most educated city). *www.WalletHub.com, "Most and Least Educated Cities in America," July 20, 2020*

Health/Fitness Rankings

- Trulia analyzed the 100 largest U.S. metro areas to identify the nation's best cities for weight loss, based on the percentage of adults who bike or walk to work, sporting goods stores, grocery stores, access to outdoor activities, weight-loss centers, gyms, and average space reserved for parks. Charleston ranked #6. *Trulia.com, "Where to Live to Get in Shape in the New Year," January 4, 2018*

- Charleston was identified as a "2021 Spring Allergy Capital." The area ranked #32 out of 100. Three groups of factors were used to identify the most challenging cities for people with allergies during the spring season: annual spring pollen levels; over the counter medicine use; number of board-certified allergy specialists. *Asthma and Allergy Foundation of America, "Spring Allergy Capitals 2021," February 23, 2021*

- Charleston was identified as a "2021 Fall Allergy Capital." The area ranked #42 out of 100. Three groups of factors were used to identify the most challenging cities for people with allergies during the fall season: annual fall pollen levels; over the counter medicine use; number of board-certified allergy specialists. *Asthma and Allergy Foundation of America, "Fall Allergy Capitals 2021," February 23, 2021*

- Charleston was identified as a "2019 Asthma Capital." The area ranked #33 out of the nation's 100 largest metropolitan areas. Criteria: estimated asthma prevalence; crude death rate from asthma; and ER visits due to asthma. Risk factors analyzed but not factored in the rankings: annual pollen score; annual air quality; public smoking laws; number of board-certified asthma specialists; rescue medication use; controller medication use; uninsured rate; poverty rate. *Asthma and Allergy Foundation of America, "Asthma Capitals 2019: The Most Challenging Places to Live With Asthma," May 7, 2019*

Real Estate Rankings

- *WalletHub* compared the most populated U.S. cities to determine which had the best markets for real estate agents. Charleston ranked #50 where demand was high and pay was the best. Criteria: sales per agent; annual median wage for real-estate agents; monthly average starting salary for real estate agents; real estate job density and competition; unemployment rate; home turnover rate; housing-market health index; and other relevant metrics. *www.WalletHub.com, "2019's Best Places to Be a Real Estate Agent," April 24, 2019*

- According to Penske Truck Rental, the Charleston metro area was named the #6 moving destination in 2019, based on one-way consumer truck rental reservations made through Penske's website, rental locations, and reservations call center. *gopenske.com/blog, "Penske Truck Rental's 2019 Top Moving Destinations," January 22, 2020*

- Charleston was ranked #156 out of 268 metro areas in terms of housing affordability in 2020 by the National Association of Home Builders (#1 = most affordable). Criteria: the share of homes sold in that area affordable to a family earning the local median income, based on standard mortgage underwriting criteria. *National Association of Home Builders®, NAHB-Wells Fargo Housing Opportunity Index, 4th Quarter 2020*

Safety Rankings

- Allstate ranked the 200 largest cities in America in terms of driver safety. Charleston ranked #80. Criteria: internal property damage claims over a two-year period from January 2016 to December 2017. The report helps increase the importance of safety and awareness behind the wheel. *Allstate, "Allstate America's Best Drivers Report, 2019" June 24, 2019*

- The National Insurance Crime Bureau ranked 384 metro areas in the U.S. in terms of per capita rates of vehicle theft. The Charleston metro area ranked #56 (#1 = highest rate). Criteria: number of vehicle theft offenses per 100,000 inhabitants in 2019. *National Insurance Crime Bureau, "Hot Spots 2019," July 21, 2020*

Seniors/Retirement Rankings

- From its Best Cities for Successful Aging indexes, the Milken Institute generated rankings for metropolitan areas, weighing data in nine categories—health care, wellness, living arrangements, transportation and convenience, financial characteristics, education, employment, community engagement, and overall livability. The Charleston metro area was ranked #39 overall in the large metro area category. *Milken Institute, "Best Cities for Successful Aging, 2017" March 14, 2017*

- Charleston was identified as #9 of 20 most popular places to retire in the Southeast region by *Topretirements.com*. The site separated its annual "Best Places to Retire" list by major U.S. regions for 2019. The list reflects the 20 cities that visitors to the website are most interested in for retirement, based on the number of times a city's review was viewed on the website. *Topretirements.com, "20 Most Popular Places to Retire in the Southeast: 2019," October 16, 2019*

Women/Minorities Rankings

- *Travel + Leisure* listed the best cities in and around the US for a memorable and fun girls' trip, even on a budget. Whether it is for a special occasion or just to get away, Charleston is sure to have something for all the ladies in your tribe. *Travel + Leisure, "25 Girls' Weekend Getaways That Won't Break the Bank," June 8, 2020*

- Personal finance website *WalletHub* compared more than 180 U.S. cities across two key dimensions, "Hispanic Business-Friendliness" and "Hispanic Purchasing Power," to arrive at the most favorable conditions for Hispanic entrepreneurs. Charleston was ranked #81 out of 182. Criteria includes: share of Hispanic-Owned Businesses; Hispanic entrepreneurship rate to median annual income of Hispanics; Small Business-Friendliness score; cost of living; and number of Hispanics with at least a bachelor's degree. *WalletHub.com, "2019's Best Cities for Hispanic Entrepreneurs," May 1, 2019*

Miscellaneous Rankings

- In *Condé Nast Traveler* magazine's 2020 Readers' Choice Survey, Charleston made the top ten list of friendliest American cities. Charleston ranked #2. *www.cntraveler.com, "The Friendliest Cities in the U.S.," November 30, 2020*

- *WalletHub* compared the 150 most populated U.S. cities to determine their operating efficiency. A "Quality of City Services" score was constructed for each city and then divided by the total budget per capita to reveal which were managed the best. Charleston ranked #47. Criteria: financial stability; economy; education; safety; health; infrastructure and pollution. *www.WalletHub.com, "2020's Best- & Worst-Run Cities in America," June 29, 2020*

Business Environment

DEMOGRAPHICS

Population Growth

Area	1990 Census	2000 Census	2010 Census	2019* Estimate	Population Growth (%) 1990-2019	Population Growth (%) 2010-2019
City	96,102	96,650	120,083	135,257	40.7	12.6
MSA[1]	506,875	549,033	664,607	774,508	52.8	16.5
U.S.	248,709,873	281,421,906	308,745,538	324,697,795	30.6	5.2

Note: (1) Figures cover the Charleston-North Charleston, SC Metropolitan Statistical Area; (*) 2015-2019 5-year estimated population
Source: U.S. Census Bureau, 1990 Census, Census 2000, Census 2010, 2015-2019 American Community Survey 5-Year Estimates

Household Size

Area	One	Two	Three	Four	Five	Six	Seven or More	Average Household Size
City	35.5	37.9	14.3	9.0	2.5	0.7	0.2	2.30
MSA[1]	29.1	35.6	16.5	11.8	4.7	1.6	0.7	2.60
U.S.	27.9	33.9	15.6	12.9	6.0	2.3	1.4	2.60

Note: (1) Figures cover the Charleston-North Charleston, SC Metropolitan Statistical Area
Source: U.S. Census Bureau, 2015-2019 American Community Survey 5-Year Estimates

Race

Area	White Alone[2] (%)	Black Alone[2] (%)	Asian Alone[2] (%)	AIAN[3] Alone[2] (%)	NHOPI[4] Alone[2] (%)	Other Race Alone[2] (%)	Two or More Races (%)
City	74.1	21.7	1.9	0.1	0.1	0.6	1.5
MSA[1]	67.6	25.6	1.8	0.3	0.1	1.9	2.7
U.S.	72.5	12.7	5.5	0.8	0.2	4.9	3.3

Note: (1) Figures cover the Charleston-North Charleston, SC Metropolitan Statistical Area; (2) Alone is defined as not being in combination with one or more other races; (3) American Indian and Alaska Native; (4) Native Hawaiian and Other Pacific Islander
Source: U.S. Census Bureau, 2015-2019 American Community Survey 5-Year Estimates

Hispanic or Latino Origin

Area	Total (%)	Mexican (%)	Puerto Rican (%)	Cuban (%)	Other (%)
City	3.2	1.3	0.5	0.2	1.2
MSA[1]	5.6	2.7	0.8	0.1	2.0
U.S.	18.0	11.2	1.7	0.7	4.3

Note: Persons of Hispanic or Latino origin can be of any race; (1) Figures cover the Charleston-North Charleston, SC Metropolitan Statistical Area
Source: U.S. Census Bureau, 2015-2019 American Community Survey 5-Year Estimates

Ancestry

Area	German	Irish	English	American	Italian	Polish	French[2]	Scottish	Dutch
City	10.4	9.9	9.9	23.1	4.4	1.9	2.2	2.7	0.7
MSA[1]	9.9	9.7	8.2	13.3	3.7	1.9	2.0	2.5	0.8
U.S.	13.3	9.7	7.2	6.2	5.1	2.8	2.3	1.7	1.2

Note: Figures are the percentage of the total population reporting a particular ancestry. The nine most commonly reported ancestries in the U.S. are shown. Figures include multiple ancestries (e.g. if a person reported being Irish and Italian, they were included in both columns); (1) Figures cover the Charleston-North Charleston, SC Metropolitan Statistical Area; (2) Excludes Basque
Source: U.S. Census Bureau, 2015-2019 American Community Survey 5-Year Estimates

Foreign-born Population

Area	Any Foreign Country	Asia	Mexico	Europe	Caribbean	Central America[2]	South America	Africa	Canada
City	4.8	1.7	0.6	1.3	0.4	0.1	0.3	0.2	0.2
MSA[1]	5.4	1.5	1.1	1.0	0.3	0.5	0.5	0.2	0.2
U.S.	13.6	4.2	3.5	1.5	1.3	1.1	1.0	0.7	0.2

Note: (1) Figures cover the Charleston-North Charleston, SC Metropolitan Statistical Area; (2) Excludes Mexico.
Source: U.S. Census Bureau, 2015-2019 American Community Survey 5-Year Estimates

Charleston, South Carolina

Marital Status

Area	Never Married	Now Married[2]	Separated	Widowed	Divorced
City	41.9	41.6	1.5	5.2	9.7
MSA[1]	34.5	46.9	2.4	5.5	10.7
U.S.	33.4	48.1	1.9	5.8	10.9

Note: Figures are percentages and cover the population 15 years of age and older; (1) Figures cover the Charleston-North Charleston, SC Metropolitan Statistical Area; (2) Excludes separated
Source: U.S. Census Bureau, 2015-2019 American Community Survey 5-Year Estimates

Disability by Age

Area	All Ages	Under 18 Years Old	18 to 64 Years Old	65 Years and Over
City	9.9	2.8	7.2	30.6
MSA[1]	12.2	4.0	10.0	33.9
U.S.	12.6	4.2	10.3	34.5

Note: Figures show percent of the civilian noninstitutionalized population that reported having a disability. Disability status is determined from six types of difficulty: vision, hearing, cognitive, ambulatory, self-care, and independent living. For children under 5 years old, hearing and vision difficulty are used to determine disability status. For children between the ages of 5 and 14, disability status is determined from hearing, vision, cognitive, ambulatory, and self-care difficulties. For people aged 15 years and older, they are considered to have a disability if they have difficulty with any one of the six difficulty types; Note: (1) Figures cover the Charleston-North Charleston, SC Metropolitan Statistical Area
Source: U.S. Census Bureau, 2015-2019 American Community Survey 5-Year Estimates

Age

Area	Under Age 5	Age 5–19	Age 20–34	Age 35–44	Age 45–54	Age 55–64	Age 65–74	Age 75–84	Age 85+	Median Age
City	6.0	14.5	29.8	12.4	10.7	11.9	9.0	3.7	1.9	34.8
MSA[1]	6.1	18.5	22.1	13.2	12.7	12.8	9.3	3.9	1.5	37.2
U.S.	6.1	19.1	20.7	12.6	13.0	12.9	9.1	4.6	1.9	38.1

Note: (1) Figures cover the Charleston-North Charleston, SC Metropolitan Statistical Area
Source: U.S. Census Bureau, 2015-2019 American Community Survey 5-Year Estimates

Gender

Area	Males	Females	Males per 100 Females
City	63,863	71,394	89.5
MSA[1]	378,374	396,134	95.5
U.S.	159,886,919	164,810,876	97.0

Note: (1) Figures cover the Charleston-North Charleston, SC Metropolitan Statistical Area
Source: U.S. Census Bureau, 2015-2019 American Community Survey 5-Year Estimates

Religious Groups by Family

Area	Catholic	Baptist	Non-Den.	Methodist[2]	Lutheran	LDS[3]	Pentecostal	Presbyterian[4]	Muslim[5]	Judaism
MSA[1]	6.2	12.4	7.1	10.0	1.1	1.0	2.0	2.4	0.2	0.3
U.S.	19.1	9.3	4.0	4.0	2.3	2.0	1.9	1.6	0.8	0.7

Note: Figures are the number of adherents as a percentage of the total population; (1) Figures cover the Charleston-North Charleston, SC Metropolitan Statistical Area; (2) Methodist/Pietist; (3) Latter Day Saints; (4) Reformed; (5) Figures are estimates
Source: Association of Statisticians of American Religious Bodies, 2010 U.S. Religion Census: Religious Congregations & Membership Study

Religious Groups by Tradition

Area	Catholic	Evangelical Protestant	Mainline Protestant	Other Tradition	Black Protestant	Orthodox
MSA[1]	6.2	19.7	11.2	1.9	7.3	0.1
U.S.	19.1	16.2	7.3	4.3	1.6	0.3

Note: Figures are the number of adherents as a percentage of the total population; (1) Figures cover the Charleston-North Charleston, SC Metropolitan Statistical Area
Source: Association of Statisticians of American Religious Bodies, 2010 U.S. Religion Census: Religious Congregations & Membership Study

ECONOMY

Gross Metropolitan Product

Area	2017	2018	2019	2020	Rank[2]
MSA[1]	42.5	44.6	46.7	49.0	67

Note: Figures are in billions of dollars; (1) Figures cover the Charleston-North Charleston, SC Metropolitan Statistical Area; (2) Rank is based on 2018 data and ranges from 1 to 381
Source: U.S. Conference of Mayors, U.S. Metro Economies: GMP & Employment 2018-2020, September 2019

Charleston, South Carolina

Economic Growth

Area	2015-17 (%)	2018 (%)	2019 (%)	2020 (%)	Rank[2]
MSA[1]	5.0	2.4	2.9	2.6	16
U.S.	1.9	2.9	2.3	2.1	—

Note: Figures are real gross metropolitan product (GMP) growth rates and represent average annual percent change; (1) Figures cover the Charleston-North Charleston, SC Metropolitan Statistical Area; (2) Rank is based on 2017 2-year average annual percent change and ranges from 1 to 381
Source: U.S. Conference of Mayors, U.S. Metro Economies: GMP & Employment 2018-2020, September 2019

Metropolitan Area Exports

Area	2014	2015	2016	2017	2018	2019	Rank[2]
MSA[1]	5,866.7	6,457.5	9,508.1	8,845.2	10,943.2	16,337.9	23

Note: Figures are in millions of dollars; (1) Figures cover the Charleston-North Charleston, SC Metropolitan Statistical Area; (2) Rank is based on 2019 data and ranges from 1 to 386
Source: U.S. Department of Commerce, International Trade Administration, Office of Trade and Economic Analysis, Industry and Analysis, Exports by Metropolitan Area, data extracted March 24, 2021

Building Permits

Area	Single-Family 2018	Single-Family 2019	Pct. Chg.	Multi-Family 2018	Multi-Family 2019	Pct. Chg.	Total 2018	Total 2019	Pct. Chg.
City	810	828	2.2	354	360	1.7	1,164	1,188	2.1
MSA[1]	4,787	4,758	-0.6	2,215	1,937	-12.6	7,002	6,695	-4.4
U.S.	855,300	862,100	0.7	473,500	523,900	10.6	1,328,800	1,386,000	4.3

Note: (1) Figures cover the Charleston-North Charleston, SC Metropolitan Statistical Area; Figures represent new, privately-owned housing units authorized (unadjusted data); All permit data are based on estimates with imputation
Source: U.S. Census Bureau, Manufacturing, Mining, and Construction Statistics, Building Permits, 2018, 2019

Bankruptcy Filings

Area	Business Filings 2019	Business Filings 2020	% Chg.	Nonbusiness Filings 2019	Nonbusiness Filings 2020	% Chg.
Charleston County	19	21	10.5	356	261	-26.7
U.S.	22,780	21,655	-4.9	752,160	522,808	-30.5

Note: Business filings include Chapter 7, Chapter 9, Chapter 11, Chapter 12, Chapter 13, Chapter 15, and Section 304; Nonbusiness filings include Chapter 7, Chapter 11, and Chapter 13
Source: Administrative Office of the U.S. Courts, Business and Nonbusiness Bankruptcy, County Cases Commenced by Chapter of the Bankruptcy Code, During the 12-Month Period Ending December 31, 2019 and Business and Nonbusiness Bankruptcy, County Cases Commenced by Chapter of the Bankruptcy Code, During the 12-Month Period Ending December 31, 2020

Housing Vacancy Rates

Area	Gross Vacancy Rate[2] (%) 2018	2019	2020	Year-Round Vacancy Rate[3] (%) 2018	2019	2020	Rental Vacancy Rate[4] (%) 2018	2019	2020	Homeowner Vacancy Rate[5] (%) 2018	2019	2020
MSA[1]	16.0	18.4	18.1	14.5	16.6	16.5	17.0	16.7	27.7	3.4	2.2	2.3
U.S.	12.3	12.0	10.6	9.7	9.5	8.2	6.9	6.7	6.3	1.5	1.4	1.0

Note: (1) Figures cover the Charleston-North Charleston, SC Metropolitan Statistical Area; (2) The percentage of the total housing inventory that is vacant; (3) The percentage of the housing inventory (excluding seasonal units) that is year-round vacant; (4) The percentage of rental inventory that is vacant for rent; (5) The percentage of homeowner inventory that is vacant for sale
Source: U.S. Census Bureau, Housing Vacancies and Homeownership Annual Statistics: 2018, 2019, 2020

INCOME

Income

Area	Per Capita ($)	Median Household ($)	Average Household ($)
City	42,872	68,438	98,288
MSA[1]	35,011	63,649	88,023
U.S.	34,103	62,843	88,607

Note: (1) Figures cover the Charleston-North Charleston, SC Metropolitan Statistical Area
Source: U.S. Census Bureau, 2015-2019 American Community Survey 5-Year Estimates

Household Income Distribution

Area	Under $15,000	$15,000 -$24,999	$25,000 -$34,999	$35,000 -$49,999	$50,000 -$74,999	$75,000 -$99,999	$100,000 -$149,999	$150,000 and up
City	11.2	7.7	7.0	10.7	17.0	12.8	17.4	16.1
MSA[1]	10.0	8.4	8.5	12.1	18.4	13.5	15.6	13.6
U.S.	10.3	8.9	8.9	12.3	17.2	12.7	15.1	14.5

Note: (1) Figures cover the Charleston-North Charleston, SC Metropolitan Statistical Area
Source: U.S. Census Bureau, 2015-2019 American Community Survey 5-Year Estimates

Poverty Rate

Area	All Ages	Under 18 Years Old	18 to 64 Years Old	65 Years and Over
City	13.2	14.7	13.8	8.8
MSA[1]	12.9	18.9	11.7	8.7
U.S.	13.4	18.5	12.6	9.3

Note: Figures are percentage of people whose income during the past 12 months was below the poverty level;
(1) Figures cover the Charleston-North Charleston, SC Metropolitan Statistical Area
Source: U.S. Census Bureau, 2015-2019 American Community Survey 5-Year Estimates

CITY FINANCES

City Government Finances

Component	2017 ($000)	2017 ($ per capita)
Total Revenues	382,743	2,886
Total Expenditures	277,977	2,096
Debt Outstanding	26,301	198
Cash and Securities[1]	282,009	2,127

Note: (1) Cash and security holdings of a government at the close of its fiscal year, including those of its dependent agencies, utilities, and liquor stores.
Source: U.S. Census Bureau, State & Local Government Finances 2017

City Government Revenue by Source

Source	2017 ($000)	2017 ($ per capita)	2017 (%)
General Revenue			
From Federal Government	6,758	51	1.8
From State Government	5,592	42	1.5
From Local Governments	0	0	0.0
Taxes			
Property	76,387	576	20.0
Sales and Gross Receipts	48,528	366	12.7
Personal Income	0	0	0.0
Corporate Income	0	0	0.0
Motor Vehicle License	0	0	0.0
Other Taxes	51,709	390	13.5
Current Charges	41,101	310	10.7
Liquor Store	0	0	0.0
Utility	119,937	904	31.3
Employee Retirement	0	0	0.0

Source: U.S. Census Bureau, State & Local Government Finances 2017

City Government Expenditures by Function

Function	2017 ($000)	2017 ($ per capita)	2017 (%)
General Direct Expenditures			
Air Transportation	0	0	0.0
Corrections	0	0	0.0
Education	0	0	0.0
Employment Security Administration	0	0	0.0
Financial Administration	9,240	69	3.3
Fire Protection	28,955	218	10.4
General Public Buildings	149	1	0.1
Governmental Administration, Other	4,686	35	1.7
Health	0	0	0.0
Highways	8,190	61	2.9
Hospitals	0	0	0.0
Housing and Community Development	4,042	30	1.5
Interest on General Debt	1,011	7	0.4
Judicial and Legal	2,489	18	0.9
Libraries	0	0	0.0
Parking	11,844	89	4.3
Parks and Recreation	17,360	130	6.2
Police Protection	49,085	370	17.7
Public Welfare	556	4	0.2
Sewerage	3,327	25	1.2
Solid Waste Management	6,241	47	2.2
Veterans' Services	0	0	0.0
Liquor Store	0	0	0.0
Utility	101,110	762	36.4
Employee Retirement	0	0	0.0

Source: U.S. Census Bureau, State & Local Government Finances 2017

Charleston, South Carolina

EMPLOYMENT

Labor Force and Employment

Area	Civilian Labor Force Dec. 2019	Civilian Labor Force Dec. 2020	% Chg.	Workers Employed Dec. 2019	Workers Employed Dec. 2020	% Chg.
City	75,308	72,571	-3.6	73,919	69,583	-5.9
MSA[1]	395,683	381,666	-3.5	387,938	365,144	-5.9
U.S.	164,007,000	160,017,000	-2.4	158,504,000	149,613,000	-5.6

Note: Data is not seasonally adjusted and covers workers 16 years of age and older; (1) Figures cover the Charleston-North Charleston, SC Metropolitan Statistical Area
Source: Bureau of Labor Statistics, Local Area Unemployment Statistics

Unemployment Rate

Area	Jan.	Feb.	Mar.	Apr.	May	Jun.	Jul.	Aug.	Sep.	Oct.	Nov.	Dec.
City	2.2	2.3	2.5	14.6	14.0	9.9	9.7	7.1	5.0	3.9	3.9	4.1
MSA[1]	2.4	2.5	2.6	12.1	12.2	9.0	9.2	6.9	5.0	4.0	4.0	4.3
U.S.	4.0	3.8	4.5	14.4	13.0	11.2	10.5	8.5	7.7	6.6	6.4	6.5

Note: Data is not seasonally adjusted and covers workers 16 years of age and older; (1) Figures cover the Charleston-North Charleston, SC Metropolitan Statistical Area
Source: Bureau of Labor Statistics, Local Area Unemployment Statistics

Average Wages

Occupation	$/Hr.	Occupation	$/Hr.
Accountants and Auditors	32.90	Maintenance and Repair Workers	19.60
Automotive Mechanics	23.70	Marketing Managers	60.30
Bookkeepers	18.30	Network and Computer Systems Admin.	41.70
Carpenters	28.30	Nurses, Licensed Practical	23.20
Cashiers	11.60	Nurses, Registered	33.50
Computer Programmers	39.20	Nursing Assistants	14.90
Computer Systems Analysts	41.10	Office Clerks, General	15.20
Computer User Support Specialists	26.70	Physical Therapists	37.60
Construction Laborers	16.80	Physicians	134.80
Cooks, Restaurant	13.20	Plumbers, Pipefitters and Steamfitters	26.00
Customer Service Representatives	18.80	Police and Sheriff's Patrol Officers	24.30
Dentists	70.80	Postal Service Mail Carriers	25.10
Electricians	22.40	Real Estate Sales Agents	24.20
Engineers, Electrical	47.80	Retail Salespersons	14.30
Fast Food and Counter Workers	10.80	Sales Representatives, Technical/Scientific	31.30
Financial Managers	69.90	Secretaries, Exc. Legal/Medical/Executive	18.00
First-Line Supervisors of Office Workers	27.70	Security Guards	15.40
General and Operations Managers	59.90	Surgeons	n/a
Hairdressers/Cosmetologists	15.80	Teacher Assistants, Exc. Postsecondary*	12.40
Home Health and Personal Care Aides	12.20	Teachers, Secondary School, Exc. Sp. Ed.*	28.30
Janitors and Cleaners	11.90	Telemarketers	9.30
Landscaping/Groundskeeping Workers	15.20	Truck Drivers, Heavy/Tractor-Trailer	20.10
Lawyers	52.10	Truck Drivers, Light/Delivery Services	17.40
Maids and Housekeeping Cleaners	11.60	Waiters and Waitresses	9.80

Note: Wage data covers the Charleston-North Charleston, SC Metropolitan Statistical Area; (*) Hourly wages were calculated from annual wage data based on a 40 hour work week; n/a not available.
Source: Bureau of Labor Statistics, Metro Area Occupational Employment & Wage Estimates, May 2020

Employment by Industry

Sector	MSA[1] Number of Employees	MSA[1] Percent of Total	U.S. Percent of Total
Construction, Mining, and Logging	20,700	5.7	5.5
Education and Health Services	43,100	11.9	16.3
Financial Activities	16,100	4.4	6.1
Government	66,000	18.2	15.2
Information	5,500	1.5	1.9
Leisure and Hospitality	41,900	11.6	9.0
Manufacturing	27,800	7.7	8.5
Other Services	13,800	3.8	3.8
Professional and Business Services	56,300	15.6	14.4
Retail Trade	44,600	12.3	10.9
Transportation, Warehousing, and Utilities	15,400	4.3	4.6
Wholesale Trade	10,700	3.0	3.9

Note: Figures are non-farm employment as of December 2020. Figures are not seasonally adjusted and include workers 16 years of age and older; (1) Figures cover the Charleston-North Charleston, SC Metropolitan Statistical Area
Source: Bureau of Labor Statistics, Current Employment Statistics, Employment, Hours, and Earnings

Employment by Occupation

Occupation Classification	City (%)	MSA[1] (%)	U.S. (%)
Management, Business, Science, and Arts	49.0	39.5	38.5
Natural Resources, Construction, and Maintenance	5.5	9.1	8.9
Production, Transportation, and Material Moving	7.0	11.4	13.2
Sales and Office	21.3	22.0	21.6
Service	17.0	17.9	17.8

Note: Figures cover employed civilians 16 years of age and older; (1) Figures cover the Charleston-North Charleston, SC Metropolitan Statistical Area
Source: U.S. Census Bureau, 2015-2019 American Community Survey 5-Year Estimates

Occupations with Greatest Projected Employment Growth: 2020 – 2022

Occupation[1]	2020 Employment	2022 Projected Employment	Numeric Employment Change	Percent Employment Change
Stockers and Order Fillers	28,530	29,560	1,030	3.6
Real Estate Sales Agents	13,120	13,440	320	2.4
Laborers and Freight, Stock, and Material Movers, Hand	64,390	64,670	280	0.4
Construction Laborers	23,860	24,130	270	1.1
Industrial Machinery Mechanics	9,530	9,740	210	2.2
Software Developers and Software Quality Assurance Analysts and Testers	7,930	8,120	190	2.4
Insurance Sales Agents	8,210	8,400	190	2.3
Medical and Health Services Managers	6,180	6,320	140	2.3
Industrial Engineers	7,510	7,650	140	1.9
Nurse Practitioners	2,580	2,720	140	5.4

Note: Projections cover South Carolina; (1) Sorted by numeric employment change
Source: www.projectionscentral.com, State Occupational Projections, 2020–2022 Short-Term Projections

Fastest-Growing Occupations: 2020 – 2022

Occupation[1]	2020 Employment	2022 Projected Employment	Numeric Employment Change	Percent Employment Change
Butchers and Meat Cutters	1,610	1,720	110	6.8
Nurse Practitioners	2,580	2,720	140	5.4
Information Security Analysts (SOC 2018)	1,640	1,700	60	3.7
Stockers and Order Fillers	28,530	29,560	1,030	3.6
Multiple Machine Tool Setters, Operators, and Tenders, Metal and Plastic	4,450	4,580	130	2.9
Personal Financial Advisors	2,520	2,590	70	2.8
Meat, Poultry, and Fish Cutters and Trimmers	4,700	4,830	130	2.8
Software Developers and Software Quality Assurance Analysts and Testers	7,930	8,120	190	2.4
Real Estate Sales Agents	13,120	13,440	320	2.4
Bakers	2,080	2,130	50	2.4

Note: Projections cover South Carolina; (1) Sorted by percent employment change and excludes occupations with numeric employment change less than 50
Source: www.projectionscentral.com, State Occupational Projections, 2020–2022 Short-Term Projections

TAXES

State Corporate Income Tax Rates

State	Tax Rate (%)	Income Brackets ($)	Num. of Brackets	Financial Institution Tax Rate (%)[a]	Federal Income Tax Ded.
South Carolina	5.0	Flat rate	1	4.5 (v)	No

Note: Tax rates as of January 1, 2021; (a) Rates listed are the corporate income tax rate applied to financial institutions or excise taxes based on income. Some states have other taxes based upon the value of deposits or shares; (v) South Carolina taxes savings and loans at a 6% rate.
Source: Federation of Tax Administrators, State Corporate Income Tax Rates, January 1, 2021

State Individual Income Tax Rates

State	Tax Rate (%)	Income Brackets ($)	Personal Exemptions ($) Single	Personal Exemptions ($) Married	Personal Exemptions ($) Depend.	Standard Ded. ($) Single	Standard Ded. ($) Married
South Carolina (a)	0.0 - 7.0	3,110 - 15,560	(d)	(d)	(d)	12,550	25,100 (d)

Note: Tax rates as of January 1, 2021; Local- and county-level taxes are not included; Federal income tax is not deductible on state income tax returns; (a) 19 states have statutory provision for automatically adjusting to the rate of inflation the dollar values of the income tax brackets, standard deductions, and/or personal exemptions. Michigan indexes the personal exemption only. Oregon does not index the income brackets for $125,000 and over; (d) These states use the personal exemption/standard deduction amounts provided in the federal Internal Revenue Code.
Source: Federation of Tax Administrators, State Individual Income Tax Rates, January 1, 2021

Various State Sales and Excise Tax Rates

State	State Sales Tax (%)	Gasoline[1] (¢/gal.)	Cigarette[2] ($/pack)	Spirits[3] ($/gal.)	Wine[4] ($/gal.)	Beer[5] ($/gal.)	Recreational Marijuana (%)
South Carolina	6	22.75	0.57	5.42	1.08	0.77	Not legal

Note: All tax rates as of January 1, 2021; (1) The American Petroleum Institute has developed a methodology for determining the average tax rate on a gallon of fuel. Rates may include any of the following: excise taxes, environmental fees, storage tank fees, other fees or taxes, general sales tax, and local taxes; (2) The federal excise tax of $1.0066 per pack and local taxes are not included; (3) Rates are those applicable to off-premise sales of 40% alcohol by volume (a.b.v.) distilled spirits in 750ml containers. Local excise taxes are excluded; (4) Rates are those applicable to off-premise sales of 11% a.b.v. non-carbonated wine in 750ml containers; (5) Rates are those applicable to off-premise sales of 4.7% a.b.v. beer in 12 ounce containers.
Source: Tax Foundation, 2021 Facts & Figures: How Does Your State Compare?

State Business Tax Climate Index Rankings

State	Overall Rank	Corporate Tax Rank	Individual Income Tax Rank	Sales Tax Rank	Property Tax Rank	Unemployment Insurance Tax Rank
South Carolina	33	5	34	31	34	24

Note: The index is a measure of how each state's tax laws affect economic performance. The lower the rank, the more favorable a state's tax system is for business. States without a given tax are given a ranking of 1. The scores/rankings for the District of Columbia do not affect other states. The 2021 index represents the tax climate as of July 1, 2020.
Source: Tax Foundation, State Business Tax Climate Index 2021

TRANSPORTATION

Means of Transportation to Work

Area	Car/Truck/Van Drove Alone	Car/Truck/Van Car-pooled	Public Transportation Bus	Public Transportation Subway	Public Transportation Railroad	Bicycle	Walked	Other Means	Worked at Home
City	76.4	7.0	0.8	0.0	0.0	2.4	5.0	1.7	6.8
MSA[1]	81.1	8.2	0.7	0.0	0.0	0.7	2.3	1.2	5.8
U.S.	76.3	9.0	2.4	1.9	0.6	0.5	2.7	1.4	5.2

Note: Figures are percentages and cover workers 16 years of age and older; (1) Figures cover the Charleston-North Charleston, SC Metropolitan Statistical Area
Source: U.S. Census Bureau, 2015-2019 American Community Survey 5-Year Estimates

Travel Time to Work

Area	Less Than 10 Minutes	10 to 19 Minutes	20 to 29 Minutes	30 to 44 Minutes	45 to 59 Minutes	60 to 89 Minutes	90 Minutes or More
City	11.4	31.9	26.3	21.1	6.5	1.5	1.3
MSA[1]	8.7	25.6	24.3	26.0	9.3	4.4	1.7
U.S.	12.2	28.4	20.8	20.8	8.3	6.4	2.9

Note: Note: Figures are percentages and include workers 16 years old and over; (1) Figures cover the Charleston-North Charleston, SC Metropolitan Statistical Area
Source: U.S. Census Bureau, 2015-2019 American Community Survey 5-Year Estimates

Key Congestion Measures

Measure	1982	1992	2002	2012	2017
Annual Hours of Delay, Total (000)	3,012	7,239	12,103	18,939	21,087
Annual Hours of Delay, Per Auto Commuter	15	28	37	47	51
Annual Congestion Cost, Total (million $)	23	76	163	339	388
Annual Congestion Cost, Per Auto Commuter ($)	303	501	653	801	865

Note: Covers the Charleston-North Charleston SC urban area
Source: Texas A&M Transportation Institute, 2019 Urban Mobility Report

Freeway Travel Time Index

Measure	1982	1987	1992	1997	2002	2007	2012	2017
Urban Area Index[1]	1.08	1.12	1.15	1.19	1.21	1.23	1.23	1.23
Urban Area Rank[1,2]	28	26	26	26	31	31	31	30

Note: Freeway Travel Time Index—the ratio of travel time in the peak period to the travel time at free-flow conditions. For example, a value of 1.30 indicates a 20-minute free-flow trip takes 26 minutes in the peak (20 minutes x 1.30 = 26 minutes); (1) Covers the Charleston-North Charleston SC urban area; (2) Rank is based on 101 larger urban areas (#1 = highest travel time index)
Source: Texas A&M Transportation Institute, 2019 Urban Mobility Report

Public Transportation

Agency Name / Mode of Transportation	Vehicles Operated in Maximum Service[1]	Annual Unlinked Passenger Trips[2] (in thous.)	Annual Passenger Miles[3] (in thous.)
Charleston Area Regional Transportation (CARTA)			
Bus (purchased transportation)	53	2,991.2	13,939.1
Commuter Bus (purchased transportation)	8	133.7	2,015.4
Demand Response (purchased transportation)	22	75.8	651.3

Note: (1) Number of revenue vehicles operated by the given mode and type of service to meet the annual maximum service requirement. This is the revenue vehicle count during the peak season of the year; on the week and day that maximum service is provided. Vehicles operated in maximum service (VOMS) exclude atypical days and one-time special events; (2) Number of passengers who boarded public transportation vehicles. Passengers are counted each time they board a vehicle no matter how many vehicles they use to travel from their origin to their destination. (3) Sum of the distances ridden by all passengers during the entire fiscal year.
Source: Federal Transit Administration, National Transit Database, 2019

Air Transportation

Airport Name and Code / Type of Service	Passenger Airlines[1]	Passenger Enplanements	Freight Carriers[2]	Freight (lbs)
Charleston International Airport (CHS)				
Domestic service (U.S. carriers - 2020)	29	944,535	11	24,372,905
International service (U.S. carriers - 2019)	2	228	2	7,039,894

Note: (1) Includes all U.S.-based major, minor and commuter airlines that carried at least one passenger during the year; (2) Includes all U.S.-based airlines and freight carriers that transported at least one pound of freight during the year.
Source: Bureau of Transportation Statistics, The Intermodal Transportation Database, Air Carriers: T-100 Domestic Market (U.S. Carriers), 2020; Bureau of Transportation Statistics, The Intermodal Transportation Database, Air Carriers: T-100 International Market (U.S. Carriers), 2019

BUSINESSES

Major Business Headquarters

Company Name	Industry	Rankings Fortune[1]	Forbes[2]
No companies listed	-	-	-

Note: (1) Companies that produce a 10-K are ranked 1 to 500 based on 2019 revenue; (2) All private companies with at least $2 billion in annual revenue through the end of their most current fiscal year are ranked 1 to 219; companies listed are headquartered in the city; dashes indicate no ranking
Source: Fortune, "Fortune 500," June/July 2020; Forbes, "America's Largest Private Companies," 2020

Living Environment

COST OF LIVING

Cost of Living Index

Composite Index	Groceries	Housing	Utilities	Transportation	Health Care	Misc. Goods/Services
100.0	104.2	97.6	121.6	93.8	99.0	96.2

Note: The Cost of Living Index measures regional differences in the cost of consumer goods and services, excluding taxes and non-consumer expenditures, for professional and managerial households in the top income quintile. It is based on more than 50,000 prices covering almost 60 different items for which prices are collected three times a year by chambers of commerce, economic development organizations or university applied economic centers in each participating urban area. The numbers shown should be read as a percentage above or below the national average of 100. For example, a value of 115.4 in the groceries column indicates that grocery prices are 15.4% higher than the national average. Small differences in the index numbers should not be interpreted as significant; Figures cover the Charleston-N Charleston SC urban area.
Source: The Council for Community and Economic Research, Cost of Living Index, 2020

Grocery Prices

Area[1]	T-Bone Steak ($/pound)	Frying Chicken ($/pound)	Whole Milk ($/half gal.)	Eggs ($/dozen)	Orange Juice ($/64 oz.)	Coffee ($/11.5 oz.)
City[2]	12.80	1.27	2.25	1.26	3.53	4.42
Avg.	11.78	1.39	2.05	1.47	3.57	4.34
Min.	8.03	0.94	1.03	0.74	2.94	3.02
Max.	15.86	2.65	4.31	3.77	5.44	8.69

Note: (1) Values for the local area are compared with the average, minimum and maximum values for all 284 areas in the Cost of Living Index; (2) Figures cover the Charleston-N Charleston SC urban area; **T-Bone Steak** (price per pound); **Frying Chicken** (price per pound, whole fryer); **Whole Milk** (half gallon carton); **Eggs** (price per dozen, Grade A, large); **Orange Juice** (64 oz. Tropicana or Florida Natural); **Coffee** (11.5 oz. can, vacuum-packed, Maxwell House, Hills Bros, or Folgers).
Source: The Council for Community and Economic Research, Cost of Living Index, 2020

Housing and Utility Costs

Area[1]	New Home Price ($)	Apartment Rent ($/month)	All Electric ($/month)	Part Electric ($/month)	Other Energy ($/month)	Telephone ($/month)
City[2]	325,960	1,372	228.13	-	-	187.30
Avg.	368,594	1,168	170.86	100.47	65.28	184.30
Min.	190,567	502	91.58	31.42	26.08	169.60
Max.	2,227,806	4,738	470.38	280.31	280.06	206.50

Note: (1) Values for the local area are compared with the average, minimum and maximum values for all 284 areas in the Cost of Living Index; (2) Figures cover the Charleston-N Charleston SC urban area; **New Home Price** (2,400 sf living area, 8,000 sf lot, in urban area with full utilities); **Apartment Rent** (950 sf 2 bedroom/1.5 or 2 bath, unfurnished, excluding all utilities except water); **All Electric** (average monthly cost for an all-electric home); **Part Electric** (average monthly cost for a part-electric home); **Other Energy** (average monthly cost for natural gas, fuel oil, coal, wood, and any other forms of energy except electricity); **Telephone** (price includes the base monthly rate plus taxes and fees for three lines of mobile phone service).
Source: The Council for Community and Economic Research, Cost of Living Index, 2020

Health Care, Transportation, and Other Costs

Area[1]	Doctor ($/visit)	Dentist ($/visit)	Optometrist ($/visit)	Gasoline ($/gallon)	Beauty Salon ($/visit)	Men's Shirt ($)
City[2]	131.23	102.76	81.87	2.06	57.83	27.44
Avg.	115.44	99.32	108.10	2.21	39.27	31.37
Min.	36.68	59.00	51.36	1.71	19.00	11.00
Max.	219.00	153.10	250.97	3.46	82.05	58.33

Note: (1) Values for the local area are compared with the average, minimum and maximum values for all 284 areas in the Cost of Living Index; (2) Figures cover the Charleston-N Charleston SC urban area; **Doctor** (general practitioners routine exam of an established patient); **Dentist** (adult teeth cleaning and periodic oral examination); **Optometrist** (full vision eye exam for established adult patient); **Gasoline** (one gallon regular unleaded, national brand, including all taxes, cash price at self-service pump if available); **Beauty Salon** (woman's shampoo, trim, and blow-dry); **Men's Shirt** (cotton/polyester dress shirt, pinpoint weave, long sleeves).
Source: The Council for Community and Economic Research, Cost of Living Index, 2020

HOUSING

Homeownership Rate

Area	2012 (%)	2013 (%)	2014 (%)	2015 (%)	2016 (%)	2017 (%)	2018 (%)	2019 (%)	2020 (%)
MSA[1]	n/a	n/a	n/a	65.8	62.1	67.7	68.8	70.7	75.5
U.S.	65.4	65.1	64.5	63.7	63.4	63.9	64.4	64.6	66.6

Note: (1) Figures cover the Charleston-North Charleston, SC Metropolitan Statistical Area
Source: U.S. Census Bureau, Housing Vacancies and Homeownership Annual Statistics: 2012-2020

House Price Index (HPI)

Area	National Ranking[2]	Quarterly Change (%)	One-Year Change (%)	Five-Year Change (%)	Since 1991Q1 (%)
MSA[1]	130	1.32	6.11	36.39	284.93
U.S.[3]	—	3.81	10.77	38.99	205.12

Note: The HPI is a weighted repeat sales index. It measures average price changes in repeat sales or refinancings on the same properties. This information is obtained by reviewing repeat mortgage transactions on single-family properties whose mortgages have been purchased or securitized by Fannie Mae or Freddie Mac since January 1975; (1) Figures cover the Charleston-North Charleston, SC Metropolitan Statistical Area; (2) Rankings are based on annual percentage change for all metro areas containing at least 15,000 transactions over the last 10 years and ranges from 1 to 253; (3) figures based on a weighted average of Census Division estimates using a seasonally adjusted, purchase-only index; all figures are for the period ending December 31, 2020
Source: Federal Housing Finance Agency, Change in Metropolitan Area House Price Indexes, April 7, 2021

Median Single-Family Home Prices

Area	2018	2019	2020p	Percent Change 2019 to 2020
MSA[1]	283.0	293.5	324.4	10.5
U.S. Average	261.6	274.6	299.9	9.2

Note: Figures are median sales prices of existing single-family homes in thousands of dollars; (p) preliminary; (1) Figures cover the Charleston-North Charleston, SC Metropolitan Statistical Area
Source: National Association of Realtors, Median Sales Price of Existing Single-Family Homes for Metropolitan Areas, 4th Quarter 2020

Qualifying Income Based on Median Sales Price of Existing Single-Family Homes

Area	With 5% Down ($)	With 10% Down ($)	With 20% Down ($)
MSA[1]	64,176	60,798	54,043
U.S. Average	59,266	56,147	49,908

Note: Figures are preliminary; Qualifying income is based on a mortgage rate of 2.81%. Monthly principal and interest payment is limited to 25% of income; (1) Figures cover the Charleston-North Charleston, SC Metropolitan Statistical Area
Source: National Association of Realtors, Qualifying Income Based on Median Sales Price of Existing Single-Family Homes for Metropolitan Areas, 4th Quarter 2020

Home Value Distribution

Area	Under $50,000	$50,000 -$99,999	$100,000 -$149,999	$150,000 -$199,999	$200,000 -$299,999	$300,000 -$499,999	$500,000 -$999,999	$1,000,000 or more
City	1.5	2.6	4.6	8.2	26.4	31.1	19.0	6.6
MSA[1]	6.0	7.5	11.6	15.3	23.1	21.1	11.7	3.7
U.S.	6.9	12.0	13.3	14.0	19.6	19.3	11.4	3.4

Note: Figures are percentages and cover owner-occupied housing units; (1) Figures cover the Charleston-North Charleston, SC Metropolitan Statistical Area
Source: U.S. Census Bureau, 2015-2019 American Community Survey 5-Year Estimates

Year Housing Structure Built

Area	2010 or Later	2000 -2009	1990 -1999	1980 -1989	1970 -1979	1960 -1969	1950 -1959	1940 -1949	Before 1940	Median Year
City	12.3	20.3	12.8	13.8	10.2	8.3	6.1	4.1	12.2	1987
MSA[1]	11.9	21.4	16.6	16.4	14.2	8.2	5.2	2.4	3.6	1990
U.S.	5.2	14.0	13.9	13.4	15.2	10.6	10.3	4.9	12.6	1978

Note: Figures are percentages except for Median Year; Note: (1) Figures cover the Charleston-North Charleston, SC Metropolitan Statistical Area
Source: U.S. Census Bureau, 2015-2019 American Community Survey 5-Year Estimates

Gross Monthly Rent

Area	Under $500	$500 -$999	$1,000 -$1,499	$1,500 -$1,999	$2,000 -$2,499	$2,500 -$2,999	$3,000 and up	Median ($)
City	6.4	20.8	40.8	22.1	5.9	1.8	2.2	1,257
MSA[1]	6.1	29.6	40.2	17.0	4.2	1.5	1.4	1,156
U.S.	9.4	36.2	30.0	14.0	5.6	2.4	2.4	1,062

Note: Figures are percentages except for Median; Gross rent is the contract rent plus the estimated average monthly cost of utilities (electricity, gas, and water and sewer) and fuels (oil, coal, kerosene, wood, etc.) if these are paid by the renter (or paid for the renter by someone else); (1) Figures cover the Charleston-North Charleston, SC Metropolitan Statistical Area
Source: U.S. Census Bureau, 2015-2019 American Community Survey 5-Year Estimates

HEALTH

Health Risk Factors

Category	MSA[1] (%)	U.S. (%)
Adults aged 18–64 who have any kind of health care coverage	82.3	87.3
Adults who reported being in good or better health	83.9	82.4
Adults who have been told they have high blood cholesterol	33.8	33.0
Adults who have been told they have high blood pressure	33.1	32.3
Adults who are current smokers	18.9	17.1
Adults who currently use E-cigarettes	4.3	4.6
Adults who currently use chewing tobacco, snuff, or snus	3.4	4.0
Adults who are heavy drinkers[2]	10.4	6.3
Adults who are binge drinkers[3]	22.6	17.4
Adults who are overweight (BMI 25.0 - 29.9)	34.9	35.3
Adults who are obese (BMI 30.0 - 99.8)	32.1	31.3
Adults who participated in any physical activities in the past month	75.5	74.4
Adults who always or nearly always wears a seat belt	95.4	94.3

Note: (1) Figures cover the Charleston-North Charleston, SC Metropolitan Statistical Area; (2) Heavy drinkers are classified as adult men having more than 14 drinks per week and adult women having more than 7 drinks per week; (3) Binge drinkers are classified as males having five or more drinks on one occasion or females having four or more drinks on one occasion
Source: Centers for Disease Control and Prevention, Behavioral Risk Factor Surveillance System, SMART: Selected Metropolitan Area Risk Trends, 2017

Acute and Chronic Health Conditions

Category	MSA[1] (%)	U.S. (%)
Adults who have ever been told they had a heart attack	3.4	4.2
Adults who have ever been told they have angina or coronary heart disease	3.9	3.9
Adults who have ever been told they had a stroke	3.1	3.0
Adults who have ever been told they have asthma	15.7	14.2
Adults who have ever been told they have arthritis	24.7	24.9
Adults who have ever been told they have diabetes[2]	12.7	10.5
Adults who have ever been told they had skin cancer	7.4	6.2
Adults who have ever been told they had any other types of cancer	7.5	7.1
Adults who have ever been told they have COPD	6.0	6.5
Adults who have ever been told they have kidney disease	2.5	3.0
Adults who have ever been told they have a form of depression	22.5	20.5

Note: (1) Figures cover the Charleston-North Charleston, SC Metropolitan Statistical Area; (2) Figures do not include pregnancy-related, borderline, or pre-diabetes
Source: Centers for Disease Control and Prevention, Behavioral Risk Factor Surveillance System, SMART: Selected Metropolitan Area Risk Trends, 2017

Health Screening and Vaccination Rates

Category	MSA[1] (%)	U.S. (%)
Adults aged 65+ who have had flu shot within the past year	63.9	60.7
Adults aged 65+ who have ever had a pneumonia vaccination	77.0	75.4
Adults who have ever been tested for HIV	44.7	36.1
Adults who have ever had the shingles or zoster vaccine?	26.4	28.9
Adults who have had their blood cholesterol checked within the last five years	86.0	85.9

Note: n/a not available; (1) Figures cover the Charleston-North Charleston, SC Metropolitan Statistical Area.
Source: Centers for Disease Control and Prevention, Behavioral Risk Factor Surveillance System, SMART: Selected Metropolitan Area Risk Trends, 2017

Disability Status

Category	MSA[1] (%)	U.S. (%)
Adults who reported being deaf	4.9	6.7
Are you blind or have serious difficulty seeing, even when wearing glasses?	3.5	4.5
Are you limited in any way in any of your usual activities due of arthritis?	10.8	12.9
Do you have difficulty doing errands alone?	5.9	6.8
Do you have difficulty dressing or bathing?	4.1	3.6
Do you have serious difficulty concentrating/remembering/making decisions?	13.0	10.7
Do you have serious difficulty walking or climbing stairs?	13.0	13.6

Note: (1) Figures cover the Charleston-North Charleston, SC Metropolitan Statistical Area.
Source: Centers for Disease Control and Prevention, Behavioral Risk Factor Surveillance System, SMART: Selected Metropolitan Area Risk Trends, 2017

Mortality Rates for the Top 10 Causes of Death in the U.S.

ICD-10[a] Sub-Chapter	ICD-10[a] Code	Age-Adjusted Mortality Rate[1] per 100,000 population County[2]	U.S.
Malignant neoplasms	C00-C97	148.6	149.2
Ischaemic heart diseases	I20-I25	72.1	90.5
Other forms of heart disease	I30-I51	46.5	52.2
Chronic lower respiratory diseases	J40-J47	32.9	39.6
Other degenerative diseases of the nervous system	G30-G31	50.1	37.6
Cerebrovascular diseases	I60-I69	40.5	37.2
Other external causes of accidental injury	W00-X59	36.6	36.1
Organic, including symptomatic, mental disorders	F01-F09	30.9	29.4
Hypertensive diseases	I10-I15	18.3	24.1
Diabetes mellitus	E10-E14	21.9	21.5

Note: (a) ICD-10 = International Classification of Diseases 10th Revision; (1) Mortality rates are a three-year average covering 2017-2019; (2) Figures cover Charleston County.
Source: Centers for Disease Control and Prevention, National Center for Health Statistics. Underlying Cause of Death 1999-2019 on CDC WONDER Online Database

Mortality Rates for Selected Causes of Death

ICD-10[a] Sub-Chapter	ICD-10[a] Code	Age-Adjusted Mortality Rate[1] per 100,000 population County[2]	U.S.
Assault	X85-Y09	12.6	6.0
Diseases of the liver	K70-K76	16.4	14.4
Human immunodeficiency virus (HIV) disease	B20-B24	2.3	1.5
Influenza and pneumonia	J09-J18	9.9	13.8
Intentional self-harm	X60-X84	14.7	14.1
Malnutrition	E40-E46	5.4	2.3
Obesity and other hyperalimentation	E65-E68	1.8	2.1
Renal failure	N17-N19	11.3	12.6
Transport accidents	V01-V99	15.5	12.3
Viral hepatitis	B15-B19	Unreliable	1.2

Note: (a) ICD-10 = International Classification of Diseases 10th Revision; (1) Mortality rates are a three-year average covering 2017-2019; (2) Figures cover Charleston County; Data are suppressed when the data meet the criteria for confidentiality constraints; Mortality rates are flagged as unreliable when the rate would be calculated with a numerator of 20 or less.
Source: Centers for Disease Control and Prevention, National Center for Health Statistics. Underlying Cause of Death 1999-2019 on CDC WONDER Online Database

Health Insurance Coverage

Area	With Health Insurance	With Private Health Insurance	With Public Health Insurance	Without Health Insurance	Population Under Age 19 Without Health Insurance
City	91.9	78.0	25.5	8.1	3.3
MSA[1]	89.5	71.1	31.4	10.5	5.7
U.S.	91.2	67.9	35.1	8.8	5.1

Note: Figures are percentages that cover the civilian noninstitutionalized population; (1) Figures cover the Charleston-North Charleston, SC Metropolitan Statistical Area
Source: U.S. Census Bureau, 2015-2019 American Community Survey 5-Year Estimates

Number of Medical Professionals

Area	MDs[3]	DOs[3,4]	Dentists	Podiatrists	Chiropractors	Optometrists
County[1] (number)	3,237	126	451	20	209	90
County[1] (rate[2])	796.9	31.0	109.6	4.9	50.8	21.9
U.S. (rate[2])	282.9	22.7	71.2	6.2	28.1	16.9

45019
Note: Data as of 2019 unless noted; (1) Data covers Charleston County; (2) Rate per 100,000 population; (3) Data as of 2018 and includes all active, non-federal physicians; (4) Doctor of Osteopathic Medicine
Source: U.S. Department of Health and Human Services, Health Resources and Services Administration, Bureau of Health Professions, Area Resource File (ARF) 2019-2020

Best Hospitals

According to *U.S. News*, the Charleston-North Charleston, SC metro area is home to one of the best hospitals in the U.S.: **MUSC Health-University Medical Center** (3 adult specialties and 4 pediatric specialties). The hospital listed was nationally ranked in at least one of 16 adult or 10 pediatric specialties. Only 134 hospitals nationwide were nationally ranked in one or more adult or pediatric specialty; this number increases to 178 counting specialized centers within hospitals. Twenty hospitals in the U.S. made the Honor Roll. The Best Hospitals Honor Roll takes both the national rankings and the procedure and condition ratings into account. Hospitals received points if they were nationally ranked in one of the 16 adult specialties—the higher they ranked, the more points they got—and how many ratings of "high performing" they earned in the 10 procedures and conditions. *U.S. News Online, "America's Best Hospitals 2020-21"*

According to *U.S. News*, the Charleston-North Charleston, SC metro area is home to one of the best children's hospitals in the U.S.: **MUSC Shawn Jenkins Children's Hospital** (4 pediatric specialties). The hospital listed was highly ranked in at least one of 10 pediatric specialties. Eighty-eight children's hospitals in the U.S. were nationally ranked in at least one specialty. Hospitals received points for being ranked in a specialty, and the 10 hospitals with the most points across the 10 specialties make up the Honor Roll. *U.S. News Online, "America's Best Children's Hospitals 2020-21"*

EDUCATION

Public School District Statistics

District Name	Schls	Pupils	Pupil/Teacher Ratio	Minority Pupils[1] (%)	Free Lunch Eligible[2] (%)	IEP[3] (%)
Charleston 01	82	49,769	14.5	51.7	55.8	10.3

Note: Table includes school districts with 2,000 or more students; (1) Percentage of students that are not non-Hispanic white; (2) Percentage of students that are eligible for the free lunch program; (3) Percentage of students that have an Individualized Education Program.
Source: U.S. Department of Education, National Center for Education Statistics, Common Core of Data, Local Education Agency (School District) Universe Survey: School Year 2018-2019; U.S. Department of Education, National Center for Education Statistics, Common Core of Data, Public Elementary/Secondary School Universe Survey: School Year 2018-2019

Highest Level of Education

Area	Less than H.S.	H.S. Diploma	Some College, No Deg.	Associate Degree	Bachelor's Degree	Master's Degree	Prof. School Degree	Doctorate Degree
City	5.1	17.6	16.3	7.9	33.8	12.6	4.5	2.2
MSA[1]	9.3	25.4	20.1	9.5	23.0	8.9	2.4	1.2
U.S.	12.0	27.0	20.4	8.5	19.8	8.8	2.1	1.4

Note: Figures cover persons age 25 and over; (1) Figures cover the Charleston-North Charleston, SC Metropolitan Statistical Area
Source: U.S. Census Bureau, 2015-2019 American Community Survey 5-Year Estimates

Educational Attainment by Race

Area	High School Graduate or Higher (%)					Bachelor's Degree or Higher (%)				
	Total	White	Black	Asian	Hisp.[2]	Total	White	Black	Asian	Hisp.[2]
City	94.9	97.4	86.9	93.5	91.4	53.1	61.0	22.3	67.3	45.6
MSA[1]	90.7	93.7	84.4	86.3	71.1	35.6	42.6	16.5	49.0	20.5
U.S.	88.0	89.9	86.0	87.1	68.7	32.1	33.5	21.6	54.3	16.4

Note: Figures shown cover persons 25 years old and over; (1) Figures cover the Charleston-North Charleston, SC Metropolitan Statistical Area; (2) People of Hispanic origin can be of any race
Source: U.S. Census Bureau, 2015-2019 American Community Survey 5-Year Estimates

School Enrollment by Grade and Control

Area	Preschool (%)		Kindergarten (%)		Grades 1 - 4 (%)		Grades 5 - 8 (%)		Grades 9 - 12 (%)	
	Public	Private	Public	Private	Public	Private	Public	Private	Public	Private
City	41.2	58.9	78.8	21.2	83.4	16.6	78.9	21.1	78.9	21.1
MSA[1]	51.2	48.8	86.2	13.8	89.8	10.2	89.3	10.7	90.4	9.6
U.S.	59.1	40.9	87.6	12.4	89.5	10.5	89.4	10.6	90.1	9.9

Note: Figures shown cover persons 3 years old and over; (1) Figures cover the Charleston-North Charleston, SC Metropolitan Statistical Area
Source: U.S. Census Bureau, 2015-2019 American Community Survey 5-Year Estimates

Higher Education

Four-Year Colleges			Two-Year Colleges			Medical Schools[1]	Law Schools[2]	Voc/Tech[3]
Public	Private Non-profit	Private For-profit	Public	Private Non-profit	Private For-profit			
3	2	1	1	0	1	1	1	3

Note: Figures cover institutions located within the city limits and include main campuses only; (1) includes schools accredited by the Liaison Committee on Medical Education and the American Osteopathic Association's Commission on Osteopathic College Accreditation; (2) includes ABA-accredited schools, schools with provisional ABA accreditation, and state accredited schools; (3) includes all schools with programs that are less than 2 years.
Source: National Center for Education Statistics, Integrated Postsecondary Education System (IPEDS), 2019-20; Wikipedia, List of Medical Schools in the United States, accessed April 2, 2021; Wikipedia, List of Law Schools in the United States, accessed April 2, 2021

EMPLOYERS

Major Employers

Company Name	Industry
Bi-Lo Stores	Grocery stores
Boeing South Carolina	Commercial aircraft
Charleston County Government	County government
Charleston County School District	Public elementary & secondary schools
City of Charleston	Municipal government
College of Charleston	Higher education
Evening Post Publishing Co.	Newspapers, publishing & printing
Force Protection	Mine-protected vehicle manufacturing
JEM Restaurant Group	Restaurants/hospitality
Joint Base Charleston	U.S. military
Medical University of South Carolina	State's teaching hospital, medical higher education
Piggly Wiggly Carolina Co	Grocery stores
Roper St. Francis Healthcare	Private hospital system
SAIC	Advanced security
Trident Health System	Hospital system
U.S. Postal Service	Federal mail delivery service
Verizon Wireless Call Center	Call center
Wal-Mart Stores	Retail merchandising

Note: Companies shown are located within the Charleston-North Charleston, SC Metropolitan Statistical Area.
Source: Hoovers.com; Wikipedia

PUBLIC SAFETY

Crime Rate

Area	All Crimes	Violent Crimes				Property Crimes		
		Murder	Rape[3]	Robbery	Aggrav. Assault	Burglary	Larceny-Theft	Motor Vehicle Theft
City	2,632.8	5.8	36.9	68.7	261.8	211.2	1,688.9	359.5
Suburbs[1]	3,168.8	9.6	42.3	61.1	290.1	419.0	2,025.9	320.8
Metro[2]	3,076.7	8.9	41.4	62.4	285.2	383.3	1,968.0	327.5
U.S.	2,489.3	5.0	42.6	81.6	250.2	340.5	1,549.5	219.9

Note: Figures are crimes per 100,000 population; (1) All areas within the metro area that are located outside the city limits; (2) Figures cover the Charleston-North Charleston, SC Metropolitan Statistical Area; (3) All figures shown were reported using the revised Uniform Crime Reporting (UCR) definition of rape.
Source: FBI Uniform Crime Reports, 2019

Hate Crimes

Area	Number of Quarters Reported	Number of Incidents per Bias Motivation					
		Race/Ethnicity/Ancestry	Religion	Sexual Orientation	Disability	Gender	Gender Identity
City	4	1	1	2	0	0	0
U.S.	4	3,963	1,521	1,195	157	69	198

Source: Federal Bureau of Investigation, Hate Crime Statistics 2019

Identity Theft Consumer Reports

Area	Reports	Reports per 100,000 Population	Rank[2]
MSA[1]	3,203	399	74
U.S.	1,387,615	423	-

Note: (1) Figures cover the Charleston-North Charleston, SC Metropolitan Statistical Area; (2) Rank ranges from 1 to 391 where 1 indicates greatest number of identity theft reports per 100,000 population
Source: Federal Trade Commission, Consumer Sentinel Network Data Book 2020

Fraud and Other Consumer Reports

Area	Reports	Reports per 100,000 Population	Rank[2]
MSA[1]	7,184	896	52
U.S.	3,385,133	1,031	-

Note: (1) Figures cover the Charleston-North Charleston, SC Metropolitan Statistical Area; (2) Rank ranges from 1 to 391 where 1 indicates greatest number of fraud and other consumer reports per 100,000 population
Source: Federal Trade Commission, Consumer Sentinel Network Data Book 2020

POLITICS

2020 Presidential Election Results

Area	Biden	Trump	Jorgensen	Hawkins	Other
Charleston County	55.5	42.6	1.5	0.3	0.1
U.S.	51.3	46.8	1.2	0.3	0.5

Note: Results are percentages and may not add to 100% due to rounding
Source: Dave Leip's Atlas of U.S. Presidential Elections

SPORTS

Professional Sports Teams

Team Name	League	Year Established
No teams are located in the metro area		

Source: Wikipedia, Major Professional Sports Teams of the United States and Canada, April 6, 2021

CLIMATE

Average and Extreme Temperatures

Temperature	Jan	Feb	Mar	Apr	May	Jun	Jul	Aug	Sep	Oct	Nov	Dec	Yr.
Extreme High (°F)	83	87	90	94	98	101	104	102	97	94	88	83	104
Average High (°F)	59	62	68	76	83	88	90	89	85	77	69	61	76
Average Temp. (°F)	49	51	57	65	73	78	81	81	76	67	58	51	66
Average Low (°F)	38	40	46	53	62	69	72	72	67	56	46	39	55
Extreme Low (°F)	6	12	15	30	36	50	58	56	42	27	15	8	6

Note: Figures cover the years 1945-1995
Source: National Climatic Data Center, International Station Meteorological Climate Summary, 9/96

Average Precipitation/Snowfall/Humidity

Precip./Humidity	Jan	Feb	Mar	Apr	May	Jun	Jul	Aug	Sep	Oct	Nov	Dec	Yr.
Avg. Precip. (in.)	3.5	3.1	4.4	2.8	4.1	6.0	7.2	6.9	5.6	3.1	2.5	3.1	52.1
Avg. Snowfall (in.)	Tr	Tr	Tr	0	0	0	0	0	0	0	Tr	Tr	1
Avg. Rel. Hum. 7am (%)	83	81	83	84	85	86	88	90	91	89	86	83	86
Avg. Rel. Hum. 4pm (%)	55	52	51	51	56	62	66	66	65	58	56	55	58

Note: Figures cover the years 1945-1995; Tr = Trace amounts (<0.05 in. of rain; <0.5 in. of snow)
Source: National Climatic Data Center, International Station Meteorological Climate Summary, 9/96

Weather Conditions

Temperature			Daytime Sky			Precipitation		
10°F & below	32°F & below	90°F & above	Clear	Partly cloudy	Cloudy	0.01 inch or more precip.	0.1 inch or more snow/ice	Thunder-storms
< 1	33	53	89	162	114	114	1	59

Note: Figures are average number of days per year and cover the years 1945-1995
Source: National Climatic Data Center, International Station Meteorological Climate Summary, 9/96

HAZARDOUS WASTE

Superfund Sites

The Charleston-North Charleston, SC metro area is home to two sites on the EPA's Superfund National Priorities List: **Koppers Co., Inc. (Charleston Plant)** (final); **Macalloy Corporation** (final). There are a total of 1,375 Superfund sites with a status of proposed or final on the list in the U.S. *U.S. Environmental Protection Agency, National Priorities List, April 7, 2021*

AIR QUALITY

Air Quality Trends: Ozone

	1990	1995	2000	2005	2010	2015	2016	2017	2018	2019
MSA[1]	0.068	0.071	0.078	0.073	0.067	0.054	0.059	0.062	0.058	0.064
U.S.	0.088	0.089	0.082	0.080	0.073	0.068	0.069	0.068	0.069	0.065

Note: (1) Data covers the Charleston-North Charleston, SC Metropolitan Statistical Area. The values shown are the composite ozone concentration averages among trend sites based on the highest fourth daily maximum 8-hour concentration in parts per million. These trends are based on sites having an adequate record of monitoring data during the trend period. Data from exceptional events are included.
Source: U.S. Environmental Protection Agency, Air Quality Monitoring Information, "Air Quality Trends by City, 1990-2019"

Air Quality Index

Area	Percent of Days when Air Quality was...[2]					AQI Statistics[2]	
	Good	Moderate	Unhealthy for Sensitive Groups	Unhealthy	Very Unhealthy	Maximum	Median
MSA[1]	84.3	15.4	0.3	0.0	0.0	140	38

Note: (1) Data covers the Charleston-North Charleston, SC Metropolitan Statistical Area; (2) Based on 357 days with AQI data in 2019. Air Quality Index (AQI) is an index for reporting daily air quality. EPA calculates the AQI for five major air pollutants regulated by the Clean Air Act: ground-level ozone, particle pollution (aka particulate matter), carbon monoxide, sulfur dioxide, and nitrogen dioxide. The AQI runs from 0 to 500. The higher the AQI value, the greater the level of air pollution and the greater the health concern. There are six AQI categories: "Good" AQI is between 0 and 50. Air quality is considered satisfactory; "Moderate" AQI is between 51 and 100. Air quality is acceptable; "Unhealthy for Sensitive Groups" When AQI values are between 101 and 150, members of sensitive groups may experience health effects; "Unhealthy" When AQI values are between 151 and 200 everyone may begin to experience health effects; "Very Unhealthy" AQI values between 201 and 300 trigger a health alert; "Hazardous" AQI values over 300 trigger warnings of emergency conditions (not shown).
Source: U.S. Environmental Protection Agency, Air Quality Index Report, 2019

Air Quality Index Pollutants

Area	Percent of Days when AQI Pollutant was...[2]					
	Carbon Monoxide	Nitrogen Dioxide	Ozone	Sulfur Dioxide	Particulate Matter 2.5	Particulate Matter 10
MSA[1]	0.0	0.0	67.2	0.0	32.5	0.3

Note: (1) Data covers the Charleston-North Charleston, SC Metropolitan Statistical Area; (2) Based on 357 days with AQI data in 2019. The Air Quality Index (AQI) is an index for reporting daily air quality. EPA calculates the AQI for five major air pollutants regulated by the Clean Air Act: ground-level ozone, particle pollution (also known as particulate matter), carbon monoxide, sulfur dioxide, and nitrogen dioxide. The AQI runs from 0 to 500. The higher the AQI value, the greater the level of air pollution and the greater the health concern.
Source: U.S. Environmental Protection Agency, Air Quality Index Report, 2019

Maximum Air Pollutant Concentrations: Particulate Matter, Ozone, CO and Lead

	Particulate Matter 10 (ug/m³)	Particulate Matter 2.5 Wtd AM (ug/m³)	Particulate Matter 2.5 24-Hr (ug/m³)	Ozone (ppm)	Carbon Monoxide (ppm)	Lead (ug/m³)
MSA[1] Level	54	6.9	14	0.064	n/a	n/a
NAAQS[2]	150	15	35	0.075	9	0.15
Met NAAQS[2]	Yes	Yes	Yes	Yes	n/a	n/a

Note: (1) Data covers the Charleston-North Charleston, SC Metropolitan Statistical Area; Data from exceptional events are included; (2) National Ambient Air Quality Standards; ppm = parts per million; ug/m³ = micrograms per cubic meter; n/a not available.
Concentrations: Particulate Matter 10 (coarse particulate)—highest second maximum 24-hour concentration; Particulate Matter 2.5 Wtd AM (fine particulate)—highest weighted annual mean concentration; Particulate Matter 2.5 24-Hour (fine particulate)—highest 98th percentile 24-hour concentration; Ozone—highest fourth daily maximum 8-hour concentration; Carbon Monoxide—highest second maximum non-overlapping 8-hour concentration; Lead—maximum running 3-month average
Source: U.S. Environmental Protection Agency, Air Quality Monitoring Information, "Air Quality Statistics by City, 2019"

Maximum Air Pollutant Concentrations: Nitrogen Dioxide and Sulfur Dioxide

	Nitrogen Dioxide AM (ppb)	Nitrogen Dioxide 1-Hr (ppb)	Sulfur Dioxide AM (ppb)	Sulfur Dioxide 1-Hr (ppb)	Sulfur Dioxide 24-Hr (ppb)
MSA[1] Level	n/a	n/a	n/a	14	n/a
NAAQS[2]	53	100	30	75	140
Met NAAQS[2]	n/a	n/a	n/a	Yes	n/a

Note: (1) Data covers the Charleston-North Charleston, SC Metropolitan Statistical Area; Data from exceptional events are included; (2) National Ambient Air Quality Standards; ppm = parts per million; ug/m³ = micrograms per cubic meter; n/a not available.
Concentrations: Nitrogen Dioxide AM—highest arithmetic mean concentration; Nitrogen Dioxide 1-Hr—highest 98th percentile 1-hour daily maximum concentration; Sulfur Dioxide AM—highest annual mean concentration; Sulfur Dioxide 1-Hr—highest 99th percentile 1-hour daily maximum concentration; Sulfur Dioxide 24-Hr—highest second maximum 24-hour concentration
Source: U.S. Environmental Protection Agency, Air Quality Monitoring Information, "Air Quality Statistics by City, 2019"

Clarksville, Tennessee

Background

Located just south of the Kentucky border and 47 miles north of Nashville, Clarksville is Tennessee's fifth-largest town and has seen significant growth in recent years. Named for Gen. George Rogers Clark, a decorated veteran of the Indian and Revolutionary Wars, the city was founded in 1784, and became incorporated by the state of Tennessee when it joined the union in 1796.

Located near the confluence of Red and Cumberland rivers, Clarksville was the site of three Confederate forts that the Union defeated in 1862. Fort Defiance transferred hands and became known as a place where fleeing or freed slaves could find refuge—and jobs. In the 1980s the well-preserved fort passed from the private hands of a local judge to the city itself, and in 2011 an interpretive center and walking trails were unveiled at what is now called Fort Defiance Civil War Park and Interpretive Center. The site features walking trails as well as the 1,500+ square foot center.

Clarksville is home to the 105,000-acre Fort Campbell, established as Camp Campbell in 1942, with nearly two-thirds of its land mass in Tennessee and the rest—including the post office—located in Kentucky. It is home to the world's only air assault division, known as the Screaming Eagles. Two special ops command units, a combat support hospital, and far more make this home to the U.S. Army's most-deployed contingency forces and the its fifth-largest military population. With more than 4,000 civilian jobs, it's the area's largest employer with services on the post ranging from bowling to the commissary to the Fort Campbell Credit Union, as well as medical services and child care.

Austin Peay State University's main campus is in Clarksville, another of the city's major employers, and named for a local son who became governor. The four-year public master's-level university saw its enrollment climb steadily throughout the last twenty years. Austin Peay also operates a center at Fort Campbell with fifteen associate, bachelor and master's level programs.

In 2012, Hemlock Semiconductor Corp, a subsidiary of Dow Corning, opened a $1.2 billion plant in the city, and the state funded a new educational center at APSU to train workers.

A 146-acre Liberty Park and Marina redevelopment project was completed in 2012, replete with pavilions, sports fields, picnic shelters, a dog park, and a ten-acre pond with a boardwalk and fishing piers. The Wilma Rudolph Pavilion and Great lawn is named for the great Olympic runner, Clarksville's native daughter. Another recent development came when the city created an Indoor Aquatic Center with an inflatable dome that allows for water sports in winter.

On the cultural side of Clarksville's quality of life, the popular Clarksville Downtown Market—with produce and arts and crafts—is a popular summer event.

> When COVID-19 cancelled her church picnic, Alexis Wall came up with the "Un-picnic," a food donation program to help feed local families.

Clarksville is also home to the state's second largest general museum, called the Customs House Museum and Cultural Center, which has seen a recent facelift. Model trains, a gallery devoted to sports champions, and even a bubble cave are all part of the experience.

The climate in Clarksville means hot summers but relatively moderate winters with average lows reaching 25 degrees in January. Precipitation stays fairly steady year round, getting no higher than 5.39 in March and bottoming out at 3.27 inches in October.

Rankings

General Rankings

- For its "Best for Vets: Places to Live 2019" rankings, *Military Times* evaluated 599 cities (83 large, 234 medium, 282 small) and compared the locations across three broad categories: veteran and military culture/services; economic indicators; and livability factors such as health, crime, traffic, and school quality. Clarksville ranked #12 out of the top 50, in the medium-sized city category (population of 100,000-249,999). Data points more specific to veterans and the military weighed more heavily than others. *rebootcamp.militarytimes.com, "Military Times Best Places to Live 2019," September 10, 2018*

Business/Finance Rankings

- The Clarksville metro area appeared on the Milken Institute "2021 Best Performing Cities" list. Rank: #134 out of 200 large metro areas (population over 250,000). Criteria: job growth; wage and salary growth; high-tech output growth; housing affordability; household broadband access. *Milken Institute, "Best-Performing Cities 2021," February 16, 2021*

- *Forbes* ranked the 200 most populous metro areas to determine the nation's "Best Places for Business and Careers." The Clarksville metro area was ranked #130. Criteria: costs (business and living); job growth (past and projected); income growth; quality of life; educational attainment (college and high school); projected economic growth; cultural and leisure opportunities; workplace tolerance laws; net migration patterns. *Forbes, "The Best Places for Business and Careers 2019: Seattle Still On Top," October 30, 2019*

Environmental Rankings

- Clarksville was highlighted as one of the cleanest metro areas for ozone air pollution in the U.S. during 2016 through 2018. The list represents cities with no monitored ozone air pollution in unhealthful ranges. *American Lung Association, "State of the Air 2020," April 21, 2020*

- Clarksville was highlighted as one of the top 98 cleanest metro areas for short-term particle pollution (24-hour PM 2.5) in the U.S. during 2016 through 2018. Monitors in these cities reported no days with unhealthful PM 2.5 levels. *American Lung Association, "State of the Air 2020," April 21, 2020*

Real Estate Rankings

- The Clarksville metro area was identified as one of the top 15 housing markets to invest in for 2021 by *Forbes*. Criteria: home price appreciation; percentage of home sales within a 2-week time frame; available inventory; number of home sales; and other factors. *Forbes.com, "Top Housing Markets To Watch In 2021," December 15, 2020*

Safety Rankings

- Allstate ranked the 200 largest cities in America in terms of driver safety. Clarksville ranked #47. Criteria: internal property damage claims over a two-year period from January 2016 to December 2017. The report helps increase the importance of safety and awareness behind the wheel. *Allstate, "Allstate America's Best Drivers Report, 2019" June 24, 2019*

- The National Insurance Crime Bureau ranked 384 metro areas in the U.S. in terms of per capita rates of vehicle theft. The Clarksville metro area ranked #156 (#1 = highest rate). Criteria: number of vehicle theft offenses per 100,000 inhabitants in 2019. *National Insurance Crime Bureau, "Hot Spots 2019," July 21, 2020*

Seniors/Retirement Rankings

- From its Best Cities for Successful Aging indexes, the Milken Institute generated rankings for metropolitan areas, weighing data in nine categories—health care, wellness, living arrangements, transportation and convenience, financial characteristics, education, employment, community engagement, and overall livability. The Clarksville metro area was ranked #185 overall in the small metro area category. *Milken Institute, "Best Cities for Successful Aging, 2017" March 14, 2017*

Business Environment

DEMOGRAPHICS

Population Growth

Area	1990 Census	2000 Census	2010 Census	2019* Estimate	Population Growth (%) 1990-2019	Population Growth (%) 2010-2019
City	78,569	103,455	132,929	152,934	94.6	15.0
MSA[1]	189,277	232,000	273,949	299,470	58.2	9.3
U.S.	248,709,873	281,421,906	308,745,538	324,697,795	30.6	5.2

Note: (1) Figures cover the Clarksville, TN-KY Metropolitan Statistical Area; (*) 2015-2019 5-year estimated population
Source: U.S. Census Bureau, 1990 Census, Census 2000, Census 2010, 2015-2019 American Community Survey 5-Year Estimates

Household Size

Area	One	Two	Three	Four	Five	Six	Seven or More	Average Household Size
City	24.7	30.8	19.7	15.2	5.9	2.3	1.4	2.70
MSA[1]	25.0	32.3	18.4	14.3	6.3	2.6	1.3	2.60
U.S.	27.9	33.9	15.6	12.9	6.0	2.3	1.4	2.60

Note: (1) Figures cover the Clarksville, TN-KY Metropolitan Statistical Area
Source: U.S. Census Bureau, 2015-2019 American Community Survey 5-Year Estimates

Race

Area	White Alone[2] (%)	Black Alone[2] (%)	Asian Alone[2] (%)	AIAN[3] Alone[2] (%)	NHOPI[4] Alone[2] (%)	Other Race Alone[2] (%)	Two or More Races (%)
City	65.1	24.3	2.5	0.7	0.5	1.8	5.2
MSA[1]	72.7	19.1	1.9	0.6	0.4	1.3	4.1
U.S.	72.5	12.7	5.5	0.8	0.2	4.9	3.3

Note: (1) Figures cover the Clarksville, TN-KY Metropolitan Statistical Area; (2) Alone is defined as not being in combination with one or more other races; (3) American Indian and Alaska Native; (4) Native Hawaiian and Other Pacific Islander
Source: U.S. Census Bureau, 2015-2019 American Community Survey 5-Year Estimates

Hispanic or Latino Origin

Area	Total (%)	Mexican (%)	Puerto Rican (%)	Cuban (%)	Other (%)
City	11.5	5.2	3.7	0.3	2.3
MSA[1]	8.8	4.2	2.7	0.2	1.7
U.S.	18.0	11.2	1.7	0.7	4.3

Note: Persons of Hispanic or Latino origin can be of any race; (1) Figures cover the Clarksville, TN-KY Metropolitan Statistical Area
Source: U.S. Census Bureau, 2015-2019 American Community Survey 5-Year Estimates

Ancestry

Area	German	Irish	English	American	Italian	Polish	French[2]	Scottish	Dutch
City	10.7	8.3	5.6	7.8	3.5	1.5	1.8	1.3	1.1
MSA[1]	11.1	9.0	6.4	9.3	2.8	1.4	1.8	1.6	0.9
U.S.	13.3	9.7	7.2	6.2	5.1	2.8	2.3	1.7	1.2

Note: Figures are the percentage of the total population reporting a particular ancestry. The nine most commonly reported ancestries in the U.S. are shown. Figures include multiple ancestries (e.g. if a person reported being Irish and Italian, they were included in both columns); (1) Figures cover the Clarksville, TN-KY Metropolitan Statistical Area; (2) Excludes Basque
Source: U.S. Census Bureau, 2015-2019 American Community Survey 5-Year Estimates

Foreign-born Population

Area	Any Foreign Country	Asia	Mexico	Europe	Caribbean	Central America[2]	South America	Africa	Canada
City	5.3	1.7	1.1	0.9	0.4	0.4	0.4	0.3	0.1
MSA[1]	4.1	1.3	0.7	0.7	0.3	0.3	0.3	0.3	0.1
U.S.	13.6	4.2	3.5	1.5	1.3	1.1	1.0	0.7	0.2

Note: (1) Figures cover the Clarksville, TN-KY Metropolitan Statistical Area; (2) Excludes Mexico.
Source: U.S. Census Bureau, 2015-2019 American Community Survey 5-Year Estimates

Marital Status

Area	Never Married	Now Married[2]	Separated	Widowed	Divorced
City	30.2	50.9	2.2	4.0	12.6
MSA[1]	28.3	52.5	2.0	5.1	12.0
U.S.	33.4	48.1	1.9	5.8	10.9

Note: Figures are percentages and cover the population 15 years of age and older; (1) Figures cover the Clarksville, TN-KY Metropolitan Statistical Area; (2) Excludes separated
Source: U.S. Census Bureau, 2015-2019 American Community Survey 5-Year Estimates

Disability by Age

Area	All Ages	Under 18 Years Old	18 to 64 Years Old	65 Years and Over
City	14.9	4.7	16.1	41.1
MSA[1]	16.5	5.7	16.6	43.2
U.S.	12.6	4.2	10.3	34.5

Note: Figures show percent of the civilian noninstitutionalized population that reported having a disability. Disability status is determined from six types of difficulty: vision, hearing, cognitive, ambulatory, self-care, and independent living. For children under 5 years old, hearing and vision difficulty are used to determine disability status. For children between the ages of 5 and 14, disability status is determined from hearing, vision, cognitive, ambulatory, and self-care difficulties. For people aged 15 years and older, they are considered to have a disability if they have difficulty with any one of the six difficulty types; Note: (1) Figures cover the Clarksville, TN-KY Metropolitan Statistical Area
Source: U.S. Census Bureau, 2015-2019 American Community Survey 5-Year Estimates

Age

Area	Under Age 5	Age 5–19	Age 20–34	Age 35–44	Age 45–54	Age 55–64	Age 65–74	Age 75–84	Age 85+	Median Age
City	9.0	20.6	30.7	13.0	10.0	8.5	5.2	2.1	0.9	29.6
MSA[1]	8.4	20.8	27.0	12.4	10.8	9.8	6.6	3.2	1.2	31.1
U.S.	6.1	19.1	20.7	12.6	13.0	12.9	9.1	4.6	1.9	38.1

Note: (1) Figures cover the Clarksville, TN-KY Metropolitan Statistical Area
Source: U.S. Census Bureau, 2015-2019 American Community Survey 5-Year Estimates

Gender

Area	Males	Females	Males per 100 Females
City	76,399	76,535	99.8
MSA[1]	151,723	147,747	102.7
U.S.	159,886,919	164,810,876	97.0

Note: (1) Figures cover the Clarksville, TN-KY Metropolitan Statistical Area
Source: U.S. Census Bureau, 2015-2019 American Community Survey 5-Year Estimates

Religious Groups by Family

Area	Catholic	Baptist	Non-Den.	Methodist[2]	Lutheran	LDS[3]	Pentecostal	Presbyterian[4]	Muslim[5]	Judaism
MSA[1]	4.1	30.9	2.3	6.2	0.6	1.5	1.8	1.1	0.1	<0.1
U.S.	19.1	9.3	4.0	4.0	2.3	2.0	1.9	1.6	0.8	0.7

Note: Figures are the number of adherents as a percentage of the total population; (1) Figures cover the Clarksville, TN-KY Metropolitan Statistical Area; (2) Methodist/Pietist; (3) Latter Day Saints; (4) Reformed; (5) Figures are estimates
Source: Association of Statisticians of American Religious Bodies, 2010 U.S. Religion Census: Religious Congregations & Membership Study

Religious Groups by Tradition

Area	Catholic	Evangelical Protestant	Mainline Protestant	Other Tradition	Black Protestant	Orthodox
MSA[1]	4.1	35.4	7.3	1.7	2.4	<0.1
U.S.	19.1	16.2	7.3	4.3	1.6	0.3

Note: Figures are the number of adherents as a percentage of the total population; (1) Figures cover the Clarksville, TN-KY Metropolitan Statistical Area
Source: Association of Statisticians of American Religious Bodies, 2010 U.S. Religion Census: Religious Congregations & Membership Study

ECONOMY

Gross Metropolitan Product

Area	2017	2018	2019	2020	Rank[2]
MSA[1]	11.0	11.6	12.2	12.6	194

Note: Figures are in billions of dollars; (1) Figures cover the Clarksville, TN-KY Metropolitan Statistical Area; (2) Rank is based on 2018 data and ranges from 1 to 381
Source: U.S. Conference of Mayors, U.S. Metro Economies: GMP & Employment 2018-2020, September 2019

Clarksville, Tennessee

Economic Growth

Area	2015-17 (%)	2018 (%)	2019 (%)	2020 (%)	Rank[2]
MSA[1]	-0.6	3.0	3.0	1.6	331
U.S.	1.9	2.9	2.3	2.1	—

Note: Figures are real gross metropolitan product (GMP) growth rates and represent average annual percent change; (1) Figures cover the Clarksville, TN-KY Metropolitan Statistical Area; (2) Rank is based on 2017 2-year average annual percent change and ranges from 1 to 381
Source: U.S. Conference of Mayors, U.S. Metro Economies: GMP & Employment 2018-2020, September 2019

Metropolitan Area Exports

Area	2014	2015	2016	2017	2018	2019	Rank[2]
MSA[1]	323.7	296.5	376.1	360.2	435.5	341.8	241

Note: Figures are in millions of dollars; (1) Figures cover the Clarksville, TN-KY Metropolitan Statistical Area; (2) Rank is based on 2019 data and ranges from 1 to 386
Source: U.S. Department of Commerce, International Trade Administration, Office of Trade and Economic Analysis, Industry and Analysis, Exports by Metropolitan Area, data extracted March 24, 2021

Building Permits

Area	Single-Family 2018	Single-Family 2019	Pct. Chg.	Multi-Family 2018	Multi-Family 2019	Pct. Chg.	Total 2018	Total 2019	Pct. Chg.
City	669	1,428	113.5	269	160	-40.5	938	1,588	69.3
MSA[1]	1,516	2,332	53.8	287	325	13.2	1,803	2,657	47.4
U.S.	855,300	862,100	0.7	473,500	523,900	10.6	1,328,800	1,386,000	4.3

Note: (1) Figures cover the Clarksville, TN-KY Metropolitan Statistical Area; Figures represent new, privately-owned housing units authorized (unadjusted data); All permit data are based on estimates with imputation
Source: U.S. Census Bureau, Manufacturing, Mining, and Construction Statistics, Building Permits, 2018, 2019

Bankruptcy Filings

Area	Business Filings 2019	Business Filings 2020	% Chg.	Nonbusiness Filings 2019	Nonbusiness Filings 2020	% Chg.
Montgomery County	11	6	-45.5	829	579	-30.2
U.S.	22,780	21,655	-4.9	752,160	522,808	-30.5

Note: Business filings include Chapter 7, Chapter 9, Chapter 11, Chapter 12, Chapter 13, Chapter 15, and Section 304; Nonbusiness filings include Chapter 7, Chapter 11, and Chapter 13
Source: Administrative Office of the U.S. Courts, Business and Nonbusiness Bankruptcy, County Cases Commenced by Chapter of the Bankruptcy Code, During the 12-Month Period Ending December 31, 2019 and Business and Nonbusiness Bankruptcy, County Cases Commenced by Chapter of the Bankruptcy Code, During the 12-Month Period Ending December 31, 2020

Housing Vacancy Rates

Area	Gross Vacancy Rate[2] (%) 2018	2019	2020	Year-Round Vacancy Rate[3] (%) 2018	2019	2020	Rental Vacancy Rate[4] (%) 2018	2019	2020	Homeowner Vacancy Rate[5] (%) 2018	2019	2020
MSA[1]	n/a	n/a	n/a	n/a	n/a	n/a	n/a	n/a	n/a	n/a	n/a	n/a
U.S.	12.3	12.0	10.6	9.7	9.5	8.2	6.9	6.7	6.3	1.5	1.4	1.0

Note: (1) Figures cover the Clarksville, TN-KY Metropolitan Statistical Area; (2) The percentage of the total housing inventory that is vacant; (3) The percentage of the housing inventory (excluding seasonal units) that is year-round vacant; (4) The percentage of rental inventory that is vacant for rent; (5) The percentage of homeowner inventory that is vacant for sale; n/a not available
Source: U.S. Census Bureau, Housing Vacancies and Homeownership Annual Statistics: 2018, 2019, 2020

INCOME

Income

Area	Per Capita ($)	Median Household ($)	Average Household ($)
City	25,239	53,604	65,458
MSA[1]	25,931	53,027	67,368
U.S.	34,103	62,843	88,607

Note: (1) Figures cover the Clarksville, TN-KY Metropolitan Statistical Area
Source: U.S. Census Bureau, 2015-2019 American Community Survey 5-Year Estimates

Household Income Distribution

Area	Under $15,000	$15,000 -$24,999	$25,000 -$34,999	$35,000 -$49,999	$50,000 -$74,999	$75,000 -$99,999	$100,000 -$149,999	$150,000 and up
City	10.4	8.7	11.3	16.2	20.8	14.2	12.7	5.6
MSA[1]	11.4	9.1	10.8	16.0	19.7	13.7	12.4	6.8
U.S.	10.3	8.9	8.9	12.3	17.2	12.7	15.1	14.5

Note: (1) Figures cover the Clarksville, TN-KY Metropolitan Statistical Area
Source: U.S. Census Bureau, 2015-2019 American Community Survey 5-Year Estimates

Poverty Rate

Area	All Ages	Under 18 Years Old	18 to 64 Years Old	65 Years and Over
City	14.5	18.5	13.5	9.0
MSA[1]	14.7	19.0	13.7	9.7
U.S.	13.4	18.5	12.6	9.3

Note: Figures are percentage of people whose income during the past 12 months was below the poverty level;
(1) Figures cover the Clarksville, TN-KY Metropolitan Statistical Area
Source: U.S. Census Bureau, 2015-2019 American Community Survey 5-Year Estimates

CITY FINANCES

City Government Finances

Component	2017 ($000)	2017 ($ per capita)
Total Revenues	372,292	2,496
Total Expenditures	349,310	2,342
Debt Outstanding	795,269	5,331
Cash and Securities[1]	419,025	2,809

Note: (1) Cash and security holdings of a government at the close of its fiscal year, including those of its dependent agencies, utilities, and liquor stores.
Source: U.S. Census Bureau, State & Local Government Finances 2017

City Government Revenue by Source

Source	2017 ($000)	2017 ($ per capita)	2017 (%)
General Revenue			
From Federal Government	0	0	0.0
From State Government	37,480	251	10.1
From Local Governments	16,506	111	4.4
Taxes			
Property	33,749	226	9.1
Sales and Gross Receipts	8,206	55	2.2
Personal Income	0	0	0.0
Corporate Income	0	0	0.0
Motor Vehicle License	0	0	0.0
Other Taxes	109	1	0.0
Current Charges	59,490	399	16.0
Liquor Store	0	0	0.0
Utility	213,652	1,432	57.4
Employee Retirement	0	0	0.0

Source: U.S. Census Bureau, State & Local Government Finances 2017

City Government Expenditures by Function

Function	2017 ($000)	2017 ($ per capita)	2017 (%)
General Direct Expenditures			
Air Transportation	0	0	0.0
Corrections	0	0	0.0
Education	0	0	0.0
Employment Security Administration	0	0	0.0
Financial Administration	1,773	11	0.5
Fire Protection	17,023	114	4.9
General Public Buildings	497	3	0.1
Governmental Administration, Other	1,927	12	0.6
Health	0	0	0.0
Highways	12,851	86	3.7
Hospitals	0	0	0.0
Housing and Community Development	1,789	12	0.5
Interest on General Debt	0	0	0.0
Judicial and Legal	406	2	0.1
Libraries	0	0	0.0
Parking	306	2	0.1
Parks and Recreation	7,426	49	2.1
Police Protection	27,577	184	7.9
Public Welfare	0	0	0.0
Sewerage	26,281	176	7.5
Solid Waste Management	0	0	0.0
Veterans' Services	0	0	0.0
Liquor Store	0	0	0.0
Utility	226,053	1,515	64.7
Employee Retirement	0	0	0.0

Source: U.S. Census Bureau, State & Local Government Finances 2017

EMPLOYMENT

Labor Force and Employment

Area	Civilian Labor Force Dec. 2019	Civilian Labor Force Dec. 2020	% Chg.	Workers Employed Dec. 2019	Workers Employed Dec. 2020	% Chg.
City	63,787	65,851	3.2	61,432	60,949	-0.8
MSA[1]	118,102	120,516	2.0	113,647	112,488	-1.0
U.S.	164,007,000	160,017,000	-2.4	158,504,000	149,613,000	-5.6

Note: Data is not seasonally adjusted and covers workers 16 years of age and older; (1) Figures cover the Clarksville, TN-KY Metropolitan Statistical Area
Source: Bureau of Labor Statistics, Local Area Unemployment Statistics

Unemployment Rate

Area	Jan.	Feb.	Mar.	Apr.	May	Jun.	Jul.	Aug.	Sep.	Oct.	Nov.	Dec.
City	4.4	4.3	3.8	17.2	11.3	11.2	11.4	9.9	7.3	8.4	5.8	7.4
MSA[1]	4.6	4.4	4.3	16.1	10.5	8.8	9.0	8.5	6.2	7.5	5.4	6.7
U.S.	4.0	3.8	4.5	14.4	13.0	11.2	10.5	8.5	7.7	6.6	6.4	6.5

Note: Data is not seasonally adjusted and covers workers 16 years of age and older; (1) Figures cover the Clarksville, TN-KY Metropolitan Statistical Area
Source: Bureau of Labor Statistics, Local Area Unemployment Statistics

Average Wages

Occupation	$/Hr.	Occupation	$/Hr.
Accountants and Auditors	30.20	Maintenance and Repair Workers	21.40
Automotive Mechanics	18.80	Marketing Managers	n/a
Bookkeepers	18.20	Network and Computer Systems Admin.	33.30
Carpenters	18.80	Nurses, Licensed Practical	20.90
Cashiers	11.10	Nurses, Registered	31.30
Computer Programmers	n/a	Nursing Assistants	13.30
Computer Systems Analysts	37.00	Office Clerks, General	15.40
Computer User Support Specialists	20.90	Physical Therapists	43.20
Construction Laborers	15.30	Physicians	113.80
Cooks, Restaurant	10.90	Plumbers, Pipefitters and Steamfitters	24.00
Customer Service Representatives	16.80	Police and Sheriff's Patrol Officers	22.20
Dentists	n/a	Postal Service Mail Carriers	25.30
Electricians	23.70	Real Estate Sales Agents	13.80
Engineers, Electrical	42.60	Retail Salespersons	13.10
Fast Food and Counter Workers	9.40	Sales Representatives, Technical/Scientific	28.40
Financial Managers	50.30	Secretaries, Exc. Legal/Medical/Executive	16.50
First-Line Supervisors of Office Workers	22.50	Security Guards	17.00
General and Operations Managers	45.80	Surgeons	n/a
Hairdressers/Cosmetologists	11.70	Teacher Assistants, Exc. Postsecondary*	13.60
Home Health and Personal Care Aides	11.10	Teachers, Secondary School, Exc. Sp. Ed.*	33.50
Janitors and Cleaners	13.50	Telemarketers	n/a
Landscaping/Groundskeeping Workers	14.10	Truck Drivers, Heavy/Tractor-Trailer	19.80
Lawyers	38.90	Truck Drivers, Light/Delivery Services	19.60
Maids and Housekeeping Cleaners	11.40	Waiters and Waitresses	10.90

Note: Wage data covers the Clarksville, TN-KY Metropolitan Statistical Area; (*) Hourly wages were calculated from annual wage data based on a 40 hour work week; n/a not available.
Source: Bureau of Labor Statistics, Metro Area Occupational Employment & Wage Estimates, May 2020

Employment by Industry

Sector	MSA[1] Number of Employees	MSA[1] Percent of Total	U.S. Percent of Total
Construction, Mining, and Logging	3,600	3.9	5.5
Education and Health Services	12,000	12.9	16.3
Financial Activities	3,100	3.3	6.1
Government	19,200	20.7	15.2
Information	1,000	1.1	1.9
Leisure and Hospitality	11,300	12.2	9.0
Manufacturing	10,900	11.7	8.5
Other Services	3,200	3.4	3.8
Professional and Business Services	9,900	10.7	14.4
Retail Trade	12,900	13.9	10.9
Transportation, Warehousing, and Utilities	2,700	2.9	4.6
Wholesale Trade	n/a	n/a	3.9

Note: Figures are non-farm employment as of December 2020. Figures are not seasonally adjusted and include workers 16 years of age and older; (1) Figures cover the Clarksville, TN-KY Metropolitan Statistical Area; n/a not available
Source: Bureau of Labor Statistics, Current Employment Statistics, Employment, Hours, and Earnings

Employment by Occupation

Occupation Classification	City (%)	MSA[1] (%)	U.S. (%)
Management, Business, Science, and Arts	30.8	31.3	38.5
Natural Resources, Construction, and Maintenance	9.4	10.0	8.9
Production, Transportation, and Material Moving	18.1	18.4	13.2
Sales and Office	22.7	21.9	21.6
Service	18.9	18.4	17.8

Note: Figures cover employed civilians 16 years of age and older; (1) Figures cover the Clarksville, TN-KY Metropolitan Statistical Area
Source: U.S. Census Bureau, 2015-2019 American Community Survey 5-Year Estimates

Occupations with Greatest Projected Employment Growth: 2020 – 2022

Occupation[1]	2020 Employment	2022 Projected Employment	Numeric Employment Change	Percent Employment Change
Heavy and Tractor-Trailer Truck Drivers	72,760	75,530	2,770	3.8
Laborers and Freight, Stock, and Material Movers, Hand	99,970	101,640	1,670	1.7
General and Operations Managers	44,540	45,510	970	2.2
Janitors and Cleaners, Except Maids and Housekeeping Cleaners	44,140	45,030	890	2.0
Construction Laborers	28,960	29,800	840	2.9
Managers, All Other	34,220	35,050	830	2.4
Retail Salespersons	88,170	88,970	800	0.9
Stock Clerks and Order Fillers	58,210	58,980	770	1.3
Farmers, Ranchers, and Other Agricultural Managers	23,960	24,700	740	3.1
Light Truck or Delivery Services Drivers	20,800	21,500	700	3.4

Note: Projections cover Tennessee; (1) Sorted by numeric employment change
Source: www.projectionscentral.com, State Occupational Projections, 2020–2022 Short-Term Projections

Fastest-Growing Occupations: 2020 – 2022

Occupation[1]	2020 Employment	2022 Projected Employment	Numeric Employment Change	Percent Employment Change
Athletes and Sports Competitors	390	510	120	30.8
Audio and Video Equipment Technicians	1,960	2,090	130	6.6
Software Developers, Applications	6,750	7,190	440	6.5
Sailors and Marine Oilers	920	980	60	6.5
Captains, Mates, and Pilots of Water Vessels	790	840	50	6.3
Operations Research Analysts	1,510	1,600	90	6.0
Massage Therapists	2,370	2,510	140	5.9
Agricultural Equipment Operators	2,790	2,950	160	5.7
Tire Repairers and Changers	2,830	2,990	160	5.7
Nonfarm Animal Caretakers	5,100	5,370	270	5.3

Note: Projections cover Tennessee; (1) Sorted by percent employment change and excludes occupations with numeric employment change less than 50
Source: www.projectionscentral.com, State Occupational Projections, 2020–2022 Short-Term Projections

TAXES

State Corporate Income Tax Rates

State	Tax Rate (%)	Income Brackets ($)	Num. of Brackets	Financial Institution Tax Rate (%)[a]	Federal Income Tax Ded.
Tennessee	6.5	Flat rate	1	6.5	No

Note: Tax rates as of January 1, 2021; (a) Rates listed are the corporate income tax rate applied to financial institutions or excise taxes based on income. Some states have other taxes based upon the value of deposits or shares.
Source: Federation of Tax Administrators, State Corporate Income Tax Rates, January 1, 2021

State Individual Income Tax Rates

State	Tax Rate (%)	Income Brackets ($)	Personal Exemptions ($) Single	Married	Depend.	Standard Ded. ($) Single	Married
Tennessee					– No state income tax (x) –		

Note: Tax rates as of January 1, 2021; Local- and county-level taxes are not included; (x) Tennessee Hall Tax Rate on Dividends and Interest has been repealed in 2021.
Source: Federation of Tax Administrators, State Individual Income Tax Rates, January 1, 2021

Various State Sales and Excise Tax Rates

State	State Sales Tax (%)	Gasoline[1] (¢/gal.)	Cigarette[2] ($/pack)	Spirits[3] ($/gal.)	Wine[4] ($/gal.)	Beer[5] ($/gal.)	Recreational Marijuana (%)
Tennessee	7	27.4	0.62	4.46	1.27	1.29	Not legal

Note: All tax rates as of January 1, 2021; (1) The American Petroleum Institute has developed a methodology for determining the average tax rate on a gallon of fuel. Rates may include any of the following: excise taxes, environmental fees, storage tank fees, other fees or taxes, general sales tax, and local taxes; (2) The federal excise tax of $1.0066 per pack and local taxes are not included; (3) Rates are those applicable to off-premise sales of 40% alcohol by volume (a.b.v.) distilled spirits in 750ml containers. Local excise taxes are excluded; (4) Rates are those applicable to off-premise sales of 11% a.b.v. non-carbonated wine in 750ml containers; (5) Rates are those applicable to off-premise sales of 4.7% a.b.v. beer in 12 ounce containers.
Source: Tax Foundation, 2021 Facts & Figures: How Does Your State Compare?

State Business Tax Climate Index Rankings

State	Overall Rank	Corporate Tax Rank	Individual Income Tax Rank	Sales Tax Rank	Property Tax Rank	Unemployment Insurance Tax Rank
Tennessee	18	24	8	47	33	26

Note: The index is a measure of how each state's tax laws affect economic performance. The lower the rank, the more favorable a state's tax system is for business. States without a given tax are given a ranking of 1. The scores/rankings for the District of Columbia do not affect other states. The 2021 index represents the tax climate as of July 1, 2020.
Source: Tax Foundation, State Business Tax Climate Index 2021

TRANSPORTATION

Means of Transportation to Work

Area	Drove Alone	Car-pooled	Bus	Subway	Railroad	Bicycle	Walked	Other Means	Worked at Home
City	85.9	7.8	0.9	0.0	0.0	0.0	1.3	1.3	2.7
MSA[1]	84.0	8.1	0.7	0.0	0.0	0.1	3.1	1.3	2.7
U.S.	76.3	9.0	2.4	1.9	0.6	0.5	2.7	1.4	5.2

Note: Figures are percentages and cover workers 16 years of age and older; (1) Figures cover the Clarksville, TN-KY Metropolitan Statistical Area
Source: U.S. Census Bureau, 2015-2019 American Community Survey 5-Year Estimates

Travel Time to Work

Area	Less Than 10 Minutes	10 to 19 Minutes	20 to 29 Minutes	30 to 44 Minutes	45 to 59 Minutes	60 to 89 Minutes	90 Minutes or More
City	10.8	34.3	24.5	15.6	5.7	7.4	1.7
MSA[1]	15.2	32.1	21.1	17.4	6.1	6.0	2.1
U.S.	12.2	28.4	20.8	20.8	8.3	6.4	2.9

Note: Note: Figures are percentages and include workers 16 years old and over; (1) Figures cover the Clarksville, TN-KY Metropolitan Statistical Area
Source: U.S. Census Bureau, 2015-2019 American Community Survey 5-Year Estimates

Key Congestion Measures

Measure	1982	1992	2002	2012	2017
Annual Hours of Delay, Total (000)	n/a	n/a	n/a	n/a	3,723
Annual Hours of Delay, Per Auto Commuter	n/a	n/a	n/a	n/a	21
Annual Congestion Cost, Total (million $)	n/a	n/a	n/a	n/a	80
Annual Congestion Cost, Per Auto Commuter ($)	n/a	n/a	n/a	n/a	462

Note: n/a not available
Source: Texas A&M Transportation Institute, 2019 Urban Mobility Report

Freeway Travel Time Index

Measure	1982	1987	1992	1997	2002	2007	2012	2017
Urban Area Index[1]	n/a	n/a	n/a	n/a	n/a	n/a	n/a	1.12
Urban Area Rank[1,2]	n/a	n/a	n/a	n/a	n/a	n/a	n/a	n/a

Note: Freeway Travel Time Index—the ratio of travel time in the peak period to the travel time at free-flow conditions. For example, a value of 1.30 indicates a 20-minute free-flow trip takes 26 minutes in the peak (20 minutes x 1.30 = 26 minutes); (1) Covers the Clarksville TN-KY urban area; (2) Rank is based on 101 larger urban areas (#1 = highest travel time index); n/a not available
Source: Texas A&M Transportation Institute, 2019 Urban Mobility Report

Public Transportation

Agency Name / Mode of Transportation	Vehicles Operated in Maximum Service[1]	Annual Unlinked Passenger Trips[2] (in thous.)	Annual Passenger Miles[3] (in thous.)
Clarksville Transit System (CTS)			
Bus (directly operated)	18	648.5	n/a
Demand Response (directly operated)	11	39.0	n/a

Note: (1) Number of revenue vehicles operated by the given mode and type of service to meet the annual maximum service requirement. This is the revenue vehicle count during the peak season of the year; on the week and day that maximum service is provided. Vehicles operated in maximum service (VOMS) exclude atypical days and one-time special events; (2) Number of passengers who boarded public transportation vehicles. Passengers are counted each time they board a vehicle no matter how many vehicles they use to travel from their origin to their destination. (3) Sum of the distances ridden by all passengers during the entire fiscal year.
Source: Federal Transit Administration, National Transit Database, 2019

Air Transportation

Airport Name and Code / Type of Service	Passenger Airlines[1]	Passenger Enplanements	Freight Carriers[2]	Freight (lbs)
Nashville International (53 miles) (BNA)				
Domestic service (U.S. carriers - 2020)	35	3,992,738	15	56,435,779
International service (U.S. carriers - 2019)	8	10,520	1	1,394

Note: (1) Includes all U.S.-based major, minor and commuter airlines that carried at least one passenger during the year; (2) Includes all U.S.-based airlines and freight carriers that transported at least one pound of freight during the year.
Source: Bureau of Transportation Statistics, The Intermodal Transportation Database, Air Carriers: T-100 Domestic Market (U.S. Carriers), 2020; Bureau of Transportation Statistics, The Intermodal Transportation Database, Air Carriers: T-100 International Market (U.S. Carriers), 2019

BUSINESSES

Major Business Headquarters

Company Name	Industry	Rankings Fortune[1]	Forbes[2]
No companies listed	-	-	-

Note: (1) Companies that produce a 10-K are ranked 1 to 500 based on 2019 revenue; (2) All private companies with at least $2 billion in annual revenue through the end of their most current fiscal year are ranked 1 to 219; companies listed are headquartered in the city; dashes indicate no ranking
Source: Fortune, "Fortune 500," June/July 2020; Forbes, "America's Largest Private Companies," 2020

Living Environment

COST OF LIVING

Cost of Living Index

	Composite Index	Groceries	Housing	Utilities	Transportation	Health Care	Misc. Goods/Services
	n/a	n/a	n/a	n/a	n/a	n/a	n/a

Note: The Cost of Living Index measures regional differences in the cost of consumer goods and services, excluding taxes and non-consumer expenditures, for professional and managerial households in the top income quintile. It is based on more than 50,000 prices covering almost 60 different items for which prices are collected three times a year by chambers of commerce, economic development organizations or university applied economic centers in each participating urban area. The numbers shown should be read as a percentage above or below the national average of 100. For example, a value of 115.4 in the groceries column indicates that grocery prices are 15.4% higher than the national average. Small differences in the index numbers should not be interpreted as significant; n/a not available.
Source: The Council for Community and Economic Research, Cost of Living Index, 2020

Grocery Prices

Area[1]	T-Bone Steak ($/pound)	Frying Chicken ($/pound)	Whole Milk ($/half gal.)	Eggs ($/dozen)	Orange Juice ($/64 oz.)	Coffee ($/11.5 oz.)
City[2]	n/a	n/a	n/a	n/a	n/a	n/a
Avg.	11.78	1.39	2.05	1.47	3.57	4.34
Min.	8.03	0.94	1.03	0.74	2.94	3.02
Max.	15.86	2.65	4.31	3.77	5.44	8.69

Note: (1) Values for the local area are compared with the average, minimum and maximum values for all 284 areas in the Cost of Living Index; (2) Figures cover the Clarksville TN urban area; n/a not available; **T-Bone Steak** (price per pound); **Frying Chicken** (price per pound, whole fryer); **Whole Milk** (half gallon carton); **Eggs** (price per dozen, Grade A, large); **Orange Juice** (64 oz. Tropicana or Florida Natural); **Coffee** (11.5 oz. can, vacuum-packed, Maxwell House, Hills Bros, or Folgers).
Source: The Council for Community and Economic Research, Cost of Living Index, 2020

Housing and Utility Costs

Area[1]	New Home Price ($)	Apartment Rent ($/month)	All Electric ($/month)	Part Electric ($/month)	Other Energy ($/month)	Telephone ($/month)
City[2]	n/a	n/a	n/a	n/a	n/a	n/a
Avg.	368,594	1,168	170.86	100.47	65.28	184.30
Min.	190,567	502	91.58	31.42	26.08	169.60
Max.	2,227,806	4,738	470.38	280.31	280.06	206.50

Note: (1) Values for the local area are compared with the average, minimum and maximum values for all 284 areas in the Cost of Living Index; (2) Figures cover the Clarksville TN urban area; n/a not available; **New Home Price** (2,400 sf living area, 8,000 sf lot, in urban area with full utilities); **Apartment Rent** (950 sf 2 bedroom/1.5 or 2 bath, unfurnished, excluding all utilities except water); **All Electric** (average monthly cost for an all-electric home); **Part Electric** (average monthly cost for a part-electric home); **Other Energy** (average monthly cost for natural gas, fuel oil, coal, wood, and any other forms of energy except electricity); **Telephone** (price includes the base monthly rate plus taxes and fees for three lines of mobile phone service).
Source: The Council for Community and Economic Research, Cost of Living Index, 2020

Health Care, Transportation, and Other Costs

Area[1]	Doctor ($/visit)	Dentist ($/visit)	Optometrist ($/visit)	Gasoline ($/gallon)	Beauty Salon ($/visit)	Men's Shirt ($)
City[2]	n/a	n/a	n/a	n/a	n/a	n/a
Avg.	115.44	99.32	108.10	2.21	39.27	31.37
Min.	36.68	59.00	51.36	1.71	19.00	11.00
Max.	219.00	153.10	250.97	3.46	82.05	58.33

Note: (1) Values for the local area are compared with the average, minimum and maximum values for all 284 areas in the Cost of Living Index; (2) Figures cover the Clarksville TN urban area; n/a not available; **Doctor** (general practitioners routine exam of an established patient); **Dentist** (adult teeth cleaning and periodic oral examination); **Optometrist** (full vision eye exam for established adult patient); **Gasoline** (one gallon regular unleaded, national brand, including all taxes, cash price at self-service pump if available); **Beauty Salon** (woman's shampoo, trim, and blow-dry); **Men's Shirt** (cotton/polyester dress shirt, pinpoint weave, long sleeves).
Source: The Council for Community and Economic Research, Cost of Living Index, 2020

HOUSING

Homeownership Rate

Area	2012 (%)	2013 (%)	2014 (%)	2015 (%)	2016 (%)	2017 (%)	2018 (%)	2019 (%)	2020 (%)
MSA[1]	n/a	n/a	n/a	n/a	n/a	n/a	n/a	n/a	n/a
U.S.	65.4	65.1	64.5	63.7	63.4	63.9	64.4	64.6	66.6

Note: (1) Figures cover the Clarksville, TN-KY Metropolitan Statistical Area; n/a not available
Source: U.S. Census Bureau, Housing Vacancies and Homeownership Annual Statistics: 2012-2020

House Price Index (HPI)

Area	National Ranking[2]	Quarterly Change (%)	One-Year Change (%)	Five-Year Change (%)	Since 1991Q1 (%)
MSA[1]	n/a	n/a	n/a	n/a	n/a
U.S.[3]	—	3.81	10.77	38.99	205.12

Note: The HPI is a weighted repeat sales index. It measures average price changes in repeat sales or refinancings on the same properties. This information is obtained by reviewing repeat mortgage transactions on single-family properties whose mortgages have been purchased or securitized by Fannie Mae or Freddie Mac since January 1975; (1) Figures cover the , Metropolitan Statistical Area; (2) Rankings are based on annual percentage change for all metro areas containing at least 15,000 transactions over the last 10 years and ranges from 1 to 253; (3) figures based on a weighted average of Census Division estimates using a seasonally adjusted, purchase-only index; all figures are for the period ending December 31, 2020; n/a not available
Source: Federal Housing Finance Agency, Change in Metropolitan Area House Price Indexes, April 7, 2021

Median Single-Family Home Prices

Area	2018	2019	2020p	Percent Change 2019 to 2020
MSA[1]	n/a	n/a	n/a	n/a
U.S. Average	261.6	274.6	299.9	9.2

Note: Figures are median sales prices of existing single-family homes in thousands of dollars; (p) preliminary; n/a not available; (1) Figures cover the Clarksville, TN-KY Metropolitan Statistical Area
Source: National Association of Realtors, Median Sales Price of Existing Single-Family Homes for Metropolitan Areas, 4th Quarter 2020

Qualifying Income Based on Median Sales Price of Existing Single-Family Homes

Area	With 5% Down ($)	With 10% Down ($)	With 20% Down ($)
MSA[1]	n/a	n/a	n/a
U.S. Average	59,266	56,147	49,908

Note: Figures are preliminary; Qualifying income is based on a mortgage rate of 2.81%. Monthly principal and interest payment is limited to 25% of income; n/a not available; (1) Figures cover the Clarksville, TN-KY Metropolitan Statistical Area
Source: National Association of Realtors, Qualifying Income Based on Median Sales Price of Existing Single-Family Homes for Metropolitan Areas, 4th Quarter 2020

Home Value Distribution

Area	Under $50,000	$50,000 -$99,999	$100,000 -$149,999	$150,000 -$199,999	$200,000 -$299,999	$300,000 -$499,999	$500,000 -$999,999	$1,000,000 or more
City	4.3	14.1	28.9	26.6	19.0	5.6	0.9	0.5
MSA[1]	6.6	17.3	23.7	21.4	19.5	9.0	1.8	0.7
U.S.	6.9	12.0	13.3	14.0	19.6	19.3	11.4	3.4

Note: Figures are percentages and cover owner-occupied housing units; (1) Figures cover the Clarksville, TN-KY Metropolitan Statistical Area
Source: U.S. Census Bureau, 2015-2019 American Community Survey 5-Year Estimates

Year Housing Structure Built

Area	2010 or Later	2000 -2009	1990 -1999	1980 -1989	1970 -1979	1960 -1969	1950 -1959	1940 -1949	Before 1940	Median Year
City	13.0	22.8	20.9	13.2	12.4	8.6	4.7	2.5	2.0	1993
MSA[1]	10.7	20.0	20.9	12.1	15.2	9.2	6.2	2.5	3.1	1991
U.S.	5.2	14.0	13.9	13.4	15.2	10.6	10.3	4.9	12.6	1978

Note: Figures are percentages except for Median Year; Note: (1) Figures cover the Clarksville, TN-KY Metropolitan Statistical Area
Source: U.S. Census Bureau, 2015-2019 American Community Survey 5-Year Estimates

Gross Monthly Rent

Area	Under $500	$500 -$999	$1,000 -$1,499	$1,500 -$1,999	$2,000 -$2,499	$2,500 -$2,999	$3,000 and up	Median ($)
City	5.8	48.7	35.6	7.8	1.8	0.1	0.1	961
MSA[1]	8.7	49.9	32.7	7.3	1.3	0.2	0.0	919
U.S.	9.4	36.2	30.0	14.0	5.6	2.4	2.4	1,062

Note: Figures are percentages except for Median; Gross rent is the contract rent plus the estimated average monthly cost of utilities (electricity, gas, and water and sewer) and fuels (oil, coal, kerosene, wood, etc.) if these are paid by the renter (or paid for the renter by someone else); (1) Figures cover the Clarksville, TN-KY Metropolitan Statistical Area
Source: U.S. Census Bureau, 2015-2019 American Community Survey 5-Year Estimates

HEALTH

Health Risk Factors

Category	MSA[1] (%)	U.S. (%)
Adults aged 18–64 who have any kind of health care coverage	n/a	87.3
Adults who reported being in good or better health	n/a	82.4
Adults who have been told they have high blood cholesterol	n/a	33.0
Adults who have been told they have high blood pressure	n/a	32.3
Adults who are current smokers	n/a	17.1
Adults who currently use E-cigarettes	n/a	4.6
Adults who currently use chewing tobacco, snuff, or snus	n/a	4.0
Adults who are heavy drinkers[2]	n/a	6.3
Adults who are binge drinkers[3]	n/a	17.4
Adults who are overweight (BMI 25.0 - 29.9)	n/a	35.3
Adults who are obese (BMI 30.0 - 99.8)	n/a	31.3
Adults who participated in any physical activities in the past month	n/a	74.4
Adults who always or nearly always wears a seat belt	n/a	94.3

Note: n/a not available; (1) Figures cover the Clarksville, TN-KY Metropolitan Statistical Area; (2) Heavy drinkers are classified as adult men having more than 14 drinks per week and adult women having more than 7 drinks per week; (3) Binge drinkers are classified as males having five or more drinks on one occasion or females having four or more drinks on one occasion
Source: Centers for Disease Control and Prevention, Behaviorial Risk Factor Surveillance System, SMART: Selected Metropolitan Area Risk Trends, 2017

Acute and Chronic Health Conditions

Category	MSA[1] (%)	U.S. (%)
Adults who have ever been told they had a heart attack	n/a	4.2
Adults who have ever been told they have angina or coronary heart disease	n/a	3.9
Adults who have ever been told they had a stroke	n/a	3.0
Adults who have ever been told they have asthma	n/a	14.2
Adults who have ever been told they have arthritis	n/a	24.9
Adults who have ever been told they have diabetes[2]	n/a	10.5
Adults who have ever been told they had skin cancer	n/a	6.2
Adults who have ever been told they had any other types of cancer	n/a	7.1
Adults who have ever been told they have COPD	n/a	6.5
Adults who have ever been told they have kidney disease	n/a	3.0
Adults who have ever been told they have a form of depression	n/a	20.5

Note: n/a not available; (1) Figures cover the Clarksville, TN-KY Metropolitan Statistical Area; (2) Figures do not include pregnancy-related, borderline, or pre-diabetes
Source: Centers for Disease Control and Prevention, Behaviorial Risk Factor Surveillance System, SMART: Selected Metropolitan Area Risk Trends, 2017

Health Screening and Vaccination Rates

Category	MSA[1] (%)	U.S. (%)
Adults aged 65+ who have had flu shot within the past year	n/a	60.7
Adults aged 65+ who have ever had a pneumonia vaccination	n/a	75.4
Adults who have ever been tested for HIV	n/a	36.1
Adults who have ever had the shingles or zoster vaccine?	n/a	28.9
Adults who have had their blood cholesterol checked within the last five years	n/a	85.9

Note: n/a not available; (1) Figures cover the Clarksville, TN-KY Metropolitan Statistical Area.
Source: Centers for Disease Control and Prevention, Behaviorial Risk Factor Surveillance System, SMART: Selected Metropolitan Area Risk Trends, 2017

Disability Status

Category	MSA[1] (%)	U.S. (%)
Adults who reported being deaf	n/a	6.7
Are you blind or have serious difficulty seeing, even when wearing glasses?	n/a	4.5
Are you limited in any way in any of your usual activities due of arthritis?	n/a	12.9
Do you have difficulty doing errands alone?	n/a	6.8
Do you have difficulty dressing or bathing?	n/a	3.6
Do you have serious difficulty concentrating/remembering/making decisions?	n/a	10.7
Do you have serious difficulty walking or climbing stairs?	n/a	13.6

Note: n/a not available; (1) Figures cover the Clarksville, TN-KY Metropolitan Statistical Area.
Source: Centers for Disease Control and Prevention, Behaviorial Risk Factor Surveillance System, SMART: Selected Metropolitan Area Risk Trends, 2017

Mortality Rates for the Top 10 Causes of Death in the U.S.

ICD-10[a] Sub-Chapter	ICD-10[a] Code	County[2]	U.S.
Malignant neoplasms	C00-C97	186.2	149.2
Ischaemic heart diseases	I20-I25	113.9	90.5
Other forms of heart disease	I30-I51	45.6	52.2
Chronic lower respiratory diseases	J40-J47	81.3	39.6
Other degenerative diseases of the nervous system	G30-G31	53.5	37.6
Cerebrovascular diseases	I60-I69	56.3	37.2
Other external causes of accidental injury	W00-X59	51.7	36.1
Organic, including symptomatic, mental disorders	F01-F09	28.0	29.4
Hypertensive diseases	I10-I15	27.3	24.1
Diabetes mellitus	E10-E14	33.9	21.5

Age-Adjusted Mortality Rate[1] per 100,000 population

Note: (a) ICD-10 = International Classification of Diseases 10th Revision; (1) Mortality rates are a three-year average covering 2017-2019; (2) Figures cover Montgomery County.
Source: Centers for Disease Control and Prevention, National Center for Health Statistics. Underlying Cause of Death 1999-2019 on CDC WONDER Online Database

Mortality Rates for Selected Causes of Death

ICD-10[a] Sub-Chapter	ICD-10[a] Code	County[2]	U.S.
Assault	X85-Y09	8.8	6.0
Diseases of the liver	K70-K76	16.4	14.4
Human immunodeficiency virus (HIV) disease	B20-B24	Suppressed	1.5
Influenza and pneumonia	J09-J18	14.2	13.8
Intentional self-harm	X60-X84	20.3	14.1
Malnutrition	E40-E46	Unreliable	2.3
Obesity and other hyperalimentation	E65-E68	5.0	2.1
Renal failure	N17-N19	11.5	12.6
Transport accidents	V01-V99	17.7	12.3
Viral hepatitis	B15-B19	Suppressed	1.2

Age-Adjusted Mortality Rate[1] per 100,000 population

Note: (a) ICD-10 = International Classification of Diseases 10th Revision; (1) Mortality rates are a three-year average covering 2017-2019; (2) Figures cover Montgomery County; Data are suppressed when the data meet the criteria for confidentiality constraints; Mortality rates are flagged as unreliable when the rate would be calculated with a numerator of 20 or less.
Source: Centers for Disease Control and Prevention, National Center for Health Statistics. Underlying Cause of Death 1999-2019 on CDC WONDER Online Database

Health Insurance Coverage

Area	With Health Insurance	With Private Health Insurance	With Public Health Insurance	Without Health Insurance	Population Under Age 19 Without Health Insurance
City	91.6	71.5	33.7	8.4	3.4
MSA[1]	91.8	69.1	37.2	8.2	5.3
U.S.	91.2	67.9	35.1	8.8	5.1

Note: Figures are percentages that cover the civilian noninstitutionalized population; (1) Figures cover the Clarksville, TN-KY Metropolitan Statistical Area
Source: U.S. Census Bureau, 2015-2019 American Community Survey 5-Year Estimates

Number of Medical Professionals

Area	MDs[3]	DOs[3,4]	Dentists	Podiatrists	Chiropractors	Optometrists
County[1] (number)	196	30	98	5	28	27
County[1] (rate[2])	95.5	14.6	46.9	2.4	13.4	12.9
U.S. (rate[2])	282.9	22.7	71.2	6.2	28.1	16.9

47125

Note: Data as of 2019 unless noted; (1) Data covers Montgomery County; (2) Rate per 100,000 population; (3) Data as of 2018 and includes all active, non-federal physicians; (4) Doctor of Osteopathic Medicine
Source: U.S. Department of Health and Human Services, Health Resources and Services Administration, Bureau of Health Professions, Area Resource File (ARF) 2019-2020

EDUCATION

Public School District Statistics

District Name	Schls	Pupils	Pupil/Teacher Ratio	Minority Pupils[1] (%)	Free Lunch Eligible[2] (%)	IEP[3] (%)
Montgomery County	39	35,366	16.4	47.9	n/a	13.7

Note: Table includes school districts with 2,000 or more students; (1) Percentage of students that are not non-Hispanic white; (2) Percentage of students that are eligible for the free lunch program; (3) Percentage of students that have an Individualized Education Program.
Source: U.S. Department of Education, National Center for Education Statistics, Common Core of Data, Local Education Agency (School District) Universe Survey: School Year 2018-2019; U.S. Department of Education, National Center for Education Statistics, Common Core of Data, Public Elementary/Secondary School Universe Survey: School Year 2018-2019

Highest Level of Education

Area	Less than H.S.	H.S. Diploma	Some College, No Deg.	Associate Degree	Bachelor's Degree	Master's Degree	Prof. School Degree	Doctorate Degree
City	7.1	27.9	26.9	10.5	18.7	6.9	0.8	1.2
MSA[1]	9.3	30.2	25.4	10.3	16.1	6.8	1.1	0.9
U.S.	12.0	27.0	20.4	8.5	19.8	8.8	2.1	1.4

Note: Figures cover persons age 25 and over; (1) Figures cover the Clarksville, TN-KY Metropolitan Statistical Area
Source: U.S. Census Bureau, 2015-2019 American Community Survey 5-Year Estimates

Educational Attainment by Race

Area	High School Graduate or Higher (%) Total	White	Black	Asian	Hisp.[2]	Bachelor's Degree or Higher (%) Total	White	Black	Asian	Hisp.[2]
City	92.9	93.5	92.6	85.2	87.2	27.6	28.1	24.7	41.9	18.2
MSA[1]	90.7	91.2	89.6	85.6	86.2	24.8	24.9	22.2	43.3	19.1
U.S.	88.0	89.9	86.0	87.1	68.7	32.1	33.5	21.6	54.3	16.4

Note: Figures shown cover persons 25 years old and over; (1) Figures cover the Clarksville, TN-KY Metropolitan Statistical Area; (2) People of Hispanic origin can be of any race
Source: U.S. Census Bureau, 2015-2019 American Community Survey 5-Year Estimates

School Enrollment by Grade and Control

Area	Preschool (%) Public	Private	Kindergarten (%) Public	Private	Grades 1 - 4 (%) Public	Private	Grades 5 - 8 (%) Public	Private	Grades 9 - 12 (%) Public	Private
City	57.3	42.7	90.6	9.4	93.7	6.3	92.5	7.5	92.4	7.6
MSA[1]	62.9	37.1	92.1	7.9	88.8	11.2	89.5	10.5	89.0	11.0
U.S.	59.1	40.9	87.6	12.4	89.5	10.5	89.4	10.6	90.1	9.9

Note: Figures shown cover persons 3 years old and over; (1) Figures cover the Clarksville, TN-KY Metropolitan Statistical Area
Source: U.S. Census Bureau, 2015-2019 American Community Survey 5-Year Estimates

Higher Education

Four-Year Colleges Public	Private Non-profit	Private For-profit	Two-Year Colleges Public	Private Non-profit	Private For-profit	Medical Schools[1]	Law Schools[2]	Voc/Tech[3]
1	0	1	0	0	1	0	0	2

Note: Figures cover institutions located within the city limits and include main campuses only; (1) includes schools accredited by the Liaison Committee on Medical Education and the American Osteopathic Association's Commission on Osteopathic College Accreditation; (2) includes ABA-accredited schools, schools with provisional ABA accreditation, and state accredited schools; (3) includes all schools with programs that are less than 2 years.
Source: National Center for Education Statistics, Integrated Postsecondary Education System (IPEDS), 2019-20; Wikipedia, List of Medical Schools in the United States, accessed April 2, 2021; Wikipedia, List of Law Schools in the United States, accessed April 2, 2021

EMPLOYERS

Major Employers

Company Name	Industry
Agero	Call center
Akebono	Hubs, rotors
AT&T	Engineering services
Austin Peay State University	University
Bridgestone Metalpha U.S.A.	Steel tire cords & tire cord fabrics
City of Clarksville	Municipal government
Clarksville-Montgomery School System	Education
Gateway Medical Center	General medical & surgical hospitals
Jennie Stuart Medical Center	General medical & surgical hospitals
Jostens	Yearbooks & commercial printing
Montgomery County Government	Government
Trane Company	Heating & air conditioners
Trigg County Board of Education	Elementary & secondary schools
U.S. Army	U.S. military
Wal-Mart Stores	Department stores, discount

Note: Companies shown are located within the Clarksville, TN-KY Metropolitan Statistical Area.
Source: Hoovers.com; Wikipedia

PUBLIC SAFETY

Crime Rate

Area	All Crimes	Murder	Rape[3]	Robbery	Aggrav. Assault	Burglary	Larceny-Theft	Motor Vehicle Theft
City	3,370.7	8.8	64.4	72.5	433.1	339.4	2,160.7	291.9
Suburbs[1]	1,876.6	4.7	31.4	23.3	124.1	401.6	1,146.8	144.8
Metro[2]	2,648.0	6.8	48.4	48.7	283.6	369.5	1,670.2	220.7
U.S.	2,489.3	5.0	42.6	81.6	250.2	340.5	1,549.5	219.9

Note: Figures are crimes per 100,000 population; (1) All areas within the metro area that are located outside the city limits; (2) Figures cover the Clarksville, TN-KY Metropolitan Statistical Area; (3) All figures shown were reported using the revised Uniform Crime Reporting (UCR) definition of rape.
Source: FBI Uniform Crime Reports, 2019

Hate Crimes

Area	Number of Quarters Reported	Race/Ethnicity/Ancestry	Religion	Sexual Orientation	Disability	Gender	Gender Identity
City	4	0	0	0	0	0	0
U.S.	4	3,963	1,521	1,195	157	69	198

Source: Federal Bureau of Investigation, Hate Crime Statistics 2019

Identity Theft Consumer Reports

Area	Reports	Reports per 100,000 Population	Rank[2]
MSA[1]	1,354	440	62
U.S.	1,387,615	423	-

Note: (1) Figures cover the Clarksville, TN-KY Metropolitan Statistical Area; (2) Rank ranges from 1 to 391 where 1 indicates greatest number of identity theft reports per 100,000 population
Source: Federal Trade Commission, Consumer Sentinel Network Data Book 2020

Fraud and Other Consumer Reports

Area	Reports	Reports per 100,000 Population	Rank[2]
MSA[1]	2,466	801	98
U.S.	3,385,133	1,031	-

Note: (1) Figures cover the Clarksville, TN-KY Metropolitan Statistical Area; (2) Rank ranges from 1 to 391 where 1 indicates greatest number of fraud and other consumer reports per 100,000 population
Source: Federal Trade Commission, Consumer Sentinel Network Data Book 2020

POLITICS

2020 Presidential Election Results

Area	Biden	Trump	Jorgensen	Hawkins	Other
Montgomery County	42.3	55.0	1.9	0.2	0.7
U.S.	51.3	46.8	1.2	0.3	0.5

Note: Results are percentages and may not add to 100% due to rounding
Source: Dave Leip's Atlas of U.S. Presidential Elections

SPORTS

Professional Sports Teams

Team Name	League	Year Established

No teams are located in the metro area
Source: Wikipedia, Major Professional Sports Teams of the United States and Canada, April 6, 2021

CLIMATE

Average and Extreme Temperatures

Temperature	Jan	Feb	Mar	Apr	May	Jun	Jul	Aug	Sep	Oct	Nov	Dec	Yr.
Extreme High (°F)	78	84	86	91	95	106	107	104	105	94	84	79	107
Average High (°F)	47	51	60	71	79	87	90	89	83	72	60	50	70
Average Temp. (°F)	38	41	50	60	68	76	80	79	72	61	49	41	60
Average Low (°F)	28	31	39	48	57	65	69	68	61	48	39	31	49
Extreme Low (°F)	-17	-13	2	23	34	42	54	49	36	26	-1	-10	-17

Note: Figures cover the years 1948-1990
Source: National Climatic Data Center, International Station Meteorological Climate Summary, 9/96

Average Precipitation/Snowfall/Humidity

Precip./Humidity	Jan	Feb	Mar	Apr	May	Jun	Jul	Aug	Sep	Oct	Nov	Dec	Yr.
Avg. Precip. (in.)	4.4	4.2	5.0	4.1	4.6	3.7	3.8	3.3	3.2	2.6	3.9	4.6	47.4
Avg. Snowfall (in.)	4	3	1	Tr	0	0	0	0	0	Tr	1	1	11
Avg. Rel. Hum. 6am (%)	81	81	80	81	86	86	88	90	90	87	83	82	85
Avg. Rel. Hum. 3pm (%)	61	57	51	48	52	52	54	53	52	49	55	59	54

Note: Figures cover the years 1948-1990; Tr = Trace amounts (<0.05 in. of rain; <0.5 in. of snow)
Source: National Climatic Data Center, International Station Meteorological Climate Summary, 9/96

Weather Conditions

Temperature			Daytime Sky			Precipitation		
10°F & below	32°F & below	90°F & above	Clear	Partly cloudy	Cloudy	0.01 inch or more precip.	0.1 inch or more snow/ice	Thunderstorms
5	76	51	98	135	132	119	8	54

Note: Figures are average number of days per year and cover the years 1948-1990
Source: National Climatic Data Center, International Station Meteorological Climate Summary, 9/96

HAZARDOUS WASTE

Superfund Sites

The Clarksville, TN-KY metro area has no sites on the EPA's Superfund Final National Priorities List. There are a total of 1,375 Superfund sites with a status of proposed or final on the list in the U.S. *U.S. Environmental Protection Agency, National Priorities List, April 7, 2021*

AIR QUALITY

Air Quality Trends: Ozone

	1990	1995	2000	2005	2010	2015	2016	2017	2018	2019
MSA[1]	n/a	n/a	n/a	n/a	n/a	n/a	n/a	n/a	n/a	n/a
U.S.	0.088	0.089	0.082	0.080	0.073	0.068	0.069	0.068	0.069	0.065

Note: (1) Data covers the Clarksville, TN-KY Metropolitan Statistical Area; n/a not available. The values shown are the composite ozone concentration averages among trend sites based on the highest fourth daily maximum 8-hour concentration in parts per million. These trends are based on sites having an adequate record of monitoring data during the trend period. Data from exceptional events are included.
Source: U.S. Environmental Protection Agency, Air Quality Monitoring Information, "Air Quality Trends by City, 1990-2019"

Air Quality Index

Area	Percent of Days when Air Quality was...[2]					AQI Statistics[2]	
	Good	Moderate	Unhealthy for Sensitive Groups	Unhealthy	Very Unhealthy	Maximum	Median
MSA[1]	84.1	15.9	0.0	0.0	0.0	87	40

Note: (1) Data covers the Clarksville, TN-KY Metropolitan Statistical Area; (2) Based on 365 days with AQI data in 2019. Air Quality Index (AQI) is an index for reporting daily air quality. EPA calculates the AQI for five major air pollutants regulated by the Clean Air Act: ground-level ozone, particle pollution (aka particulate matter), carbon monoxide, sulfur dioxide, and nitrogen dioxide. The AQI runs from 0 to 500. The higher the AQI value, the greater the level of air pollution and the greater the health concern. There are six AQI categories: "Good" AQI is between 0 and 50. Air quality is considered satisfactory; "Moderate" AQI is between 51 and 100. Air quality is acceptable; "Unhealthy for Sensitive Groups" When AQI values are between 101 and 150, members of sensitive groups may experience health effects; "Unhealthy" When AQI values are between 151 and 200 everyone may begin to experience health effects; "Very Unhealthy" AQI values between 201 and 300 trigger a health alert; "Hazardous" AQI values over 300 trigger warnings of emergency conditions (not shown).
Source: U.S. Environmental Protection Agency, Air Quality Index Report, 2019

Air Quality Index Pollutants

Area	Percent of Days when AQI Pollutant was...[2]					
	Carbon Monoxide	Nitrogen Dioxide	Ozone	Sulfur Dioxide	Particulate Matter 2.5	Particulate Matter 10
MSA[1]	0.0	0.0	72.9	0.0	27.1	0.0

Note: (1) Data covers the Clarksville, TN-KY Metropolitan Statistical Area; (2) Based on 365 days with AQI data in 2019. The Air Quality Index (AQI) is an index for reporting daily air quality. EPA calculates the AQI for five major air pollutants regulated by the Clean Air Act: ground-level ozone, particle pollution (also known as particulate matter), carbon monoxide, sulfur dioxide, and nitrogen dioxide. The AQI runs from 0 to 500. The higher the AQI value, the greater the level of air pollution and the greater the health concern.
Source: U.S. Environmental Protection Agency, Air Quality Index Report, 2019

Maximum Air Pollutant Concentrations: Particulate Matter, Ozone, CO and Lead

	Particulate Matter 10 (ug/m^3)	Particulate Matter 2.5 Wtd AM (ug/m^3)	Particulate Matter 2.5 24-Hr (ug/m^3)	Ozone (ppm)	Carbon Monoxide (ppm)	Lead (ug/m^3)
MSA[1] Level	n/a	n/a	n/a	0.061	n/a	n/a
NAAQS[2]	150	15	35	0.075	9	0.15
Met NAAQS[2]	n/a	n/a	n/a	Yes	n/a	n/a

Note: (1) Data covers the Clarksville, TN-KY Metropolitan Statistical Area; Data from exceptional events are included; (2) National Ambient Air Quality Standards; ppm = parts per million; ug/m^3 = micrograms per cubic meter; n/a not available.
Concentrations: Particulate Matter 10 (coarse particulate)—highest second maximum 24-hour concentration; Particulate Matter 2.5 Wtd AM (fine particulate)—highest weighted annual mean concentration; Particulate Matter 2.5 24-Hour (fine particulate)—highest 98th percentile 24-hour concentration; Ozone—highest fourth daily maximum 8-hour concentration; Carbon Monoxide—highest second maximum non-overlapping 8-hour concentration; Lead—maximum running 3-month average
Source: U.S. Environmental Protection Agency, Air Quality Monitoring Information, "Air Quality Statistics by City, 2019"

Maximum Air Pollutant Concentrations: Nitrogen Dioxide and Sulfur Dioxide

	Nitrogen Dioxide AM (ppb)	Nitrogen Dioxide 1-Hr (ppb)	Sulfur Dioxide AM (ppb)	Sulfur Dioxide 1-Hr (ppb)	Sulfur Dioxide 24-Hr (ppb)
MSA[1] Level	n/a	n/a	n/a	n/a	n/a
NAAQS[2]	53	100	30	75	140
Met NAAQS[2]	n/a	n/a	n/a	n/a	n/a

Note: (1) Data covers the Clarksville, TN-KY Metropolitan Statistical Area; Data from exceptional events are included; (2) National Ambient Air Quality Standards; ppm = parts per million; ug/m^3 = micrograms per cubic meter; n/a not available.
Concentrations: Nitrogen Dioxide AM—highest arithmetic mean concentration; Nitrogen Dioxide 1-Hr—highest 98th percentile 1-hour daily maximum concentration; Sulfur Dioxide AM—highest annual mean concentration; Sulfur Dioxide 1-Hr—highest 99th percentile 1-hour daily maximum concentration; Sulfur Dioxide 24-Hr—highest second maximum 24-hour concentration
Source: U.S. Environmental Protection Agency, Air Quality Monitoring Information, "Air Quality Statistics by City, 2019"

College Station, Texas

Background

College Station is located 367 feet above sea level in the center of the Texas Triangle within Brazos County, and shares a border with the city of Bryan to the northwest. Named the most educated city in Texas, College Station was built alongside the prestigious Texas A&M University during the nation's centennial in 1876. The city's origins date back to 1860, when Houston and Texas Central Railway began to build through the region during the height of railroad expansion in the mid-1800s. Though this railway no longer exists, College Station's location and the university make it important to the state.

Although College Station has always been upheld by Texas A&M, the city was not incorporated until 1938. In 1942, the so-called "Father of College Station," Mayor Ernest Langford, gave the community its own, unique identity over his 26-year run. During Langford's first term, the city also adopted a council-manager system of government.

College Station is comprised of three major districts. Northgate, Wolf Pen Creek District, and Wellborn District combine to create a bustling city populated by students, professors, and their families. The city's population is young, mostly comprised of college-age individuals.

The economy of the city largely relies on the university itself, with many of its employees doing double time both attending the school and working in the city's shops or restaurants. Unemployment was among the lowest in Texas in recent years; however, underemployment continues to be an issue among the overqualified college students. Post Oak Mall provides much of the business within College Station, being the first to have opened in the area and the largest mall in Brazos Valley. Over 75 percent of retail sales in the Brazos Valley are within this mall.

The largest employer of the city is Texas A&M University. Previously known as the Agricultural and Mechanical College of Texas, TAMU is known for its triple designation as a Land-, Sea-, and Space-Grant institution, housing ongoing research projects funded by the likes of NASA, the National Institutes of Health, and the National Science Foundation.

> Researchers at Texas A&M detected the UK variant of COVID-19 in animals, a dog and cat from the same Texas household.

The city's nightlife and entertainment attract its young crowd to events such as the four-day Northgate Music Festival and the live music at Church Street BBQ and Hurricane Harry's. The Texas country music scene thrives here, with many notable musicians getting their starts at these smaller stages. Among them are Robert Earl Keen, Grammy-award winner Lyle Lovett, and Roger Creager.

Alongside these celebrities are important landmarks and areas within College Station, as well. These include Church Street, made famous by the Lyle Lovett/Robert Earl Keen duet "The Front Porch Song," and the George Bush Presidential Library, which was dedicated in 1997 in honor of President George H.W. Bush. The population and popularity of this relatively small city continues to grow every year, with predictions of the population doubling by the year 2030.

With the climate sitting comfortably in the subtropical and temperate zone, College Station enjoys mild winters with its low-temperature period lasting less than two months. While snow and ice during winter months are very rare, February 2021 saw unprecedented frigid temperatures and snowfall that led to days-long power outages. In turn, the summers are hot with occasional rain showers are the only variation in summer weather. The city's average temperature is 69 degrees with annual rainfall averaging 39 inches.

Rankings

General Rankings

- In their seventh annual survey, Livability.com looked at data for more than 1,000 small to mid-sized U.S. cities to determine the rankings for Livability's "Top 100 Best Places to Live" in 2020. College Station ranked #58. Criteria: housing and affordable living; vibrant economy; social and civic engagement; education; demographics; health care options; transportation & infrastructure; and abundant lifestyle amenities. *Livability.com, "Top 100 Best Places to Live 2020" October 2020*

Business/Finance Rankings

- The College Station metro area appeared on the Milken Institute "2021 Best Performing Cities" list. Rank: #21 out of 201 small metro areas (population over 60,000). Criteria: job growth; wage and salary growth; high-tech output growth; housing affordability; household broadband access. *Milken Institute, "Best-Performing Cities 2021," February 16, 2021*
- *Forbes* ranked 203 smaller metro areas (population under 268,000) to determine the nation's "Best Small Places for Business and Careers." The College Station metro area was ranked #2. Criteria: costs (business and living); job growth (past and projected); income growth; quality of life; educational attainment (college and high school); projected economic growth; cultural and leisure opportunities; workplace tolerance laws; net migration patterns. *Forbes, "The Best Small Places for Business and Careers 2019," October 30, 2019*

Real Estate Rankings

- College Station was ranked #201 out of 268 metro areas in terms of housing affordability in 2020 by the National Association of Home Builders (#1 = most affordable). Criteria: the share of homes sold in that area affordable to a family earning the local median income, based on standard mortgage underwriting criteria. *National Association of Home Builders®, NAHB-Wells Fargo Housing Opportunity Index, 4th Quarter 2020*

Safety Rankings

- To identify the safest cities in America, 24/7 Wall Street focused on violent crime categories—murder, non-negligent manslaughter, rape, robbery, and aggravated assault—and property crime as reported in the FBI's 2018 annual Uniform Crime Report. Criteria also included median income from American Community Survey and unemployment figures from Bureau of Labor Statistics. For cities with populations over 100,000, College Station was ranked #49. *247wallst.com, "America's Safest Cities" January 15, 2020*
- The National Insurance Crime Bureau ranked 384 metro areas in the U.S. in terms of per capita rates of vehicle theft. The College Station metro area ranked #218 (#1 = highest rate). Criteria: number of vehicle theft offenses per 100,000 inhabitants in 2019. *National Insurance Crime Bureau, "Hot Spots 2019," July 21, 2020*

Seniors/Retirement Rankings

- From its Best Cities for Successful Aging indexes, the Milken Institute generated rankings for metropolitan areas, weighing data in nine categories—health care, wellness, living arrangements, transportation and convenience, financial characteristics, education, employment, community engagement, and overall livability. The College Station metro area was ranked #28 overall in the small metro area category. *Milken Institute, "Best Cities for Successful Aging, 2017" March 14, 2017*

Sports/Recreation Rankings

- College Station was chosen as a bicycle friendly community by the League of American Bicyclists. A "Bicycle Friendly Community" welcomes cyclists by providing safe and supportive accommodation for cycling and encouraging people to bike for transportation and recreation. There are five award levels: Diamond; Platinum; Gold; Silver; and Bronze. The community achieved an award level of Bronze. *League of American Bicyclists, "Fall 2020 Awards-New & Renewing Bicycle Friendly Communities List," December 16, 2020*

Business Environment

DEMOGRAPHICS

Population Growth

Area	1990 Census	2000 Census	2010 Census	2019* Estimate	Population Growth (%) 1990-2019	Population Growth (%) 2010-2019
City	53,318	67,890	93,857	113,686	113.2	21.1
MSA[1]	150,998	184,885	228,660	258,029	70.9	12.8
U.S.	248,709,873	281,421,906	308,745,538	324,697,795	30.6	5.2

Note: (1) Figures cover the College Station-Bryan, TX Metropolitan Statistical Area; (*) 2015-2019 5-year estimated population
Source: U.S. Census Bureau, 1990 Census, Census 2000, Census 2010, 2015-2019 American Community Survey 5-Year Estimates

Household Size

Area	One	Two	Three	Four	Five	Six	Seven or More	Average Household Size
City	29.7	33.8	16.5	14.1	3.5	1.8	0.4	2.50
MSA[1]	28.1	33.9	15.8	13.2	5.1	2.6	1.3	2.60
U.S.	27.9	33.9	15.6	12.9	6.0	2.3	1.4	2.60

Note: (1) Figures cover the College Station-Bryan, TX Metropolitan Statistical Area
Source: U.S. Census Bureau, 2015-2019 American Community Survey 5-Year Estimates

Race

Area	White Alone[2] (%)	Black Alone[2] (%)	Asian Alone[2] (%)	AIAN[3] Alone[2] (%)	NHOPI[4] Alone[2] (%)	Other Race Alone[2] (%)	Two or More Races (%)
City	77.8	7.6	10.1	0.3	0.0	1.5	2.7
MSA[1]	77.0	11.5	5.3	0.4	0.1	3.0	2.8
U.S.	72.5	12.7	5.5	0.8	0.2	4.9	3.3

Note: (1) Figures cover the College Station-Bryan, TX Metropolitan Statistical Area; (2) Alone is defined as not being in combination with one or more other races; (3) American Indian and Alaska Native; (4) Native Hawaiian and Other Pacific Islander
Source: U.S. Census Bureau, 2015-2019 American Community Survey 5-Year Estimates

Hispanic or Latino Origin

Area	Total (%)	Mexican (%)	Puerto Rican (%)	Cuban (%)	Other (%)
City	15.8	11.2	0.3	0.4	3.9
MSA[1]	24.9	21.4	0.2	0.2	3.0
U.S.	18.0	11.2	1.7	0.7	4.3

Note: Persons of Hispanic or Latino origin can be of any race; (1) Figures cover the College Station-Bryan, TX Metropolitan Statistical Area
Source: U.S. Census Bureau, 2015-2019 American Community Survey 5-Year Estimates

Ancestry

Area	German	Irish	English	American	Italian	Polish	French[2]	Scottish	Dutch
City	16.9	8.9	7.7	3.5	3.5	2.3	3.5	2.3	0.7
MSA[1]	14.0	8.0	6.6	3.9	2.9	2.0	2.5	2.0	0.6
U.S.	13.3	9.7	7.2	6.2	5.1	2.8	2.3	1.7	1.2

Note: Figures are the percentage of the total population reporting a particular ancestry. The nine most commonly reported ancestries in the U.S. are shown. Figures include multiple ancestries (e.g. if a person reported being Irish and Italian, they were included in both columns); (1) Figures cover the College Station-Bryan, TX Metropolitan Statistical Area; (2) Excludes Basque
Source: U.S. Census Bureau, 2015-2019 American Community Survey 5-Year Estimates

Foreign-born Population

Area	Any Foreign Country	Asia	Mexico	Europe	Caribbean	Central America[2]	South America	Africa	Canada
City	13.4	7.9	1.6	1.0	0.1	0.5	1.2	0.9	0.2
MSA[1]	12.5	4.2	5.5	0.7	0.1	0.5	0.7	0.7	0.1
U.S.	13.6	4.2	3.5	1.5	1.3	1.1	1.0	0.7	0.2

Note: (1) Figures cover the College Station-Bryan, TX Metropolitan Statistical Area; (2) Excludes Mexico.
Source: U.S. Census Bureau, 2015-2019 American Community Survey 5-Year Estimates

Marital Status

Area	Never Married	Now Married[2]	Separated	Widowed	Divorced
City	59.7	32.4	0.8	2.1	5.0
MSA[1]	46.3	40.1	1.9	3.8	7.9
U.S.	33.4	48.1	1.9	5.8	10.9

Note: Figures are percentages and cover the population 15 years of age and older; (1) Figures cover the College Station-Bryan, TX Metropolitan Statistical Area; (2) Excludes separated
Source: U.S. Census Bureau, 2015-2019 American Community Survey 5-Year Estimates

Disability by Age

Area	All Ages	Under 18 Years Old	18 to 64 Years Old	65 Years and Over
City	6.3	3.8	4.9	28.7
MSA[1]	9.5	4.1	7.3	35.2
U.S.	12.6	4.2	10.3	34.5

Note: Figures show percent of the civilian noninstitutionalized population that reported having a disability. Disability status is determined from six types of difficulty: vision, hearing, cognitive, ambulatory, self-care, and independent living. For children under 5 years old, hearing and vision difficulty are used to determine disability status. For children between the ages of 5 and 14, disability status is determined from hearing, vision, cognitive, ambulatory, and self-care difficulties. For people aged 15 years and older, they are considered to have a disability if they have difficulty with any one of the six difficulty types; Note: (1) Figures cover the College Station-Bryan, TX Metropolitan Statistical Area
Source: U.S. Census Bureau, 2015-2019 American Community Survey 5-Year Estimates

Age

Area	Under Age 5	Age 5–19	Age 20–34	Age 35–44	Age 45–54	Age 55–64	Age 65–74	Age 75–84	Age 85+	Median Age
City	5.1	22.9	42.6	9.9	6.8	6.0	4.3	1.9	0.6	23.0
MSA[1]	6.1	20.9	32.9	11.0	9.5	9.2	6.1	3.0	1.2	27.8
U.S.	6.1	19.1	20.7	12.6	13.0	12.9	9.1	4.6	1.9	38.1

Note: (1) Figures cover the College Station-Bryan, TX Metropolitan Statistical Area
Source: U.S. Census Bureau, 2015-2019 American Community Survey 5-Year Estimates

Gender

Area	Males	Females	Males per 100 Females
City	58,117	55,569	104.6
MSA[1]	129,895	128,134	101.4
U.S.	159,886,919	164,810,876	97.0

Note: (1) Figures cover the College Station-Bryan, TX Metropolitan Statistical Area
Source: U.S. Census Bureau, 2015-2019 American Community Survey 5-Year Estimates

Religious Groups by Family

Area	Catholic	Baptist	Non-Den.	Methodist[2]	Lutheran	LDS[3]	Pentecostal	Presbyterian[4]	Muslim[5]	Judaism
MSA[1]	11.7	15.7	4.0	4.8	1.5	1.2	0.7	0.9	1.1	0.1
U.S.	19.1	9.3	4.0	4.0	2.3	2.0	1.9	1.6	0.8	0.7

Note: Figures are the number of adherents as a percentage of the total population; (1) Figures cover the College Station-Bryan, TX Metropolitan Statistical Area; (2) Methodist/Pietist; (3) Latter Day Saints; (4) Reformed; (5) Figures are estimates
Source: Association of Statisticians of American Religious Bodies, 2010 U.S. Religion Census: Religious Congregations & Membership Study

Religious Groups by Tradition

Area	Catholic	Evangelical Protestant	Mainline Protestant	Other Tradition	Black Protestant	Orthodox
MSA[1]	11.7	20.7	6.6	2.6	1.0	<0.1
U.S.	19.1	16.2	7.3	4.3	1.6	0.3

Note: Figures are the number of adherents as a percentage of the total population; (1) Figures cover the College Station-Bryan, TX Metropolitan Statistical Area
Source: Association of Statisticians of American Religious Bodies, 2010 U.S. Religion Census: Religious Congregations & Membership Study

ECONOMY

Gross Metropolitan Product

Area	2017	2018	2019	2020	Rank[2]
MSA[1]	9.9	10.6	11.2	11.7	204

Note: Figures are in billions of dollars; (1) Figures cover the College Station-Bryan, TX Metropolitan Statistical Area; (2) Rank is based on 2018 data and ranges from 1 to 381
Source: U.S. Conference of Mayors, U.S. Metro Economies: GMP & Employment 2018-2020, September 2019

College Station, Texas

Economic Growth

Area	2015-17 (%)	2018 (%)	2019 (%)	2020 (%)	Rank[2]
MSA[1]	1.0	3.4	3.3	1.4	224
U.S.	1.9	2.9	2.3	2.1	—

Note: Figures are real gross metropolitan product (GMP) growth rates and represent average annual percent change; (1) Figures cover the College Station-Bryan, TX Metropolitan Statistical Area; (2) Rank is based on 2017 2-year average annual percent change and ranges from 1 to 381
Source: U.S. Conference of Mayors, U.S. Metro Economies: GMP & Employment 2018-2020, September 2019

Metropolitan Area Exports

Area	2014	2015	2016	2017	2018	2019	Rank[2]
MSA[1]	129.7	122.5	113.2	145.4	153.0	160.5	313

Note: Figures are in millions of dollars; (1) Figures cover the College Station-Bryan, TX Metropolitan Statistical Area; (2) Rank is based on 2019 data and ranges from 1 to 386
Source: U.S. Department of Commerce, International Trade Administration, Office of Trade and Economic Analysis, Industry and Analysis, Exports by Metropolitan Area, data extracted March 24, 2021

Building Permits

Area	Single-Family 2018	Single-Family 2019	Pct. Chg.	Multi-Family 2018	Multi-Family 2019	Pct. Chg.	Total 2018	Total 2019	Pct. Chg.
City	459	398	-13.3	572	219	-61.7	1,031	617	-40.2
MSA[1]	1,023	1,091	6.6	833	389	-53.3	1,856	1,480	-20.3
U.S.	855,300	862,100	0.7	473,500	523,900	10.6	1,328,800	1,386,000	4.3

Note: (1) Figures cover the College Station-Bryan, TX Metropolitan Statistical Area; Figures represent new, privately-owned housing units authorized (unadjusted data); All permit data are based on estimates with imputation
Source: U.S. Census Bureau, Manufacturing, Mining, and Construction Statistics, Building Permits, 2018, 2019

Bankruptcy Filings

Area	Business Filings 2019	Business Filings 2020	% Chg.	Nonbusiness Filings 2019	Nonbusiness Filings 2020	% Chg.
Brazos County	7	6	-14.3	105	87	-17.1
U.S.	22,780	21,655	-4.9	752,160	522,808	-30.5

Note: Business filings include Chapter 7, Chapter 9, Chapter 11, Chapter 12, Chapter 13, Chapter 15, and Section 304; Nonbusiness filings include Chapter 7, Chapter 11, and Chapter 13
Source: Administrative Office of the U.S. Courts, Business and Nonbusiness Bankruptcy, County Cases Commenced by Chapter of the Bankruptcy Code, During the 12-Month Period Ending December 31, 2019 and Business and Nonbusiness Bankruptcy, County Cases Commenced by Chapter of the Bankruptcy Code, During the 12-Month Period Ending December 31, 2020

Housing Vacancy Rates

Area	Gross Vacancy Rate[2] (%) 2018	2019	2020	Year-Round Vacancy Rate[3] (%) 2018	2019	2020	Rental Vacancy Rate[4] (%) 2018	2019	2020	Homeowner Vacancy Rate[5] (%) 2018	2019	2020
MSA[1]	n/a	n/a	n/a	n/a	n/a	n/a	n/a	n/a	n/a	n/a	n/a	n/a
U.S.	12.3	12.0	10.6	9.7	9.5	8.2	6.9	6.7	6.3	1.5	1.4	1.0

Note: (1) Figures cover the College Station-Bryan, TX Metropolitan Statistical Area; (2) The percentage of the total housing inventory that is vacant; (3) The percentage of the housing inventory (excluding seasonal units) that is year-round vacant; (4) The percentage of rental inventory that is vacant for rent; (5) The percentage of homeowner inventory that is vacant for sale; n/a not available
Source: U.S. Census Bureau, Housing Vacancies and Homeownership Annual Statistics: 2018, 2019, 2020

INCOME

Income

Area	Per Capita ($)	Median Household ($)	Average Household ($)
City	27,541	45,820	73,853
MSA[1]	27,698	50,240	73,129
U.S.	34,103	62,843	88,607

Note: (1) Figures cover the College Station-Bryan, TX Metropolitan Statistical Area
Source: U.S. Census Bureau, 2015-2019 American Community Survey 5-Year Estimates

Household Income Distribution

Area	Under $15,000	$15,000 -$24,999	$25,000 -$34,999	$35,000 -$49,999	$50,000 -$74,999	$75,000 -$99,999	$100,000 -$149,999	$150,000 and up
City	21.3	11.1	9.2	11.2	12.4	10.9	12.5	11.4
MSA[1]	16.3	11.0	9.8	12.7	15.8	11.5	12.8	10.2
U.S.	10.3	8.9	8.9	12.3	17.2	12.7	15.1	14.5

Note: (1) Figures cover the College Station-Bryan, TX Metropolitan Statistical Area
Source: U.S. Census Bureau, 2015-2019 American Community Survey 5-Year Estimates

Poverty Rate

Area	All Ages	Under 18 Years Old	18 to 64 Years Old	65 Years and Over
City	29.6	12.3	35.9	7.9
MSA[1]	22.7	20.1	25.8	9.1
U.S.	13.4	18.5	12.6	9.3

Note: Figures are percentage of people whose income during the past 12 months was below the poverty level;
(1) Figures cover the College Station-Bryan, TX Metropolitan Statistical Area
Source: U.S. Census Bureau, 2015-2019 American Community Survey 5-Year Estimates

CITY FINANCES

City Government Finances

Component	2017 ($000)	2017 ($ per capita)
Total Revenues	227,689	2,110
Total Expenditures	204,723	1,898
Debt Outstanding	278,939	2,585
Cash and Securities[1]	200,868	1,862

Note: (1) Cash and security holdings of a government at the close of its fiscal year, including those of its dependent agencies, utilities, and liquor stores.
Source: U.S. Census Bureau, State & Local Government Finances 2017

City Government Revenue by Source

Source	2017 ($000)	2017 ($ per capita)	2017 (%)
General Revenue			
From Federal Government	1,833	17	0.8
From State Government	1,100	10	0.5
From Local Governments	114	1	0.1
Taxes			
Property	32,359	300	14.2
Sales and Gross Receipts	35,120	326	15.4
Personal Income	0	0	0.0
Corporate Income	0	0	0.0
Motor Vehicle License	0	0	0.0
Other Taxes	2,092	19	0.9
Current Charges	32,087	297	14.1
Liquor Store	0	0	0.0
Utility	116,565	1,080	51.2
Employee Retirement	0	0	0.0

Source: U.S. Census Bureau, State & Local Government Finances 2017

City Government Expenditures by Function

Function	2017 ($000)	2017 ($ per capita)	2017 (%)
General Direct Expenditures			
Air Transportation	0	0	0.0
Corrections	0	0	0.0
Education	0	0	0.0
Employment Security Administration	0	0	0.0
Financial Administration	2,856	26	1.4
Fire Protection	13,339	123	6.5
General Public Buildings	1,805	16	0.9
Governmental Administration, Other	9,483	87	4.6
Health	0	0	0.0
Highways	16,136	149	7.9
Hospitals	0	0	0.0
Housing and Community Development	1,385	12	0.7
Interest on General Debt	3,770	34	1.8
Judicial and Legal	2,051	19	1.0
Libraries	1,099	10	0.5
Parking	570	5	0.3
Parks and Recreation	9,316	86	4.6
Police Protection	15,473	143	7.6
Public Welfare	0	0	0.0
Sewerage	12,899	119	6.3
Solid Waste Management	6,376	59	3.1
Veterans' Services	0	0	0.0
Liquor Store	0	0	0.0
Utility	100,098	927	48.9
Employee Retirement	0	0	0.0

Source: U.S. Census Bureau, State & Local Government Finances 2017

EMPLOYMENT

Labor Force and Employment

Area	Civilian Labor Force Dec. 2019	Civilian Labor Force Dec. 2020	% Chg.	Workers Employed Dec. 2019	Workers Employed Dec. 2020	% Chg.
City	62,425	62,445	0.0	60,916	59,698	-2.0
MSA[1]	137,059	137,930	0.6	133,696	130,968	-2.0
U.S.	164,007,000	160,017,000	-2.4	158,504,000	149,613,000	-5.6

Note: Data is not seasonally adjusted and covers workers 16 years of age and older; (1) Figures cover the College Station-Bryan, TX Metropolitan Statistical Area
Source: Bureau of Labor Statistics, Local Area Unemployment Statistics

Unemployment Rate

Area	2020 Jan.	Feb.	Mar.	Apr.	May	Jun.	Jul.	Aug.	Sep.	Oct.	Nov.	Dec.
City	2.8	2.6	3.7	8.2	8.1	5.9	5.3	4.2	4.7	3.9	4.9	4.4
MSA[1]	2.9	2.7	3.9	8.7	8.7	6.3	5.8	4.7	5.5	4.5	5.5	5.0
U.S.	4.0	3.8	4.5	14.4	13.0	11.2	10.5	8.5	7.7	6.6	6.4	6.5

Note: Data is not seasonally adjusted and covers workers 16 years of age and older; (1) Figures cover the College Station-Bryan, TX Metropolitan Statistical Area
Source: Bureau of Labor Statistics, Local Area Unemployment Statistics

Average Wages

Occupation	$/Hr.	Occupation	$/Hr.
Accountants and Auditors	29.40	Maintenance and Repair Workers	17.30
Automotive Mechanics	25.20	Marketing Managers	77.70
Bookkeepers	17.40	Network and Computer Systems Admin.	33.50
Carpenters	20.30	Nurses, Licensed Practical	23.40
Cashiers	11.70	Nurses, Registered	33.70
Computer Programmers	48.30	Nursing Assistants	12.90
Computer Systems Analysts	38.10	Office Clerks, General	15.40
Computer User Support Specialists	21.70	Physical Therapists	40.60
Construction Laborers	15.90	Physicians	n/a
Cooks, Restaurant	11.20	Plumbers, Pipefitters and Steamfitters	20.40
Customer Service Representatives	14.70	Police and Sheriff's Patrol Officers	31.50
Dentists	n/a	Postal Service Mail Carriers	25.70
Electricians	24.80	Real Estate Sales Agents	26.10
Engineers, Electrical	19.70	Retail Salespersons	12.40
Fast Food and Counter Workers	10.10	Sales Representatives, Technical/Scientific	38.40
Financial Managers	63.70	Secretaries, Exc. Legal/Medical/Executive	16.70
First-Line Supervisors of Office Workers	26.20	Security Guards	13.00
General and Operations Managers	45.80	Surgeons	n/a
Hairdressers/Cosmetologists	13.80	Teacher Assistants, Exc. Postsecondary*	9.90
Home Health and Personal Care Aides	10.60	Teachers, Secondary School, Exc. Sp. Ed.*	23.50
Janitors and Cleaners	13.30	Telemarketers	n/a
Landscaping/Groundskeeping Workers	14.60	Truck Drivers, Heavy/Tractor-Trailer	18.20
Lawyers	61.50	Truck Drivers, Light/Delivery Services	17.70
Maids and Housekeeping Cleaners	12.00	Waiters and Waitresses	9.90

Note: Wage data covers the College Station-Bryan, TX Metropolitan Statistical Area; (*) Hourly wages were calculated from annual wage data based on a 40 hour work week; n/a not available.
Source: Bureau of Labor Statistics, Metro Area Occupational Employment & Wage Estimates, May 2020

Employment by Industry

Sector	MSA[1] Number of Employees	MSA[1] Percent of Total	U.S. Percent of Total
Construction, Mining, and Logging	6,800	5.7	5.5
Education and Health Services	12,100	10.2	16.3
Financial Activities	3,700	3.1	6.1
Government	45,100	38.0	15.2
Information	1,400	1.2	1.9
Leisure and Hospitality	13,500	11.4	9.0
Manufacturing	5,300	4.5	8.5
Other Services	3,000	2.5	3.8
Professional and Business Services	10,700	9.0	14.4
Retail Trade	12,400	10.4	10.9
Transportation, Warehousing, and Utilities	2,100	1.8	4.6
Wholesale Trade	2,700	2.3	3.9

Note: Figures are non-farm employment as of December 2020. Figures are not seasonally adjusted and include workers 16 years of age and older; (1) Figures cover the College Station-Bryan, TX Metropolitan Statistical Area
Source: Bureau of Labor Statistics, Current Employment Statistics, Employment, Hours, and Earnings

Employment by Occupation

Occupation Classification	City (%)	MSA[1] (%)	U.S. (%)
Management, Business, Science, and Arts	51.3	41.3	38.5
Natural Resources, Construction, and Maintenance	4.0	9.5	8.9
Production, Transportation, and Material Moving	7.4	11.0	13.2
Sales and Office	21.2	21.3	21.6
Service	16.2	16.8	17.8

Note: Figures cover employed civilians 16 years of age and older; (1) Figures cover the College Station-Bryan, TX Metropolitan Statistical Area
Source: U.S. Census Bureau, 2015-2019 American Community Survey 5-Year Estimates

Occupations with Greatest Projected Employment Growth: 2020 – 2022

Occupation[1]	2020 Employment	2022 Projected Employment	Numeric Employment Change	Percent Employment Change
Fast Food and Counter Workers	336,530	411,690	75,160	22.3
Waiters and Waitresses	165,570	206,920	41,350	25.0
Home Health and Personal Care Aides	303,520	344,240	40,720	13.4
Retail Salespersons	315,590	349,820	34,230	10.8
Heavy and Tractor-Trailer Truck Drivers	199,460	228,650	29,190	14.6
Laborers and Freight, Stock, and Material Movers, Hand	193,000	219,670	26,670	13.8
Cooks, Restaurant	88,540	114,250	25,710	29.0
Customer Service Representatives	276,080	295,790	19,710	7.1
General and Operations Managers	197,410	216,580	19,170	9.7
Office Clerks, General	310,080	327,500	17,420	5.6

Note: Projections cover Texas; (1) Sorted by numeric employment change
Source: www.projectionscentral.com, State Occupational Projections, 2020–2022 Short-Term Projections

Fastest-Growing Occupations: 2020 – 2022

Occupation[1]	2020 Employment	2022 Projected Employment	Numeric Employment Change	Percent Employment Change
Motion Picture Projectionists	150	300	150	100.0
Ushers, Lobby Attendants, and Ticket Takers	5,740	8,920	3,180	55.4
Locker Room, Coatroom, and Dressing Room Attendants	340	510	170	50.0
Athletes and Sports Competitors	270	400	130	48.1
Amusement and Recreation Attendants	13,130	19,400	6,270	47.8
Hotel, Motel, and Resort Desk Clerks	16,140	23,160	7,020	43.5
Sound Engineering Technicians	330	460	130	39.4
Gaming Dealers	220	300	80	36.4
Baggage Porters and Bellhops	1,250	1,670	420	33.6
Lodging Managers	3,300	4,330	1,030	31.2

Note: Projections cover Texas; (1) Sorted by percent employment change and excludes occupations with numeric employment change less than 50
Source: www.projectionscentral.com, State Occupational Projections, 2020–2022 Short-Term Projections

TAXES

State Corporate Income Tax Rates

State	Tax Rate (%)	Income Brackets ($)	Num. of Brackets	Financial Institution Tax Rate (%)[a]	Federal Income Tax Ded.
Texas	(w)	–	–	(w)	No

Note: Tax rates as of January 1, 2021; (a) Rates listed are the corporate income tax rate applied to financial institutions or excise taxes based on income. Some states have other taxes based upon the value of deposits or shares; (w) Texas imposes a Franchise Tax, otherwise known as margin tax, imposed on entities with more than $1,130,000 total revenues at rate of 0.75%, or 0.375% for entities primarily engaged in retail or wholesale trade, on lesser of 70% of total revenues or 100% of gross receipts after deductions for either compensation or cost of goods sold.
Source: Federation of Tax Administrators, State Corporate Income Tax Rates, January 1, 2021

State Individual Income Tax Rates

State	Tax Rate (%)	Income Brackets ($)	Personal Exemptions ($) Single	Married	Depend.	Standard Ded. ($) Single	Married
Texas				– No state income tax –			

Note: Tax rates as of January 1, 2021; Local- and county-level taxes are not included
Source: Federation of Tax Administrators, State Individual Income Tax Rates, January 1, 2021

Various State Sales and Excise Tax Rates

State	State Sales Tax (%)	Gasoline[1] (¢/gal.)	Cigarette[2] ($/pack)	Spirits[3] ($/gal.)	Wine[4] ($/gal.)	Beer[5] ($/gal.)	Recreational Marijuana (%)
Texas	6.25	20	1.41	2.4	0.2	0.2	Not legal

Note: All tax rates as of January 1, 2021; (1) The American Petroleum Institute has developed a methodology for determining the average tax rate on a gallon of fuel. Rates may include any of the following: excise taxes, environmental fees, storage tank fees, other fees or taxes, general sales tax, and local taxes; (2) The federal excise tax of $1.0066 per pack and local taxes are not included; (3) Rates are those applicable to off-premise sales of 40% alcohol by volume (a.b.v.) distilled spirits in 750ml containers. Local excise taxes are excluded; (4) Rates are those applicable to off-premise sales of 11% a.b.v. non-carbonated wine in 750ml containers; (5) Rates are those applicable to off-premise sales of 4.7% a.b.v. beer in 12 ounce containers.
Source: Tax Foundation, 2021 Facts & Figures: How Does Your State Compare?

State Business Tax Climate Index Rankings

State	Overall Rank	Corporate Tax Rank	Individual Income Tax Rank	Sales Tax Rank	Property Tax Rank	Unemployment Insurance Tax Rank
Texas	11	47	6	35	36	16

Note: The index is a measure of how each state's tax laws affect economic performance. The lower the rank, the more favorable a state's tax system is for business. States without a given tax are given a ranking of 1. The scores/rankings for the District of Columbia do not affect other states. The 2021 index represents the tax climate as of July 1, 2020.
Source: Tax Foundation, State Business Tax Climate Index 2021

TRANSPORTATION

Means of Transportation to Work

Area	Car/Truck/Van Drove Alone	Car/Truck/Van Carpooled	Public Transportation Bus	Public Transportation Subway	Public Transportation Railroad	Bicycle	Walked	Other Means	Worked at Home
City	78.2	9.3	2.8	0.0	0.0	2.1	2.7	1.0	3.8
MSA[1]	79.8	10.7	1.7	0.0	0.0	1.3	1.9	1.1	3.5
U.S.	76.3	9.0	2.4	1.9	0.6	0.5	2.7	1.4	5.2

Note: Figures are percentages and cover workers 16 years of age and older; (1) Figures cover the College Station-Bryan, TX Metropolitan Statistical Area
Source: U.S. Census Bureau, 2015-2019 American Community Survey 5-Year Estimates

Travel Time to Work

Area	Less Than 10 Minutes	10 to 19 Minutes	20 to 29 Minutes	30 to 44 Minutes	45 to 59 Minutes	60 to 89 Minutes	90 Minutes or More
City	16.5	56.7	17.6	5.9	0.5	1.8	1.2
MSA[1]	15.6	49.4	19.1	10.1	2.3	2.1	1.5
U.S.	12.2	28.4	20.8	20.8	8.3	6.4	2.9

Note: Note: Figures are percentages and include workers 16 years old and over; (1) Figures cover the College Station-Bryan, TX Metropolitan Statistical Area
Source: U.S. Census Bureau, 2015-2019 American Community Survey 5-Year Estimates

Key Congestion Measures

Measure	1982	1992	2002	2012	2017
Annual Hours of Delay, Total (000)	n/a	n/a	n/a	n/a	5,453
Annual Hours of Delay, Per Auto Commuter	n/a	n/a	n/a	n/a	32
Annual Congestion Cost, Total (million $)	n/a	n/a	n/a	n/a	114
Annual Congestion Cost, Per Auto Commuter ($)	n/a	n/a	n/a	n/a	658

Note: n/a not available
Source: Texas A&M Transportation Institute, 2019 Urban Mobility Report

Freeway Travel Time Index

Measure	1982	1987	1992	1997	2002	2007	2012	2017
Urban Area Index[1]	n/a	n/a	n/a	n/a	n/a	n/a	n/a	1.16
Urban Area Rank[1,2]	n/a	n/a	n/a	n/a	n/a	n/a	n/a	n/a

Note: Freeway Travel Time Index—the ratio of travel time in the peak period to the travel time at free-flow conditions. For example, a value of 1.30 indicates a 20-minute free-flow trip takes 26 minutes in the peak (20 minutes x 1.30 = 26 minutes); (1) Covers the College Station-Bryan TX urban area; (2) Rank is based on 101 larger urban areas (#1 = highest travel time index); n/a not available
Source: Texas A&M Transportation Institute, 2019 Urban Mobility Report

Public Transportation

Agency Name / Mode of Transportation	Vehicles Operated in Maximum Service[1]	Annual Unlinked Passenger Trips[2] (in thous.)	Annual Passenger Miles[3] (in thous.)
Brazos Transit District			
Bus (directly operated)	29	370.4	2,366.9
Demand Response (directly operated)	48	68.6	1,062.2

Note: (1) Number of revenue vehicles operated by the given mode and type of service to meet the annual maximum service requirement. This is the revenue vehicle count during the peak season of the year; on the week and day that maximum service is provided. Vehicles operated in maximum service (VOMS) exclude atypical days and one-time special events; (2) Number of passengers who boarded public transportation vehicles. Passengers are counted each time they board a vehicle no matter how many vehicles they use to travel from their origin to their destination. (3) Sum of the distances ridden by all passengers during the entire fiscal year.
Source: Federal Transit Administration, National Transit Database, 2019

Air Transportation

Airport Name and Code / Type of Service	Passenger Airlines[1]	Passenger Enplanements	Freight Carriers[2]	Freight (lbs)
Easterwood Airport (CLL)				
Domestic service (U.S. carriers - 2020)	10	41,790	3	167,465
International service (U.S. carriers - 2019)	0	0	0	0

Note: (1) Includes all U.S.-based major, minor and commuter airlines that carried at least one passenger during the year; (2) Includes all U.S.-based airlines and freight carriers that transported at least one pound of freight during the year.
Source: Bureau of Transportation Statistics, The Intermodal Transportation Database, Air Carriers: T-100 Domestic Market (U.S. Carriers), 2020; Bureau of Transportation Statistics, The Intermodal Transportation Database, Air Carriers: T-100 International Market (U.S. Carriers), 2019

BUSINESSES

Major Business Headquarters

Company Name	Industry	Rankings Fortune[1]	Forbes[2]
No companies listed	-	-	-

Note: (1) Companies that produce a 10-K are ranked 1 to 500 based on 2019 revenue; (2) All private companies with at least $2 billion in annual revenue through the end of their most current fiscal year are ranked 1 to 219; companies listed are headquartered in the city; dashes indicate no ranking
Source: Fortune, "Fortune 500," June/July 2020; Forbes, "America's Largest Private Companies," 2020

Living Environment

COST OF LIVING

Cost of Living Index

Composite Index	Groceries	Housing	Utilities	Transportation	Health Care	Misc. Goods/Services
n/a	n/a	n/a	n/a	n/a	n/a	n/a

Note: The Cost of Living Index measures regional differences in the cost of consumer goods and services, excluding taxes and non-consumer expenditures, for professional and managerial households in the top income quintile. It is based on more than 50,000 prices covering almost 60 different items for which prices are collected three times a year by chambers of commerce, economic development organizations or university applied economic centers in each participating urban area. The numbers shown should be read as a percentage above or below the national average of 100. For example, a value of 115.4 in the groceries column indicates that grocery prices are 15.4% higher than the national average. Small differences in the index numbers should not be interpreted as significant; n/a not available.
Source: The Council for Community and Economic Research, Cost of Living Index, 2020

Grocery Prices

Area[1]	T-Bone Steak ($/pound)	Frying Chicken ($/pound)	Whole Milk ($/half gal.)	Eggs ($/dozen)	Orange Juice ($/64 oz.)	Coffee ($/11.5 oz.)
City[2]	n/a	n/a	n/a	n/a	n/a	n/a
Avg.	11.78	1.39	2.05	1.47	3.57	4.34
Min.	8.03	0.94	1.03	0.74	2.94	3.02
Max.	15.86	2.65	4.31	3.77	5.44	8.69

Note: (1) Values for the local area are compared with the average, minimum and maximum values for all 284 areas in the Cost of Living Index; (2) Figures cover the College Station TX urban area; n/a not available; **T-Bone Steak** (price per pound); **Frying Chicken** (price per pound, whole fryer); **Whole Milk** (half gallon carton); **Eggs** (price per dozen, Grade A, large); **Orange Juice** (64 oz. Tropicana or Florida Natural); **Coffee** (11.5 oz. can, vacuum-packed, Maxwell House, Hills Bros, or Folgers).
Source: The Council for Community and Economic Research, Cost of Living Index, 2020

Housing and Utility Costs

Area[1]	New Home Price ($)	Apartment Rent ($/month)	All Electric ($/month)	Part Electric ($/month)	Other Energy ($/month)	Telephone ($/month)
City[2]	n/a	n/a	n/a	n/a	n/a	n/a
Avg.	368,594	1,168	170.86	100.47	65.28	184.30
Min.	190,567	502	91.58	31.42	26.08	169.60
Max.	2,227,806	4,738	470.38	280.31	280.06	206.50

Note: (1) Values for the local area are compared with the average, minimum and maximum values for all 284 areas in the Cost of Living Index; (2) Figures cover the College Station TX urban area; n/a not available; **New Home Price** (2,400 sf living area, 8,000 sf lot, in urban area with full utilities); **Apartment Rent** (950 sf 2 bedroom/1.5 or 2 bath, unfurnished, excluding all utilities except water); **All Electric** (average monthly cost for an all-electric home); **Part Electric** (average monthly cost for a part-electric home); **Other Energy** (average monthly cost for natural gas, fuel oil, coal, wood, and any other forms of energy except electricity); **Telephone** (price includes the base monthly rate plus taxes and fees for three lines of mobile phone service).
Source: The Council for Community and Economic Research, Cost of Living Index, 2020

Health Care, Transportation, and Other Costs

Area[1]	Doctor ($/visit)	Dentist ($/visit)	Optometrist ($/visit)	Gasoline ($/gallon)	Beauty Salon ($/visit)	Men's Shirt ($)
City[2]	n/a	n/a	n/a	n/a	n/a	n/a
Avg.	115.44	99.32	108.10	2.21	39.27	31.37
Min.	36.68	59.00	51.36	1.71	19.00	11.00
Max.	219.00	153.10	250.97	3.46	82.05	58.33

Note: (1) Values for the local area are compared with the average, minimum and maximum values for all 284 areas in the Cost of Living Index; (2) Figures cover the College Station TX urban area; n/a not available; **Doctor** (general practitioners routine exam of an established patient); **Dentist** (adult teeth cleaning and periodic oral examination); **Optometrist** (full vision eye exam for established adult patient); **Gasoline** (one gallon regular unleaded, national brand, including all taxes, cash price at self-service pump if available); **Beauty Salon** (woman's shampoo, trim, and blow-dry); **Men's Shirt** (cotton/polyester dress shirt, pinpoint weave, long sleeves).
Source: The Council for Community and Economic Research, Cost of Living Index, 2020

HOUSING

Homeownership Rate

Area	2012 (%)	2013 (%)	2014 (%)	2015 (%)	2016 (%)	2017 (%)	2018 (%)	2019 (%)	2020 (%)
MSA[1]	n/a	n/a	n/a	n/a	n/a	n/a	n/a	n/a	n/a
U.S.	65.4	65.1	64.5	63.7	63.4	63.9	64.4	64.6	66.6

Note: (1) Figures cover the College Station-Bryan, TX Metropolitan Statistical Area; n/a not available
Source: U.S. Census Bureau, Housing Vacancies and Homeownership Annual Statistics: 2012-2020

House Price Index (HPI)

Area	National Ranking[2]	Quarterly Change (%)	One-Year Change (%)	Five-Year Change (%)	Since 1991Q1 (%)
MSA[1]	n/a	n/a	n/a	n/a	n/a
U.S.[3]	—	3.81	10.77	38.99	205.12

Note: The HPI is a weighted repeat sales index. It measures average price changes in repeat sales or refinancings on the same properties. This information is obtained by reviewing repeat mortgage transactions on single-family properties whose mortgages have been purchased or securitized by Fannie Mae or Freddie Mac since January 1975; (1) Figures cover the , Metropolitan Statistical Area; (2) Rankings are based on annual percentage change for all metro areas containing at least 15,000 transactions over the last 10 years and ranges from 1 to 253; (3) figures based on a weighted average of Census Division estimates using a seasonally adjusted, purchase-only index; all figures are for the period ending December 31, 2020; n/a not available
Source: Federal Housing Finance Agency, Change in Metropolitan Area House Price Indexes, April 7, 2021

Median Single-Family Home Prices

Area	2018	2019	2020p	Percent Change 2019 to 2020
MSA[1]	n/a	n/a	n/a	n/a
U.S. Average	261.6	274.6	299.9	9.2

Note: Figures are median sales prices of existing single-family homes in thousands of dollars; (p) preliminary; n/a not available; (1) Figures cover the College Station-Bryan, TX Metropolitan Statistical Area
Source: National Association of Realtors, Median Sales Price of Existing Single-Family Homes for Metropolitan Areas, 4th Quarter 2020

Qualifying Income Based on Median Sales Price of Existing Single-Family Homes

Area	With 5% Down ($)	With 10% Down ($)	With 20% Down ($)
MSA[1]	n/a	n/a	n/a
U.S. Average	59,266	56,147	49,908

Note: Figures are preliminary; Qualifying income is based on a mortgage rate of 2.81%. Monthly principal and interest payment is limited to 25% of income; n/a not available; (1) Figures cover the College Station-Bryan, TX Metropolitan Statistical Area
Source: National Association of Realtors, Qualifying Income Based on Median Sales Price of Existing Single-Family Homes for Metropolitan Areas, 4th Quarter 2020

Home Value Distribution

Area	Under $50,000	$50,000 -$99,999	$100,000 -$149,999	$150,000 -$199,999	$200,000 -$299,999	$300,000 -$499,999	$500,000 -$999,999	$1,000,000 or more
City	2.1	1.3	7.4	21.9	35.6	24.9	6.1	0.9
MSA[1]	10.0	13.0	13.2	18.1	23.3	16.1	5.3	1.0
U.S.	6.9	12.0	13.3	14.0	19.6	19.3	11.4	3.4

Note: Figures are percentages and cover owner-occupied housing units; (1) Figures cover the College Station-Bryan, TX Metropolitan Statistical Area
Source: U.S. Census Bureau, 2015-2019 American Community Survey 5-Year Estimates

Year Housing Structure Built

Area	2010 or Later	2000 -2009	1990 -1999	1980 -1989	1970 -1979	1960 -1969	1950 -1959	1940 -1949	Before 1940	Median Year
City	16.2	24.0	19.8	16.0	16.5	4.0	2.2	0.7	0.6	1995
MSA[1]	12.7	21.0	17.7	17.0	15.8	6.1	5.2	2.0	2.4	1991
U.S.	5.2	14.0	13.9	13.4	15.2	10.6	10.3	4.9	12.6	1978

Note: Figures are percentages except for Median Year; Note: (1) Figures cover the College Station-Bryan, TX Metropolitan Statistical Area
Source: U.S. Census Bureau, 2015-2019 American Community Survey 5-Year Estimates

Gross Monthly Rent

Area	Under $500	$500 -$999	$1,000 -$1,499	$1,500 -$1,999	$2,000 -$2,499	$2,500 -$2,999	$3,000 and up	Median ($)
City	3.2	48.7	27.6	14.1	5.0	1.0	0.5	983
MSA[1]	6.3	51.7	26.5	10.6	3.6	0.8	0.5	935
U.S.	9.4	36.2	30.0	14.0	5.6	2.4	2.4	1,062

Note: Figures are percentages except for Median; Gross rent is the contract rent plus the estimated average monthly cost of utilities (electricity, gas, and water and sewer) and fuels (oil, coal, kerosene, wood, etc.) if these are paid by the renter (or paid for the renter by someone else); (1) Figures cover the College Station-Bryan, TX Metropolitan Statistical Area
Source: U.S. Census Bureau, 2015-2019 American Community Survey 5-Year Estimates

HEALTH

Health Risk Factors

Category	MSA[1] (%)	U.S. (%)
Adults aged 18–64 who have any kind of health care coverage	83.7	87.3
Adults who reported being in good or better health	91.7	82.4
Adults who have been told they have high blood cholesterol	31.2	33.0
Adults who have been told they have high blood pressure	26.1	32.3
Adults who are current smokers	n/a	17.1
Adults who currently use E-cigarettes	n/a	4.6
Adults who currently use chewing tobacco, snuff, or snus	7.6	4.0
Adults who are heavy drinkers[2]	n/a	6.3
Adults who are binge drinkers[3]	24.2	17.4
Adults who are overweight (BMI 25.0 - 29.9)	34.5	35.3
Adults who are obese (BMI 30.0 - 99.8)	30.8	31.3
Adults who participated in any physical activities in the past month	80.2	74.4
Adults who always or nearly always wears a seat belt	92.1	94.3

Note: n/a not available; (1) Figures cover the College Station-Bryan, TX Metropolitan Statistical Area; (2) Heavy drinkers are classified as adult men having more than 14 drinks per week and adult women having more than 7 drinks per week; (3) Binge drinkers are classified as males having five or more drinks on one occasion or females having four or more drinks on one occasion
Source: Centers for Disease Control and Prevention, Behavioral Risk Factor Surveillance System, SMART: Selected Metropolitan Area Risk Trends, 2017

Acute and Chronic Health Conditions

Category	MSA[1] (%)	U.S. (%)
Adults who have ever been told they had a heart attack	n/a	4.2
Adults who have ever been told they have angina or coronary heart disease	1.6	3.9
Adults who have ever been told they had a stroke	n/a	3.0
Adults who have ever been told they have asthma	15.9	14.2
Adults who have ever been told they have arthritis	19.1	24.9
Adults who have ever been told they have diabetes[2]	7.5	10.5
Adults who have ever been told they had skin cancer	n/a	6.2
Adults who have ever been told they had any other types of cancer	7.7	7.1
Adults who have ever been told they have COPD	n/a	6.5
Adults who have ever been told they have kidney disease	n/a	3.0
Adults who have ever been told they have a form of depression	13.4	20.5

Note: n/a not available; (1) Figures cover the College Station-Bryan, TX Metropolitan Statistical Area; (2) Figures do not include pregnancy-related, borderline, or pre-diabetes
Source: Centers for Disease Control and Prevention, Behavioral Risk Factor Surveillance System, SMART: Selected Metropolitan Area Risk Trends, 2017

Health Screening and Vaccination Rates

Category	MSA[1] (%)	U.S. (%)
Adults aged 65+ who have had flu shot within the past year	70.7	60.7
Adults aged 65+ who have ever had a pneumonia vaccination	89.7	75.4
Adults who have ever been tested for HIV	33.6	36.1
Adults who have ever had the shingles or zoster vaccine?	33.8	28.9
Adults who have had their blood cholesterol checked within the last five years	77.5	85.9

Note: n/a not available; (1) Figures cover the College Station-Bryan, TX Metropolitan Statistical Area.
Source: Centers for Disease Control and Prevention, Behavioral Risk Factor Surveillance System, SMART: Selected Metropolitan Area Risk Trends, 2017

Disability Status

Category	MSA[1] (%)	U.S. (%)
Adults who reported being deaf	n/a	6.7
Are you blind or have serious difficulty seeing, even when wearing glasses?	n/a	4.5
Are you limited in any way in any of your usual activities due of arthritis?	12.5	12.9
Do you have difficulty doing errands alone?	n/a	6.8
Do you have difficulty dressing or bathing?	n/a	3.6
Do you have serious difficulty concentrating/remembering/making decisions?	n/a	10.7
Do you have serious difficulty walking or climbing stairs?	10.0	13.6

Note: n/a not available; (1) Figures cover the College Station-Bryan, TX Metropolitan Statistical Area.
Source: Centers for Disease Control and Prevention, Behavioral Risk Factor Surveillance System, SMART: Selected Metropolitan Area Risk Trends, 2017

Mortality Rates for the Top 10 Causes of Death in the U.S.

ICD-10[a] Sub-Chapter	ICD-10[a] Code	Age-Adjusted Mortality Rate[1] per 100,000 population County[2]	U.S.
Malignant neoplasms	C00-C97	120.8	149.2
Ischaemic heart diseases	I20-I25	74.8	90.5
Other forms of heart disease	I30-I51	63.3	52.2
Chronic lower respiratory diseases	J40-J47	29.7	39.6
Other degenerative diseases of the nervous system	G30-G31	48.9	37.6
Cerebrovascular diseases	I60-I69	37.4	37.2
Other external causes of accidental injury	W00-X59	15.1	36.1
Organic, including symptomatic, mental disorders	F01-F09	30.8	29.4
Hypertensive diseases	I10-I15	31.2	24.1
Diabetes mellitus	E10-E14	18.6	21.5

Note: (a) ICD-10 = International Classification of Diseases 10th Revision; (1) Mortality rates are a three-year average covering 2017-2019; (2) Figures cover Brazos County.
Source: Centers for Disease Control and Prevention, National Center for Health Statistics. Underlying Cause of Death 1999-2019 on CDC WONDER Online Database

Mortality Rates for Selected Causes of Death

ICD-10[a] Sub-Chapter	ICD-10[a] Code	Age-Adjusted Mortality Rate[1] per 100,000 population County[2]	U.S.
Assault	X85-Y09	Unreliable	6.0
Diseases of the liver	K70-K76	13.3	14.4
Human immunodeficiency virus (HIV) disease	B20-B24	Suppressed	1.5
Influenza and pneumonia	J09-J18	9.9	13.8
Intentional self-harm	X60-X84	9.1	14.1
Malnutrition	E40-E46	Unreliable	2.3
Obesity and other hyperalimentation	E65-E68	Unreliable	2.1
Renal failure	N17-N19	11.5	12.6
Transport accidents	V01-V99	11.5	12.3
Viral hepatitis	B15-B19	Unreliable	1.2

Note: (a) ICD-10 = International Classification of Diseases 10th Revision; (1) Mortality rates are a three-year average covering 2017-2019; (2) Figures cover Brazos County; Data are suppressed when the data meet the criteria for confidentiality constraints; Mortality rates are flagged as unreliable when the rate would be calculated with a numerator of 20 or less.
Source: Centers for Disease Control and Prevention, National Center for Health Statistics. Underlying Cause of Death 1999-2019 on CDC WONDER Online Database

Health Insurance Coverage

Area	With Health Insurance	With Private Health Insurance	With Public Health Insurance	Without Health Insurance	Population Under Age 19 Without Health Insurance
City	92.0	85.0	13.7	8.0	4.9
MSA[1]	87.4	73.5	23.1	12.6	8.4
U.S.	91.2	67.9	35.1	8.8	5.1

Note: Figures are percentages that cover the civilian noninstitutionalized population; (1) Figures cover the College Station-Bryan, TX Metropolitan Statistical Area
Source: U.S. Census Bureau, 2015-2019 American Community Survey 5-Year Estimates

Number of Medical Professionals

Area	MDs[3]	DOs[3,4]	Dentists	Podiatrists	Chiropractors	Optometrists
County[1] (number)	584	43	120	7	40	36
County[1] (rate[2])	258.7	19.0	52.4	3.1	17.5	15.7
U.S. (rate[2])	282.9	22.7	71.2	6.2	28.1	16.9

48041
Note: Data as of 2019 unless noted; (1) Data covers Brazos County; (2) Rate per 100,000 population; (3) Data as of 2018 and includes all active, non-federal physicians; (4) Doctor of Osteopathic Medicine
Source: U.S. Department of Health and Human Services, Health Resources and Services Administration, Bureau of Health Professions, Area Resource File (ARF) 2019-2020

EDUCATION

Public School District Statistics

District Name	Schls	Pupils	Pupil/Teacher Ratio	Minority Pupils[1] (%)	Free Lunch Eligible[2] (%)	IEP[3] (%)
College Station ISD	20	13,540	14.0	47.2	30.3	11.0

Note: Table includes school districts with 2,000 or more students; (1) Percentage of students that are not non-Hispanic white; (2) Percentage of students that are eligible for the free lunch program; (3) Percentage of students that have an Individualized Education Program.
Source: U.S. Department of Education, National Center for Education Statistics, Common Core of Data, Local Education Agency (School District) Universe Survey: School Year 2018-2019; U.S. Department of Education, National Center for Education Statistics, Common Core of Data, Public Elementary/Secondary School Universe Survey: School Year 2018-2019

Highest Level of Education

Area	Less than H.S.	H.S. Diploma	Some College, No Deg.	Associate Degree	Bachelor's Degree	Master's Degree	Prof. School Degree	Doctorate Degree
City	5.6	11.4	17.0	7.4	29.3	15.7	3.3	10.3
MSA[1]	13.4	22.2	20.4	6.5	20.6	9.6	2.2	5.1
U.S.	12.0	27.0	20.4	8.5	19.8	8.8	2.1	1.4

Note: Figures cover persons age 25 and over; (1) Figures cover the College Station-Bryan, TX Metropolitan Statistical Area
Source: U.S. Census Bureau, 2015-2019 American Community Survey 5-Year Estimates

Educational Attainment by Race

Area	High School Graduate or Higher (%)					Bachelor's Degree or Higher (%)				
	Total	White	Black	Asian	Hisp.[2]	Total	White	Black	Asian	Hisp.[2]
City	94.4	95.1	87.8	95.2	85.6	58.6	58.8	29.4	80.9	45.8
MSA[1]	86.6	87.3	85.3	94.0	63.3	37.5	39.3	16.5	78.4	15.9
U.S.	88.0	89.9	86.0	87.1	68.7	32.1	33.5	21.6	54.3	16.4

Note: Figures shown cover persons 25 years old and over; (1) Figures cover the College Station-Bryan, TX Metropolitan Statistical Area; (2) People of Hispanic origin can be of any race
Source: U.S. Census Bureau, 2015-2019 American Community Survey 5-Year Estimates

School Enrollment by Grade and Control

Area	Preschool (%)		Kindergarten (%)		Grades 1 - 4 (%)		Grades 5 - 8 (%)		Grades 9 - 12 (%)	
	Public	Private	Public	Private	Public	Private	Public	Private	Public	Private
City	46.9	53.1	85.1	14.9	86.5	13.5	93.5	6.5	92.7	7.3
MSA[1]	60.1	39.9	86.1	13.9	88.9	11.1	92.4	7.6	93.3	6.7
U.S.	59.1	40.9	87.6	12.4	89.5	10.5	89.4	10.6	90.1	9.9

Note: Figures shown cover persons 3 years old and over; (1) Figures cover the College Station-Bryan, TX Metropolitan Statistical Area
Source: U.S. Census Bureau, 2015-2019 American Community Survey 5-Year Estimates

Higher Education

Four-Year Colleges			Two-Year Colleges			Medical Schools[1]	Law Schools[2]	Voc/Tech[3]
Public	Private Non-profit	Private For-profit	Public	Private Non-profit	Private For-profit			
1	0	0	0	0	0	1	0	0

Note: Figures cover institutions located within the city limits and include main campuses only; (1) includes schools accredited by the Liaison Committee on Medical Education and the American Osteopathic Association's Commission on Osteopathic College Accreditation; (2) includes ABA-accredited schools, schools with provisional ABA accreditation, and state accredited schools; (3) includes all schools with programs that are less than 2 years.
Source: National Center for Education Statistics, Integrated Postsecondary Education System (IPEDS), 2019-20; Wikipedia, List of Medical Schools in the United States, accessed April 2, 2021; Wikipedia, List of Law Schools in the United States, accessed April 2, 2021

According to *U.S. News & World Report,* the College Station-Bryan, TX metro area is home to one of the top 200 national universities in the U.S.: **Texas A&M University** (#66 tie). The indicators used to capture academic quality fall into a number of categories: assessment by administrators at peer institutions; retention of students; faculty resources; student selectivity; financial resources; alumni giving; high school counselor ratings of colleges; and graduation rate. *U.S. News & World Report, "America's Best Colleges 2021"*

According to *U.S. News & World Report,* the College Station-Bryan, TX metro area is home to one of the top 75 medical schools for research in the U.S.: **Texas A&M University** (#75 tie). The rankings are based on a weighted average of 11 measures of quality: quality assessment; peer assessment score; assessment score by residency directors; research activity; total research activity; average research activity per faculty member; student selectivity; median MCAT total score; median undergraduate GPA; acceptance rate; and faculty resources. *U.S. News & World Report, "America's Best Graduate Schools, Medical, 2022"*

According to *U.S. News & World Report,* the College Station-Bryan, TX metro area is home to one of the top 75 business schools in the U.S.: **Texas A&M University—College Station (Mays)** (#38). The rankings are based on a weighted average of the following nine measures: quality assessment; peer assessment; recruiter assessment; placement success; mean starting salary and bonus; student selectivity; mean GMAT and GRE scores; mean undergraduate GPA; and acceptance rate. *U.S. News & World Report,* "America's Best Graduate Schools, Business, 2022"

EMPLOYERS

Major Employers

Company Name	Industry
Bryan Independent School District	Education
City of Bryan	Municipal government
City of College Station	Municipal government
College Station ISD	Education
H-E-B Grocery	Grocery stores
New Alenco Windows	Fabricated metal products
Reynolds and Reynolds/Rentsys	Computer hardware/software
Sanderson Farms	Poultry processing
St. Joseph Regional Health Center	Health services
Texas A&M University System	Education
Wal-Mart Stores	Retail

Note: Companies shown are located within the College Station-Bryan, TX Metropolitan Statistical Area.
Source: Hoovers.com; Wikipedia

PUBLIC SAFETY

Crime Rate

Area	All Crimes	Murder	Rape[3]	Robbery	Aggrav. Assault	Burglary	Larceny-Theft	Motor Vehicle Theft
City	1,948.1	0.8	40.3	36.1	111.5	327.9	1,282.2	149.3
Suburbs[1]	2,466.8	2.7	79.5	46.6	193.9	419.9	1,565.3	158.9
Metro[2]	2,233.6	1.9	61.8	41.9	156.8	378.5	1,438.0	154.6
U.S.	2,489.3	5.0	42.6	81.6	250.2	340.5	1,549.5	219.9

Note: Figures are crimes per 100,000 population; (1) All areas within the metro area that are located outside the city limits; (2) Figures cover the College Station-Bryan, TX Metropolitan Statistical Area; (3) All figures shown were reported using the revised Uniform Crime Reporting (UCR) definition of rape.
Source: FBI Uniform Crime Reports, 2019

Hate Crimes

Area	Number of Quarters Reported	Race/Ethnicity/Ancestry	Religion	Sexual Orientation	Disability	Gender	Gender Identity
City	4	1	0	0	0	0	0
U.S.	4	3,963	1,521	1,195	157	69	198

Source: Federal Bureau of Investigation, Hate Crime Statistics 2019

Identity Theft Consumer Reports

Area	Reports	Reports per 100,000 Population	Rank[2]
MSA[1]	582	220	182
U.S.	1,387,615	423	-

Note: (1) Figures cover the College Station-Bryan, TX Metropolitan Statistical Area; (2) Rank ranges from 1 to 391 where 1 indicates greatest number of identity theft reports per 100,000 population
Source: Federal Trade Commission, Consumer Sentinel Network Data Book 2020

Fraud and Other Consumer Reports

Area	Reports	Reports per 100,000 Population	Rank[2]
MSA[1]	2,003	757	134
U.S.	3,385,133	1,031	-

Note: (1) Figures cover the College Station-Bryan, TX Metropolitan Statistical Area; (2) Rank ranges from 1 to 391 where 1 indicates greatest number of fraud and other consumer reports per 100,000 population
Source: Federal Trade Commission, Consumer Sentinel Network Data Book 2020

POLITICS

2020 Presidential Election Results

Area	Biden	Trump	Jorgensen	Hawkins	Other
Brazos County	41.6	55.9	2.1	0.3	0.1
U.S.	51.3	46.8	1.2	0.3	0.5

Note: Results are percentages and may not add to 100% due to rounding
Source: Dave Leip's Atlas of U.S. Presidential Elections

SPORTS

Professional Sports Teams

Team Name	League	Year Established
No teams are located in the metro area		

Source: Wikipedia, Major Professional Sports Teams of the United States and Canada, April 6, 2021

CLIMATE

Average and Extreme Temperatures

Temperature	Jan	Feb	Mar	Apr	May	Jun	Jul	Aug	Sep	Oct	Nov	Dec	Yr.
Extreme High (°F)	90	97	98	98	100	105	109	106	104	98	91	90	109
Average High (°F)	60	64	72	79	85	91	95	96	90	81	70	63	79
Average Temp. (°F)	50	53	61	69	75	82	85	85	80	70	60	52	69
Average Low (°F)	39	43	50	58	65	72	74	74	69	59	49	41	58
Extreme Low (°F)	-2	7	18	35	43	53	64	61	47	32	20	4	-2

Note: Figures cover the years 1948-1990
Source: National Climatic Data Center, International Station Meteorological Climate Summary, 9/96

Average Precipitation/Snowfall/Humidity

Precip./Humidity	Jan	Feb	Mar	Apr	May	Jun	Jul	Aug	Sep	Oct	Nov	Dec	Yr.
Avg. Precip. (in.)	1.6	2.3	1.8	2.9	4.3	3.5	1.9	1.9	3.3	3.5	2.1	1.9	31.1
Avg. Snowfall (in.)	1	Tr	Tr	0	0	0	0	0	0	0	Tr	Tr	1
Avg. Rel. Hum. 6am (%)	79	80	79	83	88	89	88	87	86	84	81	79	84
Avg. Rel. Hum. 3pm (%)	53	51	47	50	53	49	43	42	47	47	49	51	48

Note: Figures cover the years 1948-1990; Tr = Trace amounts (<0.05 in. of rain; <0.5 in. of snow)
Source: National Climatic Data Center, International Station Meteorological Climate Summary, 9/96

Weather Conditions

Temperature			Daytime Sky			Precipitation		
10°F & below	32°F & below	90°F & above	Clear	Partly cloudy	Cloudy	0.01 inch or more precip.	0.1 inch or more snow/ice	Thunderstorms
< 1	20	111	105	148	112	83	1	41

Note: Figures are average number of days per year and cover the years 1948-1990
Source: National Climatic Data Center, International Station Meteorological Climate Summary, 9/96

HAZARDOUS WASTE

Superfund Sites

The College Station-Bryan, TX metro area has no sites on the EPA's Superfund Final National Priorities List. There are a total of 1,375 Superfund sites with a status of proposed or final on the list in the U.S. *U.S. Environmental Protection Agency, National Priorities List, April 7, 2021*

AIR QUALITY

Air Quality Trends: Ozone

	1990	1995	2000	2005	2010	2015	2016	2017	2018	2019
MSA[1]	n/a	n/a	n/a	n/a	n/a	n/a	n/a	n/a	n/a	n/a
U.S.	0.088	0.089	0.082	0.080	0.073	0.068	0.069	0.068	0.069	0.065

Note: (1) Data covers the College Station-Bryan, TX Metropolitan Statistical Area; n/a not available. The values shown are the composite ozone concentration averages among trend sites based on the highest fourth daily maximum 8-hour concentration in parts per million. These trends are based on sites having an adequate record of monitoring data during the trend period. Data from exceptional events are included.
Source: U.S. Environmental Protection Agency, Air Quality Monitoring Information, "Air Quality Trends by City, 1990-2019"

Air Quality Index

Area	Percent of Days when Air Quality was...[2]					AQI Statistics[2]	
	Good	Moderate	Unhealthy for Sensitive Groups	Unhealthy	Very Unhealthy	Maximum	Median
MSA[1]	100.0	0.0	0.0	0.0	0.0	17	0

Note: (1) Data covers the College Station-Bryan, TX Metropolitan Statistical Area; (2) Based on 352 days with AQI data in 2019. Air Quality Index (AQI) is an index for reporting daily air quality. EPA calculates the AQI for five major air pollutants regulated by the Clean Air Act: ground-level ozone, particle pollution (aka particulate matter), carbon monoxide, sulfur dioxide, and nitrogen dioxide. The AQI runs from 0 to 500. The higher the AQI value, the greater the level of air pollution and the greater the health concern. There are six AQI categories: "Good" AQI is between 0 and 50. Air quality is considered satisfactory; "Moderate" AQI is between 51 and 100. Air quality is acceptable; "Unhealthy for Sensitive Groups" When AQI values are between 101 and 150, members of sensitive groups may experience health effects; "Unhealthy" When AQI values are between 151 and 200 everyone may begin to experience health effects; "Very Unhealthy" AQI values between 201 and 300 trigger a health alert; "Hazardous" AQI values over 300 trigger warnings of emergency conditions (not shown).
Source: U.S. Environmental Protection Agency, Air Quality Index Report, 2019

Air Quality Index Pollutants

Area	Percent of Days when AQI Pollutant was...[2]					
	Carbon Monoxide	Nitrogen Dioxide	Ozone	Sulfur Dioxide	Particulate Matter 2.5	Particulate Matter 10
MSA[1]	0.0	0.0	0.0	100.0	0.0	0.0

Note: (1) Data covers the College Station-Bryan, TX Metropolitan Statistical Area; (2) Based on 352 days with AQI data in 2019. The Air Quality Index (AQI) is an index for reporting daily air quality. EPA calculates the AQI for five major air pollutants regulated by the Clean Air Act: ground-level ozone, particle pollution (also known as particulate matter), carbon monoxide, sulfur dioxide, and nitrogen dioxide. The AQI runs from 0 to 500. The higher the AQI value, the greater the level of air pollution and the greater the health concern.
Source: U.S. Environmental Protection Agency, Air Quality Index Report, 2019

Maximum Air Pollutant Concentrations: Particulate Matter, Ozone, CO and Lead

	Particulate Matter 10 (ug/m³)	Particulate Matter 2.5 Wtd AM (ug/m³)	Particulate Matter 2.5 24-Hr (ug/m³)	Ozone (ppm)	Carbon Monoxide (ppm)	Lead (ug/m³)
MSA[1] Level	n/a	n/a	n/a	n/a	n/a	n/a
NAAQS[2]	150	15	35	0.075	9	0.15
Met NAAQS[2]	n/a	n/a	n/a	n/a	n/a	n/a

Note: (1) Data covers the College Station-Bryan, TX Metropolitan Statistical Area; Data from exceptional events are included; (2) National Ambient Air Quality Standards; ppm = parts per million; ug/m³ = micrograms per cubic meter; n/a not available.
Concentrations: Particulate Matter 10 (coarse particulate)—highest second maximum 24-hour concentration; Particulate Matter 2.5 Wtd AM (fine particulate)—highest weighted annual mean concentration; Particulate Matter 2.5 24-Hour (fine particulate)—highest 98th percentile 24-hour concentration; Ozone—highest fourth daily maximum 8-hour concentration; Carbon Monoxide—highest second maximum non-overlapping 8-hour concentration; Lead—maximum running 3-month average
Source: U.S. Environmental Protection Agency, Air Quality Monitoring Information, "Air Quality Statistics by City, 2019"

Maximum Air Pollutant Concentrations: Nitrogen Dioxide and Sulfur Dioxide

	Nitrogen Dioxide AM (ppb)	Nitrogen Dioxide 1-Hr (ppb)	Sulfur Dioxide AM (ppb)	Sulfur Dioxide 1-Hr (ppb)	Sulfur Dioxide 24-Hr (ppb)
MSA[1] Level	n/a	n/a	n/a	8	n/a
NAAQS[2]	53	100	30	75	140
Met NAAQS[2]	n/a	n/a	n/a	Yes	n/a

Note: (1) Data covers the College Station-Bryan, TX Metropolitan Statistical Area; Data from exceptional events are included; (2) National Ambient Air Quality Standards; ppm = parts per million; ug/m³ = micrograms per cubic meter; n/a not available.
Concentrations: Nitrogen Dioxide AM—highest arithmetic mean concentration; Nitrogen Dioxide 1-Hr—highest 98th percentile 1-hour daily maximum concentration; Sulfur Dioxide AM—highest annual mean concentration; Sulfur Dioxide 1-Hr—highest 99th percentile 1-hour daily maximum concentration; Sulfur Dioxide 24-Hr—highest second maximum 24-hour concentration
Source: U.S. Environmental Protection Agency, Air Quality Monitoring Information, "Air Quality Statistics by City, 2019"

Columbia, South Carolina

Background

Located on the Congaree River, Columbia is South Carolina's capital and largest city, and the seat of Richland County. It is a center for local and state government, and an important financial, insurance, and medical center.

The region has been a trade center since a trading post opened south of the present-day city in 1718. In 1786, Columbia was chosen as the new state's capital due to its location in the center of South Carolina, a compromise between residents on the coast and those living further inland.

The nation's second planned city, Columbia was originally 400 acres along the river. The main thoroughfares were designed 150 feet wide and other streets were also wider than most. Much of this spacious layout survives, lending an expansive feel to the city. Columbia was chartered as a town in 1805. Its first mayor—or "intendent"—John Taylor, later served in the state general assembly, in the U.S. Congress, and as governor of the state. Columbia was staunchly Confederate during the Civil War, attacked in 1865 by General Sherman's troops and set ablaze by both Union attackers and Confederate evacuees. After the war and Reconstruction, Columbia was revitalized as the state's industrial and farm products hub.

Today, a brisk renewal continues in Columbia's formerly moribund downtown thanks to the state's first Business Improvement District. The City Center Partnership, Inc., manages the district and works to bring businesses and residents into the area, via, among other things, the free ZeRover shuttle. The area's Central Business District has seen record office space occupancy. A major CanalSide mixed use development on the Congaree River was completed in 2018, bringing 750 residential apartments to the area.

Columbia is home to the University of South Carolina, a major employer alongside BlueCross BlueShield of SC. The USC/Columbia Technology Incubator companies generated more than $30 million in gross revenue in recent years. The university has also created the 500-acre Innovista Research District to provide office and lab space to tech and innovation businesses and startups. The health care industry is also significant. The Medical University of South Carolina and the area's largest employer, Palmetto Health, merged their medical practices in 2016 under the banner of Palmetto Health-USC Medical Group. The city's two venerable Providence Hospitals—operated by the Sisters of Charity since 1938—were recently acquired by LifePoint Health, a Tennessee-based for-profit company that operates health care facilities in 22 states.

Other large employers include Fort Jackson, the U.S. Army's largest initial entry training installation (and also home to Fort Jackson National Cemetery), and the United Parcel Service, which operates a freight service center in West Columbia.

Columbia is the cultural center for the area, known as South Carolina's Midlands. The Columbia Museum of Art, with its collection of Renaissance and Baroque art, is a major regional museum. The performing arts are onstage year-round at the Koger Center for the Arts at USC. The city's Town Theatre, nearing 100, is the country's oldest community theatre in continuous use. The South Carolina State Museum "Windows to New Worlds" includes a planetarium, observatory and 4-D theater. Major historic architecture in Columbia includes the City Hall, designed by President Ulysses S. Grant's federal architect, Alfred B. Mullet, and the Lutheran Survey Print Building.

In addition to USC, Columbia's other institutions of higher learning are Lutheran Theological Seminary, Columbia College, Benedict College, Allen University, and Columbia International University.

In March, 2015, the Confederate battle flag was removed from the state house flagpole by a protester motivated by the Charleston Massacre. Although the flag was raised again minutes after this action, it was permanently removed in July of that year.

Located about 150 miles southeast of the Appalachian Mountains, Columbia has a relatively temperate climate. Summers are long and often hot and humid with frequent thunderstorms, thanks to the Bermuda high-pressure force. Winters are mild with little snow, while spring is changeable and can include infrequent tornadoes or hail. Fall is considered the most pleasant season.

Rankings

General Rankings

- For its "Best for Vets: Places to Live 2019" rankings, *Military Times* evaluated 599 cities (83 large, 234 medium, 282 small) and compared the locations across three broad categories: veteran and military culture/services; economic indicators; and livability factors such as health, crime, traffic, and school quality. Columbia ranked #39 out of the top 50, in the medium-sized city category (population of 100,000-249,999). Data points more specific to veterans and the military weighed more heavily than others. *rebootcamp.militarytimes.com, "Military Times Best Places to Live 2019," September 10, 2018*

- In their seventh annual survey, Livability.com looked at data for more than 1,000 small to mid-sized U.S. cities to determine the rankings for Livability's "Top 100 Best Places to Live" in 2020. Columbia ranked #87. Criteria: housing and affordable living; vibrant economy; social and civic engagement; education; demographics; health care options; transportation & infrastructure; and abundant lifestyle amenities. *Livability.com, "Top 100 Best Places to Live 2020" October 2020*

Business/Finance Rankings

- The Brookings Institution ranked the nation's largest cities based on income inequality. Columbia was ranked #38 (#1 = greatest inequality). Criteria: the "95/20 ratio," a figure representing the income at which a household earns more than 95 percent of all other households, divided by the income at which a household earns more than only 20 percent of all other households. *Brookings Institution, "Household Income Inequality, Largest Cities of 97 Large U.S. Metro Areas, 2014-2016," February 5, 2018*

- The Brookings Institution ranked the 100 largest metro areas in the U.S. based on income inequality. Columbia was ranked #63 (#1 = greatest inequality). Criteria: the "95/20 ratio," a figure representing the income at which a household earns more than 95 percent of all other households, divided by the income at which a household earns more than only 20 percent of all other households. *Brookings Institution, "Household Income Inequality, 100 Largest U.S. Metro Areas, 2014-2016," February 5, 2018*

- The Columbia metro area appeared on the Milken Institute "2021 Best Performing Cities" list. Rank: #77 out of 200 large metro areas (population over 250,000). Criteria: job growth; wage and salary growth; high-tech output growth; housing affordability; household broadband access. *Milken Institute, "Best-Performing Cities 2021," February 16, 2021*

- *Forbes* ranked the 200 most populous metro areas to determine the nation's "Best Places for Business and Careers." The Columbia metro area was ranked #102. Criteria: costs (business and living); job growth (past and projected); income growth; quality of life; educational attainment (college and high school); projected economic growth; cultural and leisure opportunities; workplace tolerance laws; net migration patterns. *Forbes, "The Best Places for Business and Careers 2019: Seattle Still On Top," October 30, 2019*

Children/Family Rankings

- Columbia was selected as one of the most playful cities in the U.S. by KaBOOM! The organization's Playful City USA initiative honors cities and towns across the nation that have made their communities more playable. Criteria: pledging to integrate play as a solution to challenges in their communities; making it easy for children to get active and balanced play; creating more family-friendly and innovative communities as a result. *KaBOOM! National Campaign for Play, "2017 Playful City USA Communities"*

Dating/Romance Rankings

- Columbia was selected as one of the nation's most romantic cities with 100,000 or more residents by Amazon.com. The city ranked #11 of 20. Criteria: per capita sales of romance novels, relationship books, romantic comedy movies, romantic music, and sexual wellness products. *Amazon.com, "Top 20 Most Romantic Cities in the U.S.," February 1, 2017*

Education Rankings

- Personal finance website *WalletHub* analyzed the 150 largest U.S. metropolitan statistical areas to determine where the most educated Americans are putting their degrees to work. Criteria: education levels; percentage of workers with degrees; education quality and attainment gap; public school quality rankings; quality and enrollment of each metro area's universities. Columbia was ranked #66 (#1 = most educated city). *www.WalletHub.com, "Most and Least Educated Cities in America," July 20, 2020*

Health/Fitness Rankings

- Columbia was identified as a "2021 Spring Allergy Capital." The area ranked #18 out of 100. Three groups of factors were used to identify the most challenging cities for people with allergies during the spring season: annual spring pollen levels; over the counter medicine use; number of board-certified allergy specialists. *Asthma and Allergy Foundation of America, "Spring Allergy Capitals 2021," February 23, 2021*

- Columbia was identified as a "2021 Fall Allergy Capital." The area ranked #27 out of 100. Three groups of factors were used to identify the most challenging cities for people with allergies during the fall season: annual fall pollen levels; over the counter medicine use; number of board-certified allergy specialists. *Asthma and Allergy Foundation of America, "Fall Allergy Capitals 2021," February 23, 2021*

- Columbia was identified as a "2019 Asthma Capital." The area ranked #34 out of the nation's 100 largest metropolitan areas. Criteria: estimated asthma prevalence; crude death rate from asthma; and ER visits due to asthma. Risk factors analyzed but not factored in the rankings: annual pollen score; annual air quality; public smoking laws; number of board-certified asthma specialists; rescue medication use; controller medication use; uninsured rate; poverty rate. *Asthma and Allergy Foundation of America, "Asthma Capitals 2019: The Most Challenging Places to Live With Asthma," May 7, 2019*

Real Estate Rankings

- *WalletHub* compared the most populated U.S. cities to determine which had the best markets for real estate agents. Columbia ranked #148 where demand was high and pay was the best. Criteria: sales per agent; annual median wage for real-estate agents; monthly average starting salary for real estate agents; real estate job density and competition; unemployment rate; home turnover rate; housing-market health index; and other relevant metrics. *www.WalletHub.com, "2019's Best Places to Be a Real Estate Agent," April 24, 2019*

- Columbia was ranked #47 out of 268 metro areas in terms of housing affordability in 2020 by the National Association of Home Builders (#1 = most affordable). Criteria: the share of homes sold in that area affordable to a family earning the local median income, based on standard mortgage underwriting criteria. *National Association of Home Builders®, NAHB-Wells Fargo Housing Opportunity Index, 4th Quarter 2020*

Safety Rankings

- The National Insurance Crime Bureau ranked 384 metro areas in the U.S. in terms of per capita rates of vehicle theft. The Columbia metro area ranked #29 (#1 = highest rate). Criteria: number of vehicle theft offenses per 100,000 inhabitants in 2019. *National Insurance Crime Bureau, "Hot Spots 2019," July 21, 2020*

Seniors/Retirement Rankings

- From its Best Cities for Successful Aging indexes, the Milken Institute generated rankings for metropolitan areas, weighing data in nine categories—health care, wellness, living arrangements, transportation and convenience, financial characteristics, education, employment, community engagement, and overall livability. The Columbia metro area was ranked #54 overall in the large metro area category. *Milken Institute, "Best Cities for Successful Aging, 2017" March 14, 2017*

Sports/Recreation Rankings

- Columbia was chosen as a bicycle friendly community by the League of American Bicyclists. A "Bicycle Friendly Community" welcomes cyclists by providing safe and supportive accommodation for cycling and encouraging people to bike for transportation and recreation. There are five award levels: Diamond; Platinum; Gold; Silver; and Bronze. The community achieved an award level of Bronze. *League of American Bicyclists, "Fall 2020 Awards-New & Renewing Bicycle Friendly Communities List," December 16, 2020*

Women/Minorities Rankings

- Personal finance website *WalletHub* compared more than 180 U.S. cities across two key dimensions, "Hispanic Business-Friendliness" and "Hispanic Purchasing Power," to arrive at the most favorable conditions for Hispanic entrepreneurs. Columbia was ranked #149 out of 182. Criteria includes: share of Hispanic-Owned Businesses; Hispanic entrepreneurship rate to median annual income of Hispanics; Small Business-Friendliness score; cost of living; and number of Hispanics with at least a bachelor's degree. *WalletHub.com, "2019's Best Cities for Hispanic Entrepreneurs," May 1, 2019*

Miscellaneous Rankings

- *WalletHub* compared the 150 most populated U.S. cities to determine their operating efficiency. A "Quality of City Services" score was constructed for each city and then divided by the total budget per capita to reveal which were managed the best. Columbia ranked #90. Criteria: financial stability; economy; education; safety; health; infrastructure and pollution. *www.WalletHub.com, "2020's Best- & Worst-Run Cities in America," June 29, 2020*

Business Environment

DEMOGRAPHICS

Population Growth

Area	1990 Census	2000 Census	2010 Census	2019* Estimate	Population Growth (%) 1990-2019	Population Growth (%) 2010-2019
City	115,475	116,278	129,272	133,273	15.4	3.1
MSA[1]	548,325	647,158	767,598	824,278	50.3	7.4
U.S.	248,709,873	281,421,906	308,745,538	324,697,795	30.6	5.2

Note: (1) Figures cover the Columbia, SC Metropolitan Statistical Area; (*) 2015-2019 5-year estimated population
Source: U.S. Census Bureau, 1990 Census, Census 2000, Census 2010, 2015-2019 American Community Survey 5-Year Estimates

Household Size

Area	One	Two	Three	Four	Five	Six	Seven or More	Average Household Size
City	40.6	33.0	12.3	9.0	3.6	0.9	0.6	2.20
MSA[1]	29.8	34.3	15.7	12.2	5.3	1.8	0.9	2.50
U.S.	27.9	33.9	15.6	12.9	6.0	2.3	1.4	2.60

Note: (1) Figures cover the Columbia, SC Metropolitan Statistical Area
Source: U.S. Census Bureau, 2015-2019 American Community Survey 5-Year Estimates

Race

Area	White Alone[2] (%)	Black Alone[2] (%)	Asian Alone[2] (%)	AIAN[3] Alone[2] (%)	NHOPI[4] Alone[2] (%)	Other Race Alone[2] (%)	Two or More Races (%)
City	53.4	39.8	2.7	0.1	0.2	1.0	2.8
MSA[1]	59.6	33.4	2.1	0.2	0.1	1.8	2.7
U.S.	72.5	12.7	5.5	0.8	0.2	4.9	3.3

Note: (1) Figures cover the Columbia, SC Metropolitan Statistical Area; (2) Alone is defined as not being in combination with one or more other races; (3) American Indian and Alaska Native; (4) Native Hawaiian and Other Pacific Islander
Source: U.S. Census Bureau, 2015-2019 American Community Survey 5-Year Estimates

Hispanic or Latino Origin

Area	Total (%)	Mexican (%)	Puerto Rican (%)	Cuban (%)	Other (%)
City	5.5	2.1	1.3	0.3	1.7
MSA[1]	5.5	2.8	1.1	0.2	1.4
U.S.	18.0	11.2	1.7	0.7	4.3

Note: Persons of Hispanic or Latino origin can be of any race; (1) Figures cover the Columbia, SC Metropolitan Statistical Area
Source: U.S. Census Bureau, 2015-2019 American Community Survey 5-Year Estimates

Ancestry

Area	German	Irish	English	American	Italian	Polish	French[2]	Scottish	Dutch
City	9.9	6.9	8.3	5.3	2.9	1.3	2.0	2.2	0.8
MSA[1]	10.0	7.4	7.3	8.5	2.3	1.1	1.7	2.0	0.7
U.S.	13.3	9.7	7.2	6.2	5.1	2.8	2.3	1.7	1.2

Note: Figures are the percentage of the total population reporting a particular ancestry. The nine most commonly reported ancestries in the U.S. are shown. Figures include multiple ancestries (e.g. if a person reported being Irish and Italian, they were included in both columns); (1) Figures cover the Columbia, SC Metropolitan Statistical Area; (2) Excludes Basque
Source: U.S. Census Bureau, 2015-2019 American Community Survey 5-Year Estimates

Foreign-born Population

Area	Any Foreign Country	Asia	Mexico	Europe	Caribbean	Central America[2]	South America	Africa	Canada
City	5.0	2.1	0.5	0.8	0.3	0.3	0.5	0.4	0.1
MSA[1]	5.0	1.6	1.1	0.7	0.3	0.5	0.3	0.4	0.1
U.S.	13.6	4.2	3.5	1.5	1.3	1.1	1.0	0.7	0.2

Note: (1) Figures cover the Columbia, SC Metropolitan Statistical Area; (2) Excludes Mexico.
Source: U.S. Census Bureau, 2015-2019 American Community Survey 5-Year Estimates

Columbia, South Carolina

Marital Status

Area	Never Married	Now Married[2]	Separated	Widowed	Divorced
City	55.8	27.8	2.6	4.4	9.4
MSA[1]	36.6	44.2	2.8	5.7	10.7
U.S.	33.4	48.1	1.9	5.8	10.9

Note: Figures are percentages and cover the population 15 years of age and older; (1) Figures cover the Columbia, SC Metropolitan Statistical Area; (2) Excludes separated
Source: U.S. Census Bureau, 2015-2019 American Community Survey 5-Year Estimates

Disability by Age

Area	All Ages	Under 18 Years Old	18 to 64 Years Old	65 Years and Over
City	12.6	5.4	10.8	35.7
MSA[1]	14.1	4.6	12.2	36.8
U.S.	12.6	4.2	10.3	34.5

Note: Figures show percent of the civilian noninstitutionalized population that reported having a disability. Disability status is determined from six types of difficulty: vision, hearing, cognitive, ambulatory, self-care, and independent living. For children under 5 years old, hearing and vision difficulty are used to determine disability status. For children between the ages of 5 and 14, disability status is determined from hearing, vision, cognitive, ambulatory, and self-care difficulties. For people aged 15 years and older, they are considered to have a disability if they have difficulty with any one of the six difficulty types; Note: (1) Figures cover the Columbia, SC Metropolitan Statistical Area
Source: U.S. Census Bureau, 2015-2019 American Community Survey 5-Year Estimates

Age

Area	Under Age 5	Age 5–19	Age 20–34	Age 35–44	Age 45–54	Age 55–64	Age 65–74	Age 75–84	Age 85+	Median Age
City	5.1	23.2	31.9	10.1	10.1	9.4	6.2	2.8	1.2	28.5
MSA[1]	5.8	20.2	21.6	12.5	12.7	12.7	8.9	4.1	1.5	36.6
U.S.	6.1	19.1	20.7	12.6	13.0	12.9	9.1	4.6	1.9	38.1

Note: (1) Figures cover the Columbia, SC Metropolitan Statistical Area
Source: U.S. Census Bureau, 2015-2019 American Community Survey 5-Year Estimates

Gender

Area	Males	Females	Males per 100 Females
City	67,638	65,635	103.1
MSA[1]	399,998	424,280	94.3
U.S.	159,886,919	164,810,876	97.0

Note: (1) Figures cover the Columbia, SC Metropolitan Statistical Area
Source: U.S. Census Bureau, 2015-2019 American Community Survey 5-Year Estimates

Religious Groups by Family

Area	Catholic	Baptist	Non-Den.	Methodist[2]	Lutheran	LDS[3]	Pentecostal	Presbyterian[4]	Muslim[5]	Judaism
MSA[1]	3.1	18.1	5.2	9.4	3.4	1.1	2.7	3.3	0.1	0.2
U.S.	19.1	9.3	4.0	4.0	2.3	2.0	1.9	1.6	0.8	0.7

Note: Figures are the number of adherents as a percentage of the total population; (1) Figures cover the Columbia, SC Metropolitan Statistical Area; (2) Methodist/Pietist; (3) Latter Day Saints; (4) Reformed; (5) Figures are estimates
Source: Association of Statisticians of American Religious Bodies, 2010 U.S. Religion Census: Religious Congregations & Membership Study

Religious Groups by Tradition

Area	Catholic	Evangelical Protestant	Mainline Protestant	Other Tradition	Black Protestant	Orthodox
MSA[1]	3.1	25.6	13.5	2.1	5.5	0.1
U.S.	19.1	16.2	7.3	4.3	1.6	0.3

Note: Figures are the number of adherents as a percentage of the total population; (1) Figures cover the Columbia, SC Metropolitan Statistical Area
Source: Association of Statisticians of American Religious Bodies, 2010 U.S. Religion Census: Religious Congregations & Membership Study

ECONOMY

Gross Metropolitan Product

Area	2017	2018	2019	2020	Rank[2]
MSA[1]	41.4	42.3	43.9	45.8	73

Note: Figures are in billions of dollars; (1) Figures cover the Columbia, SC Metropolitan Statistical Area; (2) Rank is based on 2018 data and ranges from 1 to 381
Source: U.S. Conference of Mayors, U.S. Metro Economies: GMP & Employment 2018-2020, September 2019

Columbia, South Carolina 169

Economic Growth

Area	2015-17 (%)	2018 (%)	2019 (%)	2020 (%)	Rank[2]
MSA[1]	0.8	-0.1	1.9	2.3	245
U.S.	1.9	2.9	2.3	2.1	—

Note: Figures are real gross metropolitan product (GMP) growth rates and represent average annual percent change; (1) Figures cover the Columbia, SC Metropolitan Statistical Area; (2) Rank is based on 2017 2-year average annual percent change and ranges from 1 to 381
Source: U.S. Conference of Mayors, U.S. Metro Economies: GMP & Employment 2018-2020, September 2019

Metropolitan Area Exports

Area	2014	2015	2016	2017	2018	2019	Rank[2]
MSA[1]	2,007.9	2,011.8	2,007.7	2,123.9	2,083.8	2,184.6	97

Note: Figures are in millions of dollars; (1) Figures cover the Columbia, SC Metropolitan Statistical Area; (2) Rank is based on 2019 data and ranges from 1 to 386
Source: U.S. Department of Commerce, International Trade Administration, Office of Trade and Economic Analysis, Industry and Analysis, Exports by Metropolitan Area, data extracted March 24, 2021

Building Permits

Area	Single-Family 2018	Single-Family 2019	Pct. Chg.	Multi-Family 2018	Multi-Family 2019	Pct. Chg.	Total 2018	Total 2019	Pct. Chg.
City	449	464	3.3	28	10	-64.3	477	474	-0.6
MSA[1]	4,478	4,209	-6.0	474	215	-54.6	4,952	4,424	-10.7
U.S.	855,300	862,100	0.7	473,500	523,900	10.6	1,328,800	1,386,000	4.3

Note: (1) Figures cover the Columbia, SC Metropolitan Statistical Area; Figures represent new, privately-owned housing units authorized (unadjusted data); All permit data are based on estimates with imputation
Source: U.S. Census Bureau, Manufacturing, Mining, and Construction Statistics, Building Permits, 2018, 2019

Bankruptcy Filings

Area	Business Filings 2019	Business Filings 2020	% Chg.	Nonbusiness Filings 2019	Nonbusiness Filings 2020	% Chg.
Richland County	11	12	9.1	837	520	-37.9
U.S.	22,780	21,655	-4.9	752,160	522,808	-30.5

Note: Business filings include Chapter 7, Chapter 9, Chapter 11, Chapter 12, Chapter 13, Chapter 15, and Section 304; Nonbusiness filings include Chapter 7, Chapter 11, and Chapter 13
Source: Administrative Office of the U.S. Courts, Business and Nonbusiness Bankruptcy, County Cases Commenced by Chapter of the Bankruptcy Code, During the 12-Month Period Ending December 31, 2019 and Business and Nonbusiness Bankruptcy, County Cases Commenced by Chapter of the Bankruptcy Code, During the 12-Month Period Ending December 31, 2020

Housing Vacancy Rates

Area	Gross Vacancy Rate[2] (%) 2018	2019	2020	Year-Round Vacancy Rate[3] (%) 2018	2019	2020	Rental Vacancy Rate[4] (%) 2018	2019	2020	Homeowner Vacancy Rate[5] (%) 2018	2019	2020
MSA[1]	8.9	10.6	7.2	8.8	10.4	7.1	9.4	9.3	4.5	1.9	1.5	0.7
U.S.	12.3	12.0	10.6	9.7	9.5	8.2	6.9	6.7	6.3	1.5	1.4	1.0

Note: (1) Figures cover the Columbia, SC Metropolitan Statistical Area; (2) The percentage of the total housing inventory that is vacant; (3) The percentage of the housing inventory (excluding seasonal units) that is year-round vacant; (4) The percentage of rental inventory that is vacant for rent; (5) The percentage of homeowner inventory that is vacant for sale
Source: U.S. Census Bureau, Housing Vacancies and Homeownership Annual Statistics: 2018, 2019, 2020

INCOME

Income

Area	Per Capita ($)	Median Household ($)	Average Household ($)
City	30,461	47,286	76,118
MSA[1]	29,894	55,971	75,154
U.S.	34,103	62,843	88,607

Note: (1) Figures cover the Columbia, SC Metropolitan Statistical Area
Source: U.S. Census Bureau, 2015-2019 American Community Survey 5-Year Estimates

Household Income Distribution

Area	Under $15,000	$15,000 -$24,999	$25,000 -$34,999	$35,000 -$49,999	$50,000 -$74,999	$75,000 -$99,999	$100,000 -$149,999	$150,000 and up
City	17.9	11.5	10.8	11.7	15.6	10.9	10.4	11.2
MSA[1]	12.2	9.1	10.1	13.4	18.4	13.4	13.6	9.8
U.S.	10.3	8.9	8.9	12.3	17.2	12.7	15.1	14.5

Note: (1) Figures cover the Columbia, SC Metropolitan Statistical Area
Source: U.S. Census Bureau, 2015-2019 American Community Survey 5-Year Estimates

Poverty Rate

Area	All Ages	Under 18 Years Old	18 to 64 Years Old	65 Years and Over
City	21.8	26.8	21.9	13.2
MSA[1]	15.0	20.2	14.3	9.5
U.S.	13.4	18.5	12.6	9.3

Note: Figures are percentage of people whose income during the past 12 months was below the poverty level;
(1) Figures cover the Columbia, SC Metropolitan Statistical Area
Source: U.S. Census Bureau, 2015-2019 American Community Survey 5-Year Estimates

CITY FINANCES

City Government Finances

Component	2017 ($000)	2017 ($ per capita)
Total Revenues	346,982	2,593
Total Expenditures	391,414	2,925
Debt Outstanding	595,015	4,447
Cash and Securities[1]	416,875	3,116

Note: (1) Cash and security holdings of a government at the close of its fiscal year, including those of its dependent agencies, utilities, and liquor stores.
Source: U.S. Census Bureau, State & Local Government Finances 2017

City Government Revenue by Source

Source	2017 ($000)	2017 ($ per capita)	2017 (%)
General Revenue			
From Federal Government	6,574	49	1.9
From State Government	26,823	200	7.7
From Local Governments	32,769	245	9.4
Taxes			
Property	40,027	299	11.5
Sales and Gross Receipts	18,719	140	5.4
Personal Income	0	0	0.0
Corporate Income	0	0	0.0
Motor Vehicle License	0	0	0.0
Other Taxes	40,194	300	11.6
Current Charges	78,892	590	22.7
Liquor Store	0	0	0.0
Utility	84,070	628	24.2
Employee Retirement	0	0	0.0

Source: U.S. Census Bureau, State & Local Government Finances 2017

City Government Expenditures by Function

Function	2017 ($000)	2017 ($ per capita)	2017 (%)
General Direct Expenditures			
Air Transportation	0	0	0.0
Corrections	0	0	0.0
Education	0	0	0.0
Employment Security Administration	0	0	0.0
Financial Administration	4,977	37	1.3
Fire Protection	47,765	357	12.2
General Public Buildings	3,545	26	0.9
Governmental Administration, Other	9,854	73	2.5
Health	1,712	12	0.4
Highways	10,300	77	2.6
Hospitals	0	0	0.0
Housing and Community Development	8,310	62	2.1
Interest on General Debt	0	0	0.0
Judicial and Legal	4,318	32	1.1
Libraries	0	0	0.0
Parking	3,805	28	1.0
Parks and Recreation	13,787	103	3.5
Police Protection	43,924	328	11.2
Public Welfare	19	<1	<0.1
Sewerage	112,004	837	28.6
Solid Waste Management	11,519	86	2.9
Veterans' Services	0	0	0.0
Liquor Store	0	0	0.0
Utility	82,458	616	21.1
Employee Retirement	0	0	0.0

Source: U.S. Census Bureau, State & Local Government Finances 2017

EMPLOYMENT

Labor Force and Employment

Area	Civilian Labor Force Dec. 2019	Civilian Labor Force Dec. 2020	% Chg.	Workers Employed Dec. 2019	Workers Employed Dec. 2020	% Chg.
City	58,665	58,030	-1.1	57,222	55,091	-3.7
MSA[1]	403,325	396,126	-1.8	394,519	379,089	-3.9
U.S.	164,007,000	160,017,000	-2.4	158,504,000	149,613,000	-5.6

Note: Data is not seasonally adjusted and covers workers 16 years of age and older; (1) Figures cover the Columbia, SC Metropolitan Statistical Area
Source: Bureau of Labor Statistics, Local Area Unemployment Statistics

Unemployment Rate

Area	Jan.	Feb.	Mar.	Apr.	May	Jun.	Jul.	Aug.	Sep.	Oct.	Nov.	Dec.
City	3.1	3.1	3.1	8.9	10.2	9.1	9.1	6.9	5.1	4.4	4.6	5.1
MSA[1]	2.7	2.8	2.8	8.5	9.3	7.8	7.8	6.0	4.4	3.7	3.8	4.3
U.S.	4.0	3.8	4.5	14.4	13.0	11.2	10.5	8.5	7.7	6.6	6.4	6.5

Note: Data is not seasonally adjusted and covers workers 16 years of age and older; (1) Figures cover the Columbia, SC Metropolitan Statistical Area
Source: Bureau of Labor Statistics, Local Area Unemployment Statistics

Average Wages

Occupation	$/Hr.	Occupation	$/Hr.
Accountants and Auditors	29.40	Maintenance and Repair Workers	19.20
Automotive Mechanics	21.10	Marketing Managers	57.60
Bookkeepers	18.00	Network and Computer Systems Admin.	38.30
Carpenters	23.20	Nurses, Licensed Practical	21.20
Cashiers	10.60	Nurses, Registered	31.90
Computer Programmers	43.50	Nursing Assistants	13.60
Computer Systems Analysts	37.50	Office Clerks, General	13.80
Computer User Support Specialists	24.60	Physical Therapists	42.60
Construction Laborers	16.90	Physicians	92.50
Cooks, Restaurant	11.80	Plumbers, Pipefitters and Steamfitters	20.00
Customer Service Representatives	16.90	Police and Sheriff's Patrol Officers	21.60
Dentists	63.00	Postal Service Mail Carriers	25.00
Electricians	25.80	Real Estate Sales Agents	21.40
Engineers, Electrical	44.60	Retail Salespersons	13.30
Fast Food and Counter Workers	9.30	Sales Representatives, Technical/Scientific	35.50
Financial Managers	58.40	Secretaries, Exc. Legal/Medical/Executive	19.70
First-Line Supervisors of Office Workers	27.60	Security Guards	15.90
General and Operations Managers	54.30	Surgeons	n/a
Hairdressers/Cosmetologists	17.80	Teacher Assistants, Exc. Postsecondary*	12.30
Home Health and Personal Care Aides	11.20	Teachers, Secondary School, Exc. Sp. Ed.*	28.00
Janitors and Cleaners	12.20	Telemarketers	16.20
Landscaping/Groundskeeping Workers	13.80	Truck Drivers, Heavy/Tractor-Trailer	21.90
Lawyers	57.80	Truck Drivers, Light/Delivery Services	17.50
Maids and Housekeeping Cleaners	11.30	Waiters and Waitresses	9.40

Note: Wage data covers the Columbia, SC Metropolitan Statistical Area; (*) Hourly wages were calculated from annual wage data based on a 40 hour work week; n/a not available.
Source: Bureau of Labor Statistics, Metro Area Occupational Employment & Wage Estimates, May 2020

Employment by Industry

Sector	MSA[1] Number of Employees	MSA[1] Percent of Total	U.S. Percent of Total
Construction, Mining, and Logging	17,400	4.4	5.5
Education and Health Services	48,000	12.2	16.3
Financial Activities	32,000	8.2	6.1
Government	85,400	21.8	15.2
Information	4,900	1.2	1.9
Leisure and Hospitality	35,100	9.0	9.0
Manufacturing	31,200	8.0	8.5
Other Services	14,900	3.8	3.8
Professional and Business Services	48,900	12.5	14.4
Retail Trade	42,700	10.9	10.9
Transportation, Warehousing, and Utilities	17,500	4.5	4.6
Wholesale Trade	14,100	3.6	3.9

Note: Figures are non-farm employment as of December 2020. Figures are not seasonally adjusted and include workers 16 years of age and older; (1) Figures cover the Columbia, SC Metropolitan Statistical Area
Source: Bureau of Labor Statistics, Current Employment Statistics, Employment, Hours, and Earnings

Employment by Occupation

Occupation Classification	City (%)	MSA[1] (%)	U.S. (%)
Management, Business, Science, and Arts	42.8	38.3	38.5
Natural Resources, Construction, and Maintenance	4.9	8.0	8.9
Production, Transportation, and Material Moving	10.1	13.4	13.2
Sales and Office	23.7	23.3	21.6
Service	18.5	16.9	17.8

Note: Figures cover employed civilians 16 years of age and older; (1) Figures cover the Columbia, SC Metropolitan Statistical Area
Source: U.S. Census Bureau, 2015-2019 American Community Survey 5-Year Estimates

Occupations with Greatest Projected Employment Growth: 2020 – 2022

Occupation[1]	2020 Employment	2022 Projected Employment	Numeric Employment Change	Percent Employment Change
Stockers and Order Fillers	28,530	29,560	1,030	3.6
Real Estate Sales Agents	13,120	13,440	320	2.4
Laborers and Freight, Stock, and Material Movers, Hand	64,390	64,670	280	0.4
Construction Laborers	23,860	24,130	270	1.1
Industrial Machinery Mechanics	9,530	9,740	210	2.2
Software Developers and Software Quality Assurance Analysts and Testers	7,930	8,120	190	2.4
Insurance Sales Agents	8,210	8,400	190	2.3
Medical and Health Services Managers	6,180	6,320	140	2.3
Industrial Engineers	7,510	7,650	140	1.9
Nurse Practitioners	2,580	2,720	140	5.4

Note: Projections cover South Carolina; (1) Sorted by numeric employment change
Source: www.projectionscentral.com, State Occupational Projections, 2020–2022 Short-Term Projections

Fastest-Growing Occupations: 2020 – 2022

Occupation[1]	2020 Employment	2022 Projected Employment	Numeric Employment Change	Percent Employment Change
Butchers and Meat Cutters	1,610	1,720	110	6.8
Nurse Practitioners	2,580	2,720	140	5.4
Information Security Analysts (SOC 2018)	1,640	1,700	60	3.7
Stockers and Order Fillers	28,530	29,560	1,030	3.6
Multiple Machine Tool Setters, Operators, and Tenders, Metal and Plastic	4,450	4,580	130	2.9
Personal Financial Advisors	2,520	2,590	70	2.8
Meat, Poultry, and Fish Cutters and Trimmers	4,700	4,830	130	2.8
Software Developers and Software Quality Assurance Analysts and Testers	7,930	8,120	190	2.4
Real Estate Sales Agents	13,120	13,440	320	2.4
Bakers	2,080	2,130	50	2.4

Note: Projections cover South Carolina; (1) Sorted by percent employment change and excludes occupations with numeric employment change less than 50
Source: www.projectionscentral.com, State Occupational Projections, 2020–2022 Short-Term Projections

TAXES

State Corporate Income Tax Rates

State	Tax Rate (%)	Income Brackets ($)	Num. of Brackets	Financial Institution Tax Rate (%)[a]	Federal Income Tax Ded.
South Carolina	5.0	Flat rate	1	4.5 (v)	No

Note: Tax rates as of January 1, 2021; (a) Rates listed are the corporate income tax rate applied to financial institutions or excise taxes based on income. Some states have other taxes based upon the value of deposits or shares; (v) South Carolina taxes savings and loans at a 6% rate.
Source: Federation of Tax Administrators, State Corporate Income Tax Rates, January 1, 2021

State Individual Income Tax Rates

State	Tax Rate (%)	Income Brackets ($)	Personal Exemptions ($) Single	Personal Exemptions ($) Married	Personal Exemptions ($) Depend.	Standard Ded. ($) Single	Standard Ded. ($) Married
South Carolina (a)	0.0 - 7.0	3,110 - 15,560	(d)	(d)	(d)	12,550	25,100 (d)

Note: Tax rates as of January 1, 2021; Local- and county-level taxes are not included; Federal income tax is not deductible on state income tax returns; (a) 19 states have statutory provision for automatically adjusting to the rate of inflation the dollar values of the income tax brackets, standard deductions, and/or personal exemptions. Michigan indexes the personal exemption only. Oregon does not index the income brackets for $125,000 and over; (d) These states use the personal exemption/standard deduction amounts provided in the federal Internal Revenue Code.
Source: Federation of Tax Administrators, State Individual Income Tax Rates, January 1, 2021

Various State Sales and Excise Tax Rates

State	State Sales Tax (%)	Gasoline[1] (¢/gal.)	Cigarette[2] ($/pack)	Spirits[3] ($/gal.)	Wine[4] ($/gal.)	Beer[5] ($/gal.)	Recreational Marijuana (%)
South Carolina	6	22.75	0.57	5.42	1.08	0.77	Not legal

Note: All tax rates as of January 1, 2021; (1) The American Petroleum Institute has developed a methodology for determining the average tax rate on a gallon of fuel. Rates may include any of the following: excise taxes, environmental fees, storage tank fees, other fees or taxes, general sales tax, and local taxes; (2) The federal excise tax of $1.0066 per pack and local taxes are not included; (3) Rates are those applicable to off-premise sales of 40% alcohol by volume (a.b.v.) distilled spirits in 750ml containers. Local excise taxes are excluded; (4) Rates are those applicable to off-premise sales of 11% a.b.v. non-carbonated wine in 750ml containers; (5) Rates are those applicable to off-premise sales of 4.7% a.b.v. beer in 12 ounce containers.
Source: Tax Foundation, 2021 Facts & Figures: How Does Your State Compare?

State Business Tax Climate Index Rankings

State	Overall Rank	Corporate Tax Rank	Individual Income Tax Rank	Sales Tax Rank	Property Tax Rank	Unemployment Insurance Tax Rank
South Carolina	33	5	34	31	34	24

Note: The index is a measure of how each state's tax laws affect economic performance. The lower the rank, the more favorable a state's tax system is for business. States without a given tax are given a ranking of 1. The scores/rankings for the District of Columbia do not affect other states. The 2021 index represents the tax climate as of July 1, 2020.
Source: Tax Foundation, State Business Tax Climate Index 2021

TRANSPORTATION

Means of Transportation to Work

Area	Drove Alone	Car-pooled	Bus	Subway	Railroad	Bicycle	Walked	Other Means	Worked at Home
City	64.1	6.1	1.8	0.0	0.0	0.5	21.9	2.2	3.4
MSA[1]	80.7	8.6	0.6	0.0	0.0	0.1	4.4	1.9	3.6
U.S.	76.3	9.0	2.4	1.9	0.6	0.5	2.7	1.4	5.2

Note: Figures are percentages and cover workers 16 years of age and older; (1) Figures cover the Columbia, SC Metropolitan Statistical Area
Source: U.S. Census Bureau, 2015-2019 American Community Survey 5-Year Estimates

Travel Time to Work

Area	Less Than 10 Minutes	10 to 19 Minutes	20 to 29 Minutes	30 to 44 Minutes	45 to 59 Minutes	60 to 89 Minutes	90 Minutes or More
City	31.3	36.6	17.6	9.7	1.8	1.8	1.2
MSA[1]	12.5	29.6	23.5	22.3	6.8	3.4	1.9
U.S.	12.2	28.4	20.8	20.8	8.3	6.4	2.9

Note: Note: Figures are percentages and include workers 16 years old and over; (1) Figures cover the Columbia, SC Metropolitan Statistical Area
Source: U.S. Census Bureau, 2015-2019 American Community Survey 5-Year Estimates

Key Congestion Measures

Measure	1982	1992	2002	2012	2017
Annual Hours of Delay, Total (000)	1,113	3,645	7,937	14,674	16,331
Annual Hours of Delay, Per Auto Commuter	7	20	31	42	44
Annual Congestion Cost, Total (million $)	8	38	107	263	301
Annual Congestion Cost, Per Auto Commuter ($)	117	263	448	648	699

Note: Covers the Columbia SC urban area
Source: Texas A&M Transportation Institute, 2019 Urban Mobility Report

Freeway Travel Time Index

Measure	1982	1987	1992	1997	2002	2007	2012	2017
Urban Area Index[1]	1.03	1.06	1.08	1.10	1.13	1.16	1.15	1.15
Urban Area Rank[1,2]	76	66	76	80	75	63	71	71

Note: Freeway Travel Time Index—the ratio of travel time in the peak period to the travel time at free-flow conditions. For example, a value of 1.30 indicates a 20-minute free-flow trip takes 26 minutes in the peak (20 minutes x 1.30 = 26 minutes); (1) Covers the Columbia SC urban area; (2) Rank is based on 101 larger urban areas (#1 = highest travel time index)
Source: Texas A&M Transportation Institute, 2019 Urban Mobility Report

Public Transportation

Agency Name / Mode of Transportation	Vehicles Operated in Maximum Service[1]	Annual Unlinked Passenger Trips[2] (in thous.)	Annual Passenger Miles[3] (in thous.)
Central Midlands Regional Transit Authority			
Bus (purchased transportation)	46	2,654.9	6,789.8
Demand Response (purchased transportation)	21	71.3	911.1
Demand Response Taxi (purchased transportation)	28	6.2	52.8
Vanpool (purchased transportation)	2	1.1	11.9

Note: (1) Number of revenue vehicles operated by the given mode and type of service to meet the annual maximum service requirement. This is the revenue vehicle count during the peak season of the year; on the week and day that maximum service is provided. Vehicles operated in maximum service (VOMS) exclude atypical days and one-time special events; (2) Number of passengers who boarded public transportation vehicles. Passengers are counted each time they board a vehicle no matter how many vehicles they use to travel from their origin to their destination. (3) Sum of the distances ridden by all passengers during the entire fiscal year.
Source: Federal Transit Administration, National Transit Database, 2019

Air Transportation

Airport Name and Code / Type of Service	Passenger Airlines[1]	Passenger Enplanements	Freight Carriers[2]	Freight (lbs)
Columbia Metropolitan (CAE)				
Domestic service (U.S. carriers - 2020)	20	268,735	13	71,777,833
International service (U.S. carriers - 2019)	0	0	1	5,311

Note: (1) Includes all U.S.-based major, minor and commuter airlines that carried at least one passenger during the year; (2) Includes all U.S.-based airlines and freight carriers that transported at least one pound of freight during the year.
Source: Bureau of Transportation Statistics, The Intermodal Transportation Database, Air Carriers: T-100 Domestic Market (U.S. Carriers), 2020; Bureau of Transportation Statistics, The Intermodal Transportation Database, Air Carriers: T-100 International Market (U.S. Carriers), 2019

BUSINESSES

Major Business Headquarters

Company Name	Industry	Rankings Fortune[1]	Forbes[2]
No companies listed	-	-	-

Note: (1) Companies that produce a 10-K are ranked 1 to 500 based on 2019 revenue; (2) All private companies with at least $2 billion in annual revenue through the end of their most current fiscal year are ranked 1 to 219; companies listed are headquartered in the city; dashes indicate no ranking
Source: Fortune, "Fortune 500," June/July 2020; Forbes, "America's Largest Private Companies," 2020

Living Environment

COST OF LIVING

Cost of Living Index

Composite Index	Groceries	Housing	Utilities	Transportation	Health Care	Misc. Goods/Services
90.6	105.5	71.9	128.2	87.3	73.4	92.7

Note: The Cost of Living Index measures regional differences in the cost of consumer goods and services, excluding taxes and non-consumer expenditures, for professional and managerial households in the top income quintile. It is based on more than 50,000 prices covering almost 60 different items for which prices are collected three times a year by chambers of commerce, economic development organizations or university applied economic centers in each participating urban area. The numbers shown should be read as a percentage above or below the national average of 100. For example, a value of 115.4 in the groceries column indicates that grocery prices are 15.4% higher than the national average. Small differences in the index numbers should not be interpreted as significant; Figures cover the Columbia SC urban area.
Source: The Council for Community and Economic Research, Cost of Living Index, 2020

Grocery Prices

Area[1]	T-Bone Steak ($/pound)	Frying Chicken ($/pound)	Whole Milk ($/half gal.)	Eggs ($/dozen)	Orange Juice ($/64 oz.)	Coffee ($/11.5 oz.)
City[2]	12.24	1.40	2.19	1.31	3.54	4.28
Avg.	11.78	1.39	2.05	1.47	3.57	4.34
Min.	8.03	0.94	1.03	0.74	2.94	3.02
Max.	15.86	2.65	4.31	3.77	5.44	8.69

Note: (1) Values for the local area are compared with the average, minimum and maximum values for all 284 areas in the Cost of Living Index; (2) Figures cover the Columbia SC urban area; **T-Bone Steak** (price per pound); **Frying Chicken** (price per pound, whole fryer); **Whole Milk** (half gallon carton); **Eggs** (price per dozen, Grade A, large); **Orange Juice** (64 oz. Tropicana or Florida Natural); **Coffee** (11.5 oz. can, vacuum-packed, Maxwell House, Hills Bros, or Folgers).
Source: The Council for Community and Economic Research, Cost of Living Index, 2020

Housing and Utility Costs

Area[1]	New Home Price ($)	Apartment Rent ($/month)	All Electric ($/month)	Part Electric ($/month)	Other Energy ($/month)	Telephone ($/month)
City[2]	258,420	885	-	116.56	131.89	185.80
Avg.	368,594	1,168	170.86	100.47	65.28	184.30
Min.	190,567	502	91.58	31.42	26.08	169.60
Max.	2,227,806	4,738	470.38	280.31	280.06	206.50

Note: (1) Values for the local area are compared with the average, minimum and maximum values for all 284 areas in the Cost of Living Index; (2) Figures cover the Columbia SC urban area; **New Home Price** (2,400 sf living area, 8,000 sf lot, in urban area with full utilities); **Apartment Rent** (950 sf 2 bedroom/1.5 or 2 bath, unfurnished, excluding all utilities except water); **All Electric** (average monthly cost for an all-electric home); **Part Electric** (average monthly cost for a part-electric home); **Other Energy** (average monthly cost for natural gas, fuel oil, coal, wood, and any other forms of energy except electricity); **Telephone** (price includes the base monthly rate plus taxes and fees for three lines of mobile phone service).
Source: The Council for Community and Economic Research, Cost of Living Index, 2020

Health Care, Transportation, and Other Costs

Area[1]	Doctor ($/visit)	Dentist ($/visit)	Optometrist ($/visit)	Gasoline ($/gallon)	Beauty Salon ($/visit)	Men's Shirt ($)
City[2]	102.00	59.00	51.67	2.00	41.63	20.62
Avg.	115.44	99.32	108.10	2.21	39.27	31.37
Min.	36.68	59.00	51.36	1.71	19.00	11.00
Max.	219.00	153.10	250.97	3.46	82.05	58.33

Note: (1) Values for the local area are compared with the average, minimum and maximum values for all 284 areas in the Cost of Living Index; (2) Figures cover the Columbia SC urban area; **Doctor** (general practitioners routine exam of an established patient); **Dentist** (adult teeth cleaning and periodic oral examination); **Optometrist** (full vision eye exam for established adult patient); **Gasoline** (one gallon regular unleaded, national brand, including all taxes, cash price at self-service pump if available); **Beauty Salon** (woman's shampoo, trim, and blow-dry); **Men's Shirt** (cotton/polyester dress shirt, pinpoint weave, long sleeves).
Source: The Council for Community and Economic Research, Cost of Living Index, 2020

HOUSING

Homeownership Rate

Area	2012 (%)	2013 (%)	2014 (%)	2015 (%)	2016 (%)	2017 (%)	2018 (%)	2019 (%)	2020 (%)
MSA[1]	65.6	68.9	69.5	66.1	63.9	70.7	69.3	65.9	69.7
U.S.	65.4	65.1	64.5	63.7	63.4	63.9	64.4	64.6	66.6

Note: (1) Figures cover the Columbia, SC Metropolitan Statistical Area
Source: U.S. Census Bureau, Housing Vacancies and Homeownership Annual Statistics: 2012-2020

House Price Index (HPI)

Area	National Ranking[2]	Quarterly Change (%)	One-Year Change (%)	Five-Year Change (%)	Since 1991Q1 (%)
MSA[1]	181	1.37	5.23	24.67	125.47
U.S.[3]	–	3.81	10.77	38.99	205.12

Note: The HPI is a weighted repeat sales index. It measures average price changes in repeat sales or refinancings on the same properties. This information is obtained by reviewing repeat mortgage transactions on single-family properties whose mortgages have been purchased or securitized by Fannie Mae or Freddie Mac since January 1975; (1) Figures cover the Columbia, SC Metropolitan Statistical Area; (2) Rankings are based on annual percentage change for all metro areas containing at least 15,000 transactions over the last 10 years and ranges from 1 to 253; (3) figures based on a weighted average of Census Division estimates using a seasonally adjusted, purchase-only index; all figures are for the period ending December 31, 2020
Source: Federal Housing Finance Agency, Change in Metropolitan Area House Price Indexes, April 7, 2021

Median Single-Family Home Prices

Area	2018	2019	2020[p]	Percent Change 2019 to 2020
MSA[1]	171.6	185.0	202.9	9.7
U.S. Average	261.6	274.6	299.9	9.2

Note: Figures are median sales prices of existing single-family homes in thousands of dollars; (p) preliminary; (1) Figures cover the Columbia, SC Metropolitan Statistical Area
Source: National Association of Realtors, Median Sales Price of Existing Single-Family Homes for Metropolitan Areas, 4th Quarter 2020

Qualifying Income Based on Median Sales Price of Existing Single-Family Homes

Area	With 5% Down ($)	With 10% Down ($)	With 20% Down ($)
MSA[1]	40,306	38,185	33,942
U.S. Average	59,266	56,147	49,908

Note: Figures are preliminary; Qualifying income is based on a mortgage rate of 2.81%. Monthly principal and interest payment is limited to 25% of income; (1) Figures cover the Columbia, SC Metropolitan Statistical Area
Source: National Association of Realtors, Qualifying Income Based on Median Sales Price of Existing Single-Family Homes for Metropolitan Areas, 4th Quarter 2020

Home Value Distribution

Area	Under $50,000	$50,000 -$99,999	$100,000 -$149,999	$150,000 -$199,999	$200,000 -$299,999	$300,000 -$499,999	$500,000 -$999,999	$1,000,000 or more
City	4.5	15.3	19.7	16.0	15.6	16.5	10.9	1.6
MSA[1]	8.6	16.9	22.6	18.7	17.1	11.2	4.2	0.8
U.S.	6.9	12.0	13.3	14.0	19.6	19.3	11.4	3.4

Note: Figures are percentages and cover owner-occupied housing units; (1) Figures cover the Columbia, SC Metropolitan Statistical Area
Source: U.S. Census Bureau, 2015-2019 American Community Survey 5-Year Estimates

Year Housing Structure Built

Area	2010 or Later	2000 -2009	1990 -1999	1980 -1989	1970 -1979	1960 -1969	1950 -1959	1940 -1949	Before 1940	Median Year
City	6.1	15.8	11.6	8.9	10.1	11.9	13.6	11.2	10.8	1972
MSA[1]	8.0	19.5	18.5	14.3	15.9	9.7	7.0	3.3	3.8	1987
U.S.	5.2	14.0	13.9	13.4	15.2	10.6	10.3	4.9	12.6	1978

Note: Figures are percentages except for Median Year; Note: (1) Figures cover the Columbia, SC Metropolitan Statistical Area
Source: U.S. Census Bureau, 2015-2019 American Community Survey 5-Year Estimates

Gross Monthly Rent

Area	Under $500	$500 -$999	$1,000 -$1,499	$1,500 -$1,999	$2,000 -$2,499	$2,500 -$2,999	$3,000 and up	Median ($)
City	10.1	48.2	31.9	7.6	1.6	0.1	0.5	933
MSA[1]	7.6	50.4	32.4	7.2	1.5	0.5	0.4	933
U.S.	9.4	36.2	30.0	14.0	5.6	2.4	2.4	1,062

Note: Figures are percentages except for Median; Gross rent is the contract rent plus the estimated average monthly cost of utilities (electricity, gas, and water and sewer) and fuels (oil, coal, kerosene, wood, etc.) if these are paid by the renter (or paid for the renter by someone else); (1) Figures cover the Columbia, SC Metropolitan Statistical Area
Source: U.S. Census Bureau, 2015-2019 American Community Survey 5-Year Estimates

HEALTH

Health Risk Factors

Category	MSA[1] (%)	U.S. (%)
Adults aged 18–64 who have any kind of health care coverage	85.6	87.3
Adults who reported being in good or better health	82.3	82.4
Adults who have been told they have high blood cholesterol	33.3	33.0
Adults who have been told they have high blood pressure	38.1	32.3
Adults who are current smokers	16.9	17.1
Adults who currently use E-cigarettes	4.6	4.6
Adults who currently use chewing tobacco, snuff, or snus	2.8	4.0
Adults who are heavy drinkers[2]	8.7	6.3
Adults who are binge drinkers[3]	17.2	17.4
Adults who are overweight (BMI 25.0 - 29.9)	34.7	35.3
Adults who are obese (BMI 30.0 - 99.8)	35.7	31.3
Adults who participated in any physical activities in the past month	73.1	74.4
Adults who always or nearly always wears a seat belt	95.8	94.3

Note: (1) Figures cover the Columbia, SC Metropolitan Statistical Area; (2) Heavy drinkers are classified as adult men having more than 14 drinks per week and adult women having more than 7 drinks per week; (3) Binge drinkers are classified as males having five or more drinks on one occasion or females having four or more drinks on one occasion
Source: Centers for Disease Control and Prevention, Behavioral Risk Factor Surveillance System, SMART: Selected Metropolitan Area Risk Trends, 2017

Acute and Chronic Health Conditions

Category	MSA[1] (%)	U.S. (%)
Adults who have ever been told they had a heart attack	3.8	4.2
Adults who have ever been told they have angina or coronary heart disease	3.8	3.9
Adults who have ever been told they had a stroke	3.1	3.0
Adults who have ever been told they have asthma	15.2	14.2
Adults who have ever been told they have arthritis	25.6	24.9
Adults who have ever been told they have diabetes[2]	12.4	10.5
Adults who have ever been told they had skin cancer	5.6	6.2
Adults who have ever been told they had any other types of cancer	6.7	7.1
Adults who have ever been told they have COPD	7.1	6.5
Adults who have ever been told they have kidney disease	2.4	3.0
Adults who have ever been told they have a form of depression	20.0	20.5

Note: (1) Figures cover the Columbia, SC Metropolitan Statistical Area; (2) Figures do not include pregnancy-related, borderline, or pre-diabetes
Source: Centers for Disease Control and Prevention, Behavioral Risk Factor Surveillance System, SMART: Selected Metropolitan Area Risk Trends, 2017

Health Screening and Vaccination Rates

Category	MSA[1] (%)	U.S. (%)
Adults aged 65+ who have had flu shot within the past year	65.0	60.7
Adults aged 65+ who have ever had a pneumonia vaccination	78.0	75.4
Adults who have ever been tested for HIV	43.6	36.1
Adults who have ever had the shingles or zoster vaccine?	26.0	28.9
Adults who have had their blood cholesterol checked within the last five years	89.1	85.9

Note: n/a not available; (1) Figures cover the Columbia, SC Metropolitan Statistical Area.
Source: Centers for Disease Control and Prevention, Behavioral Risk Factor Surveillance System, SMART: Selected Metropolitan Area Risk Trends, 2017

Disability Status

Category	MSA[1] (%)	U.S. (%)
Adults who reported being deaf	5.5	6.7
Are you blind or have serious difficulty seeing, even when wearing glasses?	4.2	4.5
Are you limited in any way in any of your usual activities due of arthritis?	12.8	12.9
Do you have difficulty doing errands alone?	5.0	6.8
Do you have difficulty dressing or bathing?	3.2	3.6
Do you have serious difficulty concentrating/remembering/making decisions?	10.0	10.7
Do you have serious difficulty walking or climbing stairs?	14.5	13.6

Note: (1) Figures cover the Columbia, SC Metropolitan Statistical Area.
Source: Centers for Disease Control and Prevention, Behavioral Risk Factor Surveillance System, SMART: Selected Metropolitan Area Risk Trends, 2017

Mortality Rates for the Top 10 Causes of Death in the U.S.

ICD-10[a] Sub-Chapter	ICD-10[a] Code	Age-Adjusted Mortality Rate[1] per 100,000 population County[2]	U.S.
Malignant neoplasms	C00-C97	165.9	149.2
Ischaemic heart diseases	I20-I25	91.2	90.5
Other forms of heart disease	I30-I51	47.2	52.2
Chronic lower respiratory diseases	J40-J47	29.2	39.6
Other degenerative diseases of the nervous system	G30-G31	48.9	37.6
Cerebrovascular diseases	I60-I69	33.6	37.2
Other external causes of accidental injury	W00-X59	33.7	36.1
Organic, including symptomatic, mental disorders	F01-F09	42.5	29.4
Hypertensive diseases	I10-I15	34.5	24.1
Diabetes mellitus	E10-E14	26.7	21.5

Note: (a) ICD-10 = International Classification of Diseases 10th Revision; (1) Mortality rates are a three-year average covering 2017-2019; (2) Figures cover Richland County.
Source: Centers for Disease Control and Prevention, National Center for Health Statistics. Underlying Cause of Death 1999-2019 on CDC WONDER Online Database

Mortality Rates for Selected Causes of Death

ICD-10[a] Sub-Chapter	ICD-10[a] Code	Age-Adjusted Mortality Rate[1] per 100,000 population County[2]	U.S.
Assault	X85-Y09	11.9	6.0
Diseases of the liver	K70-K76	14.2	14.4
Human immunodeficiency virus (HIV) disease	B20-B24	4.0	1.5
Influenza and pneumonia	J09-J18	10.2	13.8
Intentional self-harm	X60-X84	13.3	14.1
Malnutrition	E40-E46	5.6	2.3
Obesity and other hyperalimentation	E65-E68	1.8	2.1
Renal failure	N17-N19	17.2	12.6
Transport accidents	V01-V99	14.8	12.3
Viral hepatitis	B15-B19	Unreliable	1.2

Note: (a) ICD-10 = International Classification of Diseases 10th Revision; (1) Mortality rates are a three-year average covering 2017-2019; (2) Figures cover Richland County; Data are suppressed when the data meet the criteria for confidentiality constraints; Mortality rates are flagged as unreliable when the rate would be calculated with a numerator of 20 or less.
Source: Centers for Disease Control and Prevention, National Center for Health Statistics. Underlying Cause of Death 1999-2019 on CDC WONDER Online Database

Health Insurance Coverage

Area	With Health Insurance	With Private Health Insurance	With Public Health Insurance	Without Health Insurance	Population Under Age 19 Without Health Insurance
City	91.2	72.0	29.7	8.8	2.7
MSA[1]	90.5	70.4	33.6	9.5	3.7
U.S.	91.2	67.9	35.1	8.8	5.1

Note: Figures are percentages that cover the civilian noninstitutionalized population; (1) Figures cover the Columbia, SC Metropolitan Statistical Area
Source: U.S. Census Bureau, 2015-2019 American Community Survey 5-Year Estimates

Number of Medical Professionals

Area	MDs[3]	DOs[3,4]	Dentists	Podiatrists	Chiropractors	Optometrists
County[1] (number)	1,476	66	381	30	99	82
County[1] (rate[2])	356.3	15.9	91.6	7.2	23.8	19.7
U.S. (rate[2])	282.9	22.7	71.2	6.2	28.1	16.9

45079
Note: Data as of 2019 unless noted; (1) Data covers Richland County; (2) Rate per 100,000 population; (3) Data as of 2018 and includes all active, non-federal physicians; (4) Doctor of Osteopathic Medicine
Source: U.S. Department of Health and Human Services, Health Resources and Services Administration, Bureau of Health Professions, Area Resource File (ARF) 2019-2020

EDUCATION

Public School District Statistics

District Name	Schls	Pupils	Pupil/Teacher Ratio	Minority Pupils[1] (%)	Free Lunch Eligible[2] (%)	IEP[3] (%)
Charter Institute at Erskine	13	8,457	21.4	37.1	40.9	11.8
Richland 01	48	23,711	12.3	81.0	100.0	14.0
Richland 02	33	28,394	14.6	78.8	44.3	13.2
SC Public Charter School District	35	20,247	17.6	39.6	31.1	11.2

Note: Table includes school districts with 2,000 or more students; (1) Percentage of students that are not non-Hispanic white; (2) Percentage of students that are eligible for the free lunch program; (3) Percentage of students that have an Individualized Education Program.
Source: U.S. Department of Education, National Center for Education Statistics, Common Core of Data, Local Education Agency (School District) Universe Survey: School Year 2018-2019; U.S. Department of Education, National Center for Education Statistics, Common Core of Data, Public Elementary/Secondary School Universe Survey: School Year 2018-2019

Highest Level of Education

Area	Less than H.S.	H.S. Diploma	Some College, No Deg.	Associate Degree	Bachelor's Degree	Master's Degree	Prof. School Degree	Doctorate Degree
City	10.6	20.1	18.6	6.9	24.4	12.8	3.9	2.7
MSA[1]	10.1	26.9	21.2	9.0	20.1	9.2	1.8	1.5
U.S.	12.0	27.0	20.4	8.5	19.8	8.8	2.1	1.4

Note: Figures cover persons age 25 and over; (1) Figures cover the Columbia, SC Metropolitan Statistical Area
Source: U.S. Census Bureau, 2015-2019 American Community Survey 5-Year Estimates

Educational Attainment by Race

Area	High School Graduate or Higher (%) Total	White	Black	Asian	Hisp.[2]	Bachelor's Degree or Higher (%) Total	White	Black	Asian	Hisp.[2]
City	89.4	95.4	81.8	96.8	86.4	43.8	62.6	19.6	78.1	35.2
MSA[1]	89.9	91.7	87.9	90.5	65.1	32.7	37.3	23.2	58.9	20.0
U.S.	88.0	89.9	86.0	87.1	68.7	32.1	33.5	21.6	54.3	16.4

Note: Figures shown cover persons 25 years old and over; (1) Figures cover the Columbia, SC Metropolitan Statistical Area; (2) People of Hispanic origin can be of any race
Source: U.S. Census Bureau, 2015-2019 American Community Survey 5-Year Estimates

School Enrollment by Grade and Control

Area	Preschool (%) Public	Private	Kindergarten (%) Public	Private	Grades 1-4 (%) Public	Private	Grades 5-8 (%) Public	Private	Grades 9-12 (%) Public	Private
City	57.2	42.8	74.3	25.7	88.1	11.9	87.7	12.3	86.7	13.3
MSA[1]	57.9	42.1	88.4	11.6	91.0	9.0	92.1	7.9	92.9	7.1
U.S.	59.1	40.9	87.6	12.4	89.5	10.5	89.4	10.6	90.1	9.9

Note: Figures shown cover persons 3 years old and over; (1) Figures cover the Columbia, SC Metropolitan Statistical Area
Source: U.S. Census Bureau, 2015-2019 American Community Survey 5-Year Estimates

Higher Education

Four-Year Colleges Public	Private Non-profit	Private For-profit	Two-Year Colleges Public	Private Non-profit	Private For-profit	Medical Schools[1]	Law Schools[2]	Voc/Tech[3]
1	5	1	0	0	3	1	1	6

Note: Figures cover institutions located within the city limits and include main campuses only; (1) includes schools accredited by the Liaison Committee on Medical Education and the American Osteopathic Association's Commission on Osteopathic College Accreditation; (2) includes ABA-accredited schools, schools with provisional ABA accreditation, and state accredited schools; (3) includes all schools with programs that are less than 2 years.
Source: National Center for Education Statistics, Integrated Postsecondary Education System (IPEDS), 2019-20; Wikipedia, List of Medical Schools in the United States, accessed April 2, 2021; Wikipedia, List of Law Schools in the United States, accessed April 2, 2021

According to *U.S. News & World Report,* the Columbia, SC metro area is home to one of the top 200 national universities in the U.S.: **University of South Carolina** (#118 tie). The indicators used to capture academic quality fall into a number of categories: assessment by administrators at peer institutions; retention of students; faculty resources; student selectivity; financial resources; alumni giving; high school counselor ratings of colleges; and graduation rate. *U.S. News & World Report, "America's Best Colleges 2021"*

According to *U.S. News & World Report,* the Columbia, SC metro area is home to one of the top 100 law schools in the U.S.: **University of South Carolina** (#96 tie). The rankings are based on a weighted average of 12 measures of quality: peer assessment score; assessment score by lawyers/judges; median LSAT scores; median undergrad GPA; acceptance rate; employment rates for graduates; placement success; bar passage rate; faculty resources; expenditures per student; student/faculty ratio; and library resources. *U.S. News & World Report, "America's Best Graduate Schools, Law, 2022"*

According to *U.S. News & World Report,* the Columbia, SC metro area is home to one of the top 75 business schools in the U.S.: **University of South Carolina (Moore)** (#55 tie). The rankings are based on a weighted average of the following nine measures: quality assessment; peer assessment; recruiter assessment; placement success; mean starting salary and bonus; student selectivity; mean GMAT and GRE scores; mean undergraduate GPA; and acceptance rate. *U.S. News & World Report, "America's Best Graduate Schools, Business, 2022"*

EMPLOYERS

Major Employers

Company Name	Industry
AnMed Health	Healthcare
Baldor Electric Co	Utilities
Ben Arnold Beverage Co	Beverages
Berkeley County School Dist	Education
BlueCross BlueShield of SC	Finance, insurance and real estate
BMW Manufacturing Co	Manufacturing
Bon Secours St Francis Hosp	Healthcare
Charleston AIR Force Base	U.S. military
City of Columbia	Municipal government
Clemson University Research	Healthcare
Continental Tire North America	Wholesaling/manufacturing
Corrections Dept.	Government
Crescent Moon Diving	Professional, scientific, technical
Fluor Enterprises Inc	Engineering services
Greenville Memorial Hospital	Healthcare
Lexington Medical Ctr	Healthcare
McLeod Health	Healthcare
Medical University of SC	Healthcare/university
Palmetto Health	Health care & social assistance
Piggly Wiggly	Grocery stores
Pilgrim's Pride Corp	Poultry processing
Richland County	Government
Richland School District 1 & 2	Education
Robert Bosch	Manufacturing
Shaw Air Force Base	U.S. military
Sonoco Plastics Inc	Manufacturing
Spartanburg Regional Healthcre	Healthcare
University of South Carolina	Education
Women's Imaging Center	Healthcare

Note: Companies shown are located within the Columbia, SC Metropolitan Statistical Area.
Source: Hoovers.com; Wikipedia

PUBLIC SAFETY

Crime Rate

Area	All Crimes	Violent Crimes				Property Crimes		
		Murder	Rape[3]	Robbery	Aggrav. Assault	Burglary	Larceny -Theft	Motor Vehicle Theft
City	6,027.4	21.7	65.8	164.4	523.2	684.7	3,898.6	669.0
Suburbs[1]	3,564.0	5.9	45.8	67.3	428.2	503.6	2,152.4	360.8
Metro[2]	3,955.7	8.4	49.0	82.7	443.3	532.4	2,430.1	409.8
U.S.	2,489.3	5.0	42.6	81.6	250.2	340.5	1,549.5	219.9

Note: Figures are crimes per 100,000 population; (1) All areas within the metro area that are located outside the city limits; (2) Figures cover the Columbia, SC Metropolitan Statistical Area; (3) All figures shown were reported using the revised Uniform Crime Reporting (UCR) definition of rape.
Source: FBI Uniform Crime Reports, 2019

Hate Crimes

Area	Number of Quarters Reported	Number of Incidents per Bias Motivation					
		Race/Ethnicity/ Ancestry	Religion	Sexual Orientation	Disability	Gender	Gender Identity
City	4	0	0	0	0	0	0
U.S.	4	3,963	1,521	1,195	157	69	198

Source: Federal Bureau of Investigation, Hate Crime Statistics 2019

Identity Theft Consumer Reports

Area	Reports	Reports per 100,000 Population	Rank[2]
MSA[1]	4,918	587	41
U.S.	1,387,615	423	-

Note: (1) Figures cover the Columbia, SC Metropolitan Statistical Area; (2) Rank ranges from 1 to 391 where 1 indicates greatest number of identity theft reports per 100,000 population
Source: Federal Trade Commission, Consumer Sentinel Network Data Book 2020

Fraud and Other Consumer Reports

Area	Reports	Reports per 100,000 Population	Rank[2]
MSA[1]	8,150	972	25
U.S.	3,385,133	1,031	-

Note: (1) Figures cover the Columbia, SC Metropolitan Statistical Area; (2) Rank ranges from 1 to 391 where 1 indicates greatest number of fraud and other consumer reports per 100,000 population
Source: Federal Trade Commission, Consumer Sentinel Network Data Book 2020

POLITICS

2020 Presidential Election Results

Area	Biden	Trump	Jorgensen	Hawkins	Other
Richland County	68.4	30.1	1.0	0.4	0.1
U.S.	51.3	46.8	1.2	0.3	0.5

Note: Results are percentages and may not add to 100% due to rounding
Source: Dave Leip's Atlas of U.S. Presidential Elections

SPORTS

Professional Sports Teams

Team Name	League	Year Established

No teams are located in the metro area
Source: Wikipedia, Major Professional Sports Teams of the United States and Canada, April 6, 2021

CLIMATE

Average and Extreme Temperatures

Temperature	Jan	Feb	Mar	Apr	May	Jun	Jul	Aug	Sep	Oct	Nov	Dec	Yr.
Extreme High (°F)	84	84	91	94	101	107	107	107	101	101	90	83	107
Average High (°F)	56	60	67	77	84	90	92	91	85	77	67	59	75
Average Temp. (°F)	45	48	55	64	72	78	82	80	75	64	54	47	64
Average Low (°F)	33	35	42	50	59	66	70	69	64	51	41	35	51
Extreme Low (°F)	-1	5	4	26	34	44	54	53	40	23	12	4	-1

Note: Figures cover the years 1948-1990
Source: National Climatic Data Center, International Station Meteorological Climate Summary, 9/96

Average Precipitation/Snowfall/Humidity

Precip./Humidity	Jan	Feb	Mar	Apr	May	Jun	Jul	Aug	Sep	Oct	Nov	Dec	Yr.
Avg. Precip. (in.)	4.0	4.0	4.7	3.4	3.6	4.2	5.5	5.9	4.0	2.9	2.7	3.4	48.3
Avg. Snowfall (in.)	1	1	Tr	0	0	0	0	0	0	0	Tr	Tr	2
Avg. Rel. Hum. 7am (%)	83	83	84	82	84	85	88	91	91	90	88	84	86
Avg. Rel. Hum. 4pm (%)	51	47	44	41	46	50	54	56	54	49	48	51	49

Note: Figures cover the years 1948-1990; Tr = Trace amounts (<0.05 in. of rain; <0.5 in. of snow)
Source: National Climatic Data Center, International Station Meteorological Climate Summary, 9/96

Weather Conditions

Temperature			Daytime Sky			Precipitation		
10°F & below	32°F & below	90°F & above	Clear	Partly cloudy	Cloudy	0.01 inch or more precip.	0.1 inch or more snow/ice	Thunderstorms
<1	58	77	97	149	119	110	1	53

Note: Figures are average number of days per year and cover the years 1948-1990
Source: National Climatic Data Center, International Station Meteorological Climate Summary, 9/96

HAZARDOUS WASTE

Superfund Sites

The Columbia, SC metro area is home to five sites on the EPA's Superfund National Priorities List: **Lexington County Landfill Area** (final); **Palmetto Wood Preserving** (final); **SCRDI Bluff Road** (final); **SCRDI Dixiana** (final); **Townsend Saw Chain Co.** (final). There are a total of 1,375 Superfund sites with a status of proposed or final on the list in the U.S. *U.S. Environmental Protection Agency, National Priorities List, April 7, 2021*

AIR QUALITY

Air Quality Trends: Ozone

	1990	1995	2000	2005	2010	2015	2016	2017	2018	2019
MSA[1]	0.093	0.079	0.096	0.082	0.070	0.056	0.065	0.059	0.060	0.066
U.S.	0.088	0.089	0.082	0.080	0.073	0.068	0.069	0.068	0.069	0.065

Note: (1) Data covers the Columbia, SC Metropolitan Statistical Area. The values shown are the composite ozone concentration averages among trend sites based on the highest fourth daily maximum 8-hour concentration in parts per million. These trends are based on sites having an adequate record of monitoring data during the trend period. Data from exceptional events are included.
Source: U.S. Environmental Protection Agency, Air Quality Monitoring Information, "Air Quality Trends by City, 1990-2019"

Air Quality Index

Area	Percent of Days when Air Quality was...[2]					AQI Statistics[2]	
	Good	Moderate	Unhealthy for Sensitive Groups	Unhealthy	Very Unhealthy	Maximum	Median
MSA[1]	72.3	27.1	0.5	0.0	0.0	136	43

Note: (1) Data covers the Columbia, SC Metropolitan Statistical Area; (2) Based on 365 days with AQI data in 2019. Air Quality Index (AQI) is an index for reporting daily air quality. EPA calculates the AQI for five major air pollutants regulated by the Clean Air Act: ground-level ozone, particle pollution (aka particulate matter), carbon monoxide, sulfur dioxide, and nitrogen dioxide. The AQI runs from 0 to 500. The higher the AQI value, the greater the level of air pollution and the greater the health concern. There are six AQI categories: "Good" AQI is between 0 and 50. Air quality is considered satisfactory; "Moderate" AQI is between 51 and 100. Air quality is acceptable; "Unhealthy for Sensitive Groups" When AQI values are between 101 and 150, members of sensitive groups may experience health effects; "Unhealthy" When AQI values are between 151 and 200 everyone may begin to experience health effects; "Very Unhealthy" AQI values between 201 and 300 trigger a health alert; "Hazardous" AQI values over 300 trigger warnings of emergency conditions (not shown).
Source: U.S. Environmental Protection Agency, Air Quality Index Report, 2019

Air Quality Index Pollutants

Area	Percent of Days when AQI Pollutant was...[2]					
	Carbon Monoxide	Nitrogen Dioxide	Ozone	Sulfur Dioxide	Particulate Matter 2.5	Particulate Matter 10
MSA[1]	0.0	0.0	71.8	0.0	28.2	0.0

Note: (1) Data covers the Columbia, SC Metropolitan Statistical Area; (2) Based on 365 days with AQI data in 2019. The Air Quality Index (AQI) is an index for reporting daily air quality. EPA calculates the AQI for five major air pollutants regulated by the Clean Air Act: ground-level ozone, particle pollution (also known as particulate matter), carbon monoxide, sulfur dioxide, and nitrogen dioxide. The AQI runs from 0 to 500. The higher the AQI value, the greater the level of air pollution and the greater the health concern.
Source: U.S. Environmental Protection Agency, Air Quality Index Report, 2019

Maximum Air Pollutant Concentrations: Particulate Matter, Ozone, CO and Lead

	Particulate Matter 10 (ug/m^3)	Particulate Matter 2.5 Wtd AM (ug/m^3)	Particulate Matter 2.5 24-Hr (ug/m^3)	Ozone (ppm)	Carbon Monoxide (ppm)	Lead (ug/m^3)
MSA[1] Level	35	7.2	15	0.067	1	n/a
NAAQS[2]	150	15	35	0.075	9	0.15
Met NAAQS[2]	Yes	Yes	Yes	Yes	Yes	n/a

Note: (1) Data covers the Columbia, SC Metropolitan Statistical Area; Data from exceptional events are included; (2) National Ambient Air Quality Standards; ppm = parts per million; ug/m^3 = micrograms per cubic meter; n/a not available.
Concentrations: Particulate Matter 10 (coarse particulate)—highest second maximum 24-hour concentration; Particulate Matter 2.5 Wtd AM (fine particulate)—highest weighted annual mean concentration; Particulate Matter 2.5 24-Hour (fine particulate)—highest 98th percentile 24-hour concentration; Ozone—highest fourth daily maximum 8-hour concentration; Carbon Monoxide—highest second maximum non-overlapping 8-hour concentration; Lead—maximum running 3-month average
Source: U.S. Environmental Protection Agency, Air Quality Monitoring Information, "Air Quality Statistics by City, 2019"

Maximum Air Pollutant Concentrations: Nitrogen Dioxide and Sulfur Dioxide

	Nitrogen Dioxide AM (ppb)	Nitrogen Dioxide 1-Hr (ppb)	Sulfur Dioxide AM (ppb)	Sulfur Dioxide 1-Hr (ppb)	Sulfur Dioxide 24-Hr (ppb)
MSA[1] Level	3	31	n/a	3	n/a
NAAQS[2]	53	100	30	75	140
Met NAAQS[2]	Yes	Yes	n/a	Yes	n/a

Note: (1) Data covers the Columbia, SC Metropolitan Statistical Area; Data from exceptional events are included; (2) National Ambient Air Quality Standards; ppm = parts per million; ug/m³ = micrograms per cubic meter; n/a not available.
Concentrations: Nitrogen Dioxide AM—highest arithmetic mean concentration; Nitrogen Dioxide 1-Hr—highest 98th percentile 1-hour daily maximum concentration; Sulfur Dioxide AM—highest annual mean concentration; Sulfur Dioxide 1-Hr—highest 99th percentile 1-hour daily maximum concentration; Sulfur Dioxide 24-Hr—highest second maximum 24-hour concentration
Source: U.S. Environmental Protection Agency, Air Quality Monitoring Information, "Air Quality Statistics by City, 2019"

Dallas, Texas

Background

Dallas is one of those cities that offer everything. Founded in 1841 by Tennessee lawyer and trader, John Neely Bryan, Dallas has come to symbolize in modern times all that is big, exciting, and affluent. The city itself is in the top ten worldwide among cities with the most billionaires. When combined with those billionaires who live in Dallas's neighboring city of Fort Worth, the area has one of the greatest concentrations of billionaires in the world.

Originally one of the largest markets for cotton in the U.S., Dallas moved on to become one of the largest markets for oil in the country. In the 1930s, oil was struck on the eastern fields of Texas. As a result, oil companies were founded and millions, then billions, were made, creating the face we now associate with Dallas and the state of Texas.

Today, oil still plays a dominant role in the Dallas economy. Outside of Alaska, Texas holds most of the U.S. oil reserves. For that reason, many oil companies choose to headquarter in the silver skyscrapers of Dallas.

In addition to employment opportunities in the oil industry, the Dallas branch of the Federal Reserve Bank, and a host of other banks and investment firms clustering around the Federal Reserve hub employ thousands. Other opportunities are offered in the aircraft, advertising, motion picture, and publishing industries. The city is sometimes referred to as Texas's "Silicon Prairie" because of a high concentration of telecommunications companies.

The Dallas Convention Center, with more than two million square feet of space, is the largest convention center in Texas with more than 1 million square feet of exhibit area, including nearly 800,000 square feet of same level, contiguous prime exhibit space with more than 3.8 million people attending more than 3,600 conventions and spending more than $4.2 billion annually.

Dallas also has a significant cultural presence: many independent theater groups are sponsored by Southern Methodist University; Museum of Art houses an excellent collection of modern art, especially American paintings; Winspear Opera House and three other venues comprise the AT&T Performing Arts Center; Dallas Opera has showcased Maria Callas, Joan Sutherland, and Monserrat Caballe; Winspear Opera House, Wyly Theatre, Nasher Sculpture Center, and Meyerson Symphony Center make Dallas the only city in the world with four buildings within one contiguous block that are designed by Pritzker Architecture Prize winners. The city also contains many historical districts such as the Swiss Avenue District, and elegant buildings such as the City Hall Building designed by I.M. Pei. A notable city event is the State Fair of Texas, which has been held annually at Fair Park since 1886. A massive event for the state, the fair brings an estimated $350 million to the city's economy annually.

> Lt. Governor Dan Patrick covered a fine owed by salon owner Shelley Luther, who violated statewide stay-at-home orders when she reopened her business.

The area's high concentration of wealth undoubtedly contributes to Dallas's wide array of shopping centers and high-end boutiques. Downtown Dallas is home to many cafes, restaurants and clubs. The city's centrally located "Arts District" is appropriately named for the independent theaters and art galleries located in the neighborhood. Northern districts of the city and the central downtown have seen much urban revival in the last 30 years.

Colleges and universities in the Dallas area include Southern Methodist University, University of Dallas, and University of Texas at Dallas. In 2006, University of North Texas opened a branch in the southern part of the city, in part, to help accelerate development south of downtown Dallas. The city maintains 21,000 acres of park land, with over 400 parks.

The climate of Dallas is generally temperate. Occasional periods of extreme cold are short-lived, and extremely high temperatures that sometimes occur in summer usually do not last for extended periods. However, in February 2021, a series of severe winter storms caused record low temperatures in Dallas, causing a massive power disruption in the state.

Rankings

General Rankings

- As part of its *Next Stop* series, *Insider* listed 10 places in the U.S. that were either a classic vacation destination experiencing a renaissance or a new up-and-coming hot spot. That could mean the exploding food scene, experiencing the great outdoors, where cool people are moving to, or not overrun with tourists, according to the website insider.com Dallas is a place to visit in 2020. *Insider,* "10 Places in the U.S. You Need to Visit in 2020," December 23, 2019

- The Dallas metro area was identified as one of America's fastest-growing areas in terms of population and business growth by *MagnifyMoney*. The area ranked #7 out of 35. The 100 most populous metro areas in the U.S. were evaluated on their change from 2011-2016 in the following categories: people and housing; workforce and employment opportunities; growing industry. *www.businessinsider.com,* "The 35 Cities in the US with the Biggest Influx of People, the Most Work Opportunities, and the Hottest Business Growth," August 12, 2018

- The Dallas metro area was identified as one of America's fastest-growing areas in terms of population and economy by *Forbes*. The area ranked #3 out of 25. The 100 most populous metro areas in the U.S. were evaluated on the following criteria: estimated population growth; employment; economic output; wages; home values. *Forbes,* "America's Fastest-Growing Cities 2018," February 28, 2018

- The human resources consulting firm Mercer ranked 231 major cities worldwide in terms of overall quality of life. Dallas ranked #63. Criteria: political, social, economic, and socio-cultural factors; medical and health considerations; schools and education; public services and transportation; recreation; consumer goods; housing; and natural environment. *Mercer, "Mercer 2019 Quality of Living Survey,"* March 13, 2019

Business/Finance Rankings

- Based on metro area social media reviews, the employment opinion group Glassdoor surveyed 50 of the most populous U.S. metro areas and equally weighed cost of living, hiring opportunity, and job satisfaction to compose a list of "25 Best Cities for Jobs." Median pay and home value, and number of active job openings were also factored in. The Dallas metro area was ranked #25 in overall job satisfaction. *www.glassdoor.com,* "Best Cities for Jobs," February 25, 2020

- The Brookings Institution ranked the nation's largest cities based on income inequality. Dallas was ranked #33 (#1 = greatest inequality). Criteria: the "95/20 ratio," a figure representing the income at which a household earns more than 95 percent of all other households, divided by the income at which a household earns more than only 20 percent of all other households. *Brookings Institution, "Household Income Inequality, Largest Cities of 97 Large U.S. Metro Areas, 2014-2016,"* February 5, 2018

- The Brookings Institution ranked the 100 largest metro areas in the U.S. based on income inequality. Dallas was ranked #60 (#1 = greatest inequality). Criteria: the "95/20 ratio," a figure representing the income at which a household earns more than 95 percent of all other households, divided by the income at which a household earns more than only 20 percent of all other households. *Brookings Institution, "Household Income Inequality, 100 Largest U.S. Metro Areas, 2014-2016,"* February 5, 2018

- *Forbes* ranked the 100 largest metro areas in the U.S. in terms of the "Best Cities for Young Professionals." The Dallas metro area ranked #5 out of 25. Criteria: median rent of a two-bedroom apartment; job growth and unemployment rate; median salary of college graduates with 5 or less years of work experience; networking opportunities; social outlook; percentage of population 25 years of age and older with college degrees. *Forbes.com, "America's 25 Best Cities for Young Professionals in 2017,"* May 22, 2017

- The Dallas metro area was identified as one of the most debt-ridden places in America by the finance site Credit.com. The metro area was ranked #2. Criteria: residents' average credit card debt as well as median income. *Credit.com, "25 Cities With the Most Credit Card Debt,"* February 28, 2018

- Dallas was identified as one of America's most frugal metro areas by *Coupons.com*. The city ranked #2 out of 25. Criteria: digital coupon usage. *Coupons.com, "America's Most Frugal Cities of 2017,"* March 22, 2018

- *Forbes* ranked the 200 most populous metro areas to determine the nation's "Best Places for Business and Careers." The Dallas metro area was ranked #2. Criteria: costs (business and living); job growth (past and projected); income growth; quality of life; educational attainment (college and high school); projected economic growth; cultural and leisure opportunities; workplace tolerance laws; net migration patterns. *Forbes, "The Best Places for Business and Careers 2019: Seattle Still On Top,"* October 30, 2019

- Mercer Human Resources Consulting ranked 209 cities worldwide in terms of cost-of-living. Dallas ranked #52 (the lower the ranking, the higher the cost-of-living). The survey measured the comparative cost of over 200 items (such as housing, food, clothing, household goods, transportation, and entertainment) in each location. *Mercer, "2020 Cost of Living Survey," June 9, 2020*

Culture/Performing Arts Rankings

- Dallas was selected as one of the 25 best cities for moviemakers in North America. COVID-19 has spurred a quest for great film cities that offer more creative space, lower costs, and more great outdoors. NYC & LA were intentionally excluded. Criteria: longstanding reputations as film-friendly communities; efforts to deal with pandemic-specific challenges; and establish appropriate COVID-19 guidelines. The city was ranked #12. *MovieMaker Magazine, "Best Places to Live and Work as a Moviemaker, 2021," January 26, 2021*

Dating/Romance Rankings

- Dallas was selected as one of the best cities for post grads by *Rent.com*. The city ranked among the top 10. Criteria: jobs per capita; unemployment rate; mean annual income; cost of living; rental inventory. *Rent.com, "Best Cities for College Grads," December 11, 2018*

Education Rankings

- Dallas was selected as one of America's most literate cities. The city ranked #36 out of the 84 largest U.S. cities. Criteria: number of booksellers; library resources; Internet resources; educational attainment; periodical publishing resources; newspaper circulation. *Central Connecticut State University, "America's Most Literate Cities, 2018," February 2019*

Environmental Rankings

- Sperling's BestPlaces assessed the 50 largest metropolitan areas of the United States for the likelihood of dangerously extreme weather events or earthquakes. In general the Southeast and South-Central regions have the highest risk of weather extremes and earthquakes, while the Pacific Northwest enjoys the lowest risk. Of the most risky metropolitan areas, the Dallas metro area was ranked #4. *www.bestplaces.net, "Avoid Natural Disasters: BestPlaces Reveals The Top 10 Safest Places to Live," October 25, 2017*

- The U.S. Environmental Protection Agency (EPA) released a list of U.S. metropolitan areas with the most ENERGY STAR certified buildings in 2019. The Dallas metro area was ranked #4 out of 25. *U.S. Environmental Protection Agency, "2020 Energy Star Top Cities," March 2020*

- Dallas was highlighted as one of the 25 most ozone-polluted metro areas in the U.S. during 2016 through 2018. The area ranked #21. *American Lung Association, "State of the Air 2020," April 21, 2020*

Food/Drink Rankings

- Globe Life Park was selected as one of PETA's "Top 10 Vegan-Friendly Ballparks" for 2019. The park ranked #1. *People for the Ethical Treatment of Animals, "Top 10 Vegan-Friendly Ballparks," May 23, 2019*

Health/Fitness Rankings

- For each of the 100 largest cities in the United States, the American Fitness Index®, published by the American College of Sports Medicine and the Anthem Foundation, evaluated community infrastructure and 33 health behaviors including preventive health, levels of chronic disease conditions, pedestrian safety, air quality, and community resources that support physical activity. Dallas ranked #56 for "community fitness." *americanfitnessindex.org, "2020 ACSM American Fitness Index Summary Report," July 14, 2020*

- Dallas was identified as a "2021 Spring Allergy Capital." The area ranked #19 out of 100. Three groups of factors were used to identify the most challenging cities for people with allergies during the spring season: annual spring pollen levels; over the counter medicine use; number of board-certified allergy specialists. *Asthma and Allergy Foundation of America, "Spring Allergy Capitals 2021," February 23, 2021*

- Dallas was identified as a "2021 Fall Allergy Capital." The area ranked #21 out of 100. Three groups of factors were used to identify the most challenging cities for people with allergies during the fall season: annual fall pollen levels; over the counter medicine use; number of board-certified allergy specialists. *Asthma and Allergy Foundation of America, "Fall Allergy Capitals 2021," February 23, 2021*

- Dallas was identified as a "2019 Asthma Capital." The area ranked #76 out of the nation's 100 largest metropolitan areas. Criteria: estimated asthma prevalence; crude death rate from asthma; and ER visits due to asthma. Risk factors analyzed but not factored in the rankings: annual pollen score; annual air quality; public smoking laws; number of board-certified asthma specialists; rescue medication use; controller medication use; uninsured rate; poverty rate. *Asthma and Allergy Foundation of America, "Asthma Capitals 2019: The Most Challenging Places to Live With Asthma," May 7, 2019*

Pet Rankings

- Dallas appeared on *The Dogington Post* site as one of the top cities for dog lovers, ranking #17 out of 20. The real estate brokerage, Redfin and Rover, the largest pet sitter and dog walker network, compiled a list from over 14,000 U.S. cities to come up with a "Rover Rank." Criteria: highest count of dog walks, the city's Walk Score®, for-sale home listings that mention "dog," number of dog walkers and pet sitters and the hours spent and distance logged. *www.dogingtonpost.com, "The 20 Most Dog-Friendly Cities of 2019," April 4, 2019*

Real Estate Rankings

- FitSmallBusiness looked at 50 of the largest metropolitan areas in the U.S. to determine which metro was the best to start a real estate business. Data was compiled from such sources as: Zillow, Trulia, U.S. Census Bureau, and the Bureau of Labor Statistics. Criteria: location; inventory; annual wages; median sales price of homes; days on the market; median price cut percentage; and other factors that would influence real estate professional growth. The Dallas metro area ranked #19. *fitsmallbusiness.com, "The Best Cities to Become a Real Estate Agent in 2018," January 30, 2018*

- *WalletHub* compared the most populated U.S. cities to determine which had the best markets for real estate agents. Dallas ranked #52 where demand was high and pay was the best. Criteria: sales per agent; annual median wage for real-estate agents; monthly average starting salary for real estate agents; real estate job density and competition; unemployment rate; home turnover rate; housing-market health index; and other relevant metrics. *www.WalletHub.com, "2019's Best Places to Be a Real Estate Agent," April 24, 2019*

Safety Rankings

- To identify the most dangerous cities in America, 24/7 Wall Street focused on violent crime categories—murder, non-negligent manslaughter, rape, robbery, and aggravated assault—and property crime as reported in the FBI's 2019 annual Uniform Crime Report. Criteria also included median income from American Community Survey and unemployment figures from Bureau of Labor Statistics. For cities with populations over 100,000, Dallas was ranked #42. *247wallst.com, "America's 50 Most Dangerous Cities" November 16, 2020*

- Allstate ranked the 200 largest cities in America in terms of driver safety. Dallas ranked #172. Criteria: internal property damage claims over a two-year period from January 2016 to December 2017. The report helps increase the importance of safety and awareness behind the wheel. *Allstate, "Allstate America's Best Drivers Report, 2019" June 24, 2019*

- Dallas was identified as one of the most dangerous cities in America by NeighborhoodScout. The city ranked #89 out of 100 (#1 = most dangerous). Criteria: number of violent crimes per 1,000 residents. The editors evaluated cities with 25,000 or more residents. *NeighborhoodScout.com, "2021 Top 100 Most Dangerous Cities in the U.S.," January 2, 2021*

Seniors/Retirement Rankings

- Dallas made the 2020 *Forbes* list of "25 Best Places to Retire." Criteria, focused on high-quality retirement living at an affordable price, include: housing/living costs compared to the national average and state taxes; air quality; crime rates; good economic outlook; home price appreciation; risk associated with climate-change; availability of medical care; bikeability; walkability; healthy living. *Forbes.com, "The Best Places to Retire in 2020," August 14, 2020*

Women/Minorities Rankings

- The *Houston Chronicle* listed the Dallas metro area as #7 in top places for young Latinos to live in the U.S. Research was largely based on housing and occupational data from the largest metropolitan areas performed by *Forbes* and NBC Universo. Criteria: percentage of 18-34 year-olds; Latino college grad rates; and diversity. *blog.chron.com, "The 15 Best Big Cities for Latino Millenials," January 26, 2016*

- Personal finance website *WalletHub* compared more than 180 U.S. cities across two key dimensions, "Hispanic Business-Friendliness" and "Hispanic Purchasing Power," to arrive at the most favorable conditions for Hispanic entrepreneurs. Dallas was ranked #28 out of 182. Criteria includes: share of Hispanic-Owned Businesses; Hispanic entrepreneurship rate to median annual income of Hispanics; Small Business-Friendliness score; cost of living; and number of Hispanics with at least a bachelor's degree. *WalletHub.com, "2019's Best Cities for Hispanic Entrepreneurs," May 1, 2019*

Miscellaneous Rankings

- While the majority of travel ground to a halt in 2020, plugged-in travel influencers and experts were able to rediscover their local regions. Dallas appeared on a *Forbes* list of 15 U.S. cities that provided solace as well as local inspiration. Whether it be quirky things to see and do, delicious take out, outdoor exploring and daytrips, these places are must-see destinations. *Forbes, "Bucket List Travel: The 15 Best U.S. Destinations For 2021," January 1, 2021*

- The watchdog site, Charity Navigator, conducted a study of charities in major markets both to analyze statistical differences in their financial, accountability, and transparency practices and to track year-to-year variations in individual philanthropic communities. The Dallas metro area was ranked #5 among the 30 metro markets in the rating category of Overall Score. *www.charitynavigator.org, "2017 Metro Market Study," May 1, 2017*

- *WalletHub* compared the 150 most populated U.S. cities to determine their operating efficiency. A "Quality of City Services" score was constructed for each city and then divided by the total budget per capita to reveal which were managed the best. Dallas ranked #99. Criteria: financial stability; economy; education; safety; health; infrastructure and pollution. *www.WalletHub.com, "2020's Best- & Worst-Run Cities in America," June 29, 2020*

Business Environment

DEMOGRAPHICS

Population Growth

Area	1990 Census	2000 Census	2010 Census	2019* Estimate	Population Growth (%) 1990-2019	Population Growth (%) 2010-2019
City	1,006,971	1,188,580	1,197,816	1,330,612	32.1	11.1
MSA[1]	3,989,294	5,161,544	6,371,773	7,320,663	83.5	14.9
U.S.	248,709,873	281,421,906	308,745,538	324,697,795	30.6	5.2

Note: (1) Figures cover the Dallas-Fort Worth-Arlington, TX Metropolitan Statistical Area; (*) 2015-2019 5-year estimated population
Source: U.S. Census Bureau, 1990 Census, Census 2000, Census 2010, 2015-2019 American Community Survey 5-Year Estimates

Household Size

Area	One	Two	Three	Four	Five	Six	Seven or More	Average Household Size
City	35.3	29.2	13.8	11.2	6.2	2.6	1.8	2.60
MSA[1]	25.0	30.6	16.8	15.2	7.6	2.9	1.8	2.80
U.S.	27.9	33.9	15.6	12.9	6.0	2.3	1.4	2.60

Note: (1) Figures cover the Dallas-Fort Worth-Arlington, TX Metropolitan Statistical Area
Source: U.S. Census Bureau, 2015-2019 American Community Survey 5-Year Estimates

Race

Area	White Alone[2] (%)	Black Alone[2] (%)	Asian Alone[2] (%)	AIAN[3] Alone[2] (%)	NHOPI[4] Alone[2] (%)	Other Race Alone[2] (%)	Two or More Races (%)
City	62.7	24.3	3.4	0.3	0.0	6.9	2.4
MSA[1]	68.3	15.8	6.9	0.5	0.1	5.4	3.0
U.S.	72.5	12.7	5.5	0.8	0.2	4.9	3.3

Note: (1) Figures cover the Dallas-Fort Worth-Arlington, TX Metropolitan Statistical Area; (2) Alone is defined as not being in combination with one or more other races; (3) American Indian and Alaska Native; (4) Native Hawaiian and Other Pacific Islander
Source: U.S. Census Bureau, 2015-2019 American Community Survey 5-Year Estimates

Hispanic or Latino Origin

Area	Total (%)	Mexican (%)	Puerto Rican (%)	Cuban (%)	Other (%)
City	41.8	35.4	0.5	0.3	5.5
MSA[1]	28.9	23.9	0.7	0.3	4.0
U.S.	18.0	11.2	1.7	0.7	4.3

Note: Persons of Hispanic or Latino origin can be of any race; (1) Figures cover the Dallas-Fort Worth-Arlington, TX Metropolitan Statistical Area
Source: U.S. Census Bureau, 2015-2019 American Community Survey 5-Year Estimates

Ancestry

Area	German	Irish	English	American	Italian	Polish	French[2]	Scottish	Dutch
City	5.1	4.0	4.5	3.8	1.5	0.8	1.2	1.1	0.4
MSA[1]	8.6	6.5	6.7	6.3	2.1	1.1	1.7	1.6	0.7
U.S.	13.3	9.7	7.2	6.2	5.1	2.8	2.3	1.7	1.2

Note: Figures are the percentage of the total population reporting a particular ancestry. The nine most commonly reported ancestries in the U.S. are shown. Figures include multiple ancestries (e.g. if a person reported being Irish and Italian, they were included in both columns); (1) Figures cover the Dallas-Fort Worth-Arlington, TX Metropolitan Statistical Area; (2) Excludes Basque
Source: U.S. Census Bureau, 2015-2019 American Community Survey 5-Year Estimates

Foreign-born Population

Area	Any Foreign Country	Asia	Mexico	Europe	Caribbean	Central America[2]	South America	Africa	Canada
City	24.8	2.8	15.4	0.7	0.4	2.6	0.6	1.9	0.2
MSA[1]	18.7	5.3	8.4	0.8	0.3	1.5	0.6	1.5	0.2
U.S.	13.6	4.2	3.5	1.5	1.3	1.1	1.0	0.7	0.2

Note: (1) Figures cover the Dallas-Fort Worth-Arlington, TX Metropolitan Statistical Area; (2) Excludes Mexico.
Source: U.S. Census Bureau, 2015-2019 American Community Survey 5-Year Estimates

Marital Status

Area	Never Married	Now Married[2]	Separated	Widowed	Divorced
City	41.6	40.4	3.2	4.5	10.4
MSA[1]	32.8	50.3	2.1	4.4	10.5
U.S.	33.4	48.1	1.9	5.8	10.9

Note: Figures are percentages and cover the population 15 years of age and older; (1) Figures cover the Dallas-Fort Worth-Arlington, TX Metropolitan Statistical Area; (2) Excludes separated
Source: U.S. Census Bureau, 2015-2019 American Community Survey 5-Year Estimates

Disability by Age

Area	All Ages	Under 18 Years Old	18 to 64 Years Old	65 Years and Over
City	9.6	3.3	8.1	35.0
MSA[1]	9.5	3.4	7.9	33.7
U.S.	12.6	4.2	10.3	34.5

Note: Figures show percent of the civilian noninstitutionalized population that reported having a disability. Disability status is determined from six types of difficulty: vision, hearing, cognitive, ambulatory, self-care, and independent living. For children under 5 years old, hearing and vision difficulty are used to determine disability status. For children between the ages of 5 and 14, disability status is determined from hearing, vision, cognitive, ambulatory, and self-care difficulties. For people aged 15 years and older, they are considered to have a disability if they have difficulty with any one of the six difficulty types; Note: (1) Figures cover the Dallas-Fort Worth-Arlington, TX Metropolitan Statistical Area
Source: U.S. Census Bureau, 2015-2019 American Community Survey 5-Year Estimates

Age

Area	Under Age 5	Age 5–19	Age 20–34	Age 35–44	Age 45–54	Age 55–64	Age 65–74	Age 75–84	Age 85+	Median Age
City	7.5	19.9	26.4	13.7	11.8	10.4	6.1	2.9	1.2	32.7
MSA[1]	7.0	21.8	21.5	14.2	13.4	11.2	6.8	3.1	1.1	34.8
U.S.	6.1	19.1	20.7	12.6	13.0	12.9	9.1	4.6	1.9	38.1

Note: (1) Figures cover the Dallas-Fort Worth-Arlington, TX Metropolitan Statistical Area
Source: U.S. Census Bureau, 2015-2019 American Community Survey 5-Year Estimates

Gender

Area	Males	Females	Males per 100 Females
City	657,714	672,898	97.7
MSA[1]	3,601,569	3,719,094	96.8
U.S.	159,886,919	164,810,876	97.0

Note: (1) Figures cover the Dallas-Fort Worth-Arlington, TX Metropolitan Statistical Area
Source: U.S. Census Bureau, 2015-2019 American Community Survey 5-Year Estimates

Religious Groups by Family

Area	Catholic	Baptist	Non-Den.	Methodist[2]	Lutheran	LDS[3]	Pentecostal	Presbyterian[4]	Muslim[5]	Judaism
MSA[1]	13.3	18.7	7.8	5.3	0.8	1.2	2.2	1.0	2.4	0.4
U.S.	19.1	9.3	4.0	4.0	2.3	2.0	1.9	1.6	0.8	0.7

Note: Figures are the number of adherents as a percentage of the total population; (1) Figures cover the Dallas-Fort Worth-Arlington, TX Metropolitan Statistical Area; (2) Methodist/Pietist; (3) Latter Day Saints; (4) Reformed; (5) Figures are estimates
Source: Association of Statisticians of American Religious Bodies, 2010 U.S. Religion Census: Religious Congregations & Membership Study

Religious Groups by Tradition

Area	Catholic	Evangelical Protestant	Mainline Protestant	Other Tradition	Black Protestant	Orthodox
MSA[1]	13.3	28.3	7.0	4.8	1.8	0.2
U.S.	19.1	16.2	7.3	4.3	1.6	0.3

Note: Figures are the number of adherents as a percentage of the total population; (1) Figures cover the Dallas-Fort Worth-Arlington, TX Metropolitan Statistical Area
Source: Association of Statisticians of American Religious Bodies, 2010 U.S. Religion Census: Religious Congregations & Membership Study

ECONOMY

Gross Metropolitan Product

Area	2017	2018	2019	2020	Rank[2]
MSA[1]	522.3	556.9	586.7	620.6	5

Note: Figures are in billions of dollars; (1) Figures cover the Dallas-Fort Worth-Arlington, TX Metropolitan Statistical Area; (2) Rank is based on 2018 data and ranges from 1 to 381
Source: U.S. Conference of Mayors, U.S. Metro Economies: GMP & Employment 2018-2020, September 2019

Economic Growth

Area	2015-17 (%)	2018 (%)	2019 (%)	2020 (%)	Rank[2]
MSA[1]	2.7	2.8	3.7	2.7	87
U.S.	1.9	2.9	2.3	2.1	—

Note: Figures are real gross metropolitan product (GMP) growth rates and represent average annual percent change; (1) Figures cover the Dallas-Fort Worth-Arlington, TX Metropolitan Statistical Area; (2) Rank is based on 2017 2-year average annual percent change and ranges from 1 to 381
Source: U.S. Conference of Mayors, U.S. Metro Economies: GMP & Employment 2018-2020, September 2019

Metropolitan Area Exports

Area	2014	2015	2016	2017	2018	2019	Rank[2]
MSA[1]	28,669.4	27,372.9	27,187.8	30,269.1	36,260.9	39,474.0	7

Note: Figures are in millions of dollars; (1) Figures cover the Dallas-Fort Worth-Arlington, TX Metropolitan Statistical Area; (2) Rank is based on 2019 data and ranges from 1 to 386
Source: U.S. Department of Commerce, International Trade Administration, Office of Trade and Economic Analysis, Industry and Analysis, Exports by Metropolitan Area, data extracted March 24, 2021

Building Permits

Area	Single-Family 2018	Single-Family 2019	Pct. Chg.	Multi-Family 2018	Multi-Family 2019	Pct. Chg.	Total 2018	Total 2019	Pct. Chg.
City	2,009	2,093	4.2	6,038	6,000	-0.6	8,047	8,093	0.6
MSA[1]	36,832	34,939	-5.1	27,061	27,769	2.6	63,893	62,708	-1.9
U.S.	855,300	862,100	0.7	473,500	523,900	10.6	1,328,800	1,386,000	4.3

Note: (1) Figures cover the Dallas-Fort Worth-Arlington, TX Metropolitan Statistical Area; Figures represent new, privately-owned housing units authorized (unadjusted data); All permit data are based on estimates with imputation
Source: U.S. Census Bureau, Manufacturing, Mining, and Construction Statistics, Building Permits, 2018, 2019

Bankruptcy Filings

Area	Business Filings 2019	Business Filings 2020	% Chg.	Nonbusiness Filings 2019	Nonbusiness Filings 2020	% Chg.
Dallas County	355	568	60.0	3,572	2,452	-31.4
U.S.	22,780	21,655	-4.9	752,160	522,808	-30.5

Note: Business filings include Chapter 7, Chapter 9, Chapter 11, Chapter 12, Chapter 13, Chapter 15, and Section 304; Nonbusiness filings include Chapter 7, Chapter 11, and Chapter 13
Source: Administrative Office of the U.S. Courts, Business and Nonbusiness Bankruptcy, County Cases Commenced by Chapter of the Bankruptcy Code, During the 12-Month Period Ending December 31, 2019 and Business and Nonbusiness Bankruptcy, County Cases Commenced by Chapter of the Bankruptcy Code, During the 12-Month Period Ending December 31, 2020

Housing Vacancy Rates

Area	Gross Vacancy Rate[2] (%) 2018	2019	2020	Year-Round Vacancy Rate[3] (%) 2018	2019	2020	Rental Vacancy Rate[4] (%) 2018	2019	2020	Homeowner Vacancy Rate[5] (%) 2018	2019	2020
MSA[1]	7.8	7.6	6.4	7.6	7.3	6.4	7.4	6.9	7.2	1.4	1.5	0.7
U.S.	12.3	12.0	10.6	9.7	9.5	8.2	6.9	6.7	6.3	1.5	1.4	1.0

Note: (1) Figures cover the Dallas-Fort Worth-Arlington, TX Metropolitan Statistical Area; (2) The percentage of the total housing inventory that is vacant; (3) The percentage of the housing inventory (excluding seasonal units) that is year-round vacant; (4) The percentage of rental inventory that is vacant for rent; (5) The percentage of homeowner inventory that is vacant for sale
Source: U.S. Census Bureau, Housing Vacancies and Homeownership Annual Statistics: 2018, 2019, 2020

INCOME

Income

Area	Per Capita ($)	Median Household ($)	Average Household ($)
City	34,479	52,580	86,393
MSA[1]	35,278	70,281	97,589
U.S.	34,103	62,843	88,607

Note: (1) Figures cover the Dallas-Fort Worth-Arlington, TX Metropolitan Statistical Area
Source: U.S. Census Bureau, 2015-2019 American Community Survey 5-Year Estimates

Household Income Distribution

Area	Under $15,000	$15,000 -$24,999	$25,000 -$34,999	$35,000 -$49,999	$50,000 -$74,999	$75,000 -$99,999	$100,000 -$149,999	$150,000 and up
City	11.8	10.4	10.7	14.7	17.9	10.6	10.8	13.1
MSA[1]	7.7	7.1	8.3	12.0	17.8	13.2	16.7	17.2
U.S.	10.3	8.9	8.9	12.3	17.2	12.7	15.1	14.5

Note: (1) Figures cover the Dallas-Fort Worth-Arlington, TX Metropolitan Statistical Area
Source: U.S. Census Bureau, 2015-2019 American Community Survey 5-Year Estimates

Poverty Rate

Area	All Ages	Under 18 Years Old	18 to 64 Years Old	65 Years and Over
City	18.9	29.3	15.6	14.4
MSA[1]	11.7	16.6	10.1	8.5
U.S.	13.4	18.5	12.6	9.3

Note: Figures are percentage of people whose income during the past 12 months was below the poverty level;
(1) Figures cover the Dallas-Fort Worth-Arlington, TX Metropolitan Statistical Area
Source: U.S. Census Bureau, 2015-2019 American Community Survey 5-Year Estimates

CITY FINANCES

City Government Finances

Component	2017 ($000)	2017 ($ per capita)
Total Revenues	4,121,897	3,170
Total Expenditures	4,183,756	3,218
Debt Outstanding	10,912,691	8,394
Cash and Securities[1]	10,437,232	8,028

Note: (1) Cash and security holdings of a government at the close of its fiscal year, including those of its dependent agencies, utilities, and liquor stores.
Source: U.S. Census Bureau, State & Local Government Finances 2017

City Government Revenue by Source

Source	2017 ($000)	2017 ($ per capita)	2017 (%)
General Revenue			
From Federal Government	44,857	35	1.1
From State Government	88,501	68	2.1
From Local Governments	8,606	7	0.2
Taxes			
Property	828,813	638	20.1
Sales and Gross Receipts	453,013	348	11.0
Personal Income	0	0	0.0
Corporate Income	0	0	0.0
Motor Vehicle License	0	0	0.0
Other Taxes	47,453	37	1.2
Current Charges	1,532,202	1,179	37.2
Liquor Store	0	0	0.0
Utility	367,892	283	8.9
Employee Retirement	625,683	481	15.2

Source: U.S. Census Bureau, State & Local Government Finances 2017

City Government Expenditures by Function

Function	2017 ($000)	2017 ($ per capita)	2017 (%)
General Direct Expenditures			
Air Transportation	1,026,003	789	24.5
Corrections	1,656	1	0.0
Education	0	0	0.0
Employment Security Administration	0	0	0.0
Financial Administration	40,747	31	1.0
Fire Protection	216,085	166	5.2
General Public Buildings	32,664	25	0.8
Governmental Administration, Other	28,055	21	0.7
Health	30,675	23	0.7
Highways	218,670	168	5.2
Hospitals	0	0	0.0
Housing and Community Development	40,008	30	1.0
Interest on General Debt	346,481	266	8.3
Judicial and Legal	30,198	23	0.7
Libraries	31,937	24	0.8
Parking	113	<1	<0.1
Parks and Recreation	192,836	148	4.6
Police Protection	410,867	316	9.8
Public Welfare	8,912	6	0.2
Sewerage	310,023	238	7.4
Solid Waste Management	82,128	63	2.0
Veterans' Services	0	0	0.0
Liquor Store	0	0	0.0
Utility	455,415	350	10.9
Employee Retirement	492,705	379	11.8

Source: U.S. Census Bureau, State & Local Government Finances 2017

Dallas, Texas

EMPLOYMENT

Labor Force and Employment

Area	Civilian Labor Force			Workers Employed		
	Dec. 2019	Dec. 2020	% Chg.	Dec. 2019	Dec. 2020	% Chg.
City	703,081	714,931	1.7	681,628	663,820	-2.6
MD[1]	2,719,675	2,742,810	0.9	2,640,356	2,571,653	-2.6
U.S.	164,007,000	160,017,000	-2.4	158,504,000	149,613,000	-5.6

Note: Data is not seasonally adjusted and covers workers 16 years of age and older; (1) Figures cover the Dallas-Plano-Irving, TX Metropolitan Division
Source: Bureau of Labor Statistics, Local Area Unemployment Statistics

Unemployment Rate

Area	2020											
	Jan.	Feb.	Mar.	Apr.	May	Jun.	Jul.	Aug.	Sep.	Oct.	Nov.	Dec.
City	3.4	3.3	4.8	13.0	12.8	8.9	8.4	7.1	8.4	6.9	8.0	7.1
MD[1]	3.3	3.2	4.6	12.6	12.1	8.1	7.5	6.2	7.3	5.9	7.1	6.2
U.S.	4.0	3.8	4.5	14.4	13.0	11.2	10.5	8.5	7.7	6.6	6.4	6.5

Note: Data is not seasonally adjusted and covers workers 16 years of age and older; (1) Figures cover the Dallas-Plano-Irving, TX Metropolitan Division
Source: Bureau of Labor Statistics, Local Area Unemployment Statistics

Average Wages

Occupation	$/Hr.	Occupation	$/Hr.
Accountants and Auditors	40.30	Maintenance and Repair Workers	21.10
Automotive Mechanics	23.50	Marketing Managers	75.00
Bookkeepers	21.30	Network and Computer Systems Admin.	43.20
Carpenters	19.90	Nurses, Licensed Practical	25.10
Cashiers	11.40	Nurses, Registered	37.50
Computer Programmers	53.90	Nursing Assistants	14.90
Computer Systems Analysts	49.60	Office Clerks, General	18.30
Computer User Support Specialists	24.80	Physical Therapists	46.10
Construction Laborers	17.40	Physicians	98.80
Cooks, Restaurant	13.00	Plumbers, Pipefitters and Steamfitters	24.40
Customer Service Representatives	18.60	Police and Sheriff's Patrol Officers	35.20
Dentists	110.90	Postal Service Mail Carriers	25.80
Electricians	24.00	Real Estate Sales Agents	32.40
Engineers, Electrical	51.10	Retail Salespersons	14.20
Fast Food and Counter Workers	11.00	Sales Representatives, Technical/Scientific	42.10
Financial Managers	77.10	Secretaries, Exc. Legal/Medical/Executive	19.20
First-Line Supervisors of Office Workers	30.70	Security Guards	16.00
General and Operations Managers	62.20	Surgeons	96.20
Hairdressers/Cosmetologists	12.80	Teacher Assistants, Exc. Postsecondary*	11.50
Home Health and Personal Care Aides	10.70	Teachers, Secondary School, Exc. Sp. Ed.*	28.30
Janitors and Cleaners	14.30	Telemarketers	17.10
Landscaping/Groundskeeping Workers	16.50	Truck Drivers, Heavy/Tractor-Trailer	24.30
Lawyers	72.20	Truck Drivers, Light/Delivery Services	20.70
Maids and Housekeeping Cleaners	12.10	Waiters and Waitresses	9.50

Note: Wage data covers the Dallas-Fort Worth-Arlington, TX Metropolitan Statistical Area; (*) Hourly wages were calculated from annual wage data based on a 40 hour work week; n/a not available.
Source: Bureau of Labor Statistics, Metro Area Occupational Employment & Wage Estimates, May 2020

Employment by Industry

Sector	MD[1]		U.S.
	Number of Employees	Percent of Total	Percent of Total
Construction, Mining, and Logging	146,000	5.5	5.5
Education and Health Services	315,500	11.8	16.3
Financial Activities	260,200	9.7	6.1
Government	318,900	11.9	15.2
Information	69,400	2.6	1.9
Leisure and Hospitality	229,300	8.6	9.0
Manufacturing	181,600	6.8	8.5
Other Services	75,900	2.8	3.8
Professional and Business Services	521,900	19.5	14.4
Retail Trade	256,100	9.6	10.9
Transportation, Warehousing, and Utilities	150,900	5.6	4.6
Wholesale Trade	151,400	5.7	3.9

Note: Figures are non-farm employment as of December 2020. Figures are not seasonally adjusted and include workers 16 years of age and older; (1) Figures cover the Dallas-Plano-Irving, TX Metropolitan Division
Source: Bureau of Labor Statistics, Current Employment Statistics, Employment, Hours, and Earnings

Employment by Occupation

Occupation Classification	City (%)	MSA[1] (%)	U.S. (%)
Management, Business, Science, and Arts	35.3	39.5	38.5
Natural Resources, Construction, and Maintenance	12.3	9.5	8.9
Production, Transportation, and Material Moving	13.2	12.9	13.2
Sales and Office	21.6	22.8	21.6
Service	17.7	15.3	17.8

Note: Figures cover employed civilians 16 years of age and older; (1) Figures cover the Dallas-Fort Worth-Arlington, TX Metropolitan Statistical Area
Source: U.S. Census Bureau, 2015-2019 American Community Survey 5-Year Estimates

Occupations with Greatest Projected Employment Growth: 2020 – 2022

Occupation[1]	2020 Employment	2022 Projected Employment	Numeric Employment Change	Percent Employment Change
Fast Food and Counter Workers	336,530	411,690	75,160	22.3
Waiters and Waitresses	165,570	206,920	41,350	25.0
Home Health and Personal Care Aides	303,520	344,240	40,720	13.4
Retail Salespersons	315,590	349,820	34,230	10.8
Heavy and Tractor-Trailer Truck Drivers	199,460	228,650	29,190	14.6
Laborers and Freight, Stock, and Material Movers, Hand	193,000	219,670	26,670	13.8
Cooks, Restaurant	88,540	114,250	25,710	29.0
Customer Service Representatives	276,080	295,790	19,710	7.1
General and Operations Managers	197,410	216,580	19,170	9.7
Office Clerks, General	310,080	327,500	17,420	5.6

Note: Projections cover Texas; (1) Sorted by numeric employment change
Source: www.projectionscentral.com, State Occupational Projections, 2020–2022 Short-Term Projections

Fastest-Growing Occupations: 2020 – 2022

Occupation[1]	2020 Employment	2022 Projected Employment	Numeric Employment Change	Percent Employment Change
Motion Picture Projectionists	150	300	150	100.0
Ushers, Lobby Attendants, and Ticket Takers	5,740	8,920	3,180	55.4
Locker Room, Coatroom, and Dressing Room Attendants	340	510	170	50.0
Athletes and Sports Competitors	270	400	130	48.1
Amusement and Recreation Attendants	13,130	19,400	6,270	47.8
Hotel, Motel, and Resort Desk Clerks	16,140	23,160	7,020	43.5
Sound Engineering Technicians	330	460	130	39.4
Gaming Dealers	220	300	80	36.4
Baggage Porters and Bellhops	1,250	1,670	420	33.6
Lodging Managers	3,300	4,330	1,030	31.2

Note: Projections cover Texas; (1) Sorted by percent employment change and excludes occupations with numeric employment change less than 50
Source: www.projectionscentral.com, State Occupational Projections, 2020–2022 Short-Term Projections

TAXES

State Corporate Income Tax Rates

State	Tax Rate (%)	Income Brackets ($)	Num. of Brackets	Financial Institution Tax Rate (%)[a]	Federal Income Tax Ded.
Texas	(w)	–	–	(w)	No

Note: Tax rates as of January 1, 2021; (a) Rates listed are the corporate income tax rate applied to financial institutions or excise taxes based on income. Some states have other taxes based upon the value of deposits or shares; (w) Texas imposes a Franchise Tax, otherwise known as margin tax, imposed on entities with more than $1,130,000 total revenues at rate of 0.75%, or 0.375% for entities primarily engaged in retail or wholesale trade, on lesser of 70% of total revenues or 100% of gross receipts after deductions for either compensation or cost of goods sold.
Source: Federation of Tax Administrators, State Corporate Income Tax Rates, January 1, 2021

State Individual Income Tax Rates

State	Tax Rate (%)	Income Brackets ($)	Personal Exemptions ($) Single	Married	Depend.	Standard Ded. ($) Single	Married
Texas				– No state income tax –			

Note: Tax rates as of January 1, 2021; Local- and county-level taxes are not included
Source: Federation of Tax Administrators, State Individual Income Tax Rates, January 1, 2021

Various State Sales and Excise Tax Rates

State	State Sales Tax (%)	Gasoline[1] (¢/gal.)	Cigarette[2] ($/pack)	Spirits[3] ($/gal.)	Wine[4] ($/gal.)	Beer[5] ($/gal.)	Recreational Marijuana (%)
Texas	6.25	20	1.41	2.4	0.2	0.2	Not legal

Note: All tax rates as of January 1, 2021; (1) The American Petroleum Institute has developed a methodology for determining the average tax rate on a gallon of fuel. Rates may include any of the following: excise taxes, environmental fees, storage tank fees, other fees or taxes, general sales tax, and local taxes; (2) The federal excise tax of $1.0066 per pack and local taxes are not included; (3) Rates are those applicable to off-premise sales of 40% alcohol by volume (a.b.v.) distilled spirits in 750ml containers. Local excise taxes are excluded; (4) Rates are those applicable to off-premise sales of 11% a.b.v. non-carbonated wine in 750ml containers; (5) Rates are those applicable to off-premise sales of 4.7% a.b.v. beer in 12 ounce containers.
Source: Tax Foundation, 2021 Facts & Figures: How Does Your State Compare?

State Business Tax Climate Index Rankings

State	Overall Rank	Corporate Tax Rank	Individual Income Tax Rank	Sales Tax Rank	Property Tax Rank	Unemployment Insurance Tax Rank
Texas	11	47	6	35	36	16

Note: The index is a measure of how each state's tax laws affect economic performance. The lower the rank, the more favorable a state's tax system is for business. States without a given tax are given a ranking of 1. The scores/rankings for the District of Columbia do not affect other states. The 2021 index represents the tax climate as of July 1, 2020.
Source: Tax Foundation, State Business Tax Climate Index 2021

TRANSPORTATION

Means of Transportation to Work

Area	Car/Truck/Van Drove Alone	Car/Truck/Van Car-pooled	Public Transportation Bus	Public Transportation Subway	Public Transportation Railroad	Bicycle	Walked	Other Means	Worked at Home
City	76.7	11.0	2.9	0.4	0.3	0.2	2.1	1.5	4.9
MSA[1]	80.6	9.7	0.9	0.2	0.2	0.1	1.2	1.2	5.8
U.S.	76.3	9.0	2.4	1.9	0.6	0.5	2.7	1.4	5.2

Note: Figures are percentages and cover workers 16 years of age and older; (1) Figures cover the Dallas-Fort Worth-Arlington, TX Metropolitan Statistical Area
Source: U.S. Census Bureau, 2015-2019 American Community Survey 5-Year Estimates

Travel Time to Work

Area	Less Than 10 Minutes	10 to 19 Minutes	20 to 29 Minutes	30 to 44 Minutes	45 to 59 Minutes	60 to 89 Minutes	90 Minutes or More
City	7.9	26.6	23.0	26.5	8.0	5.9	2.0
MSA[1]	8.6	25.0	21.3	25.6	10.5	7.0	2.1
U.S.	12.2	28.4	20.8	20.8	8.3	6.4	2.9

Note: Note: Figures are percentages and include workers 16 years old and over; (1) Figures cover the Dallas-Fort Worth-Arlington, TX Metropolitan Statistical Area
Source: U.S. Census Bureau, 2015-2019 American Community Survey 5-Year Estimates

Key Congestion Measures

Measure	1982	1992	2002	2012	2017
Annual Hours of Delay, Total (000)	50,235	85,300	137,340	198,340	224,883
Annual Hours of Delay, Per Auto Commuter	36	42	46	57	67
Annual Congestion Cost, Total (million $)	376	896	1,844	3,517	4,116
Annual Congestion Cost, Per Auto Commuter ($)	636	742	932	1,055	1,161

Note: Covers the Dallas-Fort Worth-Arlington TX urban area
Source: Texas A&M Transportation Institute, 2019 Urban Mobility Report

Freeway Travel Time Index

Measure	1982	1987	1992	1997	2002	2007	2012	2017
Urban Area Index[1]	1.18	1.19	1.21	1.23	1.23	1.27	1.26	1.26
Urban Area Rank[1,2]	5	8	11	15	26	20	21	23

Note: Freeway Travel Time Index—the ratio of travel time in the peak period to the travel time at free-flow conditions. For example, a value of 1.30 indicates a 20-minute free-flow trip takes 26 minutes in the peak (20 minutes x 1.30 = 26 minutes); (1) Covers the Dallas-Fort Worth-Arlington TX urban area; (2) Rank is based on 101 larger urban areas (#1 = highest travel time index)
Source: Texas A&M Transportation Institute, 2019 Urban Mobility Report

Public Transportation

Agency Name / Mode of Transportation	Vehicles Operated in Maximum Service[1]	Annual Unlinked Passenger Trips[2] (in thous.)	Annual Passenger Miles[3] (in thous.)
Dallas Area Rapid Transit Authority (DART)			
Bus (directly operated)	561	37,230.8	146,291.3
Commuter Rail (purchased transportation)	23	2,007.0	35,381.6
Demand Response (purchased transportation)	107	415.0	4,153.8
Demand Response Taxi (purchased transportation)	115	590.6	7,396.6
Light Rail (directly operated)	117	28,335.8	227,090.3
Streetcar Rail (directly operated)	2	226.5	355.7
Vanpool (purchased transportation)	167	495.9	18,228.2

Note: (1) Number of revenue vehicles operated by the given mode and type of service to meet the annual maximum service requirement. This is the revenue vehicle count during the peak season of the year; on the week and day that maximum service is provided. Vehicles operated in maximum service (VOMS) exclude atypical days and one-time special events; (2) Number of passengers who boarded public transportation vehicles. Passengers are counted each time they board a vehicle no matter how many vehicles they use to travel from their origin to their destination. (3) Sum of the distances ridden by all passengers during the entire fiscal year.
Source: Federal Transit Administration, National Transit Database, 2019

Air Transportation

Airport Name and Code / Type of Service	Passenger Airlines[1]	Passenger Enplanements	Freight Carriers[2]	Freight (lbs)
Dallas-Fort Worth International (DFW)				
Domestic service (U.S. carriers - 2020)	24	16,962,314	20	585,663,631
International service (U.S. carriers - 2019)	10	3,735,113	6	74,097,599
Dallas Love Field (DAL)				
Domestic service (U.S. carriers - 2020)	19	3,666,889	7	14,081,611
International service (U.S. carriers - 2019)	3	975	1	54,209

Note: (1) Includes all U.S.-based major, minor and commuter airlines that carried at least one passenger during the year; (2) Includes all U.S.-based airlines and freight carriers that transported at least one pound of freight during the year.
Source: Bureau of Transportation Statistics, The Intermodal Transportation Database, Air Carriers: T-100 Domestic Market (U.S. Carriers), 2020; Bureau of Transportation Statistics, The Intermodal Transportation Database, Air Carriers: T-100 International Market (U.S. Carriers), 2019

BUSINESSES

Major Business Headquarters

Company Name	Industry	Fortune[1]	Forbes[2]
AT&T	Telecommunications	9	-
Austin Industries	Construction	-	179
Builders FirstSource	Building Materials, Glass	425	-
Dean Foods	Food Consumer Products	421	-
EnLink Midstream	Pipelines	483	-
Energy Transfer	Pipelines	59	-
HollyFrontier	Petroleum Refining	184	-
Hunt Consolidated/Hunt Oil	Oil & Gas Operations	-	111
Neiman Marcus Group	Retailing	-	168
Sammons Enterprises	Multicompany	-	73
Southwest Airlines	Airlines	141	-
Tenet Healthcare	Health Care, Medical Facilities	174	-
Texas Instruments	Semiconductors and Other Electronic Components	222	-
Vistra Energy	Energy	270	-

Note: (1) Companies that produce a 10-K are ranked 1 to 500 based on 2019 revenue; (2) All private companies with at least $2 billion in annual revenue through the end of their most current fiscal year are ranked 1 to 219; companies listed are headquartered in the city; dashes indicate no ranking
Source: Fortune, "Fortune 500," June/July 2020; Forbes, "America's Largest Private Companies," 2020

Fastest-Growing Businesses

According to *Inc.*, Dallas is home to six of America's 500 fastest-growing private companies: **Case Energy Partners** (#7); **Allata** (#52); **Almaguer Logistics** (#264); **Embark** (#327); **Go Energistics** (#335); **Integra Mission Critical** (#414). Criteria: must be an independent, privately-held, for-profit, U.S. corporation, proprietorship or partnership as of December 31, 2019; revenues must be at least $100,000 in 2016 and $2 million in 2019; must have four-year operating/sales history. *Inc., "America's 500 Fastest-Growing Private Companies," 2020*

According to *Fortune*, Dallas is home to three of the 100 fastest-growing companies in the world: **Texas Pacific Land Trust** (#3); **Copart** (#74); **Veritex Holdings** (#75). Companies were ranked by their revenue growth rate; their EPS growth rate; and their three-year annualized total return to investors for the period ending June 30, 2020. Criteria for inclusion: a company, foreign or domestic, must trade on a major U.S. stock exchange; must file quarterly reports with the SEC; must have a minimum market capitalization of $250 million; must have a stock price of at least $5 on June 30, 2020; must have been trading continuously since June 30, 2017; must have revenue and net income for the four quarters ended on or before April 30, 2020, of at least $50 million and $10 million, respectively; and must have posted a compound annual growth in revenue and earnings per share of at least 15% annually over the three years ending on or before April 30, 2020. Real estate investment trusts, limited-liability companies, limited parterships, business development companies, closed-end investment firms, companies about to be acquired, and companies that lost money in the quarter ending April 30, 2020 were excluded. *Fortune, "100 Fastest-Growing Companies," 2020*

According to *Initiative for a Competitive Inner City (ICIC)*, Dallas is home to one of America's 100 fastest-growing "inner city" companies: **OrderMyGear** (#16). Criteria for inclusion: company must be headquartered in or have 51 percent or more of its physical operations in an economically distressed urban area; must be an independent, for-profit corporation, partnership or proprietorship; must have 10 or more employees and have a five-year sales history that includes sales of at least $200,000 in the base year and at least $1 million in the current year with no decrease in sales over the two most recent years. Companies were ranked overall by revenue growth over the five-year period between 2015 and 2019. *Initiative for a Competitive Inner City (ICIC), "Inner City 100 Companies," 2020*

According to Deloitte, Dallas is home to three of North America's 500 fastest-growing high-technology companies: **Qentelli** (#194); **o9 Solutions, Inc.** (#235); **Zix Corp** (#477). Companies are ranked by percentage growth in revenue over a four-year period. Criteria for inclusion: company must be headquartered within North America; must own proprietary intellectual property or technology that is sold to customers in products that contributes to a significant portion of the company's operating revenue; must have been in business for a minumum of four years with 2016 operating revenues of at least $50,000 USD/CD and 2019 operating revenues of at least $5 million USD/CD. *Deloitte, 2020 Technology Fast 500™*

Minority Business Opportunity

Dallas is home to one company which is on the *Black Enterprise* Industrial/Service list (100 largest companies based on gross sales): **Parrish Restaurants Ltd.** (#55). Criteria: operational in previous calendar year; at least 51% black-owned and manufactures/owns the product it sells or provides industrial or consumer services. Brokerages, real estate firms and firms that provide professional services are not eligible. *Black Enterprise, B.E. 100s, 2019*

Dallas is home to one company which is on the *Black Enterprise* Private Equity list (10 largest private equity firms based on capital under management): **Pharos Capital Group** (#8). Criteria: company must be operational in previous calendar year and be at least 51% black-owned. *Black Enterprise, B.E. 100s, 2019*

Living Environment

COST OF LIVING

Cost of Living Index

Composite Index	Groceries	Housing	Utilities	Transportation	Health Care	Misc. Goods/Services
107.9	99.9	116.4	107.8	93.3	114.0	107.2

Note: The Cost of Living Index measures regional differences in the cost of consumer goods and services, excluding taxes and non-consumer expenditures, for professional and managerial households in the top income quintile. It is based on more than 50,000 prices covering almost 60 different items for which prices are collected three times a year by chambers of commerce, economic development organizations or university applied economic centers in each participating urban area. The numbers shown should be read as a percentage above or below the national average of 100. For example, a value of 115.4 in the groceries column indicates that grocery prices are 15.4% higher than the national average. Small differences in the index numbers should not be interpreted as significant; Figures cover the Dallas TX urban area.
Source: The Council for Community and Economic Research, Cost of Living Index, 2020

Grocery Prices

Area[1]	T-Bone Steak ($/pound)	Frying Chicken ($/pound)	Whole Milk ($/half gal.)	Eggs ($/dozen)	Orange Juice ($/64 oz.)	Coffee ($/11.5 oz.)
City[2]	10.44	1.48	1.97	1.15	3.45	4.51
Avg.	11.78	1.39	2.05	1.47	3.57	4.34
Min.	8.03	0.94	1.03	0.74	2.94	3.02
Max.	15.86	2.65	4.31	3.77	5.44	8.69

Note: (1) Values for the local area are compared with the average, minimum and maximum values for all 284 areas in the Cost of Living Index; (2) Figures cover the Dallas TX urban area; **T-Bone Steak** (price per pound); **Frying Chicken** (price per pound, whole fryer); **Whole Milk** (half gallon carton); **Eggs** (price per dozen, Grade A, large); **Orange Juice** (64 oz. Tropicana or Florida Natural); **Coffee** (11.5 oz. can, vacuum-packed, Maxwell House, Hills Bros, or Folgers).
Source: The Council for Community and Economic Research, Cost of Living Index, 2020

Housing and Utility Costs

Area[1]	New Home Price ($)	Apartment Rent ($/month)	All Electric ($/month)	Part Electric ($/month)	Other Energy ($/month)	Telephone ($/month)
City[2]	371,745	1,705	-	133.58	55.19	185.50
Avg.	368,594	1,168	170.86	100.47	65.28	184.30
Min.	190,567	502	91.58	31.42	26.08	169.60
Max.	2,227,806	4,738	470.38	280.31	280.06	206.50

Note: (1) Values for the local area are compared with the average, minimum and maximum values for all 284 areas in the Cost of Living Index; (2) Figures cover the Dallas TX urban area; **New Home Price** (2,400 sf living area, 8,000 sf lot, in urban area with full utilities); **Apartment Rent** (950 sf 2 bedroom/1.5 or 2 bath, unfurnished, excluding all utilities except water); **All Electric** (average monthly cost for an all-electric home); **Part Electric** (average monthly cost for a part-electric home); **Other Energy** (average monthly cost for natural gas, fuel oil, coal, wood, and any other forms of energy except electricity); **Telephone** (price includes the base monthly rate plus taxes and fees for three lines of mobile phone service).
Source: The Council for Community and Economic Research, Cost of Living Index, 2020

Health Care, Transportation, and Other Costs

Area[1]	Doctor ($/visit)	Dentist ($/visit)	Optometrist ($/visit)	Gasoline ($/gallon)	Beauty Salon ($/visit)	Men's Shirt ($)
City[2]	121.08	133.84	97.86	1.92	44.45	38.73
Avg.	115.44	99.32	108.10	2.21	39.27	31.37
Min.	36.68	59.00	51.36	1.71	19.00	11.00
Max.	219.00	153.10	250.97	3.46	82.05	58.33

Note: (1) Values for the local area are compared with the average, minimum and maximum values for all 284 areas in the Cost of Living Index; (2) Figures cover the Dallas TX urban area; **Doctor** (general practitioners routine exam of an established patient); **Dentist** (adult teeth cleaning and periodic oral examination); **Optometrist** (full vision eye exam for established adult patient); **Gasoline** (one gallon regular unleaded, national brand, including all taxes, cash price at self-service pump if available); **Beauty Salon** (woman's shampoo, trim, and blow-dry); **Men's Shirt** (cotton/polyester dress shirt, pinpoint weave, long sleeves).
Source: The Council for Community and Economic Research, Cost of Living Index, 2020

HOUSING

Homeownership Rate

Area	2012 (%)	2013 (%)	2014 (%)	2015 (%)	2016 (%)	2017 (%)	2018 (%)	2019 (%)	2020 (%)
MSA[1]	61.8	59.9	57.7	57.8	59.7	61.8	62.0	60.6	64.7
U.S.	65.4	65.1	64.5	63.7	63.4	63.9	64.4	64.6	66.6

Note: (1) Figures cover the Dallas-Fort Worth-Arlington, TX Metropolitan Statistical Area
Source: U.S. Census Bureau, Housing Vacancies and Homeownership Annual Statistics: 2012-2020

House Price Index (HPI)

Area	National Ranking[2]	Quarterly Change (%)	One-Year Change (%)	Five-Year Change (%)	Since 1991Q1 (%)
MD[1]	206	2.07	4.81	38.75	203.48
U.S.[3]	–	3.81	10.77	38.99	205.12

Note: The HPI is a weighted repeat sales index. It measures average price changes in repeat sales or refinancings on the same properties. This information is obtained by reviewing repeat mortgage transactions on single-family properties whose mortgages have been purchased or securitized by Fannie Mae or Freddie Mac since January 1975; (1) Figures cover the Dallas-Plano-Irving, TX Metropolitan Division; (2) Rankings are based on annual percentage change for all metro areas containing at least 15,000 transactions over the last 10 years and ranges from 1 to 253; (3) figures based on a weighted average of Census Division estimates using a seasonally adjusted, purchase-only index; all figures are for the period ending December 31, 2020
Source: Federal Housing Finance Agency, Change in Metropolitan Area House Price Indexes, April 7, 2021

Median Single-Family Home Prices

Area	2018	2019	2020p	Percent Change 2019 to 2020
MSA[1]	260.0	268.6	287.2	6.9
U.S. Average	261.6	274.6	299.9	9.2

Note: Figures are median sales prices of existing single-family homes in thousands of dollars; (p) preliminary; (1) Figures cover the Dallas-Fort Worth-Arlington, TX Metropolitan Statistical Area
Source: National Association of Realtors, Median Sales Price of Existing Single-Family Homes for Metropolitan Areas, 4th Quarter 2020

Qualifying Income Based on Median Sales Price of Existing Single-Family Homes

Area	With 5% Down ($)	With 10% Down ($)	With 20% Down ($)
MSA[1]	56,156	53,201	47,290
U.S. Average	59,266	56,147	49,908

Note: Figures are preliminary; Qualifying income is based on a mortgage rate of 2.81%. Monthly principal and interest payment is limited to 25% of income; (1) Figures cover the Dallas-Fort Worth-Arlington, TX Metropolitan Statistical Area
Source: National Association of Realtors, Qualifying Income Based on Median Sales Price of Existing Single-Family Homes for Metropolitan Areas, 4th Quarter 2020

Home Value Distribution

Area	Under $50,000	$50,000 -$99,999	$100,000 -$149,999	$150,000 -$199,999	$200,000 -$299,999	$300,000 -$499,999	$500,000 -$999,999	$1,000,000 or more
City	6.7	19.2	15.4	10.7	12.6	17.6	13.2	4.6
MSA[1]	4.5	11.1	14.5	15.9	23.1	20.9	7.9	1.9
U.S.	6.9	12.0	13.3	14.0	19.6	19.3	11.4	3.4

Note: Figures are percentages and cover owner-occupied housing units; (1) Figures cover the Dallas-Fort Worth-Arlington, TX Metropolitan Statistical Area
Source: U.S. Census Bureau, 2015-2019 American Community Survey 5-Year Estimates

Year Housing Structure Built

Area	2010 or Later	2000 -2009	1990 -1999	1980 -1989	1970 -1979	1960 -1969	1950 -1959	1940 -1949	Before 1940	Median Year
City	7.1	10.6	10.3	17.2	17.3	13.4	13.7	5.2	5.2	1977
MSA[1]	10.0	20.0	16.1	18.1	14.2	8.7	7.5	2.7	2.7	1988
U.S.	5.2	14.0	13.9	13.4	15.2	10.6	10.3	4.9	12.6	1978

Note: Figures are percentages except for Median Year; Note: (1) Figures cover the Dallas-Fort Worth-Arlington, TX Metropolitan Statistical Area
Source: U.S. Census Bureau, 2015-2019 American Community Survey 5-Year Estimates

Gross Monthly Rent

Area	Under $500	$500 -$999	$1,000 -$1,499	$1,500 -$1,999	$2,000 -$2,499	$2,500 -$2,999	$3,000 and up	Median ($)
City	4.3	41.0	36.7	11.7	3.6	1.4	1.1	1,052
MSA[1]	3.4	33.2	40.0	16.3	4.7	1.4	1.0	1,139
U.S.	9.4	36.2	30.0	14.0	5.6	2.4	2.4	1,062

Note: Figures are percentages except for Median; Gross rent is the contract rent plus the estimated average monthly cost of utilities (electricity, gas, and water and sewer) and fuels (oil, coal, kerosene, wood, etc.) if these are paid by the renter (or paid for the renter by someone else); (1) Figures cover the Dallas-Fort Worth-Arlington, TX Metropolitan Statistical Area
Source: U.S. Census Bureau, 2015-2019 American Community Survey 5-Year Estimates

HEALTH

Health Risk Factors

Category	MD[1] (%)	U.S. (%)
Adults aged 18–64 who have any kind of health care coverage	80.1	87.3
Adults who reported being in good or better health	83.9	82.4
Adults who have been told they have high blood cholesterol	30.9	33.0
Adults who have been told they have high blood pressure	31.0	32.3
Adults who are current smokers	13.1	17.1
Adults who currently use E-cigarettes	3.1	4.6
Adults who currently use chewing tobacco, snuff, or snus	2.5	4.0
Adults who are heavy drinkers[2]	7.6	6.3
Adults who are binge drinkers[3]	16.9	17.4
Adults who are overweight (BMI 25.0 - 29.9)	37.2	35.3
Adults who are obese (BMI 30.0 - 99.8)	28.4	31.3
Adults who participated in any physical activities in the past month	71.2	74.4
Adults who always or nearly always wears a seat belt	96.3	94.3

Note: (1) Figures cover the Dallas-Plano-Irving, TX Metropolitan Division; (2) Heavy drinkers are classified as adult men having more than 14 drinks per week and adult women having more than 7 drinks per week; (3) Binge drinkers are classified as males having five or more drinks on one occasion or females having four or more drinks on one occasion
Source: Centers for Disease Control and Prevention, Behaviorial Risk Factor Surveillance System, SMART: Selected Metropolitan Area Risk Trends, 2017

Acute and Chronic Health Conditions

Category	MD[1] (%)	U.S. (%)
Adults who have ever been told they had a heart attack	n/a	4.2
Adults who have ever been told they have angina or coronary heart disease	n/a	3.9
Adults who have ever been told they had a stroke	n/a	3.0
Adults who have ever been told they have asthma	13.7	14.2
Adults who have ever been told they have arthritis	17.7	24.9
Adults who have ever been told they have diabetes[2]	10.8	10.5
Adults who have ever been told they had skin cancer	5.7	6.2
Adults who have ever been told they had any other types of cancer	3.9	7.1
Adults who have ever been told they have COPD	2.8	6.5
Adults who have ever been told they have kidney disease	n/a	3.0
Adults who have ever been told they have a form of depression	14.2	20.5

Note: n/a not available; (1) Figures cover the Dallas-Plano-Irving, TX Metropolitan Division; (2) Figures do not include pregnancy-related, borderline, or pre-diabetes
Source: Centers for Disease Control and Prevention, Behaviorial Risk Factor Surveillance System, SMART: Selected Metropolitan Area Risk Trends, 2017

Health Screening and Vaccination Rates

Category	MD[1] (%)	U.S. (%)
Adults aged 65+ who have had flu shot within the past year	53.7	60.7
Adults aged 65+ who have ever had a pneumonia vaccination	78.1	75.4
Adults who have ever been tested for HIV	42.6	36.1
Adults who have ever had the shingles or zoster vaccine?	29.0	28.9
Adults who have had their blood cholesterol checked within the last five years	86.9	85.9

Note: n/a not available; (1) Figures cover the Dallas-Plano-Irving, TX Metropolitan Division.
Source: Centers for Disease Control and Prevention, Behaviorial Risk Factor Surveillance System, SMART: Selected Metropolitan Area Risk Trends, 2017

Disability Status

Category	MD[1] (%)	U.S. (%)
Adults who reported being deaf	n/a	6.7
Are you blind or have serious difficulty seeing, even when wearing glasses?	4.4	4.5
Are you limited in any way in any of your usual activities due of arthritis?	10.1	12.9
Do you have difficulty doing errands alone?	7.1	6.8
Do you have difficulty dressing or bathing?	n/a	3.6
Do you have serious difficulty concentrating/remembering/making decisions?	7.2	10.7
Do you have serious difficulty walking or climbing stairs?	11.7	13.6

Note: n/a not available; (1) Figures cover the Dallas-Plano-Irving, TX Metropolitan Division.
Source: Centers for Disease Control and Prevention, Behaviorial Risk Factor Surveillance System, SMART: Selected Metropolitan Area Risk Trends, 2017

Mortality Rates for the Top 10 Causes of Death in the U.S.

ICD-10[a] Sub-Chapter	ICD-10[a] Code	Age-Adjusted Mortality Rate[1] per 100,000 population County[2]	U.S.
Malignant neoplasms	C00-C97	144.6	149.2
Ischaemic heart diseases	I20-I25	86.1	90.5
Other forms of heart disease	I30-I51	48.0	52.2
Chronic lower respiratory diseases	J40-J47	33.8	39.6
Other degenerative diseases of the nervous system	G30-G31	54.9	37.6
Cerebrovascular diseases	I60-I69	47.2	37.2
Other external causes of accidental injury	W00-X59	26.1	36.1
Organic, including symptomatic, mental disorders	F01-F09	24.0	29.4
Hypertensive diseases	I10-I15	31.6	24.1
Diabetes mellitus	E10-E14	19.9	21.5

Note: (a) ICD-10 = International Classification of Diseases 10th Revision; (1) Mortality rates are a three-year average covering 2017-2019; (2) Figures cover Dallas County.
Source: Centers for Disease Control and Prevention, National Center for Health Statistics. Underlying Cause of Death 1999-2019 on CDC WONDER Online Database

Mortality Rates for Selected Causes of Death

ICD-10[a] Sub-Chapter	ICD-10[a] Code	Age-Adjusted Mortality Rate[1] per 100,000 population County[2]	U.S.
Assault	X85-Y09	8.3	6.0
Diseases of the liver	K70-K76	14.9	14.4
Human immunodeficiency virus (HIV) disease	B20-B24	3.2	1.5
Influenza and pneumonia	J09-J18	12.5	13.8
Intentional self-harm	X60-X84	11.6	14.1
Malnutrition	E40-E46	3.1	2.3
Obesity and other hyperalimentation	E65-E68	1.9	2.1
Renal failure	N17-N19	16.4	12.6
Transport accidents	V01-V99	11.8	12.3
Viral hepatitis	B15-B19	1.4	1.2

Note: (a) ICD-10 = International Classification of Diseases 10th Revision; (1) Mortality rates are a three-year average covering 2017-2019; (2) Figures cover Dallas County; Data are suppressed when the data meet the criteria for confidentiality constraints; Mortality rates are flagged as unreliable when the rate would be calculated with a numerator of 20 or less.
Source: Centers for Disease Control and Prevention, National Center for Health Statistics. Underlying Cause of Death 1999-2019 on CDC WONDER Online Database

Health Insurance Coverage

Area	With Health Insurance	With Private Health Insurance	With Public Health Insurance	Without Health Insurance	Population Under Age 19 Without Health Insurance
City	76.4	51.8	30.3	23.6	14.8
MSA[1]	83.6	66.0	24.9	16.4	11.0
U.S.	91.2	67.9	35.1	8.8	5.1

Note: Figures are percentages that cover the civilian noninstitutionalized population; (1) Figures cover the Dallas-Fort Worth-Arlington, TX Metropolitan Statistical Area
Source: U.S. Census Bureau, 2015-2019 American Community Survey 5-Year Estimates

Number of Medical Professionals

Area	MDs[3]	DOs[3,4]	Dentists	Podiatrists	Chiropractors	Optometrists
County[1] (number)	8,821	538	2,288	105	963	356
County[1] (rate[2])	335.5	20.5	86.8	4.0	36.5	13.5
U.S. (rate[2])	282.9	22.7	71.2	6.2	28.1	16.9

48113
Note: Data as of 2019 unless noted; (1) Data covers Dallas County; (2) Rate per 100,000 population; (3) Data as of 2018 and includes all active, non-federal physicians; (4) Doctor of Osteopathic Medicine
Source: U.S. Department of Health and Human Services, Health Resources and Services Administration, Bureau of Health Professions, Area Resource File (ARF) 2019-2020

Best Hospitals

According to *U.S. News,* the Dallas-Plano-Irving, TX metro area is home to four of the best hospitals in the U.S.: **Baylor Scott and White The Heart Hospital Plano** (1 adult specialty); **Baylor University Medical Center** (2 adult specialties); **Parkland Health and Hospital System-Dallas** (1 adult specialty); **UT Southwestern Medical Center** (10 adult specialties). The hospitals listed were nationally ranked in at least one of 16 adult or 10 pediatric specialties. Only 134 hospitals nationwide were nationally ranked in one or more adult or pediatric specialty; this number increases to 178 counting specialized centers within hospitals. Twenty hospitals in the U.S. made the Honor Roll. The Best Hospitals Honor Roll takes both the national rankings and the procedure and condition ratings into account. Hospitals received points if they were nationally ranked in one of the 16 adult specialties—the higher they ranked, the more points they got—and how many ratings of "high performing" they earned in the 10 procedures and conditions. *U.S. News Online, "America's Best Hospitals 2020-21"*

According to *U.S. News*, the Dallas-Plano-Irving, TX metro area is home to one of the best children's hospitals in the U.S.: **Children's Medical Center Dallas** (10 pediatric specialties). The hospital listed was highly ranked in at least one of 10 pediatric specialties. Eighty-eight children's hospitals in the U.S. were nationally ranked in at least one specialty. Hospitals received points for being ranked in a specialty, and the 10 hospitals with the most points across the 10 specialties make up the Honor Roll. *U.S. News Online, "America's Best Children's Hospitals 2020-21"*

EDUCATION

Public School District Statistics

District Name	Schls	Pupils	Pupil/Teacher Ratio	Minority Pupils[1] (%)	Free Lunch Eligible[2] (%)	IEP[3] (%)
A W Brown Leadership Academy	2	2,084	18.0	99.7	58.0	4.8
Dallas ISD	240	155,119	15.5	94.3	86.2	8.9
Harmony Science Academy (Waco)	16	9,763	14.9	81.8	53.0	8.0
Highland Park ISD	7	6,840	15.5	17.0	n/a	9.3
Texans Can Academies	13	5,071	21.1	92.6	78.4	8.7
Trinity Basin Preparatory	2	3,496	16.8	98.9	79.8	7.9

Note: Table includes school districts with 2,000 or more students; (1) Percentage of students that are not non-Hispanic white; (2) Percentage of students that are eligible for the free lunch program; (3) Percentage of students that have an Individualized Education Program.
Source: U.S. Department of Education, National Center for Education Statistics, Common Core of Data, Local Education Agency (School District) Universe Survey: School Year 2018-2019; U.S. Department of Education, National Center for Education Statistics, Common Core of Data, Public Elementary/Secondary School Universe Survey: School Year 2018-2019

Best High Schools

According to *U.S. News*, Dallas is home to 11 of the top 500 high schools in the U.S.: **The School for the Talented and Gifted (TAG)** (#6); **Irma Lerma Rangel Young Women's Leadership School** (#10); **Science and Engineering Magnet School (SEM)** (#17); **Judge Barefoot Sanders Law Magnet** (#165); **Booker T. Washington SPVA** (#172); **Highland Park High School** (#238); **Rosie Sorrells Education and Social Services High School** (#244); **School of Health Professions** (#270); **Trinidad Garza Early College at Mt View** (#322); **Dr. Wright L Lassiter Jr Early College High School** (#335); **School of Business and Management** (#337). Nearly 18,000 public, magnet and charter schools were ranked based on their performance on state assessments and how well they prepare students for college. *U.S. News & World Report, "Best High Schools 2020"*

Highest Level of Education

Area	Less than H.S.	H.S. Diploma	Some College, No Deg.	Associate Degree	Bachelor's Degree	Master's Degree	Prof. School Degree	Doctorate Degree
City	22.5	21.7	17.8	4.6	21.0	8.3	2.9	1.1
MSA[1]	14.4	22.3	21.1	7.0	23.0	9.2	1.9	1.1
U.S.	12.0	27.0	20.4	8.5	19.8	8.8	2.1	1.4

Note: Figures cover persons age 25 and over; (1) Figures cover the Dallas-Fort Worth-Arlington, TX Metropolitan Statistical Area
Source: U.S. Census Bureau, 2015-2019 American Community Survey 5-Year Estimates

Educational Attainment by Race

Area	High School Graduate or Higher (%)					Bachelor's Degree or Higher (%)				
	Total	White	Black	Asian	Hisp.[2]	Total	White	Black	Asian	Hisp.[2]
City	77.5	75.2	86.8	85.5	51.1	33.4	38.9	19.4	65.8	11.0
MSA[1]	85.6	85.9	91.0	88.8	60.3	35.2	35.8	27.4	62.0	14.0
U.S.	88.0	89.9	86.0	87.1	68.7	32.1	33.5	21.6	54.3	16.4

Note: Figures shown cover persons 25 years old and over; (1) Figures cover the Dallas-Fort Worth-Arlington, TX Metropolitan Statistical Area; (2) People of Hispanic origin can be of any race
Source: U.S. Census Bureau, 2015-2019 American Community Survey 5-Year Estimates

School Enrollment by Grade and Control

Area	Preschool (%)		Kindergarten (%)		Grades 1 - 4 (%)		Grades 5 - 8 (%)		Grades 9 - 12 (%)	
	Public	Private	Public	Private	Public	Private	Public	Private	Public	Private
City	69.2	30.8	91.0	9.0	92.0	8.0	91.7	8.3	91.6	8.4
MSA[1]	58.9	41.1	90.2	9.8	92.6	7.4	92.3	7.7	92.4	7.6
U.S.	59.1	40.9	87.6	12.4	89.5	10.5	89.4	10.6	90.1	9.9

Note: Figures shown cover persons 3 years old and over; (1) Figures cover the Dallas-Fort Worth-Arlington, TX Metropolitan Statistical Area
Source: U.S. Census Bureau, 2015-2019 American Community Survey 5-Year Estimates

Higher Education

Four-Year Colleges			Two-Year Colleges			Medical Schools[1]	Law Schools[2]	Voc/ Tech[3]
Public	Private Non-profit	Private For-profit	Public	Private Non-profit	Private For-profit			
2	8	4	3	1	5	1	2	8

Note: Figures cover institutions located within the city limits and include main campuses only; (1) includes schools accredited by the Liaison Committee on Medical Education and the American Osteopathic Association's Commission on Osteopathic College Accreditation; (2) includes ABA-accredited schools, schools with provisional ABA accreditation, and state accredited schools; (3) includes all schools with programs that are less than 2 years.
Source: National Center for Education Statistics, Integrated Postsecondary Education System (IPEDS), 2019-20; Wikipedia, List of Medical Schools in the United States, accessed April 2, 2021; Wikipedia, List of Law Schools in the United States, accessed April 2, 2021

According to *U.S. News & World Report*, the Dallas-Plano-Irving, TX metro division is home to two of the top 200 national universities in the U.S.: **Southern Methodist University** (#66 tie); **University of Texas at Dallas** (#143 tie). The indicators used to capture academic quality fall into a number of categories: assessment by administrators at peer institutions; retention of students; faculty resources; student selectivity; financial resources; alumni giving; high school counselor ratings of colleges; and graduation rate. *U.S. News & World Report*, "America's Best Colleges 2021"

According to *U.S. News & World Report*, the Dallas-Plano-Irving, TX metro division is home to one of the top 100 law schools in the U.S.: **Southern Methodist University (Dedman)** (#52). The rankings are based on a weighted average of 12 measures of quality: peer assessment score; assessment score by lawyers/judges; median LSAT scores; median undergrad GPA; acceptance rate; employment rates for graduates; placement success; bar passage rate; faculty resources; expenditures per student; student/faculty ratio; and library resources. *U.S. News & World Report*, "America's Best Graduate Schools, Law, 2022"

According to *U.S. News & World Report*, the Dallas-Plano-Irving, TX metro division is home to one of the top 75 medical schools for research in the U.S.: **University of Texas Southwestern Medical Center** (#26). The rankings are based on a weighted average of 11 measures of quality: quality assessment; peer assessment score; assessment score by residency directors; research activity; total research activity; average research activity per faculty member; student selectivity; median MCAT total score; median undergraduate GPA; acceptance rate; and faculty resources. *U.S. News & World Report*, "America's Best Graduate Schools, Medical, 2022"

According to *U.S. News & World Report*, the Dallas-Plano-Irving, TX metro division is home to two of the top 75 business schools in the U.S.: **University of Texas—Dallas** (#31 tie); **Southern Methodist University (Cox)** (#44 tie). The rankings are based on a weighted average of the following nine measures: quality assessment; peer assessment; recruiter assessment; placement success; mean starting salary and bonus; student selectivity; mean GMAT and GRE scores; mean undergraduate GPA; and acceptance rate. *U.S. News & World Report*, "America's Best Graduate Schools, Business, 2022"

EMPLOYERS

Major Employers

Company Name	Industry
AMR Corporation	Air transportation, scheduled
Associates First Capital Corporation	Mortgage bankers
Baylor University Medical Center	General medical & surgical hospitals
Children's Medical Center Dallas	Specialty hospitals, except psychiatric
Combat Support Associates	Engineering services
County of Dallas	County government
Dallas County Hospital District	General medical & surgical hospitals
Fort Worth Independent School District	Public elementary & secondary schools
Housewares Holding Company	Toasters, electric: household
HP Enterprise Services	Computer integrated systems design
J.C. Penney Company	Department stores
JCP Publications Corp.	Department stores
L-3 Communications Corporation	Business economic service
Odyssey HealthCare	Home health care services
Romano's Macaroni Grill	Italian restaurant
SFG Management	Milk processing (pasteurizing, homogenizing, bottling)
Texas Instruments Incorporated	Semiconductors & related devices
University of North Texas	Colleges & universities
University of Texas SW Medical Center	Accident & health insurance
Verizon Business Global	Telephone communication, except radio

Note: Companies shown are located within the Dallas-Fort Worth-Arlington, TX Metropolitan Statistical Area.
Source: Hoovers.com; Wikipedia

Best Companies to Work For

Encompass Health Home Health & Hospice; Ryan, headquartered in Dallas, are among "The 100 Best Companies to Work For." To pick the best companies, *Fortune* partnered with the Great Place to Work Institute. Two-thirds of a company's score is based on the results of the Institute's Trust Index survey, which is sent to a random sample of employees from each company. The questions related to attitudes about management's credibility, job satisfaction, and camaraderie. The other third of the scoring is based on the company's responses to the Institute's Culture Audit, which includes detailed questions about pay and benefit programs, and a series of open-ended questions about hiring practices, internal communication, training, recognition programs, and diversity efforts. Any company that is at least five years old with more than 1,000 U.S. employees is eligible. *Fortune, "The 100 Best Companies to Work For," 2020*

Texas Instruments, headquartered in Dallas, is among the "100 Best Companies for Working Mothers." Criteria: paid time off and leaves; workforce profile; benefits; women's issues and advancement; flexible work; company culture and work life programs. *Working Mother, "100 Best Companies for Working Mothers," 2020*

JCPenney, headquartered in Dallas, is among the "Best Companies for Multicultural Women." *Working Mother* selected 50 companies based on a detailed application completed by public and private firms based in the United States, excluding government agencies, companies in the human resources field and non-autonomous divisions. Companies supplied data about the hiring, pay, and promotion of multicultural employees. Applications focused on representation of multicultural women, recruitment, retention and advancement programs, and company culture. *Working Mother, "Best Companies for Multicultural Women," 2020*

Axxess, headquartered in Dallas, is among the "100 Best Places to Work in IT." To qualify, companies had to be U.S.-based organizations or be non-U.S.-based employers that met the following criteria: have a minimum of 300 total employees at a U.S. headquarters and a minimum of 30 IT employees in the U.S., with at least 50% of their IT employees based in the U.S. The best places to work were selected based on compensation, benefits, work/life balance, employee morale, and satisfaction with training and development programs. In addition, *InsiderPro* and *Computerworld* looked at retention efforts, programs for recognizing and rewarding outstanding performances, and benefits such as flextime, elder care and child care, and reimbursement for college tuition and the cost of pursuing technology certifications. *InsiderPro and Computerworld, "100 Best Places to Work in IT," 2020*

Texas Instruments, headquartered in Dallas, is among the "Top Companies for Executive Women." This list is determined by organizations filling out an in-depth survey that measures female demographics at every level, but with an emphasis on women in senior corporate roles, with profit & loss (P&L) responsibility, and those earning in the top 20 percent of the organization. *Working Mother* defines P&L as having responsibility that involves monitoring the net income after expenses for a department or entire organization, with direct influence on how company resources are allocated. *Working Mother, "Top Companies for Executive Women," 2020+*

Texas Instruments, headquartered in Dallas, is among the "Best Companies for Dads." *Working Mother's* newest list recognizes the growing importance companies place on giving dads time off and support for their families. Rankings are determined by measuring gender-neutral or paternity leave offered, as well as actual time taken, phase-back policies, child- and dependent-care benefits, and corporate support groups for men and dads. *Working Mother, "Best Companies for Dads," 2020*

PUBLIC SAFETY

Crime Rate

Area	All Crimes	Violent Crimes				Property Crimes		
		Murder	Rape[3]	Robbery	Aggrav. Assault	Burglary	Larceny-Theft	Motor Vehicle Theft
City	4,184.2	14.5	58.5	322.7	467.2	675.6	1,893.4	752.4
Suburbs[1]	n/a	n/a	n/a	n/a	n/a	n/a	n/a	n/a
Metro[2]	n/a	n/a	n/a	n/a	n/a	n/a	n/a	n/a
U.S.	2,489.3	5.0	42.6	81.6	250.2	340.5	1,549.5	219.9

Note: Figures are crimes per 100,000 population; (1) All areas within the metro area that are located outside the city limits; (2) Figures cover the Dallas-Plano-Irving, TX Metropolitan Division; n/a not available; (3) All figures shown were reported using the revised Uniform Crime Reporting (UCR) definition of rape.
Source: FBI Uniform Crime Reports, 2019

Hate Crimes

Area	Number of Quarters Reported	Race/Ethnicity/Ancestry	Religion	Sexual Orientation	Disability	Gender	Gender Identity
City	4	13	3	13	0	0	1
U.S.	4	3,963	1,521	1,195	157	69	198

Source: Federal Bureau of Investigation, Hate Crime Statistics 2019

Identity Theft Consumer Reports

Area	Reports	Reports per 100,000 Population	Rank[2]
MSA[1]	45,242	597	37
U.S.	1,387,615	423	-

Note: (1) Figures cover the Dallas-Fort Worth-Arlington, TX Metropolitan Statistical Area; (2) Rank ranges from 1 to 391 where 1 indicates greatest number of identity theft reports per 100,000 population
Source: Federal Trade Commission, Consumer Sentinel Network Data Book 2020

Fraud and Other Consumer Reports

Area	Reports	Reports per 100,000 Population	Rank[2]
MSA[1]	70,481	931	39
U.S.	3,385,133	1,031	-

Note: (1) Figures cover the Dallas-Fort Worth-Arlington, TX Metropolitan Statistical Area; (2) Rank ranges from 1 to 391 where 1 indicates greatest number of fraud and other consumer reports per 100,000 population
Source: Federal Trade Commission, Consumer Sentinel Network Data Book 2020

POLITICS

2020 Presidential Election Results

Area	Biden	Trump	Jorgensen	Hawkins	Other
Dallas County	64.9	33.3	1.0	0.4	0.4
U.S.	51.3	46.8	1.2	0.3	0.5

Note: Results are percentages and may not add to 100% due to rounding
Source: Dave Leip's Atlas of U.S. Presidential Elections

SPORTS

Professional Sports Teams

Team Name	League	Year Established
Dallas Cowboys	National Football League (NFL)	1960
Dallas Mavericks	National Basketball Association (NBA)	1980
Dallas Stars	National Hockey League (NHL)	1993
FC Dallas	Major League Soccer (MLS)	1996
Texas Rangers	Major League Baseball (MLB)	1972

Note: Includes teams located in the Dallas-Fort Worth-Arlington, TX Metropolitan Statistical Area.
Source: Wikipedia, Major Professional Sports Teams of the United States and Canada, April 6, 2021

CLIMATE

Average and Extreme Temperatures

Temperature	Jan	Feb	Mar	Apr	May	Jun	Jul	Aug	Sep	Oct	Nov	Dec	Yr.
Extreme High (°F)	85	90	100	100	101	112	111	109	107	101	91	87	112
Average High (°F)	55	60	68	76	84	92	96	96	89	79	67	58	77
Average Temp. (°F)	45	50	57	66	74	82	86	86	79	68	56	48	67
Average Low (°F)	35	39	47	56	64	72	76	75	68	57	46	38	56
Extreme Low (°F)	-2	9	12	30	39	53	58	58	42	24	16	0	-2

Note: Figures cover the years 1945-1993
Source: National Climatic Data Center, International Station Meteorological Climate Summary, 9/96

Average Precipitation/Snowfall/Humidity

Precip./Humidity	Jan	Feb	Mar	Apr	May	Jun	Jul	Aug	Sep	Oct	Nov	Dec	Yr.
Avg. Precip. (in.)	1.9	2.3	2.6	3.8	4.9	3.4	2.1	2.3	2.9	3.3	2.3	2.1	33.9
Avg. Snowfall (in.)	1	1	Tr	Tr	0	0	0	0	0	Tr	Tr	Tr	3
Avg. Rel. Hum. 6am (%)	78	77	75	77	82	81	77	76	80	79	78	77	78
Avg. Rel. Hum. 3pm (%)	53	51	47	49	51	48	43	41	46	46	48	51	48

Note: Figures cover the years 1945-1993; Tr = Trace amounts (<0.05 in. of rain; <0.5 in. of snow)
Source: National Climatic Data Center, International Station Meteorological Climate Summary, 9/96

Weather Conditions

Temperature			Daytime Sky			Precipitation		
10°F & below	32°F & below	90°F & above	Clear	Partly cloudy	Cloudy	0.01 inch or more precip.	0.1 inch or more snow/ice	Thunderstorms
1	34	102	108	160	97	78	2	49

Note: Figures are average number of days per year and cover the years 1945-1993
Source: National Climatic Data Center, International Station Meteorological Climate Summary, 9/96

HAZARDOUS WASTE

Superfund Sites

The Dallas-Plano-Irving, TX metro division is home to four sites on the EPA's Superfund National Priorities List: **Delfasco Forge** (final); **Lane Plating Works, Inc** (final); **RSR Corporation** (final); **Van Der Horst USA Corporation** (final). There are a total of 1,375 Superfund sites with a status of proposed or final on the list in the U.S. *U.S. Environmental Protection Agency, National Priorities List, April 7, 2021*

AIR QUALITY

Air Quality Trends: Ozone

	1990	1995	2000	2005	2010	2015	2016	2017	2018	2019
MSA[1]	0.095	0.105	0.096	0.097	0.080	0.077	0.070	0.073	0.078	0.071
U.S.	0.088	0.089	0.082	0.080	0.073	0.068	0.069	0.068	0.069	0.065

Note: (1) Data covers the Dallas-Fort Worth-Arlington, TX Metropolitan Statistical Area. The values shown are the composite ozone concentration averages among trend sites based on the highest fourth daily maximum 8-hour concentration in parts per million. These trends are based on sites having an adequate record of monitoring data during the trend period. Data from exceptional events are included.
Source: U.S. Environmental Protection Agency, Air Quality Monitoring Information, "Air Quality Trends by City, 1990-2019"

Air Quality Index

Area	Percent of Days when Air Quality was...[2]					AQI Statistics[2]	
	Good	Moderate	Unhealthy for Sensitive Groups	Unhealthy	Very Unhealthy	Maximum	Median
MSA[1]	49.6	42.5	7.7	0.3	0.0	156	51

Note: (1) Data covers the Dallas-Fort Worth-Arlington, TX Metropolitan Statistical Area; (2) Based on 365 days with AQI data in 2019. Air Quality Index (AQI) is an index for reporting daily air quality. EPA calculates the AQI for five major air pollutants regulated by the Clean Air Act: ground-level ozone, particle pollution (aka particulate matter), carbon monoxide, sulfur dioxide, and nitrogen dioxide. The AQI runs from 0 to 500. The higher the AQI value, the greater the level of air pollution and the greater the health concern. There are six AQI categories: "Good" AQI is between 0 and 50. Air quality is considered satisfactory; "Moderate" AQI is between 51 and 100. Air quality is acceptable; "Unhealthy for Sensitive Groups" When AQI values are between 101 and 150, members of sensitive groups may experience health effects; "Unhealthy" When AQI values are between 151 and 200 everyone may begin to experience health effects; "Very Unhealthy" AQI values between 201 and 300 trigger a health alert; "Hazardous" AQI values over 300 trigger warnings of emergency conditions (not shown).
Source: U.S. Environmental Protection Agency, Air Quality Index Report, 2019

Air Quality Index Pollutants

Area	Percent of Days when AQI Pollutant was...[2]					
	Carbon Monoxide	Nitrogen Dioxide	Ozone	Sulfur Dioxide	Particulate Matter 2.5	Particulate Matter 10
MSA[1]	0.0	3.0	56.2	0.0	40.8	0.0

Note: (1) Data covers the Dallas-Fort Worth-Arlington, TX Metropolitan Statistical Area; (2) Based on 365 days with AQI data in 2019. The Air Quality Index (AQI) is an index for reporting daily air quality. EPA calculates the AQI for five major air pollutants regulated by the Clean Air Act: ground-level ozone, particle pollution (also known as particulate matter), carbon monoxide, sulfur dioxide, and nitrogen dioxide. The AQI runs from 0 to 500. The higher the AQI value, the greater the level of air pollution and the greater the health concern.
Source: U.S. Environmental Protection Agency, Air Quality Index Report, 2019

Maximum Air Pollutant Concentrations: Particulate Matter, Ozone, CO and Lead

	Particulate Matter 10 (ug/m³)	Particulate Matter 2.5 Wtd AM (ug/m³)	Particulate Matter 2.5 24-Hr (ug/m³)	Ozone (ppm)	Carbon Monoxide (ppm)	Lead (ug/m³)
MSA[1] Level	40	9.0	19	0.076	1	0.23
NAAQS[2]	150	15	35	0.075	9	0.15
Met NAAQS[2]	Yes	Yes	Yes	No	Yes	No

Note: (1) Data covers the Dallas-Fort Worth-Arlington, TX Metropolitan Statistical Area; Data from exceptional events are included; (2) National Ambient Air Quality Standards; ppm = parts per million; ug/m³ = micrograms per cubic meter; n/a not available.
Concentrations: Particulate Matter 10 (coarse particulate)—highest second maximum 24-hour concentration; Particulate Matter 2.5 Wtd AM (fine particulate)—highest weighted annual mean concentration; Particulate Matter 2.5 24-Hour (fine particulate)—highest 98th percentile 24-hour concentration; Ozone—highest fourth daily maximum 8-hour concentration; Carbon Monoxide—highest second maximum non-overlapping 8-hour concentration; Lead—maximum running 3-month average
Source: U.S. Environmental Protection Agency, Air Quality Monitoring Information, "Air Quality Statistics by City, 2019"

Maximum Air Pollutant Concentrations: Nitrogen Dioxide and Sulfur Dioxide

	Nitrogen Dioxide AM (ppb)	Nitrogen Dioxide 1-Hr (ppb)	Sulfur Dioxide AM (ppb)	Sulfur Dioxide 1-Hr (ppb)	Sulfur Dioxide 24-Hr (ppb)
MSA[1] Level	12	46	n/a	7	n/a
NAAQS[2]	53	100	30	75	140
Met NAAQS[2]	Yes	Yes	n/a	Yes	n/a

Note: (1) Data covers the Dallas-Fort Worth-Arlington, TX Metropolitan Statistical Area; Data from exceptional events are included; (2) National Ambient Air Quality Standards; ppm = parts per million; ug/m³ = micrograms per cubic meter; n/a not available.
Concentrations: Nitrogen Dioxide AM—highest arithmetic mean concentration; Nitrogen Dioxide 1-Hr—highest 98th percentile 1-hour daily maximum concentration; Sulfur Dioxide AM—highest annual mean concentration; Sulfur Dioxide 1-Hr—highest 99th percentile 1-hour daily maximum concentration; Sulfur Dioxide 24-Hr—highest second maximum 24-hour concentration
Source: U.S. Environmental Protection Agency, Air Quality Monitoring Information, "Air Quality Statistics by City, 2019"

El Paso, Texas

Background

El Paso is so named because it sits in a spectacular pass through the Franklin Mountains, at an average elevation of 3,700 feet and in direct view of peaks that rise to 7,200 feet. El Paso is the fourth-largest city in Texas. It lies just south of New Mexico on the Rio Grande and just north of Juarez, Mexico.

The early Spanish explorer Alvar Nunez Cabeza de Vaca (circa 1530) probably passed through this area, but the city was named in 1598 by Juan de Onante, who dubbed it El Paso del Rio del Norte, or The Pass at the River of the North. It was also Onante who declared the area Spanish, on the authority of King Philip II, but a mission was not established until 1649. For some time, El Paso del Norte was the seat of government for northern Mexico, but settlement in and around the present-day city was sparse for many years.

This changed considerably by 1807, when Zebulon A. Pike, a United States Army officer, was interned in El Paso after being convicted of trespassing on Spanish territory. He found the area pleasant and well tended, with many irrigated fields and vineyards and a thriving trade in brandy and wine. In spite of Pike's stay there, though, El Paso remained for many years a largely Mexican region, escaping most of the military action connected to the Texas Revolution.

In the wake of the Mexican War (1846-1848) and in response to the California gold rush in 1849, El Paso emerged as a significant way station on the road west. A federal garrison, Fort Bliss, was established there in 1849, and was briefly occupied by Confederate sympathizers in 1862. Federal forces quickly reoccupied the fort, however, and the area was firmly controlled by Union armies. El Paso was incorporated in 1873, and after 1881, growth accelerated considerably with the building of rail links through the city, giving rise to ironworks, mills, and breweries.

During the Mexican Revolution (1911), El Paso was an important and disputed city, with Pancho Villa himself a frequent visitor, and many of his followers residents of the town. Mexico's national history, in fact, continued to affect El Paso until 1967 when, by way of settling a historic border dispute, 437 acres of the city was ceded to Mexico. Much of the disputed area on both sides of the border was made into parkland. The U.S. National Parks Service maintains the Chamizal Park on the U.S. side and it plays host to a variety of community events during the year including the Chamizal Film Festival and the summer concert series, Music Under the Stars.

One of the major points of entry to the U.S. from Mexico, El Paso is a vitally important international city and a burgeoning center of rail, road, and air transportation. During the 1990s, the city's economy shifted more toward a service-oriented economy and away from a manufacturing base. In 2020, Amazon announced plans to build a 625,000 square-foot fulfillment center in the city.

Transportation services and tourism are growing segments of the economy. Government and military are also sources of employment, with Ft. Bliss being the largest Air Defense Artillery Training Center in the world. The city hosts the University of Texas at El Paso, and a community college. Cultural amenities include the Tigua Indian Cultural Center, a Wilderness Park Museum, the El Paso Zoo, museums, a symphony orchestra, a ballet company, and many theaters. The city's "Wild West" qualities have long made it a popular destination for musicians, many of whom have recorded albums at El Paso's Sonic Ranch recording studio.

> Educators and students organized the Everyone Games West 2021 Tournament, providing students a chance to socialize as well as acquainting them with leaders in the gaming industry.

In 2019, El Paso was awarded its own United Soccer League team.

El Paso's revitalized downtown has increased the city's aesthetic appeal. It includes an open-air mall and "lifestyle center" in the city's central area, Doubletree by Hilton Hotel, and renovations of several historic downtown buildings.

El Paso is home to the world's largest inland desalination plant, designed to produce 27.5 million gallons of fresh water daily making it a critical component of the region's water portfolio.

The weather in El Paso is of the mountain-desert type, with very little precipitation. Summers are hot, humidity is low and winters are mild. However, temperatures in the flat Rio Grande Valley nearby are notably cooler at night year-round. There is plenty of sunshine and clear skies generally more than 200 days of the year.

Rankings

General Rankings

- For its "Best for Vets: Places to Live 2019" rankings, *Military Times* evaluated 599 cities (83 large, 234 medium, 282 small) and compared the locations across three broad categories: veteran and military culture/services; economic indicators; and livability factors such as health, crime, traffic, and school quality. El Paso ranked #20 out of the top 25, in the large city category (population of more than 250,000). Data points more specific to veterans and the military weighed more heavily than others. *rebootcamp.militarytimes.com, "Military Times Best Places to Live 2019," September 10, 2018*

- The El Paso metro area was identified as one of America's fastest-growing areas in terms of population and business growth by *MagnifyMoney*. The area ranked #24 out of 35. The 100 most populous metro areas in the U.S. were evaluated on their change from 2011-2016 in the following categories: people and housing; workforce and employment opportunities; growing industry. *www.businessinsider.com, "The 35 Cities in the US with the Biggest Influx of People, the Most Work Opportunities, and the Hottest Business Growth," August 12, 2018*

- El Paso was selected as an "All-America City" by the National Civic League. The All-America City Award recognizes civic excellence and in 2020 honored 10 communities that best exemplify the spirit of grassroots citizen involvement and cross-sector collaborative problem solving to collectively tackle pressing and complex issues. This year's focus was on enhancing health and wellness by means of civic engagement. *National Civic League, 2020 All-America City Awards, August 19, 2020*

Business/Finance Rankings

- El Paso was the #1-ranked city for savers, according to a study by the finance site GOBankingRates, which considered the prospects for people trying to save money. Criteria: average monthly cost of grocery items; median home listing price; median rent; median income; transportation costs; gas prices; and the cost of eating out for an inexpensive and mid-range meal in 100 U.S. cities. *www.gobankingrates.com, "The 20 Best (and Worst) Places to Live If You're Trying to Save Money," August 27, 2019*

- El Paso was ranked #1 among 100 U.S. cities for most difficult conditions for savers, according to a study by the finance site GOBankingRates. Criteria: average monthly cost of grocery items; median home listing price; median rent; median income; transportation costs; gas prices; and the cost of eating out for an inexpensive and mid-range meal. *www.gobankingrates.com, "The 20 Best (and Worst) Places to Live If You're Trying to Save Money," August 27, 2019*

- The Brookings Institution ranked the nation's largest cities based on income inequality. El Paso was ranked #59 (#1 = greatest inequality). Criteria: the "95/20 ratio," a figure representing the income at which a household earns more than 95 percent of all other households, divided by the income at which a household earns more than only 20 percent of all other households. *Brookings Institution, "Household Income Inequality, Largest Cities of 97 Large U.S. Metro Areas, 2014-2016," February 5, 2018*

- The Brookings Institution ranked the 100 largest metro areas in the U.S. based on income inequality. El Paso was ranked #39 (#1 = greatest inequality). Criteria: the "95/20 ratio," a figure representing the income at which a household earns more than 95 percent of all other households, divided by the income at which a household earns more than only 20 percent of all other households. *Brookings Institution, "Household Income Inequality, 100 Largest U.S. Metro Areas, 2014-2016," February 5, 2018*

- The El Paso metro area appeared on the Milken Institute "2021 Best Performing Cities" list. Rank: #111 out of 200 large metro areas (population over 250,000). Criteria: job growth; wage and salary growth; high-tech output growth; housing affordability; household broadband access. *Milken Institute, "Best-Performing Cities 2021," February 16, 2021*

- *Forbes* ranked the 200 most populous metro areas to determine the nation's "Best Places for Business and Careers." The El Paso metro area was ranked #171. Criteria: costs (business and living); job growth (past and projected); income growth; quality of life; educational attainment (college and high school); projected economic growth; cultural and leisure opportunities; workplace tolerance laws; net migration patterns. *Forbes, "The Best Places for Business and Careers 2019: Seattle Still On Top," October 30, 2019*

Education Rankings

- Personal finance website *WalletHub* analyzed the 150 largest U.S. metropolitan statistical areas to determine where the most educated Americans are putting their degrees to work. Criteria: education levels; percentage of workers with degrees; education quality and attainment gap; public school quality rankings; quality and enrollment of each metro area's universities. El Paso was ranked #135 (#1 = most educated city). *www.WalletHub.com, "Most and Least Educated Cities in America," July 20, 2020*

- El Paso was selected as one of America's most literate cities. The city ranked #80 out of the 84 largest U.S. cities. Criteria: number of booksellers; library resources; Internet resources; educational attainment; periodical publishing resources; newspaper circulation. *Central Connecticut State University, "America's Most Literate Cities, 2018," February 2019*

Environmental Rankings

- El Paso was highlighted as one of the 25 most ozone-polluted metro areas in the U.S. during 2016 through 2018. The area ranked #17. *American Lung Association, "State of the Air 2020," April 21, 2020*

Health/Fitness Rankings

- For each of the 100 largest cities in the United States, the American Fitness Index®, published by the American College of Sports Medicine and the Anthem Foundation, evaluated community infrastructure and 33 health behaviors including preventive health, levels of chronic disease conditions, pedestrian safety, air quality, and community resources that support physical activity. El Paso ranked #77 for "community fitness." *americanfitnessindex.org, "2020 ACSM American Fitness Index Summary Report," July 14, 2020*

- El Paso was identified as a "2021 Spring Allergy Capital." The area ranked #36 out of 100. Three groups of factors were used to identify the most challenging cities for people with allergies during the spring season: annual spring pollen levels; over the counter medicine use; number of board-certified allergy specialists. *Asthma and Allergy Foundation of America, "Spring Allergy Capitals 2021," February 23, 2021*

- El Paso was identified as a "2021 Fall Allergy Capital." The area ranked #32 out of 100. Three groups of factors were used to identify the most challenging cities for people with allergies during the fall season: annual fall pollen levels; over the counter medicine use; number of board-certified allergy specialists. *Asthma and Allergy Foundation of America, "Fall Allergy Capitals 2021," February 23, 2021*

- El Paso was identified as a "2019 Asthma Capital." The area ranked #95 out of the nation's 100 largest metropolitan areas. Criteria: estimated asthma prevalence; crude death rate from asthma; and ER visits due to asthma. Risk factors analyzed but not factored in the rankings: annual pollen score; annual air quality; public smoking laws; number of board-certified asthma specialists; rescue medication use; controller medication use; uninsured rate; poverty rate. *Asthma and Allergy Foundation of America, "Asthma Capitals 2019: The Most Challenging Places to Live With Asthma," May 7, 2019*

Real Estate Rankings

- *WalletHub* compared the most populated U.S. cities to determine which had the best markets for real estate agents. El Paso ranked #177 where demand was high and pay was the best. Criteria: sales per agent; annual median wage for real-estate agents; monthly average starting salary for real estate agents; real estate job density and competition; unemployment rate; home turnover rate; housing-market health index; and other relevant metrics. *www.WalletHub.com, "2019's Best Places to Be a Real Estate Agent," April 24, 2019*

- El Paso was ranked #181 out of 268 metro areas in terms of housing affordability in 2020 by the National Association of Home Builders (#1 = most affordable). Criteria: the share of homes sold in that area affordable to a family earning the local median income, based on standard mortgage underwriting criteria. *National Association of Home Builders®, NAHB-Wells Fargo Housing Opportunity Index, 4th Quarter 2020*

Safety Rankings

- Allstate ranked the 200 largest cities in America in terms of driver safety. El Paso ranked #48. Criteria: internal property damage claims over a two-year period from January 2016 to December 2017. The report helps increase the importance of safety and awareness behind the wheel. *Allstate, "Allstate America's Best Drivers Report, 2019" June 24, 2019*

- The National Insurance Crime Bureau ranked 384 metro areas in the U.S. in terms of per capita rates of vehicle theft. The El Paso metro area ranked #184 (#1 = highest rate). Criteria: number of vehicle theft offenses per 100,000 inhabitants in 2019. *National Insurance Crime Bureau, "Hot Spots 2019," July 21, 2020*

Seniors/Retirement Rankings

- From its Best Cities for Successful Aging indexes, the Milken Institute generated rankings for metropolitan areas, weighing data in nine categories—health care, wellness, living arrangements, transportation and convenience, financial characteristics, education, employment, community engagement, and overall livability. The El Paso metro area was ranked #80 overall in the large metro area category. *Milken Institute, "Best Cities for Successful Aging, 2017" March 14, 2017*

Women/Minorities Rankings

- The *Houston Chronicle* listed the El Paso metro area as #14 in top places for young Latinos to live in the U.S. Research was largely based on housing and occupational data from the largest metropolitan areas performed by *Forbes* and NBC Universo. Criteria: percentage of 18-34 year-olds; Latino college grad rates; and diversity. *blog.chron.com, "The 15 Best Big Cities for Latino Millenials," January 26, 2016*

- Personal finance website *WalletHub* compared more than 180 U.S. cities across two key dimensions, "Hispanic Business-Friendliness" and "Hispanic Purchasing Power," to arrive at the most favorable conditions for Hispanic entrepreneurs. El Paso was ranked #9 out of 182. Criteria includes: share of Hispanic-Owned Businesses; Hispanic entrepreneurship rate to median annual income of Hispanics; Small Business-Friendliness score; cost of living; and number of Hispanics with at least a bachelor's degree. *WalletHub.com, "2019's Best Cities for Hispanic Entrepreneurs," May 1, 2019*

Miscellaneous Rankings

- El Paso was selected as a 2020 Digital Cities Survey winner. The city ranked #7 in the large city (500,000 or more population) category. The survey examined and assessed how city governments are utilizing technology to improve transparency, enhance cybersecurity, and respond to the pandemic. Survey questions focused on ten initiatives: cybersecurity, citizen experience, disaster recovery, business intelligence, IT personnel, data governance, collaboration, infrastructure modernization, cloud computing, and mobile applications. *Center for Digital Government, "2020 Digital Cities Survey," November 10, 2020*

- The financial planning site SmartAsset has compiled its sixth annual study on the best places to trick or treat in 2019. More than 256 cities were compared to determine that El Paso ranked #6 out of 25 for rewarding those that hit the streets with candy. Criteria: neighborhood density, crime rate per 100,000 residents, average temperature and precipitation, median home values, and trick or treat age population. *www.smartasset.com, "Best Places to Trick-or-Treat in 2019," October 15, 2019*

- *WalletHub* compared the 150 most populated U.S. cities to determine their operating efficiency. A "Quality of City Services" score was constructed for each city and then divided by the total budget per capita to reveal which were managed the best. El Paso ranked #40. Criteria: financial stability; economy; education; safety; health; infrastructure and pollution. *www.WalletHub.com, "2020's Best- & Worst-Run Cities in America," June 29, 2020*

Business Environment

DEMOGRAPHICS

Population Growth

Area	1990 Census	2000 Census	2010 Census	2019* Estimate	Population Growth (%) 1990-2019	Population Growth (%) 2010-2019
City	515,541	563,662	649,121	679,813	31.9	4.7
MSA[1]	591,610	679,622	800,647	840,477	42.1	5.0
U.S.	248,709,873	281,421,906	308,745,538	324,697,795	30.6	5.2

Note: (1) Figures cover the El Paso, TX Metropolitan Statistical Area; (*) 2015-2019 5-year estimated population
Source: U.S. Census Bureau, 1990 Census, Census 2000, Census 2010, 2015-2019 American Community Survey 5-Year Estimates

Household Size

Area	One	Two	Three	Four	Five	Six	Seven or More	Average Household Size
City	25.6	28.5	17.8	15.9	7.6	3.3	1.3	3.00
MSA[1]	23.9	28.2	17.9	16.5	8.3	3.6	1.7	3.10
U.S.	27.9	33.9	15.6	12.9	6.0	2.3	1.4	2.60

Note: (1) Figures cover the El Paso, TX Metropolitan Statistical Area
Source: U.S. Census Bureau, 2015-2019 American Community Survey 5-Year Estimates

Race

Area	White Alone[2] (%)	Black Alone[2] (%)	Asian Alone[2] (%)	AIAN[3] Alone[2] (%)	NHOPI[4] Alone[2] (%)	Other Race Alone[2] (%)	Two or More Races (%)
City	80.1	3.6	1.4	0.6	0.2	11.4	2.7
MSA[1]	79.6	3.3	1.2	0.6	0.1	12.4	2.7
U.S.	72.5	12.7	5.5	0.8	0.2	4.9	3.3

Note: (1) Figures cover the El Paso, TX Metropolitan Statistical Area; (2) Alone is defined as not being in combination with one or more other races; (3) American Indian and Alaska Native; (4) Native Hawaiian and Other Pacific Islander
Source: U.S. Census Bureau, 2015-2019 American Community Survey 5-Year Estimates

Hispanic or Latino Origin

Area	Total (%)	Mexican (%)	Puerto Rican (%)	Cuban (%)	Other (%)
City	81.4	76.9	1.1	0.1	3.2
MSA[1]	82.5	78.2	1.0	0.1	3.2
U.S.	18.0	11.2	1.7	0.7	4.3

Note: Persons of Hispanic or Latino origin can be of any race; (1) Figures cover the El Paso, TX Metropolitan Statistical Area
Source: U.S. Census Bureau, 2015-2019 American Community Survey 5-Year Estimates

Ancestry

Area	German	Irish	English	American	Italian	Polish	French[2]	Scottish	Dutch
City	3.6	2.3	1.7	2.4	1.2	0.5	0.8	0.4	0.2
MSA[1]	3.4	2.2	1.6	2.3	1.1	0.5	0.8	0.4	0.2
U.S.	13.3	9.7	7.2	6.2	5.1	2.8	2.3	1.7	1.2

Note: Figures are the percentage of the total population reporting a particular ancestry. The nine most commonly reported ancestries in the U.S. are shown. Figures include multiple ancestries (e.g. if a person reported being Irish and Italian, they were included in both columns); (1) Figures cover the El Paso, TX Metropolitan Statistical Area; (2) Excludes Basque
Source: U.S. Census Bureau, 2015-2019 American Community Survey 5-Year Estimates

Foreign-born Population

Area	Any Foreign Country	Asia	Mexico	Europe	Caribbean	Central America[2]	South America	Africa	Canada
City	23.1	1.1	20.7	0.5	0.1	0.3	0.2	0.2	0.0
MSA[1]	24.2	1.0	22.0	0.4	0.1	0.3	0.2	0.2	0.0
U.S.	13.6	4.2	3.5	1.5	1.3	1.1	1.0	0.7	0.2

Note: (1) Figures cover the El Paso, TX Metropolitan Statistical Area; (2) Excludes Mexico.
Source: U.S. Census Bureau, 2015-2019 American Community Survey 5-Year Estimates

Marital Status

Area	Never Married	Now Married[2]	Separated	Widowed	Divorced
City	35.3	44.5	3.5	5.8	10.8
MSA[1]	35.4	45.2	3.5	5.5	10.3
U.S.	33.4	48.1	1.9	5.8	10.9

Note: Figures are percentages and cover the population 15 years of age and older; (1) Figures cover the El Paso, TX Metropolitan Statistical Area; (2) Excludes separated
Source: U.S. Census Bureau, 2015-2019 American Community Survey 5-Year Estimates

Disability by Age

Area	All Ages	Under 18 Years Old	18 to 64 Years Old	65 Years and Over
City	13.7	5.0	11.3	43.4
MSA[1]	13.8	5.5	11.5	44.6
U.S.	12.6	4.2	10.3	34.5

Note: Figures show percent of the civilian noninstitutionalized population that reported having a disability. Disability status is determined from six types of difficulty: vision, hearing, cognitive, ambulatory, self-care, and independent living. For children under 5 years old, hearing and vision difficulty are used to determine disability status. For children between the ages of 5 and 14, disability status is determined from hearing, vision, cognitive, ambulatory, and self-care difficulties. For people aged 15 years and older, they are considered to have a disability if they have difficulty with any one of the six difficulty types; Note: (1) Figures cover the El Paso, TX Metropolitan Statistical Area
Source: U.S. Census Bureau, 2015-2019 American Community Survey 5-Year Estimates

Age

Area	Under Age 5	Age 5–19	Age 20–34	Age 35–44	Age 45–54	Age 55–64	Age 65–74	Age 75–84	Age 85+	Median Age
City	7.4	22.2	23.2	12.4	11.7	10.6	7.1	3.9	1.7	32.9
MSA[1]	7.6	22.8	23.3	12.5	11.5	10.4	6.7	3.7	1.5	32.2
U.S.	6.1	19.1	20.7	12.6	13.0	12.9	9.1	4.6	1.9	38.1

Note: (1) Figures cover the El Paso, TX Metropolitan Statistical Area
Source: U.S. Census Bureau, 2015-2019 American Community Survey 5-Year Estimates

Gender

Area	Males	Females	Males per 100 Females
City	332,917	346,896	96.0
MSA[1]	413,883	426,594	97.0
U.S.	159,886,919	164,810,876	97.0

Note: (1) Figures cover the El Paso, TX Metropolitan Statistical Area
Source: U.S. Census Bureau, 2015-2019 American Community Survey 5-Year Estimates

Religious Groups by Family

Area	Catholic	Baptist	Non-Den.	Methodist[2]	Lutheran	LDS[3]	Pentecostal	Presbyterian[4]	Muslim[5]	Judaism
MSA[1]	43.2	3.8	5.0	0.9	0.3	1.6	1.4	0.2	0.1	0.2
U.S.	19.1	9.3	4.0	4.0	2.3	2.0	1.9	1.6	0.8	0.7

Note: Figures are the number of adherents as a percentage of the total population; (1) Figures cover the El Paso, TX Metropolitan Statistical Area; (2) Methodist/Pietist; (3) Latter Day Saints; (4) Reformed; (5) Figures are estimates
Source: Association of Statisticians of American Religious Bodies, 2010 U.S. Religion Census: Religious Congregations & Membership Study

Religious Groups by Tradition

Area	Catholic	Evangelical Protestant	Mainline Protestant	Other Tradition	Black Protestant	Orthodox
MSA[1]	43.2	10.9	1.3	2.1	0.2	0.1
U.S.	19.1	16.2	7.3	4.3	1.6	0.3

Note: Figures are the number of adherents as a percentage of the total population; (1) Figures cover the El Paso, TX Metropolitan Statistical Area
Source: Association of Statisticians of American Religious Bodies, 2010 U.S. Religion Census: Religious Congregations & Membership Study

ECONOMY

Gross Metropolitan Product

Area	2017	2018	2019	2020	Rank[2]
MSA[1]	28.3	29.4	30.5	31.5	97

Note: Figures are in billions of dollars; (1) Figures cover the El Paso, TX Metropolitan Statistical Area; (2) Rank is based on 2018 data and ranges from 1 to 381
Source: U.S. Conference of Mayors, U.S. Metro Economies: GMP & Employment 2018-2020, September 2019

Economic Growth

Area	2015-17 (%)	2018 (%)	2019 (%)	2020 (%)	Rank[2]
MSA[1]	0.9	1.5	1.6	1.4	244
U.S.	1.9	2.9	2.3	2.1	—

Note: Figures are real gross metropolitan product (GMP) growth rates and represent average annual percent change; (1) Figures cover the El Paso, TX Metropolitan Statistical Area; (2) Rank is based on 2017 2-year average annual percent change and ranges from 1 to 381
Source: U.S. Conference of Mayors, U.S. Metro Economies: GMP & Employment 2018-2020, September 2019

Metropolitan Area Exports

Area	2014	2015	2016	2017	2018	2019	Rank[2]
MSA[1]	20,079.3	24,560.9	26,452.8	25,814.1	30,052.0	32,749.6	10

Note: Figures are in millions of dollars; (1) Figures cover the El Paso, TX Metropolitan Statistical Area; (2) Rank is based on 2019 data and ranges from 1 to 386
Source: U.S. Department of Commerce, International Trade Administration, Office of Trade and Economic Analysis, Industry and Analysis, Exports by Metropolitan Area, data extracted March 24, 2021

Building Permits

Area	Single-Family 2018	Single-Family 2019	Pct. Chg.	Multi-Family 2018	Multi-Family 2019	Pct. Chg.	Total 2018	Total 2019	Pct. Chg.
City	1,588	1,873	17.9	621	413	-33.5	2,209	2,286	3.5
MSA[1]	1,751	2,433	38.9	665	633	-4.8	2,416	3,066	26.9
U.S.	855,300	862,100	0.7	473,500	523,900	10.6	1,328,800	1,386,000	4.3

Note: (1) Figures cover the El Paso, TX Metropolitan Statistical Area; Figures represent new, privately-owned housing units authorized (unadjusted data); All permit data are based on estimates with imputation
Source: U.S. Census Bureau, Manufacturing, Mining, and Construction Statistics, Building Permits, 2018, 2019

Bankruptcy Filings

Area	Business Filings 2019	Business Filings 2020	% Chg.	Nonbusiness Filings 2019	Nonbusiness Filings 2020	% Chg.
El Paso County	63	42	-33.3	2,079	1,290	-38.0
U.S.	22,780	21,655	-4.9	752,160	522,808	-30.5

Note: Business filings include Chapter 7, Chapter 9, Chapter 11, Chapter 12, Chapter 13, Chapter 15, and Section 304; Nonbusiness filings include Chapter 7, Chapter 11, and Chapter 13
Source: Administrative Office of the U.S. Courts, Business and Nonbusiness Bankruptcy, County Cases Commenced by Chapter of the Bankruptcy Code, During the 12-Month Period Ending December 31, 2019 and Business and Nonbusiness Bankruptcy, County Cases Commenced by Chapter of the Bankruptcy Code, During the 12-Month Period Ending December 31, 2020

Housing Vacancy Rates

Area	Gross Vacancy Rate[2] (%) 2018	2019	2020	Year-Round Vacancy Rate[3] (%) 2018	2019	2020	Rental Vacancy Rate[4] (%) 2018	2019	2020	Homeowner Vacancy Rate[5] (%) 2018	2019	2020
MSA[1]	n/a	n/a	n/a	n/a	n/a	n/a	n/a	n/a	n/a	n/a	n/a	n/a
U.S.	12.3	12.0	10.6	9.7	9.5	8.2	6.9	6.7	6.3	1.5	1.4	1.0

Note: (1) Figures cover the El Paso, TX Metropolitan Statistical Area; (2) The percentage of the total housing inventory that is vacant; (3) The percentage of the housing inventory (excluding seasonal units) that is year-round vacant; (4) The percentage of rental inventory that is vacant for rent; (5) The percentage of homeowner inventory that is vacant for sale; n/a not available
Source: U.S. Census Bureau, Housing Vacancies and Homeownership Annual Statistics: 2018, 2019, 2020

INCOME

Income

Area	Per Capita ($)	Median Household ($)	Average Household ($)
City	22,734	47,568	64,025
MSA[1]	21,644	46,795	62,663
U.S.	34,103	62,843	88,607

Note: (1) Figures cover the El Paso, TX Metropolitan Statistical Area
Source: U.S. Census Bureau, 2015-2019 American Community Survey 5-Year Estimates

Household Income Distribution

Area	Under $15,000	$15,000 -$24,999	$25,000 -$34,999	$35,000 -$49,999	$50,000 -$74,999	$75,000 -$99,999	$100,000 -$149,999	$150,000 and up
City	14.3	12.2	11.1	14.3	19.1	10.8	11.5	6.7
MSA[1]	14.6	12.2	11.4	14.5	19.0	10.8	11.2	6.3
U.S.	10.3	8.9	8.9	12.3	17.2	12.7	15.1	14.5

Note: (1) Figures cover the El Paso, TX Metropolitan Statistical Area
Source: U.S. Census Bureau, 2015-2019 American Community Survey 5-Year Estimates

Poverty Rate

Area	All Ages	Under 18 Years Old	18 to 64 Years Old	65 Years and Over
City	19.1	27.1	15.9	17.6
MSA[1]	20.2	28.6	16.7	18.6
U.S.	13.4	18.5	12.6	9.3

Note: Figures are percentage of people whose income during the past 12 months was below the poverty level;
(1) Figures cover the El Paso, TX Metropolitan Statistical Area
Source: U.S. Census Bureau, 2015-2019 American Community Survey 5-Year Estimates

CITY FINANCES

City Government Finances

Component	2017 ($000)	2017 ($ per capita)
Total Revenues	1,191,979	1,750
Total Expenditures	1,201,949	1,765
Debt Outstanding	2,275,124	3,340
Cash and Securities[1]	2,878,774	4,227

Note: (1) Cash and security holdings of a government at the close of its fiscal year, including those of its dependent agencies, utilities, and liquor stores.
Source: U.S. Census Bureau, State & Local Government Finances 2017

City Government Revenue by Source

Source	2017 ($000)	2017 ($ per capita)	2017 (%)
General Revenue			
From Federal Government	50,974	75	4.3
From State Government	31,275	46	2.6
From Local Governments	4,758	7	0.4
Taxes			
Property	240,099	353	20.1
Sales and Gross Receipts	202,818	298	17.0
Personal Income	0	0	0.0
Corporate Income	0	0	0.0
Motor Vehicle License	0	0	0.0
Other Taxes	15,544	23	1.3
Current Charges	272,018	399	22.8
Liquor Store	0	0	0.0
Utility	150,154	220	12.6
Employee Retirement	173,575	255	14.6

Source: U.S. Census Bureau, State & Local Government Finances 2017

City Government Expenditures by Function

Function	2017 ($000)	2017 ($ per capita)	2017 (%)
General Direct Expenditures			
Air Transportation	63,565	93	5.3
Corrections	0	0	0.0
Education	0	0	0.0
Employment Security Administration	0	0	0.0
Financial Administration	6,584	9	0.5
Fire Protection	97,691	143	8.1
General Public Buildings	23,136	34	1.9
Governmental Administration, Other	15,769	23	1.3
Health	20,182	29	1.7
Highways	38,237	56	3.2
Hospitals	0	0	0.0
Housing and Community Development	16,462	24	1.4
Interest on General Debt	87,512	128	7.3
Judicial and Legal	6,780	10	0.6
Libraries	8,979	13	0.7
Parking	0	0	0.0
Parks and Recreation	59,372	87	4.9
Police Protection	119,609	175	10.0
Public Welfare	389	< 1	< 0.1
Sewerage	89,790	131	7.5
Solid Waste Management	53,229	78	4.4
Veterans' Services	0	0	0.0
Liquor Store	0	0	0.0
Utility	323,218	474	26.9
Employee Retirement	134,086	196	11.2

Source: U.S. Census Bureau, State & Local Government Finances 2017

EMPLOYMENT

Labor Force and Employment

Area	Civilian Labor Force Dec. 2019	Dec. 2020	% Chg.	Workers Employed Dec. 2019	Dec. 2020	% Chg.
City	305,478	303,471	-0.7	295,039	280,221	-5.0
MSA[1]	367,648	366,204	-0.4	354,536	336,718	-5.0
U.S.	164,007,000	160,017,000	-2.4	158,504,000	149,613,000	-5.6

Note: Data is not seasonally adjusted and covers workers 16 years of age and older; (1) Figures cover the El Paso, TX Metropolitan Statistical Area
Source: Bureau of Labor Statistics, Local Area Unemployment Statistics

Unemployment Rate

Area	2020 Jan.	Feb.	Mar.	Apr.	May	Jun.	Jul.	Aug.	Sep.	Oct.	Nov.	Dec.
City	3.8	3.6	5.1	14.5	14.0	9.1	8.4	6.9	8.1	6.7	8.9	7.7
MSA[1]	4.0	3.8	5.4	14.9	14.6	9.5	8.8	7.3	8.6	7.1	9.4	8.1
U.S.	4.0	3.8	4.5	14.4	13.0	11.2	10.5	8.5	7.7	6.6	6.4	6.5

Note: Data is not seasonally adjusted and covers workers 16 years of age and older; (1) Figures cover the El Paso, TX Metropolitan Statistical Area
Source: Bureau of Labor Statistics, Local Area Unemployment Statistics

Average Wages

Occupation	$/Hr.	Occupation	$/Hr.
Accountants and Auditors	31.60	Maintenance and Repair Workers	15.20
Automotive Mechanics	16.30	Marketing Managers	54.70
Bookkeepers	16.10	Network and Computer Systems Admin.	33.00
Carpenters	16.70	Nurses, Licensed Practical	23.70
Cashiers	10.50	Nurses, Registered	35.10
Computer Programmers	40.20	Nursing Assistants	13.00
Computer Systems Analysts	37.40	Office Clerks, General	15.10
Computer User Support Specialists	20.30	Physical Therapists	46.20
Construction Laborers	13.70	Physicians	113.80
Cooks, Restaurant	11.30	Plumbers, Pipefitters and Steamfitters	18.20
Customer Service Representatives	12.80	Police and Sheriff's Patrol Officers	30.60
Dentists	92.60	Postal Service Mail Carriers	25.50
Electricians	18.20	Real Estate Sales Agents	28.80
Engineers, Electrical	41.50	Retail Salespersons	11.80
Fast Food and Counter Workers	9.40	Sales Representatives, Technical/Scientific	n/a
Financial Managers	51.60	Secretaries, Exc. Legal/Medical/Executive	15.50
First-Line Supervisors of Office Workers	24.20	Security Guards	12.90
General and Operations Managers	45.00	Surgeons	n/a
Hairdressers/Cosmetologists	11.60	Teacher Assistants, Exc. Postsecondary*	13.10
Home Health and Personal Care Aides	9.00	Teachers, Secondary School, Exc. Sp. Ed.*	30.30
Janitors and Cleaners	11.00	Telemarketers	10.40
Landscaping/Groundskeeping Workers	11.20	Truck Drivers, Heavy/Tractor-Trailer	23.40
Lawyers	60.80	Truck Drivers, Light/Delivery Services	17.30
Maids and Housekeeping Cleaners	9.80	Waiters and Waitresses	9.90

Note: Wage data covers the El Paso, TX Metropolitan Statistical Area; (*) Hourly wages were calculated from annual wage data based on a 40 hour work week; n/a not available.
Source: Bureau of Labor Statistics, Metro Area Occupational Employment & Wage Estimates, May 2020

Employment by Industry

Sector	MSA[1] Number of Employees	Percent of Total	U.S. Percent of Total
Construction, Mining, and Logging	17,600	5.6	5.5
Education and Health Services	47,000	14.8	16.3
Financial Activities	13,200	4.2	6.1
Government	70,500	22.2	15.2
Information	4,500	1.4	1.9
Leisure and Hospitality	33,400	10.5	9.0
Manufacturing	16,300	5.1	8.5
Other Services	8,100	2.6	3.8
Professional and Business Services	37,600	11.9	14.4
Retail Trade	39,300	12.4	10.9
Transportation, Warehousing, and Utilities	17,700	5.6	4.6
Wholesale Trade	11,900	3.8	3.9

Note: Figures are non-farm employment as of December 2020. Figures are not seasonally adjusted and include workers 16 years of age and older; (1) Figures cover the El Paso, TX Metropolitan Statistical Area
Source: Bureau of Labor Statistics, Current Employment Statistics, Employment, Hours, and Earnings

Employment by Occupation

Occupation Classification	City (%)	MSA[1] (%)	U.S. (%)
Management, Business, Science, and Arts	32.6	31.0	38.5
Natural Resources, Construction, and Maintenance	8.1	9.2	8.9
Production, Transportation, and Material Moving	12.4	13.5	13.2
Sales and Office	25.9	25.3	21.6
Service	20.9	21.1	17.8

Note: Figures cover employed civilians 16 years of age and older; (1) Figures cover the El Paso, TX Metropolitan Statistical Area
Source: U.S. Census Bureau, 2015-2019 American Community Survey 5-Year Estimates

Occupations with Greatest Projected Employment Growth: 2020 – 2022

Occupation[1]	2020 Employment	2022 Projected Employment	Numeric Employment Change	Percent Employment Change
Fast Food and Counter Workers	336,530	411,690	75,160	22.3
Waiters and Waitresses	165,570	206,920	41,350	25.0
Home Health and Personal Care Aides	303,520	344,240	40,720	13.4
Retail Salespersons	315,590	349,820	34,230	10.8
Heavy and Tractor-Trailer Truck Drivers	199,460	228,650	29,190	14.6
Laborers and Freight, Stock, and Material Movers, Hand	193,000	219,670	26,670	13.8
Cooks, Restaurant	88,540	114,250	25,710	29.0
Customer Service Representatives	276,080	295,790	19,710	7.1
General and Operations Managers	197,410	216,580	19,170	9.7
Office Clerks, General	310,080	327,500	17,420	5.6

Note: Projections cover Texas; (1) Sorted by numeric employment change
Source: www.projectionscentral.com, State Occupational Projections, 2020–2022 Short-Term Projections

Fastest-Growing Occupations: 2020 – 2022

Occupation[1]	2020 Employment	2022 Projected Employment	Numeric Employment Change	Percent Employment Change
Motion Picture Projectionists	150	300	150	100.0
Ushers, Lobby Attendants, and Ticket Takers	5,740	8,920	3,180	55.4
Locker Room, Coatroom, and Dressing Room Attendants	340	510	170	50.0
Athletes and Sports Competitors	270	400	130	48.1
Amusement and Recreation Attendants	13,130	19,400	6,270	47.8
Hotel, Motel, and Resort Desk Clerks	16,140	23,160	7,020	43.5
Sound Engineering Technicians	330	460	130	39.4
Gaming Dealers	220	300	80	36.4
Baggage Porters and Bellhops	1,250	1,670	420	33.6
Lodging Managers	3,300	4,330	1,030	31.2

Note: Projections cover Texas; (1) Sorted by percent employment change and excludes occupations with numeric employment change less than 50
Source: www.projectionscentral.com, State Occupational Projections, 2020–2022 Short-Term Projections

TAXES

State Corporate Income Tax Rates

State	Tax Rate (%)	Income Brackets ($)	Num. of Brackets	Financial Institution Tax Rate (%)[a]	Federal Income Tax Ded.
Texas	(w)	–	–	(w)	No

Note: Tax rates as of January 1, 2021; (a) Rates listed are the corporate income tax rate applied to financial institutions or excise taxes based on income. Some states have other taxes based upon the value of deposits or shares; (w) Texas imposes a Franchise Tax, otherwise known as margin tax, imposed on entities with more than $1,130,000 total revenues at rate of 0.75%, or 0.375% for entities primarily engaged in retail or wholesale trade, on lesser of 70% of total revenues or 100% of gross receipts after deductions for either compensation or cost of goods sold.
Source: Federation of Tax Administrators, State Corporate Income Tax Rates, January 1, 2021

State Individual Income Tax Rates

State	Tax Rate (%)	Income Brackets ($)	Personal Exemptions ($) Single	Married	Depend.	Standard Ded. ($) Single	Married
Texas				– No state income tax –			

Note: Tax rates as of January 1, 2021; Local- and county-level taxes are not included
Source: Federation of Tax Administrators, State Individual Income Tax Rates, January 1, 2021

Various State Sales and Excise Tax Rates

State	State Sales Tax (%)	Gasoline[1] (¢/gal.)	Cigarette[2] ($/pack)	Spirits[3] ($/gal.)	Wine[4] ($/gal.)	Beer[5] ($/gal.)	Recreational Marijuana (%)
Texas	6.25	20	1.41	2.4	0.2	0.2	Not legal

Note: All tax rates as of January 1, 2021; (1) The American Petroleum Institute has developed a methodology for determining the average tax rate on a gallon of fuel. Rates may include any of the following: excise taxes, environmental fees, storage tank fees, other fees or taxes, general sales tax, and local taxes; (2) The federal excise tax of $1.0066 per pack and local taxes are not included; (3) Rates are those applicable to off-premise sales of 40% alcohol by volume (a.b.v.) distilled spirits in 750ml containers. Local excise taxes are excluded; (4) Rates are those applicable to off-premise sales of 11% a.b.v. non-carbonated wine in 750ml containers; (5) Rates are those applicable to off-premise sales of 4.7% a.b.v. beer in 12 ounce containers.
Source: Tax Foundation, 2021 Facts & Figures: How Does Your State Compare?

State Business Tax Climate Index Rankings

State	Overall Rank	Corporate Tax Rank	Individual Income Tax Rank	Sales Tax Rank	Property Tax Rank	Unemployment Insurance Tax Rank
Texas	11	47	6	35	36	16

Note: The index is a measure of how each state's tax laws affect economic performance. The lower the rank, the more favorable a state's tax system is for business. States without a given tax are given a ranking of 1. The scores/rankings for the District of Columbia do not affect other states. The 2021 index represents the tax climate as of July 1, 2020.
Source: Tax Foundation, State Business Tax Climate Index 2021

TRANSPORTATION

Means of Transportation to Work

Area	Drove Alone	Car-pooled	Bus	Subway	Railroad	Bicycle	Walked	Other Means	Worked at Home
City	81.1	10.6	1.6	0.0	0.0	0.2	1.4	1.9	3.2
MSA[1]	80.7	10.6	1.3	0.0	0.0	0.1	1.6	2.1	3.5
U.S.	76.3	9.0	2.4	1.9	0.6	0.5	2.7	1.4	5.2

Note: Figures are percentages and cover workers 16 years of age and older; (1) Figures cover the El Paso, TX Metropolitan Statistical Area
Source: U.S. Census Bureau, 2015-2019 American Community Survey 5-Year Estimates

Travel Time to Work

Area	Less Than 10 Minutes	10 to 19 Minutes	20 to 29 Minutes	30 to 44 Minutes	45 to 59 Minutes	60 to 89 Minutes	90 Minutes or More
City	9.8	34.4	27.7	19.6	4.4	2.2	1.9
MSA[1]	10.7	32.6	26.8	20.6	4.9	2.4	2.0
U.S.	12.2	28.4	20.8	20.8	8.3	6.4	2.9

Note: Note: Figures are percentages and include workers 16 years old and over; (1) Figures cover the El Paso, TX Metropolitan Statistical Area
Source: U.S. Census Bureau, 2015-2019 American Community Survey 5-Year Estimates

Key Congestion Measures

Measure	1982	1992	2002	2012	2017
Annual Hours of Delay, Total (000)	2,209	8,391	15,064	20,106	22,711
Annual Hours of Delay, Per Auto Commuter	9	24	34	38	41
Annual Congestion Cost, Total (million $)	17	89	204	360	418
Annual Congestion Cost, Per Auto Commuter ($)	173	451	632	661	724

Note: Covers the El Paso TX-NM urban area
Source: Texas A&M Transportation Institute, 2019 Urban Mobility Report

Freeway Travel Time Index

Measure	1982	1987	1992	1997	2002	2007	2012	2017
Urban Area Index[1]	1.03	1.06	1.12	1.14	1.17	1.18	1.17	1.16
Urban Area Rank[1,2]	76	66	40	47	41	44	50	61

Note: Freeway Travel Time Index—the ratio of travel time in the peak period to the travel time at free-flow conditions. For example, a value of 1.30 indicates a 20-minute free-flow trip takes 26 minutes in the peak (20 minutes x 1.30 = 26 minutes); (1) Covers the El Paso TX-NM urban area; (2) Rank is based on 101 larger urban areas (#1 = highest travel time index)
Source: Texas A&M Transportation Institute, 2019 Urban Mobility Report

Public Transportation

Agency Name / Mode of Transportation	Vehicles Operated in Maximum Service[1]	Annual Unlinked Passenger Trips[2] (in thous.)	Annual Passenger Miles[3] (in thous.)
Mass Transit Department-City of El Paso (Sun Metro)			
Bus (directly operated)	125	10,969.7	73,773.5
Demand Response (purchased transportation)	61	321.4	3,026.6
Streetcar Rail (directly operated)	4	222.8	343.1

Note: (1) Number of revenue vehicles operated by the given mode and type of service to meet the annual maximum service requirement. This is the revenue vehicle count during the peak season of the year; on the week and day that maximum service is provided. Vehicles operated in maximum service (VOMS) exclude atypical days and one-time special events; (2) Number of passengers who boarded public transportation vehicles. Passengers are counted each time they board a vehicle no matter how many vehicles they use to travel from their origin to their destination. (3) Sum of the distances ridden by all passengers during the entire fiscal year.
Source: Federal Transit Administration, National Transit Database, 2019

Air Transportation

Airport Name and Code / Type of Service	Passenger Airlines[1]	Passenger Enplanements	Freight Carriers[2]	Freight (lbs)
El Paso International (ELP)				
Domestic service (U.S. carriers - 2020)	23	726,707	20	99,796,419
International service (U.S. carriers - 2019)	3	2,574	5	1,213,077

Note: (1) Includes all U.S.-based major, minor and commuter airlines that carried at least one passenger during the year; (2) Includes all U.S.-based airlines and freight carriers that transported at least one pound of freight during the year.
Source: Bureau of Transportation Statistics, The Intermodal Transportation Database, Air Carriers: T-100 Domestic Market (U.S. Carriers), 2020; Bureau of Transportation Statistics, The Intermodal Transportation Database, Air Carriers: T-100 International Market (U.S. Carriers), 2019

BUSINESSES

Major Business Headquarters

Company Name	Industry	Rankings Fortune[1]	Forbes[2]
No companies listed	-	-	-

Note: (1) Companies that produce a 10-K are ranked 1 to 500 based on 2019 revenue; (2) All private companies with at least $2 billion in annual revenue through the end of their most current fiscal year are ranked 1 to 219; companies listed are headquartered in the city; dashes indicate no ranking
Source: Fortune, "Fortune 500," June/July 2020; Forbes, "America's Largest Private Companies," 2020

Living Environment

COST OF LIVING

Cost of Living Index

Composite Index	Groceries	Housing	Utilities	Transportation	Health Care	Misc. Goods/Services
90.9	108.3	69.0	90.9	99.6	97.7	98.1

Note: The Cost of Living Index measures regional differences in the cost of consumer goods and services, excluding taxes and non-consumer expenditures, for professional and managerial households in the top income quintile. It is based on more than 50,000 prices covering almost 60 different items for which prices are collected three times a year by chambers of commerce, economic development organizations or university applied economic centers in each participating urban area. The numbers shown should be read as a percentage above or below the national average of 100. For example, a value of 115.4 in the groceries column indicates that grocery prices are 15.4% higher than the national average. Small differences in the index numbers should not be interpreted as significant; Figures cover the El Paso TX urban area.
Source: The Council for Community and Economic Research, Cost of Living Index, 2020

Grocery Prices

Area[1]	T-Bone Steak ($/pound)	Frying Chicken ($/pound)	Whole Milk ($/half gal.)	Eggs ($/dozen)	Orange Juice ($/64 oz.)	Coffee ($/11.5 oz.)
City[2]	10.83	2.02	2.67	1.85	3.93	5.38
Avg.	11.78	1.39	2.05	1.47	3.57	4.34
Min.	8.03	0.94	1.03	0.74	2.94	3.02
Max.	15.86	2.65	4.31	3.77	5.44	8.69

Note: (1) Values for the local area are compared with the average, minimum and maximum values for all 284 areas in the Cost of Living Index; (2) Figures cover the El Paso TX urban area; **T-Bone Steak** (price per pound); **Frying Chicken** (price per pound, whole fryer); **Whole Milk** (half gallon carton); **Eggs** (price per dozen, Grade A, large); **Orange Juice** (64 oz. Tropicana or Florida Natural); **Coffee** (11.5 oz. can, vacuum-packed, Maxwell House, Hills Bros, or Folgers).
Source: The Council for Community and Economic Research, Cost of Living Index, 2020

Housing and Utility Costs

Area[1]	New Home Price ($)	Apartment Rent ($/month)	All Electric ($/month)	Part Electric ($/month)	Other Energy ($/month)	Telephone ($/month)
City[2]	242,558	908	-	93.81	45.21	185.50
Avg.	368,594	1,168	170.86	100.47	65.28	184.30
Min.	190,567	502	91.58	31.42	26.08	169.60
Max.	2,227,806	4,738	470.38	280.31	280.06	206.50

Note: (1) Values for the local area are compared with the average, minimum and maximum values for all 284 areas in the Cost of Living Index; (2) Figures cover the El Paso TX urban area; **New Home Price** (2,400 sf living area, 8,000 sf lot, in urban area with full utilities); **Apartment Rent** (950 sf 2 bedroom/1.5 or 2 bath, unfurnished, excluding all utilities except water); **All Electric** (average monthly cost for an all-electric home); **Part Electric** (average monthly cost for a part-electric home); **Other Energy** (average monthly cost for natural gas, fuel oil, coal, wood, and any other forms of energy except electricity); **Telephone** (price includes the base monthly rate plus taxes and fees for three lines of mobile phone service).
Source: The Council for Community and Economic Research, Cost of Living Index, 2020

Health Care, Transportation, and Other Costs

Area[1]	Doctor ($/visit)	Dentist ($/visit)	Optometrist ($/visit)	Gasoline ($/gallon)	Beauty Salon ($/visit)	Men's Shirt ($)
City[2]	133.61	82.94	87.16	2.15	30.42	28.66
Avg.	115.44	99.32	108.10	2.21	39.27	31.37
Min.	36.68	59.00	51.36	1.71	19.00	11.00
Max.	219.00	153.10	250.97	3.46	82.05	58.33

Note: (1) Values for the local area are compared with the average, minimum and maximum values for all 284 areas in the Cost of Living Index; (2) Figures cover the El Paso TX urban area; **Doctor** (general practitioners routine exam of an established patient); **Dentist** (adult teeth cleaning and periodic oral examination); **Optometrist** (full vision eye exam for established adult patient); **Gasoline** (one gallon regular unleaded, national brand, including all taxes, cash price at self-service pump if available); **Beauty Salon** (woman's shampoo, trim, and blow-dry); **Men's Shirt** (cotton/polyester dress shirt, pinpoint weave, long sleeves).
Source: The Council for Community and Economic Research, Cost of Living Index, 2020

HOUSING

Homeownership Rate

Area	2012 (%)	2013 (%)	2014 (%)	2015 (%)	2016 (%)	2017 (%)	2018 (%)	2019 (%)	2020 (%)
MSA[1]	n/a	n/a	n/a	n/a	n/a	n/a	n/a	n/a	n/a
U.S.	65.4	65.1	64.5	63.7	63.4	63.9	64.4	64.6	66.6

Note: (1) Figures cover the El Paso, TX Metropolitan Statistical Area; n/a not available
Source: U.S. Census Bureau, Housing Vacancies and Homeownership Annual Statistics: 2012-2020

House Price Index (HPI)

Area	National Ranking[2]	Quarterly Change (%)	One-Year Change (%)	Five-Year Change (%)	Since 1991Q1 (%)
MSA[1]	158	1.05	5.68	18.03	118.41
U.S.[3]	–	3.81	10.77	38.99	205.12

Note: The HPI is a weighted repeat sales index. It measures average price changes in repeat sales or refinancings on the same properties. This information is obtained by reviewing repeat mortgage transactions on single-family properties whose mortgages have been purchased or securitized by Fannie Mae or Freddie Mac since January 1975; (1) Figures cover the El Paso, TX Metropolitan Statistical Area; (2) Rankings are based on annual percentage change for all metro areas containing at least 15,000 transactions over the last 10 years and ranges from 1 to 253; (3) figures based on a weighted average of Census Division estimates using a seasonally adjusted, purchase-only index; all figures are for the period ending December 31, 2020
Source: Federal Housing Finance Agency, Change in Metropolitan Area House Price Indexes, April 7, 2021

Median Single-Family Home Prices

Area	2018	2019	2020p	Percent Change 2019 to 2020
MSA[1]	155.8	164.4	177.8	8.2
U.S. Average	261.6	274.6	299.9	9.2

Note: Figures are median sales prices of existing single-family homes in thousands of dollars; (p) preliminary; (1) Figures cover the El Paso, TX Metropolitan Statistical Area
Source: National Association of Realtors, Median Sales Price of Existing Single-Family Homes for Metropolitan Areas, 4th Quarter 2020

Qualifying Income Based on Median Sales Price of Existing Single-Family Homes

Area	With 5% Down ($)	With 10% Down ($)	With 20% Down ($)
MSA[1]	35,199	33,347	29,642
U.S. Average	59,266	56,147	49,908

Note: Figures are preliminary; Qualifying income is based on a mortgage rate of 2.81%. Monthly principal and interest payment is limited to 25% of income; (1) Figures cover the El Paso, TX Metropolitan Statistical Area
Source: National Association of Realtors, Qualifying Income Based on Median Sales Price of Existing Single-Family Homes for Metropolitan Areas, 4th Quarter 2020

Home Value Distribution

Area	Under $50,000	$50,000 -$99,999	$100,000 -$149,999	$150,000 -$199,999	$200,000 -$299,999	$300,000 -$499,999	$500,000 -$999,999	$1,000,000 or more
City	5.1	25.0	32.7	18.5	12.5	4.8	1.2	0.3
MSA[1]	7.7	26.8	31.4	17.2	11.2	4.3	1.1	0.2
U.S.	6.9	12.0	13.3	14.0	19.6	19.3	11.4	3.4

Note: Figures are percentages and cover owner-occupied housing units; (1) Figures cover the El Paso, TX Metropolitan Statistical Area
Source: U.S. Census Bureau, 2015-2019 American Community Survey 5-Year Estimates

Year Housing Structure Built

Area	2010 or Later	2000 -2009	1990 -1999	1980 -1989	1970 -1979	1960 -1969	1950 -1959	1940 -1949	Before 1940	Median Year
City	9.8	15.2	13.4	14.0	16.5	10.8	11.5	4.1	4.6	1982
MSA[1]	11.0	16.5	14.6	14.5	15.7	9.7	10.1	3.6	4.2	1985
U.S.	5.2	14.0	13.9	13.4	15.2	10.6	10.3	4.9	12.6	1978

Note: Figures are percentages except for Median Year; Note: (1) Figures cover the El Paso, TX Metropolitan Statistical Area
Source: U.S. Census Bureau, 2015-2019 American Community Survey 5-Year Estimates

Gross Monthly Rent

Area	Under $500	$500 -$999	$1,000 -$1,499	$1,500 -$1,999	$2,000 -$2,499	$2,500 -$2,999	$3,000 and up	Median ($)
City	15.2	53.4	25.4	4.9	0.5	0.3	0.2	837
MSA[1]	15.0	53.4	25.4	5.2	0.5	0.3	0.2	837
U.S.	9.4	36.2	30.0	14.0	5.6	2.4	2.4	1,062

Note: Figures are percentages except for Median; Gross rent is the contract rent plus the estimated average monthly cost of utilities (electricity, gas, and water and sewer) and fuels (oil, coal, kerosene, wood, etc.) if these are paid by the renter (or paid for the renter by someone else); (1) Figures cover the El Paso, TX Metropolitan Statistical Area
Source: U.S. Census Bureau, 2015-2019 American Community Survey 5-Year Estimates

HEALTH

Health Risk Factors

Category	MSA[1] (%)	U.S. (%)
Adults aged 18–64 who have any kind of health care coverage	65.5	87.3
Adults who reported being in good or better health	74.5	82.4
Adults who have been told they have high blood cholesterol	23.7	33.0
Adults who have been told they have high blood pressure	26.9	32.3
Adults who are current smokers	10.9	17.1
Adults who currently use E-cigarettes	n/a	4.6
Adults who currently use chewing tobacco, snuff, or snus	1.4	4.0
Adults who are heavy drinkers[2]	n/a	6.3
Adults who are binge drinkers[3]	19.2	17.4
Adults who are overweight (BMI 25.0 - 29.9)	33.8	35.3
Adults who are obese (BMI 30.0 - 99.8)	34.7	31.3
Adults who participated in any physical activities in the past month	74.5	74.4
Adults who always or nearly always wears a seat belt	97.5	94.3

Note: n/a not available; (1) Figures cover the El Paso, TX Metropolitan Statistical Area; (2) Heavy drinkers are classified as adult men having more than 14 drinks per week and adult women having more than 7 drinks per week; (3) Binge drinkers are classified as males having five or more drinks on one occasion or females having four or more drinks on one occasion
Source: Centers for Disease Control and Prevention, Behaviorial Risk Factor Surveillance System, SMART: Selected Metropolitan Area Risk Trends, 2017

Acute and Chronic Health Conditions

Category	MSA[1] (%)	U.S. (%)
Adults who have ever been told they had a heart attack	n/a	4.2
Adults who have ever been told they have angina or coronary heart disease	2.6	3.9
Adults who have ever been told they had a stroke	n/a	3.0
Adults who have ever been told they have asthma	10.9	14.2
Adults who have ever been told they have arthritis	18.1	24.9
Adults who have ever been told they have diabetes[2]	14.6	10.5
Adults who have ever been told they had skin cancer	n/a	6.2
Adults who have ever been told they had any other types of cancer	n/a	7.1
Adults who have ever been told they have COPD	n/a	6.5
Adults who have ever been told they have kidney disease	n/a	3.0
Adults who have ever been told they have a form of depression	15.8	20.5

Note: n/a not available; (1) Figures cover the El Paso, TX Metropolitan Statistical Area; (2) Figures do not include pregnancy-related, borderline, or pre-diabetes
Source: Centers for Disease Control and Prevention, Behaviorial Risk Factor Surveillance System, SMART: Selected Metropolitan Area Risk Trends, 2017

Health Screening and Vaccination Rates

Category	MSA[1] (%)	U.S. (%)
Adults aged 65+ who have had flu shot within the past year	61.6	60.7
Adults aged 65+ who have ever had a pneumonia vaccination	68.5	75.4
Adults who have ever been tested for HIV	39.2	36.1
Adults who have ever had the shingles or zoster vaccine?	16.8	28.9
Adults who have had their blood cholesterol checked within the last five years	88.8	85.9

Note: n/a not available; (1) Figures cover the El Paso, TX Metropolitan Statistical Area.
Source: Centers for Disease Control and Prevention, Behaviorial Risk Factor Surveillance System, SMART: Selected Metropolitan Area Risk Trends, 2017

Disability Status

Category	MSA[1] (%)	U.S. (%)
Adults who reported being deaf	3.7	6.7
Are you blind or have serious difficulty seeing, even when wearing glasses?	6.4	4.5
Are you limited in any way in any of your usual activities due of arthritis?	8.2	12.9
Do you have difficulty doing errands alone?	5.9	6.8
Do you have difficulty dressing or bathing?	4.0	3.6
Do you have serious difficulty concentrating/remembering/making decisions?	11.1	10.7
Do you have serious difficulty walking or climbing stairs?	13.4	13.6

Note: (1) Figures cover the El Paso, TX Metropolitan Statistical Area.
Source: Centers for Disease Control and Prevention, Behaviorial Risk Factor Surveillance System, SMART: Selected Metropolitan Area Risk Trends, 2017

Mortality Rates for the Top 10 Causes of Death in the U.S.

ICD-10[a] Sub-Chapter	ICD-10[a] Code	Age-Adjusted Mortality Rate[1] per 100,000 population County[2]	U.S.
Malignant neoplasms	C00-C97	130.3	149.2
Ischaemic heart diseases	I20-I25	82.2	90.5
Other forms of heart disease	I30-I51	30.8	52.2
Chronic lower respiratory diseases	J40-J47	28.7	39.6
Other degenerative diseases of the nervous system	G30-G31	43.1	37.6
Cerebrovascular diseases	I60-I69	29.1	37.2
Other external causes of accidental injury	W00-X59	23.8	36.1
Organic, including symptomatic, mental disorders	F01-F09	20.3	29.4
Hypertensive diseases	I10-I15	36.7	24.1
Diabetes mellitus	E10-E14	35.2	21.5

Note: (a) ICD-10 = International Classification of Diseases 10th Revision; (1) Mortality rates are a three-year average covering 2017-2019; (2) Figures cover El Paso County.
Source: Centers for Disease Control and Prevention, National Center for Health Statistics. Underlying Cause of Death 1999-2019 on CDC WONDER Online Database

Mortality Rates for Selected Causes of Death

ICD-10[a] Sub-Chapter	ICD-10[a] Code	Age-Adjusted Mortality Rate[1] per 100,000 population County[2]	U.S.
Assault	X85-Y09	3.4	6.0
Diseases of the liver	K70-K76	29.9	14.4
Human immunodeficiency virus (HIV) disease	B20-B24	2.0	1.5
Influenza and pneumonia	J09-J18	8.9	13.8
Intentional self-harm	X60-X84	11.2	14.1
Malnutrition	E40-E46	2.0	2.3
Obesity and other hyperalimentation	E65-E68	1.7	2.1
Renal failure	N17-N19	17.2	12.6
Transport accidents	V01-V99	12.9	12.3
Viral hepatitis	B15-B19	2.1	1.2

Note: (a) ICD-10 = International Classification of Diseases 10th Revision; (1) Mortality rates are a three-year average covering 2017-2019; (2) Figures cover El Paso County; Data are suppressed when the data meet the criteria for confidentiality constraints; Mortality rates are flagged as unreliable when the rate would be calculated with a numerator of 20 or less.
Source: Centers for Disease Control and Prevention, National Center for Health Statistics. Underlying Cause of Death 1999-2019 on CDC WONDER Online Database

Health Insurance Coverage

Area	With Health Insurance	With Private Health Insurance	With Public Health Insurance	Without Health Insurance	Population Under Age 19 Without Health Insurance
City	80.9	54.7	33.8	19.1	9.1
MSA[1]	79.7	52.6	33.9	20.3	9.8
U.S.	91.2	67.9	35.1	8.8	5.1

Note: Figures are percentages that cover the civilian noninstitutionalized population; (1) Figures cover the El Paso, TX Metropolitan Statistical Area
Source: U.S. Census Bureau, 2015-2019 American Community Survey 5-Year Estimates

Number of Medical Professionals

Area	MDs[3]	DOs[3,4]	Dentists	Podiatrists	Chiropractors	Optometrists
County[1] (number)	1,632	108	390	33	73	85
County[1] (rate[2])	195.0	12.9	46.5	3.9	8.7	10.1
U.S. (rate[2])	282.9	22.7	71.2	6.2	28.1	16.9

48141
Note: Data as of 2019 unless noted; (1) Data covers El Paso County; (2) Rate per 100,000 population; (3) Data as of 2018 and includes all active, non-federal physicians; (4) Doctor of Osteopathic Medicine
Source: U.S. Department of Health and Human Services, Health Resources and Services Administration, Bureau of Health Professions, Area Resource File (ARF) 2019-2020

EDUCATION

Public School District Statistics

District Name	Schls	Pupils	Pupil/Teacher Ratio	Minority Pupils[1] (%)	Free Lunch Eligible[2] (%)	IEP[3] (%)
Canutillo ISD	10	6,246	15.0	95.4	53.4	9.6
Clint ISD	14	11,388	17.4	96.4	86.6	8.7
El Paso ISD	93	57,315	14.7	90.6	71.0	11.1
Harmony Science Acad. (El Paso)	5	3,565	14.3	81.6	59.7	9.9
Socorro ISD	51	46,814	16.7	96.2	62.0	10.5
Ysleta ISD	61	41,064	15.0	96.9	73.4	12.6

Note: Table includes school districts with 2,000 or more students; (1) Percentage of students that are not non-Hispanic white; (2) Percentage of students that are eligible for the free lunch program; (3) Percentage of students that have an Individualized Education Program.
Source: U.S. Department of Education, National Center for Education Statistics, Common Core of Data, Local Education Agency (School District) Universe Survey: School Year 2018-2019; U.S. Department of Education, National Center for Education Statistics, Common Core of Data, Public Elementary/Secondary School Universe Survey: School Year 2018-2019

Best High Schools

According to *U.S. News*, El Paso is home to two of the top 500 high schools in the U.S.: **Harmony Science Academy (El Paso)** (#311); **Valle Verde Early College High School** (#453). Nearly 18,000 public, magnet and charter schools were ranked based on their performance on state assessments and how well they prepare students for college. *U.S. News & World Report, "Best High Schools 2020"*

Highest Level of Education

Area	Less than H.S.	H.S. Diploma	Some College, No Deg.	Associate Degree	Bachelor's Degree	Master's Degree	Prof. School Degree	Doctorate Degree
City	19.7	23.0	24.0	8.2	16.7	6.4	1.2	0.8
MSA[1]	21.7	23.7	23.1	8.2	15.7	5.7	1.1	0.7
U.S.	12.0	27.0	20.4	8.5	19.8	8.8	2.1	1.4

Note: Figures cover persons age 25 and over; (1) Figures cover the El Paso, TX Metropolitan Statistical Area
Source: U.S. Census Bureau, 2015-2019 American Community Survey 5-Year Estimates

Educational Attainment by Race

Area	High School Graduate or Higher (%)					Bachelor's Degree or Higher (%)				
	Total	White	Black	Asian	Hisp.[2]	Total	White	Black	Asian	Hisp.[2]
City	80.3	81.1	95.7	90.1	76.4	25.1	25.7	30.5	54.0	20.7
MSA[1]	78.3	79.5	95.3	90.1	74.4	23.2	24.0	29.9	52.6	19.2
U.S.	88.0	89.9	86.0	87.1	68.7	32.1	33.5	21.6	54.3	16.4

Note: Figures shown cover persons 25 years old and over; (1) Figures cover the El Paso, TX Metropolitan Statistical Area; (2) People of Hispanic origin can be of any race
Source: U.S. Census Bureau, 2015-2019 American Community Survey 5-Year Estimates

School Enrollment by Grade and Control

Area	Preschool (%)		Kindergarten (%)		Grades 1 - 4 (%)		Grades 5 - 8 (%)		Grades 9 - 12 (%)	
	Public	Private	Public	Private	Public	Private	Public	Private	Public	Private
City	78.5	21.5	93.3	6.7	95.0	5.0	94.6	5.4	96.2	3.8
MSA[1]	81.0	19.0	93.9	6.1	95.1	4.9	94.8	5.2	96.4	3.6
U.S.	59.1	40.9	87.6	12.4	89.5	10.5	89.4	10.6	90.1	9.9

Note: Figures shown cover persons 3 years old and over; (1) Figures cover the El Paso, TX Metropolitan Statistical Area
Source: U.S. Census Bureau, 2015-2019 American Community Survey 5-Year Estimates

Higher Education

Four-Year Colleges			Two-Year Colleges			Medical Schools[1]	Law Schools[2]	Voc/Tech[3]
Public	Private Non-profit	Private For-profit	Public	Private Non-profit	Private For-profit			
2	0	3	1	0	4	1	0	5

Note: Figures cover institutions located within the city limits and include main campuses only; (1) includes schools accredited by the Liaison Committee on Medical Education and the American Osteopathic Association's Commission on Osteopathic College Accreditation; (2) includes ABA-accredited schools, schools with provisional ABA accreditation, and state accredited schools; (3) includes all schools with programs that are less than 2 years.
Source: National Center for Education Statistics, Integrated Postsecondary Education System (IPEDS), 2019-20; Wikipedia, List of Medical Schools in the United States, accessed April 2, 2021; Wikipedia, List of Law Schools in the United States, accessed April 2, 2021

EMPLOYERS

Major Employers

Company Name	Industry
Alorica	Inbound customer service
Automatic Data Processing	Contact center - private
Coca-Cola Enterprises	Bottling & distributing
Datamark	Data processing & related service
Del Sol Medical Center	Health care - private
Dish Network	Technical support center
El Paso Electric Corporation	Electric utilities
GC Services	Inbound customer service
Las Palmas Medical Center	Health care - private
Redcats USA	Inbound customer service
RM Personnel	Employment services
T&T Staff Management	Employment services
Texas Tech University Health Sci Ctr	Higher education & health care
Union Pacific Railroad Co.	Transportation
University Medical Center	Health care - public
Visiting Nurse Association of El Paso	Health care & social assistance
West Customer Management Group	Inbound customer service
Western Refining	Corporate headquarters petro chemical refinery

Note: Companies shown are located within the El Paso, TX Metropolitan Statistical Area.
Source: Hoovers.com; Wikipedia

PUBLIC SAFETY

Crime Rate

Area	All Crimes	Violent Crimes				Property Crimes		
		Murder	Rape[3]	Robbery	Aggrav. Assault	Burglary	Larceny -Theft	Motor Vehicle Theft
City	1,863.7	5.8	45.1	49.2	252.5	152.6	1,234.6	123.9
Suburbs[1]	1,251.9	0.6	37.2	15.8	195.1	156.6	746.2	100.4
Metro[2]	1,749.1	4.9	43.7	42.9	241.7	153.3	1,143.1	119.5
U.S.	2,489.3	5.0	42.6	81.6	250.2	340.5	1,549.5	219.9

Note: Figures are crimes per 100,000 population; (1) All areas within the metro area that are located outside the city limits; (2) Figures cover the El Paso, TX Metropolitan Statistical Area; (3) All figures shown were reported using the revised Uniform Crime Reporting (UCR) definition of rape.
Source: FBI Uniform Crime Reports, 2019

Hate Crimes

Area	Number of Quarters Reported	Race/Ethnicity/ Ancestry	Religion	Sexual Orientation	Disability	Gender	Gender Identity
City	4	3	0	0	0	0	0
U.S.	4	3,963	1,521	1,195	157	69	198

Source: Federal Bureau of Investigation, Hate Crime Statistics 2019

Identity Theft Consumer Reports

Area	Reports	Reports per 100,000 Population	Rank[2]
MSA[1]	1,505	178	243
U.S.	1,387,615	423	-

Note: (1) Figures cover the El Paso, TX Metropolitan Statistical Area; (2) Rank ranges from 1 to 391 where 1 indicates greatest number of identity theft reports per 100,000 population
Source: Federal Trade Commission, Consumer Sentinel Network Data Book 2020

Fraud and Other Consumer Reports

Area	Reports	Reports per 100,000 Population	Rank[2]
MSA[1]	4,778	566	322
U.S.	3,385,133	1,031	-

Note: (1) Figures cover the El Paso, TX Metropolitan Statistical Area; (2) Rank ranges from 1 to 391 where 1 indicates greatest number of fraud and other consumer reports per 100,000 population
Source: Federal Trade Commission, Consumer Sentinel Network Data Book 2020

POLITICS

2020 Presidential Election Results

Area	Biden	Trump	Jorgensen	Hawkins	Other
El Paso County	66.7	31.6	1.0	0.5	0.2
U.S.	51.3	46.8	1.2	0.3	0.5

Note: Results are percentages and may not add to 100% due to rounding
Source: Dave Leip's Atlas of U.S. Presidential Elections

SPORTS

Professional Sports Teams

Team Name	League	Year Established
No teams are located in the metro area		

Source: Wikipedia, Major Professional Sports Teams of the United States and Canada, April 6, 2021

CLIMATE

Average and Extreme Temperatures

Temperature	Jan	Feb	Mar	Apr	May	Jun	Jul	Aug	Sep	Oct	Nov	Dec	Yr.
Extreme High (°F)	80	83	89	98	104	114	112	108	104	96	87	80	114
Average High (°F)	57	63	70	79	87	96	95	93	88	79	66	58	78
Average Temp. (°F)	44	49	56	64	73	81	83	81	75	65	52	45	64
Average Low (°F)	31	35	41	49	58	66	70	68	62	50	38	32	50
Extreme Low (°F)	-8	8	14	23	31	46	57	56	42	25	1	5	-8

Note: Figures cover the years 1948-1995
Source: National Climatic Data Center, International Station Meteorological Climate Summary, 9/96

Average Precipitation/Snowfall/Humidity

Precip./Humidity	Jan	Feb	Mar	Apr	May	Jun	Jul	Aug	Sep	Oct	Nov	Dec	Yr.
Avg. Precip. (in.)	0.4	0.4	0.3	0.2	0.3	0.7	1.6	1.5	1.4	0.7	0.3	0.6	8.6
Avg. Snowfall (in.)	1	1	Tr	Tr	0	0	0	0	0	Tr	1	2	6
Avg. Rel. Hum. 6am (%)	68	60	50	43	44	46	63	69	72	66	63	68	59
Avg. Rel. Hum. 3pm (%)	34	27	21	17	17	17	28	30	32	29	30	36	26

Note: Figures cover the years 1948-1995; Tr = Trace amounts (<0.05 in. of rain; <0.5 in. of snow)
Source: National Climatic Data Center, International Station Meteorological Climate Summary, 9/96

Weather Conditions

Temperature			Daytime Sky			Precipitation		
10°F & below	32°F & below	90°F & above	Clear	Partly cloudy	Cloudy	0.01 inch or more precip.	0.1 inch or more snow/ice	Thunderstorms
1	59	106	147	164	54	49	3	35

Note: Figures are average number of days per year and cover the years 1948-1995
Source: National Climatic Data Center, International Station Meteorological Climate Summary, 9/96

HAZARDOUS WASTE

Superfund Sites

The El Paso, TX metro area has no sites on the EPA's Superfund Final National Priorities List. There are a total of 1,375 Superfund sites with a status of proposed or final on the list in the U.S. *U.S. Environmental Protection Agency, National Priorities List, April 7, 2021*

AIR QUALITY

Air Quality Trends: Ozone

	1990	1995	2000	2005	2010	2015	2016	2017	2018	2019
MSA[1]	0.080	0.078	0.082	0.074	0.072	0.071	0.068	0.073	0.077	0.074
U.S.	0.088	0.089	0.082	0.080	0.073	0.068	0.069	0.068	0.069	0.065

Note: (1) Data covers the El Paso, TX Metropolitan Statistical Area. The values shown are the composite ozone concentration averages among trend sites based on the highest fourth daily maximum 8-hour concentration in parts per million. These trends are based on sites having an adequate record of monitoring data during the trend period. Data from exceptional events are included.
Source: U.S. Environmental Protection Agency, Air Quality Monitoring Information, "Air Quality Trends by City, 1990-2019"

Air Quality Index

Area	Percent of Days when Air Quality was...[2]					AQI Statistics[2]	
	Good	Moderate	Unhealthy for Sensitive Groups	Unhealthy	Very Unhealthy	Maximum	Median
MSA[1]	40.3	56.2	3.0	0.5	0.0	157	53

Note: (1) Data covers the El Paso, TX Metropolitan Statistical Area; (2) Based on 365 days with AQI data in 2019. Air Quality Index (AQI) is an index for reporting daily air quality. EPA calculates the AQI for five major air pollutants regulated by the Clean Air Act: ground-level ozone, particle pollution (aka particulate matter), carbon monoxide, sulfur dioxide, and nitrogen dioxide. The AQI runs from 0 to 500. The higher the AQI value, the greater the level of air pollution and the greater the health concern. There are six AQI categories: "Good" AQI is between 0 and 50. Air quality is considered satisfactory; "Moderate" AQI is between 51 and 100. Air quality is acceptable; "Unhealthy for Sensitive Groups" When AQI values are between 101 and 150, members of sensitive groups may experience health effects; "Unhealthy" When AQI values are between 151 and 200 everyone may begin to experience health effects; "Very Unhealthy" AQI values between 201 and 300 trigger a health alert; "Hazardous" AQI values over 300 trigger warnings of emergency conditions (not shown).
Source: U.S. Environmental Protection Agency, Air Quality Index Report, 2019

Air Quality Index Pollutants

Area	Percent of Days when AQI Pollutant was...[2]					
	Carbon Monoxide	Nitrogen Dioxide	Ozone	Sulfur Dioxide	Particulate Matter 2.5	Particulate Matter 10
MSA[1]	0.0	5.8	55.9	0.0	37.5	0.8

Note: (1) Data covers the El Paso, TX Metropolitan Statistical Area; (2) Based on 365 days with AQI data in 2019. The Air Quality Index (AQI) is an index for reporting daily air quality. EPA calculates the AQI for five major air pollutants regulated by the Clean Air Act: ground-level ozone, particle pollution (also known as particulate matter), carbon monoxide, sulfur dioxide, and nitrogen dioxide. The AQI runs from 0 to 500. The higher the AQI value, the greater the level of air pollution and the greater the health concern.
Source: U.S. Environmental Protection Agency, Air Quality Index Report, 2019

Maximum Air Pollutant Concentrations: Particulate Matter, Ozone, CO and Lead

	Particulate Matter 10 (ug/m^3)	Particulate Matter 2.5 Wtd AM (ug/m^3)	Particulate Matter 2.5 24-Hr (ug/m^3)	Ozone (ppm)	Carbon Monoxide (ppm)	Lead (ug/m^3)
MSA[1] Level	79	8.5	25	0.075	2	0.01
NAAQS[2]	150	15	35	0.075	9	0.15
Met NAAQS[2]	Yes	Yes	Yes	Yes	Yes	Yes

Note: (1) Data covers the El Paso, TX Metropolitan Statistical Area; Data from exceptional events are included; (2) National Ambient Air Quality Standards; ppm = parts per million; ug/m^3 = micrograms per cubic meter; n/a not available.
Concentrations: Particulate Matter 10 (coarse particulate)—highest second maximum 24-hour concentration; Particulate Matter 2.5 Wtd AM (fine particulate)—highest weighted annual mean concentration; Particulate Matter 2.5 24-Hour (fine particulate)—highest 98th percentile 24-hour concentration; Ozone—highest fourth daily maximum 8-hour concentration; Carbon Monoxide—highest second maximum non-overlapping 8-hour concentration; Lead—maximum running 3-month average
Source: U.S. Environmental Protection Agency, Air Quality Monitoring Information, "Air Quality Statistics by City, 2019"

Maximum Air Pollutant Concentrations: Nitrogen Dioxide and Sulfur Dioxide

	Nitrogen Dioxide AM (ppb)	Nitrogen Dioxide 1-Hr (ppb)	Sulfur Dioxide AM (ppb)	Sulfur Dioxide 1-Hr (ppb)	Sulfur Dioxide 24-Hr (ppb)
MSA[1] Level	14	n/a	n/a	n/a	n/a
NAAQS[2]	53	100	30	75	140
Met NAAQS[2]	Yes	n/a	n/a	n/a	n/a

Note: (1) Data covers the El Paso, TX Metropolitan Statistical Area; Data from exceptional events are included; (2) National Ambient Air Quality Standards; ppm = parts per million; ug/m^3 = micrograms per cubic meter; n/a not available.
Concentrations: Nitrogen Dioxide AM—highest arithmetic mean concentration; Nitrogen Dioxide 1-Hr—highest 98th percentile 1-hour daily maximum concentration; Sulfur Dioxide AM—highest annual mean concentration; Sulfur Dioxide 1-Hr—highest 99th percentile 1-hour daily maximum concentration; Sulfur Dioxide 24-Hr—highest second maximum 24-hour concentration
Source: U.S. Environmental Protection Agency, Air Quality Monitoring Information, "Air Quality Statistics by City, 2019"

Fort Worth, Texas

Background

Fort Worth lies in north central Texas near the headwaters of the Trinity River. Despite its modern skyscrapers, multiple freeways, shopping malls, and extensive industry, the city is known for its easy-going, Western atmosphere.

The area has seen many travelers. Nomadic Native Americans of the plains rode through on horses bred from those brought by Spanish explorers. The 1840s saw American-Anglos settle in the region. On June 6, 1849, Major Ripley A. Arnold and his U.S. Cavalry troop established an outpost on the Trinity River to protect settlers moving westward. The fort was named for General William J. Worth, Commander of the U.S. Army's Texas department. When the fort was abandoned in 1853, settlers moved in and converted the vacant barracks into trading establishments and homes, stealing the county seat from Birdville (an act made legal in the 1860 election).

In the 1860s, Fort Worth, which was close to the Chisholm Trail, became an oasis for cowboys traveling to and from Kansas. Although the town's growth virtually stopped during the Civil War, Fort Worth was incorporated as a city in 1873. In a race against time, the final 26 miles of the Texas & Pacific Line were completed and Fort Worth survived to be a part of the West Texas oil boom in 1917.

Real prosperity followed at the end of World War II, when the city became a center for several military installations. Aviation is the city's principal source of economic growth. Its leading industries include the manufacture of aircraft, automobiles, machinery, and containers, as well as food processing and brewing. Emerging economic sectors in the 21st century include semiconductor manufacturing, and communications equipment manufacturing and distribution.

Since it first began testing DNA samples in 2003, the DNA Identity Laboratory at the University of North Texas Health Science Center has made over 100 matches, helping to solve missing-persons cases and close criminal cases. The university is also home to the national Osteopathic Research Center, the only academic DNA Lab qualified to work with the FBI, the Texas Center for Health Disparities and the Health Institutes of Texas. Other colleges in Fort Worth include Texas Christian University, Southwestern Baptist Seminary, and Texas Wesleyan University.

> The Dallas-Fort Worth metro area hosted five college football bowl games, due to fewer COVID-19 restrictions than in other areas.

Fort Worth's most comprehensive mixed-use project at Walsh Ranch was completed in 2017 with space for residential, commercial, office and retail. The 7,275-acre planned community is named after the original owners of the property, F. Howard and Mary D. Walsh, who were well-known ranchers, philanthropists and civic leaders. Walsh Ranch has room for 50,000 Fort Worth residents.

The Omni Fort Worth Hotel was host to the 2011 AFC champion Pittsburgh Steelers during Super Bowl XLV, and the city's 3,600-acre Greer Island Nature Center and Refuge is coming up on its 60th anniversary.

Winter temperatures and rainfall are both modified by the northeast-northwest mountain barrier, which prevents shallow cold air masses from crossing over from the west. Summer temperatures vary with cloud and shower activity, but are generally mild. Summer precipitation is largely from local thunderstorms and varies from year to year. Damaging rains are infrequent. Hurricanes have produced heavy rainfall, but are usually not accompanied by destructive winds. In February 2021, record-breaking low temperature (-2) caused icy roads and a 133-car pile-up, as well as a major disruption in electricity across the state.

Rankings

General Rankings

- For its "Best for Vets: Places to Live 2019" rankings, *Military Times* evaluated 599 cities (83 large, 234 medium, 282 small) and compared the locations across three broad categories: veteran and military culture/services; economic indicators; and livability factors such as health, crime, traffic, and school quality. Fort Worth ranked #22 out of the top 25, in the large city category (population of more than 250,000). Data points more specific to veterans and the military weighed more heavily than others. *rebootcamp.militarytimes.com, "Military Times Best Places to Live 2019," September 10, 2018*

- The Dallas metro area was identified as one of America's fastest-growing areas in terms of population and business growth by *MagnifyMoney*. The area ranked #7 out of 35. The 100 most populous metro areas in the U.S. were evaluated on their change from 2011-2016 in the following categories: people and housing; workforce and employment opportunities; growing industry. *www.businessinsider.com, "The 35 Cities in the US with the Biggest Influx of People, the Most Work Opportunities, and the Hottest Business Growth," August 12, 2018*

- The Fort Worth metro area was identified as one of America's fastest-growing areas in terms of population and economy by *Forbes*. The area ranked #5 out of 25. The 100 most populous metro areas in the U.S. were evaluated on the following criteria: estimated population growth; employment; economic output; wages; home values. *Forbes, "America's Fastest-Growing Cities 2018," February 28, 2018*

- In its eighth annual survey, *Travel + Leisure* readers nominated their favorite small cities and towns in America—those with 100,000 or fewer residents—voting on numerous attractive features in categories including culture, food and drink, quality of life, style, and people. After 50,000 votes, Fort Worth was ranked #18 among the proposed favorites. *www.travelandleisure.com, "America's Favorite Cities," October 20, 2017*

Business/Finance Rankings

- Based on metro area social media reviews, the employment opinion group Glassdoor surveyed 50 of the most populous U.S. metro areas and equally weighed cost of living, hiring opportunity, and job satisfaction to compose a list of "25 Best Cities for Jobs." Median pay and home value, and number of active job openings were also factored in. The Dallas metro area was ranked #25 in overall job satisfaction. *www.glassdoor.com, "Best Cities for Jobs," February 25, 2020*

- The Brookings Institution ranked the 100 largest metro areas in the U.S. based on income inequality. Dallas was ranked #60 (#1 = greatest inequality). Criteria: the "95/20 ratio," a figure representing the income at which a household earns more than 95 percent of all other households, divided by the income at which a household earns more than only 20 percent of all other households. *Brookings Institution, "Household Income Inequality, 100 Largest U.S. Metro Areas, 2014-2016," February 5, 2018*

- *Forbes* ranked the 100 largest metro areas in the U.S. in terms of the "Best Cities for Young Professionals." The Dallas metro area ranked #5 out of 25. Criteria: median rent of a two-bedroom apartment; job growth and unemployment rate; median salary of college graduates with 5 or less years of work experience; networking opportunities; social outlook; percentage of population 25 years of age and older with college degrees. *Forbes.com, "America's 25 Best Cities for Young Professionals in 2017," May 22, 2017*

- The Dallas metro area was identified as one of the most debt-ridden places in America by the finance site Credit.com. The metro area was ranked #2. Criteria: residents' average credit card debt as well as median income. *Credit.com, "25 Cities With the Most Credit Card Debt," February 28, 2018*

- Dallas was identified as one of America's most frugal metro areas by *Coupons.com*. The city ranked #2 out of 25. Criteria: digital coupon usage. *Coupons.com, "America's Most Frugal Cities of 2017," March 22, 2018*

- Fort Worth was identified as one of the unhappiest cities to work in by CareerBliss.com, an online community for career advancement. The city ranked #2 out of 5. Criteria: an employee's relationship with his or her boss and co-workers; general work environment; compensation; opportunities for advancement; company culture and job reputation; and resources. *Businesswire.com, "CareerBliss Unhappiest Cities to Work 2019," February 12, 2019*

- The Fort Worth metro area appeared on the Milken Institute "2021 Best Performing Cities" list. Rank: #35 out of 200 large metro areas (population over 250,000). Criteria: job growth; wage and salary growth; high-tech output growth; housing affordability; household broadband access. *Milken Institute, "Best-Performing Cities 2021," February 16, 2021*

- *Forbes* ranked the 200 most populous metro areas to determine the nation's "Best Places for Business and Careers." The Fort Worth metro area was ranked #20. Criteria: costs (business and living); job growth (past and projected); income growth; quality of life; educational attainment (college and high school); projected economic growth; cultural and leisure opportunities; workplace tolerance laws; net migration patterns. *Forbes, "The Best Places for Business and Careers 2019: Seattle Still On Top," October 30, 2019*

Culture/Performing Arts Rankings

- Fort Worth was selected as one of "America's Favorite Cities." The city ranked #15 in the "Architecture" category. Respondents to an online survey were asked to rate their favorite place (population over 100,000) in over 65 categories. *Travelandleisure.com, "America's Favorite Cities for Architecture 2016," March 2, 2017*

Education Rankings

- Fort Worth was selected as one of America's most literate cities. The city ranked #65 out of the 84 largest U.S. cities. Criteria: number of booksellers; library resources; Internet resources; educational attainment; periodical publishing resources; newspaper circulation. *Central Connecticut State University, "America's Most Literate Cities, 2018," February 2019*

Environmental Rankings

- Sperling's BestPlaces assessed the 50 largest metropolitan areas of the United States for the likelihood of dangerously extreme weather events or earthquakes. In general the Southeast and South-Central regions have the highest risk of weather extremes and earthquakes, while the Pacific Northwest enjoys the lowest risk. Of the most risky metropolitan areas, the Fort Worth metro area was ranked #4. *www.bestplaces.net, "Avoid Natural Disasters: BestPlaces Reveals The Top 10 Safest Places to Live," October 25, 2017*

- The U.S. Environmental Protection Agency (EPA) released a list of U.S. metropolitan areas with the most ENERGY STAR certified buildings in 2019. The Dallas metro area was ranked #4 out of 25. *U.S. Environmental Protection Agency, "2020 Energy Star Top Cities," March 2020*

- Dallas was highlighted as one of the 25 most ozone-polluted metro areas in the U.S. during 2016 through 2018. The area ranked #21. *American Lung Association, "State of the Air 2020," April 21, 2020*

Food/Drink Rankings

- Globe Life Park was selected as one of PETA's "Top 10 Vegan-Friendly Ballparks" for 2019. The park ranked #1. *People for the Ethical Treatment of Animals, "Top 10 Vegan-Friendly Ballparks," May 23, 2019*

Health/Fitness Rankings

- For each of the 100 largest cities in the United States, the American Fitness Index®, published by the American College of Sports Medicine and the Anthem Foundation, evaluated community infrastructure and 33 health behaviors including preventive health, levels of chronic disease conditions, pedestrian safety, air quality, and community resources that support physical activity. Fort Worth ranked #90 for "community fitness." *americanfitnessindex.org, "2020 ACSM American Fitness Index Summary Report," July 14, 2020*

- Dallas was identified as a "2021 Spring Allergy Capital." The area ranked #19 out of 100. Three groups of factors were used to identify the most challenging cities for people with allergies during the spring season: annual spring pollen levels; over the counter medicine use; number of board-certified allergy specialists. *Asthma and Allergy Foundation of America, "Spring Allergy Capitals 2021," February 23, 2021*

- Dallas was identified as a "2021 Fall Allergy Capital." The area ranked #21 out of 100. Three groups of factors were used to identify the most challenging cities for people with allergies during the fall season: annual fall pollen levels; over the counter medicine use; number of board-certified allergy specialists. *Asthma and Allergy Foundation of America, "Fall Allergy Capitals 2021," February 23, 2021*

- Dallas was identified as a "2019 Asthma Capital." The area ranked #76 out of the nation's 100 largest metropolitan areas. Criteria: estimated asthma prevalence; crude death rate from asthma; and ER visits due to asthma. Risk factors analyzed but not factored in the rankings: annual pollen score; annual air quality; public smoking laws; number of board-certified asthma specialists; rescue medication use; controller medication use; uninsured rate; poverty rate. *Asthma and Allergy Foundation of America, "Asthma Capitals 2019: The Most Challenging Places to Live With Asthma," May 7, 2019*

Real Estate Rankings

- FitSmallBusiness looked at 50 of the largest metropolitan areas in the U.S. to determine which metro was the best to start a real estate business. Data was compiled from such sources as: Zillow, Trulia, U.S. Census Bureau, and the Bureau of Labor Statistics. Criteria: location; inventory; annual wages; median sales price of homes; days on the market; median price cut percentage; and other factors that would influence real estate professional growth. The Dallas metro area ranked #19. *fitsmallbusiness.com, "The Best Cities to Become a Real Estate Agent in 2018," January 30, 2018*

- *WalletHub* compared the most populated U.S. cities to determine which had the best markets for real estate agents. Fort Worth ranked #43 where demand was high and pay was the best. Criteria: sales per agent; annual median wage for real-estate agents; monthly average starting salary for real estate agents; real estate job density and competition; unemployment rate; home turnover rate; housing-market health index; and other relevant metrics. *www.WalletHub.com, "2019's Best Places to Be a Real Estate Agent," April 24, 2019*

- Fort Worth was ranked #165 out of 268 metro areas in terms of housing affordability in 2020 by the National Association of Home Builders (#1 = most affordable). Criteria: the share of homes sold in that area affordable to a family earning the local median income, based on standard mortgage underwriting criteria. *National Association of Home Builders®, NAHB-Wells Fargo Housing Opportunity Index, 4th Quarter 2020*

Safety Rankings

- Allstate ranked the 200 largest cities in America in terms of driver safety. Fort Worth ranked #139. Criteria: internal property damage claims over a two-year period from January 2016 to December 2017. The report helps increase the importance of safety and awareness behind the wheel. *Allstate, "Allstate America's Best Drivers Report, 2019" June 24, 2019*

Women/Minorities Rankings

- The *Houston Chronicle* listed the Dallas metro area as #7 in top places for young Latinos to live in the U.S. Research was largely based on housing and occupational data from the largest metropolitan areas performed by *Forbes* and NBC Universo. Criteria: percentage of 18-34 year-olds; Latino college grad rates; and diversity. *blog.chron.com, "The 15 Best Big Cities for Latino Millenials," January 26, 2016*

- Personal finance website *WalletHub* compared more than 180 U.S. cities across two key dimensions, "Hispanic Business-Friendliness" and "Hispanic Purchasing Power," to arrive at the most favorable conditions for Hispanic entrepreneurs. Fort Worth was ranked #14 out of 182. Criteria includes: share of Hispanic-Owned Businesses; Hispanic entrepreneurship rate to median annual income of Hispanics; Small Business-Friendliness score; cost of living; and number of Hispanics with at least a bachelor's degree. *WalletHub.com, "2019's Best Cities for Hispanic Entrepreneurs," May 1, 2019*

Miscellaneous Rankings

- The watchdog site, Charity Navigator, conducted a study of charities in major markets both to analyze statistical differences in their financial, accountability, and transparency practices and to track year-to-year variations in individual philanthropic communities. The Dallas metro area was ranked #5 among the 30 metro markets in the rating category of Overall Score. *www.charitynavigator.org, "2017 Metro Market Study," May 1, 2017*

- *WalletHub* compared the 150 most populated U.S. cities to determine their operating efficiency. A "Quality of City Services" score was constructed for each city and then divided by the total budget per capita to reveal which were managed the best. Fort Worth ranked #51. Criteria: financial stability; economy; education; safety; health; infrastructure and pollution. *www.WalletHub.com, "2020's Best- & Worst-Run Cities in America," June 29, 2020*

- Fort Worth was selected as one of "America's Friendliest Cities." The city ranked #9 in the "Friendliest" category. Respondents to an online survey were asked to rate 38 top urban destinations in the United States as to general friendliness, as well as manners, politeness and warm disposition. *Travel + Leisure, "America's Friendliest Cities," October 20, 2017*

Business Environment

DEMOGRAPHICS

Population Growth

Area	1990 Census	2000 Census	2010 Census	2019* Estimate	Population Growth (%) 1990-2019	Population Growth (%) 2010-2019
City	448,311	534,694	741,206	874,401	95.0	18.0
MSA[1]	3,989,294	5,161,544	6,371,773	7,320,663	83.5	14.9
U.S.	248,709,873	281,421,906	308,745,538	324,697,795	30.6	5.2

Note: (1) Figures cover the Dallas-Fort Worth-Arlington, TX Metropolitan Statistical Area; (*) 2015-2019 5-year estimated population
Source: U.S. Census Bureau, 1990 Census, Census 2000, Census 2010, 2015-2019 American Community Survey 5-Year Estimates

Household Size

Area	One	Two	Three	Four	Five	Six	Seven or More	Average Household Size
City	26.1	28.9	16.5	15.2	7.8	3.4	2.1	2.90
MSA[1]	25.0	30.6	16.8	15.2	7.6	2.9	1.8	2.80
U.S.	27.9	33.9	15.6	12.9	6.0	2.3	1.4	2.60

Note: (1) Figures cover the Dallas-Fort Worth-Arlington, TX Metropolitan Statistical Area
Source: U.S. Census Bureau, 2015-2019 American Community Survey 5-Year Estimates

Race

Area	White Alone[2] (%)	Black Alone[2] (%)	Asian Alone[2] (%)	AIAN[3] Alone[2] (%)	NHOPI[4] Alone[2] (%)	Other Race Alone[2] (%)	Two or More Races (%)
City	63.8	18.9	4.6	0.5	0.1	9.0	3.2
MSA[1]	68.3	15.8	6.9	0.5	0.1	5.4	3.0
U.S.	72.5	12.7	5.5	0.8	0.2	4.9	3.3

Note: (1) Figures cover the Dallas-Fort Worth-Arlington, TX Metropolitan Statistical Area; (2) Alone is defined as not being in combination with one or more other races; (3) American Indian and Alaska Native; (4) Native Hawaiian and Other Pacific Islander
Source: U.S. Census Bureau, 2015-2019 American Community Survey 5-Year Estimates

Hispanic or Latino Origin

Area	Total (%)	Mexican (%)	Puerto Rican (%)	Cuban (%)	Other (%)
City	35.1	30.6	1.1	0.3	3.1
MSA[1]	28.9	23.9	0.7	0.3	4.0
U.S.	18.0	11.2	1.7	0.7	4.3

Note: Persons of Hispanic or Latino origin can be of any race; (1) Figures cover the Dallas-Fort Worth-Arlington, TX Metropolitan Statistical Area
Source: U.S. Census Bureau, 2015-2019 American Community Survey 5-Year Estimates

Ancestry

Area	German	Irish	English	American	Italian	Polish	French[2]	Scottish	Dutch
City	7.4	6.0	5.6	5.0	1.9	0.9	1.5	1.4	0.7
MSA[1]	8.6	6.5	6.7	6.3	2.1	1.1	1.7	1.6	0.7
U.S.	13.3	9.7	7.2	6.2	5.1	2.8	2.3	1.7	1.2

Note: Figures are the percentage of the total population reporting a particular ancestry. The nine most commonly reported ancestries in the U.S. are shown. Figures include multiple ancestries (e.g. if a person reported being Irish and Italian, they were included in both columns); (1) Figures cover the Dallas-Fort Worth-Arlington, TX Metropolitan Statistical Area; (2) Excludes Basque
Source: U.S. Census Bureau, 2015-2019 American Community Survey 5-Year Estimates

Foreign-born Population

Area	Any Foreign Country	Asia	Mexico	Europe	Caribbean	Central America[2]	South America	Africa	Canada
City	16.8	3.4	9.8	0.6	0.3	0.9	0.5	1.2	0.2
MSA[1]	18.7	5.3	8.4	0.8	0.3	1.5	0.6	1.5	0.2
U.S.	13.6	4.2	3.5	1.5	1.3	1.1	1.0	0.7	0.2

Note: (1) Figures cover the Dallas-Fort Worth-Arlington, TX Metropolitan Statistical Area; (2) Excludes Mexico.
Source: U.S. Census Bureau, 2015-2019 American Community Survey 5-Year Estimates

Marital Status

Area	Never Married	Now Married[2]	Separated	Widowed	Divorced
City	35.4	46.3	2.3	4.5	11.4
MSA[1]	32.8	50.3	2.1	4.4	10.5
U.S.	33.4	48.1	1.9	5.8	10.9

Note: Figures are percentages and cover the population 15 years of age and older; (1) Figures cover the Dallas-Fort Worth-Arlington, TX Metropolitan Statistical Area; (2) Excludes separated
Source: U.S. Census Bureau, 2015-2019 American Community Survey 5-Year Estimates

Disability by Age

Area	All Ages	Under 18 Years Old	18 to 64 Years Old	65 Years and Over
City	10.2	3.8	9.1	35.9
MSA[1]	9.5	3.4	7.9	33.7
U.S.	12.6	4.2	10.3	34.5

Note: Figures show percent of the civilian noninstitutionalized population that reported having a disability. Disability status is determined from six types of difficulty: vision, hearing, cognitive, ambulatory, self-care, and independent living. For children under 5 years old, hearing and vision difficulty are used to determine disability status. For children between the ages of 5 and 14, disability status is determined from hearing, vision, cognitive, ambulatory, and self-care difficulties. For people aged 15 years and older, they are considered to have a disability if they have difficulty with any one of the six difficulty types; Note: (1) Figures cover the Dallas-Fort Worth-Arlington, TX Metropolitan Statistical Area
Source: U.S. Census Bureau, 2015-2019 American Community Survey 5-Year Estimates

Age

Area	Under Age 5	Age 5–19	Age 20–34	Age 35–44	Age 45–54	Age 55–64	Age 65–74	Age 75–84	Age 85+	Median Age
City	8.0	22.5	23.3	14.0	12.4	10.1	5.9	2.6	1.2	32.6
MSA[1]	7.0	21.8	21.5	14.2	13.4	11.2	6.8	3.1	1.1	34.8
U.S.	6.1	19.1	20.7	12.6	13.0	12.9	9.1	4.6	1.9	38.1

Note: (1) Figures cover the Dallas-Fort Worth-Arlington, TX Metropolitan Statistical Area
Source: U.S. Census Bureau, 2015-2019 American Community Survey 5-Year Estimates

Gender

Area	Males	Females	Males per 100 Females
City	428,238	446,163	96.0
MSA[1]	3,601,569	3,719,094	96.8
U.S.	159,886,919	164,810,876	97.0

Note: (1) Figures cover the Dallas-Fort Worth-Arlington, TX Metropolitan Statistical Area
Source: U.S. Census Bureau, 2015-2019 American Community Survey 5-Year Estimates

Religious Groups by Family

Area	Catholic	Baptist	Non-Den.	Methodist[2]	Lutheran	LDS[3]	Pentecostal	Presbyterian[4]	Muslim[5]	Judaism
MSA[1]	13.3	18.7	7.8	5.3	0.8	1.2	2.2	1.0	2.4	0.4
U.S.	19.1	9.3	4.0	4.0	2.3	2.0	1.9	1.6	0.8	0.7

Note: Figures are the number of adherents as a percentage of the total population; (1) Figures cover the Dallas-Fort Worth-Arlington, TX Metropolitan Statistical Area; (2) Methodist/Pietist; (3) Latter Day Saints; (4) Reformed; (5) Figures are estimates
Source: Association of Statisticians of American Religious Bodies, 2010 U.S. Religion Census: Religious Congregations & Membership Study

Religious Groups by Tradition

Area	Catholic	Evangelical Protestant	Mainline Protestant	Other Tradition	Black Protestant	Orthodox
MSA[1]	13.3	28.3	7.0	4.8	1.8	0.2
U.S.	19.1	16.2	7.3	4.3	1.6	0.3

Note: Figures are the number of adherents as a percentage of the total population; (1) Figures cover the Dallas-Fort Worth-Arlington, TX Metropolitan Statistical Area
Source: Association of Statisticians of American Religious Bodies, 2010 U.S. Religion Census: Religious Congregations & Membership Study

ECONOMY

Gross Metropolitan Product

Area	2017	2018	2019	2020	Rank[2]
MSA[1]	522.3	556.9	586.7	620.6	5

Note: Figures are in billions of dollars; (1) Figures cover the Dallas-Fort Worth-Arlington, TX Metropolitan Statistical Area; (2) Rank is based on 2018 data and ranges from 1 to 381
Source: U.S. Conference of Mayors, U.S. Metro Economies: GMP & Employment 2018-2020, September 2019

Economic Growth

Area	2015-17 (%)	2018 (%)	2019 (%)	2020 (%)	Rank[2]
MSA[1]	2.7	2.8	3.7	2.7	87
U.S.	1.9	2.9	2.3	2.1	—

Note: Figures are real gross metropolitan product (GMP) growth rates and represent average annual percent change; (1) Figures cover the Dallas-Fort Worth-Arlington, TX Metropolitan Statistical Area; (2) Rank is based on 2017 2-year average annual percent change and ranges from 1 to 381
Source: U.S. Conference of Mayors, U.S. Metro Economies: GMP & Employment 2018-2020, September 2019

Metropolitan Area Exports

Area	2014	2015	2016	2017	2018	2019	Rank[2]
MSA[1]	28,669.4	27,372.9	27,187.8	30,269.1	36,260.9	39,474.0	7

Note: Figures are in millions of dollars; (1) Figures cover the Dallas-Fort Worth-Arlington, TX Metropolitan Statistical Area; (2) Rank is based on 2019 data and ranges from 1 to 386
Source: U.S. Department of Commerce, International Trade Administration, Office of Trade and Economic Analysis, Industry and Analysis, Exports by Metropolitan Area, data extracted March 24, 2021

Building Permits

Area	Single-Family 2018	Single-Family 2019	Pct. Chg.	Multi-Family 2018	Multi-Family 2019	Pct. Chg.	Total 2018	Total 2019	Pct. Chg.
City	5,477	5,063	-7.6	3,833	6,276	63.7	9,310	11,339	21.8
MSA[1]	36,832	34,939	-5.1	27,061	27,769	2.6	63,893	62,708	-1.9
U.S.	855,300	862,100	0.7	473,500	523,900	10.6	1,328,800	1,386,000	4.3

Note: (1) Figures cover the Dallas-Fort Worth-Arlington, TX Metropolitan Statistical Area; Figures represent new, privately-owned housing units authorized (unadjusted data); All permit data are based on estimates with imputation
Source: U.S. Census Bureau, Manufacturing, Mining, and Construction Statistics, Building Permits, 2018, 2019

Bankruptcy Filings

Area	Business Filings 2019	Business Filings 2020	% Chg.	Nonbusiness Filings 2019	Nonbusiness Filings 2020	% Chg.
Tarrant County	242	271	12.0	4,040	2,937	-27.3
U.S.	22,780	21,655	-4.9	752,160	522,808	-30.5

Note: Business filings include Chapter 7, Chapter 9, Chapter 11, Chapter 12, Chapter 13, Chapter 15, and Section 304; Nonbusiness filings include Chapter 7, Chapter 11, and Chapter 13
Source: Administrative Office of the U.S. Courts, Business and Nonbusiness Bankruptcy, County Cases Commenced by Chapter of the Bankruptcy Code, During the 12-Month Period Ending December 31, 2019 and Business and Nonbusiness Bankruptcy, County Cases Commenced by Chapter of the Bankruptcy Code, During the 12-Month Period Ending December 31, 2020

Housing Vacancy Rates

Area	Gross Vacancy Rate[2] (%) 2018	2019	2020	Year-Round Vacancy Rate[3] (%) 2018	2019	2020	Rental Vacancy Rate[4] (%) 2018	2019	2020	Homeowner Vacancy Rate[5] (%) 2018	2019	2020
MSA[1]	7.8	7.6	6.4	7.6	7.3	6.4	7.4	6.9	7.2	1.4	1.5	0.7
U.S.	12.3	12.0	10.6	9.7	9.5	8.2	6.9	6.7	6.3	1.5	1.4	1.0

Note: (1) Figures cover the Dallas-Fort Worth-Arlington, TX Metropolitan Statistical Area; (2) The percentage of the total housing inventory that is vacant; (3) The percentage of the housing inventory (excluding seasonal units) that is year-round vacant; (4) The percentage of rental inventory that is vacant for rent; (5) The percentage of homeowner inventory that is vacant for sale
Source: U.S. Census Bureau, Housing Vacancies and Homeownership Annual Statistics: 2018, 2019, 2020

INCOME

Income

Area	Per Capita ($)	Median Household ($)	Average Household ($)
City	29,531	62,187	82,977
MSA[1]	35,278	70,281	97,589
U.S.	34,103	62,843	88,607

Note: (1) Figures cover the Dallas-Fort Worth-Arlington, TX Metropolitan Statistical Area
Source: U.S. Census Bureau, 2015-2019 American Community Survey 5-Year Estimates

Household Income Distribution

Area	Under $15,000	$15,000 -$24,999	$25,000 -$34,999	$35,000 -$49,999	$50,000 -$74,999	$75,000 -$99,999	$100,000 -$149,999	$150,000 and up
City	10.2	8.3	9.5	12.0	18.8	13.4	15.5	12.3
MSA[1]	7.7	7.1	8.3	12.0	17.8	13.2	16.7	17.2
U.S.	10.3	8.9	8.9	12.3	17.2	12.7	15.1	14.5

Note: (1) Figures cover the Dallas-Fort Worth-Arlington, TX Metropolitan Statistical Area
Source: U.S. Census Bureau, 2015-2019 American Community Survey 5-Year Estimates

Poverty Rate

Area	All Ages	Under 18 Years Old	18 to 64 Years Old	65 Years and Over
City	14.5	20.0	12.5	11.4
MSA[1]	11.7	16.6	10.1	8.5
U.S.	13.4	18.5	12.6	9.3

Note: Figures are percentage of people whose income during the past 12 months was below the poverty level;
(1) Figures cover the Dallas-Fort Worth-Arlington, TX Metropolitan Statistical Area
Source: U.S. Census Bureau, 2015-2019 American Community Survey 5-Year Estimates

CITY FINANCES

City Government Finances

Component	2017 ($000)	2017 ($ per capita)
Total Revenues	1,834,325	2,201
Total Expenditures	1,696,675	2,036
Debt Outstanding	1,482,277	1,779
Cash and Securities[1]	4,035,387	4,843

Note: (1) Cash and security holdings of a government at the close of its fiscal year, including those of its dependent agencies, utilities, and liquor stores.
Source: U.S. Census Bureau, State & Local Government Finances 2017

City Government Revenue by Source

Source	2017 ($000)	2017 ($ per capita)	2017 (%)
General Revenue			
From Federal Government	30,969	37	1.7
From State Government	71,530	86	3.9
From Local Governments	416	0	0.0
Taxes			
Property	440,172	528	24.0
Sales and Gross Receipts	302,191	363	16.5
Personal Income	0	0	0.0
Corporate Income	0	0	0.0
Motor Vehicle License	0	0	0.0
Other Taxes	23,157	28	1.3
Current Charges	306,318	368	16.7
Liquor Store	0	0	0.0
Utility	228,874	275	12.5
Employee Retirement	294,143	353	16.0

Source: U.S. Census Bureau, State & Local Government Finances 2017

City Government Expenditures by Function

Function	2017 ($000)	2017 ($ per capita)	2017 (%)
General Direct Expenditures			
Air Transportation	30,296	36	1.8
Corrections	0	0	0.0
Education	0	0	0.0
Employment Security Administration	0	0	0.0
Financial Administration	11,855	14	0.7
Fire Protection	135,743	162	8.0
General Public Buildings	6,981	8	0.4
Governmental Administration, Other	28,208	33	1.7
Health	12,575	15	0.7
Highways	138,291	166	8.2
Hospitals	0	0	0.0
Housing and Community Development	20,629	24	1.2
Interest on General Debt	67,519	81	4.0
Judicial and Legal	24,287	29	1.4
Libraries	20,986	25	1.2
Parking	3,672	4	0.2
Parks and Recreation	91,314	109	5.4
Police Protection	284,917	341	16.8
Public Welfare	0	0	0.0
Sewerage	210,311	252	12.4
Solid Waste Management	52,835	63	3.1
Veterans' Services	0	0	0.0
Liquor Store	0	0	0.0
Utility	220,313	264	13.0
Employee Retirement	176,776	212	10.4

Source: U.S. Census Bureau, State & Local Government Finances 2017

EMPLOYMENT

Labor Force and Employment

Area	Civilian Labor Force Dec. 2019	Civilian Labor Force Dec. 2020	% Chg.	Workers Employed Dec. 2019	Workers Employed Dec. 2020	% Chg.
City	444,954	448,335	0.8	431,424	417,064	-3.3
MD[1]	1,311,941	1,316,316	0.3	1,273,454	1,230,725	-3.4
U.S.	164,007,000	160,017,000	-2.4	158,504,000	149,613,000	-5.6

Note: Data is not seasonally adjusted and covers workers 16 years of age and older; (1) Figures cover the Fort Worth-Arlington, TX Metropolitan Division
Source: Bureau of Labor Statistics, Local Area Unemployment Statistics

Unemployment Rate

Area	Jan.	Feb.	Mar.	Apr.	May	Jun.	Jul.	Aug.	Sep.	Oct.	Nov.	Dec.
City	3.5	3.3	5.0	13.5	13.1	8.9	8.3	7.1	8.1	6.7	7.9	7.0
MD[1]	3.3	3.2	4.7	13.1	12.6	8.3	7.7	6.5	7.5	6.1	7.3	6.5
U.S.	4.0	3.8	4.5	14.4	13.0	11.2	10.5	8.5	7.7	6.6	6.4	6.5

Note: Data is not seasonally adjusted and covers workers 16 years of age and older; (1) Figures cover the Fort Worth-Arlington, TX Metropolitan Division
Source: Bureau of Labor Statistics, Local Area Unemployment Statistics

Average Wages

Occupation	$/Hr.	Occupation	$/Hr.
Accountants and Auditors	40.30	Maintenance and Repair Workers	21.10
Automotive Mechanics	23.50	Marketing Managers	75.00
Bookkeepers	21.30	Network and Computer Systems Admin.	43.20
Carpenters	19.90	Nurses, Licensed Practical	25.10
Cashiers	11.40	Nurses, Registered	37.50
Computer Programmers	53.90	Nursing Assistants	14.90
Computer Systems Analysts	49.60	Office Clerks, General	18.30
Computer User Support Specialists	24.80	Physical Therapists	46.10
Construction Laborers	17.40	Physicians	98.80
Cooks, Restaurant	13.00	Plumbers, Pipefitters and Steamfitters	24.40
Customer Service Representatives	18.60	Police and Sheriff's Patrol Officers	35.20
Dentists	110.90	Postal Service Mail Carriers	25.80
Electricians	24.00	Real Estate Sales Agents	32.40
Engineers, Electrical	51.10	Retail Salespersons	14.20
Fast Food and Counter Workers	11.00	Sales Representatives, Technical/Scientific	42.10
Financial Managers	77.10	Secretaries, Exc. Legal/Medical/Executive	19.20
First-Line Supervisors of Office Workers	30.70	Security Guards	16.00
General and Operations Managers	62.20	Surgeons	96.20
Hairdressers/Cosmetologists	12.80	Teacher Assistants, Exc. Postsecondary*	11.50
Home Health and Personal Care Aides	10.70	Teachers, Secondary School, Exc. Sp. Ed.*	28.30
Janitors and Cleaners	14.30	Telemarketers	17.10
Landscaping/Groundskeeping Workers	16.50	Truck Drivers, Heavy/Tractor-Trailer	24.30
Lawyers	72.20	Truck Drivers, Light/Delivery Services	20.70
Maids and Housekeeping Cleaners	12.10	Waiters and Waitresses	9.50

Note: Wage data covers the Dallas-Fort Worth-Arlington, TX Metropolitan Statistical Area; (*) Hourly wages were calculated from annual wage data based on a 40 hour work week; n/a not available.
Source: Bureau of Labor Statistics, Metro Area Occupational Employment & Wage Estimates, May 2020

Employment by Industry

Sector	MD[1] Number of Employees	MD[1] Percent of Total	U.S. Percent of Total
Construction, Mining, and Logging	73,300	6.8	5.5
Education and Health Services	138,600	12.9	16.3
Financial Activities	68,200	6.3	6.1
Government	138,300	12.8	15.2
Information	9,500	0.9	1.9
Leisure and Hospitality	109,100	10.1	9.0
Manufacturing	99,400	9.2	8.5
Other Services	38,700	3.6	3.8
Professional and Business Services	124,100	11.5	14.4
Retail Trade	127,200	11.8	10.9
Transportation, Warehousing, and Utilities	97,800	9.1	4.6
Wholesale Trade	53,700	5.0	3.9

Note: Figures are non-farm employment as of December 2020. Figures are not seasonally adjusted and include workers 16 years of age and older; (1) Figures cover the Fort Worth-Arlington, TX Metropolitan Division
Source: Bureau of Labor Statistics, Current Employment Statistics, Employment, Hours, and Earnings

Employment by Occupation

Occupation Classification	City (%)	MSA[1] (%)	U.S. (%)
Management, Business, Science, and Arts	35.5	39.5	38.5
Natural Resources, Construction, and Maintenance	10.6	9.5	8.9
Production, Transportation, and Material Moving	15.9	12.9	13.2
Sales and Office	21.6	22.8	21.6
Service	16.5	15.3	17.8

Note: Figures cover employed civilians 16 years of age and older; (1) Figures cover the Dallas-Fort Worth-Arlington, TX Metropolitan Statistical Area
Source: U.S. Census Bureau, 2015-2019 American Community Survey 5-Year Estimates

Occupations with Greatest Projected Employment Growth: 2020 – 2022

Occupation[1]	2020 Employment	2022 Projected Employment	Numeric Employment Change	Percent Employment Change
Fast Food and Counter Workers	336,530	411,690	75,160	22.3
Waiters and Waitresses	165,570	206,920	41,350	25.0
Home Health and Personal Care Aides	303,520	344,240	40,720	13.4
Retail Salespersons	315,590	349,820	34,230	10.8
Heavy and Tractor-Trailer Truck Drivers	199,460	228,650	29,190	14.6
Laborers and Freight, Stock, and Material Movers, Hand	193,000	219,670	26,670	13.8
Cooks, Restaurant	88,540	114,250	25,710	29.0
Customer Service Representatives	276,080	295,790	19,710	7.1
General and Operations Managers	197,410	216,580	19,170	9.7
Office Clerks, General	310,080	327,500	17,420	5.6

Note: Projections cover Texas; (1) Sorted by numeric employment change
Source: www.projectionscentral.com, State Occupational Projections, 2020–2022 Short-Term Projections

Fastest-Growing Occupations: 2020 – 2022

Occupation[1]	2020 Employment	2022 Projected Employment	Numeric Employment Change	Percent Employment Change
Motion Picture Projectionists	150	300	150	100.0
Ushers, Lobby Attendants, and Ticket Takers	5,740	8,920	3,180	55.4
Locker Room, Coatroom, and Dressing Room Attendants	340	510	170	50.0
Athletes and Sports Competitors	270	400	130	48.1
Amusement and Recreation Attendants	13,130	19,400	6,270	47.8
Hotel, Motel, and Resort Desk Clerks	16,140	23,160	7,020	43.5
Sound Engineering Technicians	330	460	130	39.4
Gaming Dealers	220	300	80	36.4
Baggage Porters and Bellhops	1,250	1,670	420	33.6
Lodging Managers	3,300	4,330	1,030	31.2

Note: Projections cover Texas; (1) Sorted by percent employment change and excludes occupations with numeric employment change less than 50
Source: www.projectionscentral.com, State Occupational Projections, 2020–2022 Short-Term Projections

TAXES

State Corporate Income Tax Rates

State	Tax Rate (%)	Income Brackets ($)	Num. of Brackets	Financial Institution Tax Rate (%)[a]	Federal Income Tax Ded.
Texas	(w)	–	–	(w)	No

Note: Tax rates as of January 1, 2021; (a) Rates listed are the corporate income tax rate applied to financial institutions or excise taxes based on income. Some states have other taxes based upon the value of deposits or shares; (w) Texas imposes a Franchise Tax, otherwise known as margin tax, imposed on entities with more than $1,130,000 total revenues at rate of 0.75%, or 0.375% for entities primarily engaged in retail or wholesale trade, on lesser of 70% of total revenues or 100% of gross receipts after deductions for either compensation or cost of goods sold.
Source: Federation of Tax Administrators, State Corporate Income Tax Rates, January 1, 2021

State Individual Income Tax Rates

State	Tax Rate (%)	Income Brackets ($)	Personal Exemptions ($) Single	Married	Depend.	Standard Ded. ($) Single	Married
Texas					– No state income tax –		

Note: Tax rates as of January 1, 2021; Local- and county-level taxes are not included
Source: Federation of Tax Administrators, State Individual Income Tax Rates, January 1, 2021

Various State Sales and Excise Tax Rates

State	State Sales Tax (%)	Gasoline[1] (¢/gal.)	Cigarette[2] ($/pack)	Spirits[3] ($/gal.)	Wine[4] ($/gal.)	Beer[5] ($/gal.)	Recreational Marijuana (%)
Texas	6.25	20	1.41	2.4	0.2	0.2	Not legal

Note: All tax rates as of January 1, 2021; (1) The American Petroleum Institute has developed a methodology for determining the average tax rate on a gallon of fuel. Rates may include any of the following: excise taxes, environmental fees, storage tank fees, other fees or taxes, general sales tax, and local taxes; (2) The federal excise tax of $1.0066 per pack and local taxes are not included; (3) Rates are those applicable to off-premise sales of 40% alcohol by volume (a.b.v.) distilled spirits in 750ml containers. Local excise taxes are excluded; (4) Rates are those applicable to off-premise sales of 11% a.b.v. non-carbonated wine in 750ml containers; (5) Rates are those applicable to off-premise sales of 4.7% a.b.v. beer in 12 ounce containers.
Source: Tax Foundation, 2021 Facts & Figures: How Does Your State Compare?

State Business Tax Climate Index Rankings

State	Overall Rank	Corporate Tax Rank	Individual Income Tax Rank	Sales Tax Rank	Property Tax Rank	Unemployment Insurance Tax Rank
Texas	11	47	6	35	36	16

Note: The index is a measure of how each state's tax laws affect economic performance. The lower the rank, the more favorable a state's tax system is for business. States without a given tax are given a ranking of 1. The scores/rankings for the District of Columbia do not affect other states. The 2021 index represents the tax climate as of July 1, 2020.
Source: Tax Foundation, State Business Tax Climate Index 2021

TRANSPORTATION

Means of Transportation to Work

Area	Car/Truck/Van Drove Alone	Car/Truck/Van Carpooled	Public Transportation Bus	Public Transportation Subway	Public Transportation Railroad	Bicycle	Walked	Other Means	Worked at Home
City	81.5	11.4	0.6	0.0	0.2	0.2	1.2	0.8	4.1
MSA[1]	80.6	9.7	0.9	0.2	0.2	0.1	1.2	1.2	5.8
U.S.	76.3	9.0	2.4	1.9	0.6	0.5	2.7	1.4	5.2

Note: Figures are percentages and cover workers 16 years of age and older; (1) Figures cover the Dallas-Fort Worth-Arlington, TX Metropolitan Statistical Area
Source: U.S. Census Bureau, 2015-2019 American Community Survey 5-Year Estimates

Travel Time to Work

Area	Less Than 10 Minutes	10 to 19 Minutes	20 to 29 Minutes	30 to 44 Minutes	45 to 59 Minutes	60 to 89 Minutes	90 Minutes or More
City	8.4	28.3	22.5	23.9	8.7	6.2	2.0
MSA[1]	8.6	25.0	21.3	25.6	10.5	7.0	2.1
U.S.	12.2	28.4	20.8	20.8	8.3	6.4	2.9

Note: Note: Figures are percentages and include workers 16 years old and over; (1) Figures cover the Dallas-Fort Worth-Arlington, TX Metropolitan Statistical Area
Source: U.S. Census Bureau, 2015-2019 American Community Survey 5-Year Estimates

Key Congestion Measures

Measure	1982	1992	2002	2012	2017
Annual Hours of Delay, Total (000)	50,235	85,300	137,340	198,340	224,883
Annual Hours of Delay, Per Auto Commuter	36	42	46	57	67
Annual Congestion Cost, Total (million $)	376	896	1,844	3,517	4,116
Annual Congestion Cost, Per Auto Commuter ($)	636	742	932	1,055	1,161

Note: Covers the Dallas-Fort Worth-Arlington TX urban area
Source: Texas A&M Transportation Institute, 2019 Urban Mobility Report

Freeway Travel Time Index

Measure	1982	1987	1992	1997	2002	2007	2012	2017
Urban Area Index[1]	1.18	1.19	1.21	1.23	1.23	1.27	1.26	1.26
Urban Area Rank[1,2]	5	8	11	15	26	20	21	23

Note: Freeway Travel Time Index—the ratio of travel time in the peak period to the travel time at free-flow conditions. For example, a value of 1.30 indicates a 20-minute free-flow trip takes 26 minutes in the peak (20 minutes x 1.30 = 26 minutes); (1) Covers the Dallas-Fort Worth-Arlington TX urban area; (2) Rank is based on 101 larger urban areas (#1 = highest travel time index)
Source: Texas A&M Transportation Institute, 2019 Urban Mobility Report

Public Transportation

Agency Name / Mode of Transportation	Vehicles Operated in Maximum Service[1]	Annual Unlinked Passenger Trips[2] (in thous.)	Annual Passenger Miles[3] (in thous.)
Fort Worth Transportation Authority (The T)			
Bus (directly operated)	127	4,983.3	20,533.9
Bus (purchased transportation)	5	83.0	507.8
Commuter Rail (purchased transportation)	20	407.4	6,558.7
Demand Response (directly operated)	35	132.1	1,549.6
Demand Response (purchased transportation)	52	220.3	2,358.8
Vanpool (purchased transportation)	75	190.5	7,789.2

Note: (1) Number of revenue vehicles operated by the given mode and type of service to meet the annual maximum service requirement. This is the revenue vehicle count during the peak season of the year; on the week and day that maximum service is provided. Vehicles operated in maximum service (VOMS) exclude atypical days and one-time special events; (2) Number of passengers who boarded public transportation vehicles. Passengers are counted each time they board a vehicle no matter how many vehicles they use to travel from their origin to their destination. (3) Sum of the distances ridden by all passengers during the entire fiscal year.
Source: Federal Transit Administration, National Transit Database, 2019

Air Transportation

Airport Name and Code / Type of Service	Passenger Airlines[1]	Passenger Enplanements	Freight Carriers[2]	Freight (lbs)
Dallas-Fort Worth International (DFW)				
Domestic service (U.S. carriers - 2020)	24	16,962,314	20	585,663,631
International service (U.S. carriers - 2019)	10	3,735,113	6	74,097,599
Dallas Love Field (DAL)				
Domestic service (U.S. carriers - 2020)	19	3,666,889	7	14,081,611
International service (U.S. carriers - 2019)	3	975	1	54,209

Note: (1) Includes all U.S.-based major, minor and commuter airlines that carried at least one passenger during the year; (2) Includes all U.S.-based airlines and freight carriers that transported at least one pound of freight during the year.
Source: Bureau of Transportation Statistics, The Intermodal Transportation Database, Air Carriers: T-100 Domestic Market (U.S. Carriers), 2020; Bureau of Transportation Statistics, The Intermodal Transportation Database, Air Carriers: T-100 International Market (U.S. Carriers), 2019

BUSINESSES

Major Business Headquarters

Company Name	Industry	Fortune[1]	Forbes[2]
American Airlines Group	Airlines	70	-
Ben E Keith	Food, Drink & Tobacco	-	112
D.R. Horton	Homebuilders	183	-

Note: (1) Companies that produce a 10-K are ranked 1 to 500 based on 2019 revenue; (2) All private companies with at least $2 billion in annual revenue through the end of their most current fiscal year are ranked 1 to 219; companies listed are headquartered in the city; dashes indicate no ranking
Source: Fortune, "Fortune 500," June/July 2020; Forbes, "America's Largest Private Companies," 2020

Fastest-Growing Businesses

According to *Inc.*, Fort Worth is home to six of America's 500 fastest-growing private companies: **Case Energy Partners** (#7); **Allata** (#52); **Almaguer Logistics** (#264); **Embark** (#327); **Go Energistics** (#335); **Integra Mission Critical** (#414). Criteria: must be an independent, privately-held, for-profit, U.S. corporation, proprietorship or partnership as of December 31, 2019; revenues must be at least $100,000 in 2016 and $2 million in 2019; must have four-year operating/sales history. *Inc., "America's 500 Fastest-Growing Private Companies," 2020*

According to *Initiative for a Competitive Inner City (ICIC)*, Fort Worth is home to two of America's 100 fastest-growing "inner city" companies: **Fort Worth Gasket & Supply** (#89); **JODesign** (#91). Criteria for inclusion: company must be headquartered in or have 51 percent or more of its physical operations in an economically distressed urban area; must be an independent, for-profit corporation, partnership or proprietorship; must have 10 or more employees and have a five-year sales history that includes sales of at least $200,000 in the base year and at least $1 million in the current year with no decrease in sales over the two most recent years. Companies were ranked overall by revenue growth over the five-year period between 2015 and 2019. *Initiative for a Competitive Inner City (ICIC), "Inner City 100 Companies," 2020*

Living Environment

COST OF LIVING

Cost of Living Index

Composite Index	Groceries	Housing	Utilities	Transportation	Health Care	Misc. Goods/Services
93.8	97.2	80.2	107.4	86.9	97.5	100.9

Note: The Cost of Living Index measures regional differences in the cost of consumer goods and services, excluding taxes and non-consumer expenditures, for professional and managerial households in the top income quintile. It is based on more than 50,000 prices covering almost 60 different items for which prices are collected three times a year by chambers of commerce, economic development organizations or university applied economic centers in each participating urban area. The numbers shown should be read as a percentage above or below the national average of 100. For example, a value of 115.4 in the groceries column indicates that grocery prices are 15.4% higher than the national average. Small differences in the index numbers should not be interpreted as significant; Figures cover the Fort Worth TX urban area.
Source: The Council for Community and Economic Research, Cost of Living Index, 2020

Grocery Prices

Area[1]	T-Bone Steak ($/pound)	Frying Chicken ($/pound)	Whole Milk ($/half gal.)	Eggs ($/dozen)	Orange Juice ($/64 oz.)	Coffee ($/11.5 oz.)
City[2]	9.35	1.87	1.92	1.26	3.55	4.49
Avg.	11.78	1.39	2.05	1.47	3.57	4.34
Min.	8.03	0.94	1.03	0.74	2.94	3.02
Max.	15.86	2.65	4.31	3.77	5.44	8.69

Note: (1) Values for the local area are compared with the average, minimum and maximum values for all 284 areas in the Cost of Living Index; (2) Figures cover the Fort Worth TX urban area; **T-Bone Steak** (price per pound); **Frying Chicken** (price per pound, whole fryer); **Whole Milk** (half gallon carton); **Eggs** (price per dozen, Grade A, large); **Orange Juice** (64 oz. Tropicana or Florida Natural); **Coffee** (11.5 oz. can, vacuum-packed, Maxwell House, Hills Bros, or Folgers).
Source: The Council for Community and Economic Research, Cost of Living Index, 2020

Housing and Utility Costs

Area[1]	New Home Price ($)	Apartment Rent ($/month)	All Electric ($/month)	Part Electric ($/month)	Other Energy ($/month)	Telephone ($/month)
City[2]	258,331	1,164	-	133.52	54.42	184.70
Avg.	368,594	1,168	170.86	100.47	65.28	184.30
Min.	190,567	502	91.58	31.42	26.08	169.60
Max.	2,227,806	4,738	470.38	280.31	280.06	206.50

Note: (1) Values for the local area are compared with the average, minimum and maximum values for all 284 areas in the Cost of Living Index; (2) Figures cover the Fort Worth TX urban area; **New Home Price** (2,400 sf living area, 8,000 sf lot, in urban area with full utilities); **Apartment Rent** (950 sf 2 bedroom/1.5 or 2 bath, unfurnished, excluding all utilities except water); **All Electric** (average monthly cost for an all-electric home); **Part Electric** (average monthly cost for a part-electric home); **Other Energy** (average monthly cost for natural gas, fuel oil, coal, wood, and any other forms of energy except electricity); **Telephone** (price includes the base monthly rate plus taxes and fees for three lines of mobile phone service).
Source: The Council for Community and Economic Research, Cost of Living Index, 2020

Health Care, Transportation, and Other Costs

Area[1]	Doctor ($/visit)	Dentist ($/visit)	Optometrist ($/visit)	Gasoline ($/gallon)	Beauty Salon ($/visit)	Men's Shirt ($)
City[2]	91.05	108.33	92.25	1.83	53.57	39.58
Avg.	115.44	99.32	108.10	2.21	39.27	31.37
Min.	36.68	59.00	51.36	1.71	19.00	11.00
Max.	219.00	153.10	250.97	3.46	82.05	58.33

Note: (1) Values for the local area are compared with the average, minimum and maximum values for all 284 areas in the Cost of Living Index; (2) Figures cover the Fort Worth TX urban area; **Doctor** (general practitioners routine exam of an established patient); **Dentist** (adult teeth cleaning and periodic oral examination); **Optometrist** (full vision eye exam for established adult patient); **Gasoline** (one gallon regular unleaded, national brand, including all taxes, cash price at self-service pump if available); **Beauty Salon** (woman's shampoo, trim, and blow-dry); **Men's Shirt** (cotton/polyester dress shirt, pinpoint weave, long sleeves).
Source: The Council for Community and Economic Research, Cost of Living Index, 2020

HOUSING

Homeownership Rate

Area	2012 (%)	2013 (%)	2014 (%)	2015 (%)	2016 (%)	2017 (%)	2018 (%)	2019 (%)	2020 (%)
MSA[1]	61.8	59.9	57.7	57.8	59.7	61.8	62.0	60.6	64.7
U.S.	65.4	65.1	64.5	63.7	63.4	63.9	64.4	64.6	66.6

Note: (1) Figures cover the Dallas-Fort Worth-Arlington, TX Metropolitan Statistical Area
Source: U.S. Census Bureau, Housing Vacancies and Homeownership Annual Statistics: 2012-2020

House Price Index (HPI)

Area	National Ranking[2]	Quarterly Change (%)	One-Year Change (%)	Five-Year Change (%)	Since 1991Q1 (%)
MD[1]	191	2.39	5.13	42.54	191.04
U.S.[3]	—	3.81	10.77	38.99	205.12

Note: The HPI is a weighted repeat sales index. It measures average price changes in repeat sales or refinancings on the same properties. This information is obtained by reviewing repeat mortgage transactions on single-family properties whose mortgages have been purchased or securitized by Fannie Mae or Freddie Mac since January 1975; (1) Figures cover the Fort Worth-Arlington, TX Metropolitan Division; (2) Rankings are based on annual percentage change for all metro areas containing at least 15,000 transactions over the last 10 years and ranges from 1 to 253; (3) figures based on a weighted average of Census Division estimates using a seasonally adjusted, purchase-only index; all figures are for the period ending December 31, 2020
Source: Federal Housing Finance Agency, Change in Metropolitan Area House Price Indexes, April 7, 2021

Median Single-Family Home Prices

Area	2018	2019	2020p	Percent Change 2019 to 2020
MSA[1]	260.0	268.6	287.2	6.9
U.S. Average	261.6	274.6	299.9	9.2

Note: Figures are median sales prices of existing single-family homes in thousands of dollars; (p) preliminary; (1) Figures cover the Dallas-Fort Worth-Arlington, TX Metropolitan Statistical Area
Source: National Association of Realtors, Median Sales Price of Existing Single-Family Homes for Metropolitan Areas, 4th Quarter 2020

Qualifying Income Based on Median Sales Price of Existing Single-Family Homes

Area	With 5% Down ($)	With 10% Down ($)	With 20% Down ($)
MSA[1]	56,156	53,201	47,290
U.S. Average	59,266	56,147	49,908

Note: Figures are preliminary; Qualifying income is based on a mortgage rate of 2.81%. Monthly principal and interest payment is limited to 25% of income; (1) Figures cover the Dallas-Fort Worth-Arlington, TX Metropolitan Statistical Area
Source: National Association of Realtors, Qualifying Income Based on Median Sales Price of Existing Single-Family Homes for Metropolitan Areas, 4th Quarter 2020

Home Value Distribution

Area	Under $50,000	$50,000 -$99,999	$100,000 -$149,999	$150,000 -$199,999	$200,000 -$299,999	$300,000 -$499,999	$500,000 -$999,999	$1,000,000 or more
City	6.2	17.3	17.6	19.3	22.9	11.9	4.0	0.8
MSA[1]	4.5	11.1	14.5	15.9	23.1	20.9	7.9	1.9
U.S.	6.9	12.0	13.3	14.0	19.6	19.3	11.4	3.4

Note: Figures are percentages and cover owner-occupied housing units; (1) Figures cover the Dallas-Fort Worth-Arlington, TX Metropolitan Statistical Area
Source: U.S. Census Bureau, 2015-2019 American Community Survey 5-Year Estimates

Year Housing Structure Built

Area	2010 or Later	2000 -2009	1990 -1999	1980 -1989	1970 -1979	1960 -1969	1950 -1959	1940 -1949	Before 1940	Median Year
City	9.9	24.5	11.5	13.2	9.8	8.2	11.3	5.3	6.3	1987
MSA[1]	10.0	20.0	16.1	18.1	14.2	8.7	7.5	2.7	2.7	1988
U.S.	5.2	14.0	13.9	13.4	15.2	10.6	10.3	4.9	12.6	1978

Note: Figures are percentages except for Median Year; Note: (1) Figures cover the Dallas-Fort Worth-Arlington, TX Metropolitan Statistical Area
Source: U.S. Census Bureau, 2015-2019 American Community Survey 5-Year Estimates

Gross Monthly Rent

Area	Under $500	$500 -$999	$1,000 -$1,499	$1,500 -$1,999	$2,000 -$2,499	$2,500 -$2,999	$3,000 and up	Median ($)
City	4.9	39.7	35.0	15.5	3.1	0.9	0.9	1,060
MSA[1]	3.4	33.2	40.0	16.3	4.7	1.4	1.0	1,139
U.S.	9.4	36.2	30.0	14.0	5.6	2.4	2.4	1,062

Note: Figures are percentages except for Median; Gross rent is the contract rent plus the estimated average monthly cost of utilities (electricity, gas, and water and sewer) and fuels (oil, coal, kerosene, wood, etc.) if these are paid by the renter (or paid for the renter by someone else); (1) Figures cover the Dallas-Fort Worth-Arlington, TX Metropolitan Statistical Area
Source: U.S. Census Bureau, 2015-2019 American Community Survey 5-Year Estimates

HEALTH

Health Risk Factors

Category	MD[1] (%)	U.S. (%)
Adults aged 18–64 who have any kind of health care coverage	77.1	87.3
Adults who reported being in good or better health	77.7	82.4
Adults who have been told they have high blood cholesterol	34.3	33.0
Adults who have been told they have high blood pressure	34.6	32.3
Adults who are current smokers	15.8	17.1
Adults who currently use E-cigarettes	5.0	4.6
Adults who currently use chewing tobacco, snuff, or snus	3.9	4.0
Adults who are heavy drinkers[2]	6.3	6.3
Adults who are binge drinkers[3]	16.7	17.4
Adults who are overweight (BMI 25.0 - 29.9)	34.0	35.3
Adults who are obese (BMI 30.0 - 99.8)	36.7	31.3
Adults who participated in any physical activities in the past month	68.8	74.4
Adults who always or nearly always wears a seat belt	97.0	94.3

Note: (1) Figures cover the Fort Worth-Arlington, TX Metropolitan Division; (2) Heavy drinkers are classified as adult men having more than 14 drinks per week and adult women having more than 7 drinks per week; (3) Binge drinkers are classified as males having five or more drinks on one occasion or females having four or more drinks on one occasion
Source: Centers for Disease Control and Prevention, Behaviorial Risk Factor Surveillance System, SMART: Selected Metropolitan Area Risk Trends, 2017

Acute and Chronic Health Conditions

Category	MD[1] (%)	U.S. (%)
Adults who have ever been told they had a heart attack	4.3	4.2
Adults who have ever been told they have angina or coronary heart disease	4.3	3.9
Adults who have ever been told they had a stroke	n/a	3.0
Adults who have ever been told they have asthma	14.1	14.2
Adults who have ever been told they have arthritis	20.8	24.9
Adults who have ever been told they have diabetes[2]	9.7	10.5
Adults who have ever been told they had skin cancer	6.3	6.2
Adults who have ever been told they had any other types of cancer	4.3	7.1
Adults who have ever been told they have COPD	6.0	6.5
Adults who have ever been told they have kidney disease	3.3	3.0
Adults who have ever been told they have a form of depression	17.6	20.5

Note: n/a not available; (1) Figures cover the Fort Worth-Arlington, TX Metropolitan Division; (2) Figures do not include pregnancy-related, borderline, or pre-diabetes
Source: Centers for Disease Control and Prevention, Behaviorial Risk Factor Surveillance System, SMART: Selected Metropolitan Area Risk Trends, 2017

Health Screening and Vaccination Rates

Category	MD[1] (%)	U.S. (%)
Adults aged 65+ who have had flu shot within the past year	62.1	60.7
Adults aged 65+ who have ever had a pneumonia vaccination	76.8	75.4
Adults who have ever been tested for HIV	42.1	36.1
Adults who have ever had the shingles or zoster vaccine?	24.1	28.9
Adults who have had their blood cholesterol checked within the last five years	89.6	85.9

Note: n/a not available; (1) Figures cover the Fort Worth-Arlington, TX Metropolitan Division.
Source: Centers for Disease Control and Prevention, Behaviorial Risk Factor Surveillance System, SMART: Selected Metropolitan Area Risk Trends, 2017

Disability Status

Category	MD[1] (%)	U.S. (%)
Adults who reported being deaf	5.8	6.7
Are you blind or have serious difficulty seeing, even when wearing glasses?	5.5	4.5
Are you limited in any way in any of your usual activities due of arthritis?	9.8	12.9
Do you have difficulty doing errands alone?	6.8	6.8
Do you have difficulty dressing or bathing?	3.9	3.6
Do you have serious difficulty concentrating/remembering/making decisions?	10.1	10.7
Do you have serious difficulty walking or climbing stairs?	13.1	13.6

Note: (1) Figures cover the Fort Worth-Arlington, TX Metropolitan Division.
Source: Centers for Disease Control and Prevention, Behaviorial Risk Factor Surveillance System, SMART: Selected Metropolitan Area Risk Trends, 2017

Mortality Rates for the Top 10 Causes of Death in the U.S.

ICD-10[a] Sub-Chapter	ICD-10[a] Code	Age-Adjusted Mortality Rate[1] per 100,000 population County[2]	U.S.
Malignant neoplasms	C00-C97	147.8	149.2
Ischaemic heart diseases	I20-I25	76.8	90.5
Other forms of heart disease	I30-I51	45.5	52.2
Chronic lower respiratory diseases	J40-J47	40.2	39.6
Other degenerative diseases of the nervous system	G30-G31	60.5	37.6
Cerebrovascular diseases	I60-I69	46.4	37.2
Other external causes of accidental injury	W00-X59	21.0	36.1
Organic, including symptomatic, mental disorders	F01-F09	24.0	29.4
Hypertensive diseases	I10-I15	39.4	24.1
Diabetes mellitus	E10-E14	22.2	21.5

Note: (a) ICD-10 = International Classification of Diseases 10th Revision; (1) Mortality rates are a three-year average covering 2017-2019; (2) Figures cover Tarrant County.
Source: Centers for Disease Control and Prevention, National Center for Health Statistics. Underlying Cause of Death 1999-2019 on CDC WONDER Online Database

Mortality Rates for Selected Causes of Death

ICD-10[a] Sub-Chapter	ICD-10[a] Code	Age-Adjusted Mortality Rate[1] per 100,000 population County[2]	U.S.
Assault	X85-Y09	5.2	6.0
Diseases of the liver	K70-K76	15.5	14.4
Human immunodeficiency virus (HIV) disease	B20-B24	1.6	1.5
Influenza and pneumonia	J09-J18	12.1	13.8
Intentional self-harm	X60-X84	13.0	14.1
Malnutrition	E40-E46	4.2	2.3
Obesity and other hyperalimentation	E65-E68	2.3	2.1
Renal failure	N17-N19	16.2	12.6
Transport accidents	V01-V99	10.7	12.3
Viral hepatitis	B15-B19	1.3	1.2

Note: (a) ICD-10 = International Classification of Diseases 10th Revision; (1) Mortality rates are a three-year average covering 2017-2019; (2) Figures cover Tarrant County; Data are suppressed when the data meet the criteria for confidentiality constraints; Mortality rates are flagged as unreliable when the rate would be calculated with a numerator of 20 or less.
Source: Centers for Disease Control and Prevention, National Center for Health Statistics. Underlying Cause of Death 1999-2019 on CDC WONDER Online Database

Health Insurance Coverage

Area	With Health Insurance	With Private Health Insurance	With Public Health Insurance	Without Health Insurance	Population Under Age 19 Without Health Insurance
City	81.7	60.6	27.5	18.3	11.7
MSA[1]	83.6	66.0	24.9	16.4	11.0
U.S.	91.2	67.9	35.1	8.8	5.1

Note: Figures are percentages that cover the civilian noninstitutionalized population; (1) Figures cover the Dallas-Fort Worth-Arlington, TX Metropolitan Statistical Area
Source: U.S. Census Bureau, 2015-2019 American Community Survey 5-Year Estimates

Number of Medical Professionals

Area	MDs[3]	DOs[3,4]	Dentists	Podiatrists	Chiropractors	Optometrists
County[1] (number)	3,812	716	1,270	92	567	334
County[1] (rate[2])	183.1	34.4	60.4	4.4	27.0	15.9
U.S. (rate[2])	282.9	22.7	71.2	6.2	28.1	16.9

48439
Note: Data as of 2019 unless noted; (1) Data covers Tarrant County; (2) Rate per 100,000 population; (3) Data as of 2018 and includes all active, non-federal physicians; (4) Doctor of Osteopathic Medicine
Source: U.S. Department of Health and Human Services, Health Resources and Services Administration, Bureau of Health Professions, Area Resource File (ARF) 2019-2020

Best Hospitals

According to *U.S. News*, the Fort Worth-Arlington, TX metro area is home to one of the best children's hospitals in the U.S.: **Cook Children's Medical Center** (1 pediatric specialty). The hospital listed was highly ranked in at least one of 10 pediatric specialties. Eighty-eight children's hospitals in the U.S. were nationally ranked in at least one specialty. Hospitals received points for being ranked in a specialty, and the 10 hospitals with the most points across the 10 specialties make up the Honor Roll. *U.S. News Online*, "America's Best Children's Hospitals 2020-21"

EDUCATION

Public School District Statistics

District Name	Schls	Pupils	Pupil/Teacher Ratio	Minority Pupils[1] (%)	Free Lunch Eligible[2] (%)	IEP[3] (%)
Castleberry ISD	7	3,783	15.6	84.0	75.2	9.7
Eagle Mt-Saginaw ISD	27	20,054	16.4	59.7	37.1	9.5
Everman ISD	10	6,174	16.7	96.1	80.0	8.8
Fort Worth ISD	144	84,510	14.6	88.7	85.4	9.2
Uplift Education	38	18,709	15.5	96.5	71.3	7.2

Note: Table includes school districts with 2,000 or more students; (1) Percentage of students that are not non-Hispanic white; (2) Percentage of students that are eligible for the free lunch program; (3) Percentage of students that have an Individualized Education Program.
Source: U.S. Department of Education, National Center for Education Statistics, Common Core of Data, Local Education Agency (School District) Universe Survey: School Year 2018-2019; U.S. Department of Education, National Center for Education Statistics, Common Core of Data, Public Elementary/Secondary School Universe Survey: School Year 2018-2019

Best High Schools

According to *U.S. News*, Fort Worth is home to three of the top 500 high schools in the U.S.: **Young Women's Leadership Academy** (#82); **Texas Academy of Biomedical** (#393); **Harmony School of Innovation - Fort Worth** (#409). Nearly 18,000 public, magnet and charter schools were ranked based on their performance on state assessments and how well they prepare students for college. *U.S. News & World Report, "Best High Schools 2020"*

Highest Level of Education

Area	Less than H.S.	H.S. Diploma	Some College, No Deg.	Associate Degree	Bachelor's Degree	Master's Degree	Prof. School Degree	Doctorate Degree
City	17.8	24.9	20.8	6.9	20.0	7.1	1.5	1.1
MSA[1]	14.4	22.3	21.1	7.0	23.0	9.2	1.9	1.1
U.S.	12.0	27.0	20.4	8.5	19.8	8.8	2.1	1.4

Note: Figures cover persons age 25 and over; (1) Figures cover the Dallas-Fort Worth-Arlington, TX Metropolitan Statistical Area
Source: U.S. Census Bureau, 2015-2019 American Community Survey 5-Year Estimates

Educational Attainment by Race

Area	High School Graduate or Higher (%)						Bachelor's Degree or Higher (%)				
	Total	White	Black	Asian	Hisp.[2]	Total	White	Black	Asian	Hisp.[2]
City	82.2	84.4	88.6	80.8	59.2	29.7	33.8	21.5	42.8	12.2
MSA[1]	85.6	85.9	91.0	88.8	60.3	35.2	35.8	27.4	62.0	14.0
U.S.	88.0	89.9	86.0	87.1	68.7	32.1	33.5	21.6	54.3	16.4

Note: Figures shown cover persons 25 years old and over; (1) Figures cover the Dallas-Fort Worth-Arlington, TX Metropolitan Statistical Area; (2) People of Hispanic origin can be of any race
Source: U.S. Census Bureau, 2015-2019 American Community Survey 5-Year Estimates

School Enrollment by Grade and Control

Area	Preschool (%)		Kindergarten (%)		Grades 1 - 4 (%)		Grades 5 - 8 (%)		Grades 9 - 12 (%)	
	Public	Private	Public	Private	Public	Private	Public	Private	Public	Private
City	62.0	38.0	87.1	12.9	92.6	7.4	90.7	9.3	92.8	7.2
MSA[1]	58.9	41.1	90.2	9.8	92.6	7.4	92.3	7.7	92.4	7.6
U.S.	59.1	40.9	87.6	12.4	89.5	10.5	89.4	10.6	90.1	9.9

Note: Figures shown cover persons 3 years old and over; (1) Figures cover the Dallas-Fort Worth-Arlington, TX Metropolitan Statistical Area
Source: U.S. Census Bureau, 2015-2019 American Community Survey 5-Year Estimates

Higher Education

Four-Year Colleges			Two-Year Colleges			Medical Schools[1]	Law Schools[2]	Voc/Tech[3]
Public	Private Non-profit	Private For-profit	Public	Private Non-profit	Private For-profit			
1	5	0	1	0	1	2	1	2

Note: Figures cover institutions located within the city limits and include main campuses only; (1) includes schools accredited by the Liaison Committee on Medical Education and the American Osteopathic Association's Commission on Osteopathic College Accreditation; (2) includes ABA-accredited schools, schools with provisional ABA accreditation, and state accredited schools; (3) includes all schools with programs that are less than 2 years.
Source: National Center for Education Statistics, Integrated Postsecondary Education System (IPEDS), 2019-20; Wikipedia, List of Medical Schools in the United States, accessed April 2, 2021; Wikipedia, List of Law Schools in the United States, accessed April 2, 2021

According to *U.S. News & World Report*, the Fort Worth-Arlington, TX metro division is home to one of the top 200 national universities in the U.S.: **Texas Christian University** (#80 tie). The indicators used to capture academic quality fall into a number of categories: assessment by administrators at peer institutions; retention of students; faculty resources; student selectivity; financial resources; alumni giving; high school counselor ratings of colleges; and graduation rate. *U.S. News & World Report, "America's Best Colleges 2021"*

According to *U.S. News & World Report*, the Fort Worth-Arlington, TX metro division is home to one of the top 100 law schools in the U.S.: **Texas A&M University** (#53 tie). The rankings are based on a weighted average of 12 measures of quality: peer assessment score; assessment score by lawyers/judges; median LSAT scores; median undergrad GPA; acceptance rate; employment rates for graduates; placement success; bar passage rate; faculty resources; expenditures per student; student/faculty ratio; and library resources. *U.S. News & World Report, "America's Best Graduate Schools, Law, 2022"*

According to *U.S. News & World Report*, the Fort Worth-Arlington, TX metro division is home to one of the top 75 business schools in the U.S.: **Texas Christian University (Neeley)** (#57 tie). The rankings are based on a weighted average of the following nine measures: quality assessment; peer assessment; recruiter assessment; placement success; mean starting salary and bonus; student selectivity; mean GMAT and GRE scores; mean undergraduate GPA; and acceptance rate. *U.S. News & World Report, "America's Best Graduate Schools, Business, 2022"*

EMPLOYERS

Major Employers

Company Name	Industry
AMR Corporation	Air transportation, scheduled
Associates First Capital Corporation	Mortgage bankers
Baylor University Medical Center	General medical & surgical hospitals
Children's Medical Center Dallas	Specialty hospitals, except psychiatric
Combat Support Associates	Engineering services
County of Dallas	County government
Dallas County Hospital District	General medical & surgical hospitals
Fort Worth Independent School District	Public elementary & secondary schools
Housewares Holding Company	Toasters, electric: household
HP Enterprise Services	Computer integrated systems design
J.C. Penney Company	Department stores
JCP Publications Corp.	Department stores
L-3 Communications Corporation	Business economic service
Odyssey HealthCare	Home health care services
Romano's Macaroni Grill	Italian restaurant
SFG Management	Milk processing (pasteurizing, homogenizing, bottling)
Texas Instruments Incorporated	Semiconductors & related devices
University of North Texas	Colleges & universities
University of Texas SW Medical Center	Accident & health insurance
Verizon Business Global	Telephone communication, except radio

Note: Companies shown are located within the Dallas-Fort Worth-Arlington, TX Metropolitan Statistical Area.
Source: Hoovers.com; Wikipedia

PUBLIC SAFETY

Crime Rate

Area	All Crimes	Violent Crimes					Property Crimes		
		Murder	Rape[3]	Robbery	Aggrav. Assault	Burglary	Larceny -Theft	Motor Vehicle Theft
City	3,132.8	7.5	51.4	106.2	279.4	433.7	1,890.3	364.4
Suburbs[1]	n/a	n/a	n/a	n/a	n/a	n/a	n/a	n/a
Metro[2]	n/a	n/a	n/a	n/a	n/a	n/a	n/a	n/a
U.S.	2,489.3	5.0	42.6	81.6	250.2	340.5	1,549.5	219.9

Note: Figures are crimes per 100,000 population; (1) All areas within the metro area that are located outside the city limits; (2) Figures cover the Fort Worth-Arlington, TX Metropolitan Division; n/a not available; (3) All figures shown were reported using the revised Uniform Crime Reporting (UCR) definition of rape.
Source: FBI Uniform Crime Reports, 2019

Hate Crimes

Area	Number of Quarters Reported	Number of Incidents per Bias Motivation					
		Race/Ethnicity/ Ancestry	Religion	Sexual Orientation	Disability	Gender	Gender Identity
City[1]	4	8	2	5	0	0	0
U.S.	4	3,963	1,521	1,195	157	69	198

Note: (1) Figures include one incident reported with more than one bias motivation.
Source: Federal Bureau of Investigation, Hate Crime Statistics 2019

Identity Theft Consumer Reports

Area	Reports	Reports per 100,000 Population	Rank[2]
MSA[1]	45,242	597	37
U.S.	1,387,615	423	-

Note: (1) Figures cover the Dallas-Fort Worth-Arlington, TX Metropolitan Statistical Area; (2) Rank ranges from 1 to 391 where 1 indicates greatest number of identity theft reports per 100,000 population
Source: Federal Trade Commission, Consumer Sentinel Network Data Book 2020

Fraud and Other Consumer Reports

Area	Reports	Reports per 100,000 Population	Rank[2]
MSA[1]	70,481	931	39
U.S.	3,385,133	1,031	-

Note: (1) Figures cover the Dallas-Fort Worth-Arlington, TX Metropolitan Statistical Area; (2) Rank ranges from 1 to 391 where 1 indicates greatest number of fraud and other consumer reports per 100,000 population
Source: Federal Trade Commission, Consumer Sentinel Network Data Book 2020

POLITICS

2020 Presidential Election Results

Area	Biden	Trump	Jorgensen	Hawkins	Other
Tarrant County	49.3	49.1	1.2	0.3	0.0
U.S.	51.3	46.8	1.2	0.3	0.5

Note: Results are percentages and may not add to 100% due to rounding
Source: Dave Leip's Atlas of U.S. Presidential Elections

SPORTS

Professional Sports Teams

Team Name	League	Year Established
Dallas Cowboys	National Football League (NFL)	1960
Dallas Mavericks	National Basketball Association (NBA)	1980
Dallas Stars	National Hockey League (NHL)	1993
FC Dallas	Major League Soccer (MLS)	1996
Texas Rangers	Major League Baseball (MLB)	1972

Note: Includes teams located in the Dallas-Fort Worth-Arlington, TX Metropolitan Statistical Area.
Source: Wikipedia, Major Professional Sports Teams of the United States and Canada, April 6, 2021

CLIMATE

Average and Extreme Temperatures

Temperature	Jan	Feb	Mar	Apr	May	Jun	Jul	Aug	Sep	Oct	Nov	Dec	Yr.
Extreme High (°F)	88	88	96	98	103	113	110	108	107	106	89	90	113
Average High (°F)	54	59	67	76	83	92	96	96	88	79	67	58	76
Average Temp. (°F)	44	49	57	66	73	81	85	85	78	68	56	47	66
Average Low (°F)	33	38	45	54	63	71	75	74	67	56	45	37	55
Extreme Low (°F)	4	6	11	29	41	51	59	56	43	29	19	-1	-1

Note: Figures cover the years 1953-1990
Source: National Climatic Data Center, International Station Meteorological Climate Summary, 9/96

Average Precipitation/Snowfall/Humidity

Precip./Humidity	Jan	Feb	Mar	Apr	May	Jun	Jul	Aug	Sep	Oct	Nov	Dec	Yr.
Avg. Precip. (in.)	1.8	2.2	2.6	3.7	4.9	2.8	2.1	1.9	3.0	3.3	2.1	1.7	32.3
Avg. Snowfall (in.)	1	1	Tr	0	0	0	0	0	0	0	Tr	Tr	3
Avg. Rel. Hum. 6am (%)	79	79	79	81	86	85	80	79	83	82	80	79	81
Avg. Rel. Hum. 3pm (%)	52	51	48	50	53	47	42	41	46	47	49	51	48

Note: Figures cover the years 1953-1990; Tr = Trace amounts (<0.05 in. of rain; <0.5 in. of snow)
Source: National Climatic Data Center, International Station Meteorological Climate Summary, 9/96

Weather Conditions

Temperature			Daytime Sky			Precipitation		
10°F & below	32°F & below	90°F & above	Clear	Partly cloudy	Cloudy	0.01 inch or more precip.	0.1 inch or more snow/ice	Thunder-storms
1	40	100	123	136	106	79	3	47

Note: Figures are average number of days per year and cover the years 1953-1990
Source: National Climatic Data Center, International Station Meteorological Climate Summary, 9/96

HAZARDOUS WASTE

Superfund Sites

The Fort Worth-Arlington, TX metro division is home to three sites on the EPA's Superfund National Priorities List: **Air Force Plant #4 (General Dynamics)** (final); **Circle Court Ground Water Plume** (final); **Sandy Beach Road Ground Water Plume** (final). There are a total of 1,375

Superfund sites with a status of proposed or final on the list in the U.S. *U.S. Environmental Protection Agency, National Priorities List, April 7, 2021*

AIR QUALITY

Air Quality Trends: Ozone

	1990	1995	2000	2005	2010	2015	2016	2017	2018	2019
MSA[1]	0.095	0.105	0.096	0.097	0.080	0.077	0.070	0.073	0.078	0.071
U.S.	0.088	0.089	0.082	0.080	0.073	0.068	0.069	0.068	0.069	0.065

Note: (1) Data covers the Dallas-Fort Worth-Arlington, TX Metropolitan Statistical Area. The values shown are the composite ozone concentration averages among trend sites based on the highest fourth daily maximum 8-hour concentration in parts per million. These trends are based on sites having an adequate record of monitoring data during the trend period. Data from exceptional events are included.
Source: U.S. Environmental Protection Agency, Air Quality Monitoring Information, "Air Quality Trends by City, 1990-2019"

Air Quality Index

Area	Percent of Days when Air Quality was...[2]					AQI Statistics[2]	
	Good	Moderate	Unhealthy for Sensitive Groups	Unhealthy	Very Unhealthy	Maximum	Median
MSA[1]	49.6	42.5	7.7	0.3	0.0	156	51

Note: (1) Data covers the Dallas-Fort Worth-Arlington, TX Metropolitan Statistical Area; (2) Based on 365 days with AQI data in 2019. Air Quality Index (AQI) is an index for reporting daily air quality. EPA calculates the AQI for five major air pollutants regulated by the Clean Air Act: ground-level ozone, particle pollution (aka particulate matter), carbon monoxide, sulfur dioxide, and nitrogen dioxide. The AQI runs from 0 to 500. The higher the AQI value, the greater the level of air pollution and the greater the health concern. There are six AQI categories: "Good" AQI is between 0 and 50. Air quality is considered satisfactory; "Moderate" AQI is between 51 and 100. Air quality is acceptable; "Unhealthy for Sensitive Groups" When AQI values are between 101 and 150, members of sensitive groups may experience health effects; "Unhealthy" When AQI values are between 151 and 200 everyone may begin to experience health effects; "Very Unhealthy" AQI values between 201 and 300 trigger a health alert; "Hazardous" AQI values over 300 trigger warnings of emergency conditions (not shown).
Source: U.S. Environmental Protection Agency, Air Quality Index Report, 2019

Air Quality Index Pollutants

Area	Percent of Days when AQI Pollutant was...[2]					
	Carbon Monoxide	Nitrogen Dioxide	Ozone	Sulfur Dioxide	Particulate Matter 2.5	Particulate Matter 10
MSA[1]	0.0	3.0	56.2	0.0	40.8	0.0

Note: (1) Data covers the Dallas-Fort Worth-Arlington, TX Metropolitan Statistical Area; (2) Based on 365 days with AQI data in 2019. The Air Quality Index (AQI) is an index for reporting daily air quality. EPA calculates the AQI for five major air pollutants regulated by the Clean Air Act: ground-level ozone, particle pollution (also known as particulate matter), carbon monoxide, sulfur dioxide, and nitrogen dioxide. The AQI runs from 0 to 500. The higher the AQI value, the greater the level of air pollution and the greater the health concern.
Source: U.S. Environmental Protection Agency, Air Quality Index Report, 2019

Maximum Air Pollutant Concentrations: Particulate Matter, Ozone, CO and Lead

	Particulate Matter 10 (ug/m^3)	Particulate Matter 2.5 Wtd AM (ug/m^3)	Particulate Matter 2.5 24-Hr (ug/m^3)	Ozone (ppm)	Carbon Monoxide (ppm)	Lead (ug/m^3)
MSA[1] Level	40	9.0	19	0.076	1	0.23
NAAQS[2]	150	15	35	0.075	9	0.15
Met NAAQS[2]	Yes	Yes	Yes	No	Yes	No

Note: (1) Data covers the Dallas-Fort Worth-Arlington, TX Metropolitan Statistical Area; Data from exceptional events are included; (2) National Ambient Air Quality Standards; ppm = parts per million; ug/m^3 = micrograms per cubic meter; n/a not available.
Concentrations: Particulate Matter 10 (coarse particulate)—highest second maximum 24-hour concentration; Particulate Matter 2.5 Wtd AM (fine particulate)—highest weighted annual mean concentration; Particulate Matter 2.5 24-Hour (fine particulate)—highest 98th percentile 24-hour concentration; Ozone—highest fourth daily maximum 8-hour concentration; Carbon Monoxide—highest second maximum non-overlapping 8-hour concentration; Lead—maximum running 3-month average
Source: U.S. Environmental Protection Agency, Air Quality Monitoring Information, "Air Quality Statistics by City, 2019"

Maximum Air Pollutant Concentrations: Nitrogen Dioxide and Sulfur Dioxide

	Nitrogen Dioxide AM (ppb)	Nitrogen Dioxide 1-Hr (ppb)	Sulfur Dioxide AM (ppb)	Sulfur Dioxide 1-Hr (ppb)	Sulfur Dioxide 24-Hr (ppb)
MSA[1] Level	12	46	n/a	7	n/a
NAAQS[2]	53	100	30	75	140
Met NAAQS[2]	Yes	Yes	n/a	Yes	n/a

Note: (1) Data covers the Dallas-Fort Worth-Arlington, TX Metropolitan Statistical Area; Data from exceptional events are included; (2) National Ambient Air Quality Standards; ppm = parts per million; ug/m^3 = micrograms per cubic meter; n/a not available.
Concentrations: Nitrogen Dioxide AM—highest arithmetic mean concentration; Nitrogen Dioxide 1-Hr—highest 98th percentile 1-hour daily maximum concentration; Sulfur Dioxide AM—highest annual mean concentration; Sulfur Dioxide 1-Hr—highest 99th percentile 1-hour daily maximum concentration; Sulfur Dioxide 24-Hr—highest second maximum 24-hour concentration
Source: U.S. Environmental Protection Agency, Air Quality Monitoring Information, "Air Quality Statistics by City, 2019"

Houston, Texas

Background

In 1836, brothers John K. and Augustus C. Allen bought a 6,642-acre tract of marshy, mosquito-infested land 56 miles north of the Gulf of Mexico and named it Houston, after the hero of San Jacinto. From that moment on, Houston has experienced continued growth.

By the end of its first year in the Republic of Texas, Houston claimed 1,500 residents and one theater. The first churches came three years later. By the end of its second year, Houston saw its first steamship, establishing its position as one of the top-ranking ports in the country.

Certainly, Houston owes much to the Houston ship channel, the "golden strip" on which oil refineries, chemical plants, cement factories, and grain elevators conduct their bustling economic activity. The diversity of these industries is a testament to Houston's economy in general.

Tonnage through the Port of Houston has grown to number one in the nation for foreign tonnage. The port is important to the cruise industry as well, and the Norwegian Cruise Line sails out of Houston.

As Texas' biggest city, Houston has also enjoyed manufacturing expansion in its diversified economy. The city is home to the second largest number of Fortune 500 companies, second only to New York City.

Houston is also one of the major scientific research areas in the world. The presence of the Johnson Space Center has spawned a number of related industries in medical and technological research. The Texas Medical Center oversees a network of 45 medical institutions, including St. Luke's Episcopal Hospital, the Texas Children's Hospital, and the Methodist Hospital. As a city whose reputation rests upon advanced research, Houston is also devoted to education and the arts. Rice University, for example, whose admission standards rank as one of the highest in the nation, is located in Houston, as are Dominican College and the University of St. Thomas.

Today, this relatively young city is home to a diverse range of ethnicities, including Mexican-American, Nigerian, American-Indian and Pakistani.

Houston also is patron to the Museum of Fine Arts, the Contemporary Arts Museum, and the Houston Ballet and Grand Opera. A host of smaller cultural institutions, such as the Gilbert and Sullivan Society, the Virtuoso Quartet, and the Houston Harpsichord Society enliven the scene. Two privately funded museums, the Holocaust Museum Houston and the Houston Museum of Natural Science, are historical and educational attractions, and baseball's Minute Maid Park sits in the city's downtown.

Houstonians eagerly embrace continued revitalization. Recent years have seen a virtual explosion of dining and entertainment options in the heart of the city. The opening of the Bayou Place, Houston's largest entertainment complex, has especially generated excitement, providing a variety of restaurants and entertainment options in one facility. An active urban park sits on 12 acres in front of the George R. Brown Convention Center. Reliant Stadium in downtown Houston and home to the NFL's Houston Texans, hosted Superbowl XXXVIII in 2004 and LI in 2017, and WrestleMania XXV in 2009. Major league baseball team Houston Astros won the 2017 World Series. In fact, the city has sports teams for every major professional league except the National Hockey League.

> Vivid Gentleman's Club moved its stripping and exotic dance performances outdoors, creating the state's first drive-thru strip club.

Located in the flat coastal plains, Houston's climate is predominantly marine. The terrain includes many small streams and bayous which, together with the nearness to Galveston Bay, favor the development of fog. Temperatures are moderated by the influence of winds from the Gulf of Mexico, which is 50 miles away. Mild winters are the norm, as is abundant rainfall. Polar air penetrates the area frequently enough to provide variability in the weather.

In August 2017, Hurricane Harvey caused severe flooding in the Houston area, with some regions receiving over 50 inches of rain. Damage from the hurricane is estimated at $125 billion. It is considered one of the worst natural disasters in the history of the United States. In 2018, Houston City Council forgave the large water bills thousands of households faced in the aftermath of Hurricane Harvey. In February 2021, record-low temperatures and severe winter weather caused major power outages across the state.

Rankings

General Rankings

- The Houston metro area was identified as one of America's fastest-growing areas in terms of population and business growth by *MagnifyMoney*. The area ranked #11 out of 35. The 100 most populous metro areas in the U.S. were evaluated on their change from 2011-2016 in the following categories: people and housing; workforce and employment opportunities; growing industry. www.businessinsider.com, "The 35 Cities in the US with the Biggest Influx of People, the Most Work Opportunities, and the Hottest Business Growth," August 12, 2018

- The human resources consulting firm Mercer ranked 231 major cities worldwide in terms of overall quality of life. Houston ranked #66. Criteria: political, social, economic, and socio-cultural factors; medical and health considerations; schools and education; public services and transportation; recreation; consumer goods; housing; and natural environment. *Mercer, "Mercer 2019 Quality of Living Survey," March 13, 2019*

Business/Finance Rankings

- The Brookings Institution ranked the nation's largest cities based on income inequality. Houston was ranked #25 (#1 = greatest inequality). Criteria: the "95/20 ratio," a figure representing the income at which a household earns more than 95 percent of all other households, divided by the income at which a household earns more than only 20 percent of all other households. *Brookings Institution, "Household Income Inequality, Largest Cities of 97 Large U.S. Metro Areas, 2014-2016," February 5, 2018*

- The Brookings Institution ranked the 100 largest metro areas in the U.S. based on income inequality. Houston was ranked #8 (#1 = greatest inequality). Criteria: the "95/20 ratio," a figure representing the income at which a household earns more than 95 percent of all other households, divided by the income at which a household earns more than only 20 percent of all other households. *Brookings Institution, "Household Income Inequality, 100 Largest U.S. Metro Areas, 2014-2016," February 5, 2018*

- Payscale.com ranked the 32 largest metro areas in terms of wage growth. The Houston metro area ranked #31. Criteria: private-sector and education professional wage growth between the 4th quarter of 2019 and the 4th quarter of 2020. *PayScale, "Wage Trends by Metro Area-4th Quarter," January 11, 2021*

- The Houston metro area was identified as one of the most debt-ridden places in America by the finance site Credit.com. The metro area was ranked #4. Criteria: residents' average credit card debt as well as median income. *Credit.com, "25 Cities With the Most Credit Card Debt," February 28, 2018*

- Houston was identified as one of America's most frugal metro areas by *Coupons.com*. The city ranked #19 out of 25. Criteria: digital coupon usage. *Coupons.com, "America's Most Frugal Cities of 2017," March 22, 2018*

- Houston was cited as one of America's top metros for new and expanded facility projects in 2020. The area ranked #3 in the large metro area category (population over 1 million). *Site Selection, "Top Metros of 2020," March 2021*

- The Houston metro area appeared on the Milken Institute "2021 Best Performing Cities" list. Rank: #112 out of 200 large metro areas (population over 250,000). Criteria: job growth; wage and salary growth; high-tech output growth; housing affordability; household broadband access. *Milken Institute, "Best-Performing Cities 2021," February 16, 2021*

- *Forbes* ranked the 200 most populous metro areas to determine the nation's "Best Places for Business and Careers." The Houston metro area was ranked #34. Criteria: costs (business and living); job growth (past and projected); income growth; quality of life; educational attainment (college and high school); projected economic growth; cultural and leisure opportunities; workplace tolerance laws; net migration patterns. *Forbes, "The Best Places for Business and Careers 2019: Seattle Still On Top," October 30, 2019*

- Mercer Human Resources Consulting ranked 209 cities worldwide in terms of cost-of-living. Houston ranked #51 (the lower the ranking, the higher the cost-of-living). The survey measured the comparative cost of over 200 items (such as housing, food, clothing, household goods, transportation, and entertainment) in each location. *Mercer, "2020 Cost of Living Survey," June 9, 2020*

Dating/Romance Rankings

- *Apartment List* conducted its annual survey of renters for cities that have the best opportunities for dating. More than 11,000 single respondents rated their current city or neighborhood for opportunities to date. Houston ranked #8 out of 86 where single residents were very satisfied or somewhat satisfied, making it among the ten best areas for dating opportunities. Other criteria analyzed included gender and education levels of renters. *Apartment List, "The Best & Worst Metros for Dating 2020," February 4, 2020*

- Houston was selected as one of the best cities for post grads by *Rent.com*. The city ranked among the top 10. Criteria: jobs per capita; unemployment rate; mean annual income; cost of living; rental inventory. *Rent.com, "Best Cities for College Grads," December 11, 2018*

Education Rankings

- Personal finance website *WalletHub* analyzed the 150 largest U.S. metropolitan statistical areas to determine where the most educated Americans are putting their degrees to work. Criteria: education levels; percentage of workers with degrees; education quality and attainment gap; public school quality rankings; quality and enrollment of each metro area's universities. Houston was ranked #89 (#1 = most educated city). *www.WalletHub.com, "Most and Least Educated Cities in America," July 20, 2020*

- Houston was selected as one of America's most literate cities. The city ranked #68 out of the 84 largest U.S. cities. Criteria: number of booksellers; library resources; Internet resources; educational attainment; periodical publishing resources; newspaper circulation. *Central Connecticut State University, "America's Most Literate Cities, 2018," February 2019*

Environmental Rankings

- Sperling's BestPlaces assessed the 50 largest metropolitan areas of the United States for the likelihood of dangerously extreme weather events or earthquakes. In general the Southeast and South-Central regions have the highest risk of weather extremes and earthquakes, while the Pacific Northwest enjoys the lowest risk. Of the most risky metropolitan areas, the Houston metro area was ranked #5. *www.bestplaces.net, "Avoid Natural Disasters: BestPlaces Reveals The Top 10 Safest Places to Live," October 25, 2017*

- The U.S. Environmental Protection Agency (EPA) released a list of U.S. metropolitan areas with the most ENERGY STAR certified buildings in 2019. The Houston metro area was ranked #10 out of 25. *U.S. Environmental Protection Agency, "2020 Energy Star Top Cities," March 2020*

- Houston was highlighted as one of the 25 most ozone-polluted metro areas in the U.S. during 2016 through 2018. The area ranked #14. *American Lung Association, "State of the Air 2020," April 21, 2020*

- Houston was highlighted as one of the 25 metro areas most polluted by year-round particle pollution (Annual PM 2.5) in the U.S. during 2016 through 2018. The area ranked #22. *American Lung Association, "State of the Air 2020," April 21, 2020*

Food/Drink Rankings

- The U.S. Chamber of Commerce Foundation conducted an in-depth study on local food truck regulations, surveyed 288 food truck owners, and ranked 20 major American cities based on how friendly they are for operating a food truck. The compiled index assessed the following: procedures for obtaining permits and licenses; complying with restrictions; and financial obligations associated with operating a food truck. Houston ranked #6 overall (1 being the best). *www.foodtrucknation.us, "Food Truck Nation," March 20, 2018*

Health/Fitness Rankings

- For each of the 100 largest cities in the United States, the American Fitness Index®, published by the American College of Sports Medicine and the Anthem Foundation, evaluated community infrastructure and 33 health behaviors including preventive health, levels of chronic disease conditions, pedestrian safety, air quality, and community resources that support physical activity. Houston ranked #69 for "community fitness." *americanfitnessindex.org, "2020 ACSM American Fitness Index Summary Report," July 14, 2020*

- The Houston metro area was identified as one of the worst cities for bed bugs in America by pest control company Orkin. The area ranked #37 out of 50 based on the number of bed bug treatments Orkin performed from December 2019 to November 2020. *Orkin, "New Year, New Top City on Orkin's 2021 Bed Bug Cities List: Chicago," February 1, 2021*

- Houston was identified as a "2021 Spring Allergy Capital." The area ranked #51 out of 100. Three groups of factors were used to identify the most challenging cities for people with allergies during the spring season: annual spring pollen levels; over the counter medicine use; number of board-certified allergy specialists. *Asthma and Allergy Foundation of America, "Spring Allergy Capitals 2021," February 23, 2021*

- Houston was identified as a "2021 Fall Allergy Capital." The area ranked #55 out of 100. Three groups of factors were used to identify the most challenging cities for people with allergies during the fall season: annual fall pollen levels; over the counter medicine use; number of board-certified allergy specialists. *Asthma and Allergy Foundation of America, "Fall Allergy Capitals 2021," February 23, 2021*

- Houston was identified as a "2019 Asthma Capital." The area ranked #98 out of the nation's 100 largest metropolitan areas. Criteria: estimated asthma prevalence; crude death rate from asthma; and ER visits due to asthma. Risk factors analyzed but not factored in the rankings: annual pollen score; annual air quality; public smoking laws; number of board-certified asthma specialists; rescue medication use; controller medication use; uninsured rate; poverty rate. *Asthma and Allergy Foundation of America, "Asthma Capitals 2019: The Most Challenging Places to Live With Asthma," May 7, 2019*

Pet Rankings

- Houston appeared on *The Dogington Post* site as one of the top cities for dog lovers, ranking #12 out of 20. The real estate brokerage, Redfin and Rover, the largest pet sitter and dog walker network, compiled a list from over 14,000 U.S. cities to come up with a "Rover Rank." Criteria: highest count of dog walks, the city's Walk Score®, for-sale home listings that mention "dog," number of dog walkers and pet sitters and the hours spent and distance logged. *www.dogingtonpost.com, "The 20 Most Dog-Friendly Cities of 2019," April 4, 2019*

Real Estate Rankings

- FitSmallBusiness looked at 50 of the largest metropolitan areas in the U.S. to determine which metro was the best to start a real estate business. Data was compiled from such sources as: Zillow, Trulia, U.S. Census Bureau, and the Bureau of Labor Statistics. Criteria: location; inventory; annual wages; median sales price of homes; days on the market; median price cut percentage; and other factors that would influence real estate professional growth. The Houston metro area ranked #38. *fitsmallbusiness.com, "The Best Cities to Become a Real Estate Agent in 2018," January 30, 2018*

- *WalletHub* compared the most populated U.S. cities to determine which had the best markets for real estate agents. Houston ranked #136 where demand was high and pay was the best. Criteria: sales per agent; annual median wage for real-estate agents; monthly average starting salary for real estate agents; real estate job density and competition; unemployment rate; home turnover rate; housing-market health index; and other relevant metrics. *www.WalletHub.com, "2019's Best Places to Be a Real Estate Agent," April 24, 2019*

- Houston was ranked #167 out of 268 metro areas in terms of housing affordability in 2020 by the National Association of Home Builders (#1 = most affordable). Criteria: the share of homes sold in that area affordable to a family earning the local median income, based on standard mortgage underwriting criteria. *National Association of Home Builders®, NAHB-Wells Fargo Housing Opportunity Index, 4th Quarter 2020*

Safety Rankings

- To identify the most dangerous cities in America, 24/7 Wall Street focused on violent crime categories—murder, non-negligent manslaughter, rape, robbery, and aggravated assault—and property crime as reported in the FBI's 2019 annual Uniform Crime Report. Criteria also included median income from American Community Survey and unemployment figures from Bureau of Labor Statistics. For cities with populations over 100,000, Houston was ranked #21. *247wallst.com, "America's 50 Most Dangerous Cities" November 16, 2020*

- Allstate ranked the 200 largest cities in America in terms of driver safety. Houston ranked #158. Criteria: internal property damage claims over a two-year period from January 2016 to December 2017. The report helps increase the importance of safety and awareness behind the wheel. *Allstate, "Allstate America's Best Drivers Report, 2019" June 24, 2019*

- Houston was identified as one of the most dangerous cities in America by NeighborhoodScout. The city ranked #43 out of 100 (#1 = most dangerous). Criteria: number of violent crimes per 1,000 residents. The editors evaluated cities with 25,000 or more residents. *NeighborhoodScout.com, "2021 Top 100 Most Dangerous Cities in the U.S.," January 2, 2021*

- The National Insurance Crime Bureau ranked 384 metro areas in the U.S. in terms of per capita rates of vehicle theft. The Houston metro area ranked #43 (#1 = highest rate). Criteria: number of vehicle theft offenses per 100,000 inhabitants in 2019. *National Insurance Crime Bureau, "Hot Spots 2019," July 21, 2020*

Seniors/Retirement Rankings

- From its Best Cities for Successful Aging indexes, the Milken Institute generated rankings for metropolitan areas, weighing data in nine categories—health care, wellness, living arrangements, transportation and convenience, financial characteristics, education, employment, community engagement, and overall livability. The Houston metro area was ranked #25 overall in the large metro area category. *Milken Institute, "Best Cities for Successful Aging, 2017" March 14, 2017*

Transportation Rankings

- Houston was identified as one of the most congested metro areas in the U.S. The area ranked #9 out of 10. Criteria: yearly delay per auto commuter in hours. *Texas A&M Transportation Institute, "2019 Urban Mobility Report," December 2019*

Women/Minorities Rankings

- The *Houston Chronicle* listed the Houston metro area as #11 in top places for young Latinos to live in the U.S. Research was largely based on housing and occupational data from the largest metropolitan areas performed by *Forbes* and NBC Universo. Criteria: percentage of 18-34 year-olds; Latino college grad rates; and diversity. *blog.chron.com, "The 15 Best Big Cities for Latino Millenials," January 26, 2016*

- Personal finance website *WalletHub* compared more than 180 U.S. cities across two key dimensions, "Hispanic Business-Friendliness" and "Hispanic Purchasing Power," to arrive at the most favorable conditions for Hispanic entrepreneurs. Houston was ranked #27 out of 182. Criteria includes: share of Hispanic-Owned Businesses; Hispanic entrepreneurship rate to median annual income of Hispanics; Small Business-Friendliness score; cost of living; and number of Hispanics with at least a bachelor's degree. *WalletHub.com, "2019's Best Cities for Hispanic Entrepreneurs," May 1, 2019*

Miscellaneous Rankings

- The watchdog site, Charity Navigator, conducted a study of charities in major markets both to analyze statistical differences in their financial, accountability, and transparency practices and to track year-to-year variations in individual philanthropic communities. The Houston metro area was ranked #2 among the 30 metro markets in the rating category of Overall Score. *www.charitynavigator.org, "2017 Metro Market Study," May 1, 2017*

- *WalletHub* compared the 150 most populated U.S. cities to determine their operating efficiency. A "Quality of City Services" score was constructed for each city and then divided by the total budget per capita to reveal which were managed the best. Houston ranked #72. Criteria: financial stability; economy; education; safety; health; infrastructure and pollution. *www.WalletHub.com, "2020's Best- & Worst-Run Cities in America," June 29, 2020*

- The National Alliance to End Homelessness listed the 25 most populous metro areas with the highest rate of homelessness. The Houston metro area had a high rate of homelessness. Criteria: number of homeless people per 10,000 population in 2016. *National Alliance to End Homelessness, "Homelessness in the 25 Most Populous U.S. Metro Areas," September 1, 2017*

Business Environment

DEMOGRAPHICS

Population Growth

Area	1990 Census	2000 Census	2010 Census	2019* Estimate	Population Growth (%) 1990-2019	Population Growth (%) 2010-2019
City	1,697,610	1,953,631	2,099,451	2,310,432	36.1	10.0
MSA[1]	3,767,335	4,715,407	5,946,800	6,884,138	82.7	15.8
U.S.	248,709,873	281,421,906	308,745,538	324,697,795	30.6	5.2

Note: (1) Figures cover the Houston-The Woodlands-Sugar Land, TX Metropolitan Statistical Area; (*) 2015-2019 5-year estimated population
Source: U.S. Census Bureau, 1990 Census, Census 2000, Census 2010, 2015-2019 American Community Survey 5-Year Estimates

Household Size

Area	One	Two	Three	Four	Five	Six	Seven or More	Average Household Size
City	32.3	28.9	15.2	12.3	6.6	2.8	1.8	2.70
MSA[1]	24.1	29.7	17.2	15.7	8.2	3.2	2.0	2.90
U.S.	27.9	33.9	15.6	12.9	6.0	2.3	1.4	2.60

Note: (1) Figures cover the Houston-The Woodlands-Sugar Land, TX Metropolitan Statistical Area
Source: U.S. Census Bureau, 2015-2019 American Community Survey 5-Year Estimates

Race

Area	White Alone[2] (%)	Black Alone[2] (%)	Asian Alone[2] (%)	AIAN[3] Alone[2] (%)	NHOPI[4] Alone[2] (%)	Other Race Alone[2] (%)	Two or More Races (%)
City	57.0	22.6	6.8	0.3	0.1	11.1	2.2
MSA[1]	65.0	17.3	7.7	0.4	0.1	7.0	2.5
U.S.	72.5	12.7	5.5	0.8	0.2	4.9	3.3

Note: (1) Figures cover the Houston-The Woodlands-Sugar Land, TX Metropolitan Statistical Area; (2) Alone is defined as not being in combination with one or more other races; (3) American Indian and Alaska Native; (4) Native Hawaiian and Other Pacific Islander
Source: U.S. Census Bureau, 2015-2019 American Community Survey 5-Year Estimates

Hispanic or Latino Origin

Area	Total (%)	Mexican (%)	Puerto Rican (%)	Cuban (%)	Other (%)
City	45.0	31.8	0.6	0.8	11.7
MSA[1]	37.3	27.8	0.7	0.6	8.3
U.S.	18.0	11.2	1.7	0.7	4.3

Note: Persons of Hispanic or Latino origin can be of any race; (1) Figures cover the Houston-The Woodlands-Sugar Land, TX Metropolitan Statistical Area
Source: U.S. Census Bureau, 2015-2019 American Community Survey 5-Year Estimates

Ancestry

Area	German	Irish	English	American	Italian	Polish	French[2]	Scottish	Dutch
City	4.8	3.6	3.7	4.0	1.5	0.8	1.6	0.9	0.4
MSA[1]	7.8	5.3	5.2	4.3	2.0	1.2	2.1	1.2	0.6
U.S.	13.3	9.7	7.2	6.2	5.1	2.8	2.3	1.7	1.2

Note: Figures are the percentage of the total population reporting a particular ancestry. The nine most commonly reported ancestries in the U.S. are shown. Figures include multiple ancestries (e.g. if a person reported being Irish and Italian, they were included in both columns); (1) Figures cover the Houston-The Woodlands-Sugar Land, TX Metropolitan Statistical Area; (2) Excludes Basque
Source: U.S. Census Bureau, 2015-2019 American Community Survey 5-Year Estimates

Foreign-born Population

Area	Any Foreign Country	Asia	Mexico	Europe	Caribbean	Central America[2]	South America	Africa	Canada
City	29.3	6.0	11.4	1.1	1.1	6.3	1.3	1.9	0.2
MSA[1]	23.4	6.0	8.9	1.0	0.8	3.6	1.3	1.4	0.3
U.S.	13.6	4.2	3.5	1.5	1.3	1.1	1.0	0.7	0.2

Note: (1) Figures cover the Houston-The Woodlands-Sugar Land, TX Metropolitan Statistical Area; (2) Excludes Mexico.
Source: U.S. Census Bureau, 2015-2019 American Community Survey 5-Year Estimates

Marital Status

Area	Never Married	Now Married[2]	Separated	Widowed	Divorced
City	41.0	41.3	3.2	4.6	9.9
MSA[1]	33.7	49.8	2.5	4.5	9.6
U.S.	33.4	48.1	1.9	5.8	10.9

Note: Figures are percentages and cover the population 15 years of age and older; (1) Figures cover the Houston-The Woodlands-Sugar Land, TX Metropolitan Statistical Area; (2) Excludes separated
Source: U.S. Census Bureau, 2015-2019 American Community Survey 5-Year Estimates

Disability by Age

Area	All Ages	Under 18 Years Old	18 to 64 Years Old	65 Years and Over
City	9.5	3.2	7.7	35.6
MSA[1]	9.4	3.3	7.8	34.0
U.S.	12.6	4.2	10.3	34.5

Note: Figures show percent of the civilian noninstitutionalized population that reported having a disability. Disability status is determined from six types of difficulty: vision, hearing, cognitive, ambulatory, self-care, and independent living. For children under 5 years old, hearing and vision difficulty are used to determine disability status. For children between the ages of 5 and 14, disability status is determined from hearing, vision, cognitive, ambulatory, and self-care difficulties. For people aged 15 years and older, they are considered to have a disability if they have difficulty with any one of the six difficulty types; Note: (1) Figures cover the Houston-The Woodlands-Sugar Land, TX Metropolitan Statistical Area
Source: U.S. Census Bureau, 2015-2019 American Community Survey 5-Year Estimates

Age

Area	Under Age 5	Age 5–19	Age 20–34	Age 35–44	Age 45–54	Age 55–64	Age 65–74	Age 75–84	Age 85+	Median Age
City	7.6	19.9	25.9	14.0	11.7	10.4	6.3	3.0	1.2	33.0
MSA[1]	7.3	21.9	21.7	14.2	12.8	11.2	6.8	3.0	1.0	34.3
U.S.	6.1	19.1	20.7	12.6	13.0	12.9	9.1	4.6	1.9	38.1

Note: (1) Figures cover the Houston-The Woodlands-Sugar Land, TX Metropolitan Statistical Area
Source: U.S. Census Bureau, 2015-2019 American Community Survey 5-Year Estimates

Gender

Area	Males	Females	Males per 100 Females
City	1,153,417	1,157,015	99.7
MSA[1]	3,417,036	3,467,102	98.6
U.S.	159,886,919	164,810,876	97.0

Note: (1) Figures cover the Houston-The Woodlands-Sugar Land, TX Metropolitan Statistical Area
Source: U.S. Census Bureau, 2015-2019 American Community Survey 5-Year Estimates

Religious Groups by Family

Area	Catholic	Baptist	Non-Den.	Methodist[2]	Lutheran	LDS[3]	Pentecostal	Presbyterian[4]	Muslim[5]	Judaism
MSA[1]	17.1	16.0	7.3	4.9	1.1	1.1	1.5	0.9	2.7	0.4
U.S.	19.1	9.3	4.0	4.0	2.3	2.0	1.9	1.6	0.8	0.7

Note: Figures are the number of adherents as a percentage of the total population; (1) Figures cover the Houston-The Woodlands-Sugar Land, TX Metropolitan Statistical Area; (2) Methodist/Pietist; (3) Latter Day Saints; (4) Reformed; (5) Figures are estimates
Source: Association of Statisticians of American Religious Bodies, 2010 U.S. Religion Census: Religious Congregations & Membership Study

Religious Groups by Tradition

Area	Catholic	Evangelical Protestant	Mainline Protestant	Other Tradition	Black Protestant	Orthodox
MSA[1]	17.1	24.9	6.7	4.9	1.3	0.2
U.S.	19.1	16.2	7.3	4.3	1.6	0.3

Note: Figures are the number of adherents as a percentage of the total population; (1) Figures cover the Houston-The Woodlands-Sugar Land, TX Metropolitan Statistical Area
Source: Association of Statisticians of American Religious Bodies, 2010 U.S. Religion Census: Religious Congregations & Membership Study

ECONOMY

Gross Metropolitan Product

Area	2017	2018	2019	2020	Rank[2]
MSA[1]	478.1	513.9	546.1	583.7	7

Note: Figures are in billions of dollars; (1) Figures cover the Houston-The Woodlands-Sugar Land, TX Metropolitan Statistical Area; (2) Rank is based on 2018 data and ranges from 1 to 381
Source: U.S. Conference of Mayors, U.S. Metro Economies: GMP & Employment 2018-2020, September 2019

Economic Growth

Area	2015-17 (%)	2018 (%)	2019 (%)	2020 (%)	Rank[2]
MSA[1]	-1.7	2.9	4.6	3.1	360
U.S.	1.9	2.9	2.3	2.1	—

Note: Figures are real gross metropolitan product (GMP) growth rates and represent average annual percent change; (1) Figures cover the Houston-The Woodlands-Sugar Land, TX Metropolitan Statistical Area; (2) Rank is based on 2017 2-year average annual percent change and ranges from 1 to 381
Source: U.S. Conference of Mayors, U.S. Metro Economies: GMP & Employment 2018-2020, September 2019

Metropolitan Area Exports

Area	2014	2015	2016	2017	2018	2019	Rank[2]
MSA[1]	118,966.0	97,054.3	84,105.5	95,760.3	120,714.3	129,656.0	1

Note: Figures are in millions of dollars; (1) Figures cover the Houston-The Woodlands-Sugar Land, TX Metropolitan Statistical Area; (2) Rank is based on 2019 data and ranges from 1 to 386
Source: U.S. Department of Commerce, International Trade Administration, Office of Trade and Economic Analysis, Industry and Analysis, Exports by Metropolitan Area, data extracted March 24, 2021

Building Permits

Area	Single-Family 2018	Single-Family 2019	Pct. Chg.	Multi-Family 2018	Multi-Family 2019	Pct. Chg.	Total 2018	Total 2019	Pct. Chg.
City	5,417	5,120	-5.5	7,820	10,343	32.3	13,237	15,463	16.8
MSA[1]	40,321	39,507	-2.0	16,967	24,165	42.4	57,288	63,672	11.1
U.S.	855,300	862,100	0.7	473,500	523,900	10.6	1,328,800	1,386,000	4.3

Note: (1) Figures cover the Houston-The Woodlands-Sugar Land, TX Metropolitan Statistical Area; Figures represent new, privately-owned housing units authorized (unadjusted data); All permit data are based on estimates with imputation
Source: U.S. Census Bureau, Manufacturing, Mining, and Construction Statistics, Building Permits, 2018, 2019

Bankruptcy Filings

Area	Business Filings 2019	Business Filings 2020	% Chg.	Nonbusiness Filings 2019	Nonbusiness Filings 2020	% Chg.
Harris County	411	608	47.9	4,527	2,967	-34.5
U.S.	22,780	21,655	-4.9	752,160	522,808	-30.5

Note: Business filings include Chapter 7, Chapter 9, Chapter 11, Chapter 12, Chapter 13, Chapter 15, and Section 304; Nonbusiness filings include Chapter 7, Chapter 11, and Chapter 13
Source: Administrative Office of the U.S. Courts, Business and Nonbusiness Bankruptcy, County Cases Commenced by Chapter of the Bankruptcy Code, During the 12-Month Period Ending December 31, 2019 and Business and Nonbusiness Bankruptcy, County Cases Commenced by Chapter of the Bankruptcy Code, During the 12-Month Period Ending December 31, 2020

Housing Vacancy Rates

Area	Gross Vacancy Rate[2] (%) 2018	2019	2020	Year-Round Vacancy Rate[3] (%) 2018	2019	2020	Rental Vacancy Rate[4] (%) 2018	2019	2020	Homeowner Vacancy Rate[5] (%) 2018	2019	2020
MSA[1]	8.8	9.8	6.8	8.2	9.1	6.3	8.8	11.4	9.7	2.0	1.9	1.1
U.S.	12.3	12.0	10.6	9.7	9.5	8.2	6.9	6.7	6.3	1.5	1.4	1.0

Note: (1) Figures cover the Houston-The Woodlands-Sugar Land, TX Metropolitan Statistical Area; (2) The percentage of the total housing inventory that is vacant; (3) The percentage of the housing inventory (excluding seasonal units) that is year-round vacant; (4) The percentage of rental inventory that is vacant for rent; (5) The percentage of homeowner inventory that is vacant for sale
Source: U.S. Census Bureau, Housing Vacancies and Homeownership Annual Statistics: 2018, 2019, 2020

INCOME

Income

Area	Per Capita ($)	Median Household ($)	Average Household ($)
City	32,521	52,338	84,179
MSA[1]	34,400	67,516	97,410
U.S.	34,103	62,843	88,607

Note: (1) Figures cover the Houston-The Woodlands-Sugar Land, TX Metropolitan Statistical Area
Source: U.S. Census Bureau, 2015-2019 American Community Survey 5-Year Estimates

Household Income Distribution

Area	Under $15,000	$15,000-$24,999	$25,000-$34,999	$35,000-$49,999	$50,000-$74,999	$75,000-$99,999	$100,000-$149,999	$150,000 and up
City	12.6	11.1	10.8	13.5	16.7	10.6	11.3	13.5
MSA[1]	8.8	8.3	8.7	11.7	16.8	12.3	15.8	17.7
U.S.	10.3	8.9	8.9	12.3	17.2	12.7	15.1	14.5

Note: (1) Figures cover the Houston-The Woodlands-Sugar Land, TX Metropolitan Statistical Area
Source: U.S. Census Bureau, 2015-2019 American Community Survey 5-Year Estimates

Poverty Rate

Area	All Ages	Under 18 Years Old	18 to 64 Years Old	65 Years and Over
City	20.1	31.2	16.6	14.2
MSA[1]	13.7	19.8	11.7	10.0
U.S.	13.4	18.5	12.6	9.3

Note: Figures are percentage of people whose income during the past 12 months was below the poverty level;
(1) Figures cover the Houston-The Woodlands-Sugar Land, TX Metropolitan Statistical Area
Source: U.S. Census Bureau, 2015-2019 American Community Survey 5-Year Estimates

CITY FINANCES

City Government Finances

Component	2017 ($000)	2017 ($ per capita)
Total Revenues	6,614,771	2,881
Total Expenditures	5,180,259	2,256
Debt Outstanding	14,092,369	6,137
Cash and Securities[1]	16,559,621	7,212

Note: (1) Cash and security holdings of a government at the close of its fiscal year, including those of its dependent agencies, utilities, and liquor stores.
Source: U.S. Census Bureau, State & Local Government Finances 2017

City Government Revenue by Source

Source	2017 ($000)	2017 ($ per capita)	2017 (%)
General Revenue			
From Federal Government	102,519	45	1.5
From State Government	114,596	50	1.7
From Local Governments	103,772	45	1.6
Taxes			
Property	1,443,701	629	21.8
Sales and Gross Receipts	908,372	396	13.7
Personal Income	0	0	0.0
Corporate Income	0	0	0.0
Motor Vehicle License	0	0	0.0
Other Taxes	149,389	65	2.3
Current Charges	1,302,944	567	19.7
Liquor Store	0	0	0.0
Utility	543,034	236	8.2
Employee Retirement	1,503,210	655	22.7

Source: U.S. Census Bureau, State & Local Government Finances 2017

City Government Expenditures by Function

Function	2017 ($000)	2017 ($ per capita)	2017 (%)
General Direct Expenditures			
Air Transportation	363,125	158	7.0
Corrections	0	0	0.0
Education	0	0	0.0
Employment Security Administration	0	0	0.0
Financial Administration	46,175	20	0.9
Fire Protection	400,048	174	7.7
General Public Buildings	40,218	17	0.8
Governmental Administration, Other	311,390	135	6.0
Health	123,674	53	2.4
Highways	181,534	79	3.5
Hospitals	0	0	0.0
Housing and Community Development	65,380	28	1.3
Interest on General Debt	702,189	305	13.6
Judicial and Legal	49,076	21	0.9
Libraries	44,755	19	0.9
Parking	10,466	4	0.2
Parks and Recreation	104,626	45	2.0
Police Protection	728,467	317	14.1
Public Welfare	0	0	0.0
Sewerage	550,264	239	10.6
Solid Waste Management	61,770	26	1.2
Veterans' Services	0	0	0.0
Liquor Store	0	0	0.0
Utility	428,561	186	8.3
Employee Retirement	685,147	298	13.2

Source: U.S. Census Bureau, State & Local Government Finances 2017

EMPLOYMENT

Labor Force and Employment

Area	Civilian Labor Force Dec. 2019	Civilian Labor Force Dec. 2020	% Chg.	Workers Employed Dec. 2019	Workers Employed Dec. 2020	% Chg.
City	1,168,794	1,162,957	-0.5	1,128,145	1,071,532	-5.0
MSA[1]	3,462,635	3,445,575	-0.5	3,336,616	3,169,170	-5.0
U.S.	164,007,000	160,017,000	-2.4	158,504,000	149,613,000	-5.6

Note: Data is not seasonally adjusted and covers workers 16 years of age and older; (1) Figures cover the Houston-The Woodlands-Sugar Land, TX Metropolitan Statistical Area
Source: Bureau of Labor Statistics, Local Area Unemployment Statistics

Unemployment Rate

Area	Jan.	Feb.	Mar.	Apr.	May	Jun.	Jul.	Aug.	Sep.	Oct.	Nov.	Dec.
City	3.9	3.7	5.4	14.4	14.1	10.0	9.8	8.4	9.8	7.7	8.8	7.9
MSA[1]	4.1	3.9	5.5	14.3	13.9	9.7	9.5	8.1	9.6	7.7	8.9	8.0
U.S.	4.0	3.8	4.5	14.4	13.0	11.2	10.5	8.5	7.7	6.6	6.4	6.5

Note: Data is not seasonally adjusted and covers workers 16 years of age and older; (1) Figures cover the Houston-The Woodlands-Sugar Land, TX Metropolitan Statistical Area
Source: Bureau of Labor Statistics, Local Area Unemployment Statistics

Average Wages

Occupation	$/Hr.	Occupation	$/Hr.
Accountants and Auditors	40.30	Maintenance and Repair Workers	21.00
Automotive Mechanics	23.00	Marketing Managers	78.50
Bookkeepers	21.70	Network and Computer Systems Admin.	46.20
Carpenters	21.50	Nurses, Licensed Practical	23.50
Cashiers	11.60	Nurses, Registered	40.90
Computer Programmers	49.80	Nursing Assistants	14.10
Computer Systems Analysts	59.70	Office Clerks, General	20.20
Computer User Support Specialists	24.90	Physical Therapists	40.60
Construction Laborers	17.90	Physicians	97.10
Cooks, Restaurant	12.00	Plumbers, Pipefitters and Steamfitters	26.70
Customer Service Representatives	17.50	Police and Sheriff's Patrol Officers	32.60
Dentists	69.50	Postal Service Mail Carriers	25.50
Electricians	25.60	Real Estate Sales Agents	30.10
Engineers, Electrical	54.60	Retail Salespersons	13.10
Fast Food and Counter Workers	10.40	Sales Representatives, Technical/Scientific	45.60
Financial Managers	74.00	Secretaries, Exc. Legal/Medical/Executive	19.10
First-Line Supervisors of Office Workers	29.80	Security Guards	14.70
General and Operations Managers	61.00	Surgeons	109.60
Hairdressers/Cosmetologists	11.90	Teacher Assistants, Exc. Postsecondary*	10.90
Home Health and Personal Care Aides	10.20	Teachers, Secondary School, Exc. Sp. Ed.*	29.20
Janitors and Cleaners	12.50	Telemarketers	14.80
Landscaping/Groundskeeping Workers	14.70	Truck Drivers, Heavy/Tractor-Trailer	23.20
Lawyers	70.00	Truck Drivers, Light/Delivery Services	20.40
Maids and Housekeeping Cleaners	11.40	Waiters and Waitresses	11.40

Note: Wage data covers the Houston-The Woodlands-Sugar Land, TX Metropolitan Statistical Area; (*) Hourly wages were calculated from annual wage data based on a 40 hour work week; n/a not available.
Source: Bureau of Labor Statistics, Metro Area Occupational Employment & Wage Estimates, May 2020

Employment by Industry

Sector	MSA[1] Number of Employees	MSA[1] Percent of Total	U.S. Percent of Total
Construction	200,900	6.7	5.1
Education and Health Services	398,000	13.3	16.3
Financial Activities	163,300	5.5	6.1
Government	420,100	14.0	15.2
Information	29,000	1.0	1.9
Leisure and Hospitality	287,200	9.6	9.0
Manufacturing	208,700	7.0	8.5
Mining and Logging	66,300	2.2	0.4
Other Services	104,800	3.5	3.8
Professional and Business Services	483,800	16.1	14.4
Retail Trade	303,500	10.1	10.9
Transportation, Warehousing, and Utilities	171,600	5.7	4.6
Wholesale Trade	158,500	5.3	3.9

Note: Figures are non-farm employment as of December 2020. Figures are not seasonally adjusted and include workers 16 years of age and older; (1) Figures cover the Houston-The Woodlands-Sugar Land, TX Metropolitan Statistical Area
Source: Bureau of Labor Statistics, Current Employment Statistics, Employment, Hours, and Earnings

Employment by Occupation

Occupation Classification	City (%)	MSA[1] (%)	U.S. (%)
Management, Business, Science, and Arts	35.8	38.6	38.5
Natural Resources, Construction, and Maintenance	12.1	10.9	8.9
Production, Transportation, and Material Moving	13.3	13.1	13.2
Sales and Office	19.8	21.1	21.6
Service	18.9	16.2	17.8

Note: Figures cover employed civilians 16 years of age and older; (1) Figures cover the Houston-The Woodlands-Sugar Land, TX Metropolitan Statistical Area
Source: U.S. Census Bureau, 2015-2019 American Community Survey 5-Year Estimates

Occupations with Greatest Projected Employment Growth: 2020 – 2022

Occupation[1]	2020 Employment	2022 Projected Employment	Numeric Employment Change	Percent Employment Change
Fast Food and Counter Workers	336,530	411,690	75,160	22.3
Waiters and Waitresses	165,570	206,920	41,350	25.0
Home Health and Personal Care Aides	303,520	344,240	40,720	13.4
Retail Salespersons	315,590	349,820	34,230	10.8
Heavy and Tractor-Trailer Truck Drivers	199,460	228,650	29,190	14.6
Laborers and Freight, Stock, and Material Movers, Hand	193,000	219,670	26,670	13.8
Cooks, Restaurant	88,540	114,250	25,710	29.0
Customer Service Representatives	276,080	295,790	19,710	7.1
General and Operations Managers	197,410	216,580	19,170	9.7
Office Clerks, General	310,080	327,500	17,420	5.6

Note: Projections cover Texas; (1) Sorted by numeric employment change
Source: www.projectionscentral.com, State Occupational Projections, 2020–2022 Short-Term Projections

Fastest-Growing Occupations: 2020 – 2022

Occupation[1]	2020 Employment	2022 Projected Employment	Numeric Employment Change	Percent Employment Change
Motion Picture Projectionists	150	300	150	100.0
Ushers, Lobby Attendants, and Ticket Takers	5,740	8,920	3,180	55.4
Locker Room, Coatroom, and Dressing Room Attendants	340	510	170	50.0
Athletes and Sports Competitors	270	400	130	48.1
Amusement and Recreation Attendants	13,130	19,400	6,270	47.8
Hotel, Motel, and Resort Desk Clerks	16,140	23,160	7,020	43.5
Sound Engineering Technicians	330	460	130	39.4
Gaming Dealers	220	300	80	36.4
Baggage Porters and Bellhops	1,250	1,670	420	33.6
Lodging Managers	3,300	4,330	1,030	31.2

Note: Projections cover Texas; (1) Sorted by percent employment change and excludes occupations with numeric employment change less than 50
Source: www.projectionscentral.com, State Occupational Projections, 2020–2022 Short-Term Projections

TAXES

State Corporate Income Tax Rates

State	Tax Rate (%)	Income Brackets ($)	Num. of Brackets	Financial Institution Tax Rate (%)[a]	Federal Income Tax Ded.
Texas	(w)	–	–	(w)	No

Note: Tax rates as of January 1, 2021; (a) Rates listed are the corporate income tax rate applied to financial institutions or excise taxes based on income. Some states have other taxes based upon the value of deposits or shares; (w) Texas imposes a Franchise Tax, otherwise known as margin tax, imposed on entities with more than $1,130,000 total revenues at rate of 0.75%, or 0.375% for entities primarily engaged in retail or wholesale trade, on lesser of 70% of total revenues or 100% of gross receipts after deductions for either compensation or cost of goods sold.
Source: Federation of Tax Administrators, State Corporate Income Tax Rates, January 1, 2021

State Individual Income Tax Rates

State	Tax Rate (%)	Income Brackets ($)	Personal Exemptions ($) Single	Personal Exemptions ($) Married	Personal Exemptions ($) Depend.	Standard Ded. ($) Single	Standard Ded. ($) Married
Texas			– No state income tax –				

Note: Tax rates as of January 1, 2021; Local- and county-level taxes are not included
Source: Federation of Tax Administrators, State Individual Income Tax Rates, January 1, 2021

Various State Sales and Excise Tax Rates

State	State Sales Tax (%)	Gasoline[1] (¢/gal.)	Cigarette[2] ($/pack)	Spirits[3] ($/gal.)	Wine[4] ($/gal.)	Beer[5] ($/gal.)	Recreational Marijuana (%)
Texas	6.25	20	1.41	2.4	0.2	0.2	Not legal

Note: All tax rates as of January 1, 2021; (1) The American Petroleum Institute has developed a methodology for determining the average tax rate on a gallon of fuel. Rates may include any of the following: excise taxes, environmental fees, storage tank fees, other fees or taxes, general sales tax, and local taxes; (2) The federal excise tax of $1.0066 per pack and local taxes are not included; (3) Rates are those applicable to off-premise sales of 40% alcohol by volume (a.b.v.) distilled spirits in 750ml containers. Local excise taxes are excluded; (4) Rates are those applicable to off-premise sales of 11% a.b.v. non-carbonated wine in 750ml containers; (5) Rates are those applicable to off-premise sales of 4.7% a.b.v. beer in 12 ounce containers.
Source: Tax Foundation, 2021 Facts & Figures: How Does Your State Compare?

State Business Tax Climate Index Rankings

State	Overall Rank	Corporate Tax Rank	Individual Income Tax Rank	Sales Tax Rank	Property Tax Rank	Unemployment Insurance Tax Rank
Texas	11	47	6	35	36	16

Note: The index is a measure of how each state's tax laws affect economic performance. The lower the rank, the more favorable a state's tax system is for business. States without a given tax are given a ranking of 1. The scores/rankings for the District of Columbia do not affect other states. The 2021 index represents the tax climate as of July 1, 2020.
Source: Tax Foundation, State Business Tax Climate Index 2021

TRANSPORTATION

Means of Transportation to Work

Area	Drove Alone	Car-pooled	Bus	Subway	Railroad	Bicycle	Walked	Other Means	Worked at Home
City	77.7	10.4	3.5	0.1	0.0	0.4	2.0	2.0	4.0
MSA[1]	80.8	9.8	1.9	0.0	0.0	0.2	1.3	1.4	4.5
U.S.	76.3	9.0	2.4	1.9	0.6	0.5	2.7	1.4	5.2

Note: Figures are percentages and cover workers 16 years of age and older; (1) Figures cover the Houston-The Woodlands-Sugar Land, TX Metropolitan Statistical Area
Source: U.S. Census Bureau, 2015-2019 American Community Survey 5-Year Estimates

Travel Time to Work

Area	Less Than 10 Minutes	10 to 19 Minutes	20 to 29 Minutes	30 to 44 Minutes	45 to 59 Minutes	60 to 89 Minutes	90 Minutes or More
City	7.3	25.5	22.2	27.8	8.9	6.4	1.9
MSA[1]	7.7	23.3	19.4	26.5	11.8	8.9	2.5
U.S.	12.2	28.4	20.8	20.8	8.3	6.4	2.9

Note: Note: Figures are percentages and include workers 16 years old and over; (1) Figures cover the Houston-The Woodlands-Sugar Land, TX Metropolitan Statistical Area
Source: U.S. Census Bureau, 2015-2019 American Community Survey 5-Year Estimates

Key Congestion Measures

Measure	1982	1992	2002	2012	2017
Annual Hours of Delay, Total (000)	62,747	74,455	131,719	209,742	247,440
Annual Hours of Delay, Per Auto Commuter	42	40	47	64	75
Annual Congestion Cost, Total (million $)	473	785	1,775	3,744	4,547
Annual Congestion Cost, Per Auto Commuter ($)	856	698	964	1,203	1,376

Note: Covers the Houston TX urban area
Source: Texas A&M Transportation Institute, 2019 Urban Mobility Report

Freeway Travel Time Index

Measure	1982	1987	1992	1997	2002	2007	2012	2017
Urban Area Index[1]	1.23	1.22	1.22	1.23	1.25	1.29	1.31	1.34
Urban Area Rank[1,2]	3	4	6	15	19	15	13	11

Note: Freeway Travel Time Index—the ratio of travel time in the peak period to the travel time at free-flow conditions. For example, a value of 1.30 indicates a 20-minute free-flow trip takes 26 minutes in the peak (20 minutes x 1.30 = 26 minutes); (1) Covers the Houston TX urban area; (2) Rank is based on 101 larger urban areas (#1 = highest travel time index)
Source: Texas A&M Transportation Institute, 2019 Urban Mobility Report

Public Transportation

Agency Name / Mode of Transportation	Vehicles Operated in Maximum Service[1]	Annual Unlinked Passenger Trips[2] (in thous.)	Annual Passenger Miles[3] (in thous.)
Metropolitan Transit Authority of Harris County (METRO)			
Bus (directly operated)	613	50,413.1	266,982.5
Bus (purchased transportation)	99	9,130.9	39,149.2
Commuter Bus (directly operated)	248	6,082.4	108,607.4
Commuter Bus (purchased transportation)	64	1,877.9	36,498.9
Demand Response (purchased transportation)	340	1,786.4	19,905.0
Demand Response Taxi (purchased transportation)	160	312.2	2,530.6
Light Rail (directly operated)	54	18,556.6	52,243.1
Vanpool (directly operated)	553	1,791.7	55,659.3

Note: (1) Number of revenue vehicles operated by the given mode and type of service to meet the annual maximum service requirement. This is the revenue vehicle count during the peak season of the year; on the week and day that maximum service is provided. Vehicles operated in maximum service (VOMS) exclude atypical days and one-time special events; (2) Number of passengers who boarded public transportation vehicles. Passengers are counted each time they board a vehicle no matter how many vehicles they use to travel from their origin to their destination. (3) Sum of the distances ridden by all passengers during the entire fiscal year.
Source: Federal Transit Administration, National Transit Database, 2019

Air Transportation

Airport Name and Code / Type of Service	Passenger Airlines[1]	Passenger Enplanements	Freight Carriers[2]	Freight (lbs)
George Bush Intercontinental (IAH)				
Domestic service (U.S. carriers - 2020)	24	6,939,066	19	290,120,059
International service (U.S. carriers - 2019)	11	3,849,758	8	56,139,560
William P. Hobby (HOU)				
Domestic service (U.S. carriers - 2020)	18	2,966,674	6	12,706,724
International service (U.S. carriers - 2019)	3	427,825	1	22,697

Note: (1) Includes all U.S.-based major, minor and commuter airlines that carried at least one passenger during the year; (2) Includes all U.S.-based airlines and freight carriers that transported at least one pound of freight during the year.
Source: Bureau of Transportation Statistics, The Intermodal Transportation Database, Air Carriers: T-100 Domestic Market (U.S. Carriers), 2020; Bureau of Transportation Statistics, The Intermodal Transportation Database, Air Carriers: T-100 International Market (U.S. Carriers), 2019

BUSINESSES

Major Business Headquarters

Company Name	Industry	Fortune[1]	Forbes[2]
APA	Mining, Crude-Oil Production	465	-
BMC Software	IT Software & Services	-	211
Baker Hughes	Oil and Gas Equipment, Services	129	-
Calpine	Energy	319	39
CenterPoint Energy	Utilities, Gas and Electric	260	-
Cheniere Energy	Energy	329	-
ConocoPhillips	Mining, Crude-Oil Production	93	-
Crown Castle International	Real Estate	496	-
EOG Resources	Mining, Crude-Oil Production	186	-
Enterprise Products Partners	Pipelines	101	-
Fertitta Entertainment	Hotels, Restaurants & Leisure	-	93
Group 1 Automotive	Automotive Retailing, Services	264	-
Gulf States Toyota	Consumer Durables	-	43
Halliburton	Oil and Gas Equipment, Services	142	-
Kinder Morgan	Pipelines	242	-
NOV	Oil and Gas Equipment, Services	374	-
Occidental Petroleum	Mining, Crude-Oil Production	148	-
Phillips 66	Petroleum Refining	27	-
Plains GP Holdings	Pipelines	98	-
Quanta Services	Engineering, Construction	261	-
Sysco	Wholesalers, Food and Grocery	56	-
Targa Resources	Pipelines	365	-
Tauber Oil	Oil & Gas Operations	-	56
Waste Management	Waste Management	207	-
Westlake Chemical	Chemicals	391	-

Note: (1) Companies that produce a 10-K are ranked 1 to 500 based on 2019 revenue; (2) All private companies with at least $2 billion in annual revenue through the end of their most current fiscal year are ranked 1 to 219; companies listed are headquartered in the city; dashes indicate no ranking
Source: Fortune, "Fortune 500," June/July 2020; Forbes, "America's Largest Private Companies," 2020

Fastest-Growing Businesses

According to *Inc.*, Houston is home to seven of America's 500 fastest-growing private companies: **Advance LED Solution** (#147); **SIA Solutions** (#286); **Sarvicus** (#324); **ChangeStaffing** (#379); **Garrison Construction Group** (#424); **Integrate Agency** (#462); **Eagle Pipe** (#466). Criteria: must be an independent, privately-held, for-profit, U.S. corporation, proprietorship or partnership as of December 31, 2019; revenues must be at least $100,000 in 2016 and $2 million in 2019; must have four-year operating/sales history. *Inc., "America's 500 Fastest-Growing Private Companies," 2020*

According to *Fortune*, Houston is home to two of the 100 fastest-growing companies in the world: **Cabot Oil & Gas** (#68); **Comfort Systems USA** (#100). Companies were ranked by their revenue growth rate; their EPS growth rate; and their three-year annualized total return to investors for the period ending June 30, 2020. Criteria for inclusion: a company, foreign or domestic, must trade on a major U.S. stock exchange; must file quarterly reports with the SEC; must have a minimum market capitalization of $250 million; must have a stock price of at least $5 on June 30, 2020; must have been trading continuously since June 30, 2017; must have revenue and net income for the four quarters ended on or before April 30, 2020, of at least $50 million and $10 million, respectively; and must have posted a compound annual growth in revenue and earnings per share of at least 15% annually over the three years ending on or before April 30, 2020. Real estate investment trusts, limited-liability companies, limited partersips, business development companies, closed-end investment firms, companies about to be acquired, and companies that lost money in the quarter ending April 30, 2020 were excluded. *Fortune, "100 Fastest-Growing Companies," 2020*

According to *Initiative for a Competitive Inner City (ICIC)*, Houston is home to three of America's 100 fastest-growing "inner city" companies: **Green Light Safety** (#45); **UYL Color** (#63); **Classy Art** (#66). Criteria for inclusion: company must be headquartered in or have 51 percent or more of its physical operations in an economically distressed urban area; must be an independent, for-profit corporation, partnership or proprietorship; must have 10 or more employees and have a five-year sales history that includes sales of at least $200,000 in the base year and at least $1 million in the current year with no decrease in sales over the two most recent years. Companies were ranked overall by revenue growth over the five-year period between 2015 and 2019. *Initiative for a Competitive Inner City (ICIC), "Inner City 100 Companies," 2020*

According to Deloitte, Houston is home to three of North America's 500 fastest-growing high-technology companies: **NatGasHub.com** (#37); **Onit** (#190); **symplr** (#425). Companies are ranked by percentage growth in revenue over a four-year period. Criteria for inclusion: company must be headquartered within North America; must own proprietary intellectual property or technology that is sold to customers in products that contributes to a significant portion of the company's operating revenue; must have been in business for a minumum of four years with 2016 operating revenues of at least $50,000 USD/CD and 2019 operating revenues of at least $5 million USD/CD. *Deloitte, 2020 Technology Fast 500*™

Minority Business Opportunity

Houston is home to two companies which are on the *Black Enterprise* Industrial/Service list (100 largest companies based on gross sales): **The Lewis Group** (#36); **ChaseSource** (#82). Criteria: operational in previous calendar year; at least 51% black-owned and manufactures/owns the product it sells or provides industrial or consumer services. Brokerages, real estate firms and firms that provide professional services are not eligible. *Black Enterprise, B.E. 100s, 2019*

Houston is home to one company which is on the *Black Enterprise* Auto Dealer list (45 largest dealers based on gross sales): **J. Davis Automotive Group** (#16). Criteria: company must be operational in previous calendar year and be at least 51% black-owned. *Black Enterprise, B.E. 100s, 2019*

Houston is home to one company which is on the *Black Enterprise* Bank list (15 largest banks based on total assets, capital, deposits and loans, including mortgage-backed securities for the calendar year): **Unity National Bank** (#13). Only commercial banks or savings and loans that are classified by the Federal Reserve as black institutions and have been fully operational for the previous calendar year were considered. *Black Enterprise, B.E. 100s, 2019*

Houston is home to one company which is on the *Black Enterprise* Asset Manager list (10 largest asset management firms based on assets under management): **Smith, Graham & Co. Investment Advisors** (#6). Criteria: company must have been operational in previous calendar year and be at least 51% black-owned. *Black Enterprise, B.E. 100s, 2019*

Living Environment

COST OF LIVING

Cost of Living Index

Composite Index	Groceries	Housing	Utilities	Transportation	Health Care	Misc. Goods/Services
95.3	92.0	85.6	111.3	95.5	98.6	99.5

Note: The Cost of Living Index measures regional differences in the cost of consumer goods and services, excluding taxes and non-consumer expenditures, for professional and managerial households in the top income quintile. It is based on more than 50,000 prices covering almost 60 different items for which prices are collected three times a year by chambers of commerce, economic development organizations or university applied economic centers in each participating urban area. The numbers shown should be read as a percentage above or below the national average of 100. For example, a value of 115.4 in the groceries column indicates that grocery prices are 15.4% higher than the national average. Small differences in the index numbers should not be interpreted as significant; Figures cover the Houston TX urban area.
Source: The Council for Community and Economic Research, Cost of Living Index, 2020

Grocery Prices

Area[1]	T-Bone Steak ($/pound)	Frying Chicken ($/pound)	Whole Milk ($/half gal.)	Eggs ($/dozen)	Orange Juice ($/64 oz.)	Coffee ($/11.5 oz.)
City[2]	11.29	1.13	1.58	1.42	3.50	3.84
Avg.	11.78	1.39	2.05	1.47	3.57	4.34
Min.	8.03	0.94	1.03	0.74	2.94	3.02
Max.	15.86	2.65	4.31	3.77	5.44	8.69

Note: (1) Values for the local area are compared with the average, minimum and maximum values for all 284 areas in the Cost of Living Index; (2) Figures cover the Houston TX urban area; **T-Bone Steak** (price per pound); **Frying Chicken** (price per pound, whole fryer); **Whole Milk** (half gallon carton); **Eggs** (price per dozen, Grade A, large); **Orange Juice** (64 oz. Tropicana or Florida Natural); **Coffee** (11.5 oz. can, vacuum-packed, Maxwell House, Hills Bros, or Folgers).
Source: The Council for Community and Economic Research, Cost of Living Index, 2020

Housing and Utility Costs

Area[1]	New Home Price ($)	Apartment Rent ($/month)	All Electric ($/month)	Part Electric ($/month)	Other Energy ($/month)	Telephone ($/month)
City[2]	297,296	1,119	-	161.68	38.31	184.00
Avg.	368,594	1,168	170.86	100.47	65.28	184.30
Min.	190,567	502	91.58	31.42	26.08	169.60
Max.	2,227,806	4,738	470.38	280.31	280.06	206.50

Note: (1) Values for the local area are compared with the average, minimum and maximum values for all 284 areas in the Cost of Living Index; (2) Figures cover the Houston TX urban area; **New Home Price** (2,400 sf living area, 8,000 sf lot, in urban area with full utilities); **Apartment Rent** (950 sf 2 bedroom/1.5 or 2 bath, unfurnished, excluding all utilities except water); **All Electric** (average monthly cost for an all-electric home); **Part Electric** (average monthly cost for a part-electric home); **Other Energy** (average monthly cost for natural gas, fuel oil, coal, wood, and any other forms of energy except electricity); **Telephone** (price includes the base monthly rate plus taxes and fees for three lines of mobile phone service).
Source: The Council for Community and Economic Research, Cost of Living Index, 2020

Health Care, Transportation, and Other Costs

Area[1]	Doctor ($/visit)	Dentist ($/visit)	Optometrist ($/visit)	Gasoline ($/gallon)	Beauty Salon ($/visit)	Men's Shirt ($)
City[2]	88.11	111.03	119.84	1.92	61.37	33.46
Avg.	115.44	99.32	108.10	2.21	39.27	31.37
Min.	36.68	59.00	51.36	1.71	19.00	11.00
Max.	219.00	153.10	250.97	3.46	82.05	58.33

Note: (1) Values for the local area are compared with the average, minimum and maximum values for all 284 areas in the Cost of Living Index; (2) Figures cover the Houston TX urban area; **Doctor** (general practitioners routine exam of an established patient); **Dentist** (adult teeth cleaning and periodic oral examination); **Optometrist** (full vision eye exam for established adult patient); **Gasoline** (one gallon regular unleaded, national brand, including all taxes, cash price at self-service pump if available); **Beauty Salon** (woman's shampoo, trim, and blow-dry); **Men's Shirt** (cotton/polyester dress shirt, pinpoint weave, long sleeves).
Source: The Council for Community and Economic Research, Cost of Living Index, 2020

HOUSING

Homeownership Rate

Area	2012 (%)	2013 (%)	2014 (%)	2015 (%)	2016 (%)	2017 (%)	2018 (%)	2019 (%)	2020 (%)
MSA[1]	62.1	60.5	60.4	60.3	59.0	58.9	60.1	61.3	65.3
U.S.	65.4	65.1	64.5	63.7	63.4	63.9	64.4	64.6	66.6

Note: (1) Figures cover the Houston-The Woodlands-Sugar Land, TX Metropolitan Statistical Area
Source: U.S. Census Bureau, Housing Vacancies and Homeownership Annual Statistics: 2012-2020

House Price Index (HPI)

Area	National Ranking[2]	Quarterly Change (%)	One-Year Change (%)	Five-Year Change (%)	Since 1991Q1 (%)
MSA[1]	211	1.45	4.53	23.50	211.24
U.S.[3]	–	3.81	10.77	38.99	205.12

Note: The HPI is a weighted repeat sales index. It measures average price changes in repeat sales or refinancings on the same properties. This information is obtained by reviewing repeat mortgage transactions on single-family properties whose mortgages have been purchased or securitized by Fannie Mae or Freddie Mac since January 1975; (1) Figures cover the Houston-The Woodlands-Sugar Land, TX Metropolitan Statistical Area; (2) Rankings are based on annual percentage change for all metro areas containing at least 15,000 transactions over the last 10 years and ranges from 1 to 253; (3) figures based on a weighted average of Census Division estimates using a seasonally adjusted, purchase-only index; all figures are for the period ending December 31, 2020
Source: Federal Housing Finance Agency, Change in Metropolitan Area House Price Indexes, April 7, 2021

Median Single-Family Home Prices

Area	2018	2019	2020p	Percent Change 2019 to 2020
MSA[1]	238.8	245.8	263.8	7.3
U.S. Average	261.6	274.6	299.9	9.2

Note: Figures are median sales prices of existing single-family homes in thousands of dollars; (p) preliminary; (1) Figures cover the Houston-The Woodlands-Sugar Land, TX Metropolitan Statistical Area
Source: National Association of Realtors, Median Sales Price of Existing Single-Family Homes for Metropolitan Areas, 4th Quarter 2020

Qualifying Income Based on Median Sales Price of Existing Single-Family Homes

Area	With 5% Down ($)	With 10% Down ($)	With 20% Down ($)
MSA[1]	51,768	49,044	43,594
U.S. Average	59,266	56,147	49,908

Note: Figures are preliminary; Qualifying income is based on a mortgage rate of 2.81%. Monthly principal and interest payment is limited to 25% of income; (1) Figures cover the Houston-The Woodlands-Sugar Land, TX Metropolitan Statistical Area
Source: National Association of Realtors, Qualifying Income Based on Median Sales Price of Existing Single-Family Homes for Metropolitan Areas, 4th Quarter 2020

Home Value Distribution

Area	Under $50,000	$50,000 -$99,999	$100,000 -$149,999	$150,000 -$199,999	$200,000 -$299,999	$300,000 -$499,999	$500,000 -$999,999	$1,000,000 or more
City	5.4	19.6	18.1	13.0	14.5	15.8	10.0	3.6
MSA[1]	5.3	12.1	16.7	17.8	22.0	16.9	6.9	2.3
U.S.	6.9	12.0	13.3	14.0	19.6	19.3	11.4	3.4

Note: Figures are percentages and cover owner-occupied housing units; (1) Figures cover the Houston-The Woodlands-Sugar Land, TX Metropolitan Statistical Area
Source: U.S. Census Bureau, 2015-2019 American Community Survey 5-Year Estimates

Year Housing Structure Built

Area	2010 or Later	2000 -2009	1990 -1999	1980 -1989	1970 -1979	1960 -1969	1950 -1959	1940 -1949	Before 1940	Median Year
City	8.6	13.4	9.9	14.6	21.1	13.4	10.3	4.5	4.3	1978
MSA[1]	11.9	21.5	14.4	15.5	16.9	8.4	6.2	2.6	2.4	1989
U.S.	5.2	14.0	13.9	13.4	15.2	10.6	10.3	4.9	12.6	1978

Note: Figures are percentages except for Median Year; Note: (1) Figures cover the Houston-The Woodlands-Sugar Land, TX Metropolitan Statistical Area
Source: U.S. Census Bureau, 2015-2019 American Community Survey 5-Year Estimates

Gross Monthly Rent

Area	Under $500	$500 -$999	$1,000 -$1,499	$1,500 -$1,999	$2,000 -$2,499	$2,500 -$2,999	$3,000 and up	Median ($)
City	3.8	42.7	34.6	12.8	3.3	1.4	1.4	1,041
MSA[1]	3.8	37.0	37.0	15.6	4.0	1.4	1.2	1,101
U.S.	9.4	36.2	30.0	14.0	5.6	2.4	2.4	1,062

Note: Figures are percentages except for Median; Gross rent is the contract rent plus the estimated average monthly cost of utilities (electricity, gas, and water and sewer) and fuels (oil, coal, kerosene, wood, etc.) if these are paid by the renter (or paid for the renter by someone else); (1) Figures cover the Houston-The Woodlands-Sugar Land, TX Metropolitan Statistical Area
Source: U.S. Census Bureau, 2015-2019 American Community Survey 5-Year Estimates

HEALTH

Health Risk Factors

Category	MSA[1] (%)	U.S. (%)
Adults aged 18–64 who have any kind of health care coverage	66.8	87.3
Adults who reported being in good or better health	79.0	82.4
Adults who have been told they have high blood cholesterol	36.1	33.0
Adults who have been told they have high blood pressure	31.4	32.3
Adults who are current smokers	15.1	17.1
Adults who currently use E-cigarettes	3.3	4.6
Adults who currently use chewing tobacco, snuff, or snus	4.2	4.0
Adults who are heavy drinkers[2]	6.7	6.3
Adults who are binge drinkers[3]	18.8	17.4
Adults who are overweight (BMI 25.0 - 29.9)	42.7	35.3
Adults who are obese (BMI 30.0 - 99.8)	31.0	31.3
Adults who participated in any physical activities in the past month	70.6	74.4
Adults who always or nearly always wears a seat belt	95.8	94.3

Note: (1) Figures cover the Houston-The Woodlands-Sugar Land, TX Metropolitan Statistical Area; (2) Heavy drinkers are classified as adult men having more than 14 drinks per week and adult women having more than 7 drinks per week; (3) Binge drinkers are classified as males having five or more drinks on one occasion or females having four or more drinks on one occasion
Source: Centers for Disease Control and Prevention, Behaviorial Risk Factor Surveillance System, SMART: Selected Metropolitan Area Risk Trends, 2017

Acute and Chronic Health Conditions

Category	MSA[1] (%)	U.S. (%)
Adults who have ever been told they had a heart attack	3.3	4.2
Adults who have ever been told they have angina or coronary heart disease	3.5	3.9
Adults who have ever been told they had a stroke	3.7	3.0
Adults who have ever been told they have asthma	10.7	14.2
Adults who have ever been told they have arthritis	24.0	24.9
Adults who have ever been told they have diabetes[2]	10.0	10.5
Adults who have ever been told they had skin cancer	3.9	6.2
Adults who have ever been told they had any other types of cancer	4.9	7.1
Adults who have ever been told they have COPD	4.0	6.5
Adults who have ever been told they have kidney disease	2.5	3.0
Adults who have ever been told they have a form of depression	16.1	20.5

Note: (1) Figures cover the Houston-The Woodlands-Sugar Land, TX Metropolitan Statistical Area; (2) Figures do not include pregnancy-related, borderline, or pre-diabetes
Source: Centers for Disease Control and Prevention, Behaviorial Risk Factor Surveillance System, SMART: Selected Metropolitan Area Risk Trends, 2017

Health Screening and Vaccination Rates

Category	MSA[1] (%)	U.S. (%)
Adults aged 65+ who have had flu shot within the past year	63.2	60.7
Adults aged 65+ who have ever had a pneumonia vaccination	72.4	75.4
Adults who have ever been tested for HIV	45.5	36.1
Adults who have ever had the shingles or zoster vaccine?	23.0	28.9
Adults who have had their blood cholesterol checked within the last five years	86.2	85.9

Note: n/a not available; (1) Figures cover the Houston-The Woodlands-Sugar Land, TX Metropolitan Statistical Area.
Source: Centers for Disease Control and Prevention, Behaviorial Risk Factor Surveillance System, SMART: Selected Metropolitan Area Risk Trends, 2017

Disability Status

Category	MSA[1] (%)	U.S. (%)
Adults who reported being deaf	4.8	6.7
Are you blind or have serious difficulty seeing, even when wearing glasses?	5.2	4.5
Are you limited in any way in any of your usual activities due of arthritis?	13.3	12.9
Do you have difficulty doing errands alone?	8.1	6.8
Do you have difficulty dressing or bathing?	4.7	3.6
Do you have serious difficulty concentrating/remembering/making decisions?	12.1	10.7
Do you have serious difficulty walking or climbing stairs?	12.4	13.6

Note: (1) Figures cover the Houston-The Woodlands-Sugar Land, TX Metropolitan Statistical Area.
Source: Centers for Disease Control and Prevention, Behaviorial Risk Factor Surveillance System, SMART: Selected Metropolitan Area Risk Trends, 2017

Mortality Rates for the Top 10 Causes of Death in the U.S.

ICD-10[a] Sub-Chapter	ICD-10[a] Code	Age-Adjusted Mortality Rate[1] per 100,000 population County[2]	U.S.
Malignant neoplasms	C00-C97	137.8	149.2
Ischaemic heart diseases	I20-I25	85.3	90.5
Other forms of heart disease	I30-I51	51.4	52.2
Chronic lower respiratory diseases	J40-J47	28.1	39.6
Other degenerative diseases of the nervous system	G30-G31	40.6	37.6
Cerebrovascular diseases	I60-I69	40.6	37.2
Other external causes of accidental injury	W00-X59	27.8	36.1
Organic, including symptomatic, mental disorders	F01-F09	19.2	29.4
Hypertensive diseases	I10-I15	24.3	24.1
Diabetes mellitus	E10-E14	20.4	21.5

Note: (a) ICD-10 = International Classification of Diseases 10th Revision; (1) Mortality rates are a three-year average covering 2017-2019; (2) Figures cover Harris County.
Source: Centers for Disease Control and Prevention, National Center for Health Statistics. Underlying Cause of Death 1999-2019 on CDC WONDER Online Database

Mortality Rates for Selected Causes of Death

ICD-10[a] Sub-Chapter	ICD-10[a] Code	Age-Adjusted Mortality Rate[1] per 100,000 population County[2]	U.S.
Assault	X85-Y09	8.4	6.0
Diseases of the liver	K70-K76	14.0	14.4
Human immunodeficiency virus (HIV) disease	B20-B24	3.6	1.5
Influenza and pneumonia	J09-J18	12.1	13.8
Intentional self-harm	X60-X84	10.5	14.1
Malnutrition	E40-E46	4.3	2.3
Obesity and other hyperalimentation	E65-E68	1.8	2.1
Renal failure	N17-N19	17.6	12.6
Transport accidents	V01-V99	11.1	12.3
Viral hepatitis	B15-B19	1.3	1.2

Note: (a) ICD-10 = International Classification of Diseases 10th Revision; (1) Mortality rates are a three-year average covering 2017-2019; (2) Figures cover Harris County; Data are suppressed when the data meet the criteria for confidentiality constraints; Mortality rates are flagged as unreliable when the rate would be calculated with a numerator of 20 or less.
Source: Centers for Disease Control and Prevention, National Center for Health Statistics. Underlying Cause of Death 1999-2019 on CDC WONDER Online Database

Health Insurance Coverage

Area	With Health Insurance	With Private Health Insurance	With Public Health Insurance	Without Health Insurance	Population Under Age 19 Without Health Insurance
City	76.9	51.9	30.8	23.1	13.1
MSA[1]	81.9	62.1	26.6	18.1	11.1
U.S.	91.2	67.9	35.1	8.8	5.1

Note: Figures are percentages that cover the civilian noninstitutionalized population; (1) Figures cover the Houston-The Woodlands-Sugar Land, TX Metropolitan Statistical Area
Source: U.S. Census Bureau, 2015-2019 American Community Survey 5-Year Estimates

Number of Medical Professionals

Area	MDs[3]	DOs[3,4]	Dentists	Podiatrists	Chiropractors	Optometrists
County[1] (number)	15,609	539	3,333	222	1,052	963
County[1] (rate[2])	333.5	11.5	70.7	4.7	22.3	20.4
U.S. (rate[2])	282.9	22.7	71.2	6.2	28.1	16.9

48201
Note: Data as of 2019 unless noted; (1) Data covers Harris County; (2) Rate per 100,000 population; (3) Data as of 2018 and includes all active, non-federal physicians; (4) Doctor of Osteopathic Medicine
Source: U.S. Department of Health and Human Services, Health Resources and Services Administration, Bureau of Health Professions, Area Resource File (ARF) 2019-2020

Best Hospitals

According to *U.S. News,* the Houston-The Woodlands-Sugar Land, TX metro area is home to nine of the best hospitals in the U.S.: **Baylor St. Luke's Medical Center** (5 adult specialties); **Blanton Eye Institute, Houston Methodist Hospital** (11 adult specialties); **Cullen Eye Institute at Baylor St. Luke's Medical Center** (5 adult specialties); **Dan L Duncan Comprehensive Cancer Center at Baylor St. Luke's Medical** (5 adult specialties); **Houston Methodist Hospital** (Honor Roll/11 adult specialties); **Memorial Hermann-Texas Medical Center** (1 adult specialty and 2 pediatric specialties); **TIRR Memorial Hermann** (1 adult specialty); **Texas Heart Institute at Baylor St. Luke's Medical Center** (5 adult specialties); **University of Texas MD Anderson Cancer Center** (7 adult specialties and 1 pediatric specialty). The hospitals listed were nationally ranked in at least one of 16 adult or 10 pediatric specialties. Only 134 hospitals nationwide were nationally ranked in one or more adult or pediatric specialty; this number increases to 178 counting specialized centers within hospitals. Twenty hospitals in the U.S. made the Honor Roll. The Best Hospitals Honor Roll takes both the national rankings and the procedure and condition ratings into account. Hospitals received points if they were nationally ranked in one of the 16 adult specialties—the higher they ranked, the more points they got—and how many ratings of "high performing" they earned in the 10 procedures and conditions. *U.S. News Online, "America's Best Hospitals 2020-21"*

According to *U.S. News,* the Houston-The Woodlands-Sugar Land, TX metro area is home to three of the best children's hospitals in the U.S.: **Children's Cancer Hospital-University of Texas M.D. Anderson Cancer Center** (1 pediatric specialty); **Children's Memorial Hermann Hospital** (2 pediatric specialties); **Texas Children's Hospital** (Honor Roll/10 pediatric specialties). The hospitals listed were highly ranked in at least one of 10 pediatric specialties. Eighty-eight children's hospitals in the U.S. were nationally ranked in at least one specialty. Hospitals received points for being ranked in a specialty, and the 10 hospitals with the most points across the 10 specialties make up the Honor Roll. *U.S. News Online, "America's Best Children's Hospitals 2020-21"*

EDUCATION

Public School District Statistics

District Name	Schls	Pupils	Pupil/Teacher Ratio	Minority Pupils[1] (%)	Free Lunch Eligible[2] (%)	IEP[3] (%)
Aldine ISD	86	66,854	16.2	97.7	81.2	8.2
Alief ISD	46	45,436	13.9	96.2	77.9	7.8
Cypress-Fairbanks ISD	89	116,512	16.0	75.8	47.1	8.6
Galena Park ISD	25	22,289	16.4	95.9	85.4	9.0
Harmony School of Excellence	8	5,026	15.1	90.3	58.4	6.3
Houston Gateway Academy Inc	4	2,409	20.6	99.1	n/a	3.0
Houston ISD	280	209,772	17.5	91.0	79.4	7.5
Kipp Texas Public Schools	51	27,048	19.9	98.4	82.5	7.6
Sheldon ISD	13	9,401	16.9	94.4	74.6	8.0
Spring Branch ISD	50	34,681	15.1	73.1	57.9	8.2
Spring ISD	39	35,385	16.4	92.5	61.2	8.9
Yes Prep Public Schools Inc	14	11,405	15.8	98.7	77.6	5.9

Note: Table includes school districts with 2,000 or more students; (1) Percentage of students that are not non-Hispanic white; (2) Percentage of students that are eligible for the free lunch program; (3) Percentage of students that have an Individualized Education Program.
Source: U.S. Department of Education, National Center for Education Statistics, Common Core of Data, Local Education Agency (School District) Universe Survey: School Year 2018-2019; U.S. Department of Education, National Center for Education Statistics, Common Core of Data, Public Elementary/Secondary School Universe Survey: School Year 2018-2019

Best High Schools

According to *U.S. News,* Houston is home to 20 of the top 500 high schools in the U.S.: **DeBakey High School for Health Professions** (#29); **Carnegie Vanguard High School** (#44); **Eastwood Academy** (#97); **Challenge Early College High School** (#123); **Kerr High School** (#182); **Clear Horizons Early College High School** (#222); **The High School for the Performing and Visual Arts** (#234); **YES Prep - Southwest** (#252); **YES Prep - North Central** (#266); **YES Prep - Southeast** (#269); **North Houston Early College High School** (#271); **Victory Early College High School** (#287); **Early College Academy at Southridge** (#305); **East Early College High School** (#342); **YES Prep - West** (#350); **YES Prep - East End** (#365); **Alief Early College High School** (#381); **Young Women's College Prep Academy** (#412); **Mickey Leland College Prep Acad For Young Men** (#481); **KIPP Houston High School** (#487). Nearly 18,000 public, magnet and charter schools were ranked based on their performance on state assessments and how well they prepare students for college. *U.S. News & World Report, "Best High Schools 2020"*

Highest Level of Education

Area	Less than H.S.	H.S. Diploma	Some College, No Deg.	Associate Degree	Bachelor's Degree	Master's Degree	Prof. School Degree	Doctorate Degree
City	21.1	22.8	17.8	5.5	20.0	8.6	2.6	1.6
MSA[1]	16.3	23.2	20.6	7.1	21.0	8.4	2.0	1.5
U.S.	12.0	27.0	20.4	8.5	19.8	8.8	2.1	1.4

Note: Figures cover persons age 25 and over; (1) Figures cover the Houston-The Woodlands-Sugar Land, TX Metropolitan Statistical Area
Source: U.S. Census Bureau, 2015-2019 American Community Survey 5-Year Estimates

Educational Attainment by Race

Area	High School Graduate or Higher (%)					Bachelor's Degree or Higher (%)				
	Total	White	Black	Asian	Hisp.[2]	Total	White	Black	Asian	Hisp.[2]
City	78.9	78.0	88.8	86.9	58.5	32.9	37.4	22.6	58.9	13.6
MSA[1]	83.7	83.6	91.0	87.8	64.1	32.8	33.3	27.5	56.6	15.0
U.S.	88.0	89.9	86.0	87.1	68.7	32.1	33.5	21.6	54.3	16.4

Note: Figures shown cover persons 25 years old and over; (1) Figures cover the Houston-The Woodlands-Sugar Land, TX Metropolitan Statistical Area; (2) People of Hispanic origin can be of any race
Source: U.S. Census Bureau, 2015-2019 American Community Survey 5-Year Estimates

School Enrollment by Grade and Control

Area	Preschool (%)		Kindergarten (%)		Grades 1 - 4 (%)		Grades 5 - 8 (%)		Grades 9 - 12 (%)	
	Public	Private	Public	Private	Public	Private	Public	Private	Public	Private
City	66.9	33.1	90.8	9.2	94.2	5.8	92.7	7.3	93.5	6.5
MSA[1]	58.1	41.9	90.2	9.8	93.1	6.9	93.0	7.0	93.3	6.7
U.S.	59.1	40.9	87.6	12.4	89.5	10.5	89.4	10.6	90.1	9.9

Note: Figures shown cover persons 3 years old and over; (1) Figures cover the Houston-The Woodlands-Sugar Land, TX Metropolitan Statistical Area
Source: U.S. Census Bureau, 2015-2019 American Community Survey 5-Year Estimates

Higher Education

Four-Year Colleges			Two-Year Colleges			Medical Schools[1]	Law Schools[2]	Voc/Tech[3]
Public	Private Non-profit	Private For-profit	Public	Private Non-profit	Private For-profit			
6	10	6	1	3	15	3	3	21

Note: Figures cover institutions located within the city limits and include main campuses only; (1) includes schools accredited by the Liaison Committee on Medical Education and the American Osteopathic Association's Commission on Osteopathic College Accreditation; (2) includes ABA-accredited schools, schools with provisional ABA accreditation, and state accredited schools; (3) includes all schools with programs that are less than 2 years.
Source: National Center for Education Statistics, Integrated Postsecondary Education System (IPEDS), 2019-20; Wikipedia, List of Medical Schools in the United States, accessed April 2, 2021; Wikipedia, List of Law Schools in the United States, accessed April 2, 2021

According to *U.S. News & World Report*, the Houston-The Woodlands-Sugar Land, TX metro area is home to two of the top 200 national universities in the U.S.: **Rice University** (#16 tie); **University of Houston** (#176 tie). The indicators used to capture academic quality fall into a number of categories: assessment by administrators at peer institutions; retention of students; faculty resources; student selectivity; financial resources; alumni giving; high school counselor ratings of colleges; and graduation rate. *U.S. News & World Report, "America's Best Colleges 2021"*

According to *U.S. News & World Report*, the Houston-The Woodlands-Sugar Land, TX metro area is home to one of the top 100 law schools in the U.S.: **University of Houston** (#60 tie). The rankings are based on a weighted average of 12 measures of quality: peer assessment score; assessment score by lawyers/judges; median LSAT scores; median undergrad GPA; acceptance rate; employment rates for graduates; placement success; bar passage rate; faculty resources; expenditures per student; student/faculty ratio; and library resources. *U.S. News & World Report, "America's Best Graduate Schools, Law, 2022"*

According to *U.S. News & World Report*, the Houston-The Woodlands-Sugar Land, TX metro area is home to two of the top 75 medical schools for research in the U.S.: **Baylor College of Medicine** (#22 tie); **University of Texas Health Science Center—Houston (McGovern)** (#53). The rankings are based on a weighted average of 11 measures of quality: quality assessment; peer assessment score; assessment score by residency directors; research activity; total research activity; average research activity per faculty member; student selectivity; median MCAT total score; median undergraduate GPA; acceptance rate; and faculty resources. *U.S. News & World Report, "America's Best Graduate Schools, Medical, 2022"*

According to *U.S. News & World Report*, the Houston-The Woodlands-Sugar Land, TX metro area is home to one of the top 75 business schools in the U.S.: **Rice University (Jones)** (#25). The rankings are based on a weighted average of the following nine measures: quality assessment; peer assessment; recruiter assessment; placement success; mean starting salary and bonus; student selectivity; mean GMAT and GRE scores; mean undergraduate GPA; and acceptance rate. *U.S. News & World Report, "America's Best Graduate Schools, Business, 2022"*

Houston, Texas

EMPLOYERS

Major Employers

Company Name	Industry
Christus Health Gulf Coast	Management consulting services
Conoco Phillips	Petroleum refining
Continental Airlines	Air transportation, scheduled
Dibellos Dynamic Orthotics & Prosthetics	Surgical appliances & supplies
El Paso E&P Company	Petroleum refining
F Charles Brunicardi MD	Accounting, auditing, & bookkeeping
Grey Wolf	Drilling oil & gas wells
Kellogg Brown &Root	Industrial plant construction
Mustang Engineers and Constructors	Construction management consultant
Philip Industrial Services	Environmental consultant
Philips Petroleum Company	Oil & gas exploration services
Quaker State Corp	Lubricating oils & greases
St. Lukes Episcopal Health System	General medical & surgical hospitals
Texas Childrens Hospital	Specialty hospitals, except psychiatric
The Methodist Hospital	General medical & surgical hospitals
Tracer Industries	Plumbing
U.S. Dept of Veteran Affairs	Administration of veterans' affairs
Univ of Texas Medical Branch at Galveston	Accident & health insurance
University of Houston System	University
University of Texas System	General medical & surgical hospitals
Veterans Health Administration	Administration of veterans' affairs

Note: Companies shown are located within the Houston-The Woodlands-Sugar Land, TX Metropolitan Statistical Area.
Source: Hoovers.com; Wikipedia

Best Companies to Work For

Camden Property Trust; David Weekley Homes; Hilcorp, headquartered in Houston, are among "The 100 Best Companies to Work For." To pick the best companies, *Fortune* partnered with the Great Place to Work Institute. Two-thirds of a company's score is based on the results of the Institute's Trust Index survey, which is sent to a random sample of employees from each company. The questions related to attitudes about management's credibility, job satisfaction, and camaraderie. The other third of the scoring is based on the company's responses to the Institute's Culture Audit, which includes detailed questions about pay and benefit programs, and a series of open-ended questions about hiring practices, internal communication, training, recognition programs, and diversity efforts. Any company that is at least five years old with more than 1,000 U.S. employees is eligible. *Fortune*, "The 100 Best Companies to Work For," 2020

PUBLIC SAFETY

Crime Rate

Area	All Crimes	Violent Crimes				Property Crimes		
		Murder	Rape[3]	Robbery	Aggrav. Assault	Burglary	Larceny-Theft	Motor Vehicle Theft
City	5,391.7	11.7	53.0	388.3	619.2	723.3	3,040.2	556.0
Suburbs[1]	n/a	n/a	n/a	n/a	n/a	n/a	n/a	n/a
Metro[2]	n/a	n/a	n/a	n/a	n/a	n/a	n/a	n/a
U.S.	2,489.3	5.0	42.6	81.6	250.2	340.5	1,549.5	219.9

Note: Figures are crimes per 100,000 population; (1) All areas within the metro area that are located outside the city limits; (2) Figures cover the Houston-The Woodlands-Sugar Land, TX Metropolitan Statistical Area; n/a not available; (3) All figures shown were reported using the revised Uniform Crime Reporting (UCR) definition of rape.
Source: FBI Uniform Crime Reports, 2019

Hate Crimes

Area	Number of Quarters Reported	Race/Ethnicity/Ancestry	Religion	Sexual Orientation	Disability	Gender	Gender Identity
City	4	13	2	9	2	0	3
U.S.	4	3,963	1,521	1,195	157	69	198

Source: Federal Bureau of Investigation, Hate Crime Statistics 2019

Identity Theft Consumer Reports

Area	Reports	Reports per 100,000 Population	Rank[2]
MSA[1]	51,165	724	23
U.S.	1,387,615	423	-

Note: (1) Figures cover the Houston-The Woodlands-Sugar Land, TX Metropolitan Statistical Area; (2) Rank ranges from 1 to 391 where 1 indicates greatest number of identity theft reports per 100,000 population
Source: Federal Trade Commission, Consumer Sentinel Network Data Book 2020

Fraud and Other Consumer Reports

Area	Reports	Reports per 100,000 Population	Rank[2]
MSA[1]	67,231	951	33
U.S.	3,385,133	1,031	-

Note: (1) Figures cover the Houston-The Woodlands-Sugar Land, TX Metropolitan Statistical Area; (2) Rank ranges from 1 to 391 where 1 indicates greatest number of fraud and other consumer reports per 100,000 population
Source: Federal Trade Commission, Consumer Sentinel Network Data Book 2020

POLITICS

2020 Presidential Election Results

Area	Biden	Trump	Jorgensen	Hawkins	Other
Harris County	56.0	42.7	1.0	0.3	0.0
U.S.	51.3	46.8	1.2	0.3	0.5

Note: Results are percentages and may not add to 100% due to rounding
Source: Dave Leip's Atlas of U.S. Presidential Elections

SPORTS

Professional Sports Teams

Team Name	League	Year Established
Houston Astros	Major League Baseball (MLB)	1962
Houston Dynamo	Major League Soccer (MLS)	2006
Houston Rockets	National Basketball Association (NBA)	1971
Houston Texans	National Football League (NFL)	2002

Note: Includes teams located in the Houston-The Woodlands-Sugar Land, TX Metropolitan Statistical Area.
Source: Wikipedia, Major Professional Sports Teams of the United States and Canada, April 6, 2021

CLIMATE

Average and Extreme Temperatures

Temperature	Jan	Feb	Mar	Apr	May	Jun	Jul	Aug	Sep	Oct	Nov	Dec	Yr.
Extreme High (°F)	84	91	91	95	97	103	104	107	102	94	89	83	107
Average High (°F)	61	65	73	79	85	91	93	93	89	81	72	65	79
Average Temp. (°F)	51	54	62	69	75	81	83	83	79	70	61	54	69
Average Low (°F)	41	43	51	58	65	71	73	73	68	58	50	43	58
Extreme Low (°F)	12	20	22	31	44	52	62	62	48	32	19	7	7

Note: Figures cover the years 1969-1990
Source: National Climatic Data Center, International Station Meteorological Climate Summary, 9/96

Average Precipitation/Snowfall/Humidity

Precip./Humidity	Jan	Feb	Mar	Apr	May	Jun	Jul	Aug	Sep	Oct	Nov	Dec	Yr.
Avg. Precip. (in.)	3.3	2.7	3.3	3.3	5.6	4.9	3.7	3.7	4.8	4.7	3.7	3.3	46.9
Avg. Snowfall (in.)	Tr	Tr	0	0	0	0	0	0	0	0	Tr	Tr	Tr
Avg. Rel. Hum. 6am (%)	85	86	87	89	91	92	93	93	93	91	89	86	90
Avg. Rel. Hum. 3pm (%)	58	55	54	54	57	56	55	55	57	53	55	57	55

Note: Figures cover the years 1969-1990; Tr = Trace amounts (<0.05 in. of rain; <0.5 in. of snow)
Source: National Climatic Data Center, International Station Meteorological Climate Summary, 9/96

Weather Conditions

Temperature			Daytime Sky			Precipitation		
32°F & below	45°F & below	90°F & above	Clear	Partly cloudy	Cloudy	0.01 inch or more precip.	0.1 inch or more snow/ice	Thunder-storms
21	87	96	83	167	115	101	1	62

Note: Figures are average number of days per year and cover the years 1969-1990
Source: National Climatic Data Center, International Station Meteorological Climate Summary, 9/96

HAZARDOUS WASTE

Superfund Sites

The Houston-The Woodlands-Sugar Land, TX metro area is home to 21 sites on the EPA's Superfund National Priorities List: **Conroe Creosoting Co.** (final); **Crystal Chemical Co.** (final); **French, Ltd.** (final); **Geneva Industries/Fuhrmann Energy** (final); **Gulfco Marine Maintenance** (final); **Highlands Acid Pit** (final); **Jones Road Ground Water Plume** (final); **Malone Service Co - Swan Lake Plant** (final); **Many Diversified Interests, Inc.** (final); **Motco, Inc.** (final); **North Cavalcade Street** (final); **Patrick Bayou** (final); **Petro-Chemical Systems, Inc. (Turtle Bayou)** (final); **San Jacinto River Waste Pits** (final); **Sheridan Disposal Services** (final); **Sikes Disposal Pits** (final); **Sol Lynn/Industrial Transformers** (final); **South Cavalcade Street** (final); **Tex-Tin Corp.** (final); **United Creosoting Co.** (final); **US Oil Recovery** (final). There are a total of 1,375 Superfund sites with a status of proposed or final on the list in the U.S. *U.S. Environmental Protection Agency, National Priorities List, April 7, 2021*

AIR QUALITY

Air Quality Trends: Ozone

	1990	1995	2000	2005	2010	2015	2016	2017	2018	2019
MSA[1]	0.119	0.114	0.102	0.087	0.079	0.083	0.066	0.070	0.073	0.074
U.S.	0.088	0.089	0.082	0.080	0.073	0.068	0.069	0.068	0.069	0.065

Note: (1) Data covers the Houston-The Woodlands-Sugar Land, TX Metropolitan Statistical Area. The values shown are the composite ozone concentration averages among trend sites based on the highest fourth daily maximum 8-hour concentration in parts per million. These trends are based on sites having an adequate record of monitoring data during the trend period. Data from exceptional events are included.
Source: U.S. Environmental Protection Agency, Air Quality Monitoring Information, "Air Quality Trends by City, 1990-2019"

Air Quality Index

Area	Percent of Days when Air Quality was...[2]					AQI Statistics[2]	
	Good	Moderate	Unhealthy for Sensitive Groups	Unhealthy	Very Unhealthy	Maximum	Median
MSA[1]	46.8	44.7	7.1	1.1	0.3	202	52

Note: (1) Data covers the Houston-The Woodlands-Sugar Land, TX Metropolitan Statistical Area; (2) Based on 365 days with AQI data in 2019. Air Quality Index (AQI) is an index for reporting daily air quality. EPA calculates the AQI for five major air pollutants regulated by the Clean Air Act: ground-level ozone, particle pollution (aka particulate matter), carbon monoxide, sulfur dioxide, and nitrogen dioxide. The AQI runs from 0 to 500. The higher the AQI value, the greater the level of air pollution and the greater the health concern. There are six AQI categories: "Good" AQI is between 0 and 50. Air quality is considered satisfactory; "Moderate" AQI is between 51 and 100. Air quality is acceptable; "Unhealthy for Sensitive Groups" When AQI values are between 101 and 150, members of sensitive groups may experience health effects; "Unhealthy" When AQI values are between 151 and 200 everyone may begin to experience health effects; "Very Unhealthy" AQI values between 201 and 300 trigger a health alert; "Hazardous" AQI values over 300 trigger warnings of emergency conditions (not shown).
Source: U.S. Environmental Protection Agency, Air Quality Index Report, 2019

Air Quality Index Pollutants

Area	Percent of Days when AQI Pollutant was...[2]					
	Carbon Monoxide	Nitrogen Dioxide	Ozone	Sulfur Dioxide	Particulate Matter 2.5	Particulate Matter 10
MSA[1]	0.0	4.4	47.1	0.5	47.1	0.8

Note: (1) Data covers the Houston-The Woodlands-Sugar Land, TX Metropolitan Statistical Area; (2) Based on 365 days with AQI data in 2019. The Air Quality Index (AQI) is an index for reporting daily air quality. EPA calculates the AQI for five major air pollutants regulated by the Clean Air Act: ground-level ozone, particle pollution (also known as particulate matter), carbon monoxide, sulfur dioxide, and nitrogen dioxide. The AQI runs from 0 to 500. The higher the AQI value, the greater the level of air pollution and the greater the health concern.
Source: U.S. Environmental Protection Agency, Air Quality Index Report, 2019

Maximum Air Pollutant Concentrations: Particulate Matter, Ozone, CO and Lead

	Particulate Matter 10 (ug/m^3)	Particulate Matter 2.5 Wtd AM (ug/m^3)	Particulate Matter 2.5 24-Hr (ug/m^3)	Ozone (ppm)	Carbon Monoxide (ppm)	Lead (ug/m^3)
MSA[1] Level	63	10.7	27	0.081	2	n/a
NAAQS[2]	150	15	35	0.075	9	0.15
Met NAAQS[2]	Yes	Yes	Yes	No	Yes	n/a

Note: (1) Data covers the Houston-The Woodlands-Sugar Land, TX Metropolitan Statistical Area; Data from exceptional events are included; (2) National Ambient Air Quality Standards; ppm = parts per million; ug/m^3 = micrograms per cubic meter; n/a not available.
Concentrations: Particulate Matter 10 (coarse particulate)—highest second maximum 24-hour concentration; Particulate Matter 2.5 Wtd AM (fine particulate)—highest weighted annual mean concentration; Particulate Matter 2.5 24-Hour (fine particulate)—highest 98th percentile 24-hour concentration; Ozone—highest fourth daily maximum 8-hour concentration; Carbon Monoxide—highest second maximum non-overlapping 8-hour concentration; Lead—maximum running 3-month average
Source: U.S. Environmental Protection Agency, Air Quality Monitoring Information, "Air Quality Statistics by City, 2019"

Maximum Air Pollutant Concentrations: Nitrogen Dioxide and Sulfur Dioxide

	Nitrogen Dioxide AM (ppb)	Nitrogen Dioxide 1-Hr (ppb)	Sulfur Dioxide AM (ppb)	Sulfur Dioxide 1-Hr (ppb)	Sulfur Dioxide 24-Hr (ppb)
MSA[1] Level	17	56	n/a	14	n/a
NAAQS[2]	53	100	30	75	140
Met NAAQS[2]	Yes	Yes	n/a	Yes	n/a

Note: (1) Data covers the Houston-The Woodlands-Sugar Land, TX Metropolitan Statistical Area; Data from exceptional events are included; (2) National Ambient Air Quality Standards; ppm = parts per million; ug/m³ = micrograms per cubic meter; n/a not available.
Concentrations: Nitrogen Dioxide AM—highest arithmetic mean concentration; Nitrogen Dioxide 1-Hr—highest 98th percentile 1-hour daily maximum concentration; Sulfur Dioxide AM—highest annual mean concentration; Sulfur Dioxide 1-Hr—highest 99th percentile 1-hour daily maximum concentration; Sulfur Dioxide 24-Hr—highest second maximum 24-hour concentration
Source: U.S. Environmental Protection Agency, Air Quality Monitoring Information, "Air Quality Statistics by City, 2019"

Huntsville, Alabama

Background

The seat of Madison County, Huntsville is richly evocative of the antebellum Deep South. It is also a uniquely cosmopolitan town that remains one of the South's fastest growing, with the highest per capita income in the Southeast.

Huntsville is the seat of Madison County, named for President James Madison. Originally home to Cherokee and Chickasaw Indians, Huntsville was rich in forests and game animals. The town is named for John Hunt, a Virginia Revolutionary War veteran who built a cabin in 1805 on today's corner of Bank Street and Oak Avenue.

The fertility of the valley attracted both smaller farmers and wealthy plantation investors. Leroy Pope, having donated land to the municipality, wanted to rename it Twickenham, after a London suburb home to his kin, poet Alexander Pope, but resentment against all things British, prevented it.

Huntsville was the largest town in the Alabama Territory by 1819, the year Alabama received statehood. It was the site of the state's first constitutional convention and, briefly, the capital. It quickly became a hub for processing corn, tobacco, and cotton, which became its economic mainstay. In 1852, the Memphis and Charleston Railway was completed, and planters, merchants, and shippers transformed Huntsville into a main commercial southern city.

Because many wealthy residents had remained loyal to the Union at the outset of the Civil War, the town was largely undamaged by occupying forces and, as a result, Huntsville boasts one of the largest collections of antebellum houses in the South. Walking tours of the Twickenham historic district offer the 1819 Weeden House Museum and the 1860 Huntsville Depot Museum. Restored nineteenth-century cabins and farm buildings are displayed at the mountaintop Burritt Museum and Park.

Huntsville's U.S. Space and Rocket Center, the state's largest tourist attraction, showcases space technology and houses Space Camp, opportunities for children and adults that promote science, engineering, aviation and exploration. The Huntsville Botanical Garden features year-long floral and aquatic gardens, and the Huntsville Museum of Art features both contemporary and classical exhibits.

In 2020, Huntsville released a master plan to construct a 70-mile long biking and waking trail throughout the city.

The city's modern Von Braun Center hosts national and international trade shows, local sports teams, concerts and theater. The city has an outstanding symphony orchestra.

More than 25 biotechnology firms are in the city due to the Huntsville Biotech Initiative. The HudsonAlpha Institute for Biotechnology is the centerpiece of the Cummings Research Park Biotech Campus, and contributes genomics and genetics work to the Encyclopedia of DNA Elements (ENCODE). The University of Alabama in Huntsville's (UAH) doctoral program in biotechnology supports HudsonAlpha and the emerging biotechnology economy in Huntsville. A new Mazda Toyota manufacturing facility, scheduled to open in 2021, will employ up to 4,000.

Huntsville's institutions of higher learning include a campus of the University of Alabama, Oakwood College, and Alabama A&M University in nearby Normal, Alabama.

Redstone Arsenal, home to U.S. Army Aviation and Missile Command, propelled Huntsville into a high-tech hub, and is a strategic research site for rocketry, aviation, and related programs. In 1950, German rocket scientists, most notably the famous Wernher von Braun developed rockets for the U.S. Army here. The Redstone complex developed the rocket that launched America's first satellite into space, and rockets that put astronauts into space and landed them on the moon.

Huntsville enjoys a mild, temperate climate. Only four to five weeks during the middle of winter see temperatures below freezing. Huntsville has now gone about 15 years without significant snowfall. Rainfall is fairly abundant.

Rankings

General Rankings

- *US News & World Report* conducted a survey of more than 3,000 people and analyzed the 150 largest metropolitan areas to determine what matters most when selecting the next place to live. Huntsville ranked #15 out of the top 25 as having the best combination of desirable factors. Criteria: cost of living; quality of life; net migration; job market; desirability; and other factors. *realestate.usnews.com, "The 25 Best Places to Live in the U.S. in 2020-21," October 13, 2020*

- In their seventh annual survey, Livability.com looked at data for more than 1,000 small to mid-sized U.S. cities to determine the rankings for Livability's "Top 100 Best Places to Live" in 2020. Huntsville ranked #100. Criteria: housing and affordable living; vibrant economy; social and civic engagement; education; demographics; health care options; transportation & infrastructure; and abundant lifestyle amenities. *Livability.com, "Top 100 Best Places to Live 2020" October 2020*

Business/Finance Rankings

- According to *Business Insider*, the Huntsville metro area is a prime place to run a startup or move an existing business to. The area ranked #22. Nearly 190 metro areas were analyzed on overall economic health and investments. Data was based on the 2019 U.S. Census Bureau American Community Survey, the marketing company PitchBook, Bureau of Labor Statistics employment report, and Zillow. Criteria: percentage of change in typical home values and employment rates; quarterly venture capital investment activity; and median household income. *www.businessinsider.com, "The 25 Best Cities to Start a Business-Or Move Your Current One," January 12, 2021*

- 24/7 Wall Street used metro data from the Bureau of Labor Statistics' Occupational Employment database to identify the cities with the highest percentage of those employed in jobs requiring knowledge in the science, technology, engineering, and math (STEM) fields as well as average wages for STEM jobs. The Huntsville metro area was #3. *247wallst.com, "15 Cities with the Most High-Tech Jobs," January 11, 2020*

- Huntsville was cited as one of America's top metros for new and expanded facility projects in 2020. The area ranked #7 in the mid-sized metro area category (population 200,000 to 1 million). *Site Selection, "Top Metros of 2020," March 2021*

- The Huntsville metro area appeared on the Milken Institute "2021 Best Performing Cities" list. Rank: #10 out of 200 large metro areas (population over 250,000). Criteria: job growth; wage and salary growth; high-tech output growth; housing affordability; household broadband access. *Milken Institute, "Best-Performing Cities 2021," February 16, 2021*

- *Forbes* ranked the 200 most populous metro areas to determine the nation's "Best Places for Business and Careers." The Huntsville metro area was ranked #93. Criteria: costs (business and living); job growth (past and projected); income growth; quality of life; educational attainment (college and high school); projected economic growth; cultural and leisure opportunities; workplace tolerance laws; net migration patterns. *Forbes, "The Best Places for Business and Careers 2019: Seattle Still On Top," October 30, 2019*

Education Rankings

- Personal finance website *WalletHub* analyzed the 150 largest U.S. metropolitan statistical areas to determine where the most educated Americans are putting their degrees to work. Criteria: education levels; percentage of workers with degrees; education quality and attainment gap; public school quality rankings; quality and enrollment of each metro area's universities. Huntsville was ranked #27 (#1 = most educated city). *www.WalletHub.com, "Most and Least Educated Cities in America," July 20, 2020*

Environmental Rankings

- Huntsville was highlighted as one of the top 98 cleanest metro areas for short-term particle pollution (24-hour PM 2.5) in the U.S. during 2016 through 2018. Monitors in these cities reported no days with unhealthful PM 2.5 levels. *American Lung Association, "State of the Air 2020," April 21, 2020*

Real Estate Rankings

- *WalletHub* compared the most populated U.S. cities to determine which had the best markets for real estate agents. Huntsville ranked #106 where demand was high and pay was the best. Criteria: sales per agent; annual median wage for real-estate agents; monthly average starting salary for real estate agents; real estate job density and competition; unemployment rate; home turnover rate; housing-market health index; and other relevant metrics. *www.WalletHub.com, "2019's Best Places to Be a Real Estate Agent," April 24, 2019*

- The Huntsville metro area was identified as one of the 20 worst housing markets in the U.S. in 2020. The area ranked #180 out of 180 markets. Criteria: year-over-year change of median sales price of existing single-family homes between the 4th quarter of 2019 and the 4th quarter of 2020. *National Association of Realtors®, Median Sales Price of Existing Single-Family Homes for Metropolitan Areas, 4th Quarter 2020*

Safety Rankings

- Allstate ranked the 200 largest cities in America in terms of driver safety. Huntsville ranked #3. Criteria: internal property damage claims over a two-year period from January 2016 to December 2017. The report helps increase the importance of safety and awareness behind the wheel. *Allstate, "Allstate America's Best Drivers Report, 2019" June 24, 2019*

- The National Insurance Crime Bureau ranked 384 metro areas in the U.S. in terms of per capita rates of vehicle theft. The Huntsville metro area ranked #167 (#1 = highest rate). Criteria: number of vehicle theft offenses per 100,000 inhabitants in 2019. *National Insurance Crime Bureau, "Hot Spots 2019," July 21, 2020*

Seniors/Retirement Rankings

- From its Best Cities for Successful Aging indexes, the Milken Institute generated rankings for metropolitan areas, weighing data in nine categories—health care, wellness, living arrangements, transportation and convenience, financial characteristics, education, employment, community engagement, and overall livability. The Huntsville metro area was ranked #207 overall in the small metro area category. *Milken Institute, "Best Cities for Successful Aging, 2017" March 14, 2017*

Women/Minorities Rankings

- Personal finance website *WalletHub* compared more than 180 U.S. cities across two key dimensions, "Hispanic Business-Friendliness" and "Hispanic Purchasing Power," to arrive at the most favorable conditions for Hispanic entrepreneurs. Huntsville was ranked #128 out of 182. Criteria includes: share of Hispanic-Owned Businesses; Hispanic entrepreneurship rate to median annual income of Hispanics; Small Business-Friendliness score; cost of living; and number of Hispanics with at least a bachelor's degree. *WalletHub.com, "2019's Best Cities for Hispanic Entrepreneurs," May 1, 2019*

Huntsville, Alabama

Business Environment

DEMOGRAPHICS

Population Growth

Area	1990 Census	2000 Census	2010 Census	2019* Estimate	Population Growth (%) 1990-2019	Population Growth (%) 2010-2019
City	161,842	158,216	180,105	196,219	21.2	8.9
MSA[1]	293,047	342,376	417,593	457,003	55.9	9.4
U.S.	248,709,873	281,421,906	308,745,538	324,697,795	30.6	5.2

Note: (1) Figures cover the Huntsville, AL Metropolitan Statistical Area; (*) 2015-2019 5-year estimated population
Source: U.S. Census Bureau, 1990 Census, Census 2000, Census 2010, 2015-2019 American Community Survey 5-Year Estimates

Household Size

Area	One	Two	Three	Four	Five	Six	Seven or More	Average Household Size
City	35.7	34.4	14.5	9.5	4.2	1.3	0.4	2.20
MSA[1]	29.5	35.2	15.6	12.2	5.2	1.7	0.6	2.50
U.S.	27.9	33.9	15.6	12.9	6.0	2.3	1.4	2.60

Note: (1) Figures cover the Huntsville, AL Metropolitan Statistical Area
Source: U.S. Census Bureau, 2015-2019 American Community Survey 5-Year Estimates

Race

Area	White Alone[2] (%)	Black Alone[2] (%)	Asian Alone[2] (%)	AIAN[3] Alone[2] (%)	NHOPI[4] Alone[2] (%)	Other Race Alone[2] (%)	Two or More Races (%)
City	61.3	30.7	2.6	0.4	0.1	2.0	2.8
MSA[1]	70.5	22.1	2.4	0.6	0.1	1.5	2.8
U.S.	72.5	12.7	5.5	0.8	0.2	4.9	3.3

Note: (1) Figures cover the Huntsville, AL Metropolitan Statistical Area; (2) Alone is defined as not being in combination with one or more other races; (3) American Indian and Alaska Native; (4) Native Hawaiian and Other Pacific Islander
Source: U.S. Census Bureau, 2015-2019 American Community Survey 5-Year Estimates

Hispanic or Latino Origin

Area	Total (%)	Mexican (%)	Puerto Rican (%)	Cuban (%)	Other (%)
City	6.2	3.8	0.9	0.2	1.4
MSA[1]	5.2	3.2	0.7	0.2	1.0
U.S.	18.0	11.2	1.7	0.7	4.3

Note: Persons of Hispanic or Latino origin can be of any race; (1) Figures cover the Huntsville, AL Metropolitan Statistical Area
Source: U.S. Census Bureau, 2015-2019 American Community Survey 5-Year Estimates

Ancestry

Area	German	Irish	English	American	Italian	Polish	French[2]	Scottish	Dutch
City	8.6	8.8	8.7	11.4	2.4	0.9	1.8	2.0	0.9
MSA[1]	8.9	9.5	9.3	12.2	2.2	1.1	1.8	2.1	1.0
U.S.	13.3	9.7	7.2	6.2	5.1	2.8	2.3	1.7	1.2

Note: Figures are the percentage of the total population reporting a particular ancestry. The nine most commonly reported ancestries in the U.S. are shown. Figures include multiple ancestries (e.g. if a person reported being Irish and Italian, they were included in both columns); (1) Figures cover the Huntsville, AL Metropolitan Statistical Area; (2) Excludes Basque
Source: U.S. Census Bureau, 2015-2019 American Community Survey 5-Year Estimates

Foreign-born Population

Area	Any Foreign Country	Asia	Mexico	Europe	Caribbean	Central America[2]	South America	Africa	Canada
City	6.6	2.3	1.7	0.7	0.4	0.5	0.2	0.6	0.1
MSA[1]	5.1	1.9	1.2	0.7	0.3	0.4	0.2	0.4	0.2
U.S.	13.6	4.2	3.5	1.5	1.3	1.1	1.0	0.7	0.2

Note: (1) Figures cover the Huntsville, AL Metropolitan Statistical Area; (2) Excludes Mexico.
Source: U.S. Census Bureau, 2015-2019 American Community Survey 5-Year Estimates

Marital Status

Area	Never Married	Now Married[2]	Separated	Widowed	Divorced
City	34.9	44.8	2.0	6.0	12.3
MSA[1]	30.1	50.8	1.7	5.6	11.8
U.S.	33.4	48.1	1.9	5.8	10.9

Note: Figures are percentages and cover the population 15 years of age and older; (1) Figures cover the Huntsville, AL Metropolitan Statistical Area; (2) Excludes separated
Source: U.S. Census Bureau, 2015-2019 American Community Survey 5-Year Estimates

Disability by Age

Area	All Ages	Under 18 Years Old	18 to 64 Years Old	65 Years and Over
City	13.7	4.8	11.2	34.7
MSA[1]	13.7	4.9	11.3	37.7
U.S.	12.6	4.2	10.3	34.5

Note: Figures show percent of the civilian noninstitutionalized population that reported having a disability. Disability status is determined from six types of difficulty: vision, hearing, cognitive, ambulatory, self-care, and independent living. For children under 5 years old, hearing and vision difficulty are used to determine disability status. For children between the ages of 5 and 14, disability status is determined from hearing, vision, cognitive, ambulatory, and self-care difficulties. For people aged 15 years and older, they are considered to have a disability if they have difficulty with any one of the six difficulty types; Note: (1) Figures cover the Huntsville, AL Metropolitan Statistical Area
Source: U.S. Census Bureau, 2015-2019 American Community Survey 5-Year Estimates

Age

Area	Under Age 5	Age 5–19	Age 20–34	Age 35–44	Age 45–54	Age 55–64	Age 65–74	Age 75–84	Age 85+	Median Age
City	6.1	17.6	23.8	11.6	12.1	12.7	8.9	5.2	2.1	36.9
MSA[1]	5.8	19.0	20.3	12.4	14.1	13.5	8.6	4.5	1.6	38.7
U.S.	6.1	19.1	20.7	12.6	13.0	12.9	9.1	4.6	1.9	38.1

Note: (1) Figures cover the Huntsville, AL Metropolitan Statistical Area
Source: U.S. Census Bureau, 2015-2019 American Community Survey 5-Year Estimates

Gender

Area	Males	Females	Males per 100 Females
City	94,803	101,416	93.5
MSA[1]	224,226	232,777	96.3
U.S.	159,886,919	164,810,876	97.0

Note: (1) Figures cover the Huntsville, AL Metropolitan Statistical Area
Source: U.S. Census Bureau, 2015-2019 American Community Survey 5-Year Estimates

Religious Groups by Family

Area	Catholic	Baptist	Non-Den.	Methodist[2]	Lutheran	LDS[3]	Pentecostal	Presbyterian[4]	Muslim[5]	Judaism
MSA[1]	4.0	27.6	3.2	7.5	0.7	1.2	1.2	1.7	0.2	0.2
U.S.	19.1	9.3	4.0	4.0	2.3	2.0	1.9	1.6	0.8	0.7

Note: Figures are the number of adherents as a percentage of the total population; (1) Figures cover the Huntsville, AL Metropolitan Statistical Area; (2) Methodist/Pietist; (3) Latter Day Saints; (4) Reformed; (5) Figures are estimates
Source: Association of Statisticians of American Religious Bodies, 2010 U.S. Religion Census: Religious Congregations & Membership Study

Religious Groups by Tradition

Area	Catholic	Evangelical Protestant	Mainline Protestant	Other Tradition	Black Protestant	Orthodox
MSA[1]	4.0	33.3	9.7	1.9	1.8	0.1
U.S.	19.1	16.2	7.3	4.3	1.6	0.3

Note: Figures are the number of adherents as a percentage of the total population; (1) Figures cover the Huntsville, AL Metropolitan Statistical Area
Source: Association of Statisticians of American Religious Bodies, 2010 U.S. Religion Census: Religious Congregations & Membership Study

ECONOMY

Gross Metropolitan Product

Area	2017	2018	2019	2020	Rank[2]
MSA[1]	25.9	27.2	28.4	29.8	106

Note: Figures are in billions of dollars; (1) Figures cover the Huntsville, AL Metropolitan Statistical Area; (2) Rank is based on 2018 data and ranges from 1 to 381
Source: U.S. Conference of Mayors, U.S. Metro Economies: GMP & Employment 2018-2020, September 2019

Economic Growth

Area	2015-17 (%)	2018 (%)	2019 (%)	2020 (%)	Rank[2]
MSA[1]	1.8	3.0	2.5	2.7	155
U.S.	1.9	2.9	2.3	2.1	—

Note: Figures are real gross metropolitan product (GMP) growth rates and represent average annual percent change; (1) Figures cover the Huntsville, AL Metropolitan Statistical Area; (2) Rank is based on 2017 2-year average annual percent change and ranges from 1 to 381
Source: U.S. Conference of Mayors, U.S. Metro Economies: GMP & Employment 2018-2020, September 2019

Metropolitan Area Exports

Area	2014	2015	2016	2017	2018	2019	Rank[2]
MSA[1]	1,440.4	1,344.7	1,827.3	1,889.2	1,608.7	1,534.2	122

Note: Figures are in millions of dollars; (1) Figures cover the Huntsville, AL Metropolitan Statistical Area; (2) Rank is based on 2019 data and ranges from 1 to 386
Source: U.S. Department of Commerce, International Trade Administration, Office of Trade and Economic Analysis, Industry and Analysis, Exports by Metropolitan Area, data extracted March 24, 2021

Building Permits

Area	Single-Family 2018	Single-Family 2019	Pct. Chg.	Multi-Family 2018	Multi-Family 2019	Pct. Chg.	Total 2018	Total 2019	Pct. Chg.
City	1,241	1,436	15.7	71	167	135.2	1,312	1,603	22.2
MSA[1]	2,870	3,399	18.4	71	167	135.2	2,941	3,566	21.3
U.S.	855,300	862,100	0.7	473,500	523,900	10.6	1,328,800	1,386,000	4.3

Note: (1) Figures cover the Huntsville, AL Metropolitan Statistical Area; Figures represent new, privately-owned housing units authorized (unadjusted data); All permit data are based on estimates with imputation
Source: U.S. Census Bureau, Manufacturing, Mining, and Construction Statistics, Building Permits, 2018, 2019

Bankruptcy Filings

Area	Business Filings 2019	Business Filings 2020	% Chg.	Nonbusiness Filings 2019	Nonbusiness Filings 2020	% Chg.
Madison County	20	42	110.0	1,463	1,024	-30.0
U.S.	22,780	21,655	-4.9	752,160	522,808	-30.5

Note: Business filings include Chapter 7, Chapter 9, Chapter 11, Chapter 12, Chapter 13, Chapter 15, and Section 304; Nonbusiness filings include Chapter 7, Chapter 11, and Chapter 13
Source: Administrative Office of the U.S. Courts, Business and Nonbusiness Bankruptcy, County Cases Commenced by Chapter of the Bankruptcy Code, During the 12-Month Period Ending December 31, 2019 and Business and Nonbusiness Bankruptcy, County Cases Commenced by Chapter of the Bankruptcy Code, During the 12-Month Period Ending December 31, 2020

Housing Vacancy Rates

Area	Gross Vacancy Rate[2] (%) 2018	2019	2020	Year-Round Vacancy Rate[3] (%) 2018	2019	2020	Rental Vacancy Rate[4] (%) 2018	2019	2020	Homeowner Vacancy Rate[5] (%) 2018	2019	2020
MSA[1]	n/a	n/a	n/a	n/a	n/a	n/a	n/a	n/a	n/a	n/a	n/a	n/a
U.S.	12.3	12.0	10.6	9.7	9.5	8.2	6.9	6.7	6.3	1.5	1.4	1.0

Note: (1) Figures cover the Huntsville, AL Metropolitan Statistical Area; (2) The percentage of the total housing inventory that is vacant; (3) The percentage of the housing inventory (excluding seasonal units) that is year-round vacant; (4) The percentage of rental inventory that is vacant for rent; (5) The percentage of homeowner inventory that is vacant for sale; n/a not available
Source: U.S. Census Bureau, Housing Vacancies and Homeownership Annual Statistics: 2018, 2019, 2020

INCOME

Income

Area	Per Capita ($)	Median Household ($)	Average Household ($)
City	35,634	55,305	80,877
MSA[1]	34,918	64,483	86,328
U.S.	34,103	62,843	88,607

Note: (1) Figures cover the Huntsville, AL Metropolitan Statistical Area
Source: U.S. Census Bureau, 2015-2019 American Community Survey 5-Year Estimates

Household Income Distribution

Area	Under $15,000	$15,000-$24,999	$25,000-$34,999	$35,000-$49,999	$50,000-$74,999	$75,000-$99,999	$100,000-$149,999	$150,000 and up
City	13.7	10.7	10.0	11.8	15.2	10.9	13.9	13.8
MSA[1]	10.4	9.2	8.8	11.5	16.1	12.5	16.4	15.0
U.S.	10.3	8.9	8.9	12.3	17.2	12.7	15.1	14.5

Note: (1) Figures cover the Huntsville, AL Metropolitan Statistical Area
Source: U.S. Census Bureau, 2015-2019 American Community Survey 5-Year Estimates

Poverty Rate

Area	All Ages	Under 18 Years Old	18 to 64 Years Old	65 Years and Over
City	16.8	25.5	16.2	7.9
MSA[1]	12.7	18.5	11.8	7.7
U.S.	13.4	18.5	12.6	9.3

Note: Figures are percentage of people whose income during the past 12 months was below the poverty level;
(1) Figures cover the Huntsville, AL Metropolitan Statistical Area
Source: U.S. Census Bureau, 2015-2019 American Community Survey 5-Year Estimates

CITY FINANCES

City Government Finances

Component	2017 ($000)	2017 ($ per capita)
Total Revenues	998,368	5,239
Total Expenditures	1,011,067	5,305
Debt Outstanding	983,357	5,160
Cash and Securities[1]	446,923	2,345

Note: (1) Cash and security holdings of a government at the close of its fiscal year, including those of its dependent agencies, utilities, and liquor stores.
Source: U.S. Census Bureau, State & Local Government Finances 2017

City Government Revenue by Source

Source	2017 ($000)	2017 ($ per capita)	2017 (%)
General Revenue			
From Federal Government	2,294	12	0.2
From State Government	33,548	176	3.4
From Local Governments	0	0	0.0
Taxes			
Property	57,851	304	5.8
Sales and Gross Receipts	225,010	1,181	22.5
Personal Income	0	0	0.0
Corporate Income	0	0	0.0
Motor Vehicle License	0	0	0.0
Other Taxes	24,902	131	2.5
Current Charges	71,679	376	7.2
Liquor Store	0	0	0.0
Utility	558,141	2,929	55.9
Employee Retirement	0	0	0.0

Source: U.S. Census Bureau, State & Local Government Finances 2017

City Government Expenditures by Function

Function	2017 ($000)	2017 ($ per capita)	2017 (%)
General Direct Expenditures			
Air Transportation	0	0	0.0
Corrections	0	0	0.0
Education	0	0	0.0
Employment Security Administration	0	0	0.0
Financial Administration	6,035	31	0.6
Fire Protection	38,625	202	3.8
General Public Buildings	0	0	0.0
Governmental Administration, Other	10,518	55	1.0
Health	2,115	11	0.2
Highways	36,727	192	3.6
Hospitals	0	0	0.0
Housing and Community Development	5,215	27	0.5
Interest on General Debt	32,366	169	3.2
Judicial and Legal	7,333	38	0.7
Libraries	5,911	31	0.6
Parking	1,555	8	0.2
Parks and Recreation	38,867	203	3.8
Police Protection	46,667	244	4.6
Public Welfare	0	0	0.0
Sewerage	22,213	116	2.2
Solid Waste Management	0	0	0.0
Veterans' Services	0	0	0.0
Liquor Store	0	0	0.0
Utility	597,297	3,134	59.1
Employee Retirement	0	0	0.0

Source: U.S. Census Bureau, State & Local Government Finances 2017

EMPLOYMENT

Labor Force and Employment

Area	Civilian Labor Force Dec. 2019	Civilian Labor Force Dec. 2020	% Chg.	Workers Employed Dec. 2019	Workers Employed Dec. 2020	% Chg.
City	99,396	97,639	-1.8	97,185	94,305	-3.0
MSA[1]	229,898	224,806	-2.2	225,028	218,441	-2.9
U.S.	164,007,000	160,017,000	-2.4	158,504,000	149,613,000	-5.6

Note: Data is not seasonally adjusted and covers workers 16 years of age and older; (1) Figures cover the Huntsville, AL Metropolitan Statistical Area
Source: Bureau of Labor Statistics, Local Area Unemployment Statistics

Unemployment Rate

Area	Jan.	Feb.	Mar.	Apr.	May	Jun.	Jul.	Aug.	Sep.	Oct.	Nov.	Dec.
City	2.8	2.4	2.6	11.8	8.6	7.5	7.8	5.6	6.4	5.3	3.8	3.4
MSA[1]	2.7	2.3	2.5	10.7	7.4	6.4	6.4	4.5	5.1	4.2	3.1	2.8
U.S.	4.0	3.8	4.5	14.4	13.0	11.2	10.5	8.5	7.7	6.6	6.4	6.5

Note: Data is not seasonally adjusted and covers workers 16 years of age and older; (1) Figures cover the Huntsville, AL Metropolitan Statistical Area
Source: Bureau of Labor Statistics, Local Area Unemployment Statistics

Average Wages

Occupation	$/Hr.	Occupation	$/Hr.
Accountants and Auditors	36.00	Maintenance and Repair Workers	18.00
Automotive Mechanics	23.40	Marketing Managers	72.20
Bookkeepers	20.50	Network and Computer Systems Admin.	40.00
Carpenters	20.60	Nurses, Licensed Practical	20.00
Cashiers	11.00	Nurses, Registered	28.20
Computer Programmers	41.90	Nursing Assistants	13.40
Computer Systems Analysts	49.70	Office Clerks, General	12.60
Computer User Support Specialists	24.20	Physical Therapists	41.60
Construction Laborers	15.90	Physicians	126.00
Cooks, Restaurant	12.70	Plumbers, Pipefitters and Steamfitters	26.10
Customer Service Representatives	17.50	Police and Sheriff's Patrol Officers	26.00
Dentists	78.90	Postal Service Mail Carriers	25.10
Electricians	23.80	Real Estate Sales Agents	n/a
Engineers, Electrical	51.90	Retail Salespersons	14.20
Fast Food and Counter Workers	9.30	Sales Representatives, Technical/Scientific	40.50
Financial Managers	65.70	Secretaries, Exc. Legal/Medical/Executive	17.90
First-Line Supervisors of Office Workers	27.00	Security Guards	15.10
General and Operations Managers	71.80	Surgeons	n/a
Hairdressers/Cosmetologists	11.30	Teacher Assistants, Exc. Postsecondary*	10.10
Home Health and Personal Care Aides	9.90	Teachers, Secondary School, Exc. Sp. Ed.*	26.10
Janitors and Cleaners	12.50	Telemarketers	n/a
Landscaping/Groundskeeping Workers	15.70	Truck Drivers, Heavy/Tractor-Trailer	19.60
Lawyers	56.40	Truck Drivers, Light/Delivery Services	17.60
Maids and Housekeeping Cleaners	10.50	Waiters and Waitresses	9.20

Note: Wage data covers the Huntsville, AL Metropolitan Statistical Area; (*) Hourly wages were calculated from annual wage data based on a 40 hour work week; n/a not available.
Source: Bureau of Labor Statistics, Metro Area Occupational Employment & Wage Estimates, May 2020

Employment by Industry

Sector	MSA[1] Number of Employees	MSA[1] Percent of Total	U.S. Percent of Total
Construction, Mining, and Logging	10,000	4.1	5.5
Education and Health Services	21,500	8.7	16.3
Financial Activities	7,200	2.9	6.1
Government	52,500	21.3	15.2
Information	2,200	0.9	1.9
Leisure and Hospitality	19,900	8.1	9.0
Manufacturing	26,300	10.7	8.5
Other Services	8,100	3.3	3.8
Professional and Business Services	63,000	25.5	14.4
Retail Trade	25,700	10.4	10.9
Transportation, Warehousing, and Utilities	4,000	1.6	4.6
Wholesale Trade	6,300	2.6	3.9

Note: Figures are non-farm employment as of December 2020. Figures are not seasonally adjusted and include workers 16 years of age and older; (1) Figures cover the Huntsville, AL Metropolitan Statistical Area
Source: Bureau of Labor Statistics, Current Employment Statistics, Employment, Hours, and Earnings

Employment by Occupation

Occupation Classification	City (%)	MSA[1] (%)	U.S. (%)
Management, Business, Science, and Arts	47.1	45.6	38.5
Natural Resources, Construction, and Maintenance	5.4	7.2	8.9
Production, Transportation, and Material Moving	11.1	12.5	13.2
Sales and Office	19.4	19.7	21.6
Service	16.9	15.0	17.8

Note: Figures cover employed civilians 16 years of age and older; (1) Figures cover the Huntsville, AL Metropolitan Statistical Area
Source: U.S. Census Bureau, 2015-2019 American Community Survey 5-Year Estimates

Occupations with Greatest Projected Employment Growth: 2020 – 2022

Occupation[1]	2020 Employment	2022 Projected Employment	Numeric Employment Change	Percent Employment Change
Total,, All Occupations	2,160,690	2,237,520	76,830	3.6
Combined Food Preparation and Serving Workers, Including Fast Food	45,650	49,410	3,760	8.2
Registered Nurses	54,730	57,080	2,350	4.3
Waiters and Waitresses	34,050	36,120	2,070	6.1
Assemblers and Fabricators, All Other, Including Team Assemblers	31,130	32,950	1,820	5.8
Laborers and Freight, Stock, and Material Movers, Hand	41,600	43,250	1,650	4.0
Retail Salespersons	64,450	65,910	1,460	2.3
Janitors and Cleaners, Except Maids and Housekeeping Cleaners	30,990	32,430	1,440	4.6
Cooks, Restaurant	15,690	17,120	1,430	9.1
Heavy and Tractor-Trailer Truck Drivers	33,560	34,980	1,420	4.2

Note: Projections cover Alabama; (1) Sorted by numeric employment change
Source: www.projectionscentral.com, State Occupational Projections, 2020–2022 Short-Term Projections

Fastest-Growing Occupations: 2020 – 2022

Occupation[1]	2020 Employment	2022 Projected Employment	Numeric Employment Change	Percent Employment Change
Dental Laboratory Technicians	1,000	1,230	230	23.0
Chemical Plant and System Operators	1,110	1,250	140	12.6
Chemical Equipment Operators and Tenders	1,910	2,140	230	12.0
Chemical Engineers	670	740	70	10.4
Information Security Analysts	980	1,070	90	9.2
Cooks, Restaurant	15,690	17,120	1,430	9.1
Molders, Shapers, and Casters, Except Metal and Plastic	550	600	50	9.1
Directors, Religious Activities and Education	4,630	5,020	390	8.4
Clergy	6,710	7,260	550	8.2
Combined Food Preparation and Serving Workers, Including Fast Food	45,650	49,410	3,760	8.2

Note: Projections cover Alabama; (1) Sorted by percent employment change and excludes occupations with numeric employment change less than 50
Source: www.projectionscentral.com, State Occupational Projections, 2020–2022 Short-Term Projections

TAXES

State Corporate Income Tax Rates

State	Tax Rate (%)	Income Brackets ($)	Num. of Brackets	Financial Institution Tax Rate (%)[a]	Federal Income Tax Ded.
Alabama	6.5	Flat rate	1	6.5	Yes

Note: Tax rates as of January 1, 2021; (a) Rates listed are the corporate income tax rate applied to financial institutions or excise taxes based on income. Some states have other taxes based upon the value of deposits or shares.
Source: Federation of Tax Administrators, State Corporate Income Tax Rates, January 1, 2021

State Individual Income Tax Rates

State	Tax Rate (%)	Income Brackets ($)	Personal Exemptions ($) Single	Personal Exemptions ($) Married	Personal Exemptions ($) Depend.	Standard Ded. ($) Single	Standard Ded. ($) Married
Alabama	2.0 - 5.0	500 - 3,001 (b)	1,500	3,000	500 (e)	2,500	7,500 (y)

Note: Tax rates as of January 1, 2021; Local- and county-level taxes are not included; Federal income tax is deductible on state income tax returns; (b) For joint returns, taxes are twice the tax on half the couple's income; (e) In Alabama, the per-dependent exemption is $1,000 for taxpayers with state AGI of $20,000 or less, $500 with AGI from $20,001 to $100,000, and $300 with AGI over $100,000; (y) Alabama standard deduction is phased out for incomes over $23,000. Rhode Island exemptions & standard deductions phased out for incomes over $207,700; Wisconsin standard deduciton phases out for income over $16,149.
Source: Federation of Tax Administrators, State Individual Income Tax Rates, January 1, 2021

Various State Sales and Excise Tax Rates

State	State Sales Tax (%)	Gasoline[1] (¢/gal.)	Cigarette[2] ($/pack)	Spirits[3] ($/gal.)	Wine[4] ($/gal.)	Beer[5] ($/gal.)	Recreational Marijuana (%)
Alabama	4	29.21	0.675	19.11	1.7	0.53	Not legal

Note: All tax rates as of January 1, 2021; (1) The American Petroleum Institute has developed a methodology for determining the average tax rate on a gallon of fuel. Rates may include any of the following: excise taxes, environmental fees, storage tank fees, other fees or taxes, general sales tax, and local taxes; (2) The federal excise tax of $1.0066 per pack and local taxes are not included; (3) Rates are those applicable to off-premise sales of 40% alcohol by volume (a.b.v.) distilled spirits in 750ml containers. Local excise taxes are excluded; (4) Rates are those applicable to off-premise sales of 11% a.b.v. non-carbonated wine in 750ml containers; (5) Rates are those applicable to off-premise sales of 4.7% a.b.v. beer in 12 ounce containers.
Source: Tax Foundation, 2021 Facts & Figures: How Does Your State Compare?

State Business Tax Climate Index Rankings

State	Overall Rank	Corporate Tax Rank	Individual Income Tax Rank	Sales Tax Rank	Property Tax Rank	Unemployment Insurance Tax Rank
Alabama	41	23	30	50	19	14

Note: The index is a measure of how each state's tax laws affect economic performance. The lower the rank, the more favorable a state's tax system is for business. States without a given tax are given a ranking of 1. The scores/rankings for the District of Columbia do not affect other states. The 2021 index represents the tax climate as of July 1, 2020.
Source: Tax Foundation, State Business Tax Climate Index 2021

TRANSPORTATION

Means of Transportation to Work

Area	Car/Truck/Van Drove Alone	Car/Truck/Van Carpooled	Public Transportation Bus	Public Transportation Subway	Public Transportation Railroad	Bicycle	Walked	Other Means	Worked at Home
City	86.1	7.0	0.4	0.0	0.0	0.2	1.3	1.1	4.0
MSA[1]	88.0	6.2	0.2	0.0	0.0	0.1	0.8	1.0	3.7
U.S.	76.3	9.0	2.4	1.9	0.6	0.5	2.7	1.4	5.2

Note: Figures are percentages and cover workers 16 years of age and older; (1) Figures cover the Huntsville, AL Metropolitan Statistical Area
Source: U.S. Census Bureau, 2015-2019 American Community Survey 5-Year Estimates

Travel Time to Work

Area	Less Than 10 Minutes	10 to 19 Minutes	20 to 29 Minutes	30 to 44 Minutes	45 to 59 Minutes	60 to 89 Minutes	90 Minutes or More
City	12.8	41.7	26.3	15.2	2.3	0.7	0.9
MSA[1]	10.3	32.1	27.8	21.7	5.6	1.6	1.0
U.S.	12.2	28.4	20.8	20.8	8.3	6.4	2.9

Note: Note: Figures are percentages and include workers 16 years old and over; (1) Figures cover the Huntsville, AL Metropolitan Statistical Area
Source: U.S. Census Bureau, 2015-2019 American Community Survey 5-Year Estimates

Key Congestion Measures

Measure	1982	1992	2002	2012	2017
Annual Hours of Delay, Total (000)	n/a	n/a	n/a	n/a	7,384
Annual Hours of Delay, Per Auto Commuter	n/a	n/a	n/a	n/a	24
Annual Congestion Cost, Total (million $)	n/a	n/a	n/a	n/a	148
Annual Congestion Cost, Per Auto Commuter ($)	n/a	n/a	n/a	n/a	473

Note: n/a not available
Source: Texas A&M Transportation Institute, 2019 Urban Mobility Report

Living Environment

COST OF LIVING

Cost of Living Index

Composite Index	Groceries	Housing	Utilities	Transportation	Health Care	Misc. Goods/Services
91.9	96.9	70.4	96.0	96.2	97.6	104.1

Note: The Cost of Living Index measures regional differences in the cost of consumer goods and services, excluding taxes and non-consumer expenditures, for professional and managerial households in the top income quintile. It is based on more than 50,000 prices covering almost 60 different items for which prices are collected three times a year by chambers of commerce, economic development organizations or university applied economic centers in each participating urban area. The numbers shown should be read as a percentage above or below the national average of 100. For example, a value of 115.4 in the groceries column indicates that grocery prices are 15.4% higher than the national average. Small differences in the index numbers should not be interpreted as significant; Figures cover the Huntsville AL urban area.
Source: The Council for Community and Economic Research, Cost of Living Index, 2020

Grocery Prices

Area[1]	T-Bone Steak ($/pound)	Frying Chicken ($/pound)	Whole Milk ($/half gal.)	Eggs ($/dozen)	Orange Juice ($/64 oz.)	Coffee ($/11.5 oz.)
City[2]	13.10	1.45	1.62	0.95	3.75	4.36
Avg.	11.78	1.39	2.05	1.47	3.57	4.34
Min.	8.03	0.94	1.03	0.74	2.94	3.02
Max.	15.86	2.65	4.31	3.77	5.44	8.69

Note: (1) Values for the local area are compared with the average, minimum and maximum values for all 284 areas in the Cost of Living Index; (2) Figures cover the Huntsville AL urban area; **T-Bone Steak** (price per pound); **Frying Chicken** (price per pound, whole fryer); **Whole Milk** (half gallon carton); **Eggs** (price per dozen, Grade A, large); **Orange Juice** (64 oz. Tropicana or Florida Natural); **Coffee** (11.5 oz. can, vacuum-packed, Maxwell House, Hills Bros, or Folgers).
Source: The Council for Community and Economic Research, Cost of Living Index, 2020

Housing and Utility Costs

Area[1]	New Home Price ($)	Apartment Rent ($/month)	All Electric ($/month)	Part Electric ($/month)	Other Energy ($/month)	Telephone ($/month)
City[2]	256,311	792	156.41	-	-	181.80
Avg.	368,594	1,168	170.86	100.47	65.28	184.30
Min.	190,567	502	91.58	31.42	26.08	169.60
Max.	2,227,806	4,738	470.38	280.31	280.06	206.50

Note: (1) Values for the local area are compared with the average, minimum and maximum values for all 284 areas in the Cost of Living Index; (2) Figures cover the Huntsville AL urban area; **New Home Price** (2,400 sf living area, 8,000 sf lot, in urban area with full utilities); **Apartment Rent** (950 sf 2 bedroom/1.5 or 2 bath, unfurnished, excluding all utilities except water); **All Electric** (average monthly cost for an all-electric home); **Part Electric** (average monthly cost for a part-electric home); **Other Energy** (average monthly cost for natural gas, fuel oil, coal, wood, and any other forms of energy except electricity); **Telephone** (price includes the base monthly rate plus taxes and fees for three lines of mobile phone service).
Source: The Council for Community and Economic Research, Cost of Living Index, 2020

Health Care, Transportation, and Other Costs

Area[1]	Doctor ($/visit)	Dentist ($/visit)	Optometrist ($/visit)	Gasoline ($/gallon)	Beauty Salon ($/visit)	Men's Shirt ($)
City[2]	112.22	100.06	109.44	2.06	33.33	31.87
Avg.	115.44	99.32	108.10	2.21	39.27	31.37
Min.	36.68	59.00	51.36	1.71	19.00	11.00
Max.	219.00	153.10	250.97	3.46	82.05	58.33

Note: (1) Values for the local area are compared with the average, minimum and maximum values for all 284 areas in the Cost of Living Index; (2) Figures cover the Huntsville AL urban area; **Doctor** (general practitioners routine exam of an established patient); **Dentist** (adult teeth cleaning and periodic oral examination); **Optometrist** (full vision eye exam for established adult patient); **Gasoline** (one gallon regular unleaded, national brand, including all taxes, cash price at self-service pump if available); **Beauty Salon** (woman's shampoo, trim, and blow-dry); **Men's Shirt** (cotton/polyester dress shirt, pinpoint weave, long sleeves).
Source: The Council for Community and Economic Research, Cost of Living Index, 2020

HOUSING

Homeownership Rate

Area	2012 (%)	2013 (%)	2014 (%)	2015 (%)	2016 (%)	2017 (%)	2018 (%)	2019 (%)	2020 (%)
MSA[1]	n/a	n/a	n/a	n/a	n/a	n/a	n/a	n/a	n/a
U.S.	65.4	65.1	64.5	63.7	63.4	63.9	64.4	64.6	66.6

Note: (1) Figures cover the Huntsville, AL Metropolitan Statistical Area; n/a not available
Source: U.S. Census Bureau, Housing Vacancies and Homeownership Annual Statistics: 2012-2020

Freeway Travel Time Index

Measure	1982	1987	1992	1997	2002	2007	2012	2017
Urban Area Index[1]	n/a	n/a	n/a	n/a	n/a	n/a	n/a	1.11
Urban Area Rank[1,2]	n/a	n/a	n/a	n/a	n/a	n/a	n/a	n/a

Note: Freeway Travel Time Index—the ratio of travel time in the peak period to the travel time at free-flow conditions. For example, a value of 1.30 indicates a 20-minute free-flow trip takes 26 minutes in the peak (20 minutes x 1.30 = 26 minutes); (1) Covers the Huntsville AL urban area; (2) Rank is based on 101 larger urban areas (#1 = highest travel time index); n/a not available
Source: Texas A&M Transportation Institute, 2019 Urban Mobility Report

Public Transportation

Agency Name / Mode of Transportation	Vehicles Operated in Maximum Service[1]	Annual Unlinked Passenger Trips[2] (in thous.)	Annual Passenger Miles[3] (in thous.)
City of Huntsville - Public Transportation Division			
Bus (directly operated)	13	644.9	3,168.1
Demand Response (directly operated)	19	104.1	647.7

Note: (1) Number of revenue vehicles operated by the given mode and type of service to meet the annual maximum service requirement. This is the revenue vehicle count during the peak season of the year; on the week and day that maximum service is provided. Vehicles operated in maximum service (VOMS) exclude atypical days and one-time special events; (2) Number of passengers who boarded public transportation vehicles. Passengers are counted each time they board a vehicle no matter how many vehicles they use to travel from their origin to their destination. (3) Sum of the distances ridden by all passengers during the entire fiscal year.
Source: Federal Transit Administration, National Transit Database, 2019

Air Transportation

Airport Name and Code / Type of Service	Passenger Airlines[1]	Passenger Enplanements	Freight Carriers[2]	Freight (lbs)
Huntsville International (HSV)				
Domestic service (U.S. carriers - 2020)	18	268,657	8	37,829,297
International service (U.S. carriers - 2019)	0	0	3	65,698,423

Note: (1) Includes all U.S.-based major, minor and commuter airlines that carried at least one passenger during the year; (2) Includes all U.S.-based airlines and freight carriers that transported at least one pound of freight during the year.
Source: Bureau of Transportation Statistics, The Intermodal Transportation Database, Air Carriers: T-100 Domestic Market (U.S. Carriers), 2020; Bureau of Transportation Statistics, The Intermodal Transportation Database, Air Carriers: T-100 International Market (U.S. Carriers), 2019

BUSINESSES

Major Business Headquarters

Company Name	Industry	Rankings Fortune[1]	Forbes[2]
No companies listed	-	-	-

Note: (1) Companies that produce a 10-K are ranked 1 to 500 based on 2019 revenue; (2) All private companies with at least $2 billion in annual revenue through the end of their most current fiscal year are ranked 1 to 219; companies listed are headquartered in the city; dashes indicate no ranking
Source: Fortune, "Fortune 500," June/July 2020; Forbes, "America's Largest Private Companies," 2020

Minority Business Opportunity

Huntsville is home to one company which is on the *Black Enterprise* Auto Dealer list (45 largest dealers based on gross sales): **Lexus of Huntsville** (#34). Criteria: company must be operational in previous calendar year and be at least 51% black-owned. *Black Enterprise, B.E. 100s, 2019*

House Price Index (HPI)

Area	National Ranking[2]	Quarterly Change (%)	One-Year Change (%)	Five-Year Change (%)	Since 1991Q1 (%)
MSA[1]	9	3.60	9.98	30.56	124.28
U.S.[3]	–	3.81	10.77	38.99	205.12

Note: The HPI is a weighted repeat sales index. It measures average price changes in repeat sales or refinancings on the same properties. This information is obtained by reviewing repeat mortgage transactions on single-family properties whose mortgages have been purchased or securitized by Fannie Mae or Freddie Mac since January 1975; (1) Figures cover the Huntsville, AL Metropolitan Statistical Area; (2) Rankings are based on annual percentage change for all metro areas containing at least 15,000 transactions over the last 10 years and ranges from 1 to 253; (3) figures based on a weighted average of Census Division estimates using a seasonally adjusted, purchase-only index; all figures are for the period ending December 31, 2020
Source: Federal Housing Finance Agency, Change in Metropolitan Area House Price Indexes, April 7, 2021

Median Single-Family Home Prices

Area	2018	2019	2020p	Percent Change 2019 to 2020
MSA[1]	205.4	223.5	248.0	11.0
U.S. Average	261.6	274.6	299.9	9.2

Note: Figures are median sales prices of existing single-family homes in thousands of dollars; (p) preliminary; (1) Figures cover the Huntsville, AL Metropolitan Statistical Area
Source: National Association of Realtors, Median Sales Price of Existing Single-Family Homes for Metropolitan Areas, 4th Quarter 2020

Qualifying Income Based on Median Sales Price of Existing Single-Family Homes

Area	With 5% Down ($)	With 10% Down ($)	With 20% Down ($)
MSA[1]	47,815	45,299	40,265
U.S. Average	59,266	56,147	49,908

Note: Figures are preliminary; Qualifying income is based on a mortgage rate of 2.81%. Monthly principal and interest payment is limited to 25% of income; (1) Figures cover the Huntsville, AL Metropolitan Statistical Area
Source: National Association of Realtors, Qualifying Income Based on Median Sales Price of Existing Single-Family Homes for Metropolitan Areas, 4th Quarter 2020

Home Value Distribution

Area	Under $50,000	$50,000 -$99,999	$100,000 -$149,999	$150,000 -$199,999	$200,000 -$299,999	$300,000 -$499,999	$500,000 -$999,999	$1,000,000 or more
City	5.3	17.9	15.0	16.6	22.8	16.6	4.6	1.1
MSA[1]	6.4	13.8	17.3	19.0	23.7	15.1	3.9	0.8
U.S.	6.9	12.0	13.3	14.0	19.6	19.3	11.4	3.4

Note: Figures are percentages and cover owner-occupied housing units; (1) Figures cover the Huntsville, AL Metropolitan Statistical Area
Source: U.S. Census Bureau, 2015-2019 American Community Survey 5-Year Estimates

Year Housing Structure Built

Area	2010 or Later	2000 -2009	1990 -1999	1980 -1989	1970 -1979	1960 -1969	1950 -1959	1940 -1949	Before 1940	Median Year
City	11.8	12.9	10.8	15.6	13.2	21.0	9.5	2.4	2.8	1981
MSA[1]	10.8	19.7	17.8	16.1	11.3	13.7	6.4	1.9	2.2	1989
U.S.	5.2	14.0	13.9	13.4	15.2	10.6	10.3	4.9	12.6	1978

Note: Figures are percentages except for Median Year; Note: (1) Figures cover the Huntsville, AL Metropolitan Statistical Area
Source: U.S. Census Bureau, 2015-2019 American Community Survey 5-Year Estimates

Gross Monthly Rent

Area	Under $500	$500 -$999	$1,000 -$1,499	$1,500 -$1,999	$2,000 -$2,499	$2,500 -$2,999	$3,000 and up	Median ($)
City	11.3	59.9	24.2	3.2	0.5	0.6	0.4	827
MSA[1]	10.9	59.8	24.0	3.9	0.6	0.5	0.3	836
U.S.	9.4	36.2	30.0	14.0	5.6	2.4	2.4	1,062

Note: Figures are percentages except for Median; Gross rent is the contract rent plus the estimated average monthly cost of utilities (electricity, gas, and water and sewer) and fuels (oil, coal, kerosene, wood, etc.) if these are paid by the renter (or paid for the renter by someone else); (1) Figures cover the Huntsville, AL Metropolitan Statistical Area
Source: U.S. Census Bureau, 2015-2019 American Community Survey 5-Year Estimates

HEALTH

Health Risk Factors

Category	MSA[1] (%)	U.S. (%)
Adults aged 18–64 who have any kind of health care coverage	n/a	87.3
Adults who reported being in good or better health	n/a	82.4
Adults who have been told they have high blood cholesterol	n/a	33.0
Adults who have been told they have high blood pressure	n/a	32.3
Adults who are current smokers	n/a	17.1
Adults who currently use E-cigarettes	n/a	4.6
Adults who currently use chewing tobacco, snuff, or snus	n/a	4.0
Adults who are heavy drinkers[2]	n/a	6.3
Adults who are binge drinkers[3]	n/a	17.4
Adults who are overweight (BMI 25.0 - 29.9)	n/a	35.3
Adults who are obese (BMI 30.0 - 99.8)	n/a	31.3
Adults who participated in any physical activities in the past month	n/a	74.4
Adults who always or nearly always wears a seat belt	n/a	94.3

Note: n/a not available; (1) Figures cover the Huntsville, AL Metropolitan Statistical Area; (2) Heavy drinkers are classified as adult men having more than 14 drinks per week and adult women having more than 7 drinks per week; (3) Binge drinkers are classified as males having five or more drinks on one occasion or females having four or more drinks on one occasion
Source: Centers for Disease Control and Prevention, Behaviorial Risk Factor Surveillance System, SMART: Selected Metropolitan Area Risk Trends, 2017

Acute and Chronic Health Conditions

Category	MSA[1] (%)	U.S. (%)
Adults who have ever been told they had a heart attack	n/a	4.2
Adults who have ever been told they have angina or coronary heart disease	n/a	3.9
Adults who have ever been told they had a stroke	n/a	3.0
Adults who have ever been told they have asthma	n/a	14.2
Adults who have ever been told they have arthritis	n/a	24.9
Adults who have ever been told they have diabetes[2]	n/a	10.5
Adults who have ever been told they had skin cancer	n/a	6.2
Adults who have ever been told they had any other types of cancer	n/a	7.1
Adults who have ever been told they have COPD	n/a	6.5
Adults who have ever been told they have kidney disease	n/a	3.0
Adults who have ever been told they have a form of depression	n/a	20.5

Note: n/a not available; (1) Figures cover the Huntsville, AL Metropolitan Statistical Area; (2) Figures do not include pregnancy-related, borderline, or pre-diabetes
Source: Centers for Disease Control and Prevention, Behaviorial Risk Factor Surveillance System, SMART: Selected Metropolitan Area Risk Trends, 2017

Health Screening and Vaccination Rates

Category	MSA[1] (%)	U.S. (%)
Adults aged 65+ who have had flu shot within the past year	n/a	60.7
Adults aged 65+ who have ever had a pneumonia vaccination	n/a	75.4
Adults who have ever been tested for HIV	n/a	36.1
Adults who have ever had the shingles or zoster vaccine?	n/a	28.9
Adults who have had their blood cholesterol checked within the last five years	n/a	85.9

Note: n/a not available; (1) Figures cover the Huntsville, AL Metropolitan Statistical Area.
Source: Centers for Disease Control and Prevention, Behaviorial Risk Factor Surveillance System, SMART: Selected Metropolitan Area Risk Trends, 2017

Disability Status

Category	MSA[1] (%)	U.S. (%)
Adults who reported being deaf	n/a	6.7
Are you blind or have serious difficulty seeing, even when wearing glasses?	n/a	4.5
Are you limited in any way in any of your usual activities due of arthritis?	n/a	12.9
Do you have difficulty doing errands alone?	n/a	6.8
Do you have difficulty dressing or bathing?	n/a	3.6
Do you have serious difficulty concentrating/remembering/making decisions?	n/a	10.7
Do you have serious difficulty walking or climbing stairs?	n/a	13.6

Note: n/a not available; (1) Figures cover the Huntsville, AL Metropolitan Statistical Area.
Source: Centers for Disease Control and Prevention, Behaviorial Risk Factor Surveillance System, SMART: Selected Metropolitan Area Risk Trends, 2017

Mortality Rates for the Top 10 Causes of Death in the U.S.

ICD-10[a] Sub-Chapter	ICD-10[a] Code	Age-Adjusted Mortality Rate[1] per 100,000 population County[2]	U.S.
Malignant neoplasms	C00-C97	149.3	149.2
Ischaemic heart diseases	I20-I25	56.1	90.5
Other forms of heart disease	I30-I51	109.8	52.2
Chronic lower respiratory diseases	J40-J47	47.7	39.6
Other degenerative diseases of the nervous system	G30-G31	57.0	37.6
Cerebrovascular diseases	I60-I69	45.5	37.2
Other external causes of accidental injury	W00-X59	28.7	36.1
Organic, including symptomatic, mental disorders	F01-F09	23.7	29.4
Hypertensive diseases	I10-I15	37.0	24.1
Diabetes mellitus	E10-E14	13.8	21.5

Note: (a) ICD-10 = International Classification of Diseases 10th Revision; (1) Mortality rates are a three-year average covering 2017-2019; (2) Figures cover Madison County.
Source: Centers for Disease Control and Prevention, National Center for Health Statistics. Underlying Cause of Death 1999-2019 on CDC WONDER Online Database

Mortality Rates for Selected Causes of Death

ICD-10[a] Sub-Chapter	ICD-10[a] Code	Age-Adjusted Mortality Rate[1] per 100,000 population County[2]	U.S.
Assault	X85-Y09	9.6	6.0
Diseases of the liver	K70-K76	16.7	14.4
Human immunodeficiency virus (HIV) disease	B20-B24	Suppressed	1.5
Influenza and pneumonia	J09-J18	13.5	13.8
Intentional self-harm	X60-X84	16.3	14.1
Malnutrition	E40-E46	3.9	2.3
Obesity and other hyperalimentation	E65-E68	Unreliable	2.1
Renal failure	N17-N19	14.4	12.6
Transport accidents	V01-V99	15.3	12.3
Viral hepatitis	B15-B19	Unreliable	1.2

Note: (a) ICD-10 = International Classification of Diseases 10th Revision; (1) Mortality rates are a three-year average covering 2017-2019; (2) Figures cover Madison County; Data are suppressed when the data meet the criteria for confidentiality constraints; Mortality rates are flagged as unreliable when the rate would be calculated with a numerator of 20 or less.
Source: Centers for Disease Control and Prevention, National Center for Health Statistics. Underlying Cause of Death 1999-2019 on CDC WONDER Online Database

Health Insurance Coverage

Area	With Health Insurance	With Private Health Insurance	With Public Health Insurance	Without Health Insurance	Population Under Age 19 Without Health Insurance
City	90.2	72.8	32.9	9.8	4.2
MSA[1]	91.4	76.2	29.9	8.6	3.3
U.S.	91.2	67.9	35.1	8.8	5.1

Note: Figures are percentages that cover the civilian noninstitutionalized population; (1) Figures cover the Huntsville, AL Metropolitan Statistical Area
Source: U.S. Census Bureau, 2015-2019 American Community Survey 5-Year Estimates

Number of Medical Professionals

Area	MDs[3]	DOs[3,4]	Dentists	Podiatrists	Chiropractors	Optometrists
County[1] (number)	1,011	44	211	14	87	71
County[1] (rate[2])	275.5	12.0	56.6	3.8	23.3	19.0
U.S. (rate[2])	282.9	22.7	71.2	6.2	28.1	16.9

01089
Note: Data as of 2019 unless noted; (1) Data covers Madison County; (2) Rate per 100,000 population; (3) Data as of 2018 and includes all active, non-federal physicians; (4) Doctor of Osteopathic Medicine
Source: U.S. Department of Health and Human Services, Health Resources and Services Administration, Bureau of Health Professions, Area Resource File (ARF) 2019-2020

EDUCATION

Public School District Statistics

District Name	Schls	Pupils	Pupil/Teacher Ratio	Minority Pupils[1] (%)	Free Lunch Eligible[2] (%)	IEP[3] (%)
Huntsville City	39	23,993	16.7	61.8	44.6	12.5
Madison County	29	19,093	18.8	36.1	29.6	12.2

Note: Table includes school districts with 2,000 or more students; (1) Percentage of students that are not non-Hispanic white; (2) Percentage of students that are eligible for the free lunch program; (3) Percentage of students that have an Individualized Education Program.
Source: U.S. Department of Education, National Center for Education Statistics, Common Core of Data, Local Education Agency (School District) Universe Survey: School Year 2018-2019; U.S. Department of Education, National Center for Education Statistics, Common Core of Data, Public Elementary/Secondary School Universe Survey: School Year 2018-2019

Best High Schools

According to *U.S. News*, Huntsville is home to one of the top 500 high schools in the U.S.: **New Century Tech Demo High School** (#156). Nearly 18,000 public, magnet and charter schools were ranked based on their performance on state assessments and how well they prepare students for college. *U.S. News & World Report, "Best High Schools 2020"*

Highest Level of Education

Area	Less than H.S.	H.S. Diploma	Some College, No Deg.	Associate Degree	Bachelor's Degree	Master's Degree	Prof. School Degree	Doctorate Degree
City	9.0	18.7	20.3	7.9	26.4	13.8	1.8	2.2
MSA[1]	9.8	22.7	20.2	8.1	24.2	11.9	1.4	1.7
U.S.	12.0	27.0	20.4	8.5	19.8	8.8	2.1	1.4

Note: Figures cover persons age 25 and over; (1) Figures cover the Huntsville, AL Metropolitan Statistical Area
Source: U.S. Census Bureau, 2015-2019 American Community Survey 5-Year Estimates

Educational Attainment by Race

Area	High School Graduate or Higher (%)					Bachelor's Degree or Higher (%)				
	Total	White	Black	Asian	Hisp.[2]	Total	White	Black	Asian	Hisp.[2]
City	91.0	94.0	85.4	91.1	63.8	44.1	50.3	28.4	59.3	22.8
MSA[1]	90.2	91.6	86.8	92.7	66.6	39.2	40.9	31.4	61.9	24.3
U.S.	88.0	89.9	86.0	87.1	68.7	32.1	33.5	21.6	54.3	16.4

Note: Figures shown cover persons 25 years old and over; (1) Figures cover the Huntsville, AL Metropolitan Statistical Area; (2) People of Hispanic origin can be of any race
Source: U.S. Census Bureau, 2015-2019 American Community Survey 5-Year Estimates

School Enrollment by Grade and Control

Area	Preschool (%)		Kindergarten (%)		Grades 1 - 4 (%)		Grades 5 - 8 (%)		Grades 9 - 12 (%)	
	Public	Private	Public	Private	Public	Private	Public	Private	Public	Private
City	59.4	40.6	87.2	12.8	80.1	19.9	82.9	17.1	84.8	15.2
MSA[1]	54.3	45.7	85.8	14.2	82.9	17.1	82.7	17.3	86.0	14.0
U.S.	59.1	40.9	87.6	12.4	89.5	10.5	89.4	10.6	90.1	9.9

Note: Figures shown cover persons 3 years old and over; (1) Figures cover the Huntsville, AL Metropolitan Statistical Area
Source: U.S. Census Bureau, 2015-2019 American Community Survey 5-Year Estimates

Higher Education

Four-Year Colleges			Two-Year Colleges			Medical Schools[1]	Law Schools[2]	Voc/Tech[3]
Public	Private Non-profit	Private For-profit	Public	Private Non-profit	Private For-profit			
1	2	0	1	0	0	0	0	2

Note: Figures cover institutions located within the city limits and include main campuses only; (1) includes schools accredited by the Liaison Committee on Medical Education and the American Osteopathic Association's Commission on Osteopathic College Accreditation; (2) includes ABA-accredited schools, schools with provisional ABA accreditation, and state accredited schools; (3) includes all schools with programs that are less than 2 years.
Source: National Center for Education Statistics, Integrated Postsecondary Education System (IPEDS), 2019-20; Wikipedia, List of Medical Schools in the United States, accessed April 2, 2021; Wikipedia, List of Law Schools in the United States, accessed April 2, 2021

EMPLOYERS

Major Employers

Company Name	Industry
Avocent Corporation	Computer peripheral equip
City of Huntsville	Municipal government
City of Huntsville	Municipal government
COLSA Corporation	Commercial research laboratory
County of Madison	County government
Dynetics	Engineering laboratory/except testing
General Dynamics C4 Systems	Defense systems equipment
Healthcare Auth - City of Huntsville	General government
Intergraph Process & Bldg Solutions	Systems software development
Qualitest Products	Drugs & drug proprietaries
Science Applications Int'l Corporation	Computer processing services/commercial research lab
Teledyne Brown Engineering	Energy research
The Boeing Company	Aircraft/guided missiles/space vehicles
U.S. Army	U.S. military
United States Department of the Army	Army

Note: Companies shown are located within the Huntsville, AL Metropolitan Statistical Area.
Source: Hoovers.com; Wikipedia

PUBLIC SAFETY

Crime Rate

Area	All Crimes	Murder	Rape[3]	Robbery	Aggrav. Assault	Burglary	Larceny-Theft	Motor Vehicle Theft
City	5,635.0	11.3	88.1	184.5	621.0	731.7	3,462.6	535.9
Suburbs[1]	2,220.1	4.2	32.4	31.2	227.3	432.2	1,337.1	155.6
Metro[2]	3,685.7	7.3	56.3	97.0	396.3	560.7	2,249.3	318.9
U.S.	2,757.7	5.3	41.7	98.6	249.2	429.7	1,695.5	237.7

(Violent Crimes: Murder, Rape, Robbery, Aggrav. Assault; Property Crimes: Burglary, Larceny-Theft, Motor Vehicle Theft)

Note: Figures are crimes per 100,000 population; (1) All areas within the metro area that are located outside the city limits; (2) Figures cover the Huntsville, AL Metropolitan Statistical Area; (3) All figures shown were reported using the revised Uniform Crime Reporting (UCR) definition of rape.
Source: FBI Uniform Crime Reports, 2017 (data for 2019 was not available)

Hate Crimes

Area	Number of Quarters Reported	Race/Ethnicity/Ancestry	Religion	Sexual Orientation	Disability	Gender	Gender Identity
City	n/a	n/a	n/a	n/a	n/a	n/a	n/a
U.S.	4	3,963	1,521	1,195	157	69	198

Note: n/a not available.
Source: Federal Bureau of Investigation, Hate Crime Statistics 2019

Identity Theft Consumer Reports

Area	Reports	Reports per 100,000 Population	Rank[2]
MSA[1]	1,185	251	158
U.S.	1,387,615	423	-

Note: (1) Figures cover the Huntsville, AL Metropolitan Statistical Area; (2) Rank ranges from 1 to 391 where 1 indicates greatest number of identity theft reports per 100,000 population
Source: Federal Trade Commission, Consumer Sentinel Network Data Book 2020

Fraud and Other Consumer Reports

Area	Reports	Reports per 100,000 Population	Rank[2]
MSA[1]	4,282	908	46
U.S.	3,385,133	1,031	-

Note: (1) Figures cover the Huntsville, AL Metropolitan Statistical Area; (2) Rank ranges from 1 to 391 where 1 indicates greatest number of fraud and other consumer reports per 100,000 population
Source: Federal Trade Commission, Consumer Sentinel Network Data Book 2020

POLITICS

2020 Presidential Election Results

Area	Biden	Trump	Jorgensen	Hawkins	Other
Madison County	44.8	52.8	1.9	0.0	0.5
U.S.	51.3	46.8	1.2	0.3	0.5

Note: Results are percentages and may not add to 100% due to rounding
Source: Dave Leip's Atlas of U.S. Presidential Elections

SPORTS

Professional Sports Teams

Team Name	League	Year Established
No teams are located in the metro area		

Source: Wikipedia, Major Professional Sports Teams of the United States and Canada, April 6, 2021

CLIMATE

Average and Extreme Temperatures

Temperature	Jan	Feb	Mar	Apr	May	Jun	Jul	Aug	Sep	Oct	Nov	Dec	Yr.
Extreme High (°F)	76	82	88	92	96	101	104	103	101	91	84	77	104
Average High (°F)	49	54	63	73	80	87	90	89	83	73	62	52	71
Average Temp. (°F)	39	44	52	61	69	76	80	79	73	62	51	43	61
Average Low (°F)	30	33	41	49	58	65	69	68	62	50	40	33	50
Extreme Low (°F)	-11	5	6	26	36	45	53	52	37	28	15	-3	-11

Note: Figures cover the years 1958-1995
Source: National Climatic Data Center, International Station Meteorological Climate Summary, 9/96

Average Precipitation/Snowfall/Humidity

Precip./Humidity	Jan	Feb	Mar	Apr	May	Jun	Jul	Aug	Sep	Oct	Nov	Dec	Yr.
Avg. Precip. (in.)	5.0	5.0	6.6	4.8	5.1	4.3	4.6	3.5	4.1	3.3	4.7	5.7	56.8
Avg. Snowfall (in.)	2	1	1	Tr	0	0	0	0	0	Tr	Tr	1	4
Avg. Rel. Hum. 7am (%)	82	81	79	78	79	81	84	86	85	86	84	81	82
Avg. Rel. Hum. 4pm (%)	60	56	51	46	51	53	56	55	54	51	55	60	54

Note: Figures cover the years 1958-1995; Tr = Trace amounts (<0.05 in. of rain; <0.5 in. of snow)
Source: National Climatic Data Center, International Station Meteorological Climate Summary, 9/96

Weather Conditions

Temperature			Daytime Sky			Precipitation		
10°F & below	32°F & below	90°F & above	Clear	Partly cloudy	Cloudy	0.01 inch or more precip.	0.1 inch or more snow/ice	Thunder-storms
2	66	49	70	118	177	116	2	54

Note: Figures are average number of days per year and cover the years 1958-1995
Source: National Climatic Data Center, International Station Meteorological Climate Summary, 9/96

HAZARDOUS WASTE

Superfund Sites

The Huntsville, AL metro area is home to one site on the EPA's Superfund National Priorities List: **USARMY/NASA Redstone Arsenal** (final). There are a total of 1,375 Superfund sites with a status of proposed or final on the list in the U.S. *U.S. Environmental Protection Agency, National Priorities List, April 7, 2021*

AIR QUALITY

Air Quality Trends: Ozone

	1990	1995	2000	2005	2010	2015	2016	2017	2018	2019
MSA[1]	0.079	0.080	0.088	0.075	0.071	0.063	0.066	0.063	0.065	0.063
U.S.	0.088	0.089	0.082	0.080	0.073	0.068	0.069	0.068	0.069	0.065

Note: (1) Data covers the Huntsville, AL Metropolitan Statistical Area. The values shown are the composite ozone concentration averages among trend sites based on the highest fourth daily maximum 8-hour concentration in parts per million. These trends are based on sites having an adequate record of monitoring data during the trend period. Data from exceptional events are included.
Source: U.S. Environmental Protection Agency, Air Quality Monitoring Information, "Air Quality Trends by City, 1990-2019"

Air Quality Index

Area	Percent of Days when Air Quality was...[2]					AQI Statistics[2]	
	Good	Moderate	Unhealthy for Sensitive Groups	Unhealthy	Very Unhealthy	Maximum	Median
MSA[1]	70.6	29.4	0.0	0.0	0.0	93	44

Note: (1) Data covers the Huntsville, AL Metropolitan Statistical Area; (2) Based on 361 days with AQI data in 2019. Air Quality Index (AQI) is an index for reporting daily air quality. EPA calculates the AQI for five major air pollutants regulated by the Clean Air Act: ground-level ozone, particle pollution (aka particulate matter), carbon monoxide, sulfur dioxide, and nitrogen dioxide. The AQI runs from 0 to 500. The higher the AQI value, the greater the level of air pollution and the greater the health concern. There are six AQI categories: "Good" AQI is between 0 and 50. Air quality is considered satisfactory; "Moderate" AQI is between 51 and 100. Air quality is acceptable; "Unhealthy for Sensitive Groups" When AQI values are between 101 and 150, members of sensitive groups may experience health effects; "Unhealthy" When AQI values are between 151 and 200 everyone may begin to experience health effects; "Very Unhealthy" AQI values between 201 and 300 trigger a health alert; "Hazardous" AQI values over 300 trigger warnings of emergency conditions (not shown).
Source: U.S. Environmental Protection Agency, Air Quality Index Report, 2019

Air Quality Index Pollutants

Area	Percent of Days when AQI Pollutant was...[2]					
	Carbon Monoxide	Nitrogen Dioxide	Ozone	Sulfur Dioxide	Particulate Matter 2.5	Particulate Matter 10
MSA[1]	0.0	0.0	42.9	0.0	55.1	1.9

Note: (1) Data covers the Huntsville, AL Metropolitan Statistical Area; (2) Based on 361 days with AQI data in 2019. The Air Quality Index (AQI) is an index for reporting daily air quality. EPA calculates the AQI for five major air pollutants regulated by the Clean Air Act: ground-level ozone, particle pollution (also known as particulate matter), carbon monoxide, sulfur dioxide, and nitrogen dioxide. The AQI runs from 0 to 500. The higher the AQI value, the greater the level of air pollution and the greater the health concern.
Source: U.S. Environmental Protection Agency, Air Quality Index Report, 2019

Maximum Air Pollutant Concentrations: Particulate Matter, Ozone, CO and Lead

	Particulate Matter 10 (ug/m^3)	Particulate Matter 2.5 Wtd AM (ug/m^3)	Particulate Matter 2.5 24-Hr (ug/m^3)	Ozone (ppm)	Carbon Monoxide (ppm)	Lead (ug/m^3)
MSA[1] Level	34	7.4	14	0.063	n/a	n/a
NAAQS[2]	150	15	35	0.075	9	0.15
Met NAAQS[2]	Yes	Yes	Yes	Yes	n/a	n/a

Note: (1) Data covers the Huntsville, AL Metropolitan Statistical Area; Data from exceptional events are included; (2) National Ambient Air Quality Standards; ppm = parts per million; ug/m^3 = micrograms per cubic meter; n/a not available.
Concentrations: Particulate Matter 10 (coarse particulate)—highest second maximum 24-hour concentration; Particulate Matter 2.5 Wtd AM (fine particulate)—highest weighted annual mean concentration; Particulate Matter 2.5 24-Hour (fine particulate)—highest 98th percentile 24-hour concentration; Ozone—highest fourth daily maximum 8-hour concentration; Carbon Monoxide—highest second maximum non-overlapping 8-hour concentration; Lead—maximum running 3-month average
Source: U.S. Environmental Protection Agency, Air Quality Monitoring Information, "Air Quality Statistics by City, 2019"

Maximum Air Pollutant Concentrations: Nitrogen Dioxide and Sulfur Dioxide

	Nitrogen Dioxide AM (ppb)	Nitrogen Dioxide 1-Hr (ppb)	Sulfur Dioxide AM (ppb)	Sulfur Dioxide 1-Hr (ppb)	Sulfur Dioxide 24-Hr (ppb)
MSA[1] Level	n/a	n/a	n/a	n/a	n/a
NAAQS[2]	53	100	30	75	140
Met NAAQS[2]	n/a	n/a	n/a	n/a	n/a

Note: (1) Data covers the Huntsville, AL Metropolitan Statistical Area; Data from exceptional events are included; (2) National Ambient Air Quality Standards; ppm = parts per million; ug/m^3 = micrograms per cubic meter; n/a not available.
Concentrations: Nitrogen Dioxide AM—highest arithmetic mean concentration; Nitrogen Dioxide 1-Hr—highest 98th percentile 1-hour daily maximum concentration; Sulfur Dioxide AM—highest annual mean concentration; Sulfur Dioxide 1-Hr—highest 99th percentile 1-hour daily maximum concentration; Sulfur Dioxide 24-Hr—highest second maximum 24-hour concentration
Source: U.S. Environmental Protection Agency, Air Quality Monitoring Information, "Air Quality Statistics by City, 2019"

Jacksonville, Florida

Background

Modern day Jacksonville is largely a product of the reconstruction that occurred during the 1940s after a fire razed 147 city blocks a few decades earlier. Lying under the modern structures, however, is a history that dates back earlier than the settlement of Plymouth by the Pilgrims.

Located in the northeast part of Florida on the St. John's River, Jacksonville, the largest city in land area in the contiguous United States, was settled by English, Spanish, and French explorers from the sixteenth through the eighteenth centuries. Sites commemorating their presence include: Fort Caroline National Monument, marking the French settlement led by René de Goulaine Laudonnière in 1564; Spanish Pond one-quarter of a mile east of Fort Caroline, where Spanish forces led by Pedro Menendez captured the Fort; and Fort George Island, from which General James Oglethorpe led English attacks against the Spanish during the eighteenth century.

Jacksonville was attractive to these early settlers because of its easy access to the Atlantic Ocean, which meant a favorable port. Today, Jacksonville remains a military and civilian deep-water port. The city is home to Naval Station Mayport, Naval Air Station Jacksonville, the U.S. Marine Corps Bount Island command, and the Port of Jacksonville, Florida's third largest seaport. Jacksonville's military bases and the nearby Naval Submarine Base Kings Bay form the third largest military presence in the United States.

Jacksonville is the financial hub of Florida, and many business and financial companies are headquartered in the city. As with much of Florida, tourism is important to Jacksonville, particularly tourism related to golf.

Jacksonville voters approved The Better Jacksonville Plan in 2000, which authorized a half-penny sales tax that generated revenue for major improvement city projects, environmental protection and economic development. Recent improvements to the city's highway system are designed to reduce congestion.

On the cultural front, Jacksonville boasts a range of options, including the Children's Museum, the Jacksonville Symphony Orchestra, the Gator Bowl, and beach facilities. The Jacksonville Jazz Festival, held every April, is the second-largest jazz festival in the nation. The city is home to several theaters, including Little Theatre, which, operating since 1919, is one of the oldest operating community theaters in the nation.

In 2005, the city hosted Super Bowl XXXIX at the former Alltel Stadium (now Jacksonville Municipal Stadium), home of the NFL's Jacksonville Jaguars.

The city also boasts the largest urban park system in the United States, providing services at more than 337 locations on more than 80,000 acres located throughout the city. Most recently, The Jacksonville Arboretum and Gardens was opened in 2008.

Summers are long, warm, and relatively humid. Winters are generally mild, although periodic invasions of cold northern air bring the temperature down. Temperatures along the beaches rarely rise above 90 degrees. Summer coastal thunderstorms usually occur before noon, and move inland in the afternoons. The greatest rainfall, as localized thundershowers, occurs during the summer months. Although in the hurricane belt, this section of the coast has escaped hurricane-force winds in recent history until 2016, when Hurricane Matthew caused major flooding and damage to the city, Jacksonville Beach, Atlantic Beach and Neptune Beach. In September 2017, Hurricane Irma caused record breaking floods in Jacksonville not seen since 1846.

Rankings

General Rankings

- For its "Best for Vets: Places to Live 2019" rankings, *Military Times* evaluated 599 cities (83 large, 234 medium, 282 small) and compared the locations across three broad categories: veteran and military culture/services; economic indicators; and livability factors such as health, crime, traffic, and school quality. Jacksonville ranked #10 out of the top 25, in the large city category (population of more than 250,000). Data points more specific to veterans and the military weighed more heavily than others. *rebootcamp.militarytimes.com, "Military Times Best Places to Live 2019," September 10, 2018*

- The Jacksonville metro area was identified as one of America's fastest-growing areas in terms of population and economy by *Forbes*. The area ranked #16 out of 25. The 100 most populous metro areas in the U.S. were evaluated on the following criteria: estimated population growth; employment; economic output; wages; home values. *Forbes, "America's Fastest-Growing Cities 2018," February 28, 2018*

- In their seventh annual survey, Livability.com looked at data for more than 1,000 small to mid-sized U.S. cities to determine the rankings for Livability's "Top 100 Best Places to Live" in 2020. Jacksonville ranked #99. Criteria: housing and affordable living; vibrant economy; social and civic engagement; education; demographics; health care options; transportation & infrastructure; and abundant lifestyle amenities. *Livability.com, "Top 100 Best Places to Live 2020" October 2020*

Business/Finance Rankings

- The Brookings Institution ranked the nation's largest cities based on income inequality. Jacksonville was ranked #91 (#1 = greatest inequality). Criteria: the "95/20 ratio," a figure representing the income at which a household earns more than 95 percent of all other households, divided by the income at which a household earns more than only 20 percent of all other households. *Brookings Institution, "Household Income Inequality, Largest Cities of 97 Large U.S. Metro Areas, 2014-2016," February 5, 2018*

- The Brookings Institution ranked the 100 largest metro areas in the U.S. based on income inequality. Jacksonville was ranked #77 (#1 = greatest inequality). Criteria: the "95/20 ratio," a figure representing the income at which a household earns more than 95 percent of all other households, divided by the income at which a household earns more than only 20 percent of all other households. *Brookings Institution, "Household Income Inequality, 100 Largest U.S. Metro Areas, 2014-2016," February 5, 2018*

- The Jacksonville metro area appeared on the Milken Institute "2021 Best Performing Cities" list. Rank: #39 out of 200 large metro areas (population over 250,000). Criteria: job growth; wage and salary growth; high-tech output growth; housing affordability; household broadband access. *Milken Institute, "Best-Performing Cities 2021," February 16, 2021*

- *Forbes* ranked the 200 most populous metro areas to determine the nation's "Best Places for Business and Careers." The Jacksonville metro area was ranked #22. Criteria: costs (business and living); job growth (past and projected); income growth; quality of life; educational attainment (college and high school); projected economic growth; cultural and leisure opportunities; workplace tolerance laws; net migration patterns. *Forbes, "The Best Places for Business and Careers 2019: Seattle Still On Top," October 30, 2019*

Dating/Romance Rankings

- Jacksonville was ranked #10 out of 25 cities that stood out for inspiring romance and attracting diners on the website OpenTable.com. Criteria: percentage of people who dined out on Valentine's Day in 2018; percentage of romantic restaurants as rated by OpenTable diner reviews; and percentage of tables seated for two. *OpenTable, "25 Most Romantic Cities in America for 2019," February 7, 2019*

Education Rankings

- Personal finance website *WalletHub* analyzed the 150 largest U.S. metropolitan statistical areas to determine where the most educated Americans are putting their degrees to work. Criteria: education levels; percentage of workers with degrees; education quality and attainment gap; public school quality rankings; quality and enrollment of each metro area's universities. Jacksonville was ranked #73 (#1 = most educated city). *www.WalletHub.com, "Most and Least Educated Cities in America," July 20, 2020*

- Jacksonville was selected as one of America's most literate cities. The city ranked #64 out of the 84 largest U.S. cities. Criteria: number of booksellers; library resources; Internet resources; educational attainment; periodical publishing resources; newspaper circulation. *Central Connecticut State University, "America's Most Literate Cities, 2018," February 2019*

Health/Fitness Rankings

- For each of the 100 largest cities in the United States, the American Fitness Index®, published by the American College of Sports Medicine and the Anthem Foundation, evaluated community infrastructure and 33 health behaviors including preventive health, levels of chronic disease conditions, pedestrian safety, air quality, and community resources that support physical activity. Jacksonville ranked #82 for "community fitness." *americanfitnessindex.org, "2020 ACSM American Fitness Index Summary Report," July 14, 2020*

- Jacksonville was identified as a "2021 Spring Allergy Capital." The area ranked #28 out of 100. Three groups of factors were used to identify the most challenging cities for people with allergies during the spring season: annual spring pollen levels; over the counter medicine use; number of board-certified allergy specialists. *Asthma and Allergy Foundation of America, "Spring Allergy Capitals 2021," February 23, 2021*

- Jacksonville was identified as a "2021 Fall Allergy Capital." The area ranked #33 out of 100. Three groups of factors were used to identify the most challenging cities for people with allergies during the fall season: annual fall pollen levels; over the counter medicine use; number of board-certified allergy specialists. *Asthma and Allergy Foundation of America, "Fall Allergy Capitals 2021," February 23, 2021*

- Jacksonville was identified as a "2019 Asthma Capital." The area ranked #67 out of the nation's 100 largest metropolitan areas. Criteria: estimated asthma prevalence; crude death rate from asthma; and ER visits due to asthma. Risk factors analyzed but not factored in the rankings: annual pollen score; annual air quality; public smoking laws; number of board-certified asthma specialists; rescue medication use; controller medication use; uninsured rate; poverty rate. *Asthma and Allergy Foundation of America, "Asthma Capitals 2019: The Most Challenging Places to Live With Asthma," May 7, 2019*

Real Estate Rankings

- FitSmallBusiness looked at 50 of the largest metropolitan areas in the U.S. to determine which metro was the best to start a real estate business. Data was compiled from such sources as: Zillow, Trulia, U.S. Census Bureau, and the Bureau of Labor Statistics. Criteria: location; inventory; annual wages; median sales price of homes; days on the market; median price cut percentage; and other factors that would influence real estate professional growth. The Jacksonville metro area ranked #42. *fitsmallbusiness.com, "The Best Cities to Become a Real Estate Agent in 2018," January 30, 2018*

- *WalletHub* compared the most populated U.S. cities to determine which had the best markets for real estate agents. Jacksonville ranked #58 where demand was high and pay was the best. Criteria: sales per agent; annual median wage for real-estate agents; monthly average starting salary for real estate agents; real estate job density and competition; unemployment rate; home turnover rate; housing-market health index; and other relevant metrics. *www.WalletHub.com, "2019's Best Places to Be a Real Estate Agent," April 24, 2019*

- Jacksonville was ranked #170 out of 268 metro areas in terms of housing affordability in 2020 by the National Association of Home Builders (#1 = most affordable). Criteria: the share of homes sold in that area affordable to a family earning the local median income, based on standard mortgage underwriting criteria. *National Association of Home Builders®, NAHB-Wells Fargo Housing Opportunity Index, 4th Quarter 2020*

Safety Rankings

- Allstate ranked the 200 largest cities in America in terms of driver safety. Jacksonville ranked #69. Criteria: internal property damage claims over a two-year period from January 2016 to December 2017. The report helps increase the importance of safety and awareness behind the wheel. *Allstate, "Allstate America's Best Drivers Report, 2019" June 24, 2019*

- The National Insurance Crime Bureau ranked 384 metro areas in the U.S. in terms of per capita rates of vehicle theft. The Jacksonville metro area ranked #123 (#1 = highest rate). Criteria: number of vehicle theft offenses per 100,000 inhabitants in 2019. *National Insurance Crime Bureau, "Hot Spots 2019," July 21, 2020*

Seniors/Retirement Rankings

- From its Best Cities for Successful Aging indexes, the Milken Institute generated rankings for metropolitan areas, weighing data in nine categories—health care, wellness, living arrangements, transportation and convenience, financial characteristics, education, employment, community engagement, and overall livability. The Jacksonville metro area was ranked #63 overall in the large metro area category. *Milken Institute, "Best Cities for Successful Aging, 2017" March 14, 2017*

- Jacksonville made the 2020 *Forbes* list of "25 Best Places to Retire." Criteria, focused on high-quality retirement living at an affordable price, include: housing/living costs compared to the national average and state taxes; air quality; crime rates; good economic outlook; home price appreciation; risk associated with climate-change; availability of medical care; bikeability; walkability; healthy living. *Forbes.com, "The Best Places to Retire in 2020," August 14, 2020*

Women/Minorities Rankings

- Personal finance website *WalletHub* compared more than 180 U.S. cities across two key dimensions, "Hispanic Business-Friendliness" and "Hispanic Purchasing Power," to arrive at the most favorable conditions for Hispanic entrepreneurs. Jacksonville was ranked #32 out of 182. Criteria includes: share of Hispanic-Owned Businesses; Hispanic entrepreneurship rate to median annual income of Hispanics; Small Business-Friendliness score; cost of living; and number of Hispanics with at least a bachelor's degree. *WalletHub.com, "2019's Best Cities for Hispanic Entrepreneurs," May 1, 2019*

Miscellaneous Rankings

- *WalletHub* compared the 150 most populated U.S. cities to determine their operating efficiency. A "Quality of City Services" score was constructed for each city and then divided by the total budget per capita to reveal which were managed the best. Jacksonville ranked #103. Criteria: financial stability; economy; education; safety; health; infrastructure and pollution. *www.WalletHub.com, "2020's Best- & Worst-Run Cities in America," June 29, 2020*

Business Environment

DEMOGRAPHICS

Population Growth

Area	1990 Census	2000 Census	2010 Census	2019* Estimate	Population Growth (%) 1990-2019	Population Growth (%) 2010-2019
City	635,221	735,617	821,784	890,467	40.2	8.4
MSA[1]	925,213	1,122,750	1,345,596	1,503,574	62.5	11.7
U.S.	248,709,873	281,421,906	308,745,538	324,697,795	30.6	5.2

Note: (1) Figures cover the Jacksonville, FL Metropolitan Statistical Area; (*) 2015-2019 5-year estimated population
Source: U.S. Census Bureau, 1990 Census, Census 2000, Census 2010, 2015-2019 American Community Survey 5-Year Estimates

Household Size

Area	One	Two	Three	Four	Five	Six	Seven or More	Average Household Size
City	30.4	33.7	16.7	11.4	5.1	1.7	0.9	2.60
MSA[1]	27.2	35.7	16.7	12.4	5.3	1.9	0.9	2.60
U.S.	27.9	33.9	15.6	12.9	6.0	2.3	1.4	2.60

Note: (1) Figures cover the Jacksonville, FL Metropolitan Statistical Area
Source: U.S. Census Bureau, 2015-2019 American Community Survey 5-Year Estimates

Race

Area	White Alone[2] (%)	Black Alone[2] (%)	Asian Alone[2] (%)	AIAN[3] Alone[2] (%)	NHOPI[4] Alone[2] (%)	Other Race Alone[2] (%)	Two or More Races (%)
City	58.2	31.0	4.8	0.2	0.1	2.1	3.6
MSA[1]	69.3	21.5	3.8	0.3	0.1	1.8	3.4
U.S.	72.5	12.7	5.5	0.8	0.2	4.9	3.3

Note: (1) Figures cover the Jacksonville, FL Metropolitan Statistical Area; (2) Alone is defined as not being in combination with one or more other races; (3) American Indian and Alaska Native; (4) Native Hawaiian and Other Pacific Islander
Source: U.S. Census Bureau, 2015-2019 American Community Survey 5-Year Estimates

Hispanic or Latino Origin

Area	Total (%)	Mexican (%)	Puerto Rican (%)	Cuban (%)	Other (%)
City	10.0	2.0	3.0	1.2	3.7
MSA[1]	8.9	1.8	2.8	1.2	3.1
U.S.	18.0	11.2	1.7	0.7	4.3

Note: Persons of Hispanic or Latino origin can be of any race; (1) Figures cover the Jacksonville, FL Metropolitan Statistical Area
Source: U.S. Census Bureau, 2015-2019 American Community Survey 5-Year Estimates

Ancestry

Area	German	Irish	English	American	Italian	Polish	French[2]	Scottish	Dutch
City	7.9	7.8	6.0	5.4	3.8	1.5	1.4	1.5	0.8
MSA[1]	10.0	9.6	7.9	7.9	4.6	1.9	1.9	2.0	0.9
U.S.	13.3	9.7	7.2	6.2	5.1	2.8	2.3	1.7	1.2

Note: Figures are the percentage of the total population reporting a particular ancestry. The nine most commonly reported ancestries in the U.S. are shown. Figures include multiple ancestries (e.g. if a person reported being Irish and Italian, they were included in both columns); (1) Figures cover the Jacksonville, FL Metropolitan Statistical Area; (2) Excludes Basque
Source: U.S. Census Bureau, 2015-2019 American Community Survey 5-Year Estimates

Foreign-born Population

Area	Any Foreign Country	Asia	Mexico	Europe	Caribbean	Central America[2]	South America	Africa	Canada
City	11.3	4.0	0.6	1.8	2.0	0.8	1.3	0.6	0.2
MSA[1]	9.3	3.1	0.5	1.7	1.5	0.6	1.1	0.4	0.3
U.S.	13.6	4.2	3.5	1.5	1.3	1.1	1.0	0.7	0.2

Note: (1) Figures cover the Jacksonville, FL Metropolitan Statistical Area; (2) Excludes Mexico.
Source: U.S. Census Bureau, 2015-2019 American Community Survey 5-Year Estimates

Marital Status

Area	Never Married	Now Married[2]	Separated	Widowed	Divorced
City	35.5	42.6	2.2	5.6	14.0
MSA[1]	31.4	47.8	1.9	5.8	13.2
U.S.	33.4	48.1	1.9	5.8	10.9

Note: Figures are percentages and cover the population 15 years of age and older; (1) Figures cover the Jacksonville, FL Metropolitan Statistical Area; (2) Excludes separated
Source: U.S. Census Bureau, 2015-2019 American Community Survey 5-Year Estimates

Disability by Age

Area	All Ages	Under 18 Years Old	18 to 64 Years Old	65 Years and Over
City	13.5	5.0	11.5	37.6
MSA[1]	13.2	4.7	11.0	34.7
U.S.	12.6	4.2	10.3	34.5

Note: Figures show percent of the civilian noninstitutionalized population that reported having a disability. Disability status is determined from six types of difficulty: vision, hearing, cognitive, ambulatory, self-care, and independent living. For children under 5 years old, hearing and vision difficulty are used to determine disability status. For children between the ages of 5 and 14, disability status is determined from hearing, vision, cognitive, ambulatory, and self-care difficulties. For people aged 15 years and older, they are considered to have a disability if they have difficulty with any one of the six difficulty types; Note: (1) Figures cover the Jacksonville, FL Metropolitan Statistical Area
Source: U.S. Census Bureau, 2015-2019 American Community Survey 5-Year Estimates

Age

Area	Under Age 5	Age 5–19	Age 20–34	Age 35–44	Age 45–54	Age 55–64	Age 65–74	Age 75–84	Age 85+	Median Age
City	6.9	18.3	23.3	12.7	12.8	12.5	8.2	3.8	1.5	35.9
MSA[1]	6.2	18.5	20.7	12.7	13.3	13.2	9.5	4.3	1.6	38.3
U.S.	6.1	19.1	20.7	12.6	13.0	12.9	9.1	4.6	1.9	38.1

Note: (1) Figures cover the Jacksonville, FL Metropolitan Statistical Area
Source: U.S. Census Bureau, 2015-2019 American Community Survey 5-Year Estimates

Gender

Area	Males	Females	Males per 100 Females
City	431,133	459,334	93.9
MSA[1]	733,355	770,219	95.2
U.S.	159,886,919	164,810,876	97.0

Note: (1) Figures cover the Jacksonville, FL Metropolitan Statistical Area
Source: U.S. Census Bureau, 2015-2019 American Community Survey 5-Year Estimates

Religious Groups by Family

Area	Catholic	Baptist	Non-Den.	Methodist[2]	Lutheran	LDS[3]	Pentecostal	Presbyterian[4]	Muslim[5]	Judaism
MSA[1]	9.9	18.5	7.8	4.5	0.7	1.1	1.9	1.6	0.6	0.4
U.S.	19.1	9.3	4.0	4.0	2.3	2.0	1.9	1.6	0.8	0.7

Note: Figures are the number of adherents as a percentage of the total population; (1) Figures cover the Jacksonville, FL Metropolitan Statistical Area; (2) Methodist/Pietist; (3) Latter Day Saints; (4) Reformed; (5) Figures are estimates
Source: Association of Statisticians of American Religious Bodies, 2010 U.S. Religion Census: Religious Congregations & Membership Study

Religious Groups by Tradition

Area	Catholic	Evangelical Protestant	Mainline Protestant	Other Tradition	Black Protestant	Orthodox
MSA[1]	9.9	27.1	5.7	2.9	4.2	0.3
U.S.	19.1	16.2	7.3	4.3	1.6	0.3

Note: Figures are the number of adherents as a percentage of the total population; (1) Figures cover the Jacksonville, FL Metropolitan Statistical Area
Source: Association of Statisticians of American Religious Bodies, 2010 U.S. Religion Census: Religious Congregations & Membership Study

ECONOMY

Gross Metropolitan Product

Area	2017	2018	2019	2020	Rank[2]
MSA[1]	77.6	82.8	86.5	90.6	45

Note: Figures are in billions of dollars; (1) Figures cover the Jacksonville, FL Metropolitan Statistical Area; (2) Rank is based on 2018 data and ranges from 1 to 381
Source: U.S. Conference of Mayors, U.S. Metro Economies: GMP & Employment 2018-2020, September 2019

Economic Growth

Area	2015-17 (%)	2018 (%)	2019 (%)	2020 (%)	Rank[2]
MSA[1]	4.1	4.3	2.6	2.5	34
U.S.	1.9	2.9	2.3	2.1	—

Note: Figures are real gross metropolitan product (GMP) growth rates and represent average annual percent change; (1) Figures cover the Jacksonville, FL Metropolitan Statistical Area; (2) Rank is based on 2017 2-year average annual percent change and ranges from 1 to 381
Source: U.S. Conference of Mayors, U.S. Metro Economies: GMP & Employment 2018-2020, September 2019

Metropolitan Area Exports

Area	2014	2015	2016	2017	2018	2019	Rank[2]
MSA[1]	2,473.7	2,564.4	2,159.0	2,141.7	2,406.7	2,975.5	79

Note: Figures are in millions of dollars; (1) Figures cover the Jacksonville, FL Metropolitan Statistical Area; (2) Rank is based on 2019 data and ranges from 1 to 386
Source: U.S. Department of Commerce, International Trade Administration, Office of Trade and Economic Analysis, Industry and Analysis, Exports by Metropolitan Area, data extracted March 24, 2021

Building Permits

Area	Single-Family 2018	Single-Family 2019	Pct. Chg.	Multi-Family 2018	Multi-Family 2019	Pct. Chg.	Total 2018	Total 2019	Pct. Chg.
City	3,780	4,155	9.9	3,223	2,650	-17.8	7,003	6,805	-2.8
MSA[1]	10,755	11,583	7.7	4,695	3,104	-33.9	15,450	14,687	-4.9
U.S.	855,300	862,100	0.7	473,500	523,900	10.6	1,328,800	1,386,000	4.3

Note: (1) Figures cover the Jacksonville, FL Metropolitan Statistical Area; Figures represent new, privately-owned housing units authorized (unadjusted data); All permit data are based on estimates with imputation
Source: U.S. Census Bureau, Manufacturing, Mining, and Construction Statistics, Building Permits, 2018, 2019

Bankruptcy Filings

Area	Business Filings 2019	Business Filings 2020	% Chg.	Nonbusiness Filings 2019	Nonbusiness Filings 2020	% Chg.
Duval County	75	57	-24.0	2,349	1,604	-31.7
U.S.	22,780	21,655	-4.9	752,160	522,808	-30.5

Note: Business filings include Chapter 7, Chapter 9, Chapter 11, Chapter 12, Chapter 13, Chapter 15, and Section 304; Nonbusiness filings include Chapter 7, Chapter 11, and Chapter 13
Source: Administrative Office of the U.S. Courts, Business and Nonbusiness Bankruptcy, County Cases Commenced by Chapter of the Bankruptcy Code, During the 12-Month Period Ending December 31, 2019 and Business and Nonbusiness Bankruptcy, County Cases Commenced by Chapter of the Bankruptcy Code, During the 12-Month Period Ending December 31, 2020

Housing Vacancy Rates

Area	Gross Vacancy Rate[2] (%) 2018	2019	2020	Year-Round Vacancy Rate[3] (%) 2018	2019	2020	Rental Vacancy Rate[4] (%) 2018	2019	2020	Homeowner Vacancy Rate[5] (%) 2018	2019	2020
MSA[1]	10.1	10.1	9.5	9.3	9.8	9.3	5.6	5.2	7.5	1.3	1.0	1.5
U.S.	12.3	12.0	10.6	9.7	9.5	8.2	6.9	6.7	6.3	1.5	1.4	1.0

Note: (1) Figures cover the Jacksonville, FL Metropolitan Statistical Area; (2) The percentage of the total housing inventory that is vacant; (3) The percentage of the housing inventory (excluding seasonal units) that is year-round vacant; (4) The percentage of rental inventory that is vacant for rent; (5) The percentage of homeowner inventory that is vacant for sale
Source: U.S. Census Bureau, Housing Vacancies and Homeownership Annual Statistics: 2018, 2019, 2020

INCOME

Income

Area	Per Capita ($)	Median Household ($)	Average Household ($)
City	30,064	54,701	74,873
MSA[1]	33,304	61,723	84,690
U.S.	34,103	62,843	88,607

Note: (1) Figures cover the Jacksonville, FL Metropolitan Statistical Area
Source: U.S. Census Bureau, 2015-2019 American Community Survey 5-Year Estimates

Household Income Distribution

Area	Under $15,000	$15,000 -$24,999	$25,000 -$34,999	$35,000 -$49,999	$50,000 -$74,999	$75,000 -$99,999	$100,000 -$149,999	$150,000 and up
City	11.3	9.4	10.1	14.6	19.4	13.2	12.9	9.2
MSA[1]	9.5	8.3	9.2	13.4	18.8	13.6	14.7	12.4
U.S.	10.3	8.9	8.9	12.3	17.2	12.7	15.1	14.5

Note: (1) Figures cover the Jacksonville, FL Metropolitan Statistical Area
Source: U.S. Census Bureau, 2015-2019 American Community Survey 5-Year Estimates

Poverty Rate

Area	All Ages	Under 18 Years Old	18 to 64 Years Old	65 Years and Over
City	14.9	21.9	13.0	11.3
MSA[1]	12.6	17.7	11.6	8.9
U.S.	13.4	18.5	12.6	9.3

Note: Figures are percentage of people whose income during the past 12 months was below the poverty level;
(1) Figures cover the Jacksonville, FL Metropolitan Statistical Area
Source: U.S. Census Bureau, 2015-2019 American Community Survey 5-Year Estimates

CITY FINANCES

City Government Finances

Component	2017 ($000)	2017 ($ per capita)
Total Revenues	4,268,774	4,918
Total Expenditures	3,826,298	4,408
Debt Outstanding	8,768,858	10,102
Cash and Securities[1]	5,899,723	6,797

Note: (1) Cash and security holdings of a government at the close of its fiscal year, including those of its dependent agencies, utilities, and liquor stores.
Source: U.S. Census Bureau, State & Local Government Finances 2017

City Government Revenue by Source

Source	2017 ($000)	2017 ($ per capita)	2017 (%)
General Revenue			
From Federal Government	88,893	102	2.1
From State Government	218,264	251	5.1
From Local Governments	251,314	290	5.9
Taxes			
Property	557,918	643	13.1
Sales and Gross Receipts	326,978	377	7.7
Personal Income	0	0	0.0
Corporate Income	0	0	0.0
Motor Vehicle License	0	0	0.0
Other Taxes	108,509	125	2.5
Current Charges	573,197	660	13.4
Liquor Store	0	0	0.0
Utility	1,542,231	1,777	36.1
Employee Retirement	462,100	532	10.8

Source: U.S. Census Bureau, State & Local Government Finances 2017

City Government Expenditures by Function

Function	2017 ($000)	2017 ($ per capita)	2017 (%)
General Direct Expenditures			
Air Transportation	76,050	87	2.0
Corrections	54,374	62	1.4
Education	0	0	0.0
Employment Security Administration	0	0	0.0
Financial Administration	85,848	98	2.2
Fire Protection	159,560	183	4.2
General Public Buildings	0	0	0.0
Governmental Administration, Other	21,415	24	0.6
Health	82,540	95	2.2
Highways	47,466	54	1.2
Hospitals	0	0	0.0
Housing and Community Development	18,240	21	0.5
Interest on General Debt	111,855	128	2.9
Judicial and Legal	41,298	47	1.1
Libraries	33,086	38	0.9
Parking	3,495	4	0.1
Parks and Recreation	113,383	130	3.0
Police Protection	352,863	406	9.2
Public Welfare	12,021	13	0.3
Sewerage	90,975	104	2.4
Solid Waste Management	73,652	84	1.9
Veterans' Services	0	0	0.0
Liquor Store	0	0	0.0
Utility	1,786,851	2,058	46.7
Employee Retirement	359,038	413	9.4

Source: U.S. Census Bureau, State & Local Government Finances 2017

EMPLOYMENT

Labor Force and Employment

Area	Civilian Labor Force Dec. 2019	Dec. 2020	% Chg.	Workers Employed Dec. 2019	Dec. 2020	% Chg.
City	469,934	463,646	-1.3	457,089	438,293	-4.1
MSA[1]	794,684	779,448	-1.9	774,172	742,219	-4.1
U.S.	164,007,000	160,017,000	-2.4	158,504,000	149,613,000	-5.6

Note: Data is not seasonally adjusted and covers workers 16 years of age and older; (1) Figures cover the Jacksonville, FL Metropolitan Statistical Area
Source: Bureau of Labor Statistics, Local Area Unemployment Statistics

Unemployment Rate

Area	Jan.	Feb.	Mar.	Apr.	May	Jun.	Jul.	Aug.	Sep.	Oct.	Nov.	Dec.
City	3.3	3.1	4.6	11.5	11.0	8.4	9.7	6.4	5.5	5.6	5.7	5.5
MSA[1]	3.1	3.0	4.3	11.2	10.4	7.8	8.8	5.7	4.8	4.8	5.0	4.8
U.S.	4.0	3.8	4.5	14.4	13.0	11.2	10.5	8.5	7.7	6.6	6.4	6.5

Note: Data is not seasonally adjusted and covers workers 16 years of age and older; (1) Figures cover the Jacksonville, FL Metropolitan Statistical Area
Source: Bureau of Labor Statistics, Local Area Unemployment Statistics

Average Wages

Occupation	$/Hr.	Occupation	$/Hr.
Accountants and Auditors	32.50	Maintenance and Repair Workers	20.00
Automotive Mechanics	20.50	Marketing Managers	68.70
Bookkeepers	20.30	Network and Computer Systems Admin.	37.70
Carpenters	19.10	Nurses, Licensed Practical	22.70
Cashiers	11.30	Nurses, Registered	32.50
Computer Programmers	38.40	Nursing Assistants	13.40
Computer Systems Analysts	37.90	Office Clerks, General	17.00
Computer User Support Specialists	24.80	Physical Therapists	40.00
Construction Laborers	16.90	Physicians	120.40
Cooks, Restaurant	13.00	Plumbers, Pipefitters and Steamfitters	22.40
Customer Service Representatives	17.90	Police and Sheriff's Patrol Officers	28.70
Dentists	72.90	Postal Service Mail Carriers	26.40
Electricians	21.40	Real Estate Sales Agents	32.80
Engineers, Electrical	46.00	Retail Salespersons	12.90
Fast Food and Counter Workers	10.30	Sales Representatives, Technical/Scientific	55.80
Financial Managers	63.50	Secretaries, Exc. Legal/Medical/Executive	18.30
First-Line Supervisors of Office Workers	28.50	Security Guards	13.00
General and Operations Managers	52.10	Surgeons	n/a
Hairdressers/Cosmetologists	16.50	Teacher Assistants, Exc. Postsecondary*	12.80
Home Health and Personal Care Aides	12.40	Teachers, Secondary School, Exc. Sp. Ed.*	30.70
Janitors and Cleaners	12.10	Telemarketers	12.90
Landscaping/Groundskeeping Workers	14.60	Truck Drivers, Heavy/Tractor-Trailer	21.70
Lawyers	61.20	Truck Drivers, Light/Delivery Services	18.80
Maids and Housekeeping Cleaners	12.60	Waiters and Waitresses	12.20

Note: Wage data covers the Jacksonville, FL Metropolitan Statistical Area; (*) Hourly wages were calculated from annual wage data based on a 40 hour work week; n/a not available.
Source: Bureau of Labor Statistics, Metro Area Occupational Employment & Wage Estimates, May 2020

Employment by Industry

Sector	MSA[1] Number of Employees	Percent of Total	U.S. Percent of Total
Construction	47,500	6.6	5.1
Education and Health Services	111,900	15.5	16.3
Financial Activities	69,500	9.6	6.1
Government	78,800	10.9	15.2
Information	8,900	1.2	1.9
Leisure and Hospitality	75,400	10.4	9.0
Manufacturing	32,400	4.5	8.5
Mining and Logging	400	0.1	0.4
Other Services	25,000	3.5	3.8
Professional and Business Services	113,100	15.6	14.4
Retail Trade	81,800	11.3	10.9
Transportation, Warehousing, and Utilities	51,900	7.2	4.6
Wholesale Trade	26,700	3.7	3.9

Note: Figures are non-farm employment as of December 2020. Figures are not seasonally adjusted and include workers 16 years of age and older; (1) Figures cover the Jacksonville, FL Metropolitan Statistical Area
Source: Bureau of Labor Statistics, Current Employment Statistics, Employment, Hours, and Earnings

Employment by Occupation

Occupation Classification	City (%)	MSA[1] (%)	U.S. (%)
Management, Business, Science, and Arts	36.4	38.2	38.5
Natural Resources, Construction, and Maintenance	8.5	8.4	8.9
Production, Transportation, and Material Moving	12.1	11.3	13.2
Sales and Office	24.5	24.4	21.6
Service	18.4	17.7	17.8

Note: Figures cover employed civilians 16 years of age and older; (1) Figures cover the Jacksonville, FL Metropolitan Statistical Area
Source: U.S. Census Bureau, 2015-2019 American Community Survey 5-Year Estimates

Occupations with Greatest Projected Employment Growth: 2020 – 2022

Occupation[1]	2020 Employment	2022 Projected Employment	Numeric Employment Change	Percent Employment Change
Fast Food and Counter Workers	172,590	214,590	42,000	24.3
Waiters and Waitresses	141,990	180,530	38,540	27.1
Retail Salespersons	264,490	292,340	27,850	10.5
Cooks, Restaurant	79,150	103,770	24,620	31.1
Maids and Housekeeping Cleaners	63,280	81,030	17,750	28.0
Cashiers	204,540	221,530	16,990	8.3
Registered Nurses	189,240	202,880	13,640	7.2
Laborers and Freight, Stock, and Material Movers, Hand	147,740	160,650	12,910	8.7
First-Line Supervisors of Food Preparation and Serving Workers	51,820	64,080	12,260	23.7
Stockers and Order Fillers	130,980	142,780	11,800	9.0

Note: Projections cover Florida; (1) Sorted by numeric employment change
Source: www.projectionscentral.com, State Occupational Projections, 2020–2022 Short-Term Projections

Fastest-Growing Occupations: 2020 – 2022

Occupation[1]	2020 Employment	2022 Projected Employment	Numeric Employment Change	Percent Employment Change
Hotel, Motel, and Resort Desk Clerks	11,930	18,100	6,170	51.7
Locker Room, Coatroom, and Dressing Room Attendants	930	1,360	430	46.2
Lodging Managers	3,190	4,420	1,230	38.6
Manicurists and Pedicurists	2,640	3,580	940	35.6
Bartenders	31,430	42,540	11,110	35.3
Gaming Cage Workers	320	430	110	34.4
Parking Lot Attendants	11,200	15,040	3,840	34.3
Gaming Dealers	2,660	3,560	900	33.8
Baggage Porters and Bellhops	3,520	4,670	1,150	32.7
Cooks, Restaurant	79,150	103,770	24,620	31.1

Note: Projections cover Florida; (1) Sorted by percent employment change and excludes occupations with numeric employment change less than 50
Source: www.projectionscentral.com, State Occupational Projections, 2020–2022 Short-Term Projections

TAXES

State Corporate Income Tax Rates

State	Tax Rate (%)	Income Brackets ($)	Num. of Brackets	Financial Institution Tax Rate (%)[a]	Federal Income Tax Ded.
Florida	4.458 (e)	Flat rate	1	4.458 (e)	No

Note: Tax rates as of January 1, 2021; (a) Rates listed are the corporate income tax rate applied to financial institutions or excise taxes based on income. Some states have other taxes based upon the value of deposits or shares; (e) The Florida tax rate may be adjusted downward if certain revenue targets are met.
Source: Federation of Tax Administrators, State Corporate Income Tax Rates, January 1, 2021

State Individual Income Tax Rates

State	Tax Rate (%)	Income Brackets ($)	Personal Exemptions ($) Single	Personal Exemptions ($) Married	Personal Exemptions ($) Depend.	Standard Ded. ($) Single	Standard Ded. ($) Married
Florida	– No state income tax –						

Note: Tax rates as of January 1, 2021; Local- and county-level taxes are not included
Source: Federation of Tax Administrators, State Individual Income Tax Rates, January 1, 2021

Various State Sales and Excise Tax Rates

State	State Sales Tax (%)	Gasoline[1] (¢/gal.)	Cigarette[2] ($/pack)	Spirits[3] ($/gal.)	Wine[4] ($/gal.)	Beer[5] ($/gal.)	Recreational Marijuana (%)
Florida	6	42.46	1.339	6.5	2.25	0.48	Not legal

Note: All tax rates as of January 1, 2021; (1) The American Petroleum Institute has developed a methodology for determining the average tax rate on a gallon of fuel. Rates may include any of the following: excise taxes, environmental fees, storage tank fees, other fees or taxes, general sales tax, and local taxes; (2) The federal excise tax of $1.0066 per pack and local taxes are not included; (3) Rates are those applicable to off-premise sales of 40% alcohol by volume (a.b.v.) distilled spirits in 750ml containers. Local excise taxes are excluded; (4) Rates are those applicable to off-premise sales of 11% a.b.v. non-carbonated wine in 750ml containers; (5) Rates are those applicable to off-premise sales of 4.7% a.b.v. beer in 12 ounce containers.
Source: Tax Foundation, 2021 Facts & Figures: How Does Your State Compare?

State Business Tax Climate Index Rankings

State	Overall Rank	Corporate Tax Rank	Individual Income Tax Rank	Sales Tax Rank	Property Tax Rank	Unemployment Insurance Tax Rank
Florida	4	6	1	21	13	2

Note: The index is a measure of how each state's tax laws affect economic performance. The lower the rank, the more favorable a state's tax system is for business. States without a given tax are given a ranking of 1. The scores/rankings for the District of Columbia do not affect other states. The 2021 index represents the tax climate as of July 1, 2020.
Source: Tax Foundation, State Business Tax Climate Index 2021

TRANSPORTATION

Means of Transportation to Work

Area	Car/Truck/Van Drove Alone	Car/Truck/Van Car-pooled	Public Transportation Bus	Public Transportation Subway	Public Transportation Railroad	Bicycle	Walked	Other Means	Worked at Home
City	80.3	9.2	1.8	0.0	0.0	0.5	1.7	1.6	4.8
MSA[1]	80.9	8.2	1.2	0.0	0.0	0.5	1.5	1.7	6.0
U.S.	76.3	9.0	2.4	1.9	0.6	0.5	2.7	1.4	5.2

Note: Figures are percentages and cover workers 16 years of age and older; (1) Figures cover the Jacksonville, FL Metropolitan Statistical Area
Source: U.S. Census Bureau, 2015-2019 American Community Survey 5-Year Estimates

Travel Time to Work

Area	Less Than 10 Minutes	10 to 19 Minutes	20 to 29 Minutes	30 to 44 Minutes	45 to 59 Minutes	60 to 89 Minutes	90 Minutes or More
City	8.3	27.7	27.5	25.6	6.5	2.9	1.6
MSA[1]	8.8	25.4	24.4	26.0	9.0	4.5	1.8
U.S.	12.2	28.4	20.8	20.8	8.3	6.4	2.9

Note: Note: Figures are percentages and include workers 16 years old and over; (1) Figures cover the Jacksonville, FL Metropolitan Statistical Area
Source: U.S. Census Bureau, 2015-2019 American Community Survey 5-Year Estimates

Key Congestion Measures

Measure	1982	1992	2002	2012	2017
Annual Hours of Delay, Total (000)	5,022	12,305	23,556	31,106	34,792
Annual Hours of Delay, Per Auto Commuter	14	27	39	41	46
Annual Congestion Cost, Total (million $)	37	129	317	552	637
Annual Congestion Cost, Per Auto Commuter ($)	288	486	726	751	814

Note: Covers the Jacksonville FL urban area
Source: Texas A&M Transportation Institute, 2019 Urban Mobility Report

Freeway Travel Time Index

Measure	1982	1987	1992	1997	2002	2007	2012	2017
Urban Area Index[1]	1.07	1.09	1.12	1.16	1.18	1.20	1.17	1.19
Urban Area Rank[1,2]	35	40	40	36	37	38	50	41

Note: Freeway Travel Time Index—the ratio of travel time in the peak period to the travel time at free-flow conditions. For example, a value of 1.30 indicates a 20-minute free-flow trip takes 26 minutes in the peak (20 minutes x 1.30 = 26 minutes); (1) Covers the Jacksonville FL urban area; (2) Rank is based on 101 larger urban areas (#1 = highest travel time index)
Source: Texas A&M Transportation Institute, 2019 Urban Mobility Report

Public Transportation

Agency Name / Mode of Transportation	Vehicles Operated in Maximum Service[1]	Annual Unlinked Passenger Trips[2] (in thous.)	Annual Passenger Miles[3] (in thous.)
Jacksonville Transportation Authority (JTA)			
Bus (directly operated)	159	9,968.3	60,863.6
Bus (purchased transportation)	6	13.9	202.0
Demand Response (purchased transportation)	126	412.4	4,623.9
Ferryboat (purchased transportation)	1	423.8	190.7
Monorail and Automated Guideway (directly operated)	5	796.1	660.7

Note: (1) Number of revenue vehicles operated by the given mode and type of service to meet the annual maximum service requirement. This is the revenue vehicle count during the peak season of the year; on the week and day that maximum service is provided. Vehicles operated in maximum service (VOMS) exclude atypical days and one-time special events; (2) Number of passengers who boarded public transportation vehicles. Passengers are counted each time they board a vehicle no matter how many vehicles they use to travel from their origin to their destination. (3) Sum of the distances ridden by all passengers during the entire fiscal year.
Source: Federal Transit Administration, National Transit Database, 2019

Air Transportation

Airport Name and Code / Type of Service	Passenger Airlines[1]	Passenger Enplanements	Freight Carriers[2]	Freight (lbs)
Jacksonville International (JAX)				
Domestic service (U.S. carriers - 2020)	23	1,368,514	9	91,630,105
International service (U.S. carriers - 2019)	7	239	0	0

Note: (1) Includes all U.S.-based major, minor and commuter airlines that carried at least one passenger during the year; (2) Includes all U.S.-based airlines and freight carriers that transported at least one pound of freight during the year.
Source: Bureau of Transportation Statistics, The Intermodal Transportation Database, Air Carriers: T-100 Domestic Market (U.S. Carriers), 2020; Bureau of Transportation Statistics, The Intermodal Transportation Database, Air Carriers: T-100 International Market (U.S. Carriers), 2019

BUSINESSES

Major Business Headquarters

Company Name	Industry	Fortune[1]	Forbes[2]
CSX	Railroads	267	-
Crowley Maritime	Transportation	-	193
Fidelity National Financial	Insurance, Property and Casualty (Stock)	375	-
Fidelity National Information Services	Financial Data Services	303	-
Southeastern Grocer	Food Markets	-	52

Note: (1) Companies that produce a 10-K are ranked 1 to 500 based on 2019 revenue; (2) All private companies with at least $2 billion in annual revenue through the end of their most current fiscal year are ranked 1 to 219; companies listed are headquartered in the city; dashes indicate no ranking
Source: Fortune, "Fortune 500," June/July 2020; Forbes, "America's Largest Private Companies," 2020

Fastest-Growing Businesses

According to *Inc.*, Jacksonville is home to three of America's 500 fastest-growing private companies: **BHRS Companies** (#161); **Wellbox** (#201); **Restore Masters Contracting** (#238). Criteria: must be an independent, privately-held, for-profit, U.S. corporation, proprietorship or partnership as of December 31, 2019; revenues must be at least $100,000 in 2016 and $2 million in 2019; must have four-year operating/sales history. *Inc., "America's 500 Fastest-Growing Private Companies," 2020*

Minority Business Opportunity

Jacksonville is home to one company which is on the *Black Enterprise* Industrial/Service list (100 largest companies based on gross sales): **Raven Transport Co.** (#47). Criteria: operational in previous calendar year; at least 51% black-owned and manufactures/owns the product it sells or provides industrial or consumer services. Brokerages, real estate firms and firms that provide professional services are not eligible. *Black Enterprise, B.E. 100s, 2019*

Living Environment

COST OF LIVING

Cost of Living Index

Composite Index	Groceries	Housing	Utilities	Transportation	Health Care	Misc. Goods/Services
91.3	99.9	84.7	98.3	86.6	84.8	93.4

Note: The Cost of Living Index measures regional differences in the cost of consumer goods and services, excluding taxes and non-consumer expenditures, for professional and managerial households in the top income quintile. It is based on more than 50,000 prices covering almost 60 different items for which prices are collected three times a year by chambers of commerce, economic development organizations or university applied economic centers in each participating urban area. The numbers shown should be read as a percentage above or below the national average of 100. For example, a value of 115.4 in the groceries column indicates that grocery prices are 15.4% higher than the national average. Small differences in the index numbers should not be interpreted as significant; Figures cover the Jacksonville FL urban area.
Source: The Council for Community and Economic Research, Cost of Living Index, 2020

Grocery Prices

Area[1]	T-Bone Steak ($/pound)	Frying Chicken ($/pound)	Whole Milk ($/half gal.)	Eggs ($/dozen)	Orange Juice ($/64 oz.)	Coffee ($/11.5 oz.)
City[2]	12.36	1.49	2.21	1.46	3.30	3.86
Avg.	11.78	1.39	2.05	1.47	3.57	4.34
Min.	8.03	0.94	1.03	0.74	2.94	3.02
Max.	15.86	2.65	4.31	3.77	5.44	8.69

Note: (1) Values for the local area are compared with the average, minimum and maximum values for all 284 areas in the Cost of Living Index; (2) Figures cover the Jacksonville FL urban area; **T-Bone Steak** (price per pound); **Frying Chicken** (price per pound, whole fryer); **Whole Milk** (half gallon carton); **Eggs** (price per dozen, Grade A, large); **Orange Juice** (64 oz. Tropicana or Florida Natural); **Coffee** (11.5 oz. can, vacuum-packed, Maxwell House, Hills Bros, or Folgers).
Source: The Council for Community and Economic Research, Cost of Living Index, 2020

Housing and Utility Costs

Area[1]	New Home Price ($)	Apartment Rent ($/month)	All Electric ($/month)	Part Electric ($/month)	Other Energy ($/month)	Telephone ($/month)
City[2]	275,940	1,277	158.65	-	-	188.30
Avg.	368,594	1,168	170.86	100.47	65.28	184.30
Min.	190,567	502	91.58	31.42	26.08	169.60
Max.	2,227,806	4,738	470.38	280.31	280.06	206.50

Note: (1) Values for the local area are compared with the average, minimum and maximum values for all 284 areas in the Cost of Living Index; (2) Figures cover the Jacksonville FL urban area; **New Home Price** (2,400 sf living area, 8,000 sf lot, in urban area with full utilities); **Apartment Rent** (950 sf 2 bedroom/1.5 or 2 bath, unfurnished, excluding all utilities except water); **All Electric** (average monthly cost for an all-electric home); **Part Electric** (average monthly cost for a part-electric home); **Other Energy** (average monthly cost for natural gas, fuel oil, coal, wood, and any other forms of energy except electricity); **Telephone** (price includes the base monthly rate plus taxes and fees for three lines of mobile phone service).
Source: The Council for Community and Economic Research, Cost of Living Index, 2020

Health Care, Transportation, and Other Costs

Area[1]	Doctor ($/visit)	Dentist ($/visit)	Optometrist ($/visit)	Gasoline ($/gallon)	Beauty Salon ($/visit)	Men's Shirt ($)
City[2]	77.42	94.87	70.67	2.20	56.67	23.45
Avg.	115.44	99.32	108.10	2.21	39.27	31.37
Min.	36.68	59.00	51.36	1.71	19.00	11.00
Max.	219.00	153.10	250.97	3.46	82.05	58.33

Note: (1) Values for the local area are compared with the average, minimum and maximum values for all 284 areas in the Cost of Living Index; (2) Figures cover the Jacksonville FL urban area; **Doctor** (general practitioners routine exam of an established patient); **Dentist** (adult teeth cleaning and periodic oral examination); **Optometrist** (full vision eye exam for established adult patient); **Gasoline** (one gallon regular unleaded, national brand, including all taxes, cash price at self-service pump if available); **Beauty Salon** (woman's shampoo, trim, and blow-dry); **Men's Shirt** (cotton/polyester dress shirt, pinpoint weave, long sleeves).
Source: The Council for Community and Economic Research, Cost of Living Index, 2020

HOUSING

Homeownership Rate

Area	2012 (%)	2013 (%)	2014 (%)	2015 (%)	2016 (%)	2017 (%)	2018 (%)	2019 (%)	2020 (%)
MSA[1]	66.6	69.9	65.3	62.5	61.8	65.2	61.4	63.1	64.8
U.S.	65.4	65.1	64.5	63.7	63.4	63.9	64.4	64.6	66.6

Note: (1) Figures cover the Jacksonville, FL Metropolitan Statistical Area
Source: U.S. Census Bureau, Housing Vacancies and Homeownership Annual Statistics: 2012-2020

House Price Index (HPI)

Area	National Ranking[2]	Quarterly Change (%)	One-Year Change (%)	Five-Year Change (%)	Since 1991Q1 (%)
MSA[1]	136	2.34	6.06	43.85	224.14
U.S.[3]	–	3.81	10.77	38.99	205.12

Note: The HPI is a weighted repeat sales index. It measures average price changes in repeat sales or refinancings on the same properties. This information is obtained by reviewing repeat mortgage transactions on single-family properties whose mortgages have been purchased or securitized by Fannie Mae or Freddie Mac since January 1975; (1) Figures cover the Jacksonville, FL Metropolitan Statistical Area; (2) Rankings are based on annual percentage change for all metro areas containing at least 15,000 transactions over the last 10 years and ranges from 1 to 253; (3) figures based on a weighted average of Census Division estimates using a seasonally adjusted, purchase-only index; all figures are for the period ending December 31, 2020
Source: Federal Housing Finance Agency, Change in Metropolitan Area House Price Indexes, April 7, 2021

Median Single-Family Home Prices

Area	2018	2019	2020p	Percent Change 2019 to 2020
MSA[1]	247.0	225.7	279.0	23.6
U.S. Average	261.6	274.6	299.9	9.2

Note: Figures are median sales prices of existing single-family homes in thousands of dollars; (p) preliminary; (1) Figures cover the Jacksonville, FL Metropolitan Statistical Area
Source: National Association of Realtors, Median Sales Price of Existing Single-Family Homes for Metropolitan Areas, 4th Quarter 2020

Qualifying Income Based on Median Sales Price of Existing Single-Family Homes

Area	With 5% Down ($)	With 10% Down ($)	With 20% Down ($)
MSA[1]	54,851	51,964	46,190
U.S. Average	59,266	56,147	49,908

Note: Figures are preliminary; Qualifying income is based on a mortgage rate of 2.81%. Monthly principal and interest payment is limited to 25% of income; (1) Figures cover the Jacksonville, FL Metropolitan Statistical Area
Source: National Association of Realtors, Qualifying Income Based on Median Sales Price of Existing Single-Family Homes for Metropolitan Areas, 4th Quarter 2020

Home Value Distribution

Area	Under $50,000	$50,000 -$99,999	$100,000 -$149,999	$150,000 -$199,999	$200,000 -$299,999	$300,000 -$499,999	$500,000 -$999,999	$1,000,000 or more
City	7.4	15.2	17.4	19.0	24.0	11.9	3.9	1.2
MSA[1]	5.8	12.0	14.1	16.8	24.6	18.1	6.7	1.8
U.S.	6.9	12.0	13.3	14.0	19.6	19.3	11.4	3.4

Note: Figures are percentages and cover owner-occupied housing units; (1) Figures cover the Jacksonville, FL Metropolitan Statistical Area
Source: U.S. Census Bureau, 2015-2019 American Community Survey 5-Year Estimates

Year Housing Structure Built

Area	2010 or Later	2000 -2009	1990 -1999	1980 -1989	1970 -1979	1960 -1969	1950 -1959	1940 -1949	Before 1940	Median Year
City	6.2	19.3	15.3	15.5	12.7	10.0	11.1	4.8	5.1	1984
MSA[1]	8.6	22.7	16.6	16.6	12.4	8.0	8.0	3.4	3.9	1989
U.S.	5.2	14.0	13.9	13.4	15.2	10.6	10.3	4.9	12.6	1978

Note: Figures are percentages except for Median Year; Note: (1) Figures cover the Jacksonville, FL Metropolitan Statistical Area
Source: U.S. Census Bureau, 2015-2019 American Community Survey 5-Year Estimates

Gross Monthly Rent

Area	Under $500	$500 -$999	$1,000 -$1,499	$1,500 -$1,999	$2,000 -$2,499	$2,500 -$2,999	$3,000 and up	Median ($)
City	6.6	36.6	42.2	11.8	2.2	0.3	0.4	1,065
MSA[1]	5.9	34.8	41.3	13.6	3.2	0.7	0.6	1,093
U.S.	9.4	36.2	30.0	14.0	5.6	2.4	2.4	1,062

Note: Figures are percentages except for Median; Gross rent is the contract rent plus the estimated average monthly cost of utilities (electricity, gas, and water and sewer) and fuels (oil, coal, kerosene, wood, etc.) if these are paid by the renter (or paid for the renter by someone else); (1) Figures cover the Jacksonville, FL Metropolitan Statistical Area
Source: U.S. Census Bureau, 2015-2019 American Community Survey 5-Year Estimates

HEALTH

Health Risk Factors

Category	MSA[1] (%)	U.S. (%)
Adults aged 18–64 who have any kind of health care coverage	85.9	87.3
Adults who reported being in good or better health	78.0	82.4
Adults who have been told they have high blood cholesterol	34.1	33.0
Adults who have been told they have high blood pressure	36.1	32.3
Adults who are current smokers	18.4	17.1
Adults who currently use E-cigarettes	3.6	4.6
Adults who currently use chewing tobacco, snuff, or snus	3.4	4.0
Adults who are heavy drinkers[2]	6.6	6.3
Adults who are binge drinkers[3]	17.3	17.4
Adults who are overweight (BMI 25.0 - 29.9)	33.5	35.3
Adults who are obese (BMI 30.0 - 99.8)	33.2	31.3
Adults who participated in any physical activities in the past month	70.3	74.4
Adults who always or nearly always wears a seat belt	95.3	94.3

Note: (1) Figures cover the Jacksonville, FL Metropolitan Statistical Area; (2) Heavy drinkers are classified as adult men having more than 14 drinks per week and adult women having more than 7 drinks per week; (3) Binge drinkers are classified as males having five or more drinks on one occasion or females having four or more drinks on one occasion
Source: Centers for Disease Control and Prevention, Behaviorial Risk Factor Surveillance System, SMART: Selected Metropolitan Area Risk Trends, 2017

Acute and Chronic Health Conditions

Category	MSA[1] (%)	U.S. (%)
Adults who have ever been told they had a heart attack	3.9	4.2
Adults who have ever been told they have angina or coronary heart disease	5.5	3.9
Adults who have ever been told they had a stroke	2.9	3.0
Adults who have ever been told they have asthma	16.2	14.2
Adults who have ever been told they have arthritis	27.7	24.9
Adults who have ever been told they have diabetes[2]	12.7	10.5
Adults who have ever been told they had skin cancer	8.8	6.2
Adults who have ever been told they had any other types of cancer	7.4	7.1
Adults who have ever been told they have COPD	11.3	6.5
Adults who have ever been told they have kidney disease	3.5	3.0
Adults who have ever been told they have a form of depression	22.5	20.5

Note: (1) Figures cover the Jacksonville, FL Metropolitan Statistical Area; (2) Figures do not include pregnancy-related, borderline, or pre-diabetes
Source: Centers for Disease Control and Prevention, Behaviorial Risk Factor Surveillance System, SMART: Selected Metropolitan Area Risk Trends, 2017

Health Screening and Vaccination Rates

Category	MSA[1] (%)	U.S. (%)
Adults aged 65+ who have had flu shot within the past year	65.3	60.7
Adults aged 65+ who have ever had a pneumonia vaccination	74.1	75.4
Adults who have ever been tested for HIV	54.7	36.1
Adults who have ever had the shingles or zoster vaccine?	29.6	28.9
Adults who have had their blood cholesterol checked within the last five years	89.4	85.9

Note: n/a not available; (1) Figures cover the Jacksonville, FL Metropolitan Statistical Area.
Source: Centers for Disease Control and Prevention, Behaviorial Risk Factor Surveillance System, SMART: Selected Metropolitan Area Risk Trends, 2017

Disability Status

Category	MSA[1] (%)	U.S. (%)
Adults who reported being deaf	7.1	6.7
Are you blind or have serious difficulty seeing, even when wearing glasses?	5.5	4.5
Are you limited in any way in any of your usual activities due of arthritis?	14.1	12.9
Do you have difficulty doing errands alone?	9.9	6.8
Do you have difficulty dressing or bathing?	4.1	3.6
Do you have serious difficulty concentrating/remembering/making decisions?	14.6	10.7
Do you have serious difficulty walking or climbing stairs?	17.2	13.6

Note: (1) Figures cover the Jacksonville, FL Metropolitan Statistical Area.
Source: Centers for Disease Control and Prevention, Behaviorial Risk Factor Surveillance System, SMART: Selected Metropolitan Area Risk Trends, 2017

Mortality Rates for the Top 10 Causes of Death in the U.S.

ICD-10[a] Sub-Chapter	ICD-10[a] Code	Age-Adjusted Mortality Rate[1] per 100,000 population County[2]	U.S.
Malignant neoplasms	C00-C97	172.3	149.2
Ischaemic heart diseases	I20-I25	94.2	90.5
Other forms of heart disease	I30-I51	51.8	52.2
Chronic lower respiratory diseases	J40-J47	42.4	39.6
Other degenerative diseases of the nervous system	G30-G31	40.9	37.6
Cerebrovascular diseases	I60-I69	54.5	37.2
Other external causes of accidental injury	W00-X59	55.7	36.1
Organic, including symptomatic, mental disorders	F01-F09	36.9	29.4
Hypertensive diseases	I10-I15	30.0	24.1
Diabetes mellitus	E10-E14	24.7	21.5

Note: (a) ICD-10 = International Classification of Diseases 10th Revision; (1) Mortality rates are a three-year average covering 2017-2019; (2) Figures cover Duval County.
Source: Centers for Disease Control and Prevention, National Center for Health Statistics. Underlying Cause of Death 1999-2019 on CDC WONDER Online Database

Mortality Rates for Selected Causes of Death

ICD-10[a] Sub-Chapter	ICD-10[a] Code	Age-Adjusted Mortality Rate[1] per 100,000 population County[2]	U.S.
Assault	X85-Y09	14.6	6.0
Diseases of the liver	K70-K76	18.2	14.4
Human immunodeficiency virus (HIV) disease	B20-B24	4.7	1.5
Influenza and pneumonia	J09-J18	13.2	13.8
Intentional self-harm	X60-X84	17.0	14.1
Malnutrition	E40-E46	4.6	2.3
Obesity and other hyperalimentation	E65-E68	2.8	2.1
Renal failure	N17-N19	16.9	12.6
Transport accidents	V01-V99	16.4	12.3
Viral hepatitis	B15-B19	1.5	1.2

Note: (a) ICD-10 = International Classification of Diseases 10th Revision; (1) Mortality rates are a three-year average covering 2017-2019; (2) Figures cover Duval County; Data are suppressed when the data meet the criteria for confidentiality constraints; Mortality rates are flagged as unreliable when the rate would be calculated with a numerator of 20 or less.
Source: Centers for Disease Control and Prevention, National Center for Health Statistics. Underlying Cause of Death 1999-2019 on CDC WONDER Online Database

Health Insurance Coverage

Area	With Health Insurance	With Private Health Insurance	With Public Health Insurance	Without Health Insurance	Population Under Age 19 Without Health Insurance
City	88.0	64.7	33.9	12.0	6.8
MSA[1]	89.1	68.7	32.7	10.9	6.6
U.S.	91.2	67.9	35.1	8.8	5.1

Note: Figures are percentages that cover the civilian noninstitutionalized population; (1) Figures cover the Jacksonville, FL Metropolitan Statistical Area
Source: U.S. Census Bureau, 2015-2019 American Community Survey 5-Year Estimates

Number of Medical Professionals

Area	MDs[3]	DOs[3,4]	Dentists	Podiatrists	Chiropractors	Optometrists
County[1] (number)	3,331	217	798	80	239	155
County[1] (rate[2])	351.1	22.9	83.3	8.4	25.0	16.2
U.S. (rate[2])	282.9	22.7	71.2	6.2	28.1	16.9

12031
Note: Data as of 2019 unless noted; (1) Data covers Duval County; (2) Rate per 100,000 population; (3) Data as of 2018 and includes all active, non-federal physicians; (4) Doctor of Osteopathic Medicine
Source: U.S. Department of Health and Human Services, Health Resources and Services Administration, Bureau of Health Professions, Area Resource File (ARF) 2019-2020

Best Hospitals

According to *U.S. News,* the Jacksonville, FL metro area is home to three of the best hospitals in the U.S.: **Baptist Medical Center Jacksonville** (1 adult specialty and 3 pediatric specialties); **Mayo Clinic-Jacksonville** (7 adult specialties); **UF Health Jacksonville** (1 adult specialty). The hospitals listed were nationally ranked in at least one of 16 adult or 10 pediatric specialties. Only 134 hospitals nationwide were nationally ranked in one or more adult or pediatric specialty; this number increases to 178 counting specialized centers within hospitals. Twenty hospitals in the U.S. made the Honor Roll. The Best Hospitals Honor Roll takes both the national rankings and the procedure and condition ratings into account. Hospitals received points if they were nationally ranked in one of the 16 adult specialties—the higher they ranked, the more points they got—and how many ratings of "high performing" they earned in the 10 procedures and conditions. *U.S. News Online, "America's Best Hospitals 2020-21"*

According to *U.S. News*, the Jacksonville, FL metro area is home to one of the best children's hospitals in the U.S.: **Wolfson Children's Hospital** (3 pediatric specialties). The hospital listed was highly ranked in at least one of 10 pediatric specialties. Eighty-eight children's hospitals in the U.S. were nationally ranked in at least one specialty. Hospitals received points for being ranked in a specialty, and the 10 hospitals with the most points across the 10 specialties make up the Honor Roll. *U.S. News Online, "America's Best Children's Hospitals 2020-21"*

EDUCATION

Public School District Statistics

District Name	Schls	Pupils	Pupil/Teacher Ratio	Minority Pupils[1] (%)	Free Lunch Eligible[2] (%)	IEP[3] (%)
Duval	205	130,229	18.4	66.4	48.4	15.7

Note: Table includes school districts with 2,000 or more students; (1) Percentage of students that are not non-Hispanic white; (2) Percentage of students that are eligible for the free lunch program; (3) Percentage of students that have an Individualized Education Program.
Source: U.S. Department of Education, National Center for Education Statistics, Common Core of Data, Local Education Agency (School District) Universe Survey: School Year 2018-2019; U.S. Department of Education, National Center for Education Statistics, Common Core of Data, Public Elementary/Secondary School Universe Survey: School Year 2018-2019

Best High Schools

According to *U.S. News*, Jacksonville is home to four of the top 500 high schools in the U.S.: **Stanton College Preparatory School** (#62); **Paxon School/Advanced Studies** (#195); **Darnell Cookman Middle/High School** (#250); **Douglas Anderson School of the Arts** (#261). Nearly 18,000 public, magnet and charter schools were ranked based on their performance on state assessments and how well they prepare students for college. *U.S. News & World Report, "Best High Schools 2020"*

Highest Level of Education

Area	Less than H.S.	H.S. Diploma	Some College, No Deg.	Associate Degree	Bachelor's Degree	Master's Degree	Prof. School Degree	Doctorate Degree
City	10.5	28.4	22.3	10.1	19.1	7.0	1.7	0.8
MSA[1]	9.1	27.7	21.8	10.0	20.6	7.9	1.9	1.1
U.S.	12.0	27.0	20.4	8.5	19.8	8.8	2.1	1.4

Note: Figures cover persons age 25 and over; (1) Figures cover the Jacksonville, FL Metropolitan Statistical Area
Source: U.S. Census Bureau, 2015-2019 American Community Survey 5-Year Estimates

Educational Attainment by Race

Area	High School Graduate or Higher (%)						Bachelor's Degree or Higher (%)				
	Total	White	Black	Asian	Hisp.[2]	Total	White	Black	Asian	Hisp.[2]
City	89.5	91.0	86.7	88.7	82.3	28.6	31.5	19.1	49.5	24.6
MSA[1]	90.9	92.2	87.2	89.4	84.3	31.4	33.8	19.7	49.7	27.0
U.S.	88.0	89.9	86.0	87.1	68.7	32.1	33.5	21.6	54.3	16.4

Note: Figures shown cover persons 25 years old and over; (1) Figures cover the Jacksonville, FL Metropolitan Statistical Area; (2) People of Hispanic origin can be of any race
Source: U.S. Census Bureau, 2015-2019 American Community Survey 5-Year Estimates

School Enrollment by Grade and Control

Area	Preschool (%)		Kindergarten (%)		Grades 1 - 4 (%)		Grades 5 - 8 (%)		Grades 9 - 12 (%)	
	Public	Private	Public	Private	Public	Private	Public	Private	Public	Private
City	57.5	42.5	84.3	15.7	84.3	15.7	81.7	18.3	83.5	16.5
MSA[1]	55.1	44.9	86.2	13.8	86.3	13.7	84.3	15.7	86.7	13.3
U.S.	59.1	40.9	87.6	12.4	89.5	10.5	89.4	10.6	90.1	9.9

Note: Figures shown cover persons 3 years old and over; (1) Figures cover the Jacksonville, FL Metropolitan Statistical Area
Source: U.S. Census Bureau, 2015-2019 American Community Survey 5-Year Estimates

Higher Education

Four-Year Colleges			Two-Year Colleges			Medical Schools[1]	Law Schools[2]	Voc/ Tech[3]
Public	Private Non-profit	Private For-profit	Public	Private Non-profit	Private For-profit			
2	3	2	0	1	2	0	1	9

Note: Figures cover institutions located within the city limits and include main campuses only; (1) includes schools accredited by the Liaison Committee on Medical Education and the American Osteopathic Association's Commission on Osteopathic College Accreditation; (2) includes ABA-accredited schools, schools with provisional ABA accreditation, and state accredited schools; (3) includes all schools with programs that are less than 2 years.
Source: National Center for Education Statistics, Integrated Postsecondary Education System (IPEDS), 2019-20; Wikipedia, List of Medical Schools in the United States, accessed April 2, 2021; Wikipedia, List of Law Schools in the United States, accessed April 2, 2021

EMPLOYERS

Major Employers

Company Name	Industry
Bank of America, Merrill Lynch	Financial services
Baptist Health	Healthcare
Citi	Financial services
Fleet Readiness Center SE	Aviation & aerospace
Florida Blue	Financial services
Mayo Clinic	Healthcare
St. Vincent's Medical Center - Riverside	Healthcare
UF Health	Healthcare

Note: Companies shown are located within the Jacksonville, FL Metropolitan Statistical Area.
Source: Hoovers.com; Wikipedia

Best Companies to Work For

Suddath; VyStar Credit Union, headquartered in Jacksonville, are among the "100 Best Places to Work in IT." To qualify, companies had to be U.S.-based organizations or be non-U.S.-based employers that met the following criteria: have a minimum of 300 total employees at a U.S. headquarters and a minimum of 30 IT employees in the U.S., with at least 50% of their IT employees based in the U.S. The best places to work were selected based on compensation, benefits, work/life balance, employee morale, and satisfaction with training and development programs. In addition, *InsiderPro* and *Computerworld* looked at retention efforts, programs for recognizing and rewarding outstanding performances, and benefits such as flextime, elder care and child care, and reimbursement for college tuition and the cost of pursuing technology certifications. *InsiderPro and Computerworld, "100 Best Places to Work in IT," 2020*

PUBLIC SAFETY

Crime Rate

Area	All Crimes	Violent Crimes				Property Crimes		
		Murder	Rape[3]	Robbery	Aggrav. Assault	Burglary	Larceny -Theft	Motor Vehicle Theft
City	3,956.9	14.2	60.9	142.3	430.0	539.6	2,460.9	309.0
Suburbs[1]	1,592.3	2.2	35.2	25.3	166.6	235.0	1,031.9	96.1
Metro[2]	2,980.1	9.2	50.3	94.0	321.2	413.8	1,870.6	221.0
U.S.	2,489.3	5.0	42.6	81.6	250.2	340.5	1,549.5	219.9

Note: Figures are crimes per 100,000 population; (1) All areas within the metro area that are located outside the city limits; (2) Figures cover the Jacksonville, FL Metropolitan Statistical Area; (3) All figures shown were reported using the revised Uniform Crime Reporting (UCR) definition of rape.
Source: FBI Uniform Crime Reports, 2019

Hate Crimes

Area	Number of Quarters Reported	Number of Incidents per Bias Motivation					
		Race/Ethnicity/ Ancestry	Religion	Sexual Orientation	Disability	Gender	Gender Identity
City	4	4	0	0	0	0	0
U.S.	4	3,963	1,521	1,195	157	69	198

Source: Federal Bureau of Investigation, Hate Crime Statistics 2019

Identity Theft Consumer Reports

Area	Reports	Reports per 100,000 Population	Rank[2]
MSA[1]	5,799	372	83
U.S.	1,387,615	423	-

Note: (1) Figures cover the Jacksonville, FL Metropolitan Statistical Area; (2) Rank ranges from 1 to 391 where 1 indicates greatest number of identity theft reports per 100,000 population
Source: Federal Trade Commission, Consumer Sentinel Network Data Book 2020

Fraud and Other Consumer Reports

Area	Reports	Reports per 100,000 Population	Rank[2]
MSA[1]	17,719	1,136	9
U.S.	3,385,133	1,031	-

Note: (1) Figures cover the Jacksonville, FL Metropolitan Statistical Area; (2) Rank ranges from 1 to 391 where 1 indicates greatest number of fraud and other consumer reports per 100,000 population
Source: Federal Trade Commission, Consumer Sentinel Network Data Book 2020

POLITICS

2020 Presidential Election Results

Area	Biden	Trump	Jorgensen	Hawkins	Other
Duval County	51.1	47.3	1.0	0.2	0.5
U.S.	51.3	46.8	1.2	0.3	0.5

Note: Results are percentages and may not add to 100% due to rounding
Source: Dave Leip's Atlas of U.S. Presidential Elections

SPORTS

Professional Sports Teams

Team Name	League	Year Established
Jacksonville Jaguars	National Football League (NFL)	1995

Note: Includes teams located in the Jacksonville, FL Metropolitan Statistical Area.
Source: Wikipedia, Major Professional Sports Teams of the United States and Canada, April 6, 2021

CLIMATE

Average and Extreme Temperatures

Temperature	Jan	Feb	Mar	Apr	May	Jun	Jul	Aug	Sep	Oct	Nov	Dec	Yr.
Extreme High (°F)	84	88	91	95	100	103	103	102	98	96	88	84	103
Average High (°F)	65	68	74	80	86	90	92	91	87	80	73	67	79
Average Temp. (°F)	54	57	62	69	75	80	83	82	79	71	62	56	69
Average Low (°F)	43	45	51	57	64	70	73	73	70	61	51	44	58
Extreme Low (°F)	7	22	23	34	45	47	61	63	48	36	21	11	7

Note: Figures cover the years 1948-1990
Source: National Climatic Data Center, International Station Meteorological Climate Summary, 9/96

Average Precipitation/Snowfall/Humidity

Precip./Humidity	Jan	Feb	Mar	Apr	May	Jun	Jul	Aug	Sep	Oct	Nov	Dec	Yr.
Avg. Precip. (in.)	3.0	3.7	3.8	3.0	3.6	5.3	6.2	7.4	7.8	3.7	2.0	2.6	52.0
Avg. Snowfall (in.)	Tr	Tr	Tr	0	0	0	0	0	0	0	0	Tr	0
Avg. Rel. Hum. 7am (%)	86	86	87	86	86	88	89	91	92	91	89	88	88
Avg. Rel. Hum. 4pm (%)	56	53	50	49	54	61	64	65	66	62	58	58	58

Note: Figures cover the years 1948-1990; Tr = Trace amounts (<0.05 in. of rain; <0.5 in. of snow)
Source: National Climatic Data Center, International Station Meteorological Climate Summary, 9/96

Weather Conditions

Temperature			Daytime Sky			Precipitation		
10°F & below	32°F & below	90°F & above	Clear	Partly cloudy	Cloudy	0.01 inch or more precip.	0.1 inch or more snow/ice	Thunderstorms
< 1	16	83	86	181	98	114	1	65

Note: Figures are average number of days per year and cover the years 1948-1990
Source: National Climatic Data Center, International Station Meteorological Climate Summary, 9/96

HAZARDOUS WASTE

Superfund Sites

The Jacksonville, FL metro area is home to four sites on the EPA's Superfund National Priorities List: **Jacksonville Naval Air Station** (final); **Kerr-Mcgee Chemical Corp - Jacksonville** (final); **Pickettville Road Landfill** (final); **USN Air Station Cecil Field** (final). There are a total of 1,375 Superfund sites with a status of proposed or final on the list in the U.S. *U.S. Environmental Protection Agency, National Priorities List, April 7, 2021*

AIR QUALITY

Air Quality Trends: Ozone

	1990	1995	2000	2005	2010	2015	2016	2017	2018	2019
MSA[1]	0.080	0.068	0.072	0.076	0.068	0.060	0.057	0.059	0.060	0.062
U.S.	0.088	0.089	0.082	0.080	0.073	0.068	0.069	0.068	0.069	0.065

Note: (1) Data covers the Jacksonville, FL Metropolitan Statistical Area. The values shown are the composite ozone concentration averages among trend sites based on the highest fourth daily maximum 8-hour concentration in parts per million. These trends are based on sites having an adequate record of monitoring data during the trend period. Data from exceptional events are included.
Source: U.S. Environmental Protection Agency, Air Quality Monitoring Information, "Air Quality Trends by City, 1990-2019"

Air Quality Index

Area	Percent of Days when Air Quality was...[2]					AQI Statistics[2]	
	Good	Moderate	Unhealthy for Sensitive Groups	Unhealthy	Very Unhealthy	Maximum	Median
MSA[1]	67.1	32.6	0.3	0.0	0.0	114	43

Note: (1) Data covers the Jacksonville, FL Metropolitan Statistical Area; (2) Based on 365 days with AQI data in 2019. Air Quality Index (AQI) is an index for reporting daily air quality. EPA calculates the AQI for five major air pollutants regulated by the Clean Air Act: ground-level ozone, particle pollution (aka particulate matter), carbon monoxide, sulfur dioxide, and nitrogen dioxide. The AQI runs from 0 to 500. The higher the AQI value, the greater the level of air pollution and the greater the health concern. There are six AQI categories: "Good" AQI is between 0 and 50. Air quality is considered satisfactory; "Moderate" AQI is between 51 and 100. Air quality is acceptable; "Unhealthy for Sensitive Groups" When AQI values are between 101 and 150, members of sensitive groups may experience health effects; "Unhealthy" When AQI values are between 151 and 200 everyone may begin to experience health effects; "Very Unhealthy" AQI values between 201 and 300 trigger a health alert; "Hazardous" AQI values over 300 trigger warnings of emergency conditions (not shown).
Source: U.S. Environmental Protection Agency, Air Quality Index Report, 2019

Air Quality Index Pollutants

Area	Percent of Days when AQI Pollutant was...[2]					
	Carbon Monoxide	Nitrogen Dioxide	Ozone	Sulfur Dioxide	Particulate Matter 2.5	Particulate Matter 10
MSA[1]	0.0	0.0	48.2	2.7	49.0	0.0

Note: (1) Data covers the Jacksonville, FL Metropolitan Statistical Area; (2) Based on 365 days with AQI data in 2019. The Air Quality Index (AQI) is an index for reporting daily air quality. EPA calculates the AQI for five major air pollutants regulated by the Clean Air Act: ground-level ozone, particle pollution (also known as particulate matter), carbon monoxide, sulfur dioxide, and nitrogen dioxide. The AQI runs from 0 to 500. The higher the AQI value, the greater the level of air pollution and the greater the health concern.
Source: U.S. Environmental Protection Agency, Air Quality Index Report, 2019

Maximum Air Pollutant Concentrations: Particulate Matter, Ozone, CO and Lead

	Particulate Matter 10 (ug/m³)	Particulate Matter 2.5 Wtd AM (ug/m³)	Particulate Matter 2.5 24-Hr (ug/m³)	Ozone (ppm)	Carbon Monoxide (ppm)	Lead (ug/m³)
MSA[1] Level	57	8.6	20	0.065	1	n/a
NAAQS[2]	150	15	35	0.075	9	0.15
Met NAAQS[2]	Yes	Yes	Yes	Yes	Yes	n/a

Note: (1) Data covers the Jacksonville, FL Metropolitan Statistical Area; Data from exceptional events are included; (2) National Ambient Air Quality Standards; ppm = parts per million; ug/m³ = micrograms per cubic meter; n/a not available.
Concentrations: Particulate Matter 10 (coarse particulate)—highest second maximum 24-hour concentration; Particulate Matter 2.5 Wtd AM (fine particulate)—highest weighted annual mean concentration; Particulate Matter 2.5 24-Hour (fine particulate)—highest 98th percentile 24-hour concentration; Ozone—highest fourth daily maximum 8-hour concentration; Carbon Monoxide—highest second maximum non-overlapping 8-hour concentration; Lead—maximum running 3-month average
Source: U.S. Environmental Protection Agency, Air Quality Monitoring Information, "Air Quality Statistics by City, 2019"

Maximum Air Pollutant Concentrations: Nitrogen Dioxide and Sulfur Dioxide

	Nitrogen Dioxide AM (ppb)	Nitrogen Dioxide 1-Hr (ppb)	Sulfur Dioxide AM (ppb)	Sulfur Dioxide 1-Hr (ppb)	Sulfur Dioxide 24-Hr (ppb)
MSA[1] Level	11	39	n/a	41	n/a
NAAQS[2]	53	100	30	75	140
Met NAAQS[2]	Yes	Yes	n/a	Yes	n/a

Note: (1) Data covers the Jacksonville, FL Metropolitan Statistical Area; Data from exceptional events are included; (2) National Ambient Air Quality Standards; ppm = parts per million; ug/m³ = micrograms per cubic meter; n/a not available.
Concentrations: Nitrogen Dioxide AM—highest arithmetic mean concentration; Nitrogen Dioxide 1-Hr—highest 98th percentile 1-hour daily maximum concentration; Sulfur Dioxide AM—highest annual mean concentration; Sulfur Dioxide 1-Hr—highest 99th percentile 1-hour daily maximum concentration; Sulfur Dioxide 24-Hr—highest second maximum 24-hour concentration
Source: U.S. Environmental Protection Agency, Air Quality Monitoring Information, "Air Quality Statistics by City, 2019"

Lafayette, Louisiana

Background

Lafayette's cultural origins originated far north of the city, to Nova Scotia, Canada. In 1755, the British governor, Charles Lawrence, expelled the entire population of Canadians known as the Acadians, whose roots were French and Catholic, when they refused to pledge loyalty to the British crown. Many lost their lives in their quest for a new home, as they settled all along the eastern seaboard of the United States. A large majority of Acadians settled in southern Louisiana, in the area surrounding New Orleans.

Prior to the Acadian expulsion, southern Louisiana had remained fairly unsettled. The first known inhabitants were the Attakapas, a much-feared and brutal tribe of Native Americans. A sparse population of French trappers, traders, and ranchers occupied the region until the Spanish occupation of 1766. The 1789 French Revolution brought teams of French immigrants fleeing the brutal conditions at home. In 1803, the French sold the Louisiana territory to the United States—a transaction known as the Louisiana Purchase.

The most important early event for Lafayette was the donation of land by an Acadian named Jean Mouton, to the Catholic Church. The population began to grow in the parish then known as St. John the Evangelist of Vermillion. Lafayette's original name was Vermillionville, but it was renamed in 1884 in honor of the French Marquis de Lafayette, a Frenchman who fought under General George Washington in the American Revolution. Lafayette has been credited with bringing some of the ideals of the American Revolution to the French, partly precipitating the French Revolution. By his death, Lafayette had visited all 24 of the United States, and was an American citizen.

The word "cajun," is derived from the early Acadian settlers. In French, "Les Acadians" became "le Cadiens," which later became just "'Cadien." The French pronunciation was difficult for non-French Americans to say, so Cadien became Cajun. A primary characteristic of the Acadian/Cajun culture is what's known as "joie de vivre"—joy of living. The Cajun reputation is one of hard work and hard play, full of passion that can turn on a dime. Their greatest contribution to the fabric of America has been their food and their music—both are decidedly spicy.

Geographically, Lafayette is about 40 miles north of the Gulf of Mexico, and 100 miles west of New Orleans. The city is often referred to as the center of Cajun culture not because of its geography, but because of the strong Cajun influence in everyday life. Celebration is a major part of the Cajun culture, and this is reflected in Lafayette's many festivals and cultural traditions. The most famous of dozens of annual festivals is Mari Gras. The Festival International de Louisiana celebrates the French-speaking heritage of much of the population. Festival Acadians celebrates everything that is uniquely Cajun.

The 2018 Christmas film *The Christmas Contract* was set in the city.

While Lafayette is known for its oil and natural gas industries, with over 600 oil-related businesses in Lafayette Parish alone, jobs in healthcare are not far behind. Education is also a big industry in Lafayette, home of the University of Louisiana's Ragin' Cajuns. UL started out as a small agricultural college with about 100 students, and today, over 17,000 students roam the 1,300-acre campus. It is the second largest public university in the state. The university's main focus is hands-on research—dubbed "research for a reason"—meaning that all students are given the opportunity to have a meaningful impact in their area of study. The University of Louisiana is considered among the top universities in computer science, engineering and nursing.

Lafayette's climate is humid and subtropical. It is typical of areas along the Gulf of Mexico with hot, humid summers and mild winters.

Rankings

Business/Finance Rankings

- The Lafayette metro area appeared on the Milken Institute "2021 Best Performing Cities" list. Rank: #176 out of 200 large metro areas (population over 250,000). Criteria: job growth; wage and salary growth; high-tech output growth; housing affordability; household broadband access. *Milken Institute, "Best-Performing Cities 2021," February 16, 2021*

- *Forbes* ranked the 200 most populous metro areas to determine the nation's "Best Places for Business and Careers." The Lafayette metro area was ranked #194. Criteria: costs (business and living); job growth (past and projected); income growth; quality of life; educational attainment (college and high school); projected economic growth; cultural and leisure opportunities; workplace tolerance laws; net migration patterns. *Forbes, "The Best Places for Business and Careers 2019: Seattle Still On Top," October 30, 2019*

Education Rankings

- Personal finance website *WalletHub* analyzed the 150 largest U.S. metropolitan statistical areas to determine where the most educated Americans are putting their degrees to work. Criteria: education levels; percentage of workers with degrees; education quality and attainment gap; public school quality rankings; quality and enrollment of each metro area's universities. Lafayette was ranked #136 (#1 = most educated city). *www.WalletHub.com, "Most and Least Educated Cities in America," July 20, 2020*

Environmental Rankings

- Lafayette was highlighted as one of the top 98 cleanest metro areas for short-term particle pollution (24-hour PM 2.5) in the U.S. during 2016 through 2018. Monitors in these cities reported no days with unhealthful PM 2.5 levels. *American Lung Association, "State of the Air 2020," April 21, 2020*

Safety Rankings

- The National Insurance Crime Bureau ranked 384 metro areas in the U.S. in terms of per capita rates of vehicle theft. The Lafayette metro area ranked #194 (#1 = highest rate). Criteria: number of vehicle theft offenses per 100,000 inhabitants in 2019. *National Insurance Crime Bureau, "Hot Spots 2019," July 21, 2020*

Seniors/Retirement Rankings

- From its Best Cities for Successful Aging indexes, the Milken Institute generated rankings for metropolitan areas, weighing data in nine categories—health care, wellness, living arrangements, transportation and convenience, financial characteristics, education, employment, community engagement, and overall livability. The Lafayette metro area was ranked #85 overall in the small metro area category. *Milken Institute, "Best Cities for Successful Aging, 2017" March 14, 2017*

Business Environment

DEMOGRAPHICS

Population Growth

Area	1990 Census	2000 Census	2010 Census	2019* Estimate	Population Growth (%) 1990-2019	Population Growth (%) 2010-2019
City	104,735	110,257	120,623	126,666	20.9	5.0
MSA[1]	208,740	239,086	273,738	489,914	134.7	79.0
U.S.	248,709,873	281,421,906	308,745,538	324,697,795	30.6	5.2

Note: (1) Figures cover the Lafayette, LA Metropolitan Statistical Area; (*) 2015-2019 5-year estimated population
Source: U.S. Census Bureau, 1990 Census, Census 2000, Census 2010, 2015-2019 American Community Survey 5-Year Estimates

Household Size

Area	One	Two	Three	Four	Five	Six	Seven or More	Average Household Size
City	35.2	34.5	13.9	9.6	4.0	1.8	1.0	2.40
MSA[1]	26.9	34.1	16.7	13.0	6.2	2.2	1.0	2.70
U.S.	27.9	33.9	15.6	12.9	6.0	2.3	1.4	2.60

Note: (1) Figures cover the Lafayette, LA Metropolitan Statistical Area
Source: U.S. Census Bureau, 2015-2019 American Community Survey 5-Year Estimates

Race

Area	White Alone[2] (%)	Black Alone[2] (%)	Asian Alone[2] (%)	AIAN[3] Alone[2] (%)	NHOPI[4] Alone[2] (%)	Other Race Alone[2] (%)	Two or More Races (%)
City	64.0	30.9	2.2	0.3	0.0	0.6	2.1
MSA[1]	70.6	24.6	1.7	0.3	0.0	0.8	2.0
U.S.	72.5	12.7	5.5	0.8	0.2	4.9	3.3

Note: (1) Figures cover the Lafayette, LA Metropolitan Statistical Area; (2) Alone is defined as not being in combination with one or more other races; (3) American Indian and Alaska Native; (4) Native Hawaiian and Other Pacific Islander
Source: U.S. Census Bureau, 2015-2019 American Community Survey 5-Year Estimates

Hispanic or Latino Origin

Area	Total (%)	Mexican (%)	Puerto Rican (%)	Cuban (%)	Other (%)
City	3.6	1.4	0.2	0.2	1.7
MSA[1]	4.0	2.1	0.2	0.2	1.5
U.S.	18.0	11.2	1.7	0.7	4.3

Note: Persons of Hispanic or Latino origin can be of any race; (1) Figures cover the Lafayette, LA Metropolitan Statistical Area
Source: U.S. Census Bureau, 2015-2019 American Community Survey 5-Year Estimates

Ancestry

Area	German	Irish	English	American	Italian	Polish	French[2]	Scottish	Dutch
City	7.4	5.5	5.7	6.4	3.8	0.4	17.8	1.1	0.5
MSA[1]	6.3	4.2	3.8	9.0	2.4	0.4	18.4	0.7	0.3
U.S.	13.3	9.7	7.2	6.2	5.1	2.8	2.3	1.7	1.2

Note: Figures are the percentage of the total population reporting a particular ancestry. The nine most commonly reported ancestries in the U.S. are shown. Figures include multiple ancestries (e.g. if a person reported being Irish and Italian, they were included in both columns); (1) Figures cover the Lafayette, LA Metropolitan Statistical Area; (2) Excludes Basque
Source: U.S. Census Bureau, 2015-2019 American Community Survey 5-Year Estimates

Foreign-born Population

Area	Any Foreign Country	Asia	Mexico	Europe	Caribbean	Central America[2]	South America	Africa	Canada
City	4.3	1.8	0.5	0.7	0.2	0.4	0.2	0.2	0.1
MSA[1]	3.3	1.2	0.7	0.3	0.2	0.5	0.1	0.2	0.1
U.S.	13.6	4.2	3.5	1.5	1.3	1.1	1.0	0.7	0.2

Note: (1) Figures cover the Lafayette, LA Metropolitan Statistical Area; (2) Excludes Mexico.
Source: U.S. Census Bureau, 2015-2019 American Community Survey 5-Year Estimates

Lafayette, Louisiana

Marital Status

Area	Never Married	Now Married[2]	Separated	Widowed	Divorced
City	42.2	38.8	1.7	6.0	11.2
MSA[1]	34.7	46.2	1.9	6.0	11.3
U.S.	33.4	48.1	1.9	5.8	10.9

Note: Figures are percentages and cover the population 15 years of age and older; (1) Figures cover the Lafayette, LA Metropolitan Statistical Area; (2) Excludes separated
Source: U.S. Census Bureau, 2015-2019 American Community Survey 5-Year Estimates

Disability by Age

Area	All Ages	Under 18 Years Old	18 to 64 Years Old	65 Years and Over
City	12.4	3.7	10.7	32.7
MSA[1]	14.5	5.0	12.9	39.1
U.S.	12.6	4.2	10.3	34.5

Note: Figures show percent of the civilian noninstitutionalized population that reported having a disability. Disability status is determined from six types of difficulty: vision, hearing, cognitive, ambulatory, self-care, and independent living. For children under 5 years old, hearing and vision difficulty are used to determine disability status. For children between the ages of 5 and 14, disability status is determined from hearing, vision, cognitive, ambulatory, and self-care difficulties. For people aged 15 years and older, they are considered to have a disability if they have difficulty with any one of the six difficulty types; Note: (1) Figures cover the Lafayette, LA Metropolitan Statistical Area
Source: U.S. Census Bureau, 2015-2019 American Community Survey 5-Year Estimates

Age

Area	Under Age 5	Age 5–19	Age 20–34	Age 35–44	Age 45–54	Age 55–64	Age 65–74	Age 75–84	Age 85+	Median Age
City	5.7	18.5	24.4	11.5	11.5	13.5	8.9	4.2	1.7	35.8
MSA[1]	6.9	20.2	21.3	12.6	12.4	12.9	8.1	4.0	1.6	36.0
U.S.	6.1	19.1	20.7	12.6	13.0	12.9	9.1	4.6	1.9	38.1

Note: (1) Figures cover the Lafayette, LA Metropolitan Statistical Area
Source: U.S. Census Bureau, 2015-2019 American Community Survey 5-Year Estimates

Gender

Area	Males	Females	Males per 100 Females
City	61,742	64,924	95.1
MSA[1]	238,957	250,957	95.2
U.S.	159,886,919	164,810,876	97.0

Note: (1) Figures cover the Lafayette, LA Metropolitan Statistical Area
Source: U.S. Census Bureau, 2015-2019 American Community Survey 5-Year Estimates

Religious Groups by Family

Area	Catholic	Baptist	Non-Den.	Methodist[2]	Lutheran	LDS[3]	Pentecostal	Presbyterian[4]	Muslim[5]	Judaism
MSA[1]	47.0	14.8	4.0	2.6	0.2	0.4	2.9	0.2	0.1	0.1
U.S.	19.1	9.3	4.0	4.0	2.3	2.0	1.9	1.6	0.8	0.7

Note: Figures are the number of adherents as a percentage of the total population; (1) Figures cover the Lafayette, LA Metropolitan Statistical Area; (2) Methodist/Pietist; (3) Latter Day Saints; (4) Reformed; (5) Figures are estimates
Source: Association of Statisticians of American Religious Bodies, 2010 U.S. Religion Census: Religious Congregations & Membership Study

Religious Groups by Tradition

Area	Catholic	Evangelical Protestant	Mainline Protestant	Other Tradition	Black Protestant	Orthodox
MSA[1]	47.0	12.8	3.2	0.8	9.3	0.1
U.S.	19.1	16.2	7.3	4.3	1.6	0.3

Note: Figures are the number of adherents as a percentage of the total population; (1) Figures cover the Lafayette, LA Metropolitan Statistical Area
Source: Association of Statisticians of American Religious Bodies, 2010 U.S. Religion Census: Religious Congregations & Membership Study

ECONOMY

Gross Metropolitan Product

Area	2017	2018	2019	2020	Rank[2]
MSA[1]	21.4	23.0	24.0	25.4	116

Note: Figures are in billions of dollars; (1) Figures cover the Lafayette, LA Metropolitan Statistical Area; (2) Rank is based on 2018 data and ranges from 1 to 381
Source: U.S. Conference of Mayors, U.S. Metro Economies: GMP & Employment 2018-2020, September 2019

Economic Growth

Area	2015-17 (%)	2018 (%)	2019 (%)	2020 (%)	Rank[2]
MSA[1]	-4.9	2.6	3.0	2.0	380
U.S.	1.9	2.9	2.3	2.1	—

Note: Figures are real gross metropolitan product (GMP) growth rates and represent average annual percent change; (1) Figures cover the Lafayette, LA Metropolitan Statistical Area; (2) Rank is based on 2017 2-year average annual percent change and ranges from 1 to 381
Source: U.S. Conference of Mayors, U.S. Metro Economies: GMP & Employment 2018-2020, September 2019

Metropolitan Area Exports

Area	2014	2015	2016	2017	2018	2019	Rank[2]
MSA[1]	1,532.7	1,165.2	1,335.2	954.8	1,001.7	1,086.2	148

Note: Figures are in millions of dollars; (1) Figures cover the Lafayette, LA Metropolitan Statistical Area; (2) Rank is based on 2019 data and ranges from 1 to 386
Source: U.S. Department of Commerce, International Trade Administration, Office of Trade and Economic Analysis, Industry and Analysis, Exports by Metropolitan Area, data extracted March 24, 2021

Building Permits

Area	Single-Family 2018	Single-Family 2019	Pct. Chg.	Multi-Family 2018	Multi-Family 2019	Pct. Chg.	Total 2018	Total 2019	Pct. Chg.
City	n/a	n/a	n/a	n/a	n/a	n/a	n/a	n/a	n/a
MSA[1]	1,657	1,632	-1.5	30	34	13.3	1,687	1,666	-1.2
U.S.	855,300	862,100	0.7	473,500	523,900	10.6	1,328,800	1,386,000	4.3

Note: (1) Figures cover the Lafayette, LA Metropolitan Statistical Area; Figures represent new, privately-owned housing units authorized (unadjusted data); All permit data are based on estimates with imputation
Source: U.S. Census Bureau, Manufacturing, Mining, and Construction Statistics, Building Permits, 2018, 2019

Bankruptcy Filings

Area	Business Filings 2019	Business Filings 2020	% Chg.	Nonbusiness Filings 2019	Nonbusiness Filings 2020	% Chg.
Lafayette Parish	44	22	-50.0	560	306	-45.4
U.S.	22,780	21,655	-4.9	752,160	522,808	-30.5

Note: Business filings include Chapter 7, Chapter 9, Chapter 11, Chapter 12, Chapter 13, Chapter 15, and Section 304; Nonbusiness filings include Chapter 7, Chapter 11, and Chapter 13
Source: Administrative Office of the U.S. Courts, Business and Nonbusiness Bankruptcy, County Cases Commenced by Chapter of the Bankruptcy Code, During the 12-Month Period Ending December 31, 2019 and Business and Nonbusiness Bankruptcy, County Cases Commenced by Chapter of the Bankruptcy Code, During the 12-Month Period Ending December 31, 2020

Housing Vacancy Rates

Area	Gross Vacancy Rate[2] (%) 2018	2019	2020	Year-Round Vacancy Rate[3] (%) 2018	2019	2020	Rental Vacancy Rate[4] (%) 2018	2019	2020	Homeowner Vacancy Rate[5] (%) 2018	2019	2020
MSA[1]	n/a	n/a	n/a	n/a	n/a	n/a	n/a	n/a	n/a	n/a	n/a	n/a
U.S.	12.3	12.0	10.6	9.7	9.5	8.2	6.9	6.7	6.3	1.5	1.4	1.0

Note: (1) Figures cover the Lafayette, LA Metropolitan Statistical Area; (2) The percentage of the total housing inventory that is vacant; (3) The percentage of the housing inventory (excluding seasonal units) that is year-round vacant; (4) The percentage of rental inventory that is vacant for rent; (5) The percentage of homeowner inventory that is vacant for sale; n/a not available
Source: U.S. Census Bureau, Housing Vacancies and Homeownership Annual Statistics: 2018, 2019, 2020

INCOME

Income

Area	Per Capita ($)	Median Household ($)	Average Household ($)
City	32,998	51,264	78,055
MSA[1]	27,955	51,955	72,041
U.S.	34,103	62,843	88,607

Note: (1) Figures cover the Lafayette, LA Metropolitan Statistical Area
Source: U.S. Census Bureau, 2015-2019 American Community Survey 5-Year Estimates

Household Income Distribution

Area	Under $15,000	$15,000-$24,999	$25,000-$34,999	$35,000-$49,999	$50,000-$74,999	$75,000-$99,999	$100,000-$149,999	$150,000 and up
City	15.8	11.1	10.1	12.0	17.1	10.2	11.1	12.7
MSA[1]	14.4	11.5	10.3	12.4	16.1	12.4	13.4	9.6
U.S.	10.3	8.9	8.9	12.3	17.2	12.7	15.1	14.5

Note: (1) Figures cover the Lafayette, LA Metropolitan Statistical Area
Source: U.S. Census Bureau, 2015-2019 American Community Survey 5-Year Estimates

Poverty Rate

Area	All Ages	Under 18 Years Old	18 to 64 Years Old	65 Years and Over
City	19.7	27.7	18.9	11.4
MSA[1]	19.1	26.4	17.4	13.7
U.S.	13.4	18.5	12.6	9.3

Note: Figures are percentage of people whose income during the past 12 months was below the poverty level;
(1) Figures cover the Lafayette, LA Metropolitan Statistical Area
Source: U.S. Census Bureau, 2015-2019 American Community Survey 5-Year Estimates

CITY FINANCES

City Government Finances

Component	2017 ($000)	2017 ($ per capita)
Total Revenues	624,295	4,890
Total Expenditures	633,821	4,965
Debt Outstanding	484,080	3,792
Cash and Securities[1]	691,358	5,416

Note: (1) Cash and security holdings of a government at the close of its fiscal year, including those of its dependent agencies, utilities, and liquor stores.
Source: U.S. Census Bureau, State & Local Government Finances 2017

City Government Revenue by Source

Source	2017 ($000)	2017 ($ per capita)	2017 (%)
General Revenue			
From Federal Government	28,664	225	4.6
From State Government	7,273	57	1.2
From Local Governments	1,927	15	0.3
Taxes			
Property	126,302	989	20.2
Sales and Gross Receipts	102,180	800	16.4
Personal Income	0	0	0.0
Corporate Income	0	0	0.0
Motor Vehicle License	0	0	0.0
Other Taxes	5,175	41	0.8
Current Charges	89,224	699	14.3
Liquor Store	0	0	0.0
Utility	246,314	1,929	39.5
Employee Retirement	0	0	0.0

Source: U.S. Census Bureau, State & Local Government Finances 2017

City Government Expenditures by Function

Function	2017 ($000)	2017 ($ per capita)	2017 (%)
General Direct Expenditures			
Air Transportation	21,906	171	3.5
Corrections	8,245	64	1.3
Education	0	0	0.0
Employment Security Administration	0	0	0.0
Financial Administration	9,770	76	1.5
Fire Protection	22,867	179	3.6
General Public Buildings	5,058	39	0.8
Governmental Administration, Other	8,968	70	1.4
Health	1,790	14	0.3
Highways	47,769	374	7.5
Hospitals	0	0	0.0
Housing and Community Development	16,916	132	2.7
Interest on General Debt	15,733	123	2.5
Judicial and Legal	17,845	139	2.8
Libraries	9,995	78	1.6
Parking	679	5	0.1
Parks and Recreation	30,118	235	4.8
Police Protection	95,013	744	15.0
Public Welfare	1,107	8	0.2
Sewerage	22,212	174	3.5
Solid Waste Management	13,544	106	2.1
Veterans' Services	0	0	0.0
Liquor Store	0	0	0.0
Utility	234,226	1,834	37.0
Employee Retirement	0	0	0.0

Source: U.S. Census Bureau, State & Local Government Finances 2017

EMPLOYMENT

Labor Force and Employment

Area	Civilian Labor Force			Workers Employed		
	Dec. 2019	Dec. 2020	% Chg.	Dec. 2019	Dec. 2020	% Chg.
City	59,376	59,649	0.5	56,669	56,144	-0.9
MSA[1]	210,923	212,283	0.6	200,667	199,150	-0.8
U.S.	164,007,000	160,017,000	-2.4	158,504,000	149,613,000	-5.6

Note: Data is not seasonally adjusted and covers workers 16 years of age and older; (1) Figures cover the Lafayette, LA Metropolitan Statistical Area
Source: Bureau of Labor Statistics, Local Area Unemployment Statistics

Unemployment Rate

Area	2020											
	Jan.	Feb.	Mar.	Apr.	May	Jun.	Jul.	Aug.	Sep.	Oct.	Nov.	Dec.
City	5.4	4.0	6.1	13.5	12.8	9.3	9.1	7.2	7.0	7.9	7.0	5.9
MSA[1]	5.7	4.3	6.4	13.0	12.4	9.2	9.1	7.4	7.3	8.2	7.3	6.2
U.S.	4.0	3.8	4.5	14.4	13.0	11.2	10.5	8.5	7.7	6.6	6.4	6.5

Note: Data is not seasonally adjusted and covers workers 16 years of age and older; (1) Figures cover the Lafayette, LA Metropolitan Statistical Area
Source: Bureau of Labor Statistics, Local Area Unemployment Statistics

Average Wages

Occupation	$/Hr.	Occupation	$/Hr.
Accountants and Auditors	31.80	Maintenance and Repair Workers	17.60
Automotive Mechanics	18.70	Marketing Managers	43.80
Bookkeepers	18.10	Network and Computer Systems Admin.	34.50
Carpenters	19.40	Nurses, Licensed Practical	19.10
Cashiers	10.00	Nurses, Registered	n/a
Computer Programmers	35.30	Nursing Assistants	10.90
Computer Systems Analysts	39.80	Office Clerks, General	13.10
Computer User Support Specialists	26.20	Physical Therapists	41.10
Construction Laborers	17.60	Physicians	97.20
Cooks, Restaurant	13.20	Plumbers, Pipefitters and Steamfitters	26.70
Customer Service Representatives	16.10	Police and Sheriff's Patrol Officers	20.10
Dentists	n/a	Postal Service Mail Carriers	25.60
Electricians	23.40	Real Estate Sales Agents	20.00
Engineers, Electrical	43.40	Retail Salespersons	13.20
Fast Food and Counter Workers	9.60	Sales Representatives, Technical/Scientific	41.30
Financial Managers	50.00	Secretaries, Exc. Legal/Medical/Executive	15.00
First-Line Supervisors of Office Workers	24.40	Security Guards	11.60
General and Operations Managers	59.00	Surgeons	n/a
Hairdressers/Cosmetologists	11.40	Teacher Assistants, Exc. Postsecondary*	11.30
Home Health and Personal Care Aides	10.00	Teachers, Secondary School, Exc. Sp. Ed.*	25.20
Janitors and Cleaners	11.00	Telemarketers	n/a
Landscaping/Groundskeeping Workers	15.40	Truck Drivers, Heavy/Tractor-Trailer	20.90
Lawyers	45.40	Truck Drivers, Light/Delivery Services	14.70
Maids and Housekeeping Cleaners	9.90	Waiters and Waitresses	9.80

Note: Wage data covers the Lafayette, LA Metropolitan Statistical Area; (*) Hourly wages were calculated from annual wage data based on a 40 hour work week; n/a not available.
Source: Bureau of Labor Statistics, Metro Area Occupational Employment & Wage Estimates, May 2020

Employment by Industry

Sector	MSA[1]		U.S.
	Number of Employees	Percent of Total	Percent of Total
Construction	9,400	5.0	5.1
Education and Health Services	31,900	16.8	16.3
Financial Activities	9,900	5.2	6.1
Government	25,500	13.4	15.2
Information	2,000	1.1	1.9
Leisure and Hospitality	19,200	10.1	9.0
Manufacturing	13,400	7.1	8.5
Mining and Logging	9,900	5.2	0.4
Other Services	6,600	3.5	3.8
Professional and Business Services	21,200	11.2	14.4
Retail Trade	26,700	14.1	10.9
Transportation, Warehousing, and Utilities	6,200	3.3	4.6
Wholesale Trade	8,000	4.2	3.9

Note: Figures are non-farm employment as of December 2020. Figures are not seasonally adjusted and include workers 16 years of age and older; (1) Figures cover the Lafayette, LA Metropolitan Statistical Area
Source: Bureau of Labor Statistics, Current Employment Statistics, Employment, Hours, and Earnings

Employment by Occupation

Occupation Classification	City (%)	MSA[1] (%)	U.S. (%)
Management, Business, Science, and Arts	38.7	32.7	38.5
Natural Resources, Construction, and Maintenance	7.0	12.4	8.9
Production, Transportation, and Material Moving	9.5	14.0	13.2
Sales and Office	23.8	22.7	21.6
Service	21.1	18.2	17.8

Note: Figures cover employed civilians 16 years of age and older; (1) Figures cover the Lafayette, LA Metropolitan Statistical Area
Source: U.S. Census Bureau, 2015-2019 American Community Survey 5-Year Estimates

Occupations with Greatest Projected Employment Growth: 2020 – 2022

Occupation[1]	2020 Employment	2022 Projected Employment	Numeric Employment Change	Percent Employment Change
Fast Food and Counter Workers	21,880	22,580	700	3.2
Home Health and Personal Care Aides	35,530	36,200	670	1.9
Registered Nurses	40,540	41,050	510	1.3
Cooks, Restaurant	11,020	11,530	510	4.6
Stockers and Order Fillers	20,590	21,030	440	2.1
Medical Assistants	8,110	8,440	330	4.1
Nurse Practitioners	3,080	3,390	310	10.1
Medical and Health Services Managers	4,970	5,230	260	5.2
Licensed Practical and Licensed Vocational Nurses	18,340	18,580	240	1.3
Waiters and Waitresses	24,100	24,340	240	1.0

Note: Projections cover Louisiana; (1) Sorted by numeric employment change
Source: www.projectionscentral.com, State Occupational Projections, 2020–2022 Short-Term Projections

Fastest-Growing Occupations: 2020 – 2022

Occupation[1]	2020 Employment	2022 Projected Employment	Numeric Employment Change	Percent Employment Change
Nurse Practitioners	3,080	3,390	310	10.1
Occupational Therapy Assistants	670	730	60	9.0
Physician Assistants	1,130	1,210	80	7.1
Physical Therapist Assistants	1,410	1,510	100	7.1
Speech-Language Pathologists	1,240	1,310	70	5.6
Medical and Health Services Managers	4,970	5,230	260	5.2
Cooks, Restaurant	11,020	11,530	510	4.6
Respiratory Therapists	2,480	2,590	110	4.4
Physical Therapist Aides	1,630	1,700	70	4.3
Medical Assistants	8,110	8,440	330	4.1

Note: Projections cover Louisiana; (1) Sorted by percent employment change and excludes occupations with numeric employment change less than 50
Source: www.projectionscentral.com, State Occupational Projections, 2020–2022 Short-Term Projections

TAXES

State Corporate Income Tax Rates

State	Tax Rate (%)	Income Brackets ($)	Num. of Brackets	Financial Institution Tax Rate (%)[a]	Federal Income Tax Ded.
Louisiana	4.0 - 8.0	25,000 - 200,001	5	4.0 - 8.0	Yes

Note: Tax rates as of January 1, 2021; (a) Rates listed are the corporate income tax rate applied to financial institutions or excise taxes based on income. Some states have other taxes based upon the value of deposits or shares.
Source: Federation of Tax Administrators, State Corporate Income Tax Rates, January 1, 2021

State Individual Income Tax Rates

State	Tax Rate (%)	Income Brackets ($)	Personal Exemptions ($) Single	Personal Exemptions ($) Married	Personal Exemptions ($) Depend.	Standard Ded. ($) Single	Standard Ded. ($) Married
Louisiana	2.0 - 6.0	12,500 - 50,001 (b)	4,500	9,000 (k)	1,000	(k)	(k)

Note: Tax rates as of January 1, 2021; Local- and county-level taxes are not included; Federal income tax is deductible on state income tax returns; (b) For joint returns, taxes are twice the tax on half the couple's income; (k) The amounts reported for Louisiana are a combined personal exemption-standard deduction.
Source: Federation of Tax Administrators, State Individual Income Tax Rates, January 1, 2021

Various State Sales and Excise Tax Rates

State	State Sales Tax (%)	Gasoline[1] (¢/gal.)	Cigarette[2] ($/pack)	Spirits[3] ($/gal.)	Wine[4] ($/gal.)	Beer[5] ($/gal.)	Recreational Marijuana (%)
Louisiana	4.45	20.01	1.08	3.03	0.76	0.4	Not legal

Note: All tax rates as of January 1, 2021; (1) The American Petroleum Institute has developed a methodology for determining the average tax rate on a gallon of fuel. Rates may include any of the following: excise taxes, environmental fees, storage tank fees, other fees or taxes, general sales tax, and local taxes; (2) The federal excise tax of $1.0066 per pack and local taxes are not included; (3) Rates are those applicable to off-premise sales of 40% alcohol by volume (a.b.v.) distilled spirits in 750ml containers. Local excise taxes are excluded; (4) Rates are those applicable to off-premise sales of 11% a.b.v. non-carbonated wine in 750ml containers; (5) Rates are those applicable to off-premise sales of 4.7% a.b.v. beer in 12 ounce containers.
Source: Tax Foundation, 2021 Facts & Figures: How Does Your State Compare?

State Business Tax Climate Index Rankings

State	Overall Rank	Corporate Tax Rank	Individual Income Tax Rank	Sales Tax Rank	Property Tax Rank	Unemployment Insurance Tax Rank
Louisiana	42	35	32	49	23	4

Note: The index is a measure of how each state's tax laws affect economic performance. The lower the rank, the more favorable a state's tax system is for business. States without a given tax are given a ranking of 1. The scores/rankings for the District of Columbia do not affect other states. The 2021 index represents the tax climate as of July 1, 2020.
Source: Tax Foundation, State Business Tax Climate Index 2021

TRANSPORTATION

Means of Transportation to Work

Area	Drove Alone	Car-pooled	Bus	Subway	Railroad	Bicycle	Walked	Other Means	Worked at Home
City	84.3	6.7	1.2	0.0	0.0	1.2	2.3	0.9	3.5
MSA[1]	84.8	8.2	0.5	0.0	0.0	0.4	1.9	1.1	3.0
U.S.	76.3	9.0	2.4	1.9	0.6	0.5	2.7	1.4	5.2

Note: Figures are percentages and cover workers 16 years of age and older; (1) Figures cover the Lafayette, LA Metropolitan Statistical Area
Source: U.S. Census Bureau, 2015-2019 American Community Survey 5-Year Estimates

Travel Time to Work

Area	Less Than 10 Minutes	10 to 19 Minutes	20 to 29 Minutes	30 to 44 Minutes	45 to 59 Minutes	60 to 89 Minutes	90 Minutes or More
City	16.4	42.1	20.4	12.5	2.5	2.8	3.3
MSA[1]	15.1	32.4	21.0	18.4	5.2	3.7	4.3
U.S.	12.2	28.4	20.8	20.8	8.3	6.4	2.9

Note: Note: Figures are percentages and include workers 16 years old and over; (1) Figures cover the Lafayette, LA Metropolitan Statistical Area
Source: U.S. Census Bureau, 2015-2019 American Community Survey 5-Year Estimates

Key Congestion Measures

Measure	1982	1992	2002	2012	2017
Annual Hours of Delay, Total (000)	n/a	n/a	n/a	n/a	8,375
Annual Hours of Delay, Per Auto Commuter	n/a	n/a	n/a	n/a	31
Annual Congestion Cost, Total (million $)	n/a	n/a	n/a	n/a	187
Annual Congestion Cost, Per Auto Commuter ($)	n/a	n/a	n/a	n/a	691

Note: n/a not available
Source: Texas A&M Transportation Institute, 2019 Urban Mobility Report

Freeway Travel Time Index

Measure	1982	1987	1992	1997	2002	2007	2012	2017
Urban Area Index[1]	n/a	n/a	n/a	n/a	n/a	n/a	n/a	1.13
Urban Area Rank[1,2]	n/a	n/a	n/a	n/a	n/a	n/a	n/a	n/a

Note: Freeway Travel Time Index—the ratio of travel time in the peak period to the travel time at free-flow conditions. For example, a value of 1.30 indicates a 20-minute free-flow trip takes 26 minutes in the peak (20 minutes x 1.30 = 26 minutes); (1) Covers the Lafayette LA urban area; (2) Rank is based on 101 larger urban areas (#1 = highest travel time index); n/a not available
Source: Texas A&M Transportation Institute, 2019 Urban Mobility Report

Public Transportation

Agency Name / Mode of Transportation	Vehicles Operated in Maximum Service[1]	Annual Unlinked Passenger Trips[2] (in thous.)	Annual Passenger Miles[3] (in thous.)
Lafayette Transit System			
Bus (directly operated)	14	1,323.6	9,668.6
Demand Response (purchased transportation)	6	34.8	369.7

Note: (1) Number of revenue vehicles operated by the given mode and type of service to meet the annual maximum service requirement. This is the revenue vehicle count during the peak season of the year; on the week and day that maximum service is provided. Vehicles operated in maximum service (VOMS) exclude atypical days and one-time special events; (2) Number of passengers who boarded public transportation vehicles. Passengers are counted each time they board a vehicle no matter how many vehicles they use to travel from their origin to their destination. (3) Sum of the distances ridden by all passengers during the entire fiscal year.
Source: Federal Transit Administration, National Transit Database, 2019

Air Transportation

Airport Name and Code / Type of Service	Passenger Airlines[1]	Passenger Enplanements	Freight Carriers[2]	Freight (lbs)
Lafayette Regional Airport (LFT)				
Domestic service (U.S. carriers - 2020)	12	119,205	5	9,453,603
International service (U.S. carriers - 2019)	0	0	0	0

Note: (1) Includes all U.S.-based major, minor and commuter airlines that carried at least one passenger during the year; (2) Includes all U.S.-based airlines and freight carriers that transported at least one pound of freight during the year.
Source: Bureau of Transportation Statistics, The Intermodal Transportation Database, Air Carriers: T-100 Domestic Market (U.S. Carriers), 2020; Bureau of Transportation Statistics, The Intermodal Transportation Database, Air Carriers: T-100 International Market (U.S. Carriers), 2019

BUSINESSES

Major Business Headquarters

Company Name	Industry	Rankings Fortune[1]	Forbes[2]
No companies listed	-	-	-

Note: (1) Companies that produce a 10-K are ranked 1 to 500 based on 2019 revenue; (2) All private companies with at least $2 billion in annual revenue through the end of their most current fiscal year are ranked 1 to 219; companies listed are headquartered in the city; dashes indicate no ranking
Source: Fortune, "Fortune 500," June/July 2020; Forbes, "America's Largest Private Companies," 2020

Fastest-Growing Businesses

According to *Inc.*, Lafayette is home to two of America's 500 fastest-growing private companies: **360ia** (#50); **Adeline Clothing Boutique** (#166). Criteria: must be an independent, privately-held, for-profit, U.S. corporation, proprietorship or partnership as of December 31, 2019; revenues must be at least $100,000 in 2016 and $2 million in 2019; must have four-year operating/sales history. *Inc.,* "America's 500 Fastest-Growing Private Companies," 2020

Living Environment

COST OF LIVING

Cost of Living Index

Composite Index	Groceries	Housing	Utilities	Transportation	Health Care	Misc. Goods/Services
90.6	100.6	72.9	90.4	100.2	93.9	97.7

Note: The Cost of Living Index measures regional differences in the cost of consumer goods and services, excluding taxes and non-consumer expenditures, for professional and managerial households in the top income quintile. It is based on more than 50,000 prices covering almost 60 different items for which prices are collected three times a year by chambers of commerce, economic development organizations or university applied economic centers in each participating urban area. The numbers shown should be read as a percentage above or below the national average of 100. For example, a value of 115.4 in the groceries column indicates that grocery prices are 15.4% higher than the national average. Small differences in the index numbers should not be interpreted as significant; Figures cover the Lafayette LA urban area.
Source: The Council for Community and Economic Research, Cost of Living Index, 2020

Grocery Prices

Area[1]	T-Bone Steak ($/pound)	Frying Chicken ($/pound)	Whole Milk ($/half gal.)	Eggs ($/dozen)	Orange Juice ($/64 oz.)	Coffee ($/11.5 oz.)
City[2]	11.14	1.16	2.19	1.69	3.82	4.26
Avg.	11.78	1.39	2.05	1.47	3.57	4.34
Min.	8.03	0.94	1.03	0.74	2.94	3.02
Max.	15.86	2.65	4.31	3.77	5.44	8.69

Note: (1) Values for the local area are compared with the average, minimum and maximum values for all 284 areas in the Cost of Living Index; (2) Figures cover the Lafayette LA urban area; **T-Bone Steak** (price per pound); **Frying Chicken** (price per pound, whole fryer); **Whole Milk** (half gallon carton); **Eggs** (price per dozen, Grade A, large); **Orange Juice** (64 oz. Tropicana or Florida Natural); **Coffee** (11.5 oz. can, vacuum-packed, Maxwell House, Hills Bros, or Folgers).
Source: The Council for Community and Economic Research, Cost of Living Index, 2020

Housing and Utility Costs

Area[1]	New Home Price ($)	Apartment Rent ($/month)	All Electric ($/month)	Part Electric ($/month)	Other Energy ($/month)	Telephone ($/month)
City[2]	244,456	952	-	88.34	52.94	180.20
Avg.	368,594	1,168	170.86	100.47	65.28	184.30
Min.	190,567	502	91.58	31.42	26.08	169.60
Max.	2,227,806	4,738	470.38	280.31	280.06	206.50

Note: (1) Values for the local area are compared with the average, minimum and maximum values for all 284 areas in the Cost of Living Index; (2) Figures cover the Lafayette LA urban area; **New Home Price** (2,400 sf living area, 8,000 sf lot, in urban area with full utilities); **Apartment Rent** (950 sf 2 bedroom/1.5 or 2 bath, unfurnished, excluding all utilities except water); **All Electric** (average monthly cost for an all-electric home); **Part Electric** (average monthly cost for a part-electric home); **Other Energy** (average monthly cost for natural gas, fuel oil, coal, wood, and any other forms of energy except electricity); **Telephone** (price includes the base monthly rate plus taxes and fees for three lines of mobile phone service).
Source: The Council for Community and Economic Research, Cost of Living Index, 2020

Health Care, Transportation, and Other Costs

Area[1]	Doctor ($/visit)	Dentist ($/visit)	Optometrist ($/visit)	Gasoline ($/gallon)	Beauty Salon ($/visit)	Men's Shirt ($)
City[2]	113.42	79.60	103.22	1.92	40.73	32.66
Avg.	115.44	99.32	108.10	2.21	39.27	31.37
Min.	36.68	59.00	51.36	1.71	19.00	11.00
Max.	219.00	153.10	250.97	3.46	82.05	58.33

Note: (1) Values for the local area are compared with the average, minimum and maximum values for all 284 areas in the Cost of Living Index; (2) Figures cover the Lafayette LA urban area; **Doctor** (general practitioners routine exam of an established patient); **Dentist** (adult teeth cleaning and periodic oral examination); **Optometrist** (full vision eye exam for established adult patient); **Gasoline** (one gallon regular unleaded, national brand, including all taxes, cash price at self-service pump if available); **Beauty Salon** (woman's shampoo, trim, and blow-dry); **Men's Shirt** (cotton/polyester dress shirt, pinpoint weave, long sleeves).
Source: The Council for Community and Economic Research, Cost of Living Index, 2020

HOUSING

Homeownership Rate

Area	2012 (%)	2013 (%)	2014 (%)	2015 (%)	2016 (%)	2017 (%)	2018 (%)	2019 (%)	2020 (%)
MSA[1]	n/a	n/a	n/a	n/a	n/a	n/a	n/a	n/a	n/a
U.S.	65.4	65.1	64.5	63.7	63.4	63.9	64.4	64.6	66.6

Note: (1) Figures cover the Lafayette, LA Metropolitan Statistical Area; n/a not available
Source: U.S. Census Bureau, Housing Vacancies and Homeownership Annual Statistics: 2012-2020

House Price Index (HPI)

Area	National Ranking[2]	Quarterly Change (%)	One-Year Change (%)	Five-Year Change (%)	Since 1991Q1 (%)
MSA[1]	221	0.62	3.89	8.70	180.99
U.S.[3]	–	3.81	10.77	38.99	205.12

Note: The HPI is a weighted repeat sales index. It measures average price changes in repeat sales or refinancings on the same properties. This information is obtained by reviewing repeat mortgage transactions on single-family properties whose mortgages have been purchased or securitized by Fannie Mae or Freddie Mac since January 1975; (1) Figures cover the Lafayette, LA Metropolitan Statistical Area; (2) Rankings are based on annual percentage change for all metro areas containing at least 15,000 transactions over the last 10 years and ranges from 1 to 253; (3) figures based on a weighted average of Census Division estimates using a seasonally adjusted, purchase-only index; all figures are for the period ending December 31, 2020
Source: Federal Housing Finance Agency, Change in Metropolitan Area House Price Indexes, April 7, 2021

Median Single-Family Home Prices

Area	2018	2019	2020p	Percent Change 2019 to 2020
MSA[1]	n/a	n/a	n/a	n/a
U.S. Average	261.6	274.6	299.9	9.2

Note: Figures are median sales prices of existing single-family homes in thousands of dollars; (p) preliminary; n/a not available; (1) Figures cover the Lafayette, LA Metropolitan Statistical Area
Source: National Association of Realtors, Median Sales Price of Existing Single-Family Homes for Metropolitan Areas, 4th Quarter 2020

Qualifying Income Based on Median Sales Price of Existing Single-Family Homes

Area	With 5% Down ($)	With 10% Down ($)	With 20% Down ($)
MSA[1]	n/a	n/a	n/a
U.S. Average	59,266	56,147	49,908

Note: Figures are preliminary; Qualifying income is based on a mortgage rate of 2.81%. Monthly principal and interest payment is limited to 25% of income; n/a not available; (1) Figures cover the Lafayette, LA Metropolitan Statistical Area
Source: National Association of Realtors, Qualifying Income Based on Median Sales Price of Existing Single-Family Homes for Metropolitan Areas, 4th Quarter 2020

Home Value Distribution

Area	Under $50,000	$50,000 -$99,999	$100,000 -$149,999	$150,000 -$199,999	$200,000 -$299,999	$300,000 -$499,999	$500,000 -$999,999	$1,000,000 or more
City	5.5	8.2	14.9	23.2	23.8	16.0	6.5	1.9
MSA[1]	14.7	16.0	16.1	19.5	19.3	10.1	3.5	0.8
U.S.	6.9	12.0	13.3	14.0	19.6	19.3	11.4	3.4

Note: Figures are percentages and cover owner-occupied housing units; (1) Figures cover the Lafayette, LA Metropolitan Statistical Area
Source: U.S. Census Bureau, 2015-2019 American Community Survey 5-Year Estimates

Year Housing Structure Built

Area	2010 or Later	2000 -2009	1990 -1999	1980 -1989	1970 -1979	1960 -1969	1950 -1959	1940 -1949	Before 1940	Median Year
City	7.2	13.3	10.4	18.0	21.7	13.4	9.0	3.9	3.1	1979
MSA[1]	9.5	16.6	12.9	15.5	16.4	10.4	9.3	4.1	5.2	1983
U.S.	5.2	14.0	13.9	13.4	15.2	10.6	10.3	4.9	12.6	1978

Note: Figures are percentages except for Median Year; Note: (1) Figures cover the Lafayette, LA Metropolitan Statistical Area
Source: U.S. Census Bureau, 2015-2019 American Community Survey 5-Year Estimates

Gross Monthly Rent

Area	Under $500	$500 -$999	$1,000 -$1,499	$1,500 -$1,999	$2,000 -$2,499	$2,500 -$2,999	$3,000 and up	Median ($)
City	9.9	54.6	27.8	6.1	1.3	0.3	0.1	890
MSA[1]	15.3	57.0	21.5	4.8	1.2	0.1	0.1	811
U.S.	9.4	36.2	30.0	14.0	5.6	2.4	2.4	1,062

Note: Figures are percentages except for Median; Gross rent is the contract rent plus the estimated average monthly cost of utilities (electricity, gas, and water and sewer) and fuels (oil, coal, kerosene, wood, etc.) if these are paid by the renter (or paid for the renter by someone else); (1) Figures cover the Lafayette, LA Metropolitan Statistical Area
Source: U.S. Census Bureau, 2015-2019 American Community Survey 5-Year Estimates

HEALTH

Health Risk Factors

Category	MSA[1] (%)	U.S. (%)
Adults aged 18–64 who have any kind of health care coverage	n/a	87.3
Adults who reported being in good or better health	n/a	82.4
Adults who have been told they have high blood cholesterol	n/a	33.0
Adults who have been told they have high blood pressure	n/a	32.3
Adults who are current smokers	n/a	17.1
Adults who currently use E-cigarettes	n/a	4.6
Adults who currently use chewing tobacco, snuff, or snus	n/a	4.0
Adults who are heavy drinkers[2]	n/a	6.3
Adults who are binge drinkers[3]	n/a	17.4
Adults who are overweight (BMI 25.0 - 29.9)	n/a	35.3
Adults who are obese (BMI 30.0 - 99.8)	n/a	31.3
Adults who participated in any physical activities in the past month	n/a	74.4
Adults who always or nearly always wears a seat belt	n/a	94.3

Note: n/a not available; (1) Figures cover the Lafayette, LA Metropolitan Statistical Area; (2) Heavy drinkers are classified as adult men having more than 14 drinks per week and adult women having more than 7 drinks per week; (3) Binge drinkers are classified as males having five or more drinks on one occasion or females having four or more drinks on one occasion
Source: Centers for Disease Control and Prevention, Behaviorial Risk Factor Surveillance System, SMART: Selected Metropolitan Area Risk Trends, 2017

Acute and Chronic Health Conditions

Category	MSA[1] (%)	U.S. (%)
Adults who have ever been told they had a heart attack	n/a	4.2
Adults who have ever been told they have angina or coronary heart disease	n/a	3.9
Adults who have ever been told they had a stroke	n/a	3.0
Adults who have ever been told they have asthma	n/a	14.2
Adults who have ever been told they have arthritis	n/a	24.9
Adults who have ever been told they have diabetes[2]	n/a	10.5
Adults who have ever been told they had skin cancer	n/a	6.2
Adults who have ever been told they had any other types of cancer	n/a	7.1
Adults who have ever been told they have COPD	n/a	6.5
Adults who have ever been told they have kidney disease	n/a	3.0
Adults who have ever been told they have a form of depression	n/a	20.5

Note: n/a not available; (1) Figures cover the Lafayette, LA Metropolitan Statistical Area; (2) Figures do not include pregnancy-related, borderline, or pre-diabetes
Source: Centers for Disease Control and Prevention, Behaviorial Risk Factor Surveillance System, SMART: Selected Metropolitan Area Risk Trends, 2017

Health Screening and Vaccination Rates

Category	MSA[1] (%)	U.S. (%)
Adults aged 65+ who have had flu shot within the past year	n/a	60.7
Adults aged 65+ who have ever had a pneumonia vaccination	n/a	75.4
Adults who have ever been tested for HIV	n/a	36.1
Adults who have ever had the shingles or zoster vaccine?	n/a	28.9
Adults who have had their blood cholesterol checked within the last five years	n/a	85.9

Note: n/a not available; (1) Figures cover the Lafayette, LA Metropolitan Statistical Area.
Source: Centers for Disease Control and Prevention, Behaviorial Risk Factor Surveillance System, SMART: Selected Metropolitan Area Risk Trends, 2017

Disability Status

Category	MSA[1] (%)	U.S. (%)
Adults who reported being deaf	n/a	6.7
Are you blind or have serious difficulty seeing, even when wearing glasses?	n/a	4.5
Are you limited in any way in any of your usual activities due of arthritis?	n/a	12.9
Do you have difficulty doing errands alone?	n/a	6.8
Do you have difficulty dressing or bathing?	n/a	3.6
Do you have serious difficulty concentrating/remembering/making decisions?	n/a	10.7
Do you have serious difficulty walking or climbing stairs?	n/a	13.6

Note: n/a not available; (1) Figures cover the Lafayette, LA Metropolitan Statistical Area.
Source: Centers for Disease Control and Prevention, Behaviorial Risk Factor Surveillance System, SMART: Selected Metropolitan Area Risk Trends, 2017

Mortality Rates for the Top 10 Causes of Death in the U.S.

ICD-10[a] Sub-Chapter	ICD-10[a] Code	Age-Adjusted Mortality Rate[1] per 100,000 population County[2]	U.S.
Malignant neoplasms	C00-C97	159.1	149.2
Ischaemic heart diseases	I20-I25	84.6	90.5
Other forms of heart disease	I30-I51	65.5	52.2
Chronic lower respiratory diseases	J40-J47	36.5	39.6
Other degenerative diseases of the nervous system	G30-G31	60.8	37.6
Cerebrovascular diseases	I60-I69	45.4	37.2
Other external causes of accidental injury	W00-X59	32.8	36.1
Organic, including symptomatic, mental disorders	F01-F09	7.4	29.4
Hypertensive diseases	I10-I15	45.2	24.1
Diabetes mellitus	E10-E14	22.9	21.5

Note: (a) ICD-10 = International Classification of Diseases 10th Revision; (1) Mortality rates are a three-year average covering 2017-2019; (2) Figures cover Lafayette Parish.
Source: Centers for Disease Control and Prevention, National Center for Health Statistics. Underlying Cause of Death 1999-2019 on CDC WONDER Online Database

Mortality Rates for Selected Causes of Death

ICD-10[a] Sub-Chapter	ICD-10[a] Code	Age-Adjusted Mortality Rate[1] per 100,000 population County[2]	U.S.
Assault	X85-Y09	9.1	6.0
Diseases of the liver	K70-K76	10.6	14.4
Human immunodeficiency virus (HIV) disease	B20-B24	Unreliable	1.5
Influenza and pneumonia	J09-J18	9.5	13.8
Intentional self-harm	X60-X84	14.1	14.1
Malnutrition	E40-E46	2.8	2.3
Obesity and other hyperalimentation	E65-E68	7.8	2.1
Renal failure	N17-N19	15.8	12.6
Transport accidents	V01-V99	10.6	12.3
Viral hepatitis	B15-B19	Suppressed	1.2

Note: (a) ICD-10 = International Classification of Diseases 10th Revision; (1) Mortality rates are a three-year average covering 2017-2019; (2) Figures cover Lafayette Parish; Data are suppressed when the data meet the criteria for confidentiality constraints; Mortality rates are flagged as unreliable when the rate would be calculated with a numerator of 20 or less.
Source: Centers for Disease Control and Prevention, National Center for Health Statistics. Underlying Cause of Death 1999-2019 on CDC WONDER Online Database

Health Insurance Coverage

Area	With Health Insurance	With Private Health Insurance	With Public Health Insurance	Without Health Insurance	Population Under Age 19 Without Health Insurance
City	91.3	67.0	35.3	8.7	3.1
MSA[1]	90.1	62.1	38.5	9.9	3.6
U.S.	91.2	67.9	35.1	8.8	5.1

Note: Figures are percentages that cover the civilian noninstitutionalized population; (1) Figures cover the Lafayette, LA Metropolitan Statistical Area
Source: U.S. Census Bureau, 2015-2019 American Community Survey 5-Year Estimates

Number of Medical Professionals

Area	MDs[3]	DOs[3,4]	Dentists	Podiatrists	Chiropractors	Optometrists
Parish[1] (number)	894	24	168	9	80	32
Parish[1] (rate[2])	367.7	9.9	68.7	3.7	32.7	13.1
U.S. (rate[2])	282.9	22.7	71.2	6.2	28.1	16.9

22055
Note: Data as of 2019 unless noted; (1) Data covers Lafayette Parish; (2) Rate per 100,000 population; (3) Data as of 2018 and includes all active, non-federal physicians; (4) Doctor of Osteopathic Medicine
Source: U.S. Department of Health and Human Services, Health Resources and Services Administration, Bureau of Health Professions, Area Resource File (ARF) 2019-2020

EDUCATION

Public School District Statistics

District Name	Schls	Pupils	Pupil/Teacher Ratio	Minority Pupils[1] (%)	Free Lunch Eligible[2] (%)	IEP[3] (%)
Lafayette Parish	44	30,897	19.0	53.6	45.8	8.6

Note: Table includes school districts with 2,000 or more students; (1) Percentage of students that are not non-Hispanic white; (2) Percentage of students that are eligible for the free lunch program; (3) Percentage of students that have an Individualized Education Program.
Source: U.S. Department of Education, National Center for Education Statistics, Common Core of Data, Local Education Agency (School District) Universe Survey: School Year 2018-2019; U.S. Department of Education, National Center for Education Statistics, Common Core of Data, Public Elementary/Secondary School Universe Survey: School Year 2018-2019

Highest Level of Education

Area	Less than H.S.	H.S. Diploma	Some College, No Deg.	Associate Degree	Bachelor's Degree	Master's Degree	Prof. School Degree	Doctorate Degree
City	10.5	27.0	20.0	4.3	25.6	8.5	2.7	1.4
MSA[1]	15.9	36.4	18.6	5.7	16.4	5.0	1.3	0.7
U.S.	12.0	27.0	20.4	8.5	19.8	8.8	2.1	1.4

Note: Figures cover persons age 25 and over; (1) Figures cover the Lafayette, LA Metropolitan Statistical Area
Source: U.S. Census Bureau, 2015-2019 American Community Survey 5-Year Estimates

Educational Attainment by Race

Area	High School Graduate or Higher (%) Total	White	Black	Asian	Hisp.[2]	Bachelor's Degree or Higher (%) Total	White	Black	Asian	Hisp.[2]
City	89.5	93.6	79.4	94.8	57.4	38.2	47.0	15.1	56.8	21.2
MSA[1]	84.1	87.0	76.3	73.1	63.9	23.4	26.4	13.0	34.9	12.3
U.S.	88.0	89.9	86.0	87.1	68.7	32.1	33.5	21.6	54.3	16.4

Note: Figures shown cover persons 25 years old and over; (1) Figures cover the Lafayette, LA Metropolitan Statistical Area; (2) People of Hispanic origin can be of any race
Source: U.S. Census Bureau, 2015-2019 American Community Survey 5-Year Estimates

School Enrollment by Grade and Control

Area	Preschool (%) Public	Private	Kindergarten (%) Public	Private	Grades 1 - 4 (%) Public	Private	Grades 5 - 8 (%) Public	Private	Grades 9 - 12 (%) Public	Private
City	60.7	39.3	64.2	35.8	74.4	25.6	73.3	26.7	80.6	19.4
MSA[1]	66.9	33.1	79.2	20.8	81.0	19.0	79.8	20.2	81.3	18.7
U.S.	59.1	40.9	87.6	12.4	89.5	10.5	89.4	10.6	90.1	9.9

Note: Figures shown cover persons 3 years old and over; (1) Figures cover the Lafayette, LA Metropolitan Statistical Area
Source: U.S. Census Bureau, 2015-2019 American Community Survey 5-Year Estimates

Higher Education

Four-Year Colleges Public	Private Non-profit	Private For-profit	Two-Year Colleges Public	Private Non-profit	Private For-profit	Medical Schools[1]	Law Schools[2]	Voc/Tech[3]
1	0	0	1	2	1	0	0	5

Note: Figures cover institutions located within the city limits and include main campuses only; (1) includes schools accredited by the Liaison Committee on Medical Education and the American Osteopathic Association's Commission on Osteopathic College Accreditation; (2) includes ABA-accredited schools, schools with provisional ABA accreditation, and state accredited schools; (3) includes all schools with programs that are less than 2 years.
Source: National Center for Education Statistics, Integrated Postsecondary Education System (IPEDS), 2019-20; Wikipedia, List of Medical Schools in the United States, accessed April 2, 2021; Wikipedia, List of Law Schools in the United States, accessed April 2, 2021

EMPLOYERS

Major Employers

Company Name	Industry
Acadian Companies	Health care
American Legion Hospital	Health care
AT&T Wireless	Telecommunications
Baker Hughes	Oil field service
Cal Dive Intl Inc	Diving instruction
Cameron Valves & Measurement	Valves, manufacturers
Cheveron USA Production Co.	Oil & gas
Fieldwood Energy	Oil & gas
Frank's Casing Crew & Rental	Oil field service
Halliburton Energy SVC	Oil field service
Lafayette General Medical Ctr	Health care
LHC Group Inc	Health care
McDonald's of Acadiana	Services
Offshore Energy Inc	Oil field service
Opelousas Health Systems	Health care
Our Lady of Lourdes Regional Medical Ctr	Health care
Petroleum Helicopters	Transportation
Quality Construction & Production	General contractors
Regional Medical Center-Acadiana	Health care
Schlumberger	Oil field service
Stuller Inc	Jewelry-manufacturers
Superior Energy Svc	Oil field service
Wal-Mart Stores	Retail
Walmart Distribution Center	Distribution centers
Weatherford	Oil field service

Note: Companies shown are located within the Lafayette, LA Metropolitan Statistical Area.
Source: Hoovers.com; Wikipedia

PUBLIC SAFETY

Crime Rate

Area	All Crimes	Violent Crimes				Property Crimes		
		Murder	Rape[3]	Robbery	Aggrav. Assault	Burglary	Larceny-Theft	Motor Vehicle Theft
City	4,829.0	11.1	12.6	116.8	383.6	814.6	3,236.9	253.4
Suburbs[1]	2,832.6	6.6	29.8	51.6	358.4	551.2	1,694.4	140.6
Metro[2]	3,349.4	7.8	25.3	68.5	365.0	619.4	2,093.7	169.8
U.S.	2,489.3	5.0	42.6	81.6	250.2	340.5	1,549.5	219.9

Note: Figures are crimes per 100,000 population; (1) All areas within the metro area that are located outside the city limits; (2) Figures cover the Lafayette, LA Metropolitan Statistical Area; (3) All figures shown were reported using the revised Uniform Crime Reporting (UCR) definition of rape.
Source: FBI Uniform Crime Reports, 2019

Hate Crimes

Area	Number of Quarters Reported	Number of Incidents per Bias Motivation					
		Race/Ethnicity/Ancestry	Religion	Sexual Orientation	Disability	Gender	Gender Identity
City	4	0	0	0	0	0	0
U.S.	4	3,963	1,521	1,195	157	69	198

Source: Federal Bureau of Investigation, Hate Crime Statistics 2019

Identity Theft Consumer Reports

Area	Reports	Reports per 100,000 Population	Rank[2]
MSA[1]	2,805	573	44
U.S.	1,387,615	423	-

Note: (1) Figures cover the Lafayette, LA Metropolitan Statistical Area; (2) Rank ranges from 1 to 391 where 1 indicates greatest number of identity theft reports per 100,000 population
Source: Federal Trade Commission, Consumer Sentinel Network Data Book 2020

Fraud and Other Consumer Reports

Area	Reports	Reports per 100,000 Population	Rank[2]
MSA[1]	2,965	606	277
U.S.	3,385,133	1,031	-

Note: (1) Figures cover the Lafayette, LA Metropolitan Statistical Area; (2) Rank ranges from 1 to 391 where 1 indicates greatest number of fraud and other consumer reports per 100,000 population
Source: Federal Trade Commission, Consumer Sentinel Network Data Book 2020

POLITICS

2020 Presidential Election Results

Area	Biden	Trump	Jorgensen	Hawkins	Other
Lafayette Parish	34.7	63.3	1.3	0.0	0.7
U.S.	51.3	46.8	1.2	0.3	0.5

Note: Results are percentages and may not add to 100% due to rounding
Source: Dave Leip's Atlas of U.S. Presidential Elections

SPORTS

Professional Sports Teams

Team Name	League	Year Established
No teams are located in the metro area		

Source: Wikipedia, Major Professional Sports Teams of the United States and Canada, April 6, 2021

CLIMATE

Average and Extreme Temperatures

Temperature	Jan	Feb	Mar	Apr	May	Jun	Jul	Aug	Sep	Oct	Nov	Dec	Yr.
Extreme High (°F)	82	85	91	92	98	103	101	102	99	94	87	85	103
Average High (°F)	61	65	71	79	85	90	91	91	87	80	70	64	78
Average Temp. (°F)	51	54	61	68	75	81	82	82	78	69	59	53	68
Average Low (°F)	41	44	50	57	64	70	73	72	68	57	48	43	57
Extreme Low (°F)	9	13	20	32	44	53	58	59	43	30	21	8	8

Note: Figures cover the years 1948-1995
Source: National Climatic Data Center, International Station Meteorological Climate Summary, 9/96

Average Precipitation/Snowfall/Humidity

Precip./Humidity	Jan	Feb	Mar	Apr	May	Jun	Jul	Aug	Sep	Oct	Nov	Dec	Yr.
Avg. Precip. (in.)	4.9	5.1	4.8	5.5	5.0	4.4	6.6	5.4	4.1	3.1	4.2	5.3	58.5
Avg. Snowfall (in.)	Tr	Tr	Tr	0	0	0	0	0	0	Tr	Tr	Tr	Tr
Avg. Rel. Hum. 6am (%)	85	85	86	89	91	91	92	93	91	89	88	86	89
Avg. Rel. Hum. 3pm (%)	59	55	52	52	54	57	62	61	59	51	53	57	56

Note: Figures cover the years 1948-1995; Tr = Trace amounts (<0.05 in. of rain; <0.5 in. of snow)
Source: National Climatic Data Center, International Station Meteorological Climate Summary, 9/96

Weather Conditions

Temperature			Daytime Sky			Precipitation		
10°F & below	32°F & below	90°F & above	Clear	Partly cloudy	Cloudy	0.01 inch or more precip.	0.1 inch or more snow/ice	Thunderstorms
< 1	21	86	99	150	116	113	< 1	73

Note: Figures are average number of days per year and cover the years 1948-1995
Source: National Climatic Data Center, International Station Meteorological Climate Summary, 9/96

HAZARDOUS WASTE

Superfund Sites

The Lafayette, LA metro area is home to one site on the EPA's Superfund National Priorities List: **Evr-Wood Treating/Evangeline Refining Company** (final). There are a total of 1,375 Superfund sites with a status of proposed or final on the list in the U.S. *U.S. Environmental Protection Agency, National Priorities List, April 7, 2021*

AIR QUALITY

Air Quality Trends: Ozone

	1990	1995	2000	2005	2010	2015	2016	2017	2018	2019
MSA[1]	n/a	n/a	n/a	n/a	n/a	n/a	n/a	n/a	n/a	n/a
U.S.	0.088	0.089	0.082	0.080	0.073	0.068	0.069	0.068	0.069	0.065

Note: (1) Data covers the Lafayette, LA Metropolitan Statistical Area; n/a not available. The values shown are the composite ozone concentration averages among trend sites based on the highest fourth daily maximum 8-hour concentration in parts per million. These trends are based on sites having an adequate record of monitoring data during the trend period. Data from exceptional events are included.
Source: U.S. Environmental Protection Agency, Air Quality Monitoring Information, "Air Quality Trends by City, 1990-2019"

Air Quality Index

Area	Percent of Days when Air Quality was...[2]					AQI Statistics[2]	
	Good	Moderate	Unhealthy for Sensitive Groups	Unhealthy	Very Unhealthy	Maximum	Median
MSA[1]	76.7	23.3	0.0	0.0	0.0	84	41

Note: (1) Data covers the Lafayette, LA Metropolitan Statistical Area; (2) Based on 365 days with AQI data in 2019. Air Quality Index (AQI) is an index for reporting daily air quality. EPA calculates the AQI for five major air pollutants regulated by the Clean Air Act: ground-level ozone, particle pollution (aka particulate matter), carbon monoxide, sulfur dioxide, and nitrogen dioxide. The AQI runs from 0 to 500. The higher the AQI value, the greater the level of air pollution and the greater the health concern. There are six AQI categories: "Good" AQI is between 0 and 50. Air quality is considered satisfactory; "Moderate" AQI is between 51 and 100. Air quality is acceptable; "Unhealthy for Sensitive Groups" When AQI values are between 101 and 150, members of sensitive groups may experience health effects; "Unhealthy" When AQI values are between 151 and 200 everyone may begin to experience health effects; "Very Unhealthy" AQI values between 201 and 300 trigger a health alert; "Hazardous" AQI values over 300 trigger warnings of emergency conditions (not shown).
Source: U.S. Environmental Protection Agency, Air Quality Index Report, 2019

Air Quality Index Pollutants

Area	Percent of Days when AQI Pollutant was...[2]					
	Carbon Monoxide	Nitrogen Dioxide	Ozone	Sulfur Dioxide	Particulate Matter 2.5	Particulate Matter 10
MSA[1]	0.0	0.0	58.4	0.0	41.6	0.0

Note: (1) Data covers the Lafayette, LA Metropolitan Statistical Area; (2) Based on 365 days with AQI data in 2019. The Air Quality Index (AQI) is an index for reporting daily air quality. EPA calculates the AQI for five major air pollutants regulated by the Clean Air Act: ground-level ozone, particle pollution (also known as particulate matter), carbon monoxide, sulfur dioxide, and nitrogen dioxide. The AQI runs from 0 to 500. The higher the AQI value, the greater the level of air pollution and the greater the health concern.
Source: U.S. Environmental Protection Agency, Air Quality Index Report, 2019

Maximum Air Pollutant Concentrations: Particulate Matter, Ozone, CO and Lead

	Particulate Matter 10 (ug/m^3)	Particulate Matter 2.5 Wtd AM (ug/m^3)	Particulate Matter 2.5 24-Hr (ug/m^3)	Ozone (ppm)	Carbon Monoxide (ppm)	Lead (ug/m^3)
MSA[1] Level	52	7.9	17	0.063	n/a	n/a
NAAQS[2]	150	15	35	0.075	9	0.15
Met NAAQS[2]	Yes	Yes	Yes	Yes	n/a	n/a

Note: (1) Data covers the Lafayette, LA Metropolitan Statistical Area; Data from exceptional events are included; (2) National Ambient Air Quality Standards; ppm = parts per million; ug/m^3 = micrograms per cubic meter; n/a not available.
Concentrations: Particulate Matter 10 (coarse particulate)—highest second maximum 24-hour concentration; Particulate Matter 2.5 Wtd AM (fine particulate)—highest weighted annual mean concentration; Particulate Matter 2.5 24-Hour (fine particulate)—highest 98th percentile 24-hour concentration; Ozone—highest fourth daily maximum 8-hour concentration; Carbon Monoxide—highest second maximum non-overlapping 8-hour concentration; Lead—maximum running 3-month average
Source: U.S. Environmental Protection Agency, Air Quality Monitoring Information, "Air Quality Statistics by City, 2019"

Maximum Air Pollutant Concentrations: Nitrogen Dioxide and Sulfur Dioxide

	Nitrogen Dioxide AM (ppb)	Nitrogen Dioxide 1-Hr (ppb)	Sulfur Dioxide AM (ppb)	Sulfur Dioxide 1-Hr (ppb)	Sulfur Dioxide 24-Hr (ppb)
MSA[1] Level	n/a	n/a	n/a	n/a	n/a
NAAQS[2]	53	100	30	75	140
Met NAAQS[2]	n/a	n/a	n/a	n/a	n/a

Note: (1) Data covers the Lafayette, LA Metropolitan Statistical Area; Data from exceptional events are included; (2) National Ambient Air Quality Standards; ppm = parts per million; ug/m^3 = micrograms per cubic meter; n/a not available.
Concentrations: Nitrogen Dioxide AM—highest arithmetic mean concentration; Nitrogen Dioxide 1-Hr—highest 98th percentile 1-hour daily maximum concentration; Sulfur Dioxide AM—highest annual mean concentration; Sulfur Dioxide 1-Hr—highest 99th percentile 1-hour daily maximum concentration; Sulfur Dioxide 24-Hr—highest second maximum 24-hour concentration
Source: U.S. Environmental Protection Agency, Air Quality Monitoring Information, "Air Quality Statistics by City, 2019"

Lakeland, Florida

Background

Lakeland is located along Interstate 4 in central Florida. The westernmost city in Polk County, it is one of the principal cities of the Lakeland-Winter Haven area as well as part of the larger Tampa Bay area. It is part of the Central Florida Highlands and its geography is marked by flatlands, low hills, and true to its name, many lakes.

Occupied by the Seminole Indian tribe through the early 19th century, the area that would become Lakeland began to be settled by European Americans in the 1870s, following the defeat and removal of the earlier inhabitants in the Second Seminole War of 1835-1842 and the conclusion of the American Civil War. The railroad reached the area in 1884, spurring an increase in population and Lakeland was officially incorporated the following year. When the Spanish-American War broke out in 1898, 9,000 troops were stationed in Lakeland and a resulting boom occurred, resulting in the construction of new structures, including hotels, theaters, libraries, and museums, and a vastly increased population. This new population, with residents attracted by the phosphate mining and citrus industries, doubled between 1890 and 1900, tripled between 1900 and 1910, and has continued to increase steadily since. Although the city's economic history has been continually marked by booms and busts, the 1930s proved to be a particularly auspicious decade as the Detroit Tigers baseball team began their spring training in Lakeland, the Lakeland Municipal Airport was built, and the president of Florida Southern College commissioned Frank Lloyd Wright to re-design the campus.

While Lakeland's traditional industries of citrus farming and phosphate mining continue to employ numerous residents, the city has significantly diversified its economy. Today, tourism, medicine, insurance, transportation, and music have all become notable industries. Transportation in particular employs a large number of Lakeland residents, with FedEx and the Saddle Creek Corporation among the region's largest corporate presences. The biggest employer headquartered in the area is Publix Supermarkets with 6,500 employees in the region. Other major employers include Amazon, GEICO, and Lakeland Regional Health. The city's proximity to Orlando and Tampa provides its residents with additional employment opportunities.

In 2019, Lakeland Electric presented a plan to phase out the CD McIntosh Power Plant, which uses a coal/gas combination, by 2024.

A picturesque city with numerous designated historical districts, Lakeland is also home to a number of highly regarded cultural institutions. Among the most notable are the Polk Museum of Art, continually ranked among Florida's top museums, and the 1,400-seat Polk Theatre, founded in 1928. Lakeland is the site of several colleges and universities, including the Christian liberal arts school Southeastern University. Others include Florida Southern College and Florida Polytechnic University.

Publix Field at Joker Marchant Stadium continues to host spring training for the Detroit Tigers and is also home to two minor league baseball teams, the Lakeland Flying Tigers and the Gulf Coast Tigers. Other local sports franchises include the Florida Tropics SC, an indoor soccer team, and the Lakeland Magic, a basketball team that is part of the N.B.A. Both teams play at RP Funding Center, the city's multipurpose entertainment complex. Southeastern University also features a number of sports programs, and alum Dee Gordon went on to star for Major League Baseball's Dodgers, Marlins, and Mariners.

Lakeland is located in the humid subtropical zone and is noted for its hot summers when the high temperature rarely falls below 90 degrees Fahrenheit. The temperature almost never dips below freezing at any time of the year, with wintertime highs usually in the low 70s. Thunderstorms are a frequent occurrence in Lakeland, particularly during the summer. In June, the city experiences an average of 8.74 inches of precipitation.

Rankings

General Rankings

- The Lakeland metro area was identified as one of America's fastest-growing areas in terms of population and economy by *Forbes*. The area ranked #14 out of 25. The 100 most populous metro areas in the U.S. were evaluated on the following criteria: estimated population growth; employment; economic output; wages; home values. *Forbes, "America's Fastest-Growing Cities 2018," February 28, 2018*

Business/Finance Rankings

- The Brookings Institution ranked the nation's largest cities based on income inequality. Lakeland was ranked #81 (#1 = greatest inequality). Criteria: the "95/20 ratio," a figure representing the income at which a household earns more than 95 percent of all other households, divided by the income at which a household earns more than only 20 percent of all other households. *Brookings Institution, "Household Income Inequality, Largest Cities of 97 Large U.S. Metro Areas, 2014-2016," February 5, 2018*

- The Brookings Institution ranked the 100 largest metro areas in the U.S. based on income inequality. Lakeland was ranked #92 (#1 = greatest inequality). Criteria: the "95/20 ratio," a figure representing the income at which a household earns more than 95 percent of all other households, divided by the income at which a household earns more than only 20 percent of all other households. *Brookings Institution, "Household Income Inequality, 100 Largest U.S. Metro Areas, 2014-2016," February 5, 2018*

- The Lakeland metro area appeared on the Milken Institute "2021 Best Performing Cities" list. Rank: #25 out of 200 large metro areas (population over 250,000). Criteria: job growth; wage and salary growth; high-tech output growth; housing affordability; household broadband access. *Milken Institute, "Best-Performing Cities 2021," February 16, 2021*

- *Forbes* ranked the 200 most populous metro areas to determine the nation's "Best Places for Business and Careers." The Lakeland metro area was ranked #138. Criteria: costs (business and living); job growth (past and projected); income growth; quality of life; educational attainment (college and high school); projected economic growth; cultural and leisure opportunities; workplace tolerance laws; net migration patterns. *Forbes, "The Best Places for Business and Careers 2019: Seattle Still On Top," October 30, 2019*

Children/Family Rankings

- Lakeland was selected as one of the most playful cities in the U.S. by KaBOOM! The organization's Playful City USA initiative honors cities and towns across the nation that have made their communities more playable. Criteria: pledging to integrate play as a solution to challenges in their communities; making it easy for children to get active and balanced play; creating more family-friendly and innovative communities as a result. *KaBOOM! National Campaign for Play, "2017 Playful City USA Communities"*

Dating/Romance Rankings

- *Apartment List* conducted its annual survey of renters to for cities that have the best opportunities for dating. More than 11,000 single respondents rated their current city or neighborhood for opportunities to date. Lakeland ranked #3 out of 86 where single residents were very satisfied or somewhat satisfied, making it among the ten worst areas for dating opportunities. Other criteria analyzed included gender and education levels of renters. *Apartment List, "The Best & Worst Metros for Dating 2020," February 4, 2020*

Education Rankings

- Personal finance website *WalletHub* analyzed the 150 largest U.S. metropolitan statistical areas to determine where the most educated Americans are putting their degrees to work. Criteria: education levels; percentage of workers with degrees; education quality and attainment gap; public school quality rankings; quality and enrollment of each metro area's universities. Lakeland was ranked #138 (#1 = most educated city). *www.WalletHub.com, "Most and Least Educated Cities in America," July 20, 2020*

Health/Fitness Rankings

- Lakeland was identified as a "2021 Spring Allergy Capital." The area ranked #60 out of 100. Three groups of factors were used to identify the most challenging cities for people with allergies during the spring season: annual spring pollen levels; over the counter medicine use; number of board-certified allergy specialists. *Asthma and Allergy Foundation of America, "Spring Allergy Capitals 2021," February 23, 2021*

- Lakeland was identified as a "2021 Fall Allergy Capital." The area ranked #62 out of 100. Three groups of factors were used to identify the most challenging cities for people with allergies during the fall season: annual fall pollen levels; over the counter medicine use; number of board-certified allergy specialists. *Asthma and Allergy Foundation of America, "Fall Allergy Capitals 2021," February 23, 2021*
- Lakeland was identified as a "2019 Asthma Capital." The area ranked #86 out of the nation's 100 largest metropolitan areas. Criteria: estimated asthma prevalence; crude death rate from asthma; and ER visits due to asthma. Risk factors analyzed but not factored in the rankings: annual pollen score; annual air quality; public smoking laws; number of board-certified asthma specialists; rescue medication use; controller medication use; uninsured rate; poverty rate. *Asthma and Allergy Foundation of America, "Asthma Capitals 2019: The Most Challenging Places to Live With Asthma," May 7, 2019*

Real Estate Rankings

- Lakeland was ranked #169 out of 268 metro areas in terms of housing affordability in 2020 by the National Association of Home Builders (#1 = most affordable). Criteria: the share of homes sold in that area affordable to a family earning the local median income, based on standard mortgage underwriting criteria. *National Association of Home Builders®, NAHB-Wells Fargo Housing Opportunity Index, 4th Quarter 2020*

Safety Rankings

- The National Insurance Crime Bureau ranked 384 metro areas in the U.S. in terms of per capita rates of vehicle theft. The Lakeland metro area ranked #254 (#1 = highest rate). Criteria: number of vehicle theft offenses per 100,000 inhabitants in 2019. *National Insurance Crime Bureau, "Hot Spots 2019," July 21, 2020*

Seniors/Retirement Rankings

- From its Best Cities for Successful Aging indexes, the Milken Institute generated rankings for metropolitan areas, weighing data in nine categories—health care, wellness, living arrangements, transportation and convenience, financial characteristics, education, employment, community engagement, and overall livability. The Lakeland metro area was ranked #99 overall in the large metro area category. *Milken Institute, "Best Cities for Successful Aging, 2017" March 14, 2017*

Business Environment

DEMOGRAPHICS

Population Growth

Area	1990 Census	2000 Census	2010 Census	2019* Estimate	Population Growth (%) 1990-2019	Population Growth (%) 2010-2019
City	73,375	78,452	97,422	107,922	47.1	10.8
MSA[1]	405,382	483,924	602,095	686,218	69.3	14.0
U.S.	248,709,873	281,421,906	308,745,538	324,697,795	30.6	5.2

Note: (1) Figures cover the Lakeland-Winter Haven, FL Metropolitan Statistical Area; (*) 2015-2019 5-year estimated population
Source: U.S. Census Bureau, 1990 Census, Census 2000, Census 2010, 2015-2019 American Community Survey 5-Year Estimates

Household Size

Area	One	Two	Three	Four	Five	Six	Seven or More	Average Household Size
City	33.2	37.5	14.4	8.9	3.6	1.6	0.7	2.50
MSA[1]	25.3	37.9	15.2	11.7	5.9	2.5	1.5	2.90
U.S.	27.9	33.9	15.6	12.9	6.0	2.3	1.4	2.60

Note: (1) Figures cover the Lakeland-Winter Haven, FL Metropolitan Statistical Area
Source: U.S. Census Bureau, 2015-2019 American Community Survey 5-Year Estimates

Race

Area	White Alone[2] (%)	Black Alone[2] (%)	Asian Alone[2] (%)	AIAN[3] Alone[2] (%)	NHOPI[4] Alone[2] (%)	Other Race Alone[2] (%)	Two or More Races (%)
City	72.3	20.5	2.2	0.4	0.1	2.8	1.8
MSA[1]	77.1	15.3	1.8	0.3	0.0	3.0	2.5
U.S.	72.5	12.7	5.5	0.8	0.2	4.9	3.3

Note: (1) Figures cover the Lakeland-Winter Haven, FL Metropolitan Statistical Area; (2) Alone is defined as not being in combination with one or more other races; (3) American Indian and Alaska Native; (4) Native Hawaiian and Other Pacific Islander
Source: U.S. Census Bureau, 2015-2019 American Community Survey 5-Year Estimates

Hispanic or Latino Origin

Area	Total (%)	Mexican (%)	Puerto Rican (%)	Cuban (%)	Other (%)
City	16.4	3.5	6.3	2.5	4.0
MSA[1]	22.5	7.5	9.3	1.6	4.0
U.S.	18.0	11.2	1.7	0.7	4.3

Note: Persons of Hispanic or Latino origin can be of any race; (1) Figures cover the Lakeland-Winter Haven, FL Metropolitan Statistical Area
Source: U.S. Census Bureau, 2015-2019 American Community Survey 5-Year Estimates

Ancestry

Area	German	Irish	English	American	Italian	Polish	French[2]	Scottish	Dutch
City	10.1	8.1	8.7	8.1	4.5	1.8	2.6	1.7	1.4
MSA[1]	8.9	7.4	7.3	13.2	3.6	1.7	2.0	1.5	1.0
U.S.	13.3	9.7	7.2	6.2	5.1	2.8	2.3	1.7	1.2

Note: Figures are the percentage of the total population reporting a particular ancestry. The nine most commonly reported ancestries in the U.S. are shown. Figures include multiple ancestries (e.g. if a person reported being Irish and Italian, they were included in both columns); (1) Figures cover the Lakeland-Winter Haven, FL Metropolitan Statistical Area; (2) Excludes Basque
Source: U.S. Census Bureau, 2015-2019 American Community Survey 5-Year Estimates

Foreign-born Population

Area	Any Foreign Country	Asia	Mexico	Europe	Caribbean	Central America[2]	South America	Africa	Canada
City	10.9	1.8	1.3	0.8	4.0	0.5	1.4	0.2	0.9
MSA[1]	10.0	1.3	2.3	0.9	2.8	0.6	1.4	0.2	0.5
U.S.	13.6	4.2	3.5	1.5	1.3	1.1	1.0	0.7	0.2

Note: (1) Figures cover the Lakeland-Winter Haven, FL Metropolitan Statistical Area; (2) Excludes Mexico.
Source: U.S. Census Bureau, 2015-2019 American Community Survey 5-Year Estimates

Marital Status

Area	Never Married	Now Married[2]	Separated	Widowed	Divorced
City	34.9	41.7	2.1	8.2	13.1
MSA[1]	31.8	46.9	2.1	7.2	12.1
U.S.	33.4	48.1	1.9	5.8	10.9

Note: Figures are percentages and cover the population 15 years of age and older; (1) Figures cover the Lakeland-Winter Haven, FL Metropolitan Statistical Area; (2) Excludes separated
Source: U.S. Census Bureau, 2015-2019 American Community Survey 5-Year Estimates

Disability by Age

Area	All Ages	Under 18 Years Old	18 to 64 Years Old	65 Years and Over
City	15.8	4.3	11.8	37.1
MSA[1]	15.4	5.7	12.4	34.7
U.S.	12.6	4.2	10.3	34.5

Note: Figures show percent of the civilian noninstitutionalized population that reported having a disability. Disability status is determined from six types of difficulty: vision, hearing, cognitive, ambulatory, self-care, and independent living. For children under 5 years old, hearing and vision difficulty are used to determine disability status. For children between the ages of 5 and 14, disability status is determined from hearing, vision, cognitive, ambulatory, and self-care difficulties. For people aged 15 years and older, they are considered to have a disability if they have difficulty with any one of the six difficulty types; Note: (1) Figures cover the Lakeland-Winter Haven, FL Metropolitan Statistical Area
Source: U.S. Census Bureau, 2015-2019 American Community Survey 5-Year Estimates

Age

Area	Under Age 5	Age 5–19	Age 20–34	Age 35–44	Age 45–54	Age 55–64	Age 65–74	Age 75–84	Age 85+	Median Age
City	4.9	17.8	19.9	11.9	11.4	11.9	11.8	7.2	3.2	41.1
MSA[1]	5.8	18.8	19.0	11.8	12.1	12.3	11.4	6.7	2.1	40.2
U.S.	6.1	19.1	20.7	12.6	13.0	12.9	9.1	4.6	1.9	38.1

Note: (1) Figures cover the Lakeland-Winter Haven, FL Metropolitan Statistical Area
Source: U.S. Census Bureau, 2015-2019 American Community Survey 5-Year Estimates

Gender

Area	Males	Females	Males per 100 Females
City	51,105	56,817	89.9
MSA[1]	336,279	349,939	96.1
U.S.	159,886,919	164,810,876	97.0

Note: (1) Figures cover the Lakeland-Winter Haven, FL Metropolitan Statistical Area
Source: U.S. Census Bureau, 2015-2019 American Community Survey 5-Year Estimates

Religious Groups by Family

Area	Catholic	Baptist	Non-Den.	Methodist[2]	Lutheran	LDS[3]	Pentecostal	Presbyterian[4]	Muslim[5]	Judaism
MSA[1]	7.5	13.6	5.0	4.0	0.9	0.8	4.0	1.7	0.5	0.1
U.S.	19.1	9.3	4.0	4.0	2.3	2.0	1.9	1.6	0.8	0.7

Note: Figures are the number of adherents as a percentage of the total population; (1) Figures cover the Lakeland-Winter Haven, FL Metropolitan Statistical Area; (2) Methodist/Pietist; (3) Latter Day Saints; (4) Reformed; (5) Figures are estimates
Source: Association of Statisticians of American Religious Bodies, 2010 U.S. Religion Census: Religious Congregations & Membership Study

Religious Groups by Tradition

Area	Catholic	Evangelical Protestant	Mainline Protestant	Other Tradition	Black Protestant	Orthodox
MSA[1]	7.5	24.7	5.2	1.4	1.8	0.1
U.S.	19.1	16.2	7.3	4.3	1.6	0.3

Note: Figures are the number of adherents as a percentage of the total population; (1) Figures cover the Lakeland-Winter Haven, FL Metropolitan Statistical Area
Source: Association of Statisticians of American Religious Bodies, 2010 U.S. Religion Census: Religious Congregations & Membership Study

ECONOMY

Gross Metropolitan Product

Area	2017	2018	2019	2020	Rank[2]
MSA[1]	21.4	22.6	23.6	24.6	119

Note: Figures are in billions of dollars; (1) Figures cover the Lakeland-Winter Haven, FL Metropolitan Statistical Area; (2) Rank is based on 2018 data and ranges from 1 to 381
Source: U.S. Conference of Mayors, U.S. Metro Economies: GMP & Employment 2018-2020, September 2019

Economic Growth

Area	2015-17 (%)	2018 (%)	2019 (%)	2020 (%)	Rank[2]
MSA[1]	2.7	3.2	2.5	2.4	82
U.S.	1.9	2.9	2.3	2.1	—

Note: Figures are real gross metropolitan product (GMP) growth rates and represent average annual percent change; (1) Figures cover the Lakeland-Winter Haven, FL Metropolitan Statistical Area; (2) Rank is based on 2017 2-year average annual percent change and ranges from 1 to 381
Source: U.S. Conference of Mayors, U.S. Metro Economies: GMP & Employment 2018-2020, September 2019

Metropolitan Area Exports

Area	2014	2015	2016	2017	2018	2019	Rank[2]
MSA[1]	2,151.9	1,318.6	995.5	1,147.2	1,299.8	1,141.5	143

Note: Figures are in millions of dollars; (1) Figures cover the Lakeland-Winter Haven, FL Metropolitan Statistical Area; (2) Rank is based on 2019 data and ranges from 1 to 386
Source: U.S. Department of Commerce, International Trade Administration, Office of Trade and Economic Analysis, Industry and Analysis, Exports by Metropolitan Area, data extracted March 24, 2021

Building Permits

Area	Single-Family 2018	Single-Family 2019	Pct. Chg.	Multi-Family 2018	Multi-Family 2019	Pct. Chg.	Total 2018	Total 2019	Pct. Chg.
City	435	606	39.3	0	953	–	435	1,559	258.4
MSA[1]	5,331	6,435	20.7	0	2,291	–	5,331	8,726	63.7
U.S.	855,300	862,100	0.7	473,500	523,900	10.6	1,328,800	1,386,000	4.3

Note: (1) Figures cover the Lakeland-Winter Haven, FL Metropolitan Statistical Area; Figures represent new, privately-owned housing units authorized (unadjusted data); All permit data are based on estimates with imputation
Source: U.S. Census Bureau, Manufacturing, Mining, and Construction Statistics, Building Permits, 2018, 2019

Bankruptcy Filings

Area	Business Filings 2019	Business Filings 2020	% Chg.	Nonbusiness Filings 2019	Nonbusiness Filings 2020	% Chg.
Polk County	31	53	71.0	1,466	1,168	-20.3
U.S.	22,780	21,655	-4.9	752,160	522,808	-30.5

Note: Business filings include Chapter 7, Chapter 9, Chapter 11, Chapter 12, Chapter 13, Chapter 15, and Section 304; Nonbusiness filings include Chapter 7, Chapter 11, and Chapter 13
Source: Administrative Office of the U.S. Courts, Business and Nonbusiness Bankruptcy, County Cases Commenced by Chapter of the Bankruptcy Code, During the 12-Month Period Ending December 31, 2019 and Business and Nonbusiness Bankruptcy, County Cases Commenced by Chapter of the Bankruptcy Code, During the 12-Month Period Ending December 31, 2020

Housing Vacancy Rates

Area	Gross Vacancy Rate[2] (%) 2018	2019	2020	Year-Round Vacancy Rate[3] (%) 2018	2019	2020	Rental Vacancy Rate[4] (%) 2018	2019	2020	Homeowner Vacancy Rate[5] (%) 2018	2019	2020
MSA[1]	n/a	n/a	n/a	n/a	n/a	n/a	n/a	n/a	n/a	n/a	n/a	n/a
U.S.	12.3	12.0	10.6	9.7	9.5	8.2	6.9	6.7	6.3	1.5	1.4	1.0

Note: (1) Figures cover the Lakeland-Winter Haven, FL Metropolitan Statistical Area; (2) The percentage of the total housing inventory that is vacant; (3) The percentage of the housing inventory (excluding seasonal units) that is year-round vacant; (4) The percentage of rental inventory that is vacant for rent; (5) The percentage of homeowner inventory that is vacant for sale; n/a not available
Source: U.S. Census Bureau, Housing Vacancies and Homeownership Annual Statistics: 2018, 2019, 2020

INCOME

Income

Area	Per Capita ($)	Median Household ($)	Average Household ($)
City	28,042	47,511	67,899
MSA[1]	24,864	50,584	66,810
U.S.	34,103	62,843	88,607

Note: (1) Figures cover the Lakeland-Winter Haven, FL Metropolitan Statistical Area
Source: U.S. Census Bureau, 2015-2019 American Community Survey 5-Year Estimates

Household Income Distribution

Area	Under $15,000	$15,000 -$24,999	$25,000 -$34,999	$35,000 -$49,999	$50,000 -$74,999	$75,000 -$99,999	$100,000 -$149,999	$150,000 and up
City	12.5	11.9	12.5	15.3	19.2	11.7	9.9	7.1
MSA[1]	11.1	11.2	11.2	16.0	19.9	12.6	11.3	6.8
U.S.	10.3	8.9	8.9	12.3	17.2	12.7	15.1	14.5

Note: (1) Figures cover the Lakeland-Winter Haven, FL Metropolitan Statistical Area
Source: U.S. Census Bureau, 2015-2019 American Community Survey 5-Year Estimates

Lakeland, Florida

Poverty Rate

Area	All Ages	Under 18 Years Old	18 to 64 Years Old	65 Years and Over
City	16.4	23.5	15.5	12.3
MSA[1]	15.8	24.7	14.5	9.9
U.S.	13.4	18.5	12.6	9.3

Note: Figures are percentage of people whose income during the past 12 months was below the poverty level;
(1) Figures cover the Lakeland-Winter Haven, FL Metropolitan Statistical Area
Source: U.S. Census Bureau, 2015-2019 American Community Survey 5-Year Estimates

CITY FINANCES

City Government Finances

Component	2017 ($000)	2017 ($ per capita)
Total Revenues	643,093	6,160
Total Expenditures	611,523	5,857
Debt Outstanding	987,999	9,464
Cash and Securities[1]	1,304,590	12,496

Note: (1) Cash and security holdings of a government at the close of its fiscal year, including those of its dependent agencies, utilities, and liquor stores.
Source: U.S. Census Bureau, State & Local Government Finances 2017

City Government Revenue by Source

Source	2017 ($000)	2017 ($ per capita)	2017 (%)
General Revenue			
From Federal Government	6,644	64	1.0
From State Government	17,649	169	2.7
From Local Governments	1,944	19	0.3
Taxes			
Property	31,166	299	4.8
Sales and Gross Receipts	20,586	197	3.2
Personal Income	0	0	0.0
Corporate Income	0	0	0.0
Motor Vehicle License	0	0	0.0
Other Taxes	5,201	50	0.8
Current Charges	65,152	624	10.1
Liquor Store	0	0	0.0
Utility	326,936	3,132	50.8
Employee Retirement	86,118	825	13.4

Source: U.S. Census Bureau, State & Local Government Finances 2017

City Government Expenditures by Function

Function	2017 ($000)	2017 ($ per capita)	2017 (%)
General Direct Expenditures			
Air Transportation	8,033	76	1.3
Corrections	0	0	0.0
Education	0	0	0.0
Employment Security Administration	0	0	0.0
Financial Administration	9,239	88	1.5
Fire Protection	17,425	166	2.8
General Public Buildings	0	0	0.0
Governmental Administration, Other	3,954	37	0.6
Health	0	0	0.0
Highways	16,649	159	2.7
Hospitals	0	0	0.0
Housing and Community Development	2,207	21	0.4
Interest on General Debt	737	7	0.1
Judicial and Legal	255	2	0.0
Libraries	3,742	35	0.6
Parking	1,043	10	0.2
Parks and Recreation	54,372	520	8.9
Police Protection	38,626	370	6.3
Public Welfare	0	0	0.0
Sewerage	20,735	198	3.4
Solid Waste Management	12,300	117	2.0
Veterans' Services	0	0	0.0
Liquor Store	0	0	0.0
Utility	328,134	3,143	53.7
Employee Retirement	52,781	505	8.6

Source: U.S. Census Bureau, State & Local Government Finances 2017

Lakeland, Florida

EMPLOYMENT

Labor Force and Employment

Area	Civilian Labor Force Dec. 2019	Dec. 2020	% Chg.	Workers Employed Dec. 2019	Dec. 2020	% Chg.
City	47,582	47,525	-0.1	46,092	44,428	-3.6
MSA[1]	308,057	308,560	0.2	298,597	287,817	-3.6
U.S.	164,007,000	160,017,000	-2.4	158,504,000	149,613,000	-5.6

Note: Data is not seasonally adjusted and covers workers 16 years of age and older; (1) Figures cover the Lakeland-Winter Haven, FL Metropolitan Statistical Area
Source: Bureau of Labor Statistics, Local Area Unemployment Statistics

Unemployment Rate

Area	Jan.	Feb.	Mar.	Apr.	May	Jun.	Jul.	Aug.	Sep.	Oct.	Nov.	Dec.
City	3.8	3.5	4.9	11.4	12.0	9.4	10.7	7.3	6.4	6.5	6.9	6.5
MSA[1]	3.7	3.5	4.9	14.0	17.6	13.6	13.2	9.2	7.9	7.1	7.0	6.7
U.S.	4.0	3.8	4.5	14.4	13.0	11.2	10.5	8.5	7.7	6.6	6.4	6.5

Note: Data is not seasonally adjusted and covers workers 16 years of age and older; (1) Figures cover the Lakeland-Winter Haven, FL Metropolitan Statistical Area
Source: Bureau of Labor Statistics, Local Area Unemployment Statistics

Average Wages

Occupation	$/Hr.	Occupation	$/Hr.
Accountants and Auditors	36.20	Maintenance and Repair Workers	20.60
Automotive Mechanics	22.40	Marketing Managers	62.00
Bookkeepers	18.60	Network and Computer Systems Admin.	36.30
Carpenters	18.80	Nurses, Licensed Practical	21.00
Cashiers	12.00	Nurses, Registered	31.80
Computer Programmers	31.50	Nursing Assistants	13.40
Computer Systems Analysts	37.50	Office Clerks, General	17.00
Computer User Support Specialists	26.20	Physical Therapists	45.90
Construction Laborers	16.50	Physicians	111.80
Cooks, Restaurant	12.90	Plumbers, Pipefitters and Steamfitters	21.30
Customer Service Representatives	15.50	Police and Sheriff's Patrol Officers	28.10
Dentists	97.40	Postal Service Mail Carriers	25.70
Electricians	19.90	Real Estate Sales Agents	24.70
Engineers, Electrical	43.20	Retail Salespersons	14.00
Fast Food and Counter Workers	10.40	Sales Representatives, Technical/Scientific	50.70
Financial Managers	52.80	Secretaries, Exc. Legal/Medical/Executive	16.80
First-Line Supervisors of Office Workers	26.80	Security Guards	13.70
General and Operations Managers	46.20	Surgeons	125.70
Hairdressers/Cosmetologists	12.90	Teacher Assistants, Exc. Postsecondary*	11.20
Home Health and Personal Care Aides	11.90	Teachers, Secondary School, Exc. Sp. Ed.*	24.20
Janitors and Cleaners	12.30	Telemarketers	12.40
Landscaping/Groundskeeping Workers	14.40	Truck Drivers, Heavy/Tractor-Trailer	22.00
Lawyers	44.80	Truck Drivers, Light/Delivery Services	22.50
Maids and Housekeeping Cleaners	11.50	Waiters and Waitresses	11.40

Note: Wage data covers the Lakeland-Winter Haven, FL Metropolitan Statistical Area; (*) Hourly wages were calculated from annual wage data based on a 40 hour work week; n/a not available.
Source: Bureau of Labor Statistics, Metro Area Occupational Employment & Wage Estimates, May 2020

Employment by Industry

Sector	MSA[1] Number of Employees	Percent of Total	U.S. Percent of Total
Construction, Mining, and Logging	15,500	6.3	5.5
Education and Health Services	35,900	14.6	16.3
Financial Activities	14,400	5.9	6.1
Government	28,800	11.7	15.2
Information	1,900	0.8	1.9
Leisure and Hospitality	21,500	8.8	9.0
Manufacturing	17,900	7.3	8.5
Other Services	6,300	2.6	3.8
Professional and Business Services	34,200	13.9	14.4
Retail Trade	33,300	13.6	10.9
Transportation, Warehousing, and Utilities	24,700	10.1	4.6
Wholesale Trade	11,200	4.6	3.9

Note: Figures are non-farm employment as of December 2020. Figures are not seasonally adjusted and include workers 16 years of age and older; (1) Figures cover the Lakeland-Winter Haven, FL Metropolitan Statistical Area
Source: Bureau of Labor Statistics, Current Employment Statistics, Employment, Hours, and Earnings

Employment by Occupation

Occupation Classification	City (%)	MSA[1] (%)	U.S. (%)
Management, Business, Science, and Arts	33.4	29.5	38.5
Natural Resources, Construction, and Maintenance	8.4	10.9	8.9
Production, Transportation, and Material Moving	15.4	14.9	13.2
Sales and Office	25.9	24.3	21.6
Service	16.9	20.4	17.8

Note: Figures cover employed civilians 16 years of age and older; (1) Figures cover the Lakeland-Winter Haven, FL Metropolitan Statistical Area
Source: U.S. Census Bureau, 2015-2019 American Community Survey 5-Year Estimates

Occupations with Greatest Projected Employment Growth: 2020 – 2022

Occupation[1]	2020 Employment	2022 Projected Employment	Numeric Employment Change	Percent Employment Change
Fast Food and Counter Workers	172,590	214,590	42,000	24.3
Waiters and Waitresses	141,990	180,530	38,540	27.1
Retail Salespersons	264,490	292,340	27,850	10.5
Cooks, Restaurant	79,150	103,770	24,620	31.1
Maids and Housekeeping Cleaners	63,280	81,030	17,750	28.0
Cashiers	204,540	221,530	16,990	8.3
Registered Nurses	189,240	202,880	13,640	7.2
Laborers and Freight, Stock, and Material Movers, Hand	147,740	160,650	12,910	8.7
First-Line Supervisors of Food Preparation and Serving Workers	51,820	64,080	12,260	23.7
Stockers and Order Fillers	130,980	142,780	11,800	9.0

Note: Projections cover Florida; (1) Sorted by numeric employment change
Source: www.projectionscentral.com, State Occupational Projections, 2020–2022 Short-Term Projections

Fastest-Growing Occupations: 2020 – 2022

Occupation[1]	2020 Employment	2022 Projected Employment	Numeric Employment Change	Percent Employment Change
Hotel, Motel, and Resort Desk Clerks	11,930	18,100	6,170	51.7
Locker Room, Coatroom, and Dressing Room Attendants	930	1,360	430	46.2
Lodging Managers	3,190	4,420	1,230	38.6
Manicurists and Pedicurists	2,640	3,580	940	35.6
Bartenders	31,430	42,540	11,110	35.3
Gaming Cage Workers	320	430	110	34.4
Parking Lot Attendants	11,200	15,040	3,840	34.3
Gaming Dealers	2,660	3,560	900	33.8
Baggage Porters and Bellhops	3,520	4,670	1,150	32.7
Cooks, Restaurant	79,150	103,770	24,620	31.1

Note: Projections cover Florida; (1) Sorted by percent employment change and excludes occupations with numeric employment change less than 50
Source: www.projectionscentral.com, State Occupational Projections, 2020–2022 Short-Term Projections

TAXES

State Corporate Income Tax Rates

State	Tax Rate (%)	Income Brackets ($)	Num. of Brackets	Financial Institution Tax Rate (%)[a]	Federal Income Tax Ded.
Florida	4.458 (e)	Flat rate	1	4.458 (e)	No

Note: Tax rates as of January 1, 2021; (a) Rates listed are the corporate income tax rate applied to financial institutions or excise taxes based on income. Some states have other taxes based upon the value of deposits or shares; (e) The Florida tax rate may be adjusted downward if certain revenue targets are met.
Source: Federation of Tax Administrators, State Corporate Income Tax Rates, January 1, 2021

State Individual Income Tax Rates

State	Tax Rate (%)	Income Brackets ($)	Personal Exemptions ($) Single	Personal Exemptions ($) Married	Personal Exemptions ($) Depend.	Standard Ded. ($) Single	Standard Ded. ($) Married
Florida				– No state income tax –			

Note: Tax rates as of January 1, 2021; Local- and county-level taxes are not included
Source: Federation of Tax Administrators, State Individual Income Tax Rates, January 1, 2021

Various State Sales and Excise Tax Rates

State	State Sales Tax (%)	Gasoline[1] (¢/gal.)	Cigarette[2] ($/pack)	Spirits[3] ($/gal.)	Wine[4] ($/gal.)	Beer[5] ($/gal.)	Recreational Marijuana (%)
Florida	6	42.46	1.339	6.5	2.25	0.48	Not legal

Note: All tax rates as of January 1, 2021; (1) The American Petroleum Institute has developed a methodology for determining the average tax rate on a gallon of fuel. Rates may include any of the following: excise taxes, environmental fees, storage tank fees, other fees or taxes, general sales tax, and local taxes; (2) The federal excise tax of $1.0066 per pack and local taxes are not included; (3) Rates are those applicable to off-premise sales of 40% alcohol by volume (a.b.v.) distilled spirits in 750ml containers. Local excise taxes are excluded; (4) Rates are those applicable to off-premise sales of 11% a.b.v. non-carbonated wine in 750ml containers; (5) Rates are those applicable to off-premise sales of 4.7% a.b.v. beer in 12 ounce containers.
Source: Tax Foundation, 2021 Facts & Figures: How Does Your State Compare?

State Business Tax Climate Index Rankings

State	Overall Rank	Corporate Tax Rank	Individual Income Tax Rank	Sales Tax Rank	Property Tax Rank	Unemployment Insurance Tax Rank
Florida	4	6	1	21	13	2

Note: The index is a measure of how each state's tax laws affect economic performance. The lower the rank, the more favorable a state's tax system is for business. States without a given tax are given a ranking of 1. The scores/rankings for the District of Columbia do not affect other states. The 2021 index represents the tax climate as of July 1, 2020.
Source: Tax Foundation, State Business Tax Climate Index 2021

TRANSPORTATION

Means of Transportation to Work

Area	Car/Truck/Van Drove Alone	Car/Truck/Van Carpooled	Public Transportation Bus	Public Transportation Subway	Public Transportation Railroad	Bicycle	Walked	Other Means	Worked at Home
City	80.5	10.5	0.8	0.0	0.0	0.3	1.6	1.8	4.6
MSA[1]	83.4	9.4	0.5	0.0	0.0	0.4	1.0	1.4	4.0
U.S.	76.3	9.0	2.4	1.9	0.6	0.5	2.7	1.4	5.2

Note: Figures are percentages and cover workers 16 years of age and older; (1) Figures cover the Lakeland-Winter Haven, FL Metropolitan Statistical Area
Source: U.S. Census Bureau, 2015-2019 American Community Survey 5-Year Estimates

Travel Time to Work

Area	Less Than 10 Minutes	10 to 19 Minutes	20 to 29 Minutes	30 to 44 Minutes	45 to 59 Minutes	60 to 89 Minutes	90 Minutes or More
City	10.8	43.4	20.1	14.4	5.8	3.5	2.0
MSA[1]	8.4	30.0	21.7	21.0	9.9	6.3	2.7
U.S.	12.2	28.4	20.8	20.8	8.3	6.4	2.9

Note: Note: Figures are percentages and include workers 16 years old and over; (1) Figures cover the Lakeland-Winter Haven, FL Metropolitan Statistical Area
Source: U.S. Census Bureau, 2015-2019 American Community Survey 5-Year Estimates

Key Congestion Measures

Measure	1982	1992	2002	2012	2017
Annual Hours of Delay, Total (000)	n/a	n/a	n/a	n/a	4,773
Annual Hours of Delay, Per Auto Commuter	n/a	n/a	n/a	n/a	16
Annual Congestion Cost, Total (million $)	n/a	n/a	n/a	n/a	102
Annual Congestion Cost, Per Auto Commuter ($)	n/a	n/a	n/a	n/a	351

Note: n/a not available
Source: Texas A&M Transportation Institute, 2019 Urban Mobility Report

Freeway Travel Time Index

Measure	1982	1987	1992	1997	2002	2007	2012	2017
Urban Area Index[1]	n/a	n/a	n/a	n/a	n/a	n/a	n/a	1.09
Urban Area Rank[1,2]	n/a	n/a	n/a	n/a	n/a	n/a	n/a	n/a

Note: Freeway Travel Time Index—the ratio of travel time in the peak period to the travel time at free-flow conditions. For example, a value of 1.30 indicates a 20-minute free-flow trip takes 26 minutes in the peak (20 minutes x 1.30 = 26 minutes); (1) Covers the Lakeland FL urban area; (2) Rank is based on 101 larger urban areas (#1 = highest travel time index); n/a not available
Source: Texas A&M Transportation Institute, 2019 Urban Mobility Report

Public Transportation

Agency Name / Mode of Transportation	Vehicles Operated in Maximum Service[1]	Annual Unlinked Passenger Trips[2] (in thous.)	Annual Passenger Miles[3] (in thous.)
Lakeland Area Mass Transit District			
Bus (directly operated)	30	1,187.0	6,722.8
Demand Response (directly operated)	35	107.7	705.6

Note: (1) Number of revenue vehicles operated by the given mode and type of service to meet the annual maximum service requirement. This is the revenue vehicle count during the peak season of the year; on the week and day that maximum service is provided. Vehicles operated in maximum service (VOMS) exclude atypical days and one-time special events; (2) Number of passengers who boarded public transportation vehicles. Passengers are counted each time they board a vehicle no matter how many vehicles they use to travel from their origin to their destination. (3) Sum of the distances ridden by all passengers during the entire fiscal year.
Source: Federal Transit Administration, National Transit Database, 2019

Air Transportation

Airport Name and Code / Type of Service	Passenger Airlines[1]	Passenger Enplanements	Freight Carriers[2]	Freight (lbs)
Tampa International Airport (TPA)				
Domestic service (U.S. carriers - 2020)	25	4,821,157	12	230,581,855
International service (U.S. carriers - 2019)	12	96,232	3	2,417,945

Note: (1) Includes all U.S.-based major, minor and commuter airlines that carried at least one passenger during the year; (2) Includes all U.S.-based airlines and freight carriers that transported at least one pound of freight during the year.
Source: Bureau of Transportation Statistics, The Intermodal Transportation Database, Air Carriers: T-100 Domestic Market (U.S. Carriers), 2020; Bureau of Transportation Statistics, The Intermodal Transportation Database, Air Carriers: T-100 International Market (U.S. Carriers), 2019

BUSINESSES

Major Business Headquarters

Company Name	Industry	Rankings Fortune[1]	Forbes[2]
Publix Super Markets	Food and Drug Stores	87	5

Note: (1) Companies that produce a 10-K are ranked 1 to 500 based on 2019 revenue; (2) All private companies with at least $2 billion in annual revenue through the end of their most current fiscal year are ranked 1 to 219; companies listed are headquartered in the city; dashes indicate no ranking
Source: Fortune, "Fortune 500," June/July 2020; Forbes, "America's Largest Private Companies," 2020

Living Environment

COST OF LIVING

Cost of Living Index

Composite Index	Groceries	Housing	Utilities	Transportation	Health Care	Misc. Goods/Services
n/a	n/a	n/a	n/a	n/a	n/a	n/a

Note: The Cost of Living Index measures regional differences in the cost of consumer goods and services, excluding taxes and non-consumer expenditures, for professional and managerial households in the top income quintile. It is based on more than 50,000 prices covering almost 60 different items for which prices are collected three times a year by chambers of commerce, economic development organizations or university applied economic centers in each participating urban area. The numbers shown should be read as a percentage above or below the national average of 100. For example, a value of 115.4 in the groceries column indicates that grocery prices are 15.4% higher than the national average. Small differences in the index numbers should not be interpreted as significant; n/a not available.
Source: The Council for Community and Economic Research, Cost of Living Index, 2020

Grocery Prices

Area[1]	T-Bone Steak ($/pound)	Frying Chicken ($/pound)	Whole Milk ($/half gal.)	Eggs ($/dozen)	Orange Juice ($/64 oz.)	Coffee ($/11.5 oz.)
City[2]	n/a	n/a	n/a	n/a	n/a	n/a
Avg.	11.78	1.39	2.05	1.47	3.57	4.34
Min.	8.03	0.94	1.03	0.74	2.94	3.02
Max.	15.86	2.65	4.31	3.77	5.44	8.69

Note: (1) Values for the local area are compared with the average, minimum and maximum values for all 284 areas in the Cost of Living Index; (2) Figures cover the Lakeland FL urban area; n/a not available; **T-Bone Steak** (price per pound); **Frying Chicken** (price per pound, whole fryer); **Whole Milk** (half gallon carton); **Eggs** (price per dozen, Grade A, large); **Orange Juice** (64 oz. Tropicana or Florida Natural); **Coffee** (11.5 oz. can, vacuum-packed, Maxwell House, Hills Bros, or Folgers).
Source: The Council for Community and Economic Research, Cost of Living Index, 2020

Housing and Utility Costs

Area[1]	New Home Price ($)	Apartment Rent ($/month)	All Electric ($/month)	Part Electric ($/month)	Other Energy ($/month)	Telephone ($/month)
City[2]	n/a	n/a	n/a	n/a	n/a	n/a
Avg.	368,594	1,168	170.86	100.47	65.28	184.30
Min.	190,567	502	91.58	31.42	26.08	169.60
Max.	2,227,806	4,738	470.38	280.31	280.06	206.50

Note: (1) Values for the local area are compared with the average, minimum and maximum values for all 284 areas in the Cost of Living Index; (2) Figures cover the Lakeland FL urban area; n/a not available; **New Home Price** (2,400 sf living area, 8,000 sf lot, in urban area with full utilities); **Apartment Rent** (950 sf 2 bedroom/1.5 or 2 bath, unfurnished, excluding all utilities except water); **All Electric** (average monthly cost for an all-electric home); **Part Electric** (average monthly cost for a part-electric home); **Other Energy** (average monthly cost for natural gas, fuel oil, coal, wood, and any other forms of energy except electricity); **Telephone** (price includes the base monthly rate plus taxes and fees for three lines of mobile phone service).
Source: The Council for Community and Economic Research, Cost of Living Index, 2020

Health Care, Transportation, and Other Costs

Area[1]	Doctor ($/visit)	Dentist ($/visit)	Optometrist ($/visit)	Gasoline ($/gallon)	Beauty Salon ($/visit)	Men's Shirt ($)
City[2]	n/a	n/a	n/a	n/a	n/a	n/a
Avg.	115.44	99.32	108.10	2.21	39.27	31.37
Min.	36.68	59.00	51.36	1.71	19.00	11.00
Max.	219.00	153.10	250.97	3.46	82.05	58.33

Note: (1) Values for the local area are compared with the average, minimum and maximum values for all 284 areas in the Cost of Living Index; (2) Figures cover the Lakeland FL urban area; n/a not available; **Doctor** (general practitioners routine exam of an established patient); **Dentist** (adult teeth cleaning and periodic oral examination); **Optometrist** (full vision eye exam for established adult patient); **Gasoline** (one gallon regular unleaded, national brand, including all taxes, cash price at self-service pump if available); **Beauty Salon** (woman's shampoo, trim, and blow-dry); **Men's Shirt** (cotton/polyester dress shirt, pinpoint weave, long sleeves).
Source: The Council for Community and Economic Research, Cost of Living Index, 2020

HOUSING

Homeownership Rate

Area	2012 (%)	2013 (%)	2014 (%)	2015 (%)	2016 (%)	2017 (%)	2018 (%)	2019 (%)	2020 (%)
MSA[1]	n/a	n/a	n/a	n/a	n/a	n/a	n/a	n/a	n/a
U.S.	65.4	65.1	64.5	63.7	63.4	63.9	64.4	64.6	66.6

Note: (1) Figures cover the Lakeland-Winter Haven, FL Metropolitan Statistical Area; n/a not available
Source: U.S. Census Bureau, Housing Vacancies and Homeownership Annual Statistics: 2012-2020

House Price Index (HPI)

Area	National Ranking[2]	Quarterly Change (%)	One-Year Change (%)	Five-Year Change (%)	Since 1991Q1 (%)
MSA[1]	8	4.29	10.11	53.44	194.73
U.S.[3]	—	3.81	10.77	38.99	205.12

Note: The HPI is a weighted repeat sales index. It measures average price changes in repeat sales or refinancings on the same properties. This information is obtained by reviewing repeat mortgage transactions on single-family properties whose mortgages have been purchased or securitized by Fannie Mae or Freddie Mac since January 1975; (1) Figures cover the Lakeland-Winter Haven, FL Metropolitan Statistical Area; (2) Rankings are based on annual percentage change for all metro areas containing at least 15,000 transactions over the last 10 years and ranges from 1 to 253; (3) figures based on a weighted average of Census Division estimates using a seasonally adjusted, purchase-only index; all figures are for the period ending December 31, 2020
Source: Federal Housing Finance Agency, Change in Metropolitan Area House Price Indexes, April 7, 2021

Median Single-Family Home Prices

Area	2018	2019	2020p	Percent Change 2019 to 2020
MSA[1]	196.0	210.0	230.0	9.5
U.S. Average	261.6	274.6	299.9	9.2

Note: Figures are median sales prices of existing single-family homes in thousands of dollars; (p) preliminary; (1) Figures cover the Lakeland-Winter Haven, FL Metropolitan Statistical Area
Source: National Association of Realtors, Median Sales Price of Existing Single-Family Homes for Metropolitan Areas, 4th Quarter 2020

Qualifying Income Based on Median Sales Price of Existing Single-Family Homes

Area	With 5% Down ($)	With 10% Down ($)	With 20% Down ($)
MSA[1]	45,394	43,005	38,227
U.S. Average	59,266	56,147	49,908

Note: Figures are preliminary; Qualifying income is based on a mortgage rate of 2.81%. Monthly principal and interest payment is limited to 25% of income; (1) Figures cover the Lakeland-Winter Haven, FL Metropolitan Statistical Area
Source: National Association of Realtors, Qualifying Income Based on Median Sales Price of Existing Single-Family Homes for Metropolitan Areas, 4th Quarter 2020

Home Value Distribution

Area	Under $50,000	$50,000 -$99,999	$100,000 -$149,999	$150,000 -$199,999	$200,000 -$299,999	$300,000 -$499,999	$500,000 -$999,999	$1,000,000 or more
City	18.2	15.4	16.7	19.4	18.7	8.6	2.6	0.5
MSA[1]	14.7	18.2	16.8	18.6	20.6	8.3	2.2	0.6
U.S.	6.9	12.0	13.3	14.0	19.6	19.3	11.4	3.4

Note: Figures are percentages and cover owner-occupied housing units; (1) Figures cover the Lakeland-Winter Haven, FL Metropolitan Statistical Area
Source: U.S. Census Bureau, 2015-2019 American Community Survey 5-Year Estimates

Year Housing Structure Built

Area	2010 or Later	2000 -2009	1990 -1999	1980 -1989	1970 -1979	1960 -1969	1950 -1959	1940 -1949	Before 1940	Median Year
City	3.4	15.1	13.2	19.6	20.2	10.4	8.8	3.3	6.0	1981
MSA[1]	5.8	23.8	17.7	18.2	15.1	7.7	6.5	2.1	3.2	1989
U.S.	5.2	14.0	13.9	13.4	15.2	10.6	10.3	4.9	12.6	1978

Note: Figures are percentages except for Median Year; Note: (1) Figures cover the Lakeland-Winter Haven, FL Metropolitan Statistical Area
Source: U.S. Census Bureau, 2015-2019 American Community Survey 5-Year Estimates

Gross Monthly Rent

Area	Under $500	$500 -$999	$1,000 -$1,499	$1,500 -$1,999	$2,000 -$2,499	$2,500 -$2,999	$3,000 and up	Median ($)
City	5.6	44.6	39.6	7.9	1.4	0.6	0.3	999
MSA[1]	6.7	45.8	33.6	11.3	1.8	0.5	0.3	978
U.S.	9.4	36.2	30.0	14.0	5.6	2.4	2.4	1,062

Note: Figures are percentages except for Median; Gross rent is the contract rent plus the estimated average monthly cost of utilities (electricity, gas, and water and sewer) and fuels (oil, coal, kerosene, wood, etc.) if these are paid by the renter (or paid for the renter by someone else); (1) Figures cover the Lakeland-Winter Haven, FL Metropolitan Statistical Area
Source: U.S. Census Bureau, 2015-2019 American Community Survey 5-Year Estimates

HEALTH

Health Risk Factors

Category	MSA[1] (%)	U.S. (%)
Adults aged 18–64 who have any kind of health care coverage	n/a	87.3
Adults who reported being in good or better health	n/a	82.4
Adults who have been told they have high blood cholesterol	n/a	33.0
Adults who have been told they have high blood pressure	n/a	32.3
Adults who are current smokers	n/a	17.1
Adults who currently use E-cigarettes	n/a	4.6
Adults who currently use chewing tobacco, snuff, or snus	n/a	4.0
Adults who are heavy drinkers[2]	n/a	6.3
Adults who are binge drinkers[3]	n/a	17.4
Adults who are overweight (BMI 25.0 - 29.9)	n/a	35.3
Adults who are obese (BMI 30.0 - 99.8)	n/a	31.3
Adults who participated in any physical activities in the past month	n/a	74.4
Adults who always or nearly always wears a seat belt	n/a	94.3

Note: n/a not available; (1) Figures cover the Lakeland-Winter Haven, FL Metropolitan Statistical Area; (2) Heavy drinkers are classified as adult men having more than 14 drinks per week and adult women having more than 7 drinks per week; (3) Binge drinkers are classified as males having five or more drinks on one occasion or females having four or more drinks on one occasion
Source: Centers for Disease Control and Prevention, Behaviorial Risk Factor Surveillance System, SMART: Selected Metropolitan Area Risk Trends, 2017

Acute and Chronic Health Conditions

Category	MSA[1] (%)	U.S. (%)
Adults who have ever been told they had a heart attack	n/a	4.2
Adults who have ever been told they have angina or coronary heart disease	n/a	3.9
Adults who have ever been told they had a stroke	n/a	3.0
Adults who have ever been told they have asthma	n/a	14.2
Adults who have ever been told they have arthritis	n/a	24.9
Adults who have ever been told they have diabetes[2]	n/a	10.5
Adults who have ever been told they had skin cancer	n/a	6.2
Adults who have ever been told they had any other types of cancer	n/a	7.1
Adults who have ever been told they have COPD	n/a	6.5
Adults who have ever been told they have kidney disease	n/a	3.0
Adults who have ever been told they have a form of depression	n/a	20.5

Note: n/a not available; (1) Figures cover the Lakeland-Winter Haven, FL Metropolitan Statistical Area; (2) Figures do not include pregnancy-related, borderline, or pre-diabetes
Source: Centers for Disease Control and Prevention, Behaviorial Risk Factor Surveillance System, SMART: Selected Metropolitan Area Risk Trends, 2017

Health Screening and Vaccination Rates

Category	MSA[1] (%)	U.S. (%)
Adults aged 65+ who have had flu shot within the past year	n/a	60.7
Adults aged 65+ who have ever had a pneumonia vaccination	n/a	75.4
Adults who have ever been tested for HIV	n/a	36.1
Adults who have ever had the shingles or zoster vaccine?	n/a	28.9
Adults who have had their blood cholesterol checked within the last five years	n/a	85.9

Note: n/a not available; (1) Figures cover the Lakeland-Winter Haven, FL Metropolitan Statistical Area.
Source: Centers for Disease Control and Prevention, Behaviorial Risk Factor Surveillance System, SMART: Selected Metropolitan Area Risk Trends, 2017

Disability Status

Category	MSA[1] (%)	U.S. (%)
Adults who reported being deaf	n/a	6.7
Are you blind or have serious difficulty seeing, even when wearing glasses?	n/a	4.5
Are you limited in any way in any of your usual activities due of arthritis?	n/a	12.9
Do you have difficulty doing errands alone?	n/a	6.8
Do you have difficulty dressing or bathing?	n/a	3.6
Do you have serious difficulty concentrating/remembering/making decisions?	n/a	10.7
Do you have serious difficulty walking or climbing stairs?	n/a	13.6

Note: n/a not available; (1) Figures cover the Lakeland-Winter Haven, FL Metropolitan Statistical Area.
Source: Centers for Disease Control and Prevention, Behaviorial Risk Factor Surveillance System, SMART: Selected Metropolitan Area Risk Trends, 2017

Mortality Rates for the Top 10 Causes of Death in the U.S.

ICD-10[a] Sub-Chapter	ICD-10[a] Code	Age-Adjusted Mortality Rate[1] per 100,000 population County[2]	U.S.
Malignant neoplasms	C00-C97	147.3	149.2
Ischaemic heart diseases	I20-I25	92.5	90.5
Other forms of heart disease	I30-I51	43.9	52.2
Chronic lower respiratory diseases	J40-J47	50.1	39.6
Other degenerative diseases of the nervous system	G30-G31	30.5	37.6
Cerebrovascular diseases	I60-I69	50.9	37.2
Other external causes of accidental injury	W00-X59	34.5	36.1
Organic, including symptomatic, mental disorders	F01-F09	24.5	29.4
Hypertensive diseases	I10-I15	23.6	24.1
Diabetes mellitus	E10-E14	23.8	21.5

Note: (a) ICD-10 = International Classification of Diseases 10th Revision; (1) Mortality rates are a three-year average covering 2017-2019; (2) Figures cover Polk County.
Source: Centers for Disease Control and Prevention, National Center for Health Statistics. Underlying Cause of Death 1999-2019 on CDC WONDER Online Database

Mortality Rates for Selected Causes of Death

ICD-10[a] Sub-Chapter	ICD-10[a] Code	Age-Adjusted Mortality Rate[1] per 100,000 population County[2]	U.S.
Assault	X85-Y09	4.6	6.0
Diseases of the liver	K70-K76	15.0	14.4
Human immunodeficiency virus (HIV) disease	B20-B24	2.5	1.5
Influenza and pneumonia	J09-J18	16.2	13.8
Intentional self-harm	X60-X84	15.2	14.1
Malnutrition	E40-E46	2.0	2.3
Obesity and other hyperalimentation	E65-E68	2.5	2.1
Renal failure	N17-N19	11.4	12.6
Transport accidents	V01-V99	19.0	12.3
Viral hepatitis	B15-B19	1.3	1.2

Note: (a) ICD-10 = International Classification of Diseases 10th Revision; (1) Mortality rates are a three-year average covering 2017-2019; (2) Figures cover Polk County; Data are suppressed when the data meet the criteria for confidentiality constraints; Mortality rates are flagged as unreliable when the rate would be calculated with a numerator of 20 or less.
Source: Centers for Disease Control and Prevention, National Center for Health Statistics. Underlying Cause of Death 1999-2019 on CDC WONDER Online Database

Health Insurance Coverage

Area	With Health Insurance	With Private Health Insurance	With Public Health Insurance	Without Health Insurance	Population Under Age 19 Without Health Insurance
City	90.0	62.2	41.4	10.0	5.2
MSA[1]	87.3	59.0	41.4	12.7	7.2
U.S.	91.2	67.9	35.1	8.8	5.1

Note: Figures are percentages that cover the civilian noninstitutionalized population; (1) Figures cover the Lakeland-Winter Haven, FL Metropolitan Statistical Area
Source: U.S. Census Bureau, 2015-2019 American Community Survey 5-Year Estimates

Number of Medical Professionals

Area	MDs[3]	DOs[3,4]	Dentists	Podiatrists	Chiropractors	Optometrists
County[1] (number)	880	71	247	31	131	70
County[1] (rate[2])	124.5	10.0	34.1	4.3	18.1	9.7
U.S. (rate[2])	282.9	22.7	71.2	6.2	28.1	16.9

12105
Note: Data as of 2019 unless noted; (1) Data covers Polk County; (2) Rate per 100,000 population; (3) Data as of 2018 and includes all active, non-federal physicians; (4) Doctor of Osteopathic Medicine
Source: U.S. Department of Health and Human Services, Health Resources and Services Administration, Bureau of Health Professions, Area Resource File (ARF) 2019-2020

EDUCATION

Public School District Statistics

District Name	Schls	Pupils	Pupil/Teacher Ratio	Minority Pupils[1] (%)	Free Lunch Eligible[2] (%)	IEP[3] (%)
Polk	163	101,408	17.5	61.5	51.4	13.6

Note: Table includes school districts with 2,000 or more students; (1) Percentage of students that are not non-Hispanic white; (2) Percentage of students that are eligible for the free lunch program; (3) Percentage of students that have an Individualized Education Program.
Source: U.S. Department of Education, National Center for Education Statistics, Common Core of Data, Local Education Agency (School District) Universe Survey: School Year 2018-2019; U.S. Department of Education, National Center for Education Statistics, Common Core of Data, Public Elementary/Secondary School Universe Survey: School Year 2018-2019

Highest Level of Education

Area	Less than H.S.	H.S. Diploma	Some College, No Deg.	Associate Degree	Bachelor's Degree	Master's Degree	Prof. School Degree	Doctorate Degree
City	12.0	33.0	19.5	9.6	16.8	6.7	1.6	0.9
MSA[1]	15.0	34.7	20.9	9.2	13.2	5.2	1.1	0.7
U.S.	12.0	27.0	20.4	8.5	19.8	8.8	2.1	1.4

Note: Figures cover persons age 25 and over; (1) Figures cover the Lakeland-Winter Haven, FL Metropolitan Statistical Area
Source: U.S. Census Bureau, 2015-2019 American Community Survey 5-Year Estimates

Educational Attainment by Race

Area	High School Graduate or Higher (%)					Bachelor's Degree or Higher (%)				
	Total	White	Black	Asian	Hisp.[2]	Total	White	Black	Asian	Hisp.[2]
City	88.0	89.3	83.3	81.6	78.8	25.9	27.5	15.7	51.0	19.5
MSA[1]	85.0	86.1	82.2	80.4	73.1	20.2	20.6	15.0	41.5	14.6
U.S.	88.0	89.9	86.0	87.1	68.7	32.1	33.5	21.6	54.3	16.4

Note: Figures shown cover persons 25 years old and over; (1) Figures cover the Lakeland-Winter Haven, FL Metropolitan Statistical Area; (2) People of Hispanic origin can be of any race
Source: U.S. Census Bureau, 2015-2019 American Community Survey 5-Year Estimates

School Enrollment by Grade and Control

Area	Preschool (%)		Kindergarten (%)		Grades 1 - 4 (%)		Grades 5 - 8 (%)		Grades 9 - 12 (%)	
	Public	Private	Public	Private	Public	Private	Public	Private	Public	Private
City	61.7	38.3	85.0	15.0	83.6	16.4	83.7	16.3	88.0	12.0
MSA[1]	69.5	30.5	85.9	14.1	89.0	11.0	86.1	13.9	90.5	9.5
U.S.	59.1	40.9	87.6	12.4	89.5	10.5	89.4	10.6	90.1	9.9

Note: Figures shown cover persons 3 years old and over; (1) Figures cover the Lakeland-Winter Haven, FL Metropolitan Statistical Area
Source: U.S. Census Bureau, 2015-2019 American Community Survey 5-Year Estimates

Higher Education

Four-Year Colleges			Two-Year Colleges			Medical Schools[1]	Law Schools[2]	Voc/Tech[3]
Public	Private Non-profit	Private For-profit	Public	Private Non-profit	Private For-profit			
1	2	0	0	0	0	0	0	3

Note: Figures cover institutions located within the city limits and include main campuses only; (1) includes schools accredited by the Liaison Committee on Medical Education and the American Osteopathic Association's Commission on Osteopathic College Accreditation; (2) includes ABA-accredited schools, schools with provisional ABA accreditation, and state accredited schools; (3) includes all schools with programs that are less than 2 years.
Source: National Center for Education Statistics, Integrated Postsecondary Education System (IPEDS), 2019-20; Wikipedia, List of Medical Schools in the United States, accessed April 2, 2021; Wikipedia, List of Law Schools in the United States, accessed April 2, 2021

EMPLOYERS

Major Employers

Company Name	Industry
Amazon	Online retailer
City of Lakeland	Municipal government
GC Services	Business processes outsourcing
GEICO	Insurance
Lakeland Regional Health	Health care system
Publix	Food distributor & retailer
Rooms To Go	Furniture retailer
Saddle Creek Logistics Services	Supply chain solutions
Southeastern University	Educational services
Watson Clinic	Medical services

Note: Companies shown are located within the Lakeland-Winter Haven, FL Metropolitan Statistical Area.
Source: Hoovers.com; Wikipedia

Best Companies to Work For

Publix Super Markets, headquartered in Lakeland, is among "The 100 Best Companies to Work For." To pick the best companies, *Fortune* partnered with the Great Place to Work Institute. Two-thirds of a company's score is based on the results of the Institute's Trust Index survey, which is sent to a random sample of employees from each company. The questions related to attitudes about management's credibility, job satisfaction, and camaraderie. The other third of the scoring is based on the company's responses to the Institute's Culture Audit, which includes detailed questions about pay and benefit programs, and a series of open-ended questions about hiring practices, internal communication, training, recognition programs, and diversity efforts. Any company that is at least five years old with more than 1,000 U.S. employees is eligible. *Fortune, "The 100 Best Companies to Work For," 2020*

PUBLIC SAFETY

Crime Rate

Area	All Crimes	Violent Crimes				Property Crimes		
		Murder	Rape[3]	Robbery	Aggrav. Assault	Burglary	Larceny -Theft	Motor Vehicle Theft
City	3,189.7	6.2	56.1	86.4	163.0	390.2	2,306.7	180.9
Suburbs[1]	1,687.2	2.6	17.0	33.6	217.9	249.4	1,045.5	121.2
Metro[2]	1,922.4	3.2	23.1	41.8	209.3	271.5	1,242.9	130.5
U.S.	2,489.3	5.0	42.6	81.6	250.2	340.5	1,549.5	219.9

Note: Figures are crimes per 100,000 population; (1) All areas within the metro area that are located outside the city limits; (2) Figures cover the Lakeland-Winter Haven, FL Metropolitan Statistical Area; (3) All figures shown were reported using the revised Uniform Crime Reporting (UCR) definition of rape.
Source: FBI Uniform Crime Reports, 2019

Hate Crimes

Area	Number of Quarters Reported	Number of Incidents per Bias Motivation					
		Race/Ethnicity/ Ancestry	Religion	Sexual Orientation	Disability	Gender	Gender Identity
City	4	0	0	0	0	0	0
U.S.	4	3,963	1,521	1,195	157	69	198

Source: Federal Bureau of Investigation, Hate Crime Statistics 2019

Identity Theft Consumer Reports

Area	Reports	Reports per 100,000 Population	Rank[2]
MSA[1]	2,568	354	95
U.S.	1,387,615	423	-

Note: (1) Figures cover the Lakeland-Winter Haven, FL Metropolitan Statistical Area; (2) Rank ranges from 1 to 391 where 1 indicates greatest number of identity theft reports per 100,000 population
Source: Federal Trade Commission, Consumer Sentinel Network Data Book 2020

Fraud and Other Consumer Reports

Area	Reports	Reports per 100,000 Population	Rank[2]
MSA[1]	6,099	842	78
U.S.	3,385,133	1,031	-

Note: (1) Figures cover the Lakeland-Winter Haven, FL Metropolitan Statistical Area; (2) Rank ranges from 1 to 391 where 1 indicates greatest number of fraud and other consumer reports per 100,000 population
Source: Federal Trade Commission, Consumer Sentinel Network Data Book 2020

POLITICS

2020 Presidential Election Results

Area	Biden	Trump	Jorgensen	Hawkins	Other
Polk County	42.2	56.6	0.8	0.1	0.4
U.S.	51.3	46.8	1.2	0.3	0.5

Note: Results are percentages and may not add to 100% due to rounding
Source: Dave Leip's Atlas of U.S. Presidential Elections

SPORTS

Professional Sports Teams

Team Name	League	Year Established
No teams are located in the metro area		

Source: Wikipedia, Major Professional Sports Teams of the United States and Canada, April 6, 2021

CLIMATE

Average and Extreme Temperatures

Temperature	Jan	Feb	Mar	Apr	May	Jun	Jul	Aug	Sep	Oct	Nov	Dec	Yr.
Extreme High (°F)	85	88	91	93	98	99	97	98	96	94	90	86	99
Average High (°F)	70	72	76	82	87	90	90	90	89	84	77	72	82
Average Temp. (°F)	60	62	67	72	78	81	82	83	81	75	68	62	73
Average Low (°F)	50	52	56	61	67	73	74	74	73	66	57	52	63
Extreme Low (°F)	21	24	29	40	49	53	63	67	57	40	23	18	18

Note: Figures cover the years 1948-1990
Source: National Climatic Data Center, International Station Meteorological Climate Summary, 9/96

Average Precipitation/Snowfall/Humidity

Precip./Humidity	Jan	Feb	Mar	Apr	May	Jun	Jul	Aug	Sep	Oct	Nov	Dec	Yr.
Avg. Precip. (in.)	2.1	2.8	3.5	1.8	3.0	5.6	7.3	7.9	6.5	2.3	1.8	2.1	46.7
Avg. Snowfall (in.)	Tr	Tr	Tr	0	0	0	0	0	0	0	0	Tr	Tr
Avg. Rel. Hum. 7am (%)	87	87	86	86	85	86	88	90	91	89	88	87	88
Avg. Rel. Hum. 4pm (%)	56	55	54	51	52	60	65	66	64	57	56	57	58

Note: Figures cover the years 1948-1990; Tr = Trace amounts (<0.05 in. of rain; <0.5 in. of snow)
Source: National Climatic Data Center, International Station Meteorological Climate Summary, 9/96

Weather Conditions

Temperature			Daytime Sky			Precipitation		
32°F & below	45°F & below	90°F & above	Clear	Partly cloudy	Cloudy	0.01 inch or more precip.	0.1 inch or more snow/ice	Thunder-storms
3	35	85	81	204	80	107	< 1	87

Note: Figures are average number of days per year and cover the years 1948-1990
Source: National Climatic Data Center, International Station Meteorological Climate Summary, 9/96

HAZARDOUS WASTE

Superfund Sites

The Lakeland-Winter Haven, FL metro area is home to one site on the EPA's Superfund National Priorities List: **Landia Chemical Company** (final). There are a total of 1,375 Superfund sites with a status of proposed or final on the list in the U.S. *U.S. Environmental Protection Agency, National Priorities List, April 7, 2021*

AIR QUALITY

Air Quality Trends: Ozone

	1990	1995	2000	2005	2010	2015	2016	2017	2018	2019
MSA[1]	0.066	0.071	0.079	0.074	0.064	0.062	0.064	0.072	0.065	0.066
U.S.	0.088	0.089	0.082	0.080	0.073	0.068	0.069	0.068	0.069	0.065

Note: (1) Data covers the Lakeland-Winter Haven, FL Metropolitan Statistical Area. The values shown are the composite ozone concentration averages among trend sites based on the highest fourth daily maximum 8-hour concentration in parts per million. These trends are based on sites having an adequate record of monitoring data during the trend period. Data from exceptional events are included.
Source: U.S. Environmental Protection Agency, Air Quality Monitoring Information, "Air Quality Trends by City, 1990-2019"

Air Quality Index

Area	Percent of Days when Air Quality was...[2]					AQI Statistics[2]	
	Good	Moderate	Unhealthy for Sensitive Groups	Unhealthy	Very Unhealthy	Maximum	Median
MSA[1]	86.0	14.0	0.0	0.0	0.0	100	36

Note: (1) Data covers the Lakeland-Winter Haven, FL Metropolitan Statistical Area; (2) Based on 365 days with AQI data in 2019. Air Quality Index (AQI) is an index for reporting daily air quality. EPA calculates the AQI for five major air pollutants regulated by the Clean Air Act: ground-level ozone, particle pollution (aka particulate matter), carbon monoxide, sulfur dioxide, and nitrogen dioxide. The AQI runs from 0 to 500. The higher the AQI value, the greater the level of air pollution and the greater the health concern. There are six AQI categories: "Good" AQI is between 0 and 50. Air quality is considered satisfactory; "Moderate" AQI is between 51 and 100. Air quality is acceptable; "Unhealthy for Sensitive Groups" When AQI values are between 101 and 150, members of sensitive groups may experience health effects; "Unhealthy" When AQI values are between 151 and 200 everyone may begin to experience health effects; "Very Unhealthy" AQI values between 201 and 300 trigger a health alert; "Hazardous" AQI values over 300 trigger warnings of emergency conditions (not shown).
Source: U.S. Environmental Protection Agency, Air Quality Index Report, 2019

Air Quality Index Pollutants

Area	Percent of Days when AQI Pollutant was...[2]					
	Carbon Monoxide	Nitrogen Dioxide	Ozone	Sulfur Dioxide	Particulate Matter 2.5	Particulate Matter 10
MSA[1]	0.0	0.0	67.9	0.5	31.5	0.0

Note: (1) Data covers the Lakeland-Winter Haven, FL Metropolitan Statistical Area; (2) Based on 365 days with AQI data in 2019. The Air Quality Index (AQI) is an index for reporting daily air quality. EPA calculates the AQI for five major air pollutants regulated by the Clean Air Act: ground-level ozone, particle pollution (also known as particulate matter), carbon monoxide, sulfur dioxide, and nitrogen dioxide. The AQI runs from 0 to 500. The higher the AQI value, the greater the level of air pollution and the greater the health concern.
Source: U.S. Environmental Protection Agency, Air Quality Index Report, 2019

Maximum Air Pollutant Concentrations: Particulate Matter, Ozone, CO and Lead

	Particulate Matter 10 (ug/m^3)	Particulate Matter 2.5 Wtd AM (ug/m^3)	Particulate Matter 2.5 24-Hr (ug/m^3)	Ozone (ppm)	Carbon Monoxide (ppm)	Lead (ug/m^3)
MSA[1] Level	57	7.7	19	0.067	n/a	n/a
NAAQS[2]	150	15	35	0.075	9	0.15
Met NAAQS[2]	Yes	Yes	Yes	Yes	n/a	n/a

Note: (1) Data covers the Lakeland-Winter Haven, FL Metropolitan Statistical Area; Data from exceptional events are included; (2) National Ambient Air Quality Standards; ppm = parts per million; ug/m^3 = micrograms per cubic meter; n/a not available.
Concentrations: Particulate Matter 10 (coarse particulate)—highest second maximum 24-hour concentration; Particulate Matter 2.5 Wtd AM (fine particulate)—highest weighted annual mean concentration; Particulate Matter 2.5 24-Hour (fine particulate)—highest 98th percentile 24-hour concentration; Ozone—highest fourth daily maximum 8-hour concentration; Carbon Monoxide—highest second maximum non-overlapping 8-hour concentration; Lead—maximum running 3-month average
Source: U.S. Environmental Protection Agency, Air Quality Monitoring Information, "Air Quality Statistics by City, 2019"

Maximum Air Pollutant Concentrations: Nitrogen Dioxide and Sulfur Dioxide

	Nitrogen Dioxide AM (ppb)	Nitrogen Dioxide 1-Hr (ppb)	Sulfur Dioxide AM (ppb)	Sulfur Dioxide 1-Hr (ppb)	Sulfur Dioxide 24-Hr (ppb)
MSA[1] Level	n/a	n/a	n/a	26	n/a
NAAQS[2]	53	100	30	75	140
Met NAAQS[2]	n/a	n/a	n/a	Yes	n/a

Note: (1) Data covers the Lakeland-Winter Haven, FL Metropolitan Statistical Area; Data from exceptional events are included; (2) National Ambient Air Quality Standards; ppm = parts per million; ug/m^3 = micrograms per cubic meter; n/a not available.
Concentrations: Nitrogen Dioxide AM—highest arithmetic mean concentration; Nitrogen Dioxide 1-Hr—highest 98th percentile 1-hour daily maximum concentration; Sulfur Dioxide AM—highest annual mean concentration; Sulfur Dioxide 1-Hr—highest 99th percentile 1-hour daily maximum concentration; Sulfur Dioxide 24-Hr—highest second maximum 24-hour concentration
Source: U.S. Environmental Protection Agency, Air Quality Monitoring Information, "Air Quality Statistics by City, 2019"

Memphis, Tennessee

Background

Memphis, named after the ancient city in Egypt, has had a long and illustrious history. Inhabited for centuries by the Chickasaws, it came to the attention of early white explorers, and was visited by Hernando de Soto in 1541. French explorers followed. By the Treaty of Paris of 1783 the western lands up to the Mississippi claimed by the British crown passed to the newly independent United States, and the Chickasaws gave up their claim to the area of Memphis in 1818. The next year a trio of American citizens, James Winchester, John Overton, and General Andrew Jackson, the last fresh from his victory at the Battle of New Orleans, in 1815, organized a settlement.

In the years before the Civil War, Memphis flourished, serving as a natural inland port because of its advantageous location on the Mississippi. At the opening of the Civil War, it was a prize of both Northern and Southern armies. As the war lengthened and the North drew a cordon around its Southern foes, Memphis fell, but the city survived. And by the end of the nineteenth century, it was clearly flourishing. In the next century, Memphis took its place as the virtual economic capital of Tennessee and the state's largest city. The driving forces in the early expansion of Memphis were cotton, and, by the end of the nineteenth century, the rapidly expanding lumber trade. After World War II, the city's industry saw a rapid expansion, including food stuffs, chemicals, and electrical goods.

Livestock and meatpacking have proved highly profitable, and the city has attracted such agricultural products from across the Upper South, earning the sobriquet America's Distribution Center. Medical care has been a principal occupation of many residents, with a large hospital complex, the Memphis Medical Center, including the famous St. Jude Children's Research Hospital, located in the city. FedEx, AutoZone, and International Paper have their corporate headquarters here.

The recording industry, too, has flourished in Memphis, for music has long been important. The composer W.C. Handy developed the blues in Memphis, and, of course, the late rock-and-roll idol Elvis Presley and his home Graceland have brought renown to the city.

For some time, the city seemed to be decaying at its core, in that buildings were being vacated or even razed. But in the late 1970s, the city fathers undertook to revive the core area, and launched a project that, by the 1990s, had spent three-quarters of a billion dollars in reviving buildings and in new construction. A convention center and a theme park (Mud Island River Park) have been built, the latter connected by monorail to the downtown area, as part of an ongoing riverfront development effort. In the course of renovation the Orpheum Theater and the Peabody Hotel, both early landmarks, have been restored to their previous grandeur.

> The 2020 Miss USA and Miss Teen USA competitions aired live from Elvis's iconic home, Graceland, complete with health screenings, social distancing, and limited audience.

Fabled Beale Street, with its history as a place to hear the blues, fell into decay in the mid-20th century; it has seen a comeback as a center for blues and music over the last 30 years and is now a major tourist draw.

The Memphis Medical District has been the site of extensive investment and development, employing as it does over 20,000 people. The University of Tennessee designed a new College of Pharmacy building and a modern bio-containment laboratory which was completed in 2008. Other projects include the University of Tennessee Cancer Institute, and Methodist University Hospital. The Medical District, increasingly called the Biomedical District, is served by new Memphis Area Transit Authority (MATA) rail links.

The $250 million NBA FedEx Forum, the catalyst for new growth and development in the Sports and Entertainment District and home to the Memphis Grizzlies basketball team, opened in the fall of 2004, along with the newly expanded and renovated Memphis Cook Convention Center and state-of-the-art Cannon Center for the Performing Arts.

The climate of Memphis is mild. Most precipitation occurs during winter and spring, with a secondary surge in rainfall due to thunderstorm activity. Severe storms are relatively infrequent.

Rankings

Business/Finance Rankings

- Memphis was the #14-ranked city for savers, according to a study by the finance site GOBankingRates, which considered the prospects for people trying to save money. Criteria: average monthly cost of grocery items; median home listing price; median rent; median income; transportation costs; gas prices; and the cost of eating out for an inexpensive and mid-range meal in 100 U.S. cities. *www.gobankingrates.com, "The 20 Best (and Worst) Places to Live If You're Trying to Save Money," August 27, 2019*

- Memphis was ranked #14 among 100 U.S. cities for most difficult conditions for savers, according to a study by the finance site GOBankingRates. Criteria: average monthly cost of grocery items; median home listing price; median rent; median income; transportation costs; gas prices; and the cost of eating out for an inexpensive and mid-range meal. *www.gobankingrates.com, "The 20 Best (and Worst) Places to Live If You're Trying to Save Money," August 27, 2019*

- Based on metro area social media reviews, the employment opinion group Glassdoor surveyed 50 of the most populous U.S. metro areas and equally weighed cost of living, hiring opportunity, and job satisfaction to compose a list of "25 Best Cities for Jobs." Median pay and home value, and number of active job openings were also factored in. The Memphis metro area was ranked #4 in overall job satisfaction. *www.glassdoor.com, "Best Cities for Jobs," February 25, 2020*

- The Brookings Institution ranked the nation's largest cities based on income inequality. Memphis was ranked #40 (#1 = greatest inequality). Criteria: the "95/20 ratio," a figure representing the income at which a household earns more than 95 percent of all other households, divided by the income at which a household earns more than only 20 percent of all other households. *Brookings Institution, "Household Income Inequality, Largest Cities of 97 Large U.S. Metro Areas, 2014-2016," February 5, 2018*

- The Brookings Institution ranked the 100 largest metro areas in the U.S. based on income inequality. Memphis was ranked #14 (#1 = greatest inequality). Criteria: the "95/20 ratio," a figure representing the income at which a household earns more than 95 percent of all other households, divided by the income at which a household earns more than only 20 percent of all other households. *Brookings Institution, "Household Income Inequality, 100 Largest U.S. Metro Areas, 2014-2016," February 5, 2018*

- For its annual survey of the "Cheapest U.S. Cities to Live In," Kiplinger applied Cost of Living Index statistics developed by the Council for Community and Economic Research to U.S. Census Bureau population and median household income data for 270 urban areas. In the resulting ranking, Memphis ranked #6. *Kiplinger.com, "The 25 Cheapest U.S. Cities to Live In," October 1, 2020*

- The Memphis metro area appeared on the Milken Institute "2021 Best Performing Cities" list. Rank: #166 out of 200 large metro areas (population over 250,000). Criteria: job growth; wage and salary growth; high-tech output growth; housing affordability; household broadband access. *Milken Institute, "Best-Performing Cities 2021," February 16, 2021*

- *Forbes* ranked the 200 most populous metro areas to determine the nation's "Best Places for Business and Careers." The Memphis metro area was ranked #111. Criteria: costs (business and living); job growth (past and projected); income growth; quality of life; educational attainment (college and high school); projected economic growth; cultural and leisure opportunities; workplace tolerance laws; net migration patterns. *Forbes, "The Best Places for Business and Careers 2019: Seattle Still On Top," October 30, 2019*

Culture/Performing Arts Rankings

- Memphis was selected as one of the 25 best cities for moviemakers in North America. COVID-19 has spurred a quest for great film cities that offer more creative space, lower costs, and more great outdoors. NYC & LA were intentionally excluded. Criteria: longstanding reputations as film-friendly communities; efforts to deal with pandemic-specific challenges; and establish appropriate COVID-19 guidelines. The city was ranked #16. *MovieMaker Magazine, "Best Places to Live and Work as a Moviemaker, 2021," January 26, 2021*

Dating/Romance Rankings

- Memphis was ranked #16 out of 25 cities that stood out for inspiring romance and attracting diners on the website OpenTable.com. Criteria: percentage of people who dined out on Valentine's Day in 2018; percentage of romantic restaurants as rated by OpenTable diner reviews; and percentage of tables seated for two. *OpenTable, "25 Most Romantic Cities in America for 2019," February 7, 2019*

Education Rankings

- Personal finance website *WalletHub* analyzed the 150 largest U.S. metropolitan statistical areas to determine where the most educated Americans are putting their degrees to work. Criteria: education levels; percentage of workers with degrees; education quality and attainment gap; public school quality rankings; quality and enrollment of each metro area's universities. Memphis was ranked #110 (#1 = most educated city). *www.WalletHub.com, "Most and Least Educated Cities in America," July 20, 2020*

- Memphis was selected as one of America's most literate cities. The city ranked #67 out of the 84 largest U.S. cities. Criteria: number of booksellers; library resources; Internet resources; educational attainment; periodical publishing resources; newspaper circulation. *Central Connecticut State University, "America's Most Literate Cities, 2018," February 2019*

Environmental Rankings

- Sperling's BestPlaces assessed the 50 largest metropolitan areas of the United States for the likelihood of dangerously extreme weather events or earthquakes. In general the Southeast and South-Central regions have the highest risk of weather extremes and earthquakes, while the Pacific Northwest enjoys the lowest risk. Of the most risky metropolitan areas, the Memphis metro area was ranked #7. *www.bestplaces.net, "Avoid Natural Disasters: BestPlaces Reveals The Top 10 Safest Places to Live," October 25, 2017*

- Memphis was highlighted as one of the top 98 cleanest metro areas for short-term particle pollution (24-hour PM 2.5) in the U.S. during 2016 through 2018. Monitors in these cities reported no days with unhealthful PM 2.5 levels. *American Lung Association, "State of the Air 2020," April 21, 2020*

Health/Fitness Rankings

- For each of the 100 largest cities in the United States, the American Fitness Index®, published by the American College of Sports Medicine and the Anthem Foundation, evaluated community infrastructure and 33 health behaviors including preventive health, levels of chronic disease conditions, pedestrian safety, air quality, and community resources that support physical activity. Memphis ranked #96 for "community fitness." *americanfitnessindex.org, "2020 ACSM American Fitness Index Summary Report," July 14, 2020*

- Memphis was identified as a "2021 Spring Allergy Capital." The area ranked #20 out of 100. Three groups of factors were used to identify the most challenging cities for people with allergies during the spring season: annual spring pollen levels; over the counter medicine use; number of board-certified allergy specialists. *Asthma and Allergy Foundation of America, "Spring Allergy Capitals 2021," February 23, 2021*

- Memphis was identified as a "2021 Fall Allergy Capital." The area ranked #18 out of 100. Three groups of factors were used to identify the most challenging cities for people with allergies during the fall season: annual fall pollen levels; over the counter medicine use; number of board-certified allergy specialists. *Asthma and Allergy Foundation of America, "Fall Allergy Capitals 2021," February 23, 2021*

- Memphis was identified as a "2019 Asthma Capital." The area ranked #29 out of the nation's 100 largest metropolitan areas. Criteria: estimated asthma prevalence; crude death rate from asthma; and ER visits due to asthma. Risk factors analyzed but not factored in the rankings: annual pollen score; annual air quality; public smoking laws; number of board-certified asthma specialists; rescue medication use; controller medication use; uninsured rate; poverty rate. *Asthma and Allergy Foundation of America, "Asthma Capitals 2019: The Most Challenging Places to Live With Asthma," May 7, 2019*

Real Estate Rankings

- FitSmallBusiness looked at 50 of the largest metropolitan areas in the U.S. to determine which metro was the best to start a real estate business. Data was compiled from such sources as: Zillow, Trulia, U.S. Census Bureau, and the Bureau of Labor Statistics. Criteria: location; inventory; annual wages; median sales price of homes; days on the market; median price cut percentage; and other factors that would influence real estate professional growth. The Memphis metro area ranked #33. *fitsmallbusiness.com, "The Best Cities to Become a Real Estate Agent in 2018," January 30, 2018*

- *WalletHub* compared the most populated U.S. cities to determine which had the best markets for real estate agents. Memphis ranked #134 where demand was high and pay was the best. Criteria: sales per agent; annual median wage for real-estate agents; monthly average starting salary for real estate agents; real estate job density and competition; unemployment rate; home turnover rate; housing-market health index; and other relevant metrics. *www.WalletHub.com, "2019's Best Places to Be a Real Estate Agent," April 24, 2019*

- The Memphis metro area was identified as one of the 20 best housing markets in the U.S. in 2020. The area ranked #19 out of 180 markets. Criteria: year-over-year change of median sales price of existing single-family homes between the 4th quarter of 2019 and the 4th quarter of 2020. *National Association of Realtors®, Median Sales Price of Existing Single-Family Homes for Metropolitan Areas, 4th Quarter 2020*
- Memphis was ranked #148 out of 268 metro areas in terms of housing affordability in 2020 by the National Association of Home Builders (#1 = most affordable). Criteria: the share of homes sold in that area affordable to a family earning the local median income, based on standard mortgage underwriting criteria. *National Association of Home Builders®, NAHB-Wells Fargo Housing Opportunity Index, 4th Quarter 2020*

Safety Rankings

- To identify the most dangerous cities in America, 24/7 Wall Street focused on violent crime categories—murder, non-negligent manslaughter, rape, robbery, and aggravated assault—and property crime as reported in the FBI's 2019 annual Uniform Crime Report. Criteria also included median income from American Community Survey and unemployment figures from Bureau of Labor Statistics. For cities with populations over 100,000, Memphis was ranked #3. *247wallst.com, "America's 50 Most Dangerous Cities" November 16, 2020*
- Allstate ranked the 200 largest cities in America in terms of driver safety. Memphis ranked #100. Criteria: internal property damage claims over a two-year period from January 2016 to December 2017. The report helps increase the importance of safety and awareness behind the wheel. *Allstate, "Allstate America's Best Drivers Report, 2019" June 24, 2019*
- Memphis was identified as one of the most dangerous cities in America by NeighborhoodScout. The city ranked #3 out of 100 (#1 = most dangerous). Criteria: number of violent crimes per 1,000 residents. The editors evaluated cities with 25,000 or more residents. *NeighborhoodScout.com, "2021 Top 100 Most Dangerous Cities in the U.S.," January 2, 2021*
- The National Insurance Crime Bureau ranked 384 metro areas in the U.S. in terms of per capita rates of vehicle theft. The Memphis metro area ranked #31 (#1 = highest rate). Criteria: number of vehicle theft offenses per 100,000 inhabitants in 2019. *National Insurance Crime Bureau, "Hot Spots 2019," July 21, 2020*

Seniors/Retirement Rankings

- From its Best Cities for Successful Aging indexes, the Milken Institute generated rankings for metropolitan areas, weighing data in nine categories—health care, wellness, living arrangements, transportation and convenience, financial characteristics, education, employment, community engagement, and overall livability. The Memphis metro area was ranked #76 overall in the large metro area category. *Milken Institute, "Best Cities for Successful Aging, 2017" March 14, 2017*

Sports/Recreation Rankings

- Memphis was chosen as one of America's best cities for bicycling. The city ranked #31 out of 50. Criteria: cycling infrastructure that is safe and friendly for all ages; energy and bike culture. The editors evaluated cities with populations of 100,000 or more. *Bicycling, "The 50 Best Bike Cities in America," October 10, 2018*

Women/Minorities Rankings

- Personal finance website *WalletHub* compared more than 180 U.S. cities across two key dimensions, "Hispanic Business-Friendliness" and "Hispanic Purchasing Power," to arrive at the most favorable conditions for Hispanic entrepreneurs. Memphis was ranked #127 out of 182. Criteria includes: share of Hispanic-Owned Businesses; Hispanic entrepreneurship rate to median annual income of Hispanics; Small Business-Friendliness score; cost of living; and number of Hispanics with at least a bachelor's degree. *WalletHub.com, "2019's Best Cities for Hispanic Entrepreneurs," May 1, 2019*

Miscellaneous Rankings

- Memphis was selected as a 2020 Digital Cities Survey winner. The city ranked #10 in the large city (500,000 or more population) category. The survey examined and assessed how city governments are utilizing technology to improve transparency, enhance cybersecurity, and respond to the pandemic. Survey questions focused on ten initiatives: cybersecurity, citizen experience, disaster recovery, business intelligence, IT personnel, data governance, collaboration, infrastructure modernization, cloud computing, and mobile applications. *Center for Digital Government, "2020 Digital Cities Survey," November 10, 2020*

- *WalletHub* compared the 150 most populated U.S. cities to determine their operating efficiency. A "Quality of City Services" score was constructed for each city and then divided by the total budget per capita to reveal which were managed the best. Memphis ranked #138. Criteria: financial stability; economy; education; safety; health; infrastructure and pollution. *www.WalletHub.com, "2020's Best- & Worst-Run Cities in America," June 29, 2020*

Business Environment

DEMOGRAPHICS

Population Growth

Area	1990 Census	2000 Census	2010 Census	2019* Estimate	Population Growth (%) 1990-2019	Population Growth (%) 2010-2019
City	660,536	650,100	646,889	651,932	-1.3	0.8
MSA[1]	1,067,263	1,205,204	1,316,100	1,339,623	25.5	1.8
U.S.	248,709,873	281,421,906	308,745,538	324,697,795	30.6	5.2

Note: (1) Figures cover the Memphis, TN-MS-AR Metropolitan Statistical Area; (*) 2015-2019 5-year estimated population
Source: U.S. Census Bureau, 1990 Census, Census 2000, Census 2010, 2015-2019 American Community Survey 5-Year Estimates

Household Size

Area	One	Two	Three	Four	Five	Six	Seven or More	Average Household Size
City	37.1	30.4	14.8	9.9	4.2	2.2	1.4	2.50
MSA[1]	29.8	32.5	16.3	12.4	5.4	2.2	1.4	2.60
U.S.	27.9	33.9	15.6	12.9	6.0	2.3	1.4	2.60

Note: (1) Figures cover the Memphis, TN-MS-AR Metropolitan Statistical Area
Source: U.S. Census Bureau, 2015-2019 American Community Survey 5-Year Estimates

Race

Area	White Alone[2] (%)	Black Alone[2] (%)	Asian Alone[2] (%)	AIAN[3] Alone[2] (%)	NHOPI[4] Alone[2] (%)	Other Race Alone[2] (%)	Two or More Races (%)
City	29.2	64.1	1.7	0.2	0.0	3.3	1.5
MSA[1]	46.3	47.1	2.1	0.2	0.0	2.3	1.9
U.S.	72.5	12.7	5.5	0.8	0.2	4.9	3.3

Note: (1) Figures cover the Memphis, TN-MS-AR Metropolitan Statistical Area; (2) Alone is defined as not being in combination with one or more other races; (3) American Indian and Alaska Native; (4) Native Hawaiian and Other Pacific Islander
Source: U.S. Census Bureau, 2015-2019 American Community Survey 5-Year Estimates

Hispanic or Latino Origin

Area	Total (%)	Mexican (%)	Puerto Rican (%)	Cuban (%)	Other (%)
City	7.2	5.1	0.3	0.2	1.6
MSA[1]	5.6	4.0	0.2	0.1	1.2
U.S.	18.0	11.2	1.7	0.7	4.3

Note: Persons of Hispanic or Latino origin can be of any race; (1) Figures cover the Memphis, TN-MS-AR Metropolitan Statistical Area
Source: U.S. Census Bureau, 2015-2019 American Community Survey 5-Year Estimates

Ancestry

Area	German	Irish	English	American	Italian	Polish	French[2]	Scottish	Dutch
City	3.4	4.2	3.9	3.9	1.6	0.7	1.0	1.0	0.3
MSA[1]	5.2	6.3	6.0	7.1	2.1	0.7	1.2	1.4	0.5
U.S.	13.3	9.7	7.2	6.2	5.1	2.8	2.3	1.7	1.2

Note: Figures are the percentage of the total population reporting a particular ancestry. The nine most commonly reported ancestries in the U.S. are shown. Figures include multiple ancestries (e.g. if a person reported being Irish and Italian, they were included in both columns); (1) Figures cover the Memphis, TN-MS-AR Metropolitan Statistical Area; (2) Excludes Basque
Source: U.S. Census Bureau, 2015-2019 American Community Survey 5-Year Estimates

Foreign-born Population

Area	Any Foreign Country	Asia	Mexico	Europe	Caribbean	Central America[2]	South America	Africa	Canada
City	6.2	1.5	2.2	0.3	0.2	0.9	0.2	0.8	0.1
MSA[1]	5.3	1.7	1.6	0.4	0.2	0.5	0.2	0.6	0.1
U.S.	13.6	4.2	3.5	1.5	1.3	1.1	1.0	0.7	0.2

Note: (1) Figures cover the Memphis, TN-MS-AR Metropolitan Statistical Area; (2) Excludes Mexico.
Source: U.S. Census Bureau, 2015-2019 American Community Survey 5-Year Estimates

Marital Status

Area	Never Married	Now Married[2]	Separated	Widowed	Divorced
City	47.8	31.3	3.7	5.8	11.4
MSA[1]	38.4	42.0	2.9	5.7	11.0
U.S.	33.4	48.1	1.9	5.8	10.9

Note: Figures are percentages and cover the population 15 years of age and older; (1) Figures cover the Memphis, TN-MS-AR Metropolitan Statistical Area; (2) Excludes separated
Source: U.S. Census Bureau, 2015-2019 American Community Survey 5-Year Estimates

Disability by Age

Area	All Ages	Under 18 Years Old	18 to 64 Years Old	65 Years and Over
City	13.5	5.1	12.0	37.8
MSA[1]	12.9	4.5	11.2	36.4
U.S.	12.6	4.2	10.3	34.5

Note: Figures show percent of the civilian noninstitutionalized population that reported having a disability. Disability status is determined from six types of difficulty: vision, hearing, cognitive, ambulatory, self-care, and independent living. For children under 5 years old, hearing and vision difficulty are used to determine disability status. For children between the ages of 5 and 14, disability status is determined from hearing, vision, cognitive, ambulatory, and self-care difficulties. For people aged 15 years and older, they are considered to have a disability if they have difficulty with any one of the six difficulty types; Note: (1) Figures cover the Memphis, TN-MS-AR Metropolitan Statistical Area
Source: U.S. Census Bureau, 2015-2019 American Community Survey 5-Year Estimates

Age

Area	Under Age 5	Age 5–19	Age 20–34	Age 35–44	Age 45–54	Age 55–64	Age 65–74	Age 75–84	Age 85+	Median Age
City	7.6	19.9	23.7	12.0	11.8	12.0	7.7	3.6	1.5	34.0
MSA[1]	6.8	20.7	20.8	12.7	12.9	12.5	8.3	3.8	1.4	36.3
U.S.	6.1	19.1	20.7	12.6	13.0	12.9	9.1	4.6	1.9	38.1

Note: (1) Figures cover the Memphis, TN-MS-AR Metropolitan Statistical Area
Source: U.S. Census Bureau, 2015-2019 American Community Survey 5-Year Estimates

Gender

Area	Males	Females	Males per 100 Females
City	308,460	343,472	89.8
MSA[1]	640,257	699,366	91.5
U.S.	159,886,919	164,810,876	97.0

Note: (1) Figures cover the Memphis, TN-MS-AR Metropolitan Statistical Area
Source: U.S. Census Bureau, 2015-2019 American Community Survey 5-Year Estimates

Religious Groups by Family

Area	Catholic	Baptist	Non-Den.	Methodist[2]	Lutheran	LDS[3]	Pentecostal	Presbyterian[4]	Muslim[5]	Judaism
MSA[1]	5.3	30.8	5.4	6.2	0.4	0.6	4.8	2.4	0.3	0.6
U.S.	19.1	9.3	4.0	4.0	2.3	2.0	1.9	1.6	0.8	0.7

Note: Figures are the number of adherents as a percentage of the total population; (1) Figures cover the Memphis, TN-MS-AR Metropolitan Statistical Area; (2) Methodist/Pietist; (3) Latter Day Saints; (4) Reformed; (5) Figures are estimates
Source: Association of Statisticians of American Religious Bodies, 2010 U.S. Religion Census: Religious Congregations & Membership Study

Religious Groups by Tradition

Area	Catholic	Evangelical Protestant	Mainline Protestant	Other Tradition	Black Protestant	Orthodox
MSA[1]	5.3	29.4	8.4	2.2	13.5	0.1
U.S.	19.1	16.2	7.3	4.3	1.6	0.3

Note: Figures are the number of adherents as a percentage of the total population; (1) Figures cover the Memphis, TN-MS-AR Metropolitan Statistical Area
Source: Association of Statisticians of American Religious Bodies, 2010 U.S. Religion Census: Religious Congregations & Membership Study

ECONOMY

Gross Metropolitan Product

Area	2017	2018	2019	2020	Rank[2]
MSA[1]	72.9	76.2	79.4	82.2	49

Note: Figures are in billions of dollars; (1) Figures cover the Memphis, TN-MS-AR Metropolitan Statistical Area; (2) Rank is based on 2018 data and ranges from 1 to 381
Source: U.S. Conference of Mayors, U.S. Metro Economies: GMP & Employment 2018-2020, September 2019

Economic Growth

Area	2015-17 (%)	2018 (%)	2019 (%)	2020 (%)	Rank[2]
MSA[1]	0.1	2.3	2.3	1.4	299
U.S.	1.9	2.9	2.3	2.1	—

Note: Figures are real gross metropolitan product (GMP) growth rates and represent average annual percent change; (1) Figures cover the Memphis, TN-MS-AR Metropolitan Statistical Area; (2) Rank is based on 2017 2-year average annual percent change and ranges from 1 to 381
Source: U.S. Conference of Mayors, U.S. Metro Economies: GMP & Employment 2018-2020, September 2019

Metropolitan Area Exports

Area	2014	2015	2016	2017	2018	2019	Rank[2]
MSA[1]	11,002.0	11,819.5	11,628.7	11,233.9	12,695.4	13,751.7	28

Note: Figures are in millions of dollars; (1) Figures cover the Memphis, TN-MS-AR Metropolitan Statistical Area; (2) Rank is based on 2019 data and ranges from 1 to 386
Source: U.S. Department of Commerce, International Trade Administration, Office of Trade and Economic Analysis, Industry and Analysis, Exports by Metropolitan Area, data extracted March 24, 2021

Building Permits

Area	Single-Family 2018	Single-Family 2019	Pct. Chg.	Multi-Family 2018	Multi-Family 2019	Pct. Chg.	Total 2018	Total 2019	Pct. Chg.
City	n/a	n/a	n/a	n/a	n/a	n/a	n/a	n/a	n/a
MSA[1]	3,185	3,319	4.2	1,307	355	-72.8	4,492	3,674	-18.2
U.S.	855,300	862,100	0.7	473,500	523,900	10.6	1,328,800	1,386,000	4.3

Note: (1) Figures cover the Memphis, TN-MS-AR Metropolitan Statistical Area; Figures represent new, privately-owned housing units authorized (unadjusted data); All permit data are based on estimates with imputation
Source: U.S. Census Bureau, Manufacturing, Mining, and Construction Statistics, Building Permits, 2018, 2019

Bankruptcy Filings

Area	Business Filings 2019	Business Filings 2020	% Chg.	Nonbusiness Filings 2019	Nonbusiness Filings 2020	% Chg.
Shelby County	72	41	-43.1	9,622	5,523	-42.6
U.S.	22,780	21,655	-4.9	752,160	522,808	-30.5

Note: Business filings include Chapter 7, Chapter 9, Chapter 11, Chapter 12, Chapter 13, Chapter 15, and Section 304; Nonbusiness filings include Chapter 7, Chapter 11, and Chapter 13
Source: Administrative Office of the U.S. Courts, Business and Nonbusiness Bankruptcy, County Cases Commenced by Chapter of the Bankruptcy Code, During the 12-Month Period Ending December 31, 2019 and Business and Nonbusiness Bankruptcy, County Cases Commenced by Chapter of the Bankruptcy Code, During the 12-Month Period Ending December 31, 2020

Housing Vacancy Rates

Area	Gross Vacancy Rate[2] (%) 2018	2019	2020	Year-Round Vacancy Rate[3] (%) 2018	2019	2020	Rental Vacancy Rate[4] (%) 2018	2019	2020	Homeowner Vacancy Rate[5] (%) 2018	2019	2020
MSA[1]	12.6	9.9	7.3	12.5	9.9	7.0	11.7	10.6	6.6	1.6	1.4	1.0
U.S.	12.3	12.0	10.6	9.7	9.5	8.2	6.9	6.7	6.3	1.5	1.4	1.0

Note: (1) Figures cover the Memphis, TN-MS-AR Metropolitan Statistical Area; (2) The percentage of the total housing inventory that is vacant; (3) The percentage of the housing inventory (excluding seasonal units) that is year-round vacant; (4) The percentage of rental inventory that is vacant for rent; (5) The percentage of homeowner inventory that is vacant for sale
Source: U.S. Census Bureau, Housing Vacancies and Homeownership Annual Statistics: 2018, 2019, 2020

INCOME

Income

Area	Per Capita ($)	Median Household ($)	Average Household ($)
City	25,605	41,228	62,588
MSA[1]	29,453	53,209	76,187
U.S.	34,103	62,843	88,607

Note: (1) Figures cover the Memphis, TN-MS-AR Metropolitan Statistical Area
Source: U.S. Census Bureau, 2015-2019 American Community Survey 5-Year Estimates

Household Income Distribution

Area	Under $15,000	$15,000 -$24,999	$25,000 -$34,999	$35,000 -$49,999	$50,000 -$74,999	$75,000 -$99,999	$100,000 -$149,999	$150,000 and up
City	18.3	13.5	11.8	14.6	16.5	9.4	8.8	7.0
MSA[1]	13.2	10.6	10.2	13.4	17.4	11.8	13.0	10.4
U.S.	10.3	8.9	8.9	12.3	17.2	12.7	15.1	14.5

Note: (1) Figures cover the Memphis, TN-MS-AR Metropolitan Statistical Area
Source: U.S. Census Bureau, 2015-2019 American Community Survey 5-Year Estimates

Poverty Rate

Area	All Ages	Under 18 Years Old	18 to 64 Years Old	65 Years and Over
City	25.1	40.8	21.1	13.6
MSA[1]	17.6	27.8	15.0	10.1
U.S.	13.4	18.5	12.6	9.3

Note: Figures are percentage of people whose income during the past 12 months was below the poverty level; (1) Figures cover the Memphis, TN-MS-AR Metropolitan Statistical Area
Source: U.S. Census Bureau, 2015-2019 American Community Survey 5-Year Estimates

CITY FINANCES

City Government Finances

Component	2017 ($000)	2017 ($ per capita)
Total Revenues	3,248,477	4,954
Total Expenditures	3,107,579	4,739
Debt Outstanding	2,006,045	3,059
Cash and Securities[1]	4,531,462	6,910

Note: (1) Cash and security holdings of a government at the close of its fiscal year, including those of its dependent agencies, utilities, and liquor stores.
Source: U.S. Census Bureau, State & Local Government Finances 2017

City Government Revenue by Source

Source	2017 ($000)	2017 ($ per capita)	2017 (%)
General Revenue			
From Federal Government	59,784	91	1.8
From State Government	108,933	166	3.4
From Local Governments	150,048	229	4.6
Taxes			
Property	382,507	583	11.8
Sales and Gross Receipts	55,039	84	1.7
Personal Income	0	0	0.0
Corporate Income	0	0	0.0
Motor Vehicle License	12,423	19	0.4
Other Taxes	3,002	5	0.1
Current Charges	237,236	362	7.3
Liquor Store	0	0	0.0
Utility	1,563,115	2,384	48.1
Employee Retirement	443,303	676	13.6

Source: U.S. Census Bureau, State & Local Government Finances 2017

City Government Expenditures by Function

Function	2017 ($000)	2017 ($ per capita)	2017 (%)
General Direct Expenditures			
Air Transportation	0	0	0.0
Corrections	0	0	0.0
Education	0	0	0.0
Employment Security Administration	0	0	0.0
Financial Administration	38,430	58	1.2
Fire Protection	171,852	262	5.5
General Public Buildings	9,817	15	0.3
Governmental Administration, Other	26,659	40	0.9
Health	181	< 1	< 0.1
Highways	21,696	33	0.7
Hospitals	0	0	0.0
Housing and Community Development	27,083	41	0.9
Interest on General Debt	81,946	125	2.6
Judicial and Legal	22,036	33	0.7
Libraries	18,384	28	0.6
Parking	1,870	2	0.1
Parks and Recreation	48,430	73	1.6
Police Protection	253,043	385	8.1
Public Welfare	0	0	0.0
Sewerage	51,480	78	1.7
Solid Waste Management	70,010	106	2.3
Veterans' Services	0	0	0.0
Liquor Store	0	0	0.0
Utility	1,771,305	2,701	57.0
Employee Retirement	287,489	438	9.3

Source: U.S. Census Bureau, State & Local Government Finances 2017

EMPLOYMENT

Labor Force and Employment

Area	Civilian Labor Force Dec. 2019	Civilian Labor Force Dec. 2020	% Chg.	Workers Employed Dec. 2019	Workers Employed Dec. 2020	% Chg.
City	299,167	316,351	5.7	287,040	285,384	-0.6
MSA[1]	647,507	668,382	3.2	622,648	618,793	-0.6
U.S.	164,007,000	160,017,000	-2.4	158,504,000	149,613,000	-5.6

Note: Data is not seasonally adjusted and covers workers 16 years of age and older; (1) Figures cover the Memphis, TN-MS-AR Metropolitan Statistical Area
Source: Bureau of Labor Statistics, Local Area Unemployment Statistics

Unemployment Rate

Area	Jan.	Feb.	Mar.	Apr.	May	Jun.	Jul.	Aug.	Sep.	Oct.	Nov.	Dec.
City	4.9	4.9	4.2	14.5	12.9	15.3	17.4	16.3	12.5	13.1	8.7	9.8
MSA[1]	4.4	4.4	3.8	12.8	10.7	11.9	13.1	11.9	9.2	9.6	6.7	7.4
U.S.	4.0	3.8	4.5	14.4	13.0	11.2	10.5	8.5	7.7	6.6	6.4	6.5

Note: Data is not seasonally adjusted and covers workers 16 years of age and older; (1) Figures cover the Memphis, TN-MS-AR Metropolitan Statistical Area
Source: Bureau of Labor Statistics, Local Area Unemployment Statistics

Average Wages

Occupation	$/Hr.	Occupation	$/Hr.
Accountants and Auditors	34.50	Maintenance and Repair Workers	19.60
Automotive Mechanics	26.00	Marketing Managers	47.60
Bookkeepers	21.20	Network and Computer Systems Admin.	36.30
Carpenters	21.40	Nurses, Licensed Practical	21.50
Cashiers	10.80	Nurses, Registered	32.80
Computer Programmers	41.10	Nursing Assistants	14.00
Computer Systems Analysts	39.90	Office Clerks, General	16.60
Computer User Support Specialists	23.10	Physical Therapists	44.10
Construction Laborers	15.90	Physicians	61.00
Cooks, Restaurant	12.50	Plumbers, Pipefitters and Steamfitters	25.60
Customer Service Representatives	18.10	Police and Sheriff's Patrol Officers	25.00
Dentists	71.00	Postal Service Mail Carriers	25.90
Electricians	24.90	Real Estate Sales Agents	28.50
Engineers, Electrical	46.50	Retail Salespersons	14.10
Fast Food and Counter Workers	10.00	Sales Representatives, Technical/Scientific	42.80
Financial Managers	56.30	Secretaries, Exc. Legal/Medical/Executive	18.30
First-Line Supervisors of Office Workers	27.60	Security Guards	13.20
General and Operations Managers	55.80	Surgeons	n/a
Hairdressers/Cosmetologists	14.50	Teacher Assistants, Exc. Postsecondary*	12.20
Home Health and Personal Care Aides	10.90	Teachers, Secondary School, Exc. Sp. Ed.*	27.00
Janitors and Cleaners	12.40	Telemarketers	15.50
Landscaping/Groundskeeping Workers	13.90	Truck Drivers, Heavy/Tractor-Trailer	22.90
Lawyers	51.20	Truck Drivers, Light/Delivery Services	19.10
Maids and Housekeeping Cleaners	11.40	Waiters and Waitresses	9.80

Note: Wage data covers the Memphis, TN-MS-AR Metropolitan Statistical Area; (*) Hourly wages were calculated from annual wage data based on a 40 hour work week; n/a not available.
Source: Bureau of Labor Statistics, Metro Area Occupational Employment & Wage Estimates, May 2020

Employment by Industry

Sector	MSA[1] Number of Employees	MSA[1] Percent of Total	U.S. Percent of Total
Construction, Mining, and Logging	23,700	3.7	5.5
Education and Health Services	94,300	14.6	16.3
Financial Activities	29,300	4.5	6.1
Government	83,600	13.0	15.2
Information	5,100	0.8	1.9
Leisure and Hospitality	57,400	8.9	9.0
Manufacturing	44,000	6.8	8.5
Other Services	27,100	4.2	3.8
Professional and Business Services	99,300	15.4	14.4
Retail Trade	64,700	10.0	10.9
Transportation, Warehousing, and Utilities	81,400	12.6	4.6
Wholesale Trade	34,200	5.3	3.9

Note: Figures are non-farm employment as of December 2020. Figures are not seasonally adjusted and include workers 16 years of age and older; (1) Figures cover the Memphis, TN-MS-AR Metropolitan Statistical Area
Source: Bureau of Labor Statistics, Current Employment Statistics, Employment, Hours, and Earnings

Employment by Occupation

Occupation Classification	City (%)	MSA[1] (%)	U.S. (%)
Management, Business, Science, and Arts	30.8	34.4	38.5
Natural Resources, Construction, and Maintenance	7.0	7.9	8.9
Production, Transportation, and Material Moving	20.0	18.0	13.2
Sales and Office	22.3	22.5	21.6
Service	19.9	17.2	17.8

Note: Figures cover employed civilians 16 years of age and older; (1) Figures cover the Memphis, TN-MS-AR Metropolitan Statistical Area
Source: U.S. Census Bureau, 2015-2019 American Community Survey 5-Year Estimates

Occupations with Greatest Projected Employment Growth: 2020 – 2022

Occupation[1]	2020 Employment	2022 Projected Employment	Numeric Employment Change	Percent Employment Change
Heavy and Tractor-Trailer Truck Drivers	72,760	75,530	2,770	3.8
Laborers and Freight, Stock, and Material Movers, Hand	99,970	101,640	1,670	1.7
General and Operations Managers	44,540	45,510	970	2.2
Janitors and Cleaners, Except Maids and Housekeeping Cleaners	44,140	45,030	890	2.0
Construction Laborers	28,960	29,800	840	2.9
Managers, All Other	34,220	35,050	830	2.4
Retail Salespersons	88,170	88,970	800	0.9
Stock Clerks and Order Fillers	58,210	58,980	770	1.3
Farmers, Ranchers, and Other Agricultural Managers	23,960	24,700	740	3.1
Light Truck or Delivery Services Drivers	20,800	21,500	700	3.4

Note: Projections cover Tennessee; (1) Sorted by numeric employment change
Source: www.projectionscentral.com, State Occupational Projections, 2020–2022 Short-Term Projections

Fastest-Growing Occupations: 2020 – 2022

Occupation[1]	2020 Employment	2022 Projected Employment	Numeric Employment Change	Percent Employment Change
Athletes and Sports Competitors	390	510	120	30.8
Audio and Video Equipment Technicians	1,960	2,090	130	6.6
Software Developers, Applications	6,750	7,190	440	6.5
Sailors and Marine Oilers	920	980	60	6.5
Captains, Mates, and Pilots of Water Vessels	790	840	50	6.3
Operations Research Analysts	1,510	1,600	90	6.0
Massage Therapists	2,370	2,510	140	5.9
Agricultural Equipment Operators	2,790	2,950	160	5.7
Tire Repairers and Changers	2,830	2,990	160	5.7
Nonfarm Animal Caretakers	5,100	5,370	270	5.3

Note: Projections cover Tennessee; (1) Sorted by percent employment change and excludes occupations with numeric employment change less than 50
Source: www.projectionscentral.com, State Occupational Projections, 2020–2022 Short-Term Projections

TAXES

State Corporate Income Tax Rates

State	Tax Rate (%)	Income Brackets ($)	Num. of Brackets	Financial Institution Tax Rate (%)[a]	Federal Income Tax Ded.
Tennessee	6.5	Flat rate	1	6.5	No

Note: Tax rates as of January 1, 2021; (a) Rates listed are the corporate income tax rate applied to financial institutions or excise taxes based on income. Some states have other taxes based upon the value of deposits or shares.
Source: Federation of Tax Administrators, State Corporate Income Tax Rates, January 1, 2021

State Individual Income Tax Rates

State	Tax Rate (%)	Income Brackets ($)	Personal Exemptions ($) Single	Personal Exemptions ($) Married	Personal Exemptions ($) Depend.	Standard Ded. ($) Single	Standard Ded. ($) Married
Tennessee	– No state income tax (x) –						

Note: Tax rates as of January 1, 2021; Local- and county-level taxes are not included; (x) Tennessee Hall Tax Rate on Dividends and Interest has been repealed in 2021.
Source: Federation of Tax Administrators, State Individual Income Tax Rates, January 1, 2021

Various State Sales and Excise Tax Rates

State	State Sales Tax (%)	Gasoline[1] (¢/gal.)	Cigarette[2] ($/pack)	Spirits[3] ($/gal.)	Wine[4] ($/gal.)	Beer[5] ($/gal.)	Recreational Marijuana (%)
Tennessee	7	27.4	0.62	4.46	1.27	1.29	Not legal

Note: All tax rates as of January 1, 2021; (1) The American Petroleum Institute has developed a methodology for determining the average tax rate on a gallon of fuel. Rates may include any of the following: excise taxes, environmental fees, storage tank fees, other fees or taxes, general sales tax, and local taxes; (2) The federal excise tax of $1.0066 per pack and local taxes are not included; (3) Rates are those applicable to off-premise sales of 40% alcohol by volume (a.b.v.) distilled spirits in 750ml containers. Local excise taxes are excluded; (4) Rates are those applicable to off-premise sales of 11% a.b.v. non-carbonated wine in 750ml containers; (5) Rates are those applicable to off-premise sales of 4.7% a.b.v. beer in 12 ounce containers.
Source: Tax Foundation, 2021 Facts & Figures: How Does Your State Compare?

State Business Tax Climate Index Rankings

State	Overall Rank	Corporate Tax Rank	Individual Income Tax Rank	Sales Tax Rank	Property Tax Rank	Unemployment Insurance Tax Rank
Tennessee	18	24	8	47	33	26

Note: The index is a measure of how each state's tax laws affect economic performance. The lower the rank, the more favorable a state's tax system is for business. States without a given tax are given a ranking of 1. The scores/rankings for the District of Columbia do not affect other states. The 2021 index represents the tax climate as of July 1, 2020.
Source: Tax Foundation, State Business Tax Climate Index 2021

TRANSPORTATION

Means of Transportation to Work

Area	Car/Truck/Van Drove Alone	Car/Truck/Van Carpooled	Public Transportation Bus	Public Transportation Subway	Public Transportation Railroad	Bicycle	Walked	Other Means	Worked at Home
City	82.0	10.5	1.4	0.0	0.0	0.2	1.6	1.3	2.9
MSA[1]	84.6	9.2	0.7	0.0	0.0	0.1	1.0	1.1	3.3
U.S.	76.3	9.0	2.4	1.9	0.6	0.5	2.7	1.4	5.2

Note: Figures are percentages and cover workers 16 years of age and older; (1) Figures cover the Memphis, TN-MS-AR Metropolitan Statistical Area
Source: U.S. Census Bureau, 2015-2019 American Community Survey 5-Year Estimates

Travel Time to Work

Area	Less Than 10 Minutes	10 to 19 Minutes	20 to 29 Minutes	30 to 44 Minutes	45 to 59 Minutes	60 to 89 Minutes	90 Minutes or More
City	10.2	32.9	30.2	20.5	3.6	1.6	1.0
MSA[1]	10.2	28.3	26.7	24.1	6.8	2.7	1.2
U.S.	12.2	28.4	20.8	20.8	8.3	6.4	2.9

Note: Note: Figures are percentages and include workers 16 years old and over; (1) Figures cover the Memphis, TN-MS-AR Metropolitan Statistical Area
Source: U.S. Census Bureau, 2015-2019 American Community Survey 5-Year Estimates

Key Congestion Measures

Measure	1982	1992	2002	2012	2017
Annual Hours of Delay, Total (000)	3,149	10,322	19,385	24,364	28,015
Annual Hours of Delay, Per Auto Commuter	10	27	35	42	48
Annual Congestion Cost, Total (million $)	24	109	262	437	516
Annual Congestion Cost, Per Auto Commuter ($)	164	369	541	532	594

Note: Covers the Memphis TN-MS-AR urban area
Source: Texas A&M Transportation Institute, 2019 Urban Mobility Report

Freeway Travel Time Index

Measure	1982	1987	1992	1997	2002	2007	2012	2017
Urban Area Index[1]	1.04	1.07	1.12	1.15	1.17	1.17	1.17	1.18
Urban Area Rank[1,2]	61	55	40	41	41	56	50	45

Note: Freeway Travel Time Index—the ratio of travel time in the peak period to the travel time at free-flow conditions. For example, a value of 1.30 indicates a 20-minute free-flow trip takes 26 minutes in the peak (20 minutes x 1.30 = 26 minutes); (1) Covers the Memphis TN-MS-AR urban area; (2) Rank is based on 101 larger urban areas (#1 = highest travel time index)
Source: Texas A&M Transportation Institute, 2019 Urban Mobility Report

Public Transportation

Agency Name / Mode of Transportation	Vehicles Operated in Maximum Service[1]	Annual Unlinked Passenger Trips[2] (in thous.)	Annual Passenger Miles[3] (in thous.)
Memphis Area Transit Authority (MATA)			
Bus (directly operated)	93	5,846.4	32,537.7
Demand Response (directly operated)	40	192.9	2,190.8
Streetcar Rail (directly operated)	4	371.0	452.2

Note: (1) Number of revenue vehicles operated by the given mode and type of service to meet the annual maximum service requirement. This is the revenue vehicle count during the peak season of the year; on the week and day that maximum service is provided. Vehicles operated in maximum service (VOMS) exclude atypical days and one-time special events; (2) Number of passengers who boarded public transportation vehicles. Passengers are counted each time they board a vehicle no matter how many vehicles they use to travel from their origin to their destination. (3) Sum of the distances ridden by all passengers during the entire fiscal year.
Source: Federal Transit Administration, National Transit Database, 2019

Air Transportation

Airport Name and Code / Type of Service	Passenger Airlines[1]	Passenger Enplanements	Freight Carriers[2]	Freight (lbs)
Memphis International (MEM)				
Domestic service (U.S. carriers - 2020)	26	1,017,653	20	4,662,403,753
International service (U.S. carriers - 2019)	4	125	6	369,729,764

Note: (1) Includes all U.S.-based major, minor and commuter airlines that carried at least one passenger during the year; (2) Includes all U.S.-based airlines and freight carriers that transported at least one pound of freight during the year.
Source: Bureau of Transportation Statistics, The Intermodal Transportation Database, Air Carriers: T-100 Domestic Market (U.S. Carriers), 2020; Bureau of Transportation Statistics, The Intermodal Transportation Database, Air Carriers: T-100 International Market (U.S. Carriers), 2019

BUSINESSES

Major Business Headquarters

Company Name	Industry	Rankings Fortune[1]	Forbes[2]
AutoZone	Specialty Retailers, Other	268	-
FedEx	Mail, Package, and Freight Delivery	47	-
International Paper	Packaging, Containers	144	-

Note: (1) Companies that produce a 10-K are ranked 1 to 500 based on 2019 revenue; (2) All private companies with at least $2 billion in annual revenue through the end of their most current fiscal year are ranked 1 to 219; companies listed are headquartered in the city; dashes indicate no ranking
Source: Fortune, "Fortune 500," June/July 2020; Forbes, "America's Largest Private Companies," 2020

Fastest-Growing Businesses

According to *Initiative for a Competitive Inner City (ICIC)*, Memphis is home to five of America's 100 fastest-growing "inner city" companies: **neMarc Professional Services** (#24); **ER2** (#32); **AHA Mechanical Contractors** (#41); **Medford Roofing** (#67); **Karen Adams Designs** (#99). Criteria for inclusion: company must be headquartered in or have 51 percent or more of its physical operations in an economically distressed urban area; must be an independent, for-profit corporation, partnership or proprietorship; must have 10 or more employees and have a five-year sales history that includes sales of at least $200,000 in the base year and at least $1 million in the current year with no decrease in sales over the two most recent years. Companies were ranked overall by revenue growth over the five-year period between 2015 and 2019. *Initiative for a Competitive Inner City (ICIC), "Inner City 100 Companies," 2020*

Minority Business Opportunity

Memphis is home to one company which is on the *Black Enterprise* Industrial/Service list (100 largest companies based on gross sales): **Castle Black Construction** (#100). Criteria: operational in previous calendar year; at least 51% black-owned and manufactures/owns the product it sells or provides industrial or consumer services. Brokerages, real estate firms and firms that provide professional services are not eligible. *Black Enterprise, B.E. 100s, 2019*

Memphis is home to one company which is on the *Black Enterprise* Bank list (15 largest banks based on total assets, capital, deposits and loans, including mortgage-backed securities for the calendar year): **Tri-State Bank of Memphis** (#14). Only commercial banks or savings and loans that are classified by the Federal Reserve as black institutions and have been fully operational for the previous calendar year were considered. *Black Enterprise, B.E. 100s, 2019*

Living Environment

COST OF LIVING

Cost of Living Index

Composite Index	Groceries	Housing	Utilities	Trans-portation	Health Care	Misc. Goods/Services
85.1	88.7	74.5	89.1	85.7	81.0	91.3

Note: The Cost of Living Index measures regional differences in the cost of consumer goods and services, excluding taxes and non-consumer expenditures, for professional and managerial households in the top income quintile. It is based on more than 50,000 prices covering almost 60 different items for which prices are collected three times a year by chambers of commerce, economic development organizations or university applied economic centers in each participating urban area. The numbers shown should be read as a percentage above or below the national average of 100. For example, a value of 115.4 in the groceries column indicates that grocery prices are 15.4% higher than the national average. Small differences in the index numbers should not be interpreted as significant; Figures cover the Memphis TN urban area.
Source: The Council for Community and Economic Research, Cost of Living Index, 2020

Grocery Prices

Area[1]	T-Bone Steak ($/pound)	Frying Chicken ($/pound)	Whole Milk ($/half gal.)	Eggs ($/dozen)	Orange Juice ($/64 oz.)	Coffee ($/11.5 oz.)
City[2]	9.64	0.98	1.79	1.27	3.09	4.05
Avg.	11.78	1.39	2.05	1.47	3.57	4.34
Min.	8.03	0.94	1.03	0.74	2.94	3.02
Max.	15.86	2.65	4.31	3.77	5.44	8.69

Note: (1) Values for the local area are compared with the average, minimum and maximum values for all 284 areas in the Cost of Living Index; (2) Figures cover the Memphis TN urban area; **T-Bone Steak** (price per pound); **Frying Chicken** (price per pound, whole fryer); **Whole Milk** (half gallon carton); **Eggs** (price per dozen, Grade A, large); **Orange Juice** (64 oz. Tropicana or Florida Natural); **Coffee** (11.5 oz. can, vacuum-packed, Maxwell House, Hills Bros, or Folgers).
Source: The Council for Community and Economic Research, Cost of Living Index, 2020

Housing and Utility Costs

Area[1]	New Home Price ($)	Apartment Rent ($/month)	All Electric ($/month)	Part Electric ($/month)	Other Energy ($/month)	Telephone ($/month)
City[2]	273,404	903	-	90.75	43.22	185.00
Avg.	368,594	1,168	170.86	100.47	65.28	184.30
Min.	190,567	502	91.58	31.42	26.08	169.60
Max.	2,227,806	4,738	470.38	280.31	280.06	206.50

Note: (1) Values for the local area are compared with the average, minimum and maximum values for all 284 areas in the Cost of Living Index; (2) Figures cover the Memphis TN urban area; **New Home Price** (2,400 sf living area, 8,000 sf lot, in urban area with full utilities); **Apartment Rent** (950 sf 2 bedroom/1.5 or 2 bath, unfurnished, excluding all utilities except water); **All Electric** (average monthly cost for an all-electric home); **Part Electric** (average monthly cost for a part-electric home); **Other Energy** (average monthly cost for natural gas, fuel oil, coal, wood, and any other forms of energy except electricity); **Telephone** (price includes the base monthly rate plus taxes and fees for three lines of mobile phone service).
Source: The Council for Community and Economic Research, Cost of Living Index, 2020

Health Care, Transportation, and Other Costs

Area[1]	Doctor ($/visit)	Dentist ($/visit)	Optometrist ($/visit)	Gasoline ($/gallon)	Beauty Salon ($/visit)	Men's Shirt ($)
City[2]	84.25	77.68	74.47	1.94	36.63	25.89
Avg.	115.44	99.32	108.10	2.21	39.27	31.37
Min.	36.68	59.00	51.36	1.71	19.00	11.00
Max.	219.00	153.10	250.97	3.46	82.05	58.33

Note: (1) Values for the local area are compared with the average, minimum and maximum values for all 284 areas in the Cost of Living Index; (2) Figures cover the Memphis TN urban area; **Doctor** (general practitioners routine exam of an established patient); **Dentist** (adult teeth cleaning and periodic oral examination); **Optometrist** (full vision eye exam for established adult patient); **Gasoline** (one gallon regular unleaded, national brand, including all taxes, cash price at self-service pump if available); **Beauty Salon** (woman's shampoo, trim, and blow-dry); **Men's Shirt** (cotton/polyester dress shirt, pinpoint weave, long sleeves).
Source: The Council for Community and Economic Research, Cost of Living Index, 2020

HOUSING

Homeownership Rate

Area	2012 (%)	2013 (%)	2014 (%)	2015 (%)	2016 (%)	2017 (%)	2018 (%)	2019 (%)	2020 (%)
MSA[1]	60.5	56.2	57.2	59.6	61.8	62.4	63.5	63.7	62.5
U.S.	65.4	65.1	64.5	63.7	63.4	63.9	64.4	64.6	66.6

Note: (1) Figures cover the Memphis, TN-MS-AR Metropolitan Statistical Area
Source: U.S. Census Bureau, Housing Vacancies and Homeownership Annual Statistics: 2012-2020

House Price Index (HPI)

Area	National Ranking[2]	Quarterly Change (%)	One-Year Change (%)	Five-Year Change (%)	Since 1991Q1 (%)
MSA[1]	90	1.82	6.94	33.17	120.34
U.S.[3]	–	3.81	10.77	38.99	205.12

Note: The HPI is a weighted repeat sales index. It measures average price changes in repeat sales or refinancings on the same properties. This information is obtained by reviewing repeat mortgage transactions on single-family properties whose mortgages have been purchased or securitized by Fannie Mae or Freddie Mac since January 1975; (1) Figures cover the Memphis, TN-MS-AR Metropolitan Statistical Area; (2) Rankings are based on annual percentage change for all metro areas containing at least 15,000 transactions over the last 10 years and ranges from 1 to 253; (3) figures based on a weighted average of Census Division estimates using a seasonally adjusted, purchase-only index; all figures are for the period ending December 31, 2020
Source: Federal Housing Finance Agency, Change in Metropolitan Area House Price Indexes, April 7, 2021

Median Single-Family Home Prices

Area	2018	2019	2020p	Percent Change 2019 to 2020
MSA[1]	177.9	188.7	221.2	17.2
U.S. Average	261.6	274.6	299.9	9.2

Note: Figures are median sales prices of existing single-family homes in thousands of dollars; (p) preliminary; (1) Figures cover the Memphis, TN-MS-AR Metropolitan Statistical Area
Source: National Association of Realtors, Median Sales Price of Existing Single-Family Homes for Metropolitan Areas, 4th Quarter 2020

Qualifying Income Based on Median Sales Price of Existing Single-Family Homes

Area	With 5% Down ($)	With 10% Down ($)	With 20% Down ($)
MSA[1]	43,332	41,052	36,490
U.S. Average	59,266	56,147	49,908

Note: Figures are preliminary; Qualifying income is based on a mortgage rate of 2.81%. Monthly principal and interest payment is limited to 25% of income; (1) Figures cover the Memphis, TN-MS-AR Metropolitan Statistical Area
Source: National Association of Realtors, Qualifying Income Based on Median Sales Price of Existing Single-Family Homes for Metropolitan Areas, 4th Quarter 2020

Home Value Distribution

Area	Under $50,000	$50,000 -$99,999	$100,000 -$149,999	$150,000 -$199,999	$200,000 -$299,999	$300,000 -$499,999	$500,000 -$999,999	$1,000,000 or more
City	14.5	34.7	17.4	12.4	9.9	6.8	3.3	1.0
MSA[1]	9.1	21.8	18.2	16.5	18.6	11.2	3.6	0.9
U.S.	6.9	12.0	13.3	14.0	19.6	19.3	11.4	3.4

Note: Figures are percentages and cover owner-occupied housing units; (1) Figures cover the Memphis, TN-MS-AR Metropolitan Statistical Area
Source: U.S. Census Bureau, 2015-2019 American Community Survey 5-Year Estimates

Year Housing Structure Built

Area	2010 or Later	2000 -2009	1990 -1999	1980 -1989	1970 -1979	1960 -1969	1950 -1959	1940 -1949	Before 1940	Median Year
City	2.0	7.0	10.0	12.4	18.2	14.9	19.1	8.7	7.7	1970
MSA[1]	4.2	15.7	17.1	13.7	16.2	10.8	11.9	5.3	5.1	1980
U.S.	5.2	14.0	13.9	13.4	15.2	10.6	10.3	4.9	12.6	1978

Note: Figures are percentages except for Median Year; Note: (1) Figures cover the Memphis, TN-MS-AR Metropolitan Statistical Area
Source: U.S. Census Bureau, 2015-2019 American Community Survey 5-Year Estimates

Gross Monthly Rent

Area	Under $500	$500 -$999	$1,000 -$1,499	$1,500 -$1,999	$2,000 -$2,499	$2,500 -$2,999	$3,000 and up	Median ($)
City	8.1	54.6	31.2	4.7	0.9	0.2	0.2	901
MSA[1]	7.8	50.9	32.8	6.4	1.5	0.3	0.3	930
U.S.	9.4	36.2	30.0	14.0	5.6	2.4	2.4	1,062

Note: Figures are percentages except for Median; Gross rent is the contract rent plus the estimated average monthly cost of utilities (electricity, gas, and water and sewer) and fuels (oil, coal, kerosene, wood, etc.) if these are paid by the renter (or paid for the renter by someone else); (1) Figures cover the Memphis, TN-MS-AR Metropolitan Statistical Area
Source: U.S. Census Bureau, 2015-2019 American Community Survey 5-Year Estimates

HEALTH

Health Risk Factors

Category	MSA[1] (%)	U.S. (%)
Adults aged 18–64 who have any kind of health care coverage	80.3	87.3
Adults who reported being in good or better health	80.8	82.4
Adults who have been told they have high blood cholesterol	32.3	33.0
Adults who have been told they have high blood pressure	36.6	32.3
Adults who are current smokers	20.1	17.1
Adults who currently use E-cigarettes	4.8	4.6
Adults who currently use chewing tobacco, snuff, or snus	3.9	4.0
Adults who are heavy drinkers[2]	6.4	6.3
Adults who are binge drinkers[3]	12.1	17.4
Adults who are overweight (BMI 25.0 - 29.9)	35.3	35.3
Adults who are obese (BMI 30.0 - 99.8)	37.2	31.3
Adults who participated in any physical activities in the past month	68.1	74.4
Adults who always or nearly always wears a seat belt	92.3	94.3

Note: (1) Figures cover the Memphis, TN-MS-AR Metropolitan Statistical Area; (2) Heavy drinkers are classified as adult men having more than 14 drinks per week and adult women having more than 7 drinks per week; (3) Binge drinkers are classified as males having five or more drinks on one occasion or females having four or more drinks on one occasion
Source: Centers for Disease Control and Prevention, Behaviorial Risk Factor Surveillance System, SMART: Selected Metropolitan Area Risk Trends, 2017

Acute and Chronic Health Conditions

Category	MSA[1] (%)	U.S. (%)
Adults who have ever been told they had a heart attack	2.9	4.2
Adults who have ever been told they have angina or coronary heart disease	2.9	3.9
Adults who have ever been told they had a stroke	5.0	3.0
Adults who have ever been told they have asthma	14.6	14.2
Adults who have ever been told they have arthritis	25.4	24.9
Adults who have ever been told they have diabetes[2]	11.6	10.5
Adults who have ever been told they had skin cancer	4.2	6.2
Adults who have ever been told they had any other types of cancer	5.8	7.1
Adults who have ever been told they have COPD	6.0	6.5
Adults who have ever been told they have kidney disease	2.7	3.0
Adults who have ever been told they have a form of depression	17.5	20.5

Note: (1) Figures cover the Memphis, TN-MS-AR Metropolitan Statistical Area; (2) Figures do not include pregnancy-related, borderline, or pre-diabetes
Source: Centers for Disease Control and Prevention, Behaviorial Risk Factor Surveillance System, SMART: Selected Metropolitan Area Risk Trends, 2017

Health Screening and Vaccination Rates

Category	MSA[1] (%)	U.S. (%)
Adults aged 65+ who have had flu shot within the past year	49.3	60.7
Adults aged 65+ who have ever had a pneumonia vaccination	67.8	75.4
Adults who have ever been tested for HIV	47.7	36.1
Adults who have ever had the shingles or zoster vaccine?	19.7	28.9
Adults who have had their blood cholesterol checked within the last five years	86.7	85.9

Note: n/a not available; (1) Figures cover the Memphis, TN-MS-AR Metropolitan Statistical Area.
Source: Centers for Disease Control and Prevention, Behaviorial Risk Factor Surveillance System, SMART: Selected Metropolitan Area Risk Trends, 2017

Disability Status

Category	MSA[1] (%)	U.S. (%)
Adults who reported being deaf	4.3	6.7
Are you blind or have serious difficulty seeing, even when wearing glasses?	6.2	4.5
Are you limited in any way in any of your usual activities due of arthritis?	12.9	12.9
Do you have difficulty doing errands alone?	8.4	6.8
Do you have difficulty dressing or bathing?	4.2	3.6
Do you have serious difficulty concentrating/remembering/making decisions?	11.4	10.7
Do you have serious difficulty walking or climbing stairs?	14.0	13.6

Note: (1) Figures cover the Memphis, TN-MS-AR Metropolitan Statistical Area.
Source: Centers for Disease Control and Prevention, Behaviorial Risk Factor Surveillance System, SMART: Selected Metropolitan Area Risk Trends, 2017

Mortality Rates for the Top 10 Causes of Death in the U.S.

ICD-10[a] Sub-Chapter	ICD-10[a] Code	Age-Adjusted Mortality Rate[1] per 100,000 population County[2]	U.S.
Malignant neoplasms	C00-C97	166.3	149.2
Ischaemic heart diseases	I20-I25	102.8	90.5
Other forms of heart disease	I30-I51	54.4	52.2
Chronic lower respiratory diseases	J40-J47	35.7	39.6
Other degenerative diseases of the nervous system	G30-G31	50.7	37.6
Cerebrovascular diseases	I60-I69	50.7	37.2
Other external causes of accidental injury	W00-X59	38.0	36.1
Organic, including symptomatic, mental disorders	F01-F09	26.5	29.4
Hypertensive diseases	I10-I15	46.5	24.1
Diabetes mellitus	E10-E14	26.7	21.5

Note: (a) ICD-10 = International Classification of Diseases 10th Revision; (1) Mortality rates are a three-year average covering 2017-2019; (2) Figures cover Shelby County.
Source: Centers for Disease Control and Prevention, National Center for Health Statistics. Underlying Cause of Death 1999-2019 on CDC WONDER Online Database

Mortality Rates for Selected Causes of Death

ICD-10[a] Sub-Chapter	ICD-10[a] Code	Age-Adjusted Mortality Rate[1] per 100,000 population County[2]	U.S.
Assault	X85-Y09	23.7	6.0
Diseases of the liver	K70-K76	12.5	14.4
Human immunodeficiency virus (HIV) disease	B20-B24	4.9	1.5
Influenza and pneumonia	J09-J18	18.1	13.8
Intentional self-harm	X60-X84	11.2	14.1
Malnutrition	E40-E46	4.8	2.3
Obesity and other hyperalimentation	E65-E68	3.4	2.1
Renal failure	N17-N19	15.3	12.6
Transport accidents	V01-V99	16.9	12.3
Viral hepatitis	B15-B19	1.4	1.2

Note: (a) ICD-10 = International Classification of Diseases 10th Revision; (1) Mortality rates are a three-year average covering 2017-2019; (2) Figures cover Shelby County; Data are suppressed when the data meet the criteria for confidentiality constraints; Mortality rates are flagged as unreliable when the rate would be calculated with a numerator of 20 or less.
Source: Centers for Disease Control and Prevention, National Center for Health Statistics. Underlying Cause of Death 1999-2019 on CDC WONDER Online Database

Health Insurance Coverage

Area	With Health Insurance	With Private Health Insurance	With Public Health Insurance	Without Health Insurance	Population Under Age 19 Without Health Insurance
City	86.3	55.7	41.0	13.7	6.3
MSA[1]	89.2	64.7	35.4	10.8	5.0
U.S.	91.2	67.9	35.1	8.8	5.1

Note: Figures are percentages that cover the civilian noninstitutionalized population; (1) Figures cover the Memphis, TN-MS-AR Metropolitan Statistical Area
Source: U.S. Census Bureau, 2015-2019 American Community Survey 5-Year Estimates

Number of Medical Professionals

Area	MDs[3]	DOs[3,4]	Dentists	Podiatrists	Chiropractors	Optometrists
County[1] (number)	3,780	96	690	34	124	296
County[1] (rate[2])	403.7	10.3	73.6	3.6	13.2	31.6
U.S. (rate[2])	282.9	22.7	71.2	6.2	28.1	16.9

47157
Note: Data as of 2019 unless noted; (1) Data covers Shelby County; (2) Rate per 100,000 population; (3) Data as of 2018 and includes all active, non-federal physicians; (4) Doctor of Osteopathic Medicine
Source: U.S. Department of Health and Human Services, Health Resources and Services Administration, Bureau of Health Professions, Area Resource File (ARF) 2019-2020

Best Hospitals

According to *U.S. News,* the Memphis, TN-MS-AR metro area is home to two of the best children's hospitals in the U.S.: **Le Bonheur Children's Hospital** (8 pediatric specialties); **St. Jude Children's Research Hospital** (1 pediatric specialty). The hospitals listed were highly ranked in at least one of 10 pediatric specialties. Eighty-eight children's hospitals in the U.S. were nationally ranked in at least one specialty. Hospitals received points for being ranked in a specialty, and the 10 hospitals with the most points across the 10 specialties make up the Honor Roll. *U.S. News Online,* "America's Best Children's Hospitals 2020-21"

EDUCATION

Public School District Statistics

District Name	Schls	Pupils	Pupil/Teacher Ratio	Minority Pupils[1] (%)	Free Lunch Eligible[2] (%)	IEP[3] (%)
Shelby County	219	112,125	16.3	92.8	n/a	11.1

Note: Table includes school districts with 2,000 or more students; (1) Percentage of students that are not non-Hispanic white; (2) Percentage of students that are eligible for the free lunch program; (3) Percentage of students that have an Individualized Education Program.
Source: U.S. Department of Education, National Center for Education Statistics, Common Core of Data, Local Education Agency (School District) Universe Survey: School Year 2018-2019; U.S. Department of Education, National Center for Education Statistics, Common Core of Data, Public Elementary/Secondary School Universe Survey: School Year 2018-2019

Highest Level of Education

Area	Less than H.S.	H.S. Diploma	Some College, No Deg.	Associate Degree	Bachelor's Degree	Master's Degree	Prof. School Degree	Doctorate Degree
City	14.3	30.6	23.3	5.6	15.7	7.1	2.0	1.3
MSA[1]	12.0	29.2	23.5	7.1	17.4	7.9	1.9	1.2
U.S.	12.0	27.0	20.4	8.5	19.8	8.8	2.1	1.4

Note: Figures cover persons age 25 and over; (1) Figures cover the Memphis, TN-MS-AR Metropolitan Statistical Area
Source: U.S. Census Bureau, 2015-2019 American Community Survey 5-Year Estimates

Educational Attainment by Race

Area	High School Graduate or Higher (%)					Bachelor's Degree or Higher (%)				
	Total	White	Black	Asian	Hisp.[2]	Total	White	Black	Asian	Hisp.[2]
City	85.7	91.7	84.1	87.0	49.5	26.2	44.5	15.9	57.0	11.2
MSA[1]	88.0	91.9	85.2	87.9	57.7	28.3	35.7	19.1	58.2	14.8
U.S.	88.0	89.9	86.0	87.1	68.7	32.1	33.5	21.6	54.3	16.4

Note: Figures shown cover persons 25 years old and over; (1) Figures cover the Memphis, TN-MS-AR Metropolitan Statistical Area; (2) People of Hispanic origin can be of any race
Source: U.S. Census Bureau, 2015-2019 American Community Survey 5-Year Estimates

School Enrollment by Grade and Control

Area	Preschool (%)		Kindergarten (%)		Grades 1-4 (%)		Grades 5-8 (%)		Grades 9-12 (%)	
	Public	Private	Public	Private	Public	Private	Public	Private	Public	Private
City	67.2	32.8	87.3	12.7	87.9	12.1	87.2	12.8	85.5	14.5
MSA[1]	61.4	38.6	86.2	13.8	86.6	13.4	86.3	13.7	84.7	15.3
U.S.	59.1	40.9	87.6	12.4	89.5	10.5	89.4	10.6	90.1	9.9

Note: Figures shown cover persons 3 years old and over; (1) Figures cover the Memphis, TN-MS-AR Metropolitan Statistical Area
Source: U.S. Census Bureau, 2015-2019 American Community Survey 5-Year Estimates

Higher Education

Four-Year Colleges			Two-Year Colleges			Medical Schools[1]	Law Schools[2]	Voc/Tech[3]
Public	Private Non-profit	Private For-profit	Public	Private Non-profit	Private For-profit			
2	10	1	2	1	1	1	1	7

Note: Figures cover institutions located within the city limits and include main campuses only; (1) includes schools accredited by the Liaison Committee on Medical Education and the American Osteopathic Association's Commission on Osteopathic College Accreditation; (2) includes ABA-accredited schools, schools with provisional ABA accreditation, and state accredited schools; (3) includes all schools with programs that are less than 2 years.
Source: National Center for Education Statistics, Integrated Postsecondary Education System (IPEDS), 2019-20; Wikipedia, List of Medical Schools in the United States, accessed April 2, 2021; Wikipedia, List of Law Schools in the United States, accessed April 2, 2021

According to *U.S. News & World Report,* the Memphis, TN-MS-AR metro area is home to one of the top 100 liberal arts colleges in the U.S.: **Rhodes College** (#54 tie). The indicators used to capture academic quality fall into a number of categories: assessment by administrators at peer institutions; retention of students; faculty resources; student selectivity; financial resources; alumni giving; high school counselor ratings of colleges; and graduation rate. *U.S. News & World Report, "America's Best Colleges 2021"*

EMPLOYERS

Major Employers

Company Name	Industry
Baptist Memorial Healthcare Corp.	Health care system
Baptist Memorial Healthcare Corp.	Integrated health care delivery system
City of Memphis	Municipal government
FedEx Corp.	Transportation
First Tennessee Bank	Commercial banking
Horseshoe Casino & Hotel	Casinos & hotel resorts
International Paper	Printing & writing paper
Kroger Delta Marketing	Grocery stores
Memphis City Schools	Primary & secondary education
Memphis Light	Gas & Water
Methodist Le Bonheur Healthcare	Integrated health care delivery system
Naval Support Activity Mid-South	Federal government
Park Place Entertainment	Casinos & hotel resorts
Shelby County Government	County government
Shelby County Schools	Primary & secondary education
St. Jude Children's Research Hospital	Specialty hospital
Tennessee State Government	State government
United States Government	Federal government
University of Memphis	Colleges & universities
University of Tennessee	Memphis
Wal-Mart Stores	Retail stores

Note: Companies shown are located within the Memphis, TN-MS-AR Metropolitan Statistical Area.
Source: Hoovers.com; Wikipedia

Best Companies to Work For

First Horizon National, headquartered in Memphis, is among the "Best Companies for Multicultural Women." *Working Mother* selected 50 companies based on a detailed application completed by public and private firms based in the United States, excluding government agencies, companies in the human resources field and non-autonomous divisions. Companies supplied data about the hiring, pay, and promotion of multicultural employees. Applications focused on representation of multicultural women, recruitment, retention and advancement programs, and company culture. *Working Mother*, "Best Companies for Multicultural Women," 2020

FedEx; International Paper, headquartered in Memphis, are among the "100 Best Places to Work in IT." To qualify, companies had to be U.S.-based organizations or be non-U.S.-based employers that met the following criteria: have a minimum of 300 total employees at a U.S. headquarters and a minimum of 30 IT employees in the U.S., with at least 50% of their IT employees based in the U.S. The best places to work were selected based on compensation, benefits, work/life balance, employee morale, and satisfaction with training and development programs. In addition, *InsiderPro* and *Computerworld* looked at retention efforts, programs for recognizing and rewarding outstanding performances, and benefits such as flextime, elder care and child care, and reimbursement for college tuition and the cost of pursuing technology certifications. *InsiderPro and Computerworld*, "100 Best Places to Work in IT," 2020

PUBLIC SAFETY

Crime Rate

Area	All Crimes	Violent Crimes				Property Crimes		
		Murder	Rape[3]	Robbery	Aggrav. Assault	Burglary	Larceny-Theft	Motor Vehicle Theft
City	8,029.9	29.2	72.0	373.9	1,426.3	1,204.3	4,302.1	622.1
Suburbs[1]	2,498.8	6.8	34.3	50.8	297.1	361.2	1,515.0	233.6
Metro[2]	5,173.9	17.6	52.5	207.1	843.3	769.0	2,863.0	421.5
U.S.	2,489.3	5.0	42.6	81.6	250.2	340.5	1,549.5	219.9

Note: Figures are crimes per 100,000 population; (1) All areas within the metro area that are located outside the city limits; (2) Figures cover the Memphis, TN-MS-AR Metropolitan Statistical Area; (3) All figures shown were reported using the revised Uniform Crime Reporting (UCR) definition of rape.
Source: FBI Uniform Crime Reports, 2019

Hate Crimes

Area	Number of Quarters Reported	Number of Incidents per Bias Motivation					
		Race/Ethnicity/Ancestry	Religion	Sexual Orientation	Disability	Gender	Gender Identity
City	4	4	0	1	0	0	0
U.S.	4	3,963	1,521	1,195	157	69	198

Source: Federal Bureau of Investigation, Hate Crime Statistics 2019

Identity Theft Consumer Reports

Area	Reports	Reports per 100,000 Population	Rank[2]
MSA[1]	12,136	902	13
U.S.	1,387,615	423	-

Note: (1) Figures cover the Memphis, TN-MS-AR Metropolitan Statistical Area; (2) Rank ranges from 1 to 391 where 1 indicates greatest number of identity theft reports per 100,000 population
Source: Federal Trade Commission, Consumer Sentinel Network Data Book 2020

Fraud and Other Consumer Reports

Area	Reports	Reports per 100,000 Population	Rank[2]
MSA[1]	18,322	1,361	4
U.S.	3,385,133	1,031	-

Note: (1) Figures cover the Memphis, TN-MS-AR Metropolitan Statistical Area; (2) Rank ranges from 1 to 391 where 1 indicates greatest number of fraud and other consumer reports per 100,000 population
Source: Federal Trade Commission, Consumer Sentinel Network Data Book 2020

POLITICS

2020 Presidential Election Results

Area	Biden	Trump	Jorgensen	Hawkins	Other
Shelby County	64.4	34.0	0.6	0.2	0.8
U.S.	51.3	46.8	1.2	0.3	0.5

Note: Results are percentages and may not add to 100% due to rounding
Source: Dave Leip's Atlas of U.S. Presidential Elections

SPORTS

Professional Sports Teams

Team Name	League	Year Established
Memphis Grizzlies	National Basketball Association (NBA)	2001

Note: Includes teams located in the Memphis, TN-MS-AR Metropolitan Statistical Area.
Source: Wikipedia, Major Professional Sports Teams of the United States and Canada, April 6, 2021

CLIMATE

Average and Extreme Temperatures

Temperature	Jan	Feb	Mar	Apr	May	Jun	Jul	Aug	Sep	Oct	Nov	Dec	Yr.
Extreme High (°F)	83	85	90	95	99	104	107	104	105	97	86	82	107
Average High (°F)	57	62	69	78	84	90	92	92	87	78	68	60	77
Average Temp. (°F)	46	50	57	65	72	79	81	81	76	65	55	48	65
Average Low (°F)	34	37	44	51	59	67	70	69	64	51	42	36	52
Extreme Low (°F)	0	8	15	28	38	42	55	53	34	24	16	2	0

Note: Figures cover the years 1948-1990
Source: National Climatic Data Center, International Station Meteorological Climate Summary, 9/96

Average Precipitation/Snowfall/Humidity

Precip./Humidity	Jan	Feb	Mar	Apr	May	Jun	Jul	Aug	Sep	Oct	Nov	Dec	Yr.
Avg. Precip. (in.)	4.9	5.1	6.6	5.2	4.3	3.7	5.3	3.5	3.6	2.7	4.2	5.6	54.8
Avg. Snowfall (in.)	1	Tr	Tr	Tr	0	0	0	0	0	0	Tr	Tr	1
Avg. Rel. Hum. 6am (%)	87	86	87	90	91	91	93	93	92	91	88	87	90
Avg. Rel. Hum. 3pm (%)	56	51	47	46	50	52	57	54	54	48	49	54	51

Note: Figures cover the years 1948-1990; Tr = Trace amounts (<0.05 in. of rain; <0.5 in. of snow)
Source: National Climatic Data Center, International Station Meteorological Climate Summary, 9/96

Weather Conditions

Temperature			Daytime Sky			Precipitation		
10°F & below	32°F & below	90°F & above	Clear	Partly cloudy	Cloudy	0.01 inch or more precip.	0.1 inch or more snow/ice	Thunderstorms
1	53	86	101	152	112	104	2	59

Note: Figures are average number of days per year and cover the years 1948-1990
Source: National Climatic Data Center, International Station Meteorological Climate Summary, 9/96

HAZARDOUS WASTE

Superfund Sites

The Memphis, TN-MS-AR metro area is home to seven sites on the EPA's Superfund National Priorities List: **Arlington Blending & Packaging** (final); **Carrier Air Conditioning Co.** (final); **Former Custom Cleaners** (final); **Memphis Defense Depot (DLA)** (final); **Ross Metals Inc.** (final); **Smalley-Piper** (final); **Walker Machine Products, Inc.** (final). There are a total of 1,375 Superfund sites with a status of proposed or final on the list in the U.S. *U.S. Environmental Protection Agency, National Priorities List, April 7, 2021*

AIR QUALITY

Air Quality Trends: Ozone

	1990	1995	2000	2005	2010	2015	2016	2017	2018	2019
MSA[1]	0.088	0.095	0.092	0.086	0.076	0.065	0.069	0.063	0.069	0.065
U.S.	0.088	0.089	0.082	0.080	0.073	0.068	0.069	0.068	0.069	0.065

Note: (1) Data covers the Memphis, TN-MS-AR Metropolitan Statistical Area. The values shown are the composite ozone concentration averages among trend sites based on the highest fourth daily maximum 8-hour concentration in parts per million. These trends are based on sites having an adequate record of monitoring data during the trend period. Data from exceptional events are included.
Source: U.S. Environmental Protection Agency, Air Quality Monitoring Information, "Air Quality Trends by City, 1990-2019"

Air Quality Index

Area	\multicolumn{5}{c}{Percent of Days when Air Quality was...[2]}	\multicolumn{2}{c}{AQI Statistics[2]}
	Good	Moderate	Unhealthy for Sensitive Groups	Unhealthy	Very Unhealthy	Maximum	Median
MSA[1]	60.5	38.1	1.4	0.0	0.0	148	45

Note: (1) Data covers the Memphis, TN-MS-AR Metropolitan Statistical Area; (2) Based on 365 days with AQI data in 2019. Air Quality Index (AQI) is an index for reporting daily air quality. EPA calculates the AQI for five major air pollutants regulated by the Clean Air Act: ground-level ozone, particle pollution (aka particulate matter), carbon monoxide, sulfur dioxide, and nitrogen dioxide. The AQI runs from 0 to 500. The higher the AQI value, the greater the level of air pollution and the greater the health concern. There are six AQI categories: "Good" AQI is between 0 and 50. Air quality is considered satisfactory; "Moderate" AQI is between 51 and 100. Air quality is acceptable; "Unhealthy for Sensitive Groups" When AQI values are between 101 and 150, members of sensitive groups may experience health effects; "Unhealthy" When AQI values are between 151 and 200 everyone may begin to experience health effects; "Very Unhealthy" AQI values between 201 and 300 trigger a health alert; "Hazardous" AQI values over 300 trigger warnings of emergency conditions (not shown).
Source: U.S. Environmental Protection Agency, Air Quality Index Report, 2019

Air Quality Index Pollutants

Area	\multicolumn{6}{c}{Percent of Days when AQI Pollutant was...[2]}
	Carbon Monoxide	Nitrogen Dioxide	Ozone	Sulfur Dioxide	Particulate Matter 2.5	Particulate Matter 10
MSA[1]	0.0	2.5	51.0	0.0	46.6	0.0

Note: (1) Data covers the Memphis, TN-MS-AR Metropolitan Statistical Area; (2) Based on 365 days with AQI data in 2019. The Air Quality Index (AQI) is an index for reporting daily air quality. EPA calculates the AQI for five major air pollutants regulated by the Clean Air Act: ground-level ozone, particle pollution (also known as particulate matter), carbon monoxide, sulfur dioxide, and nitrogen dioxide. The AQI runs from 0 to 500. The higher the AQI value, the greater the level of air pollution and the greater the health concern.
Source: U.S. Environmental Protection Agency, Air Quality Index Report, 2019

Maximum Air Pollutant Concentrations: Particulate Matter, Ozone, CO and Lead

	Particulate Matter 10 (ug/m^3)	Particulate Matter 2.5 Wtd AM (ug/m^3)	Particulate Matter 2.5 24-Hr (ug/m^3)	Ozone (ppm)	Carbon Monoxide (ppm)	Lead (ug/m^3)
MSA[1] Level	54	8.8	19	0.070	1	n/a
NAAQS[2]	150	15	35	0.075	9	0.15
Met NAAQS[2]	Yes	Yes	Yes	Yes	Yes	n/a

Note: (1) Data covers the Memphis, TN-MS-AR Metropolitan Statistical Area; Data from exceptional events are included; (2) National Ambient Air Quality Standards; ppm = parts per million; ug/m^3 = micrograms per cubic meter; n/a not available.
Concentrations: Particulate Matter 10 (coarse particulate)—highest second maximum 24-hour concentration; Particulate Matter 2.5 Wtd AM (fine particulate)—highest weighted annual mean concentration; Particulate Matter 2.5 24-Hour (fine particulate)—highest 98th percentile 24-hour concentration; Ozone—highest fourth daily maximum 8-hour concentration; Carbon Monoxide—highest second maximum non-overlapping 8-hour concentration; Lead—maximum running 3-month average
Source: U.S. Environmental Protection Agency, Air Quality Monitoring Information, "Air Quality Statistics by City, 2019"

Maximum Air Pollutant Concentrations: Nitrogen Dioxide and Sulfur Dioxide

	Nitrogen Dioxide AM (ppb)	Nitrogen Dioxide 1-Hr (ppb)	Sulfur Dioxide AM (ppb)	Sulfur Dioxide 1-Hr (ppb)	Sulfur Dioxide 24-Hr (ppb)
MSA[1] Level	10	40	n/a	2	n/a
NAAQS[2]	53	100	30	75	140
Met NAAQS[2]	Yes	Yes	n/a	Yes	n/a

Note: (1) Data covers the Memphis, TN-MS-AR Metropolitan Statistical Area; Data from exceptional events are included; (2) National Ambient Air Quality Standards; ppm = parts per million; ug/m³ = micrograms per cubic meter; n/a not available.
Concentrations: Nitrogen Dioxide AM—highest arithmetic mean concentration; Nitrogen Dioxide 1-Hr—highest 98th percentile 1-hour daily maximum concentration; Sulfur Dioxide AM—highest annual mean concentration; Sulfur Dioxide 1-Hr—highest 99th percentile 1-hour daily maximum concentration; Sulfur Dioxide 24-Hr—highest second maximum 24-hour concentration
Source: U.S. Environmental Protection Agency, Air Quality Monitoring Information, "Air Quality Statistics by City, 2019"

Miami, Florida

Background

Miami is a growing city comprised mostly of Latinos. Its large numbers of Cubans, Puerto Ricans, and Haitians give the city a flavorful mix with a Latin American and Caribbean accent. The City of Miami has three official languages: English, Spanish, and Haitian Creole.

Thanks to early pioneer Julia Tuttle, railroad magnate Henry Flagler extended the East Coast Railroad beyond Palm Beach. Within 15 years of that decision, Miami became known as the "Gold Coast." The land boom of the 1920s brought wealthy socialites, as well as African-Americans in search of work. Pink- and aquamarine-hued art deco hotels were squeezed onto a tiny tract of land called Miami Beach, and the population of the Miami metro area swelled.

Miami's tourist economy is second in the U.S. only to NYC. Many of the activities in which residents engage are "leisurely," including swimming, scuba diving, golf, tennis, and boating. For those who enjoy professional sports, the city is host to the following teams: the Miami Dolphins, football; the Florida Marlins, baseball; the Miami Heat, basketball; and the Florida Panthers, hockey. Cultural activities range from the Miami City Ballet and the Coconut Grove Playhouse to numerous art galleries and museums, including the Bass Museum of Art. Visits to the Villa Vizcaya, a gorgeous palazzo built by industrialist James Deering in the Italian Renaissance style, and to the Miami MetroZoo are popular pastimes.

Miami's prime location on Biscayne Bay in the southeastern United States makes it a perfect nexus for travel and trade. The Port of Miami is a bustling center for many cruise and cargo ships. The Port is also a base for the National Oceanic and Atmospheric Administration. The Miami International Airport is a busy destination point to and from many Latin-American and Caribbean countries.

Miami is still at the trading crossroads of the Western Hemisphere as the chief shipment point for exports and imports with Latin America and the Caribbean. One out of every three North American cruise passengers sails from Miami. It is also the major U.S. coastal city most affected by climate change, with sea rise expected to total 31 inches by 2060.

> COVID-19's social distancing rules encouraged the city's first "boat-in movie theater" in 2020.

The sultry, subtropical climate against a backdrop of Spanish, art deco, and modern architecture makes Miami a uniquely cosmopolitan city. The Art Deco Historic District, known as South Beach and located on the tip of Miami Beach, has an international reputation in the fashion, film, and music industries. Greater Miami is now a national center for film, television, and print production.

In recent years Miami has witnessed its largest real estate boom since the 1920s, especially in the city's midtown, north of downtown and south of the Design District. Nearly 25,000 residential units have been added to the downtown skyline since 2005.

Long, warm summers are typical, as are mild, dry winters. The marine influence is evidenced by the narrow daily range of temperature and the rapid warming of cold air masses. During the summer months, rainfall occurs in early morning near the ocean and in early afternoon further inland. Hurricanes occasionally affect the Miami area, usually in September and October, while destructive tornadoes are quite rare. Funnel clouds are occasionally sighted and a few touch the ground briefly, but significant destruction is unusual. Waterspouts are visible from the beaches during the summer months but seldom cause any damage. During June, July, and August, there are numerous beautiful, but dangerous, lightning events.

Rankings

General Rankings

- The Miami metro area was identified as one of America's fastest-growing areas in terms of population and business growth by *MagnifyMoney*. The area ranked #29 out of 35. The 100 most populous metro areas in the U.S. were evaluated on their change from 2011-2016 in the following categories: people and housing; workforce and employment opportunities; growing industry. *www.businessinsider.com, "The 35 Cities in the US with the Biggest Influx of People, the Most Work Opportunities, and the Hottest Business Growth," August 12, 2018*

- Miami was selected as one of the best places to live in America by *Outside Magazine*. Criteria included population, park acreage, neighborhood and resident diversity, new and upcoming things of interest, and opportunities for outdoor adventure. *Outside Magazine, "The 12 Best Places to Live in 2019," July 11, 2019*

- The human resources consulting firm Mercer ranked 231 major cities worldwide in terms of overall quality of life. Miami ranked #66. Criteria: political, social, economic, and socio-cultural factors; medical and health considerations; schools and education; public services and transportation; recreation; consumer goods; housing; and natural environment. *Mercer, "Mercer 2019 Quality of Living Survey," March 13, 2019*

Business/Finance Rankings

- The Brookings Institution ranked the nation's largest cities based on income inequality. Miami was ranked #5 (#1 = greatest inequality). Criteria: the "95/20 ratio," a figure representing the income at which a household earns more than 95 percent of all other households, divided by the income at which a household earns more than only 20 percent of all other households. *Brookings Institution, "Household Income Inequality, Largest Cities of 97 Large U.S. Metro Areas, 2014-2016," February 5, 2018*

- The Brookings Institution ranked the 100 largest metro areas in the U.S. based on income inequality. Miami was ranked #7 (#1 = greatest inequality). Criteria: the "95/20 ratio," a figure representing the income at which a household earns more than 95 percent of all other households, divided by the income at which a household earns more than only 20 percent of all other households. *Brookings Institution, "Household Income Inequality, 100 Largest U.S. Metro Areas, 2014-2016," February 5, 2018*

- The Miami metro area was identified as one of the most debt-ridden places in America by the finance site Credit.com. The metro area was ranked #14. Criteria: residents' average credit card debt as well as median income. *Credit.com, "25 Cities With the Most Credit Card Debt," February 28, 2018*

- Miami was identified as one of America's most frugal metro areas by *Coupons.com*. The city ranked #12 out of 25. Criteria: digital coupon usage. *Coupons.com, "America's Most Frugal Cities of 2017," March 22, 2018*

- *Forbes* ranked the 200 most populous metro areas to determine the nation's "Best Places for Business and Careers." The Miami metro area was ranked #85. Criteria: costs (business and living); job growth (past and projected); income growth; quality of life; educational attainment (college and high school); projected economic growth; cultural and leisure opportunities; workplace tolerance laws; net migration patterns. *Forbes, "The Best Places for Business and Careers 2019: Seattle Still On Top," October 30, 2019*

- Mercer Human Resources Consulting ranked 209 cities worldwide in terms of cost-of-living. Miami ranked #37 (the lower the ranking, the higher the cost-of-living). The survey measured the comparative cost of over 200 items (such as housing, food, clothing, household goods, transportation, and entertainment) in each location. *Mercer, "2020 Cost of Living Survey," June 9, 2020*

Children/Family Rankings

- Miami was selected as one of the most playful cities in the U.S. by KaBOOM! The organization's Playful City USA initiative honors cities and towns across the nation that have made their communities more playable. Criteria: pledging to integrate play as a solution to challenges in their communities; making it easy for children to get active and balanced play; creating more family-friendly and innovative communities as a result. *KaBOOM! National Campaign for Play, "2017 Playful City USA Communities"*

Culture/Performing Arts Rankings

- Miami was selected as one of the 25 best cities for moviemakers in North America. COVID-19 has spurred a quest for great film cities that offer more creative space, lower costs, and more great outdoors. NYC & LA were intentionally excluded. Criteria: longstanding reputations as film-friendly communities; efforts to deal with pandemic-specific challenges; and establish appropriate COVID-19 guidelines. The city was ranked #8. *MovieMaker Magazine, "Best Places to Live and Work as a Moviemaker, 2021," January 26, 2021*

Dating/Romance Rankings

- Miami was selected as one of the nation's most romantic cities with 100,000 or more residents by Amazon.com. The city ranked #2 of 20. Criteria: per capita sales of romance novels, relationship books, romantic comedy movies, romantic music, and sexual wellness products. *Amazon.com, "Top 20 Most Romantic Cities in the U.S.," February 1, 2017*

Education Rankings

- Miami was selected as one of America's most literate cities. The city ranked #47 out of the 84 largest U.S. cities. Criteria: number of booksellers; library resources; Internet resources; educational attainment; periodical publishing resources; newspaper circulation. *Central Connecticut State University, "America's Most Literate Cities, 2018," February 2019*

Environmental Rankings

- Sperling's BestPlaces assessed the 50 largest metropolitan areas of the United States for the likelihood of dangerously extreme weather events or earthquakes. In general the Southeast and South-Central regions have the highest risk of weather extremes and earthquakes, while the Pacific Northwest enjoys the lowest risk. Of the most risky metropolitan areas, the Miami metro area was ranked #1. *www.bestplaces.net, "Avoid Natural Disasters: BestPlaces Reveals The Top 10 Safest Places to Live," October 25, 2017*

- The U.S. Environmental Protection Agency (EPA) released a list of U.S. metropolitan areas with the most ENERGY STAR certified buildings in 2019. The Miami metro area was ranked #21 out of 25. *U.S. Environmental Protection Agency, "2020 Energy Star Top Cities," March 2020*

Health/Fitness Rankings

- For each of the 100 largest cities in the United States, the American Fitness Index®, published by the American College of Sports Medicine and the Anthem Foundation, evaluated community infrastructure and 33 health behaviors including preventive health, levels of chronic disease conditions, pedestrian safety, air quality, and community resources that support physical activity. Miami ranked #47 for "community fitness." *americanfitnessindex.org, "2020 ACSM American Fitness Index Summary Report," July 14, 2020*

- Miami was identified as one of the 10 most walkable cities in the U.S. by Walk Score. The city ranked #5. Walk Score measures walkability by analyzing hundreds of walking routes to nearby amenities, and also measures pedestrian friendliness by analyzing population density and road metrics such as block length and intersection density. *WalkScore.com, April 13, 2021*

- Miami was identified as a "2021 Spring Allergy Capital." The area ranked #39 out of 100. Three groups of factors were used to identify the most challenging cities for people with allergies during the spring season: annual spring pollen levels; over the counter medicine use; number of board-certified allergy specialists. *Asthma and Allergy Foundation of America, "Spring Allergy Capitals 2021," February 23, 2021*

- Miami was identified as a "2021 Fall Allergy Capital." The area ranked #25 out of 100. Three groups of factors were used to identify the most challenging cities for people with allergies during the fall season: annual fall pollen levels; over the counter medicine use; number of board-certified allergy specialists. *Asthma and Allergy Foundation of America, "Fall Allergy Capitals 2021," February 23, 2021*

- Miami was identified as a "2019 Asthma Capital." The area ranked #89 out of the nation's 100 largest metropolitan areas. Criteria: estimated asthma prevalence; crude death rate from asthma; and ER visits due to asthma. Risk factors analyzed but not factored in the rankings: annual pollen score; annual air quality; public smoking laws; number of board-certified asthma specialists; rescue medication use; controller medication use; uninsured rate; poverty rate. *Asthma and Allergy Foundation of America, "Asthma Capitals 2019: The Most Challenging Places to Live With Asthma," May 7, 2019*

Real Estate Rankings

- FitSmallBusiness looked at 50 of the largest metropolitan areas in the U.S. to determine which metro was the best to start a real estate business. Data was compiled from such sources as: Zillow, Trulia, U.S. Census Bureau, and the Bureau of Labor Statistics. Criteria: location; inventory; annual wages; median sales price of homes; days on the market; median price cut percentage; and other factors that would influence real estate professional growth. The Miami metro area ranked #8. *fitsmallbusiness.com*, "The Best Cities to Become a Real Estate Agent in 2018," January 30, 2018

- *WalletHub* compared the most populated U.S. cities to determine which had the best markets for real estate agents. Miami ranked #109 where demand was high and pay was the best. Criteria: sales per agent; annual median wage for real-estate agents; monthly average starting salary for real estate agents; real estate job density and competition; unemployment rate; home turnover rate; housing-market health index; and other relevant metrics. *www.WalletHub.com*, "2019's Best Places to Be a Real Estate Agent," April 24, 2019

Safety Rankings

- Allstate ranked the 200 largest cities in America in terms of driver safety. Miami ranked #57. Criteria: internal property damage claims over a two-year period from January 2016 to December 2017. The report helps increase the importance of safety and awareness behind the wheel. *Allstate*, "Allstate America's Best Drivers Report, 2019" June 24, 2019

Sports/Recreation Rankings

- Miami was chosen as one of America's best cities for bicycling. The city ranked #50 out of 50. Criteria: cycling infrastructure that is safe and friendly for all ages; energy and bike culture. The editors evaluated cities with populations of 100,000 or more. *Bicycling*, "The 50 Best Bike Cities in America," October 10, 2018

Transportation Rankings

- Business Insider presented an AllTransit Performance Score ranking of public transportation in major U.S. cities and towns, with populations over 250,000, in which Miami earned the #11-ranked "Transit Score," awarded for frequency of service, access to jobs, quality and number of stops, and affordability. *www.businessinsider.com*, "The 17 Major U.S. Cities with the Best Public Transportation," April 17, 2018

Women/Minorities Rankings

- Miami was selected as one of the gayest cities in America by *The Advocate*. The city ranked #16 out of 25. Criteria, among many: Trans Pride parades/festivals; gay rugby teams; lesbian bars; LGBT centers; theater screenings of "Moonlight"; LGBT-inclusive nondiscrimination ordinances; and gay bowling teams. *The Advocate*, "Queerest Cities in America 2017" January 12, 2017

- Personal finance website *WalletHub* compared more than 180 U.S. cities across two key dimensions, "Hispanic Business-Friendliness" and "Hispanic Purchasing Power," to arrive at the most favorable conditions for Hispanic entrepreneurs. Miami was ranked #4 out of 182. Criteria includes: share of Hispanic-Owned Businesses; Hispanic entrepreneurship rate to median annual income of Hispanics; Small Business-Friendliness score; cost of living; and number of Hispanics with at least a bachelor's degree. *WalletHub.com*, "2019's Best Cities for Hispanic Entrepreneurs," May 1, 2019

Miscellaneous Rankings

- *MoveHub* ranked 446 hipster cities across 20 countries, using its *alternative* Hipster Index and Miami came out as #7 among the top 50. Criteria: population over 150,000; number of vintage boutiques; density of tattoo parlors; vegan places to eat; coffee shops; and density of vinyl record stores. *www.movehub.com*, "The Hipster Index: Brighton Pips Portland to Global Top Spot," February 20, 2020

- The watchdog site, Charity Navigator, conducted a study of charities in major markets both to analyze statistical differences in their financial, accountability, and transparency practices and to track year-to-year variations in individual philanthropic communities. The Miami metro area was ranked #7 among the 30 metro markets in the rating category of Overall Score. *www.charitynavigator.org*, "2017 Metro Market Study," May 1, 2017

- *WalletHub* compared the 150 most populated U.S. cities to determine their operating efficiency. A "Quality of City Services" score was constructed for each city and then divided by the total budget per capita to reveal which were managed the best. Miami ranked #83. Criteria: financial stability; economy; education; safety; health; infrastructure and pollution. *www.WalletHub.com*, "2020's Best- & Worst-Run Cities in America," June 29, 2020

Business Environment

DEMOGRAPHICS

Population Growth

Area	1990 Census	2000 Census	2010 Census	2019* Estimate	Population Growth (%) 1990-2019	Population Growth (%) 2010-2019
City	358,843	362,470	399,457	454,279	26.6	13.7
MSA[1]	4,056,100	5,007,564	5,564,635	6,090,660	50.2	9.5
U.S.	248,709,873	281,421,906	308,745,538	324,697,795	30.6	5.2

Note: (1) Figures cover the Miami-Fort Lauderdale-West Palm Beach, FL Metropolitan Statistical Area; (*) 2015-2019 5-year estimated population
Source: U.S. Census Bureau, 1990 Census, Census 2000, Census 2010, 2015-2019 American Community Survey 5-Year Estimates

Household Size

Area	One	Two	Three	Four	Five	Six	Seven or More	Average Household Size
City	37.4	31.1	16.1	8.9	4.0	1.6	1.0	2.50
MSA[1]	28.2	32.7	16.8	13.2	5.8	2.1	1.1	2.80
U.S.	27.9	33.9	15.6	12.9	6.0	2.3	1.4	2.60

Note: (1) Figures cover the Miami-Fort Lauderdale-West Palm Beach, FL Metropolitan Statistical Area
Source: U.S. Census Bureau, 2015-2019 American Community Survey 5-Year Estimates

Race

Area	White Alone[2] (%)	Black Alone[2] (%)	Asian Alone[2] (%)	AIAN[3] Alone[2] (%)	NHOPI[4] Alone[2] (%)	Other Race Alone[2] (%)	Two or More Races (%)
City	76.1	16.8	1.1	0.2	0.0	4.0	1.7
MSA[1]	70.2	21.2	2.5	0.2	0.0	3.5	2.3
U.S.	72.5	12.7	5.5	0.8	0.2	4.9	3.3

Note: (1) Figures cover the Miami-Fort Lauderdale-West Palm Beach, FL Metropolitan Statistical Area; (2) Alone is defined as not being in combination with one or more other races; (3) American Indian and Alaska Native; (4) Native Hawaiian and Other Pacific Islander
Source: U.S. Census Bureau, 2015-2019 American Community Survey 5-Year Estimates

Hispanic or Latino Origin

Area	Total (%)	Mexican (%)	Puerto Rican (%)	Cuban (%)	Other (%)
City	72.7	1.9	3.4	35.0	32.4
MSA[1]	45.2	2.5	3.9	19.0	19.8
U.S.	18.0	11.2	1.7	0.7	4.3

Note: Persons of Hispanic or Latino origin can be of any race; (1) Figures cover the Miami-Fort Lauderdale-West Palm Beach, FL Metropolitan Statistical Area
Source: U.S. Census Bureau, 2015-2019 American Community Survey 5-Year Estimates

Ancestry

Area	German	Irish	English	American	Italian	Polish	French[2]	Scottish	Dutch
City	1.5	1.2	0.8	3.3	2.3	0.7	0.9	0.2	0.2
MSA[1]	4.4	4.3	2.7	6.0	5.0	1.9	1.2	0.6	0.4
U.S.	13.3	9.7	7.2	6.2	5.1	2.8	2.3	1.7	1.2

Note: Figures are the percentage of the total population reporting a particular ancestry. The nine most commonly reported ancestries in the U.S. are shown. Figures include multiple ancestries (e.g. if a person reported being Irish and Italian, they were included in both columns); (1) Figures cover the Miami-Fort Lauderdale-West Palm Beach, FL Metropolitan Statistical Area; (2) Excludes Basque
Source: U.S. Census Bureau, 2015-2019 American Community Survey 5-Year Estimates

Foreign-born Population

Area	Any Foreign Country	Asia	Mexico	Europe	Caribbean	Central America[2]	South America	Africa	Canada
City	58.3	1.1	0.9	2.0	32.5	11.9	9.6	0.3	0.2
MSA[1]	40.7	2.1	1.1	2.3	21.2	4.2	8.8	0.4	0.5
U.S.	13.6	4.2	3.5	1.5	1.3	1.1	1.0	0.7	0.2

Note: (1) Figures cover the Miami-Fort Lauderdale-West Palm Beach, FL Metropolitan Statistical Area; (2) Excludes Mexico.
Source: U.S. Census Bureau, 2015-2019 American Community Survey 5-Year Estimates

Marital Status

Area	Never Married	Now Married[2]	Separated	Widowed	Divorced
City	40.2	36.0	3.7	6.6	13.5
MSA[1]	34.6	43.3	2.8	6.4	12.8
U.S.	33.4	48.1	1.9	5.8	10.9

Note: Figures are percentages and cover the population 15 years of age and older; (1) Figures cover the Miami-Fort Lauderdale-West Palm Beach, FL Metropolitan Statistical Area; (2) Excludes separated
Source: U.S. Census Bureau, 2015-2019 American Community Survey 5-Year Estimates

Disability by Age

Area	All Ages	Under 18 Years Old	18 to 64 Years Old	65 Years and Over
City	11.8	3.9	7.7	36.3
MSA[1]	10.9	3.4	7.2	32.1
U.S.	12.6	4.2	10.3	34.5

Note: Figures show percent of the civilian noninstitutionalized population that reported having a disability. Disability status is determined from six types of difficulty: vision, hearing, cognitive, ambulatory, self-care, and independent living. For children under 5 years old, hearing and vision difficulty are used to determine disability status. For children between the ages of 5 and 14, disability status is determined from hearing, vision, cognitive, ambulatory, and self-care difficulties. For people aged 15 years and older, they are considered to have a disability if they have difficulty with any one of the six difficulty types; Note: (1) Figures cover the Miami-Fort Lauderdale-West Palm Beach, FL Metropolitan Statistical Area
Source: U.S. Census Bureau, 2015-2019 American Community Survey 5-Year Estimates

Age

Area	Under Age 5	Age 5–19	Age 20–34	Age 35–44	Age 45–54	Age 55–64	Age 65–74	Age 75–84	Age 85+	Median Age
City	5.9	13.4	23.0	14.6	14.5	11.8	8.5	5.8	2.6	40.1
MSA[1]	5.7	17.0	19.4	13.1	14.2	12.8	9.4	5.8	2.7	41.0
U.S.	6.1	19.1	20.7	12.6	13.0	12.9	9.1	4.6	1.9	38.1

Note: (1) Figures cover the Miami-Fort Lauderdale-West Palm Beach, FL Metropolitan Statistical Area
Source: U.S. Census Bureau, 2015-2019 American Community Survey 5-Year Estimates

Gender

Area	Males	Females	Males per 100 Females
City	224,810	229,469	98.0
MSA[1]	2,959,743	3,130,917	94.5
U.S.	159,886,919	164,810,876	97.0

Note: (1) Figures cover the Miami-Fort Lauderdale-West Palm Beach, FL Metropolitan Statistical Area
Source: U.S. Census Bureau, 2015-2019 American Community Survey 5-Year Estimates

Religious Groups by Family

Area	Catholic	Baptist	Non-Den.	Methodist[2]	Lutheran	LDS[3]	Pentecostal	Presbyterian[4]	Muslim[5]	Judaism
MSA[1]	18.6	5.4	4.2	1.3	0.5	0.5	1.8	0.7	0.9	1.6
U.S.	19.1	9.3	4.0	4.0	2.3	2.0	1.9	1.6	0.8	0.7

Note: Figures are the number of adherents as a percentage of the total population; (1) Figures cover the Miami-Fort Lauderdale-West Palm Beach, FL Metropolitan Statistical Area; (2) Methodist/Pietist; (3) Latter Day Saints; (4) Reformed; (5) Figures are estimates
Source: Association of Statisticians of American Religious Bodies, 2010 U.S. Religion Census: Religious Congregations & Membership Study

Religious Groups by Tradition

Area	Catholic	Evangelical Protestant	Mainline Protestant	Other Tradition	Black Protestant	Orthodox
MSA[1]	18.6	11.4	2.5	3.5	1.7	0.3
U.S.	19.1	16.2	7.3	4.3	1.6	0.3

Note: Figures are the number of adherents as a percentage of the total population; (1) Figures cover the Miami-Fort Lauderdale-West Palm Beach, FL Metropolitan Statistical Area
Source: Association of Statisticians of American Religious Bodies, 2010 U.S. Religion Census: Religious Congregations & Membership Study

ECONOMY

Gross Metropolitan Product

Area	2017	2018	2019	2020	Rank[2]
MSA[1]	349.2	369.5	386.7	403.4	12

Note: Figures are in billions of dollars; (1) Figures cover the Miami-Fort Lauderdale-West Palm Beach, FL Metropolitan Statistical Area; (2) Rank is based on 2018 data and ranges from 1 to 381
Source: U.S. Conference of Mayors, U.S. Metro Economies: GMP & Employment 2018-2020, September 2019

Economic Growth

Area	2015-17 (%)	2018 (%)	2019 (%)	2020 (%)	Rank[2]
MSA[1]	3.2	3.5	2.9	2.1	56
U.S.	1.9	2.9	2.3	2.1	—

Note: Figures are real gross metropolitan product (GMP) growth rates and represent average annual percent change; (1) Figures cover the Miami-Fort Lauderdale-West Palm Beach, FL Metropolitan Statistical Area; (2) Rank is based on 2017 2-year average annual percent change and ranges from 1 to 381
Source: U.S. Conference of Mayors, U.S. Metro Economies: GMP & Employment 2018-2020, September 2019

Metropolitan Area Exports

Area	2014	2015	2016	2017	2018	2019	Rank[2]
MSA[1]	37,969.5	33,258.5	32,734.5	34,780.5	35,650.2	35,498.9	8

Note: Figures are in millions of dollars; (1) Figures cover the Miami-Fort Lauderdale-West Palm Beach, FL Metropolitan Statistical Area; (2) Rank is based on 2019 data and ranges from 1 to 386
Source: U.S. Department of Commerce, International Trade Administration, Office of Trade and Economic Analysis, Industry and Analysis, Exports by Metropolitan Area, data extracted March 24, 2021

Building Permits

Area	Single-Family 2018	Single-Family 2019	Pct. Chg.	Multi-Family 2018	Multi-Family 2019	Pct. Chg.	Total 2018	Total 2019	Pct. Chg.
City	80	107	33.8	4,545	4,361	-4.0	4,625	4,468	-3.4
MSA[1]	7,022	7,241	3.1	12,531	13,447	7.3	19,553	20,688	5.8
U.S.	855,300	862,100	0.7	473,500	523,900	10.6	1,328,800	1,386,000	4.3

Note: (1) Figures cover the Miami-Fort Lauderdale-West Palm Beach, FL Metropolitan Statistical Area; Figures represent new, privately-owned housing units authorized (unadjusted data); All permit data are based on estimates with imputation
Source: U.S. Census Bureau, Manufacturing, Mining, and Construction Statistics, Building Permits, 2018, 2019

Bankruptcy Filings

Area	Business Filings 2019	Business Filings 2020	% Chg.	Nonbusiness Filings 2019	Nonbusiness Filings 2020	% Chg.
Miami-Dade County	215	322	49.8	8,490	7,108	-16.3
U.S.	22,780	21,655	-4.9	752,160	522,808	-30.5

Note: Business filings include Chapter 7, Chapter 9, Chapter 11, Chapter 12, Chapter 13, Chapter 15, and Section 304; Nonbusiness filings include Chapter 7, Chapter 11, and Chapter 13
Source: Administrative Office of the U.S. Courts, Business and Nonbusiness Bankruptcy, County Cases Commenced by Chapter of the Bankruptcy Code, During the 12-Month Period Ending December 31, 2019 and Business and Nonbusiness Bankruptcy, County Cases Commenced by Chapter of the Bankruptcy Code, During the 12-Month Period Ending December 31, 2020

Housing Vacancy Rates

Area	Gross Vacancy Rate[2] (%) 2018	2019	2020	Year-Round Vacancy Rate[3] (%) 2018	2019	2020	Rental Vacancy Rate[4] (%) 2018	2019	2020	Homeowner Vacancy Rate[5] (%) 2018	2019	2020
MSA[1]	14.9	14.1	12.6	7.9	7.4	6.8	7.4	7.0	5.4	1.9	1.8	1.4
U.S.	12.3	12.0	10.6	9.7	9.5	8.2	6.9	6.7	6.3	1.5	1.4	1.0

Note: (1) Figures cover the Miami-Fort Lauderdale-West Palm Beach, FL Metropolitan Statistical Area; (2) The percentage of the total housing inventory that is vacant; (3) The percentage of the housing inventory (excluding seasonal units) that is year-round vacant; (4) The percentage of rental inventory that is vacant for rent; (5) The percentage of homeowner inventory that is vacant for sale
Source: U.S. Census Bureau, Housing Vacancies and Homeownership Annual Statistics: 2018, 2019, 2020

INCOME

Income

Area	Per Capita ($)	Median Household ($)	Average Household ($)
City	28,804	39,049	68,105
MSA[1]	32,522	56,775	86,518
U.S.	34,103	62,843	88,607

Note: (1) Figures cover the Miami-Fort Lauderdale-West Palm Beach, FL Metropolitan Statistical Area
Source: U.S. Census Bureau, 2015-2019 American Community Survey 5-Year Estimates

Household Income Distribution

Area	Under $15,000	$15,000 -$24,999	$25,000 -$34,999	$35,000 -$49,999	$50,000 -$74,999	$75,000 -$99,999	$100,000 -$149,999	$150,000 and up
City	20.8	14.1	11.6	12.3	14.5	8.8	8.6	9.4
MSA[1]	11.8	9.9	9.8	13.0	17.2	11.7	13.3	13.4
U.S.	10.3	8.9	8.9	12.3	17.2	12.7	15.1	14.5

Note: (1) Figures cover the Miami-Fort Lauderdale-West Palm Beach, FL Metropolitan Statistical Area
Source: U.S. Census Bureau, 2015-2019 American Community Survey 5-Year Estimates

Poverty Rate

Area	All Ages	Under 18 Years Old	18 to 64 Years Old	65 Years and Over
City	23.4	31.8	19.0	31.6
MSA[1]	14.6	20.2	12.6	15.1
U.S.	13.4	18.5	12.6	9.3

Note: Figures are percentage of people whose income during the past 12 months was below the poverty level;
(1) Figures cover the Miami-Fort Lauderdale-West Palm Beach, FL Metropolitan Statistical Area
Source: U.S. Census Bureau, 2015-2019 American Community Survey 5-Year Estimates

CITY FINANCES

City Government Finances

Component	2017 ($000)	2017 ($ per capita)
Total Revenues	1,186,454	2,690
Total Expenditures	1,150,578	2,609
Debt Outstanding	652,345	1,479
Cash and Securities[1]	3,248,946	7,367

Note: (1) Cash and security holdings of a government at the close of its fiscal year, including those of its dependent agencies, utilities, and liquor stores.
Source: U.S. Census Bureau, State & Local Government Finances 2017

City Government Revenue by Source

Source	2017 ($000)	2017 ($ per capita)	2017 (%)
General Revenue			
From Federal Government	63,583	144	5.4
From State Government	64,608	147	5.4
From Local Governments	45,526	103	3.8
Taxes			
Property	337,607	766	28.5
Sales and Gross Receipts	103,909	236	8.8
Personal Income	0	0	0.0
Corporate Income	0	0	0.0
Motor Vehicle License	0	0	0.0
Other Taxes	104,682	237	8.8
Current Charges	130,055	295	11.0
Liquor Store	0	0	0.0
Utility	3	0	0.0
Employee Retirement	256,529	582	21.6

Source: U.S. Census Bureau, State & Local Government Finances 2017

City Government Expenditures by Function

Function	2017 ($000)	2017 ($ per capita)	2017 (%)
General Direct Expenditures			
Air Transportation	0	0	0.0
Corrections	0	0	0.0
Education	0	0	0.0
Employment Security Administration	0	0	0.0
Financial Administration	49,650	112	4.3
Fire Protection	126,321	286	11.0
General Public Buildings	0	0	0.0
Governmental Administration, Other	52,145	118	4.5
Health	0	0	0.0
Highways	14,299	32	1.2
Hospitals	0	0	0.0
Housing and Community Development	29,888	67	2.6
Interest on General Debt	37,408	84	3.3
Judicial and Legal	7,181	16	0.6
Libraries	0	0	0.0
Parking	34,972	79	3.0
Parks and Recreation	92,163	209	8.0
Police Protection	236,255	535	20.5
Public Welfare	2,932	6	0.3
Sewerage	516	1	0.0
Solid Waste Management	37,232	84	3.2
Veterans' Services	0	0	0.0
Liquor Store	0	0	0.0
Utility	0	0	0.0
Employee Retirement	256,188	580	22.3

Source: U.S. Census Bureau, State & Local Government Finances 2017

EMPLOYMENT

Labor Force and Employment

Area	Civilian Labor Force Dec. 2019	Civilian Labor Force Dec. 2020	% Chg.	Workers Employed Dec. 2019	Workers Employed Dec. 2020	% Chg.
City	234,913	222,511	-5.3	231,476	205,346	-11.3
MD[1]	1,377,214	1,301,119	-5.5	1,353,568	1,197,859	-11.5
U.S.	164,007,000	160,017,000	-2.4	158,504,000	149,613,000	-5.6

Note: Data is not seasonally adjusted and covers workers 16 years of age and older; (1) Figures cover the Miami-Miami Beach-Kendall, FL Metropolitan Division
Source: Bureau of Labor Statistics, Local Area Unemployment Statistics

Unemployment Rate

Area	Jan.	Feb.	Mar.	Apr.	May	Jun.	Jul.	Aug.	Sep.	Oct.	Nov.	Dec.
City	1.4	1.4	3.7	12.4	12.8	12.5	15.4	8.6	13.6	9.3	8.4	7.7
MD[1]	1.8	1.6	2.2	10.3	10.3	10.1	15.2	9.1	12.6	8.5	8.2	7.9
U.S.	4.0	3.8	4.5	14.4	13.0	11.2	10.5	8.5	7.7	6.6	6.4	6.5

2020

Note: Data is not seasonally adjusted and covers workers 16 years of age and older; (1) Figures cover the Miami-Miami Beach-Kendall, FL Metropolitan Division
Source: Bureau of Labor Statistics, Local Area Unemployment Statistics

Average Wages

Occupation	$/Hr.	Occupation	$/Hr.
Accountants and Auditors	38.50	Maintenance and Repair Workers	18.60
Automotive Mechanics	21.80	Marketing Managers	65.40
Bookkeepers	21.30	Network and Computer Systems Admin.	42.00
Carpenters	20.90	Nurses, Licensed Practical	23.30
Cashiers	11.80	Nurses, Registered	34.80
Computer Programmers	41.70	Nursing Assistants	13.70
Computer Systems Analysts	44.60	Office Clerks, General	17.50
Computer User Support Specialists	26.20	Physical Therapists	39.20
Construction Laborers	16.40	Physicians	103.10
Cooks, Restaurant	15.00	Plumbers, Pipefitters and Steamfitters	22.70
Customer Service Representatives	17.40	Police and Sheriff's Patrol Officers	35.20
Dentists	100.70	Postal Service Mail Carriers	25.70
Electricians	22.70	Real Estate Sales Agents	33.10
Engineers, Electrical	46.90	Retail Salespersons	14.10
Fast Food and Counter Workers	10.90	Sales Representatives, Technical/Scientific	43.50
Financial Managers	72.90	Secretaries, Exc. Legal/Medical/Executive	18.00
First-Line Supervisors of Office Workers	30.00	Security Guards	14.30
General and Operations Managers	55.20	Surgeons	102.70
Hairdressers/Cosmetologists	13.80	Teacher Assistants, Exc. Postsecondary*	13.50
Home Health and Personal Care Aides	12.10	Teachers, Secondary School, Exc. Sp. Ed.*	31.80
Janitors and Cleaners	12.80	Telemarketers	14.10
Landscaping/Groundskeeping Workers	14.80	Truck Drivers, Heavy/Tractor-Trailer	19.60
Lawyers	81.50	Truck Drivers, Light/Delivery Services	17.20
Maids and Housekeeping Cleaners	12.00	Waiters and Waitresses	12.60

Note: Wage data covers the Miami-Fort Lauderdale-West Palm Beach, FL Metropolitan Statistical Area; (*) Hourly wages were calculated from annual wage data based on a 40 hour work week; n/a not available.
Source: Bureau of Labor Statistics, Metro Area Occupational Employment & Wage Estimates, May 2020

Employment by Industry

Sector	MD[1] Number of Employees	MD[1] Percent of Total	U.S. Percent of Total
Construction	51,100	4.5	5.1
Education and Health Services	188,200	16.6	16.3
Financial Activities	82,300	7.2	6.1
Government	137,700	12.1	15.2
Information	18,400	1.6	1.9
Leisure and Hospitality	104,700	9.2	9.0
Manufacturing	42,200	3.7	8.5
Mining and Logging	500	<0.1	0.4
Other Services	44,700	3.9	3.8
Professional and Business Services	180,900	15.9	14.4
Retail Trade	137,000	12.0	10.9
Transportation, Warehousing, and Utilities	80,800	7.1	4.6
Wholesale Trade	68,500	6.0	3.9

Note: Figures are non-farm employment as of December 2020. Figures are not seasonally adjusted and include workers 16 years of age and older; (1) Figures cover the Miami-Miami Beach-Kendall, FL Metropolitan Division
Source: Bureau of Labor Statistics, Current Employment Statistics, Employment, Hours, and Earnings

Employment by Occupation

Occupation Classification	City (%)	MSA[1] (%)	U.S. (%)
Management, Business, Science, and Arts	32.2	35.0	38.5
Natural Resources, Construction, and Maintenance	11.3	9.1	8.9
Production, Transportation, and Material Moving	10.6	10.3	13.2
Sales and Office	21.6	24.9	21.6
Service	24.3	20.8	17.8

Note: Figures cover employed civilians 16 years of age and older; (1) Figures cover the Miami-Fort Lauderdale-West Palm Beach, FL Metropolitan Statistical Area
Source: U.S. Census Bureau, 2015-2019 American Community Survey 5-Year Estimates

Occupations with Greatest Projected Employment Growth: 2020 – 2022

Occupation[1]	2020 Employment	2022 Projected Employment	Numeric Employment Change	Percent Employment Change
Fast Food and Counter Workers	172,590	214,590	42,000	24.3
Waiters and Waitresses	141,990	180,530	38,540	27.1
Retail Salespersons	264,490	292,340	27,850	10.5
Cooks, Restaurant	79,150	103,770	24,620	31.1
Maids and Housekeeping Cleaners	63,280	81,030	17,750	28.0
Cashiers	204,540	221,530	16,990	8.3
Registered Nurses	189,240	202,880	13,640	7.2
Laborers and Freight, Stock, and Material Movers, Hand	147,740	160,650	12,910	8.7
First-Line Supervisors of Food Preparation and Serving Workers	51,820	64,080	12,260	23.7
Stockers and Order Fillers	130,980	142,780	11,800	9.0

Note: Projections cover Florida; (1) Sorted by numeric employment change
Source: www.projectionscentral.com, State Occupational Projections, 2020–2022 Short-Term Projections

Fastest-Growing Occupations: 2020 – 2022

Occupation[1]	2020 Employment	2022 Projected Employment	Numeric Employment Change	Percent Employment Change
Hotel, Motel, and Resort Desk Clerks	11,930	18,100	6,170	51.7
Locker Room, Coatroom, and Dressing Room Attendants	930	1,360	430	46.2
Lodging Managers	3,190	4,420	1,230	38.6
Manicurists and Pedicurists	2,640	3,580	940	35.6
Bartenders	31,430	42,540	11,110	35.3
Gaming Cage Workers	320	430	110	34.4
Parking Lot Attendants	11,200	15,040	3,840	34.3
Gaming Dealers	2,660	3,560	900	33.8
Baggage Porters and Bellhops	3,520	4,670	1,150	32.7
Cooks, Restaurant	79,150	103,770	24,620	31.1

Note: Projections cover Florida; (1) Sorted by percent employment change and excludes occupations with numeric employment change less than 50
Source: www.projectionscentral.com, State Occupational Projections, 2020–2022 Short-Term Projections

TAXES

State Corporate Income Tax Rates

State	Tax Rate (%)	Income Brackets ($)	Num. of Brackets	Financial Institution Tax Rate (%)[a]	Federal Income Tax Ded.
Florida	4.458 (e)	Flat rate	1	4.458 (e)	No

Note: Tax rates as of January 1, 2021; (a) Rates listed are the corporate income tax rate applied to financial institutions or excise taxes based on income. Some states have other taxes based upon the value of deposits or shares; (e) The Florida tax rate may be adjusted downward if certain revenue targets are met.
Source: Federation of Tax Administrators, State Corporate Income Tax Rates, January 1, 2021

State Individual Income Tax Rates

State	Tax Rate (%)	Income Brackets ($)	Personal Exemptions ($) Single	Married	Depend.	Standard Ded. ($) Single	Married
Florida				– No state income tax –			

Note: Tax rates as of January 1, 2021; Local- and county-level taxes are not included
Source: Federation of Tax Administrators, State Individual Income Tax Rates, January 1, 2021

Various State Sales and Excise Tax Rates

State	State Sales Tax (%)	Gasoline[1] (¢/gal.)	Cigarette[2] ($/pack)	Spirits[3] ($/gal.)	Wine[4] ($/gal.)	Beer[5] ($/gal.)	Recreational Marijuana (%)
Florida	6	42.46	1.339	6.5	2.25	0.48	Not legal

Note: All tax rates as of January 1, 2021; (1) The American Petroleum Institute has developed a methodology for determining the average tax rate on a gallon of fuel. Rates may include any of the following: excise taxes, environmental fees, storage tank fees, other fees or taxes, general sales tax, and local taxes; (2) The federal excise tax of $1.0066 per pack and local taxes are not included; (3) Rates are those applicable to off-premise sales of 40% alcohol by volume (a.b.v.) distilled spirits in 750ml containers. Local excise taxes are excluded; (4) Rates are those applicable to off-premise sales of 11% a.b.v. non-carbonated wine in 750ml containers; (5) Rates are those applicable to off-premise sales of 4.7% a.b.v. beer in 12 ounce containers.
Source: Tax Foundation, 2021 Facts & Figures: How Does Your State Compare?

State Business Tax Climate Index Rankings

State	Overall Rank	Corporate Tax Rank	Individual Income Tax Rank	Sales Tax Rank	Property Tax Rank	Unemployment Insurance Tax Rank
Florida	4	6	1	21	13	2

Note: The index is a measure of how each state's tax laws affect economic performance. The lower the rank, the more favorable a state's tax system is for business. States without a given tax are given a ranking of 1. The scores/rankings for the District of Columbia do not affect other states. The 2021 index represents the tax climate as of July 1, 2020.
Source: Tax Foundation, State Business Tax Climate Index 2021

TRANSPORTATION

Means of Transportation to Work

Area	Drove Alone	Car-pooled	Bus	Subway	Railroad	Bicycle	Walked	Other Means	Worked at Home
City	69.4	8.3	7.9	1.0	0.2	0.9	4.0	3.2	5.2
MSA[1]	77.9	9.1	2.8	0.3	0.2	0.6	1.6	1.8	5.7
U.S.	76.3	9.0	2.4	1.9	0.6	0.5	2.7	1.4	5.2

Note: Figures are percentages and cover workers 16 years of age and older; (1) Figures cover the Miami-Fort Lauderdale-West Palm Beach, FL Metropolitan Statistical Area
Source: U.S. Census Bureau, 2015-2019 American Community Survey 5-Year Estimates

Travel Time to Work

Area	Less Than 10 Minutes	10 to 19 Minutes	20 to 29 Minutes	30 to 44 Minutes	45 to 59 Minutes	60 to 89 Minutes	90 Minutes or More
City	4.9	21.3	22.7	31.7	10.2	7.4	1.8
MSA[1]	6.4	22.6	22.0	27.9	10.3	8.1	2.7
U.S.	12.2	28.4	20.8	20.8	8.3	6.4	2.9

Note: Note: Figures are percentages and include workers 16 years old and over; (1) Figures cover the Miami-Fort Lauderdale-West Palm Beach, FL Metropolitan Statistical Area
Source: U.S. Census Bureau, 2015-2019 American Community Survey 5-Year Estimates

Key Congestion Measures

Measure	1982	1992	2002	2012	2017
Annual Hours of Delay, Total (000)	51,639	88,902	191,999	224,594	265,947
Annual Hours of Delay, Per Auto Commuter	26	34	52	58	69
Annual Congestion Cost, Total (million $)	389	938	2,595	4,025	4,900
Annual Congestion Cost, Per Auto Commuter ($)	614	728	1,225	1,123	1,289

Note: Covers the Miami FL urban area
Source: Texas A&M Transportation Institute, 2019 Urban Mobility Report

Freeway Travel Time Index

Measure	1982	1987	1992	1997	2002	2007	2012	2017
Urban Area Index[1]	1.14	1.17	1.19	1.24	1.29	1.29	1.29	1.31
Urban Area Rank[1,2]	12	15	17	11	10	15	17	17

Note: Freeway Travel Time Index—the ratio of travel time in the peak period to the travel time at free-flow conditions. For example, a value of 1.30 indicates a 20-minute free-flow trip takes 26 minutes in the peak (20 minutes x 1.30 = 26 minutes); (1) Covers the Miami FL urban area; (2) Rank is based on 101 larger urban areas (#1 = highest travel time index)
Source: Texas A&M Transportation Institute, 2019 Urban Mobility Report

Public Transportation

Agency Name / Mode of Transportation	Vehicles Operated in Maximum Service[1]	Annual Unlinked Passenger Trips[2] (in thous.)	Annual Passenger Miles[3] (in thous.)
Miami-Dade Transit (MDT)			
Bus (directly operated)	601	47,827.1	242,678.9
Bus (purchased transportation)	64	1,805.0	6,890.2
Commuter Bus (purchased transportation)	9	328.2	12,520.5
Demand Response (purchased transportation)	385	1,777.9	23,390.1
Heavy Rail (directly operated)	76	18,494.5	136,546.1
Monorail and Automated Guideway (directly operated)	21	8,863.8	8,325.8
Vanpool (purchased transportation)	214	482.0	15,092.0
South Florida Regional Transportation Authority (TRI-Rail)			
Bus (purchased transportation)	22	968.0	3,436.2
Commuter Rail (purchased transportation)	50	4,465.8	119,189.6

Note: (1) Number of revenue vehicles operated by the given mode and type of service to meet the annual maximum service requirement. This is the revenue vehicle count during the peak season of the year; on the week and day that maximum service is provided. Vehicles operated in maximum service (VOMS) exclude atypical days and one-time special events; (2) Number of passengers who boarded public transportation vehicles. Passengers are counted each time they board a vehicle no matter how many vehicles they use to travel from their origin to their destination. (3) Sum of the distances ridden by all passengers during the entire fiscal year.
Source: Federal Transit Administration, National Transit Database, 2019

Air Transportation

Airport Name and Code / Type of Service	Passenger Airlines[1]	Passenger Enplanements	Freight Carriers[2]	Freight (lbs)
Miami International (MIA)				
Domestic service (U.S. carriers - 2020)	23	5,254,955	23	436,080,487
International service (U.S. carriers - 2019)	15	6,171,575	15	753,437,656

Note: (1) Includes all U.S.-based major, minor and commuter airlines that carried at least one passenger during the year; (2) Includes all U.S.-based airlines and freight carriers that transported at least one pound of freight during the year.
Source: Bureau of Transportation Statistics, The Intermodal Transportation Database, Air Carriers: T-100 Domestic Market (U.S. Carriers), 2020; Bureau of Transportation Statistics, The Intermodal Transportation Database, Air Carriers: T-100 International Market (U.S. Carriers), 2019

BUSINESSES

Major Business Headquarters

Company Name	Industry	Fortune[1]	Forbes[2]
Lennar	Homebuilders	147	-
Ryder System	Trucking, Truck Leasing	354	-
Southern Glazer's Wine & Spirits	Food, Drink & Tobacco	-	17
World Fuel Services	Wholesalers, Diversified	91	-

Note: (1) Companies that produce a 10-K are ranked 1 to 500 based on 2019 revenue; (2) All private companies with at least $2 billion in annual revenue through the end of their most current fiscal year are ranked 1 to 219; companies listed are headquartered in the city; dashes indicate no ranking
Source: Fortune, "Fortune 500," June/July 2020; Forbes, "America's Largest Private Companies," 2020

Fastest-Growing Businesses

According to *Inc.*, Miami is home to seven of America's 500 fastest-growing private companies: **Cano Health** (#39); **EcoSystems** (#48); **NCM Group** (#66); **Effectus Partners** (#117); **Bore Tech Utilities** (#265); **M. Gill & Associates** (#406); **CloudTask** (#418). Criteria: must be an independent, privately-held, for-profit, U.S. corporation, proprietorship or partnership as of December 31, 2019; revenues must be at least $100,000 in 2016 and $2 million in 2019; must have four-year operating/sales history. *Inc., "America's 500 Fastest-Growing Private Companies," 2020*

According to *Fortune*, Miami is home to one of the 100 fastest-growing companies in the world: **Lennar** (#63). Companies were ranked by their revenue growth rate; their EPS growth rate; and their three-year annualized total return to investors for the period ending June 30, 2020. Criteria for inclusion: a company, foreign or domestic, must trade on a major U.S. stock exchange; must file quarterly reports with the SEC; must have a minimum market capitalization of $250 million; must have a stock price of at least $5 on June 30, 2020; must have been trading continuously since June 30, 2017; must have revenue and net income for the four quarters ended on or before April 30, 2020, of at least $50 million and $10 million, respectively; and must have posted a compound annual growth in revenue and earnings per share of at least 15% annually over the three years ending on or before April 30, 2020. Real estate investment trusts, limited-liability companies, limited partersships, business development companies, closed-end investment firms, companies about to be acquired, and companies that lost money in the quarter ending April 30, 2020 were excluded. *Fortune, "100 Fastest-Growing Companies," 2020*

According to *Initiative for a Competitive Inner City (ICIC)*, Miami is home to four of America's 100 fastest-growing "inner city" companies: **TISSINI** (#1); **Excellent Fruit & Produce** (#78); **Masterclass Automotive** (#90); **Cube Care** (#92). Criteria for inclusion: company must be headquartered in or have 51 percent or more of its physical operations in an economically distressed urban area; must be an independent, for-profit corporation, partnership or proprietorship; must have 10 or more employees and have a five-year sales history that includes sales of at least $200,000 in the base year and at least $1 million in the current year with no decrease in sales over the two most recent years. Companies were ranked overall by revenue growth over the five-year period between 2015 and 2019. *Initiative for a Competitive Inner City (ICIC), "Inner City 100 Companies," 2020*

Living Environment

COST OF LIVING

Cost of Living Index

Composite Index	Groceries	Housing	Utilities	Transportation	Health Care	Misc. Goods/Services
116.3	117.6	143.8	99.4	107.8	104.4	102.2

Note: The Cost of Living Index measures regional differences in the cost of consumer goods and services, excluding taxes and non-consumer expenditures, for professional and managerial households in the top income quintile. It is based on more than 50,000 prices covering almost 60 different items for which prices are collected three times a year by chambers of commerce, economic development organizations or university applied economic centers in each participating urban area. The numbers shown should be read as a percentage above or below the national average of 100. For example, a value of 115.4 in the groceries column indicates that grocery prices are 15.4% higher than the national average. Small differences in the index numbers should not be interpreted as significant; Figures cover the Miami-Dade County FL urban area.
Source: The Council for Community and Economic Research, Cost of Living Index, 2020

Grocery Prices

Area[1]	T-Bone Steak ($/pound)	Frying Chicken ($/pound)	Whole Milk ($/half gal.)	Eggs ($/dozen)	Orange Juice ($/64 oz.)	Coffee ($/11.5 oz.)
City[2]	12.55	1.73	3.16	1.71	3.67	4.00
Avg.	11.78	1.39	2.05	1.47	3.57	4.34
Min.	8.03	0.94	1.03	0.74	2.94	3.02
Max.	15.86	2.65	4.31	3.77	5.44	8.69

Note: (1) Values for the local area are compared with the average, minimum and maximum values for all 284 areas in the Cost of Living Index; (2) Figures cover the Miami-Dade County FL urban area; **T-Bone Steak** (price per pound); **Frying Chicken** (price per pound, whole fryer); **Whole Milk** (half gallon carton); **Eggs** (price per dozen, Grade A, large); **Orange Juice** (64 oz. Tropicana or Florida Natural); **Coffee** (11.5 oz. can, vacuum-packed, Maxwell House, Hills Bros, or Folgers).
Source: The Council for Community and Economic Research, Cost of Living Index, 2020

Housing and Utility Costs

Area[1]	New Home Price ($)	Apartment Rent ($/month)	All Electric ($/month)	Part Electric ($/month)	Other Energy ($/month)	Telephone ($/month)
City[2]	447,771	2,208	162.18	-	-	188.20
Avg.	368,594	1,168	170.86	100.47	65.28	184.30
Min.	190,567	502	91.58	31.42	26.08	169.60
Max.	2,227,806	4,738	470.38	280.31	280.06	206.50

Note: (1) Values for the local area are compared with the average, minimum and maximum values for all 284 areas in the Cost of Living Index; (2) Figures cover the Miami-Dade County FL urban area; **New Home Price** (2,400 sf living area, 8,000 sf lot, in urban area with full utilities); **Apartment Rent** (950 sf 2 bedroom/1.5 or 2 bath, unfurnished, excluding all utilities except water); **All Electric** (average monthly cost for an all-electric home); **Part Electric** (average monthly cost for a part-electric home); **Other Energy** (average monthly cost for natural gas, fuel oil, coal, wood, and any other forms of energy except electricity); **Telephone** (price includes the base monthly rate plus taxes and fees for three lines of mobile phone service).
Source: The Council for Community and Economic Research, Cost of Living Index, 2020

Health Care, Transportation, and Other Costs

Area[1]	Doctor ($/visit)	Dentist ($/visit)	Optometrist ($/visit)	Gasoline ($/gallon)	Beauty Salon ($/visit)	Men's Shirt ($)
City[2]	111.06	107.78	105.63	2.24	70.00	23.08
Avg.	115.44	99.32	108.10	2.21	39.27	31.37
Min.	36.68	59.00	51.36	1.71	19.00	11.00
Max.	219.00	153.10	250.97	3.46	82.05	58.33

Note: (1) Values for the local area are compared with the average, minimum and maximum values for all 284 areas in the Cost of Living Index; (2) Figures cover the Miami-Dade County FL urban area; **Doctor** (general practitioners routine exam of an established patient); **Dentist** (adult teeth cleaning and periodic oral examination); **Optometrist** (full vision eye exam for established adult patient); **Gasoline** (one gallon regular unleaded, national brand, including all taxes, cash price at self-service pump if available); **Beauty Salon** (woman's shampoo, trim, and blow-dry); **Men's Shirt** (cotton/polyester dress shirt, pinpoint weave, long sleeves).
Source: The Council for Community and Economic Research, Cost of Living Index, 2020

HOUSING

Homeownership Rate

Area	2012 (%)	2013 (%)	2014 (%)	2015 (%)	2016 (%)	2017 (%)	2018 (%)	2019 (%)	2020 (%)
MSA[1]	61.8	60.1	58.8	58.6	58.4	57.9	59.9	60.4	60.6
U.S.	65.4	65.1	64.5	63.7	63.4	63.9	64.4	64.6	66.6

Note: (1) Figures cover the Miami-Fort Lauderdale-West Palm Beach, FL Metropolitan Statistical Area
Source: U.S. Census Bureau, Housing Vacancies and Homeownership Annual Statistics: 2012-2020

House Price Index (HPI)

Area	National Ranking[2]	Quarterly Change (%)	One-Year Change (%)	Five-Year Change (%)	Since 1991Q1 (%)
MD[1]	124	1.83	6.32	38.91	334.89
U.S.[3]	–	3.81	10.77	38.99	205.12

Note: The HPI is a weighted repeat sales index. It measures average price changes in repeat sales or refinancings on the same properties. This information is obtained by reviewing repeat mortgage transactions on single-family properties whose mortgages have been purchased or securitized by Fannie Mae or Freddie Mac since January 1975; (1) Figures cover the Miami-Miami Beach-Kendall, FL Metropolitan Division; (2) Rankings are based on annual percentage change for all metro areas containing at least 15,000 transactions over the last 10 years and ranges from 1 to 253; (3) figures based on a weighted average of Census Division estimates using a seasonally adjusted, purchase-only index; all figures are for the period ending December 31, 2020
Source: Federal Housing Finance Agency, Change in Metropolitan Area House Price Indexes, April 7, 2021

Median Single-Family Home Prices

Area	2018	2019	2020p	Percent Change 2019 to 2020
MSA[1]	350.0	360.0	398.0	10.6
U.S. Average	261.6	274.6	299.9	9.2

Note: Figures are median sales prices of existing single-family homes in thousands of dollars; (p) preliminary; (1) Figures cover the Miami-Fort Lauderdale-West Palm Beach, FL Metropolitan Statistical Area
Source: National Association of Realtors, Median Sales Price of Existing Single-Family Homes for Metropolitan Areas, 4th Quarter 2020

Qualifying Income Based on Median Sales Price of Existing Single-Family Homes

Area	With 5% Down ($)	With 10% Down ($)	With 20% Down ($)
MSA[1]	80,385	76,155	67,693
U.S. Average	59,266	56,147	49,908

Note: Figures are preliminary; Qualifying income is based on a mortgage rate of 2.81%. Monthly principal and interest payment is limited to 25% of income; (1) Figures cover the Miami-Fort Lauderdale-West Palm Beach, FL Metropolitan Statistical Area
Source: National Association of Realtors, Qualifying Income Based on Median Sales Price of Existing Single-Family Homes for Metropolitan Areas, 4th Quarter 2020

Home Value Distribution

Area	Under $50,000	$50,000 -$99,999	$100,000 -$149,999	$150,000 -$199,999	$200,000 -$299,999	$300,000 -$499,999	$500,000 -$999,999	$1,000,000 or more
City	2.2	4.6	6.0	9.8	24.1	29.6	16.1	7.5
MSA[1]	4.0	7.1	8.7	11.9	22.9	28.5	12.5	4.5
U.S.	6.9	12.0	13.3	14.0	19.6	19.3	11.4	3.4

Note: Figures are percentages and cover owner-occupied housing units; (1) Figures cover the Miami-Fort Lauderdale-West Palm Beach, FL Metropolitan Statistical Area
Source: U.S. Census Bureau, 2015-2019 American Community Survey 5-Year Estimates

Year Housing Structure Built

Area	2010 or Later	2000 -2009	1990 -1999	1980 -1989	1970 -1979	1960 -1969	1950 -1959	1940 -1949	Before 1940	Median Year
City	7.6	19.0	6.4	8.3	13.3	9.8	14.7	11.7	9.2	1973
MSA[1]	4.1	13.0	15.1	19.4	21.4	12.3	9.8	2.8	2.1	1981
U.S.	5.2	14.0	13.9	13.4	15.2	10.6	10.3	4.9	12.6	1978

Note: Figures are percentages except for Median Year; Note: (1) Figures cover the Miami-Fort Lauderdale-West Palm Beach, FL Metropolitan Statistical Area
Source: U.S. Census Bureau, 2015-2019 American Community Survey 5-Year Estimates

Gross Monthly Rent

Area	Under $500	$500 -$999	$1,000 -$1,499	$1,500 -$1,999	$2,000 -$2,499	$2,500 -$2,999	$3,000 and up	Median ($)
City	10.7	26.3	30.0	17.0	9.3	3.8	2.9	1,183
MSA[1]	5.2	17.0	37.9	24.5	9.5	3.4	2.4	1,363
U.S.	9.4	36.2	30.0	14.0	5.6	2.4	2.4	1,062

Note: Figures are percentages except for Median; Gross rent is the contract rent plus the estimated average monthly cost of utilities (electricity, gas, and water and sewer) and fuels (oil, coal, kerosene, wood, etc.) if these are paid by the renter (or paid for the renter by someone else); (1) Figures cover the Miami-Fort Lauderdale-West Palm Beach, FL Metropolitan Statistical Area
Source: U.S. Census Bureau, 2015-2019 American Community Survey 5-Year Estimates

HEALTH

Health Risk Factors

Category	MSA[1] (%)	U.S. (%)
Adults aged 18–64 who have any kind of health care coverage	81.7	87.3
Adults who reported being in good or better health	83.4	82.4
Adults who have been told they have high blood cholesterol	34.7	33.0
Adults who have been told they have high blood pressure	30.2	32.3
Adults who are current smokers	13.6	17.1
Adults who currently use E-cigarettes	2.8	4.6
Adults who currently use chewing tobacco, snuff, or snus	1.4	4.0
Adults who are heavy drinkers[2]	4.6	6.3
Adults who are binge drinkers[3]	15.6	17.4
Adults who are overweight (BMI 25.0 - 29.9)	34.5	35.3
Adults who are obese (BMI 30.0 - 99.8)	27.0	31.3
Adults who participated in any physical activities in the past month	71.5	74.4
Adults who always or nearly always wears a seat belt	96.2	94.3

Note: (1) Figures cover the Miami-Fort Lauderdale-West Palm Beach, FL Metropolitan Statistical Area; (2) Heavy drinkers are classified as adult men having more than 14 drinks per week and adult women having more than 7 drinks per week; (3) Binge drinkers are classified as males having five or more drinks on one occasion or females having four or more drinks on one occasion
Source: Centers for Disease Control and Prevention, Behaviorial Risk Factor Surveillance System, SMART: Selected Metropolitan Area Risk Trends, 2017

Acute and Chronic Health Conditions

Category	MSA[1] (%)	U.S. (%)
Adults who have ever been told they had a heart attack	4.1	4.2
Adults who have ever been told they have angina or coronary heart disease	3.7	3.9
Adults who have ever been told they had a stroke	3.2	3.0
Adults who have ever been told they have asthma	10.2	14.2
Adults who have ever been told they have arthritis	19.4	24.9
Adults who have ever been told they have diabetes[2]	8.5	10.5
Adults who have ever been told they had skin cancer	6.4	6.2
Adults who have ever been told they had any other types of cancer	5.9	7.1
Adults who have ever been told they have COPD	4.5	6.5
Adults who have ever been told they have kidney disease	2.1	3.0
Adults who have ever been told they have a form of depression	13.3	20.5

Note: (1) Figures cover the Miami-Fort Lauderdale-West Palm Beach, FL Metropolitan Statistical Area; (2) Figures do not include pregnancy-related, borderline, or pre-diabetes
Source: Centers for Disease Control and Prevention, Behaviorial Risk Factor Surveillance System, SMART: Selected Metropolitan Area Risk Trends, 2017

Health Screening and Vaccination Rates

Category	MSA[1] (%)	U.S. (%)
Adults aged 65+ who have had flu shot within the past year	63.0	60.7
Adults aged 65+ who have ever had a pneumonia vaccination	58.0	75.4
Adults who have ever been tested for HIV	53.1	36.1
Adults who have ever had the shingles or zoster vaccine?	19.6	28.9
Adults who have had their blood cholesterol checked within the last five years	91.3	85.9

Note: n/a not available; (1) Figures cover the Miami-Fort Lauderdale-West Palm Beach, FL Metropolitan Statistical Area.
Source: Centers for Disease Control and Prevention, Behaviorial Risk Factor Surveillance System, SMART: Selected Metropolitan Area Risk Trends, 2017

Disability Status

Category	MSA[1] (%)	U.S. (%)
Adults who reported being deaf	5.8	6.7
Are you blind or have serious difficulty seeing, even when wearing glasses?	6.0	4.5
Are you limited in any way in any of your usual activities due of arthritis?	10.9	12.9
Do you have difficulty doing errands alone?	5.9	6.8
Do you have difficulty dressing or bathing?	4.4	3.6
Do you have serious difficulty concentrating/remembering/making decisions?	12.1	10.7
Do you have serious difficulty walking or climbing stairs?	14.9	13.6

Note: (1) Figures cover the Miami-Fort Lauderdale-West Palm Beach, FL Metropolitan Statistical Area.
Source: Centers for Disease Control and Prevention, Behaviorial Risk Factor Surveillance System, SMART: Selected Metropolitan Area Risk Trends, 2017

Mortality Rates for the Top 10 Causes of Death in the U.S.

ICD-10[a] Sub-Chapter	ICD-10[a] Code	Age-Adjusted Mortality Rate[1] per 100,000 population County[2]	U.S.
Malignant neoplasms	C00-C97	125.3	149.2
Ischaemic heart diseases	I20-I25	92.0	90.5
Other forms of heart disease	I30-I51	30.5	52.2
Chronic lower respiratory diseases	J40-J47	26.9	39.6
Other degenerative diseases of the nervous system	G30-G31	27.4	37.6
Cerebrovascular diseases	I60-I69	44.8	37.2
Other external causes of accidental injury	W00-X59	18.6	36.1
Organic, including symptomatic, mental disorders	F01-F09	18.3	29.4
Hypertensive diseases	I10-I15	25.7	24.1
Diabetes mellitus	E10-E14	21.2	21.5

Note: (a) ICD-10 = International Classification of Diseases 10th Revision; (1) Mortality rates are a three-year average covering 2017-2019; (2) Figures cover Miami-Dade County.
Source: Centers for Disease Control and Prevention, National Center for Health Statistics. Underlying Cause of Death 1999-2019 on CDC WONDER Online Database

Mortality Rates for Selected Causes of Death

ICD-10[a] Sub-Chapter	ICD-10[a] Code	Age-Adjusted Mortality Rate[1] per 100,000 population County[2]	U.S.
Assault	X85-Y09	7.6	6.0
Diseases of the liver	K70-K76	8.7	14.4
Human immunodeficiency virus (HIV) disease	B20-B24	4.6	1.5
Influenza and pneumonia	J09-J18	8.2	13.8
Intentional self-harm	X60-X84	8.9	14.1
Malnutrition	E40-E46	0.8	2.3
Obesity and other hyperalimentation	E65-E68	1.9	2.1
Renal failure	N17-N19	8.5	12.6
Transport accidents	V01-V99	11.2	12.3
Viral hepatitis	B15-B19	0.8	1.2

Note: (a) ICD-10 = International Classification of Diseases 10th Revision; (1) Mortality rates are a three-year average covering 2017-2019; (2) Figures cover Miami-Dade County; Data are suppressed when the data meet the criteria for confidentiality constraints; Mortality rates are flagged as unreliable when the rate would be calculated with a numerator of 20 or less.
Source: Centers for Disease Control and Prevention, National Center for Health Statistics. Underlying Cause of Death 1999-2019 on CDC WONDER Online Database

Health Insurance Coverage

Area	With Health Insurance	With Private Health Insurance	With Public Health Insurance	Without Health Insurance	Population Under Age 19 Without Health Insurance
City	80.2	46.7	36.7	19.8	8.6
MSA[1]	84.9	58.9	33.6	15.1	7.8
U.S.	91.2	67.9	35.1	8.8	5.1

Note: Figures are percentages that cover the civilian noninstitutionalized population; (1) Figures cover the Miami-Fort Lauderdale-West Palm Beach, FL Metropolitan Statistical Area
Source: U.S. Census Bureau, 2015-2019 American Community Survey 5-Year Estimates

Number of Medical Professionals

Area	MDs[3]	DOs[3,4]	Dentists	Podiatrists	Chiropractors	Optometrists
County[1] (number)	9,343	449	1,896	280	497	391
County[1] (rate[2])	344.1	16.5	69.8	10.3	18.3	14.4
U.S. (rate[2])	282.9	22.7	71.2	6.2	28.1	16.9

12086
Note: Data as of 2019 unless noted; (1) Data covers Miami-Dade County; (2) Rate per 100,000 population; (3) Data as of 2018 and includes all active, non-federal physicians; (4) Doctor of Osteopathic Medicine
Source: U.S. Department of Health and Human Services, Health Resources and Services Administration, Bureau of Health Professions, Area Resource File (ARF) 2019-2020

Best Hospitals

According to *U.S. News,* the Miami-Miami Beach-Kendall, FL metro area is home to two of the best hospitals in the U.S.: **Bascom Palmer Eye Institute-University of Miami Hospital and Clinics** (2 adult specialties); **University of Miami Hospital and Clinics-UHealth Tower** (2 adult specialties). The hospitals listed were nationally ranked in at least one of 16 adult or 10 pediatric specialties. Only 134 hospitals nationwide were nationally ranked in one or more adult or pediatric specialty; this number increases to 178 counting specialized centers within hospitals. Twenty hospitals in the U.S. made the Honor Roll. The Best Hospitals Honor Roll takes both the national rankings and the procedure and condition ratings into account. Hospitals received points if they were nationally ranked in one of the 16 adult specialties—the higher they ranked, the more points they got—and how many ratings of "high performing" they earned in the 10 procedures and conditions. *U.S. News Online, "America's Best Hospitals 2020-21"*

According to *U.S. News,* the Miami-Miami Beach-Kendall, FL metro area is home to two of the best children's hospitals in the U.S.: **Holtz Children's Hospital at UM-Jackson Memorial Medical Center** (1 pediatric specialty); **Nicklaus Children's Hospital** (5 pediatric specialties). The hospitals listed were highly ranked in at least one of 10 pediatric specialties. Eighty-eight children's hospitals in the U.S. were nationally ranked in at least one specialty. Hospitals received points for being ranked in a specialty, and the 10 hospitals with the most points across the 10 specialties make up the Honor Roll. *U.S. News Online, "America's Best Children's Hospitals 2020-21"*

EDUCATION

Public School District Statistics

District Name	Schls	Pupils	Pupil/Teacher Ratio	Minority Pupils[1] (%)	Free Lunch Eligible[2] (%)	IEP[3] (%)
Miami-Dade	510	350,434	19.2	93.3	61.7	10.7

Note: Table includes school districts with 2,000 or more students; (1) Percentage of students that are not non-Hispanic white; (2) Percentage of students that are eligible for the free lunch program; (3) Percentage of students that have an Individualized Education Program.
Source: U.S. Department of Education, National Center for Education Statistics, Common Core of Data, Local Education Agency (School District) Universe Survey: School Year 2018-2019; U.S. Department of Education, National Center for Education Statistics, Common Core of Data, Public Elementary/Secondary School Universe Survey: School Year 2018-2019

Best High Schools

According to *U.S. News,* Miami is home to 10 of the top 500 high schools in the U.S.: **School for Advanced Studies (SAS)** (#4); **Young Women's Preparatory Academy** (#52); **Design and Architecture Senior High** (#72); **Archimedean Upper Conservatory Charter School** (#74); **International Studies Charter High School** (#83); **iPrep Academy** (#104); **Terra Environmental Research Institute** (#146); **New World School of the Arts** (#248); **Coral Reef Senior High School** (#277); **Zelda Glazer Middle School** (#497). Nearly 18,000 public, magnet and charter schools were ranked based on their performance on state assessments and how well they prepare students for college. *U.S. News & World Report, "Best High Schools 2020"*

Highest Level of Education

Area	Less than H.S.	H.S. Diploma	Some College, No Deg.	Associate Degree	Bachelor's Degree	Master's Degree	Prof. School Degree	Doctorate Degree
City	22.0	28.4	12.5	7.4	17.9	7.1	3.6	1.1
MSA[1]	14.5	26.5	17.4	9.3	20.2	7.9	2.9	1.2
U.S.	12.0	27.0	20.4	8.5	19.8	8.8	2.1	1.4

Note: Figures cover persons age 25 and over; (1) Figures cover the Miami-Fort Lauderdale-West Palm Beach, FL Metropolitan Statistical Area
Source: U.S. Census Bureau, 2015-2019 American Community Survey 5-Year Estimates

Educational Attainment by Race

Area	High School Graduate or Higher (%) Total	White	Black	Asian	Hisp.[2]	Bachelor's Degree or Higher (%) Total	White	Black	Asian	Hisp.[2]
City	78.0	78.7	74.2	90.4	75.3	29.6	32.2	14.8	63.5	25.9
MSA[1]	85.5	86.9	81.4	87.5	80.0	32.3	35.4	19.8	51.6	27.7
U.S.	88.0	89.9	86.0	87.1	68.7	32.1	33.5	21.6	54.3	16.4

Note: Figures shown cover persons 25 years old and over; (1) Figures cover the Miami-Fort Lauderdale-West Palm Beach, FL Metropolitan Statistical Area; (2) People of Hispanic origin can be of any race
Source: U.S. Census Bureau, 2015-2019 American Community Survey 5-Year Estimates

School Enrollment by Grade and Control

Area	Preschool (%) Public	Private	Kindergarten (%) Public	Private	Grades 1 - 4 (%) Public	Private	Grades 5 - 8 (%) Public	Private	Grades 9 - 12 (%) Public	Private
City	56.0	44.0	86.7	13.3	88.1	11.9	85.6	14.4	90.8	9.2
MSA[1]	50.3	49.7	83.3	16.7	86.2	13.8	86.7	13.3	87.2	12.8
U.S.	59.1	40.9	87.6	12.4	89.5	10.5	89.4	10.6	90.1	9.9

Note: Figures shown cover persons 3 years old and over; (1) Figures cover the Miami-Fort Lauderdale-West Palm Beach, FL Metropolitan Statistical Area
Source: U.S. Census Bureau, 2015-2019 American Community Survey 5-Year Estimates

Higher Education

Four-Year Colleges			Two-Year Colleges			Medical Schools[1]	Law Schools[2]	Voc/Tech[3]
Public	Private Non-profit	Private For-profit	Public	Private Non-profit	Private For-profit			
2	7	4	3	1	9	2	2	17

Note: Figures cover institutions located within the city limits and include main campuses only; (1) includes schools accredited by the Liaison Committee on Medical Education and the American Osteopathic Association's Commission on Osteopathic College Accreditation; (2) includes ABA-accredited schools, schools with provisional ABA accreditation, and state accredited schools; (3) includes all schools with programs that are less than 2 years.
Source: National Center for Education Statistics, Integrated Postsecondary Education System (IPEDS), 2019-20; Wikipedia, List of Medical Schools in the United States, accessed April 2, 2021; Wikipedia, List of Law Schools in the United States, accessed April 2, 2021

According to *U.S. News & World Report,* the Miami-Miami Beach-Kendall, FL metro division is home to two of the top 200 national universities in the U.S.: **University of Miami** (#49 tie); **Florida International University** (#187 tie). The indicators used to capture academic quality fall into a number of categories: assessment by administrators at peer institutions; retention of students; faculty resources; student selectivity; financial resources; alumni giving; high school counselor ratings of colleges; and graduation rate. *U.S. News & World Report, "America's Best Colleges 2021"*

According to *U.S. News & World Report,* the Miami-Miami Beach-Kendall, FL metro division is home to two of the top 100 law schools in the U.S.: **University of Miami** (#72 tie); **Florida International University** (#88 tie). The rankings are based on a weighted average of 12 measures of quality: peer assessment score; assessment score by lawyers/judges; median LSAT scores; median undergrad GPA; acceptance rate; employment rates for graduates; placement success; bar passage rate; faculty resources; expenditures per student; student/faculty ratio; and library resources. *U.S. News & World Report, "America's Best Graduate Schools, Law, 2022"*

According to *U.S. News & World Report,* the Miami-Miami Beach-Kendall, FL metro division is home to one of the top 75 medical schools for research in the U.S.: **University of Miami (Miller)** (#45 tie). The rankings are based on a weighted average of 11 measures of quality: quality assessment; peer assessment score; assessment score by residency directors; research activity; total research activity; average research activity per faculty member; student selectivity; median MCAT total score; median undergraduate GPA; acceptance rate; and faculty resources. *U.S. News & World Report, "America's Best Graduate Schools, Medical, 2022"*

According to *U.S. News & World Report,* the Miami-Miami Beach-Kendall, FL metro division is home to one of the top 75 business schools in the U.S.: **University of Miami** (#60 tie). The rankings are based on a weighted average of the following nine measures: quality assessment; peer assessment; recruiter assessment; placement success; mean starting salary and bonus; student selectivity; mean GMAT and GRE scores; mean undergraduate GPA; and acceptance rate. *U.S. News & World Report, "America's Best Graduate Schools, Business, 2022"*

EMPLOYERS

Major Employers

Company Name	Industry
Baptist Health South Florida	General medical & surgical hospitals
Baptist Hospital of Miami	General medical & surgical hospitals
County of Miami-Dade	County government
Florida International University	Colleges & universities
Intercoastal Health Systems	Management services
Miami Dade College	Community college
Mount Sinai Medical Center of Florida	General medical & surgical hospitals
North Broward Hospital District	General medical & surgical hospitals
Palm Beach County	County government
Royal Caribbean Cruises Ltd	Deep sea passenger transportation, except ferry
School Board of Palm Beach County	Public elementary & secondary schools
Style View Products	Storm doors of windows, metal
The Answer Group	Custom computer programming services
University of Miami	Colleges & universities
Veterans Health Administration	General medical & surgical hospitals

Note: Companies shown are located within the Miami-Fort Lauderdale-West Palm Beach, FL Metropolitan Statistical Area.
Source: Hoovers.com; Wikipedia

PUBLIC SAFETY

Crime Rate

Area	All Crimes	Violent Crimes				Property Crimes		
		Murder	Rape[3]	Robbery	Aggrav. Assault	Burglary	Larceny-Theft	Motor Vehicle Theft
City	4,260.9	8.9	31.6	160.0	392.5	368.6	2,959.2	340.1
Suburbs[1]	3,417.0	6.9	35.0	125.5	289.7	268.7	2,428.8	262.4
Metro[2]	3,563.1	7.3	34.4	131.5	307.5	286.0	2,520.6	275.9
U.S.	2,489.3	5.0	42.6	81.6	250.2	340.5	1,549.5	219.9

Note: Figures are crimes per 100,000 population; (1) All areas within the metro area that are located outside the city limits; (2) Figures cover the Miami-Miami Beach-Kendall, FL Metropolitan Division; (3) All figures shown were reported using the revised Uniform Crime Reporting (UCR) definition of rape.
Source: FBI Uniform Crime Reports, 2019

Hate Crimes

Area	Number of Quarters Reported	Number of Incidents per Bias Motivation					
		Race/Ethnicity/Ancestry	Religion	Sexual Orientation	Disability	Gender	Gender Identity
City	4	0	2	0	0	0	0
U.S.	4	3,963	1,521	1,195	157	69	198

Source: Federal Bureau of Investigation, Hate Crime Statistics 2019

Identity Theft Consumer Reports

Area	Reports	Reports per 100,000 Population	Rank[2]
MSA[1]	50,341	816	18
U.S.	1,387,615	423	-

Note: (1) Figures cover the Miami-Fort Lauderdale-West Palm Beach, FL Metropolitan Statistical Area; (2) Rank ranges from 1 to 391 where 1 indicates greatest number of identity theft reports per 100,000 population
Source: Federal Trade Commission, Consumer Sentinel Network Data Book 2020

Fraud and Other Consumer Reports

Area	Reports	Reports per 100,000 Population	Rank[2]
MSA[1]	81,365	1,319	5
U.S.	3,385,133	1,031	-

Note: (1) Figures cover the Miami-Fort Lauderdale-West Palm Beach, FL Metropolitan Statistical Area; (2) Rank ranges from 1 to 391 where 1 indicates greatest number of fraud and other consumer reports per 100,000 population
Source: Federal Trade Commission, Consumer Sentinel Network Data Book 2020

POLITICS

2020 Presidential Election Results

Area	Biden	Trump	Jorgensen	Hawkins	Other
Miami-Dade County	53.3	46.0	0.3	0.1	0.3
U.S.	51.3	46.8	1.2	0.3	0.5

Note: Results are percentages and may not add to 100% due to rounding
Source: Dave Leip's Atlas of U.S. Presidential Elections

SPORTS

Professional Sports Teams

Team Name	League	Year Established
Florida Panthers	National Hockey League (NHL)	1993
Inter Miami CF	Major League Soccer (MLS)	2020
Miami Dolphins	National Football League (NFL)	1966
Miami Heat	National Basketball Association (NBA)	1988
Miami Marlins	Major League Baseball (MLB)	1993

Note: Includes teams located in the Miami-Fort Lauderdale-West Palm Beach, FL Metropolitan Statistical Area.
Source: Wikipedia, Major Professional Sports Teams of the United States and Canada, April 6, 2021

CLIMATE

Average and Extreme Temperatures

Temperature	Jan	Feb	Mar	Apr	May	Jun	Jul	Aug	Sep	Oct	Nov	Dec	Yr.
Extreme High (°F)	88	89	92	96	95	98	98	98	97	95	89	87	98
Average High (°F)	75	77	79	82	85	88	89	90	88	85	80	77	83
Average Temp. (°F)	68	69	72	75	79	82	83	83	82	78	73	69	76
Average Low (°F)	59	60	64	68	72	75	76	76	76	72	66	61	69
Extreme Low (°F)	30	35	32	42	55	60	69	68	68	53	39	30	30

Note: Figures cover the years 1948-1990
Source: National Climatic Data Center, International Station Meteorological Climate Summary, 9/96

Average Precipitation/Snowfall/Humidity

Precip./Humidity	Jan	Feb	Mar	Apr	May	Jun	Jul	Aug	Sep	Oct	Nov	Dec	Yr.
Avg. Precip. (in.)	1.9	2.0	2.3	3.0	6.2	8.7	6.1	7.5	8.2	6.6	2.7	1.8	57.1
Avg. Snowfall (in.)	0	0	0	0	0	0	0	0	0	0	0	0	0
Avg. Rel. Hum. 7am (%)	84	84	82	80	81	84	84	86	88	87	85	84	84
Avg. Rel. Hum. 4pm (%)	59	57	57	57	62	68	66	67	69	65	63	60	63

Note: Figures cover the years 1948-1990; Tr = Trace amounts (<0.05 in. of rain; <0.5 in. of snow)
Source: National Climatic Data Center, International Station Meteorological Climate Summary, 9/96

Weather Conditions

Temperature			Daytime Sky			Precipitation		
32°F & below	45°F & below	90°F & above	Clear	Partly cloudy	Cloudy	0.01 inch or more precip.	0.1 inch or more snow/ice	Thunderstorms
<1	7	55	48	263	54	128	0	74

Note: Figures are average number of days per year and cover the years 1948-1990
Source: National Climatic Data Center, International Station Meteorological Climate Summary, 9/96

HAZARDOUS WASTE

Superfund Sites

The Miami-Miami Beach-Kendall, FL metro division is home to six sites on the EPA's Superfund National Priorities List: **Airco Plating Co.** (final); **Anodyne, Inc.** (final); **Continental Cleaners** (final); **Homestead Air Force Base** (final); **Miami Drum Services** (final); **Pepper Steel & Alloys, Inc.** (final). There are a total of 1,375 Superfund sites with a status of proposed or final on the list in the U.S.
U.S. Environmental Protection Agency, National Priorities List, April 7, 2021

AIR QUALITY

Air Quality Trends: Ozone

	1990	1995	2000	2005	2010	2015	2016	2017	2018	2019
MSA[1]	0.068	0.072	0.075	0.065	0.064	0.061	0.061	0.064	0.064	0.058
U.S.	0.088	0.089	0.082	0.080	0.073	0.068	0.069	0.068	0.069	0.065

Note: (1) Data covers the Miami-Fort Lauderdale-West Palm Beach, FL Metropolitan Statistical Area. The values shown are the composite ozone concentration averages among trend sites based on the highest fourth daily maximum 8-hour concentration in parts per million. These trends are based on sites having an adequate record of monitoring data during the trend period. Data from exceptional events are included.
Source: U.S. Environmental Protection Agency, Air Quality Monitoring Information, "Air Quality Trends by City, 1990-2019"

Air Quality Index

Area	Percent of Days when Air Quality was...[2]					AQI Statistics[2]	
	Good	Moderate	Unhealthy for Sensitive Groups	Unhealthy	Very Unhealthy	Maximum	Median
MSA[1]	78.3	21.2	0.5	0.0	0.0	146	41

Note: (1) Data covers the Miami-Fort Lauderdale-West Palm Beach, FL Metropolitan Statistical Area; (2) Based on 364 days with AQI data in 2019. Air Quality Index (AQI) is an index for reporting daily air quality. EPA calculates the AQI for five major air pollutants regulated by the Clean Air Act: ground-level ozone, particle pollution (aka particulate matter), carbon monoxide, sulfur dioxide, and nitrogen dioxide. The AQI runs from 0 to 500. The higher the AQI value, the greater the level of air pollution and the greater the health concern. There are six AQI categories: "Good" AQI is between 0 and 50. Air quality is considered satisfactory; "Moderate" AQI is between 51 and 100. Air quality is acceptable; "Unhealthy for Sensitive Groups" When AQI values are between 101 and 150, members of sensitive groups may experience health effects; "Unhealthy" When AQI values are between 151 and 200 everyone may begin to experience health effects; "Very Unhealthy" AQI values between 201 and 300 trigger a health alert; "Hazardous" AQI values over 300 trigger warnings of emergency conditions (not shown).
Source: U.S. Environmental Protection Agency, Air Quality Index Report, 2019

Air Quality Index Pollutants

Area	Percent of Days when AQI Pollutant was...[2]					
	Carbon Monoxide	Nitrogen Dioxide	Ozone	Sulfur Dioxide	Particulate Matter 2.5	Particulate Matter 10
MSA[1]	0.3	3.6	37.4	0.0	58.5	0.3

Note: (1) Data covers the Miami-Fort Lauderdale-West Palm Beach, FL Metropolitan Statistical Area; (2) Based on 364 days with AQI data in 2019. The Air Quality Index (AQI) is an index for reporting daily air quality. EPA calculates the AQI for five major air pollutants regulated by the Clean Air Act: ground-level ozone, particle pollution (also known as particulate matter), carbon monoxide, sulfur dioxide, and nitrogen dioxide. The AQI runs from 0 to 500. The higher the AQI value, the greater the level of air pollution and the greater the health concern.
Source: U.S. Environmental Protection Agency, Air Quality Index Report, 2019

Maximum Air Pollutant Concentrations: Particulate Matter, Ozone, CO and Lead

	Particulate Matter 10 (ug/m³)	Particulate Matter 2.5 Wtd AM (ug/m³)	Particulate Matter 2.5 24-Hr (ug/m³)	Ozone (ppm)	Carbon Monoxide (ppm)	Lead (ug/m³)
MSA[1] Level	54	8.9	19	0.060	2	n/a
NAAQS[2]	150	15	35	0.075	9	0.15
Met NAAQS[2]	Yes	Yes	Yes	Yes	Yes	n/a

Note: (1) Data covers the Miami-Fort Lauderdale-West Palm Beach, FL Metropolitan Statistical Area; Data from exceptional events are included; (2) National Ambient Air Quality Standards; ppm = parts per million; ug/m³ = micrograms per cubic meter; n/a not available.
Concentrations: Particulate Matter 10 (coarse particulate)—highest second maximum 24-hour concentration; Particulate Matter 2.5 Wtd AM (fine particulate)—highest weighted annual mean concentration; Particulate Matter 2.5 24-Hour (fine particulate)—highest 98th percentile 24-hour concentration; Ozone—highest fourth daily maximum 8-hour concentration; Carbon Monoxide—highest second maximum non-overlapping 8-hour concentration; Lead—maximum running 3-month average
Source: U.S. Environmental Protection Agency, Air Quality Monitoring Information, "Air Quality Statistics by City, 2019"

Maximum Air Pollutant Concentrations: Nitrogen Dioxide and Sulfur Dioxide

	Nitrogen Dioxide AM (ppb)	Nitrogen Dioxide 1-Hr (ppb)	Sulfur Dioxide AM (ppb)	Sulfur Dioxide 1-Hr (ppb)	Sulfur Dioxide 24-Hr (ppb)
MSA[1] Level	15	48	n/a	1	n/a
NAAQS[2]	53	100	30	75	140
Met NAAQS[2]	Yes	Yes	n/a	Yes	n/a

Note: (1) Data covers the Miami-Fort Lauderdale-West Palm Beach, FL Metropolitan Statistical Area; Data from exceptional events are included; (2) National Ambient Air Quality Standards; ppm = parts per million; ug/m³ = micrograms per cubic meter; n/a not available.
Concentrations: Nitrogen Dioxide AM—highest arithmetic mean concentration; Nitrogen Dioxide 1-Hr—highest 98th percentile 1-hour daily maximum concentration; Sulfur Dioxide AM—highest annual mean concentration; Sulfur Dioxide 1-Hr—highest 99th percentile 1-hour daily maximum concentration; Sulfur Dioxide 24-Hr—highest second maximum 24-hour concentration
Source: U.S. Environmental Protection Agency, Air Quality Monitoring Information, "Air Quality Statistics by City, 2019"

Midland, Texas

Background

In 1881, when Midland, Texas might have appeared as a dot on a map, it would have been called the middle of nowhere. In fact, Midland was almost exactly at the midpoint between Fort Worth Texas and El Paso. Today the locals like to tease that Midland is "in the middle of somewhere." Then barely a whistle-stop, Midland provided a small shelter where Texas and Pacific Railroad crews could rest and store maintenance equipment. Ten years later, it was a vital shipping center for the cattle trade.

Little is known about the first inhabitants in the region, though they left plenty of evidence of their existence. The Pecos Trail region is rich with petroglyphs and pictographs. Anthropologists refer to these communities as the Karankawas (hunter-gatherers), and surmise these early scribes are the ancestors of the Comanche, Apache, Kiowa, and Kickapoo nations.

The first westerner to make Midland his permanent home in 1882 was Herman Garrett, a sheep rancher from California. Midland grew quickly. Within three years, 100 families lived there, and by 1900, the population was 1,000. Midland became known as the "Windmill Town," as individual homes built windmills to pump water. After several devastating fires in 1905 and 1909, the town put in a municipal water system and a fire department.

Midland would remain a center of ranching and shipping until 1923, when a new industry overtook the town. Just southeast of Midland, the Santa Rita No. 1 oil rig "blew." From then on, Midland's economy and culture was defined by the price of oil, and its roller coaster ride of market highs and lows. By 1929, there were thirty-six oil companies in Midland. Roads were paved and streetlights were raised as Midland's skyline began to rise from the wide-open landscape. The new Hogal Building was twelve stories high. By 1930, the population blossomed to 5,484. When the Great Depression hit, the demand for petroleum decreased and prices plummeted. By 1932, one third of Midland's workers were unemployed.

World War II brought an increase in oil prices, along with the new Midland Army Air Force Base, a training ground for bomber pilots, giving Midland's economy a much-needed boost. By 1950, 250 oil companies had set up shop in Midland.

In 1972, Midland Community College was founded, and later, a satellite campus in Fort Stockton opened. Twice a year, Midland College hosts free lectures by world-renowned speakers—a Who's Who list of past guest lecturers include Ken Burns, Bill Moyers, Sandra Day O'Connor, Richard Rodriguez, John Updike and Neil deGrasse Tyson.

In recent years, Midland has grabbed headlines due to its association with the Bush family. Laura Bush was born and raised in Midland. Both former presidents George W. Bush, and George H.W. Bush, as well as Barbara and Jeb Bush, lived in Midland. The George Bush Childhood Home Museum in Midland receives thousands of visitors a year.

Midland is a cultural mecca with six museums, as well as a community theater that offers fifteen shows each year. The Midland-Odessa Symphony & Chorale performs eighteen venues each year, with four masterworks, four Pops Concerts, six Chamber Concerts, two Chorale concerts and a youth concert. The Marian Blakemore planetarium offers educational shows and lectures about the history of astronomy.

Midland features a semi-arid climate with long, hot summers and short, moderate winters. The city is occasionally subject to cold waves during the winter, but it rarely sees extended periods of below-freezing cold. Midland receives approximately 14.6 inches of precipitation per year, much of which falls in the summer. Highs exceed 90 °F (32 °C) on 101 days per year, and 100 °F (38 °C) on 16 days.

Rankings

Business/Finance Rankings

- Midland was cited as one of America's top metros for new and expanded facility projects in 2020. The area ranked #6 in the small metro area category (population under 200,000). *Site Selection, "Top Metros of 2020," March 2021*

- The Midland metro area appeared on the Milken Institute "2021 Best Performing Cities" list. Rank: #55 out of 201 small metro areas (population over 60,000). Criteria: job growth; wage and salary growth; high-tech output growth; housing affordability; household broadband access. *Milken Institute, "Best-Performing Cities 2021," February 16, 2021*

- *Forbes* ranked 203 smaller metro areas (population under 268,000) to determine the nation's "Best Small Places for Business and Careers." The Midland metro area was ranked #81. Criteria: costs (business and living); job growth (past and projected); income growth; quality of life; educational attainment (college and high school); projected economic growth; cultural and leisure opportunities; workplace tolerance laws; net migration patterns. *Forbes, "The Best Small Places for Business and Careers 2019," October 30, 2019*

Real Estate Rankings

- Midland was ranked #102 out of 268 metro areas in terms of housing affordability in 2020 by the National Association of Home Builders (#1 = most affordable). Criteria: the share of homes sold in that area affordable to a family earning the local median income, based on standard mortgage underwriting criteria. *National Association of Home Builders®, NAHB-Wells Fargo Housing Opportunity Index, 4th Quarter 2020*

Safety Rankings

- The National Insurance Crime Bureau ranked 384 metro areas in the U.S. in terms of per capita rates of vehicle theft. The Midland metro area ranked #36 (#1 = highest rate). Criteria: number of vehicle theft offenses per 100,000 inhabitants in 2019. *National Insurance Crime Bureau, "Hot Spots 2019," July 21, 2020*

Seniors/Retirement Rankings

- From its Best Cities for Successful Aging indexes, the Milken Institute generated rankings for metropolitan areas, weighing data in nine categories—health care, wellness, living arrangements, transportation and convenience, financial characteristics, education, employment, community engagement, and overall livability. The Midland metro area was ranked #15 overall in the small metro area category. *Milken Institute, "Best Cities for Successful Aging, 2017" March 14, 2017*

Business Environment

DEMOGRAPHICS

Population Growth

Area	1990 Census	2000 Census	2010 Census	2019* Estimate	Population Growth (%) 1990-2019	Population Growth (%) 2010-2019
City	89,358	94,996	111,147	138,549	55.0	24.7
MSA[1]	106,611	116,009	136,872	173,816	63.0	27.0
U.S.	248,709,873	281,421,906	308,745,538	324,697,795	30.6	5.2

Note: (1) Figures cover the Midland, TX Metropolitan Statistical Area; (*) 2015-2019 5-year estimated population
Source: U.S. Census Bureau, 1990 Census, Census 2000, Census 2010, 2015-2019 American Community Survey 5-Year Estimates

Household Size

Area	One	Two	Three	Four	Five	Six	Seven or More	Average Household Size
City	26.1	31.2	16.5	14.5	7.3	3.0	1.3	2.90
MSA[1]	26.3	30.9	15.9	14.5	7.8	2.9	1.6	2.90
U.S.	27.9	33.9	15.6	12.9	6.0	2.3	1.4	2.60

Note: (1) Figures cover the Midland, TX Metropolitan Statistical Area
Source: U.S. Census Bureau, 2015-2019 American Community Survey 5-Year Estimates

Race

Area	White Alone[2] (%)	Black Alone[2] (%)	Asian Alone[2] (%)	AIAN[3] Alone[2] (%)	NHOPI[4] Alone[2] (%)	Other Race Alone[2] (%)	Two or More Races (%)
City	80.6	7.8	2.2	0.6	0.1	6.4	2.3
MSA[1]	82.1	6.5	1.9	0.6	0.1	6.4	2.4
U.S.	72.5	12.7	5.5	0.8	0.2	4.9	3.3

Note: (1) Figures cover the Midland, TX Metropolitan Statistical Area; (2) Alone is defined as not being in combination with one or more other races; (3) American Indian and Alaska Native; (4) Native Hawaiian and Other Pacific Islander
Source: U.S. Census Bureau, 2015-2019 American Community Survey 5-Year Estimates

Hispanic or Latino Origin

Area	Total (%)	Mexican (%)	Puerto Rican (%)	Cuban (%)	Other (%)
City	44.2	40.6	0.5	0.9	2.2
MSA[1]	44.7	41.6	0.5	0.7	1.9
U.S.	18.0	11.2	1.7	0.7	4.3

Note: Persons of Hispanic or Latino origin can be of any race; (1) Figures cover the Midland, TX Metropolitan Statistical Area
Source: U.S. Census Bureau, 2015-2019 American Community Survey 5-Year Estimates

Ancestry

Area	German	Irish	English	American	Italian	Polish	French[2]	Scottish	Dutch
City	6.8	6.0	6.7	4.4	1.4	0.6	1.6	1.6	0.7
MSA[1]	6.9	6.1	6.4	4.5	1.4	0.6	1.6	1.5	0.6
U.S.	13.3	9.7	7.2	6.2	5.1	2.8	2.3	1.7	1.2

Note: Figures are the percentage of the total population reporting a particular ancestry. The nine most commonly reported ancestries in the U.S. are shown. Figures include multiple ancestries (e.g. if a person reported being Irish and Italian, they were included in both columns); (1) Figures cover the Midland, TX Metropolitan Statistical Area; (2) Excludes Basque
Source: U.S. Census Bureau, 2015-2019 American Community Survey 5-Year Estimates

Foreign-born Population

Area	Any Foreign Country	Asia	Mexico	Europe	Caribbean	Central America[2]	South America	Africa	Canada
City	14.1	1.8	8.6	0.3	1.2	0.6	0.4	0.8	0.4
MSA[1]	13.4	1.6	8.8	0.3	1.0	0.5	0.3	0.6	0.3
U.S.	13.6	4.2	3.5	1.5	1.3	1.1	1.0	0.7	0.2

Note: (1) Figures cover the Midland, TX Metropolitan Statistical Area; (2) Excludes Mexico.
Source: U.S. Census Bureau, 2015-2019 American Community Survey 5-Year Estimates

Marital Status

Area	Never Married	Now Married[2]	Separated	Widowed	Divorced
City	30.1	51.1	2.1	5.1	11.6
MSA[1]	29.2	51.8	2.0	5.0	11.9
U.S.	33.4	48.1	1.9	5.8	10.9

Note: Figures are percentages and cover the population 15 years of age and older; (1) Figures cover the Midland, TX Metropolitan Statistical Area; (2) Excludes separated
Source: U.S. Census Bureau, 2015-2019 American Community Survey 5-Year Estimates

Disability by Age

Area	All Ages	Under 18 Years Old	18 to 64 Years Old	65 Years and Over
City	9.7	2.4	8.2	38.5
MSA[1]	9.8	2.3	8.3	39.5
U.S.	12.6	4.2	10.3	34.5

Note: Figures show percent of the civilian noninstitutionalized population that reported having a disability. Disability status is determined from six types of difficulty: vision, hearing, cognitive, ambulatory, self-care, and independent living. For children under 5 years old, hearing and vision difficulty are used to determine disability status. For children between the ages of 5 and 14, disability status is determined from hearing, vision, cognitive, ambulatory, and self-care difficulties. For people aged 15 years and older, they are considered to have a disability if they have difficulty with any one of the six difficulty types; Note: (1) Figures cover the Midland, TX Metropolitan Statistical Area
Source: U.S. Census Bureau, 2015-2019 American Community Survey 5-Year Estimates

Age

Area	Under Age 5	Age 5–19	Age 20–34	Age 35–44	Age 45–54	Age 55–64	Age 65–74	Age 75–84	Age 85+	Median Age
City	8.8	21.0	25.5	13.0	10.8	10.5	5.7	3.1	1.6	31.7
MSA[1]	8.8	22.1	24.4	13.1	10.6	10.8	5.8	3.1	1.5	31.7
U.S.	6.1	19.1	20.7	12.6	13.0	12.9	9.1	4.6	1.9	38.1

Note: (1) Figures cover the Midland, TX Metropolitan Statistical Area
Source: U.S. Census Bureau, 2015-2019 American Community Survey 5-Year Estimates

Gender

Area	Males	Females	Males per 100 Females
City	70,558	67,991	103.8
MSA[1]	87,984	85,832	102.5
U.S.	159,886,919	164,810,876	97.0

Note: (1) Figures cover the Midland, TX Metropolitan Statistical Area
Source: U.S. Census Bureau, 2015-2019 American Community Survey 5-Year Estimates

Religious Groups by Family

Area	Catholic	Baptist	Non-Den.	Methodist[2]	Lutheran	LDS[3]	Pentecostal	Presbyterian[4]	Muslim[5]	Judaism
MSA[1]	22.4	25.3	8.8	4.2	0.7	1.2	1.6	1.9	3.7	<0.1
U.S.	19.1	9.3	4.0	4.0	2.3	2.0	1.9	1.6	0.8	0.7

Note: Figures are the number of adherents as a percentage of the total population; (1) Figures cover the Midland, TX Metropolitan Statistical Area; (2) Methodist/Pietist; (3) Latter Day Saints; (4) Reformed; (5) Figures are estimates
Source: Association of Statisticians of American Religious Bodies, 2010 U.S. Religion Census: Religious Congregations & Membership Study

Religious Groups by Tradition

Area	Catholic	Evangelical Protestant	Mainline Protestant	Other Tradition	Black Protestant	Orthodox
MSA[1]	22.4	35.5	7.2	5.4	1.0	<0.1
U.S.	19.1	16.2	7.3	4.3	1.6	0.3

Note: Figures are the number of adherents as a percentage of the total population; (1) Figures cover the Midland, TX Metropolitan Statistical Area
Source: Association of Statisticians of American Religious Bodies, 2010 U.S. Religion Census: Religious Congregations & Membership Study

ECONOMY

Gross Metropolitan Product

Area	2017	2018	2019	2020	Rank[2]
MSA[1]	27.1	35.0	38.1	44.4	83

Note: Figures are in billions of dollars; (1) Figures cover the Midland, TX Metropolitan Statistical Area; (2) Rank is based on 2018 data and ranges from 1 to 381
Source: U.S. Conference of Mayors, U.S. Metro Economies: GMP & Employment 2018-2020, September 2019

Economic Growth

Area	2015-17 (%)	2018 (%)	2019 (%)	2020 (%)	Rank[2]
MSA[1]	1.0	13.0	9.2	3.6	231
U.S.	1.9	2.9	2.3	2.1	—

Note: Figures are real gross metropolitan product (GMP) growth rates and represent average annual percent change; (1) Figures cover the Midland, TX Metropolitan Statistical Area; (2) Rank is based on 2017 2-year average annual percent change and ranges from 1 to 381
Source: U.S. Conference of Mayors, U.S. Metro Economies: GMP & Employment 2018-2020, September 2019

Metropolitan Area Exports

Area	2014	2015	2016	2017	2018	2019	Rank[2]
MSA[1]	122.7	110.1	69.6	69.4	63.6	63.7	357

Note: Figures are in millions of dollars; (1) Figures cover the Midland, TX Metropolitan Statistical Area; (2) Rank is based on 2019 data and ranges from 1 to 386
Source: U.S. Department of Commerce, International Trade Administration, Office of Trade and Economic Analysis, Industry and Analysis, Exports by Metropolitan Area, data extracted March 24, 2021

Building Permits

Area	Single-Family 2018	Single-Family 2019	Pct. Chg.	Multi-Family 2018	Multi-Family 2019	Pct. Chg.	Total 2018	Total 2019	Pct. Chg.
City	1,222	1,290	5.6	0	0	0.0	1,222	1,290	5.6
MSA[1]	1,227	1,306	6.4	0	0	0.0	1,227	1,306	6.4
U.S.	855,300	862,100	0.7	473,500	523,900	10.6	1,328,800	1,386,000	4.3

Note: (1) Figures cover the Midland, TX Metropolitan Statistical Area; Figures represent new, privately-owned housing units authorized (unadjusted data); All permit data are based on estimates with imputation
Source: U.S. Census Bureau, Manufacturing, Mining, and Construction Statistics, Building Permits, 2018, 2019

Bankruptcy Filings

Area	Business Filings 2019	Business Filings 2020	% Chg.	Nonbusiness Filings 2019	Nonbusiness Filings 2020	% Chg.
Midland County	32	11	-65.6	72	48	-33.3
U.S.	22,780	21,655	-4.9	752,160	522,808	-30.5

Note: Business filings include Chapter 7, Chapter 9, Chapter 11, Chapter 12, Chapter 13, Chapter 15, and Section 304; Nonbusiness filings include Chapter 7, Chapter 11, and Chapter 13
Source: Administrative Office of the U.S. Courts, Business and Nonbusiness Bankruptcy, County Cases Commenced by Chapter of the Bankruptcy Code, During the 12-Month Period Ending December 31, 2019 and Business and Nonbusiness Bankruptcy, County Cases Commenced by Chapter of the Bankruptcy Code, During the 12-Month Period Ending December 31, 2020

Housing Vacancy Rates

Area	Gross Vacancy Rate[2] (%) 2018	2019	2020	Year-Round Vacancy Rate[3] (%) 2018	2019	2020	Rental Vacancy Rate[4] (%) 2018	2019	2020	Homeowner Vacancy Rate[5] (%) 2018	2019	2020
MSA[1]	n/a	n/a	n/a	n/a	n/a	n/a	n/a	n/a	n/a	n/a	n/a	n/a
U.S.	12.3	12.0	10.6	9.7	9.5	8.2	6.9	6.7	6.3	1.5	1.4	1.0

Note: (1) Figures cover the Midland, TX Metropolitan Statistical Area; (2) The percentage of the total housing inventory that is vacant; (3) The percentage of the housing inventory (excluding seasonal units) that is year-round vacant; (4) The percentage of rental inventory that is vacant for rent; (5) The percentage of homeowner inventory that is vacant for sale; n/a not available
Source: U.S. Census Bureau, Housing Vacancies and Homeownership Annual Statistics: 2018, 2019, 2020

INCOME

Income

Area	Per Capita ($)	Median Household ($)	Average Household ($)
City	40,252	79,329	112,701
MSA[1]	38,966	79,140	109,861
U.S.	34,103	62,843	88,607

Note: (1) Figures cover the Midland, TX Metropolitan Statistical Area
Source: U.S. Census Bureau, 2015-2019 American Community Survey 5-Year Estimates

Household Income Distribution

Area	Under $15,000	$15,000 -$24,999	$25,000 -$34,999	$35,000 -$49,999	$50,000 -$74,999	$75,000 -$99,999	$100,000 -$149,999	$150,000 and up
City	6.7	6.7	6.9	9.8	17.3	13.7	18.0	20.8
MSA[1]	6.9	6.9	7.1	9.9	17.1	13.5	18.1	20.6
U.S.	10.3	8.9	8.9	12.3	17.2	12.7	15.1	14.5

Note: (1) Figures cover the Midland, TX Metropolitan Statistical Area
Source: U.S. Census Bureau, 2015-2019 American Community Survey 5-Year Estimates

Poverty Rate

Area	All Ages	Under 18 Years Old	18 to 64 Years Old	65 Years and Over
City	9.2	11.5	7.7	11.8
MSA[1]	9.5	13.2	7.5	11.1
U.S.	13.4	18.5	12.6	9.3

Note: Figures are percentage of people whose income during the past 12 months was below the poverty level;
(1) Figures cover the Midland, TX Metropolitan Statistical Area
Source: U.S. Census Bureau, 2015-2019 American Community Survey 5-Year Estimates

CITY FINANCES

City Government Finances

Component	2017 ($000)	2017 ($ per capita)
Total Revenues	241,288	1,815
Total Expenditures	198,939	1,496
Debt Outstanding	78,305	589
Cash and Securities[1]	371,901	2,797

Note: (1) Cash and security holdings of a government at the close of its fiscal year, including those of its dependent agencies, utilities, and liquor stores.
Source: U.S. Census Bureau, State & Local Government Finances 2017

City Government Revenue by Source

Source	2017 ($000)	2017 ($ per capita)	2017 (%)
General Revenue			
From Federal Government	7,042	53	2.9
From State Government	2,995	23	1.2
From Local Governments	0	0	0.0
Taxes			
Property	42,512	320	17.6
Sales and Gross Receipts	85,666	644	35.5
Personal Income	0	0	0.0
Corporate Income	0	0	0.0
Motor Vehicle License	0	0	0.0
Other Taxes	3,926	30	1.6
Current Charges	42,450	319	17.6
Liquor Store	0	0	0.0
Utility	32,350	243	13.4
Employee Retirement	7,947	60	3.3

Source: U.S. Census Bureau, State & Local Government Finances 2017

City Government Expenditures by Function

Function	2017 ($000)	2017 ($ per capita)	2017 (%)
General Direct Expenditures			
Air Transportation	10,951	82	5.5
Corrections	0	0	0.0
Education	0	0	0.0
Employment Security Administration	0	0	0.0
Financial Administration	7,336	55	3.7
Fire Protection	25,102	188	12.6
General Public Buildings	1,410	10	0.7
Governmental Administration, Other	2,718	20	1.4
Health	5,318	40	2.7
Highways	7,535	56	3.8
Hospitals	0	0	0.0
Housing and Community Development	1,484	11	0.7
Interest on General Debt	2,415	18	1.2
Judicial and Legal	3,334	25	1.7
Libraries	0	0	0.0
Parking	0	0	0.0
Parks and Recreation	19,955	150	10.0
Police Protection	27,398	206	13.8
Public Welfare	0	0	0.0
Sewerage	11,163	84	5.6
Solid Waste Management	12,337	92	6.2
Veterans' Services	0	0	0.0
Liquor Store	0	0	0.0
Utility	37,328	280	18.8
Employee Retirement	7,004	52	3.5

Source: U.S. Census Bureau, State & Local Government Finances 2017

EMPLOYMENT

Labor Force and Employment

Area	Civilian Labor Force Dec. 2019	Dec. 2020	% Chg.	Workers Employed Dec. 2019	Dec. 2020	% Chg.
City	88,858	84,069	-5.4	87,068	77,687	-10.8
MSA[1]	110,792	105,257	-5.0	108,522	96,833	-10.8
U.S.	164,007,000	160,017,000	-2.4	158,504,000	149,613,000	-5.6

Note: Data is not seasonally adjusted and covers workers 16 years of age and older; (1) Figures cover the Midland, TX Metropolitan Statistical Area
Source: Bureau of Labor Statistics, Local Area Unemployment Statistics

Unemployment Rate

Area	Jan.	Feb.	Mar.	Apr.	May	Jun.	Jul.	Aug.	Sep.	Oct.	Nov.	Dec.
City	2.3	2.3	3.3	9.9	12.3	9.2	9.1	7.8	9.2	7.7	8.8	7.6
MSA[1]	2.4	2.3	3.4	10.1	12.6	9.5	9.5	8.1	9.5	8.0	9.3	8.0
U.S.	4.0	3.8	4.5	14.4	13.0	11.2	10.5	8.5	7.7	6.6	6.4	6.5

Note: Data is not seasonally adjusted and covers workers 16 years of age and older; (1) Figures cover the Midland, TX Metropolitan Statistical Area
Source: Bureau of Labor Statistics, Local Area Unemployment Statistics

Average Wages

Occupation	$/Hr.	Occupation	$/Hr.
Accountants and Auditors	49.60	Maintenance and Repair Workers	19.90
Automotive Mechanics	30.40	Marketing Managers	81.10
Bookkeepers	23.20	Network and Computer Systems Admin.	44.10
Carpenters	20.50	Nurses, Licensed Practical	25.00
Cashiers	13.30	Nurses, Registered	32.90
Computer Programmers	57.40	Nursing Assistants	15.50
Computer Systems Analysts	n/a	Office Clerks, General	19.20
Computer User Support Specialists	24.70	Physical Therapists	51.30
Construction Laborers	17.40	Physicians	n/a
Cooks, Restaurant	13.10	Plumbers, Pipefitters and Steamfitters	22.40
Customer Service Representatives	17.40	Police and Sheriff's Patrol Officers	32.00
Dentists	n/a	Postal Service Mail Carriers	24.10
Electricians	28.90	Real Estate Sales Agents	43.90
Engineers, Electrical	52.80	Retail Salespersons	15.70
Fast Food and Counter Workers	11.30	Sales Representatives, Technical/Scientific	47.50
Financial Managers	68.90	Secretaries, Exc. Legal/Medical/Executive	18.70
First-Line Supervisors of Office Workers	32.20	Security Guards	17.50
General and Operations Managers	66.40	Surgeons	n/a
Hairdressers/Cosmetologists	12.70	Teacher Assistants, Exc. Postsecondary*	10.40
Home Health and Personal Care Aides	11.10	Teachers, Secondary School, Exc. Sp. Ed.*	28.60
Janitors and Cleaners	12.70	Telemarketers	n/a
Landscaping/Groundskeeping Workers	16.70	Truck Drivers, Heavy/Tractor-Trailer	24.50
Lawyers	79.50	Truck Drivers, Light/Delivery Services	21.90
Maids and Housekeeping Cleaners	13.00	Waiters and Waitresses	9.30

Note: Wage data covers the Midland, TX Metropolitan Statistical Area; (*) Hourly wages were calculated from annual wage data based on a 40 hour work week; n/a not available.
Source: Bureau of Labor Statistics, Metro Area Occupational Employment & Wage Estimates, May 2020

Employment by Industry

Sector	MSA[1] Number of Employees	MSA[1] Percent of Total	U.S. Percent of Total
Construction, Mining, and Logging	26,500	28.0	5.5
Education and Health Services	6,900	7.3	16.3
Financial Activities	4,600	4.9	6.1
Government	10,600	11.2	15.2
Information	700	0.7	1.9
Leisure and Hospitality	9,600	10.2	9.0
Manufacturing	3,200	3.4	8.5
Other Services	3,500	3.7	3.8
Professional and Business Services	8,900	9.4	14.4
Retail Trade	10,000	10.6	10.9
Transportation, Warehousing, and Utilities	5,000	5.3	4.6
Wholesale Trade	5,000	5.3	3.9

Note: Figures are non-farm employment as of December 2020. Figures are not seasonally adjusted and include workers 16 years of age and older; (1) Figures cover the Midland, TX Metropolitan Statistical Area
Source: Bureau of Labor Statistics, Current Employment Statistics, Employment, Hours, and Earnings

Employment by Occupation

Occupation Classification	City (%)	MSA[1] (%)	U.S. (%)
Management, Business, Science, and Arts	35.9	35.6	38.5
Natural Resources, Construction, and Maintenance	14.1	14.7	8.9
Production, Transportation, and Material Moving	13.2	12.9	13.2
Sales and Office	21.5	22.0	21.6
Service	15.3	14.7	17.8

Note: Figures cover employed civilians 16 years of age and older; (1) Figures cover the Midland, TX Metropolitan Statistical Area
Source: U.S. Census Bureau, 2015-2019 American Community Survey 5-Year Estimates

Occupations with Greatest Projected Employment Growth: 2020 – 2022

Occupation[1]	2020 Employment	2022 Projected Employment	Numeric Employment Change	Percent Employment Change
Fast Food and Counter Workers	336,530	411,690	75,160	22.3
Waiters and Waitresses	165,570	206,920	41,350	25.0
Home Health and Personal Care Aides	303,520	344,240	40,720	13.4
Retail Salespersons	315,590	349,820	34,230	10.8
Heavy and Tractor-Trailer Truck Drivers	199,460	228,650	29,190	14.6
Laborers and Freight, Stock, and Material Movers, Hand	193,000	219,670	26,670	13.8
Cooks, Restaurant	88,540	114,250	25,710	29.0
Customer Service Representatives	276,080	295,790	19,710	7.1
General and Operations Managers	197,410	216,580	19,170	9.7
Office Clerks, General	310,080	327,500	17,420	5.6

Note: Projections cover Texas; (1) Sorted by numeric employment change
Source: www.projectionscentral.com, State Occupational Projections, 2020–2022 Short-Term Projections

Fastest-Growing Occupations: 2020 – 2022

Occupation[1]	2020 Employment	2022 Projected Employment	Numeric Employment Change	Percent Employment Change
Motion Picture Projectionists	150	300	150	100.0
Ushers, Lobby Attendants, and Ticket Takers	5,740	8,920	3,180	55.4
Locker Room, Coatroom, and Dressing Room Attendants	340	510	170	50.0
Athletes and Sports Competitors	270	400	130	48.1
Amusement and Recreation Attendants	13,130	19,400	6,270	47.8
Hotel, Motel, and Resort Desk Clerks	16,140	23,160	7,020	43.5
Sound Engineering Technicians	330	460	130	39.4
Gaming Dealers	220	300	80	36.4
Baggage Porters and Bellhops	1,250	1,670	420	33.6
Lodging Managers	3,300	4,330	1,030	31.2

Note: Projections cover Texas; (1) Sorted by percent employment change and excludes occupations with numeric employment change less than 50
Source: www.projectionscentral.com, State Occupational Projections, 2020–2022 Short-Term Projections

TAXES

State Corporate Income Tax Rates

State	Tax Rate (%)	Income Brackets ($)	Num. of Brackets	Financial Institution Tax Rate (%)[a]	Federal Income Tax Ded.
Texas	(w)	–	–	(w)	No

Note: Tax rates as of January 1, 2021; (a) Rates listed are the corporate income tax rate applied to financial institutions or excise taxes based on income. Some states have other taxes based upon the value of deposits or shares; (w) Texas imposes a Franchise Tax, otherwise known as margin tax, imposed on entities with more than $1,130,000 total revenues at rate of 0.75%, or 0.375% for entities primarily engaged in retail or wholesale trade, on lesser of 70% of total revenues or 100% of gross receipts after deductions for either compensation or cost of goods sold.
Source: Federation of Tax Administrators, State Corporate Income Tax Rates, January 1, 2021

State Individual Income Tax Rates

State	Tax Rate (%)	Income Brackets ($)	Personal Exemptions ($) Single	Married	Depend.	Standard Ded. ($) Single	Married
Texas				– No state income tax –			

Note: Tax rates as of January 1, 2021; Local- and county-level taxes are not included
Source: Federation of Tax Administrators, State Individual Income Tax Rates, January 1, 2021

Various State Sales and Excise Tax Rates

State	State Sales Tax (%)	Gasoline[1] (¢/gal.)	Cigarette[2] ($/pack)	Spirits[3] ($/gal.)	Wine[4] ($/gal.)	Beer[5] ($/gal.)	Recreational Marijuana (%)
Texas	6.25	20	1.41	2.4	0.2	0.2	Not legal

Note: All tax rates as of January 1, 2021; (1) The American Petroleum Institute has developed a methodology for determining the average tax rate on a gallon of fuel. Rates may include any of the following: excise taxes, environmental fees, storage tank fees, other fees or taxes, general sales tax, and local taxes; (2) The federal excise tax of $1.0066 per pack and local taxes are not included; (3) Rates are those applicable to off-premise sales of 40% alcohol by volume (a.b.v.) distilled spirits in 750ml containers. Local excise taxes are excluded; (4) Rates are those applicable to off-premise sales of 11% a.b.v. non-carbonated wine in 750ml containers; (5) Rates are those applicable to off-premise sales of 4.7% a.b.v. beer in 12 ounce containers.
Source: Tax Foundation, 2021 Facts & Figures: How Does Your State Compare?

State Business Tax Climate Index Rankings

State	Overall Rank	Corporate Tax Rank	Individual Income Tax Rank	Sales Tax Rank	Property Tax Rank	Unemployment Insurance Tax Rank
Texas	11	47	6	35	36	16

Note: The index is a measure of how each state's tax laws affect economic performance. The lower the rank, the more favorable a state's tax system is for business. States without a given tax are given a ranking of 1. The scores/rankings for the District of Columbia do not affect other states. The 2021 index represents the tax climate as of July 1, 2020.
Source: Tax Foundation, State Business Tax Climate Index 2021

TRANSPORTATION

Means of Transportation to Work

Area	Drove Alone	Car-pooled	Bus	Subway	Railroad	Bicycle	Walked	Other Means	Worked at Home
City	85.1	10.1	0.2	0.0	0.0	0.1	0.6	1.0	2.8
MSA[1]	84.8	9.7	0.2	0.0	0.0	0.1	1.1	0.8	3.3
U.S.	76.3	9.0	2.4	1.9	0.6	0.5	2.7	1.4	5.2

Note: Figures are percentages and cover workers 16 years of age and older; (1) Figures cover the Midland, TX Metropolitan Statistical Area
Source: U.S. Census Bureau, 2015-2019 American Community Survey 5-Year Estimates

Travel Time to Work

Area	Less Than 10 Minutes	10 to 19 Minutes	20 to 29 Minutes	30 to 44 Minutes	45 to 59 Minutes	60 to 89 Minutes	90 Minutes or More
City	16.1	49.1	17.2	11.1	2.6	2.0	1.9
MSA[1]	15.8	46.2	17.9	12.5	3.1	2.6	1.8
U.S.	12.2	28.4	20.8	20.8	8.3	6.4	2.9

Note: Note: Figures are percentages and include workers 16 years old and over; (1) Figures cover the Midland, TX Metropolitan Statistical Area
Source: U.S. Census Bureau, 2015-2019 American Community Survey 5-Year Estimates

Key Congestion Measures

Measure	1982	1992	2002	2012	2017
Annual Hours of Delay, Total (000)	n/a	n/a	n/a	n/a	2,950
Annual Hours of Delay, Per Auto Commuter	n/a	n/a	n/a	n/a	22
Annual Congestion Cost, Total (million $)	n/a	n/a	n/a	n/a	63
Annual Congestion Cost, Per Auto Commuter ($)	n/a	n/a	n/a	n/a	473

Note: n/a not available
Source: Texas A&M Transportation Institute, 2019 Urban Mobility Report

Freeway Travel Time Index

Measure	1982	1987	1992	1997	2002	2007	2012	2017
Urban Area Index[1]	n/a	n/a	n/a	n/a	n/a	n/a	n/a	1.09
Urban Area Rank[1,2]	n/a	n/a	n/a	n/a	n/a	n/a	n/a	n/a

Note: Freeway Travel Time Index—the ratio of travel time in the peak period to the travel time at free-flow conditions. For example, a value of 1.30 indicates a 20-minute free-flow trip takes 26 minutes in the peak (20 minutes x 1.30 = 26 minutes); (1) Covers the Midland TX urban area; (2) Rank is based on 101 larger urban areas (#1 = highest travel time index); n/a not available
Source: Texas A&M Transportation Institute, 2019 Urban Mobility Report

Public Transportation

Agency Name / Mode of Transportation	Vehicles Operated in Maximum Service[1]	Annual Unlinked Passenger Trips[2] (in thous.)	Annual Passenger Miles[3] (in thous.)
Midland-Odessa Urban Transit District			
Bus (directly operated)	12	268.7	n/a
Commuter Bus (directly operated)	2	15.2	n/a
Demand Response (directly operated)	12	44.6	n/a

Note: (1) Number of revenue vehicles operated by the given mode and type of service to meet the annual maximum service requirement. This is the revenue vehicle count during the peak season of the year; on the week and day that maximum service is provided. Vehicles operated in maximum service (VOMS) exclude atypical days and one-time special events; (2) Number of passengers who boarded public transportation vehicles. Passengers are counted each time they board a vehicle no matter how many vehicles they use to travel from their origin to their destination. (3) Sum of the distances ridden by all passengers during the entire fiscal year.
Source: Federal Transit Administration, National Transit Database, 2019

Air Transportation

Airport Name and Code / Type of Service	Passenger Airlines[1]	Passenger Enplanements	Freight Carriers[2]	Freight (lbs)
Midland International Airport (MAF)				
Domestic service (U.S. carriers - 2020)	11	319,538	5	2,682,938
International service (U.S. carriers - 2019)	0	0	0	0

Note: (1) Includes all U.S.-based major, minor and commuter airlines that carried at least one passenger during the year; (2) Includes all U.S.-based airlines and freight carriers that transported at least one pound of freight during the year.
Source: Bureau of Transportation Statistics, The Intermodal Transportation Database, Air Carriers: T-100 Domestic Market (U.S. Carriers), 2020; Bureau of Transportation Statistics, The Intermodal Transportation Database, Air Carriers: T-100 International Market (U.S. Carriers), 2019

BUSINESSES

Major Business Headquarters

Company Name	Industry	Rankings Fortune[1]	Forbes[2]
No companies listed	-	-	-

Note: (1) Companies that produce a 10-K are ranked 1 to 500 based on 2019 revenue; (2) All private companies with at least $2 billion in annual revenue through the end of their most current fiscal year are ranked 1 to 219; companies listed are headquartered in the city; dashes indicate no ranking
Source: Fortune, "Fortune 500," June/July 2020; Forbes, "America's Largest Private Companies," 2020

Living Environment

COST OF LIVING

Cost of Living Index

Composite Index	Groceries	Housing	Utilities	Transportation	Health Care	Misc. Goods/Services
96.7	90.3	84.5	99.5	97.7	98.9	107.6

Note: The Cost of Living Index measures regional differences in the cost of consumer goods and services, excluding taxes and non-consumer expenditures, for professional and managerial households in the top income quintile. It is based on more than 50,000 prices covering almost 60 different items for which prices are collected three times a year by chambers of commerce, economic development organizations or university applied economic centers in each participating urban area. The numbers shown should be read as a percentage above or below the national average of 100. For example, a value of 115.4 in the groceries column indicates that grocery prices are 15.4% higher than the national average. Small differences in the index numbers should not be interpreted as significant; Figures cover the Midland TX urban area.
Source: The Council for Community and Economic Research, Cost of Living Index, 2020

Grocery Prices

Area[1]	T-Bone Steak ($/pound)	Frying Chicken ($/pound)	Whole Milk ($/half gal.)	Eggs ($/dozen)	Orange Juice ($/64 oz.)	Coffee ($/11.5 oz.)
City[2]	10.05	1.16	1.51	1.47	3.37	4.14
Avg.	11.78	1.39	2.05	1.47	3.57	4.34
Min.	8.03	0.94	1.03	0.74	2.94	3.02
Max.	15.86	2.65	4.31	3.77	5.44	8.69

Note: (1) Values for the local area are compared with the average, minimum and maximum values for all 284 areas in the Cost of Living Index; (2) Figures cover the Midland TX urban area; **T-Bone Steak** (price per pound); **Frying Chicken** (price per pound, whole fryer); **Whole Milk** (half gallon carton); **Eggs** (price per dozen, Grade A, large); **Orange Juice** (64 oz. Tropicana or Florida Natural); **Coffee** (11.5 oz. can, vacuum-packed, Maxwell House, Hills Bros, or Folgers).
Source: The Council for Community and Economic Research, Cost of Living Index, 2020

Housing and Utility Costs

Area[1]	New Home Price ($)	Apartment Rent ($/month)	All Electric ($/month)	Part Electric ($/month)	Other Energy ($/month)	Telephone ($/month)
City[2]	301,432	1,078	-	125.29	39.71	184.40
Avg.	368,594	1,168	170.86	100.47	65.28	184.30
Min.	190,567	502	91.58	31.42	26.08	169.60
Max.	2,227,806	4,738	470.38	280.31	280.06	206.50

Note: (1) Values for the local area are compared with the average, minimum and maximum values for all 284 areas in the Cost of Living Index; (2) Figures cover the Midland TX urban area; **New Home Price** (2,400 sf living area, 8,000 sf lot, in urban area with full utilities); **Apartment Rent** (950 sf 2 bedroom/1.5 or 2 bath, unfurnished, excluding all utilities except water); **All Electric** (average monthly cost for an all-electric home); **Part Electric** (average monthly cost for a part-electric home); **Other Energy** (average monthly cost for natural gas, fuel oil, coal, wood, and any other forms of energy except electricity); **Telephone** (price includes the base monthly rate plus taxes and fees for three lines of mobile phone service).
Source: The Council for Community and Economic Research, Cost of Living Index, 2020

Health Care, Transportation, and Other Costs

Area[1]	Doctor ($/visit)	Dentist ($/visit)	Optometrist ($/visit)	Gasoline ($/gallon)	Beauty Salon ($/visit)	Men's Shirt ($)
City[2]	98.67	109.17	103.22	2.03	33.61	25.58
Avg.	115.44	99.32	108.10	2.21	39.27	31.37
Min.	36.68	59.00	51.36	1.71	19.00	11.00
Max.	219.00	153.10	250.97	3.46	82.05	58.33

Note: (1) Values for the local area are compared with the average, minimum and maximum values for all 284 areas in the Cost of Living Index; (2) Figures cover the Midland TX urban area; **Doctor** (general practitioners routine exam of an established patient); **Dentist** (adult teeth cleaning and periodic oral examination); **Optometrist** (full vision eye exam for established adult patient); **Gasoline** (one gallon regular unleaded, national brand, including all taxes, cash price at self-service pump if available); **Beauty Salon** (woman's shampoo, trim, and blow-dry); **Men's Shirt** (cotton/polyester dress shirt, pinpoint weave, long sleeves).
Source: The Council for Community and Economic Research, Cost of Living Index, 2020

HOUSING

Homeownership Rate

Area	2012 (%)	2013 (%)	2014 (%)	2015 (%)	2016 (%)	2017 (%)	2018 (%)	2019 (%)	2020 (%)
MSA[1]	n/a	n/a	n/a	n/a	n/a	n/a	n/a	n/a	n/a
U.S.	65.4	65.1	64.5	63.7	63.4	63.9	64.4	64.6	66.6

Note: (1) Figures cover the Midland, TX Metropolitan Statistical Area; n/a not available
Source: U.S. Census Bureau, Housing Vacancies and Homeownership Annual Statistics: 2012-2020

House Price Index (HPI)

Area	National Ranking[2]	Quarterly Change (%)	One-Year Change (%)	Five-Year Change (%)	Since 1991Q1 (%)
MSA[1]	n/a	n/a	n/a	n/a	n/a
U.S.[3]	—	3.81	10.77	38.99	205.12

Note: The HPI is a weighted repeat sales index. It measures average price changes in repeat sales or refinancings on the same properties. This information is obtained by reviewing repeat mortgage transactions on single-family properties whose mortgages have been purchased or securitized by Fannie Mae or Freddie Mac since January 1975; (1) Figures cover the , Metropolitan Statistical Area; (2) Rankings are based on annual percentage change for all metro areas containing at least 15,000 transactions over the last 10 years and ranges from 1 to 253; (3) figures based on a weighted average of Census Division estimates using a seasonally adjusted, purchase-only index; all figures are for the period ending December 31, 2020; n/a not available
Source: Federal Housing Finance Agency, Change in Metropolitan Area House Price Indexes, April 7, 2021

Median Single-Family Home Prices

Area	2018	2019	2020p	Percent Change 2019 to 2020
MSA[1]	n/a	n/a	n/a	n/a
U.S. Average	261.6	274.6	299.9	9.2

Note: Figures are median sales prices of existing single-family homes in thousands of dollars; (p) preliminary; n/a not available; (1) Figures cover the Midland, TX Metropolitan Statistical Area
Source: National Association of Realtors, Median Sales Price of Existing Single-Family Homes for Metropolitan Areas, 4th Quarter 2020

Qualifying Income Based on Median Sales Price of Existing Single-Family Homes

Area	With 5% Down ($)	With 10% Down ($)	With 20% Down ($)
MSA[1]	n/a	n/a	n/a
U.S. Average	59,266	56,147	49,908

Note: Figures are preliminary; Qualifying income is based on a mortgage rate of 2.81%. Monthly principal and interest payment is limited to 25% of income; n/a not available; (1) Figures cover the Midland, TX Metropolitan Statistical Area
Source: National Association of Realtors, Qualifying Income Based on Median Sales Price of Existing Single-Family Homes for Metropolitan Areas, 4th Quarter 2020

Home Value Distribution

Area	Under $50,000	$50,000 -$99,999	$100,000 -$149,999	$150,000 -$199,999	$200,000 -$299,999	$300,000 -$499,999	$500,000 -$999,999	$1,000,000 or more
City	4.9	9.0	12.7	17.4	28.4	18.3	7.8	1.4
MSA[1]	8.7	10.4	11.9	15.9	26.2	17.9	7.5	1.3
U.S.	6.9	12.0	13.3	14.0	19.6	19.3	11.4	3.4

Note: Figures are percentages and cover owner-occupied housing units; (1) Figures cover the Midland, TX Metropolitan Statistical Area
Source: U.S. Census Bureau, 2015-2019 American Community Survey 5-Year Estimates

Year Housing Structure Built

Area	2010 or Later	2000 -2009	1990 -1999	1980 -1989	1970 -1979	1960 -1969	1950 -1959	1940 -1949	Before 1940	Median Year
City	12.9	8.5	13.8	18.4	11.7	11.6	18.5	3.0	1.5	1982
MSA[1]	14.0	11.4	14.5	18.0	11.2	10.5	15.9	2.8	1.7	1984
U.S.	5.2	14.0	13.9	13.4	15.2	10.6	10.3	4.9	12.6	1978

Note: Figures are percentages except for Median Year; Note: (1) Figures cover the Midland, TX Metropolitan Statistical Area
Source: U.S. Census Bureau, 2015-2019 American Community Survey 5-Year Estimates

Gross Monthly Rent

Area	Under $500	$500 -$999	$1,000 -$1,499	$1,500 -$1,999	$2,000 -$2,499	$2,500 -$2,999	$3,000 and up	Median ($)
City	1.7	26.0	41.3	19.5	7.5	2.9	1.2	1,262
MSA[1]	2.0	25.1	41.0	20.1	7.5	3.2	1.1	1,269
U.S.	9.4	36.2	30.0	14.0	5.6	2.4	2.4	1,062

Note: Figures are percentages except for Median; Gross rent is the contract rent plus the estimated average monthly cost of utilities (electricity, gas, and water and sewer) and fuels (oil, coal, kerosene, wood, etc.) if these are paid by the renter (or paid for the renter by someone else); (1) Figures cover the Midland, TX Metropolitan Statistical Area
Source: U.S. Census Bureau, 2015-2019 American Community Survey 5-Year Estimates

HEALTH

Health Risk Factors

Category	MSA[1] (%)	U.S. (%)
Adults aged 18–64 who have any kind of health care coverage	n/a	87.3
Adults who reported being in good or better health	n/a	82.4
Adults who have been told they have high blood cholesterol	n/a	33.0
Adults who have been told they have high blood pressure	n/a	32.3
Adults who are current smokers	n/a	17.1
Adults who currently use E-cigarettes	n/a	4.6
Adults who currently use chewing tobacco, snuff, or snus	n/a	4.0
Adults who are heavy drinkers[2]	n/a	6.3
Adults who are binge drinkers[3]	n/a	17.4
Adults who are overweight (BMI 25.0 - 29.9)	n/a	35.3
Adults who are obese (BMI 30.0 - 99.8)	n/a	31.3
Adults who participated in any physical activities in the past month	n/a	74.4
Adults who always or nearly always wears a seat belt	n/a	94.3

Note: n/a not available; (1) Figures cover the Midland, TX Metropolitan Statistical Area; (2) Heavy drinkers are classified as adult men having more than 14 drinks per week and adult women having more than 7 drinks per week; (3) Binge drinkers are classified as males having five or more drinks on one occasion or females having four or more drinks on one occasion
Source: Centers for Disease Control and Prevention, Behaviorial Risk Factor Surveillance System, SMART: Selected Metropolitan Area Risk Trends, 2017

Acute and Chronic Health Conditions

Category	MSA[1] (%)	U.S. (%)
Adults who have ever been told they had a heart attack	n/a	4.2
Adults who have ever been told they have angina or coronary heart disease	n/a	3.9
Adults who have ever been told they had a stroke	n/a	3.0
Adults who have ever been told they have asthma	n/a	14.2
Adults who have ever been told they have arthritis	n/a	24.9
Adults who have ever been told they have diabetes[2]	n/a	10.5
Adults who have ever been told they had skin cancer	n/a	6.2
Adults who have ever been told they had any other types of cancer	n/a	7.1
Adults who have ever been told they have COPD	n/a	6.5
Adults who have ever been told they have kidney disease	n/a	3.0
Adults who have ever been told they have a form of depression	n/a	20.5

Note: n/a not available; (1) Figures cover the Midland, TX Metropolitan Statistical Area; (2) Figures do not include pregnancy-related, borderline, or pre-diabetes
Source: Centers for Disease Control and Prevention, Behaviorial Risk Factor Surveillance System, SMART: Selected Metropolitan Area Risk Trends, 2017

Health Screening and Vaccination Rates

Category	MSA[1] (%)	U.S. (%)
Adults aged 65+ who have had flu shot within the past year	n/a	60.7
Adults aged 65+ who have ever had a pneumonia vaccination	n/a	75.4
Adults who have ever been tested for HIV	n/a	36.1
Adults who have ever had the shingles or zoster vaccine?	n/a	28.9
Adults who have had their blood cholesterol checked within the last five years	n/a	85.9

Note: n/a not available; (1) Figures cover the Midland, TX Metropolitan Statistical Area.
Source: Centers for Disease Control and Prevention, Behaviorial Risk Factor Surveillance System, SMART: Selected Metropolitan Area Risk Trends, 2017

Disability Status

Category	MSA[1] (%)	U.S. (%)
Adults who reported being deaf	n/a	6.7
Are you blind or have serious difficulty seeing, even when wearing glasses?	n/a	4.5
Are you limited in any way in any of your usual activities due of arthritis?	n/a	12.9
Do you have difficulty doing errands alone?	n/a	6.8
Do you have difficulty dressing or bathing?	n/a	3.6
Do you have serious difficulty concentrating/remembering/making decisions?	n/a	10.7
Do you have serious difficulty walking or climbing stairs?	n/a	13.6

Note: n/a not available; (1) Figures cover the Midland, TX Metropolitan Statistical Area.
Source: Centers for Disease Control and Prevention, Behaviorial Risk Factor Surveillance System, SMART: Selected Metropolitan Area Risk Trends, 2017

Mortality Rates for the Top 10 Causes of Death in the U.S.

ICD-10[a] Sub-Chapter	ICD-10[a] Code	County[2]	U.S.
Malignant neoplasms	C00-C97	146.3	149.2
Ischaemic heart diseases	I20-I25	113.7	90.5
Other forms of heart disease	I30-I51	48.5	52.2
Chronic lower respiratory diseases	J40-J47	53.3	39.6
Other degenerative diseases of the nervous system	G30-G31	63.1	37.6
Cerebrovascular diseases	I60-I69	36.7	37.2
Other external causes of accidental injury	W00-X59	16.5	36.1
Organic, including symptomatic, mental disorders	F01-F09	18.3	29.4
Hypertensive diseases	I10-I15	12.5	24.1
Diabetes mellitus	E10-E14	14.2	21.5

Age-Adjusted Mortality Rate[1] per 100,000 population

Note: (a) ICD-10 = International Classification of Diseases 10th Revision; (1) Mortality rates are a three-year average covering 2017-2019; (2) Figures cover Midland County.
Source: Centers for Disease Control and Prevention, National Center for Health Statistics. Underlying Cause of Death 1999-2019 on CDC WONDER Online Database

Mortality Rates for Selected Causes of Death

ICD-10[a] Sub-Chapter	ICD-10[a] Code	County[2]	U.S.
Assault	X85-Y09	4.3	6.0
Diseases of the liver	K70-K76	18.0	14.4
Human immunodeficiency virus (HIV) disease	B20-B24	Suppressed	1.5
Influenza and pneumonia	J09-J18	19.8	13.8
Intentional self-harm	X60-X84	17.8	14.1
Malnutrition	E40-E46	5.1	2.3
Obesity and other hyperalimentation	E65-E68	Unreliable	2.1
Renal failure	N17-N19	11.2	12.6
Transport accidents	V01-V99	23.6	12.3
Viral hepatitis	B15-B19	Suppressed	1.2

Age-Adjusted Mortality Rate[1] per 100,000 population

Note: (a) ICD-10 = International Classification of Diseases 10th Revision; (1) Mortality rates are a three-year average covering 2017-2019; (2) Figures cover Midland County; Data are suppressed when the data meet the criteria for confidentiality constraints; Mortality rates are flagged as unreliable when the rate would be calculated with a numerator of 20 or less.
Source: Centers for Disease Control and Prevention, National Center for Health Statistics. Underlying Cause of Death 1999-2019 on CDC WONDER Online Database

Health Insurance Coverage

Area	With Health Insurance	With Private Health Insurance	With Public Health Insurance	Without Health Insurance	Population Under Age 19 Without Health Insurance
City	83.3	71.1	19.7	16.7	14.7
MSA[1]	83.6	71.1	20.2	16.4	14.0
U.S.	91.2	67.9	35.1	8.8	5.1

Note: Figures are percentages that cover the civilian noninstitutionalized population; (1) Figures cover the Midland, TX Metropolitan Statistical Area
Source: U.S. Census Bureau, 2015-2019 American Community Survey 5-Year Estimates

Number of Medical Professionals

Area	MDs[3]	DOs[3,4]	Dentists	Podiatrists	Chiropractors	Optometrists
County[1] (number)	259	16	97	4	24	21
County[1] (rate[2])	150.1	9.3	54.9	2.3	13.6	11.9
U.S. (rate[2])	282.9	22.7	71.2	6.2	28.1	16.9

48329
Note: Data as of 2019 unless noted; (1) Data covers Midland County; (2) Rate per 100,000 population; (3) Data as of 2018 and includes all active, non-federal physicians; (4) Doctor of Osteopathic Medicine
Source: U.S. Department of Health and Human Services, Health Resources and Services Administration, Bureau of Health Professions, Area Resource File (ARF) 2019-2020

EDUCATION

Public School District Statistics

District Name	Schls	Pupils	Pupil/Teacher Ratio	Minority Pupils[1] (%)	Free Lunch Eligible[2] (%)	IEP[3] (%)
Greenwood ISD	3	2,844	16.6	51.7	33.4	7.0
Midland ISD	39	26,183	16.7	75.2	40.3	7.2

Note: Table includes school districts with 2,000 or more students; (1) Percentage of students that are not non-Hispanic white; (2) Percentage of students that are eligible for the free lunch program; (3) Percentage of students that have an Individualized Education Program.
Source: U.S. Department of Education, National Center for Education Statistics, Common Core of Data, Local Education Agency (School District) Universe Survey: School Year 2018-2019; U.S. Department of Education, National Center for Education Statistics, Common Core of Data, Public Elementary/Secondary School Universe Survey: School Year 2018-2019

Highest Level of Education

Area	Less than H.S.	H.S. Diploma	Some College, No Deg.	Associate Degree	Bachelor's Degree	Master's Degree	Prof. School Degree	Doctorate Degree
City	14.9	25.2	23.2	7.7	20.7	5.9	1.7	0.7
MSA[1]	15.7	25.9	23.5	7.8	19.3	5.8	1.4	0.6
U.S.	12.0	27.0	20.4	8.5	19.8	8.8	2.1	1.4

Note: Figures cover persons age 25 and over; (1) Figures cover the Midland, TX Metropolitan Statistical Area
Source: U.S. Census Bureau, 2015-2019 American Community Survey 5-Year Estimates

Educational Attainment by Race

Area	High School Graduate or Higher (%) Total	White	Black	Asian	Hisp.[2]	Bachelor's Degree or Higher (%) Total	White	Black	Asian	Hisp.[2]
City	85.1	85.8	85.6	81.7	71.3	28.9	30.3	18.1	51.7	11.9
MSA[1]	84.3	84.9	85.7	83.4	69.6	27.1	28.3	18.3	54.5	10.6
U.S.	88.0	89.9	86.0	87.1	68.7	32.1	33.5	21.6	54.3	16.4

Note: Figures shown cover persons 25 years old and over; (1) Figures cover the Midland, TX Metropolitan Statistical Area; (2) People of Hispanic origin can be of any race
Source: U.S. Census Bureau, 2015-2019 American Community Survey 5-Year Estimates

School Enrollment by Grade and Control

Area	Preschool (%) Public	Private	Kindergarten (%) Public	Private	Grades 1 - 4 (%) Public	Private	Grades 5 - 8 (%) Public	Private	Grades 9 - 12 (%) Public	Private
City	64.4	35.6	89.1	10.9	86.0	14.0	88.3	11.7	89.9	10.1
MSA[1]	64.3	35.7	89.1	10.9	86.9	13.1	90.0	10.0	90.3	9.7
U.S.	59.1	40.9	87.6	12.4	89.5	10.5	89.4	10.6	90.1	9.9

Note: Figures shown cover persons 3 years old and over; (1) Figures cover the Midland, TX Metropolitan Statistical Area
Source: U.S. Census Bureau, 2015-2019 American Community Survey 5-Year Estimates

Higher Education

Four-Year Colleges Public	Private Non-profit	Private For-profit	Two-Year Colleges Public	Private Non-profit	Private For-profit	Medical Schools[1]	Law Schools[2]	Voc/Tech[3]
1	0	0	0	0	0	0	0	0

Note: Figures cover institutions located within the city limits and include main campuses only; (1) includes schools accredited by the Liaison Committee on Medical Education and the American Osteopathic Association's Commission on Osteopathic College Accreditation; (2) includes ABA-accredited schools, schools with provisional ABA accreditation, and state accredited schools; (3) includes all schools with programs that are less than 2 years.
Source: National Center for Education Statistics, Integrated Postsecondary Education System (IPEDS), 2019-20; Wikipedia, List of Medical Schools in the United States, accessed April 2, 2021; Wikipedia, List of Law Schools in the United States, accessed April 2, 2021

EMPLOYERS

Major Employers

Company Name	Industry
Albertsons Companies	Grocery stores
Bobby Cox Companies	Retail, restaurants
City of Odessa	Municipal government
Cudd Energy	Oil & gas
Dixie Electric	Electric
Ector County	Government
Ector County ISD	Public education
Family Dollar	Distribution
Halliburton Services	Oil & gas
HEB	Grocery stores
Holloman Construction	Oil field construction
Investment Corp. of America	Financial services
Lithia Motors	Automotive
Medical Center Hospital	County hospital
Nurses Unlimited	Medical
Odessa College	Education
Odessa Regional Medical Center	Medical
REXtac	Manufacturer
Saulsbury Companies	Electric & construction
Sewell Family of Dealerships	Automotive
Southwest Convenience Stores	Retail, service
Texas Tech University Health Sci Ctr	Education/medical
The University of Texas Permian Basin	Education
Wal-Mart Stores	Retail
Weatherford	Oil & gas

Note: Companies shown are located within the Midland, TX Metropolitan Statistical Area.
Source: Hoovers.com; Wikipedia

PUBLIC SAFETY

Crime Rate

Area	All Crimes	Violent Crimes				Property Crimes		
		Murder	Rape[3]	Robbery	Aggrav. Assault	Burglary	Larceny -Theft	Motor Vehicle Theft
City	2,261.0	3.6	42.8	42.1	199.2	269.9	1,504.9	198.5
Suburbs[1]	2,400.0	11.5	25.9	31.7	368.8	299.6	1,293.6	368.8
Metro[2]	2,288.6	5.1	39.5	40.1	232.9	275.8	1,463.0	232.3
U.S.	2,593.1	5.0	44.0	86.1	248.2	378.0	1,601.6	230.2

Note: Figures are crimes per 100,000 population; (1) All areas within the metro area that are located outside the city limits; (2) Figures cover the Midland, TX Metropolitan Statistical Area; (3) All figures shown were reported using the revised Uniform Crime Reporting (UCR) definition of rape.
Source: FBI Uniform Crime Reports, 2018 (data for 2019 was not available)

Hate Crimes

Area	Number of Quarters Reported	Number of Incidents per Bias Motivation					
		Race/Ethnicity/ Ancestry	Religion	Sexual Orientation	Disability	Gender	Gender Identity
City	2	0	0	0	0	0	0
U.S.	4	3,963	1,521	1,195	157	69	198

Source: Federal Bureau of Investigation, Hate Crime Statistics 2019

Identity Theft Consumer Reports

Area	Reports	Reports per 100,000 Population	Rank[2]
MSA[1]	399	219	186
U.S.	1,387,615	423	-

Note: (1) Figures cover the Midland, TX Metropolitan Statistical Area; (2) Rank ranges from 1 to 391 where 1 indicates greatest number of identity theft reports per 100,000 population
Source: Federal Trade Commission, Consumer Sentinel Network Data Book 2020

Fraud and Other Consumer Reports

Area	Reports	Reports per 100,000 Population	Rank[2]
MSA[1]	1,089	596	287
U.S.	3,385,133	1,031	-

Note: (1) Figures cover the Midland, TX Metropolitan Statistical Area; (2) Rank ranges from 1 to 391 where 1 indicates greatest number of fraud and other consumer reports per 100,000 population
Source: Federal Trade Commission, Consumer Sentinel Network Data Book 2020

POLITICS

2020 Presidential Election Results

Area	Biden	Trump	Jorgensen	Hawkins	Other
Midland County	20.9	77.3	1.3	0.2	0.2
U.S.	51.3	46.8	1.2	0.3	0.5

Note: Results are percentages and may not add to 100% due to rounding
Source: Dave Leip's Atlas of U.S. Presidential Elections

SPORTS

Professional Sports Teams

Team Name	League	Year Established
No teams are located in the metro area		

Source: Wikipedia, Major Professional Sports Teams of the United States and Canada, April 6, 2021

CLIMATE

Average and Extreme Temperatures

Temperature	Jan	Feb	Mar	Apr	May	Jun	Jul	Aug	Sep	Oct	Nov	Dec	Yr.
Extreme High (°F)	84	90	95	101	108	116	112	107	107	100	89	85	116
Average High (°F)	57	62	70	79	86	93	94	93	86	78	66	59	77
Average Temp. (°F)	43	48	55	64	73	80	82	81	74	65	53	46	64
Average Low (°F)	30	34	40	49	59	67	69	68	62	51	39	32	50
Extreme Low (°F)	-8	-11	9	20	34	47	53	54	36	24	13	-1	-11

Note: Figures cover the years 1948-1995
Source: National Climatic Data Center, International Station Meteorological Climate Summary, 9/96

Average Precipitation/Snowfall/Humidity

Precip./Humidity	Jan	Feb	Mar	Apr	May	Jun	Jul	Aug	Sep	Oct	Nov	Dec	Yr.
Avg. Precip. (in.)	0.6	0.6	0.5	0.8	2.1	1.6	1.9	1.7	2.1	1.6	0.6	0.5	14.6
Avg. Snowfall (in.)	2	1	Tr	Tr	0	0	0	0	0	Tr	Tr	1	4
Avg. Rel. Hum. 6am (%)	72	72	65	67	75	76	73	74	79	78	74	71	73
Avg. Rel. Hum. 3pm (%)	38	35	27	27	31	32	34	34	40	37	35	37	34

Note: Figures cover the years 1948-1995; Tr = Trace amounts (<0.05 in. of rain; <0.5 in. of snow)
Source: National Climatic Data Center, International Station Meteorological Climate Summary, 9/96

Weather Conditions

Temperature			Daytime Sky			Precipitation		
10°F & below	32°F & below	90°F & above	Clear	Partly cloudy	Cloudy	0.01 inch or more precip.	0.1 inch or more snow/ice	Thunder-storms
1	62	102	144	138	83	52	3	38

Note: Figures are average number of days per year and cover the years 1948-1995
Source: National Climatic Data Center, International Station Meteorological Climate Summary, 9/96

HAZARDOUS WASTE

Superfund Sites

The Midland, TX metro area is home to two sites on the EPA's Superfund National Priorities List: **Midessa Ground Water Plume** (final); **West County Road 112 Ground Water** (final). There are a total of 1,375 Superfund sites with a status of proposed or final on the list in the U.S. *U.S. Environmental Protection Agency, National Priorities List, April 7, 2021*

AIR QUALITY

Air Quality Trends: Ozone

	1990	1995	2000	2005	2010	2015	2016	2017	2018	2019
MSA[1]	n/a	n/a	n/a	n/a	n/a	n/a	n/a	n/a	n/a	n/a
U.S.	0.088	0.089	0.082	0.080	0.073	0.068	0.069	0.068	0.069	0.065

Note: (1) Data covers the Midland, TX Metropolitan Statistical Area; n/a not available. The values shown are the composite ozone concentration averages among trend sites based on the highest fourth daily maximum 8-hour concentration in parts per million. These trends are based on sites having an adequate record of monitoring data during the trend period. Data from exceptional events are included.
Source: U.S. Environmental Protection Agency, Air Quality Monitoring Information, "Air Quality Trends by City, 1990-2019"

Air Quality Index

Area	Percent of Days when Air Quality was...[2]					AQI Statistics[2]	
	Good	Moderate	Unhealthy for Sensitive Groups	Unhealthy	Very Unhealthy	Maximum	Median
MSA[1]	n/a	n/a	n/a	n/a	n/a	n/a	n/a

Note: (1) Data covers the Midland, TX Metropolitan Statistical Area; (2) Based on days with AQI data in 2019. Air Quality Index (AQI) is an index for reporting daily air quality. EPA calculates the AQI for five major air pollutants regulated by the Clean Air Act: ground-level ozone, particle pollution (aka particulate matter), carbon monoxide, sulfur dioxide, and nitrogen dioxide. The AQI runs from 0 to 500. The higher the AQI value, the greater the level of air pollution and the greater the health concern. There are six AQI categories: "Good" AQI is between 0 and 50. Air quality is considered satisfactory; "Moderate" AQI is between 51 and 100. Air quality is acceptable; "Unhealthy for Sensitive Groups" When AQI values are between 101 and 150, members of sensitive groups may experience health effects; "Unhealthy" When AQI values are between 151 and 200 everyone may begin to experience health effects; "Very Unhealthy" AQI values between 201 and 300 trigger a health alert; "Hazardous" AQI values over 300 trigger warnings of emergency conditions (not shown).
Source: U.S. Environmental Protection Agency, Air Quality Index Report, 2019

Air Quality Index Pollutants

Area	Percent of Days when AQI Pollutant was...[2]					
	Carbon Monoxide	Nitrogen Dioxide	Ozone	Sulfur Dioxide	Particulate Matter 2.5	Particulate Matter 10
MSA[1]	n/a	n/a	n/a	n/a	n/a	n/a

Note: (1) Data covers the Midland, TX Metropolitan Statistical Area; (2) Based on days with AQI data in 2019. The Air Quality Index (AQI) is an index for reporting daily air quality. EPA calculates the AQI for five major air pollutants regulated by the Clean Air Act: ground-level ozone, particle pollution (also known as particulate matter), carbon monoxide, sulfur dioxide, and nitrogen dioxide. The AQI runs from 0 to 500. The higher the AQI value, the greater the level of air pollution and the greater the health concern.
Source: U.S. Environmental Protection Agency, Air Quality Index Report, 2019

Maximum Air Pollutant Concentrations: Particulate Matter, Ozone, CO and Lead

	Particulate Matter 10 (ug/m^3)	Particulate Matter 2.5 Wtd AM (ug/m^3)	Particulate Matter 2.5 24-Hr (ug/m^3)	Ozone (ppm)	Carbon Monoxide (ppm)	Lead (ug/m^3)
MSA[1] Level	n/a	n/a	n/a	n/a	n/a	n/a
NAAQS[2]	150	15	35	0.075	9	0.15
Met NAAQS[2]	Yes	Yes	Yes	Yes	Yes	Yes

Note: (1) Data covers the Midland, TX Metropolitan Statistical Area; Data from exceptional events are included; (2) National Ambient Air Quality Standards; ppm = parts per million; ug/m^3 = micrograms per cubic meter; n/a not available.
Concentrations: Particulate Matter 10 (coarse particulate)—highest second maximum 24-hour concentration; Particulate Matter 2.5 Wtd AM (fine particulate)—highest weighted annual mean concentration; Particulate Matter 2.5 24-Hour (fine particulate)—highest 98th percentile 24-hour concentration; Ozone—highest fourth daily maximum 8-hour concentration; Carbon Monoxide—highest second maximum non-overlapping 8-hour concentration; Lead—maximum running 3-month average
Source: U.S. Environmental Protection Agency, Air Quality Monitoring Information, "Air Quality Statistics by City, 2019"

Maximum Air Pollutant Concentrations: Nitrogen Dioxide and Sulfur Dioxide

	Nitrogen Dioxide AM (ppb)	Nitrogen Dioxide 1-Hr (ppb)	Sulfur Dioxide AM (ppb)	Sulfur Dioxide 1-Hr (ppb)	Sulfur Dioxide 24-Hr (ppb)
MSA[1] Level	n/a	n/a	n/a	n/a	n/a
NAAQS[2]	53	100	30	75	140
Met NAAQS[2]	Yes	Yes	Yes	Yes	Yes

Note: (1) Data covers the Midland, TX Metropolitan Statistical Area; Data from exceptional events are included; (2) National Ambient Air Quality Standards; ppm = parts per million; ug/m^3 = micrograms per cubic meter; n/a not available.
Concentrations: Nitrogen Dioxide AM—highest arithmetic mean concentration; Nitrogen Dioxide 1-Hr—highest 98th percentile 1-hour daily maximum concentration; Sulfur Dioxide AM—highest annual mean concentration; Sulfur Dioxide 1-Hr—highest 99th percentile 1-hour daily maximum concentration; Sulfur Dioxide 24-Hr—highest second maximum 24-hour concentration
Source: U.S. Environmental Protection Agency, Air Quality Monitoring Information, "Air Quality Statistics by City, 2019"

Nashville, Tennessee

Background

Nashville, the capital of Tennessee, was founded on Christmas Day in 1779 by James Robertson and John Donelson, and considered the country music capital of the world. It is home to the Grand Ole Opry—the longest-running radio show in the country—with millions of devoted listeners. It is no wonder, given how profoundly this industry has touched people, names like Dolly, Chet, Loretta, Hank, and Johnny are more familiar than the city's true native sons—Andrew Jackson, James Polk, and Sam Houston, that is.

Nashville is home to Music Row, an area just to the southwest of downtown with hundreds of businesses related to the country music, gospel music, and contemporary Christian music industries. The USA Network's *Nashville Star*, a country music singing competition, is held in the Acuff Theatre. The magnitude of Nashville's recording industry is impressive, but other industries important to the city include health care management, automobile production, and printing and publishing.

The city has is consistently ranked a high job-growth region, and has been called "Nowville" and "It City." Nashville's first female mayor, Megan Barry, performed the city's first same-sex wedding in Nashville. The city recently received accolades for its economy and robust housing market.

In 2018, Amazon announced plans to build an operations center in the city. In 2019, Alliance Bernstein built new offices in Nashville with plans to move its HQ from NYC to Nashville by 2024.

Nashville is a devoted patron of education. The Davidson Academy, forerunner of the George Peabody College for Teachers, was founded in Nashville, as were Vanderbilt and Fisk universities, the latter being the first private black university in the United States. Vanderbilt University and Medical Center is the region's largest non-governmental employer.

Nashville citizens take pride in their museums, including the Adventure Science Center, with its Sudekum Planetarium; the Aaron Douglas Gallery at Fisk University, which features a remarkable collection of African-American art; and the Carl Van Vechten Gallery, also at Fisk University, home to works by Alfred Stieglitz, Picasso, Cezanne, and Georgia O'Keefe. The Cheekwood Botanical Garden and Museum of Art includes 55 acres of gardens and contemporary art galleries.

The city's majestic mansions and plantations testify to the nineteenth-century splendor for which the South is famous. The Belle Meade Plantation is an 1853 Greek Revival mansion crowning a 5,400-acre thoroughbred stud farm and nursery. The Belmont Mansion, built in 1850 by Adelicia Acklen, one of the wealthiest women in America, is constructed in the style of an Italian villa and was originally intended to be the summer home of the Acklens. Travelers' Rest Plantation still served as a haven for weary travelers, and is Nashville's oldest plantation home open to the public. Carnton Plantation was the site of the Civil War's Battle of Franklin, and The Hermitage was the home of Andrew Jackson, the seventh president of the United States. Tennessee's historic State Capitol Building, completed in 1859, has had much of its interior restored to its nineteenth-century appearance.

The Nashville area comprises many urban, suburban, rural, and historic districts, which differ immensely from each other. Many restaurants, clubs, and shops are on the west side of the Cumberland River, while the east side encompasses fine neighborhoods, interesting homes, and upscale shopping. A new club, CabaRay, opened in 2018, as a performance venue for American singer/songwriter Ray Stevens.

In 2020, Amtrak announced that it was considering connecting serviced between Atlanta and Nashville.

Outdoor activities include camping, fishing, hiking, and biking at the many scenic and accessible lakes in the region. Sports action in the city include the Tennessee Titans winning their fourth division championship in 2020, and the Nashville Super Speedway hosting their first NASCAR Cup Series in 2021.

Located on the Cumberland River in central Tennessee, Nashville's average relative humidity is moderate, as is its weather, with great temperature extremes a rarity. The city is not in the common path of storms that cross the country, but a tornado killed 25 in 2020.

Rankings

General Rankings

- *US News & World Report* conducted a survey of more than 3,000 people and analyzed the 150 largest metropolitan areas to determine what matters most when selecting the next place to live. Nashville ranked #17 out of the top 25 as having the best combination of desirable factors. Criteria: cost of living; quality of life; net migration; job market; desirability; and other factors. *realestate.usnews.com, "The 25 Best Places to Live in the U.S. in 2020-21," October 13, 2020*

- The Nashville metro area was identified as one of America's fastest-growing areas in terms of population and business growth by *MagnifyMoney*. The area ranked #5 out of 35. The 100 most populous metro areas in the U.S. were evaluated on their change from 2011-2016 in the following categories: people and housing; workforce and employment opportunities; growing industry. *www.businessinsider.com, "The 35 Cities in the US with the Biggest Influx of People, the Most Work Opportunities, and the Hottest Business Growth," August 12, 2018*

- The Nashville metro area was identified as one of America's fastest-growing areas in terms of population and economy by *Forbes*. The area ranked #7 out of 25. The 100 most populous metro areas in the U.S. were evaluated on the following criteria: estimated population growth; employment; economic output; wages; home values. *Forbes, "America's Fastest-Growing Cities 2018," February 28, 2018*

- In its eighth annual survey, *Travel + Leisure* readers nominated their favorite small cities and towns in America—those with 100,000 or fewer residents—voting on numerous attractive features in categories including culture, food and drink, quality of life, style, and people. After 50,000 votes, Nashville was ranked #8 among the proposed favorites. *www.travelandleisure.com, "America's Favorite Cities," October 20, 2017*

- Nashville appeared on *Travel + Leisure's* list of the 15 best cities in the United States. The city was ranked #11. Criteria: sights/landmarks; culture; food; friendliness; shopping; and overall value. *Travel + Leisure, "The World's Best Awards 2020" July 8, 2020*

- For its 33rd annual "Readers' Choice Awards" survey, *Condé Nast Traveler* ranked its readers' favorite cities in the U.S. These places brought feelings of comfort in a time of limited travel. The list was broken into large cities and cities under 250,000. Nashville ranked #8 in the big city category. *Condé Nast Traveler, Readers' Choice Awards 2020, "Best Big Cities in the U.S." October 6, 2020*

Business/Finance Rankings

- The Brookings Institution ranked the nation's largest cities based on income inequality. Nashville was ranked #83 (#1 = greatest inequality). Criteria: the "95/20 ratio," a figure representing the income at which a household earns more than 95 percent of all other households, divided by the income at which a household earns more than only 20 percent of all other households. *Brookings Institution, "Household Income Inequality, Largest Cities of 97 Large U.S. Metro Areas, 2014-2016," February 5, 2018*

- The Brookings Institution ranked the 100 largest metro areas in the U.S. based on income inequality. Nashville was ranked #78 (#1 = greatest inequality). Criteria: the "95/20 ratio," a figure representing the income at which a household earns more than 95 percent of all other households, divided by the income at which a household earns more than only 20 percent of all other households. *Brookings Institution, "Household Income Inequality, 100 Largest U.S. Metro Areas, 2014-2016," February 5, 2018*

- *Forbes* ranked the 100 largest metro areas in the U.S. in terms of the "Best Cities for Young Professionals." The Nashville metro area ranked #17 out of 25. Criteria: median rent of a two-bedroom apartment; job growth and unemployment rate; median salary of college graduates with 5 or less years of work experience; networking opportunities; social outlook; percentage of population 25 years of age and older with college degrees. *Forbes.com, "America's 25 Best Cities for Young Professionals in 2017," May 22, 2017*

- Payscale.com ranked the 32 largest metro areas in terms of wage growth. The Nashville metro area ranked #28. Criteria: private-sector and education professional wage growth between the 4th quarter of 2019 and the 4th quarter of 2020. *PayScale, "Wage Trends by Metro Area-4th Quarter," January 11, 2021*

- Nashville was identified as one of America's most frugal metro areas by *Coupons.com*. The city ranked #9 out of 25. Criteria: digital coupon usage. *Coupons.com, "America's Most Frugal Cities of 2017," March 22, 2018*

- The Nashville metro area appeared on the Milken Institute "2021 Best Performing Cities" list. Rank: #8 out of 200 large metro areas (population over 250,000). Criteria: job growth; wage and salary growth; high-tech output growth; housing affordability; household broadband access. *Milken Institute, "Best-Performing Cities 2021," February 16, 2021*

- *Forbes* ranked the 200 most populous metro areas to determine the nation's "Best Places for Business and Careers." The Nashville metro area was ranked #15. Criteria: costs (business and living); job growth (past and projected); income growth; quality of life; educational attainment (college and high school); projected economic growth; cultural and leisure opportunities; workplace tolerance laws; net migration patterns. *Forbes, "The Best Places for Business and Careers 2019: Seattle Still On Top," October 30, 2019*

Children/Family Rankings

- Nashville was selected as one of the most playful cities in the U.S. by KaBOOM! The organization's Playful City USA initiative honors cities and towns across the nation that have made their communities more playable. Criteria: pledging to integrate play as a solution to challenges in their communities; making it easy for children to get active and balanced play; creating more family-friendly and innovative communities as a result. *KaBOOM! National Campaign for Play, "2017 Playful City USA Communities"*

Dating/Romance Rankings

- Nashville was selected as one of America's best cities for singles by the readers of *Travel + Leisure* in their annual "America's Favorite Cities" survey. Criteria included good-looking locals, cool shopping, an active bar scene and hipster-magnet coffee bars. *Travel + Leisure, "Best Cities in America for Singles," July 21, 2017*

Education Rankings

- Personal finance website *WalletHub* analyzed the 150 largest U.S. metropolitan statistical areas to determine where the most educated Americans are putting their degrees to work. Criteria: education levels; percentage of workers with degrees; education quality and attainment gap; public school quality rankings; quality and enrollment of each metro area's universities. Nashville was ranked #57 (#1 = most educated city). *www.WalletHub.com, "Most and Least Educated Cities in America," July 20, 2020*

- Nashville was selected as one of America's most literate cities. The city ranked #28 out of the 84 largest U.S. cities. Criteria: number of booksellers; library resources; Internet resources; educational attainment; periodical publishing resources; newspaper circulation. *Central Connecticut State University, "America's Most Literate Cities, 2018," February 2019*

Environmental Rankings

- The U.S. Environmental Protection Agency (EPA) released a list of mid-size U.S. metropolitan areas with the most ENERGY STAR certified buildings in 2019. The Nashville metro area was ranked #8 out of 10. *U.S. Environmental Protection Agency, "2020 Energy Star Top Cities," March 2020*

Food/Drink Rankings

- The U.S. Chamber of Commerce Foundation conducted an in-depth study on local food truck regulations, surveyed 288 food truck owners, and ranked 20 major American cities based on how friendly they are for operating a food truck. The compiled index assessed the following: procedures for obtaining permits and licenses; complying with restrictions; and financial obligations associated with operating a food truck. Nashville ranked #10 overall (1 being the best). *www.foodtrucknation.us, "Food Truck Nation," March 20, 2018*

Health/Fitness Rankings

- For each of the 100 largest cities in the United States, the American Fitness Index®, published by the American College of Sports Medicine and the Anthem Foundation, evaluated community infrastructure and 33 health behaviors including preventive health, levels of chronic disease conditions, pedestrian safety, air quality, and community resources that support physical activity. Nashville ranked #61 for "community fitness." *americanfitnessindex.org, "2020 ACSM American Fitness Index Summary Report," July 14, 2020*

- The Nashville metro area was identified as one of the worst cities for bed bugs in America by pest control company Orkin. The area ranked #31 out of 50 based on the number of bed bug treatments Orkin performed from December 2019 to November 2020. *Orkin, "New Year, New Top City on Orkin's 2021 Bed Bug Cities List: Chicago," February 1, 2021*

- Nashville was identified as a "2021 Spring Allergy Capital." The area ranked #73 out of 100. Three groups of factors were used to identify the most challenging cities for people with allergies during the spring season: annual spring pollen levels; over the counter medicine use; number of board-certified allergy specialists. *Asthma and Allergy Foundation of America, "Spring Allergy Capitals 2021," February 23, 2021*

- Nashville was identified as a "2021 Fall Allergy Capital." The area ranked #73 out of 100. Three groups of factors were used to identify the most challenging cities for people with allergies during the fall season: annual fall pollen levels; over the counter medicine use; number of board-certified allergy specialists. *Asthma and Allergy Foundation of America, "Fall Allergy Capitals 2021," February 23, 2021*

- Nashville was identified as a "2019 Asthma Capital." The area ranked #43 out of the nation's 100 largest metropolitan areas. Criteria: estimated asthma prevalence; crude death rate from asthma; and ER visits due to asthma. Risk factors analyzed but not factored in the rankings: annual pollen score; annual air quality; public smoking laws; number of board-certified asthma specialists; rescue medication use; controller medication use; uninsured rate; poverty rate. *Asthma and Allergy Foundation of America, "Asthma Capitals 2019: The Most Challenging Places to Live With Asthma," May 7, 2019*

Pet Rankings

- Nashville appeared on *The Dogington Post* site as one of the top cities for dog lovers, ranking #20 out of 20. The real estate brokerage, Redfin and Rover, the largest pet sitter and dog walker network, compiled a list from over 14,000 U.S. cities to come up with a "Rover Rank." Criteria: highest count of dog walks, the city's Walk Score®, for-sale home listings that mention "dog," number of dog walkers and pet sitters and the hours spent and distance logged. *www.dogingtonpost.com, "The 20 Most Dog-Friendly Cities of 2019," April 4, 2019*

Real Estate Rankings

- FitSmallBusiness looked at 50 of the largest metropolitan areas in the U.S. to determine which metro was the best to start a real estate business. Data was compiled from such sources as: Zillow, Trulia, U.S. Census Bureau, and the Bureau of Labor Statistics. Criteria: location; inventory; annual wages; median sales price of homes; days on the market; median price cut percentage; and other factors that would influence real estate professional growth. The Nashville metro area ranked #15. *fitsmallbusiness.com, "The Best Cities to Become a Real Estate Agent in 2018," January 30, 2018*

- *WalletHub* compared the most populated U.S. cities to determine which had the best markets for real estate agents. Nashville ranked #24 where demand was high and pay was the best. Criteria: sales per agent; annual median wage for real-estate agents; monthly average starting salary for real estate agents; real estate job density and competition; unemployment rate; home turnover rate; housing-market health index; and other relevant metrics. *www.WalletHub.com, "2019's Best Places to Be a Real Estate Agent," April 24, 2019*

- According to Penske Truck Rental, the Nashville metro area was named the #9 moving destination in 2019, based on one-way consumer truck rental reservations made through Penske's website, rental locations, and reservations call center. *gopenske.com/blog, "Penske Truck Rental's 2019 Top Moving Destinations," January 22, 2020*

Safety Rankings

- To identify the most dangerous cities in America, 24/7 Wall Street focused on violent crime categories—murder, non-negligent manslaughter, rape, robbery, and aggravated assault—and property crime as reported in the FBI's 2019 annual Uniform Crime Report. Criteria also included median income from American Community Survey and unemployment figures from Bureau of Labor Statistics. For cities with populations over 100,000, Nashville was ranked #20. *247wallst.com, "America's 50 Most Dangerous Cities" November 16, 2020*

- Allstate ranked the 200 largest cities in America in terms of driver safety. Nashville ranked #108. Criteria: internal property damage claims over a two-year period from January 2016 to December 2017. The report helps increase the importance of safety and awareness behind the wheel. *Allstate, "Allstate America's Best Drivers Report, 2019" June 24, 2019*

- Nashville was identified as one of the most dangerous cities in America by NeighborhoodScout. The city ranked #42 out of 100 (#1 = most dangerous). Criteria: number of violent crimes per 1,000 residents. The editors evaluated cities with 25,000 or more residents. *NeighborhoodScout.com, "2021 Top 100 Most Dangerous Cities in the U.S.," January 2, 2021*

- The National Insurance Crime Bureau ranked 384 metro areas in the U.S. in terms of per capita rates of vehicle theft. The Nashville metro area ranked #120 (#1 = highest rate). Criteria: number of vehicle theft offenses per 100,000 inhabitants in 2019. *National Insurance Crime Bureau, "Hot Spots 2019," July 21, 2020*

Seniors/Retirement Rankings

- From its Best Cities for Successful Aging indexes, the Milken Institute generated rankings for metropolitan areas, weighing data in nine categories—health care, wellness, living arrangements, transportation and convenience, financial characteristics, education, employment, community engagement, and overall livability. The Nashville metro area was ranked #30 overall in the large metro area category. *Milken Institute, "Best Cities for Successful Aging, 2017" March 14, 2017*

Women/Minorities Rankings

- *Travel + Leisure* listed the best cities in and around the US for a memorable and fun girls' trip, even on a budget. Whether it is for a special occasion or just to get away, Nashville is sure to have something for all the ladies in your tribe. *Travel + Leisure, "25 Girls' Weekend Getaways That Won't Break the Bank," June 8, 2020*

- Personal finance website *WalletHub* compared more than 180 U.S. cities across two key dimensions, "Hispanic Business-Friendliness" and "Hispanic Purchasing Power," to arrive at the most favorable conditions for Hispanic entrepreneurs. Nashville was ranked #48 out of 182. Criteria includes: share of Hispanic-Owned Businesses; Hispanic entrepreneurship rate to median annual income of Hispanics; Small Business-Friendliness score; cost of living; and number of Hispanics with at least a bachelor's degree. *WalletHub.com, "2019's Best Cities for Hispanic Entrepreneurs," May 1, 2019*

Miscellaneous Rankings

- The watchdog site, Charity Navigator, conducted a study of charities in major markets both to analyze statistical differences in their financial, accountability, and transparency practices and to track year-to-year variations in individual philanthropic communities. The Nashville metro area was ranked #26 among the 30 metro markets in the rating category of Overall Score. *www.charitynavigator.org, "2017 Metro Market Study," May 1, 2017*

- *WalletHub* compared the 150 most populated U.S. cities to determine their operating efficiency. A "Quality of City Services" score was constructed for each city and then divided by the total budget per capita to reveal which were managed the best. Nashville ranked #106. Criteria: financial stability; economy; education; safety; health; infrastructure and pollution. *www.WalletHub.com, "2020's Best- & Worst-Run Cities in America," June 29, 2020*

- Nashville was selected as one of "America's Friendliest Cities." The city ranked #7 in the "Friendliest" category. Respondents to an online survey were asked to rate 38 top urban destinations in the United States as to general friendliness, as well as manners, politeness and warm disposition. *Travel + Leisure, "America's Friendliest Cities," October 20, 2017*

Business Environment

DEMOGRAPHICS

Population Growth

Area	1990 Census	2000 Census	2010 Census	2019* Estimate	Population Growth (%) 1990-2019	Population Growth (%) 2010-2019
City	488,364	545,524	601,222	663,750	35.9	10.4
MSA[1]	1,048,218	1,311,789	1,589,934	1,871,903	78.6	17.7
U.S.	248,709,873	281,421,906	308,745,538	324,697,795	30.6	5.2

Note: (1) Figures cover the Nashville-Davidson—Murfreesboro—Franklin, TN Metropolitan Statistical Area; (*) 2015-2019 5-year estimated population
Source: U.S. Census Bureau, 1990 Census, Census 2000, Census 2010, 2015-2019 American Community Survey 5-Year Estimates

Household Size

Area	One	Two	Three	Four	Five	Six	Seven or More	Average Household Size
City	33.9	33.9	15.3	9.6	4.6	1.6	1.0	2.40
MSA[1]	26.1	34.9	16.7	13.4	5.8	2.1	1.1	2.60
U.S.	27.9	33.9	15.6	12.9	6.0	2.3	1.4	2.60

Note: (1) Figures cover the Nashville-Davidson—Murfreesboro—Franklin, TN Metropolitan Statistical Area
Source: U.S. Census Bureau, 2015-2019 American Community Survey 5-Year Estimates

Race

Area	White Alone[2] (%)	Black Alone[2] (%)	Asian Alone[2] (%)	AIAN[3] Alone[2] (%)	NHOPI[4] Alone[2] (%)	Other Race Alone[2] (%)	Two or More Races (%)
City	63.5	27.6	3.7	0.2	0.1	2.4	2.6
MSA[1]	77.6	15.3	2.8	0.2	0.0	1.6	2.5
U.S.	72.5	12.7	5.5	0.8	0.2	4.9	3.3

Note: (1) Figures cover the Nashville-Davidson—Murfreesboro—Franklin, TN Metropolitan Statistical Area; (2) Alone is defined as not being in combination with one or more other races; (3) American Indian and Alaska Native; (4) Native Hawaiian and Other Pacific Islander
Source: U.S. Census Bureau, 2015-2019 American Community Survey 5-Year Estimates

Hispanic or Latino Origin

Area	Total (%)	Mexican (%)	Puerto Rican (%)	Cuban (%)	Other (%)
City	10.5	6.2	0.6	0.4	3.4
MSA[1]	7.3	4.4	0.5	0.2	2.2
U.S.	18.0	11.2	1.7	0.7	4.3

Note: Persons of Hispanic or Latino origin can be of any race; (1) Figures cover the Nashville-Davidson—Murfreesboro—Franklin, TN Metropolitan Statistical Area
Source: U.S. Census Bureau, 2015-2019 American Community Survey 5-Year Estimates

Ancestry

Area	German	Irish	English	American	Italian	Polish	French[2]	Scottish	Dutch
City	8.4	7.9	7.3	8.2	2.4	1.3	1.7	1.9	0.8
MSA[1]	10.0	9.6	9.2	10.8	2.7	1.4	1.8	2.2	1.0
U.S.	13.3	9.7	7.2	6.2	5.1	2.8	2.3	1.7	1.2

Note: Figures are the percentage of the total population reporting a particular ancestry. The nine most commonly reported ancestries in the U.S. are shown. Figures include multiple ancestries (e.g. if a person reported being Irish and Italian, they were included in both columns); (1) Figures cover the Nashville-Davidson—Murfreesboro—Franklin, TN Metropolitan Statistical Area; (2) Excludes Basque
Source: U.S. Census Bureau, 2015-2019 American Community Survey 5-Year Estimates

Foreign-born Population

Area	Any Foreign Country	Asia	Mexico	Europe	Caribbean	Central America[2]	South America	Africa	Canada
City	13.3	4.0	3.1	0.9	0.4	1.9	0.3	2.5	0.2
MSA[1]	8.3	2.6	2.0	0.7	0.2	1.0	0.3	1.1	0.2
U.S.	13.6	4.2	3.5	1.5	1.3	1.1	1.0	0.7	0.2

Note: (1) Figures cover the Nashville-Davidson—Murfreesboro—Franklin, TN Metropolitan Statistical Area; (2) Excludes Mexico.
Source: U.S. Census Bureau, 2015-2019 American Community Survey 5-Year Estimates

Marital Status

Area	Never Married	Now Married[2]	Separated	Widowed	Divorced
City	40.7	40.8	1.8	4.7	11.9
MSA[1]	32.0	50.3	1.6	5.0	11.2
U.S.	33.4	48.1	1.9	5.8	10.9

Note: Figures are percentages and cover the population 15 years of age and older; (1) Figures cover the Nashville-Davidson—Murfreesboro—Franklin, TN Metropolitan Statistical Area; (2) Excludes separated
Source: U.S. Census Bureau, 2015-2019 American Community Survey 5-Year Estimates

Disability by Age

Area	All Ages	Under 18 Years Old	18 to 64 Years Old	65 Years and Over
City	11.5	4.0	9.8	35.4
MSA[1]	12.0	4.0	10.2	35.2
U.S.	12.6	4.2	10.3	34.5

Note: Figures show percent of the civilian noninstitutionalized population that reported having a disability. Disability status is determined from six types of difficulty: vision, hearing, cognitive, ambulatory, self-care, and independent living. For children under 5 years old, hearing and vision difficulty are used to determine disability status. For children between the ages of 5 and 14, disability status is determined from hearing, vision, cognitive, ambulatory, and self-care difficulties. For people aged 15 years and older, they are considered to have a disability if they have difficulty with any one of the six difficulty types; Note: (1) Figures cover the Nashville-Davidson—Murfreesboro—Franklin, TN Metropolitan Statistical Area
Source: U.S. Census Bureau, 2015-2019 American Community Survey 5-Year Estimates

Age

Area	Under Age 5	Age 5–19	Age 20–34	Age 35–44	Age 45–54	Age 55–64	Age 65–74	Age 75–84	Age 85+	Median Age
City	6.8	17.0	27.6	13.8	11.8	11.4	7.1	3.3	1.3	34.2
MSA[1]	6.4	19.4	22.1	13.7	13.3	12.3	8.0	3.6	1.3	36.4
U.S.	6.1	19.1	20.7	12.6	13.0	12.9	9.1	4.6	1.9	38.1

Note: (1) Figures cover the Nashville-Davidson—Murfreesboro—Franklin, TN Metropolitan Statistical Area
Source: U.S. Census Bureau, 2015-2019 American Community Survey 5-Year Estimates

Gender

Area	Males	Females	Males per 100 Females
City	319,844	343,906	93.0
MSA[1]	913,820	958,083	95.4
U.S.	159,886,919	164,810,876	97.0

Note: (1) Figures cover the Nashville-Davidson—Murfreesboro—Franklin, TN Metropolitan Statistical Area
Source: U.S. Census Bureau, 2015-2019 American Community Survey 5-Year Estimates

Religious Groups by Family

Area	Catholic	Baptist	Non-Den.	Methodist[2]	Lutheran	LDS[3]	Pentecostal	Presbyterian[4]	Muslim[5]	Judaism
MSA[1]	4.1	25.3	5.8	6.1	0.4	0.8	2.2	2.1	0.4	0.2
U.S.	19.1	9.3	4.0	4.0	2.3	2.0	1.9	1.6	0.8	0.7

Note: Figures are the number of adherents as a percentage of the total population; (1) Figures cover the Nashville-Davidson—Murfreesboro—Franklin, TN Metropolitan Statistical Area; (2) Methodist/Pietist; (3) Latter Day Saints; (4) Reformed; (5) Figures are estimates
Source: Association of Statisticians of American Religious Bodies, 2010 U.S. Religion Census: Religious Congregations & Membership Study

Religious Groups by Tradition

Area	Catholic	Evangelical Protestant	Mainline Protestant	Other Tradition	Black Protestant	Orthodox
MSA[1]	4.1	33.0	8.0	1.7	3.4	0.5
U.S.	19.1	16.2	7.3	4.3	1.6	0.3

Note: Figures are the number of adherents as a percentage of the total population; (1) Figures cover the Nashville-Davidson—Murfreesboro—Franklin, TN Metropolitan Statistical Area
Source: Association of Statisticians of American Religious Bodies, 2010 U.S. Religion Census: Religious Congregations & Membership Study

ECONOMY

Gross Metropolitan Product

Area	2017	2018	2019	2020	Rank[2]
MSA[1]	134.3	142.5	149.8	156.5	30

Note: Figures are in billions of dollars; (1) Figures cover the Nashville-Davidson—Murfreesboro—Franklin, TN Metropolitan Statistical Area; (2) Rank is based on 2018 data and ranges from 1 to 381
Source: U.S. Conference of Mayors, U.S. Metro Economies: GMP & Employment 2018-2020, September 2019

Economic Growth

Area	2015-17 (%)	2018 (%)	2019 (%)	2020 (%)	Rank[2]
MSA[1]	4.0	3.9	3.3	2.3	39
U.S.	1.9	2.9	2.3	2.1	—

Note: Figures are real gross metropolitan product (GMP) growth rates and represent average annual percent change; (1) Figures cover the Nashville-Davidson—Murfreesboro—Franklin, TN Metropolitan Statistical Area; (2) Rank is based on 2017 2-year average annual percent change and ranges from 1 to 381
Source: U.S. Conference of Mayors, U.S. Metro Economies: GMP & Employment 2018-2020, September 2019

Metropolitan Area Exports

Area	2014	2015	2016	2017	2018	2019	Rank[2]
MSA[1]	9,620.9	9,353.0	9,460.1	10,164.3	8,723.7	7,940.7	44

Note: Figures are in millions of dollars; (1) Figures cover the Nashville-Davidson—Murfreesboro—Franklin, TN Metropolitan Statistical Area; (2) Rank is based on 2019 data and ranges from 1 to 386
Source: U.S. Department of Commerce, International Trade Administration, Office of Trade and Economic Analysis, Industry and Analysis, Exports by Metropolitan Area, data extracted March 24, 2021

Building Permits

Area	Single-Family 2018	Single-Family 2019	Pct. Chg.	Multi-Family 2018	Multi-Family 2019	Pct. Chg.	Total 2018	Total 2019	Pct. Chg.
City	3,560	3,830	7.6	3,268	5,935	81.6	6,828	9,765	43.0
MSA[1]	13,470	14,460	7.3	5,689	8,242	44.9	19,159	22,702	18.5
U.S.	855,300	862,100	0.7	473,500	523,900	10.6	1,328,800	1,386,000	4.3

Note: (1) Figures cover the Nashville-Davidson—Murfreesboro—Franklin, TN Metropolitan Statistical Area; Figures represent new, privately-owned housing units authorized (unadjusted data); All permit data are based on estimates with imputation
Source: U.S. Census Bureau, Manufacturing, Mining, and Construction Statistics, Building Permits, 2018, 2019

Bankruptcy Filings

Area	Business Filings 2019	Business Filings 2020	% Chg.	Nonbusiness Filings 2019	Nonbusiness Filings 2020	% Chg.
Davidson County	53	60	13.2	2,051	1,330	-35.2
U.S.	22,780	21,655	-4.9	752,160	522,808	-30.5

Note: Business filings include Chapter 7, Chapter 9, Chapter 11, Chapter 12, Chapter 13, Chapter 15, and Section 304; Nonbusiness filings include Chapter 7, Chapter 11, and Chapter 13
Source: Administrative Office of the U.S. Courts, Business and Nonbusiness Bankruptcy, County Cases Commenced by Chapter of the Bankruptcy Code, During the 12-Month Period Ending December 31, 2019 and Business and Nonbusiness Bankruptcy, County Cases Commenced by Chapter of the Bankruptcy Code, During the 12-Month Period Ending December 31, 2020

Housing Vacancy Rates

Area	Gross Vacancy Rate[2] (%) 2018	2019	2020	Year-Round Vacancy Rate[3] (%) 2018	2019	2020	Rental Vacancy Rate[4] (%) 2018	2019	2020	Homeowner Vacancy Rate[5] (%) 2018	2019	2020
MSA[1]	5.9	7.8	6.5	5.8	7.5	6.1	7.5	8.6	7.3	0.8	1.2	0.7
U.S.	12.3	12.0	10.6	9.7	9.5	8.2	6.9	6.7	6.3	1.5	1.4	1.0

Note: (1) Figures cover the Nashville-Davidson—Murfreesboro—Franklin, TN Metropolitan Statistical Area; (2) The percentage of the total housing inventory that is vacant; (3) The percentage of the housing inventory (excluding seasonal units) that is year-round vacant; (4) The percentage of rental inventory that is vacant for rent; (5) The percentage of homeowner inventory that is vacant for sale
Source: U.S. Census Bureau, Housing Vacancies and Homeownership Annual Statistics: 2018, 2019, 2020

INCOME

Income

Area	Per Capita ($)	Median Household ($)	Average Household ($)
City	35,243	59,828	83,348
MSA[1]	35,479	66,347	91,202
U.S.	34,103	62,843	88,607

Note: (1) Figures cover the Nashville-Davidson—Murfreesboro—Franklin, TN Metropolitan Statistical Area
Source: U.S. Census Bureau, 2015-2019 American Community Survey 5-Year Estimates

Household Income Distribution

Area	Under $15,000	$15,000 -$24,999	$25,000 -$34,999	$35,000 -$49,999	$50,000 -$74,999	$75,000 -$99,999	$100,000 -$149,999	$150,000 and up
City	9.8	8.5	9.3	14.1	18.9	13.6	14.3	11.8
MSA[1]	8.0	7.5	8.6	13.0	18.6	14.1	16.2	14.0
U.S.	10.3	8.9	8.9	12.3	17.2	12.7	15.1	14.5

Note: (1) Figures cover the Nashville-Davidson—Murfreesboro—Franklin, TN Metropolitan Statistical Area
Source: U.S. Census Bureau, 2015-2019 American Community Survey 5-Year Estimates

Poverty Rate

Area	All Ages	Under 18 Years Old	18 to 64 Years Old	65 Years and Over
City	15.1	24.2	13.2	9.2
MSA[1]	11.4	15.7	10.6	7.6
U.S.	13.4	18.5	12.6	9.3

Note: Figures are percentage of people whose income during the past 12 months was below the poverty level;
(1) Figures cover the Nashville-Davidson—Murfreesboro—Franklin, TN Metropolitan Statistical Area
Source: U.S. Census Bureau, 2015-2019 American Community Survey 5-Year Estimates

CITY FINANCES

City Government Finances

Component	2017 ($000)	2017 ($ per capita)
Total Revenues	4,491,189	6,615
Total Expenditures	4,748,542	6,995
Debt Outstanding	14,599,158	21,504
Cash and Securities[1]	14,608,254	21,518

Note: (1) Cash and security holdings of a government at the close of its fiscal year,
including those of its dependent agencies, utilities, and liquor stores.
Source: U.S. Census Bureau, State & Local Government Finances 2017

City Government Revenue by Source

Source	2017 ($000)	2017 ($ per capita)	2017 (%)
General Revenue			
From Federal Government	35,457	52	0.8
From State Government	608,970	897	13.6
From Local Governments	509	1	0.0
Taxes			
Property	971,643	1,431	21.6
Sales and Gross Receipts	573,349	845	12.8
Personal Income	0	0	0.0
Corporate Income	0	0	0.0
Motor Vehicle License	26,253	39	0.6
Other Taxes	29,335	43	0.7
Current Charges	293,770	433	6.5
Liquor Store	0	0	0.0
Utility	1,366,898	2,013	30.4
Employee Retirement	466,545	687	10.4

Source: U.S. Census Bureau, State & Local Government Finances 2017

City Government Expenditures by Function

Function	2017 ($000)	2017 ($ per capita)	2017 (%)
General Direct Expenditures			
Air Transportation	0	0	0.0
Corrections	76,371	112	1.6
Education	1,116,230	1,644	23.5
Employment Security Administration	0	0	0.0
Financial Administration	26,420	38	0.6
Fire Protection	128,227	188	2.7
General Public Buildings	700	1	0.0
Governmental Administration, Other	70,872	104	1.5
Health	63,013	92	1.3
Highways	135,143	199	2.8
Hospitals	100,002	147	2.1
Housing and Community Development	0	0	0.0
Interest on General Debt	151,009	222	3.2
Judicial and Legal	124,387	183	2.6
Libraries	40,021	59	0.8
Parking	3,521	5	0.1
Parks and Recreation	131,430	193	2.8
Police Protection	213,301	314	4.5
Public Welfare	48,563	71	1.0
Sewerage	180,256	265	3.8
Solid Waste Management	24,170	35	0.5
Veterans' Services	0	0	0.0
Liquor Store	0	0	0.0
Utility	1,649,096	2,429	34.7
Employee Retirement	205,458	302	4.3

Source: U.S. Census Bureau, State & Local Government Finances 2017

EMPLOYMENT

Labor Force and Employment

Area	Civilian Labor Force			Workers Employed		
	Dec. 2019	Dec. 2020	% Chg.	Dec. 2019	Dec. 2020	% Chg.
City	413,927	420,401	1.6	404,589	396,582	-2.0
MSA[1]	1,102,127	1,112,635	1.0	1,076,372	1,054,820	-2.0
U.S.	164,007,000	160,017,000	-2.4	158,504,000	149,613,000	-5.6

Note: Data is not seasonally adjusted and covers workers 16 years of age and older; (1) Figures cover the Nashville-Davidson—Murfreesboro—Franklin, TN Metropolitan Statistical Area
Source: Bureau of Labor Statistics, Local Area Unemployment Statistics

Unemployment Rate

Area	2020											
	Jan.	Feb.	Mar.	Apr.	May	Jun.	Jul.	Aug.	Sep.	Oct.	Nov.	Dec.
City	2.7	2.7	2.4	16.1	12.3	12.0	12.3	10.6	7.7	6.9	4.7	5.7
MSA[1]	2.8	2.8	2.5	15.2	11.1	10.2	10.0	8.4	6.1	6.1	4.2	5.2
U.S.	4.0	3.8	4.5	14.4	13.0	11.2	10.5	8.5	7.7	6.6	6.4	6.5

Note: Data is not seasonally adjusted and covers workers 16 years of age and older; (1) Figures cover the Nashville-Davidson—Murfreesboro—Franklin, TN Metropolitan Statistical Area
Source: Bureau of Labor Statistics, Local Area Unemployment Statistics

Average Wages

Occupation	$/Hr.	Occupation	$/Hr.
Accountants and Auditors	34.70	Maintenance and Repair Workers	20.30
Automotive Mechanics	21.80	Marketing Managers	59.00
Bookkeepers	21.50	Network and Computer Systems Admin.	37.50
Carpenters	22.20	Nurses, Licensed Practical	22.00
Cashiers	11.50	Nurses, Registered	32.80
Computer Programmers	45.30	Nursing Assistants	14.00
Computer Systems Analysts	40.00	Office Clerks, General	17.10
Computer User Support Specialists	24.10	Physical Therapists	37.80
Construction Laborers	17.20	Physicians	98.60
Cooks, Restaurant	13.20	Plumbers, Pipefitters and Steamfitters	27.20
Customer Service Representatives	18.00	Police and Sheriff's Patrol Officers	25.20
Dentists	75.30	Postal Service Mail Carriers	25.70
Electricians	25.50	Real Estate Sales Agents	22.90
Engineers, Electrical	45.40	Retail Salespersons	14.60
Fast Food and Counter Workers	10.80	Sales Representatives, Technical/Scientific	38.90
Financial Managers	59.60	Secretaries, Exc. Legal/Medical/Executive	20.10
First-Line Supervisors of Office Workers	28.50	Security Guards	14.60
General and Operations Managers	60.00	Surgeons	88.00
Hairdressers/Cosmetologists	15.10	Teacher Assistants, Exc. Postsecondary*	13.10
Home Health and Personal Care Aides	11.80	Teachers, Secondary School, Exc. Sp. Ed.*	25.00
Janitors and Cleaners	14.00	Telemarketers	18.70
Landscaping/Groundskeeping Workers	14.20	Truck Drivers, Heavy/Tractor-Trailer	25.40
Lawyers	62.20	Truck Drivers, Light/Delivery Services	17.80
Maids and Housekeeping Cleaners	12.20	Waiters and Waitresses	9.90

Note: Wage data covers the Nashville-Davidson—Murfreesboro—Franklin, TN Metropolitan Statistical Area; (*) Hourly wages were calculated from annual wage data based on a 40 hour work week; n/a not available.
Source: Bureau of Labor Statistics, Metro Area Occupational Employment & Wage Estimates, May 2020

Employment by Industry

Sector	MSA[1]		U.S.
	Number of Employees	Percent of Total	Percent of Total
Construction, Mining, and Logging	49,700	4.8	5.5
Education and Health Services	152,700	14.9	16.3
Financial Activities	71,300	7.0	6.1
Government	121,400	11.8	15.2
Information	24,900	2.4	1.9
Leisure and Hospitality	95,200	9.3	9.0
Manufacturing	81,200	7.9	8.5
Other Services	39,300	3.8	3.8
Professional and Business Services	177,900	17.4	14.4
Retail Trade	103,100	10.1	10.9
Transportation, Warehousing, and Utilities	67,200	6.6	4.6
Wholesale Trade	41,400	4.0	3.9

Note: Figures are non-farm employment as of December 2020. Figures are not seasonally adjusted and include workers 16 years of age and older; (1) Figures cover the Nashville-Davidson—Murfreesboro—Franklin, TN Metropolitan Statistical Area
Source: Bureau of Labor Statistics, Current Employment Statistics, Employment, Hours, and Earnings

Employment by Occupation

Occupation Classification	City (%)	MSA[1] (%)	U.S. (%)
Management, Business, Science, and Arts	42.2	40.3	38.5
Natural Resources, Construction, and Maintenance	7.3	8.0	8.9
Production, Transportation, and Material Moving	12.2	13.8	13.2
Sales and Office	21.5	22.5	21.6
Service	16.9	15.5	17.8

Note: Figures cover employed civilians 16 years of age and older; (1) Figures cover the Nashville-Davidson—Murfreesboro—Franklin, TN Metropolitan Statistical Area
Source: U.S. Census Bureau, 2015-2019 American Community Survey 5-Year Estimates

Occupations with Greatest Projected Employment Growth: 2020 – 2022

Occupation[1]	2020 Employment	2022 Projected Employment	Numeric Employment Change	Percent Employment Change
Heavy and Tractor-Trailer Truck Drivers	72,760	75,530	2,770	3.8
Laborers and Freight, Stock, and Material Movers, Hand	99,970	101,640	1,670	1.7
General and Operations Managers	44,540	45,510	970	2.2
Janitors and Cleaners, Except Maids and Housekeeping Cleaners	44,140	45,030	890	2.0
Construction Laborers	28,960	29,800	840	2.9
Managers, All Other	34,220	35,050	830	2.4
Retail Salespersons	88,170	88,970	800	0.9
Stock Clerks and Order Fillers	58,210	58,980	770	1.3
Farmers, Ranchers, and Other Agricultural Managers	23,960	24,700	740	3.1
Light Truck or Delivery Services Drivers	20,800	21,500	700	3.4

Note: Projections cover Tennessee; (1) Sorted by numeric employment change
Source: www.projectionscentral.com, State Occupational Projections, 2020–2022 Short-Term Projections

Fastest-Growing Occupations: 2020 – 2022

Occupation[1]	2020 Employment	2022 Projected Employment	Numeric Employment Change	Percent Employment Change
Athletes and Sports Competitors	390	510	120	30.8
Audio and Video Equipment Technicians	1,960	2,090	130	6.6
Software Developers, Applications	6,750	7,190	440	6.5
Sailors and Marine Oilers	920	980	60	6.5
Captains, Mates, and Pilots of Water Vessels	790	840	50	6.3
Operations Research Analysts	1,510	1,600	90	6.0
Massage Therapists	2,370	2,510	140	5.9
Agricultural Equipment Operators	2,790	2,950	160	5.7
Tire Repairers and Changers	2,830	2,990	160	5.7
Nonfarm Animal Caretakers	5,100	5,370	270	5.3

Note: Projections cover Tennessee; (1) Sorted by percent employment change and excludes occupations with numeric employment change less than 50
Source: www.projectionscentral.com, State Occupational Projections, 2020–2022 Short-Term Projections

TAXES

State Corporate Income Tax Rates

State	Tax Rate (%)	Income Brackets ($)	Num. of Brackets	Financial Institution Tax Rate (%)[a]	Federal Income Tax Ded.
Tennessee	6.5	Flat rate	1	6.5	No

Note: Tax rates as of January 1, 2021; (a) Rates listed are the corporate income tax rate applied to financial institutions or excise taxes based on income. Some states have other taxes based upon the value of deposits or shares.
Source: Federation of Tax Administrators, State Corporate Income Tax Rates, January 1, 2021

State Individual Income Tax Rates

State	Tax Rate (%)	Income Brackets ($)	Personal Exemptions ($) Single	Married	Depend.	Standard Ded. ($) Single	Married
Tennessee				– No state income tax (x) –			

Note: Tax rates as of January 1, 2021; Local- and county-level taxes are not included; (x) Tennessee Hall Tax Rate on Dividends and Interest has been repealed in 2021.
Source: Federation of Tax Administrators, State Individual Income Tax Rates, January 1, 2021

Various State Sales and Excise Tax Rates

State	State Sales Tax (%)	Gasoline[1] (¢/gal.)	Cigarette[2] ($/pack)	Spirits[3] ($/gal.)	Wine[4] ($/gal.)	Beer[5] ($/gal.)	Recreational Marijuana (%)
Tennessee	7	27.4	0.62	4.46	1.27	1.29	Not legal

Note: All tax rates as of January 1, 2021; (1) The American Petroleum Institute has developed a methodology for determining the average tax rate on a gallon of fuel. Rates may include any of the following: excise taxes, environmental fees, storage tank fees, other fees or taxes, general sales tax, and local taxes; (2) The federal excise tax of $1.0066 per pack and local taxes are not included; (3) Rates are those applicable to off-premise sales of 40% alcohol by volume (a.b.v.) distilled spirits in 750ml containers. Local excise taxes are excluded; (4) Rates are those applicable to off-premise sales of 11% a.b.v. non-carbonated wine in 750ml containers; (5) Rates are those applicable to off-premise sales of 4.7% a.b.v. beer in 12 ounce containers.
Source: Tax Foundation, 2021 Facts & Figures: How Does Your State Compare?

State Business Tax Climate Index Rankings

State	Overall Rank	Corporate Tax Rank	Individual Income Tax Rank	Sales Tax Rank	Property Tax Rank	Unemployment Insurance Tax Rank
Tennessee	18	24	8	47	33	26

Note: The index is a measure of how each state's tax laws affect economic performance. The lower the rank, the more favorable a state's tax system is for business. States without a given tax are given a ranking of 1. The scores/rankings for the District of Columbia do not affect other states. The 2021 index represents the tax climate as of July 1, 2020.
Source: Tax Foundation, State Business Tax Climate Index 2021

TRANSPORTATION

Means of Transportation to Work

Area	Drove Alone	Car-pooled	Bus	Subway	Railroad	Bicycle	Walked	Other Means	Worked at Home
City	77.7	10.0	2.0	0.0	0.1	0.2	2.4	1.2	6.4
MSA[1]	80.8	9.4	0.9	0.0	0.1	0.1	1.3	1.1	6.3
U.S.	76.3	9.0	2.4	1.9	0.6	0.5	2.7	1.4	5.2

Note: Figures are percentages and cover workers 16 years of age and older; (1) Figures cover the Nashville-Davidson—Murfreesboro—Franklin, TN Metropolitan Statistical Area
Source: U.S. Census Bureau, 2015-2019 American Community Survey 5-Year Estimates

Travel Time to Work

Area	Less Than 10 Minutes	10 to 19 Minutes	20 to 29 Minutes	30 to 44 Minutes	45 to 59 Minutes	60 to 89 Minutes	90 Minutes or More
City	8.7	29.1	26.2	23.8	7.2	3.5	1.5
MSA[1]	9.2	26.5	21.7	23.4	10.6	6.6	2.0
U.S.	12.2	28.4	20.8	20.8	8.3	6.4	2.9

Note: Note: Figures are percentages and include workers 16 years old and over; (1) Figures cover the Nashville-Davidson—Murfreesboro—Franklin, TN Metropolitan Statistical Area
Source: U.S. Census Bureau, 2015-2019 American Community Survey 5-Year Estimates

Key Congestion Measures

Measure	1982	1992	2002	2012	2017
Annual Hours of Delay, Total (000)	6,250	11,377	30,475	45,483	52,249
Annual Hours of Delay, Per Auto Commuter	19	29	45	51	58
Annual Congestion Cost, Total (million $)	47	120	412	816	963
Annual Congestion Cost, Per Auto Commuter ($)	326	408	853	997	1,111

Note: Covers the Nashville-Davidson TN urban area
Source: Texas A&M Transportation Institute, 2019 Urban Mobility Report

Freeway Travel Time Index

Measure	1982	1987	1992	1997	2002	2007	2012	2017
Urban Area Index[1]	1.09	1.11	1.13	1.17	1.21	1.22	1.22	1.22
Urban Area Rank[1,2]	25	29	37	32	31	34	32	33

Note: Freeway Travel Time Index—the ratio of travel time in the peak period to the travel time at free-flow conditions. For example, a value of 1.30 indicates a 20-minute free-flow trip takes 26 minutes in the peak (20 minutes x 1.30 = 26 minutes); (1) Covers the Nashville-Davidson TN urban area; (2) Rank is based on 101 larger urban areas (#1 = highest travel time index)
Source: Texas A&M Transportation Institute, 2019 Urban Mobility Report

Public Transportation

Agency Name / Mode of Transportation	Vehicles Operated in Maximum Service[1]	Annual Unlinked Passenger Trips[2] (in thous.)	Annual Passenger Miles[3] (in thous.)
Metropolitan Transit Authority (MTA)			
Bus (directly operated)	157	9,285.4	40,952.3
Demand Response (directly operated)	63	306.0	3,019.4
Demand Response Taxi (purchased transportation)	55	95.5	1,041.2

Note: (1) Number of revenue vehicles operated by the given mode and type of service to meet the annual maximum service requirement. This is the revenue vehicle count during the peak season of the year; on the week and day that maximum service is provided. Vehicles operated in maximum service (VOMS) exclude atypical days and one-time special events; (2) Number of passengers who boarded public transportation vehicles. Passengers are counted each time they board a vehicle no matter how many vehicles they use to travel from their origin to their destination. (3) Sum of the distances ridden by all passengers during the entire fiscal year.
Source: Federal Transit Administration, National Transit Database, 2019

Air Transportation

Airport Name and Code / Type of Service	Passenger Airlines[1]	Passenger Enplanements	Freight Carriers[2]	Freight (lbs)
Nashville International (BNA)				
Domestic service (U.S. carriers - 2020)	35	3,992,738	15	56,435,779
International service (U.S. carriers - 2019)	8	10,520	1	1,394

Note: (1) Includes all U.S.-based major, minor and commuter airlines that carried at least one passenger during the year; (2) Includes all U.S.-based airlines and freight carriers that transported at least one pound of freight during the year.
Source: Bureau of Transportation Statistics, The Intermodal Transportation Database, Air Carriers: T-100 Domestic Market (U.S. Carriers), 2020; Bureau of Transportation Statistics, The Intermodal Transportation Database, Air Carriers: T-100 International Market (U.S. Carriers), 2019

BUSINESSES

Major Business Headquarters

Company Name	Industry	Fortune[1]	Forbes[2]
HCA Healthcare	Health Care, Medical Facilities	65	-
Ingram Industries	Multicompany	-	177

Note: (1) Companies that produce a 10-K are ranked 1 to 500 based on 2019 revenue; (2) All private companies with at least $2 billion in annual revenue through the end of their most current fiscal year are ranked 1 to 219; companies listed are headquartered in the city; dashes indicate no ranking
Source: Fortune, "Fortune 500," June/July 2020; Forbes, "America's Largest Private Companies," 2020

Fastest-Growing Businesses

According to *Inc.*, Nashville is home to two of America's 500 fastest-growing private companies: **Soundstripe** (#68); **PCE - Power of Clean Energy** (#294). Criteria: must be an independent, privately-held, for-profit, U.S. corporation, proprietorship or partnership as of December 31, 2019; revenues must be at least $100,000 in 2016 and $2 million in 2019; must have four-year operating/sales history. *Inc., "America's 500 Fastest-Growing Private Companies," 2020*

According to *Fortune*, Nashville is home to one of the 100 fastest-growing companies in the world: **Pinnacle Financial Partners** (#82). Companies were ranked by their revenue growth rate; their EPS growth rate; and their three-year annualized total return to investors for the period ending June 30, 2020. Criteria for inclusion: a company, foreign or domestic, must trade on a major U.S. stock exchange; must file quarterly reports with the SEC; must have a minimum market capitalization of $250 million; must have a stock price of at least $5 on June 30, 2020; must have been trading continuously since June 30, 2017; must have revenue and net income for the four quarters ended on or before April 30, 2020, of at least $50 million and $10 million, respectively; and must have posted a compound annual growth in revenue and earnings per share of at least 15% annually over the three years ending on or before April 30, 2020. Real estate investment trusts, limited-liability companies, limited partnerships, business development companies, closed-end investment firms, companies about to be acquired, and companies that lost money in the quarter ending April 30, 2020 were excluded. *Fortune, "100 Fastest-Growing Companies," 2020*

Minority Business Opportunity

Nashville is home to one company which is on the *Black Enterprise* Bank list (15 largest banks based on total assets, capital, deposits and loans, including mortgage-backed securities for the calendar year): **Citizens Savings Bank & Trust Co.** (#12). Only commercial banks or savings and loans that are classified by the Federal Reserve as black institutions and have been fully operational for the previous calendar year were considered. *Black Enterprise, B.E. 100s, 2019*

Living Environment

COST OF LIVING

Cost of Living Index

Composite Index	Groceries	Housing	Utilities	Transportation	Health Care	Misc. Goods/Services
96.7	100.2	92.7	92.6	94.8	95.5	100.2

Note: The Cost of Living Index measures regional differences in the cost of consumer goods and services, excluding taxes and non-consumer expenditures, for professional and managerial households in the top income quintile. It is based on more than 50,000 prices covering almost 60 different items for which prices are collected three times a year by chambers of commerce, economic development organizations or university applied economic centers in each participating urban area. The numbers shown should be read as a percentage above or below the national average of 100. For example, a value of 115.4 in the groceries column indicates that grocery prices are 15.4% higher than the national average. Small differences in the index numbers should not be interpreted as significant; Figures cover the Nashville-Murfreesboro TN urban area.
Source: The Council for Community and Economic Research, Cost of Living Index, 2020

Grocery Prices

Area[1]	T-Bone Steak ($/pound)	Frying Chicken ($/pound)	Whole Milk ($/half gal.)	Eggs ($/dozen)	Orange Juice ($/64 oz.)	Coffee ($/11.5 oz.)
City[2]	13.20	1.42	1.96	1.05	3.65	4.37
Avg.	11.78	1.39	2.05	1.47	3.57	4.34
Min.	8.03	0.94	1.03	0.74	2.94	3.02
Max.	15.86	2.65	4.31	3.77	5.44	8.69

Note: (1) Values for the local area are compared with the average, minimum and maximum values for all 284 areas in the Cost of Living Index; (2) Figures cover the Nashville-Murfreesboro TN urban area; **T-Bone Steak** (price per pound); **Frying Chicken** (price per pound, whole fryer); **Whole Milk** (half gallon carton); **Eggs** (price per dozen, Grade A, large); **Orange Juice** (64 oz. Tropicana or Florida Natural); **Coffee** (11.5 oz. can, vacuum-packed, Maxwell House, Hills Bros, or Folgers).
Source: The Council for Community and Economic Research, Cost of Living Index, 2020

Housing and Utility Costs

Area[1]	New Home Price ($)	Apartment Rent ($/month)	All Electric ($/month)	Part Electric ($/month)	Other Energy ($/month)	Telephone ($/month)
City[2]	339,380	1,130	-	88.87	55.47	185.00
Avg.	368,594	1,168	170.86	100.47	65.28	184.30
Min.	190,567	502	91.58	31.42	26.08	169.60
Max.	2,227,806	4,738	470.38	280.31	280.06	206.50

Note: (1) Values for the local area are compared with the average, minimum and maximum values for all 284 areas in the Cost of Living Index; (2) Figures cover the Nashville-Murfreesboro TN urban area; **New Home Price** (2,400 sf living area, 8,000 sf lot, in urban area with full utilities); **Apartment Rent** (950 sf 2 bedroom/1.5 or 2 bath, unfurnished, excluding all utilities except water); **All Electric** (average monthly cost for an all-electric home); **Part Electric** (average monthly cost for a part-electric home); **Other Energy** (average monthly cost for natural gas, fuel oil, coal, wood, and any other forms of energy except electricity); **Telephone** (price includes the base monthly rate plus taxes and fees for three lines of mobile phone service).
Source: The Council for Community and Economic Research, Cost of Living Index, 2020

Health Care, Transportation, and Other Costs

Area[1]	Doctor ($/visit)	Dentist ($/visit)	Optometrist ($/visit)	Gasoline ($/gallon)	Beauty Salon ($/visit)	Men's Shirt ($)
City[2]	94.18	107.94	91.08	2.05	35.67	32.97
Avg.	115.44	99.32	108.10	2.21	39.27	31.37
Min.	36.68	59.00	51.36	1.71	19.00	11.00
Max.	219.00	153.10	250.97	3.46	82.05	58.33

Note: (1) Values for the local area are compared with the average, minimum and maximum values for all 284 areas in the Cost of Living Index; (2) Figures cover the Nashville-Murfreesboro TN urban area; **Doctor** (general practitioners routine exam of an established patient); **Dentist** (adult teeth cleaning and periodic oral examination); **Optometrist** (full vision eye exam for established adult patient); **Gasoline** (one gallon regular unleaded, national brand, including all taxes, cash price at self-service pump if available); **Beauty Salon** (woman's shampoo, trim, and blow-dry); **Men's Shirt** (cotton/polyester dress shirt, pinpoint weave, long sleeves).
Source: The Council for Community and Economic Research, Cost of Living Index, 2020

HOUSING

Homeownership Rate

Area	2012 (%)	2013 (%)	2014 (%)	2015 (%)	2016 (%)	2017 (%)	2018 (%)	2019 (%)	2020 (%)
MSA[1]	64.9	63.9	67.1	67.4	65.0	69.4	68.3	69.8	69.8
U.S.	65.4	65.1	64.5	63.7	63.4	63.9	64.4	64.6	66.6

Note: (1) Figures cover the Nashville-Davidson—Murfreesboro—Franklin, TN Metropolitan Statistical Area
Source: U.S. Census Bureau, Housing Vacancies and Homeownership Annual Statistics: 2012-2020

House Price Index (HPI)

Area	National Ranking[2]	Quarterly Change (%)	One-Year Change (%)	Five-Year Change (%)	Since 1991Q1 (%)
MSA[1]	88	1.88	6.96	45.40	266.19
U.S.[3]	–	3.81	10.77	38.99	205.12

Note: The HPI is a weighted repeat sales index. It measures average price changes in repeat sales or refinancings on the same properties. This information is obtained by reviewing repeat mortgage transactions on single-family properties whose mortgages have been purchased or securitized by Fannie Mae or Freddie Mac since January 1975; (1) Figures cover the Nashville-Davidson—Murfreesboro—Franklin, TN Metropolitan Statistical Area; (2) Rankings are based on annual percentage change for all metro areas containing at least 15,000 transactions over the last 10 years and ranges from 1 to 253; (3) figures based on a weighted average of Census Division estimates using a seasonally adjusted, purchase-only index; all figures are for the period ending December 31, 2020
Source: Federal Housing Finance Agency, Change in Metropolitan Area House Price Indexes, April 7, 2021

Median Single-Family Home Prices

Area	2018	2019	2020p	Percent Change 2019 to 2020
MSA[1]	260.5	275.0	298.9	8.7
U.S. Average	261.6	274.6	299.9	9.2

Note: Figures are median sales prices of existing single-family homes in thousands of dollars; (p) preliminary; (1) Figures cover the Nashville-Davidson—Murfreesboro—Franklin, TN Metropolitan Statistical Area
Source: National Association of Realtors, Median Sales Price of Existing Single-Family Homes for Metropolitan Areas, 4th Quarter 2020

Qualifying Income Based on Median Sales Price of Existing Single-Family Homes

Area	With 5% Down ($)	With 10% Down ($)	With 20% Down ($)
MSA[1]	58,766	55,673	49,488
U.S. Average	59,266	56,147	49,908

Note: Figures are preliminary; Qualifying income is based on a mortgage rate of 2.81%. Monthly principal and interest payment is limited to 25% of income; (1) Figures cover the Nashville-Davidson—Murfreesboro—Franklin, TN Metropolitan Statistical Area
Source: National Association of Realtors, Qualifying Income Based on Median Sales Price of Existing Single-Family Homes for Metropolitan Areas, 4th Quarter 2020

Home Value Distribution

Area	Under $50,000	$50,000 -$99,999	$100,000 -$149,999	$150,000 -$199,999	$200,000 -$299,999	$300,000 -$499,999	$500,000 -$999,999	$1,000,000 or more
City	2.1	5.0	13.5	17.4	27.0	23.1	10.0	1.9
MSA[1]	2.9	6.1	13.1	16.5	25.6	23.0	10.5	2.3
U.S.	6.9	12.0	13.3	14.0	19.6	19.3	11.4	3.4

Note: Figures are percentages and cover owner-occupied housing units; (1) Figures cover the Nashville-Davidson—Murfreesboro—Franklin, TN Metropolitan Statistical Area
Source: U.S. Census Bureau, 2015-2019 American Community Survey 5-Year Estimates

Year Housing Structure Built

Area	2010 or Later	2000 -2009	1990 -1999	1980 -1989	1970 -1979	1960 -1969	1950 -1959	1940 -1949	Before 1940	Median Year
City	9.3	14.6	12.4	15.3	14.8	12.2	10.6	4.5	6.2	1981
MSA[1]	10.7	19.7	17.8	14.3	13.6	9.2	6.9	3.1	4.7	1989
U.S.	5.2	14.0	13.9	13.4	15.2	10.6	10.3	4.9	12.6	1978

Note: Figures are percentages except for Median Year; Note: (1) Figures cover the Nashville-Davidson—Murfreesboro—Franklin, TN Metropolitan Statistical Area
Source: U.S. Census Bureau, 2015-2019 American Community Survey 5-Year Estimates

Gross Monthly Rent

Area	Under $500	$500 -$999	$1,000 -$1,499	$1,500 -$1,999	$2,000 -$2,499	$2,500 -$2,999	$3,000 and up	Median ($)
City	8.7	31.5	39.8	14.1	4.0	1.1	0.8	1,100
MSA[1]	8.0	35.2	38.0	13.3	3.6	1.1	0.8	1,073
U.S.	9.4	36.2	30.0	14.0	5.6	2.4	2.4	1,062

Note: Figures are percentages except for Median; Gross rent is the contract rent plus the estimated average monthly cost of utilities (electricity, gas, and water and sewer) and fuels (oil, coal, kerosene, wood, etc.) if these are paid by the renter (or paid for the renter by someone else); (1) Figures cover the Nashville-Davidson—Murfreesboro—Franklin, TN Metropolitan Statistical Area
Source: U.S. Census Bureau, 2015-2019 American Community Survey 5-Year Estimates

HEALTH

Health Risk Factors

Category	MSA[1] (%)	U.S. (%)
Adults aged 18–64 who have any kind of health care coverage	85.8	87.3
Adults who reported being in good or better health	85.6	82.4
Adults who have been told they have high blood cholesterol	33.7	33.0
Adults who have been told they have high blood pressure	34.7	32.3
Adults who are current smokers	15.9	17.1
Adults who currently use E-cigarettes	6.2	4.6
Adults who currently use chewing tobacco, snuff, or snus	4.5	4.0
Adults who are heavy drinkers[2]	5.0	6.3
Adults who are binge drinkers[3]	14.5	17.4
Adults who are overweight (BMI 25.0 - 29.9)	37.2	35.3
Adults who are obese (BMI 30.0 - 99.8)	28.2	31.3
Adults who participated in any physical activities in the past month	74.9	74.4
Adults who always or nearly always wears a seat belt	94.0	94.3

Note: (1) Figures cover the Nashville-Davidson—Murfreesboro—Franklin, TN Metropolitan Statistical Area; (2) Heavy drinkers are classified as adult men having more than 14 drinks per week and adult women having more than 7 drinks per week; (3) Binge drinkers are classified as males having five or more drinks on one occasion or females having four or more drinks on one occasion
Source: Centers for Disease Control and Prevention, Behaviorial Risk Factor Surveillance System, SMART: Selected Metropolitan Area Risk Trends, 2017

Acute and Chronic Health Conditions

Category	MSA[1] (%)	U.S. (%)
Adults who have ever been told they had a heart attack	5.6	4.2
Adults who have ever been told they have angina or coronary heart disease	3.7	3.9
Adults who have ever been told they had a stroke	3.7	3.0
Adults who have ever been told they have asthma	15.0	14.2
Adults who have ever been told they have arthritis	25.4	24.9
Adults who have ever been told they have diabetes[2]	11.8	10.5
Adults who have ever been told they had skin cancer	5.4	6.2
Adults who have ever been told they had any other types of cancer	7.4	7.1
Adults who have ever been told they have COPD	6.4	6.5
Adults who have ever been told they have kidney disease	4.0	3.0
Adults who have ever been told they have a form of depression	21.2	20.5

Note: (1) Figures cover the Nashville-Davidson—Murfreesboro—Franklin, TN Metropolitan Statistical Area; (2) Figures do not include pregnancy-related, borderline, or pre-diabetes
Source: Centers for Disease Control and Prevention, Behaviorial Risk Factor Surveillance System, SMART: Selected Metropolitan Area Risk Trends, 2017

Health Screening and Vaccination Rates

Category	MSA[1] (%)	U.S. (%)
Adults aged 65+ who have had flu shot within the past year	53.3	60.7
Adults aged 65+ who have ever had a pneumonia vaccination	75.4	75.4
Adults who have ever been tested for HIV	40.0	36.1
Adults who have ever had the shingles or zoster vaccine?	24.8	28.9
Adults who have had their blood cholesterol checked within the last five years	91.4	85.9

Note: n/a not available; (1) Figures cover the Nashville-Davidson—Murfreesboro—Franklin, TN Metropolitan Statistical Area.
Source: Centers for Disease Control and Prevention, Behaviorial Risk Factor Surveillance System, SMART: Selected Metropolitan Area Risk Trends, 2017

Disability Status

Category	MSA[1] (%)	U.S. (%)
Adults who reported being deaf	6.9	6.7
Are you blind or have serious difficulty seeing, even when wearing glasses?	5.2	4.5
Are you limited in any way in any of your usual activities due of arthritis?	12.5	12.9
Do you have difficulty doing errands alone?	5.7	6.8
Do you have difficulty dressing or bathing?	3.3	3.6
Do you have serious difficulty concentrating/remembering/making decisions?	11.5	10.7
Do you have serious difficulty walking or climbing stairs?	15.0	13.6

Note: (1) Figures cover the Nashville-Davidson—Murfreesboro—Franklin, TN Metropolitan Statistical Area.
Source: Centers for Disease Control and Prevention, Behaviorial Risk Factor Surveillance System, SMART: Selected Metropolitan Area Risk Trends, 2017

Mortality Rates for the Top 10 Causes of Death in the U.S.

ICD-10[a] Sub-Chapter	ICD-10[a] Code	Age-Adjusted Mortality Rate[1] per 100,000 population County[2]	U.S.
Malignant neoplasms	C00-C97	155.7	149.2
Ischaemic heart diseases	I20-I25	99.3	90.5
Other forms of heart disease	I30-I51	45.1	52.2
Chronic lower respiratory diseases	J40-J47	43.8	39.6
Other degenerative diseases of the nervous system	G30-G31	61.1	37.6
Cerebrovascular diseases	I60-I69	42.8	37.2
Other external causes of accidental injury	W00-X59	61.9	36.1
Organic, including symptomatic, mental disorders	F01-F09	29.8	29.4
Hypertensive diseases	I10-I15	41.3	24.1
Diabetes mellitus	E10-E14	23.6	21.5

Note: (a) ICD-10 = International Classification of Diseases 10th Revision; (1) Mortality rates are a three-year average covering 2017-2019; (2) Figures cover Davidson County.
Source: Centers for Disease Control and Prevention, National Center for Health Statistics. Underlying Cause of Death 1999-2019 on CDC WONDER Online Database

Mortality Rates for Selected Causes of Death

ICD-10[a] Sub-Chapter	ICD-10[a] Code	Age-Adjusted Mortality Rate[1] per 100,000 population County[2]	U.S.
Assault	X85-Y09	13.1	6.0
Diseases of the liver	K70-K76	13.7	14.4
Human immunodeficiency virus (HIV) disease	B20-B24	2.4	1.5
Influenza and pneumonia	J09-J18	14.0	13.8
Intentional self-harm	X60-X84	12.9	14.1
Malnutrition	E40-E46	1.3	2.3
Obesity and other hyperalimentation	E65-E68	3.7	2.1
Renal failure	N17-N19	10.0	12.6
Transport accidents	V01-V99	12.4	12.3
Viral hepatitis	B15-B19	2.0	1.2

Note: (a) ICD-10 = International Classification of Diseases 10th Revision; (1) Mortality rates are a three-year average covering 2017-2019; (2) Figures cover Davidson County; Data are suppressed when the data meet the criteria for confidentiality constraints; Mortality rates are flagged as unreliable when the rate would be calculated with a numerator of 20 or less.
Source: Centers for Disease Control and Prevention, National Center for Health Statistics. Underlying Cause of Death 1999-2019 on CDC WONDER Online Database

Health Insurance Coverage

Area	With Health Insurance	With Private Health Insurance	With Public Health Insurance	Without Health Insurance	Population Under Age 19 Without Health Insurance
City	87.9	67.1	29.8	12.1	6.9
MSA[1]	90.7	72.1	28.7	9.3	5.1
U.S.	91.2	67.9	35.1	8.8	5.1

Note: Figures are percentages that cover the civilian noninstitutionalized population; (1) Figures cover the Nashville-Davidson—Murfreesboro—Franklin, TN Metropolitan Statistical Area
Source: U.S. Census Bureau, 2015-2019 American Community Survey 5-Year Estimates

Number of Medical Professionals

Area	MDs[3]	DOs[3,4]	Dentists	Podiatrists	Chiropractors	Optometrists
County[1] (number)	4,469	84	563	30	178	117
County[1] (rate[2])	647.2	12.2	81.1	4.3	25.6	16.9
U.S. (rate[2])	282.9	22.7	71.2	6.2	28.1	16.9

47037
Note: Data as of 2019 unless noted; (1) Data covers Davidson County; (2) Rate per 100,000 population; (3) Data as of 2018 and includes all active, non-federal physicians; (4) Doctor of Osteopathic Medicine
Source: U.S. Department of Health and Human Services, Health Resources and Services Administration, Bureau of Health Professions, Area Resource File (ARF) 2019-2020

Best Hospitals

According to *U.S. News,* the Nashville-Davidson—Murfreesboro—Franklin, TN metro area is home to one of the best hospitals in the U.S.: **Vanderbilt University Medical Center** (7 adult specialties and 10 pediatric specialties). The hospital listed was nationally ranked in at least one of 16 adult or 10 pediatric specialties. Only 134 hospitals nationwide were nationally ranked in one or more adult or pediatric specialty; this number increases to 178 counting specialized centers within hospitals. Twenty hospitals in the U.S. made the Honor Roll. The Best Hospitals Honor Roll takes both the national rankings and the procedure and condition ratings into account. Hospitals received points if they were nationally ranked in one of the 16 adult specialties—the higher they ranked, the more points they got—and how many ratings of "high performing" they earned in the 10 procedures and conditions. *U.S. News Online, "America's Best Hospitals 2020-21"*

According to *U.S. News,* the Nashville-Davidson—Murfreesboro—Franklin, TN metro area is home to one of the best children's hospitals in the U.S.: **Monroe Carell Jr. Children's Hospital at Vanderbilt** (10 pediatric specialties). The hospital listed was highly ranked in at least one of 10 pediatric specialties. Eighty-eight children's hospitals in the U.S. were nationally ranked in at least one specialty. Hospitals received points for being ranked in a specialty, and the 10 hospitals with the most points across the 10 specialties make up the Honor Roll. *U.S. News Online, "America's Best Children's Hospitals 2020-21"*

EDUCATION

Public School District Statistics

District Name	Schls	Pupils	Pupil/Teacher Ratio	Minority Pupils[1] (%)	Free Lunch Eligible[2] (%)	IEP[3] (%)
Achievement School District	30	11,031	21.2	97.6	n/a	11.0
Davidson County	169	84,667	15.2	71.9	n/a	12.3

Note: Table includes school districts with 2,000 or more students; (1) Percentage of students that are not non-Hispanic white; (2) Percentage of students that are eligible for the free lunch program; (3) Percentage of students that have an Individualized Education Program.
Source: U.S. Department of Education, National Center for Education Statistics, Common Core of Data, Local Education Agency (School District) Universe Survey: School Year 2018-2019; U.S. Department of Education, National Center for Education Statistics, Common Core of Data, Public Elementary/Secondary School Universe Survey: School Year 2018-2019

Best High Schools

According to *U.S. News,* Nashville is home to two of the top 500 high schools in the U.S.: **Hume Fogg Magnet High School** (#51); **Martin Luther King Jr. Magnet School** (#147). Nearly 18,000 public, magnet and charter schools were ranked based on their performance on state assessments and how well they prepare students for college. *U.S. News & World Report, "Best High Schools 2020"*

Highest Level of Education

Area	Less than H.S.	H.S. Diploma	Some College, No Deg.	Associate Degree	Bachelor's Degree	Master's Degree	Prof. School Degree	Doctorate Degree
City	11.2	22.3	18.9	6.4	25.8	10.3	2.9	2.1
MSA[1]	10.0	26.4	20.2	7.3	23.5	9.0	2.2	1.6
U.S.	12.0	27.0	20.4	8.5	19.8	8.8	2.1	1.4

Note: Figures cover persons age 25 and over; (1) Figures cover the Nashville-Davidson—Murfreesboro—Franklin, TN Metropolitan Statistical Area
Source: U.S. Census Bureau, 2015-2019 American Community Survey 5-Year Estimates

Educational Attainment by Race

Area	High School Graduate or Higher (%) Total	White	Black	Asian	Hisp.[2]	Bachelor's Degree or Higher (%) Total	White	Black	Asian	Hisp.[2]
City	88.8	90.4	88.2	77.9	57.0	41.1	46.5	27.6	49.2	15.4
MSA[1]	90.0	90.9	88.5	84.0	62.9	36.2	37.5	28.2	51.5	17.3
U.S.	88.0	89.9	86.0	87.1	68.7	32.1	33.5	21.6	54.3	16.4

Note: Figures shown cover persons 25 years old and over; (1) Figures cover the Nashville-Davidson—Murfreesboro—Franklin, TN Metropolitan Statistical Area; (2) People of Hispanic origin can be of any race
Source: U.S. Census Bureau, 2015-2019 American Community Survey 5-Year Estimates

School Enrollment by Grade and Control

Area	Preschool (%) Public	Private	Kindergarten (%) Public	Private	Grades 1 - 4 (%) Public	Private	Grades 5 - 8 (%) Public	Private	Grades 9 - 12 (%) Public	Private
City	50.7	49.3	87.4	12.6	85.6	14.4	83.4	16.6	82.0	18.0
MSA[1]	47.3	52.7	86.2	13.8	87.1	12.9	86.3	13.7	84.4	15.6
U.S.	59.1	40.9	87.6	12.4	89.5	10.5	89.4	10.6	90.1	9.9

Note: Figures shown cover persons 3 years old and over; (1) Figures cover the Nashville-Davidson—Murfreesboro—Franklin, TN Metropolitan Statistical Area
Source: U.S. Census Bureau, 2015-2019 American Community Survey 5-Year Estimates

Higher Education

Four-Year Colleges			Two-Year Colleges			Medical Schools[1]	Law Schools[2]	Voc/Tech[3]
Public	Private Non-profit	Private For-profit	Public	Private Non-profit	Private For-profit			
1	8	4	2	2	4	2	3	4

Note: Figures cover institutions located within the city limits and include main campuses only; (1) includes schools accredited by the Liaison Committee on Medical Education and the American Osteopathic Association's Commission on Osteopathic College Accreditation; (2) includes ABA-accredited schools, schools with provisional ABA accreditation, and state accredited schools; (3) includes all schools with programs that are less than 2 years.
Source: National Center for Education Statistics, Integrated Postsecondary Education System (IPEDS), 2019-20; Wikipedia, List of Medical Schools in the United States, accessed April 2, 2021; Wikipedia, List of Law Schools in the United States, accessed April 2, 2021

According to *U.S. News & World Report*, the Nashville-Davidson—Murfreesboro—Franklin, TN metro area is home to two of the top 200 national universities in the U.S.: **Vanderbilt University** (#14 tie); **Belmont University** (#160 tie). The indicators used to capture academic quality fall into a number of categories: assessment by administrators at peer institutions; retention of students; faculty resources; student selectivity; financial resources; alumni giving; high school counselor ratings of colleges; and graduation rate. *U.S. News & World Report, "America's Best Colleges 2021"*

According to *U.S. News & World Report*, the Nashville-Davidson—Murfreesboro—Franklin, TN metro area is home to one of the top 100 law schools in the U.S.: **Vanderbilt University** (#16 tie). The rankings are based on a weighted average of 12 measures of quality: peer assessment score; assessment score by lawyers/judges; median LSAT scores; median undergrad GPA; acceptance rate; employment rates for graduates; placement success; bar passage rate; faculty resources; expenditures per student; student/faculty ratio; and library resources. *U.S. News & World Report, "America's Best Graduate Schools, Law, 2022"*

According to *U.S. News & World Report*, the Nashville-Davidson—Murfreesboro—Franklin, TN metro area is home to one of the top 75 medical schools for research in the U.S.: **Vanderbilt University** (#13 tie). The rankings are based on a weighted average of 11 measures of quality: quality assessment; peer assessment score; assessment score by residency directors; research activity; total research activity; average research activity per faculty member; student selectivity; median MCAT total score; median undergraduate GPA; acceptance rate; and faculty resources. *U.S. News & World Report, "America's Best Graduate Schools, Medical, 2022"*

According to *U.S. News & World Report*, the Nashville-Davidson—Murfreesboro—Franklin, TN metro area is home to one of the top 75 business schools in the U.S.: **Vanderbilt University (Owen)** (#23 tie). The rankings are based on a weighted average of the following nine measures: quality assessment; peer assessment; recruiter assessment; placement success; mean starting salary and bonus; student selectivity; mean GMAT and GRE scores; mean undergraduate GPA; and acceptance rate. *U.S. News & World Report, "America's Best Graduate Schools, Business, 2022"*

EMPLOYERS

Major Employers

Company Name	Industry
AHOM Holdings	Home health care services
Asurion Corporation	Business services nec
Baptist Hospital	General medical & surgical hospitals
Cannon County Knitting Mills	Apparel & outerwear broadwoven fabrics
County of Rutherford	County government
County of Sumner	County government
Gaylord Entertainment Company	Hotels & motels
Gaylord Opryland USA	Hotels & motels
Ingram Book Company	Books, periodicals, & newspapers
International Automotive	Automotive storage garage
LifeWay Christian Resources of the SBC	Religious organizations
Middle Tennessee State University	Colleges & universities
Newspaper Printing Corporation	Newspapers, publishing & printing
Nissan North America	Motor vehicles & car bodies
Primus Automotive Financial Services	Automobile loans including insurance
Psychiatric Solutions	Psychiatric clinic
State Industries	Hot water heaters, household
State of Tennessee	State government
Tennesee Department of Transportation	Regulation, administration of transportation
Vanderbilt Childrens Hospital	General medical & surgical hospitals
Vanderbilt University	Colleges & universities

Note: Companies shown are located within the Nashville-Davidson—Murfreesboro—Franklin, TN Metropolitan Statistical Area.
Source: Hoovers.com; Wikipedia

Best Companies to Work For

Pinnacle Financial Partners, headquartered in Nashville, is among "The 100 Best Companies to Work For." To pick the best companies, *Fortune* partnered with the Great Place to Work Institute. Two-thirds of a company's score is based on the results of the Institute's Trust Index survey, which is sent to a random sample of employees from each company. The questions related to attitudes about management's credibility, job satisfaction, and camaraderie. The other third of the scoring is based on the company's responses to the Institute's Culture Audit, which includes detailed questions about pay and benefit programs, and a series of open-ended questions about hiring practices, internal communication, training, recognition programs, and diversity efforts. Any company that is at least five years old with more than 1,000 U.S. employees is eligible. *Fortune, "The 100 Best Companies to Work For," 2020*

Asurion, headquartered in Nashville, is among the "100 Best Places to Work in IT." To qualify, companies had to be U.S.-based organizations or be non-U.S.-based employers that met the following criteria: have a minimum of 300 total employees at a U.S. headquarters and a minimum of 30 IT employees in the U.S., with at least 50% of their IT employees based in the U.S. The best places to work were selected based on compensation, benefits, work/life balance, employee morale, and satisfaction with training and development programs. In addition, *InsiderPro* and *Computerworld* looked at retention efforts, programs for recognizing and rewarding outstanding performances, and benefits such as flextime, elder care and child care, and reimbursement for college tuition and the cost of pursuing technology certifications. *InsiderPro and Computerworld, "100 Best Places to Work in IT," 2020*

PUBLIC SAFETY

Crime Rate

Area	All Crimes	Violent Crimes				Property Crimes		
		Murder	Rape[3]	Robbery	Aggrav. Assault	Burglary	Larceny-Theft	Motor Vehicle Theft
City	5,114.2	12.1	63.7	287.8	709.5	490.9	3,150.5	399.8
Suburbs[1]	1,872.5	2.8	29.2	26.7	236.4	201.0	1,238.9	137.5
Metro[2]	3,020.0	6.1	41.4	119.1	403.9	303.6	1,915.5	230.4
U.S.	2,489.3	5.0	42.6	81.6	250.2	340.5	1,549.5	219.9

Note: Figures are crimes per 100,000 population; (1) All areas within the metro area that are located outside the city limits; (2) Figures cover the Nashville-Davidson—Murfreesboro—Franklin, TN Metropolitan Statistical Area; (3) All figures shown were reported using the revised Uniform Crime Reporting (UCR) definition of rape.
Source: FBI Uniform Crime Reports, 2019

Hate Crimes

Area	Number of Quarters Reported	Number of Incidents per Bias Motivation					
		Race/Ethnicity/Ancestry	Religion	Sexual Orientation	Disability	Gender	Gender Identity
City	4	3	2	1	0	0	0
U.S.	4	3,963	1,521	1,195	157	69	198

Source: Federal Bureau of Investigation, Hate Crime Statistics 2019

Identity Theft Consumer Reports

Area	Reports	Reports per 100,000 Population	Rank[2]
MSA[1]	4,236	219	185
U.S.	1,387,615	423	-

Note: (1) Figures cover the Nashville-Davidson—Murfreesboro—Franklin, TN Metropolitan Statistical Area; (2) Rank ranges from 1 to 391 where 1 indicates greatest number of identity theft reports per 100,000 population
Source: Federal Trade Commission, Consumer Sentinel Network Data Book 2020

Fraud and Other Consumer Reports

Area	Reports	Reports per 100,000 Population	Rank[2]
MSA[1]	16,583	857	67
U.S.	3,385,133	1,031	-

Note: (1) Figures cover the Nashville-Davidson—Murfreesboro—Franklin, TN Metropolitan Statistical Area; (2) Rank ranges from 1 to 391 where 1 indicates greatest number of fraud and other consumer reports per 100,000 population
Source: Federal Trade Commission, Consumer Sentinel Network Data Book 2020

POLITICS

2020 Presidential Election Results

Area	Biden	Trump	Jorgensen	Hawkins	Other
Davidson County	64.5	32.4	1.1	0.2	1.8
U.S.	51.3	46.8	1.2	0.3	0.5

Note: Results are percentages and may not add to 100% due to rounding
Source: Dave Leip's Atlas of U.S. Presidential Elections

SPORTS

Professional Sports Teams

Team Name	League	Year Established
Nashville Predators	National Hockey League (NHL)	1998
Nashville SC	Major League Soccer (MLS)	1997
Tennessee Titans	National Football League (NFL)	1997

Note: Includes teams located in the Nashville-Davidson—Murfreesboro—Franklin, TN Metropolitan Statistical Area.
Source: Wikipedia, Major Professional Sports Teams of the United States and Canada, April 6, 2021

CLIMATE

Average and Extreme Temperatures

Temperature	Jan	Feb	Mar	Apr	May	Jun	Jul	Aug	Sep	Oct	Nov	Dec	Yr.
Extreme High (°F)	78	84	86	91	95	106	107	104	105	94	84	79	107
Average High (°F)	47	51	60	71	79	87	90	89	83	72	60	50	70
Average Temp. (°F)	38	41	50	60	68	76	80	79	72	61	49	41	60
Average Low (°F)	28	31	39	48	57	65	69	68	61	48	39	31	49
Extreme Low (°F)	-17	-13	2	23	34	42	54	49	36	26	-1	-10	-17

Note: Figures cover the years 1948-1990
Source: National Climatic Data Center, International Station Meteorological Climate Summary, 9/96

Average Precipitation/Snowfall/Humidity

Precip./Humidity	Jan	Feb	Mar	Apr	May	Jun	Jul	Aug	Sep	Oct	Nov	Dec	Yr.
Avg. Precip. (in.)	4.4	4.2	5.0	4.1	4.6	3.7	3.8	3.3	3.2	2.6	3.9	4.6	47.4
Avg. Snowfall (in.)	4	3	1	Tr	0	0	0	0	0	Tr	1	1	11
Avg. Rel. Hum. 6am (%)	81	81	80	81	86	86	88	90	90	87	83	82	85
Avg. Rel. Hum. 3pm (%)	61	57	51	48	52	52	54	53	52	49	55	59	54

Note: Figures cover the years 1948-1990; Tr = Trace amounts (<0.05 in. of rain; <0.5 in. of snow)
Source: National Climatic Data Center, International Station Meteorological Climate Summary, 9/96

Weather Conditions

Temperature			Daytime Sky			Precipitation		
10°F & below	32°F & below	90°F & above	Clear	Partly cloudy	Cloudy	0.01 inch or more precip.	0.1 inch or more snow/ice	Thunder-storms
5	76	51	98	135	132	119	8	54

Note: Figures are average number of days per year and cover the years 1948-1990
Source: National Climatic Data Center, International Station Meteorological Climate Summary, 9/96

HAZARDOUS WASTE

Superfund Sites

The Nashville-Davidson—Murfreesboro—Franklin, TN metro area is home to one site on the EPA's Superfund National Priorities List: **Wrigley Charcoal Plant** (final). There are a total of 1,375 Superfund sites with a status of proposed or final on the list in the U.S. *U.S. Environmental Protection Agency, National Priorities List, April 7, 2021*

AIR QUALITY

Air Quality Trends: Ozone

	1990	1995	2000	2005	2010	2015	2016	2017	2018	2019
MSA[1]	0.089	0.092	0.084	0.078	0.073	0.065	0.067	0.063	0.068	0.064
U.S.	0.088	0.089	0.082	0.080	0.073	0.068	0.069	0.068	0.069	0.065

Note: (1) Data covers the Nashville-Davidson—Murfreesboro—Franklin, TN Metropolitan Statistical Area. The values shown are the composite ozone concentration averages among trend sites based on the highest fourth daily maximum 8-hour concentration in parts per million. These trends are based on sites having an adequate record of monitoring data during the trend period. Data from exceptional events are included.
Source: U.S. Environmental Protection Agency, Air Quality Monitoring Information, "Air Quality Trends by City, 1990-2019"

Air Quality Index

Area	Percent of Days when Air Quality was...[2]					AQI Statistics[2]	
	Good	Moderate	Unhealthy for Sensitive Groups	Unhealthy	Very Unhealthy	Maximum	Median
MSA[1]	62.7	37.0	0.3	0.0	0.0	101	45

Note: (1) Data covers the Nashville-Davidson—Murfreesboro—Franklin, TN Metropolitan Statistical Area; (2) Based on 365 days with AQI data in 2019. Air Quality Index (AQI) is an index for reporting daily air quality. EPA calculates the AQI for five major air pollutants regulated by the Clean Air Act: ground-level ozone, particle pollution (aka particulate matter), carbon monoxide, sulfur dioxide, and nitrogen dioxide. The AQI runs from 0 to 500. The higher the AQI value, the greater the level of air pollution and the greater the health concern. There are six AQI categories: "Good" AQI is between 0 and 50. Air quality is considered satisfactory; "Moderate" AQI is between 51 and 100. Air quality is acceptable; "Unhealthy for Sensitive Groups" When AQI values are between 101 and 150, members of sensitive groups may experience health effects; "Unhealthy" When AQI values are between 151 and 200 everyone may begin to experience health effects; "Very Unhealthy" AQI values between 201 and 300 trigger a health alert; "Hazardous" AQI values over 300 trigger warnings of emergency conditions (not shown).
Source: U.S. Environmental Protection Agency, Air Quality Index Report, 2019

Air Quality Index Pollutants

Area	Percent of Days when AQI Pollutant was...[2]					
	Carbon Monoxide	Nitrogen Dioxide	Ozone	Sulfur Dioxide	Particulate Matter 2.5	Particulate Matter 10
MSA[1]	0.0	6.8	40.5	0.0	52.6	0.0

Note: (1) Data covers the Nashville-Davidson—Murfreesboro—Franklin, TN Metropolitan Statistical Area; (2) Based on 365 days with AQI data in 2019. The Air Quality Index (AQI) is an index for reporting daily air quality. EPA calculates the AQI for five major air pollutants regulated by the Clean Air Act: ground-level ozone, particle pollution (also known as particulate matter), carbon monoxide, sulfur dioxide, and nitrogen dioxide. The AQI runs from 0 to 500. The higher the AQI value, the greater the level of air pollution and the greater the health concern.
Source: U.S. Environmental Protection Agency, Air Quality Index Report, 2019

Maximum Air Pollutant Concentrations: Particulate Matter, Ozone, CO and Lead

	Particulate Matter 10 (ug/m^3)	Particulate Matter 2.5 Wtd AM (ug/m^3)	Particulate Matter 2.5 24-Hr (ug/m^3)	Ozone (ppm)	Carbon Monoxide (ppm)	Lead (ug/m^3)
MSA[1] Level	32	9.2	18	0.066	1	n/a
NAAQS[2]	150	15	35	0.075	9	0.15
Met NAAQS[2]	Yes	Yes	Yes	Yes	Yes	n/a

Note: (1) Data covers the Nashville-Davidson—Murfreesboro—Franklin, TN Metropolitan Statistical Area; Data from exceptional events are included; (2) National Ambient Air Quality Standards; ppm = parts per million; ug/m^3 = micrograms per cubic meter; n/a not available.
Concentrations: Particulate Matter 10 (coarse particulate)—highest second maximum 24-hour concentration; Particulate Matter 2.5 Wtd AM (fine particulate)—highest weighted annual mean concentration; Particulate Matter 2.5 24-Hour (fine particulate)—highest 98th percentile 24-hour concentration; Ozone—highest fourth daily maximum 8-hour concentration; Carbon Monoxide—highest second maximum non-overlapping 8-hour concentration; Lead—maximum running 3-month average
Source: U.S. Environmental Protection Agency, Air Quality Monitoring Information, "Air Quality Statistics by City, 2019"

Maximum Air Pollutant Concentrations: Nitrogen Dioxide and Sulfur Dioxide

	Nitrogen Dioxide AM (ppb)	Nitrogen Dioxide 1-Hr (ppb)	Sulfur Dioxide AM (ppb)	Sulfur Dioxide 1-Hr (ppb)	Sulfur Dioxide 24-Hr (ppb)
MSA[1] Level	14	51	n/a	n/a	n/a
NAAQS[2]	53	100	30	75	140
Met NAAQS[2]	Yes	Yes	n/a	n/a	n/a

Note: (1) Data covers the Nashville-Davidson—Murfreesboro—Franklin, TN Metropolitan Statistical Area; Data from exceptional events are included; (2) National Ambient Air Quality Standards; ppm = parts per million; ug/m^3 = micrograms per cubic meter; n/a not available.
Concentrations: Nitrogen Dioxide AM—highest arithmetic mean concentration; Nitrogen Dioxide 1-Hr—highest 98th percentile 1-hour daily maximum concentration; Sulfur Dioxide AM—highest annual mean concentration; Sulfur Dioxide 1-Hr—highest 99th percentile 1-hour daily maximum concentration; Sulfur Dioxide 24-Hr—highest second maximum 24-hour concentration
Source: U.S. Environmental Protection Agency, Air Quality Monitoring Information, "Air Quality Statistics by City, 2019"

New Orleans, Louisiana

Background

New Orleans, the old port city upriver from the mouth of the Mississippi River, is one of the United States' most interesting cities. The birthplace of jazz is rich in unique local history, distinctive neighborhoods, and an unmistakably individual character.

The failure of the federal levees following Hurricane Katrina in 2005 put 80 percent of the city under floodwaters for weeks. The Crescent City's revival since then is a testament to her unique spirit, an influx of federal dollars, and an outpouring from volunteers ranging from church groups to spring breakers who returned year after year to help rebuild.

New Orleans was founded on behalf of France by the brothers Le Moyne, Sieurs d'Iberville, and de Bienville, in 1718. Despite disease, starvation, and an unwilling working class, New Orleans emerged as a genteel antebellum slave society, fashioning itself after the rigid social hierarchy of Versailles. Even after New Orleans was ceded to Spain after the French & Indian War, this unequal lifestyle, however gracious, persisted.

The port city briefly returned to French control, then became a crown jewel in the 1803 Louisiana Purchase to the U.S. The transfer of control changed New Orleans's Old World isolation. American settlers introduced aggressive business acumen to the area, as well as the idea of respect for the self-made man. As trade opened up with countries around the world, this made for a happy union. New Orleans became "Queen City of the South," growing prosperous from adventurous riverboat traders and speculators, as well as the cotton trade.

Today, much of the city's Old World charm remains, resulting from Southern, Creole, African-American, and European cultures. New Orleans' cuisine, indigenous music, unique festivals, and sultry, pleasing atmosphere, draws nearly 10 million visitors a year—a major pillar of the city's economy. The Ernest N. Morial Convention Center's numerous convention goers continuously fill more than 35,000 rooms. A second economic pillar is the Port of New Orleans, one of the nation's leading general cargo ports. In recent years, it has seen $400 million invested in new facilities.

The influx of young people who arrived after Hurricane Katrina has given rise to a new start-up spirit. State tax breaks have helped to turn New Orleans into "Hollywood South," where 35 films were produced in the last few years. New Orleans has given birth to a mother lode of cultural phenomena: Dixieland jazz, musicians Louis Armstrong, Mahalia Jackson, Dr. John, and chefs Emeril Lagasse and John Besh. The city is well aware of its "cultural economy," which employs 12.5 percent of the local workforce. Popular tourist draws include the annual Mardi Gras celebration—which spans two long spring weekends leading up to Fat Tuesday—and the annual New Orleans Jazz & Heritage Festival. The Louisiana Superdome—renovated and renamed to the Mercedes Benz Superdome, is home to the 2010 Super Bowl champion New Orleans Saints, and hosted the 2013 Super Bowl.

> Mardi Gras celebrations moved online this year with hundreds of virtual acts, including chef demonstrations, live performances, interviews, and lots of house floats.

Louis Armstrong New Orleans International Airport was made more efficient for travelers by the expansion of the Consolidated Rental Car Facility project that has also brought scattered facilities under one roof. In addition, an effort to boost a medical economy that suffered after Hurricane Katrina, the city has a new Louisiana State University teaching hospital.

Billions of dollars have been spent in recent years for bridge, airport, road, hospital, and school updates. Since Katrina, the majority of New Orleans public schools have become charter schools—a major experiment that is seeing some success. Higher education campuses include Tulane University (including a medical school and law school), Loyola University, and the University of New Orleans. Louisiana State University has a medical school campus downtown.

Cultural amenities include the New Orleans Museum of Art located in the live-oak filled City Park, the Ogden Museum of Southern Art, and Audubon Park, designed by John Charles Olmsted with its golf course and the Audubon Zoo.

The New Orleans metro area is virtually surrounded by water, which influences its climate. Between mid-June and September, temperatures are kept down by near-daily sporadic thunderstorms. Cold spells sometimes reach the area in winter but seldom last. Frequent and sometimes heavy rains are typical. Hurricane season officially runs from June 1 to November 30 but typically reaches its height in late summer.

Rankings

General Rankings

- The New Orleans metro area was identified as one of America's fastest-growing areas in terms of population and business growth by *MagnifyMoney*. The area ranked #30 out of 35. The 100 most populous metro areas in the U.S. were evaluated on their change from 2011-2016 in the following categories: people and housing; workforce and employment opportunities; growing industry. *www.businessinsider.com, "The 35 Cities in the US with the Biggest Influx of People, the Most Work Opportunities, and the Hottest Business Growth," August 12, 2018*

- In its eighth annual survey, *Travel + Leisure* readers nominated their favorite small cities and towns in America—those with 100,000 or fewer residents—voting on numerous attractive features in categories including culture, food and drink, quality of life, style, and people. After 50,000 votes, New Orleans was ranked #2 among the proposed favorites. *www.travelandleisure.com, "America's Favorite Cities," October 20, 2017*

- New Orleans appeared on *Travel + Leisure's* list of the 15 best cities in the United States. The city was ranked #2. Criteria: sights/landmarks; culture; food; friendliness; shopping; and overall value. *Travel + Leisure, "The World's Best Awards 2020" July 8, 2020*

- For its 33rd annual "Readers' Choice Awards" survey, *Condé Nast Traveler* ranked its readers' favorite cities in the U.S. These places brought feelings of comfort in a time of limited travel. The list was broken into large cities and cities under 250,000. New Orleans ranked #4 in the big city category. *Condé Nast Traveler, Readers' Choice Awards 2020, "Best Big Cities in the U.S." October 6, 2020*

Business/Finance Rankings

- The Brookings Institution ranked the nation's largest cities based on income inequality. New Orleans was ranked #4 (#1 = greatest inequality). Criteria: the "95/20 ratio," a figure representing the income at which a household earns more than 95 percent of all other households, divided by the income at which a household earns more than only 20 percent of all other households. *Brookings Institution, "Household Income Inequality, Largest Cities of 97 Large U.S. Metro Areas, 2014-2016," February 5, 2018*

- The Brookings Institution ranked the 100 largest metro areas in the U.S. based on income inequality. New Orleans was ranked #5 (#1 = greatest inequality). Criteria: the "95/20 ratio," a figure representing the income at which a household earns more than 95 percent of all other households, divided by the income at which a household earns more than only 20 percent of all other households. *Brookings Institution, "Household Income Inequality, 100 Largest U.S. Metro Areas, 2014-2016," February 5, 2018*

- The New Orleans metro area appeared on the Milken Institute "2021 Best Performing Cities" list. Rank: #195 out of 200 large metro areas (population over 250,000). Criteria: job growth; wage and salary growth; high-tech output growth; housing affordability; household broadband access. *Milken Institute, "Best-Performing Cities 2021," February 16, 2021*

- *Forbes* ranked the 200 most populous metro areas to determine the nation's "Best Places for Business and Careers." The New Orleans metro area was ranked #146. Criteria: costs (business and living); job growth (past and projected); income growth; quality of life; educational attainment (college and high school); projected economic growth; cultural and leisure opportunities; workplace tolerance laws; net migration patterns. *Forbes, "The Best Places for Business and Careers 2019: Seattle Still On Top," October 30, 2019*

Children/Family Rankings

- New Orleans was selected as one of the most playful cities in the U.S. by KaBOOM! The organization's Playful City USA initiative honors cities and towns across the nation that have made their communities more playable. Criteria: pledging to integrate play as a solution to challenges in their communities; making it easy for children to get active and balanced play; creating more family-friendly and innovative communities as a result. *KaBOOM! National Campaign for Play, "2017 Playful City USA Communities"*

Culture/Performing Arts Rankings

- New Orleans was selected as one of the ten best small North American cities and towns for moviemakers. Of cities with smaller populations, the area ranked #1. As with the 2021 list for bigger cities, pandemic challenges and COVID-19 guidelines were factored in. Other criteria: film community and culture; access to equipment and facilities; tax incentives; and standard of living. *MovieMaker Magazine, "Best Places to Live and Work as a Moviemaker, 2021," January 26, 2021*

- New Orleans was selected as one of "America's Favorite Cities." The city ranked #7 in the "Architecture" category. Respondents to an online survey were asked to rate their favorite place (population over 100,000) in over 65 categories. *Travelandleisure.com, "America's Favorite Cities for Architecture 2016," March 2, 2017*

Dating/Romance Rankings

- New Orleans was selected as one of America's best cities for singles by the readers of *Travel + Leisure* in their annual "America's Favorite Cities" survey. Criteria included good-looking locals, cool shopping, an active bar scene and hipster-magnet coffee bars. *Travel + Leisure, "Best Cities in America for Singles," July 21, 2017*

Education Rankings

- Personal finance website *WalletHub* analyzed the 150 largest U.S. metropolitan statistical areas to determine where the most educated Americans are putting their degrees to work. Criteria: education levels; percentage of workers with degrees; education quality and attainment gap; public school quality rankings; quality and enrollment of each metro area's universities. New Orleans was ranked #102 (#1 = most educated city). *www.WalletHub.com, "Most and Least Educated Cities in America," July 20, 2020*

- New Orleans was selected as one of America's most literate cities. The city ranked #28 out of the 84 largest U.S. cities. Criteria: number of booksellers; library resources; Internet resources; educational attainment; periodical publishing resources; newspaper circulation. *Central Connecticut State University, "America's Most Literate Cities, 2018," February 2019*

Environmental Rankings

- Sperling's BestPlaces assessed the 50 largest metropolitan areas of the United States for the likelihood of dangerously extreme weather events or earthquakes. In general the Southeast and South-Central regions have the highest risk of weather extremes and earthquakes, while the Pacific Northwest enjoys the lowest risk. Of the most risky metropolitan areas, the New Orleans metro area was ranked #10. *www.bestplaces.net, "Avoid Natural Disasters: BestPlaces Reveals The Top 10 Safest Places to Live," October 25, 2017*

- New Orleans was highlighted as one of the top 98 cleanest metro areas for short-term particle pollution (24-hour PM 2.5) in the U.S. during 2016 through 2018. Monitors in these cities reported no days with unhealthful PM 2.5 levels. *American Lung Association, "State of the Air 2020," April 21, 2020*

Health/Fitness Rankings

- For each of the 100 largest cities in the United States, the American Fitness Index®, published by the American College of Sports Medicine and the Anthem Foundation, evaluated community infrastructure and 33 health behaviors including preventive health, levels of chronic disease conditions, pedestrian safety, air quality, and community resources that support physical activity. New Orleans ranked #50 for "community fitness." *americanfitnessindex.org, "2020 ACSM American Fitness Index Summary Report," July 14, 2020*

- New Orleans was identified as a "2021 Spring Allergy Capital." The area ranked #52 out of 100. Three groups of factors were used to identify the most challenging cities for people with allergies during the spring season: annual spring pollen levels; over the counter medicine use; number of board-certified allergy specialists. *Asthma and Allergy Foundation of America, "Spring Allergy Capitals 2021," February 23, 2021*

- New Orleans was identified as a "2021 Fall Allergy Capital." The area ranked #41 out of 100. Three groups of factors were used to identify the most challenging cities for people with allergies during the fall season: annual fall pollen levels; over the counter medicine use; number of board-certified allergy specialists. *Asthma and Allergy Foundation of America, "Fall Allergy Capitals 2021," February 23, 2021*

- New Orleans was identified as a "2019 Asthma Capital." The area ranked #26 out of the nation's 100 largest metropolitan areas. Criteria: estimated asthma prevalence; crude death rate from asthma; and ER visits due to asthma. Risk factors analyzed but not factored in the rankings: annual pollen score; annual air quality; public smoking laws; number of board-certified asthma specialists; rescue medication use; controller medication use; uninsured rate; poverty rate. *Asthma and Allergy Foundation of America, "Asthma Capitals 2019: The Most Challenging Places to Live With Asthma," May 7, 2019*

Real Estate Rankings

- FitSmallBusiness looked at 50 of the largest metropolitan areas in the U.S. to determine which metro was the best to start a real estate business. Data was compiled from such sources as: Zillow, Trulia, U.S. Census Bureau, and the Bureau of Labor Statistics. Criteria: location; inventory; annual wages; median sales price of homes; days on the market; median price cut percentage; and other factors that would influence real estate professional growth. The New Orleans metro area ranked #47. *fitsmallbusiness.com, "The Best Cities to Become a Real Estate Agent in 2018," January 30, 2018*

- *WalletHub* compared the most populated U.S. cities to determine which had the best markets for real estate agents. New Orleans ranked #152 where demand was high and pay was the best. Criteria: sales per agent; annual median wage for real-estate agents; monthly average starting salary for real estate agents; real estate job density and competition; unemployment rate; home turnover rate; housing-market health index; and other relevant metrics. *www.WalletHub.com, "2019's Best Places to Be a Real Estate Agent," April 24, 2019*

- New Orleans was ranked #158 out of 268 metro areas in terms of housing affordability in 2020 by the National Association of Home Builders (#1 = most affordable). Criteria: the share of homes sold in that area affordable to a family earning the local median income, based on standard mortgage underwriting criteria. *National Association of Home Builders®, NAHB-Wells Fargo Housing Opportunity Index, 4th Quarter 2020*

Safety Rankings

- To identify the most dangerous cities in America, 24/7 Wall Street focused on violent crime categories—murder, non-negligent manslaughter, rape, robbery, and aggravated assault—and property crime as reported in the FBI's 2019 annual Uniform Crime Report. Criteria also included median income from American Community Survey and unemployment figures from Bureau of Labor Statistics. For cities with populations over 100,000, New Orleans was ranked #17. *247wallst.com, "America's 50 Most Dangerous Cities" November 16, 2020*

- Allstate ranked the 200 largest cities in America in terms of driver safety. New Orleans ranked #177. Criteria: internal property damage claims over a two-year period from January 2016 to December 2017. The report helps increase the importance of safety and awareness behind the wheel. *Allstate, "Allstate America's Best Drivers Report, 2019" June 24, 2019*

- New Orleans was identified as one of the most dangerous cities in America by NeighborhoodScout. The city ranked #34 out of 100 (#1 = most dangerous). Criteria: number of violent crimes per 1,000 residents. The editors evaluated cities with 25,000 or more residents. *NeighborhoodScout.com, "2021 Top 100 Most Dangerous Cities in the U.S.," January 2, 2021*

- The National Insurance Crime Bureau ranked 384 metro areas in the U.S. in terms of per capita rates of vehicle theft. The New Orleans metro area ranked #51 (#1 = highest rate). Criteria: number of vehicle theft offenses per 100,000 inhabitants in 2019. *National Insurance Crime Bureau, "Hot Spots 2019," July 21, 2020*

Seniors/Retirement Rankings

- From its Best Cities for Successful Aging indexes, the Milken Institute generated rankings for metropolitan areas, weighing data in nine categories—health care, wellness, living arrangements, transportation and convenience, financial characteristics, education, employment, community engagement, and overall livability. The New Orleans metro area was ranked #55 overall in the large metro area category. *Milken Institute, "Best Cities for Successful Aging, 2017" March 14, 2017*

Sports/Recreation Rankings

- New Orleans was chosen as one of America's best cities for bicycling. The city ranked #22 out of 50. Criteria: cycling infrastructure that is safe and friendly for all ages; energy and bike culture. The editors evaluated cities with populations of 100,000 or more. *Bicycling, "The 50 Best Bike Cities in America," October 10, 2018*

Women/Minorities Rankings

- *Travel + Leisure* listed the best cities in and around the US for a memorable and fun girls' trip, even on a budget. Whether it is for a special occasion or just to get away, New Orleans is sure to have something for all the ladies in your tribe. *Travel + Leisure, "25 Girls' Weekend Getaways That Won't Break the Bank," June 8, 2020*

- New Orleans was selected as one of the gayest cities in America by *The Advocate*. The city ranked #5 out of 25. Criteria, among many: Trans Pride parades/festivals; gay rugby teams; lesbian bars; LGBT centers; theater screenings of "Moonlight"; LGBT-inclusive nondiscrimination ordinances; and gay bowling teams. *The Advocate, "Queerest Cities in America 2017" January 12, 2017*

- Personal finance website *WalletHub* compared more than 180 U.S. cities across two key dimensions, "Hispanic Business-Friendliness" and "Hispanic Purchasing Power," to arrive at the most favorable conditions for Hispanic entrepreneurs. New Orleans was ranked #70 out of 182. Criteria includes: share of Hispanic-Owned Businesses; Hispanic entrepreneurship rate to median annual income of Hispanics; Small Business-Friendliness score; cost of living; and number of Hispanics with at least a bachelor's degree. *WalletHub.com, "2019's Best Cities for Hispanic Entrepreneurs," May 1, 2019*

Miscellaneous Rankings

- *MoveHub* ranked 446 hipster cities across 20 countries, using its *alternative* Hipster Index and New Orleans came out as #22 among the top 50. Criteria: population over 150,000; number of vintage boutiques; density of tattoo parlors; vegan places to eat; coffee shops; and density of vinyl record stores. *www.movehub.com, "The Hipster Index: Brighton Pips Portland to Global Top Spot," February 20, 2020*

- In its roundup of St. Patrick's Day parades "Gayot" listed the best festivals and parades of all things Irish. The festivities in New Orleans as among the best. *www.gayot.com, "Best St. Patrick's Day Parades," March 2020*

- *WalletHub* compared the 150 most populated U.S. cities to determine their operating efficiency. A "Quality of City Services" score was constructed for each city and then divided by the total budget per capita to reveal which were managed the best. New Orleans ranked #112. Criteria: financial stability; economy; education; safety; health; infrastructure and pollution. *www.WalletHub.com, "2020's Best- & Worst-Run Cities in America," June 29, 2020*

- New Orleans was selected as one of "America's Friendliest Cities." The city ranked #4 in the "Friendliest" category. Respondents to an online survey were asked to rate 38 top urban destinations in the United States as to general friendliness, as well as manners, politeness and warm disposition. *Travel + Leisure, "America's Friendliest Cities," October 20, 2017*

Business Environment

DEMOGRAPHICS

Population Growth

Area	1990 Census	2000 Census	2010 Census	2019* Estimate	Population Growth (%) 1990-2019	Population Growth (%) 2010-2019
City	496,938	484,674	343,829	390,845	-21.3	13.7
MSA[1]	1,264,391	1,316,510	1,167,764	1,267,777	0.3	8.6
U.S.	248,709,873	281,421,906	308,745,538	324,697,795	30.6	5.2

Note: (1) Figures cover the New Orleans-Metairie, LA Metropolitan Statistical Area; (*) 2015-2019 5-year estimated population
Source: U.S. Census Bureau, 1990 Census, Census 2000, Census 2010, 2015-2019 American Community Survey 5-Year Estimates

Household Size

Area	One	Two	Three	Four	Five	Six	Seven or More	Average Household Size
City	45.9	29.2	12.6	7.9	2.6	1.1	0.6	2.50
MSA[1]	33.5	32.3	15.5	11.5	4.6	1.7	0.9	2.60
U.S.	27.9	33.9	15.6	12.9	6.0	2.3	1.4	2.60

Note: (1) Figures cover the New Orleans-Metairie, LA Metropolitan Statistical Area
Source: U.S. Census Bureau, 2015-2019 American Community Survey 5-Year Estimates

Race

Area	White Alone[2] (%)	Black Alone[2] (%)	Asian Alone[2] (%)	AIAN[3] Alone[2] (%)	NHOPI[4] Alone[2] (%)	Other Race Alone[2] (%)	Two or More Races (%)
City	33.9	59.5	2.9	0.2	0.0	1.5	1.9
MSA[1]	57.3	35.1	2.9	0.4	0.0	2.2	2.0
U.S.	72.5	12.7	5.5	0.8	0.2	4.9	3.3

Note: (1) Figures cover the New Orleans-Metairie, LA Metropolitan Statistical Area; (2) Alone is defined as not being in combination with one or more other races; (3) American Indian and Alaska Native; (4) Native Hawaiian and Other Pacific Islander
Source: U.S. Census Bureau, 2015-2019 American Community Survey 5-Year Estimates

Hispanic or Latino Origin

Area	Total (%)	Mexican (%)	Puerto Rican (%)	Cuban (%)	Other (%)
City	5.5	1.3	0.3	0.4	3.5
MSA[1]	8.8	1.9	0.5	0.6	5.9
U.S.	18.0	11.2	1.7	0.7	4.3

Note: Persons of Hispanic or Latino origin can be of any race; (1) Figures cover the New Orleans-Metairie, LA Metropolitan Statistical Area
Source: U.S. Census Bureau, 2015-2019 American Community Survey 5-Year Estimates

Ancestry

Area	German	Irish	English	American	Italian	Polish	French[2]	Scottish	Dutch
City	6.1	5.4	4.1	2.5	3.9	0.9	5.4	1.1	0.4
MSA[1]	9.7	7.4	4.5	5.0	7.9	0.7	11.7	1.0	0.4
U.S.	13.3	9.7	7.2	6.2	5.1	2.8	2.3	1.7	1.2

Note: Figures are the percentage of the total population reporting a particular ancestry. The nine most commonly reported ancestries in the U.S. are shown. Figures include multiple ancestries (e.g. if a person reported being Irish and Italian, they were included in both columns); (1) Figures cover the New Orleans-Metairie, LA Metropolitan Statistical Area; (2) Excludes Basque
Source: U.S. Census Bureau, 2015-2019 American Community Survey 5-Year Estimates

Foreign-born Population

Area	Any Foreign Country	Asia	Mexico	Europe	Caribbean	Central America[2]	South America	Africa	Canada
City	5.5	2.0	0.3	0.8	0.3	1.5	0.3	0.2	0.1
MSA[1]	7.6	2.1	0.6	0.6	0.7	2.7	0.5	0.3	0.1
U.S.	13.6	4.2	3.5	1.5	1.3	1.1	1.0	0.7	0.2

Note: (1) Figures cover the New Orleans-Metairie, LA Metropolitan Statistical Area; (2) Excludes Mexico.
Source: U.S. Census Bureau, 2015-2019 American Community Survey 5-Year Estimates

Marital Status

Area	Never Married	Now Married[2]	Separated	Widowed	Divorced
City	49.2	29.4	2.7	5.9	12.8
MSA[1]	37.8	41.3	2.3	6.3	12.2
U.S.	33.4	48.1	1.9	5.8	10.9

Note: Figures are percentages and cover the population 15 years of age and older; (1) Figures cover the New Orleans-Metairie, LA Metropolitan Statistical Area; (2) Excludes separated
Source: U.S. Census Bureau, 2015-2019 American Community Survey 5-Year Estimates

Disability by Age

Area	All Ages	Under 18 Years Old	18 to 64 Years Old	65 Years and Over
City	14.2	5.0	12.3	36.4
MSA[1]	14.4	5.0	12.3	36.6
U.S.	12.6	4.2	10.3	34.5

Note: Figures show percent of the civilian noninstitutionalized population that reported having a disability. Disability status is determined from six types of difficulty: vision, hearing, cognitive, ambulatory, self-care, and independent living. For children under 5 years old, hearing and vision difficulty are used to determine disability status. For children between the ages of 5 and 14, disability status is determined from hearing, vision, cognitive, ambulatory, and self-care difficulties. For people aged 15 years and older, they are considered to have a disability if they have difficulty with any one of the six difficulty types; Note: (1) Figures cover the New Orleans-Metairie, LA Metropolitan Statistical Area
Source: U.S. Census Bureau, 2015-2019 American Community Survey 5-Year Estimates

Age

Area	Under Age 5	Age 5–19	Age 20–34	Age 35–44	Age 45–54	Age 55–64	Age 65–74	Age 75–84	Age 85+	Median Age
City	5.9	16.6	24.6	13.4	12.1	13.3	8.7	3.7	1.7	36.8
MSA[1]	6.2	18.3	21.0	12.8	12.8	13.7	9.3	4.3	1.7	38.3
U.S.	6.1	19.1	20.7	12.6	13.0	12.9	9.1	4.6	1.9	38.1

Note: (1) Figures cover the New Orleans-Metairie, LA Metropolitan Statistical Area
Source: U.S. Census Bureau, 2015-2019 American Community Survey 5-Year Estimates

Gender

Area	Males	Females	Males per 100 Females
City	185,513	205,332	90.3
MSA[1]	612,116	655,661	93.4
U.S.	159,886,919	164,810,876	97.0

Note: (1) Figures cover the New Orleans-Metairie, LA Metropolitan Statistical Area
Source: U.S. Census Bureau, 2015-2019 American Community Survey 5-Year Estimates

Religious Groups by Family

Area	Catholic	Baptist	Non-Den.	Methodist[2]	Lutheran	LDS[3]	Pentecostal	Presbyterian[4]	Muslim[5]	Judaism
MSA[1]	31.6	8.4	3.7	2.7	0.8	0.6	2.1	0.5	0.5	0.5
U.S.	19.1	9.3	4.0	4.0	2.3	2.0	1.9	1.6	0.8	0.7

Note: Figures are the number of adherents as a percentage of the total population; (1) Figures cover the New Orleans-Metairie, LA Metropolitan Statistical Area; (2) Methodist/Pietist; (3) Latter Day Saints; (4) Reformed; (5) Figures are estimates
Source: Association of Statisticians of American Religious Bodies, 2010 U.S. Religion Census: Religious Congregations & Membership Study

Religious Groups by Tradition

Area	Catholic	Evangelical Protestant	Mainline Protestant	Other Tradition	Black Protestant	Orthodox
MSA[1]	31.6	12.7	4.0	2.1	3.0	0.1
U.S.	19.1	16.2	7.3	4.3	1.6	0.3

Note: Figures are the number of adherents as a percentage of the total population; (1) Figures cover the New Orleans-Metairie, LA Metropolitan Statistical Area
Source: Association of Statisticians of American Religious Bodies, 2010 U.S. Religion Census: Religious Congregations & Membership Study

ECONOMY

Gross Metropolitan Product

Area	2017	2018	2019	2020	Rank[2]
MSA[1]	76.7	81.0	83.8	87.5	46

Note: Figures are in billions of dollars; (1) Figures cover the New Orleans-Metairie, LA Metropolitan Statistical Area; (2) Rank is based on 2018 data and ranges from 1 to 381
Source: U.S. Conference of Mayors, U.S. Metro Economies: GMP & Employment 2018-2020, September 2019

Economic Growth

Area	2015-17 (%)	2018 (%)	2019 (%)	2020 (%)	Rank[2]
MSA[1]	-0.6	1.2	1.3	2.0	329
U.S.	1.9	2.9	2.3	2.1	—

Note: Figures are real gross metropolitan product (GMP) growth rates and represent average annual percent change; (1) Figures cover the New Orleans-Metairie, LA Metropolitan Statistical Area; (2) Rank is based on 2017 2-year average annual percent change and ranges from 1 to 381
Source: U.S. Conference of Mayors, U.S. Metro Economies: GMP & Employment 2018-2020, September 2019

Metropolitan Area Exports

Area	2014	2015	2016	2017	2018	2019	Rank[2]
MSA[1]	34,881.5	27,023.3	29,518.8	31,648.5	36,570.4	34,109.6	9

Note: Figures are in millions of dollars; (1) Figures cover the New Orleans-Metairie, LA Metropolitan Statistical Area; (2) Rank is based on 2019 data and ranges from 1 to 386
Source: U.S. Department of Commerce, International Trade Administration, Office of Trade and Economic Analysis, Industry and Analysis, Exports by Metropolitan Area, data extracted March 24, 2021

Building Permits

Area	Single-Family 2018	Single-Family 2019	Pct. Chg.	Multi-Family 2018	Multi-Family 2019	Pct. Chg.	Total 2018	Total 2019	Pct. Chg.
City	524	558	6.5	779	748	-4.0	1,303	1,306	0.2
MSA[1]	3,046	3,241	6.4	818	785	-4.0	3,864	4,026	4.2
U.S.	855,300	862,100	0.7	473,500	523,900	10.6	1,328,800	1,386,000	4.3

Note: (1) Figures cover the New Orleans-Metairie, LA Metropolitan Statistical Area; Figures represent new, privately-owned housing units authorized (unadjusted data); All permit data are based on estimates with imputation
Source: U.S. Census Bureau, Manufacturing, Mining, and Construction Statistics, Building Permits, 2018, 2019

Bankruptcy Filings

Area	Business Filings 2019	Business Filings 2020	% Chg.	Nonbusiness Filings 2019	Nonbusiness Filings 2020	% Chg.
Orleans Parish	36	21	-41.7	683	391	-42.8
U.S.	22,780	21,655	-4.9	752,160	522,808	-30.5

Note: Business filings include Chapter 7, Chapter 9, Chapter 11, Chapter 12, Chapter 13, Chapter 15, and Section 304; Nonbusiness filings include Chapter 7, Chapter 11, and Chapter 13
Source: Administrative Office of the U.S. Courts, Business and Nonbusiness Bankruptcy, County Cases Commenced by Chapter of the Bankruptcy Code, During the 12-Month Period Ending December 31, 2019 and Business and Nonbusiness Bankruptcy, County Cases Commenced by Chapter of the Bankruptcy Code, During the 12-Month Period Ending December 31, 2020

Housing Vacancy Rates

Area	Gross Vacancy Rate[2] (%) 2018	2019	2020	Year-Round Vacancy Rate[3] (%) 2018	2019	2020	Rental Vacancy Rate[4] (%) 2018	2019	2020	Homeowner Vacancy Rate[5] (%) 2018	2019	2020
MSA[1]	11.9	12.9	10.7	11.8	12.8	9.8	9.7	9.4	6.1	1.7	1.8	1.3
U.S.	12.3	12.0	10.6	9.7	9.5	8.2	6.9	6.7	6.3	1.5	1.4	1.0

Note: (1) Figures cover the New Orleans-Metairie, LA Metropolitan Statistical Area; (2) The percentage of the total housing inventory that is vacant; (3) The percentage of the housing inventory (excluding seasonal units) that is year-round vacant; (4) The percentage of rental inventory that is vacant for rent; (5) The percentage of homeowner inventory that is vacant for sale
Source: U.S. Census Bureau, Housing Vacancies and Homeownership Annual Statistics: 2018, 2019, 2020

INCOME

Income

Area	Per Capita ($)	Median Household ($)	Average Household ($)
City	31,385	41,604	71,938
MSA[1]	31,072	53,084	76,818
U.S.	34,103	62,843	88,607

Note: (1) Figures cover the New Orleans-Metairie, LA Metropolitan Statistical Area
Source: U.S. Census Bureau, 2015-2019 American Community Survey 5-Year Estimates

Household Income Distribution

Area	Under $15,000	$15,000-$24,999	$25,000-$34,999	$35,000-$49,999	$50,000-$74,999	$75,000-$99,999	$100,000-$149,999	$150,000 and up
City	22.1	12.2	10.3	11.5	14.2	8.8	9.9	10.9
MSA[1]	14.8	10.9	9.6	12.2	16.4	11.6	13.0	11.5
U.S.	10.3	8.9	8.9	12.3	17.2	12.7	15.1	14.5

Note: (1) Figures cover the New Orleans-Metairie, LA Metropolitan Statistical Area
Source: U.S. Census Bureau, 2015-2019 American Community Survey 5-Year Estimates

Poverty Rate

Area	All Ages	Under 18 Years Old	18 to 64 Years Old	65 Years and Over
City	23.7	34.2	21.6	18.1
MSA[1]	17.3	25.2	15.7	12.5
U.S.	13.4	18.5	12.6	9.3

Note: Figures are percentage of people whose income during the past 12 months was below the poverty level;
(1) Figures cover the New Orleans-Metairie, LA Metropolitan Statistical Area
Source: U.S. Census Bureau, 2015-2019 American Community Survey 5-Year Estimates

CITY FINANCES

City Government Finances

Component	2017 ($000)	2017 ($ per capita)
Total Revenues	1,661,792	4,265
Total Expenditures	1,555,182	3,992
Debt Outstanding	2,414,117	6,196
Cash and Securities[1]	2,504,597	6,428

Note: (1) Cash and security holdings of a government at the close of its fiscal year, including those of its dependent agencies, utilities, and liquor stores.
Source: U.S. Census Bureau, State & Local Government Finances 2017

City Government Revenue by Source

Source	2017 ($000)	2017 ($ per capita)	2017 (%)
General Revenue			
From Federal Government	252,349	648	15.2
From State Government	67,369	173	4.1
From Local Governments	59,862	154	3.6
Taxes			
Property	257,721	661	15.5
Sales and Gross Receipts	272,881	700	16.4
Personal Income	0	0	0.0
Corporate Income	0	0	0.0
Motor Vehicle License	2,923	8	0.2
Other Taxes	20,895	54	1.3
Current Charges	410,162	1,053	24.7
Liquor Store	0	0	0.0
Utility	83,159	213	5.0
Employee Retirement	69,721	179	4.2

Source: U.S. Census Bureau, State & Local Government Finances 2017

City Government Expenditures by Function

Function	2017 ($000)	2017 ($ per capita)	2017 (%)
General Direct Expenditures			
Air Transportation	233,182	598	15.0
Corrections	0	0	0.0
Education	0	0	0.0
Employment Security Administration	0	0	0.0
Financial Administration	48,253	123	3.1
Fire Protection	105,342	270	6.8
General Public Buildings	0	0	0.0
Governmental Administration, Other	60,948	156	3.9
Health	0	0	0.0
Highways	57,270	147	3.7
Hospitals	45,659	117	2.9
Housing and Community Development	256,338	657	16.5
Interest on General Debt	82,538	211	5.3
Judicial and Legal	21,691	55	1.4
Libraries	0	0	0.0
Parking	0	0	0.0
Parks and Recreation	82,996	213	5.3
Police Protection	86,070	220	5.5
Public Welfare	0	0	0.0
Sewerage	96,656	248	6.2
Solid Waste Management	41,759	107	2.7
Veterans' Services	0	0	0.0
Liquor Store	0	0	0.0
Utility	84,465	216	5.4
Employee Retirement	111,629	286	7.2

Source: U.S. Census Bureau, State & Local Government Finances 2017

EMPLOYMENT

Labor Force and Employment

Area	Civilian Labor Force			Workers Employed		
	Dec. 2019	Dec. 2020	% Chg.	Dec. 2019	Dec. 2020	% Chg.
City	179,138	182,736	2.0	170,426	162,218	-4.8
MSA[1]	596,687	591,186	-0.9	570,042	542,565	-4.8
U.S.	164,007,000	160,017,000	-2.4	158,504,000	149,613,000	-5.6

Note: Data is not seasonally adjusted and covers workers 16 years of age and older; (1) Figures cover the New Orleans-Metairie, LA Metropolitan Statistical Area
Source: Bureau of Labor Statistics, Local Area Unemployment Statistics

Unemployment Rate

Area	2020											
	Jan.	Feb.	Mar.	Apr.	May	Jun.	Jul.	Aug.	Sep.	Oct.	Nov.	Dec.
City	5.5	4.2	6.3	22.2	20.7	15.9	15.1	12.6	12.4	15.1	13.6	11.2
MSA[1]	5.2	3.9	5.9	19.0	17.4	12.8	11.9	9.7	9.4	11.2	10.0	8.2
U.S.	4.0	3.8	4.5	14.4	13.0	11.2	10.5	8.5	7.7	6.6	6.4	6.5

Note: Data is not seasonally adjusted and covers workers 16 years of age and older; (1) Figures cover the New Orleans-Metairie, LA Metropolitan Statistical Area
Source: Bureau of Labor Statistics, Local Area Unemployment Statistics

Average Wages

Occupation	$/Hr.	Occupation	$/Hr.
Accountants and Auditors	33.50	Maintenance and Repair Workers	19.00
Automotive Mechanics	19.90	Marketing Managers	48.60
Bookkeepers	19.00	Network and Computer Systems Admin.	34.10
Carpenters	22.10	Nurses, Licensed Practical	21.90
Cashiers	10.50	Nurses, Registered	34.10
Computer Programmers	49.80	Nursing Assistants	12.30
Computer Systems Analysts	46.70	Office Clerks, General	13.40
Computer User Support Specialists	24.40	Physical Therapists	43.00
Construction Laborers	16.70	Physicians	105.80
Cooks, Restaurant	12.30	Plumbers, Pipefitters and Steamfitters	27.90
Customer Service Representatives	16.50	Police and Sheriff's Patrol Officers	24.00
Dentists	74.70	Postal Service Mail Carriers	25.20
Electricians	27.50	Real Estate Sales Agents	n/a
Engineers, Electrical	54.20	Retail Salespersons	12.90
Fast Food and Counter Workers	10.20	Sales Representatives, Technical/Scientific	32.30
Financial Managers	61.30	Secretaries, Exc. Legal/Medical/Executive	17.70
First-Line Supervisors of Office Workers	24.90	Security Guards	14.20
General and Operations Managers	60.80	Surgeons	n/a
Hairdressers/Cosmetologists	10.00	Teacher Assistants, Exc. Postsecondary*	12.40
Home Health and Personal Care Aides	9.90	Teachers, Secondary School, Exc. Sp. Ed.*	26.60
Janitors and Cleaners	11.80	Telemarketers	17.10
Landscaping/Groundskeeping Workers	13.10	Truck Drivers, Heavy/Tractor-Trailer	22.70
Lawyers	59.20	Truck Drivers, Light/Delivery Services	18.90
Maids and Housekeeping Cleaners	11.00	Waiters and Waitresses	9.90

Note: Wage data covers the New Orleans-Metairie, LA Metropolitan Statistical Area; (*) Hourly wages were calculated from annual wage data based on a 40 hour work week; n/a not available.
Source: Bureau of Labor Statistics, Metro Area Occupational Employment & Wage Estimates, May 2020

Employment by Industry

Sector	MSA[1]		U.S.
	Number of Employees	Percent of Total	Percent of Total
Construction	26,100	4.9	5.1
Education and Health Services	101,100	19.1	16.3
Financial Activities	27,600	5.2	6.1
Government	71,400	13.5	15.2
Information	5,400	1.0	1.9
Leisure and Hospitality	63,400	12.0	9.0
Manufacturing	29,900	5.7	8.5
Mining and Logging	3,700	0.7	0.4
Other Services	21,200	4.0	3.8
Professional and Business Services	70,200	13.3	14.4
Retail Trade	61,200	11.6	10.9
Transportation, Warehousing, and Utilities	27,600	5.2	4.6
Wholesale Trade	20,200	3.8	3.9

Note: Figures are non-farm employment as of December 2020. Figures are not seasonally adjusted and include workers 16 years of age and older; (1) Figures cover the New Orleans-Metairie, LA Metropolitan Statistical Area
Source: Bureau of Labor Statistics, Current Employment Statistics, Employment, Hours, and Earnings

Employment by Occupation

Occupation Classification	City (%)	MSA[1] (%)	U.S. (%)
Management, Business, Science, and Arts	43.1	37.9	38.5
Natural Resources, Construction, and Maintenance	6.0	10.1	8.9
Production, Transportation, and Material Moving	8.8	10.9	13.2
Sales and Office	19.4	21.4	21.6
Service	22.7	19.7	17.8

Note: Figures cover employed civilians 16 years of age and older; (1) Figures cover the New Orleans-Metairie, LA Metropolitan Statistical Area
Source: U.S. Census Bureau, 2015-2019 American Community Survey 5-Year Estimates

Occupations with Greatest Projected Employment Growth: 2020 – 2022

Occupation[1]	2020 Employment	2022 Projected Employment	Numeric Employment Change	Percent Employment Change
Fast Food and Counter Workers	21,880	22,580	700	3.2
Home Health and Personal Care Aides	35,530	36,200	670	1.9
Registered Nurses	40,540	41,050	510	1.3
Cooks, Restaurant	11,020	11,530	510	4.6
Stockers and Order Fillers	20,590	21,030	440	2.1
Medical Assistants	8,110	8,440	330	4.1
Nurse Practitioners	3,080	3,390	310	10.1
Medical and Health Services Managers	4,970	5,230	260	5.2
Licensed Practical and Licensed Vocational Nurses	18,340	18,580	240	1.3
Waiters and Waitresses	24,100	24,340	240	1.0

Note: Projections cover Louisiana; (1) Sorted by numeric employment change
Source: www.projectionscentral.com, State Occupational Projections, 2020–2022 Short-Term Projections

Fastest-Growing Occupations: 2020 – 2022

Occupation[1]	2020 Employment	2022 Projected Employment	Numeric Employment Change	Percent Employment Change
Nurse Practitioners	3,080	3,390	310	10.1
Occupational Therapy Assistants	670	730	60	9.0
Physician Assistants	1,130	1,210	80	7.1
Physical Therapist Assistants	1,410	1,510	100	7.1
Speech-Language Pathologists	1,240	1,310	70	5.6
Medical and Health Services Managers	4,970	5,230	260	5.2
Cooks, Restaurant	11,020	11,530	510	4.6
Respiratory Therapists	2,480	2,590	110	4.4
Physical Therapist Aides	1,630	1,700	70	4.3
Medical Assistants	8,110	8,440	330	4.1

Note: Projections cover Louisiana; (1) Sorted by percent employment change and excludes occupations with numeric employment change less than 50
Source: www.projectionscentral.com, State Occupational Projections, 2020–2022 Short-Term Projections

TAXES

State Corporate Income Tax Rates

State	Tax Rate (%)	Income Brackets ($)	Num. of Brackets	Financial Institution Tax Rate (%)[a]	Federal Income Tax Ded.
Louisiana	4.0 - 8.0	25,000 - 200,001	5	4.0 - 8.0	Yes

Note: Tax rates as of January 1, 2021; (a) Rates listed are the corporate income tax rate applied to financial institutions or excise taxes based on income. Some states have other taxes based upon the value of deposits or shares.
Source: Federation of Tax Administrators, State Corporate Income Tax Rates, January 1, 2021

State Individual Income Tax Rates

State	Tax Rate (%)	Income Brackets ($)	Personal Exemptions ($) Single	Personal Exemptions ($) Married	Personal Exemptions ($) Depend.	Standard Ded. ($) Single	Standard Ded. ($) Married
Louisiana	2.0 - 6.0	12,500 - 50,001 (b)	4,500	9,000 (k)	1,000	(k)	(k)

Note: Tax rates as of January 1, 2021; Local- and county-level taxes are not included; Federal income tax is deductible on state income tax returns; (b) For joint returns, taxes are twice the tax on half the couple's income; (k) The amounts reported for Louisiana are a combined personal exemption-standard deduction.
Source: Federation of Tax Administrators, State Individual Income Tax Rates, January 1, 2021

Various State Sales and Excise Tax Rates

State	State Sales Tax (%)	Gasoline[1] (¢/gal.)	Cigarette[2] ($/pack)	Spirits[3] ($/gal.)	Wine[4] ($/gal.)	Beer[5] ($/gal.)	Recreational Marijuana (%)
Louisiana	4.45	20.01	1.08	3.03	0.76	0.4	Not legal

Note: All tax rates as of January 1, 2021; (1) The American Petroleum Institute has developed a methodology for determining the average tax rate on a gallon of fuel. Rates may include any of the following: excise taxes, environmental fees, storage tank fees, other fees or taxes, general sales tax, and local taxes; (2) The federal excise tax of $1.0066 per pack and local taxes are not included; (3) Rates are those applicable to off-premise sales of 40% alcohol by volume (a.b.v.) distilled spirits in 750ml containers. Local excise taxes are excluded; (4) Rates are those applicable to off-premise sales of 11% a.b.v. non-carbonated wine in 750ml containers; (5) Rates are those applicable to off-premise sales of 4.7% a.b.v. beer in 12 ounce containers.
Source: Tax Foundation, 2021 Facts & Figures: How Does Your State Compare?

State Business Tax Climate Index Rankings

State	Overall Rank	Corporate Tax Rank	Individual Income Tax Rank	Sales Tax Rank	Property Tax Rank	Unemployment Insurance Tax Rank
Louisiana	42	35	32	49	23	4

Note: The index is a measure of how each state's tax laws affect economic performance. The lower the rank, the more favorable a state's tax system is for business. States without a given tax are given a ranking of 1. The scores/rankings for the District of Columbia do not affect other states. The 2021 index represents the tax climate as of July 1, 2020.
Source: Tax Foundation, State Business Tax Climate Index 2021

TRANSPORTATION

Means of Transportation to Work

Area	Car/Truck/Van Drove Alone	Car/Truck/Van Car-pooled	Public Transportation Bus	Public Transportation Subway	Public Transportation Railroad	Bicycle	Walked	Other Means	Worked at Home
City	68.0	9.1	5.9	0.0	0.0	3.1	5.4	2.7	5.7
MSA[1]	78.1	9.8	2.3	0.0	0.0	1.1	2.5	1.7	4.5
U.S.	76.3	9.0	2.4	1.9	0.6	0.5	2.7	1.4	5.2

Note: Figures are percentages and cover workers 16 years of age and older; (1) Figures cover the New Orleans-Metairie, LA Metropolitan Statistical Area
Source: U.S. Census Bureau, 2015-2019 American Community Survey 5-Year Estimates

Travel Time to Work

Area	Less Than 10 Minutes	10 to 19 Minutes	20 to 29 Minutes	30 to 44 Minutes	45 to 59 Minutes	60 to 89 Minutes	90 Minutes or More
City	9.9	33.9	25.4	19.7	4.5	4.2	2.3
MSA[1]	10.5	30.6	22.2	20.9	7.6	5.6	2.5
U.S.	12.2	28.4	20.8	20.8	8.3	6.4	2.9

Note: Note: Figures are percentages and include workers 16 years old and over; (1) Figures cover the New Orleans-Metairie, LA Metropolitan Statistical Area
Source: U.S. Census Bureau, 2015-2019 American Community Survey 5-Year Estimates

Key Congestion Measures

Measure	1982	1992	2002	2012	2017
Annual Hours of Delay, Total (000)	16,022	26,555	36,593	49,530	55,833
Annual Hours of Delay, Per Auto Commuter	16	23	32	49	58
Annual Congestion Cost, Total (million $)	121	281	494	888	1,029
Annual Congestion Cost, Per Auto Commuter ($)	776	885	951	1,008	1,103

Note: Covers the New Orleans LA urban area
Source: Texas A&M Transportation Institute, 2019 Urban Mobility Report

Freeway Travel Time Index

Measure	1982	1987	1992	1997	2002	2007	2012	2017
Urban Area Index[1]	1.12	1.15	1.18	1.21	1.23	1.27	1.33	1.36
Urban Area Rank[1,2]	15	17	18	23	26	20	10	6

Note: Freeway Travel Time Index—the ratio of travel time in the peak period to the travel time at free-flow conditions. For example, a value of 1.30 indicates a 20-minute free-flow trip takes 26 minutes in the peak (20 minutes x 1.30 = 26 minutes); (1) Covers the New Orleans LA urban area; (2) Rank is based on 101 larger urban areas (#1 = highest travel time index)
Source: Texas A&M Transportation Institute, 2019 Urban Mobility Report

Public Transportation

Agency Name / Mode of Transportation	Vehicles Operated in Maximum Service[1]	Annual Unlinked Passenger Trips[2] (in thous.)	Annual Passenger Miles[3] (in thous.)
New Orleans Regional Transit Authority (NORTA)			
Bus (purchased transportation)	97	9,953.1	37,136.2
Demand Response (purchased transportation)	43	229.2	1,747.5
Ferryboat (purchased transportation)	2	844.9	422.5
Streetcar Rail (purchased transportation)	31	5,289.3	12,324.1

Note: (1) Number of revenue vehicles operated by the given mode and type of service to meet the annual maximum service requirement. This is the revenue vehicle count during the peak season of the year; on the week and day that maximum service is provided. Vehicles operated in maximum service (VOMS) exclude atypical days and one-time special events; (2) Number of passengers who boarded public transportation vehicles. Passengers are counted each time they board a vehicle no matter how many vehicles they use to travel from their origin to their destination. (3) Sum of the distances ridden by all passengers during the entire fiscal year.
Source: Federal Transit Administration, National Transit Database, 2019

Air Transportation

Airport Name and Code / Type of Service	Passenger Airlines[1]	Passenger Enplanements	Freight Carriers[2]	Freight (lbs)
New Orleans International (MSY)				
Domestic service (U.S. carriers - 2020)	24	2,607,096	19	50,586,202
International service (U.S. carriers - 2019)	8	5,669	0	0

Note: (1) Includes all U.S.-based major, minor and commuter airlines that carried at least one passenger during the year; (2) Includes all U.S.-based airlines and freight carriers that transported at least one pound of freight during the year.
Source: Bureau of Transportation Statistics, The Intermodal Transportation Database, Air Carriers: T-100 Domestic Market (U.S. Carriers), 2020; Bureau of Transportation Statistics, The Intermodal Transportation Database, Air Carriers: T-100 International Market (U.S. Carriers), 2019

BUSINESSES

Major Business Headquarters

Company Name	Industry	Rankings Fortune[1]	Rankings Forbes[2]
Entergy	Utilities, Gas and Electric	293	-

Note: (1) Companies that produce a 10-K are ranked 1 to 500 based on 2019 revenue; (2) All private companies with at least $2 billion in annual revenue through the end of their most current fiscal year are ranked 1 to 219; companies listed are headquartered in the city; dashes indicate no ranking
Source: Fortune, "Fortune 500," June/July 2020; Forbes, "America's Largest Private Companies," 2020

Fastest-Growing Businesses

According to *Initiative for a Competitive Inner City (ICIC)*, New Orleans is home to one of America's 100 fastest-growing "inner city" companies: **French Truck Coffee** (#12). Criteria for inclusion: company must be headquartered in or have 51 percent or more of its physical operations in an economically distressed urban area; must be an independent, for-profit corporation, partnership or proprietorship; must have 10 or more employees and have a five-year sales history that includes sales of at least $200,000 in the base year and at least $1 million in the current year with no decrease in sales over the two most recent years. Companies were ranked overall by revenue growth over the five-year period between 2015 and 2019. *Initiative for a Competitive Inner City (ICIC), "Inner City 100 Companies," 2020*

Minority Business Opportunity

New Orleans is home to one company which is on the *Black Enterprise* Bank list (15 largest banks based on total assets, capital, deposits and loans, including mortgage-backed securities for the calendar year): **Liberty Bank and Trust Co.** (#2). Only commercial banks or savings and loans that are classified by the Federal Reserve as black institutions and have been fully operational for the previous calendar year were considered. *Black Enterprise, B.E. 100s, 2019*

Living Environment

COST OF LIVING

Cost of Living Index

Composite Index	Groceries	Housing	Utilities	Trans-portation	Health Care	Misc. Goods/Services
110.3	100.1	137.1	75.5	97.9	116.5	104.8

Note: The Cost of Living Index measures regional differences in the cost of consumer goods and services, excluding taxes and non-consumer expenditures, for professional and managerial households in the top income quintile. It is based on more than 50,000 prices covering almost 60 different items for which prices are collected three times a year by chambers of commerce, economic development organizations or university applied economic centers in each participating urban area. The numbers shown should be read as a percentage above or below the national average of 100. For example, a value of 115.4 in the groceries column indicates that grocery prices are 15.4% higher than the national average. Small differences in the index numbers should not be interpreted as significant; Figures cover the New Orleans LA urban area.
Source: The Council for Community and Economic Research, Cost of Living Index, 2020

Grocery Prices

Area[1]	T-Bone Steak ($/pound)	Frying Chicken ($/pound)	Whole Milk ($/half gal.)	Eggs ($/dozen)	Orange Juice ($/64 oz.)	Coffee ($/11.5 oz.)
City[2]	10.51	1.21	2.30	1.63	3.63	3.83
Avg.	11.78	1.39	2.05	1.47	3.57	4.34
Min.	8.03	0.94	1.03	0.74	2.94	3.02
Max.	15.86	2.65	4.31	3.77	5.44	8.69

Note: (1) Values for the local area are compared with the average, minimum and maximum values for all 284 areas in the Cost of Living Index; (2) Figures cover the New Orleans LA urban area; **T-Bone Steak** (price per pound); **Frying Chicken** (price per pound, whole fryer); **Whole Milk** (half gallon carton); **Eggs** (price per dozen, Grade A, large); **Orange Juice** (64 oz. Tropicana or Florida Natural); **Coffee** (11.5 oz. can, vacuum-packed, Maxwell House, Hills Bros, or Folgers).
Source: The Council for Community and Economic Research, Cost of Living Index, 2020

Housing and Utility Costs

Area[1]	New Home Price ($)	Apartment Rent ($/month)	All Electric ($/month)	Part Electric ($/month)	Other Energy ($/month)	Telephone ($/month)
City[2]	520,536	1,618	-	58.74	38.53	180.20
Avg.	368,594	1,168	170.86	100.47	65.28	184.30
Min.	190,567	502	91.58	31.42	26.08	169.60
Max.	2,227,806	4,738	470.38	280.31	280.06	206.50

Note: (1) Values for the local area are compared with the average, minimum and maximum values for all 284 areas in the Cost of Living Index; (2) Figures cover the New Orleans LA urban area; **New Home Price** (2,400 sf living area, 8,000 sf lot, in urban area with full utilities); **Apartment Rent** (950 sf 2 bedroom/1.5 or 2 bath, unfurnished, excluding all utilities except water); **All Electric** (average monthly cost for an all-electric home); **Part Electric** (average monthly cost for a part-electric home); **Other Energy** (average monthly cost for natural gas, fuel oil, coal, wood, and any other forms of energy except electricity); **Telephone** (price includes the base monthly rate plus taxes and fees for three lines of mobile phone service).
Source: The Council for Community and Economic Research, Cost of Living Index, 2020

Health Care, Transportation, and Other Costs

Area[1]	Doctor ($/visit)	Dentist ($/visit)	Optometrist ($/visit)	Gasoline ($/gallon)	Beauty Salon ($/visit)	Men's Shirt ($)
City[2]	156.11	111.89	94.77	2.02	48.89	27.54
Avg.	115.44	99.32	108.10	2.21	39.27	31.37
Min.	36.68	59.00	51.36	1.71	19.00	11.00
Max.	219.00	153.10	250.97	3.46	82.05	58.33

Note: (1) Values for the local area are compared with the average, minimum and maximum values for all 284 areas in the Cost of Living Index; (2) Figures cover the New Orleans LA urban area; **Doctor** (general practitioners routine exam of an established patient); **Dentist** (adult teeth cleaning and periodic oral examination); **Optometrist** (full vision eye exam for established adult patient); **Gasoline** (one gallon regular unleaded, national brand, including all taxes, cash price at self-service pump if available); **Beauty Salon** (woman's shampoo, trim, and blow-dry); **Men's Shirt** (cotton/polyester dress shirt, pinpoint weave, long sleeves).
Source: The Council for Community and Economic Research, Cost of Living Index, 2020

HOUSING

Homeownership Rate

Area	2012 (%)	2013 (%)	2014 (%)	2015 (%)	2016 (%)	2017 (%)	2018 (%)	2019 (%)	2020 (%)
MSA[1]	62.4	61.4	60.6	62.8	59.3	61.7	62.6	61.1	66.3
U.S.	65.4	65.1	64.5	63.7	63.4	63.9	64.4	64.6	66.6

Note: (1) Figures cover the New Orleans-Metairie, LA Metropolitan Statistical Area
Source: U.S. Census Bureau, Housing Vacancies and Homeownership Annual Statistics: 2012-2020

House Price Index (HPI)

Area	National Ranking[2]	Quarterly Change (%)	One-Year Change (%)	Five-Year Change (%)	Since 1991Q1 (%)
MSA[1]	174	2.09	5.37	22.52	226.15
U.S.[3]	–	3.81	10.77	38.99	205.12

Note: The HPI is a weighted repeat sales index. It measures average price changes in repeat sales or refinancings on the same properties. This information is obtained by reviewing repeat mortgage transactions on single-family properties whose mortgages have been purchased or securitized by Fannie Mae or Freddie Mac since January 1975; (1) Figures cover the New Orleans-Metairie, LA Metropolitan Statistical Area; (2) Rankings are based on annual percentage change for all metro areas containing at least 15,000 transactions over the last 10 years and ranges from 1 to 253; (3) figures based on a weighted average of Census Division estimates using a seasonally adjusted, purchase-only index; all figures are for the period ending December 31, 2020
Source: Federal Housing Finance Agency, Change in Metropolitan Area House Price Indexes, April 7, 2021

Median Single-Family Home Prices

Area	2018	2019	2020p	Percent Change 2019 to 2020
MSA[1]	210.1	222.0	240.5	8.3
U.S. Average	261.6	274.6	299.9	9.2

Note: Figures are median sales prices of existing single-family homes in thousands of dollars; (p) preliminary; (1) Figures cover the New Orleans-Metairie, LA Metropolitan Statistical Area
Source: National Association of Realtors, Median Sales Price of Existing Single-Family Homes for Metropolitan Areas, 4th Quarter 2020

Qualifying Income Based on Median Sales Price of Existing Single-Family Homes

Area	With 5% Down ($)	With 10% Down ($)	With 20% Down ($)
MSA[1]	47,475	44,976	39,979
U.S. Average	59,266	56,147	49,908

Note: Figures are preliminary; Qualifying income is based on a mortgage rate of 2.81%. Monthly principal and interest payment is limited to 25% of income; (1) Figures cover the New Orleans-Metairie, LA Metropolitan Statistical Area
Source: National Association of Realtors, Qualifying Income Based on Median Sales Price of Existing Single-Family Homes for Metropolitan Areas, 4th Quarter 2020

Home Value Distribution

Area	Under $50,000	$50,000 -$99,999	$100,000 -$149,999	$150,000 -$199,999	$200,000 -$299,999	$300,000 -$499,999	$500,000 -$999,999	$1,000,000 or more
City	2.8	7.9	13.8	18.6	19.9	20.5	13.0	3.7
MSA[1]	4.2	9.0	16.8	20.8	24.8	16.4	6.4	1.6
U.S.	6.9	12.0	13.3	14.0	19.6	19.3	11.4	3.4

Note: Figures are percentages and cover owner-occupied housing units; (1) Figures cover the New Orleans-Metairie, LA Metropolitan Statistical Area
Source: U.S. Census Bureau, 2015-2019 American Community Survey 5-Year Estimates

Year Housing Structure Built

Area	2010 or Later	2000 -2009	1990 -1999	1980 -1989	1970 -1979	1960 -1969	1950 -1959	1940 -1949	Before 1940	Median Year
City	3.4	7.1	3.5	7.3	13.7	11.1	12.1	7.7	34.0	1957
MSA[1]	3.8	11.9	9.8	13.3	19.3	13.6	10.1	4.8	13.5	1974
U.S.	5.2	14.0	13.9	13.4	15.2	10.6	10.3	4.9	12.6	1978

Note: Figures are percentages except for Median Year; Note: (1) Figures cover the New Orleans-Metairie, LA Metropolitan Statistical Area
Source: U.S. Census Bureau, 2015-2019 American Community Survey 5-Year Estimates

Gross Monthly Rent

Area	Under $500	$500 -$999	$1,000 -$1,499	$1,500 -$1,999	$2,000 -$2,499	$2,500 -$2,999	$3,000 and up	Median ($)
City	12.8	37.4	33.7	11.5	3.0	0.9	0.6	998
MSA[1]	9.3	41.9	35.6	10.0	2.2	0.6	0.5	991
U.S.	9.4	36.2	30.0	14.0	5.6	2.4	2.4	1,062

Note: Figures are percentages except for Median; Gross rent is the contract rent plus the estimated average monthly cost of utilities (electricity, gas, and water and sewer) and fuels (oil, coal, kerosene, wood, etc.) if these are paid by the renter (or paid for the renter by someone else); (1) Figures cover the New Orleans-Metairie, LA Metropolitan Statistical Area
Source: U.S. Census Bureau, 2015-2019 American Community Survey 5-Year Estimates

HEALTH

Health Risk Factors

Category	MSA[1] (%)	U.S. (%)
Adults aged 18–64 who have any kind of health care coverage	88.2	87.3
Adults who reported being in good or better health	78.9	82.4
Adults who have been told they have high blood cholesterol	38.0	33.0
Adults who have been told they have high blood pressure	39.1	32.3
Adults who are current smokers	21.7	17.1
Adults who currently use E-cigarettes	4.2	4.6
Adults who currently use chewing tobacco, snuff, or snus	3.6	4.0
Adults who are heavy drinkers[2]	8.7	6.3
Adults who are binge drinkers[3]	19.5	17.4
Adults who are overweight (BMI 25.0 - 29.9)	34.7	35.3
Adults who are obese (BMI 30.0 - 99.8)	36.1	31.3
Adults who participated in any physical activities in the past month	74.5	74.4
Adults who always or nearly always wears a seat belt	95.6	94.3

Note: (1) Figures cover the New Orleans-Metairie, LA Metropolitan Statistical Area; (2) Heavy drinkers are classified as adult men having more than 14 drinks per week and adult women having more than 7 drinks per week; (3) Binge drinkers are classified as males having five or more drinks on one occasion or females having four or more drinks on one occasion
Source: Centers for Disease Control and Prevention, Behaviorial Risk Factor Surveillance System, SMART: Selected Metropolitan Area Risk Trends, 2017

Acute and Chronic Health Conditions

Category	MSA[1] (%)	U.S. (%)
Adults who have ever been told they had a heart attack	4.2	4.2
Adults who have ever been told they have angina or coronary heart disease	4.4	3.9
Adults who have ever been told they had a stroke	3.9	3.0
Adults who have ever been told they have asthma	14.3	14.2
Adults who have ever been told they have arthritis	28.2	24.9
Adults who have ever been told they have diabetes[2]	15.3	10.5
Adults who have ever been told they had skin cancer	5.9	6.2
Adults who have ever been told they had any other types of cancer	6.4	7.1
Adults who have ever been told they have COPD	10.4	6.5
Adults who have ever been told they have kidney disease	3.8	3.0
Adults who have ever been told they have a form of depression	20.7	20.5

Note: (1) Figures cover the New Orleans-Metairie, LA Metropolitan Statistical Area; (2) Figures do not include pregnancy-related, borderline, or pre-diabetes
Source: Centers for Disease Control and Prevention, Behaviorial Risk Factor Surveillance System, SMART: Selected Metropolitan Area Risk Trends, 2017

Health Screening and Vaccination Rates

Category	MSA[1] (%)	U.S. (%)
Adults aged 65+ who have had flu shot within the past year	56.8	60.7
Adults aged 65+ who have ever had a pneumonia vaccination	76.8	75.4
Adults who have ever been tested for HIV	41.7	36.1
Adults who have ever had the shingles or zoster vaccine?	25.4	28.9
Adults who have had their blood cholesterol checked within the last five years	88.5	85.9

Note: n/a not available; (1) Figures cover the New Orleans-Metairie, LA Metropolitan Statistical Area.
Source: Centers for Disease Control and Prevention, Behaviorial Risk Factor Surveillance System, SMART: Selected Metropolitan Area Risk Trends, 2017

Disability Status

Category	MSA[1] (%)	U.S. (%)
Adults who reported being deaf	7.6	6.7
Are you blind or have serious difficulty seeing, even when wearing glasses?	6.0	4.5
Are you limited in any way in any of your usual activities due of arthritis?	15.2	12.9
Do you have difficulty doing errands alone?	10.5	6.8
Do you have difficulty dressing or bathing?	4.9	3.6
Do you have serious difficulty concentrating/remembering/making decisions?	13.3	10.7
Do you have serious difficulty walking or climbing stairs?	16.1	13.6

Note: (1) Figures cover the New Orleans-Metairie, LA Metropolitan Statistical Area.
Source: Centers for Disease Control and Prevention, Behaviorial Risk Factor Surveillance System, SMART: Selected Metropolitan Area Risk Trends, 2017

Mortality Rates for the Top 10 Causes of Death in the U.S.

ICD-10[a] Sub-Chapter	ICD-10[a] Code	Age-Adjusted Mortality Rate[1] per 100,000 population County[2]	U.S.
Malignant neoplasms	C00-C97	153.5	149.2
Ischaemic heart diseases	I20-I25	66.8	90.5
Other forms of heart disease	I30-I51	75.3	52.2
Chronic lower respiratory diseases	J40-J47	23.4	39.6
Other degenerative diseases of the nervous system	G30-G31	36.9	37.6
Cerebrovascular diseases	I60-I69	41.2	37.2
Other external causes of accidental injury	W00-X59	54.8	36.1
Organic, including symptomatic, mental disorders	F01-F09	25.3	29.4
Hypertensive diseases	I10-I15	36.7	24.1
Diabetes mellitus	E10-E14	29.0	21.5

Note: (a) ICD-10 = International Classification of Diseases 10th Revision; (1) Mortality rates are a three-year average covering 2017-2019; (2) Figures cover Orleans Parish.
Source: Centers for Disease Control and Prevention, National Center for Health Statistics. Underlying Cause of Death 1999-2019 on CDC WONDER Online Database

Mortality Rates for Selected Causes of Death

ICD-10[a] Sub-Chapter	ICD-10[a] Code	Age-Adjusted Mortality Rate[1] per 100,000 population County[2]	U.S.
Assault	X85-Y09	31.6	6.0
Diseases of the liver	K70-K76	13.8	14.4
Human immunodeficiency virus (HIV) disease	B20-B24	6.2	1.5
Influenza and pneumonia	J09-J18	7.4	13.8
Intentional self-harm	X60-X84	11.6	14.1
Malnutrition	E40-E46	5.6	2.3
Obesity and other hyperalimentation	E65-E68	Unreliable	2.1
Renal failure	N17-N19	24.2	12.6
Transport accidents	V01-V99	10.7	12.3
Viral hepatitis	B15-B19	Unreliable	1.2

Note: (a) ICD-10 = International Classification of Diseases 10th Revision; (1) Mortality rates are a three-year average covering 2017-2019; (2) Figures cover Orleans Parish; Data are suppressed when the data meet the criteria for confidentiality constraints; Mortality rates are flagged as unreliable when the rate would be calculated with a numerator of 20 or less.
Source: Centers for Disease Control and Prevention, National Center for Health Statistics. Underlying Cause of Death 1999-2019 on CDC WONDER Online Database

Health Insurance Coverage

Area	With Health Insurance	With Private Health Insurance	With Public Health Insurance	Without Health Insurance	Population Under Age 19 Without Health Insurance
City	90.8	56.3	42.9	9.2	3.4
MSA[1]	90.3	60.4	40.1	9.7	3.7
U.S.	91.2	67.9	35.1	8.8	5.1

Note: Figures are percentages that cover the civilian noninstitutionalized population; (1) Figures cover the New Orleans-Metairie, LA Metropolitan Statistical Area
Source: U.S. Census Bureau, 2015-2019 American Community Survey 5-Year Estimates

Number of Medical Professionals

Area	MDs[3]	DOs[3,4]	Dentists	Podiatrists	Chiropractors	Optometrists
Parish[1] (number)	3,160	71	290	15	37	24
Parish[1] (rate[2])	808.2	18.2	74.3	3.8	9.5	6.2
U.S. (rate[2])	282.9	22.7	71.2	6.2	28.1	16.9

22071
Note: Data as of 2019 unless noted; (1) Data covers Orleans Parish; (2) Rate per 100,000 population; (3) Data as of 2018 and includes all active, non-federal physicians; (4) Doctor of Osteopathic Medicine
Source: U.S. Department of Health and Human Services, Health Resources and Services Administration, Bureau of Health Professions, Area Resource File (ARF) 2019-2020

Best Hospitals

According to *U.S. News,* the New Orleans-Metairie, LA metro area is home to one of the best hospitals in the U.S.: **Ochsner Medical Center** (1 adult specialty and 1 pediatric specialty). The hospital listed was nationally ranked in at least one of 16 adult or 10 pediatric specialties. Only 134 hospitals nationwide were nationally ranked in one or more adult or pediatric specialty; this number increases to 178 counting specialized centers within hospitals. Twenty hospitals in the U.S. made the Honor Roll. The Best Hospitals Honor Roll takes both the national rankings and the procedure and condition ratings into account. Hospitals received points if they were nationally ranked in one of the 16 adult specialties—the higher they ranked, the more points they got—and how many ratings of "high performing" they earned in the 10 procedures and conditions. *U.S. News Online, "America's Best Hospitals 2020-21"*

According to *U.S. News,* the New Orleans-Metairie, LA metro area is home to one of the best children's hospitals in the U.S.: **Ochsner Hospital for Children** (1 pediatric specialty). The hospital listed was highly ranked in at least one of 10 pediatric specialties. Eighty-eight children's hospitals in the U.S. were nationally ranked in at least one specialty. Hospitals received points for being ranked in a specialty, and the 10 hospitals with the most points across the 10 specialties make up the Honor Roll. *U.S. News Online, "America's Best Children's Hospitals 2020-21"*

EDUCATION

Public School District Statistics

District Name	Schls	Pupils	Pupil/Teacher Ratio	Minority Pupils[1] (%)	Free Lunch Eligible[2] (%)	IEP[3] (%)
Orleans Parish	11	4,642	17.6	87.7	53.9	14.2

Note: Table includes school districts with 2,000 or more students; (1) Percentage of students that are not non-Hispanic white; (2) Percentage of students that are eligible for the free lunch program; (3) Percentage of students that have an Individualized Education Program.
Source: U.S. Department of Education, National Center for Education Statistics, Common Core of Data, Local Education Agency (School District) Universe Survey: School Year 2018-2019; U.S. Department of Education, National Center for Education Statistics, Common Core of Data, Public Elementary/Secondary School Universe Survey: School Year 2018-2019

Best High Schools

According to *U.S. News,* New Orleans is home to two of the top 500 high schools in the U.S.: **Benjamin Franklin High School** (#71); **Lusher Charter School** (#148). Nearly 18,000 public, magnet and charter schools were ranked based on their performance on state assessments and how well they prepare students for college. *U.S. News & World Report, "Best High Schools 2020"*

Highest Level of Education

Area	Less than H.S.	H.S. Diploma	Some College, No Deg.	Associate Degree	Bachelor's Degree	Master's Degree	Prof. School Degree	Doctorate Degree
City	13.5	22.8	21.5	4.7	21.2	9.9	4.4	2.0
MSA[1]	13.1	28.2	22.5	5.8	19.0	7.3	2.8	1.2
U.S.	12.0	27.0	20.4	8.5	19.8	8.8	2.1	1.4

Note: Figures cover persons age 25 and over; (1) Figures cover the New Orleans-Metairie, LA Metropolitan Statistical Area
Source: U.S. Census Bureau, 2015-2019 American Community Survey 5-Year Estimates

Educational Attainment by Race

Area	High School Graduate or Higher (%)					Bachelor's Degree or Higher (%)				
	Total	White	Black	Asian	Hisp.[2]	Total	White	Black	Asian	Hisp.[2]
City	86.5	95.7	81.0	75.8	80.9	37.6	63.9	19.7	40.4	35.9
MSA[1]	86.9	90.6	82.0	77.4	75.1	30.3	36.8	18.7	38.7	19.2
U.S.	88.0	89.9	86.0	87.1	68.7	32.1	33.5	21.6	54.3	16.4

Note: Figures shown cover persons 25 years old and over; (1) Figures cover the New Orleans-Metairie, LA Metropolitan Statistical Area; (2) People of Hispanic origin can be of any race
Source: U.S. Census Bureau, 2015-2019 American Community Survey 5-Year Estimates

School Enrollment by Grade and Control

Area	Preschool (%)		Kindergarten (%)		Grades 1 - 4 (%)		Grades 5 - 8 (%)		Grades 9 - 12 (%)	
	Public	Private	Public	Private	Public	Private	Public	Private	Public	Private
City	50.3	49.7	77.0	23.0	80.1	19.9	80.0	20.0	78.9	21.1
MSA[1]	53.6	46.4	77.3	22.7	78.1	21.9	77.7	22.3	76.0	24.0
U.S.	59.1	40.9	87.6	12.4	89.5	10.5	89.4	10.6	90.1	9.9

Note: Figures shown cover persons 3 years old and over; (1) Figures cover the New Orleans-Metairie, LA Metropolitan Statistical Area
Source: U.S. Census Bureau, 2015-2019 American Community Survey 5-Year Estimates

Higher Education

Four-Year Colleges			Two-Year Colleges			Medical Schools[1]	Law Schools[2]	Voc/Tech[3]
Public	Private Non-profit	Private For-profit	Public	Private Non-profit	Private For-profit			
3	7	0	1	0	0	2	2	5

Note: Figures cover institutions located within the city limits and include main campuses only; (1) includes schools accredited by the Liaison Committee on Medical Education and the American Osteopathic Association's Commission on Osteopathic College Accreditation; (2) includes ABA-accredited schools, schools with provisional ABA accreditation, and state accredited schools; (3) includes all schools with programs that are less than 2 years.
Source: National Center for Education Statistics, Integrated Postsecondary Education System (IPEDS), 2019-20; Wikipedia, List of Medical Schools in the United States, accessed April 2, 2021; Wikipedia, List of Law Schools in the United States, accessed April 2, 2021

According to *U.S. News & World Report,* the New Orleans-Metairie, LA metro area is home to two of the top 200 national universities in the U.S.: **Tulane University** (#41); **Loyola University New Orleans** (#196 tie). The indicators used to capture academic quality fall into a number of categories: assessment by administrators at peer institutions; retention of students; faculty resources; student selectivity; financial resources; alumni giving; high school counselor ratings of colleges; and graduation rate. *U.S. News & World Report, "America's Best Colleges 2021"*

According to *U.S. News & World Report,* the New Orleans-Metairie, LA metro area is home to one of the top 100 law schools in the U.S.: **Tulane University** (#60 tie). The rankings are based on a weighted average of 12 measures of quality: peer assessment score; assessment score by lawyers/judges; median LSAT scores; median undergrad GPA; acceptance rate; employment rates for graduates; placement success; bar passage rate; faculty resources; expenditures per student; student/faculty ratio; and library resources. *U.S. News & World Report, "America's Best Graduate Schools, Law, 2022"*

EMPLOYERS

Major Employers

Company Name	Industry
Al Copeland Investments	Restaurants & food manufacturing
Boh Bros. Construction Co.	General contractor
Capital One	Commercial banking
City of New Orleans	Municipal government
Dow Chemical Company	Chemical manufacturing
East Jefferson Hospital	Health care
Harrah's New Orleans Casino	Casinos
Jefferson Parish Government	Government
Jefferson Parish School Board	Elementary & secondary schools
Jefferson Parish Sheriff's Office	Government
Lockheed Martin Corp/Nasa Michoud	Space research & technology
LSU Health Sciences Center New Orleans	Colleges & universities
Naval Support Activity	Government
North Oaks Medical Center	Health care
Northrop Grumman	Ship building & repairing
Ochsner Health System	Health care
Saint Tammany Parish Hospital	General medical & surgical hospitals
Southeastern Louisiana University	Colleges & universities
St. Tammany Parish Public School Board	Elementary & secondary schools
Touro Infirmary	Health care
Tulane University	Colleges & universities
United States Postal Service	U.S. postal service
West Jefferson Medical Center	Health care

Note: Companies shown are located within the New Orleans-Metairie, LA Metropolitan Statistical Area.
Source: Hoovers.com; Wikipedia

PUBLIC SAFETY

Crime Rate

Area	All Crimes	Violent Crimes				Property Crimes		
		Murder	Rape[3]	Robbery	Aggrav. Assault	Burglary	Larceny -Theft	Motor Vehicle Theft
City	6,437.3	30.7	196.2	256.8	661.1	543.2	4,001.3	748.0
Suburbs[1]	2,472.9	9.3	22.9	43.8	209.1	290.9	1,767.8	129.1
Metro[2]	3,701.4	15.9	76.6	109.8	349.1	369.1	2,459.9	320.9
U.S.	2,489.3	5.0	42.6	81.6	250.2	340.5	1,549.5	219.9

Note: Figures are crimes per 100,000 population; (1) All areas within the metro area that are located outside the city limits; (2) Figures cover the New Orleans-Metairie, LA Metropolitan Statistical Area; (3) All figures shown were reported using the revised Uniform Crime Reporting (UCR) definition of rape.
Source: FBI Uniform Crime Reports, 2019

Hate Crimes

Area	Number of Quarters Reported	Race/Ethnicity/Ancestry	Religion	Sexual Orientation	Disability	Gender	Gender Identity
City	4	2	0	3	0	0	0
U.S.	4	3,963	1,521	1,195	157	69	198

Source: Federal Bureau of Investigation, Hate Crime Statistics 2019

Identity Theft Consumer Reports

Area	Reports	Reports per 100,000 Population	Rank[2]
MSA[1]	6,466	509	52
U.S.	1,387,615	423	-

Note: (1) Figures cover the New Orleans-Metairie, LA Metropolitan Statistical Area; (2) Rank ranges from 1 to 391 where 1 indicates greatest number of identity theft reports per 100,000 population
Source: Federal Trade Commission, Consumer Sentinel Network Data Book 2020

Fraud and Other Consumer Reports

Area	Reports	Reports per 100,000 Population	Rank[2]
MSA[1]	10,973	864	64
U.S.	3,385,133	1,031	-

Note: (1) Figures cover the New Orleans-Metairie, LA Metropolitan Statistical Area; (2) Rank ranges from 1 to 391 where 1 indicates greatest number of fraud and other consumer reports per 100,000 population
Source: Federal Trade Commission, Consumer Sentinel Network Data Book 2020

POLITICS

2020 Presidential Election Results

Area	Biden	Trump	Jorgensen	Hawkins	Other
Orleans Parish	83.1	15.0	0.9	0.0	1.0
U.S.	51.3	46.8	1.2	0.3	0.5

Note: Results are percentages and may not add to 100% due to rounding
Source: Dave Leip's Atlas of U.S. Presidential Elections

SPORTS

Professional Sports Teams

Team Name	League	Year Established
New Orleans Pelicans	National Basketball Association (NBA)	2002
New Orleans Saints	National Football League (NFL)	1967

Note: Includes teams located in the New Orleans-Metairie, LA Metropolitan Statistical Area.
Source: Wikipedia, Major Professional Sports Teams of the United States and Canada, April 6, 2021

CLIMATE

Average and Extreme Temperatures

Temperature	Jan	Feb	Mar	Apr	May	Jun	Jul	Aug	Sep	Oct	Nov	Dec	Yr.
Extreme High (°F)	83	85	89	92	96	100	101	102	101	92	87	84	102
Average High (°F)	62	65	71	78	85	89	91	90	87	80	71	64	78
Average Temp. (°F)	53	56	62	69	75	81	82	82	79	70	61	55	69
Average Low (°F)	43	46	52	59	66	71	73	73	70	59	51	45	59
Extreme Low (°F)	14	19	25	32	41	50	60	60	42	35	24	11	11

Note: Figures cover the years 1948-1990
Source: National Climatic Data Center, International Station Meteorological Climate Summary, 9/96

Average Precipitation/Snowfall/Humidity

Precip./Humidity	Jan	Feb	Mar	Apr	May	Jun	Jul	Aug	Sep	Oct	Nov	Dec	Yr.
Avg. Precip. (in.)	4.7	5.6	5.2	4.7	4.4	5.4	6.4	5.9	5.5	2.8	4.4	5.5	60.6
Avg. Snowfall (in.)	Tr	Tr	Tr	0	0	0	0	0	0	0	0	Tr	Tr
Avg. Rel. Hum. 6am (%)	85	84	84	88	89	89	91	91	89	87	86	85	88
Avg. Rel. Hum. 3pm (%)	62	59	57	57	58	61	66	65	63	56	59	62	60

Note: Figures cover the years 1948-1990; Tr = Trace amounts (<0.05 in. of rain; <0.5 in. of snow)
Source: National Climatic Data Center, International Station Meteorological Climate Summary, 9/96

Weather Conditions

Temperature			Daytime Sky			Precipitation	
10°F & below	32°F & below	90°F & above	Clear	Partly cloudy	Cloudy	0.01 inch or more precip.	0.1 inch or more snow/ice	Thunderstorms
0	13	70	90	169	106	114	1	69

Note: Figures are average number of days per year and cover the years 1948-1990
Source: National Climatic Data Center, International Station Meteorological Climate Summary, 9/96

HAZARDOUS WASTE

Superfund Sites

The New Orleans-Metairie, LA metro area is home to three sites on the EPA's Superfund National Priorities List: **Agriculture Street Landfill** (final); **Bayou Bonfouca** (final); **Madisonville Creosote Works** (final). There are a total of 1,375 Superfund sites with a status of proposed or final on the list in the U.S. *U.S. Environmental Protection Agency, National Priorities List, April 7, 2021*

AIR QUALITY

Air Quality Trends: Ozone

	1990	1995	2000	2005	2010	2015	2016	2017	2018	2019
MSA[1]	0.082	0.088	0.091	0.079	0.074	0.067	0.065	0.063	0.065	0.062
U.S.	0.088	0.089	0.082	0.080	0.073	0.068	0.069	0.068	0.069	0.065

Note: (1) Data covers the New Orleans-Metairie, LA Metropolitan Statistical Area. The values shown are the composite ozone concentration averages among trend sites based on the highest fourth daily maximum 8-hour concentration in parts per million. These trends are based on sites having an adequate record of monitoring data during the trend period. Data from exceptional events are included.
Source: U.S. Environmental Protection Agency, Air Quality Monitoring Information, "Air Quality Trends by City, 1990-2019"

Air Quality Index

Area	Percent of Days when Air Quality was...[2]					AQI Statistics[2]	
	Good	Moderate	Unhealthy for Sensitive Groups	Unhealthy	Very Unhealthy	Maximum	Median
MSA[1]	62.7	36.7	0.5	0.0	0.0	112	45

Note: (1) Data covers the New Orleans-Metairie, LA Metropolitan Statistical Area; (2) Based on 365 days with AQI data in 2019. Air Quality Index (AQI) is an index for reporting daily air quality. EPA calculates the AQI for five major air pollutants regulated by the Clean Air Act: ground-level ozone, particle pollution (aka particulate matter), carbon monoxide, sulfur dioxide, and nitrogen dioxide. The AQI runs from 0 to 500. The higher the AQI value, the greater the level of air pollution and the greater the health concern. There are six AQI categories: "Good" AQI is between 0 and 50. Air quality is considered satisfactory; "Moderate" AQI is between 51 and 100. Air quality is acceptable; "Unhealthy for Sensitive Groups" When AQI values are between 101 and 150, members of sensitive groups may experience health effects; "Unhealthy" When AQI values are between 151 and 200 everyone may begin to experience health effects; "Very Unhealthy" AQI values between 201 and 300 trigger a health alert; "Hazardous" AQI values over 300 trigger warnings of emergency conditions (not shown).
Source: U.S. Environmental Protection Agency, Air Quality Index Report, 2019

Air Quality Index Pollutants

Area	Percent of Days when AQI Pollutant was...[2]					
	Carbon Monoxide	Nitrogen Dioxide	Ozone	Sulfur Dioxide	Particulate Matter 2.5	Particulate Matter 10
MSA[1]	0.0	0.8	45.8	8.8	44.4	0.3

Note: (1) Data covers the New Orleans-Metairie, LA Metropolitan Statistical Area; (2) Based on 365 days with AQI data in 2019. The Air Quality Index (AQI) is an index for reporting daily air quality. EPA calculates the AQI for five major air pollutants regulated by the Clean Air Act: ground-level ozone, particle pollution (also known as particulate matter), carbon monoxide, sulfur dioxide, and nitrogen dioxide. The AQI runs from 0 to 500. The higher the AQI value, the greater the level of air pollution and the greater the health concern.
Source: U.S. Environmental Protection Agency, Air Quality Index Report, 2019

Maximum Air Pollutant Concentrations: Particulate Matter, Ozone, CO and Lead

	Particulate Matter 10 (ug/m^3)	Particulate Matter 2.5 Wtd AM (ug/m^3)	Particulate Matter 2.5 24-Hr (ug/m^3)	Ozone (ppm)	Carbon Monoxide (ppm)	Lead (ug/m^3)
MSA[1] Level	79	7.8	17	0.063	2	0.09
NAAQS[2]	150	15	35	0.075	9	0.15
Met NAAQS[2]	Yes	Yes	Yes	Yes	Yes	Yes

Note: (1) Data covers the New Orleans-Metairie, LA Metropolitan Statistical Area; Data from exceptional events are included; (2) National Ambient Air Quality Standards; ppm = parts per million; ug/m^3 = micrograms per cubic meter; n/a not available.
Concentrations: Particulate Matter 10 (coarse particulate)—highest second maximum 24-hour concentration; Particulate Matter 2.5 Wtd AM (fine particulate)—highest weighted annual mean concentration; Particulate Matter 2.5 24-Hour (fine particulate)—highest 98th percentile 24-hour concentration; Ozone—highest fourth daily maximum 8-hour concentration; Carbon Monoxide—highest second maximum non-overlapping 8-hour concentration; Lead—maximum running 3-month average
Source: U.S. Environmental Protection Agency, Air Quality Monitoring Information, "Air Quality Statistics by City, 2019"

Maximum Air Pollutant Concentrations: Nitrogen Dioxide and Sulfur Dioxide

	Nitrogen Dioxide AM (ppb)	Nitrogen Dioxide 1-Hr (ppb)	Sulfur Dioxide AM (ppb)	Sulfur Dioxide 1-Hr (ppb)	Sulfur Dioxide 24-Hr (ppb)
MSA[1] Level	10	43	n/a	53	n/a
NAAQS[2]	53	100	30	75	140
Met NAAQS[2]	Yes	Yes	n/a	Yes	n/a

Note: (1) Data covers the New Orleans-Metairie, LA Metropolitan Statistical Area; Data from exceptional events are included; (2) National Ambient Air Quality Standards; ppm = parts per million; ug/m^3 = micrograms per cubic meter; n/a not available.
Concentrations: Nitrogen Dioxide AM—highest arithmetic mean concentration; Nitrogen Dioxide 1-Hr—highest 98th percentile 1-hour daily maximum concentration; Sulfur Dioxide AM—highest annual mean concentration; Sulfur Dioxide 1-Hr—highest 99th percentile 1-hour daily maximum concentration; Sulfur Dioxide 24-Hr—highest second maximum 24-hour concentration
Source: U.S. Environmental Protection Agency, Air Quality Monitoring Information, "Air Quality Statistics by City, 2019"

Orlando, Florida

Background

The city of Orlando can hold the viewer aghast with its rampant tourism. Not only is it home to the worldwide tourist attractions of Disney World, Epcot Center, and Sea World, but Orlando and its surrounding area also host such institutions as Medieval Times Dinner & Tournament, Wet-N-Wild, Ripley's Believe It or Not Museum, and Sleuths Mystery Dinner Shows. In fact, the city is nicknamed "The Theme Park Capital of the World."

Orlando has its own high-tech corridor because of the University of Central Florida's College of Optics and Photonics. Manufacturing, government, business service, health care, high-tech research, and tourism supply significant numbers of jobs. The city is also one of the busiest American cities for conferences and conventions; the Orange County Convention Center is the second-largest convention facility in the United States, and vies with Chicago and Las Vegas for hosting the most conventions annually.

Aside from the glitz that pumps most of the money into its economy, Orlando is also called "The City Beautiful." The warm climate and abundant rains produce a variety of lush flora and fauna, which provide an attractive setting for the many young people who settle in the area, spending their nights in the numerous jazz clubs, restaurants, and pubs along Orange Avenue and Church Street. Known as the land of orange juice and sunshine, Orlando is also the city for young job seekers and professionals.

This genteel setting is a far cry from Orlando's rough-and-tumble origins. The city started out as a makeshift campsite in the middle of a cotton plantation. The Civil War and devastating rains brought an end to the cotton trade, and its settlers turned to raising livestock. The transition to a new livelihood did not insure any peace and serenity. Rustling, chaotic brawls, and senseless shootings were everyday occurrences. Martial law had to be imposed by a few large ranch families.

> Disney World guests must submit to a mandatory temperature check at the entrance, and are required to wear masks when walking around. But wait times for attractions are far shorter than usual.

The greatest impetus toward modernity came from the installation of Cape Canaveral, 50 miles away, which brought missile assembly and electronic component production to the area, and Walt Disney World, created out of 27,000 acres of unexplored swampland, which set the tone for Orlando as a tourist-oriented economy.

Orlando's University of Central Florida is the largest university campus in terms of enrollment in the United States, and was listed as a "gamma" level global city in the World Cities Study Group's inventory.

Also a major film production site, the city is home to Nickelodeon, the world's largest tele-production studio dedicated to children's television programming, the Golf Channel, Sun Sports, House of Moves, and the America Channel. Disney's biggest theme-park competitor, Universal Studios, is also based in Orlando. The city is also home to a variety of arts and entertainment facilities, including the Amway Arena, part of the Orlando Centroplex, home to the NBA's Orlando Magic and the Orlando Sharks of the Indoor Soccer League.

The city is also remembered for one of the deadliest mass shootings by a lone gunman when, in October 2016, more than 100 people were shot at a gay nightclub in Orlando.

Orlando is surrounded by many lakes. Its relative humidity remains high year-round, although winters are generally less humid. June through September is the rainy season, when scattered afternoon thunderstorms are an almost daily occurrence. During the winter months rainfall is light and the afternoons are most pleasant. Hurricanes are not usually considered a threat to the area.

Rankings

General Rankings

- The Orlando metro area was identified as one of America's fastest-growing areas in terms of population and business growth by *MagnifyMoney*. The area ranked #14 out of 35. The 100 most populous metro areas in the U.S. were evaluated on their change from 2011-2016 in the following categories: people and housing; workforce and employment opportunities; growing industry. www.businessinsider.com, "The 35 Cities in the US with the Biggest Influx of People, the Most Work Opportunities, and the Hottest Business Growth," August 12, 2018

- The Orlando metro area was identified as one of America's fastest-growing areas in terms of population and economy by *Forbes*. The area ranked #4 out of 25. The 100 most populous metro areas in the U.S. were evaluated on the following criteria: estimated population growth; employment; economic output; wages; home values. *Forbes*, "America's Fastest-Growing Cities 2018," February 28, 2018

- Orlando was selected as one of the best places in the world to "dream of now and go to later" by *National Geographic Travel* editors. The list reflects 25 of the most extraordinary and inspiring destinations that also support National Geographic's tourism goals of cultural engagement, diversity, community benefit, and value. In collaboration with its international editorial teams, the new list reports on the timeless must-see sites for 2021, framed by the five categories of Culture and History, Family, Adventure, Sustainability, and Nature. www.nationalgeographic.com/travel, "Best of the World, Destinations on the Rise for 2021," November 17, 2020

- In their seventh annual survey, Livability.com looked at data for more than 1,000 small to mid-sized U.S. cities to determine the rankings for Livability's "Top 100 Best Places to Live" in 2020. Orlando ranked #29. Criteria: housing and affordable living; vibrant economy; social and civic engagement; education; demographics; health care options; transportation & infrastructure; and abundant lifestyle amenities. *Livability.com*, "Top 100 Best Places to Live 2020" October 2020

Business/Finance Rankings

- The Brookings Institution ranked the nation's largest cities based on income inequality. Orlando was ranked #69 (#1 = greatest inequality). Criteria: the "95/20 ratio," a figure representing the income at which a household earns more than 95 percent of all other households, divided by the income at which a household earns more than only 20 percent of all other households. *Brookings Institution*, "Household Income Inequality, Largest Cities of 97 Large U.S. Metro Areas, 2014-2016," February 5, 2018

- The Brookings Institution ranked the 100 largest metro areas in the U.S. based on income inequality. Orlando was ranked #69 (#1 = greatest inequality). Criteria: the "95/20 ratio," a figure representing the income at which a household earns more than 95 percent of all other households, divided by the income at which a household earns more than only 20 percent of all other households. *Brookings Institution*, "Household Income Inequality, 100 Largest U.S. Metro Areas, 2014-2016," February 5, 2018

- Payscale.com ranked the 32 largest metro areas in terms of wage growth. The Orlando metro area ranked #15. Criteria: private-sector and education professional wage growth between the 4th quarter of 2019 and the 4th quarter of 2020. *PayScale*, "Wage Trends by Metro Area-4th Quarter," January 11, 2021

- The Orlando metro area was identified as one of the most debt-ridden places in America by the finance site Credit.com. The metro area was ranked #23. Criteria: residents' average credit card debt as well as median income. *Credit.com*, "25 Cities With the Most Credit Card Debt," February 28, 2018

- Orlando was identified as one of America's most frugal metro areas by *Coupons.com*. The city ranked #5 out of 25. Criteria: digital coupon usage. *Coupons.com*, "America's Most Frugal Cities of 2017," March 22, 2018

- Orlando was identified as one of the unhappiest cities to work in by CareerBliss.com, an online community for career advancement. The city ranked #5 out of 5. Criteria: an employee's relationship with his or her boss and co-workers; general work environment; compensation; opportunities for advancement; company culture and job reputation; and resources. *Businesswire.com*, "CareerBliss Unhappiest Cities to Work 2019," February 12, 2019

- The Orlando metro area appeared on the Milken Institute "2021 Best Performing Cities" list. Rank: #27 out of 200 large metro areas (population over 250,000). Criteria: job growth; wage and salary growth; high-tech output growth; housing affordability; household broadband access. *Milken Institute*, "Best-Performing Cities 2021," February 16, 2021

- *Forbes* ranked the 200 most populous metro areas to determine the nation's "Best Places for Business and Careers." The Orlando metro area was ranked #23. Criteria: costs (business and living); job growth (past and projected); income growth; quality of life; educational attainment (college and high school); projected economic growth; cultural and leisure opportunities; workplace tolerance laws; net migration patterns. *Forbes, "The Best Places for Business and Careers 2019: Seattle Still On Top," October 30, 2019*

Children/Family Rankings

- Orlando was selected as one of the most playful cities in the U.S. by KaBOOM! The organization's Playful City USA initiative honors cities and towns across the nation that have made their communities more playable. Criteria: pledging to integrate play as a solution to challenges in their communities; making it easy for children to get active and balanced play; creating more family-friendly and innovative communities as a result. *KaBOOM! National Campaign for Play, "2017 Playful City USA Communities"*

Dating/Romance Rankings

- Orlando was selected as one of America's best cities for singles by the readers of *Travel + Leisure* in their annual "America's Favorite Cities" survey. Criteria included good-looking locals, cool shopping, an active bar scene and hipster-magnet coffee bars. *Travel + Leisure, "Best Cities in America for Singles," July 21, 2017*

- Orlando was selected as one of the nation's most romantic cities with 100,000 or more residents by Amazon.com. The city ranked #4 of 20. Criteria: per capita sales of romance novels, relationship books, romantic comedy movies, romantic music, and sexual wellness products. *Amazon.com, "Top 20 Most Romantic Cities in the U.S.," February 1, 2017*

Education Rankings

- Personal finance website *WalletHub* analyzed the 150 largest U.S. metropolitan statistical areas to determine where the most educated Americans are putting their degrees to work. Criteria: education levels; percentage of workers with degrees; education quality and attainment gap; public school quality rankings; quality and enrollment of each metro area's universities. Orlando was ranked #61 (#1 = most educated city). *www.WalletHub.com, "Most and Least Educated Cities in America," July 20, 2020*

- Orlando was selected as one of America's most literate cities. The city ranked #41 out of the 84 largest U.S. cities. Criteria: number of booksellers; library resources; Internet resources; educational attainment; periodical publishing resources; newspaper circulation. *Central Connecticut State University, "America's Most Literate Cities, 2018," February 2019*

Environmental Rankings

- Orlando was highlighted as one of the top 98 cleanest metro areas for short-term particle pollution (24-hour PM 2.5) in the U.S. during 2016 through 2018. Monitors in these cities reported no days with unhealthful PM 2.5 levels. *American Lung Association, "State of the Air 2020," April 21, 2020*

Food/Drink Rankings

- The U.S. Chamber of Commerce Foundation conducted an in-depth study on local food truck regulations, surveyed 288 food truck owners, and ranked 20 major American cities based on how friendly they are for operating a food truck. The compiled index assessed the following: procedures for obtaining permits and licenses; complying with restrictions; and financial obligations associated with operating a food truck. Orlando ranked #3 overall (1 being the best). *www.foodtrucknation.us, "Food Truck Nation," March 20, 2018*

Health/Fitness Rankings

- For each of the 100 largest cities in the United States, the American Fitness Index®, published by the American College of Sports Medicine and the Anthem Foundation, evaluated community infrastructure and 33 health behaviors including preventive health, levels of chronic disease conditions, pedestrian safety, air quality, and community resources that support physical activity. Orlando ranked #43 for "community fitness." *americanfitnessindex.org, "2020 ACSM American Fitness Index Summary Report," July 14, 2020*

- The Orlando metro area was identified as one of the worst cities for bed bugs in America by pest control company Orkin. The area ranked #45 out of 50 based on the number of bed bug treatments Orkin performed from December 2019 to November 2020. *Orkin, "New Year, New Top City on Orkin's 2021 Bed Bug Cities List: Chicago," February 1, 2021*

- Orlando was identified as a "2021 Spring Allergy Capital." The area ranked #38 out of 100. Three groups of factors were used to identify the most challenging cities for people with allergies during the spring season: annual spring pollen levels; over the counter medicine use; number of board-certified allergy specialists. *Asthma and Allergy Foundation of America, "Spring Allergy Capitals 2021," February 23, 2021*

- Orlando was identified as a "2021 Fall Allergy Capital." The area ranked #38 out of 100. Three groups of factors were used to identify the most challenging cities for people with allergies during the fall season: annual fall pollen levels; over the counter medicine use; number of board-certified allergy specialists. *Asthma and Allergy Foundation of America, "Fall Allergy Capitals 2021," February 23, 2021*

- Orlando was identified as a "2019 Asthma Capital." The area ranked #85 out of the nation's 100 largest metropolitan areas. Criteria: estimated asthma prevalence; crude death rate from asthma; and ER visits due to asthma. Risk factors analyzed but not factored in the rankings: annual pollen score; annual air quality; public smoking laws; number of board-certified asthma specialists; rescue medication use; controller medication use; uninsured rate; poverty rate. *Asthma and Allergy Foundation of America, "Asthma Capitals 2019: The Most Challenging Places to Live With Asthma," May 7, 2019*

Real Estate Rankings

- FitSmallBusiness looked at 50 of the largest metropolitan areas in the U.S. to determine which metro was the best to start a real estate business. Data was compiled from such sources as: Zillow, Trulia, U.S. Census Bureau, and the Bureau of Labor Statistics. Criteria: location; inventory; annual wages; median sales price of homes; days on the market; median price cut percentage; and other factors that would influence real estate professional growth. The Orlando metro area ranked #18. *fitsmallbusiness.com, "The Best Cities to Become a Real Estate Agent in 2018," January 30, 2018*

- *WalletHub* compared the most populated U.S. cities to determine which had the best markets for real estate agents. Orlando ranked #68 where demand was high and pay was the best. Criteria: sales per agent; annual median wage for real-estate agents; monthly average starting salary for real estate agents; real estate job density and competition; unemployment rate; home turnover rate; housing-market health index; and other relevant metrics. *www.WalletHub.com, "2019's Best Places to Be a Real Estate Agent," April 24, 2019*

- According to Penske Truck Rental, the Orlando metro area was named the #5 moving destination in 2019, based on one-way consumer truck rental reservations made through Penske's website, rental locations, and reservations call center. *gopenske.com/blog, "Penske Truck Rental's 2019 Top Moving Destinations," January 22, 2020*

- Orlando was ranked #196 out of 268 metro areas in terms of housing affordability in 2020 by the National Association of Home Builders (#1 = most affordable). Criteria: the share of homes sold in that area affordable to a family earning the local median income, based on standard mortgage underwriting criteria. *National Association of Home Builders®, NAHB-Wells Fargo Housing Opportunity Index, 4th Quarter 2020*

Safety Rankings

- Allstate ranked the 200 largest cities in America in terms of driver safety. Orlando ranked #93. Criteria: internal property damage claims over a two-year period from January 2016 to December 2017. The report helps increase the importance of safety and awareness behind the wheel. *Allstate, "Allstate America's Best Drivers Report, 2019" June 24, 2019*

- The National Insurance Crime Bureau ranked 384 metro areas in the U.S. in terms of per capita rates of vehicle theft. The Orlando metro area ranked #115 (#1 = highest rate). Criteria: number of vehicle theft offenses per 100,000 inhabitants in 2019. *National Insurance Crime Bureau, "Hot Spots 2019," July 21, 2020*

Seniors/Retirement Rankings

- From its Best Cities for Successful Aging indexes, the Milken Institute generated rankings for metropolitan areas, weighing data in nine categories—health care, wellness, living arrangements, transportation and convenience, financial characteristics, education, employment, community engagement, and overall livability. The Orlando metro area was ranked #69 overall in the large metro area category. *Milken Institute, "Best Cities for Successful Aging, 2017" March 14, 2017*

- Orlando made the 2020 *Forbes* list of "25 Best Places to Retire." Criteria, focused on high-quality retirement living at an affordable price, include: housing/living costs compared to the national average and state taxes; air quality; crime rates; good economic outlook; home price appreciation; risk associated with climate-change; availability of medical care; bikeability; walkability; healthy living. *Forbes.com, "The Best Places to Retire in 2020," August 14, 2020*

Sports/Recreation Rankings

- Orlando was chosen as a bicycle friendly community by the League of American Bicyclists. A "Bicycle Friendly Community" welcomes cyclists by providing safe and supportive accommodation for cycling and encouraging people to bike for transportation and recreation. There are five award levels: Diamond; Platinum; Gold; Silver; and Bronze. The community achieved an award level of Bronze. *League of American Bicyclists, "Fall 2020 Awards-New & Renewing Bicycle Friendly Communities List," December 16, 2020*

Women/Minorities Rankings

- Orlando was selected as one of the gayest cities in America by *The Advocate*. The city ranked #2 out of 25. Criteria, among many: Trans Pride parades/festivals; gay rugby teams; lesbian bars; LGBT centers; theater screenings of "Moonlight"; LGBT-inclusive nondiscrimination ordinances; and gay bowling teams. *The Advocate, "Queerest Cities in America 2017" January 12, 2017*

- Personal finance website *WalletHub* compared more than 180 U.S. cities across two key dimensions, "Hispanic Business-Friendliness" and "Hispanic Purchasing Power," to arrive at the most favorable conditions for Hispanic entrepreneurs. Orlando was ranked #18 out of 182. Criteria includes: share of Hispanic-Owned Businesses; Hispanic entrepreneurship rate to median annual income of Hispanics; Small Business-Friendliness score; cost of living; and number of Hispanics with at least a bachelor's degree. *WalletHub.com, "2019's Best Cities for Hispanic Entrepreneurs," May 1, 2019*

Miscellaneous Rankings

- *MoveHub* ranked 446 hipster cities across 20 countries, using its *alternative* Hipster Index and Orlando came out as #8 among the top 50. Criteria: population over 150,000; number of vintage boutiques; density of tattoo parlors; vegan places to eat; coffee shops; and density of vinyl record stores. *www.movehub.com, "The Hipster Index: Brighton Pips Portland to Global Top Spot," February 20, 2020*

- The watchdog site, Charity Navigator, conducted a study of charities in major markets both to analyze statistical differences in their financial, accountability, and transparency practices and to track year-to-year variations in individual philanthropic communities. The Orlando metro area was ranked #15 among the 30 metro markets in the rating category of Overall Score. *www.charitynavigator.org, "2017 Metro Market Study," May 1, 2017*

- *WalletHub* compared the 150 most populated U.S. cities to determine their operating efficiency. A "Quality of City Services" score was constructed for each city and then divided by the total budget per capita to reveal which were managed the best. Orlando ranked #92. Criteria: financial stability; economy; education; safety; health; infrastructure and pollution. *www.WalletHub.com, "2020's Best- & Worst-Run Cities in America," June 29, 2020*

- The National Alliance to End Homelessness listed the 25 most populous metro areas with the highest rate of homelessness. The Orlando metro area had a high rate of homelessness. Criteria: number of homeless people per 10,000 population in 2016. *National Alliance to End Homelessness, "Homelessness in the 25 Most Populous U.S. Metro Areas," September 1, 2017*

Business Environment

DEMOGRAPHICS

Population Growth

Area	1990 Census	2000 Census	2010 Census	2019* Estimate	Population Growth (%) 1990-2019	Population Growth (%) 2010-2019
City	161,172	185,951	238,300	280,832	74.2	17.8
MSA[1]	1,224,852	1,644,561	2,134,411	2,508,970	104.8	17.5
U.S.	248,709,873	281,421,906	308,745,538	324,697,795	30.6	5.2

Note: (1) Figures cover the Orlando-Kissimmee-Sanford, FL Metropolitan Statistical Area; (*) 2015-2019 5-year estimated population
Source: U.S. Census Bureau, 1990 Census, Census 2000, Census 2010, 2015-2019 American Community Survey 5-Year Estimates

Household Size

Area	One	Two	Three	Four	Five	Six	Seven or More	Average Household Size
City	33.6	33.2	16.8	9.8	4.1	1.8	0.7	2.50
MSA[1]	24.9	34.3	17.4	14.0	6.0	2.3	1.2	2.80
U.S.	27.9	33.9	15.6	12.9	6.0	2.3	1.4	2.60

Note: (1) Figures cover the Orlando-Kissimmee-Sanford, FL Metropolitan Statistical Area
Source: U.S. Census Bureau, 2015-2019 American Community Survey 5-Year Estimates

Race

Area	White Alone[2] (%)	Black Alone[2] (%)	Asian Alone[2] (%)	AIAN[3] Alone[2] (%)	NHOPI[4] Alone[2] (%)	Other Race Alone[2] (%)	Two or More Races (%)
City	61.3	24.5	4.2	0.2	0.0	6.2	3.5
MSA[1]	69.7	16.6	4.3	0.3	0.1	5.7	3.3
U.S.	72.5	12.7	5.5	0.8	0.2	4.9	3.3

Note: (1) Figures cover the Orlando-Kissimmee-Sanford, FL Metropolitan Statistical Area; (2) Alone is defined as not being in combination with one or more other races; (3) American Indian and Alaska Native; (4) Native Hawaiian and Other Pacific Islander
Source: U.S. Census Bureau, 2015-2019 American Community Survey 5-Year Estimates

Hispanic or Latino Origin

Area	Total (%)	Mexican (%)	Puerto Rican (%)	Cuban (%)	Other (%)
City	32.6	1.9	15.6	3.0	12.0
MSA[1]	30.7	2.9	15.2	2.4	10.1
U.S.	18.0	11.2	1.7	0.7	4.3

Note: Persons of Hispanic or Latino origin can be of any race; (1) Figures cover the Orlando-Kissimmee-Sanford, FL Metropolitan Statistical Area
Source: U.S. Census Bureau, 2015-2019 American Community Survey 5-Year Estimates

Ancestry

Area	German	Irish	English	American	Italian	Polish	French[2]	Scottish	Dutch
City	6.3	5.3	4.5	5.6	4.3	1.6	1.7	1.3	0.5
MSA[1]	8.2	7.3	6.1	7.6	5.1	1.9	1.9	1.4	0.7
U.S.	13.3	9.7	7.2	6.2	5.1	2.8	2.3	1.7	1.2

Note: Figures are the percentage of the total population reporting a particular ancestry. The nine most commonly reported ancestries in the U.S. are shown. Figures include multiple ancestries (e.g. if a person reported being Irish and Italian, they were included in both columns); (1) Figures cover the Orlando-Kissimmee-Sanford, FL Metropolitan Statistical Area; (2) Excludes Basque
Source: U.S. Census Bureau, 2015-2019 American Community Survey 5-Year Estimates

Foreign-born Population

Area	Any Foreign Country	Asia	Mexico	Europe	Caribbean	Central America[2]	South America	Africa	Canada
City	22.0	2.9	0.5	1.5	6.9	1.2	8.0	0.6	0.3
MSA[1]	18.5	3.0	1.1	1.5	5.7	1.1	5.2	0.6	0.3
U.S.	13.6	4.2	3.5	1.5	1.3	1.1	1.0	0.7	0.2

Note: (1) Figures cover the Orlando-Kissimmee-Sanford, FL Metropolitan Statistical Area; (2) Excludes Mexico.
Source: U.S. Census Bureau, 2015-2019 American Community Survey 5-Year Estimates

Marital Status

Area	Never Married	Now Married[2]	Separated	Widowed	Divorced
City	43.0	36.5	3.1	4.1	13.3
MSA[1]	34.8	46.0	2.2	5.2	11.8
U.S.	33.4	48.1	1.9	5.8	10.9

Note: Figures are percentages and cover the population 15 years of age and older; (1) Figures cover the Orlando-Kissimmee-Sanford, FL Metropolitan Statistical Area; (2) Excludes separated
Source: U.S. Census Bureau, 2015-2019 American Community Survey 5-Year Estimates

Disability by Age

Area	All Ages	Under 18 Years Old	18 to 64 Years Old	65 Years and Over
City	10.1	5.4	8.2	32.5
MSA[1]	12.2	5.1	9.6	34.5
U.S.	12.6	4.2	10.3	34.5

Note: Figures show percent of the civilian noninstitutionalized population that reported having a disability. Disability status is determined from six types of difficulty: vision, hearing, cognitive, ambulatory, self-care, and independent living. For children under 5 years old, hearing and vision difficulty are used to determine disability status. For children between the ages of 5 and 14, disability status is determined from hearing, vision, cognitive, ambulatory, and self-care difficulties. For people aged 15 years and older, they are considered to have a disability if they have difficulty with any one of the six difficulty types; Note: (1) Figures cover the Orlando-Kissimmee-Sanford, FL Metropolitan Statistical Area
Source: U.S. Census Bureau, 2015-2019 American Community Survey 5-Year Estimates

Age

Area	Under Age 5	Age 5–19	Age 20–34	Age 35–44	Age 45–54	Age 55–64	Age 65–74	Age 75–84	Age 85+	Median Age
City	6.7	15.9	29.7	15.1	12.1	10.1	6.3	2.7	1.2	33.8
MSA[1]	5.9	18.7	22.2	13.7	13.3	11.7	8.5	4.3	1.7	37.2
U.S.	6.1	19.1	20.7	12.6	13.0	12.9	9.1	4.6	1.9	38.1

Note: (1) Figures cover the Orlando-Kissimmee-Sanford, FL Metropolitan Statistical Area
Source: U.S. Census Bureau, 2015-2019 American Community Survey 5-Year Estimates

Gender

Area	Males	Females	Males per 100 Females
City	134,785	146,047	92.3
MSA[1]	1,226,241	1,282,729	95.6
U.S.	159,886,919	164,810,876	97.0

Note: (1) Figures cover the Orlando-Kissimmee-Sanford, FL Metropolitan Statistical Area
Source: U.S. Census Bureau, 2015-2019 American Community Survey 5-Year Estimates

Religious Groups by Family

Area	Catholic	Baptist	Non-Den.	Methodist[2]	Lutheran	LDS[3]	Pentecostal	Presbyterian[4]	Muslim[5]	Judaism
MSA[1]	13.2	7.0	5.7	3.0	0.9	1.0	3.2	1.4	1.3	0.3
U.S.	19.1	9.3	4.0	4.0	2.3	2.0	1.9	1.6	0.8	0.7

Note: Figures are the number of adherents as a percentage of the total population; (1) Figures cover the Orlando-Kissimmee-Sanford, FL Metropolitan Statistical Area; (2) Methodist/Pietist; (3) Latter Day Saints; (4) Reformed; (5) Figures are estimates
Source: Association of Statisticians of American Religious Bodies, 2010 U.S. Religion Census: Religious Congregations & Membership Study

Religious Groups by Tradition

Area	Catholic	Evangelical Protestant	Mainline Protestant	Other Tradition	Black Protestant	Orthodox
MSA[1]	13.2	17.8	4.8	3.3	1.2	0.3
U.S.	19.1	16.2	7.3	4.3	1.6	0.3

Note: Figures are the number of adherents as a percentage of the total population; (1) Figures cover the Orlando-Kissimmee-Sanford, FL Metropolitan Statistical Area
Source: Association of Statisticians of American Religious Bodies, 2010 U.S. Religion Census: Religious Congregations & Membership Study

ECONOMY

Gross Metropolitan Product

Area	2017	2018	2019	2020	Rank[2]
MSA[1]	134.1	142.4	150.7	158.6	31

Note: Figures are in billions of dollars; (1) Figures cover the Orlando-Kissimmee-Sanford, FL Metropolitan Statistical Area; (2) Rank is based on 2018 data and ranges from 1 to 381
Source: U.S. Conference of Mayors, U.S. Metro Economies: GMP & Employment 2018-2020, September 2019

Economic Growth

Area	2015-17 (%)	2018 (%)	2019 (%)	2020 (%)	Rank[2]
MSA[1]	2.4	3.8	4.0	3.0	109
U.S.	1.9	2.9	2.3	2.1	—

Note: Figures are real gross metropolitan product (GMP) growth rates and represent average annual percent change; (1) Figures cover the Orlando-Kissimmee-Sanford, FL Metropolitan Statistical Area; (2) Rank is based on 2017 2-year average annual percent change and ranges from 1 to 381
Source: U.S. Conference of Mayors, U.S. Metro Economies: GMP & Employment 2018-2020, September 2019

Metropolitan Area Exports

Area	2014	2015	2016	2017	2018	2019	Rank[2]
MSA[1]	3,134.8	3,082.7	3,363.9	3,196.7	3,131.7	3,363.9	73

Note: Figures are in millions of dollars; (1) Figures cover the Orlando-Kissimmee-Sanford, FL Metropolitan Statistical Area; (2) Rank is based on 2019 data and ranges from 1 to 386
Source: U.S. Department of Commerce, International Trade Administration, Office of Trade and Economic Analysis, Industry and Analysis, Exports by Metropolitan Area, data extracted March 24, 2021

Building Permits

Area	Single-Family 2018	Single-Family 2019	Pct. Chg.	Multi-Family 2018	Multi-Family 2019	Pct. Chg.	Total 2018	Total 2019	Pct. Chg.
City	790	747	-5.4	2,289	1,887	-17.6	3,079	2,634	-14.5
MSA[1]	16,455	14,995	-8.9	12,427	9,475	-23.8	28,882	24,470	-15.3
U.S.	855,300	862,100	0.7	473,500	523,900	10.6	1,328,800	1,386,000	4.3

Note: (1) Figures cover the Orlando-Kissimmee-Sanford, FL Metropolitan Statistical Area; Figures represent new, privately-owned housing units authorized (unadjusted data); All permit data are based on estimates with imputation
Source: U.S. Census Bureau, Manufacturing, Mining, and Construction Statistics, Building Permits, 2018, 2019

Bankruptcy Filings

Area	Business Filings 2019	Business Filings 2020	% Chg.	Nonbusiness Filings 2019	Nonbusiness Filings 2020	% Chg.
Orange County	154	167	8.4	2,956	2,477	-16.2
U.S.	22,780	21,655	-4.9	752,160	522,808	-30.5

Note: Business filings include Chapter 7, Chapter 9, Chapter 11, Chapter 12, Chapter 13, Chapter 15, and Section 304; Nonbusiness filings include Chapter 7, Chapter 11, and Chapter 13
Source: Administrative Office of the U.S. Courts, Business and Nonbusiness Bankruptcy, County Cases Commenced by Chapter of the Bankruptcy Code, During the 12-Month Period Ending December 31, 2019 and Business and Nonbusiness Bankruptcy, County Cases Commenced by Chapter of the Bankruptcy Code, During the 12-Month Period Ending December 31, 2020

Housing Vacancy Rates

Area	Gross Vacancy Rate[2] (%) 2018	2019	2020	Year-Round Vacancy Rate[3] (%) 2018	2019	2020	Rental Vacancy Rate[4] (%) 2018	2019	2020	Homeowner Vacancy Rate[5] (%) 2018	2019	2020
MSA[1]	19.4	16.0	12.9	16.2	12.7	9.8	5.8	8.3	8.6	2.6	2.5	1.2
U.S.	12.3	12.0	10.6	9.7	9.5	8.2	6.9	6.7	6.3	1.5	1.4	1.0

Note: (1) Figures cover the Orlando-Kissimmee-Sanford, FL Metropolitan Statistical Area; (2) The percentage of the total housing inventory that is vacant; (3) The percentage of the housing inventory (excluding seasonal units) that is year-round vacant; (4) The percentage of rental inventory that is vacant for rent; (5) The percentage of homeowner inventory that is vacant for sale
Source: U.S. Census Bureau, Housing Vacancies and Homeownership Annual Statistics: 2018, 2019, 2020

INCOME

Income

Area	Per Capita ($)	Median Household ($)	Average Household ($)
City	32,085	51,757	75,669
MSA[1]	29,875	58,368	80,864
U.S.	34,103	62,843	88,607

Note: (1) Figures cover the Orlando-Kissimmee-Sanford, FL Metropolitan Statistical Area
Source: U.S. Census Bureau, 2015-2019 American Community Survey 5-Year Estimates

Household Income Distribution

Area	Under $15,000	$15,000 -$24,999	$25,000 -$34,999	$35,000 -$49,999	$50,000 -$74,999	$75,000 -$99,999	$100,000 -$149,999	$150,000 and up
City	12.5	10.4	11.1	14.2	19.8	10.9	10.8	10.3
MSA[1]	9.5	9.2	10.1	14.0	18.9	13.1	13.7	11.5
U.S.	10.3	8.9	8.9	12.3	17.2	12.7	15.1	14.5

Note: (1) Figures cover the Orlando-Kissimmee-Sanford, FL Metropolitan Statistical Area
Source: U.S. Census Bureau, 2015-2019 American Community Survey 5-Year Estimates

Poverty Rate

Area	All Ages	Under 18 Years Old	18 to 64 Years Old	65 Years and Over
City	17.2	24.4	15.4	14.8
MSA[1]	13.7	19.6	12.5	9.9
U.S.	13.4	18.5	12.6	9.3

Note: Figures are percentage of people whose income during the past 12 months was below the poverty level;
(1) Figures cover the Orlando-Kissimmee-Sanford, FL Metropolitan Statistical Area
Source: U.S. Census Bureau, 2015-2019 American Community Survey 5-Year Estimates

CITY FINANCES

City Government Finances

Component	2017 ($000)	2017 ($ per capita)
Total Revenues	945,620	3,490
Total Expenditures	966,718	3,568
Debt Outstanding	1,241,547	4,582
Cash and Securities[1]	1,831,318	6,759

Note: (1) Cash and security holdings of a government at the close of its fiscal year, including those of its dependent agencies, utilities, and liquor stores.
Source: U.S. Census Bureau, State & Local Government Finances 2017

City Government Revenue by Source

Source	2017 ($000)	2017 ($ per capita)	2017 (%)
General Revenue			
From Federal Government	21,195	78	2.2
From State Government	60,889	225	6.4
From Local Governments	172,258	636	18.2
Taxes			
Property	147,334	544	15.6
Sales and Gross Receipts	58,670	217	6.2
Personal Income	0	0	0.0
Corporate Income	0	0	0.0
Motor Vehicle License	0	0	0.0
Other Taxes	62,762	232	6.6
Current Charges	272,361	1,005	28.8
Liquor Store	0	0	0.0
Utility	45	0	0.0
Employee Retirement	71,673	265	7.6

Source: U.S. Census Bureau, State & Local Government Finances 2017

City Government Expenditures by Function

Function	2017 ($000)	2017 ($ per capita)	2017 (%)
General Direct Expenditures			
Air Transportation	0	0	0.0
Corrections	0	0	0.0
Education	0	0	0.0
Employment Security Administration	0	0	0.0
Financial Administration	24,272	89	2.5
Fire Protection	112,272	414	11.6
General Public Buildings	0	0	0.0
Governmental Administration, Other	74,930	276	7.8
Health	0	0	0.0
Highways	18,614	68	1.9
Hospitals	0	0	0.0
Housing and Community Development	9,463	34	1.0
Interest on General Debt	50,083	184	5.2
Judicial and Legal	4,814	17	0.5
Libraries	0	0	0.0
Parking	13,886	51	1.4
Parks and Recreation	107,670	397	11.1
Police Protection	149,108	550	15.4
Public Welfare	0	0	0.0
Sewerage	77,476	286	8.0
Solid Waste Management	29,560	109	3.1
Veterans' Services	0	0	0.0
Liquor Store	0	0	0.0
Utility	0	0	0.0
Employee Retirement	115,543	426	12.0

Source: U.S. Census Bureau, State & Local Government Finances 2017

EMPLOYMENT

Labor Force and Employment

Area	Civilian Labor Force Dec. 2019	Dec. 2020	% Chg.	Workers Employed Dec. 2019	Dec. 2020	% Chg.
City	170,544	162,722	-4.6	166,541	149,954	-10.0
MSA[1]	1,372,173	1,294,626	-5.7	1,337,648	1,204,999	-9.9
U.S.	164,007,000	160,017,000	-2.4	158,504,000	149,613,000	-5.6

Note: Data is not seasonally adjusted and covers workers 16 years of age and older; (1) Figures cover the Orlando-Kissimmee-Sanford, FL Metropolitan Statistical Area
Source: Bureau of Labor Statistics, Local Area Unemployment Statistics

Unemployment Rate

Area	Jan.	Feb.	Mar.	Apr.	May	Jun.	Jul.	Aug.	Sep.	Oct.	Nov.	Dec.
City	2.8	2.7	4.0	18.2	21.7	16.9	17.0	12.0	10.4	9.0	8.6	7.8
MSA[1]	3.0	2.9	4.2	16.8	21.1	16.1	15.4	10.8	9.2	7.8	7.4	6.9
U.S.	4.0	3.8	4.5	14.4	13.0	11.2	10.5	8.5	7.7	6.6	6.4	6.5

Note: Data is not seasonally adjusted and covers workers 16 years of age and older; (1) Figures cover the Orlando-Kissimmee-Sanford, FL Metropolitan Statistical Area
Source: Bureau of Labor Statistics, Local Area Unemployment Statistics

Average Wages

Occupation	$/Hr.	Occupation	$/Hr.
Accountants and Auditors	35.20	Maintenance and Repair Workers	18.10
Automotive Mechanics	19.60	Marketing Managers	58.40
Bookkeepers	20.00	Network and Computer Systems Admin.	40.80
Carpenters	21.10	Nurses, Licensed Practical	22.30
Cashiers	11.70	Nurses, Registered	32.40
Computer Programmers	41.60	Nursing Assistants	13.60
Computer Systems Analysts	44.40	Office Clerks, General	17.30
Computer User Support Specialists	24.90	Physical Therapists	41.80
Construction Laborers	16.60	Physicians	87.70
Cooks, Restaurant	14.10	Plumbers, Pipefitters and Steamfitters	21.20
Customer Service Representatives	17.00	Police and Sheriff's Patrol Officers	28.80
Dentists	81.40	Postal Service Mail Carriers	25.60
Electricians	22.30	Real Estate Sales Agents	21.90
Engineers, Electrical	50.40	Retail Salespersons	13.90
Fast Food and Counter Workers	10.40	Sales Representatives, Technical/Scientific	45.90
Financial Managers	67.60	Secretaries, Exc. Legal/Medical/Executive	17.40
First-Line Supervisors of Office Workers	27.00	Security Guards	13.40
General and Operations Managers	50.40	Surgeons	107.60
Hairdressers/Cosmetologists	14.70	Teacher Assistants, Exc. Postsecondary*	13.10
Home Health and Personal Care Aides	12.00	Teachers, Secondary School, Exc. Sp. Ed.*	28.00
Janitors and Cleaners	13.00	Telemarketers	13.00
Landscaping/Groundskeeping Workers	14.10	Truck Drivers, Heavy/Tractor-Trailer	22.30
Lawyers	58.70	Truck Drivers, Light/Delivery Services	19.10
Maids and Housekeeping Cleaners	11.90	Waiters and Waitresses	12.50

Note: Wage data covers the Orlando-Kissimmee-Sanford, FL Metropolitan Statistical Area; (*) Hourly wages were calculated from annual wage data based on a 40 hour work week; n/a not available.
Source: Bureau of Labor Statistics, Metro Area Occupational Employment & Wage Estimates, May 2020

Employment by Industry

Sector	MSA[1] Number of Employees	Percent of Total	U.S. Percent of Total
Construction	83,600	7.1	5.1
Education and Health Services	155,300	13.1	16.3
Financial Activities	77,000	6.5	6.1
Government	126,200	10.7	15.2
Information	24,600	2.1	1.9
Leisure and Hospitality	179,400	15.1	9.0
Manufacturing	47,500	4.0	8.5
Mining and Logging	200	<0.1	0.4
Other Services	39,500	3.3	3.8
Professional and Business Services	216,000	18.2	14.4
Retail Trade	145,300	12.3	10.9
Transportation, Warehousing, and Utilities	44,900	3.8	4.6
Wholesale Trade	45,200	3.8	3.9

Note: Figures are non-farm employment as of December 2020. Figures are not seasonally adjusted and include workers 16 years of age and older; (1) Figures cover the Orlando-Kissimmee-Sanford, FL Metropolitan Statistical Area
Source: Bureau of Labor Statistics, Current Employment Statistics, Employment, Hours, and Earnings

Employment by Occupation

Occupation Classification	City (%)	MSA[1] (%)	U.S. (%)
Management, Business, Science, and Arts	37.7	37.1	38.5
Natural Resources, Construction, and Maintenance	6.2	7.9	8.9
Production, Transportation, and Material Moving	10.3	10.5	13.2
Sales and Office	25.5	24.7	21.6
Service	20.3	19.8	17.8

Note: Figures cover employed civilians 16 years of age and older; (1) Figures cover the Orlando-Kissimmee-Sanford, FL Metropolitan Statistical Area
Source: U.S. Census Bureau, 2015-2019 American Community Survey 5-Year Estimates

Occupations with Greatest Projected Employment Growth: 2020 – 2022

Occupation[1]	2020 Employment	2022 Projected Employment	Numeric Employment Change	Percent Employment Change
Fast Food and Counter Workers	172,590	214,590	42,000	24.3
Waiters and Waitresses	141,990	180,530	38,540	27.1
Retail Salespersons	264,490	292,340	27,850	10.5
Cooks, Restaurant	79,150	103,770	24,620	31.1
Maids and Housekeeping Cleaners	63,280	81,030	17,750	28.0
Cashiers	204,540	221,530	16,990	8.3
Registered Nurses	189,240	202,880	13,640	7.2
Laborers and Freight, Stock, and Material Movers, Hand	147,740	160,650	12,910	8.7
First-Line Supervisors of Food Preparation and Serving Workers	51,820	64,080	12,260	23.7
Stockers and Order Fillers	130,980	142,780	11,800	9.0

Note: Projections cover Florida; (1) Sorted by numeric employment change
Source: www.projectionscentral.com, State Occupational Projections, 2020–2022 Short-Term Projections

Fastest-Growing Occupations: 2020 – 2022

Occupation[1]	2020 Employment	2022 Projected Employment	Numeric Employment Change	Percent Employment Change
Hotel, Motel, and Resort Desk Clerks	11,930	18,100	6,170	51.7
Locker Room, Coatroom, and Dressing Room Attendants	930	1,360	430	46.2
Lodging Managers	3,190	4,420	1,230	38.6
Manicurists and Pedicurists	2,640	3,580	940	35.6
Bartenders	31,430	42,540	11,110	35.3
Gaming Cage Workers	320	430	110	34.4
Parking Lot Attendants	11,200	15,040	3,840	34.3
Gaming Dealers	2,660	3,560	900	33.8
Baggage Porters and Bellhops	3,520	4,670	1,150	32.7
Cooks, Restaurant	79,150	103,770	24,620	31.1

Note: Projections cover Florida; (1) Sorted by percent employment change and excludes occupations with numeric employment change less than 50
Source: www.projectionscentral.com, State Occupational Projections, 2020–2022 Short-Term Projections

TAXES

State Corporate Income Tax Rates

State	Tax Rate (%)	Income Brackets ($)	Num. of Brackets	Financial Institution Tax Rate (%)[a]	Federal Income Tax Ded.
Florida	4.458 (e)	Flat rate	1	4.458 (e)	No

Note: Tax rates as of January 1, 2021; (a) Rates listed are the corporate income tax rate applied to financial institutions or excise taxes based on income. Some states have other taxes based upon the value of deposits or shares; (e) The Florida tax rate may be adjusted downward if certain revenue targets are met.
Source: Federation of Tax Administrators, State Corporate Income Tax Rates, January 1, 2021

State Individual Income Tax Rates

State	Tax Rate (%)	Income Brackets ($)	Personal Exemptions ($) Single	Married	Depend.	Standard Ded. ($) Single	Married
Florida				– No state income tax –			

Note: Tax rates as of January 1, 2021; Local- and county-level taxes are not included
Source: Federation of Tax Administrators, State Individual Income Tax Rates, January 1, 2021

Various State Sales and Excise Tax Rates

State	State Sales Tax (%)	Gasoline[1] (¢/gal.)	Cigarette[2] ($/pack)	Spirits[3] ($/gal.)	Wine[4] ($/gal.)	Beer[5] ($/gal.)	Recreational Marijuana (%)
Florida	6	42.46	1.339	6.5	2.25	0.48	Not legal

Note: All tax rates as of January 1, 2021; (1) The American Petroleum Institute has developed a methodology for determining the average tax rate on a gallon of fuel. Rates may include any of the following: excise taxes, environmental fees, storage tank fees, other fees or taxes, general sales tax, and local taxes; (2) The federal excise tax of $1.0066 per pack and local taxes are not included; (3) Rates are those applicable to off-premise sales of 40% alcohol by volume (a.b.v.) distilled spirits in 750ml containers. Local excise taxes are excluded; (4) Rates are those applicable to off-premise sales of 11% a.b.v. non-carbonated wine in 750ml containers; (5) Rates are those applicable to off-premise sales of 4.7% a.b.v. beer in 12 ounce containers.
Source: Tax Foundation, 2021 Facts & Figures: How Does Your State Compare?

State Business Tax Climate Index Rankings

State	Overall Rank	Corporate Tax Rank	Individual Income Tax Rank	Sales Tax Rank	Property Tax Rank	Unemployment Insurance Tax Rank
Florida	4	6	1	21	13	2

Note: The index is a measure of how each state's tax laws affect economic performance. The lower the rank, the more favorable a state's tax system is for business. States without a given tax are given a ranking of 1. The scores/rankings for the District of Columbia do not affect other states. The 2021 index represents the tax climate as of July 1, 2020.
Source: Tax Foundation, State Business Tax Climate Index 2021

TRANSPORTATION

Means of Transportation to Work

Area	Car/Truck/Van Drove Alone	Car/Truck/Van Carpooled	Public Transportation Bus	Public Transportation Subway	Public Transportation Railroad	Bicycle	Walked	Other Means	Worked at Home
City	79.0	8.0	3.4	0.1	0.0	0.6	1.8	1.9	5.3
MSA[1]	79.7	9.8	1.5	0.0	0.1	0.4	1.1	1.6	5.9
U.S.	76.3	9.0	2.4	1.9	0.6	0.5	2.7	1.4	5.2

Note: Figures are percentages and cover workers 16 years of age and older; (1) Figures cover the Orlando-Kissimmee-Sanford, FL Metropolitan Statistical Area
Source: U.S. Census Bureau, 2015-2019 American Community Survey 5-Year Estimates

Travel Time to Work

Area	Less Than 10 Minutes	10 to 19 Minutes	20 to 29 Minutes	30 to 44 Minutes	45 to 59 Minutes	60 to 89 Minutes	90 Minutes or More
City	7.8	27.2	25.9	26.7	6.8	3.4	2.2
MSA[1]	7.1	22.9	22.9	28.1	11.1	5.6	2.3
U.S.	12.2	28.4	20.8	20.8	8.3	6.4	2.9

Note: Note: Figures are percentages and include workers 16 years old and over; (1) Figures cover the Orlando-Kissimmee-Sanford, FL Metropolitan Statistical Area
Source: U.S. Census Bureau, 2015-2019 American Community Survey 5-Year Estimates

Key Congestion Measures

Measure	1982	1992	2002	2012	2017
Annual Hours of Delay, Total (000)	5,267	18,525	40,604	53,777	63,205
Annual Hours of Delay, Per Auto Commuter	15	32	47	50	57
Annual Congestion Cost, Total (million $)	40	195	548	963	1,164
Annual Congestion Cost, Per Auto Commuter ($)	206	498	851	883	1,007

Note: Covers the Orlando FL urban area
Source: Texas A&M Transportation Institute, 2019 Urban Mobility Report

Freeway Travel Time Index

Measure	1982	1987	1992	1997	2002	2007	2012	2017
Urban Area Index[1]	1.07	1.11	1.15	1.17	1.22	1.23	1.22	1.24
Urban Area Rank[1,2]	35	29	26	32	29	31	32	28

Note: Freeway Travel Time Index—the ratio of travel time in the peak period to the travel time at free-flow conditions. For example, a value of 1.30 indicates a 20-minute free-flow trip takes 26 minutes in the peak (20 minutes x 1.30 = 26 minutes); (1) Covers the Orlando FL urban area; (2) Rank is based on 101 larger urban areas (#1 = highest travel time index)
Source: Texas A&M Transportation Institute, 2019 Urban Mobility Report

Public Transportation

Agency Name / Mode of Transportation	Vehicles Operated in Maximum Service[1]	Annual Unlinked Passenger Trips[2] (in thous.)	Annual Passenger Miles[3] (in thous.)
Central Florida Regional Transportation Authority (Lynx)			
Bus (directly operated)	255	22,821.8	140,099.8
Bus (purchased transportation)	13	142.0	823.2
Bus Rapid Transit (directly operated)	13	1,040.3	718.0
Demand Response (purchased transportation)	210	582.2	7,564.2
Vanpool (purchased transportation)	190	434.3	14,022.4

Note: (1) Number of revenue vehicles operated by the given mode and type of service to meet the annual maximum service requirement. This is the revenue vehicle count during the peak season of the year; on the week and day that maximum service is provided. Vehicles operated in maximum service (VOMS) exclude atypical days and one-time special events; (2) Number of passengers who boarded public transportation vehicles. Passengers are counted each time they board a vehicle no matter how many vehicles they use to travel from their origin to their destination. (3) Sum of the distances ridden by all passengers during the entire fiscal year.
Source: Federal Transit Administration, National Transit Database, 2019

Air Transportation

Airport Name and Code / Type of Service	Passenger Airlines[1]	Passenger Enplanements	Freight Carriers[2]	Freight (lbs)
Orlando International (MCO)				
Domestic service (U.S. carriers - 2020)	23	9,697,729	18	185,731,146
International service (U.S. carriers - 2019)	11	758,022	5	1,526,115

Note: (1) Includes all U.S.-based major, minor and commuter airlines that carried at least one passenger during the year; (2) Includes all U.S.-based airlines and freight carriers that transported at least one pound of freight during the year.
Source: Bureau of Transportation Statistics, The Intermodal Transportation Database, Air Carriers: T-100 Domestic Market (U.S. Carriers), 2020; Bureau of Transportation Statistics, The Intermodal Transportation Database, Air Carriers: T-100 International Market (U.S. Carriers), 2019

BUSINESSES

Major Business Headquarters

Company Name	Industry	Fortune[1]	Forbes[2]
Darden Restaurants	Food Services	372	-
Red Lobster	Hotels, Restaurants & Leisure	-	169

Note: (1) Companies that produce a 10-K are ranked 1 to 500 based on 2019 revenue; (2) All private companies with at least $2 billion in annual revenue through the end of their most current fiscal year are ranked 1 to 219; companies listed are headquartered in the city; dashes indicate no ranking
Source: Fortune, "Fortune 500," June/July 2020; Forbes, "America's Largest Private Companies," 2020

Fastest-Growing Businesses

According to *Inc.*, Orlando is home to one of America's 500 fastest-growing private companies: **Fattmerchant** (#436). Criteria: must be an independent, privately-held, for-profit, U.S. corporation, proprietorship or partnership as of December 31, 2019; revenues must be at least $100,000 in 2016 and $2 million in 2019; must have four-year operating/sales history. *Inc., "America's 500 Fastest-Growing Private Companies," 2020*

According to Deloitte, Orlando is home to one of North America's 500 fastest-growing high-technology companies: **Fattmerchant** (#118). Companies are ranked by percentage growth in revenue over a four-year period. Criteria for inclusion: company must be headquartered within North America; must own proprietary intellectual property or technology that is sold to customers in products that contributes to a significant portion of the company's operating revenue; must have been in business for a minumum of four years with 2016 operating revenues of at least $50,000 USD/CD and 2019 operating revenues of at least $5 million USD/CD. *Deloitte, 2020 Technology Fast 500™*

Minority Business Opportunity

Orlando is home to one company which is on the *Black Enterprise* Auto Dealer list (45 largest dealers based on gross sales): **Boyland Auto Group** (#3). Criteria: company must be operational in previous calendar year and be at least 51% black-owned. *Black Enterprise, B.E. 100s, 2019*

Living Environment

COST OF LIVING

Cost of Living Index

Composite Index	Groceries	Housing	Utilities	Transportation	Health Care	Misc. Goods/Services
93.7	102.9	86.5	100.0	96.1	91.9	93.7

Note: The Cost of Living Index measures regional differences in the cost of consumer goods and services, excluding taxes and non-consumer expenditures, for professional and managerial households in the top income quintile. It is based on more than 50,000 prices covering almost 60 different items for which prices are collected three times a year by chambers of commerce, economic development organizations or university applied economic centers in each participating urban area. The numbers shown should be read as a percentage above or below the national average of 100. For example, a value of 115.4 in the groceries column indicates that grocery prices are 15.4% higher than the national average. Small differences in the index numbers should not be interpreted as significant; Figures cover the Orlando FL urban area.
Source: The Council for Community and Economic Research, Cost of Living Index, 2020

Grocery Prices

Area[1]	T-Bone Steak ($/pound)	Frying Chicken ($/pound)	Whole Milk ($/half gal.)	Eggs ($/dozen)	Orange Juice ($/64 oz.)	Coffee ($/11.5 oz.)
City[2]	11.14	1.27	2.39	1.31	3.60	3.91
Avg.	11.78	1.39	2.05	1.47	3.57	4.34
Min.	8.03	0.94	1.03	0.74	2.94	3.02
Max.	15.86	2.65	4.31	3.77	5.44	8.69

Note: (1) Values for the local area are compared with the average, minimum and maximum values for all 284 areas in the Cost of Living Index; (2) Figures cover the Orlando FL urban area; **T-Bone Steak** (price per pound); **Frying Chicken** (price per pound, whole fryer); **Whole Milk** (half gallon carton); **Eggs** (price per dozen, Grade A, large); **Orange Juice** (64 oz. Tropicana or Florida Natural); **Coffee** (11.5 oz. can, vacuum-packed, Maxwell House, Hills Bros, or Folgers).
Source: The Council for Community and Economic Research, Cost of Living Index, 2020

Housing and Utility Costs

Area[1]	New Home Price ($)	Apartment Rent ($/month)	All Electric ($/month)	Part Electric ($/month)	Other Energy ($/month)	Telephone ($/month)
City[2]	294,196	1,148	164.06	-	-	187.90
Avg.	368,594	1,168	170.86	100.47	65.28	184.30
Min.	190,567	502	91.58	31.42	26.08	169.60
Max.	2,227,806	4,738	470.38	280.31	280.06	206.50

Note: (1) Values for the local area are compared with the average, minimum and maximum values for all 284 areas in the Cost of Living Index; (2) Figures cover the Orlando FL urban area; **New Home Price** (2,400 sf living area, 8,000 sf lot, in urban area with full utilities); **Apartment Rent** (950 sf 2 bedroom/1.5 or 2 bath, unfurnished, excluding all utilities except water); **All Electric** (average monthly cost for an all-electric home); **Part Electric** (average monthly cost for a part-electric home); **Other Energy** (average monthly cost for natural gas, fuel oil, coal, wood, and any other forms of energy except electricity); **Telephone** (price includes the base monthly rate plus taxes and fees for three lines of mobile phone service).
Source: The Council for Community and Economic Research, Cost of Living Index, 2020

Health Care, Transportation, and Other Costs

Area[1]	Doctor ($/visit)	Dentist ($/visit)	Optometrist ($/visit)	Gasoline ($/gallon)	Beauty Salon ($/visit)	Men's Shirt ($)
City[2]	83.46	97.71	100.39	2.10	54.17	17.78
Avg.	115.44	99.32	108.10	2.21	39.27	31.37
Min.	36.68	59.00	51.36	1.71	19.00	11.00
Max.	219.00	153.10	250.97	3.46	82.05	58.33

Note: (1) Values for the local area are compared with the average, minimum and maximum values for all 284 areas in the Cost of Living Index; (2) Figures cover the Orlando FL urban area; **Doctor** (general practitioners routine exam of an established patient); **Dentist** (adult teeth cleaning and periodic oral examination); **Optometrist** (full vision eye exam for established adult patient); **Gasoline** (one gallon regular unleaded, national brand, including all taxes, cash price at self-service pump if available); **Beauty Salon** (woman's shampoo, trim, and blow-dry); **Men's Shirt** (cotton/polyester dress shirt, pinpoint weave, long sleeves).
Source: The Council for Community and Economic Research, Cost of Living Index, 2020

HOUSING

Homeownership Rate

Area	2012 (%)	2013 (%)	2014 (%)	2015 (%)	2016 (%)	2017 (%)	2018 (%)	2019 (%)	2020 (%)
MSA[1]	68.0	65.5	62.3	58.4	58.5	59.5	58.5	56.1	64.2
U.S.	65.4	65.1	64.5	63.7	63.4	63.9	64.4	64.6	66.6

Note: (1) Figures cover the Orlando-Kissimmee-Sanford, FL Metropolitan Statistical Area
Source: U.S. Census Bureau, Housing Vacancies and Homeownership Annual Statistics: 2012-2020

House Price Index (HPI)

Area	National Ranking[2]	Quarterly Change (%)	One-Year Change (%)	Five-Year Change (%)	Since 1991Q1 (%)
MSA[1]	119	1.83	6.36	44.80	198.33
U.S.[3]	–	3.81	10.77	38.99	205.12

Note: The HPI is a weighted repeat sales index. It measures average price changes in repeat sales or refinancings on the same properties. This information is obtained by reviewing repeat mortgage transactions on single-family properties whose mortgages have been purchased or securitized by Fannie Mae or Freddie Mac since January 1975; (1) Figures cover the Orlando-Kissimmee-Sanford, FL Metropolitan Statistical Area; (2) Rankings are based on annual percentage change for all metro areas containing at least 15,000 transactions over the last 10 years and ranges from 1 to 253; (3) figures based on a weighted average of Census Division estimates using a seasonally adjusted, purchase-only index; all figures are for the period ending December 31, 2020
Source: Federal Housing Finance Agency, Change in Metropolitan Area House Price Indexes, April 7, 2021

Median Single-Family Home Prices

Area	2018	2019	2020[p]	Percent Change 2019 to 2020
MSA[1]	265.0	276.0	301.6	9.3
U.S. Average	261.6	274.6	299.9	9.2

Note: Figures are median sales prices of existing single-family homes in thousands of dollars; (p) preliminary; (1) Figures cover the Orlando-Kissimmee-Sanford, FL Metropolitan Statistical Area
Source: National Association of Realtors, Median Sales Price of Existing Single-Family Homes for Metropolitan Areas, 4th Quarter 2020

Qualifying Income Based on Median Sales Price of Existing Single-Family Homes

Area	With 5% Down ($)	With 10% Down ($)	With 20% Down ($)
MSA[1]	59,580	56,444	50,172
U.S. Average	59,266	56,147	49,908

Note: Figures are preliminary; Qualifying income is based on a mortgage rate of 2.81%. Monthly principal and interest payment is limited to 25% of income; (1) Figures cover the Orlando-Kissimmee-Sanford, FL Metropolitan Statistical Area
Source: National Association of Realtors, Qualifying Income Based on Median Sales Price of Existing Single-Family Homes for Metropolitan Areas, 4th Quarter 2020

Home Value Distribution

Area	Under $50,000	$50,000 -$99,999	$100,000 -$149,999	$150,000 -$199,999	$200,000 -$299,999	$300,000 -$499,999	$500,000 -$999,999	$1,000,000 or more
City	2.9	10.7	13.4	13.0	24.6	24.6	8.8	2.1
MSA[1]	6.1	8.5	11.7	17.0	28.6	20.3	6.2	1.7
U.S.	6.9	12.0	13.3	14.0	19.6	19.3	11.4	3.4

Note: Figures are percentages and cover owner-occupied housing units; (1) Figures cover the Orlando-Kissimmee-Sanford, FL Metropolitan Statistical Area
Source: U.S. Census Bureau, 2015-2019 American Community Survey 5-Year Estimates

Year Housing Structure Built

Area	2010 or Later	2000 -2009	1990 -1999	1980 -1989	1970 -1979	1960 -1969	1950 -1959	1940 -1949	Before 1940	Median Year
City	9.6	21.6	16.3	16.9	13.9	7.2	8.6	2.9	3.0	1989
MSA[1]	8.8	23.8	20.6	20.2	12.8	5.9	5.2	1.2	1.5	1992
U.S.	5.2	14.0	13.9	13.4	15.2	10.6	10.3	4.9	12.6	1978

Note: Figures are percentages except for Median Year; Note: (1) Figures cover the Orlando-Kissimmee-Sanford, FL Metropolitan Statistical Area
Source: U.S. Census Bureau, 2015-2019 American Community Survey 5-Year Estimates

Gross Monthly Rent

Area	Under $500	$500 -$999	$1,000 -$1,499	$1,500 -$1,999	$2,000 -$2,499	$2,500 -$2,999	$3,000 and up	Median ($)
City	3.7	24.7	48.8	17.6	4.0	0.8	0.4	1,196
MSA[1]	2.9	25.1	46.3	19.7	4.2	1.1	0.7	1,210
U.S.	9.4	36.2	30.0	14.0	5.6	2.4	2.4	1,062

Note: Figures are percentages except for Median; Gross rent is the contract rent plus the estimated average monthly cost of utilities (electricity, gas, and water and sewer) and fuels (oil, coal, kerosene, wood, etc.) if these are paid by the renter (or paid for the renter by someone else); (1) Figures cover the Orlando-Kissimmee-Sanford, FL Metropolitan Statistical Area
Source: U.S. Census Bureau, 2015-2019 American Community Survey 5-Year Estimates

HEALTH

Health Risk Factors

Category	MSA[1] (%)	U.S. (%)
Adults aged 18–64 who have any kind of health care coverage	79.0	87.3
Adults who reported being in good or better health	80.6	82.4
Adults who have been told they have high blood cholesterol	34.5	33.0
Adults who have been told they have high blood pressure	32.2	32.3
Adults who are current smokers	12.9	17.1
Adults who currently use E-cigarettes	6.1	4.6
Adults who currently use chewing tobacco, snuff, or snus	2.7	4.0
Adults who are heavy drinkers[2]	4.1	6.3
Adults who are binge drinkers[3]	13.8	17.4
Adults who are overweight (BMI 25.0 - 29.9)	38.8	35.3
Adults who are obese (BMI 30.0 - 99.8)	26.4	31.3
Adults who participated in any physical activities in the past month	72.9	74.4
Adults who always or nearly always wears a seat belt	96.3	94.3

Note: (1) Figures cover the Orlando-Kissimmee-Sanford, FL Metropolitan Statistical Area; (2) Heavy drinkers are classified as adult men having more than 14 drinks per week and adult women having more than 7 drinks per week; (3) Binge drinkers are classified as males having five or more drinks on one occasion or females having four or more drinks on one occasion
Source: Centers for Disease Control and Prevention, Behaviorial Risk Factor Surveillance System, SMART: Selected Metropolitan Area Risk Trends, 2017

Acute and Chronic Health Conditions

Category	MSA[1] (%)	U.S. (%)
Adults who have ever been told they had a heart attack	4.1	4.2
Adults who have ever been told they have angina or coronary heart disease	4.0	3.9
Adults who have ever been told they had a stroke	3.1	3.0
Adults who have ever been told they have asthma	14.4	14.2
Adults who have ever been told they have arthritis	20.6	24.9
Adults who have ever been told they have diabetes[2]	10.2	10.5
Adults who have ever been told they had skin cancer	6.3	6.2
Adults who have ever been told they had any other types of cancer	6.8	7.1
Adults who have ever been told they have COPD	6.4	6.5
Adults who have ever been told they have kidney disease	2.3	3.0
Adults who have ever been told they have a form of depression	16.9	20.5

Note: (1) Figures cover the Orlando-Kissimmee-Sanford, FL Metropolitan Statistical Area; (2) Figures do not include pregnancy-related, borderline, or pre-diabetes
Source: Centers for Disease Control and Prevention, Behaviorial Risk Factor Surveillance System, SMART: Selected Metropolitan Area Risk Trends, 2017

Health Screening and Vaccination Rates

Category	MSA[1] (%)	U.S. (%)
Adults aged 65+ who have had flu shot within the past year	57.2	60.7
Adults aged 65+ who have ever had a pneumonia vaccination	66.2	75.4
Adults who have ever been tested for HIV	47.4	36.1
Adults who have ever had the shingles or zoster vaccine?	20.4	28.9
Adults who have had their blood cholesterol checked within the last five years	89.7	85.9

Note: n/a not available; (1) Figures cover the Orlando-Kissimmee-Sanford, FL Metropolitan Statistical Area.
Source: Centers for Disease Control and Prevention, Behaviorial Risk Factor Surveillance System, SMART: Selected Metropolitan Area Risk Trends, 2017

Disability Status

Category	MSA[1] (%)	U.S. (%)
Adults who reported being deaf	5.0	6.7
Are you blind or have serious difficulty seeing, even when wearing glasses?	6.0	4.5
Are you limited in any way in any of your usual activities due of arthritis?	11.9	12.9
Do you have difficulty doing errands alone?	7.9	6.8
Do you have difficulty dressing or bathing?	4.3	3.6
Do you have serious difficulty concentrating/remembering/making decisions?	13.0	10.7
Do you have serious difficulty walking or climbing stairs?	13.8	13.6

Note: (1) Figures cover the Orlando-Kissimmee-Sanford, FL Metropolitan Statistical Area.
Source: Centers for Disease Control and Prevention, Behaviorial Risk Factor Surveillance System, SMART: Selected Metropolitan Area Risk Trends, 2017

Mortality Rates for the Top 10 Causes of Death in the U.S.

ICD-10[a] Sub-Chapter	ICD-10[a] Code	Age-Adjusted Mortality Rate[1] per 100,000 population County[2]	U.S.
Malignant neoplasms	C00-C97	144.3	149.2
Ischaemic heart diseases	I20-I25	86.1	90.5
Other forms of heart disease	I30-I51	39.1	52.2
Chronic lower respiratory diseases	J40-J47	30.8	39.6
Other degenerative diseases of the nervous system	G30-G31	25.7	37.6
Cerebrovascular diseases	I60-I69	50.4	37.2
Other external causes of accidental injury	W00-X59	31.9	36.1
Organic, including symptomatic, mental disorders	F01-F09	23.5	29.4
Hypertensive diseases	I10-I15	22.7	24.1
Diabetes mellitus	E10-E14	20.6	21.5

Note: (a) ICD-10 = International Classification of Diseases 10th Revision; (1) Mortality rates are a three-year average covering 2017-2019; (2) Figures cover Orange County.
Source: Centers for Disease Control and Prevention, National Center for Health Statistics. Underlying Cause of Death 1999-2019 on CDC WONDER Online Database

Mortality Rates for Selected Causes of Death

ICD-10[a] Sub-Chapter	ICD-10[a] Code	Age-Adjusted Mortality Rate[1] per 100,000 population County[2]	U.S.
Assault	X85-Y09	6.7	6.0
Diseases of the liver	K70-K76	11.8	14.4
Human immunodeficiency virus (HIV) disease	B20-B24	2.9	1.5
Influenza and pneumonia	J09-J18	9.6	13.8
Intentional self-harm	X60-X84	10.1	14.1
Malnutrition	E40-E46	4.0	2.3
Obesity and other hyperalimentation	E65-E68	1.2	2.1
Renal failure	N17-N19	10.3	12.6
Transport accidents	V01-V99	12.5	12.3
Viral hepatitis	B15-B19	1.1	1.2

Note: (a) ICD-10 = International Classification of Diseases 10th Revision; (1) Mortality rates are a three-year average covering 2017-2019; (2) Figures cover Orange County; Data are suppressed when the data meet the criteria for confidentiality constraints; Mortality rates are flagged as unreliable when the rate would be calculated with a numerator of 20 or less.
Source: Centers for Disease Control and Prevention, National Center for Health Statistics. Underlying Cause of Death 1999-2019 on CDC WONDER Online Database

Health Insurance Coverage

Area	With Health Insurance	With Private Health Insurance	With Public Health Insurance	Without Health Insurance	Population Under Age 19 Without Health Insurance
City	84.8	62.3	29.4	15.2	7.5
MSA[1]	87.6	65.5	31.5	12.4	6.9
U.S.	91.2	67.9	35.1	8.8	5.1

Note: Figures are percentages that cover the civilian noninstitutionalized population; (1) Figures cover the Orlando-Kissimmee-Sanford, FL Metropolitan Statistical Area
Source: U.S. Census Bureau, 2015-2019 American Community Survey 5-Year Estimates

Number of Medical Professionals

Area	MDs[3]	DOs[3,4]	Dentists	Podiatrists	Chiropractors	Optometrists
County[1] (number)	4,301	306	707	51	370	179
County[1] (rate[2])	311.3	22.1	50.7	3.7	26.6	12.8
U.S. (rate[2])	282.9	22.7	71.2	6.2	28.1	16.9

12095
Note: Data as of 2019 unless noted; (1) Data covers Orange County; (2) Rate per 100,000 population; (3) Data as of 2018 and includes all active, non-federal physicians; (4) Doctor of Osteopathic Medicine
Source: U.S. Department of Health and Human Services, Health Resources and Services Administration, Bureau of Health Professions, Area Resource File (ARF) 2019-2020

Best Hospitals

According to *U.S. News*, the Orlando-Kissimmee-Sanford, FL metro area is home to one of the best hospitals in the U.S.: **AdventHealth Orlando** (4 adult specialties and 1 pediatric specialty). The hospital listed was nationally ranked in at least one of 16 adult or 10 pediatric specialties. Only 134 hospitals nationwide were nationally ranked in one or more adult or pediatric specialty; this number increases to 178 counting specialized centers within hospitals. Twenty hospitals in the U.S. made the Honor Roll. The Best Hospitals Honor Roll takes both the national rankings and the procedure and condition ratings into account. Hospitals received points if they were nationally ranked in one of the 16 adult specialties—the higher they ranked, the more points they got—and how many ratings of "high performing" they earned in the 10 procedures and conditions. *U.S. News Online, "America's Best Hospitals 2020-21"*

According to *U.S. News,* the Orlando-Kissimmee-Sanford, FL metro area is home to two of the best children's hospitals in the U.S.: **AdventHealth for Children** (1 pediatric specialty); **Arnold Palmer Hospital for Children** (4 pediatric specialties). The hospitals listed were highly ranked in at least one of 10 pediatric specialties. Eighty-eight children's hospitals in the U.S. were nationally ranked in at least one specialty. Hospitals received points for being ranked in a specialty, and the 10 hospitals with the most points across the 10 specialties make up the Honor Roll. *U.S. News Online, "America's Best Children's Hospitals 2020-21"*

EDUCATION

Public School District Statistics

District Name	Schls	Pupils	Pupil/Teacher Ratio	Minority Pupils[1] (%)	Free Lunch Eligible[2] (%)	IEP[3] (%)
Orange	258	208,203	17.5	74.7	46.3	10.4

Note: Table includes school districts with 2,000 or more students; (1) Percentage of students that are not non-Hispanic white; (2) Percentage of students that are eligible for the free lunch program; (3) Percentage of students that have an Individualized Education Program.
Source: U.S. Department of Education, National Center for Education Statistics, Common Core of Data, Local Education Agency (School District) Universe Survey: School Year 2018-2019; U.S. Department of Education, National Center for Education Statistics, Common Core of Data, Public Elementary/Secondary School Universe Survey: School Year 2018-2019

Best High Schools

According to *U.S. News,* Orlando is home to one of the top 500 high schools in the U.S.: **Orlando Science Middle High Charter** (#358). Nearly 18,000 public, magnet and charter schools were ranked based on their performance on state assessments and how well they prepare students for college. *U.S. News & World Report, "Best High Schools 2020"*

Highest Level of Education

Area	Less than H.S.	H.S. Diploma	Some College, No Deg.	Associate Degree	Bachelor's Degree	Master's Degree	Prof. School Degree	Doctorate Degree
City	9.6	23.2	18.4	10.8	25.4	8.3	3.0	1.3
MSA[1]	10.5	25.8	19.9	11.5	21.3	7.8	2.0	1.0
U.S.	12.0	27.0	20.4	8.5	19.8	8.8	2.1	1.4

Note: Figures cover persons age 25 and over; (1) Figures cover the Orlando-Kissimmee-Sanford, FL Metropolitan Statistical Area
Source: U.S. Census Bureau, 2015-2019 American Community Survey 5-Year Estimates

Educational Attainment by Race

Area	High School Graduate or Higher (%)					Bachelor's Degree or Higher (%)				
	Total	White	Black	Asian	Hisp.[2]	Total	White	Black	Asian	Hisp.[2]
City	90.4	92.8	84.6	92.6	86.8	38.1	43.3	21.8	60.3	28.8
MSA[1]	89.5	91.1	85.8	88.8	83.6	32.2	33.9	22.8	52.3	23.2
U.S.	88.0	89.9	86.0	87.1	68.7	32.1	33.5	21.6	54.3	16.4

Note: Figures shown cover persons 25 years old and over; (1) Figures cover the Orlando-Kissimmee-Sanford, FL Metropolitan Statistical Area; (2) People of Hispanic origin can be of any race
Source: U.S. Census Bureau, 2015-2019 American Community Survey 5-Year Estimates

School Enrollment by Grade and Control

Area	Preschool (%)		Kindergarten (%)		Grades 1 - 4 (%)		Grades 5 - 8 (%)		Grades 9 - 12 (%)	
	Public	Private	Public	Private	Public	Private	Public	Private	Public	Private
City	62.2	37.8	86.4	13.6	91.2	8.8	85.0	15.0	93.3	6.7
MSA[1]	55.2	44.8	81.0	19.0	86.3	13.7	85.6	14.4	89.6	10.4
U.S.	59.1	40.9	87.6	12.4	89.5	10.5	89.4	10.6	90.1	9.9

Note: Figures shown cover persons 3 years old and over; (1) Figures cover the Orlando-Kissimmee-Sanford, FL Metropolitan Statistical Area
Source: U.S. Census Bureau, 2015-2019 American Community Survey 5-Year Estimates

Higher Education

Four-Year Colleges			Two-Year Colleges			Medical Schools[1]	Law Schools[2]	Voc/Tech[3]
Public	Private Non-profit	Private For-profit	Public	Private Non-profit	Private For-profit			
2	2	3	2	0	6	1	2	1

Note: Figures cover institutions located within the city limits and include main campuses only; (1) includes schools accredited by the Liaison Committee on Medical Education and the American Osteopathic Association's Commission on Osteopathic College Accreditation; (2) includes ABA-accredited schools, schools with provisional ABA accreditation, and state accredited schools; (3) includes all schools with programs that are less than 2 years.
Source: National Center for Education Statistics, Integrated Postsecondary Education System (IPEDS), 2019-20; Wikipedia, List of Medical Schools in the United States, accessed April 2, 2021; Wikipedia, List of Law Schools in the United States, accessed April 2, 2021

According to *U.S. News & World Report,* the Orlando-Kissimmee-Sanford, FL metro area is home to one of the top 200 national universities in the U.S.: **University of Central Florida** (#160 tie). The indicators used to capture academic quality fall into a number of categories: assessment by administrators at peer institutions; retention of students; faculty resources; student selectivity; financial resources; alumni giving; high school counselor ratings of colleges; and graduation rate. *U.S. News & World Report, "America's Best Colleges 2021"*

EMPLOYERS

Major Employers

Company Name	Industry
Adventist Health System/Sunbelt	General medical & surgical hospitals
Airtran Airways	Air passenger carrier, scheduled
Central Florida Health Alliance	Hospital management
CNL Lifestyle Properties	Real estate agents & managers
Connextions	Communication services, nec
Florida Department of Children & Families	Individual & family services
Florida Hospital Medical Center	General medical & surgical hospitals
Gaylord Palms Resort & Conv Ctr	Hotel franchised
Leesburg Regional Medical Center	General medical & surgical hospitals
Lockheed Martin Corporation	Aircraft
Marriott International	Hotels & motels
Orlando Health	General medical & surgical hospitals
Rosen 9939	Hotels & motels
Sea World of Florida	Theme park, amusement
Sears Termite & Pest Control	Pest control in structures
Siemens Energy	Power plant construction
Universal City Florida Partners	Amusement & theme parks
University of Central Florida	Colleges & universities
Winter Park Healthcare Group	Hospital affiliated with AMA residency

Note: Companies shown are located within the Orlando-Kissimmee-Sanford, FL Metropolitan Statistical Area.
Source: Hoovers.com; Wikipedia

PUBLIC SAFETY

Crime Rate

Area	All Crimes	Violent Crimes				Property Crimes		
		Murder	Rape[3]	Robbery	Aggrav. Assault	Burglary	Larceny-Theft	Motor Vehicle Theft
City	5,565.2	8.6	69.8	183.5	476.5	501.2	3,889.5	436.1
Suburbs[1]	2,485.9	4.1	42.0	75.9	269.2	341.2	1,573.1	180.5
Metro[2]	2,829.9	4.6	45.1	87.9	292.4	359.1	1,831.9	209.0
U.S.	2,489.3	5.0	42.6	81.6	250.2	340.5	1,549.5	219.9

Note: Figures are crimes per 100,000 population; (1) All areas within the metro area that are located outside the city limits; (2) Figures cover the Orlando-Kissimmee-Sanford, FL Metropolitan Statistical Area; (3) All figures shown were reported using the revised Uniform Crime Reporting (UCR) definition of rape.
Source: FBI Uniform Crime Reports, 2019

Hate Crimes

Area	Number of Quarters Reported	Number of Incidents per Bias Motivation					
		Race/Ethnicity/Ancestry	Religion	Sexual Orientation	Disability	Gender	Gender Identity
City	4	1	1	2	0	0	0
U.S.	4	3,963	1,521	1,195	157	69	198

Source: Federal Bureau of Investigation, Hate Crime Statistics 2019

Identity Theft Consumer Reports

Area	Reports	Reports per 100,000 Population	Rank[2]
MSA[1]	12,297	471	59
U.S.	1,387,615	423	-

Note: (1) Figures cover the Orlando-Kissimmee-Sanford, FL Metropolitan Statistical Area; (2) Rank ranges from 1 to 391 where 1 indicates greatest number of identity theft reports per 100,000 population
Source: Federal Trade Commission, Consumer Sentinel Network Data Book 2020

Fraud and Other Consumer Reports

Area	Reports	Reports per 100,000 Population	Rank[2]
MSA[1]	27,956	1,072	13
U.S.	3,385,133	1,031	-

Note: (1) Figures cover the Orlando-Kissimmee-Sanford, FL Metropolitan Statistical Area; (2) Rank ranges from 1 to 391 where 1 indicates greatest number of fraud and other consumer reports per 100,000 population
Source: Federal Trade Commission, Consumer Sentinel Network Data Book 2020

POLITICS

2020 Presidential Election Results

Area	Biden	Trump	Jorgensen	Hawkins	Other
Orange County	60.9	37.8	0.7	0.2	0.4
U.S.	51.3	46.8	1.2	0.3	0.5

Note: Results are percentages and may not add to 100% due to rounding
Source: Dave Leip's Atlas of U.S. Presidential Elections

SPORTS

Professional Sports Teams

Team Name	League	Year Established
Orlando City SC	Major League Soccer (MLS)	2015
Orlando Magic	National Basketball Association (NBA)	1989

Note: Includes teams located in the Orlando-Kissimmee-Sanford, FL Metropolitan Statistical Area.
Source: Wikipedia, Major Professional Sports Teams of the United States and Canada, April 6, 2021

CLIMATE

Average and Extreme Temperatures

Temperature	Jan	Feb	Mar	Apr	May	Jun	Jul	Aug	Sep	Oct	Nov	Dec	Yr.
Extreme High (°F)	86	89	90	95	100	100	99	100	98	95	89	90	100
Average High (°F)	70	72	77	82	87	90	91	91	89	83	78	72	82
Average Temp. (°F)	59	62	67	72	77	81	82	82	81	75	68	62	72
Average Low (°F)	48	51	56	60	66	71	73	74	72	66	58	51	62
Extreme Low (°F)	19	29	25	38	51	53	64	65	57	44	32	20	19

Note: Figures cover the years 1952-1990
Source: National Climatic Data Center, International Station Meteorological Climate Summary, 9/96

Average Precipitation/Snowfall/Humidity

Precip./Humidity	Jan	Feb	Mar	Apr	May	Jun	Jul	Aug	Sep	Oct	Nov	Dec	Yr.
Avg. Precip. (in.)	2.3	2.8	3.4	2.0	3.2	7.0	7.2	5.8	5.8	2.7	3.5	2.0	47.7
Avg. Snowfall (in.)	Tr	0	0	0	0	0	0	0	0	0	0	0	Tr
Avg. Rel. Hum. 7am (%)	87	87	88	87	88	89	90	92	92	89	89	87	89
Avg. Rel. Hum. 4pm (%)	53	51	49	47	51	61	65	66	66	59	56	55	57

Note: Figures cover the years 1952-1990; Tr = Trace amounts (<0.05 in. of rain; <0.5 in. of snow)
Source: National Climatic Data Center, International Station Meteorological Climate Summary, 9/96

Weather Conditions

Temperature			Daytime Sky			Precipitation		
32°F & below	45°F & below	90°F & above	Clear	Partly cloudy	Cloudy	0.01 inch or more precip.	0.1 inch or more snow/ice	Thunder-storms
3	35	90	76	208	81	115	0	80

Note: Figures are average number of days per year and cover the years 1952-1990
Source: National Climatic Data Center, International Station Meteorological Climate Summary, 9/96

HAZARDOUS WASTE

Superfund Sites

The Orlando-Kissimmee-Sanford, FL metro area is home to six sites on the EPA's Superfund National Priorities List: **Chevron Chemical Co. (Ortho Division)** (final); **City Industries, Inc.** (final); **General Dynamics Longwood** (final); **Sanford Dry Cleaners** (final); **Tower Chemical Co.** (final); **Zellwood Ground Water Contamination** (final). There are a total of 1,375 Superfund sites with a status of proposed or final on the list in the U.S. *U.S. Environmental Protection Agency, National Priorities List, April 7, 2021*

AIR QUALITY

Air Quality Trends: Ozone

	1990	1995	2000	2005	2010	2015	2016	2017	2018	2019
MSA[1]	0.081	0.075	0.080	0.083	0.069	0.060	0.064	0.067	0.062	0.062
U.S.	0.088	0.089	0.082	0.080	0.073	0.068	0.069	0.068	0.069	0.065

Note: (1) Data covers the Orlando-Kissimmee-Sanford, FL Metropolitan Statistical Area. The values shown are the composite ozone concentration averages among trend sites based on the highest fourth daily maximum 8-hour concentration in parts per million. These trends are based on sites having an adequate record of monitoring data during the trend period. Data from exceptional events are included.
Source: U.S. Environmental Protection Agency, Air Quality Monitoring Information, "Air Quality Trends by City, 1990-2019"

Air Quality Index

Area	Percent of Days when Air Quality was...[2]					AQI Statistics[2]	
	Good	Moderate	Unhealthy for Sensitive Groups	Unhealthy	Very Unhealthy	Maximum	Median
MSA[1]	81.1	17.3	1.6	0.0	0.0	122	39

Note: (1) Data covers the Orlando-Kissimmee-Sanford, FL Metropolitan Statistical Area; (2) Based on 365 days with AQI data in 2019. Air Quality Index (AQI) is an index for reporting daily air quality. EPA calculates the AQI for five major air pollutants regulated by the Clean Air Act: ground-level ozone, particle pollution (aka particulate matter), carbon monoxide, sulfur dioxide, and nitrogen dioxide. The AQI runs from 0 to 500. The higher the AQI value, the greater the level of air pollution and the greater the health concern. There are six AQI categories: "Good" AQI is between 0 and 50. Air quality is considered satisfactory; "Moderate" AQI is between 51 and 100. Air quality is acceptable; "Unhealthy for Sensitive Groups" When AQI values are between 101 and 150, members of sensitive groups may experience health effects; "Unhealthy" When AQI values are between 151 and 200 everyone may begin to experience health effects; "Very Unhealthy" AQI values between 201 and 300 trigger a health alert; "Hazardous" AQI values over 300 trigger warnings of emergency conditions (not shown).
Source: U.S. Environmental Protection Agency, Air Quality Index Report, 2019

Air Quality Index Pollutants

Area	Percent of Days when AQI Pollutant was...[2]					
	Carbon Monoxide	Nitrogen Dioxide	Ozone	Sulfur Dioxide	Particulate Matter 2.5	Particulate Matter 10
MSA[1]	0.0	0.0	80.5	0.0	19.5	0.0

Note: (1) Data covers the Orlando-Kissimmee-Sanford, FL Metropolitan Statistical Area; (2) Based on 365 days with AQI data in 2019. The Air Quality Index (AQI) is an index for reporting daily air quality. EPA calculates the AQI for five major air pollutants regulated by the Clean Air Act: ground-level ozone, particle pollution (also known as particulate matter), carbon monoxide, sulfur dioxide, and nitrogen dioxide. The AQI runs from 0 to 500. The higher the AQI value, the greater the level of air pollution and the greater the health concern.
Source: U.S. Environmental Protection Agency, Air Quality Index Report, 2019

Maximum Air Pollutant Concentrations: Particulate Matter, Ozone, CO and Lead

	Particulate Matter 10 (ug/m^3)	Particulate Matter 2.5 Wtd AM (ug/m^3)	Particulate Matter 2.5 24-Hr (ug/m^3)	Ozone (ppm)	Carbon Monoxide (ppm)	Lead (ug/m^3)
MSA[1] Level	49	6.9	16	0.072	1	n/a
NAAQS[2]	150	15	35	0.075	9	0.15
Met NAAQS[2]	Yes	Yes	Yes	Yes	Yes	n/a

Note: (1) Data covers the Orlando-Kissimmee-Sanford, FL Metropolitan Statistical Area; Data from exceptional events are included; (2) National Ambient Air Quality Standards; ppm = parts per million; ug/m^3 = micrograms per cubic meter; n/a not available.
Concentrations: Particulate Matter 10 (coarse particulate)—highest second maximum 24-hour concentration; Particulate Matter 2.5 Wtd AM (fine particulate)—highest weighted annual mean concentration; Particulate Matter 2.5 24-Hour (fine particulate)—highest 98th percentile 24-hour concentration; Ozone—highest fourth daily maximum 8-hour concentration; Carbon Monoxide—highest second maximum non-overlapping 8-hour concentration; Lead—maximum running 3-month average
Source: U.S. Environmental Protection Agency, Air Quality Monitoring Information, "Air Quality Statistics by City, 2019"

Maximum Air Pollutant Concentrations: Nitrogen Dioxide and Sulfur Dioxide

	Nitrogen Dioxide AM (ppb)	Nitrogen Dioxide 1-Hr (ppb)	Sulfur Dioxide AM (ppb)	Sulfur Dioxide 1-Hr (ppb)	Sulfur Dioxide 24-Hr (ppb)
MSA[1] Level	4	30	n/a	3	n/a
NAAQS[2]	53	100	30	75	140
Met NAAQS[2]	Yes	Yes	n/a	Yes	n/a

Note: (1) Data covers the Orlando-Kissimmee-Sanford, FL Metropolitan Statistical Area; Data from exceptional events are included; (2) National Ambient Air Quality Standards; ppm = parts per million; ug/m^3 = micrograms per cubic meter; n/a not available.
Concentrations: Nitrogen Dioxide AM—highest arithmetic mean concentration; Nitrogen Dioxide 1-Hr—highest 98th percentile 1-hour daily maximum concentration; Sulfur Dioxide AM—highest annual mean concentration; Sulfur Dioxide 1-Hr—highest 99th percentile 1-hour daily maximum concentration; Sulfur Dioxide 24-Hr—highest second maximum 24-hour concentration
Source: U.S. Environmental Protection Agency, Air Quality Monitoring Information, "Air Quality Statistics by City, 2019"

San Antonio, Texas

Background

San Antonio is a charming preservation of its Mexican-Spanish heritage. Walking along its famous Paseo Del Rio at night, with cream-colored stucco structures, sea shell ornamented facades, and gently illuminating tiny lights is romantic and picturesque.

San Antonio began in the early eighteenth century as a cohesion of different Spanish missions, whose aim was to convert the Coahuiltecan natives to Christianity, and to European ways of farming. A debilitating epidemic, however, killed most of the natives, as well as the missions' goal, causing the city to be abandoned.

In 1836, San Antonio became the site of interest again, when a small band of American soldiers were unable to successfully defend themselves against an army of 4,000 Mexican soldiers, led by General Antonio de Lopez Santa Anna. Fighting desperately from within the walls of the Mission San Antonio de Valero, or The Alamo, all 183 men were killed. This inspired the cry "Remember the Alamo" from every American soldier led by General Sam Houston, who was determined to wrest Texas territory and independence from Mexico.

Despite the Anglo victory over the Mexicans more than 150 years ago, the Mexican culture and its influence remain strong. We see evidence of this in the architecture, the Franciscan educational system, the variety of Spanish-language media, and the racial composition of the population, in which over half the city's residents are Latino.

This blend of old and new makes San Antonio unique among American cities. It is San home to the first museum of modern art in Texas, the McNay Art Museum. Other art institutions and museums include ArtPace, Blue Star Contemporary Art Center, the Briscoe Western Art Museum, Buckhorn Saloon & Museum (heavy on the cowboy culture), San Antonio Museum of Art, formerly the Lonestar Brewery, Say Si (mentoring San Antonio artistic youth), the Southwest School of Art, Texas Rangers Museum, Texas Transportation Museum, the Witte Museum and the DoSeum. An outdoor display at North Star Mall features 40-foot tall cowboy boots.

The five missions in the city, four of which are in the San Antonio Missions National Historical Park, plus the Alamo, were named a UNESCO World Heritage Site on July 5, 2015. The San Antonio Missions became the 23rd U.S. site on the World Heritage List, which includes the Grand Canyon and the Statue of Liberty. It is the first such site in the state of Texas.

The city continues to draw tourists who come to visit not just the Alamo, but the nearby theme parks like Six Flags Fiesta Texas and SeaWorld, the famed River Walk, charming promenade of shops, restaurants, and pubs. Kelly Air Force Base, decommissioned in 2001, is now a nearly 5,000-acre business park, Kelly USA. Port San Antonio, a warehouse on the site was used to house refugees from Hurricane Katrina. Businesses at the port receive favorable property tax and pay no state, city or corporate income taxes. Sego Lily Dam was constructed in 2017 to prevent further flooding in the city.

The city's airport is undergoing a major renovation, which is scheduled to be complete in 2024.

San Antonio's location on the edge of the Gulf Coastal Plains exposes it to a modified subtropical climate. Summers are hot, although extremely high temperatures are rare. Winters are mild. Since the city is only 140 miles from the Gulf of Mexico, tropical storms occasionally occur, bringing strong winds and heavy rains. In 2020, the city experienced a 5.7 magnitude earthquake. Relative humidity is high in the morning, but tends to drop by late afternoon.

Rankings

General Rankings

- For its "Best for Vets: Places to Live 2019" rankings, *Military Times* evaluated 599 cities (83 large, 234 medium, 282 small) and compared the locations across three broad categories: veteran and military culture/services; economic indicators; and livability factors such as health, crime, traffic, and school quality. San Antonio ranked #3 out of the top 25, in the large city category (population of more than 250,000). Data points more specific to veterans and the military weighed more heavily than others. *rebootcamp.militarytimes.com, "Military Times Best Places to Live 2019," September 10, 2018*

- The San Antonio metro area was identified as one of America's fastest-growing areas in terms of population and business growth by *MagnifyMoney*. The area ranked #9 out of 35. The 100 most populous metro areas in the U.S. were evaluated on their change from 2011-2016 in the following categories: people and housing; workforce and employment opportunities; growing industry. *www.businessinsider.com, "The 35 Cities in the US with the Biggest Influx of People, the Most Work Opportunities, and the Hottest Business Growth," August 12, 2018*

- The San Antonio metro area was identified as one of America's fastest-growing areas in terms of population and economy by *Forbes*. The area ranked #21 out of 25. The 100 most populous metro areas in the U.S. were evaluated on the following criteria: estimated population growth; employment; economic output; wages; home values. *Forbes, "America's Fastest-Growing Cities 2018," February 28, 2018*

- San Antonio appeared on *Travel + Leisure's* list of the 15 best cities in the United States. The city was ranked #7. Criteria: sights/landmarks; culture; food; friendliness; shopping; and overall value. *Travel + Leisure, "The World's Best Awards 2020" July 8, 2020*

- For its 33rd annual "Readers' Choice Awards" survey, *Condé Nast Traveler* ranked its readers' favorite cities in the U.S. These places brought feelings of comfort in a time of limited travel. The list was broken into large cities and cities under 250,000. San Antonio ranked #5 in the big city category. *Condé Nast Traveler, Readers' Choice Awards 2020, "Best Big Cities in the U.S." October 6, 2020*

Business/Finance Rankings

- San Antonio was the #17-ranked city for savers, according to a study by the finance site GOBankingRates, which considered the prospects for people trying to save money. Criteria: average monthly cost of grocery items; median home listing price; median rent; median income; transportation costs; gas prices; and the cost of eating out for an inexpensive and mid-range meal in 100 U.S. cities. *www.gobankingrates.com, "The 20 Best (and Worst) Places to Live If You're Trying to Save Money," August 27, 2019*

- San Antonio was ranked #17 among 100 U.S. cities for most difficult conditions for savers, according to a study by the finance site GOBankingRates. Criteria: average monthly cost of grocery items; median home listing price; median rent; median income; transportation costs; gas prices; and the cost of eating out for an inexpensive and mid-range meal. *www.gobankingrates.com, "The 20 Best (and Worst) Places to Live If You're Trying to Save Money," August 27, 2019*

- The Brookings Institution ranked the nation's largest cities based on income inequality. San Antonio was ranked #79 (#1 = greatest inequality). Criteria: the "95/20 ratio," a figure representing the income at which a household earns more than 95 percent of all other households, divided by the income at which a household earns more than only 20 percent of all other households. *Brookings Institution, "Household Income Inequality, Largest Cities of 97 Large U.S. Metro Areas, 2014-2016," February 5, 2018*

- The Brookings Institution ranked the 100 largest metro areas in the U.S. based on income inequality. San Antonio was ranked #56 (#1 = greatest inequality). Criteria: the "95/20 ratio," a figure representing the income at which a household earns more than 95 percent of all other households, divided by the income at which a household earns more than only 20 percent of all other households. *Brookings Institution, "Household Income Inequality, 100 Largest U.S. Metro Areas, 2014-2016," February 5, 2018*

- The San Antonio metro area was identified as one of the most debt-ridden places in America by the finance site Credit.com. The metro area was ranked #5. Criteria: residents' average credit card debt as well as median income. *Credit.com, "25 Cities With the Most Credit Card Debt," February 28, 2018*

- San Antonio was identified as one of the unhappiest cities to work in by CareerBliss.com, an online community for career advancement. The city ranked #4 out of 5. Criteria: an employee's relationship with his or her boss and co-workers; general work environment; compensation; opportunities for advancement; company culture and job reputation; and resources. *Businesswire.com, "CareerBliss Unhappiest Cities to Work 2019," February 12, 2019*

- The San Antonio metro area appeared on the Milken Institute "2021 Best Performing Cities" list. Rank: #48 out of 200 large metro areas (population over 250,000). Criteria: job growth; wage and salary growth; high-tech output growth; housing affordability; household broadband access. *Milken Institute, "Best-Performing Cities 2021," February 16, 2021*

- *Forbes* ranked the 200 most populous metro areas to determine the nation's "Best Places for Business and Careers." The San Antonio metro area was ranked #48. Criteria: costs (business and living); job growth (past and projected); income growth; quality of life; educational attainment (college and high school); projected economic growth; cultural and leisure opportunities; workplace tolerance laws; net migration patterns. *Forbes, "The Best Places for Business and Careers 2019: Seattle Still On Top," October 30, 2019*

Children/Family Rankings

- San Antonio was selected as one of the most playful cities in the U.S. by KaBOOM! The organization's Playful City USA initiative honors cities and towns across the nation that have made their communities more playable. Criteria: pledging to integrate play as a solution to challenges in their communities; making it easy for children to get active and balanced play; creating more family-friendly and innovative communities as a result. *KaBOOM! National Campaign for Play, "2017 Playful City USA Communities"*

Culture/Performing Arts Rankings

- San Antonio was selected as one of the 25 best cities for moviemakers in North America. COVID-19 has spurred a quest for great film cities that offer more creative space, lower costs, and more great outdoors. NYC & LA were intentionally excluded. Criteria: longstanding reputations as film-friendly communities; efforts to deal with pandemic-specific challenges; and establish appropriate COVID-19 guidelines. The city was ranked #22. *MovieMaker Magazine, "Best Places to Live and Work as a Moviemaker, 2021," January 26, 2021*

Dating/Romance Rankings

- San Antonio was selected as one of America's best cities for singles by the readers of *Travel + Leisure* in their annual "America's Favorite Cities" survey. Criteria included good-looking locals, cool shopping, an active bar scene and hipster-magnet coffee bars. *Travel + Leisure, "Best Cities in America for Singles," July 21, 2017*

- San Antonio was selected as one of the nation's most romantic cities with 100,000 or more residents by Amazon.com. The city ranked #1 of 20. Criteria: per capita sales of romance novels, relationship books, romantic comedy movies, romantic music, and sexual wellness products. *Amazon.com, "Top 20 Most Romantic Cities in the U.S.," February 1, 2017*

Education Rankings

- Personal finance website *WalletHub* analyzed the 150 largest U.S. metropolitan statistical areas to determine where the most educated Americans are putting their degrees to work. Criteria: education levels; percentage of workers with degrees; education quality and attainment gap; public school quality rankings; quality and enrollment of each metro area's universities. San Antonio was ranked #108 (#1 = most educated city). *www.WalletHub.com, "Most and Least Educated Cities in America," July 20, 2020*

- San Antonio was selected as one of America's most literate cities. The city ranked #76 out of the 84 largest U.S. cities. Criteria: number of booksellers; library resources; Internet resources; educational attainment; periodical publishing resources; newspaper circulation. *Central Connecticut State University, "America's Most Literate Cities, 2018," February 2019*

Health/Fitness Rankings

- For each of the 100 largest cities in the United States, the American Fitness Index®, published by the American College of Sports Medicine and the Anthem Foundation, evaluated community infrastructure and 33 health behaviors including preventive health, levels of chronic disease conditions, pedestrian safety, air quality, and community resources that support physical activity. San Antonio ranked #84 for "community fitness." *americanfitnessindex.org, "2020 ACSM American Fitness Index Summary Report," July 14, 2020*

- San Antonio was identified as a "2021 Spring Allergy Capital." The area ranked #16 out of 100. Three groups of factors were used to identify the most challenging cities for people with allergies during the spring season: annual spring pollen levels; over the counter medicine use; number of board-certified allergy specialists. *Asthma and Allergy Foundation of America, "Spring Allergy Capitals 2021," February 23, 2021*

- San Antonio was identified as a "2021 Fall Allergy Capital." The area ranked #12 out of 100. Three groups of factors were used to identify the most challenging cities for people with allergies during the fall season: annual fall pollen levels; over the counter medicine use; number of board-certified allergy specialists. *Asthma and Allergy Foundation of America, "Fall Allergy Capitals 2021," February 23, 2021*
- San Antonio was identified as a "2019 Asthma Capital." The area ranked #94 out of the nation's 100 largest metropolitan areas. Criteria: estimated asthma prevalence; crude death rate from asthma; and ER visits due to asthma. Risk factors analyzed but not factored in the rankings: annual pollen score; annual air quality; public smoking laws; number of board-certified asthma specialists; rescue medication use; controller medication use; uninsured rate; poverty rate. *Asthma and Allergy Foundation of America, "Asthma Capitals 2019: The Most Challenging Places to Live With Asthma," May 7, 2019*

Real Estate Rankings

- FitSmallBusiness looked at 50 of the largest metropolitan areas in the U.S. to determine which metro was the best to start a real estate business. Data was compiled from such sources as: Zillow, Trulia, U.S. Census Bureau, and the Bureau of Labor Statistics. Criteria: location; inventory; annual wages; median sales price of homes; days on the market; median price cut percentage; and other factors that would influence real estate professional growth. The San Antonio metro area ranked #12. *fitsmallbusiness.com, "The Best Cities to Become a Real Estate Agent in 2018," January 30, 2018*
- *WalletHub* compared the most populated U.S. cities to determine which had the best markets for real estate agents. San Antonio ranked #137 where demand was high and pay was the best. Criteria: sales per agent; annual median wage for real-estate agents; monthly average starting salary for real estate agents; real estate job density and competition; unemployment rate; home turnover rate; housing-market health index; and other relevant metrics. *www.WalletHub.com, "2019's Best Places to Be a Real Estate Agent," April 24, 2019*
- San Antonio was ranked #178 out of 268 metro areas in terms of housing affordability in 2020 by the National Association of Home Builders (#1 = most affordable). Criteria: the share of homes sold in that area affordable to a family earning the local median income, based on standard mortgage underwriting criteria. *National Association of Home Builders®, NAHB-Wells Fargo Housing Opportunity Index, 4th Quarter 2020*

Safety Rankings

- Allstate ranked the 200 largest cities in America in terms of driver safety. San Antonio ranked #138. Criteria: internal property damage claims over a two-year period from January 2016 to December 2017. The report helps increase the importance of safety and awareness behind the wheel. *Allstate, "Allstate America's Best Drivers Report, 2019" June 24, 2019*
- The National Insurance Crime Bureau ranked 384 metro areas in the U.S. in terms of per capita rates of vehicle theft. The San Antonio metro area ranked #59 (#1 = highest rate). Criteria: number of vehicle theft offenses per 100,000 inhabitants in 2019. *National Insurance Crime Bureau, "Hot Spots 2019," July 21, 2020*

Seniors/Retirement Rankings

- From its Best Cities for Successful Aging indexes, the Milken Institute generated rankings for metropolitan areas, weighing data in nine categories—health care, wellness, living arrangements, transportation and convenience, financial characteristics, education, employment, community engagement, and overall livability. The San Antonio metro area was ranked #64 overall in the large metro area category. *Milken Institute, "Best Cities for Successful Aging, 2017" March 14, 2017*
- San Antonio made the 2020 *Forbes* list of "25 Best Places to Retire." Criteria, focused on high-quality retirement living at an affordable price, include: housing/living costs compared to the national average and state taxes; air quality; crime rates; good economic outlook; home price appreciation; risk associated with climate-change; availability of medical care; bikeability; walkability; healthy living. *Forbes.com, "The Best Places to Retire in 2020," August 14, 2020*
- San Antonio was identified as #8 of 20 most popular places to retire in the Southwest region by *Topretirements.com*. The site separated its annual "Best Places to Retire" list by major U.S. regions for 2019. The list reflects the 20 cities that visitors to the website are most interested in for retirement, based on the number of times a city's review was viewed on the website. *Topretirements.com, "20 Most Popular Places to Retire in the Southwest for 2019," October 2, 2019*

Sports/Recreation Rankings

- San Antonio was chosen as a bicycle friendly community by the League of American Bicyclists. A "Bicycle Friendly Community" welcomes cyclists by providing safe and supportive accommodation for cycling and encouraging people to bike for transportation and recreation. There are five award levels: Diamond; Platinum; Gold; Silver; and Bronze. The community achieved an award level of Bronze. *League of American Bicyclists, "Fall 2020 Awards-New & Renewing Bicycle Friendly Communities List," December 16, 2020*

Women/Minorities Rankings

- The *Houston Chronicle* listed the San Antonio metro area as #13 in top places for young Latinos to live in the U.S. Research was largely based on housing and occupational data from the largest metropolitan areas performed by *Forbes* and NBC Universo. Criteria: percentage of 18-34 year-olds; Latino college grad rates; and diversity. *blog.chron.com, "The 15 Best Big Cities for Latino Millenials," January 26, 2016*

- Personal finance website *WalletHub* compared more than 180 U.S. cities across two key dimensions, "Hispanic Business-Friendliness" and "Hispanic Purchasing Power," to arrive at the most favorable conditions for Hispanic entrepreneurs. San Antonio was ranked #5 out of 182. Criteria includes: share of Hispanic-Owned Businesses; Hispanic entrepreneurship rate to median annual income of Hispanics; Small Business-Friendliness score; cost of living; and number of Hispanics with at least a bachelor's degree. *WalletHub.com, "2019's Best Cities for Hispanic Entrepreneurs," May 1, 2019*

Miscellaneous Rankings

- *WalletHub* compared the 150 most populated U.S. cities to determine their operating efficiency. A "Quality of City Services" score was constructed for each city and then divided by the total budget per capita to reveal which were managed the best. San Antonio ranked #96. Criteria: financial stability; economy; education; safety; health; infrastructure and pollution. *www.WalletHub.com, "2020's Best- & Worst-Run Cities in America," June 29, 2020*

- San Antonio was selected as one of "America's Friendliest Cities." The city ranked #5 in the "Friendliest" category. Respondents to an online survey were asked to rate 38 top urban destinations in the United States as to general friendliness, as well as manners, politeness and warm disposition. *Travel + Leisure, "America's Friendliest Cities," October 20, 2017*

- The National Alliance to End Homelessness listed the 25 most populous metro areas with the highest rate of homelessness. The San Antonio metro area had a high rate of homelessness. Criteria: number of homeless people per 10,000 population in 2016. *National Alliance to End Homelessness, "Homelessness in the 25 Most Populous U.S. Metro Areas," September 1, 2017*

Business Environment

DEMOGRAPHICS

Population Growth

Area	1990 Census	2000 Census	2010 Census	2019* Estimate	Population Growth (%) 1990-2019	Population Growth (%) 2010-2019
City	997,258	1,144,646	1,327,407	1,508,083	51.2	13.6
MSA[1]	1,407,745	1,711,703	2,142,508	2,468,193	75.3	15.2
U.S.	248,709,873	281,421,906	308,745,538	324,697,795	30.6	5.2

Note: (1) Figures cover the San Antonio-New Braunfels, TX Metropolitan Statistical Area; (*) 2015-2019 5-year estimated population
Source: U.S. Census Bureau, 1990 Census, Census 2000, Census 2010, 2015-2019 American Community Survey 5-Year Estimates

Household Size

Area	One	Two	Three	Four	Five	Six	Seven or More	Average Household Size
City	29.9	29.5	16.3	13.0	6.7	2.8	1.8	3.00
MSA[1]	26.4	31.3	16.6	13.8	7.2	3.0	1.7	3.00
U.S.	27.9	33.9	15.6	12.9	6.0	2.3	1.4	2.60

Note: (1) Figures cover the San Antonio-New Braunfels, TX Metropolitan Statistical Area
Source: U.S. Census Bureau, 2015-2019 American Community Survey 5-Year Estimates

Race

Area	White Alone[2] (%)	Black Alone[2] (%)	Asian Alone[2] (%)	AIAN[3] Alone[2] (%)	NHOPI[4] Alone[2] (%)	Other Race Alone[2] (%)	Two or More Races (%)
City	80.3	7.0	2.8	0.8	0.1	6.0	3.0
MSA[1]	80.7	6.8	2.5	0.6	0.1	5.9	3.4
U.S.	72.5	12.7	5.5	0.8	0.2	4.9	3.3

Note: (1) Figures cover the San Antonio-New Braunfels, TX Metropolitan Statistical Area; (2) Alone is defined as not being in combination with one or more other races; (3) American Indian and Alaska Native; (4) Native Hawaiian and Other Pacific Islander
Source: U.S. Census Bureau, 2015-2019 American Community Survey 5-Year Estimates

Hispanic or Latino Origin

Area	Total (%)	Mexican (%)	Puerto Rican (%)	Cuban (%)	Other (%)
City	64.2	56.9	1.3	0.3	5.7
MSA[1]	55.4	48.8	1.3	0.2	5.0
U.S.	18.0	11.2	1.7	0.7	4.3

Note: Persons of Hispanic or Latino origin can be of any race; (1) Figures cover the San Antonio-New Braunfels, TX Metropolitan Statistical Area
Source: U.S. Census Bureau, 2015-2019 American Community Survey 5-Year Estimates

Ancestry

Area	German	Irish	English	American	Italian	Polish	French[2]	Scottish	Dutch
City	6.8	4.3	3.6	3.1	1.6	1.0	1.3	0.9	0.4
MSA[1]	10.1	5.5	5.1	3.5	1.9	1.5	1.7	1.2	0.5
U.S.	13.3	9.7	7.2	6.2	5.1	2.8	2.3	1.7	1.2

Note: Figures are the percentage of the total population reporting a particular ancestry. The nine most commonly reported ancestries in the U.S. are shown. Figures include multiple ancestries (e.g. if a person reported being Irish and Italian, they were included in both columns); (1) Figures cover the San Antonio-New Braunfels, TX Metropolitan Statistical Area; (2) Excludes Basque
Source: U.S. Census Bureau, 2015-2019 American Community Survey 5-Year Estimates

Foreign-born Population

Area	Any Foreign Country	Asia	Mexico	Europe	Caribbean	Central America[2]	South America	Africa	Canada
City	14.3	2.6	9.1	0.6	0.2	0.8	0.4	0.3	0.1
MSA[1]	11.8	2.2	7.3	0.6	0.2	0.7	0.4	0.3	0.1
U.S.	13.6	4.2	3.5	1.5	1.3	1.1	1.0	0.7	0.2

Note: (1) Figures cover the San Antonio-New Braunfels, TX Metropolitan Statistical Area; (2) Excludes Mexico.
Source: U.S. Census Bureau, 2015-2019 American Community Survey 5-Year Estimates

Marital Status

Area	Never Married	Now Married[2]	Separated	Widowed	Divorced
City	39.0	40.6	3.1	5.2	12.1
MSA[1]	35.1	45.6	2.6	5.2	11.5
U.S.	33.4	48.1	1.9	5.8	10.9

Note: Figures are percentages and cover the population 15 years of age and older; (1) Figures cover the San Antonio-New Braunfels, TX Metropolitan Statistical Area; (2) Excludes separated
Source: U.S. Census Bureau, 2015-2019 American Community Survey 5-Year Estimates

Disability by Age

Area	All Ages	Under 18 Years Old	18 to 64 Years Old	65 Years and Over
City	14.6	5.8	13.2	41.1
MSA[1]	14.0	5.3	12.5	39.2
U.S.	12.6	4.2	10.3	34.5

Note: Figures show percent of the civilian noninstitutionalized population that reported having a disability. Disability status is determined from six types of difficulty: vision, hearing, cognitive, ambulatory, self-care, and independent living. For children under 5 years old, hearing and vision difficulty are used to determine disability status. For children between the ages of 5 and 14, disability status is determined from hearing, vision, cognitive, ambulatory, and self-care difficulties. For people aged 15 years and older, they are considered to have a disability if they have difficulty with any one of the six difficulty types; Note: (1) Figures cover the San Antonio-New Braunfels, TX Metropolitan Statistical Area
Source: U.S. Census Bureau, 2015-2019 American Community Survey 5-Year Estimates

Age

Area	Under Age 5	Age 5–19	Age 20–34	Age 35–44	Age 45–54	Age 55–64	Age 65–74	Age 75–84	Age 85+	Median Age
City	6.9	21.0	24.2	13.2	12.0	10.7	7.1	3.5	1.5	33.6
MSA[1]	6.9	21.4	22.2	13.3	12.4	11.2	7.6	3.7	1.5	34.7
U.S.	6.1	19.1	20.7	12.6	13.0	12.9	9.1	4.6	1.9	38.1

Note: (1) Figures cover the San Antonio-New Braunfels, TX Metropolitan Statistical Area
Source: U.S. Census Bureau, 2015-2019 American Community Survey 5-Year Estimates

Gender

Area	Males	Females	Males per 100 Females
City	744,596	763,487	97.5
MSA[1]	1,220,720	1,247,473	97.9
U.S.	159,886,919	164,810,876	97.0

Note: (1) Figures cover the San Antonio-New Braunfels, TX Metropolitan Statistical Area
Source: U.S. Census Bureau, 2015-2019 American Community Survey 5-Year Estimates

Religious Groups by Family

Area	Catholic	Baptist	Non-Den.	Methodist[2]	Lutheran	LDS[3]	Pentecostal	Presbyterian[4]	Muslim[5]	Judaism
MSA[1]	28.4	8.5	6.0	3.1	1.7	1.4	1.3	0.8	1.0	0.2
U.S.	19.1	9.3	4.0	4.0	2.3	2.0	1.9	1.6	0.8	0.7

Note: Figures are the number of adherents as a percentage of the total population; (1) Figures cover the San Antonio-New Braunfels, TX Metropolitan Statistical Area; (2) Methodist/Pietist; (3) Latter Day Saints; (4) Reformed; (5) Figures are estimates
Source: Association of Statisticians of American Religious Bodies, 2010 U.S. Religion Census: Religious Congregations & Membership Study

Religious Groups by Tradition

Area	Catholic	Evangelical Protestant	Mainline Protestant	Other Tradition	Black Protestant	Orthodox
MSA[1]	28.4	17.0	5.0	3.2	0.4	0.1
U.S.	19.1	16.2	7.3	4.3	1.6	0.3

Note: Figures are the number of adherents as a percentage of the total population; (1) Figures cover the San Antonio-New Braunfels, TX Metropolitan Statistical Area
Source: Association of Statisticians of American Religious Bodies, 2010 U.S. Religion Census: Religious Congregations & Membership Study

ECONOMY

Gross Metropolitan Product

Area	2017	2018	2019	2020	Rank[2]
MSA[1]	126.1	134.5	140.1	148.6	35

Note: Figures are in billions of dollars; (1) Figures cover the San Antonio-New Braunfels, TX Metropolitan Statistical Area; (2) Rank is based on 2018 data and ranges from 1 to 381
Source: U.S. Conference of Mayors, U.S. Metro Economies: GMP & Employment 2018-2020, September 2019

Economic Growth

Area	2015-17 (%)	2018 (%)	2019 (%)	2020 (%)	Rank[2]
MSA[1]	4.2	2.0	2.7	1.7	30
U.S.	1.9	2.9	2.3	2.1	—

Note: Figures are real gross metropolitan product (GMP) growth rates and represent average annual percent change; (1) Figures cover the San Antonio-New Braunfels, TX Metropolitan Statistical Area; (2) Rank is based on 2017 2-year average annual percent change and ranges from 1 to 381
Source: U.S. Conference of Mayors, U.S. Metro Economies: GMP & Employment 2018-2020, September 2019

Metropolitan Area Exports

Area	2014	2015	2016	2017	2018	2019	Rank[2]
MSA[1]	25,781.8	15,919.2	5,621.2	9,184.1	11,678.1	11,668.0	32

Note: Figures are in millions of dollars; (1) Figures cover the San Antonio-New Braunfels, TX Metropolitan Statistical Area; (2) Rank is based on 2019 data and ranges from 1 to 386
Source: U.S. Department of Commerce, International Trade Administration, Office of Trade and Economic Analysis, Industry and Analysis, Exports by Metropolitan Area, data extracted March 24, 2021

Building Permits

Area	Single-Family 2018	Single-Family 2019	Pct. Chg.	Multi-Family 2018	Multi-Family 2019	Pct. Chg.	Total 2018	Total 2019	Pct. Chg.
City	3,266	3,890	19.1	2,663	5,306	99.2	5,929	9,196	55.1
MSA[1]	8,013	9,103	13.6	3,484	6,792	94.9	11,497	15,895	38.3
U.S.	855,300	862,100	0.7	473,500	523,900	10.6	1,328,800	1,386,000	4.3

Note: (1) Figures cover the San Antonio-New Braunfels, TX Metropolitan Statistical Area; Figures represent new, privately-owned housing units authorized (unadjusted data); All permit data are based on estimates with imputation
Source: U.S. Census Bureau, Manufacturing, Mining, and Construction Statistics, Building Permits, 2018, 2019

Bankruptcy Filings

Area	Business Filings 2019	Business Filings 2020	% Chg.	Nonbusiness Filings 2019	Nonbusiness Filings 2020	% Chg.
Bexar County	191	128	-33.0	2,173	1,445	-33.5
U.S.	22,780	21,655	-4.9	752,160	522,808	-30.5

Note: Business filings include Chapter 7, Chapter 9, Chapter 11, Chapter 12, Chapter 13, Chapter 15, and Section 304; Nonbusiness filings include Chapter 7, Chapter 11, and Chapter 13
Source: Administrative Office of the U.S. Courts, Business and Nonbusiness Bankruptcy, County Cases Commenced by Chapter of the Bankruptcy Code, During the 12-Month Period Ending December 31, 2019 and Business and Nonbusiness Bankruptcy, County Cases Commenced by Chapter of the Bankruptcy Code, During the 12-Month Period Ending December 31, 2020

Housing Vacancy Rates

Area	Gross Vacancy Rate[2] (%) 2018	2019	2020	Year-Round Vacancy Rate[3] (%) 2018	2019	2020	Rental Vacancy Rate[4] (%) 2018	2019	2020	Homeowner Vacancy Rate[5] (%) 2018	2019	2020
MSA[1]	6.7	9.0	7.4	5.8	8.2	6.7	7.4	10.1	7.2	0.6	2.0	1.0
U.S.	12.3	12.0	10.6	9.7	9.5	8.2	6.9	6.7	6.3	1.5	1.4	1.0

Note: (1) Figures cover the San Antonio-New Braunfels, TX Metropolitan Statistical Area; (2) The percentage of the total housing inventory that is vacant; (3) The percentage of the housing inventory (excluding seasonal units) that is year-round vacant; (4) The percentage of rental inventory that is vacant for rent; (5) The percentage of homeowner inventory that is vacant for sale
Source: U.S. Census Bureau, Housing Vacancies and Homeownership Annual Statistics: 2018, 2019, 2020

INCOME

Income

Area	Per Capita ($)	Median Household ($)	Average Household ($)
City	25,894	52,455	70,778
MSA[1]	29,071	60,327	81,852
U.S.	34,103	62,843	88,607

Note: (1) Figures cover the San Antonio-New Braunfels, TX Metropolitan Statistical Area
Source: U.S. Census Bureau, 2015-2019 American Community Survey 5-Year Estimates

Household Income Distribution

Area	Under $15,000	$15,000 -$24,999	$25,000 -$34,999	$35,000 -$49,999	$50,000 -$74,999	$75,000 -$99,999	$100,000 -$149,999	$150,000 and up
City	12.7	10.4	10.6	14.0	19.0	12.1	12.5	8.7
MSA[1]	10.3	8.9	9.4	12.8	18.7	13.2	14.8	11.9
U.S.	10.3	8.9	8.9	12.3	17.2	12.7	15.1	14.5

Note: (1) Figures cover the San Antonio-New Braunfels, TX Metropolitan Statistical Area
Source: U.S. Census Bureau, 2015-2019 American Community Survey 5-Year Estimates

Poverty Rate

Area	All Ages	Under 18 Years Old	18 to 64 Years Old	65 Years and Over
City	17.8	26.1	15.4	12.8
MSA[1]	14.4	20.6	12.7	10.4
U.S.	13.4	18.5	12.6	9.3

Note: Figures are percentage of people whose income during the past 12 months was below the poverty level; (1) Figures cover the San Antonio-New Braunfels, TX Metropolitan Statistical Area
Source: U.S. Census Bureau, 2015-2019 American Community Survey 5-Year Estimates

CITY FINANCES

City Government Finances

Component	2017 ($000)	2017 ($ per capita)
Total Revenues	5,497,860	3,740
Total Expenditures	5,364,452	3,650
Debt Outstanding	11,712,528	7,969
Cash and Securities[1]	6,976,529	4,746

Note: (1) Cash and security holdings of a government at the close of its fiscal year, including those of its dependent agencies, utilities, and liquor stores.
Source: U.S. Census Bureau, State & Local Government Finances 2017

City Government Revenue by Source

Source	2017 ($000)	2017 ($ per capita)	2017 (%)
General Revenue			
From Federal Government	124,738	85	2.3
From State Government	171,621	117	3.1
From Local Governments	168,111	114	3.1
Taxes			
Property	446,287	304	8.1
Sales and Gross Receipts	449,219	306	8.2
Personal Income	0	0	0.0
Corporate Income	0	0	0.0
Motor Vehicle License	0	0	0.0
Other Taxes	50,566	34	0.9
Current Charges	617,794	420	11.2
Liquor Store	0	0	0.0
Utility	2,852,810	1,941	51.9
Employee Retirement	316,593	215	5.8

Source: U.S. Census Bureau, State & Local Government Finances 2017

City Government Expenditures by Function

Function	2017 ($000)	2017 ($ per capita)	2017 (%)
General Direct Expenditures			
Air Transportation	147,525	100	2.8
Corrections	0	0	0.0
Education	64,391	43	1.2
Employment Security Administration	0	0	0.0
Financial Administration	43,226	29	0.8
Fire Protection	269,015	183	5.0
General Public Buildings	16,630	11	0.3
Governmental Administration, Other	9,828	6	0.2
Health	28,722	19	0.5
Highways	141,589	96	2.6
Hospitals	0	0	0.0
Housing and Community Development	50,948	34	0.9
Interest on General Debt	139,358	94	2.6
Judicial and Legal	25,927	17	0.5
Libraries	37,344	25	0.7
Parking	12,903	8	0.2
Parks and Recreation	234,005	159	4.4
Police Protection	389,142	264	7.3
Public Welfare	128,192	87	2.4
Sewerage	231,170	157	4.3
Solid Waste Management	121,953	83	2.3
Veterans' Services	0	0	0.0
Liquor Store	0	0	0.0
Utility	2,930,825	1,994	54.6
Employee Retirement	159,919	108	3.0

Source: U.S. Census Bureau, State & Local Government Finances 2017

San Antonio, Texas

EMPLOYMENT

Labor Force and Employment

Area	Civilian Labor Force Dec. 2019	Civilian Labor Force Dec. 2020	% Chg.	Workers Employed Dec. 2019	Workers Employed Dec. 2020	% Chg.
City	740,486	738,883	-0.2	720,097	690,895	-4.1
MSA[1]	1,218,568	1,213,928	-0.4	1,184,374	1,136,070	-4.1
U.S.	164,007,000	160,017,000	-2.4	158,504,000	149,613,000	-5.6

Note: Data is not seasonally adjusted and covers workers 16 years of age and older; (1) Figures cover the San Antonio-New Braunfels, TX Metropolitan Statistical Area
Source: Bureau of Labor Statistics, Local Area Unemployment Statistics

Unemployment Rate

Area	Jan.	Feb.	Mar.	Apr.	May	Jun.	Jul.	Aug.	Sep.	Oct.	Nov.	Dec.
City	3.2	3.1	4.5	13.8	13.0	8.5	8.3	6.9	7.9	6.3	7.4	6.5
MSA[1]	3.2	3.1	4.5	13.3	12.7	8.3	8.0	6.6	7.7	6.2	7.3	6.4
U.S.	4.0	3.8	4.5	14.4	13.0	11.2	10.5	8.5	7.7	6.6	6.4	6.5

(2020)

Note: Data is not seasonally adjusted and covers workers 16 years of age and older; (1) Figures cover the San Antonio-New Braunfels, TX Metropolitan Statistical Area
Source: Bureau of Labor Statistics, Local Area Unemployment Statistics

Average Wages

Occupation	$/Hr.	Occupation	$/Hr.
Accountants and Auditors	35.80	Maintenance and Repair Workers	18.50
Automotive Mechanics	20.70	Marketing Managers	71.40
Bookkeepers	21.00	Network and Computer Systems Admin.	39.00
Carpenters	20.40	Nurses, Licensed Practical	22.60
Cashiers	11.80	Nurses, Registered	36.10
Computer Programmers	46.40	Nursing Assistants	14.00
Computer Systems Analysts	47.70	Office Clerks, General	17.10
Computer User Support Specialists	23.60	Physical Therapists	41.30
Construction Laborers	16.10	Physicians	104.50
Cooks, Restaurant	12.30	Plumbers, Pipefitters and Steamfitters	21.50
Customer Service Representatives	16.80	Police and Sheriff's Patrol Officers	29.60
Dentists	72.50	Postal Service Mail Carriers	25.90
Electricians	25.40	Real Estate Sales Agents	30.90
Engineers, Electrical	45.10	Retail Salespersons	14.00
Fast Food and Counter Workers	11.00	Sales Representatives, Technical/Scientific	43.40
Financial Managers	67.10	Secretaries, Exc. Legal/Medical/Executive	17.10
First-Line Supervisors of Office Workers	26.80	Security Guards	16.40
General and Operations Managers	61.50	Surgeons	n/a
Hairdressers/Cosmetologists	12.90	Teacher Assistants, Exc. Postsecondary*	12.00
Home Health and Personal Care Aides	10.90	Teachers, Secondary School, Exc. Sp. Ed.*	28.30
Janitors and Cleaners	12.80	Telemarketers	19.60
Landscaping/Groundskeeping Workers	14.40	Truck Drivers, Heavy/Tractor-Trailer	20.50
Lawyers	61.80	Truck Drivers, Light/Delivery Services	21.20
Maids and Housekeeping Cleaners	11.80	Waiters and Waitresses	10.00

Note: Wage data covers the San Antonio-New Braunfels, TX Metropolitan Statistical Area; (*) Hourly wages were calculated from annual wage data based on a 40 hour work week; n/a not available.
Source: Bureau of Labor Statistics, Metro Area Occupational Employment & Wage Estimates, May 2020

Employment by Industry

Sector	MSA[1] Number of Employees	MSA[1] Percent of Total	U.S. Percent of Total
Construction	55,500	5.3	5.1
Education and Health Services	159,600	15.1	16.3
Financial Activities	94,600	9.0	6.1
Government	174,900	16.6	15.2
Information	18,300	1.7	1.9
Leisure and Hospitality	114,600	10.9	9.0
Manufacturing	51,000	4.8	8.5
Mining and Logging	6,200	0.6	0.4
Other Services	34,700	3.3	3.8
Professional and Business Services	155,800	14.8	14.4
Retail Trade	112,700	10.7	10.9
Transportation, Warehousing, and Utilities	40,100	3.8	4.6
Wholesale Trade	35,900	3.4	3.9

Note: Figures are non-farm employment as of December 2020. Figures are not seasonally adjusted and include workers 16 years of age and older; (1) Figures cover the San Antonio-New Braunfels, TX Metropolitan Statistical Area
Source: Bureau of Labor Statistics, Current Employment Statistics, Employment, Hours, and Earnings

Employment by Occupation

Occupation Classification	City (%)	MSA[1] (%)	U.S. (%)
Management, Business, Science, and Arts	33.5	35.4	38.5
Natural Resources, Construction, and Maintenance	10.2	10.3	8.9
Production, Transportation, and Material Moving	11.4	11.6	13.2
Sales and Office	24.0	23.6	21.6
Service	20.9	19.2	17.8

Note: Figures cover employed civilians 16 years of age and older; (1) Figures cover the San Antonio-New Braunfels, TX Metropolitan Statistical Area
Source: U.S. Census Bureau, 2015-2019 American Community Survey 5-Year Estimates

Occupations with Greatest Projected Employment Growth: 2020 – 2022

Occupation[1]	2020 Employment	2022 Projected Employment	Numeric Employment Change	Percent Employment Change
Fast Food and Counter Workers	336,530	411,690	75,160	22.3
Waiters and Waitresses	165,570	206,920	41,350	25.0
Home Health and Personal Care Aides	303,520	344,240	40,720	13.4
Retail Salespersons	315,590	349,820	34,230	10.8
Heavy and Tractor-Trailer Truck Drivers	199,460	228,650	29,190	14.6
Laborers and Freight, Stock, and Material Movers, Hand	193,000	219,670	26,670	13.8
Cooks, Restaurant	88,540	114,250	25,710	29.0
Customer Service Representatives	276,080	295,790	19,710	7.1
General and Operations Managers	197,410	216,580	19,170	9.7
Office Clerks, General	310,080	327,500	17,420	5.6

Note: Projections cover Texas; (1) Sorted by numeric employment change
Source: www.projectionscentral.com, State Occupational Projections, 2020–2022 Short-Term Projections

Fastest-Growing Occupations: 2020 – 2022

Occupation[1]	2020 Employment	2022 Projected Employment	Numeric Employment Change	Percent Employment Change
Motion Picture Projectionists	150	300	150	100.0
Ushers, Lobby Attendants, and Ticket Takers	5,740	8,920	3,180	55.4
Locker Room, Coatroom, and Dressing Room Attendants	340	510	170	50.0
Athletes and Sports Competitors	270	400	130	48.1
Amusement and Recreation Attendants	13,130	19,400	6,270	47.8
Hotel, Motel, and Resort Desk Clerks	16,140	23,160	7,020	43.5
Sound Engineering Technicians	330	460	130	39.4
Gaming Dealers	220	300	80	36.4
Baggage Porters and Bellhops	1,250	1,670	420	33.6
Lodging Managers	3,300	4,330	1,030	31.2

Note: Projections cover Texas; (1) Sorted by percent employment change and excludes occupations with numeric employment change less than 50
Source: www.projectionscentral.com, State Occupational Projections, 2020–2022 Short-Term Projections

TAXES

State Corporate Income Tax Rates

State	Tax Rate (%)	Income Brackets ($)	Num. of Brackets	Financial Institution Tax Rate (%)[a]	Federal Income Tax Ded.
Texas	(w)	–	–	(w)	No

Note: Tax rates as of January 1, 2021; (a) Rates listed are the corporate income tax rate applied to financial institutions or excise taxes based on income. Some states have other taxes based upon the value of deposits or shares; (w) Texas imposes a Franchise Tax, otherwise known as margin tax, imposed on entities with more than $1,130,000 total revenues at rate of 0.75%, or 0.375% for entities primarily engaged in retail or wholesale trade, on lesser of 70% of total revenues or 100% of gross receipts after deductions for either compensation or cost of goods sold.
Source: Federation of Tax Administrators, State Corporate Income Tax Rates, January 1, 2021

State Individual Income Tax Rates

State	Tax Rate (%)	Income Brackets ($)	Personal Exemptions ($) Single	Married	Depend.	Standard Ded. ($) Single	Married
Texas				– No state income tax –			

Note: Tax rates as of January 1, 2021; Local- and county-level taxes are not included
Source: Federation of Tax Administrators, State Individual Income Tax Rates, January 1, 2021

Various State Sales and Excise Tax Rates

State	State Sales Tax (%)	Gasoline[1] (¢/gal.)	Cigarette[2] ($/pack)	Spirits[3] ($/gal.)	Wine[4] ($/gal.)	Beer[5] ($/gal.)	Recreational Marijuana (%)
Texas	6.25	20	1.41	2.4	0.2	0.2	Not legal

Note: All tax rates as of January 1, 2021; (1) The American Petroleum Institute has developed a methodology for determining the average tax rate on a gallon of fuel. Rates may include any of the following: excise taxes, environmental fees, storage tank fees, other fees or taxes, general sales tax, and local taxes; (2) The federal excise tax of $1.0066 per pack and local taxes are not included; (3) Rates are those applicable to off-premise sales of 40% alcohol by volume (a.b.v.) distilled spirits in 750ml containers. Local excise taxes are excluded; (4) Rates are those applicable to off-premise sales of 11% a.b.v. non-carbonated wine in 750ml containers; (5) Rates are those applicable to off-premise sales of 4.7% a.b.v. beer in 12 ounce containers.
Source: Tax Foundation, 2021 Facts & Figures: How Does Your State Compare?

State Business Tax Climate Index Rankings

State	Overall Rank	Corporate Tax Rank	Individual Income Tax Rank	Sales Tax Rank	Property Tax Rank	Unemployment Insurance Tax Rank
Texas	11	47	6	35	36	16

Note: The index is a measure of how each state's tax laws affect economic performance. The lower the rank, the more favorable a state's tax system is for business. States without a given tax are given a ranking of 1. The scores/rankings for the District of Columbia do not affect other states. The 2021 index represents the tax climate as of July 1, 2020.
Source: Tax Foundation, State Business Tax Climate Index 2021

TRANSPORTATION

Means of Transportation to Work

Area	Car/Truck/Van Drove Alone	Car/Truck/Van Carpooled	Public Transportation Bus	Public Transportation Subway	Public Transportation Railroad	Bicycle	Walked	Other Means	Worked at Home
City	78.7	11.3	2.9	0.0	0.0	0.2	1.7	1.5	3.8
MSA[1]	79.5	10.7	1.9	0.0	0.0	0.2	1.7	1.3	4.7
U.S.	76.3	9.0	2.4	1.9	0.6	0.5	2.7	1.4	5.2

Note: Figures are percentages and cover workers 16 years of age and older; (1) Figures cover the San Antonio-New Braunfels, TX Metropolitan Statistical Area
Source: U.S. Census Bureau, 2015-2019 American Community Survey 5-Year Estimates

Travel Time to Work

Area	Less Than 10 Minutes	10 to 19 Minutes	20 to 29 Minutes	30 to 44 Minutes	45 to 59 Minutes	60 to 89 Minutes	90 Minutes or More
City	8.5	30.8	27.2	22.1	6.1	3.3	2.0
MSA[1]	9.0	28.1	24.3	23.2	8.5	4.7	2.2
U.S.	12.2	28.4	20.8	20.8	8.3	6.4	2.9

Note: Note: Figures are percentages and include workers 16 years old and over; (1) Figures cover the San Antonio-New Braunfels, TX Metropolitan Statistical Area
Source: U.S. Census Bureau, 2015-2019 American Community Survey 5-Year Estimates

Key Congestion Measures

Measure	1982	1992	2002	2012	2017
Annual Hours of Delay, Total (000)	9,389	18,829	42,217	60,658	69,982
Annual Hours of Delay, Per Auto Commuter	18	26	41	44	51
Annual Congestion Cost, Total (million $)	71	198	568	1,081	1,284
Annual Congestion Cost, Per Auto Commuter ($)	289	400	698	786	880

Note: Covers the San Antonio TX urban area
Source: Texas A&M Transportation Institute, 2019 Urban Mobility Report

Freeway Travel Time Index

Measure	1982	1987	1992	1997	2002	2007	2012	2017
Urban Area Index[1]	1.10	1.12	1.15	1.20	1.24	1.24	1.24	1.23
Urban Area Rank[1,2]	19	26	26	24	23	29	26	30

Note: Freeway Travel Time Index—the ratio of travel time in the peak period to the travel time at free-flow conditions. For example, a value of 1.30 indicates a 20-minute free-flow trip takes 26 minutes in the peak (20 minutes x 1.30 = 26 minutes); (1) Covers the San Antonio TX urban area; (2) Rank is based on 101 larger urban areas (#1 = highest travel time index)
Source: Texas A&M Transportation Institute, 2019 Urban Mobility Report

Public Transportation

Agency Name / Mode of Transportation	Vehicles Operated in Maximum Service[1]	Annual Unlinked Passenger Trips[2] (in thous.)	Annual Passenger Miles[3] (in thous.)
VIA Metropolitan Transit (VIA)			
Bus (directly operated)	384	40,962.6	158,505.9
Demand Response (directly operated)	159	518.2	6,343.2
Demand Response (purchased transportation)	110	498.2	6,228.0
Demand Response Taxi (purchased transportation)	66	32.4	397.9
Vanpool (purchased transportation)	214	499.3	24,570.0

Note: (1) Number of revenue vehicles operated by the given mode and type of service to meet the annual maximum service requirement. This is the revenue vehicle count during the peak season of the year; on the week and day that maximum service is provided. Vehicles operated in maximum service (VOMS) exclude atypical days and one-time special events; (2) Number of passengers who boarded public transportation vehicles. Passengers are counted each time they board a vehicle no matter how many vehicles they use to travel from their origin to their destination. (3) Sum of the distances ridden by all passengers during the entire fiscal year.
Source: Federal Transit Administration, National Transit Database, 2019

Air Transportation

Airport Name and Code / Type of Service	Passenger Airlines[1]	Passenger Enplanements	Freight Carriers[2]	Freight (lbs)
San Antonio International (SAT)				
Domestic service (U.S. carriers - 2020)	22	1,842,381	16	106,419,988
International service (U.S. carriers - 2019)	6	13,277	4	12,767,309

Note: (1) Includes all U.S.-based major, minor and commuter airlines that carried at least one passenger during the year; (2) Includes all U.S.-based airlines and freight carriers that transported at least one pound of freight during the year.
Source: Bureau of Transportation Statistics, The Intermodal Transportation Database, Air Carriers: T-100 Domestic Market (U.S. Carriers), 2020; Bureau of Transportation Statistics, The Intermodal Transportation Database, Air Carriers: T-100 International Market (U.S. Carriers), 2019

BUSINESSES

Major Business Headquarters

Company Name	Industry	Fortune[1]	Forbes[2]
H-E-B	Food Markets	-	9
USAA	Insurance, Property and Casualty (Stock)	94	-
Valero Energy	Petroleum Refining	32	-
Zachry Group	Construction	-	190

Note: (1) Companies that produce a 10-K are ranked 1 to 500 based on 2019 revenue; (2) All private companies with at least $2 billion in annual revenue through the end of their most current fiscal year are ranked 1 to 219; companies listed are headquartered in the city; dashes indicate no ranking
Source: Fortune, "Fortune 500," June/July 2020; Forbes, "America's Largest Private Companies," 2020

Fastest-Growing Businesses

According to *Inc.*, San Antonio is home to two of America's 500 fastest-growing private companies: **FactoryPure** (#208); **Nationwide Pharmaceutical** (#256). Criteria: must be an independent, privately-held, for-profit, U.S. corporation, proprietorship or partnership as of December 31, 2019; revenues must be at least $100,000 in 2016 and $2 million in 2019; must have four-year operating/sales history. *Inc., "America's 500 Fastest-Growing Private Companies," 2020*

According to Deloitte, San Antonio is home to one of North America's 500 fastest-growing high-technology companies: **CloudCommerce, Inc.** (#300). Companies are ranked by percentage growth in revenue over a four-year period. Criteria for inclusion: company must be headquartered within North America; must own proprietary intellectual property or technology that is sold to customers in products that contributes to a significant portion of the company's operating revenue; must have been in business for a minumum of four years with 2016 operating revenues of at least $50,000 USD/CD and 2019 operating revenues of at least $5 million USD/CD. *Deloitte, 2020 Technology Fast 500™*

Minority Business Opportunity

San Antonio is home to one company which is on the *Black Enterprise* Industrial/Service list (100 largest companies based on gross sales): **Millennium Steel of Texas** (#14). Criteria: operational in previous calendar year; at least 51% black-owned and manufactures/owns the product it sells or provides industrial or consumer services. Brokerages, real estate firms and firms that provide professional services are not eligible. *Black Enterprise, B.E. 100s, 2019*

Living Environment

COST OF LIVING

Cost of Living Index

Composite Index	Groceries	Housing	Utilities	Transportation	Health Care	Misc. Goods/Services
92.9	88.8	89.9	88.8	92.2	85.9	99.1

Note: The Cost of Living Index measures regional differences in the cost of consumer goods and services, excluding taxes and non-consumer expenditures, for professional and managerial households in the top income quintile. It is based on more than 50,000 prices covering almost 60 different items for which prices are collected three times a year by chambers of commerce, economic development organizations or university applied economic centers in each participating urban area. The numbers shown should be read as a percentage above or below the national average of 100. For example, a value of 115.4 in the groceries column indicates that grocery prices are 15.4% higher than the national average. Small differences in the index numbers should not be interpreted as significant; Figures cover the San Antonio TX urban area.
Source: The Council for Community and Economic Research, Cost of Living Index, 2020

Grocery Prices

Area[1]	T-Bone Steak ($/pound)	Frying Chicken ($/pound)	Whole Milk ($/half gal.)	Eggs ($/dozen)	Orange Juice ($/64 oz.)	Coffee ($/11.5 oz.)
City[2]	9.89	1.01	1.63	1.66	3.14	3.93
Avg.	11.78	1.39	2.05	1.47	3.57	4.34
Min.	8.03	0.94	1.03	0.74	2.94	3.02
Max.	15.86	2.65	4.31	3.77	5.44	8.69

Note: (1) Values for the local area are compared with the average, minimum and maximum values for all 284 areas in the Cost of Living Index; (2) Figures cover the San Antonio TX urban area; **T-Bone Steak** (price per pound); **Frying Chicken** (price per pound, whole fryer); **Whole Milk** (half gallon carton); **Eggs** (price per dozen, Grade A, large); **Orange Juice** (64 oz. Tropicana or Florida Natural); **Coffee** (11.5 oz. can, vacuum-packed, Maxwell House, Hills Bros, or Folgers).
Source: The Council for Community and Economic Research, Cost of Living Index, 2020

Housing and Utility Costs

Area[1]	New Home Price ($)	Apartment Rent ($/month)	All Electric ($/month)	Part Electric ($/month)	Other Energy ($/month)	Telephone ($/month)
City[2]	271,143	1,396	-	96.33	37.17	184.30
Avg.	368,594	1,168	170.86	100.47	65.28	184.30
Min.	190,567	502	91.58	31.42	26.08	169.60
Max.	2,227,806	4,738	470.38	280.31	280.06	206.50

Note: (1) Values for the local area are compared with the average, minimum and maximum values for all 284 areas in the Cost of Living Index; (2) Figures cover the San Antonio TX urban area; **New Home Price** (2,400 sf living area, 8,000 sf lot, in urban area with full utilities); **Apartment Rent** (950 sf 2 bedroom/1.5 or 2 bath, unfurnished, excluding all utilities except water); **All Electric** (average monthly cost for an all-electric home); **Part Electric** (average monthly cost for a part-electric home); **Other Energy** (average monthly cost for natural gas, fuel oil, coal, wood, and any other forms of energy except electricity); **Telephone** (price includes the base monthly rate plus taxes and fees for three lines of mobile phone service).
Source: The Council for Community and Economic Research, Cost of Living Index, 2020

Health Care, Transportation, and Other Costs

Area[1]	Doctor ($/visit)	Dentist ($/visit)	Optometrist ($/visit)	Gasoline ($/gallon)	Beauty Salon ($/visit)	Men's Shirt ($)
City[2]	86.07	87.61	97.83	1.90	45.96	31.37
Avg.	115.44	99.32	108.10	2.21	39.27	31.37
Min.	36.68	59.00	51.36	1.71	19.00	11.00
Max.	219.00	153.10	250.97	3.46	82.05	58.33

Note: (1) Values for the local area are compared with the average, minimum and maximum values for all 284 areas in the Cost of Living Index; (2) Figures cover the San Antonio TX urban area; **Doctor** (general practitioners routine exam of an established patient); **Dentist** (adult teeth cleaning and periodic oral examination); **Optometrist** (full vision eye exam for established adult patient); **Gasoline** (one gallon regular unleaded, national brand, including all taxes, cash price at self-service pump if available); **Beauty Salon** (woman's shampoo, trim, and blow-dry); **Men's Shirt** (cotton/polyester dress shirt, pinpoint weave, long sleeves).
Source: The Council for Community and Economic Research, Cost of Living Index, 2020

HOUSING

Homeownership Rate

Area	2012 (%)	2013 (%)	2014 (%)	2015 (%)	2016 (%)	2017 (%)	2018 (%)	2019 (%)	2020 (%)
MSA[1]	67.5	70.1	70.2	66.0	61.6	62.5	64.4	62.6	64.2
U.S.	65.4	65.1	64.5	63.7	63.4	63.9	64.4	64.6	66.6

Note: (1) Figures cover the San Antonio-New Braunfels, TX Metropolitan Statistical Area
Source: U.S. Census Bureau, Housing Vacancies and Homeownership Annual Statistics: 2012-2020

House Price Index (HPI)

Area	National Ranking[2]	Quarterly Change (%)	One-Year Change (%)	Five-Year Change (%)	Since 1991Q1 (%)
MSA[1]	149	2.10	5.83	34.99	224.63
U.S.[3]	—	3.81	10.77	38.99	205.12

Note: The HPI is a weighted repeat sales index. It measures average price changes in repeat sales or refinancings on the same properties. This information is obtained by reviewing repeat mortgage transactions on single-family properties whose mortgages have been purchased or securitized by Fannie Mae or Freddie Mac since January 1975; (1) Figures cover the San Antonio-New Braunfels, TX Metropolitan Statistical Area; (2) Rankings are based on annual percentage change for all metro areas containing at least 15,000 transactions over the last 10 years and ranges from 1 to 253; (3) figures based on a weighted average of Census Division estimates using a seasonally adjusted, purchase-only index; all figures are for the period ending December 31, 2020
Source: Federal Housing Finance Agency, Change in Metropolitan Area House Price Indexes, April 7, 2021

Median Single-Family Home Prices

Area	2018	2019	2020p	Percent Change 2019 to 2020
MSA[1]	228.1	236.6	254.3	7.5
U.S. Average	261.6	274.6	299.9	9.2

Note: Figures are median sales prices of existing single-family homes in thousands of dollars; (p) preliminary; (1) Figures cover the San Antonio-New Braunfels, TX Metropolitan Statistical Area
Source: National Association of Realtors, Median Sales Price of Existing Single-Family Homes for Metropolitan Areas, 4th Quarter 2020

Qualifying Income Based on Median Sales Price of Existing Single-Family Homes

Area	With 5% Down ($)	With 10% Down ($)	With 20% Down ($)
MSA[1]	50,104	47,467	42,193
U.S. Average	59,266	56,147	49,908

Note: Figures are preliminary; Qualifying income is based on a mortgage rate of 2.81%. Monthly principal and interest payment is limited to 25% of income; (1) Figures cover the San Antonio-New Braunfels, TX Metropolitan Statistical Area
Source: National Association of Realtors, Qualifying Income Based on Median Sales Price of Existing Single-Family Homes for Metropolitan Areas, 4th Quarter 2020

Home Value Distribution

Area	Under $50,000	$50,000 -$99,999	$100,000 -$149,999	$150,000 -$199,999	$200,000 -$299,999	$300,000 -$499,999	$500,000 -$999,999	$1,000,000 or more
City	6.8	24.5	20.0	18.4	17.9	9.4	2.5	0.6
MSA[1]	6.8	18.2	16.6	17.7	20.5	14.2	4.9	1.2
U.S.	6.9	12.0	13.3	14.0	19.6	19.3	11.4	3.4

Note: Figures are percentages and cover owner-occupied housing units; (1) Figures cover the San Antonio-New Braunfels, TX Metropolitan Statistical Area
Source: U.S. Census Bureau, 2015-2019 American Community Survey 5-Year Estimates

Year Housing Structure Built

Area	2010 or Later	2000 -2009	1990 -1999	1980 -1989	1970 -1979	1960 -1969	1950 -1959	1940 -1949	Before 1940	Median Year
City	7.3	15.9	13.7	16.6	15.0	10.2	10.1	5.7	5.6	1982
MSA[1]	11.4	20.2	14.5	15.4	13.5	8.4	7.7	4.2	4.6	1988
U.S.	5.2	14.0	13.9	13.4	15.2	10.6	10.3	4.9	12.6	1978

Note: Figures are percentages except for Median Year; Note: (1) Figures cover the San Antonio-New Braunfels, TX Metropolitan Statistical Area
Source: U.S. Census Bureau, 2015-2019 American Community Survey 5-Year Estimates

Gross Monthly Rent

Area	Under $500	$500 -$999	$1,000 -$1,499	$1,500 -$1,999	$2,000 -$2,499	$2,500 -$2,999	$3,000 and up	Median ($)
City	7.6	43.3	36.4	10.0	1.7	0.4	0.6	992
MSA[1]	7.0	40.8	36.6	11.8	2.3	0.7	0.8	1,024
U.S.	9.4	36.2	30.0	14.0	5.6	2.4	2.4	1,062

Note: Figures are percentages except for Median; Gross rent is the contract rent plus the estimated average monthly cost of utilities (electricity, gas, and water and sewer) and fuels (oil, coal, kerosene, wood, etc.) if these are paid by the renter (or paid for the renter by someone else); (1) Figures cover the San Antonio-New Braunfels, TX Metropolitan Statistical Area
Source: U.S. Census Bureau, 2015-2019 American Community Survey 5-Year Estimates

HEALTH

Health Risk Factors

Category	MSA[1] (%)	U.S. (%)
Adults aged 18–64 who have any kind of health care coverage	67.4	87.3
Adults who reported being in good or better health	78.4	82.4
Adults who have been told they have high blood cholesterol	28.9	33.0
Adults who have been told they have high blood pressure	30.6	32.3
Adults who are current smokers	17.9	17.1
Adults who currently use E-cigarettes	n/a	4.6
Adults who currently use chewing tobacco, snuff, or snus	3.8	4.0
Adults who are heavy drinkers[2]	7.5	6.3
Adults who are binge drinkers[3]	19.2	17.4
Adults who are overweight (BMI 25.0 - 29.9)	37.5	35.3
Adults who are obese (BMI 30.0 - 99.8)	30.7	31.3
Adults who participated in any physical activities in the past month	66.5	74.4
Adults who always or nearly always wears a seat belt	94.9	94.3

Note: n/a not available; (1) Figures cover the San Antonio-New Braunfels, TX Metropolitan Statistical Area; (2) Heavy drinkers are classified as adult men having more than 14 drinks per week and adult women having more than 7 drinks per week; (3) Binge drinkers are classified as males having five or more drinks on one occasion or females having four or more drinks on one occasion
Source: Centers for Disease Control and Prevention, Behavioral Risk Factor Surveillance System, SMART: Selected Metropolitan Area Risk Trends, 2017

Acute and Chronic Health Conditions

Category	MSA[1] (%)	U.S. (%)
Adults who have ever been told they had a heart attack	7.0	4.2
Adults who have ever been told they have angina or coronary heart disease	5.0	3.9
Adults who have ever been told they had a stroke	n/a	3.0
Adults who have ever been told they have asthma	9.0	14.2
Adults who have ever been told they have arthritis	20.2	24.9
Adults who have ever been told they have diabetes[2]	13.0	10.5
Adults who have ever been told they had skin cancer	4.2	6.2
Adults who have ever been told they had any other types of cancer	8.6	7.1
Adults who have ever been told they have COPD	7.2	6.5
Adults who have ever been told they have kidney disease	n/a	3.0
Adults who have ever been told they have a form of depression	21.4	20.5

Note: n/a not available; (1) Figures cover the San Antonio-New Braunfels, TX Metropolitan Statistical Area; (2) Figures do not include pregnancy-related, borderline, or pre-diabetes
Source: Centers for Disease Control and Prevention, Behavioral Risk Factor Surveillance System, SMART: Selected Metropolitan Area Risk Trends, 2017

Health Screening and Vaccination Rates

Category	MSA[1] (%)	U.S. (%)
Adults aged 65+ who have had flu shot within the past year	70.1	60.7
Adults aged 65+ who have ever had a pneumonia vaccination	76.3	75.4
Adults who have ever been tested for HIV	41.9	36.1
Adults who have ever had the shingles or zoster vaccine?	29.6	28.9
Adults who have had their blood cholesterol checked within the last five years	80.5	85.9

Note: n/a not available; (1) Figures cover the San Antonio-New Braunfels, TX Metropolitan Statistical Area.
Source: Centers for Disease Control and Prevention, Behavioral Risk Factor Surveillance System, SMART: Selected Metropolitan Area Risk Trends, 2017

Disability Status

Category	MSA[1] (%)	U.S. (%)
Adults who reported being deaf	5.0	6.7
Are you blind or have serious difficulty seeing, even when wearing glasses?	n/a	4.5
Are you limited in any way in any of your usual activities due of arthritis?	12.9	12.9
Do you have difficulty doing errands alone?	9.1	6.8
Do you have difficulty dressing or bathing?	n/a	3.6
Do you have serious difficulty concentrating/remembering/making decisions?	12.9	10.7
Do you have serious difficulty walking or climbing stairs?	13.2	13.6

Note: n/a not available; (1) Figures cover the San Antonio-New Braunfels, TX Metropolitan Statistical Area.
Source: Centers for Disease Control and Prevention, Behavioral Risk Factor Surveillance System, SMART: Selected Metropolitan Area Risk Trends, 2017

Mortality Rates for the Top 10 Causes of Death in the U.S.

ICD-10[a] Sub-Chapter	ICD-10[a] Code	Age-Adjusted Mortality Rate[1] per 100,000 population County[2]	U.S.
Malignant neoplasms	C00-C97	141.2	149.2
Ischaemic heart diseases	I20-I25	89.5	90.5
Other forms of heart disease	I30-I51	62.9	52.2
Chronic lower respiratory diseases	J40-J47	33.2	39.6
Other degenerative diseases of the nervous system	G30-G31	60.1	37.6
Cerebrovascular diseases	I60-I69	42.7	37.2
Other external causes of accidental injury	W00-X59	27.6	36.1
Organic, including symptomatic, mental disorders	F01-F09	17.0	29.4
Hypertensive diseases	I10-I15	23.6	24.1
Diabetes mellitus	E10-E14	26.5	21.5

Note: (a) ICD-10 = International Classification of Diseases 10th Revision; (1) Mortality rates are a three-year average covering 2017-2019; (2) Figures cover Bexar County.
Source: Centers for Disease Control and Prevention, National Center for Health Statistics. Underlying Cause of Death 1999-2019 on CDC WONDER Online Database

Mortality Rates for Selected Causes of Death

ICD-10[a] Sub-Chapter	ICD-10[a] Code	Age-Adjusted Mortality Rate[1] per 100,000 population County[2]	U.S.
Assault	X85-Y09	7.3	6.0
Diseases of the liver	K70-K76	22.7	14.4
Human immunodeficiency virus (HIV) disease	B20-B24	2.3	1.5
Influenza and pneumonia	J09-J18	9.6	13.8
Intentional self-harm	X60-X84	13.0	14.1
Malnutrition	E40-E46	3.9	2.3
Obesity and other hyperalimentation	E65-E68	2.1	2.1
Renal failure	N17-N19	14.9	12.6
Transport accidents	V01-V99	11.0	12.3
Viral hepatitis	B15-B19	1.6	1.2

Note: (a) ICD-10 = International Classification of Diseases 10th Revision; (1) Mortality rates are a three-year average covering 2017-2019; (2) Figures cover Bexar County; Data are suppressed when the data meet the criteria for confidentiality constraints; Mortality rates are flagged as unreliable when the rate would be calculated with a numerator of 20 or less.
Source: Centers for Disease Control and Prevention, National Center for Health Statistics. Underlying Cause of Death 1999-2019 on CDC WONDER Online Database

Health Insurance Coverage

Area	With Health Insurance	With Private Health Insurance	With Public Health Insurance	Without Health Insurance	Population Under Age 19 Without Health Insurance
City	83.3	60.1	32.7	16.7	8.6
MSA[1]	85.3	65.1	31.0	14.7	8.1
U.S.	91.2	67.9	35.1	8.8	5.1

Note: Figures are percentages that cover the civilian noninstitutionalized population; (1) Figures cover the San Antonio-New Braunfels, TX Metropolitan Statistical Area
Source: U.S. Census Bureau, 2015-2019 American Community Survey 5-Year Estimates

Number of Medical Professionals

Area	MDs[3]	DOs[3,4]	Dentists	Podiatrists	Chiropractors	Optometrists
County[1] (number)	6,432	369	1,788	106	326	363
County[1] (rate[2])	324.7	18.6	89.2	5.3	16.3	18.1
U.S. (rate[2])	282.9	22.7	71.2	6.2	28.1	16.9

48029
Note: Data as of 2019 unless noted; (1) Data covers Bexar County; (2) Rate per 100,000 population; (3) Data as of 2018 and includes all active, non-federal physicians; (4) Doctor of Osteopathic Medicine
Source: U.S. Department of Health and Human Services, Health Resources and Services Administration, Bureau of Health Professions, Area Resource File (ARF) 2019-2020

EDUCATION

Public School District Statistics

District Name	Schls	Pupils	Pupil/Teacher Ratio	Minority Pupils[1] (%)	Free Lunch Eligible[2] (%)	IEP[3] (%)
Alamo Heights ISD	5	4,864	14.1	47.3	16.9	8.4
Basis Texas	3	2,597	18.2	67.0	5.5	1.8
Brooks Academies Of Texas	4	3,322	18.7	91.5	62.3	6.7
East Central ISD	17	10,041	16.7	84.8	59.7	11.1
Edgewood ISD	22	10,234	16.1	99.4	94.7	10.2
Great Hearts Texas	5	3,615	18.0	57.1	14.4	5.7
Harlandale ISD	31	14,086	14.6	98.5	87.9	9.9
Harmony Science Academy	8	4,512	15.2	90.3	72.6	7.9
Jubilee Academies	10	5,957	17.8	92.0	67.9	6.9
North East ISD	75	65,186	15.6	74.8	43.7	10.2
Northside ISD	120	106,501	15.3	81.1	44.8	12.4
San Antonio ISD	100	48,745	15.5	97.6	89.9	11.0
School of Science and Technology	5	2,382	14.4	83.8	58.5	7.9
South San Antonio ISD	14	8,939	16.9	98.6	90.9	10.4
Southside ISD	9	5,663	15.8	93.6	82.3	10.9
Southwest ISD	18	13,759	15.0	94.8	82.3	12.5

Note: Table includes school districts with 2,000 or more students; (1) Percentage of students that are not non-Hispanic white; (2) Percentage of students that are eligible for the free lunch program; (3) Percentage of students that have an Individualized Education Program.
Source: U.S. Department of Education, National Center for Education Statistics, Common Core of Data, Local Education Agency (School District) Universe Survey: School Year 2018-2019; U.S. Department of Education, National Center for Education Statistics, Common Core of Data, Public Elementary/Secondary School Universe Survey: School Year 2018-2019

Best High Schools

According to *U.S. News,* San Antonio is home to three of the top 500 high schools in the U.S.: **Young Women's Leadership Academy** (#102); **Health Careers High School** (#117); **International School of America** (#450). Nearly 18,000 public, magnet and charter schools were ranked based on their performance on state assessments and how well they prepare students for college. *U.S. News & World Report, "Best High Schools 2020"*

Highest Level of Education

Area	Less than H.S.	H.S. Diploma	Some College, No Deg.	Associate Degree	Bachelor's Degree	Master's Degree	Prof. School Degree	Doctorate Degree
City	17.6	26.3	22.4	7.7	16.6	6.7	1.7	1.0
MSA[1]	14.9	26.3	22.6	8.0	18.0	7.5	1.7	1.0
U.S.	12.0	27.0	20.4	8.5	19.8	8.8	2.1	1.4

Note: Figures cover persons age 25 and over; (1) Figures cover the San Antonio-New Braunfels, TX Metropolitan Statistical Area
Source: U.S. Census Bureau, 2015-2019 American Community Survey 5-Year Estimates

Educational Attainment by Race

Area	High School Graduate or Higher (%)					Bachelor's Degree or Higher (%)				
	Total	White	Black	Asian	Hisp.[2]	Total	White	Black	Asian	Hisp.[2]
City	82.4	82.4	91.1	87.2	74.8	26.0	26.0	23.9	53.1	16.4
MSA[1]	85.1	85.3	92.2	87.5	76.1	28.2	28.4	28.8	51.7	17.2
U.S.	88.0	89.9	86.0	87.1	68.7	32.1	33.5	21.6	54.3	16.4

Note: Figures shown cover persons 25 years old and over; (1) Figures cover the San Antonio-New Braunfels, TX Metropolitan Statistical Area; (2) People of Hispanic origin can be of any race
Source: U.S. Census Bureau, 2015-2019 American Community Survey 5-Year Estimates

School Enrollment by Grade and Control

Area	Preschool (%)		Kindergarten (%)		Grades 1 - 4 (%)		Grades 5 - 8 (%)		Grades 9 - 12 (%)	
	Public	Private	Public	Private	Public	Private	Public	Private	Public	Private
City	70.1	29.9	90.3	9.7	93.1	6.9	92.9	7.1	92.6	7.4
MSA[1]	65.9	34.1	90.4	9.6	92.9	7.1	92.1	7.9	92.5	7.5
U.S.	59.1	40.9	87.6	12.4	89.5	10.5	89.4	10.6	90.1	9.9

Note: Figures shown cover persons 3 years old and over; (1) Figures cover the San Antonio-New Braunfels, TX Metropolitan Statistical Area
Source: U.S. Census Bureau, 2015-2019 American Community Survey 5-Year Estimates

Higher Education

Four-Year Colleges			Two-Year Colleges			Medical Schools[1]	Law Schools[2]	Voc/Tech[3]
Public	Private Non-profit	Private For-profit	Public	Private Non-profit	Private For-profit			
3	8	4	4	0	4	2	1	20

Note: Figures cover institutions located within the city limits and include main campuses only; (1) includes schools accredited by the Liaison Committee on Medical Education and the American Osteopathic Association's Commission on Osteopathic College Accreditation; (2) includes ABA-accredited schools, schools with provisional ABA accreditation, and state accredited schools; (3) includes all schools with programs that are less than 2 years.
Source: National Center for Education Statistics, Integrated Postsecondary Education System (IPEDS), 2019-20; Wikipedia, List of Medical Schools in the United States, accessed April 2, 2021; Wikipedia, List of Law Schools in the United States, accessed April 2, 2021

According to *U.S. News & World Report,* the San Antonio-New Braunfels, TX metro area is home to one of the top 75 medical schools for research in the U.S.: **University of Texas Health Science Center—San Antonio** (#52). The rankings are based on a weighted average of 11 measures of quality: quality assessment; peer assessment score; assessment score by residency directors; research activity; total research activity; average research activity per faculty member; student selectivity; median MCAT total score; median undergraduate GPA; acceptance rate; and faculty resources. *U.S. News & World Report, "America's Best Graduate Schools, Medical, 2022"*

EMPLOYERS

Major Employers

Company Name	Industry
AT&T	Phone, wireless & internet services
Baptist Health System	Health care services
Bill Miller BBQ	Restaurant chain
Christus Santa Rosa Health Care	Health care services
City of San Antonio	Municipal government
Clear Channel Communications	TV & radio stations, outdoor ads
CPS Energy	Utilities
Fort Sam Houston-U.S. Army	U.S. military
H-E-B	Super market chain
JPMorgan Chase	Financial services
Lackland Air Force Base	U.S. military
Methodist Healthcare System	Health care services
North East ISD	School districts
Northside ISD	School districts
Rackspace	IT managed hosting solutions
Randolph Air Force Base	U.S. military
San Antonio ISD	School districts
Toyota Motor Manufacturing	Manufacturing
USAA	Financial services & insurance
Wells Fargo	Financial services

Note: Companies shown are located within the San Antonio-New Braunfels, TX Metropolitan Statistical Area.
Source: Hoovers.com; Wikipedia

Best Companies to Work For

USAA, headquartered in San Antonio, is among "The 100 Best Companies to Work For." To pick the best companies, *Fortune* partnered with the Great Place to Work Institute. Two-thirds of a company's score is based on the results of the Institute's Trust Index survey, which is sent to a random sample of employees from each company. The questions related to attitudes about management's credibility, job satisfaction, and camaraderie. The other third of the scoring is based on the company's responses to the Institute's Culture Audit, which includes detailed questions about pay and benefit programs, and a series of open-ended questions about hiring practices, internal communication, training, recognition programs, and diversity efforts. Any company that is at least five years old with more than 1,000 U.S. employees is eligible. *Fortune, "The 100 Best Companies to Work For," 2020*

PUBLIC SAFETY

Crime Rate

Area	All Crimes	Violent Crimes				Property Crimes		
		Murder	Rape[3]	Robbery	Aggrav. Assault	Burglary	Larceny-Theft	Motor Vehicle Theft
City	5,032.7	6.7	104.5	126.0	471.1	524.1	3,301.1	499.0
Suburbs[1]	1,855.5	2.5	37.7	25.0	148.4	294.5	1,199.2	148.3
Metro[2]	3,796.6	5.1	78.5	86.7	345.6	434.8	2,483.3	362.6
U.S.	2,489.3	5.0	42.6	81.6	250.2	340.5	1,549.5	219.9

Note: Figures are crimes per 100,000 population; (1) All areas within the metro area that are located outside the city limits; (2) Figures cover the San Antonio-New Braunfels, TX Metropolitan Statistical Area; (3) All figures shown were reported using the revised Uniform Crime Reporting (UCR) definition of rape.
Source: FBI Uniform Crime Reports, 2019

Hate Crimes

Area	Number of Quarters Reported	Number of Incidents per Bias Motivation					
		Race/Ethnicity/Ancestry	Religion	Sexual Orientation	Disability	Gender	Gender Identity
City	4	5	0	4	0	0	0
U.S.	4	3,963	1,521	1,195	157	69	198

Source: Federal Bureau of Investigation, Hate Crime Statistics 2019

Identity Theft Consumer Reports

Area	Reports	Reports per 100,000 Population	Rank[2]
MSA[1]	7,065	277	138
U.S.	1,387,615	423	-

Note: (1) Figures cover the San Antonio-New Braunfels, TX Metropolitan Statistical Area; (2) Rank ranges from 1 to 391 where 1 indicates greatest number of identity theft reports per 100,000 population
Source: Federal Trade Commission, Consumer Sentinel Network Data Book 2020

Fraud and Other Consumer Reports

Area	Reports	Reports per 100,000 Population	Rank[2]
MSA[1]	19,074	748	145
U.S.	3,385,133	1,031	-

Note: (1) Figures cover the San Antonio-New Braunfels, TX Metropolitan Statistical Area; (2) Rank ranges from 1 to 391 where 1 indicates greatest number of fraud and other consumer reports per 100,000 population
Source: Federal Trade Commission, Consumer Sentinel Network Data Book 2020

POLITICS

2020 Presidential Election Results

Area	Biden	Trump	Jorgensen	Hawkins	Other
Bexar County	58.2	40.1	1.1	0.4	0.2
U.S.	51.3	46.8	1.2	0.3	0.5

Note: Results are percentages and may not add to 100% due to rounding
Source: Dave Leip's Atlas of U.S. Presidential Elections

SPORTS

Professional Sports Teams

Team Name	League	Year Established
San Antonio Spurs	National Basketball Association (NBA)	1973

Note: Includes teams located in the San Antonio-New Braunfels, TX Metropolitan Statistical Area.
Source: Wikipedia, Major Professional Sports Teams of the United States and Canada, April 6, 2021

CLIMATE

Average and Extreme Temperatures

Temperature	Jan	Feb	Mar	Apr	May	Jun	Jul	Aug	Sep	Oct	Nov	Dec	Yr.
Extreme High (°F)	89	97	100	100	103	105	106	108	103	98	94	90	108
Average High (°F)	62	66	74	80	86	92	95	95	90	82	71	64	80
Average Temp. (°F)	51	55	62	70	76	82	85	85	80	71	60	53	69
Average Low (°F)	39	43	50	58	66	72	74	74	69	59	49	41	58
Extreme Low (°F)	0	6	19	31	43	53	62	61	46	33	21	6	0

Note: Figures cover the years 1948-1990
Source: National Climatic Data Center, International Station Meteorological Climate Summary, 9/96

Average Precipitation/Snowfall/Humidity

Precip./Humidity	Jan	Feb	Mar	Apr	May	Jun	Jul	Aug	Sep	Oct	Nov	Dec	Yr.
Avg. Precip. (in.)	1.5	1.8	1.5	2.6	3.8	3.6	2.0	2.5	3.3	3.2	2.3	1.4	29.6
Avg. Snowfall (in.)	1	Tr	Tr	0	0	0	0	0	0	0	Tr	Tr	1
Avg. Rel. Hum. 6am (%)	79	80	79	82	87	87	87	86	85	83	81	79	83
Avg. Rel. Hum. 3pm (%)	51	48	45	48	51	48	43	42	47	46	48	49	47

Note: Figures cover the years 1948-1990; Tr = Trace amounts (<0.05 in. of rain; <0.5 in. of snow)
Source: National Climatic Data Center, International Station Meteorological Climate Summary, 9/96

Weather Conditions

Temperature			Daytime Sky			Precipitation		
32°F & below	45°F & below	90°F & above	Clear	Partly cloudy	Cloudy	0.01 inch or more precip.	0.1 inch or more snow/ice	Thunderstorms
23	91	112	97	153	115	81	1	36

Note: Figures are average number of days per year and cover the years 1948-1990
Source: National Climatic Data Center, International Station Meteorological Climate Summary, 9/96

HAZARDOUS WASTE

Superfund Sites

The San Antonio-New Braunfels, TX metro area is home to four sites on the EPA's Superfund National Priorities List: **Bandera Road Ground Water Plume** (final); **Eldorado Chemical Co., Inc.** (final); **R & H Oil/Tropicana** (proposed); **River City Metal Finishing** (final). There are a total of 1,375 Superfund sites with a status of proposed or final on the list in the U.S. *U.S. Environmental Protection Agency, National Priorities List, April 7, 2021*

AIR QUALITY

Air Quality Trends: Ozone

	1990	1995	2000	2005	2010	2015	2016	2017	2018	2019
MSA[1]	0.090	0.095	0.078	0.084	0.072	0.079	0.071	0.073	0.072	0.075
U.S.	0.088	0.089	0.082	0.080	0.073	0.068	0.069	0.068	0.069	0.065

Note: (1) Data covers the San Antonio-New Braunfels, TX Metropolitan Statistical Area. The values shown are the composite ozone concentration averages among trend sites based on the highest fourth daily maximum 8-hour concentration in parts per million. These trends are based on sites having an adequate record of monitoring data during the trend period. Data from exceptional events are included.
Source: U.S. Environmental Protection Agency, Air Quality Monitoring Information, "Air Quality Trends by City, 1990-2019"

Air Quality Index

Area	Percent of Days when Air Quality was...[2]						AQI Statistics[2]	
	Good	Moderate	Unhealthy for Sensitive Groups	Unhealthy	Very Unhealthy	Maximum	Median
MSA[1]	53.7	44.7	1.4	0.3	0.0	169	49

Note: (1) Data covers the San Antonio-New Braunfels, TX Metropolitan Statistical Area; (2) Based on 365 days with AQI data in 2019. Air Quality Index (AQI) is an index for reporting daily air quality. EPA calculates the AQI for five major air pollutants regulated by the Clean Air Act: ground-level ozone, particle pollution (aka particulate matter), carbon monoxide, sulfur dioxide, and nitrogen dioxide. The AQI runs from 0 to 500. The higher the AQI value, the greater the level of air pollution and the greater the health concern. There are six AQI categories: "Good" AQI is between 0 and 50. Air quality is considered satisfactory; "Moderate" AQI is between 51 and 100. Air quality is acceptable; "Unhealthy for Sensitive Groups" When AQI values are between 101 and 150, members of sensitive groups may experience health effects; "Unhealthy" When AQI values are between 151 and 200 everyone may begin to experience health effects; "Very Unhealthy" AQI values between 201 and 300 trigger a health alert; "Hazardous" AQI values over 300 trigger warnings of emergency conditions (not shown).
Source: U.S. Environmental Protection Agency, Air Quality Index Report, 2019

Air Quality Index Pollutants

Area	Percent of Days when AQI Pollutant was...[2]					
	Carbon Monoxide	Nitrogen Dioxide	Ozone	Sulfur Dioxide	Particulate Matter 2.5	Particulate Matter 10
MSA[1]	0.0	0.8	44.1	0.0	54.8	0.3

Note: (1) Data covers the San Antonio-New Braunfels, TX Metropolitan Statistical Area; (2) Based on 365 days with AQI data in 2019. The Air Quality Index (AQI) is an index for reporting daily air quality. EPA calculates the AQI for five major air pollutants regulated by the Clean Air Act: ground-level ozone, particle pollution (also known as particulate matter), carbon monoxide, sulfur dioxide, and nitrogen dioxide. The AQI runs from 0 to 500. The higher the AQI value, the greater the level of air pollution and the greater the health concern.
Source: U.S. Environmental Protection Agency, Air Quality Index Report, 2019

Maximum Air Pollutant Concentrations: Particulate Matter, Ozone, CO and Lead

	Particulate Matter 10 (ug/m^3)	Particulate Matter 2.5 Wtd AM (ug/m^3)	Particulate Matter 2.5 24-Hr (ug/m^3)	Ozone (ppm)	Carbon Monoxide (ppm)	Lead (ug/m^3)
MSA[1] Level	42	8.9	21	0.075	1	n/a
NAAQS[2]	150	15	35	0.075	9	0.15
Met NAAQS[2]	Yes	Yes	Yes	Yes	Yes	n/a

Note: (1) Data covers the San Antonio-New Braunfels, TX Metropolitan Statistical Area; Data from exceptional events are included; (2) National Ambient Air Quality Standards; ppm = parts per million; ug/m^3 = micrograms per cubic meter; n/a not available.
Concentrations: Particulate Matter 10 (coarse particulate)—highest second maximum 24-hour concentration; Particulate Matter 2.5 Wtd AM (fine particulate)—highest weighted annual mean concentration; Particulate Matter 2.5 24-Hour (fine particulate)—highest 98th percentile 24-hour concentration; Ozone—highest fourth daily maximum 8-hour concentration; Carbon Monoxide—highest second maximum non-overlapping 8-hour concentration; Lead—maximum running 3-month average
Source: U.S. Environmental Protection Agency, Air Quality Monitoring Information, "Air Quality Statistics by City, 2019"

Maximum Air Pollutant Concentrations: Nitrogen Dioxide and Sulfur Dioxide

	Nitrogen Dioxide AM (ppb)	Nitrogen Dioxide 1-Hr (ppb)	Sulfur Dioxide AM (ppb)	Sulfur Dioxide 1-Hr (ppb)	Sulfur Dioxide 24-Hr (ppb)
MSA[1] Level	7	40	n/a	4	n/a
NAAQS[2]	53	100	30	75	140
Met NAAQS[2]	Yes	Yes	n/a	Yes	n/a

Note: (1) Data covers the San Antonio-New Braunfels, TX Metropolitan Statistical Area; Data from exceptional events are included; (2) National Ambient Air Quality Standards; ppm = parts per million; ug/m^3 = micrograms per cubic meter; n/a not available.
Concentrations: Nitrogen Dioxide AM—highest arithmetic mean concentration; Nitrogen Dioxide 1-Hr—highest 98th percentile 1-hour daily maximum concentration; Sulfur Dioxide AM—highest annual mean concentration; Sulfur Dioxide 1-Hr—highest 99th percentile 1-hour daily maximum concentration; Sulfur Dioxide 24-Hr—highest second maximum 24-hour concentration
Source: U.S. Environmental Protection Agency, Air Quality Monitoring Information, "Air Quality Statistics by City, 2019"

Savannah, Georgia

Background

Savannah is at the mouth of the Savannah River on the border between Georgia and South Carolina. It was established in 1733 when General James Oglethorpe landed with a group of settlers in the sailing vessel *Anne, after a voyage of more than three months. City Hall now stands at the spot where Oglethorpe and his followers first camped on a small bluff overlooking the river.*

Savannah is unique among American cities in that it was extensively planned while Oglethorpe was still in England. Each new settler was given a package of property, including a town lot, a garden space, and an outlying farm area. The town was planned in quadrants, the north and south for residences, and the east and west for public buildings.

The quadrant design was inspired in part by considerations of public defense, given the unsettled character of relations with Native Americans, but in fact an early treaty between the settlers and the Creek Indian Chief Tomochichi allowed Savannah to develop quite peacefully, with little of the hostility between Europeans and Indians that marred much of the development elsewhere in the colonies.

Savannah was taken by the British during the American Revolution and, in the patriotic siege that followed, many lives were lost, including that of Revolutionary War hero Count Pulaski. Savannah was eventually retaken in 1782 by the American Generals Nathaniel Greene and Anthony Wayne. In the post-Revolutionary period, Savannah grew dramatically, its economic strength being driven in large part by Eli Whitney's cotton gin. As the world's leader in the cotton trade, Savannah also hosted a great development in export activity, and the first American steamboat built in the United States to cross the Atlantic was launched in its busy port.

Savannah's physical structure had been saved from the worst ravages of war, but the destruction of the area's infrastructure slowed its further development for an extended period. In the long period of slow recovery that followed, the Girl Scouts was established in the city in 1912 by Juliette Gordeon Low—a true Savannah success story.

> When the city's popular Earth Day festivities were canceled, it was replaced by "Earth Day Savannah Month," a month-long celebration of bird watching, oyster bagging, and socially-distanced nature walks.

In 1954, an extensive fire destroyed a large portion of the historic City Market, and the area was bulldozed to make room for a parking garage. The Historic Savannah Foundation has worked continuously since to maintain and improve Savannah's considerable architectural charms. As a result, Savannah's Historic District was designated a Registered National Historic Landmark, and the city has been a favored site for movie makers for decades. More than forty major movies have been filmed in Savannah including *Roots* (1976), *East of Eden* (1980), *Forrest Gump* (1994), *Midnight in the Garden of Good and Evil* (1997) and *The Legend of Bagger Vance* (2000), and a segment of the Colbert Report (2005).

The Port of Savannah, manufacturing, the military, and tourism are the city's major economic drivers in the twenty-first century. Its port facilities, operated by the Georgia Ports Authority, have seen notable growth in container tonnage in recent years. Garden City Terminal is the fourth largest container port in the United States, and the largest single-terminal operation in North America. In 2019, a second passenger airport, Paine Field, opened for business. Military installations in the area include Hunter Army Airfield and Fort Stewart military bases, employing nearly 50,000.

Museums include Juliette Gordon Low Museum, Flannery O'Connor Childhood Home/Museum, Telfair Museum of Art and the Mighty 8th Air Force Museum. Savannah hosted the sailing competitions during the 1996 Summer Olympics held in Atlanta, and the Savannah Book Festival is a popular annual book fair held on President's Day weekend. Football's XFL league will resume play in the city in 2022.

The city's beauty draws not just tourists, but conventioneers. The Savannah International Trade & Convention Center is a state-of-the-art facility with more than 100,000 square feet of exhibition space, accommodating nearly 10,000 people.

Colleges and universities in the city include the Savannah College of Art and Design, Savannah State University, and South University.

Savannah's climate is subtropical, and is at risk for hurricanes. With hot summers and mild winters, however, the city is ideal for all-year outside activities.

Rankings

General Rankings

- As part of its *Next Stop* series, *Insider* listed 10 places in the U.S. that were either a classic vacation destination experiencing a renaissance or a new up-and-coming hot spot. That could mean the exploding food scene, experiencing the great outdoors, where cool people are moving to, or not overrun with tourists, according to the website insider.com Savannah is a place to visit in 2020. *Insider, "10 Places in the U.S. You Need to Visit in 2020," December 23, 2019*

- Savannah appeared on *Travel + Leisure's* list of the 15 best cities in the United States. The city was ranked #4. Criteria: sights/landmarks; culture; food; friendliness; shopping; and overall value. *Travel + Leisure, "The World's Best Awards 2020" July 8, 2020*

- For its 33rd annual "Readers' Choice Awards" survey, *Condé Nast Traveler* ranked its readers' favorite cities in the U.S. These places brought feelings of comfort in a time of limited travel. The list was broken into large cities and cities under 250,000. Savannah ranked #8 in the small city category. *Condé Nast Traveler, Readers' Choice Awards 2020, "Best Small Cities in the U.S." October 6, 2020*

Business/Finance Rankings

- Savannah was cited as one of America's top metros for new and expanded facility projects in 2020. The area ranked #1 in the mid-sized metro area category (population 200,000 to 1 million). *Site Selection, "Top Metros of 2020," March 2021*

- The Savannah metro area appeared on the Milken Institute "2021 Best Performing Cities" list. Rank: #52 out of 200 large metro areas (population over 250,000). Criteria: job growth; wage and salary growth; high-tech output growth; housing affordability; household broadband access. *Milken Institute, "Best-Performing Cities 2021," February 16, 2021*

- *Forbes* ranked the 200 most populous metro areas to determine the nation's "Best Places for Business and Careers." The Savannah metro area was ranked #74. Criteria: costs (business and living); job growth (past and projected); income growth; quality of life; educational attainment (college and high school); projected economic growth; cultural and leisure opportunities; workplace tolerance laws; net migration patterns. *Forbes, "The Best Places for Business and Careers 2019: Seattle Still On Top," October 30, 2019*

Children/Family Rankings

- Savannah was selected as one of the most playful cities in the U.S. by KaBOOM! The organization's Playful City USA initiative honors cities and towns across the nation that have made their communities more playable. Criteria: pledging to integrate play as a solution to challenges in their communities; making it easy for children to get active and balanced play; creating more family-friendly and innovative communities as a result. *KaBOOM! National Campaign for Play, "2017 Playful City USA Communities"*

Culture/Performing Arts Rankings

- Savannah was selected as one of the ten best small North American cities and towns for moviemakers. Of cities with smaller populations, the area ranked #4. As with the 2021 list for bigger cities, pandemic challenges and COVID-19 guidelines were factored in. Other criteria: film community and culture; access to equipment and facilities; tax incentives; and standard of living. *MovieMaker Magazine, "Best Places to Live and Work as a Moviemaker, 2021," January 26, 2021*

- Savannah was selected as one of "America's Favorite Cities." The city ranked #2 in the "Architecture" category. Respondents to an online survey were asked to rate their favorite place (population over 100,000) in over 65 categories. *Travelandleisure.com, "America's Favorite Cities for Architecture 2016," March 2, 2017*

Education Rankings

- Personal finance website *WalletHub* analyzed the 150 largest U.S. metropolitan statistical areas to determine where the most educated Americans are putting their degrees to work. Criteria: education levels; percentage of workers with degrees; education quality and attainment gap; public school quality rankings; quality and enrollment of each metro area's universities. Savannah was ranked #77 (#1 = most educated city). *www.WalletHub.com, "Most and Least Educated Cities in America," July 20, 2020*

Environmental Rankings

- Savannah was highlighted as one of the cleanest metro areas for ozone air pollution in the U.S. during 2016 through 2018. The list represents cities with no monitored ozone air pollution in unhealthful ranges. *American Lung Association, "State of the Air 2020," April 21, 2020*

Safety Rankings

- Allstate ranked the 200 largest cities in America in terms of driver safety. Savannah ranked #157. Criteria: internal property damage claims over a two-year period from January 2016 to December 2017. The report helps increase the importance of safety and awareness behind the wheel. *Allstate, "Allstate America's Best Drivers Report, 2019" June 24, 2019*

- The National Insurance Crime Bureau ranked 384 metro areas in the U.S. in terms of per capita rates of vehicle theft. The Savannah metro area ranked #86 (#1 = highest rate). Criteria: number of vehicle theft offenses per 100,000 inhabitants in 2019. *National Insurance Crime Bureau, "Hot Spots 2019," July 21, 2020*

Seniors/Retirement Rankings

- From its Best Cities for Successful Aging indexes, the Milken Institute generated rankings for metropolitan areas, weighing data in nine categories—health care, wellness, living arrangements, transportation and convenience, financial characteristics, education, employment, community engagement, and overall livability. The Savannah metro area was ranked #99 overall in the small metro area category. *Milken Institute, "Best Cities for Successful Aging, 2017" March 14, 2017*

- Savannah made the 2020 *Forbes* list of "25 Best Places to Retire." Criteria, focused on high-quality retirement living at an affordable price, include: housing/living costs compared to the national average and state taxes; air quality; crime rates; good economic outlook; home price appreciation; risk associated with climate-change; availability of medical care; bikeability; walkability; healthy living. *Forbes.com, "The Best Places to Retire in 2020," August 14, 2020*

Miscellaneous Rankings

- In its roundup of St. Patrick's Day parades "Gayot" listed the best festivals and parades of all things Irish. The festivities in Savannah as among the best. *www.gayot.com, "Best St. Patrick's Day Parades," March 2020*

- In *Condé Nast Traveler* magazine's 2020 Readers' Choice Survey, Savannah made the top ten list of friendliest American cities. Savannah ranked #4. *www.cntraveler.com, "The Friendliest Cities in the U.S.," November 30, 2020*

Business Environment

DEMOGRAPHICS

Population Growth

Area	1990 Census	2000 Census	2010 Census	2019* Estimate	Population Growth (%) 1990-2019	Population Growth (%) 2010-2019
City	138,038	131,510	136,286	145,403	5.3	6.7
MSA[1]	258,060	293,000	347,611	386,036	49.6	11.1
U.S.	248,709,873	281,421,906	308,745,538	324,697,795	30.6	5.2

Note: (1) Figures cover the Savannah, GA Metropolitan Statistical Area; (*) 2015-2019 5-year estimated population
Source: U.S. Census Bureau, 1990 Census, Census 2000, Census 2010, 2015-2019 American Community Survey 5-Year Estimates

Household Size

Area	One	Two	Three	Four	Five	Six	Seven or More	Average Household Size
City	33.5	34.1	15.7	9.9	4.4	1.5	1.0	2.60
MSA[1]	28.0	36.0	16.2	12.2	5.0	1.6	0.9	2.60
U.S.	27.9	33.9	15.6	12.9	6.0	2.3	1.4	2.60

Note: (1) Figures cover the Savannah, GA Metropolitan Statistical Area
Source: U.S. Census Bureau, 2015-2019 American Community Survey 5-Year Estimates

Race

Area	White Alone[2] (%)	Black Alone[2] (%)	Asian Alone[2] (%)	AIAN[3] Alone[2] (%)	NHOPI[4] Alone[2] (%)	Other Race Alone[2] (%)	Two or More Races (%)
City	38.9	53.9	2.6	0.3	0.1	1.4	2.8
MSA[1]	59.6	33.3	2.2	0.3	0.1	1.5	3.0
U.S.	72.5	12.7	5.5	0.8	0.2	4.9	3.3

Note: (1) Figures cover the Savannah, GA Metropolitan Statistical Area; (2) Alone is defined as not being in combination with one or more other races; (3) American Indian and Alaska Native; (4) Native Hawaiian and Other Pacific Islander
Source: U.S. Census Bureau, 2015-2019 American Community Survey 5-Year Estimates

Hispanic or Latino Origin

Area	Total (%)	Mexican (%)	Puerto Rican (%)	Cuban (%)	Other (%)
City	5.8	2.3	1.5	0.2	1.8
MSA[1]	6.2	2.9	1.2	0.4	1.6
U.S.	18.0	11.2	1.7	0.7	4.3

Note: Persons of Hispanic or Latino origin can be of any race; (1) Figures cover the Savannah, GA Metropolitan Statistical Area
Source: U.S. Census Bureau, 2015-2019 American Community Survey 5-Year Estimates

Ancestry

Area	German	Irish	English	American	Italian	Polish	French[2]	Scottish	Dutch
City	5.5	6.7	4.6	3.6	2.8	1.2	1.6	1.6	0.7
MSA[1]	9.1	9.7	7.4	7.9	3.3	1.3	1.8	1.8	0.7
U.S.	13.3	9.7	7.2	6.2	5.1	2.8	2.3	1.7	1.2

Note: Figures are the percentage of the total population reporting a particular ancestry. The nine most commonly reported ancestries in the U.S. are shown. Figures include multiple ancestries (e.g. if a person reported being Irish and Italian, they were included in both columns); (1) Figures cover the Savannah, GA Metropolitan Statistical Area; (2) Excludes Basque
Source: U.S. Census Bureau, 2015-2019 American Community Survey 5-Year Estimates

Foreign-born Population

Area	Any Foreign Country	Asia	Mexico	Europe	Caribbean	Central America[2]	South America	Africa	Canada
City	6.2	2.7	0.7	0.9	0.4	0.4	0.5	0.3	0.1
MSA[1]	5.7	2.0	1.1	0.8	0.5	0.4	0.4	0.3	0.2
U.S.	13.6	4.2	3.5	1.5	1.3	1.1	1.0	0.7	0.2

Note: (1) Figures cover the Savannah, GA Metropolitan Statistical Area; (2) Excludes Mexico.
Source: U.S. Census Bureau, 2015-2019 American Community Survey 5-Year Estimates

Marital Status

Area	Never Married	Now Married[2]	Separated	Widowed	Divorced
City	47.5	31.2	3.0	5.9	12.4
MSA[1]	34.9	44.9	2.2	5.8	12.1
U.S.	33.4	48.1	1.9	5.8	10.9

Note: Figures are percentages and cover the population 15 years of age and older; (1) Figures cover the Savannah, GA Metropolitan Statistical Area; (2) Excludes separated
Source: U.S. Census Bureau, 2015-2019 American Community Survey 5-Year Estimates

Disability by Age

Area	All Ages	Under 18 Years Old	18 to 64 Years Old	65 Years and Over
City	15.2	6.1	12.5	43.4
MSA[1]	13.7	5.5	11.6	37.0
U.S.	12.6	4.2	10.3	34.5

Note: Figures show percent of the civilian noninstitutionalized population that reported having a disability. Disability status is determined from six types of difficulty: vision, hearing, cognitive, ambulatory, self-care, and independent living. For children under 5 years old, hearing and vision difficulty are used to determine disability status. For children between the ages of 5 and 14, disability status is determined from hearing, vision, cognitive, ambulatory, and self-care difficulties. For people aged 15 years and older, they are considered to have a disability if they have difficulty with any one of the six difficulty types; Note: (1) Figures cover the Savannah, GA Metropolitan Statistical Area
Source: U.S. Census Bureau, 2015-2019 American Community Survey 5-Year Estimates

Age

Area	Under Age 5	Age 5–19	Age 20–34	Age 35–44	Age 45–54	Age 55–64	Age 65–74	Age 75–84	Age 85+	Median Age
City	6.4	18.2	29.1	11.6	10.4	11.2	7.7	3.7	1.7	32.6
MSA[1]	6.6	19.4	23.2	12.9	12.1	11.9	8.5	4.0	1.5	35.6
U.S.	6.1	19.1	20.7	12.6	13.0	12.9	9.1	4.6	1.9	38.1

Note: (1) Figures cover the Savannah, GA Metropolitan Statistical Area
Source: U.S. Census Bureau, 2015-2019 American Community Survey 5-Year Estimates

Gender

Area	Males	Females	Males per 100 Females
City	69,220	76,183	90.9
MSA[1]	187,309	198,727	94.3
U.S.	159,886,919	164,810,876	97.0

Note: (1) Figures cover the Savannah, GA Metropolitan Statistical Area
Source: U.S. Census Bureau, 2015-2019 American Community Survey 5-Year Estimates

Religious Groups by Family

Area	Catholic	Baptist	Non-Den.	Methodist[2]	Lutheran	LDS[3]	Pentecostal	Presbyterian[4]	Muslim[5]	Judaism
MSA[1]	7.1	19.7	6.9	8.9	1.6	1.0	2.4	1.0	0.2	0.8
U.S.	19.1	9.3	4.0	4.0	2.3	2.0	1.9	1.6	0.8	0.7

Note: Figures are the number of adherents as a percentage of the total population; (1) Figures cover the Savannah, GA Metropolitan Statistical Area; (2) Methodist/Pietist; (3) Latter Day Saints; (4) Reformed; (5) Figures are estimates
Source: Association of Statisticians of American Religious Bodies, 2010 U.S. Religion Census: Religious Congregations & Membership Study

Religious Groups by Tradition

Area	Catholic	Evangelical Protestant	Mainline Protestant	Other Tradition	Black Protestant	Orthodox
MSA[1]	7.1	25.1	9.5	2.6	8.6	0.1
U.S.	19.1	16.2	7.3	4.3	1.6	0.3

Note: Figures are the number of adherents as a percentage of the total population; (1) Figures cover the Savannah, GA Metropolitan Statistical Area
Source: Association of Statisticians of American Religious Bodies, 2010 U.S. Religion Census: Religious Congregations & Membership Study

ECONOMY

Gross Metropolitan Product

Area	2017	2018	2019	2020	Rank[2]
MSA[1]	18.8	19.7	20.6	21.2	134

Note: Figures are in billions of dollars; (1) Figures cover the Savannah, GA Metropolitan Statistical Area; (2) Rank is based on 2018 data and ranges from 1 to 381
Source: U.S. Conference of Mayors, U.S. Metro Economies: GMP & Employment 2018-2020, September 2019

Economic Growth

Area	2015-17 (%)	2018 (%)	2019 (%)	2020 (%)	Rank[2]
MSA[1]	2.3	2.7	2.4	1.2	115
U.S.	1.9	2.9	2.3	2.1	—

Note: Figures are real gross metropolitan product (GMP) growth rates and represent average annual percent change; (1) Figures cover the Savannah, GA Metropolitan Statistical Area; (2) Rank is based on 2017 2-year average annual percent change and ranges from 1 to 381
Source: U.S. Conference of Mayors, U.S. Metro Economies: GMP & Employment 2018-2020, September 2019

Metropolitan Area Exports

Area	2014	2015	2016	2017	2018	2019	Rank[2]
MSA[1]	5,093.4	5,447.5	4,263.4	4,472.0	5,407.8	4,925.5	58

Note: Figures are in millions of dollars; (1) Figures cover the Savannah, GA Metropolitan Statistical Area; (2) Rank is based on 2019 data and ranges from 1 to 386
Source: U.S. Department of Commerce, International Trade Administration, Office of Trade and Economic Analysis, Industry and Analysis, Exports by Metropolitan Area, data extracted March 24, 2021

Building Permits

Area	Single-Family 2018	Single-Family 2019	Pct. Chg.	Multi-Family 2018	Multi-Family 2019	Pct. Chg.	Total 2018	Total 2019	Pct. Chg.
City	399	339	-15.0	0	0	0.0	399	339	-15.0
MSA[1]	2,080	2,151	3.4	1,078	440	-59.2	3,158	2,591	-18.0
U.S.	855,300	862,100	0.7	473,500	523,900	10.6	1,328,800	1,386,000	4.3

Note: (1) Figures cover the Savannah, GA Metropolitan Statistical Area; Figures represent new, privately-owned housing units authorized (unadjusted data); All permit data are based on estimates with imputation
Source: U.S. Census Bureau, Manufacturing, Mining, and Construction Statistics, Building Permits, 2018, 2019

Bankruptcy Filings

Area	Business Filings 2019	Business Filings 2020	% Chg.	Nonbusiness Filings 2019	Nonbusiness Filings 2020	% Chg.
Chatham County	18	13	-27.8	1,220	729	-40.2
U.S.	22,780	21,655	-4.9	752,160	522,808	-30.5

Note: Business filings include Chapter 7, Chapter 9, Chapter 11, Chapter 12, Chapter 13, Chapter 15, and Section 304; Nonbusiness filings include Chapter 7, Chapter 11, and Chapter 13
Source: Administrative Office of the U.S. Courts, Business and Nonbusiness Bankruptcy, County Cases Commenced by Chapter of the Bankruptcy Code, During the 12-Month Period Ending December 31, 2019 and Business and Nonbusiness Bankruptcy, County Cases Commenced by Chapter of the Bankruptcy Code, During the 12-Month Period Ending December 31, 2020

Housing Vacancy Rates

Area	Gross Vacancy Rate[2] (%) 2018	2019	2020	Year-Round Vacancy Rate[3] (%) 2018	2019	2020	Rental Vacancy Rate[4] (%) 2018	2019	2020	Homeowner Vacancy Rate[5] (%) 2018	2019	2020
MSA[1]	n/a	n/a	n/a	n/a	n/a	n/a	n/a	n/a	n/a	n/a	n/a	n/a
U.S.	12.3	12.0	10.6	9.7	9.5	8.2	6.9	6.7	6.3	1.5	1.4	1.0

Note: (1) Figures cover the Savannah, GA Metropolitan Statistical Area; (2) The percentage of the total housing inventory that is vacant; (3) The percentage of the housing inventory (excluding seasonal units) that is year-round vacant; (4) The percentage of rental inventory that is vacant for rent; (5) The percentage of homeowner inventory that is vacant for sale; n/a not available
Source: U.S. Census Bureau, Housing Vacancies and Homeownership Annual Statistics: 2018, 2019, 2020

INCOME

Income

Area	Per Capita ($)	Median Household ($)	Average Household ($)
City	25,664	43,307	63,984
MSA[1]	32,088	59,459	82,125
U.S.	34,103	62,843	88,607

Note: (1) Figures cover the Savannah, GA Metropolitan Statistical Area
Source: U.S. Census Bureau, 2015-2019 American Community Survey 5-Year Estimates

Household Income Distribution

Area	Under $15,000	$15,000 -$24,999	$25,000 -$34,999	$35,000 -$49,999	$50,000 -$74,999	$75,000 -$99,999	$100,000 -$149,999	$150,000 and up
City	17.5	13.1	10.9	14.8	16.5	10.9	9.7	6.7
MSA[1]	10.6	9.5	9.2	13.0	17.8	13.8	14.6	11.4
U.S.	10.3	8.9	8.9	12.3	17.2	12.7	15.1	14.5

Note: (1) Figures cover the Savannah, GA Metropolitan Statistical Area
Source: U.S. Census Bureau, 2015-2019 American Community Survey 5-Year Estimates

Poverty Rate

Area	All Ages	Under 18 Years Old	18 to 64 Years Old	65 Years and Over
City	21.9	30.9	20.8	12.4
MSA[1]	13.7	18.4	13.1	8.7
U.S.	13.4	18.5	12.6	9.3

Note: Figures are percentage of people whose income during the past 12 months was below the poverty level; (1) Figures cover the Savannah, GA Metropolitan Statistical Area
Source: U.S. Census Bureau, 2015-2019 American Community Survey 5-Year Estimates

CITY FINANCES

City Government Finances

Component	2017 ($000)	2017 ($ per capita)
Total Revenues	450,679	3,094
Total Expenditures	426,983	2,931
Debt Outstanding	158,940	1,091
Cash and Securities[1]	854,076	5,863

Note: (1) Cash and security holdings of a government at the close of its fiscal year, including those of its dependent agencies, utilities, and liquor stores.
Source: U.S. Census Bureau, State & Local Government Finances 2017

City Government Revenue by Source

Source	2017 ($000)	2017 ($ per capita)	2017 (%)
General Revenue			
From Federal Government	13,835	95	3.1
From State Government	976	7	0.2
From Local Governments	71,876	493	15.9
Taxes			
Property	65,807	452	14.6
Sales and Gross Receipts	45,446	312	10.1
Personal Income	0	0	0.0
Corporate Income	0	0	0.0
Motor Vehicle License	0	0	0.0
Other Taxes	10,979	75	2.4
Current Charges	128,012	879	28.4
Liquor Store	0	0	0.0
Utility	41,206	283	9.1
Employee Retirement	34,133	234	7.6

Source: U.S. Census Bureau, State & Local Government Finances 2017

City Government Expenditures by Function

Function	2017 ($000)	2017 ($ per capita)	2017 (%)
General Direct Expenditures			
Air Transportation	33,851	232	7.9
Corrections	0	0	0.0
Education	0	0	0.0
Employment Security Administration	0	0	0.0
Financial Administration	4,718	32	1.1
Fire Protection	32,114	220	7.5
General Public Buildings	15,264	104	3.6
Governmental Administration, Other	10,699	73	2.5
Health	0	0	0.0
Highways	41,986	288	9.8
Hospitals	0	0	0.0
Housing and Community Development	0	0	0.0
Interest on General Debt	5,089	34	1.2
Judicial and Legal	5,346	36	1.3
Libraries	0	0	0.0
Parking	7,202	49	1.7
Parks and Recreation	28,759	197	6.7
Police Protection	68,079	467	15.9
Public Welfare	13,891	95	3.3
Sewerage	33,789	231	7.9
Solid Waste Management	35,777	245	8.4
Veterans' Services	0	0	0.0
Liquor Store	0	0	0.0
Utility	22,641	155	5.3
Employee Retirement	26,149	179	6.1

Source: U.S. Census Bureau, State & Local Government Finances 2017

EMPLOYMENT

Labor Force and Employment

Area	Civilian Labor Force Dec. 2019	Dec. 2020	% Chg.	Workers Employed Dec. 2019	Dec. 2020	% Chg.
City	66,855	68,668	2.7	64,804	63,654	-1.8
MSA[1]	187,692	190,082	1.3	182,609	179,365	-1.8
U.S.	164,007,000	160,017,000	-2.4	158,504,000	149,613,000	-5.6

Note: Data is not seasonally adjusted and covers workers 16 years of age and older; (1) Figures cover the Savannah, GA Metropolitan Statistical Area
Source: Bureau of Labor Statistics, Local Area Unemployment Statistics

Unemployment Rate

Area	Jan.	Feb.	Mar.	Apr.	May	Jun.	Jul.	Aug.	Sep.	Oct.	Nov.	Dec.
City	3.7	3.7	5.1	18.5	13.7	11.3	11.0	8.8	8.8	6.3	7.5	7.3
MSA[1]	3.3	3.3	4.4	15.3	10.8	8.6	8.5	6.5	6.7	4.7	5.6	5.6
U.S.	4.0	3.8	4.5	14.4	13.0	11.2	10.5	8.5	7.7	6.6	6.4	6.5

Note: Data is not seasonally adjusted and covers workers 16 years of age and older; (1) Figures cover the Savannah, GA Metropolitan Statistical Area
Source: Bureau of Labor Statistics, Local Area Unemployment Statistics

Average Wages

Occupation	$/Hr.	Occupation	$/Hr.
Accountants and Auditors	33.10	Maintenance and Repair Workers	17.70
Automotive Mechanics	25.10	Marketing Managers	53.90
Bookkeepers	20.20	Network and Computer Systems Admin.	36.90
Carpenters	22.90	Nurses, Licensed Practical	21.50
Cashiers	10.50	Nurses, Registered	31.20
Computer Programmers	38.10	Nursing Assistants	12.90
Computer Systems Analysts	49.70	Office Clerks, General	17.10
Computer User Support Specialists	24.00	Physical Therapists	42.30
Construction Laborers	16.10	Physicians	79.70
Cooks, Restaurant	12.20	Plumbers, Pipefitters and Steamfitters	26.00
Customer Service Representatives	14.70	Police and Sheriff's Patrol Officers	22.00
Dentists	84.30	Postal Service Mail Carriers	25.30
Electricians	25.80	Real Estate Sales Agents	26.50
Engineers, Electrical	59.50	Retail Salespersons	13.10
Fast Food and Counter Workers	10.40	Sales Representatives, Technical/Scientific	42.70
Financial Managers	49.30	Secretaries, Exc. Legal/Medical/Executive	16.90
First-Line Supervisors of Office Workers	26.00	Security Guards	15.60
General and Operations Managers	50.30	Surgeons	135.00
Hairdressers/Cosmetologists	11.70	Teacher Assistants, Exc. Postsecondary*	12.50
Home Health and Personal Care Aides	11.70	Teachers, Secondary School, Exc. Sp. Ed.*	26.50
Janitors and Cleaners	12.40	Telemarketers	n/a
Landscaping/Groundskeeping Workers	14.10	Truck Drivers, Heavy/Tractor-Trailer	22.20
Lawyers	60.10	Truck Drivers, Light/Delivery Services	17.20
Maids and Housekeeping Cleaners	10.60	Waiters and Waitresses	9.30

Note: Wage data covers the Savannah, GA Metropolitan Statistical Area; (*) Hourly wages were calculated from annual wage data based on a 40 hour work week; n/a not available.
Source: Bureau of Labor Statistics, Metro Area Occupational Employment & Wage Estimates, May 2020

Employment by Industry

Sector	MSA[1] Number of Employees	Percent of Total	U.S. Percent of Total
Construction, Mining, and Logging	8,700	4.7	5.5
Education and Health Services	26,100	14.0	16.3
Financial Activities	6,000	3.2	6.1
Government	24,400	13.1	15.2
Information	1,600	0.9	1.9
Leisure and Hospitality	22,800	12.2	9.0
Manufacturing	17,500	9.4	8.5
Other Services	7,000	3.8	3.8
Professional and Business Services	26,800	14.4	14.4
Retail Trade	22,000	11.8	10.9
Transportation, Warehousing, and Utilities	17,100	9.2	4.6
Wholesale Trade	6,400	3.4	3.9

Note: Figures are non-farm employment as of December 2020. Figures are not seasonally adjusted and include workers 16 years of age and older; (1) Figures cover the Savannah, GA Metropolitan Statistical Area
Source: Bureau of Labor Statistics, Current Employment Statistics, Employment, Hours, and Earnings

Employment by Occupation

Occupation Classification	City (%)	MSA[1] (%)	U.S. (%)
Management, Business, Science, and Arts	31.6	36.4	38.5
Natural Resources, Construction, and Maintenance	6.7	8.5	8.9
Production, Transportation, and Material Moving	14.3	14.7	13.2
Sales and Office	22.2	21.1	21.6
Service	25.1	19.4	17.8

Note: Figures cover employed civilians 16 years of age and older; (1) Figures cover the Savannah, GA Metropolitan Statistical Area
Source: U.S. Census Bureau, 2015-2019 American Community Survey 5-Year Estimates

Occupations with Greatest Projected Employment Growth: 2020 – 2022

Occupation[1]	2020 Employment	2022 Projected Employment	Numeric Employment Change	Percent Employment Change
Laborers and Freight, Stock, and Material Movers, Hand	126,370	132,960	6,590	5.2
Fast Food and Counter Workers	134,770	139,200	4,430	3.3
Software Developers and Software Quality Assurance Analysts and Testers	44,810	47,890	3,080	6.9
Home Health and Personal Care Aides	47,800	50,800	3,000	6.3
General and Operations Managers	84,320	87,250	2,930	3.5
Maids and Housekeeping Cleaners	26,600	29,080	2,480	9.3
Cooks, Restaurant	38,680	41,070	2,390	6.2
Maintenance and Repair Workers, General	44,140	46,510	2,370	5.4
Registered Nurses	81,380	83,690	2,310	2.8
Customer Service Representatives	111,220	113,240	2,020	1.8

Note: Projections cover Georgia; (1) Sorted by numeric employment change
Source: www.projectionscentral.com, State Occupational Projections, 2020–2022 Short-Term Projections

Fastest-Growing Occupations: 2020 – 2022

Occupation[1]	2020 Employment	2022 Projected Employment	Numeric Employment Change	Percent Employment Change
Nurse Practitioners	8,440	9,520	1,080	12.8
Hotel, Motel, and Resort Desk Clerks	8,960	10,030	1,070	11.9
Occupational Therapy Assistants	1,220	1,350	130	10.7
Film and Video Editors	1,670	1,840	170	10.2
Lighting Technicians and Media and Communication Equipment Workers, All Other	1,010	1,110	100	9.9
Baggage Porters and Bellhops	1,020	1,120	100	9.8
Animal Trainers	1,250	1,370	120	9.6
Physical Therapist Assistants	2,790	3,050	260	9.3
Maids and Housekeeping Cleaners	26,600	29,080	2,480	9.3
Information Security Analysts (SOC 2018)	3,910	4,250	340	8.7

Note: Projections cover Georgia; (1) Sorted by percent employment change and excludes occupations with numeric employment change less than 50
Source: www.projectionscentral.com, State Occupational Projections, 2020–2022 Short-Term Projections

TAXES

State Corporate Income Tax Rates

State	Tax Rate (%)	Income Brackets ($)	Num. of Brackets	Financial Institution Tax Rate (%)[a]	Federal Income Tax Ded.
Georgia	5.75	Flat rate	1	5.75	No

Note: Tax rates as of January 1, 2021; (a) Rates listed are the corporate income tax rate applied to financial institutions or excise taxes based on income. Some states have other taxes based upon the value of deposits or shares.
Source: Federation of Tax Administrators, State Corporate Income Tax Rates, January 1, 2021

State Individual Income Tax Rates

State	Tax Rate (%)	Income Brackets ($)	Personal Exemptions ($) Single	Personal Exemptions ($) Married	Personal Exemptions ($) Depend.	Standard Ded. ($) Single	Standard Ded. ($) Married
Georgia	1.0 - 5.75	750 - 7,001 (i)	2,700	7,400	3,000	4,600	6,000

Note: Tax rates as of January 1, 2021; Local- and county-level taxes are not included; Federal income tax is not deductible on state income tax returns; (i) The Georgia income brackets reported are for single individuals. For married couples filing jointly, the same tax rates apply to income brackets ranging from $1,000, to $10,000.
Source: Federation of Tax Administrators, State Individual Income Tax Rates, January 1, 2021

Various State Sales and Excise Tax Rates

State	State Sales Tax (%)	Gasoline[1] (¢/gal.)	Cigarette[2] ($/pack)	Spirits[3] ($/gal.)	Wine[4] ($/gal.)	Beer[5] ($/gal.)	Recreational Marijuana (%)
Georgia	4	33.96	0.37	3.79	1.51	0.48	Not legal

Note: All tax rates as of January 1, 2021; (1) The American Petroleum Institute has developed a methodology for determining the average tax rate on a gallon of fuel. Rates may include any of the following: excise taxes, environmental fees, storage tank fees, other fees or taxes, general sales tax, and local taxes; (2) The federal excise tax of $1.0066 per pack and local taxes are not included; (3) Rates are those applicable to off-premise sales of 40% alcohol by volume (a.b.v.) distilled spirits in 750ml containers. Local excise taxes are excluded; (4) Rates are those applicable to off-premise sales of 11% a.b.v. non-carbonated wine in 750ml containers; (5) Rates are those applicable to off-premise sales of 4.7% a.b.v. beer in 12 ounce containers.
Source: Tax Foundation, 2021 Facts & Figures: How Does Your State Compare?

State Business Tax Climate Index Rankings

State	Overall Rank	Corporate Tax Rank	Individual Income Tax Rank	Sales Tax Rank	Property Tax Rank	Unemployment Insurance Tax Rank
Georgia	31	7	36	27	24	39

Note: The index is a measure of how each state's tax laws affect economic performance. The lower the rank, the more favorable a state's tax system is for business. States without a given tax are given a ranking of 1. The scores/rankings for the District of Columbia do not affect other states. The 2021 index represents the tax climate as of July 1, 2020.
Source: Tax Foundation, State Business Tax Climate Index 2021

TRANSPORTATION

Means of Transportation to Work

Area	Car/Truck/Van Drove Alone	Car/Truck/Van Carpooled	Public Transportation Bus	Public Transportation Subway	Public Transportation Railroad	Bicycle	Walked	Other Means	Worked at Home
City	72.0	11.0	4.4	0.1	0.0	1.7	4.7	1.9	4.2
MSA[1]	79.5	9.7	1.8	0.1	0.0	0.8	2.4	1.6	4.2
U.S.	76.3	9.0	2.4	1.9	0.6	0.5	2.7	1.4	5.2

Note: Figures are percentages and cover workers 16 years of age and older; (1) Figures cover the Savannah, GA Metropolitan Statistical Area
Source: U.S. Census Bureau, 2015-2019 American Community Survey 5-Year Estimates

Travel Time to Work

Area	Less Than 10 Minutes	10 to 19 Minutes	20 to 29 Minutes	30 to 44 Minutes	45 to 59 Minutes	60 to 89 Minutes	90 Minutes or More
City	16.0	40.0	22.3	12.8	4.4	3.2	1.4
MSA[1]	11.0	30.6	24.1	21.2	7.7	4.1	1.3
U.S.	12.2	28.4	20.8	20.8	8.3	6.4	2.9

Note: Note: Figures are percentages and include workers 16 years old and over; (1) Figures cover the Savannah, GA Metropolitan Statistical Area
Source: U.S. Census Bureau, 2015-2019 American Community Survey 5-Year Estimates

Key Congestion Measures

Measure	1982	1992	2002	2012	2017
Annual Hours of Delay, Total (000)	n/a	n/a	n/a	n/a	10,021
Annual Hours of Delay, Per Auto Commuter	n/a	n/a	n/a	n/a	35
Annual Congestion Cost, Total (million $)	n/a	n/a	n/a	n/a	206
Annual Congestion Cost, Per Auto Commuter ($)	n/a	n/a	n/a	n/a	713

Note: n/a not available
Source: Texas A&M Transportation Institute, 2019 Urban Mobility Report

Freeway Travel Time Index

Measure	1982	1987	1992	1997	2002	2007	2012	2017
Urban Area Index[1]	n/a	n/a	n/a	n/a	n/a	n/a	n/a	1.12
Urban Area Rank[1,2]	n/a	n/a	n/a	n/a	n/a	n/a	n/a	n/a

Note: Freeway Travel Time Index—the ratio of travel time in the peak period to the travel time at free-flow conditions. For example, a value of 1.30 indicates a 20-minute free-flow trip takes 26 minutes in the peak (20 minutes x 1.30 = 26 minutes); (1) Covers the Savannah GA urban area; (2) Rank is based on 101 larger urban areas (#1 = highest travel time index); n/a not available
Source: Texas A&M Transportation Institute, 2019 Urban Mobility Report

Public Transportation

Agency Name / Mode of Transportation	Vehicles Operated in Maximum Service[1]	Annual Unlinked Passenger Trips[2] (in thous.)	Annual Passenger Miles[3] (in thous.)
Chatham Area Transit Authority (CAT)			
Bus (directly operated)	49	3,168.8	10,710.5
Demand Response (directly operated)	29	111.8	1,442.3
Demand Response (purchased transportation)	3	1.2	8.1
Ferryboat (directly operated)	2	787.5	299.2

Note: (1) Number of revenue vehicles operated by the given mode and type of service to meet the annual maximum service requirement. This is the revenue vehicle count during the peak season of the year; on the week and day that maximum service is provided. Vehicles operated in maximum service (VOMS) exclude atypical days and one-time special events; (2) Number of passengers who boarded public transportation vehicles. Passengers are counted each time they board a vehicle no matter how many vehicles they use to travel from their origin to their destination. (3) Sum of the distances ridden by all passengers during the entire fiscal year.
Source: Federal Transit Administration, National Transit Database, 2019

Air Transportation

Airport Name and Code / Type of Service	Passenger Airlines[1]	Passenger Enplanements	Freight Carriers[2]	Freight (lbs)
Savannah International (SAV)				
Domestic service (U.S. carriers - 2020)	20	579,503	7	6,515,333
International service (U.S. carriers - 2019)	1	4	0	0

Note: (1) Includes all U.S.-based major, minor and commuter airlines that carried at least one passenger during the year; (2) Includes all U.S.-based airlines and freight carriers that transported at least one pound of freight during the year.
Source: Bureau of Transportation Statistics, The Intermodal Transportation Database, Air Carriers: T-100 Domestic Market (U.S. Carriers), 2020; Bureau of Transportation Statistics, The Intermodal Transportation Database, Air Carriers: T-100 International Market (U.S. Carriers), 2019

BUSINESSES

Major Business Headquarters

Company Name	Industry	Fortune[1]	Forbes[2]
Colonial Group	Oil & Gas Operations	-	180

Note: (1) Companies that produce a 10-K are ranked 1 to 500 based on 2019 revenue; (2) All private companies with at least $2 billion in annual revenue through the end of their most current fiscal year are ranked 1 to 219; companies listed are headquartered in the city; dashes indicate no ranking
Source: Fortune, "Fortune 500," June/July 2020; Forbes, "America's Largest Private Companies," 2020

Living Environment

COST OF LIVING

Cost of Living Index

Composite Index	Groceries	Housing	Utilities	Transportation	Health Care	Misc. Goods/Services
89.0	93.8	64.9	95.6	99.6	108.2	99.1

Note: The Cost of Living Index measures regional differences in the cost of consumer goods and services, excluding taxes and non-consumer expenditures, for professional and managerial households in the top income quintile. It is based on more than 50,000 prices covering almost 60 different items for which prices are collected three times a year by chambers of commerce, economic development organizations or university applied economic centers in each participating urban area. The numbers shown should be read as a percentage above or below the national average of 100. For example, a value of 115.4 in the groceries column indicates that grocery prices are 15.4% higher than the national average. Small differences in the index numbers should not be interpreted as significant; Figures cover the Savannah GA urban area.
Source: The Council for Community and Economic Research, Cost of Living Index, 2020

Grocery Prices

Area[1]	T-Bone Steak ($/pound)	Frying Chicken ($/pound)	Whole Milk ($/half gal.)	Eggs ($/dozen)	Orange Juice ($/64 oz.)	Coffee ($/11.5 oz.)
City[2]	11.65	1.51	1.76	1.50	3.22	3.92
Avg.	11.78	1.39	2.05	1.47	3.57	4.34
Min.	8.03	0.94	1.03	0.74	2.94	3.02
Max.	15.86	2.65	4.31	3.77	5.44	8.69

Note: (1) Values for the local area are compared with the average, minimum and maximum values for all 284 areas in the Cost of Living Index; (2) Figures cover the Savannah GA urban area; **T-Bone Steak** (price per pound); **Frying Chicken** (price per pound, whole fryer); **Whole Milk** (half gallon carton); **Eggs** (price per dozen, Grade A, large); **Orange Juice** (64 oz. Tropicana or Florida Natural); **Coffee** (11.5 oz. can, vacuum-packed, Maxwell House, Hills Bros, or Folgers).
Source: The Council for Community and Economic Research, Cost of Living Index, 2020

Housing and Utility Costs

Area[1]	New Home Price ($)	Apartment Rent ($/month)	All Electric ($/month)	Part Electric ($/month)	Other Energy ($/month)	Telephone ($/month)
City[2]	218,111	905	155.12	-	-	182.20
Avg.	368,594	1,168	170.86	100.47	65.28	184.30
Min.	190,567	502	91.58	31.42	26.08	169.60
Max.	2,227,806	4,738	470.38	280.31	280.06	206.50

Note: (1) Values for the local area are compared with the average, minimum and maximum values for all 284 areas in the Cost of Living Index; (2) Figures cover the Savannah GA urban area; **New Home Price** (2,400 sf living area, 8,000 sf lot, in urban area with full utilities); **Apartment Rent** (950 sf 2 bedroom/1.5 or 2 bath, unfurnished, excluding all utilities except water); **All Electric** (average monthly cost for an all-electric home); **Part Electric** (average monthly cost for a part-electric home); **Other Energy** (average monthly cost for natural gas, fuel oil, coal, wood, and any other forms of energy except electricity); **Telephone** (price includes the base monthly rate plus taxes and fees for three lines of mobile phone service).
Source: The Council for Community and Economic Research, Cost of Living Index, 2020

Health Care, Transportation, and Other Costs

Area[1]	Doctor ($/visit)	Dentist ($/visit)	Optometrist ($/visit)	Gasoline ($/gallon)	Beauty Salon ($/visit)	Men's Shirt ($)
City[2]	109.21	127.37	93.79	2.10	35.80	25.61
Avg.	115.44	99.32	108.10	2.21	39.27	31.37
Min.	36.68	59.00	51.36	1.71	19.00	11.00
Max.	219.00	153.10	250.97	3.46	82.05	58.33

Note: (1) Values for the local area are compared with the average, minimum and maximum values for all 284 areas in the Cost of Living Index; (2) Figures cover the Savannah GA urban area; **Doctor** (general practitioners routine exam of an established patient); **Dentist** (adult teeth cleaning and periodic oral examination); **Optometrist** (full vision eye exam for established adult patient); **Gasoline** (one gallon regular unleaded, national brand, including all taxes, cash price at self-service pump if available); **Beauty Salon** (woman's shampoo, trim, and blow-dry); **Men's Shirt** (cotton/polyester dress shirt, pinpoint weave, long sleeves).
Source: The Council for Community and Economic Research, Cost of Living Index, 2020

HOUSING

Homeownership Rate

Area	2012 (%)	2013 (%)	2014 (%)	2015 (%)	2016 (%)	2017 (%)	2018 (%)	2019 (%)	2020 (%)
MSA[1]	n/a	n/a	n/a	n/a	n/a	n/a	n/a	n/a	n/a
U.S.	65.4	65.1	64.5	63.7	63.4	63.9	64.4	64.6	66.6

Note: (1) Figures cover the Savannah, GA Metropolitan Statistical Area; n/a not available
Source: U.S. Census Bureau, Housing Vacancies and Homeownership Annual Statistics: 2012-2020

House Price Index (HPI)

Area	National Ranking[2]	Quarterly Change (%)	One-Year Change (%)	Five-Year Change (%)	Since 1991Q1 (%)
MSA[1]	214	0.50	4.40	33.56	221.18
U.S.[3]	–	3.81	10.77	38.99	205.12

Note: The HPI is a weighted repeat sales index. It measures average price changes in repeat sales or refinancings on the same properties. This information is obtained by reviewing repeat mortgage transactions on single-family properties whose mortgages have been purchased or securitized by Fannie Mae or Freddie Mac since January 1975; (1) Figures cover the Savannah, GA Metropolitan Statistical Area; (2) Rankings are based on annual percentage change for all metro areas containing at least 15,000 transactions over the last 10 years and ranges from 1 to 253; (3) figures based on a weighted average of Census Division estimates using a seasonally adjusted, purchase-only index; all figures are for the period ending December 31, 2020
Source: Federal Housing Finance Agency, Change in Metropolitan Area House Price Indexes, April 7, 2021

Median Single-Family Home Prices

Area	2018	2019	2020p	Percent Change 2019 to 2020
MSA[1]	n/a	n/a	n/a	n/a
U.S. Average	261.6	274.6	299.9	9.2

Note: Figures are median sales prices of existing single-family homes in thousands of dollars; (p) preliminary; n/a not available; (1) Figures cover the Savannah, GA Metropolitan Statistical Area
Source: National Association of Realtors, Median Sales Price of Existing Single-Family Homes for Metropolitan Areas, 4th Quarter 2020

Qualifying Income Based on Median Sales Price of Existing Single-Family Homes

Area	With 5% Down ($)	With 10% Down ($)	With 20% Down ($)
MSA[1]	n/a	n/a	n/a
U.S. Average	59,266	56,147	49,908

Note: Figures are preliminary; Qualifying income is based on a mortgage rate of 2.81%. Monthly principal and interest payment is limited to 25% of income; n/a not available; (1) Figures cover the Savannah, GA Metropolitan Statistical Area
Source: National Association of Realtors, Qualifying Income Based on Median Sales Price of Existing Single-Family Homes for Metropolitan Areas, 4th Quarter 2020

Home Value Distribution

Area	Under $50,000	$50,000 -$99,999	$100,000 -$149,999	$150,000 -$199,999	$200,000 -$299,999	$300,000 -$499,999	$500,000 -$999,999	$1,000,000 or more
City	6.1	20.2	20.4	19.5	18.7	9.4	4.6	1.1
MSA[1]	5.7	11.2	17.1	19.2	23.1	14.9	7.1	1.6
U.S.	6.9	12.0	13.3	14.0	19.6	19.3	11.4	3.4

Note: Figures are percentages and cover owner-occupied housing units; (1) Figures cover the Savannah, GA Metropolitan Statistical Area
Source: U.S. Census Bureau, 2015-2019 American Community Survey 5-Year Estimates

Year Housing Structure Built

Area	2010 or Later	2000 -2009	1990 -1999	1980 -1989	1970 -1979	1960 -1969	1950 -1959	1940 -1949	Before 1940	Median Year
City	6.3	11.3	7.4	9.8	12.7	12.6	15.0	8.1	16.7	1968
MSA[1]	9.0	20.7	16.3	13.8	12.0	7.8	8.1	4.3	8.0	1987
U.S.	5.2	14.0	13.9	13.4	15.2	10.6	10.3	4.9	12.6	1978

Note: Figures are percentages except for Median Year; Note: (1) Figures cover the Savannah, GA Metropolitan Statistical Area
Source: U.S. Census Bureau, 2015-2019 American Community Survey 5-Year Estimates

Gross Monthly Rent

Area	Under $500	$500 -$999	$1,000 -$1,499	$1,500 -$1,999	$2,000 -$2,499	$2,500 -$2,999	$3,000 and up	Median ($)
City	10.0	38.1	39.8	8.9	1.8	0.5	1.0	1,019
MSA[1]	7.3	33.4	43.3	12.0	2.8	0.4	0.8	1,086
U.S.	9.4	36.2	30.0	14.0	5.6	2.4	2.4	1,062

Note: Figures are percentages except for Median; Gross rent is the contract rent plus the estimated average monthly cost of utilities (electricity, gas, and water and sewer) and fuels (oil, coal, kerosene, wood, etc.) if these are paid by the renter (or paid for the renter by someone else); (1) Figures cover the Savannah, GA Metropolitan Statistical Area
Source: U.S. Census Bureau, 2015-2019 American Community Survey 5-Year Estimates

HEALTH

Health Risk Factors

Category	MSA[1] (%)	U.S. (%)
Adults aged 18–64 who have any kind of health care coverage	n/a	87.3
Adults who reported being in good or better health	n/a	82.4
Adults who have been told they have high blood cholesterol	n/a	33.0
Adults who have been told they have high blood pressure	n/a	32.3
Adults who are current smokers	n/a	17.1
Adults who currently use E-cigarettes	n/a	4.6
Adults who currently use chewing tobacco, snuff, or snus	n/a	4.0
Adults who are heavy drinkers[2]	n/a	6.3
Adults who are binge drinkers[3]	n/a	17.4
Adults who are overweight (BMI 25.0 - 29.9)	n/a	35.3
Adults who are obese (BMI 30.0 - 99.8)	n/a	31.3
Adults who participated in any physical activities in the past month	n/a	74.4
Adults who always or nearly always wears a seat belt	n/a	94.3

Note: n/a not available; (1) Figures cover the Savannah, GA Metropolitan Statistical Area; (2) Heavy drinkers are classified as adult men having more than 14 drinks per week and adult women having more than 7 drinks per week; (3) Binge drinkers are classified as males having five or more drinks on one occasion or females having four or more drinks on one occasion
Source: Centers for Disease Control and Prevention, Behavioral Risk Factor Surveillance System, SMART: Selected Metropolitan Area Risk Trends, 2017

Acute and Chronic Health Conditions

Category	MSA[1] (%)	U.S. (%)
Adults who have ever been told they had a heart attack	n/a	4.2
Adults who have ever been told they have angina or coronary heart disease	n/a	3.9
Adults who have ever been told they had a stroke	n/a	3.0
Adults who have ever been told they have asthma	n/a	14.2
Adults who have ever been told they have arthritis	n/a	24.9
Adults who have ever been told they have diabetes[2]	n/a	10.5
Adults who have ever been told they had skin cancer	n/a	6.2
Adults who have ever been told they had any other types of cancer	n/a	7.1
Adults who have ever been told they have COPD	n/a	6.5
Adults who have ever been told they have kidney disease	n/a	3.0
Adults who have ever been told they have a form of depression	n/a	20.5

Note: n/a not available; (1) Figures cover the Savannah, GA Metropolitan Statistical Area; (2) Figures do not include pregnancy-related, borderline, or pre-diabetes
Source: Centers for Disease Control and Prevention, Behavioral Risk Factor Surveillance System, SMART: Selected Metropolitan Area Risk Trends, 2017

Health Screening and Vaccination Rates

Category	MSA[1] (%)	U.S. (%)
Adults aged 65+ who have had flu shot within the past year	n/a	60.7
Adults aged 65+ who have ever had a pneumonia vaccination	n/a	75.4
Adults who have ever been tested for HIV	n/a	36.1
Adults who have ever had the shingles or zoster vaccine?	n/a	28.9
Adults who have had their blood cholesterol checked within the last five years	n/a	85.9

Note: n/a not available; (1) Figures cover the Savannah, GA Metropolitan Statistical Area.
Source: Centers for Disease Control and Prevention, Behavioral Risk Factor Surveillance System, SMART: Selected Metropolitan Area Risk Trends, 2017

Disability Status

Category	MSA[1] (%)	U.S. (%)
Adults who reported being deaf	n/a	6.7
Are you blind or have serious difficulty seeing, even when wearing glasses?	n/a	4.5
Are you limited in any way in any of your usual activities due of arthritis?	n/a	12.9
Do you have difficulty doing errands alone?	n/a	6.8
Do you have difficulty dressing or bathing?	n/a	3.6
Do you have serious difficulty concentrating/remembering/making decisions?	n/a	10.7
Do you have serious difficulty walking or climbing stairs?	n/a	13.6

Note: n/a not available; (1) Figures cover the Savannah, GA Metropolitan Statistical Area.
Source: Centers for Disease Control and Prevention, Behavioral Risk Factor Surveillance System, SMART: Selected Metropolitan Area Risk Trends, 2017

Mortality Rates for the Top 10 Causes of Death in the U.S.

ICD-10[a] Sub-Chapter	ICD-10[a] Code	Age-Adjusted Mortality Rate[1] per 100,000 population County[2]	U.S.
Malignant neoplasms	C00-C97	144.4	149.2
Ischaemic heart diseases	I20-I25	53.1	90.5
Other forms of heart disease	I30-I51	60.1	52.2
Chronic lower respiratory diseases	J40-J47	43.0	39.6
Other degenerative diseases of the nervous system	G30-G31	46.6	37.6
Cerebrovascular diseases	I60-I69	39.2	37.2
Other external causes of accidental injury	W00-X59	29.1	36.1
Organic, including symptomatic, mental disorders	F01-F09	21.8	29.4
Hypertensive diseases	I10-I15	66.8	24.1
Diabetes mellitus	E10-E14	16.9	21.5

Note: (a) ICD-10 = International Classification of Diseases 10th Revision; (1) Mortality rates are a three-year average covering 2017-2019; (2) Figures cover Chatham County.
Source: Centers for Disease Control and Prevention, National Center for Health Statistics. Underlying Cause of Death 1999-2019 on CDC WONDER Online Database

Mortality Rates for Selected Causes of Death

ICD-10[a] Sub-Chapter	ICD-10[a] Code	Age-Adjusted Mortality Rate[1] per 100,000 population County[2]	U.S.
Assault	X85-Y09	11.3	6.0
Diseases of the liver	K70-K76	13.4	14.4
Human immunodeficiency virus (HIV) disease	B20-B24	5.3	1.5
Influenza and pneumonia	J09-J18	15.2	13.8
Intentional self-harm	X60-X84	17.6	14.1
Malnutrition	E40-E46	3.6	2.3
Obesity and other hyperalimentation	E65-E68	Unreliable	2.1
Renal failure	N17-N19	18.8	12.6
Transport accidents	V01-V99	10.8	12.3
Viral hepatitis	B15-B19	Unreliable	1.2

Note: (a) ICD-10 = International Classification of Diseases 10th Revision; (1) Mortality rates are a three-year average covering 2017-2019; (2) Figures cover Chatham County; Data are suppressed when the data meet the criteria for confidentiality constraints; Mortality rates are flagged as unreliable when the rate would be calculated with a numerator of 20 or less.
Source: Centers for Disease Control and Prevention, National Center for Health Statistics. Underlying Cause of Death 1999-2019 on CDC WONDER Online Database

Health Insurance Coverage

Area	With Health Insurance	With Private Health Insurance	With Public Health Insurance	Without Health Insurance	Population Under Age 19 Without Health Insurance
City	83.0	57.3	34.5	17.0	7.7
MSA[1]	87.0	67.6	30.1	13.0	6.2
U.S.	91.2	67.9	35.1	8.8	5.1

Note: Figures are percentages that cover the civilian noninstitutionalized population; (1) Figures cover the Savannah, GA Metropolitan Statistical Area
Source: U.S. Census Bureau, 2015-2019 American Community Survey 5-Year Estimates

Number of Medical Professionals

Area	MDs[3]	DOs[3,4]	Dentists	Podiatrists	Chiropractors	Optometrists
County[1] (number)	1,018	52	202	20	55	39
County[1] (rate[2])	352.0	18.0	69.8	6.9	19.0	13.5
U.S. (rate[2])	282.9	22.7	71.2	6.2	28.1	16.9

13051
Note: Data as of 2019 unless noted; (1) Data covers Chatham County; (2) Rate per 100,000 population; (3) Data as of 2018 and includes all active, non-federal physicians; (4) Doctor of Osteopathic Medicine
Source: U.S. Department of Health and Human Services, Health Resources and Services Administration, Bureau of Health Professions, Area Resource File (ARF) 2019-2020

EDUCATION

Public School District Statistics

District Name	Schls	Pupils	Pupil/Teacher Ratio	Minority Pupils[1] (%)	Free Lunch Eligible[2] (%)	IEP[3] (%)
Savannah-Chatham County	57	37,576	14.1	75.2	57.5	12.2

Note: Table includes school districts with 2,000 or more students; (1) Percentage of students that are not non-Hispanic white; (2) Percentage of students that are eligible for the free lunch program; (3) Percentage of students that have an Individualized Education Program.
Source: U.S. Department of Education, National Center for Education Statistics, Common Core of Data, Local Education Agency (School District) Universe Survey: School Year 2018-2019; U.S. Department of Education, National Center for Education Statistics, Common Core of Data, Public Elementary/Secondary School Universe Survey: School Year 2018-2019

Best High Schools

According to *U.S. News*, Savannah is home to one of the top 500 high schools in the U.S.: **Savannah Arts Academy** (#241). Nearly 18,000 public, magnet and charter schools were ranked based on their performance on state assessments and how well they prepare students for college. *U.S. News & World Report, "Best High Schools 2020"*

Highest Level of Education

Area	Less than H.S.	H.S. Diploma	Some College, No Deg.	Associate Degree	Bachelor's Degree	Master's Degree	Prof. School Degree	Doctorate Degree
City	12.4	26.8	25.9	6.7	17.8	7.6	1.6	1.2
MSA[1]	10.2	26.3	24.2	7.9	19.5	8.4	2.2	1.3
U.S.	12.0	27.0	20.4	8.5	19.8	8.8	2.1	1.4

Note: Figures cover persons age 25 and over; (1) Figures cover the Savannah, GA Metropolitan Statistical Area
Source: U.S. Census Bureau, 2015-2019 American Community Survey 5-Year Estimates

Educational Attainment by Race

Area	High School Graduate or Higher (%)					Bachelor's Degree or Higher (%)				
	Total	White	Black	Asian	Hisp.[2]	Total	White	Black	Asian	Hisp.[2]
City	87.6	93.0	83.3	85.8	79.4	28.2	42.9	15.5	46.7	27.1
MSA[1]	89.8	92.0	86.2	84.2	81.2	31.5	36.7	19.8	45.2	26.2
U.S.	88.0	89.9	86.0	87.1	68.7	32.1	33.5	21.6	54.3	16.4

Note: Figures shown cover persons 25 years old and over; (1) Figures cover the Savannah, GA Metropolitan Statistical Area; (2) People of Hispanic origin can be of any race
Source: U.S. Census Bureau, 2015-2019 American Community Survey 5-Year Estimates

School Enrollment by Grade and Control

Area	Preschool (%)		Kindergarten (%)		Grades 1 - 4 (%)		Grades 5 - 8 (%)		Grades 9 - 12 (%)	
	Public	Private	Public	Private	Public	Private	Public	Private	Public	Private
City	67.6	32.4	93.0	7.0	90.1	9.9	91.0	9.0	89.6	10.4
MSA[1]	58.3	41.7	92.2	7.8	86.1	13.9	87.8	12.2	85.9	14.1
U.S.	59.1	40.9	87.6	12.4	89.5	10.5	89.4	10.6	90.1	9.9

Note: Figures shown cover persons 3 years old and over; (1) Figures cover the Savannah, GA Metropolitan Statistical Area
Source: U.S. Census Bureau, 2015-2019 American Community Survey 5-Year Estimates

Higher Education

Four-Year Colleges			Two-Year Colleges			Medical Schools[1]	Law Schools[2]	Voc/Tech[3]
Public	Private Non-profit	Private For-profit	Public	Private Non-profit	Private For-profit			
1	1	3	1	0	0	0	0	1

Note: Figures cover institutions located within the city limits and include main campuses only; (1) includes schools accredited by the Liaison Committee on Medical Education and the American Osteopathic Association's Commission on Osteopathic College Accreditation; (2) includes ABA-accredited schools, schools with provisional ABA accreditation, and state accredited schools; (3) includes all schools with programs that are less than 2 years.
Source: National Center for Education Statistics, Integrated Postsecondary Education System (IPEDS), 2019-20; Wikipedia, List of Medical Schools in the United States, accessed April 2, 2021; Wikipedia, List of Law Schools in the United States, accessed April 2, 2021

EMPLOYERS

Major Employers

Company Name	Industry
Ceres Marine Terminals	Marine cargo handling
Coastal Home Care	Medical care
Colonial Group	Petroleum products
CSX	Railroad
Dollar Tree	Retail
Effingham County Hospital Authority	Hospital
Georgia Power Company	Electric utility
Georgia Regional Hospital	Hospital
Goodwill Industries of the Coastal Empire	Adult vocational rehabilitation
Kroger Company	Retail food
Marine Terminals Corp.	Marine cargo handling
McDonalds	Restaurants
Memorial University Medical Center	Hospital
Publix Supermarkets	Retail grocery
SouthCoast Health	Healthcare services
SSA Cooper	Marine cargo handling
St. Joseph's/Candler	Hospital
The Landings Club	Private membership club
TMX Finance	Financial services
Trace Staffing Solutions	Employment services
UTC Overseas	Logistics solutions
Wal-Mart Stores	Retail

Note: Companies shown are located within the Savannah, GA Metropolitan Statistical Area.
Source: Hoovers.com; Wikipedia

PUBLIC SAFETY

Crime Rate

Area	All Crimes	Violent Crimes				Property Crimes		
		Murder	Rape[3]	Robbery	Aggrav. Assault	Burglary	Larceny-Theft	Motor Vehicle Theft
City	2,865.5	11.6	35.1	110.2	248.5	364.9	1,824.4	270.8
Suburbs[1]	3,497.3	5.3	37.2	67.1	245.2	497.1	2,366.1	279.1
Metro[2]	3,107.5	9.2	35.9	93.7	247.2	415.6	2,032.0	274.0
U.S.	2,593.1	5.0	44.0	86.1	248.2	378.0	1,601.6	230.2

Note: Figures are crimes per 100,000 population; (1) All areas within the metro area that are located outside the city limits; (2) Figures cover the Savannah, GA Metropolitan Statistical Area; (3) All figures shown were reported using the revised Uniform Crime Reporting (UCR) definition of rape.
Source: FBI Uniform Crime Reports, 2018 (data for 2019 was not available)

Hate Crimes

Area	Number of Quarters Reported	Number of Incidents per Bias Motivation					
		Race/Ethnicity/ Ancestry	Religion	Sexual Orientation	Disability	Gender	Gender Identity
City	3	0	0	0	0	0	0
U.S.	4	3,963	1,521	1,195	157	69	198

Source: Federal Bureau of Investigation, Hate Crime Statistics 2019

Identity Theft Consumer Reports

Area	Reports	Reports per 100,000 Population	Rank[2]
MSA[1]	1,400	356	94
U.S.	1,387,615	423	-

Note: (1) Figures cover the Savannah, GA Metropolitan Statistical Area; (2) Rank ranges from 1 to 391 where 1 indicates greatest number of identity theft reports per 100,000 population
Source: Federal Trade Commission, Consumer Sentinel Network Data Book 2020

Fraud and Other Consumer Reports

Area	Reports	Reports per 100,000 Population	Rank[2]
MSA[1]	3,750	953	30
U.S.	3,385,133	1,031	-

Note: (1) Figures cover the Savannah, GA Metropolitan Statistical Area; (2) Rank ranges from 1 to 391 where 1 indicates greatest number of fraud and other consumer reports per 100,000 population
Source: Federal Trade Commission, Consumer Sentinel Network Data Book 2020

POLITICS

2020 Presidential Election Results

Area	Biden	Trump	Jorgensen	Hawkins	Other
Chatham County	58.6	39.9	1.4	0.0	0.0
U.S.	51.3	46.8	1.2	0.3	0.5

Note: Results are percentages and may not add to 100% due to rounding
Source: Dave Leip's Atlas of U.S. Presidential Elections

SPORTS

Professional Sports Teams

Team Name	League	Year Established
No teams are located in the metro area		

Source: Wikipedia, Major Professional Sports Teams of the United States and Canada, April 6, 2021

CLIMATE

Average and Extreme Temperatures

Temperature	Jan	Feb	Mar	Apr	May	Jun	Jul	Aug	Sep	Oct	Nov	Dec	Yr.
Extreme High (°F)	84	86	91	95	100	104	105	104	98	97	89	83	105
Average High (°F)	60	64	70	78	84	89	92	90	86	78	70	62	77
Average Temp. (°F)	49	53	59	66	74	79	82	81	77	68	59	52	67
Average Low (°F)	38	41	48	54	62	69	72	72	68	57	47	40	56
Extreme Low (°F)	3	14	20	32	39	51	61	57	43	28	15	9	3

Note: Figures cover the years 1950-1995
Source: National Climatic Data Center, International Station Meteorological Climate Summary, 9/96

Average Precipitation/Snowfall/Humidity

Precip./Humidity	Jan	Feb	Mar	Apr	May	Jun	Jul	Aug	Sep	Oct	Nov	Dec	Yr.
Avg. Precip. (in.)	3.5	3.1	3.9	3.2	4.2	5.6	6.8	7.2	5.0	2.9	2.2	2.7	50.3
Avg. Snowfall (in.)	Tr	Tr	Tr	0	0	0	0	0	0	Tr	Tr	Tr	Tr
Avg. Rel. Hum. 7am (%)	83	82	83	84	85	87	88	91	91	88	86	83	86
Avg. Rel. Hum. 4pm (%)	53	50	49	48	52	58	61	63	62	55	53	54	55

Note: Figures cover the years 1950-1995; Tr = Trace amounts (<0.05 in. of rain; <0.5 in. of snow)
Source: National Climatic Data Center, International Station Meteorological Climate Summary, 9/96

Weather Conditions

Temperature			Daytime Sky			Precipitation		Thunder-storms
10°F & below	32°F & below	90°F & above	Clear	Partly cloudy	Cloudy	0.01 inch or more precip.	0.1 inch or more snow/ice	
< 1	29	70	97	155	113	111	< 1	63

Note: Figures are average number of days per year and cover the years 1950-1995
Source: National Climatic Data Center, International Station Meteorological Climate Summary, 9/96

HAZARDOUS WASTE

Superfund Sites

The Savannah, GA metro area has no sites on the EPA's Superfund Final National Priorities List. There are a total of 1,375 Superfund sites with a status of proposed or final on the list in the U.S. *U.S. Environmental Protection Agency, National Priorities List, April 7, 2021*

AIR QUALITY

Air Quality Trends: Ozone

	1990	1995	2000	2005	2010	2015	2016	2017	2018	2019
MSA[1]	n/a	n/a	n/a	n/a	n/a	n/a	n/a	n/a	n/a	n/a
U.S.	0.088	0.089	0.082	0.080	0.073	0.068	0.069	0.068	0.069	0.065

Note: (1) Data covers the Savannah, GA Metropolitan Statistical Area; n/a not available. The values shown are the composite ozone concentration averages among trend sites based on the highest fourth daily maximum 8-hour concentration in parts per million. These trends are based on sites having an adequate record of monitoring data during the trend period. Data from exceptional events are included.
Source: U.S. Environmental Protection Agency, Air Quality Monitoring Information, "Air Quality Trends by City, 1990-2019"

Air Quality Index

Area	Percent of Days when Air Quality was...[2]					AQI Statistics[2]	
	Good	Moderate	Unhealthy for Sensitive Groups	Unhealthy	Very Unhealthy	Maximum	Median
MSA[1]	80.8	19.2	0.0	0.0	0.0	87	39

Note: (1) Data covers the Savannah, GA Metropolitan Statistical Area; (2) Based on 365 days with AQI data in 2019. Air Quality Index (AQI) is an index for reporting daily air quality. EPA calculates the AQI for five major air pollutants regulated by the Clean Air Act: ground-level ozone, particle pollution (aka particulate matter), carbon monoxide, sulfur dioxide, and nitrogen dioxide. The AQI runs from 0 to 500. The higher the AQI value, the greater the level of air pollution and the greater the health concern. There are six AQI categories: "Good" AQI is between 0 and 50. Air quality is considered satisfactory; "Moderate" AQI is between 51 and 100. Air quality is acceptable; "Unhealthy for Sensitive Groups" When AQI values are between 101 and 150, members of sensitive groups may experience health effects; "Unhealthy" When AQI values are between 151 and 200 everyone may begin to experience health effects; "Very Unhealthy" AQI values between 201 and 300 trigger a health alert; "Hazardous" AQI values over 300 trigger warnings of emergency conditions (not shown).
Source: U.S. Environmental Protection Agency, Air Quality Index Report, 2019

Air Quality Index Pollutants

Area	Percent of Days when AQI Pollutant was...[2]					
	Carbon Monoxide	Nitrogen Dioxide	Ozone	Sulfur Dioxide	Particulate Matter 2.5	Particulate Matter 10
MSA[1]	0.0	0.0	40.0	15.9	44.1	0.0

Note: (1) Data covers the Savannah, GA Metropolitan Statistical Area; (2) Based on 365 days with AQI data in 2019. The Air Quality Index (AQI) is an index for reporting daily air quality. EPA calculates the AQI for five major air pollutants regulated by the Clean Air Act: ground-level ozone, particle pollution (also known as particulate matter), carbon monoxide, sulfur dioxide, and nitrogen dioxide. The AQI runs from 0 to 500. The higher the AQI value, the greater the level of air pollution and the greater the health concern.
Source: U.S. Environmental Protection Agency, Air Quality Index Report, 2019

Maximum Air Pollutant Concentrations: Particulate Matter, Ozone, CO and Lead

	Particulate Matter 10 (ug/m^3)	Particulate Matter 2.5 Wtd AM (ug/m^3)	Particulate Matter 2.5 24-Hr (ug/m^3)	Ozone (ppm)	Carbon Monoxide (ppm)	Lead (ug/m^3)
MSA[1] Level	n/a	n/a	n/a	0.060	n/a	n/a
NAAQS[2]	150	15	35	0.075	9	0.15
Met NAAQS[2]	n/a	n/a	n/a	Yes	n/a	n/a

Note: (1) Data covers the Savannah, GA Metropolitan Statistical Area; Data from exceptional events are included; (2) National Ambient Air Quality Standards; ppm = parts per million; ug/m^3 = micrograms per cubic meter; n/a not available.
Concentrations: Particulate Matter 10 (coarse particulate)—highest second maximum 24-hour concentration; Particulate Matter 2.5 Wtd AM (fine particulate)—highest weighted annual mean concentration; Particulate Matter 2.5 24-Hour (fine particulate)—highest 98th percentile 24-hour concentration; Ozone—highest fourth daily maximum 8-hour concentration; Carbon Monoxide—highest second maximum non-overlapping 8-hour concentration; Lead—maximum running 3-month average
Source: U.S. Environmental Protection Agency, Air Quality Monitoring Information, "Air Quality Statistics by City, 2019"

Maximum Air Pollutant Concentrations: Nitrogen Dioxide and Sulfur Dioxide

	Nitrogen Dioxide AM (ppb)	Nitrogen Dioxide 1-Hr (ppb)	Sulfur Dioxide AM (ppb)	Sulfur Dioxide 1-Hr (ppb)	Sulfur Dioxide 24-Hr (ppb)
MSA[1] Level	n/a	n/a	n/a	50	n/a
NAAQS[2]	53	100	30	75	140
Met NAAQS[2]	n/a	n/a	n/a	Yes	n/a

Note: (1) Data covers the Savannah, GA Metropolitan Statistical Area; Data from exceptional events are included; (2) National Ambient Air Quality Standards; ppm = parts per million; ug/m^3 = micrograms per cubic meter; n/a not available.
Concentrations: Nitrogen Dioxide AM—highest arithmetic mean concentration; Nitrogen Dioxide 1-Hr—highest 98th percentile 1-hour daily maximum concentration; Sulfur Dioxide AM—highest annual mean concentration; Sulfur Dioxide 1-Hr—highest 99th percentile 1-hour daily maximum concentration; Sulfur Dioxide 24-Hr—highest second maximum 24-hour concentration
Source: U.S. Environmental Protection Agency, Air Quality Monitoring Information, "Air Quality Statistics by City, 2019"

Tallahassee, Florida

Background

Tallahassee is the capital of Florida, located in the northern panhandle of the state in Leon County. In addition to the state government, the city is primarily known as home to Florida State University, with its 40,000 students and 16 colleges. The presence of top-ranked FSU, as well as other smaller universities, has transformed Tallahassee from a small, rural settlement to a modern metropolis.

After the state of Florida was ceded to United States from Spain in 1821, a governing body alternated meetings between St. Augustine and Pensacola. Eventually a more central, permanent location for the government was established in Tallahassee, which was incorporated in 1824. The word Tallahassee means "old town" in the language of the Creek Native American tribe that inhabited the area during the 18th century.

Florida State University (FSU) was founded in 1851, establishing Tallahassee as a city known for education. During the Civil War, Tallahassee was the only Confederate capital city east of the Mississippi not captured by the Union Army. After the war, much of the industry in the southern United States changed; cotton and tobacco production suffered without slave labor and new industries emerged, including citrus production, cattle ranching and tourism.

The first airport in the city opened in 1929. In 1961, the Tallahassee Regional Airport opened with limited service. In 1989, major passenger service was offered, and in 2000, the terminal was renamed Ivan Monroe Terminal after the first Tallahassee resident to own his own plane and to be the first manager of Dale Mabry Field—the city's original airport, which was adjacent to today's Tallahassee Regional Airport. Other transportation services in the city include the StarMetro bus lines and the CSX railroad.

Economic and population growth in recent decades has created the need for more land in the city, and about seventy-five square miles have been added by voluntary annexation. A program to fund new infrastructure and transportation projects via a one cent sales tax has yielded such public gems as the Capital Cascades Park, comprising the Capital City Amphitheater and the 5.2 mile Capital Cascades Trail.

Today, economic activity in Tallahassee is centered primarily on education and research. In addition to FSU, the city is home to A&M University, the state's only historically black university. In 2014, the 126-year-old institution hired its first woman president, Dr. Elmira Magnum. Tallahassee Community College is home to a 16,000-square foot Advanced Manufacturing Training Center, geared toward high tech and precision manufacturing training, and the Ghazvini Center for Healthcare Education. Other higher education offerings in Tallahassee include campuses of Barry University, Embry Riddle Aeronautical University, and Flagler College, among others.

> The Thanksgiving Turkey Trot went virtual, with proceeds supporting local organizations.

The high-tech industry has grown significantly with companies such as Bing Energy and SunnyLand Solar working with university-based researchers.

Major attractions in the Tallahassee area include the Alfred B. Maclay Gardens State Park, the Florida State Capitol, the Lake Jackson Mounds Archaeological State Park, the Mary Brogan Museum of Art and Science and the Tallahassee Museum.

Unlike most other cities in Florida, Tallahassee experiences four distinct seasons. Despite being located in the northern part of the state, it is generally hotter in the summer than cities in located on the Florida peninsula. The summer season also brings thunderstorms that develop on the Gulf of Mexico. Winters in the city are usually much cooler than in the rest of Florida, with occasional light snow every few years. The city's location near the Gulf of Mexico also means hurricane activity. Tallahassee was hit by Hurricane Kate in 1985, Hurricane Hermine in 2016, Hurricane Michael in 2018, and a damaging tornado early in 2021.

Rankings

General Rankings

- In their seventh annual survey, Livability.com looked at data for more than 1,000 small to mid-sized U.S. cities to determine the rankings for Livability's "Top 100 Best Places to Live" in 2020. Tallahassee ranked #81. Criteria: housing and affordable living; vibrant economy; social and civic engagement; education; demographics; health care options; transportation & infrastructure; and abundant lifestyle amenities. *Livability.com, "Top 100 Best Places to Live 2020" October 2020*

Business/Finance Rankings

- The Tallahassee metro area appeared on the Milken Institute "2021 Best Performing Cities" list. Rank: #123 out of 200 large metro areas (population over 250,000). Criteria: job growth; wage and salary growth; high-tech output growth; housing affordability; household broadband access. *Milken Institute, "Best-Performing Cities 2021," February 16, 2021*
- *Forbes* ranked the 200 most populous metro areas to determine the nation's "Best Places for Business and Careers." The Tallahassee metro area was ranked #103. Criteria: costs (business and living); job growth (past and projected); income growth; quality of life; educational attainment (college and high school); projected economic growth; cultural and leisure opportunities; workplace tolerance laws; net migration patterns. *Forbes, "The Best Places for Business and Careers 2019: Seattle Still On Top," October 30, 2019*

Education Rankings

- Personal finance website *WalletHub* analyzed the 150 largest U.S. metropolitan statistical areas to determine where the most educated Americans are putting their degrees to work. Criteria: education levels; percentage of workers with degrees; education quality and attainment gap; public school quality rankings; quality and enrollment of each metro area's universities. Tallahassee was ranked #17 (#1 = most educated city). *www.WalletHub.com, "Most and Least Educated Cities in America," July 20, 2020*

Environmental Rankings

- Tallahassee was highlighted as one of the cleanest metro areas for ozone air pollution in the U.S. during 2016 through 2018. The list represents cities with no monitored ozone air pollution in unhealthful ranges. *American Lung Association, "State of the Air 2020," April 21, 2020*
- Tallahassee was highlighted as one of the top 98 cleanest metro areas for short-term particle pollution (24-hour PM 2.5) in the U.S. during 2016 through 2018. Monitors in these cities reported no days with unhealthful PM 2.5 levels. *American Lung Association, "State of the Air 2020," April 21, 2020*

Real Estate Rankings

- *WalletHub* compared the most populated U.S. cities to determine which had the best markets for real estate agents. Tallahassee ranked #143 where demand was high and pay was the best. Criteria: sales per agent; annual median wage for real-estate agents; monthly average starting salary for real estate agents; real estate job density and competition; unemployment rate; home turnover rate; housing-market health index; and other relevant metrics. *www.WalletHub.com, "2019's Best Places to Be a Real Estate Agent," April 24, 2019*
- Tallahassee was ranked #82 out of 268 metro areas in terms of housing affordability in 2020 by the National Association of Home Builders (#1 = most affordable). Criteria: the share of homes sold in that area affordable to a family earning the local median income, based on standard mortgage underwriting criteria. *National Association of Home Builders®, NAHB-Wells Fargo Housing Opportunity Index, 4th Quarter 2020*

Safety Rankings

- Allstate ranked the 200 largest cities in America in terms of driver safety. Tallahassee ranked #42. Criteria: internal property damage claims over a two-year period from January 2016 to December 2017. The report helps increase the importance of safety and awareness behind the wheel. *Allstate, "Allstate America's Best Drivers Report, 2019" June 24, 2019*
- The National Insurance Crime Bureau ranked 384 metro areas in the U.S. in terms of per capita rates of vehicle theft. The Tallahassee metro area ranked #106 (#1 = highest rate). Criteria: number of vehicle theft offenses per 100,000 inhabitants in 2019. *National Insurance Crime Bureau, "Hot Spots 2019," July 21, 2020*

Seniors/Retirement Rankings

- From its Best Cities for Successful Aging indexes, the Milken Institute generated rankings for metropolitan areas, weighing data in nine categories—health care, wellness, living arrangements, transportation and convenience, financial characteristics, education, employment, community engagement, and overall livability. The Tallahassee metro area was ranked #123 overall in the small metro area category. *Milken Institute, "Best Cities for Successful Aging, 2017" March 14, 2017*

Sports/Recreation Rankings

- Tallahassee was chosen as one of America's best cities for bicycling. The city ranked #44 out of 50. Criteria: cycling infrastructure that is safe and friendly for all ages; energy and bike culture. The editors evaluated cities with populations of 100,000 or more. *Bicycling, "The 50 Best Bike Cities in America," October 10, 2018*

Women/Minorities Rankings

- Personal finance website *WalletHub* compared more than 180 U.S. cities across two key dimensions, "Hispanic Business-Friendliness" and "Hispanic Purchasing Power," to arrive at the most favorable conditions for Hispanic entrepreneurs. Tallahassee was ranked #124 out of 182. Criteria includes: share of Hispanic-Owned Businesses; Hispanic entrepreneurship rate to median annual income of Hispanics; Small Business-Friendliness score; cost of living; and number of Hispanics with at least a bachelor's degree. *WalletHub.com, "2019's Best Cities for Hispanic Entrepreneurs," May 1, 2019*

Miscellaneous Rankings

- Tallahassee was selected as a 2020 Digital Cities Survey winner. The city ranked #10 in the mid-sized city (125,000 to 249,999 population) category. The survey examined and assessed how city governments are utilizing technology to improve transparency, enhance cybersecurity, and respond to the pandemic. Survey questions focused on ten initiatives: cybersecurity, citizen experience, disaster recovery, business intelligence, IT personnel, data governance, collaboration, infrastructure modernization, cloud computing, and mobile applications. *Center for Digital Government, "2020 Digital Cities Survey," November 10, 2020*

- *WalletHub* compared the 150 most populated U.S. cities to determine their operating efficiency. A "Quality of City Services" score was constructed for each city and then divided by the total budget per capita to reveal which were managed the best. Tallahassee ranked #80. Criteria: financial stability; economy; education; safety; health; infrastructure and pollution. *www.WalletHub.com, "2020's Best- & Worst-Run Cities in America," June 29, 2020*

Business Environment

DEMOGRAPHICS

Population Growth

Area	1990 Census	2000 Census	2010 Census	2019* Estimate	Population Growth (%) 1990-2019	Population Growth (%) 2010-2019
City	128,014	150,624	181,376	191,279	49.4	5.5
MSA[1]	259,096	320,304	367,413	382,197	47.5	4.0
U.S.	248,709,873	281,421,906	308,745,538	324,697,795	30.6	5.2

Note: (1) Figures cover the Tallahassee, FL Metropolitan Statistical Area; (*) 2015-2019 5-year estimated population
Source: U.S. Census Bureau, 1990 Census, Census 2000, Census 2010, 2015-2019 American Community Survey 5-Year Estimates

Household Size

Area	One	Two	Three	Four	Five	Six	Seven or More	Average Household Size
City	35.1	33.1	16.8	10.3	3.6	1.0	0.2	2.30
MSA[1]	30.5	35.3	17.1	11.1	4.3	1.2	0.6	2.40
U.S.	27.9	33.9	15.6	12.9	6.0	2.3	1.4	2.60

Note: (1) Figures cover the Tallahassee, FL Metropolitan Statistical Area
Source: U.S. Census Bureau, 2015-2019 American Community Survey 5-Year Estimates

Race

Area	White Alone[2] (%)	Black Alone[2] (%)	Asian Alone[2] (%)	AIAN[3] Alone[2] (%)	NHOPI[4] Alone[2] (%)	Other Race Alone[2] (%)	Two or More Races (%)
City	56.2	35.0	4.6	0.2	0.0	1.1	2.9
MSA[1]	60.6	32.7	2.7	0.2	0.0	1.3	2.4
U.S.	72.5	12.7	5.5	0.8	0.2	4.9	3.3

Note: (1) Figures cover the Tallahassee, FL Metropolitan Statistical Area; (2) Alone is defined as not being in combination with one or more other races; (3) American Indian and Alaska Native; (4) Native Hawaiian and Other Pacific Islander
Source: U.S. Census Bureau, 2015-2019 American Community Survey 5-Year Estimates

Hispanic or Latino Origin

Area	Total (%)	Mexican (%)	Puerto Rican (%)	Cuban (%)	Other (%)
City	6.7	1.2	1.4	1.3	2.8
MSA[1]	6.6	1.9	1.3	1.0	2.4
U.S.	18.0	11.2	1.7	0.7	4.3

Note: Persons of Hispanic or Latino origin can be of any race; (1) Figures cover the Tallahassee, FL Metropolitan Statistical Area
Source: U.S. Census Bureau, 2015-2019 American Community Survey 5-Year Estimates

Ancestry

Area	German	Irish	English	American	Italian	Polish	French[2]	Scottish	Dutch
City	8.5	8.1	7.8	3.8	3.7	1.8	1.9	2.1	0.7
MSA[1]	8.4	8.2	8.0	5.2	3.3	1.6	1.9	2.3	0.9
U.S.	13.3	9.7	7.2	6.2	5.1	2.8	2.3	1.7	1.2

Note: Figures are the percentage of the total population reporting a particular ancestry. The nine most commonly reported ancestries in the U.S. are shown. Figures include multiple ancestries (e.g. if a person reported being Irish and Italian, they were included in both columns); (1) Figures cover the Tallahassee, FL Metropolitan Statistical Area; (2) Excludes Basque
Source: U.S. Census Bureau, 2015-2019 American Community Survey 5-Year Estimates

Foreign-born Population

Area	Any Foreign Country	Asia	Mexico	Europe	Caribbean	Central America[2]	South America	Africa	Canada
City	8.1	3.6	0.2	0.9	1.0	0.4	0.7	0.9	0.3
MSA[1]	6.1	2.2	0.5	0.8	0.9	0.5	0.5	0.6	0.2
U.S.	13.6	4.2	3.5	1.5	1.3	1.1	1.0	0.7	0.2

Note: (1) Figures cover the Tallahassee, FL Metropolitan Statistical Area; (2) Excludes Mexico.
Source: U.S. Census Bureau, 2015-2019 American Community Survey 5-Year Estimates

Marital Status

Area	Never Married	Now Married[2]	Separated	Widowed	Divorced
City	56.3	29.3	1.3	3.3	9.8
MSA[1]	43.9	39.0	1.6	4.6	10.9
U.S.	33.4	48.1	1.9	5.8	10.9

Note: Figures are percentages and cover the population 15 years of age and older; (1) Figures cover the Tallahassee, FL Metropolitan Statistical Area; (2) Excludes separated
Source: U.S. Census Bureau, 2015-2019 American Community Survey 5-Year Estimates

Disability by Age

Area	All Ages	Under 18 Years Old	18 to 64 Years Old	65 Years and Over
City	9.9	4.7	8.2	30.5
MSA[1]	12.7	5.9	10.2	33.9
U.S.	12.6	4.2	10.3	34.5

Note: Figures show percent of the civilian noninstitutionalized population that reported having a disability. Disability status is determined from six types of difficulty: vision, hearing, cognitive, ambulatory, self-care, and independent living. For children under 5 years old, hearing and vision difficulty are used to determine disability status. For children between the ages of 5 and 14, disability status is determined from hearing, vision, cognitive, ambulatory, and self-care difficulties. For people aged 15 years and older, they are considered to have a disability if they have difficulty with any one of the six difficulty types; Note: (1) Figures cover the Tallahassee, FL Metropolitan Statistical Area
Source: U.S. Census Bureau, 2015-2019 American Community Survey 5-Year Estimates

Age

Area	Under Age 5	Age 5–19	Age 20–34	Age 35–44	Age 45–54	Age 55–64	Age 65–74	Age 75–84	Age 85+	Median Age
City	4.9	19.2	38.0	10.0	8.8	8.7	6.3	2.8	1.2	26.9
MSA[1]	5.2	18.9	27.4	11.5	11.2	11.8	8.7	3.8	1.5	33.8
U.S.	6.1	19.1	20.7	12.6	13.0	12.9	9.1	4.6	1.9	38.1

Note: (1) Figures cover the Tallahassee, FL Metropolitan Statistical Area
Source: U.S. Census Bureau, 2015-2019 American Community Survey 5-Year Estimates

Gender

Area	Males	Females	Males per 100 Females
City	90,053	101,226	89.0
MSA[1]	184,249	197,948	93.1
U.S.	159,886,919	164,810,876	97.0

Note: (1) Figures cover the Tallahassee, FL Metropolitan Statistical Area
Source: U.S. Census Bureau, 2015-2019 American Community Survey 5-Year Estimates

Religious Groups by Family

Area	Catholic	Baptist	Non-Den.	Methodist[2]	Lutheran	LDS[3]	Pentecostal	Presbyterian[4]	Muslim[5]	Judaism
MSA[1]	4.8	16.1	6.8	9.2	0.5	1.0	2.2	1.6	0.9	0.4
U.S.	19.1	9.3	4.0	4.0	2.3	2.0	1.9	1.6	0.8	0.7

Note: Figures are the number of adherents as a percentage of the total population; (1) Figures cover the Tallahassee, FL Metropolitan Statistical Area; (2) Methodist/Pietist; (3) Latter Day Saints; (4) Reformed; (5) Figures are estimates
Source: Association of Statisticians of American Religious Bodies, 2010 U.S. Religion Census: Religious Congregations & Membership Study

Religious Groups by Tradition

Area	Catholic	Evangelical Protestant	Mainline Protestant	Other Tradition	Black Protestant	Orthodox
MSA[1]	4.8	21.9	6.4	3.0	9.2	0.2
U.S.	19.1	16.2	7.3	4.3	1.6	0.3

Note: Figures are the number of adherents as a percentage of the total population; (1) Figures cover the Tallahassee, FL Metropolitan Statistical Area
Source: Association of Statisticians of American Religious Bodies, 2010 U.S. Religion Census: Religious Congregations & Membership Study

ECONOMY

Gross Metropolitan Product

Area	2017	2018	2019	2020	Rank[2]
MSA[1]	16.4	17.1	17.9	18.7	152

Note: Figures are in billions of dollars; (1) Figures cover the Tallahassee, FL Metropolitan Statistical Area; (2) Rank is based on 2018 data and ranges from 1 to 381
Source: U.S. Conference of Mayors, U.S. Metro Economies: GMP & Employment 2018-2020, September 2019

Economic Growth

Area	2015-17 (%)	2018 (%)	2019 (%)	2020 (%)	Rank[2]
MSA[1]	3.1	2.6	2.8	1.9	61
U.S.	1.9	2.9	2.3	2.1	—

Note: Figures are real gross metropolitan product (GMP) growth rates and represent average annual percent change; (1) Figures cover the Tallahassee, FL Metropolitan Statistical Area; (2) Rank is based on 2017 2-year average annual percent change and ranges from 1 to 381
Source: U.S. Conference of Mayors, U.S. Metro Economies: GMP & Employment 2018-2020, September 2019

Metropolitan Area Exports

Area	2014	2015	2016	2017	2018	2019	Rank[2]
MSA[1]	174.0	191.2	223.1	241.1	270.8	219.7	291

Note: Figures are in millions of dollars; (1) Figures cover the Tallahassee, FL Metropolitan Statistical Area; (2) Rank is based on 2019 data and ranges from 1 to 386
Source: U.S. Department of Commerce, International Trade Administration, Office of Trade and Economic Analysis, Industry and Analysis, Exports by Metropolitan Area, data extracted March 24, 2021

Building Permits

Area	Single-Family 2018	Single-Family 2019	Pct. Chg.	Multi-Family 2018	Multi-Family 2019	Pct. Chg.	Total 2018	Total 2019	Pct. Chg.
City	396	407	2.8	1,128	1,275	13.0	1,524	1,682	10.4
MSA[1]	2,073	1,070	-48.4	1,128	1,275	13.0	3,201	2,345	-26.7
U.S.	855,300	862,100	0.7	473,500	523,900	10.6	1,328,800	1,386,000	4.3

Note: (1) Figures cover the Tallahassee, FL Metropolitan Statistical Area; Figures represent new, privately-owned housing units authorized (unadjusted data); All permit data are based on estimates with imputation
Source: U.S. Census Bureau, Manufacturing, Mining, and Construction Statistics, Building Permits, 2018, 2019

Bankruptcy Filings

Area	Business Filings 2019	Business Filings 2020	% Chg.	Nonbusiness Filings 2019	Nonbusiness Filings 2020	% Chg.
Leon County	35	17	-51.4	446	288	-35.4
U.S.	22,780	21,655	-4.9	752,160	522,808	-30.5

Note: Business filings include Chapter 7, Chapter 9, Chapter 11, Chapter 12, Chapter 13, Chapter 15, and Section 304; Nonbusiness filings include Chapter 7, Chapter 11, and Chapter 13
Source: Administrative Office of the U.S. Courts, Business and Nonbusiness Bankruptcy, County Cases Commenced by Chapter of the Bankruptcy Code, During the 12-Month Period Ending December 31, 2019 and Business and Nonbusiness Bankruptcy, County Cases Commenced by Chapter of the Bankruptcy Code, During the 12-Month Period Ending December 31, 2020

Housing Vacancy Rates

Area	Gross Vacancy Rate[2] (%) 2018	2019	2020	Year-Round Vacancy Rate[3] (%) 2018	2019	2020	Rental Vacancy Rate[4] (%) 2018	2019	2020	Homeowner Vacancy Rate[5] (%) 2018	2019	2020
MSA[1]	n/a	n/a	n/a	n/a	n/a	n/a	n/a	n/a	n/a	n/a	n/a	n/a
U.S.	12.3	12.0	10.6	9.7	9.5	8.2	6.9	6.7	6.3	1.5	1.4	1.0

Note: (1) Figures cover the Tallahassee, FL Metropolitan Statistical Area; (2) The percentage of the total housing inventory that is vacant; (3) The percentage of the housing inventory (excluding seasonal units) that is year-round vacant; (4) The percentage of rental inventory that is vacant for rent; (5) The percentage of homeowner inventory that is vacant for sale; n/a not available
Source: U.S. Census Bureau, Housing Vacancies and Homeownership Annual Statistics: 2018, 2019, 2020

INCOME

Income

Area	Per Capita ($)	Median Household ($)	Average Household ($)
City	27,677	45,734	66,889
MSA[1]	28,766	51,874	72,487
U.S.	34,103	62,843	88,607

Note: (1) Figures cover the Tallahassee, FL Metropolitan Statistical Area
Source: U.S. Census Bureau, 2015-2019 American Community Survey 5-Year Estimates

Household Income Distribution

Area	Under $15,000	$15,000 -$24,999	$25,000 -$34,999	$35,000 -$49,999	$50,000 -$74,999	$75,000 -$99,999	$100,000 -$149,999	$150,000 and up
City	16.8	10.9	11.7	13.8	17.3	10.2	10.4	8.8
MSA[1]	13.5	10.2	10.8	13.9	17.5	12.1	12.2	9.7
U.S.	10.3	8.9	8.9	12.3	17.2	12.7	15.1	14.5

Note: (1) Figures cover the Tallahassee, FL Metropolitan Statistical Area
Source: U.S. Census Bureau, 2015-2019 American Community Survey 5-Year Estimates

Poverty Rate

Area	All Ages	Under 18 Years Old	18 to 64 Years Old	65 Years and Over
City	26.4	24.3	29.3	9.9
MSA[1]	20.0	22.1	21.9	8.4
U.S.	13.4	18.5	12.6	9.3

Note: Figures are percentage of people whose income during the past 12 months was below the poverty level; (1) Figures cover the Tallahassee, FL Metropolitan Statistical Area
Source: U.S. Census Bureau, 2015-2019 American Community Survey 5-Year Estimates

CITY FINANCES

City Government Finances

Component	2017 ($000)	2017 ($ per capita)
Total Revenues	912,955	4,807
Total Expenditures	822,285	4,330
Debt Outstanding	1,413,042	7,441
Cash and Securities[1]	2,884,354	15,188

Note: (1) Cash and security holdings of a government at the close of its fiscal year, including those of its dependent agencies, utilities, and liquor stores.
Source: U.S. Census Bureau, State & Local Government Finances 2017

City Government Revenue by Source

Source	2017 ($000)	2017 ($ per capita)	2017 (%)
General Revenue			
From Federal Government	24,032	127	2.6
From State Government	38,859	205	4.3
From Local Governments	5,452	29	0.6
Taxes			
Property	39,100	206	4.3
Sales and Gross Receipts	57,169	301	6.3
Personal Income	0	0	0.0
Corporate Income	0	0	0.0
Motor Vehicle License	0	0	0.0
Other Taxes	7,168	38	0.8
Current Charges	157,292	828	17.2
Liquor Store	0	0	0.0
Utility	331,942	1,748	36.4
Employee Retirement	199,181	1,049	21.8

Source: U.S. Census Bureau, State & Local Government Finances 2017

City Government Expenditures by Function

Function	2017 ($000)	2017 ($ per capita)	2017 (%)
General Direct Expenditures			
Air Transportation	29,632	156	3.6
Corrections	0	0	0.0
Education	0	0	0.0
Employment Security Administration	0	0	0.0
Financial Administration	4,674	24	0.6
Fire Protection	40,842	215	5.0
General Public Buildings	0	0	0.0
Governmental Administration, Other	15,315	80	1.9
Health	0	0	0.0
Highways	55,470	292	6.7
Hospitals	0	0	0.0
Housing and Community Development	3,648	19	0.4
Interest on General Debt	7,161	37	0.9
Judicial and Legal	2,173	11	0.3
Libraries	0	0	0.0
Parking	0	0	0.0
Parks and Recreation	24,698	130	3.0
Police Protection	60,149	316	7.3
Public Welfare	0	0	0.0
Sewerage	39,460	207	4.8
Solid Waste Management	23,516	123	2.9
Veterans' Services	0	0	0.0
Liquor Store	0	0	0.0
Utility	347,123	1,827	42.2
Employee Retirement	124,439	655	15.1

Source: U.S. Census Bureau, State & Local Government Finances 2017

EMPLOYMENT

Labor Force and Employment

Area	Civilian Labor Force			Workers Employed		
	Dec. 2019	Dec. 2020	% Chg.	Dec. 2019	Dec. 2020	% Chg.
City	102,369	97,422	-4.8	99,536	91,619	-8.0
MSA[1]	195,372	185,262	-5.2	190,212	175,456	-7.8
U.S.	164,007,000	160,017,000	-2.4	158,504,000	149,613,000	-5.6

Note: Data is not seasonally adjusted and covers workers 16 years of age and older; (1) Figures cover the Tallahassee, FL Metropolitan Statistical Area
Source: Bureau of Labor Statistics, Local Area Unemployment Statistics

Unemployment Rate

Area	2020											
	Jan.	Feb.	Mar.	Apr.	May	Jun.	Jul.	Aug.	Sep.	Oct.	Nov.	Dec.
City	3.4	3.0	4.4	9.2	9.1	7.8	9.5	6.2	5.3	5.7	6.0	6.0
MSA[1]	3.2	2.9	4.2	8.3	8.1	7.0	8.4	5.5	4.7	5.0	5.4	5.3
U.S.	4.0	3.8	4.5	14.4	13.0	11.2	10.5	8.5	7.7	6.6	6.4	6.5

Note: Data is not seasonally adjusted and covers workers 16 years of age and older; (1) Figures cover the Tallahassee, FL Metropolitan Statistical Area
Source: Bureau of Labor Statistics, Local Area Unemployment Statistics

Average Wages

Occupation	$/Hr.	Occupation	$/Hr.
Accountants and Auditors	27.30	Maintenance and Repair Workers	17.40
Automotive Mechanics	21.80	Marketing Managers	47.00
Bookkeepers	19.50	Network and Computer Systems Admin.	31.10
Carpenters	20.10	Nurses, Licensed Practical	20.90
Cashiers	11.10	Nurses, Registered	31.80
Computer Programmers	31.00	Nursing Assistants	12.60
Computer Systems Analysts	29.10	Office Clerks, General	15.00
Computer User Support Specialists	21.80	Physical Therapists	41.00
Construction Laborers	14.30	Physicians	100.00
Cooks, Restaurant	13.50	Plumbers, Pipefitters and Steamfitters	21.60
Customer Service Representatives	16.10	Police and Sheriff's Patrol Officers	27.10
Dentists	78.70	Postal Service Mail Carriers	25.20
Electricians	21.70	Real Estate Sales Agents	26.90
Engineers, Electrical	44.40	Retail Salespersons	14.00
Fast Food and Counter Workers	10.50	Sales Representatives, Technical/Scientific	38.00
Financial Managers	47.50	Secretaries, Exc. Legal/Medical/Executive	17.30
First-Line Supervisors of Office Workers	29.70	Security Guards	13.90
General and Operations Managers	45.50	Surgeons	n/a
Hairdressers/Cosmetologists	13.90	Teacher Assistants, Exc. Postsecondary*	13.00
Home Health and Personal Care Aides	12.80	Teachers, Secondary School, Exc. Sp. Ed.*	24.50
Janitors and Cleaners	12.80	Telemarketers	14.80
Landscaping/Groundskeeping Workers	13.50	Truck Drivers, Heavy/Tractor-Trailer	20.10
Lawyers	49.00	Truck Drivers, Light/Delivery Services	17.90
Maids and Housekeeping Cleaners	10.80	Waiters and Waitresses	12.10

Note: Wage data covers the Tallahassee, FL Metropolitan Statistical Area; (*) Hourly wages were calculated from annual wage data based on a 40 hour work week; n/a not available.
Source: Bureau of Labor Statistics, Metro Area Occupational Employment & Wage Estimates, May 2020

Employment by Industry

Sector	MSA[1]		U.S.
	Number of Employees	Percent of Total	Percent of Total
Construction, Mining, and Logging	8,200	4.6	5.5
Education and Health Services	24,600	13.8	16.3
Financial Activities	7,600	4.3	6.1
Government	58,700	32.9	15.2
Information	3,100	1.7	1.9
Leisure and Hospitality	16,900	9.5	9.0
Manufacturing	3,500	2.0	8.5
Other Services	9,000	5.0	3.8
Professional and Business Services	22,900	12.8	14.4
Retail Trade	18,000	10.1	10.9
Transportation, Warehousing, and Utilities	2,400	1.3	4.6
Wholesale Trade	3,600	2.0	3.9

Note: Figures are non-farm employment as of December 2020. Figures are not seasonally adjusted and include workers 16 years of age and older; (1) Figures cover the Tallahassee, FL Metropolitan Statistical Area
Source: Bureau of Labor Statistics, Current Employment Statistics, Employment, Hours, and Earnings

Employment by Occupation

Occupation Classification	City (%)	MSA[1] (%)	U.S. (%)
Management, Business, Science, and Arts	46.1	43.7	38.5
Natural Resources, Construction, and Maintenance	3.6	6.6	8.9
Production, Transportation, and Material Moving	6.0	7.1	13.2
Sales and Office	24.9	24.1	21.6
Service	19.4	18.5	17.8

Note: Figures cover employed civilians 16 years of age and older; (1) Figures cover the Tallahassee, FL Metropolitan Statistical Area
Source: U.S. Census Bureau, 2015-2019 American Community Survey 5-Year Estimates

Occupations with Greatest Projected Employment Growth: 2020 – 2022

Occupation[1]	2020 Employment	2022 Projected Employment	Numeric Employment Change	Percent Employment Change
Fast Food and Counter Workers	172,590	214,590	42,000	24.3
Waiters and Waitresses	141,990	180,530	38,540	27.1
Retail Salespersons	264,490	292,340	27,850	10.5
Cooks, Restaurant	79,150	103,770	24,620	31.1
Maids and Housekeeping Cleaners	63,280	81,030	17,750	28.0
Cashiers	204,540	221,530	16,990	8.3
Registered Nurses	189,240	202,880	13,640	7.2
Laborers and Freight, Stock, and Material Movers, Hand	147,740	160,650	12,910	8.7
First-Line Supervisors of Food Preparation and Serving Workers	51,820	64,080	12,260	23.7
Stockers and Order Fillers	130,980	142,780	11,800	9.0

Note: Projections cover Florida; (1) Sorted by numeric employment change
Source: www.projectionscentral.com, State Occupational Projections, 2020–2022 Short-Term Projections

Fastest-Growing Occupations: 2020 – 2022

Occupation[1]	2020 Employment	2022 Projected Employment	Numeric Employment Change	Percent Employment Change
Hotel, Motel, and Resort Desk Clerks	11,930	18,100	6,170	51.7
Locker Room, Coatroom, and Dressing Room Attendants	930	1,360	430	46.2
Lodging Managers	3,190	4,420	1,230	38.6
Manicurists and Pedicurists	2,640	3,580	940	35.6
Bartenders	31,430	42,540	11,110	35.3
Gaming Cage Workers	320	430	110	34.4
Parking Lot Attendants	11,200	15,040	3,840	34.3
Gaming Dealers	2,660	3,560	900	33.8
Baggage Porters and Bellhops	3,520	4,670	1,150	32.7
Cooks, Restaurant	79,150	103,770	24,620	31.1

Note: Projections cover Florida; (1) Sorted by percent employment change and excludes occupations with numeric employment change less than 50
Source: www.projectionscentral.com, State Occupational Projections, 2020–2022 Short-Term Projections

TAXES

State Corporate Income Tax Rates

State	Tax Rate (%)	Income Brackets ($)	Num. of Brackets	Financial Institution Tax Rate (%)[a]	Federal Income Tax Ded.
Florida	4.458 (e)	Flat rate	1	4.458 (e)	No

Note: Tax rates as of January 1, 2021; (a) Rates listed are the corporate income tax rate applied to financial institutions or excise taxes based on income. Some states have other taxes based upon the value of deposits or shares; (e) The Florida tax rate may be adjusted downward if certain revenue targets are met.
Source: Federation of Tax Administrators, State Corporate Income Tax Rates, January 1, 2021

State Individual Income Tax Rates

State	Tax Rate (%)	Income Brackets ($)	Personal Exemptions ($) Single	Married	Depend.	Standard Ded. ($) Single	Married
Florida				– No state income tax –			

Note: Tax rates as of January 1, 2021; Local- and county-level taxes are not included
Source: Federation of Tax Administrators, State Individual Income Tax Rates, January 1, 2021

Various State Sales and Excise Tax Rates

State	State Sales Tax (%)	Gasoline[1] (¢/gal.)	Cigarette[2] ($/pack)	Spirits[3] ($/gal.)	Wine[4] ($/gal.)	Beer[5] ($/gal.)	Recreational Marijuana (%)
Florida	6	42.46	1.339	6.5	2.25	0.48	Not legal

Note: All tax rates as of January 1, 2021; (1) The American Petroleum Institute has developed a methodology for determining the average tax rate on a gallon of fuel. Rates may include any of the following: excise taxes, environmental fees, storage tank fees, other fees or taxes, general sales tax, and local taxes; (2) The federal excise tax of $1.0066 per pack and local taxes are not included; (3) Rates are those applicable to off-premise sales of 40% alcohol by volume (a.b.v.) distilled spirits in 750ml containers. Local excise taxes are excluded; (4) Rates are those applicable to off-premise sales of 11% a.b.v. non-carbonated wine in 750ml containers; (5) Rates are those applicable to off-premise sales of 4.7% a.b.v. beer in 12 ounce containers.
Source: Tax Foundation, 2021 Facts & Figures: How Does Your State Compare?

State Business Tax Climate Index Rankings

State	Overall Rank	Corporate Tax Rank	Individual Income Tax Rank	Sales Tax Rank	Property Tax Rank	Unemployment Insurance Tax Rank
Florida	4	6	1	21	13	2

Note: The index is a measure of how each state's tax laws affect economic performance. The lower the rank, the more favorable a state's tax system is for business. States without a given tax are given a ranking of 1. The scores/rankings for the District of Columbia do not affect other states. The 2021 index represents the tax climate as of July 1, 2020.
Source: Tax Foundation, State Business Tax Climate Index 2021

TRANSPORTATION

Means of Transportation to Work

Area	Car/Truck/Van Drove Alone	Car/Truck/Van Carpooled	Public Transportation Bus	Public Transportation Subway	Public Transportation Railroad	Bicycle	Walked	Other Means	Worked at Home
City	78.5	8.7	2.4	0.0	0.0	0.8	3.3	1.5	4.8
MSA[1]	81.1	9.2	1.4	0.0	0.0	0.6	2.0	1.3	4.3
U.S.	76.3	9.0	2.4	1.9	0.6	0.5	2.7	1.4	5.2

Note: Figures are percentages and cover workers 16 years of age and older; (1) Figures cover the Tallahassee, FL Metropolitan Statistical Area
Source: U.S. Census Bureau, 2015-2019 American Community Survey 5-Year Estimates

Travel Time to Work

Area	Less Than 10 Minutes	10 to 19 Minutes	20 to 29 Minutes	30 to 44 Minutes	45 to 59 Minutes	60 to 89 Minutes	90 Minutes or More
City	14.6	44.7	23.9	12.3	2.1	1.3	1.0
MSA[1]	11.0	34.3	24.8	20.4	5.6	2.4	1.5
U.S.	12.2	28.4	20.8	20.8	8.3	6.4	2.9

Note: Note: Figures are percentages and include workers 16 years old and over; (1) Figures cover the Tallahassee, FL Metropolitan Statistical Area
Source: U.S. Census Bureau, 2015-2019 American Community Survey 5-Year Estimates

Key Congestion Measures

Measure	1982	1992	2002	2012	2017
Annual Hours of Delay, Total (000)	n/a	n/a	n/a	n/a	7,356
Annual Hours of Delay, Per Auto Commuter	n/a	n/a	n/a	n/a	33
Annual Congestion Cost, Total (million $)	n/a	n/a	n/a	n/a	151
Annual Congestion Cost, Per Auto Commuter ($)	n/a	n/a	n/a	n/a	686

Note: n/a not available
Source: Texas A&M Transportation Institute, 2019 Urban Mobility Report

Freeway Travel Time Index

Measure	1982	1987	1992	1997	2002	2007	2012	2017
Urban Area Index[1]	n/a	n/a	n/a	n/a	n/a	n/a	n/a	1.14
Urban Area Rank[1,2]	n/a	n/a	n/a	n/a	n/a	n/a	n/a	n/a

Note: Freeway Travel Time Index—the ratio of travel time in the peak period to the travel time at free-flow conditions. For example, a value of 1.30 indicates a 20-minute free-flow trip takes 26 minutes in the peak (20 minutes x 1.30 = 26 minutes); (1) Covers the Tallahassee FL urban area; (2) Rank is based on 101 larger urban areas (#1 = highest travel time index); n/a not available
Source: Texas A&M Transportation Institute, 2019 Urban Mobility Report

Public Transportation

Agency Name / Mode of Transportation	Vehicles Operated in Maximum Service[1]	Annual Unlinked Passenger Trips[2] (in thous.)	Annual Passenger Miles[3] (in thous.)
City of Tallahassee (StarMetro)			
Bus (directly operated)	55	3,448.3	9,851.3
Bus (purchased transportation)	2	32.1	91.9
Demand Response (directly operated)	20	59.9	370.7
Demand Response (purchased transportation)	40	77.9	1,055.5
Demand Response Taxi (purchased transportation)	13	25.2	126.1

Note: (1) Number of revenue vehicles operated by the given mode and type of service to meet the annual maximum service requirement. This is the revenue vehicle count during the peak season of the year; on the week and day that maximum service is provided. Vehicles operated in maximum service (VOMS) exclude atypical days and one-time special events; (2) Number of passengers who boarded public transportation vehicles. Passengers are counted each time they board a vehicle no matter how many vehicles they use to travel from their origin to their destination. (3) Sum of the distances ridden by all passengers during the entire fiscal year.
Source: Federal Transit Administration, National Transit Database, 2019

Air Transportation

Airport Name and Code / Type of Service	Passenger Airlines[1]	Passenger Enplanements	Freight Carriers[2]	Freight (lbs)
Tallahassee Regional (TLH)				
Domestic service (U.S. carriers - 2020)	16	180,018	5	9,422,258
International service (U.S. carriers - 2019)	1	3	0	0

Note: (1) Includes all U.S.-based major, minor and commuter airlines that carried at least one passenger during the year; (2) Includes all U.S.-based airlines and freight carriers that transported at least one pound of freight during the year.
Source: Bureau of Transportation Statistics, The Intermodal Transportation Database, Air Carriers: T-100 Domestic Market (U.S. Carriers), 2020; Bureau of Transportation Statistics, The Intermodal Transportation Database, Air Carriers: T-100 International Market (U.S. Carriers), 2019

BUSINESSES

Major Business Headquarters

Company Name	Industry	Rankings Fortune[1]	Forbes[2]
No companies listed	-	-	-

Note: (1) Companies that produce a 10-K are ranked 1 to 500 based on 2019 revenue; (2) All private companies with at least $2 billion in annual revenue through the end of their most current fiscal year are ranked 1 to 219; companies listed are headquartered in the city; dashes indicate no ranking
Source: Fortune, "Fortune 500," June/July 2020; Forbes, "America's Largest Private Companies," 2020

Living Environment

COST OF LIVING

Cost of Living Index

Composite Index	Groceries	Housing	Utilities	Transportation	Health Care	Misc. Goods/Services
97.1	109.3	92.8	87.1	101.0	104.6	96.3

Note: The Cost of Living Index measures regional differences in the cost of consumer goods and services, excluding taxes and non-consumer expenditures, for professional and managerial households in the top income quintile. It is based on more than 50,000 prices covering almost 60 different items for which prices are collected three times a year by chambers of commerce, economic development organizations or university applied economic centers in each participating urban area. The numbers shown should be read as a percentage above or below the national average of 100. For example, a value of 115.4 in the groceries column indicates that grocery prices are 15.4% higher than the national average. Small differences in the index numbers should not be interpreted as significant; Figures cover the Tallahassee FL urban area.
Source: The Council for Community and Economic Research, Cost of Living Index, 2020

Grocery Prices

Area[1]	T-Bone Steak ($/pound)	Frying Chicken ($/pound)	Whole Milk ($/half gal.)	Eggs ($/dozen)	Orange Juice ($/64 oz.)	Coffee ($/11.5 oz.)
City[2]	11.54	1.56	2.71	1.70	3.95	3.85
Avg.	11.78	1.39	2.05	1.47	3.57	4.34
Min.	8.03	0.94	1.03	0.74	2.94	3.02
Max.	15.86	2.65	4.31	3.77	5.44	8.69

Note: (1) Values for the local area are compared with the average, minimum and maximum values for all 284 areas in the Cost of Living Index; (2) Figures cover the Tallahassee FL urban area; **T-Bone Steak** (price per pound); **Frying Chicken** (price per pound, whole fryer); **Whole Milk** (half gallon carton); **Eggs** (price per dozen, Grade A, large); **Orange Juice** (64 oz. Tropicana or Florida Natural); **Coffee** (11.5 oz. can, vacuum-packed, Maxwell House, Hills Bros, or Folgers).
Source: The Council for Community and Economic Research, Cost of Living Index, 2020

Housing and Utility Costs

Area[1]	New Home Price ($)	Apartment Rent ($/month)	All Electric ($/month)	Part Electric ($/month)	Other Energy ($/month)	Telephone ($/month)
City[2]	344,867	1,132	124.57	-	-	189.90
Avg.	368,594	1,168	170.86	100.47	65.28	184.30
Min.	190,567	502	91.58	31.42	26.08	169.60
Max.	2,227,806	4,738	470.38	280.31	280.06	206.50

Note: (1) Values for the local area are compared with the average, minimum and maximum values for all 284 areas in the Cost of Living Index; (2) Figures cover the Tallahassee FL urban area; **New Home Price** (2,400 sf living area, 8,000 sf lot, in urban area with full utilities); **Apartment Rent** (950 sf 2 bedroom/1.5 or 2 bath, unfurnished, excluding all utilities except water); **All Electric** (average monthly cost for an all-electric home); **Part Electric** (average monthly cost for a part-electric home); **Other Energy** (average monthly cost for natural gas, fuel oil, coal, wood, and any other forms of energy except electricity); **Telephone** (price includes the base monthly rate plus taxes and fees for three lines of mobile phone service).
Source: The Council for Community and Economic Research, Cost of Living Index, 2020

Health Care, Transportation, and Other Costs

Area[1]	Doctor ($/visit)	Dentist ($/visit)	Optometrist ($/visit)	Gasoline ($/gallon)	Beauty Salon ($/visit)	Men's Shirt ($)
City[2]	126.07	111.09	69.75	2.25	36.64	33.99
Avg.	115.44	99.32	108.10	2.21	39.27	31.37
Min.	36.68	59.00	51.36	1.71	19.00	11.00
Max.	219.00	153.10	250.97	3.46	82.05	58.33

Note: (1) Values for the local area are compared with the average, minimum and maximum values for all 284 areas in the Cost of Living Index; (2) Figures cover the Tallahassee FL urban area; **Doctor** (general practitioners routine exam of an established patient); **Dentist** (adult teeth cleaning and periodic oral examination); **Optometrist** (full vision eye exam for established adult patient); **Gasoline** (one gallon regular unleaded, national brand, including all taxes, cash price at self-service pump if available); **Beauty Salon** (woman's shampoo, trim, and blow-dry); **Men's Shirt** (cotton/polyester dress shirt, pinpoint weave, long sleeves).
Source: The Council for Community and Economic Research, Cost of Living Index, 2020

HOUSING

Homeownership Rate

Area	2012 (%)	2013 (%)	2014 (%)	2015 (%)	2016 (%)	2017 (%)	2018 (%)	2019 (%)	2020 (%)
MSA[1]	n/a	n/a	n/a	n/a	n/a	n/a	n/a	n/a	n/a
U.S.	65.4	65.1	64.5	63.7	63.4	63.9	64.4	64.6	66.6

Note: (1) Figures cover the Tallahassee, FL Metropolitan Statistical Area; n/a not available
Source: U.S. Census Bureau, Housing Vacancies and Homeownership Annual Statistics: 2012-2020

House Price Index (HPI)

Area	National Ranking[2]	Quarterly Change (%)	One-Year Change (%)	Five-Year Change (%)	Since 1991Q1 (%)
MSA[1]	186	1.55	5.20	30.45	154.52
U.S.[3]	—	3.81	10.77	38.99	205.12

Note: The HPI is a weighted repeat sales index. It measures average price changes in repeat sales or refinancings on the same properties. This information is obtained by reviewing repeat mortgage transactions on single-family properties whose mortgages have been purchased or securitized by Fannie Mae or Freddie Mac since January 1975; (1) Figures cover the Tallahassee, FL Metropolitan Statistical Area; (2) Rankings are based on annual percentage change for all metro areas containing at least 15,000 transactions over the last 10 years and ranges from 1 to 253; (3) figures based on a weighted average of Census Division estimates using a seasonally adjusted, purchase-only index; all figures are for the period ending December 31, 2020
Source: Federal Housing Finance Agency, Change in Metropolitan Area House Price Indexes, April 7, 2021

Median Single-Family Home Prices

Area	2018	2019	2020p	Percent Change 2019 to 2020
MSA[1]	215.0	227.0	248.0	9.3
U.S. Average	261.6	274.6	299.9	9.2

Note: Figures are median sales prices of existing single-family homes in thousands of dollars; (p) preliminary; (1) Figures cover the Tallahassee, FL Metropolitan Statistical Area
Source: National Association of Realtors, Median Sales Price of Existing Single-Family Homes for Metropolitan Areas, 4th Quarter 2020

Qualifying Income Based on Median Sales Price of Existing Single-Family Homes

Area	With 5% Down ($)	With 10% Down ($)	With 20% Down ($)
MSA[1]	48,591	46,033	40,918
U.S. Average	59,266	56,147	49,908

Note: Figures are preliminary; Qualifying income is based on a mortgage rate of 2.81%. Monthly principal and interest payment is limited to 25% of income; (1) Figures cover the Tallahassee, FL Metropolitan Statistical Area
Source: National Association of Realtors, Qualifying Income Based on Median Sales Price of Existing Single-Family Homes for Metropolitan Areas, 4th Quarter 2020

Home Value Distribution

Area	Under $50,000	$50,000 -$99,999	$100,000 -$149,999	$150,000 -$199,999	$200,000 -$299,999	$300,000 -$499,999	$500,000 -$999,999	$1,000,000 or more
City	2.9	9.9	16.8	19.3	26.8	19.3	4.0	1.0
MSA[1]	8.3	15.3	16.5	16.9	22.4	15.2	4.6	0.8
U.S.	6.9	12.0	13.3	14.0	19.6	19.3	11.4	3.4

Note: Figures are percentages and cover owner-occupied housing units; (1) Figures cover the Tallahassee, FL Metropolitan Statistical Area
Source: U.S. Census Bureau, 2015-2019 American Community Survey 5-Year Estimates

Year Housing Structure Built

Area	2010 or Later	2000 -2009	1990 -1999	1980 -1989	1970 -1979	1960 -1969	1950 -1959	1940 -1949	Before 1940	Median Year
City	3.9	18.2	20.8	17.7	18.0	9.2	7.5	3.2	1.5	1986
MSA[1]	4.0	18.7	22.6	19.2	16.2	8.3	6.6	2.6	1.7	1988
U.S.	5.2	14.0	13.9	13.4	15.2	10.6	10.3	4.9	12.6	1978

Note: Figures are percentages except for Median Year; Note: (1) Figures cover the Tallahassee, FL Metropolitan Statistical Area
Source: U.S. Census Bureau, 2015-2019 American Community Survey 5-Year Estimates

Gross Monthly Rent

Area	Under $500	$500 -$999	$1,000 -$1,499	$1,500 -$1,999	$2,000 -$2,499	$2,500 -$2,999	$3,000 and up	Median ($)
City	5.3	42.2	39.8	8.5	3.2	0.6	0.3	1,023
MSA[1]	6.9	44.2	36.9	8.4	2.9	0.5	0.2	991
U.S.	9.4	36.2	30.0	14.0	5.6	2.4	2.4	1,062

Note: Figures are percentages except for Median; Gross rent is the contract rent plus the estimated average monthly cost of utilities (electricity, gas, and water and sewer) and fuels (oil, coal, kerosene, wood, etc.) if these are paid by the renter (or paid for the renter by someone else); (1) Figures cover the Tallahassee, FL Metropolitan Statistical Area
Source: U.S. Census Bureau, 2015-2019 American Community Survey 5-Year Estimates

HEALTH

Health Risk Factors

Category	MSA[1] (%)	U.S. (%)
Adults aged 18–64 who have any kind of health care coverage	88.0	87.3
Adults who reported being in good or better health	87.7	82.4
Adults who have been told they have high blood cholesterol	27.7	33.0
Adults who have been told they have high blood pressure	28.4	32.3
Adults who are current smokers	14.0	17.1
Adults who currently use E-cigarettes	n/a	4.6
Adults who currently use chewing tobacco, snuff, or snus	3.3	4.0
Adults who are heavy drinkers[2]	9.0	6.3
Adults who are binge drinkers[3]	18.7	17.4
Adults who are overweight (BMI 25.0 - 29.9)	25.4	35.3
Adults who are obese (BMI 30.0 - 99.8)	32.3	31.3
Adults who participated in any physical activities in the past month	72.4	74.4
Adults who always or nearly always wears a seat belt	95.1	94.3

Note: n/a not available; (1) Figures cover the Tallahassee, FL Metropolitan Statistical Area; (2) Heavy drinkers are classified as adult men having more than 14 drinks per week and adult women having more than 7 drinks per week; (3) Binge drinkers are classified as males having five or more drinks on one occasion or females having four or more drinks on one occasion
Source: Centers for Disease Control and Prevention, Behaviorial Risk Factor Surveillance System, SMART: Selected Metropolitan Area Risk Trends, 2017

Acute and Chronic Health Conditions

Category	MSA[1] (%)	U.S. (%)
Adults who have ever been told they had a heart attack	2.6	4.2
Adults who have ever been told they have angina or coronary heart disease	3.2	3.9
Adults who have ever been told they had a stroke	2.4	3.0
Adults who have ever been told they have asthma	12.5	14.2
Adults who have ever been told they have arthritis	18.5	24.9
Adults who have ever been told they have diabetes[2]	8.7	10.5
Adults who have ever been told they had skin cancer	8.5	6.2
Adults who have ever been told they had any other types of cancer	5.1	7.1
Adults who have ever been told they have COPD	5.1	6.5
Adults who have ever been told they have kidney disease	n/a	3.0
Adults who have ever been told they have a form of depression	15.7	20.5

Note: n/a not available; (1) Figures cover the Tallahassee, FL Metropolitan Statistical Area; (2) Figures do not include pregnancy-related, borderline, or pre-diabetes
Source: Centers for Disease Control and Prevention, Behaviorial Risk Factor Surveillance System, SMART: Selected Metropolitan Area Risk Trends, 2017

Health Screening and Vaccination Rates

Category	MSA[1] (%)	U.S. (%)
Adults aged 65+ who have had flu shot within the past year	68.0	60.7
Adults aged 65+ who have ever had a pneumonia vaccination	75.7	75.4
Adults who have ever been tested for HIV	49.8	36.1
Adults who have ever had the shingles or zoster vaccine?	33.6	28.9
Adults who have had their blood cholesterol checked within the last five years	88.4	85.9

Note: n/a not available; (1) Figures cover the Tallahassee, FL Metropolitan Statistical Area.
Source: Centers for Disease Control and Prevention, Behaviorial Risk Factor Surveillance System, SMART: Selected Metropolitan Area Risk Trends, 2017

Disability Status

Category	MSA[1] (%)	U.S. (%)
Adults who reported being deaf	7.3	6.7
Are you blind or have serious difficulty seeing, even when wearing glasses?	6.3	4.5
Are you limited in any way in any of your usual activities due of arthritis?	8.9	12.9
Do you have difficulty doing errands alone?	4.8	6.8
Do you have difficulty dressing or bathing?	n/a	3.6
Do you have serious difficulty concentrating/remembering/making decisions?	8.9	10.7
Do you have serious difficulty walking or climbing stairs?	11.2	13.6

Note: n/a not available; (1) Figures cover the Tallahassee, FL Metropolitan Statistical Area.
Source: Centers for Disease Control and Prevention, Behaviorial Risk Factor Surveillance System, SMART: Selected Metropolitan Area Risk Trends, 2017

Mortality Rates for the Top 10 Causes of Death in the U.S.

ICD-10[a] Sub-Chapter	ICD-10[a] Code	Age-Adjusted Mortality Rate[1] per 100,000 population County[2]	U.S.
Malignant neoplasms	C00-C97	142.2	149.2
Ischaemic heart diseases	I20-I25	75.2	90.5
Other forms of heart disease	I30-I51	53.2	52.2
Chronic lower respiratory diseases	J40-J47	29.1	39.6
Other degenerative diseases of the nervous system	G30-G31	50.8	37.6
Cerebrovascular diseases	I60-I69	39.6	37.2
Other external causes of accidental injury	W00-X59	29.0	36.1
Organic, including symptomatic, mental disorders	F01-F09	33.9	29.4
Hypertensive diseases	I10-I15	21.2	24.1
Diabetes mellitus	E10-E14	23.1	21.5

Note: (a) ICD-10 = International Classification of Diseases 10th Revision; (1) Mortality rates are a three-year average covering 2017-2019; (2) Figures cover Leon County.
Source: Centers for Disease Control and Prevention, National Center for Health Statistics. Underlying Cause of Death 1999-2019 on CDC WONDER Online Database

Mortality Rates for Selected Causes of Death

ICD-10[a] Sub-Chapter	ICD-10[a] Code	Age-Adjusted Mortality Rate[1] per 100,000 population County[2]	U.S.
Assault	X85-Y09	5.6	6.0
Diseases of the liver	K70-K76	12.6	14.4
Human immunodeficiency virus (HIV) disease	B20-B24	4.2	1.5
Influenza and pneumonia	J09-J18	8.9	13.8
Intentional self-harm	X60-X84	11.9	14.1
Malnutrition	E40-E46	Unreliable	2.3
Obesity and other hyperalimentation	E65-E68	3.4	2.1
Renal failure	N17-N19	10.6	12.6
Transport accidents	V01-V99	10.6	12.3
Viral hepatitis	B15-B19	Suppressed	1.2

Note: (a) ICD-10 = International Classification of Diseases 10th Revision; (1) Mortality rates are a three-year average covering 2017-2019; (2) Figures cover Leon County; Data are suppressed when the data meet the criteria for confidentiality constraints; Mortality rates are flagged as unreliable when the rate would be calculated with a numerator of 20 or less.
Source: Centers for Disease Control and Prevention, National Center for Health Statistics. Underlying Cause of Death 1999-2019 on CDC WONDER Online Database

Health Insurance Coverage

Area	With Health Insurance	With Private Health Insurance	With Public Health Insurance	Without Health Insurance	Population Under Age 19 Without Health Insurance
City	91.6	76.3	25.1	8.4	4.2
MSA[1]	91.2	73.4	30.0	8.8	4.6
U.S.	91.2	67.9	35.1	8.8	5.1

Note: Figures are percentages that cover the civilian noninstitutionalized population; (1) Figures cover the Tallahassee, FL Metropolitan Statistical Area
Source: U.S. Census Bureau, 2015-2019 American Community Survey 5-Year Estimates

Number of Medical Professionals

Area	MDs[3]	DOs[3,4]	Dentists	Podiatrists	Chiropractors	Optometrists
County[1] (number)	888	41	144	10	70	55
County[1] (rate[2])	304.5	14.1	49.0	3.4	23.8	18.7
U.S. (rate[2])	282.9	22.7	71.2	6.2	28.1	16.9

12073
Note: Data as of 2019 unless noted; (1) Data covers Leon County; (2) Rate per 100,000 population; (3) Data as of 2018 and includes all active, non-federal physicians; (4) Doctor of Osteopathic Medicine
Source: U.S. Department of Health and Human Services, Health Resources and Services Administration, Bureau of Health Professions, Area Resource File (ARF) 2019-2020

EDUCATION

Public School District Statistics

District Name	Schls	Pupils	Pupil/ Teacher Ratio	Minority Pupils[1] (%)	Free Lunch Eligible[2] (%)	IEP[3] (%)
Leon	57	33,974	17.5	58.6	37.9	15.6

Note: Table includes school districts with 2,000 or more students; (1) Percentage of students that are not non-Hispanic white; (2) Percentage of students that are eligible for the free lunch program; (3) Percentage of students that have an Individualized Education Program.
Source: U.S. Department of Education, National Center for Education Statistics, Common Core of Data, Local Education Agency (School District) Universe Survey: School Year 2018-2019; U.S. Department of Education, National Center for Education Statistics, Common Core of Data, Public Elementary/Secondary School Universe Survey: School Year 2018-2019

Highest Level of Education

Area	Less than H.S.	H.S. Diploma	Some College, No Deg.	Associate Degree	Bachelor's Degree	Master's Degree	Prof. School Degree	Doctorate Degree
City	6.5	17.0	19.0	9.3	26.2	13.8	3.9	4.3
MSA[1]	9.4	23.7	19.8	8.7	22.0	10.4	2.9	3.1
U.S.	12.0	27.0	20.4	8.5	19.8	8.8	2.1	1.4

Note: Figures cover persons age 25 and over; (1) Figures cover the Tallahassee, FL Metropolitan Statistical Area
Source: U.S. Census Bureau, 2015-2019 American Community Survey 5-Year Estimates

Educational Attainment by Race

Area	High School Graduate or Higher (%)					Bachelor's Degree or Higher (%)				
	Total	White	Black	Asian	Hisp.[2]	Total	White	Black	Asian	Hisp.[2]
City	93.5	96.4	88.2	96.0	88.5	48.2	56.9	28.1	80.7	39.6
MSA[1]	90.6	93.9	83.5	96.3	82.1	38.4	44.1	23.0	79.3	30.2
U.S.	88.0	89.9	86.0	87.1	68.7	32.1	33.5	21.6	54.3	16.4

Note: Figures shown cover persons 25 years old and over; (1) Figures cover the Tallahassee, FL Metropolitan Statistical Area; (2) People of Hispanic origin can be of any race
Source: U.S. Census Bureau, 2015-2019 American Community Survey 5-Year Estimates

School Enrollment by Grade and Control

Area	Preschool (%)		Kindergarten (%)		Grades 1 - 4 (%)		Grades 5 - 8 (%)		Grades 9 - 12 (%)	
	Public	Private	Public	Private	Public	Private	Public	Private	Public	Private
City	48.6	51.4	86.3	13.7	85.9	14.1	83.3	16.7	87.4	12.6
MSA[1]	49.6	50.4	86.3	13.7	86.0	14.0	81.7	18.3	86.2	13.8
U.S.	59.1	40.9	87.6	12.4	89.5	10.5	89.4	10.6	90.1	9.9

Note: Figures shown cover persons 3 years old and over; (1) Figures cover the Tallahassee, FL Metropolitan Statistical Area
Source: U.S. Census Bureau, 2015-2019 American Community Survey 5-Year Estimates

Higher Education

Four-Year Colleges			Two-Year Colleges			Medical Schools[1]	Law Schools[2]	Voc/ Tech[3]
Public	Private Non-profit	Private For-profit	Public	Private Non-profit	Private For-profit			
3	1	0	0	0	0	1	1	4

Note: Figures cover institutions located within the city limits and include main campuses only; (1) includes schools accredited by the Liaison Committee on Medical Education and the American Osteopathic Association's Commission on Osteopathic College Accreditation; (2) includes ABA-accredited schools, schools with provisional ABA accreditation, and state accredited schools; (3) includes all schools with programs that are less than 2 years.
Source: National Center for Education Statistics, Integrated Postsecondary Education System (IPEDS), 2019-20; Wikipedia, List of Medical Schools in the United States, accessed April 2, 2021; Wikipedia, List of Law Schools in the United States, accessed April 2, 2021

According to *U.S. News & World Report,* the Tallahassee, FL metro area is home to one of the top 200 national universities in the U.S.: **Florida State University** (#58 tie). The indicators used to capture academic quality fall into a number of categories: assessment by administrators at peer institutions; retention of students; faculty resources; student selectivity; financial resources; alumni giving; high school counselor ratings of colleges; and graduation rate. *U.S. News & World Report, "America's Best Colleges 2021"*

According to *U.S. News & World Report,* the Tallahassee, FL metro area is home to one of the top 100 law schools in the U.S.: **Florida State University** (#48 tie). The rankings are based on a weighted average of 12 measures of quality: peer assessment score; assessment score by lawyers/judges; median LSAT scores; median undergrad GPA; acceptance rate; employment rates for graduates; placement success; bar passage rate; faculty resources; expenditures per student; student/faculty ratio; and library resources. *U.S. News & World Report, "America's Best Graduate Schools, Law, 2022"*

EMPLOYERS

Major Employers

Company Name	Industry
ACS, A Xerox Company	Manufacturer
Apalachee Center	Behavioral health network
Big Bend Hospice	Healthcare
Capital City Bank Group	Financial services
Capital Health Plan	Healthcare
Capital Regional Medical Center	Healthcare
CenturyLink	High speed internet, phone & TV services
City of Tallahassee	Municipal government
Danfoss Turbocor	Compressors mfg
Florida A&M University	Education
Florida Bar	Law association
Florida State University	Education
General Dynamics Lands System	Supplier of armored vehicles
Leon County	Government
Leon County Schools	Education
Publix Supermarkets	Retail grocery
St. Mark Powder, a General Dynamics Co.	Manufacturer of commercial smokeless powder
State of Florida	State government
Tallahassee Community College	Education
Tallahassee Memorial HealthCare	Healthcare
Tallahassee Primary Care Associates	Healthcare
University Center Club	Meeting & event center
Veterans of Foreign Wars	Government
Wal-Mart Stores	Retail
Westminster Oaks	Health care

Note: Companies shown are located within the Tallahassee, FL Metropolitan Statistical Area.
Source: Hoovers.com; Wikipedia

PUBLIC SAFETY

Crime Rate

Area	All Crimes	Violent Crimes				Property Crimes		
		Murder	Rape[3]	Robbery	Aggrav. Assault	Burglary	Larceny -Theft	Motor Vehicle Theft
City	4,675.5	10.3	101.0	129.2	456.2	608.4	3,022.5	348.0
Suburbs[1]	2,203.5	2.6	40.1	31.7	278.9	510.7	1,198.9	140.5
Metro[2]	3,458.0	6.5	71.0	81.2	368.9	560.3	2,124.4	245.8
U.S.	2,489.3	5.0	42.6	81.6	250.2	340.5	1,549.5	219.9

Note: Figures are crimes per 100,000 population; (1) All areas within the metro area that are located outside the city limits; (2) Figures cover the Tallahassee, FL Metropolitan Statistical Area; (3) All figures shown were reported using the revised Uniform Crime Reporting (UCR) definition of rape.
Source: FBI Uniform Crime Reports, 2019

Hate Crimes

Area	Number of Quarters Reported	Number of Incidents per Bias Motivation					
		Race/Ethnicity/ Ancestry	Religion	Sexual Orientation	Disability	Gender	Gender Identity
City	4	0	0	0	0	0	0
U.S.	4	3,963	1,521	1,195	157	69	198

Source: Federal Bureau of Investigation, Hate Crime Statistics 2019

Identity Theft Consumer Reports

Area	Reports	Reports per 100,000 Population	Rank[2]
MSA[1]	2,655	686	27
U.S.	1,387,615	423	-

Note: (1) Figures cover the Tallahassee, FL Metropolitan Statistical Area; (2) Rank ranges from 1 to 391 where 1 indicates greatest number of identity theft reports per 100,000 population
Source: Federal Trade Commission, Consumer Sentinel Network Data Book 2020

Fraud and Other Consumer Reports

Area	Reports	Reports per 100,000 Population	Rank[2]
MSA[1]	3,779	976	24
U.S.	3,385,133	1,031	-

Note: (1) Figures cover the Tallahassee, FL Metropolitan Statistical Area; (2) Rank ranges from 1 to 391 where 1 indicates greatest number of fraud and other consumer reports per 100,000 population
Source: Federal Trade Commission, Consumer Sentinel Network Data Book 2020

POLITICS

2020 Presidential Election Results

Area	Biden	Trump	Jorgensen	Hawkins	Other
Leon County	63.3	35.1	0.8	0.2	0.5
U.S.	51.3	46.8	1.2	0.3	0.5

Note: Results are percentages and may not add to 100% due to rounding
Source: Dave Leip's Atlas of U.S. Presidential Elections

SPORTS

Professional Sports Teams

Team Name	League	Year Established
No teams are located in the metro area		

Source: Wikipedia, Major Professional Sports Teams of the United States and Canada, April 6, 2021

CLIMATE

Average and Extreme Temperatures

Temperature	Jan	Feb	Mar	Apr	May	Jun	Jul	Aug	Sep	Oct	Nov	Dec	Yr.
Extreme High (°F)	83	89	90	95	102	103	103	102	99	94	88	84	103
Average High (°F)	64	67	73	80	86	90	91	91	88	81	72	66	79
Average Temp. (°F)	52	55	61	67	74	80	81	81	78	69	60	54	68
Average Low (°F)	40	42	48	53	62	69	71	72	68	57	47	41	56
Extreme Low (°F)	6	14	20	29	34	46	57	61	40	30	13	10	6

Note: Figures cover the years 1948-1990
Source: National Climatic Data Center, International Station Meteorological Climate Summary, 9/96

Average Precipitation/Snowfall/Humidity

Precip./Humidity	Jan	Feb	Mar	Apr	May	Jun	Jul	Aug	Sep	Oct	Nov	Dec	Yr.
Avg. Precip. (in.)	4.2	5.1	6.0	4.2	4.5	6.8	8.8	7.1	5.7	2.9	3.5	4.5	63.3
Avg. Snowfall (in.)	Tr	Tr	Tr	0	0	0	0	0	0	0	0	Tr	Tr
Avg. Rel. Hum. 7am (%)	86	87	88	89	89	91	93	94	93	90	89	87	90
Avg. Rel. Hum. 4pm (%)	54	51	49	46	50	58	66	64	60	51	52	55	55

Note: Figures cover the years 1948-1990; Tr = Trace amounts (<0.05 in. of rain; <0.5 in. of snow)
Source: National Climatic Data Center, International Station Meteorological Climate Summary, 9/96

Weather Conditions

Temperature			Daytime Sky			Precipitation		
10°F & below	32°F & below	90°F & above	Clear	Partly cloudy	Cloudy	0.01 inch or more precip.	0.1 inch or more snow/ice	Thunder-storms
< 1	31	86	93	175	97	114	1	83

Note: Figures are average number of days per year and cover the years 1948-1990
Source: National Climatic Data Center, International Station Meteorological Climate Summary, 9/96

HAZARDOUS WASTE

Superfund Sites

The Tallahassee, FL metro area is home to one site on the EPA's Superfund National Priorities List: **Post and Lumber Preserving Co Inc** (final). There are a total of 1,375 Superfund sites with a status of proposed or final on the list in the U.S. *U.S. Environmental Protection Agency, National Priorities List, April 7, 2021*

AIR QUALITY

Air Quality Trends: Ozone

	1990	1995	2000	2005	2010	2015	2016	2017	2018	2019
MSA[1]	n/a	n/a	n/a	n/a	n/a	n/a	n/a	n/a	n/a	n/a
U.S.	0.088	0.089	0.082	0.080	0.073	0.068	0.069	0.068	0.069	0.065

Note: (1) Data covers the Tallahassee, FL Metropolitan Statistical Area; n/a not available. The values shown are the composite ozone concentration averages among trend sites based on the highest fourth daily maximum 8-hour concentration in parts per million. These trends are based on sites having an adequate record of monitoring data during the trend period. Data from exceptional events are included.
Source: U.S. Environmental Protection Agency, Air Quality Monitoring Information, "Air Quality Trends by City, 1990-2019"

Air Quality Index

Area	Percent of Days when Air Quality was...[2]					AQI Statistics[2]	
	Good	Moderate	Unhealthy for Sensitive Groups	Unhealthy	Very Unhealthy	Maximum	Median
MSA[1]	74.5	25.2	0.3	0.0	0.0	119	40

Note: (1) Data covers the Tallahassee, FL Metropolitan Statistical Area; (2) Based on 365 days with AQI data in 2019. Air Quality Index (AQI) is an index for reporting daily air quality. EPA calculates the AQI for five major air pollutants regulated by the Clean Air Act: ground-level ozone, particle pollution (aka particulate matter), carbon monoxide, sulfur dioxide, and nitrogen dioxide. The AQI runs from 0 to 500. The higher the AQI value, the greater the level of air pollution and the greater the health concern. There are six AQI categories: "Good" AQI is between 0 and 50. Air quality is considered satisfactory; "Moderate" AQI is between 51 and 100. Air quality is acceptable; "Unhealthy for Sensitive Groups" When AQI values are between 101 and 150, members of sensitive groups may experience health effects; "Unhealthy" When AQI values are between 151 and 200 everyone may begin to experience health effects; "Very Unhealthy" AQI values between 201 and 300 trigger a health alert; "Hazardous" AQI values over 300 trigger warnings of emergency conditions (not shown).
Source: U.S. Environmental Protection Agency, Air Quality Index Report, 2019

Air Quality Index Pollutants

Area	Percent of Days when AQI Pollutant was...[2]					
	Carbon Monoxide	Nitrogen Dioxide	Ozone	Sulfur Dioxide	Particulate Matter 2.5	Particulate Matter 10
MSA[1]	0.0	0.0	47.7	0.0	52.3	0.0

Note: (1) Data covers the Tallahassee, FL Metropolitan Statistical Area; (2) Based on 365 days with AQI data in 2019. The Air Quality Index (AQI) is an index for reporting daily air quality. EPA calculates the AQI for five major air pollutants regulated by the Clean Air Act: ground-level ozone, particle pollution (also known as particulate matter), carbon monoxide, sulfur dioxide, and nitrogen dioxide. The AQI runs from 0 to 500. The higher the AQI value, the greater the level of air pollution and the greater the health concern.
Source: U.S. Environmental Protection Agency, Air Quality Index Report, 2019

Maximum Air Pollutant Concentrations: Particulate Matter, Ozone, CO and Lead

	Particulate Matter 10 (ug/m^3)	Particulate Matter 2.5 Wtd AM (ug/m^3)	Particulate Matter 2.5 24-Hr (ug/m^3)	Ozone (ppm)	Carbon Monoxide (ppm)	Lead (ug/m^3)
MSA[1] Level	n/a	7.7	20	0.063	1	n/a
NAAQS[2]	150	15	35	0.075	9	0.15
Met NAAQS[2]	n/a	Yes	Yes	Yes	Yes	n/a

Note: (1) Data covers the Tallahassee, FL Metropolitan Statistical Area; Data from exceptional events are included; (2) National Ambient Air Quality Standards; ppm = parts per million; ug/m^3 = micrograms per cubic meter; n/a not available.
Concentrations: Particulate Matter 10 (coarse particulate)—highest second maximum 24-hour concentration; Particulate Matter 2.5 Wtd AM (fine particulate)—highest weighted annual mean concentration; Particulate Matter 2.5 24-Hour (fine particulate)—highest 98th percentile 24-hour concentration; Ozone—highest fourth daily maximum 8-hour concentration; Carbon Monoxide—highest second maximum non-overlapping 8-hour concentration; Lead—maximum running 3-month average
Source: U.S. Environmental Protection Agency, Air Quality Monitoring Information, "Air Quality Statistics by City, 2019"

Maximum Air Pollutant Concentrations: Nitrogen Dioxide and Sulfur Dioxide

	Nitrogen Dioxide AM (ppb)	Nitrogen Dioxide 1-Hr (ppb)	Sulfur Dioxide AM (ppb)	Sulfur Dioxide 1-Hr (ppb)	Sulfur Dioxide 24-Hr (ppb)
MSA[1] Level	n/a	n/a	n/a	n/a	n/a
NAAQS[2]	53	100	30	75	140
Met NAAQS[2]	n/a	n/a	n/a	n/a	n/a

Note: (1) Data covers the Tallahassee, FL Metropolitan Statistical Area; Data from exceptional events are included; (2) National Ambient Air Quality Standards; ppm = parts per million; ug/m^3 = micrograms per cubic meter; n/a not available.
Concentrations: Nitrogen Dioxide AM—highest arithmetic mean concentration; Nitrogen Dioxide 1-Hr—highest 98th percentile 1-hour daily maximum concentration; Sulfur Dioxide AM—highest annual mean concentration; Sulfur Dioxide 1-Hr—highest 99th percentile 1-hour daily maximum concentration; Sulfur Dioxide 24-Hr—highest second maximum 24-hour concentration
Source: U.S. Environmental Protection Agency, Air Quality Monitoring Information, "Air Quality Statistics by City, 2019"

Tampa, Florida

Background

Although Tampa was visited by Spanish explorers, such as Ponce de Leon and Hernando de Soto as early as 1521, this city, located on the mouth of the Hillsborough River on Tampa Bay, did not see significant growth until the mid-nineteenth century.

Like many cities in northern Florida, such as Jacksonville, Tampa was a fort during the Seminole War, and during the Civil War it was captured by the Union Army. Later, Tampa enjoyed prosperity and development when the railroad transported tourists from up north to enjoy the warmth and sunshine of Florida.

Two historical events in the late nineteenth century set Tampa apart from other Florida cities. First, Tampa played a significant role during the Spanish-American War in 1898 as a chief port of embarkation for American troops to Cuba. During that time, Colonel Theodore Roosevelt occupied a Tampa hotel as his military headquarters. Second, a cigar factory in nearby Ybor City, named after owner Vicente Martinez Ybor, was where Jose Marti (the George Washington of Cuba) exhorted workers to take up arms against the tyranny of Spanish rule in the late 1800s.

By 1900, Tampa was known as the Cigar Capital of the World. In the peak year of 1929, factories in Tampa and Ybor City hand rolled an unbelievable 500 million cigars.

The city also saw its share of organized crime, with crime family alliances in New York and Cuba, from the late nineteenth century to the 1950s. Rampant and open corruption ended when crime hearings came to town, followed by the sensational misconduct of several local officials.

Today, Tampa enjoys its role as the largest port in the state, and host to many cruise ships. Major industries in and around Tampa include finance, retail, healthcare, insurance, shipping by air and sea, national defense, professional sports, and real estate. Like most of Florida, the city's economy is heavily based on tourism. Redevelopment of Tampa's downtown includes Tampa Riverwalk and Channelside, new homes in Tampa Bay History Center, the Glazer Children's Museum and Tampa Museum of Art.

Public transportation in the city includes Amtrak's Silver Star Line at Tampa Union Station and the TECO Line Streetcar System. Several sites in the Ybor and other neighborhoods have been designated historical landmarks. Tampa is also home to Big Cat Rescue, one of the largest accredited sanctuaries in the world dedicated entirely to abused and abandoned big cats, including lions, tigers, bobcats, and cougars.

Significant employers in the city include the Hillsborough County School District, WellCare Health Plan, Raymond James Financial, the University of South Florida, Hillsborough County Government, and MacDill Air Force Base. It is also home to computer servers that run Wikipedia, the online encyclopedia.

The city boasts National Football's Tampa Bay Buccaneers, Major League Baseball's Devil Rays baseball team, and National Hockey League's Lightning, which won the Stanley Cup in 2020. Other attractions include Florida's Latin Quarter known as Ybor City, Busch Gardens, and a Museum of Science and Industry. Two popular annual events are the MacDill Air Force Base air show, and the Gasparilla Pirate Festival, referred to as Tampa's "mardi gras."

> Tampa became "Canada South" when both the Toronto Raptors and Toronto Blue Jays made the city their temporary home base due to COVID-19 travel restrictions.

Winters are mild, while summers are long, warm, and humid. Freezing temperatures occur on one or two mornings per year during November through March. A dramatic feature of the Tampa climate is the summer thunderstorm season. Most occur during the late afternoon, sometimes causing temperatures to drop dramatically. The area is vulnerable to tidal surges, as the land has an elevation of less than 15 feet above sea level. The city has not experienced a direct hit from a hurricane since the 1930s, but three major hurricanes have seriously threatened Tampa—Donna in 1960, Charley in 2004 and Irma in 2017, the last of which caused significant damage, particularly to the city's electrical grid.

Rankings

General Rankings

- For its "Best for Vets: Places to Live 2019" rankings, *Military Times* evaluated 599 cities (83 large, 234 medium, 282 small) and compared the locations across three broad categories: veteran and military culture/services; economic indicators; and livability factors such as health, crime, traffic, and school quality. Tampa ranked #13 out of the top 25, in the large city category (population of more than 250,000). Data points more specific to veterans and the military weighed more heavily than others. *rebootcamp.militarytimes.com*, "Military Times Best Places to Live 2019," September 10, 2018

- The Tampa metro area was identified as one of America's fastest-growing areas in terms of population and economy by *Forbes*. The area ranked #23 out of 25. The 100 most populous metro areas in the U.S. were evaluated on the following criteria: estimated population growth; employment; economic output; wages; home values. *Forbes*, "America's Fastest-Growing Cities 2018," February 28, 2018

Business/Finance Rankings

- The Brookings Institution ranked the nation's largest cities based on income inequality. Tampa was ranked #13 (#1 = greatest inequality). Criteria: the "95/20 ratio," a figure representing the income at which a household earns more than 95 percent of all other households, divided by the income at which a household earns more than only 20 percent of all other households. *Brookings Institution*, "Household Income Inequality, Largest Cities of 97 Large U.S. Metro Areas, 2014-2016," February 5, 2018

- The Brookings Institution ranked the 100 largest metro areas in the U.S. based on income inequality. Tampa was ranked #38 (#1 = greatest inequality). Criteria: the "95/20 ratio," a figure representing the income at which a household earns more than 95 percent of all other households, divided by the income at which a household earns more than only 20 percent of all other households. *Brookings Institution*, "Household Income Inequality, 100 Largest U.S. Metro Areas, 2014-2016," February 5, 2018

- Payscale.com ranked the 32 largest metro areas in terms of wage growth. The Tampa metro area ranked #5. Criteria: private-sector and education professional wage growth between the 4th quarter of 2019 and the 4th quarter of 2020. *PayScale*, "Wage Trends by Metro Area-4th Quarter," January 11, 2021

- The Tampa metro area was identified as one of the most debt-ridden places in America by the finance site Credit.com. The metro area was ranked #19. Criteria: residents' average credit card debt as well as median income. *Credit.com*, "25 Cities With the Most Credit Card Debt," February 28, 2018

- Tampa was identified as one of America's most frugal metro areas by *Coupons.com*. The city ranked #7 out of 25. Criteria: digital coupon usage. *Coupons.com*, "America's Most Frugal Cities of 2017," March 22, 2018

- The Tampa metro area appeared on the Milken Institute "2021 Best Performing Cities" list. Rank: #32 out of 200 large metro areas (population over 250,000). Criteria: job growth; wage and salary growth; high-tech output growth; housing affordability; household broadband access. *Milken Institute*, "Best-Performing Cities 2021," February 16, 2021

- *Forbes* ranked the 200 most populous metro areas to determine the nation's "Best Places for Business and Careers." The Tampa metro area was ranked #35. Criteria: costs (business and living); job growth (past and projected); income growth; quality of life; educational attainment (college and high school); projected economic growth; cultural and leisure opportunities; workplace tolerance laws; net migration patterns. *Forbes*, "The Best Places for Business and Careers 2019: Seattle Still On Top," October 30, 2019

Children/Family Rankings

- Tampa was selected as one of the most playful cities in the U.S. by KaBOOM! The organization's Playful City USA initiative honors cities and towns across the nation that have made their communities more playable. Criteria: pledging to integrate play as a solution to challenges in their communities; making it easy for children to get active and balanced play; creating more family-friendly and innovative communities as a result. *KaBOOM! National Campaign for Play*, "2017 Playful City USA Communities"

Dating/Romance Rankings

- Tampa was selected as one of the nation's most romantic cities with 100,000 or more residents by Amazon.com. The city ranked #16 of 20. Criteria: per capita sales of romance novels, relationship books, romantic comedy movies, romantic music, and sexual wellness products. *Amazon.com*, "Top 20 Most Romantic Cities in the U.S.," February 1, 2017

Education Rankings

- Personal finance website *WalletHub* analyzed the 150 largest U.S. metropolitan statistical areas to determine where the most educated Americans are putting their degrees to work. Criteria: education levels; percentage of workers with degrees; education quality and attainment gap; public school quality rankings; quality and enrollment of each metro area's universities. Tampa was ranked #86 (#1 = most educated city). *www.WalletHub.com, "Most and Least Educated Cities in America," July 20, 2020*

- Tampa was selected as one of America's most literate cities. The city ranked #49 out of the 84 largest U.S. cities. Criteria: number of booksellers; library resources; Internet resources; educational attainment; periodical publishing resources; newspaper circulation. *Central Connecticut State University, "America's Most Literate Cities, 2018," February 2019*

Environmental Rankings

- Sperling's BestPlaces assessed the 50 largest metropolitan areas of the United States for the likelihood of dangerously extreme weather events or earthquakes. In general the Southeast and South-Central regions have the highest risk of weather extremes and earthquakes, while the Pacific Northwest enjoys the lowest risk. Of the most risky metropolitan areas, the Tampa metro area was ranked #8. *www.bestplaces.net, "Avoid Natural Disasters: BestPlaces Reveals The Top 10 Safest Places to Live," October 25, 2017*

- The U.S. Environmental Protection Agency (EPA) released a list of U.S. metropolitan areas with the most ENERGY STAR certified buildings in 2019. The Tampa metro area was ranked #11 out of 25. *U.S. Environmental Protection Agency, "2020 Energy Star Top Cities," March 2020*

- Tampa was highlighted as one of the top 98 cleanest metro areas for short-term particle pollution (24-hour PM 2.5) in the U.S. during 2016 through 2018. Monitors in these cities reported no days with unhealthful PM 2.5 levels. *American Lung Association, "State of the Air 2020," April 21, 2020*

Health/Fitness Rankings

- For each of the 100 largest cities in the United States, the American Fitness Index®, published by the American College of Sports Medicine and the Anthem Foundation, evaluated community infrastructure and 33 health behaviors including preventive health, levels of chronic disease conditions, pedestrian safety, air quality, and community resources that support physical activity. Tampa ranked #45 for "community fitness." *americanfitnessindex.org, "2020 ACSM American Fitness Index Summary Report," July 14, 2020*

- The Tampa metro area was identified as one of the worst cities for bed bugs in America by pest control company Orkin. The area ranked #39 out of 50 based on the number of bed bug treatments Orkin performed from December 2019 to November 2020. *Orkin, "New Year, New Top City on Orkin's 2021 Bed Bug Cities List: Chicago," February 1, 2021*

- Tampa was identified as a "2021 Spring Allergy Capital." The area ranked #69 out of 100. Three groups of factors were used to identify the most challenging cities for people with allergies during the spring season: annual spring pollen levels; over the counter medicine use; number of board-certified allergy specialists. *Asthma and Allergy Foundation of America, "Spring Allergy Capitals 2021," February 23, 2021*

- Tampa was identified as a "2021 Fall Allergy Capital." The area ranked #71 out of 100. Three groups of factors were used to identify the most challenging cities for people with allergies during the fall season: annual fall pollen levels; over the counter medicine use; number of board-certified allergy specialists. *Asthma and Allergy Foundation of America, "Fall Allergy Capitals 2021," February 23, 2021*

- Tampa was identified as a "2019 Asthma Capital." The area ranked #83 out of the nation's 100 largest metropolitan areas. Criteria: estimated asthma prevalence; crude death rate from asthma; and ER visits due to asthma. Risk factors analyzed but not factored in the rankings: annual pollen score; annual air quality; public smoking laws; number of board-certified asthma specialists; rescue medication use; controller medication use; uninsured rate; poverty rate. *Asthma and Allergy Foundation of America, "Asthma Capitals 2019: The Most Challenging Places to Live With Asthma," May 7, 2019*

Real Estate Rankings

- FitSmallBusiness looked at 50 of the largest metropolitan areas in the U.S. to determine which metro was the best to start a real estate business. Data was compiled from such sources as: Zillow, Trulia, U.S. Census Bureau, and the Bureau of Labor Statistics. Criteria: location; inventory; annual wages; median sales price of homes; days on the market; median price cut percentage; and other factors that would influence real estate professional growth. The Tampa metro area ranked #32. *fitsmallbusiness.com, "The Best Cities to Become a Real Estate Agent in 2018," January 30, 2018*

- *WalletHub* compared the most populated U.S. cities to determine which had the best markets for real estate agents. Tampa ranked #26 where demand was high and pay was the best. Criteria: sales per agent; annual median wage for real-estate agents; monthly average starting salary for real estate agents; real estate job density and competition; unemployment rate; home turnover rate; housing-market health index; and other relevant metrics. *www.WalletHub.com, "2019's Best Places to Be a Real Estate Agent," April 24, 2019*

- According to Penske Truck Rental, the Tampa metro area was named the #3 moving destination in 2019, based on one-way consumer truck rental reservations made through Penske's website, rental locations, and reservations call center. *gopenske.com/blog, "Penske Truck Rental's 2019 Top Moving Destinations," January 22, 2020*

- Tampa was ranked #168 out of 268 metro areas in terms of housing affordability in 2020 by the National Association of Home Builders (#1 = most affordable). Criteria: the share of homes sold in that area affordable to a family earning the local median income, based on standard mortgage underwriting criteria. *National Association of Home Builders®, NAHB-Wells Fargo Housing Opportunity Index, 4th Quarter 2020*

Safety Rankings

- Allstate ranked the 200 largest cities in America in terms of driver safety. Tampa ranked #101. Criteria: internal property damage claims over a two-year period from January 2016 to December 2017. The report helps increase the importance of safety and awareness behind the wheel. *Allstate, "Allstate America's Best Drivers Report, 2019" June 24, 2019*

- The National Insurance Crime Bureau ranked 384 metro areas in the U.S. in terms of per capita rates of vehicle theft. The Tampa metro area ranked #223 (#1 = highest rate). Criteria: number of vehicle theft offenses per 100,000 inhabitants in 2019. *National Insurance Crime Bureau, "Hot Spots 2019," July 21, 2020*

Seniors/Retirement Rankings

- From its Best Cities for Successful Aging indexes, the Milken Institute generated rankings for metropolitan areas, weighing data in nine categories—health care, wellness, living arrangements, transportation and convenience, financial characteristics, education, employment, community engagement, and overall livability. The Tampa metro area was ranked #84 overall in the large metro area category. *Milken Institute, "Best Cities for Successful Aging, 2017" March 14, 2017*

Sports/Recreation Rankings

- Tampa was chosen as one of America's best cities for bicycling. The city ranked #48 out of 50. Criteria: cycling infrastructure that is safe and friendly for all ages; energy and bike culture. The editors evaluated cities with populations of 100,000 or more. *Bicycling, "The 50 Best Bike Cities in America," October 10, 2018*

Women/Minorities Rankings

- Tampa was selected as one of the gayest cities in America by *The Advocate*. The city ranked #19 out of 25. Criteria, among many: Trans Pride parades/festivals; gay rugby teams; lesbian bars; LGBT centers; theater screenings of "Moonlight"; LGBT-inclusive nondiscrimination ordinances; and gay bowling teams. *The Advocate, "Queerest Cities in America 2017" January 12, 2017*

- Personal finance website *WalletHub* compared more than 180 U.S. cities across two key dimensions, "Hispanic Business-Friendliness" and "Hispanic Purchasing Power," to arrive at the most favorable conditions for Hispanic entrepreneurs. Tampa was ranked #7 out of 182. Criteria includes: share of Hispanic-Owned Businesses; Hispanic entrepreneurship rate to median annual income of Hispanics; Small Business-Friendliness score; cost of living; and number of Hispanics with at least a bachelor's degree. *WalletHub.com, "2019's Best Cities for Hispanic Entrepreneurs," May 1, 2019*

Miscellaneous Rankings

- *MoveHub* ranked 446 hipster cities across 20 countries, using its *alternative* Hipster Index and Tampa came out as #11 among the top 50. Criteria: population over 150,000; number of vintage boutiques; density of tattoo parlors; vegan places to eat; coffee shops; and density of vinyl record stores. *www.movehub.com, "The Hipster Index: Brighton Pips Portland to Global Top Spot," February 20, 2020*

- The watchdog site, Charity Navigator, conducted a study of charities in major markets both to analyze statistical differences in their financial, accountability, and transparency practices and to track year-to-year variations in individual philanthropic communities. The Tampa metro area was ranked #4 among the 30 metro markets in the rating category of Overall Score. *www.charitynavigator.org, "2017 Metro Market Study," May 1, 2017*

- *WalletHub* compared the 150 most populated U.S. cities to determine their operating efficiency. A "Quality of City Services" score was constructed for each city and then divided by the total budget per capita to reveal which were managed the best. Tampa ranked #88. Criteria: financial stability; economy; education; safety; health; infrastructure and pollution. *www.WalletHub.com, "2020's Best- & Worst-Run Cities in America," June 29, 2020*

- The National Alliance to End Homelessness listed the 25 most populous metro areas with the highest rate of homelessness. The Tampa metro area had a high rate of homelessness. Criteria: number of homeless people per 10,000 population in 2016. *National Alliance to End Homelessness, "Homelessness in the 25 Most Populous U.S. Metro Areas," September 1, 2017*

Business Environment

DEMOGRAPHICS

Population Growth

Area	1990 Census	2000 Census	2010 Census	2019* Estimate	Population Growth (%) 1990-2019	Population Growth (%) 2010-2019
City	279,960	303,447	335,709	387,916	38.6	15.6
MSA[1]	2,067,959	2,395,997	2,783,243	3,097,859	49.8	11.3
U.S.	248,709,873	281,421,906	308,745,538	324,697,795	30.6	5.2

Note: (1) Figures cover the Tampa-St. Petersburg-Clearwater, FL Metropolitan Statistical Area; (*) 2015-2019 5-year estimated population
Source: U.S. Census Bureau, 1990 Census, Census 2000, Census 2010, 2015-2019 American Community Survey 5-Year Estimates

Household Size

Area	One	Two	Three	Four	Five	Six	Seven or More	Average Household Size
City	35.8	31.6	15.4	10.9	4.2	1.5	0.7	2.50
MSA[1]	30.9	36.7	14.8	10.9	4.4	1.5	0.8	2.50
U.S.	27.9	33.9	15.6	12.9	6.0	2.3	1.4	2.60

Note: (1) Figures cover the Tampa-St. Petersburg-Clearwater, FL Metropolitan Statistical Area
Source: U.S. Census Bureau, 2015-2019 American Community Survey 5-Year Estimates

Race

Area	White Alone[2] (%)	Black Alone[2] (%)	Asian Alone[2] (%)	AIAN[3] Alone[2] (%)	NHOPI[4] Alone[2] (%)	Other Race Alone[2] (%)	Two or More Races (%)
City	65.4	23.6	4.3	0.3	0.1	2.5	3.9
MSA[1]	77.8	12.2	3.4	0.3	0.1	2.9	3.3
U.S.	72.5	12.7	5.5	0.8	0.2	4.9	3.3

Note: (1) Figures cover the Tampa-St. Petersburg-Clearwater, FL Metropolitan Statistical Area; (2) Alone is defined as not being in combination with one or more other races; (3) American Indian and Alaska Native; (4) Native Hawaiian and Other Pacific Islander
Source: U.S. Census Bureau, 2015-2019 American Community Survey 5-Year Estimates

Hispanic or Latino Origin

Area	Total (%)	Mexican (%)	Puerto Rican (%)	Cuban (%)	Other (%)
City	26.4	3.1	7.6	8.0	7.7
MSA[1]	19.6	3.8	6.2	4.0	5.6
U.S.	18.0	11.2	1.7	0.7	4.3

Note: Persons of Hispanic or Latino origin can be of any race; (1) Figures cover the Tampa-St. Petersburg-Clearwater, FL Metropolitan Statistical Area
Source: U.S. Census Bureau, 2015-2019 American Community Survey 5-Year Estimates

Ancestry

Area	German	Irish	English	American	Italian	Polish	French[2]	Scottish	Dutch
City	8.7	8.0	6.0	6.2	6.0	2.0	2.0	1.5	0.8
MSA[1]	12.3	10.8	7.8	8.6	7.5	3.0	2.6	1.8	1.1
U.S.	13.3	9.7	7.2	6.2	5.1	2.8	2.3	1.7	1.2

Note: Figures are the percentage of the total population reporting a particular ancestry. The nine most commonly reported ancestries in the U.S. are shown. Figures include multiple ancestries (e.g. if a person reported being Irish and Italian, they were included in both columns); (1) Figures cover the Tampa-St. Petersburg-Clearwater, FL Metropolitan Statistical Area; (2) Excludes Basque
Source: U.S. Census Bureau, 2015-2019 American Community Survey 5-Year Estimates

Foreign-born Population

Area	Any Foreign Country	Asia	Mexico	Europe	Caribbean	Central America[2]	South America	Africa	Canada
City	17.2	3.8	1.1	1.4	6.9	1.1	2.0	0.4	0.4
MSA[1]	13.9	2.8	1.3	2.2	3.7	0.8	1.9	0.5	0.6
U.S.	13.6	4.2	3.5	1.5	1.3	1.1	1.0	0.7	0.2

Note: (1) Figures cover the Tampa-St. Petersburg-Clearwater, FL Metropolitan Statistical Area; (2) Excludes Mexico.
Source: U.S. Census Bureau, 2015-2019 American Community Survey 5-Year Estimates

Marital Status

Area	Never Married	Now Married[2]	Separated	Widowed	Divorced
City	40.4	38.4	2.7	5.0	13.6
MSA[1]	31.2	45.9	2.1	7.0	13.9
U.S.	33.4	48.1	1.9	5.8	10.9

Note: Figures are percentages and cover the population 15 years of age and older; (1) Figures cover the Tampa-St. Petersburg-Clearwater, FL Metropolitan Statistical Area; (2) Excludes separated
Source: U.S. Census Bureau, 2015-2019 American Community Survey 5-Year Estimates

Disability by Age

Area	All Ages	Under 18 Years Old	18 to 64 Years Old	65 Years and Over
City	12.2	3.7	9.9	39.4
MSA[1]	14.0	4.4	10.8	34.3
U.S.	12.6	4.2	10.3	34.5

Note: Figures show percent of the civilian noninstitutionalized population that reported having a disability. Disability status is determined from six types of difficulty: vision, hearing, cognitive, ambulatory, self-care, and independent living. For children under 5 years old, hearing and vision difficulty are used to determine disability status. For children between the ages of 5 and 14, disability status is determined from hearing, vision, cognitive, ambulatory, and self-care difficulties. For people aged 15 years and older, they are considered to have a disability if they have difficulty with any one of the six difficulty types; Note: (1) Figures cover the Tampa-St. Petersburg-Clearwater, FL Metropolitan Statistical Area
Source: U.S. Census Bureau, 2015-2019 American Community Survey 5-Year Estimates

Age

Area	Under Age 5	Age 5–19	Age 20–34	Age 35–44	Age 45–54	Age 55–64	Age 65–74	Age 75–84	Age 85+	Median Age
City	6.4	18.5	24.2	13.5	13.4	11.8	7.3	3.5	1.5	35.7
MSA[1]	5.4	16.8	18.9	12.4	13.5	13.6	10.9	6.0	2.5	42.1
U.S.	6.1	19.1	20.7	12.6	13.0	12.9	9.1	4.6	1.9	38.1

Note: (1) Figures cover the Tampa-St. Petersburg-Clearwater, FL Metropolitan Statistical Area
Source: U.S. Census Bureau, 2015-2019 American Community Survey 5-Year Estimates

Gender

Area	Males	Females	Males per 100 Females
City	188,134	199,782	94.2
MSA[1]	1,502,972	1,594,887	94.2
U.S.	159,886,919	164,810,876	97.0

Note: (1) Figures cover the Tampa-St. Petersburg-Clearwater, FL Metropolitan Statistical Area
Source: U.S. Census Bureau, 2015-2019 American Community Survey 5-Year Estimates

Religious Groups by Family

Area	Catholic	Baptist	Non-Den.	Methodist[2]	Lutheran	LDS[3]	Pentecostal	Presbyterian[4]	Muslim[5]	Judaism
MSA[1]	10.9	7.1	3.8	3.5	1.0	0.6	2.1	1.0	1.3	0.5
U.S.	19.1	9.3	4.0	4.0	2.3	2.0	1.9	1.6	0.8	0.7

Note: Figures are the number of adherents as a percentage of the total population; (1) Figures cover the Tampa-St. Petersburg-Clearwater, FL Metropolitan Statistical Area; (2) Methodist/Pietist; (3) Latter Day Saints; (4) Reformed; (5) Figures are estimates
Source: Association of Statisticians of American Religious Bodies, 2010 U.S. Religion Census: Religious Congregations & Membership Study

Religious Groups by Tradition

Area	Catholic	Evangelical Protestant	Mainline Protestant	Other Tradition	Black Protestant	Orthodox
MSA[1]	10.9	13.6	5.2	3.1	1.2	0.8
U.S.	19.1	16.2	7.3	4.3	1.6	0.3

Note: Figures are the number of adherents as a percentage of the total population; (1) Figures cover the Tampa-St. Petersburg-Clearwater, FL Metropolitan Statistical Area
Source: Association of Statisticians of American Religious Bodies, 2010 U.S. Religion Census: Religious Congregations & Membership Study

ECONOMY

Gross Metropolitan Product

Area	2017	2018	2019	2020	Rank[2]
MSA[1]	148.2	156.6	164.0	172.0	24

Note: Figures are in billions of dollars; (1) Figures cover the Tampa-St. Petersburg-Clearwater, FL Metropolitan Statistical Area; (2) Rank is based on 2018 data and ranges from 1 to 381
Source: U.S. Conference of Mayors, U.S. Metro Economies: GMP & Employment 2018-2020, September 2019

Economic Growth

Area	2015-17 (%)	2018 (%)	2019 (%)	2020 (%)	Rank[2]
MSA[1]	2.7	3.5	2.9	2.6	85
U.S.	1.9	2.9	2.3	2.1	—

Note: Figures are real gross metropolitan product (GMP) growth rates and represent average annual percent change; (1) Figures cover the Tampa-St. Petersburg-Clearwater, FL Metropolitan Statistical Area; (2) Rank is based on 2017 2-year average annual percent change and ranges from 1 to 381
Source: U.S. Conference of Mayors, U.S. Metro Economies: GMP & Employment 2018-2020, September 2019

Metropolitan Area Exports

Area	2014	2015	2016	2017	2018	2019	Rank[2]
MSA[1]	5,817.3	5,660.4	5,702.9	6,256.0	4,966.7	6,219.7	50

Note: Figures are in millions of dollars; (1) Figures cover the Tampa-St. Petersburg-Clearwater, FL Metropolitan Statistical Area; (2) Rank is based on 2019 data and ranges from 1 to 386
Source: U.S. Department of Commerce, International Trade Administration, Office of Trade and Economic Analysis, Industry and Analysis, Exports by Metropolitan Area, data extracted March 24, 2021

Building Permits

Area	Single-Family 2018	Single-Family 2019	Pct. Chg.	Multi-Family 2018	Multi-Family 2019	Pct. Chg.	Total 2018	Total 2019	Pct. Chg.
City	1,109	1,159	4.5	679	3,618	432.8	1,788	4,777	167.2
MSA[1]	14,228	14,670	3.1	3,224	8,870	175.1	17,452	23,540	34.9
U.S.	855,300	862,100	0.7	473,500	523,900	10.6	1,328,800	1,386,000	4.3

Note: (1) Figures cover the Tampa-St. Petersburg-Clearwater, FL Metropolitan Statistical Area; Figures represent new, privately-owned housing units authorized (unadjusted data); All permit data are based on estimates with imputation
Source: U.S. Census Bureau, Manufacturing, Mining, and Construction Statistics, Building Permits, 2018, 2019

Bankruptcy Filings

Area	Business Filings 2019	Business Filings 2020	% Chg.	Nonbusiness Filings 2019	Nonbusiness Filings 2020	% Chg.
Hillsborough County	155	110	-29.0	3,356	2,538	-24.4
U.S.	22,780	21,655	-4.9	752,160	522,808	-30.5

Note: Business filings include Chapter 7, Chapter 9, Chapter 11, Chapter 12, Chapter 13, Chapter 15, and Section 304; Nonbusiness filings include Chapter 7, Chapter 11, and Chapter 13
Source: Administrative Office of the U.S. Courts, Business and Nonbusiness Bankruptcy, County Cases Commenced by Chapter of the Bankruptcy Code, During the 12-Month Period Ending December 31, 2019 and Business and Nonbusiness Bankruptcy, County Cases Commenced by Chapter of the Bankruptcy Code, During the 12-Month Period Ending December 31, 2020

Housing Vacancy Rates

Area	Gross Vacancy Rate[2] (%) 2018	2019	2020	Year-Round Vacancy Rate[3] (%) 2018	2019	2020	Rental Vacancy Rate[4] (%) 2018	2019	2020	Homeowner Vacancy Rate[5] (%) 2018	2019	2020
MSA[1]	16.1	16.2	13.0	11.9	12.7	10.1	9.9	10.7	8.9	2.1	1.6	1.5
U.S.	12.3	12.0	10.6	9.7	9.5	8.2	6.9	6.7	6.3	1.5	1.4	1.0

Note: (1) Figures cover the Tampa-St. Petersburg-Clearwater, FL Metropolitan Statistical Area; (2) The percentage of the total housing inventory that is vacant; (3) The percentage of the housing inventory (excluding seasonal units) that is year-round vacant; (4) The percentage of rental inventory that is vacant for rent; (5) The percentage of homeowner inventory that is vacant for sale
Source: U.S. Census Bureau, Housing Vacancies and Homeownership Annual Statistics: 2018, 2019, 2020

INCOME

Income

Area	Per Capita ($)	Median Household ($)	Average Household ($)
City	36,169	53,833	87,818
MSA[1]	32,276	55,285	78,248
U.S.	34,103	62,843	88,607

Note: (1) Figures cover the Tampa-St. Petersburg-Clearwater, FL Metropolitan Statistical Area
Source: U.S. Census Bureau, 2015-2019 American Community Survey 5-Year Estimates

Household Income Distribution

Area	Under $15,000	$15,000 -$24,999	$25,000 -$34,999	$35,000 -$49,999	$50,000 -$74,999	$75,000 -$99,999	$100,000 -$149,999	$150,000 and up
City	14.6	10.3	9.9	12.2	15.8	10.7	12.0	14.6
MSA[1]	10.9	10.0	10.3	14.0	18.0	12.4	13.2	11.1
U.S.	10.3	8.9	8.9	12.3	17.2	12.7	15.1	14.5

Note: (1) Figures cover the Tampa-St. Petersburg-Clearwater, FL Metropolitan Statistical Area
Source: U.S. Census Bureau, 2015-2019 American Community Survey 5-Year Estimates

Poverty Rate

Area	All Ages	Under 18 Years Old	18 to 64 Years Old	65 Years and Over
City	18.6	26.5	16.2	17.6
MSA[1]	13.5	18.6	12.8	10.3
U.S.	13.4	18.5	12.6	9.3

Note: Figures are percentage of people whose income during the past 12 months was below the poverty level;
(1) Figures cover the Tampa-St. Petersburg-Clearwater, FL Metropolitan Statistical Area
Source: U.S. Census Bureau, 2015-2019 American Community Survey 5-Year Estimates

CITY FINANCES

City Government Finances

Component	2017 ($000)	2017 ($ per capita)
Total Revenues	1,047,634	2,839
Total Expenditures	935,405	2,534
Debt Outstanding	1,675,263	4,539
Cash and Securities[1]	3,475,941	9,418

Note: (1) Cash and security holdings of a government at the close of its fiscal year, including those of its dependent agencies, utilities, and liquor stores.
Source: U.S. Census Bureau, State & Local Government Finances 2017

City Government Revenue by Source

Source	2017 ($000)	2017 ($ per capita)	2017 (%)
General Revenue			
From Federal Government	16,217	44	1.5
From State Government	62,333	169	5.9
From Local Governments	16,365	44	1.6
Taxes			
Property	144,295	391	13.8
Sales and Gross Receipts	108,979	295	10.4
Personal Income	0	0	0.0
Corporate Income	0	0	0.0
Motor Vehicle License	0	0	0.0
Other Taxes	56,145	152	5.4
Current Charges	260,421	706	24.9
Liquor Store	0	0	0.0
Utility	105,452	286	10.1
Employee Retirement	241,676	655	23.1

Source: U.S. Census Bureau, State & Local Government Finances 2017

City Government Expenditures by Function

Function	2017 ($000)	2017 ($ per capita)	2017 (%)
General Direct Expenditures			
Air Transportation	0	0	0.0
Corrections	0	0	0.0
Education	0	0	0.0
Employment Security Administration	0	0	0.0
Financial Administration	35,557	96	3.8
Fire Protection	80,324	217	8.6
General Public Buildings	12,147	32	1.3
Governmental Administration, Other	3,472	9	0.4
Health	0	0	0.0
Highways	33,719	91	3.6
Hospitals	0	0	0.0
Housing and Community Development	17,057	46	1.8
Interest on General Debt	14,983	40	1.6
Judicial and Legal	4,898	13	0.5
Libraries	0	0	0.0
Parking	15,477	41	1.7
Parks and Recreation	70,195	190	7.5
Police Protection	153,120	414	16.4
Public Welfare	0	0	0.0
Sewerage	122,371	331	13.1
Solid Waste Management	66,493	180	7.1
Veterans' Services	0	0	0.0
Liquor Store	0	0	0.0
Utility	110,890	300	11.9
Employee Retirement	92,004	249	9.8

Source: U.S. Census Bureau, State & Local Government Finances 2017

EMPLOYMENT

Labor Force and Employment

Area	Civilian Labor Force Dec. 2019	Civilian Labor Force Dec. 2020	% Chg.	Workers Employed Dec. 2019	Workers Employed Dec. 2020	% Chg.
City	205,639	203,778	-0.9	200,162	191,493	-4.3
MSA[1]	1,566,692	1,540,183	-1.7	1,525,133	1,459,839	-4.3
U.S.	164,007,000	160,017,000	-2.4	158,504,000	149,613,000	-5.6

Note: Data is not seasonally adjusted and covers workers 16 years of age and older; (1) Figures cover the Tampa-St. Petersburg-Clearwater, FL Metropolitan Statistical Area
Source: Bureau of Labor Statistics, Local Area Unemployment Statistics

Unemployment Rate

Area	Jan.	Feb.	Mar.	Apr.	May	Jun.	Jul.	Aug.	Sep.	Oct.	Nov.	Dec.
City	3.1	3.0	4.3	12.6	12.2	9.7	11.6	7.8	6.6	6.4	6.4	6.0
MSA[1]	3.1	3.0	4.3	13.2	12.2	9.0	10.2	6.7	5.7	5.4	5.5	5.2
U.S.	4.0	3.8	4.5	14.4	13.0	11.2	10.5	8.5	7.7	6.6	6.4	6.5

Note: Data is not seasonally adjusted and covers workers 16 years of age and older; (1) Figures cover the Tampa-St. Petersburg-Clearwater, FL Metropolitan Statistical Area
Source: Bureau of Labor Statistics, Local Area Unemployment Statistics

Average Wages

Occupation	$/Hr.	Occupation	$/Hr.
Accountants and Auditors	37.30	Maintenance and Repair Workers	18.40
Automotive Mechanics	21.60	Marketing Managers	70.10
Bookkeepers	20.90	Network and Computer Systems Admin.	40.30
Carpenters	19.30	Nurses, Licensed Practical	22.60
Cashiers	11.50	Nurses, Registered	34.30
Computer Programmers	38.80	Nursing Assistants	14.10
Computer Systems Analysts	42.80	Office Clerks, General	17.70
Computer User Support Specialists	24.80	Physical Therapists	39.90
Construction Laborers	15.90	Physicians	104.00
Cooks, Restaurant	13.00	Plumbers, Pipefitters and Steamfitters	22.00
Customer Service Representatives	17.30	Police and Sheriff's Patrol Officers	30.90
Dentists	71.80	Postal Service Mail Carriers	25.80
Electricians	22.10	Real Estate Sales Agents	27.80
Engineers, Electrical	46.50	Retail Salespersons	14.20
Fast Food and Counter Workers	10.80	Sales Representatives, Technical/Scientific	38.90
Financial Managers	67.60	Secretaries, Exc. Legal/Medical/Executive	17.90
First-Line Supervisors of Office Workers	29.20	Security Guards	16.60
General and Operations Managers	54.50	Surgeons	99.80
Hairdressers/Cosmetologists	14.10	Teacher Assistants, Exc. Postsecondary*	14.50
Home Health and Personal Care Aides	11.60	Teachers, Secondary School, Exc. Sp. Ed.*	30.10
Janitors and Cleaners	16.80	Telemarketers	13.80
Landscaping/Groundskeeping Workers	14.00	Truck Drivers, Heavy/Tractor-Trailer	20.30
Lawyers	57.70	Truck Drivers, Light/Delivery Services	17.80
Maids and Housekeeping Cleaners	11.20	Waiters and Waitresses	14.20

Note: Wage data covers the Tampa-St. Petersburg-Clearwater, FL Metropolitan Statistical Area; (*) Hourly wages were calculated from annual wage data based on a 40 hour work week; n/a not available.
Source: Bureau of Labor Statistics, Metro Area Occupational Employment & Wage Estimates, May 2020

Employment by Industry

Sector	MSA[1] Number of Employees	MSA[1] Percent of Total	U.S. Percent of Total
Construction	84,400	6.2	5.1
Education and Health Services	213,100	15.6	16.3
Financial Activities	126,600	9.3	6.1
Government	154,100	11.3	15.2
Information	23,800	1.7	1.9
Leisure and Hospitality	136,600	10.0	9.0
Manufacturing	68,100	5.0	8.5
Mining and Logging	300	<0.1	0.4
Other Services	45,400	3.3	3.8
Professional and Business Services	255,700	18.7	14.4
Retail Trade	160,000	11.7	10.9
Transportation, Warehousing, and Utilities	44,400	3.2	4.6
Wholesale Trade	54,600	4.0	3.9

Note: Figures are non-farm employment as of December 2020. Figures are not seasonally adjusted and include workers 16 years of age and older; (1) Figures cover the Tampa-St. Petersburg-Clearwater, FL Metropolitan Statistical Area
Source: Bureau of Labor Statistics, Current Employment Statistics, Employment, Hours, and Earnings

Employment by Occupation

Occupation Classification	City (%)	MSA[1] (%)	U.S. (%)
Management, Business, Science, and Arts	42.6	38.5	38.5
Natural Resources, Construction, and Maintenance	6.6	8.4	8.9
Production, Transportation, and Material Moving	8.6	9.9	13.2
Sales and Office	23.6	25.2	21.6
Service	18.6	18.0	17.8

Note: Figures cover employed civilians 16 years of age and older; (1) Figures cover the Tampa-St. Petersburg-Clearwater, FL Metropolitan Statistical Area
Source: U.S. Census Bureau, 2015-2019 American Community Survey 5-Year Estimates

Occupations with Greatest Projected Employment Growth: 2020 – 2022

Occupation[1]	2020 Employment	2022 Projected Employment	Numeric Employment Change	Percent Employment Change
Fast Food and Counter Workers	172,590	214,590	42,000	24.3
Waiters and Waitresses	141,990	180,530	38,540	27.1
Retail Salespersons	264,490	292,340	27,850	10.5
Cooks, Restaurant	79,150	103,770	24,620	31.1
Maids and Housekeeping Cleaners	63,280	81,030	17,750	28.0
Cashiers	204,540	221,530	16,990	8.3
Registered Nurses	189,240	202,880	13,640	7.2
Laborers and Freight, Stock, and Material Movers, Hand	147,740	160,650	12,910	8.7
First-Line Supervisors of Food Preparation and Serving Workers	51,820	64,080	12,260	23.7
Stockers and Order Fillers	130,980	142,780	11,800	9.0

Note: Projections cover Florida; (1) Sorted by numeric employment change
Source: www.projectionscentral.com, State Occupational Projections, 2020–2022 Short-Term Projections

Fastest-Growing Occupations: 2020 – 2022

Occupation[1]	2020 Employment	2022 Projected Employment	Numeric Employment Change	Percent Employment Change
Hotel, Motel, and Resort Desk Clerks	11,930	18,100	6,170	51.7
Locker Room, Coatroom, and Dressing Room Attendants	930	1,360	430	46.2
Lodging Managers	3,190	4,420	1,230	38.6
Manicurists and Pedicurists	2,640	3,580	940	35.6
Bartenders	31,430	42,540	11,110	35.3
Gaming Cage Workers	320	430	110	34.4
Parking Lot Attendants	11,200	15,040	3,840	34.3
Gaming Dealers	2,660	3,560	900	33.8
Baggage Porters and Bellhops	3,520	4,670	1,150	32.7
Cooks, Restaurant	79,150	103,770	24,620	31.1

Note: Projections cover Florida; (1) Sorted by percent employment change and excludes occupations with numeric employment change less than 50
Source: www.projectionscentral.com, State Occupational Projections, 2020–2022 Short-Term Projections

TAXES

State Corporate Income Tax Rates

State	Tax Rate (%)	Income Brackets ($)	Num. of Brackets	Financial Institution Tax Rate (%)[a]	Federal Income Tax Ded.
Florida	4.458 (e)	Flat rate	1	4.458 (e)	No

Note: Tax rates as of January 1, 2021; (a) Rates listed are the corporate income tax rate applied to financial institutions or excise taxes based on income. Some states have other taxes based upon the value of deposits or shares; (e) The Florida tax rate may be adjusted downward if certain revenue targets are met.
Source: Federation of Tax Administrators, State Corporate Income Tax Rates, January 1, 2021

State Individual Income Tax Rates

State	Tax Rate (%)	Income Brackets ($)	Personal Exemptions ($) Single	Married	Depend.	Standard Ded. ($) Single	Married
Florida						– No state income tax –	

Note: Tax rates as of January 1, 2021; Local- and county-level taxes are not included
Source: Federation of Tax Administrators, State Individual Income Tax Rates, January 1, 2021

Various State Sales and Excise Tax Rates

State	State Sales Tax (%)	Gasoline[1] (¢/gal.)	Cigarette[2] ($/pack)	Spirits[3] ($/gal.)	Wine[4] ($/gal.)	Beer[5] ($/gal.)	Recreational Marijuana (%)
Florida	6	42.46	1.339	6.5	2.25	0.48	Not legal

Note: All tax rates as of January 1, 2021; (1) The American Petroleum Institute has developed a methodology for determining the average tax rate on a gallon of fuel. Rates may include any of the following: excise taxes, environmental fees, storage tank fees, other fees or taxes, general sales tax, and local taxes; (2) The federal excise tax of $1.0066 per pack and local taxes are not included; (3) Rates are those applicable to off-premise sales of 40% alcohol by volume (a.b.v.) distilled spirits in 750ml containers. Local excise taxes are excluded; (4) Rates are those applicable to off-premise sales of 11% a.b.v. non-carbonated wine in 750ml containers; (5) Rates are those applicable to off-premise sales of 4.7% a.b.v. beer in 12 ounce containers.
Source: Tax Foundation, 2021 Facts & Figures: How Does Your State Compare?

State Business Tax Climate Index Rankings

State	Overall Rank	Corporate Tax Rank	Individual Income Tax Rank	Sales Tax Rank	Property Tax Rank	Unemployment Insurance Tax Rank
Florida	4	6	1	21	13	2

Note: The index is a measure of how each state's tax laws affect economic performance. The lower the rank, the more favorable a state's tax system is for business. States without a given tax are given a ranking of 1. The scores/rankings for the District of Columbia do not affect other states. The 2021 index represents the tax climate as of July 1, 2020.
Source: Tax Foundation, State Business Tax Climate Index 2021

TRANSPORTATION

Means of Transportation to Work

Area	Car/Truck/Van Drove Alone	Car/Truck/Van Carpooled	Public Transportation Bus	Public Transportation Subway	Public Transportation Railroad	Bicycle	Walked	Other Means	Worked at Home
City	77.1	8.8	2.1	0.0	0.0	1.0	2.4	1.5	6.9
MSA[1]	78.9	8.8	1.3	0.0	0.0	0.6	1.4	1.6	7.4
U.S.	76.3	9.0	2.4	1.9	0.6	0.5	2.7	1.4	5.2

Note: Figures are percentages and cover workers 16 years of age and older; (1) Figures cover the Tampa-St. Petersburg-Clearwater, FL Metropolitan Statistical Area
Source: U.S. Census Bureau, 2015-2019 American Community Survey 5-Year Estimates

Travel Time to Work

Area	Less Than 10 Minutes	10 to 19 Minutes	20 to 29 Minutes	30 to 44 Minutes	45 to 59 Minutes	60 to 89 Minutes	90 Minutes or More
City	11.1	30.5	23.6	21.8	6.7	4.3	1.9
MSA[1]	9.6	26.9	21.6	23.0	10.1	6.5	2.3
U.S.	12.2	28.4	20.8	20.8	8.3	6.4	2.9

Note: Note: Figures are percentages and include workers 16 years old and over; (1) Figures cover the Tampa-St. Petersburg-Clearwater, FL Metropolitan Statistical Area
Source: U.S. Census Bureau, 2015-2019 American Community Survey 5-Year Estimates

Key Congestion Measures

Measure	1982	1992	2002	2012	2017
Annual Hours of Delay, Total (000)	16,035	33,384	53,496	76,538	85,860
Annual Hours of Delay, Per Auto Commuter	20	32	39	44	50
Annual Congestion Cost, Total (million $)	120	352	722	1,366	1,579
Annual Congestion Cost, Per Auto Commuter ($)	413	592	739	829	901

Note: Covers the Tampa-St. Petersburg FL urban area
Source: Texas A&M Transportation Institute, 2019 Urban Mobility Report

Freeway Travel Time Index

Measure	1982	1987	1992	1997	2002	2007	2012	2017
Urban Area Index[1]	1.11	1.13	1.17	1.18	1.21	1.23	1.21	1.22
Urban Area Rank[1,2]	17	21	22	28	31	31	34	33

Note: Freeway Travel Time Index—the ratio of travel time in the peak period to the travel time at free-flow conditions. For example, a value of 1.30 indicates a 20-minute free-flow trip takes 26 minutes in the peak (20 minutes x 1.30 = 26 minutes); (1) Covers the Tampa-St. Petersburg FL urban area; (2) Rank is based on 101 larger urban areas (#1 = highest travel time index)
Source: Texas A&M Transportation Institute, 2019 Urban Mobility Report

Public Transportation

Agency Name / Mode of Transportation	Vehicles Operated in Maximum Service[1]	Annual Unlinked Passenger Trips[2] (in thous.)	Annual Passenger Miles[3] (in thous.)
Hillsborough Area Regional Transit Authority (HART)			
Bus (directly operated)	137	12,032.4	71,147.5
Demand Response (directly operated)	56	196.9	1,907.5
Streetcar Rail (directly operated)	4	878.3	1,220.9

Note: (1) Number of revenue vehicles operated by the given mode and type of service to meet the annual maximum service requirement. This is the revenue vehicle count during the peak season of the year; on the week and day that maximum service is provided. Vehicles operated in maximum service (VOMS) exclude atypical days and one-time special events; (2) Number of passengers who boarded public transportation vehicles. Passengers are counted each time they board a vehicle no matter how many vehicles they use to travel from their origin to their destination. (3) Sum of the distances ridden by all passengers during the entire fiscal year.
Source: Federal Transit Administration, National Transit Database, 2019

Air Transportation

Airport Name and Code / Type of Service	Passenger Airlines[1]	Passenger Enplanements	Freight Carriers[2]	Freight (lbs)
Tampa International (TPA)				
Domestic service (U.S. carriers - 2020)	25	4,821,157	12	230,581,855
International service (U.S. carriers - 2019)	12	96,232	3	2,417,945

Note: (1) Includes all U.S.-based major, minor and commuter airlines that carried at least one passenger during the year; (2) Includes all U.S.-based airlines and freight carriers that transported at least one pound of freight during the year.
Source: Bureau of Transportation Statistics, The Intermodal Transportation Database, Air Carriers: T-100 Domestic Market (U.S. Carriers), 2020; Bureau of Transportation Statistics, The Intermodal Transportation Database, Air Carriers: T-100 International Market (U.S. Carriers), 2019

BUSINESSES

Major Business Headquarters

Company Name	Industry	Rankings Fortune[1]	Forbes[2]
No companies listed	-	-	-

Note: (1) Companies that produce a 10-K are ranked 1 to 500 based on 2019 revenue; (2) All private companies with at least $2 billion in annual revenue through the end of their most current fiscal year are ranked 1 to 219; companies listed are headquartered in the city; dashes indicate no ranking
Source: Fortune, "Fortune 500," June/July 2020; Forbes, "America's Largest Private Companies," 2020

Fastest-Growing Businesses

According to *Inc.*, Tampa is home to seven of America's 500 fastest-growing private companies: **Avalon Healthcare Solutions** (#4); **Allied Trust Insurance Company** (#34); **Real Advisors** (#80); **Cedar Grove Group** (#108); **Web River Group** (#314); **ComplianceQuest** (#446); **Clearly Agile** (#500). Criteria: must be an independent, privately-held, for-profit, U.S. corporation, proprietorship or partnership as of December 31, 2019; revenues must be at least $100,000 in 2016 and $2 million in 2019; must have four-year operating/sales history. *Inc., "America's 500 Fastest-Growing Private Companies," 2020*

According to *Initiative for a Competitive Inner City (ICIC)*, Tampa is home to one of America's 100 fastest-growing "inner city" companies: **VetCor** (#44). Criteria for inclusion: company must be headquartered in or have 51 percent or more of its physical operations in an economically distressed urban area; must be an independent, for-profit corporation, partnership or proprietorship; must have 10 or more employees and have a five-year sales history that includes sales of at least $200,000 in the base year and at least $1 million in the current year with no decrease in sales over the two most recent years. Companies were ranked overall by revenue growth over the five-year period between 2015 and 2019. *Initiative for a Competitive Inner City (ICIC), "Inner City 100 Companies," 2020*

According to Deloitte, Tampa is home to two of North America's 500 fastest-growing high-technology companies: **ReliaQuest** (#409); **Corestream** (#431). Companies are ranked by percentage growth in revenue over a four-year period. Criteria for inclusion: company must be headquartered within North America; must own proprietary intellectual property or technology that is sold to customers in products that contributes to a significant portion of the company's operating revenue; must have been in business for a minumum of four years with 2016 operating revenues of at least $50,000 USD/CD and 2019 operating revenues of at least $5 million USD/CD. *Deloitte, 2020 Technology Fast 500™*

Minority Business Opportunity

Tampa is home to two companies which are on the *Black Enterprise* Industrial/Service list (100 largest companies based on gross sales): **Coca-Cola Beverages Florida** (#4); **Sun State International Trucks** (#28). Criteria: operational in previous calendar year; at least 51% black-owned and manufactures/owns the product it sells or provides industrial or consumer services. Brokerages, real estate firms and firms that provide professional services are not eligible. *Black Enterprise, B.E. 100s, 2019*

Tampa is home to one company which is on the *Black Enterprise* Auto Dealer list (45 largest dealers based on gross sales): **March Hodge Automotive Group** (#4). Criteria: company must be operational in previous calendar year and be at least 51% black-owned. *Black Enterprise, B.E. 100s, 2019*

Living Environment

COST OF LIVING

Cost of Living Index

Composite Index	Groceries	Housing	Utilities	Transportation	Health Care	Misc. Goods/Services
95.9	104.1	86.1	101.0	100.3	97.9	97.7

Note: The Cost of Living Index measures regional differences in the cost of consumer goods and services, excluding taxes and non-consumer expenditures, for professional and managerial households in the top income quintile. It is based on more than 50,000 prices covering almost 60 different items for which prices are collected three times a year by chambers of commerce, economic development organizations or university applied economic centers in each participating urban area. The numbers shown should be read as a percentage above or below the national average of 100. For example, a value of 115.4 in the groceries column indicates that grocery prices are 15.4% higher than the national average. Small differences in the index numbers should not be interpreted as significant; Figures cover the Tampa FL urban area.
Source: The Council for Community and Economic Research, Cost of Living Index, 2020

Grocery Prices

Area[1]	T-Bone Steak ($/pound)	Frying Chicken ($/pound)	Whole Milk ($/half gal.)	Eggs ($/dozen)	Orange Juice ($/64 oz.)	Coffee ($/11.5 oz.)
City[2]	11.11	1.74	2.66	1.68	3.43	4.28
Avg.	11.78	1.39	2.05	1.47	3.57	4.34
Min.	8.03	0.94	1.03	0.74	2.94	3.02
Max.	15.86	2.65	4.31	3.77	5.44	8.69

Note: (1) Values for the local area are compared with the average, minimum and maximum values for all 284 areas in the Cost of Living Index; (2) Figures cover the Tampa FL urban area; **T-Bone Steak** (price per pound); **Frying Chicken** (price per pound, whole fryer); **Whole Milk** (half gallon carton); **Eggs** (price per dozen, Grade A, large); **Orange Juice** (64 oz. Tropicana or Florida Natural); **Coffee** (11.5 oz. can, vacuum-packed, Maxwell House, Hills Bros, or Folgers).
Source: The Council for Community and Economic Research, Cost of Living Index, 2020

Housing and Utility Costs

Area[1]	New Home Price ($)	Apartment Rent ($/month)	All Electric ($/month)	Part Electric ($/month)	Other Energy ($/month)	Telephone ($/month)
City[2]	278,508	1,296	165.98	-	-	189.50
Avg.	368,594	1,168	170.86	100.47	65.28	184.30
Min.	190,567	502	91.58	31.42	26.08	169.60
Max.	2,227,806	4,738	470.38	280.31	280.06	206.50

Note: (1) Values for the local area are compared with the average, minimum and maximum values for all 284 areas in the Cost of Living Index; (2) Figures cover the Tampa FL urban area; **New Home Price** (2,400 sf living area, 8,000 sf lot, in urban area with full utilities); **Apartment Rent** (950 sf 2 bedroom/1.5 or 2 bath, unfurnished, excluding all utilities except water); **All Electric** (average monthly cost for an all-electric home); **Part Electric** (average monthly cost for a part-electric home); **Other Energy** (average monthly cost for natural gas, fuel oil, coal, wood, and any other forms of energy except electricity); **Telephone** (price includes the base monthly rate plus taxes and fees for three lines of mobile phone service).
Source: The Council for Community and Economic Research, Cost of Living Index, 2020

Health Care, Transportation, and Other Costs

Area[1]	Doctor ($/visit)	Dentist ($/visit)	Optometrist ($/visit)	Gasoline ($/gallon)	Beauty Salon ($/visit)	Men's Shirt ($)
City[2]	99.22	105.57	99.12	2.11	37.26	23.11
Avg.	115.44	99.32	108.10	2.21	39.27	31.37
Min.	36.68	59.00	51.36	1.71	19.00	11.00
Max.	219.00	153.10	250.97	3.46	82.05	58.33

Note: (1) Values for the local area are compared with the average, minimum and maximum values for all 284 areas in the Cost of Living Index; (2) Figures cover the Tampa FL urban area; **Doctor** (general practitioners routine exam of an established patient); **Dentist** (adult teeth cleaning and periodic oral examination); **Optometrist** (full vision eye exam for established adult patient); **Gasoline** (one gallon regular unleaded, national brand, including all taxes, cash price at self-service pump if available); **Beauty Salon** (woman's shampoo, trim, and blow-dry); **Men's Shirt** (cotton/polyester dress shirt, pinpoint weave, long sleeves).
Source: The Council for Community and Economic Research, Cost of Living Index, 2020

HOUSING

Homeownership Rate

Area	2012 (%)	2013 (%)	2014 (%)	2015 (%)	2016 (%)	2017 (%)	2018 (%)	2019 (%)	2020 (%)
MSA[1]	67.0	65.3	64.9	64.9	62.9	60.4	64.9	68.0	72.2
U.S.	65.4	65.1	64.5	63.7	63.4	63.9	64.4	64.6	66.6

Note: (1) Figures cover the Tampa-St. Petersburg-Clearwater, FL Metropolitan Statistical Area
Source: U.S. Census Bureau, Housing Vacancies and Homeownership Annual Statistics: 2012-2020

House Price Index (HPI)

Area	National Ranking[2]	Quarterly Change (%)	One-Year Change (%)	Five-Year Change (%)	Since 1991Q1 (%)
MSA[1]	33	2.36	8.17	52.43	254.29
U.S.[3]	—	3.81	10.77	38.99	205.12

Note: The HPI is a weighted repeat sales index. It measures average price changes in repeat sales or refinancings on the same properties. This information is obtained by reviewing repeat mortgage transactions on single-family properties whose mortgages have been purchased or securitized by Fannie Mae or Freddie Mac since January 1975; (1) Figures cover the Tampa-St. Petersburg-Clearwater, FL Metropolitan Statistical Area; (2) Rankings are based on annual percentage change for all metro areas containing at least 15,000 transactions over the last 10 years and ranges from 1 to 253; (3) figures based on a weighted average of Census Division estimates using a seasonally adjusted, purchase-only index; all figures are for the period ending December 31, 2020
Source: Federal Housing Finance Agency, Change in Metropolitan Area House Price Indexes, April 7, 2021

Median Single-Family Home Prices

Area	2018	2019	2020p	Percent Change 2019 to 2020
MSA[1]	235.0	245.0	272.0	11.0
U.S. Average	261.6	274.6	299.9	9.2

Note: Figures are median sales prices of existing single-family homes in thousands of dollars; (p) preliminary; (1) Figures cover the Tampa-St. Petersburg-Clearwater, FL Metropolitan Statistical Area
Source: National Association of Realtors, Median Sales Price of Existing Single-Family Homes for Metropolitan Areas, 4th Quarter 2020

Qualifying Income Based on Median Sales Price of Existing Single-Family Homes

Area	With 5% Down ($)	With 10% Down ($)	With 20% Down ($)
MSA[1]	54,284	51,427	45,713
U.S. Average	59,266	56,147	49,908

Note: Figures are preliminary; Qualifying income is based on a mortgage rate of 2.81%. Monthly principal and interest payment is limited to 25% of income; (1) Figures cover the Tampa-St. Petersburg-Clearwater, FL Metropolitan Statistical Area
Source: National Association of Realtors, Qualifying Income Based on Median Sales Price of Existing Single-Family Homes for Metropolitan Areas, 4th Quarter 2020

Home Value Distribution

Area	Under $50,000	$50,000 -$99,999	$100,000 -$149,999	$150,000 -$199,999	$200,000 -$299,999	$300,000 -$499,999	$500,000 -$999,999	$1,000,000 or more
City	3.8	10.8	11.7	14.7	20.7	20.1	13.6	4.5
MSA[1]	8.8	13.0	13.5	16.7	23.7	16.4	6.4	1.6
U.S.	6.9	12.0	13.3	14.0	19.6	19.3	11.4	3.4

Note: Figures are percentages and cover owner-occupied housing units; (1) Figures cover the Tampa-St. Petersburg-Clearwater, FL Metropolitan Statistical Area
Source: U.S. Census Bureau, 2015-2019 American Community Survey 5-Year Estimates

Year Housing Structure Built

Area	2010 or Later	2000 -2009	1990 -1999	1980 -1989	1970 -1979	1960 -1969	1950 -1959	1940 -1949	Before 1940	Median Year
City	7.8	17.9	12.4	11.8	11.9	10.0	14.4	5.2	8.7	1980
MSA[1]	5.6	16.4	14.1	20.1	21.0	9.5	8.5	2.0	2.7	1983
U.S.	5.2	14.0	13.9	13.4	15.2	10.6	10.3	4.9	12.6	1978

Note: Figures are percentages except for Median Year; Note: (1) Figures cover the Tampa-St. Petersburg-Clearwater, FL Metropolitan Statistical Area
Source: U.S. Census Bureau, 2015-2019 American Community Survey 5-Year Estimates

Gross Monthly Rent

Area	Under $500	$500 -$999	$1,000 -$1,499	$1,500 -$1,999	$2,000 -$2,499	$2,500 -$2,999	$3,000 and up	Median ($)
City	8.1	30.2	37.6	16.0	4.8	1.9	1.5	1,131
MSA[1]	4.9	33.9	40.4	14.9	3.6	1.4	1.0	1,115
U.S.	9.4	36.2	30.0	14.0	5.6	2.4	2.4	1,062

Note: Figures are percentages except for Median; Gross rent is the contract rent plus the estimated average monthly cost of utilities (electricity, gas, and water and sewer) and fuels (oil, coal, kerosene, wood, etc.) if these are paid by the renter (or paid for the renter by someone else); (1) Figures cover the Tampa-St. Petersburg-Clearwater, FL Metropolitan Statistical Area
Source: U.S. Census Bureau, 2015-2019 American Community Survey 5-Year Estimates

HEALTH

Health Risk Factors

Category	MSA[1] (%)	U.S. (%)
Adults aged 18–64 who have any kind of health care coverage	79.1	87.3
Adults who reported being in good or better health	79.4	82.4
Adults who have been told they have high blood cholesterol	36.3	33.0
Adults who have been told they have high blood pressure	33.9	32.3
Adults who are current smokers	18.4	17.1
Adults who currently use E-cigarettes	6.5	4.6
Adults who currently use chewing tobacco, snuff, or snus	2.9	4.0
Adults who are heavy drinkers[2]	6.7	6.3
Adults who are binge drinkers[3]	16.5	17.4
Adults who are overweight (BMI 25.0 - 29.9)	36.5	35.3
Adults who are obese (BMI 30.0 - 99.8)	26.0	31.3
Adults who participated in any physical activities in the past month	71.2	74.4
Adults who always or nearly always wears a seat belt	96.9	94.3

Note: (1) Figures cover the Tampa-St. Petersburg-Clearwater, FL Metropolitan Statistical Area; (2) Heavy drinkers are classified as adult men having more than 14 drinks per week and adult women having more than 7 drinks per week; (3) Binge drinkers are classified as males having five or more drinks on one occasion or females having four or more drinks on one occasion
Source: Centers for Disease Control and Prevention, Behaviorial Risk Factor Surveillance System, SMART: Selected Metropolitan Area Risk Trends, 2017

Acute and Chronic Health Conditions

Category	MSA[1] (%)	U.S. (%)
Adults who have ever been told they had a heart attack	6.0	4.2
Adults who have ever been told they have angina or coronary heart disease	5.6	3.9
Adults who have ever been told they had a stroke	4.2	3.0
Adults who have ever been told they have asthma	13.2	14.2
Adults who have ever been told they have arthritis	27.3	24.9
Adults who have ever been told they have diabetes[2]	9.2	10.5
Adults who have ever been told they had skin cancer	9.4	6.2
Adults who have ever been told they had any other types of cancer	9.9	7.1
Adults who have ever been told they have COPD	8.4	6.5
Adults who have ever been told they have kidney disease	1.9	3.0
Adults who have ever been told they have a form of depression	16.6	20.5

Note: (1) Figures cover the Tampa-St. Petersburg-Clearwater, FL Metropolitan Statistical Area; (2) Figures do not include pregnancy-related, borderline, or pre-diabetes
Source: Centers for Disease Control and Prevention, Behaviorial Risk Factor Surveillance System, SMART: Selected Metropolitan Area Risk Trends, 2017

Health Screening and Vaccination Rates

Category	MSA[1] (%)	U.S. (%)
Adults aged 65+ who have had flu shot within the past year	63.9	60.7
Adults aged 65+ who have ever had a pneumonia vaccination	75.4	75.4
Adults who have ever been tested for HIV	47.6	36.1
Adults who have ever had the shingles or zoster vaccine?	27.0	28.9
Adults who have had their blood cholesterol checked within the last five years	90.3	85.9

Note: n/a not available; (1) Figures cover the Tampa-St. Petersburg-Clearwater, FL Metropolitan Statistical Area.
Source: Centers for Disease Control and Prevention, Behaviorial Risk Factor Surveillance System, SMART: Selected Metropolitan Area Risk Trends, 2017

Disability Status

Category	MSA[1] (%)	U.S. (%)
Adults who reported being deaf	7.3	6.7
Are you blind or have serious difficulty seeing, even when wearing glasses?	6.2	4.5
Are you limited in any way in any of your usual activities due of arthritis?	15.4	12.9
Do you have difficulty doing errands alone?	9.2	6.8
Do you have difficulty dressing or bathing?	6.0	3.6
Do you have serious difficulty concentrating/remembering/making decisions?	11.8	10.7
Do you have serious difficulty walking or climbing stairs?	18.1	13.6

Note: (1) Figures cover the Tampa-St. Petersburg-Clearwater, FL Metropolitan Statistical Area.
Source: Centers for Disease Control and Prevention, Behaviorial Risk Factor Surveillance System, SMART: Selected Metropolitan Area Risk Trends, 2017

Mortality Rates for the Top 10 Causes of Death in the U.S.

ICD-10[a] Sub-Chapter	ICD-10[a] Code	County[2]	U.S.
Malignant neoplasms	C00-C97	148.1	149.2
Ischaemic heart diseases	I20-I25	94.3	90.5
Other forms of heart disease	I30-I51	33.1	52.2
Chronic lower respiratory diseases	J40-J47	39.1	39.6
Other degenerative diseases of the nervous system	G30-G31	44.7	37.6
Cerebrovascular diseases	I60-I69	29.0	37.2
Other external causes of accidental injury	W00-X59	34.1	36.1
Organic, including symptomatic, mental disorders	F01-F09	32.0	29.4
Hypertensive diseases	I10-I15	39.1	24.1
Diabetes mellitus	E10-E14	19.3	21.5

Age-Adjusted Mortality Rate[1] per 100,000 population

Note: (a) ICD-10 = International Classification of Diseases 10th Revision; (1) Mortality rates are a three-year average covering 2017-2019; (2) Figures cover Hillsborough County.
Source: Centers for Disease Control and Prevention, National Center for Health Statistics. Underlying Cause of Death 1999-2019 on CDC WONDER Online Database

Mortality Rates for Selected Causes of Death

ICD-10[a] Sub-Chapter	ICD-10[a] Code	County[2]	U.S.
Assault	X85-Y09	5.4	6.0
Diseases of the liver	K70-K76	11.8	14.4
Human immunodeficiency virus (HIV) disease	B20-B24	2.5	1.5
Influenza and pneumonia	J09-J18	11.7	13.8
Intentional self-harm	X60-X84	13.6	14.1
Malnutrition	E40-E46	1.3	2.3
Obesity and other hyperalimentation	E65-E68	1.7	2.1
Renal failure	N17-N19	8.8	12.6
Transport accidents	V01-V99	14.1	12.3
Viral hepatitis	B15-B19	1.2	1.2

Age-Adjusted Mortality Rate[1] per 100,000 population

Note: (a) ICD-10 = International Classification of Diseases 10th Revision; (1) Mortality rates are a three-year average covering 2017-2019; (2) Figures cover Hillsborough County; Data are suppressed when the data meet the criteria for confidentiality constraints; Mortality rates are flagged as unreliable when the rate would be calculated with a numerator of 20 or less.
Source: Centers for Disease Control and Prevention, National Center for Health Statistics. Underlying Cause of Death 1999-2019 on CDC WONDER Online Database

Health Insurance Coverage

Area	With Health Insurance	With Private Health Insurance	With Public Health Insurance	Without Health Insurance	Population Under Age 19 Without Health Insurance
City	88.3	62.5	32.9	11.7	5.4
MSA[1]	88.1	63.3	36.8	11.9	6.3
U.S.	91.2	67.9	35.1	8.8	5.1

Note: Figures are percentages that cover the civilian noninstitutionalized population; (1) Figures cover the Tampa-St. Petersburg-Clearwater, FL Metropolitan Statistical Area
Source: U.S. Census Bureau, 2015-2019 American Community Survey 5-Year Estimates

Number of Medical Professionals

Area	MDs[3]	DOs[3,4]	Dentists	Podiatrists	Chiropractors	Optometrists
County[1] (number)	5,007	379	867	83	389	209
County[1] (rate[2])	344.9	26.1	58.9	5.6	26.4	14.2
U.S. (rate[2])	282.9	22.7	71.2	6.2	28.1	16.9

12057
Note: Data as of 2019 unless noted; (1) Data covers Hillsborough County; (2) Rate per 100,000 population; (3) Data as of 2018 and includes all active, non-federal physicians; (4) Doctor of Osteopathic Medicine
Source: U.S. Department of Health and Human Services, Health Resources and Services Administration, Bureau of Health Professions, Area Resource File (ARF) 2019-2020

Best Hospitals

According to *U.S. News,* the Tampa-St. Petersburg-Clearwater, FL metro area is home to two of the best hospitals in the U.S.: **H. Lee Moffitt Cancer Center and Research Institute** (3 adult specialties); **Tampa General Hospital** (5 adult specialties). The hospitals listed were nationally ranked in at least one of 16 adult or 10 pediatric specialties. Only 134 hospitals nationwide were nationally ranked in one or more adult or pediatric specialty; this number increases to 178 counting specialized centers within hospitals. Twenty hospitals in the U.S. made the Honor Roll. The Best Hospitals Honor Roll takes both the national rankings and the procedure and condition ratings into account. Hospitals received points if they were nationally ranked in one of the 16 adult specialties—the higher they ranked, the more points they got—and how many ratings of "high performing" they earned in the 10 procedures and conditions. *U.S. News Online, "America's Best Hospitals 2020-21"*

According to *U.S. News,* the Tampa-St. Petersburg-Clearwater, FL metro area is home to one of the best children's hospitals in the U.S.: **Johns Hopkins All Children's Hospital** (8 pediatric specialties). The hospital listed was highly ranked in at least one of 10 pediatric specialties. Eighty-eight children's hospitals in the U.S. were nationally ranked in at least one specialty. Hospitals received points for being ranked in a specialty, and the 10 hospitals with the most points across the 10 specialties make up the Honor Roll. *U.S. News Online, "America's Best Children's Hospitals 2020-21"*

EDUCATION

Public School District Statistics

District Name	Schls	Pupils	Pupil/Teacher Ratio	Minority Pupils[1] (%)	Free Lunch Eligible[2] (%)	IEP[3] (%)
Hillsborough	297	220,252	16.7	67.1	52.0	14.4

Note: Table includes school districts with 2,000 or more students; (1) Percentage of students that are not non-Hispanic white; (2) Percentage of students that are eligible for the free lunch program; (3) Percentage of students that have an Individualized Education Program.
Source: U.S. Department of Education, National Center for Education Statistics, Common Core of Data, Local Education Agency (School District) Universe Survey: School Year 2018-2019; U.S. Department of Education, National Center for Education Statistics, Common Core of Data, Public Elementary/Secondary School Universe Survey: School Year 2018-2019

Highest Level of Education

Area	Less than H.S.	H.S. Diploma	Some College, No Deg.	Associate Degree	Bachelor's Degree	Master's Degree	Prof. School Degree	Doctorate Degree
City	12.1	25.6	16.0	7.7	23.3	9.6	3.9	1.7
MSA[1]	10.4	28.9	20.5	9.8	19.6	7.6	2.0	1.2
U.S.	12.0	27.0	20.4	8.5	19.8	8.8	2.1	1.4

Note: Figures cover persons age 25 and over; (1) Figures cover the Tampa-St. Petersburg-Clearwater, FL Metropolitan Statistical Area
Source: U.S. Census Bureau, 2015-2019 American Community Survey 5-Year Estimates

Educational Attainment by Race

Area	High School Graduate or Higher (%)					Bachelor's Degree or Higher (%)				
	Total	White	Black	Asian	Hisp.[2]	Total	White	Black	Asian	Hisp.[2]
City	87.9	90.1	82.9	86.7	78.3	38.6	44.4	16.8	63.0	23.5
MSA[1]	89.6	90.8	87.0	85.4	80.2	30.4	30.9	22.4	51.7	22.6
U.S.	88.0	89.9	86.0	87.1	68.7	32.1	33.5	21.6	54.3	16.4

Note: Figures shown cover persons 25 years old and over; (1) Figures cover the Tampa-St. Petersburg-Clearwater, FL Metropolitan Statistical Area; (2) People of Hispanic origin can be of any race
Source: U.S. Census Bureau, 2015-2019 American Community Survey 5-Year Estimates

School Enrollment by Grade and Control

Area	Preschool (%)		Kindergarten (%)		Grades 1 - 4 (%)		Grades 5 - 8 (%)		Grades 9 - 12 (%)	
	Public	Private	Public	Private	Public	Private	Public	Private	Public	Private
City	49.9	50.1	83.4	16.6	89.5	10.5	85.7	14.3	84.5	15.5
MSA[1]	57.1	42.9	84.8	15.2	86.9	13.1	87.1	12.9	88.3	11.7
U.S.	59.1	40.9	87.6	12.4	89.5	10.5	89.4	10.6	90.1	9.9

Note: Figures shown cover persons 3 years old and over; (1) Figures cover the Tampa-St. Petersburg-Clearwater, FL Metropolitan Statistical Area
Source: U.S. Census Bureau, 2015-2019 American Community Survey 5-Year Estimates

Higher Education

Four-Year Colleges			Two-Year Colleges			Medical Schools[1]	Law Schools[2]	Voc/Tech[3]
Public	Private Non-profit	Private For-profit	Public	Private Non-profit	Private For-profit			
1	2	3	3	1	2	1	0	8

Note: Figures cover institutions located within the city limits and include main campuses only; (1) includes schools accredited by the Liaison Committee on Medical Education and the American Osteopathic Association's Commission on Osteopathic College Accreditation; (2) includes ABA-accredited schools, schools with provisional ABA accreditation, and state accredited schools; (3) includes all schools with programs that are less than 2 years.
Source: National Center for Education Statistics, Integrated Postsecondary Education System (IPEDS), 2019-20; Wikipedia, List of Medical Schools in the United States, accessed April 2, 2021; Wikipedia, List of Law Schools in the United States, accessed April 2, 2021

According to *U.S. News & World Report,* the Tampa-St. Petersburg-Clearwater, FL metro area is home to one of the top 200 national universities in the U.S.: **University of South Florida** (#103 tie). The indicators used to capture academic quality fall into a number of categories: assessment by administrators at peer institutions; retention of students; faculty resources; student selectivity; financial resources; alumni giving; high school counselor ratings of colleges; and graduation rate. *U.S. News & World Report, "America's Best Colleges 2021"*

According to *U.S. News & World Report*, the Tampa-St. Petersburg-Clearwater, FL metro area is home to one of the top 75 medical schools for research in the U.S.: **University of South Florida** (#48 tie). The rankings are based on a weighted average of 11 measures of quality: quality assessment; peer assessment score; assessment score by residency directors; research activity; total research activity; average research activity per faculty member; student selectivity; median MCAT total score; median undergraduate GPA; acceptance rate; and faculty resources. *U.S. News & World Report, "America's Best Graduate Schools, Medical, 2022"*

EMPLOYERS

Major Employers

Company Name	Industry
Baycare Health System	General medical & surgical hospitals
Beall's	Manufacturing
Busch Gardens	Arts, entertainment & recreation
Caspers Company	Accommodation & food services
Citi	Finance & insurance
Florida Hospital	Health care & social assistance
Gerdau Ameristeel US	Manufacturing
HCA Healthcare	Health care & social assistance
Home Shopping Network	Information
JPMorgan Chase	Finance & insurance
MacDill Air Force Base	Public administration
Moffitt Cancer Center & Research Institute	Health care & social assistance
Progressive	Finance & insurance
Publix Supermarkets	Retail grocery
Raymond James Financial	Finance & insurance
Tampa General Hospital	Health care & social assistance
Tech Data Corp	Wholesale trade
University of South Florida	Educational services
Verizon	Information
WellCare	Finance & insurance

Note: Companies shown are located within the Tampa-St. Petersburg-Clearwater, FL Metropolitan Statistical Area.
Source: Hoovers.com; Wikipedia

Best Companies to Work For

H. Lee Moffitt Cancer Center and Research Institut, headquartered in Tampa, is among the "100 Best Places to Work in IT." To qualify, companies had to be U.S.-based organizations or be non-U.S.-based employers that met the following criteria: have a minimum of 300 total employees at a U.S. headquarters and a minimum of 30 IT employees in the U.S., with at least 50% of their IT employees based in the U.S. The best places to work were selected based on compensation, benefits, work/life balance, employee morale, and satisfaction with training and development programs. In addition, *InsiderPro* and *Computerworld* looked at retention efforts, programs for recognizing and rewarding outstanding performances, and benefits such as flextime, elder care and child care, and reimbursement for college tuition and the cost of pursuing technology certifications. *InsiderPro and Computerworld, "100 Best Places to Work in IT," 2020*

PUBLIC SAFETY

Crime Rate

Area	All Crimes	Violent Crimes				Property Crimes		
		Murder	Rape[3]	Robbery	Aggrav. Assault	Burglary	Larceny-Theft	Motor Vehicle Theft
City	2,033.7	7.7	30.0	71.2	296.1	255.2	1,242.9	130.6
Suburbs[1]	1,969.7	3.4	37.9	46.7	187.8	210.4	1,356.1	127.3
Metro[2]	1,977.8	4.0	36.9	49.8	201.5	216.1	1,341.8	127.7
U.S.	2,489.3	5.0	42.6	81.6	250.2	340.5	1,549.5	219.9

Note: Figures are crimes per 100,000 population; (1) All areas within the metro area that are located outside the city limits; (2) Figures cover the Tampa-St. Petersburg-Clearwater, FL Metropolitan Statistical Area; (3) All figures shown were reported using the revised Uniform Crime Reporting (UCR) definition of rape.
Source: FBI Uniform Crime Reports, 2019

Hate Crimes

Area	Number of Quarters Reported	Number of Incidents per Bias Motivation					
		Race/Ethnicity/Ancestry	Religion	Sexual Orientation	Disability	Gender	Gender Identity
City	4	0	2	0	0	0	0
U.S.	4	3,963	1,521	1,195	157	69	198

Source: Federal Bureau of Investigation, Hate Crime Statistics 2019

Identity Theft Consumer Reports

Area	Reports	Reports per 100,000 Population	Rank[2]
MSA[1]	10,518	329	105
U.S.	1,387,615	423	-

Note: (1) Figures cover the Tampa-St. Petersburg-Clearwater, FL Metropolitan Statistical Area; (2) Rank ranges from 1 to 391 where 1 indicates greatest number of identity theft reports per 100,000 population
Source: Federal Trade Commission, Consumer Sentinel Network Data Book 2020

Fraud and Other Consumer Reports

Area	Reports	Reports per 100,000 Population	Rank[2]
MSA[1]	34,930	1,093	11
U.S.	3,385,133	1,031	-

Note: (1) Figures cover the Tampa-St. Petersburg-Clearwater, FL Metropolitan Statistical Area; (2) Rank ranges from 1 to 391 where 1 indicates greatest number of fraud and other consumer reports per 100,000 population
Source: Federal Trade Commission, Consumer Sentinel Network Data Book 2020

POLITICS

2020 Presidential Election Results

Area	Biden	Trump	Jorgensen	Hawkins	Other
Hillsborough County	52.7	45.8	0.8	0.2	0.5
U.S.	51.3	46.8	1.2	0.3	0.5

Note: Results are percentages and may not add to 100% due to rounding
Source: Dave Leip's Atlas of U.S. Presidential Elections

SPORTS

Professional Sports Teams

Team Name	League	Year Established
Tampa Bay Buccaneers	National Football League (NFL)	1976
Tampa Bay Lightning	National Hockey League (NHL)	1993
Tampa Bay Rays	Major League Baseball (MLB)	1998

Note: Includes teams located in the Tampa-St. Petersburg-Clearwater, FL Metropolitan Statistical Area.
Source: Wikipedia, Major Professional Sports Teams of the United States and Canada, April 6, 2021

CLIMATE

Average and Extreme Temperatures

Temperature	Jan	Feb	Mar	Apr	May	Jun	Jul	Aug	Sep	Oct	Nov	Dec	Yr.
Extreme High (°F)	85	88	91	93	98	99	97	98	96	94	90	86	99
Average High (°F)	70	72	76	82	87	90	90	90	89	84	77	72	82
Average Temp. (°F)	60	62	67	72	78	81	82	83	81	75	68	62	73
Average Low (°F)	50	52	56	61	67	73	74	74	73	66	57	52	63
Extreme Low (°F)	21	24	29	40	49	53	63	67	57	40	23	18	18

Note: Figures cover the years 1948-1990
Source: National Climatic Data Center, International Station Meteorological Climate Summary, 9/96

Average Precipitation/Snowfall/Humidity

Precip./Humidity	Jan	Feb	Mar	Apr	May	Jun	Jul	Aug	Sep	Oct	Nov	Dec	Yr.
Avg. Precip. (in.)	2.1	2.8	3.5	1.8	3.0	5.6	7.3	7.9	6.5	2.3	1.8	2.1	46.7
Avg. Snowfall (in.)	Tr	Tr	Tr	0	0	0	0	0	0	0	0	Tr	Tr
Avg. Rel. Hum. 7am (%)	87	87	86	86	85	86	88	90	91	89	88	87	88
Avg. Rel. Hum. 4pm (%)	56	55	54	51	52	60	65	66	64	57	56	57	58

Note: Figures cover the years 1948-1990; Tr = Trace amounts (<0.05 in. of rain; <0.5 in. of snow)
Source: National Climatic Data Center, International Station Meteorological Climate Summary, 9/96

Weather Conditions

Temperature			Daytime Sky			Precipitation		
32°F & below	45°F & below	90°F & above	Clear	Partly cloudy	Cloudy	0.01 inch or more precip.	0.1 inch or more snow/ice	Thunderstorms
3	35	85	81	204	80	107	<1	87

Note: Figures are average number of days per year and cover the years 1948-1990
Source: National Climatic Data Center, International Station Meteorological Climate Summary, 9/96

HAZARDOUS WASTE

Superfund Sites

The Tampa-St. Petersburg-Clearwater, FL metro area is home to 14 sites on the EPA's Superfund National Priorities List: **Alaric Area Gw Plume** (final); **Arkla Terra Property** (final); **Helena Chemical Co. (Tampa Plant)** (final); **JJ Seifert Machine** (final); **MRI Corp (Tampa)** (final); **Normandy Park Apartments** (proposed); **Peak Oil Co./Bay Drum Co.** (final); **Raleigh Street Dump** (final); **Reeves Southeastern Galvanizing Corp.** (final); **Southern Solvents, Inc.** (final); **Stauffer Chemical Co (Tampa) (final); **Stauffer Chemical Co. (Tarpon Springs)** (final); **Sydney Mine Sludge Ponds** (final); **Taylor Road Landfill** (final). There are a total of 1,375 Superfund sites with a status of proposed or final on the list in the U.S. *U.S. Environmental Protection Agency, National Priorities List, April 7, 2021*

AIR QUALITY

Air Quality Trends: Ozone

	1990	1995	2000	2005	2010	2015	2016	2017	2018	2019
MSA[1]	0.080	0.075	0.081	0.075	0.067	0.062	0.064	0.064	0.065	0.065
U.S.	0.088	0.089	0.082	0.080	0.073	0.068	0.069	0.068	0.069	0.065

Note: (1) Data covers the Tampa-St. Petersburg-Clearwater, FL Metropolitan Statistical Area. The values shown are the composite ozone concentration averages among trend sites based on the highest fourth daily maximum 8-hour concentration in parts per million. These trends are based on sites having an adequate record of monitoring data during the trend period. Data from exceptional events are included.
Source: U.S. Environmental Protection Agency, Air Quality Monitoring Information, "Air Quality Trends by City, 1990-2019"

Air Quality Index

Area	Percent of Days when Air Quality was...[2]					AQI Statistics[2]	
	Good	Moderate	Unhealthy for Sensitive Groups	Unhealthy	Very Unhealthy	Maximum	Median
MSA[1]	73.2	25.2	1.6	0.0	0.0	132	43

Note: (1) Data covers the Tampa-St. Petersburg-Clearwater, FL Metropolitan Statistical Area; (2) Based on 365 days with AQI data in 2019. Air Quality Index (AQI) is an index for reporting daily air quality. EPA calculates the AQI for five major air pollutants regulated by the Clean Air Act: ground-level ozone, particle pollution (aka particulate matter), carbon monoxide, sulfur dioxide, and nitrogen dioxide. The AQI runs from 0 to 500. The higher the AQI value, the greater the level of air pollution and the greater the health concern. There are six AQI categories: "Good" AQI is between 0 and 50. Air quality is considered satisfactory; "Moderate" AQI is between 51 and 100. Air quality is acceptable; "Unhealthy for Sensitive Groups" When AQI values are between 101 and 150, members of sensitive groups may experience health effects; "Unhealthy" When AQI values are between 151 and 200 everyone may begin to experience health effects; "Very Unhealthy" AQI values between 201 and 300 trigger a health alert; "Hazardous" AQI values over 300 trigger warnings of emergency conditions (not shown).
Source: U.S. Environmental Protection Agency, Air Quality Index Report, 2019

Air Quality Index Pollutants

Area	Percent of Days when AQI Pollutant was...[2]					
	Carbon Monoxide	Nitrogen Dioxide	Ozone	Sulfur Dioxide	Particulate Matter 2.5	Particulate Matter 10
MSA[1]	0.0	0.0	58.4	1.1	39.5	1.1

Note: (1) Data covers the Tampa-St. Petersburg-Clearwater, FL Metropolitan Statistical Area; (2) Based on 365 days with AQI data in 2019. The Air Quality Index (AQI) is an index for reporting daily air quality. EPA calculates the AQI for five major air pollutants regulated by the Clean Air Act: ground-level ozone, particle pollution (also known as particulate matter), carbon monoxide, sulfur dioxide, and nitrogen dioxide. The AQI runs from 0 to 500. The higher the AQI value, the greater the level of air pollution and the greater the health concern.
Source: U.S. Environmental Protection Agency, Air Quality Index Report, 2019

Maximum Air Pollutant Concentrations: Particulate Matter, Ozone, CO and Lead

	Particulate Matter 10 (ug/m^3)	Particulate Matter 2.5 Wtd AM (ug/m^3)	Particulate Matter 2.5 24-Hr (ug/m^3)	Ozone (ppm)	Carbon Monoxide (ppm)	Lead (ug/m^3)
MSA[1] Level	64	7.7	17	0.070	1	0.09
NAAQS[2]	150	15	35	0.075	9	0.15
Met NAAQS[2]	Yes	Yes	Yes	Yes	Yes	Yes

Note: (1) Data covers the Tampa-St. Petersburg-Clearwater, FL Metropolitan Statistical Area; Data from exceptional events are included; (2) National Ambient Air Quality Standards; ppm = parts per million; ug/m^3 = micrograms per cubic meter; n/a not available.
Concentrations: Particulate Matter 10 (coarse particulate)—highest second maximum 24-hour concentration; Particulate Matter 2.5 Wtd AM (fine particulate)—highest weighted annual mean concentration; Particulate Matter 2.5 24-Hour (fine particulate)—highest 98th percentile 24-hour concentration; Ozone—highest fourth daily maximum 8-hour concentration; Carbon Monoxide—highest second maximum non-overlapping 8-hour concentration; Lead—maximum running 3-month average
Source: U.S. Environmental Protection Agency, Air Quality Monitoring Information, "Air Quality Statistics by City, 2019"

Maximum Air Pollutant Concentrations: Nitrogen Dioxide and Sulfur Dioxide

	Nitrogen Dioxide AM (ppb)	Nitrogen Dioxide 1-Hr (ppb)	Sulfur Dioxide AM (ppb)	Sulfur Dioxide 1-Hr (ppb)	Sulfur Dioxide 24-Hr (ppb)
MSA[1] Level	10	37	n/a	11	n/a
NAAQS[2]	53	100	30	75	140
Met NAAQS[2]	Yes	Yes	n/a	Yes	n/a

Note: (1) Data covers the Tampa-St. Petersburg-Clearwater, FL Metropolitan Statistical Area; Data from exceptional events are included; (2) National Ambient Air Quality Standards; ppm = parts per million; ug/m³ = micrograms per cubic meter; n/a not available.
Concentrations: Nitrogen Dioxide AM—highest arithmetic mean concentration; Nitrogen Dioxide 1-Hr—highest 98th percentile 1-hour daily maximum concentration; Sulfur Dioxide AM—highest annual mean concentration; Sulfur Dioxide 1-Hr—highest 99th percentile 1-hour daily maximum concentration; Sulfur Dioxide 24-Hr—highest second maximum 24-hour concentration
Source: U.S. Environmental Protection Agency, Air Quality Monitoring Information, "Air Quality Statistics by City, 2019"

Tuscaloosa, Alabama

Background

Tuscaloosa is located on the Black Warrior River in west central Alabama. The seat of Tuscaloosa County, it is situated on the divide between the Appalachian Highland and the Gulf Coastal Plain, giving the city a diverse geography. The city celebrated its 200th birthday in 2019.

Originally inhabited by the Creek or Muskogee people, these native inhabitants were relocated following the passage of the Indian Removal Act in 1830 and were sent to Indian Territory. The capital of Alabama, from 1826 to 1846, Tuscaloosa grew rapidly once the University of Alabama was founded there in 1831, although the removal of the capital to Montgomery in 1846 reversed a good deal of this growth. Following the Civil War in which the city was widely damaged, including the burning of the University, and the Reconstruction period in which the entire region suffered economically, in the 1890s the U.S. Army Corps of Engineers constructed a series of locks and dams on the Black Warrior River which linked Tuscaloosa to the city of Mobile and to the Gulf Coast. As a result, Tuscaloosa became active in trade and its economy finally began to flourish, with the mining and metallurgical industries also taking root in the city at this time.

Tuscaloosa continued to experience steady growth during this time with its population increasing by 75 percent between 1880 and 1890 and continuing to make steady gains in every census since. The city's economy diversified continually throughout the 20th century and into the 21st century, although mining and construction continued to form a central part of the economy, as did higher education. Nonetheless, retail trade and transportation, hospitality, government work, and finance have also become key fields of employment. Similarly, the manufacturing sector retains a healthy presence in the city, with BF Goodrich Tire Manufacturing, GAF Materials Corporation, and JVC America all having operations in Tuscaloosa, and Mercedes-Benz's U.S. International Assembly plant located in the region and employing many of the city's residents.

Tuscaloosa played a key role in the Civil Rights Movement of the 1960s, a role not always flattering to the city's image, with much of it revolving around the question of university admissions. In 1956, Autherine Lucy became the first African American admitted to a white public university in the state, when she enrolled in a graduate Library Science program at the University of Alabama. When she was transported to classes on her first day, though, she was met with a mob of more than a thousand white men who threw objects at her car and was eventually expelled by the University. In 1963, Alabama governor George Wallace stood at the entrance to the University of Alabama auditorium, attempting to physically block two enrolled African American students from entering. Despite these events, though, Tuscaloosa was home to many brave protestors who fought valiantly for civil rights. Today, the University is successfully integrated and enrolls a diverse population of students.

Although much of the cultural life of Tuscaloosa is centered on the University, the city nonetheless possesses a rich array of institutions, particularly for a municipality of its size. The Bama Theater in downtown Tuscaloosa is a world-class, 1,094-seat venue, while the massive Tuscaloosa Amphitheater hosts many of the world's biggest musical acts. Among the city's many museums are the Murphy African-American Museum, the Alabama Museum of Natural History, and the Westervelt Warner Museum of American Art.

In the world of sports, Tuscaloosa is best known for the University of Alabama's football team, the Crimson Tide. Among the most successful programs in the country, Alabama has won five national championships since 2009 and regularly turns out star N.F.L. players under Coach Nick Saban. The Tide play in the 101,821-seat Bryant-Denny stadium which it regularly fills with fans. In addition, the University features highly accomplished baseball, softball, golf, and women's gymnastics programs. Nearby Stillman College features a number of competitive programs as well.

Tuscaloosa is marked by a humid subtropical climate. Although the city experiences four distinct seasons, winter, which lasts from mid-December until late-February, is notably mild, with average daily temperatures in January reaching 44.7 degrees Fahrenheit. On average, the city records 71-72 days of temperatures 90 degrees Fahrenheit or above. Tuscaloosa is also subject to severe thunderstorms and the occasional tornado. In 2011, two tornadoes struck the city in a span of 12 days, killing over 50 people and causing much structural damage.

Rankings

Business/Finance Rankings

- The Tuscaloosa metro area appeared on the Milken Institute "2021 Best Performing Cities" list. Rank: #29 out of 201 small metro areas (population over 60,000). Criteria: job growth; wage and salary growth; high-tech output growth; housing affordability; household broadband access. *Milken Institute, "Best-Performing Cities 2021," February 16, 2021*

- *Forbes* ranked 203 smaller metro areas (population under 268,000) to determine the nation's "Best Small Places for Business and Careers." The Tuscaloosa metro area was ranked #49. Criteria: costs (business and living); job growth (past and projected); income growth; quality of life; educational attainment (college and high school); projected economic growth; cultural and leisure opportunities; workplace tolerance laws; net migration patterns. *Forbes, "The Best Small Places for Business and Careers 2019," October 30, 2019*

Environmental Rankings

- Tuscaloosa was highlighted as one of the top 98 cleanest metro areas for short-term particle pollution (24-hour PM 2.5) in the U.S. during 2016 through 2018. Monitors in these cities reported no days with unhealthful PM 2.5 levels. *American Lung Association, "State of the Air 2020," April 21, 2020*

Safety Rankings

- The National Insurance Crime Bureau ranked 384 metro areas in the U.S. in terms of per capita rates of vehicle theft. The Tuscaloosa metro area ranked #84 (#1 = highest rate). Criteria: number of vehicle theft offenses per 100,000 inhabitants in 2019. *National Insurance Crime Bureau, "Hot Spots 2019," July 21, 2020*

Seniors/Retirement Rankings

- From its Best Cities for Successful Aging indexes, the Milken Institute generated rankings for metropolitan areas, weighing data in nine categories—health care, wellness, living arrangements, transportation and convenience, financial characteristics, education, employment, community engagement, and overall livability. The Tuscaloosa metro area was ranked #129 overall in the small metro area category. *Milken Institute, "Best Cities for Successful Aging, 2017" March 14, 2017*

Business Environment

DEMOGRAPHICS

Population Growth

Area	1990 Census	2000 Census	2010 Census	2019* Estimate	Population Growth (%) 1990-2019	Population Growth (%) 2010-2019
City	81,075	77,906	90,468	99,390	22.6	9.9
MSA[1]	176,123	192,034	219,461	250,681	42.3	14.2
U.S.	248,709,873	281,421,906	308,745,538	324,697,795	30.6	5.2

Note: (1) Figures cover the Tuscaloosa, AL Metropolitan Statistical Area; (*) 2015-2019 5-year estimated population
Source: U.S. Census Bureau, 1990 Census, Census 2000, Census 2010, 2015-2019 American Community Survey 5-Year Estimates

Household Size

Area	One	Two	Three	Four	Five	Six	Seven or More	Average Household Size
City	35.4	33.8	15.9	9.9	3.4	1.0	0.4	2.60
MSA[1]	29.5	35.1	16.4	11.5	5.3	1.3	0.9	2.70
U.S.	27.9	33.9	15.6	12.9	6.0	2.3	1.4	2.60

Note: (1) Figures cover the Tuscaloosa, AL Metropolitan Statistical Area
Source: U.S. Census Bureau, 2015-2019 American Community Survey 5-Year Estimates

Race

Area	White Alone[2] (%)	Black Alone[2] (%)	Asian Alone[2] (%)	AIAN[3] Alone[2] (%)	NHOPI[4] Alone[2] (%)	Other Race Alone[2] (%)	Two or More Races (%)
City	51.2	44.0	2.5	0.3	0.1	0.9	1.0
MSA[1]	60.6	35.8	1.4	0.2	0.0	0.8	1.1
U.S.	72.5	12.7	5.5	0.8	0.2	4.9	3.3

Note: (1) Figures cover the Tuscaloosa, AL Metropolitan Statistical Area; (2) Alone is defined as not being in combination with one or more other races; (3) American Indian and Alaska Native; (4) Native Hawaiian and Other Pacific Islander
Source: U.S. Census Bureau, 2015-2019 American Community Survey 5-Year Estimates

Hispanic or Latino Origin

Area	Total (%)	Mexican (%)	Puerto Rican (%)	Cuban (%)	Other (%)
City	3.2	1.6	0.1	0.2	1.4
MSA[1]	3.5	2.2	0.2	0.1	1.0
U.S.	18.0	11.2	1.7	0.7	4.3

Note: Persons of Hispanic or Latino origin can be of any race; (1) Figures cover the Tuscaloosa, AL Metropolitan Statistical Area
Source: U.S. Census Bureau, 2015-2019 American Community Survey 5-Year Estimates

Ancestry

Area	German	Irish	English	American	Italian	Polish	French[2]	Scottish	Dutch
City	5.8	6.6	5.6	7.3	2.3	0.9	1.2	2.2	0.6
MSA[1]	5.1	6.5	5.3	11.4	1.6	0.6	1.0	1.8	0.5
U.S.	13.3	9.7	7.2	6.2	5.1	2.8	2.3	1.7	1.2

Note: Figures are the percentage of the total population reporting a particular ancestry. The nine most commonly reported ancestries in the U.S. are shown. Figures include multiple ancestries (e.g. if a person reported being Irish and Italian, they were included in both columns); (1) Figures cover the Tuscaloosa, AL Metropolitan Statistical Area; (2) Excludes Basque
Source: U.S. Census Bureau, 2015-2019 American Community Survey 5-Year Estimates

Foreign-born Population

Area	Any Foreign Country	Asia	Mexico	Europe	Caribbean	Central America[2]	South America	Africa	Canada
City	4.6	2.2	0.5	0.4	0.1	0.9	0.1	0.3	0.1
MSA[1]	3.4	1.1	0.9	0.4	0.1	0.6	0.1	0.2	0.1
U.S.	13.6	4.2	3.5	1.5	1.3	1.1	1.0	0.7	0.2

Note: (1) Figures cover the Tuscaloosa, AL Metropolitan Statistical Area; (2) Excludes Mexico.
Source: U.S. Census Bureau, 2015-2019 American Community Survey 5-Year Estimates

Marital Status

Area	Never Married	Now Married[2]	Separated	Widowed	Divorced
City	53.2	30.8	1.9	4.3	9.9
MSA[1]	40.8	41.1	2.1	5.6	10.3
U.S.	33.4	48.1	1.9	5.8	10.9

Note: Figures are percentages and cover the population 15 years of age and older; (1) Figures cover the Tuscaloosa, AL Metropolitan Statistical Area; (2) Excludes separated
Source: U.S. Census Bureau, 2015-2019 American Community Survey 5-Year Estimates

Disability by Age

Area	All Ages	Under 18 Years Old	18 to 64 Years Old	65 Years and Over
City	11.1	2.8	9.5	32.4
MSA[1]	14.4	4.0	12.4	40.2
U.S.	12.6	4.2	10.3	34.5

Note: Figures show percent of the civilian noninstitutionalized population that reported having a disability. Disability status is determined from six types of difficulty: vision, hearing, cognitive, ambulatory, self-care, and independent living. For children under 5 years old, hearing and vision difficulty are used to determine disability status. For children between the ages of 5 and 14, disability status is determined from hearing, vision, cognitive, ambulatory, and self-care difficulties. For people aged 15 years and older, they are considered to have a disability if they have difficulty with any one of the six difficulty types; Note: (1) Figures cover the Tuscaloosa, AL Metropolitan Statistical Area
Source: U.S. Census Bureau, 2015-2019 American Community Survey 5-Year Estimates

Age

Area	Under Age 5	Age 5–19	Age 20–34	Age 35–44	Age 45–54	Age 55–64	Age 65–74	Age 75–84	Age 85+	Median Age
City	5.2	22.9	29.5	10.0	9.9	10.3	6.9	3.9	1.4	29.3
MSA[1]	6.0	20.5	24.3	11.8	11.5	12.0	8.4	4.1	1.5	34.4
U.S.	6.1	19.1	20.7	12.6	13.0	12.9	9.1	4.6	1.9	38.1

Note: (1) Figures cover the Tuscaloosa, AL Metropolitan Statistical Area
Source: U.S. Census Bureau, 2015-2019 American Community Survey 5-Year Estimates

Gender

Area	Males	Females	Males per 100 Females
City	47,718	51,672	92.3
MSA[1]	120,524	130,157	92.6
U.S.	159,886,919	164,810,876	97.0

Note: (1) Figures cover the Tuscaloosa, AL Metropolitan Statistical Area
Source: U.S. Census Bureau, 2015-2019 American Community Survey 5-Year Estimates

Religious Groups by Family

Area	Catholic	Baptist	Non-Den.	Methodist[2]	Lutheran	LDS[3]	Pentecostal	Presbyterian[4]	Muslim[5]	Judaism
MSA[1]	1.7	32.3	4.6	8.4	0.1	0.6	1.5	1.4	0.1	0.1
U.S.	19.1	9.3	4.0	4.0	2.3	2.0	1.9	1.6	0.8	0.7

Note: Figures are the number of adherents as a percentage of the total population; (1) Figures cover the Tuscaloosa, AL Metropolitan Statistical Area; (2) Methodist/Pietist; (3) Latter Day Saints; (4) Reformed; (5) Figures are estimates
Source: Association of Statisticians of American Religious Bodies, 2010 U.S. Religion Census: Religious Congregations & Membership Study

Religious Groups by Tradition

Area	Catholic	Evangelical Protestant	Mainline Protestant	Other Tradition	Black Protestant	Orthodox
MSA[1]	1.7	35.2	6.5	1.0	8.6	<0.1
U.S.	19.1	16.2	7.3	4.3	1.6	0.3

Note: Figures are the number of adherents as a percentage of the total population; (1) Figures cover the Tuscaloosa, AL Metropolitan Statistical Area
Source: Association of Statisticians of American Religious Bodies, 2010 U.S. Religion Census: Religious Congregations & Membership Study

ECONOMY

Gross Metropolitan Product

Area	2017	2018	2019	2020	Rank[2]
MSA[1]	11.8	12.4	13.0	13.4	190

Note: Figures are in billions of dollars; (1) Figures cover the Tuscaloosa, AL Metropolitan Statistical Area; (2) Rank is based on 2018 data and ranges from 1 to 381
Source: U.S. Conference of Mayors, U.S. Metro Economies: GMP & Employment 2018-2020, September 2019

Economic Growth

Area	2015-17 (%)	2018 (%)	2019 (%)	2020 (%)	Rank[2]
MSA[1]	1.0	2.8	3.4	1.5	227
U.S.	1.9	2.9	2.3	2.1	—

Note: Figures are real gross metropolitan product (GMP) growth rates and represent average annual percent change; (1) Figures cover the Tuscaloosa, AL Metropolitan Statistical Area; (2) Rank is based on 2017 2-year average annual percent change and ranges from 1 to 381
Source: U.S. Conference of Mayors, U.S. Metro Economies: GMP & Employment 2018-2020, September 2019

Metropolitan Area Exports

Area	2014	2015	2016	2017	2018	2019	Rank[2]
MSA[1]	n/a	n/a	n/a	n/a	n/a	n/a	400

Note: Figures are in millions of dollars; (1) Figures cover the Tuscaloosa, AL Metropolitan Statistical Area; (2) Rank is based on 2019 data and ranges from 1 to 386
Source: U.S. Department of Commerce, International Trade Administration, Office of Trade and Economic Analysis, Industry and Analysis, Exports by Metropolitan Area, data extracted March 24, 2021

Building Permits

Area	Single-Family 2018	Single-Family 2019	Pct. Chg.	Multi-Family 2018	Multi-Family 2019	Pct. Chg.	Total 2018	Total 2019	Pct. Chg.
City	353	321	-9.1	469	844	80.0	822	1,165	41.7
MSA[1]	578	630	9.0	469	844	80.0	1,047	1,474	40.8
U.S.	855,300	862,100	0.7	473,500	523,900	10.6	1,328,800	1,386,000	4.3

Note: (1) Figures cover the Tuscaloosa, AL Metropolitan Statistical Area; Figures represent new, privately-owned housing units authorized (unadjusted data); All permit data are based on estimates with imputation
Source: U.S. Census Bureau, Manufacturing, Mining, and Construction Statistics, Building Permits, 2018, 2019

Bankruptcy Filings

Area	Business Filings 2019	Business Filings 2020	% Chg.	Nonbusiness Filings 2019	Nonbusiness Filings 2020	% Chg.
Tuscaloosa County	9	10	11.1	1,246	799	-35.9
U.S.	22,780	21,655	-4.9	752,160	522,808	-30.5

Note: Business filings include Chapter 7, Chapter 9, Chapter 11, Chapter 12, Chapter 13, Chapter 15, and Section 304; Nonbusiness filings include Chapter 7, Chapter 11, and Chapter 13
Source: Administrative Office of the U.S. Courts, Business and Nonbusiness Bankruptcy, County Cases Commenced by Chapter of the Bankruptcy Code, During the 12-Month Period Ending December 31, 2019 and Business and Nonbusiness Bankruptcy, County Cases Commenced by Chapter of the Bankruptcy Code, During the 12-Month Period Ending December 31, 2020

Housing Vacancy Rates

Area	Gross Vacancy Rate[2] (%) 2018	2019	2020	Year-Round Vacancy Rate[3] (%) 2018	2019	2020	Rental Vacancy Rate[4] (%) 2018	2019	2020	Homeowner Vacancy Rate[5] (%) 2018	2019	2020
MSA[1]	n/a	n/a	n/a	n/a	n/a	n/a	n/a	n/a	n/a	n/a	n/a	n/a
U.S.	12.3	12.0	10.6	9.7	9.5	8.2	6.9	6.7	6.3	1.5	1.4	1.0

Note: (1) Figures cover the Tuscaloosa, AL Metropolitan Statistical Area; (2) The percentage of the total housing inventory that is vacant; (3) The percentage of the housing inventory (excluding seasonal units) that is year-round vacant; (4) The percentage of rental inventory that is vacant for rent; (5) The percentage of homeowner inventory that is vacant for sale; n/a not available
Source: U.S. Census Bureau, Housing Vacancies and Homeownership Annual Statistics: 2018, 2019, 2020

INCOME

Income

Area	Per Capita ($)	Median Household ($)	Average Household ($)
City	26,437	45,268	68,837
MSA[1]	25,759	50,408	67,811
U.S.	34,103	62,843	88,607

Note: (1) Figures cover the Tuscaloosa, AL Metropolitan Statistical Area
Source: U.S. Census Bureau, 2015-2019 American Community Survey 5-Year Estimates

Household Income Distribution

Area	Under $15,000	$15,000 -$24,999	$25,000 -$34,999	$35,000 -$49,999	$50,000 -$74,999	$75,000 -$99,999	$100,000 -$149,999	$150,000 and up
City	19.4	11.0	11.0	12.3	16.5	9.4	10.2	10.2
MSA[1]	16.4	10.6	10.2	12.4	17.8	11.5	12.7	8.4
U.S.	10.3	8.9	8.9	12.3	17.2	12.7	15.1	14.5

Note: (1) Figures cover the Tuscaloosa, AL Metropolitan Statistical Area
Source: U.S. Census Bureau, 2015-2019 American Community Survey 5-Year Estimates

Tuscaloosa, Alabama

Poverty Rate

Area	All Ages	Under 18 Years Old	18 to 64 Years Old	65 Years and Over
City	24.0	24.2	26.6	10.3
MSA[1]	19.2	24.7	19.2	10.6
U.S.	13.4	18.5	12.6	9.3

Note: Figures are percentage of people whose income during the past 12 months was below the poverty level;
(1) Figures cover the Tuscaloosa, AL Metropolitan Statistical Area
Source: U.S. Census Bureau, 2015-2019 American Community Survey 5-Year Estimates

CITY FINANCES

City Government Finances

Component	2017 ($000)	2017 ($ per capita)
Total Revenues	223,745	2,275
Total Expenditures	205,871	2,094
Debt Outstanding	191,825	1,951
Cash and Securities[1]	222,639	2,264

Note: (1) Cash and security holdings of a government at the close of its fiscal year, including those of its dependent agencies, utilities, and liquor stores.
Source: U.S. Census Bureau, State & Local Government Finances 2017

City Government Revenue by Source

Source	2017 ($000)	2017 ($ per capita)	2017 (%)
General Revenue			
From Federal Government	2,898	29	1.3
From State Government	18,888	192	8.4
From Local Governments	30,382	309	13.6
Taxes			
Property	13,735	140	6.1
Sales and Gross Receipts	52,964	539	23.7
Personal Income	0	0	0.0
Corporate Income	0	0	0.0
Motor Vehicle License	0	0	0.0
Other Taxes	22,564	229	10.1
Current Charges	37,652	383	16.8
Liquor Store	0	0	0.0
Utility	13,871	141	6.2
Employee Retirement	18,677	190	8.3

Source: U.S. Census Bureau, State & Local Government Finances 2017

City Government Expenditures by Function

Function	2017 ($000)	2017 ($ per capita)	2017 (%)
General Direct Expenditures			
Air Transportation	388	3	0.2
Corrections	322	3	0.2
Education	0	0	0.0
Employment Security Administration	0	0	0.0
Financial Administration	6,031	61	2.9
Fire Protection	21,216	215	10.3
General Public Buildings	3,507	35	1.7
Governmental Administration, Other	3,511	35	1.7
Health	301	3	0.1
Highways	25,265	256	12.3
Hospitals	0	0	0.0
Housing and Community Development	2,461	25	1.2
Interest on General Debt	3,456	35	1.7
Judicial and Legal	2,735	27	1.3
Libraries	1,919	19	0.9
Parking	0	0	0.0
Parks and Recreation	9,694	98	4.7
Police Protection	30,382	309	14.8
Public Welfare	0	0	0.0
Sewerage	9,362	95	4.5
Solid Waste Management	6,739	68	3.3
Veterans' Services	0	0	0.0
Liquor Store	0	0	0.0
Utility	32,023	325	15.6
Employee Retirement	16,862	171	8.2

Source: U.S. Census Bureau, State & Local Government Finances 2017

EMPLOYMENT

Labor Force and Employment

Area	Civilian Labor Force Dec. 2019	Civilian Labor Force Dec. 2020	% Chg.	Workers Employed Dec. 2019	Workers Employed Dec. 2020	% Chg.
City	48,708	47,374	-2.7	47,449	45,126	-4.9
MSA[1]	120,183	116,579	-3.0	117,420	111,848	-4.7
U.S.	164,007,000	160,017,000	-2.4	158,504,000	149,613,000	-5.6

Note: Data is not seasonally adjusted and covers workers 16 years of age and older; (1) Figures cover the Tuscaloosa, AL Metropolitan Statistical Area
Source: Bureau of Labor Statistics, Local Area Unemployment Statistics

Unemployment Rate

Area	Jan.	Feb.	Mar.	Apr.	May	Jun.	Jul.	Aug.	Sep.	Oct.	Nov.	Dec.
City	3.2	2.7	3.0	17.9	11.9	10.4	10.6	7.6	8.6	7.0	5.0	4.7
MSA[1]	2.9	2.5	2.8	16.6	10.8	9.0	9.1	6.3	7.1	6.0	4.4	4.1
U.S.	4.0	3.8	4.5	14.4	13.0	11.2	10.5	8.5	7.7	6.6	6.4	6.5

Note: Data is not seasonally adjusted and covers workers 16 years of age and older; (1) Figures cover the Tuscaloosa, AL Metropolitan Statistical Area
Source: Bureau of Labor Statistics, Local Area Unemployment Statistics

Average Wages

Occupation	$/Hr.	Occupation	$/Hr.
Accountants and Auditors	34.40	Maintenance and Repair Workers	16.60
Automotive Mechanics	20.20	Marketing Managers	46.20
Bookkeepers	17.40	Network and Computer Systems Admin.	37.00
Carpenters	19.70	Nurses, Licensed Practical	19.30
Cashiers	10.40	Nurses, Registered	28.80
Computer Programmers	30.40	Nursing Assistants	12.80
Computer Systems Analysts	43.50	Office Clerks, General	12.80
Computer User Support Specialists	29.00	Physical Therapists	47.80
Construction Laborers	15.00	Physicians	104.40
Cooks, Restaurant	10.40	Plumbers, Pipefitters and Steamfitters	22.90
Customer Service Representatives	16.10	Police and Sheriff's Patrol Officers	26.10
Dentists	73.10	Postal Service Mail Carriers	24.90
Electricians	25.70	Real Estate Sales Agents	29.60
Engineers, Electrical	43.70	Retail Salespersons	14.20
Fast Food and Counter Workers	9.60	Sales Representatives, Technical/Scientific	n/a
Financial Managers	67.00	Secretaries, Exc. Legal/Medical/Executive	17.40
First-Line Supervisors of Office Workers	25.70	Security Guards	13.60
General and Operations Managers	56.20	Surgeons	n/a
Hairdressers/Cosmetologists	13.20	Teacher Assistants, Exc. Postsecondary*	9.50
Home Health and Personal Care Aides	9.90	Teachers, Secondary School, Exc. Sp. Ed.*	24.80
Janitors and Cleaners	13.80	Telemarketers	n/a
Landscaping/Groundskeeping Workers	14.90	Truck Drivers, Heavy/Tractor-Trailer	20.30
Lawyers	55.00	Truck Drivers, Light/Delivery Services	18.30
Maids and Housekeeping Cleaners	10.50	Waiters and Waitresses	9.00

Note: Wage data covers the Tuscaloosa, AL Metropolitan Statistical Area; (*) Hourly wages were calculated from annual wage data based on a 40 hour work week; n/a not available.
Source: Bureau of Labor Statistics, Metro Area Occupational Employment & Wage Estimates, May 2020

Employment by Industry

Sector	MSA[1] Number of Employees	MSA[1] Percent of Total	U.S. Percent of Total
Construction, Mining, and Logging	6,800	6.5	5.5
Education and Health Services	8,800	8.3	16.3
Financial Activities	4,100	3.9	6.1
Government	27,900	26.5	15.2
Information	900	0.9	1.9
Leisure and Hospitality	9,700	9.2	9.0
Manufacturing	17,400	16.5	8.5
Other Services	4,100	3.9	3.8
Professional and Business Services	9,700	9.2	14.4
Retail Trade	10,900	10.3	10.9
Transportation, Warehousing, and Utilities	3,000	2.8	4.6
Wholesale Trade	2,100	2.0	3.9

Note: Figures are non-farm employment as of December 2020. Figures are not seasonally adjusted and include workers 16 years of age and older; (1) Figures cover the Tuscaloosa, AL Metropolitan Statistical Area
Source: Bureau of Labor Statistics, Current Employment Statistics, Employment, Hours, and Earnings

Employment by Occupation

Occupation Classification	City (%)	MSA[1] (%)	U.S. (%)
Management, Business, Science, and Arts	37.4	34.7	38.5
Natural Resources, Construction, and Maintenance	5.7	8.9	8.9
Production, Transportation, and Material Moving	17.5	19.4	13.2
Sales and Office	20.7	20.4	21.6
Service	18.7	16.6	17.8

Note: Figures cover employed civilians 16 years of age and older; (1) Figures cover the Tuscaloosa, AL Metropolitan Statistical Area
Source: U.S. Census Bureau, 2015-2019 American Community Survey 5-Year Estimates

Occupations with Greatest Projected Employment Growth: 2020 – 2022

Occupation[1]	2020 Employment	2022 Projected Employment	Numeric Employment Change	Percent Employment Change
Total,, All Occupations	2,160,690	2,237,520	76,830	3.6
Combined Food Preparation and Serving Workers, Including Fast Food	45,650	49,410	3,760	8.2
Registered Nurses	54,730	57,080	2,350	4.3
Waiters and Waitresses	34,050	36,120	2,070	6.1
Assemblers and Fabricators, All Other, Including Team Assemblers	31,130	32,950	1,820	5.8
Laborers and Freight, Stock, and Material Movers, Hand	41,600	43,250	1,650	4.0
Retail Salespersons	64,450	65,910	1,460	2.3
Janitors and Cleaners, Except Maids and Housekeeping Cleaners	30,990	32,430	1,440	4.6
Cooks, Restaurant	15,690	17,120	1,430	9.1
Heavy and Tractor-Trailer Truck Drivers	33,560	34,980	1,420	4.2

Note: Projections cover Alabama; (1) Sorted by numeric employment change
Source: www.projectionscentral.com, State Occupational Projections, 2020–2022 Short-Term Projections

Fastest-Growing Occupations: 2020 – 2022

Occupation[1]	2020 Employment	2022 Projected Employment	Numeric Employment Change	Percent Employment Change
Dental Laboratory Technicians	1,000	1,230	230	23.0
Chemical Plant and System Operators	1,110	1,250	140	12.6
Chemical Equipment Operators and Tenders	1,910	2,140	230	12.0
Chemical Engineers	670	740	70	10.4
Information Security Analysts	980	1,070	90	9.2
Cooks, Restaurant	15,690	17,120	1,430	9.1
Molders, Shapers, and Casters, Except Metal and Plastic	550	600	50	9.1
Directors, Religious Activities and Education	4,630	5,020	390	8.4
Clergy	6,710	7,260	550	8.2
Combined Food Preparation and Serving Workers, Including Fast Food	45,650	49,410	3,760	8.2

Note: Projections cover Alabama; (1) Sorted by percent employment change and excludes occupations with numeric employment change less than 50
Source: www.projectionscentral.com, State Occupational Projections, 2020–2022 Short-Term Projections

TAXES

State Corporate Income Tax Rates

State	Tax Rate (%)	Income Brackets ($)	Num. of Brackets	Financial Institution Tax Rate (%)[a]	Federal Income Tax Ded.
Alabama	6.5	Flat rate	1	6.5	Yes

Note: Tax rates as of January 1, 2021; (a) Rates listed are the corporate income tax rate applied to financial institutions or excise taxes based on income. Some states have other taxes based upon the value of deposits or shares.
Source: Federation of Tax Administrators, State Corporate Income Tax Rates, January 1, 2021

State Individual Income Tax Rates

State	Tax Rate (%)	Income Brackets ($)	Personal Exemptions ($) Single	Personal Exemptions ($) Married	Personal Exemptions ($) Depend.	Standard Ded. ($) Single	Standard Ded. ($) Married
Alabama	2.0 - 5.0	500 - 3,001 (b)	1,500	3,000	500 (e)	2,500	7,500 (y)

Note: Tax rates as of January 1, 2021; Local- and county-level taxes are not included; Federal income tax is deductible on state income tax returns; (b) For joint returns, taxes are twice the tax on half the couple's income; (e) In Alabama, the per-dependent exemption is $1,000 for taxpayers with state AGI of $20,000 or less, $500 with AGI from $20,001 to $100,000, and $300 with AGI over $100,000; (y) Alabama standard deduction is phased out for incomes over $23,000. Rhode Island exemptions & standard deductions phased out for incomes over $207,700; Wisconsin standard deduciton phases out for income over $16,149.
Source: Federation of Tax Administrators, State Individual Income Tax Rates, January 1, 2021

Various State Sales and Excise Tax Rates

State	State Sales Tax (%)	Gasoline[1] (¢/gal.)	Cigarette[2] ($/pack)	Spirits[3] ($/gal.)	Wine[4] ($/gal.)	Beer[5] ($/gal.)	Recreational Marijuana (%)
Alabama	4	29.21	0.675	19.11	1.7	0.53	Not legal

Note: All tax rates as of January 1, 2021; (1) The American Petroleum Institute has developed a methodology for determining the average tax rate on a gallon of fuel. Rates may include any of the following: excise taxes, environmental fees, storage tank fees, other fees or taxes, general sales tax, and local taxes; (2) The federal excise tax of $1.0066 per pack and local taxes are not included; (3) Rates are those applicable to off-premise sales of 40% alcohol by volume (a.b.v.) distilled spirits in 750ml containers. Local excise taxes are excluded; (4) Rates are those applicable to off-premise sales of 11% a.b.v. non-carbonated wine in 750ml containers; (5) Rates are those applicable to off-premise sales of 4.7% a.b.v. beer in 12 ounce containers.
Source: Tax Foundation, 2021 Facts & Figures: How Does Your State Compare?

State Business Tax Climate Index Rankings

State	Overall Rank	Corporate Tax Rank	Individual Income Tax Rank	Sales Tax Rank	Property Tax Rank	Unemployment Insurance Tax Rank
Alabama	41	23	30	50	19	14

Note: The index is a measure of how each state's tax laws affect economic performance. The lower the rank, the more favorable a state's tax system is for business. States without a given tax are given a ranking of 1. The scores/rankings for the District of Columbia do not affect other states. The 2021 index represents the tax climate as of July 1, 2020.
Source: Tax Foundation, State Business Tax Climate Index 2021

TRANSPORTATION

Means of Transportation to Work

Area	Car/Truck/Van Drove Alone	Car/Truck/Van Car-pooled	Public Transportation Bus	Public Transportation Subway	Public Transportation Railroad	Bicycle	Walked	Other Means	Worked at Home
City	84.2	8.1	0.8	0.1	0.0	0.5	1.8	0.6	3.9
MSA[1]	85.3	9.0	0.5	0.0	0.0	0.2	1.1	0.5	3.4
U.S.	76.3	9.0	2.4	1.9	0.6	0.5	2.7	1.4	5.2

Note: Figures are percentages and cover workers 16 years of age and older; (1) Figures cover the Tuscaloosa, AL Metropolitan Statistical Area
Source: U.S. Census Bureau, 2015-2019 American Community Survey 5-Year Estimates

Travel Time to Work

Area	Less Than 10 Minutes	10 to 19 Minutes	20 to 29 Minutes	30 to 44 Minutes	45 to 59 Minutes	60 to 89 Minutes	90 Minutes or More
City	14.6	44.8	25.9	7.4	3.5	2.8	1.0
MSA[1]	11.3	32.4	26.5	16.5	6.6	5.0	1.7
U.S.	12.2	28.4	20.8	20.8	8.3	6.4	2.9

Note: Note: Figures are percentages and include workers 16 years old and over; (1) Figures cover the Tuscaloosa, AL Metropolitan Statistical Area
Source: U.S. Census Bureau, 2015-2019 American Community Survey 5-Year Estimates

Key Congestion Measures

Measure	1982	1992	2002	2012	2017
Annual Hours of Delay, Total (000)	n/a	n/a	n/a	n/a	4,600
Annual Hours of Delay, Per Auto Commuter	n/a	n/a	n/a	n/a	30
Annual Congestion Cost, Total (million $)	n/a	n/a	n/a	n/a	95
Annual Congestion Cost, Per Auto Commuter ($)	n/a	n/a	n/a	n/a	624

Note: n/a not available
Source: Texas A&M Transportation Institute, 2019 Urban Mobility Report

Tuscaloosa, Alabama

Freeway Travel Time Index

Measure	1982	1987	1992	1997	2002	2007	2012	2017
Urban Area Index[1]	n/a	n/a	n/a	n/a	n/a	n/a	n/a	1.11
Urban Area Rank[1,2]	n/a	n/a	n/a	n/a	n/a	n/a	n/a	n/a

Note: Freeway Travel Time Index—the ratio of travel time in the peak period to the travel time at free-flow conditions. For example, a value of 1.30 indicates a 20-minute free-flow trip takes 26 minutes in the peak (20 minutes x 1.30 = 26 minutes); (1) Covers the Tuscaloosa AL urban area; (2) Rank is based on 101 larger urban areas (#1 = highest travel time index); n/a not available
Source: Texas A&M Transportation Institute, 2019 Urban Mobility Report

Public Transportation

Agency Name / Mode of Transportation	Vehicles Operated in Maximum Service[1]	Annual Unlinked Passenger Trips[2] (in thous.)	Annual Passenger Miles[3] (in thous.)
Tuscaloosa County Parking and Transit Authority			
Bus (directly operated)	7	297.9	n/a
Demand Response (directly operated)	5	15.1	n/a

Note: (1) Number of revenue vehicles operated by the given mode and type of service to meet the annual maximum service requirement. This is the revenue vehicle count during the peak season of the year; on the week and day that maximum service is provided. Vehicles operated in maximum service (VOMS) exclude atypical days and one-time special events; (2) Number of passengers who boarded public transportation vehicles. Passengers are counted each time they board a vehicle no matter how many vehicles they use to travel from their origin to their destination. (3) Sum of the distances ridden by all passengers during the entire fiscal year.
Source: Federal Transit Administration, National Transit Database, 2019

Air Transportation

Airport Name and Code / Type of Service	Passenger Airlines[1]	Passenger Enplanements	Freight Carriers[2]	Freight (lbs)
Birmingham-Shuttlesworth International Airport (BHM)				
Domestic service (U.S. carriers - 2020)	19	622,097	10	19,502,208
International service (U.S. carriers - 2019)	3	634	0	0

Note: (1) Includes all U.S.-based major, minor and commuter airlines that carried at least one passenger during the year; (2) Includes all U.S.-based airlines and freight carriers that transported at least one pound of freight during the year.
Source: Bureau of Transportation Statistics, The Intermodal Transportation Database, Air Carriers: T-100 Domestic Market (U.S. Carriers), 2020; Bureau of Transportation Statistics, The Intermodal Transportation Database, Air Carriers: T-100 International Market (U.S. Carriers), 2019

BUSINESSES

Major Business Headquarters

Company Name	Industry	Fortune[1]	Forbes[2]
No companies listed	-	-	-

Note: (1) Companies that produce a 10-K are ranked 1 to 500 based on 2019 revenue; (2) All private companies with at least $2 billion in annual revenue through the end of their most current fiscal year are ranked 1 to 219; companies listed are headquartered in the city; dashes indicate no ranking
Source: Fortune, "Fortune 500," June/July 2020; Forbes, "America's Largest Private Companies," 2020

Living Environment

COST OF LIVING

Cost of Living Index

Composite Index	Groceries	Housing	Utilities	Transportation	Health Care	Misc. Goods/Services
n/a	n/a	n/a	n/a	n/a	n/a	n/a

Note: The Cost of Living Index measures regional differences in the cost of consumer goods and services, excluding taxes and non-consumer expenditures, for professional and managerial households in the top income quintile. It is based on more than 50,000 prices covering almost 60 different items for which prices are collected three times a year by chambers of commerce, economic development organizations or university applied economic centers in each participating urban area. The numbers shown should be read as a percentage above or below the national average of 100. For example, a value of 115.4 in the groceries column indicates that grocery prices are 15.4% higher than the national average. Small differences in the index numbers should not be interpreted as significant; n/a not available.
Source: The Council for Community and Economic Research, Cost of Living Index, 2020

Grocery Prices

Area[1]	T-Bone Steak ($/pound)	Frying Chicken ($/pound)	Whole Milk ($/half gal.)	Eggs ($/dozen)	Orange Juice ($/64 oz.)	Coffee ($/11.5 oz.)
City[2]	n/a	n/a	n/a	n/a	n/a	n/a
Avg.	11.78	1.39	2.05	1.47	3.57	4.34
Min.	8.03	0.94	1.03	0.74	2.94	3.02
Max.	15.86	2.65	4.31	3.77	5.44	8.69

Note: (1) Values for the local area are compared with the average, minimum and maximum values for all 284 areas in the Cost of Living Index; (2) Figures cover the Tuscaloosa AL urban area; n/a not available; **T-Bone Steak** (price per pound); **Frying Chicken** (price per pound, whole fryer); **Whole Milk** (half gallon carton); **Eggs** (price per dozen, Grade A, large); **Orange Juice** (64 oz. Tropicana or Florida Natural); **Coffee** (11.5 oz. can, vacuum-packed, Maxwell House, Hills Bros, or Folgers).
Source: The Council for Community and Economic Research, Cost of Living Index, 2020

Housing and Utility Costs

Area[1]	New Home Price ($)	Apartment Rent ($/month)	All Electric ($/month)	Part Electric ($/month)	Other Energy ($/month)	Telephone ($/month)
City[2]	n/a	n/a	n/a	n/a	n/a	n/a
Avg.	368,594	1,168	170.86	100.47	65.28	184.30
Min.	190,567	502	91.58	31.42	26.08	169.60
Max.	2,227,806	4,738	470.38	280.31	280.06	206.50

Note: (1) Values for the local area are compared with the average, minimum and maximum values for all 284 areas in the Cost of Living Index; (2) Figures cover the Tuscaloosa AL urban area; n/a not available; **New Home Price** (2,400 sf living area, 8,000 sf lot, in urban area with full utilities); **Apartment Rent** (950 sf 2 bedroom/1.5 or 2 bath, unfurnished, excluding all utilities except water); **All Electric** (average monthly cost for an all-electric home); **Part Electric** (average monthly cost for a part-electric home); **Other Energy** (average monthly cost for natural gas, fuel oil, coal, wood, and any other forms of energy except electricity); **Telephone** (price includes the base monthly rate plus taxes and fees for three lines of mobile phone service).
Source: The Council for Community and Economic Research, Cost of Living Index, 2020

Health Care, Transportation, and Other Costs

Area[1]	Doctor ($/visit)	Dentist ($/visit)	Optometrist ($/visit)	Gasoline ($/gallon)	Beauty Salon ($/visit)	Men's Shirt ($)
City[2]	n/a	n/a	n/a	n/a	n/a	n/a
Avg.	115.44	99.32	108.10	2.21	39.27	31.37
Min.	36.68	59.00	51.36	1.71	19.00	11.00
Max.	219.00	153.10	250.97	3.46	82.05	58.33

Note: (1) Values for the local area are compared with the average, minimum and maximum values for all 284 areas in the Cost of Living Index; (2) Figures cover the Tuscaloosa AL urban area; n/a not available; **Doctor** (general practitioners routine exam of an established patient); **Dentist** (adult teeth cleaning and periodic oral examination); **Optometrist** (full vision eye exam for established adult patient); **Gasoline** (one gallon regular unleaded, national brand, including all taxes, cash price at self-service pump if available); **Beauty Salon** (woman's shampoo, trim, and blow-dry); **Men's Shirt** (cotton/polyester dress shirt, pinpoint weave, long sleeves).
Source: The Council for Community and Economic Research, Cost of Living Index, 2020

HOUSING

Homeownership Rate

Area	2012 (%)	2013 (%)	2014 (%)	2015 (%)	2016 (%)	2017 (%)	2018 (%)	2019 (%)	2020 (%)
MSA[1]	n/a	n/a	n/a	n/a	n/a	n/a	n/a	n/a	n/a
U.S.	65.4	65.1	64.5	63.7	63.4	63.9	64.4	64.6	66.6

Note: (1) Figures cover the Tuscaloosa, AL Metropolitan Statistical Area; n/a not available
Source: U.S. Census Bureau, Housing Vacancies and Homeownership Annual Statistics: 2012-2020

House Price Index (HPI)

Area	National Ranking[2]	Quarterly Change (%)	One-Year Change (%)	Five-Year Change (%)	Since 1991Q1 (%)
MSA[1]	n/a	n/a	n/a	n/a	n/a
U.S.[3]	–	3.81	10.77	38.99	205.12

Note: The HPI is a weighted repeat sales index. It measures average price changes in repeat sales or refinancings on the same properties. This information is obtained by reviewing repeat mortgage transactions on single-family properties whose mortgages have been purchased or securitized by Fannie Mae or Freddie Mac since January 1975; (1) Figures cover the , Metropolitan Statistical Area; (2) Rankings are based on annual percentage change for all metro areas containing at least 15,000 transactions over the last 10 years and ranges from 1 to 253; (3) figures based on a weighted average of Census Division estimates using a seasonally adjusted, purchase-only index; all figures are for the period ending December 31, 2020; n/a not available
Source: Federal Housing Finance Agency, Change in Metropolitan Area House Price Indexes, April 7, 2021

Median Single-Family Home Prices

Area	2018	2019	2020p	Percent Change 2019 to 2020
MSA[1]	n/a	n/a	n/a	n/a
U.S. Average	261.6	274.6	299.9	9.2

Note: Figures are median sales prices of existing single-family homes in thousands of dollars; (p) preliminary; n/a not available; (1) Figures cover the Tuscaloosa, AL Metropolitan Statistical Area
Source: National Association of Realtors, Median Sales Price of Existing Single-Family Homes for Metropolitan Areas, 4th Quarter 2020

Qualifying Income Based on Median Sales Price of Existing Single-Family Homes

Area	With 5% Down ($)	With 10% Down ($)	With 20% Down ($)
MSA[1]	n/a	n/a	n/a
U.S. Average	59,266	56,147	49,908

Note: Figures are preliminary; Qualifying income is based on a mortgage rate of 2.81%. Monthly principal and interest payment is limited to 25% of income; n/a not available; (1) Figures cover the Tuscaloosa, AL Metropolitan Statistical Area
Source: National Association of Realtors, Qualifying Income Based on Median Sales Price of Existing Single-Family Homes for Metropolitan Areas, 4th Quarter 2020

Home Value Distribution

Area	Under $50,000	$50,000 -$99,999	$100,000 -$149,999	$150,000 -$199,999	$200,000 -$299,999	$300,000 -$499,999	$500,000 -$999,999	$1,000,000 or more
City	4.4	11.2	21.2	19.0	19.4	15.1	8.2	1.4
MSA[1]	13.0	14.9	17.5	20.5	19.7	9.8	3.9	0.7
U.S.	6.9	12.0	13.3	14.0	19.6	19.3	11.4	3.4

Note: Figures are percentages and cover owner-occupied housing units; (1) Figures cover the Tuscaloosa, AL Metropolitan Statistical Area
Source: U.S. Census Bureau, 2015-2019 American Community Survey 5-Year Estimates

Year Housing Structure Built

Area	2010 or Later	2000 -2009	1990 -1999	1980 -1989	1970 -1979	1960 -1969	1950 -1959	1940 -1949	Before 1940	Median Year
City	12.9	17.6	15.5	11.5	13.7	10.4	8.8	5.2	4.3	1987
MSA[1]	9.2	18.7	18.7	14.2	14.6	9.7	7.1	4.0	3.9	1988
U.S.	5.2	14.0	13.9	13.4	15.2	10.6	10.3	4.9	12.6	1978

Note: Figures are percentages except for Median Year; Note: (1) Figures cover the Tuscaloosa, AL Metropolitan Statistical Area
Source: U.S. Census Bureau, 2015-2019 American Community Survey 5-Year Estimates

Gross Monthly Rent

Area	Under $500	$500 -$999	$1,000 -$1,499	$1,500 -$1,999	$2,000 -$2,499	$2,500 -$2,999	$3,000 and up	Median ($)
City	13.1	57.0	22.2	4.6	1.9	0.3	1.0	844
MSA[1]	17.1	54.6	21.8	4.2	1.5	0.2	0.6	819
U.S.	9.4	36.2	30.0	14.0	5.6	2.4	2.4	1,062

Note: Figures are percentages except for Median; Gross rent is the contract rent plus the estimated average monthly cost of utilities (electricity, gas, and water and sewer) and fuels (oil, coal, kerosene, wood, etc.) if these are paid by the renter (or paid for the renter by someone else); (1) Figures cover the Tuscaloosa, AL Metropolitan Statistical Area
Source: U.S. Census Bureau, 2015-2019 American Community Survey 5-Year Estimates

HEALTH

Health Risk Factors

Category	MSA[1] (%)	U.S. (%)
Adults aged 18–64 who have any kind of health care coverage	83.3	87.3
Adults who reported being in good or better health	81.1	82.4
Adults who have been told they have high blood cholesterol	35.9	33.0
Adults who have been told they have high blood pressure	39.6	32.3
Adults who are current smokers	19.9	17.1
Adults who currently use E-cigarettes	5.5	4.6
Adults who currently use chewing tobacco, snuff, or snus	4.2	4.0
Adults who are heavy drinkers[2]	n/a	6.3
Adults who are binge drinkers[3]	12.5	17.4
Adults who are overweight (BMI 25.0 - 29.9)	31.7	35.3
Adults who are obese (BMI 30.0 - 99.8)	36.8	31.3
Adults who participated in any physical activities in the past month	67.7	74.4
Adults who always or nearly always wears a seat belt	96.1	94.3

Note: n/a not available; (1) Figures cover the Tuscaloosa, AL Metropolitan Statistical Area; (2) Heavy drinkers are classified as adult men having more than 14 drinks per week and adult women having more than 7 drinks per week; (3) Binge drinkers are classified as males having five or more drinks on one occasion or females having four or more drinks on one occasion
Source: Centers for Disease Control and Prevention, Behaviorial Risk Factor Surveillance System, SMART: Selected Metropolitan Area Risk Trends, 2017

Acute and Chronic Health Conditions

Category	MSA[1] (%)	U.S. (%)
Adults who have ever been told they had a heart attack	5.5	4.2
Adults who have ever been told they have angina or coronary heart disease	3.0	3.9
Adults who have ever been told they had a stroke	2.5	3.0
Adults who have ever been told they have asthma	14.8	14.2
Adults who have ever been told they have arthritis	28.5	24.9
Adults who have ever been told they have diabetes[2]	11.4	10.5
Adults who have ever been told they had skin cancer	6.2	6.2
Adults who have ever been told they had any other types of cancer	6.9	7.1
Adults who have ever been told they have COPD	10.2	6.5
Adults who have ever been told they have kidney disease	2.0	3.0
Adults who have ever been told they have a form of depression	26.3	20.5

Note: (1) Figures cover the Tuscaloosa, AL Metropolitan Statistical Area; (2) Figures do not include pregnancy-related, borderline, or pre-diabetes
Source: Centers for Disease Control and Prevention, Behaviorial Risk Factor Surveillance System, SMART: Selected Metropolitan Area Risk Trends, 2017

Health Screening and Vaccination Rates

Category	MSA[1] (%)	U.S. (%)
Adults aged 65+ who have had flu shot within the past year	59.9	60.7
Adults aged 65+ who have ever had a pneumonia vaccination	79.4	75.4
Adults who have ever been tested for HIV	44.0	36.1
Adults who have ever had the shingles or zoster vaccine?	26.5	28.9
Adults who have had their blood cholesterol checked within the last five years	85.6	85.9

Note: n/a not available; (1) Figures cover the Tuscaloosa, AL Metropolitan Statistical Area.
Source: Centers for Disease Control and Prevention, Behaviorial Risk Factor Surveillance System, SMART: Selected Metropolitan Area Risk Trends, 2017

Disability Status

Category	MSA[1] (%)	U.S. (%)
Adults who reported being deaf	5.5	6.7
Are you blind or have serious difficulty seeing, even when wearing glasses?	4.7	4.5
Are you limited in any way in any of your usual activities due of arthritis?	16.0	12.9
Do you have difficulty doing errands alone?	13.2	6.8
Do you have difficulty dressing or bathing?	3.5	3.6
Do you have serious difficulty concentrating/remembering/making decisions?	16.8	10.7
Do you have serious difficulty walking or climbing stairs?	18.1	13.6

Note: (1) Figures cover the Tuscaloosa, AL Metropolitan Statistical Area.
Source: Centers for Disease Control and Prevention, Behaviorial Risk Factor Surveillance System, SMART: Selected Metropolitan Area Risk Trends, 2017

Mortality Rates for the Top 10 Causes of Death in the U.S.

ICD-10[a] Sub-Chapter	ICD-10[a] Code	Age-Adjusted Mortality Rate[1] per 100,000 population County[2]	U.S.
Malignant neoplasms	C00-C97	148.7	149.2
Ischaemic heart diseases	I20-I25	68.8	90.5
Other forms of heart disease	I30-I51	118.8	52.2
Chronic lower respiratory diseases	J40-J47	50.1	39.6
Other degenerative diseases of the nervous system	G30-G31	71.0	37.6
Cerebrovascular diseases	I60-I69	48.4	37.2
Other external causes of accidental injury	W00-X59	26.7	36.1
Organic, including symptomatic, mental disorders	F01-F09	29.7	29.4
Hypertensive diseases	I10-I15	35.2	24.1
Diabetes mellitus	E10-E14	9.6	21.5

Note: (a) ICD-10 = International Classification of Diseases 10th Revision; (1) Mortality rates are a three-year average covering 2017-2019; (2) Figures cover Tuscaloosa County.
Source: Centers for Disease Control and Prevention, National Center for Health Statistics. Underlying Cause of Death 1999-2019 on CDC WONDER Online Database

Mortality Rates for Selected Causes of Death

ICD-10[a] Sub-Chapter	ICD-10[a] Code	Age-Adjusted Mortality Rate[1] per 100,000 population County[2]	U.S.
Assault	X85-Y09	7.7	6.0
Diseases of the liver	K70-K76	16.1	14.4
Human immunodeficiency virus (HIV) disease	B20-B24	Suppressed	1.5
Influenza and pneumonia	J09-J18	25.3	13.8
Intentional self-harm	X60-X84	12.3	14.1
Malnutrition	E40-E46	Unreliable	2.3
Obesity and other hyperalimentation	E65-E68	Suppressed	2.1
Renal failure	N17-N19	17.7	12.6
Transport accidents	V01-V99	15.8	12.3
Viral hepatitis	B15-B19	Suppressed	1.2

Note: (a) ICD-10 = International Classification of Diseases 10th Revision; (1) Mortality rates are a three-year average covering 2017-2019; (2) Figures cover Tuscaloosa County; Data are suppressed when the data meet the criteria for confidentiality constraints; Mortality rates are flagged as unreliable when the rate would be calculated with a numerator of 20 or less.
Source: Centers for Disease Control and Prevention, National Center for Health Statistics. Underlying Cause of Death 1999-2019 on CDC WONDER Online Database

Health Insurance Coverage

Area	With Health Insurance	With Private Health Insurance	With Public Health Insurance	Without Health Insurance	Population Under Age 19 Without Health Insurance
City	92.6	72.0	31.2	7.4	2.5
MSA[1]	92.3	70.5	33.7	7.7	2.5
U.S.	91.2	67.9	35.1	8.8	5.1

Note: Figures are percentages that cover the civilian noninstitutionalized population; (1) Figures cover the Tuscaloosa, AL Metropolitan Statistical Area
Source: U.S. Census Bureau, 2015-2019 American Community Survey 5-Year Estimates

Number of Medical Professionals

Area	MDs[3]	DOs[3,4]	Dentists	Podiatrists	Chiropractors	Optometrists
County[1] (number)	475	19	104	11	43	33
County[1] (rate[2])	228.0	9.1	49.7	5.3	20.5	15.8
U.S. (rate[2])	282.9	22.7	71.2	6.2	28.1	16.9

01125
Note: Data as of 2019 unless noted; (1) Data covers Tuscaloosa County; (2) Rate per 100,000 population; (3) Data as of 2018 and includes all active, non-federal physicians; (4) Doctor of Osteopathic Medicine
Source: U.S. Department of Health and Human Services, Health Resources and Services Administration, Bureau of Health Professions, Area Resource File (ARF) 2019-2020

EDUCATION

Public School District Statistics

District Name	Schls	Pupils	Pupil/Teacher Ratio	Minority Pupils[1] (%)	Free Lunch Eligible[2] (%)	IEP[3] (%)
Tuscaloosa City	20	10,538	15.9	76.7	52.9	12.6
Tuscaloosa County	35	18,709	18.5	40.1	43.5	15.1

Note: Table includes school districts with 2,000 or more students; (1) Percentage of students that are not non-Hispanic white; (2) Percentage of students that are eligible for the free lunch program; (3) Percentage of students that have an Individualized Education Program.
Source: U.S. Department of Education, National Center for Education Statistics, Common Core of Data, Local Education Agency (School District) Universe Survey: School Year 2018-2019; U.S. Department of Education, National Center for Education Statistics, Common Core of Data, Public Elementary/Secondary School Universe Survey: School Year 2018-2019

Highest Level of Education

Area	Less than H.S.	H.S. Diploma	Some College, No Deg.	Associate Degree	Bachelor's Degree	Master's Degree	Prof. School Degree	Doctorate Degree
City	10.9	27.3	19.9	5.0	21.0	10.3	2.5	3.1
MSA[1]	12.9	31.7	21.1	6.9	16.6	7.5	1.4	1.9
U.S.	12.0	27.0	20.4	8.5	19.8	8.8	2.1	1.4

Note: Figures cover persons age 25 and over; (1) Figures cover the Tuscaloosa, AL Metropolitan Statistical Area
Source: U.S. Census Bureau, 2015-2019 American Community Survey 5-Year Estimates

Educational Attainment by Race

Area	High School Graduate or Higher (%) Total	White	Black	Asian	Hisp.[2]	Bachelor's Degree or Higher (%) Total	White	Black	Asian	Hisp.[2]
City	89.1	94.4	84.1	84.5	73.8	36.9	54.1	17.6	53.0	11.5
MSA[1]	87.1	89.9	82.8	81.1	70.1	27.4	33.4	16.2	51.8	11.5
U.S.	88.0	89.9	86.0	87.1	68.7	32.1	33.5	21.6	54.3	16.4

Note: Figures shown cover persons 25 years old and over; (1) Figures cover the Tuscaloosa, AL Metropolitan Statistical Area; (2) People of Hispanic origin can be of any race
Source: U.S. Census Bureau, 2015-2019 American Community Survey 5-Year Estimates

School Enrollment by Grade and Control

Area	Preschool (%) Public	Private	Kindergarten (%) Public	Private	Grades 1 - 4 (%) Public	Private	Grades 5 - 8 (%) Public	Private	Grades 9 - 12 (%) Public	Private
City	62.5	37.5	91.8	8.2	86.2	13.8	92.2	7.8	85.1	14.9
MSA[1]	66.5	33.5	89.8	10.2	87.4	12.6	90.3	9.7	86.1	13.9
U.S.	59.1	40.9	87.6	12.4	89.5	10.5	89.4	10.6	90.1	9.9

Note: Figures shown cover persons 3 years old and over; (1) Figures cover the Tuscaloosa, AL Metropolitan Statistical Area
Source: U.S. Census Bureau, 2015-2019 American Community Survey 5-Year Estimates

Higher Education

Four-Year Colleges Public	Private Non-profit	Private For-profit	Two-Year Colleges Public	Private Non-profit	Private For-profit	Medical Schools[1]	Law Schools[2]	Voc/Tech[3]
1	1	0	1	0	0	1	1	1

Note: Figures cover institutions located within the city limits and include main campuses only; (1) includes schools accredited by the Liaison Committee on Medical Education and the American Osteopathic Association's Commission on Osteopathic College Accreditation; (2) includes ABA-accredited schools, schools with provisional ABA accreditation, and state accredited schools; (3) includes all schools with programs that are less than 2 years.
Source: National Center for Education Statistics, Integrated Postsecondary Education System (IPEDS), 2019-20; Wikipedia, List of Medical Schools in the United States, accessed April 2, 2021; Wikipedia, List of Law Schools in the United States, accessed April 2, 2021

According to *U.S. News & World Report,* the Tuscaloosa, AL metro area is home to one of the top 200 national universities in the U.S.: **University of Alabama** (#143 tie). The indicators used to capture academic quality fall into a number of categories: assessment by administrators at peer institutions; retention of students; faculty resources; student selectivity; financial resources; alumni giving; high school counselor ratings of colleges; and graduation rate. *U.S. News & World Report, "America's Best Colleges 2021"*

According to *U.S. News & World Report,* the Tuscaloosa, AL metro area is home to one of the top 100 law schools in the U.S.: **University of Alabama** (#25 tie). The rankings are based on a weighted average of 12 measures of quality: peer assessment score; assessment score by lawyers/judges; median LSAT scores; median undergrad GPA; acceptance rate; employment rates for graduates; placement success; bar passage rate; faculty resources; expenditures per student; student/faculty ratio; and library resources. *U.S. News & World Report, "America's Best Graduate Schools, Law, 2022"*

According to *U.S. News & World Report*, the Tuscaloosa, AL metro area is home to one of the top 75 business schools in the U.S.: **University of Alabama (Manderson)** (#44 tie). The rankings are based on a weighted average of the following nine measures: quality assessment; peer assessment; recruiter assessment; placement success; mean starting salary and bonus; student selectivity; mean GMAT and GRE scores; mean undergraduate GPA; and acceptance rate. *U.S. News & World Report*, "America's Best Graduate Schools, Business, 2022"

EMPLOYERS

Major Employers

Company Name	Industry
City Board of Education	Public education
City of Tuscaloosa	Municipal government
County Board of Education	Public education
DCH Regional Medical Center	Medical services
Mercedes-Benz U.S. International	Automobile manufacturing
Michelin/BFGoodrich Tire Manufacturing	Aftermarket tire manufacturing
Phifer Incorporated	Aluminum/fiberglass screening, mfg
The University of Alabama	Higher education
Veterans Administration Hospital	Specialized health care
Warrior Met Coal	Metallurgical coal mining

Note: Companies shown are located within the Tuscaloosa, AL Metropolitan Statistical Area.
Source: Hoovers.com; Wikipedia

PUBLIC SAFETY

Crime Rate

Area	All Crimes	Violent Crimes				Property Crimes		
		Murder	Rape[3]	Robbery	Aggrav. Assault	Burglary	Larceny-Theft	Motor Vehicle Theft
City	4,843.6	4.9	46.2	137.6	316.4	739.9	3,289.0	309.5
Suburbs[1]	2,503.0	3.3	28.5	41.7	249.6	518.3	1,449.1	212.5
Metro[2]	3,445.1	4.0	35.6	80.3	276.5	607.5	2,189.7	251.6
U.S.	2,593.1	5.0	44.0	86.1	248.2	378.0	1,601.6	230.2

Note: Figures are crimes per 100,000 population; (1) All areas within the metro area that are located outside the city limits; (2) Figures cover the Tuscaloosa, AL Metropolitan Statistical Area; (3) All figures shown were reported using the revised Uniform Crime Reporting (UCR) definition of rape.
Source: FBI Uniform Crime Reports, 2018 (data for 2019 was not available)

Hate Crimes

Area	Number of Quarters Reported	Number of Incidents per Bias Motivation					
		Race/Ethnicity/Ancestry	Religion	Sexual Orientation	Disability	Gender	Gender Identity
City	n/a	n/a	n/a	n/a	n/a	n/a	n/a
U.S.	4	3,963	1,521	1,195	157	69	198

Note: n/a not available.
Source: Federal Bureau of Investigation, Hate Crime Statistics 2019

Identity Theft Consumer Reports

Area	Reports	Reports per 100,000 Population	Rank[2]
MSA[1]	3,011	1,195	5
U.S.	1,387,615	423	-

Note: (1) Figures cover the Tuscaloosa, AL Metropolitan Statistical Area; (2) Rank ranges from 1 to 391 where 1 indicates greatest number of identity theft reports per 100,000 population
Source: Federal Trade Commission, Consumer Sentinel Network Data Book 2020

Fraud and Other Consumer Reports

Area	Reports	Reports per 100,000 Population	Rank[2]
MSA[1]	5,729	2,273	1
U.S.	3,385,133	1,031	-

Note: (1) Figures cover the Tuscaloosa, AL Metropolitan Statistical Area; (2) Rank ranges from 1 to 391 where 1 indicates greatest number of fraud and other consumer reports per 100,000 population
Source: Federal Trade Commission, Consumer Sentinel Network Data Book 2020

POLITICS

2020 Presidential Election Results

Area	Biden	Trump	Jorgensen	Hawkins	Other
Tuscaloosa County	41.9	56.7	1.0	0.0	0.4
U.S.	51.3	46.8	1.2	0.3	0.5

Note: Results are percentages and may not add to 100% due to rounding
Source: Dave Leip's Atlas of U.S. Presidential Elections

SPORTS

Professional Sports Teams

Team Name	League	Year Established
No teams are located in the metro area		

Source: Wikipedia, Major Professional Sports Teams of the United States and Canada, April 6, 2021

CLIMATE

Average and Extreme Temperatures

Temperature	Jan	Feb	Mar	Apr	May	Jun	Jul	Aug	Sep	Oct	Nov	Dec	Yr.
Extreme High (°F)	81	83	89	92	99	102	106	103	100	94	84	80	106
Average High (°F)	53	58	66	75	82	88	90	90	84	75	64	56	74
Average Temp. (°F)	43	47	54	63	70	77	80	80	74	63	53	46	63
Average Low (°F)	33	36	42	50	58	66	70	69	63	51	41	35	51
Extreme Low (°F)	-6	3	2	26	36	42	51	52	37	27	5	1	-6

Note: Figures cover the years 1948-1995
Source: National Climatic Data Center, International Station Meteorological Climate Summary, 9/96

Average Precipitation/Snowfall/Humidity

Precip./Humidity	Jan	Feb	Mar	Apr	May	Jun	Jul	Aug	Sep	Oct	Nov	Dec	Yr.
Avg. Precip. (in.)	5.0	4.8	5.9	4.6	4.4	3.8	5.1	3.8	4.1	2.9	4.3	4.8	53.5
Avg. Snowfall (in.)	1	Tr	Tr	Tr	0	0	0	0	0	Tr	Tr	Tr	2
Avg. Rel. Hum. 7am (%)	82	81	78	76	76	78	81	82	81	82	82	82	80
Avg. Rel. Hum. 4pm (%)	57	53	48	46	51	54	58	55	54	50	52	58	53

Note: Figures cover the years 1948-1995; Tr = Trace amounts (<0.05 in. of rain; <0.5 in. of snow)
Source: National Climatic Data Center, International Station Meteorological Climate Summary, 9/96

Weather Conditions

Temperature			Daytime Sky			Precipitation		
10°F & below	32°F & below	90°F & above	Clear	Partly cloudy	Cloudy	0.01 inch or more precip.	0.1 inch or more snow/ice	Thunderstorms
1	57	59	91	161	113	119	1	57

Note: Figures are average number of days per year and cover the years 1948-1995
Source: National Climatic Data Center, International Station Meteorological Climate Summary, 9/96

HAZARDOUS WASTE

Superfund Sites

The Tuscaloosa, AL metro area has no sites on the EPA's Superfund Final National Priorities List. There are a total of 1,375 Superfund sites with a status of proposed or final on the list in the U.S. *U.S. Environmental Protection Agency, National Priorities List, April 7, 2021*

AIR QUALITY

Air Quality Trends: Ozone

	1990	1995	2000	2005	2010	2015	2016	2017	2018	2019
MSA[1]	n/a	n/a	n/a	n/a	n/a	n/a	n/a	n/a	n/a	n/a
U.S.	0.088	0.089	0.082	0.080	0.073	0.068	0.069	0.068	0.069	0.065

Note: (1) Data covers the Tuscaloosa, AL Metropolitan Statistical Area; n/a not available. The values shown are the composite ozone concentration averages among trend sites based on the highest fourth daily maximum 8-hour concentration in parts per million. These trends are based on sites having an adequate record of monitoring data during the trend period. Data from exceptional events are included.
Source: U.S. Environmental Protection Agency, Air Quality Monitoring Information, "Air Quality Trends by City, 1990-2019"

Air Quality Index

Area	Percent of Days when Air Quality was...[2]					AQI Statistics[2]	
	Good	Moderate	Unhealthy for Sensitive Groups	Unhealthy	Very Unhealthy	Maximum	Median
MSA[1]	90.9	9.1	0.0	0.0	0.0	87	35

Note: (1) Data covers the Tuscaloosa, AL Metropolitan Statistical Area; (2) Based on 264 days with AQI data in 2019. Air Quality Index (AQI) is an index for reporting daily air quality. EPA calculates the AQI for five major air pollutants regulated by the Clean Air Act: ground-level ozone, particle pollution (aka particulate matter), carbon monoxide, sulfur dioxide, and nitrogen dioxide. The AQI runs from 0 to 500. The higher the AQI value, the greater the level of air pollution and the greater the health concern. There are six AQI categories: "Good" AQI is between 0 and 50. Air quality is considered satisfactory; "Moderate" AQI is between 51 and 100. Air quality is acceptable; "Unhealthy for Sensitive Groups" When AQI values are between 101 and 150, members of sensitive groups may experience health effects; "Unhealthy" When AQI values are between 151 and 200 everyone may begin to experience health effects; "Very Unhealthy" AQI values between 201 and 300 trigger a health alert; "Hazardous" AQI values over 300 trigger warnings of emergency conditions (not shown).
Source: U.S. Environmental Protection Agency, Air Quality Index Report, 2019

Air Quality Index Pollutants

Area	Percent of Days when AQI Pollutant was...[2]					
	Carbon Monoxide	Nitrogen Dioxide	Ozone	Sulfur Dioxide	Particulate Matter 2.5	Particulate Matter 10
MSA[1]	0.0	0.0	71.2	0.0	28.8	0.0

Note: (1) Data covers the Tuscaloosa, AL Metropolitan Statistical Area; (2) Based on 264 days with AQI data in 2019. The Air Quality Index (AQI) is an index for reporting daily air quality. EPA calculates the AQI for five major air pollutants regulated by the Clean Air Act: ground-level ozone, particle pollution (also known as particulate matter), carbon monoxide, sulfur dioxide, and nitrogen dioxide. The AQI runs from 0 to 500. The higher the AQI value, the greater the level of air pollution and the greater the health concern.
Source: U.S. Environmental Protection Agency, Air Quality Index Report, 2019

Maximum Air Pollutant Concentrations: Particulate Matter, Ozone, CO and Lead

	Particulate Matter 10 (ug/m^3)	Particulate Matter 2.5 Wtd AM (ug/m^3)	Particulate Matter 2.5 24-Hr (ug/m^3)	Ozone (ppm)	Carbon Monoxide (ppm)	Lead (ug/m^3)
MSA[1] Level	n/a	7.9	15	0.060	n/a	n/a
NAAQS[2]	150	15	35	0.075	9	0.15
Met NAAQS[2]	n/a	Yes	Yes	Yes	n/a	n/a

Note: (1) Data covers the Tuscaloosa, AL Metropolitan Statistical Area; Data from exceptional events are included; (2) National Ambient Air Quality Standards; ppm = parts per million; ug/m^3 = micrograms per cubic meter; n/a not available.
Concentrations: Particulate Matter 10 (coarse particulate)—highest second maximum 24-hour concentration; Particulate Matter 2.5 Wtd AM (fine particulate)—highest weighted annual mean concentration; Particulate Matter 2.5 24-Hour (fine particulate)—highest 98th percentile 24-hour concentration; Ozone—highest fourth daily maximum 8-hour concentration; Carbon Monoxide—highest second maximum non-overlapping 8-hour concentration; Lead—maximum running 3-month average
Source: U.S. Environmental Protection Agency, Air Quality Monitoring Information, "Air Quality Statistics by City, 2019"

Maximum Air Pollutant Concentrations: Nitrogen Dioxide and Sulfur Dioxide

	Nitrogen Dioxide AM (ppb)	Nitrogen Dioxide 1-Hr (ppb)	Sulfur Dioxide AM (ppb)	Sulfur Dioxide 1-Hr (ppb)	Sulfur Dioxide 24-Hr (ppb)
MSA[1] Level	n/a	n/a	n/a	n/a	n/a
NAAQS[2]	53	100	30	75	140
Met NAAQS[2]	n/a	n/a	n/a	n/a	n/a

Note: (1) Data covers the Tuscaloosa, AL Metropolitan Statistical Area; Data from exceptional events are included; (2) National Ambient Air Quality Standards; ppm = parts per million; ug/m^3 = micrograms per cubic meter; n/a not available.
Concentrations: Nitrogen Dioxide AM—highest arithmetic mean concentration; Nitrogen Dioxide 1-Hr—highest 98th percentile 1-hour daily maximum concentration; Sulfur Dioxide AM—highest annual mean concentration; Sulfur Dioxide 1-Hr—highest 99th percentile 1-hour daily maximum concentration; Sulfur Dioxide 24-Hr—highest second maximum 24-hour concentration
Source: U.S. Environmental Protection Agency, Air Quality Monitoring Information, "Air Quality Statistics by City, 2019"

Appendixes

Appendices

Appendix A: Comparative Statistics

Table of Contents

Demographics
- Population Growth: City A-4
- Population Growth: Metro Area A-6
- Household Size: City A-8
- Household Size: Metro Area A-10
- Race: City A-12
- Race: Metro Area A-14
- Hispanic Origin: City A-16
- Hispanic Origin: Metro Area A-18
- Age: City A-20
- Age: Metro Area A-22
- Religious Groups by Family A-24
- Religious Groups by Tradition A-26
- Ancestry: City A-28
- Ancestry: Metro Area A-30
- Foreign-born Population: City A-32
- Foreign-born Population: Metro Area A-34
- Marital Status: City A-36
- Marital Status: Metro Area A-38
- Disability by Age: City A-40
- Disability by Age: Metro Area A-42
- Male/Female Ratio: City A-44
- Male/Female Ratio: Metro Area A-46

Economy
- Gross Metropolitan Product A-48
- Economic Growth A-50
- Metropolitan Area Exports A-52
- Building Permits: City A-54
- Building Permits: Metro Area A-56
- Housing Vacancy Rates A-58
- Bankruptcy Filings A-60

Income and Poverty
- Income: City A-62
- Income: Metro Area A-64
- Household Income Distribution: City A-66
- Household Income Distribution: Metro Area A-68
- Poverty Rate: City A-70
- Poverty Rate: Metro Area A-72

Employment and Earnings
- Employment by Industry A-74
- Labor Force, Employment and Job Growth: City A-76
- Labor Force, Employment and Job Growth: Metro Area ... A-78
- Unemployment Rate: City A-80
- Unemployment Rate: Metro Area A-82
- Average Hourly Wages: Occupations A - C A-84
- Average Hourly Wages: Occupations C - E A-86
- Average Hourly Wages: Occupations F - H A-88
- Average Hourly Wages: Occupations L - N A-90
- Average Hourly Wages: Occupations P - S A-92
- Average Hourly Wages: Occupations T - W A-94
- Average Hourly Wages: Occupations T - W A-96

- Means of Transportation to Work: City A-98
- Means of Transportation to Work: Metro Area A-100
- Travel Time to Work: City A-102
- Travel Time to Work: Metro Area A-104

Election Results
- 2020 Presidential Election Results A-106

Housing
- House Price Index (HPI) A-108
- Home Value Distribution: City A-110
- Home Value Distribution: Metro Area A-112
- Homeownership Rate A-114
- Year Housing Structure Built: City A-116
- Year Housing Structure Built: Metro Area A-118
- Gross Monthly Rent: City A-120
- Gross Monthly Rent: Metro Area A-122

Education
- Highest Level of Education: City A-124
- Highest Level of Education: Metro Area A-126
- School Enrollment by Grade and Control: City A-128
- School Enrollment by Grade and Control: Metro Area ... A-130
- Educational Attainment by Race: City A-132
- Educational Attainment by Race: Metro Area A-134

Cost of Living
- Cost of Living Index A-136
- Grocery Prices A-138
- Housing and Utility Costs A-140
- Health Care, Transportation, and Other Costs A-142

Health Care
- Number of Medical Professionals A-144
- Health Insurance Coverage: City A-146
- Health Insurance Coverage: Metro Area A-148

Public Safety
- Crime Rate: City A-150
- Crime Rate: Suburbs A-152
- Crime Rate: Metro Area A-154

Climate
- Temperature & Precipitation: Yearly Averages and Extremes A-156
- Weather Conditions A-158

Air Quality
- Air Quality Index A-160
- Air Quality Index Pollutants A-162
- Air Quality Trends: Ozone A-164
- Maximum Air Pollutant Concentrations: Particulate Matter, Ozone, CO and Lead A-166
- Maximum Air Pollutant Concentrations: Nitrogen Dioxide and Sulfur Dioxide A-168

Appendix A: Comparative Statistics

Population Growth: City

Area	1990 Census	2000 Census	2010 Census	2019* Estimate	Population Growth (%) 1990-2019	Population Growth (%) 2010-2019
Albuquerque, NM	388,375	448,607	545,852	559,374	44.0	2.5
Allentown, PA	105,066	106,632	118,032	120,915	15.1	2.4
Anchorage, AK	226,338	260,283	291,826	293,531	29.7	0.6
Ann Arbor, MI	111,018	114,024	113,934	120,735	8.8	6.0
Athens, GA	86,561	100,266	115,452	124,719	44.1	8.0
Atlanta, GA	394,092	416,474	420,003	488,800	24.0	16.4
Austin, TX	499,053	656,562	790,390	950,807	90.5	20.3
Baton Rouge, LA	223,299	227,818	229,493	224,149	0.4	-2.3
Boise City, ID	144,317	185,787	205,671	226,115	56.7	9.9
Boston, MA	574,283	589,141	617,594	684,379	19.2	10.8
Boulder, CO	87,737	94,673	97,385	106,392	21.3	9.2
Cape Coral, FL	75,507	102,286	154,305	183,942	143.6	19.2
Cedar Rapids, IA	110,829	120,758	126,326	132,301	19.4	4.7
Charleston, SC	96,102	96,650	120,083	135,257	40.7	12.6
Charlotte, NC	428,283	540,828	731,424	857,425	100.2	17.2
Chicago, IL	2,783,726	2,896,016	2,695,598	2,709,534	-2.7	0.5
Cincinnati, OH	363,974	331,285	296,943	301,394	-17.2	1.5
Clarksville, TN	78,569	103,455	132,929	152,934	94.6	15.0
Cleveland, OH	505,333	478,403	396,815	385,282	-23.8	-2.9
College Station, TX	53,318	67,890	93,857	113,686	113.2	21.1
Colorado Springs, CO	283,798	360,890	416,427	464,871	63.8	11.6
Columbia, MO	71,069	84,531	108,500	121,230	70.6	11.7
Columbia, SC	115,475	116,278	129,272	133,273	15.4	3.1
Columbus, OH	648,656	711,470	787,033	878,553	35.4	11.6
Dallas, TX	1,006,971	1,188,580	1,197,816	1,330,612	32.1	11.1
Davenport, IA	95,705	98,359	99,685	102,169	6.8	2.5
Denver, CO	467,153	554,636	600,158	705,576	51.0	17.6
Des Moines, IA	193,569	198,682	203,433	215,636	11.4	6.0
Durham, NC	151,737	187,035	228,330	269,702	77.7	18.1
Edison, NJ	88,680	97,687	99,967	100,447	13.3	0.5
El Paso, TX	515,541	563,662	649,121	679,813	31.9	4.7
Fargo, ND	74,372	90,599	105,549	121,889	63.9	15.5
Fayetteville, NC	118,247	121,015	200,564	210,432	78.0	4.9
Fort Collins, CO	89,555	118,652	143,986	165,609	84.9	15.0
Fort Wayne, IN	205,671	205,727	253,691	265,752	29.2	4.8
Fort Worth, TX	448,311	534,694	741,206	874,401	95.0	18.0
Grand Rapids, MI	189,145	197,800	188,040	198,401	4.9	5.5
Greeley, CO	60,887	76,930	92,889	105,888	73.9	14.0
Green Bay, WI	96,466	102,313	104,057	104,777	8.6	0.7
Greensboro, NC	193,389	223,891	269,666	291,303	50.6	8.0
Honolulu, HI	376,465	371,657	337,256	348,985	-7.3	3.5
Houston, TX	1,697,610	1,953,631	2,099,451	2,310,432	36.1	10.0
Huntsville, AL	161,842	158,216	180,105	196,219	21.2	8.9
Indianapolis, IN	730,993	781,870	820,445	864,447	18.3	5.4
Jacksonville, FL	635,221	735,617	821,784	890,467	40.2	8.4
Kansas City, MO	434,967	441,545	459,787	486,404	11.8	5.8
Lafayette, LA	104,735	110,257	120,623	126,666	20.9	5.0
Lakeland, FL	73,375	78,452	97,422	107,922	47.1	10.8
Las Vegas, NV	261,374	478,434	583,756	634,773	142.9	8.7
Lexington, KY	225,366	260,512	295,803	320,601	42.3	8.4
Lincoln, NE	193,629	225,581	258,379	283,839	46.6	9.9
Little Rock, AR	177,519	183,133	193,524	197,958	11.5	2.3
Los Angeles, CA	3,487,671	3,694,820	3,792,621	3,966,936	13.7	4.6
Louisville, KY	269,160	256,231	597,337	617,790	129.5	3.4
Madison, WI	193,451	208,054	233,209	254,977	31.8	9.3

Table continued on following page.

Area	1990 Census	2000 Census	2010 Census	2019* Estimate	Population Growth (%) 1990-2019	Population Growth (%) 2010-2019
Manchester, NH	99,567	107,006	109,565	112,109	12.6	2.3
Memphis, TN	660,536	650,100	646,889	651,932	-1.3	0.8
Miami, FL	358,843	362,470	399,457	454,279	26.6	13.7
Midland, TX	89,358	94,996	111,147	138,549	55.0	24.7
Milwaukee, WI	628,095	596,974	594,833	594,548	-5.3	0.0
Minneapolis, MN	368,383	382,618	382,578	420,324	14.1	9.9
Nashville, TN	488,364	545,524	601,222	663,750	35.9	10.4
New Haven, CT	130,474	123,626	129,779	130,331	-0.1	0.4
New Orleans, LA	496,938	484,674	343,829	390,845	-21.3	13.7
New York, NY	7,322,552	8,008,278	8,175,133	8,419,316	15.0	3.0
Oklahoma City, OK	445,065	506,132	579,999	643,692	44.6	11.0
Omaha, NE	371,972	390,007	408,958	475,862	27.9	16.4
Orlando, FL	161,172	185,951	238,300	280,832	74.2	17.8
Peoria, IL	114,341	112,936	115,007	113,532	-0.7	-1.3
Philadelphia, PA	1,585,577	1,517,550	1,526,006	1,579,075	-0.4	3.5
Phoenix, AZ	989,873	1,321,045	1,445,632	1,633,017	65.0	13.0
Pittsburgh, PA	369,785	334,563	305,704	302,205	-18.3	-1.1
Portland, OR	485,833	529,121	583,776	645,291	32.8	10.5
Providence, RI	160,734	173,618	178,042	179,494	11.7	0.8
Provo, UT	87,148	105,166	112,488	116,403	33.6	3.5
Raleigh, NC	226,841	276,093	403,892	464,485	104.8	15.0
Reno, NV	139,950	180,480	225,221	246,500	76.1	9.4
Richmond, VA	202,783	197,790	204,214	226,622	11.8	11.0
Riverside, CA	226,232	255,166	303,871	326,414	44.3	7.4
Rochester, MN	74,151	85,806	106,769	115,557	55.8	8.2
Sacramento, CA	368,923	407,018	466,488	500,930	35.8	7.4
Salt Lake City, UT	159,796	181,743	186,440	197,756	23.8	6.1
San Antonio, TX	997,258	1,144,646	1,327,407	1,508,083	51.2	13.6
San Diego, CA	1,111,048	1,223,400	1,307,402	1,409,573	26.9	7.8
San Francisco, CA	723,959	776,733	805,235	874,961	20.9	8.7
San Jose, CA	784,324	894,943	945,942	1,027,690	31.0	8.6
Santa Rosa, CA	123,297	147,595	167,815	179,701	45.7	7.1
Savannah, GA	138,038	131,510	136,286	145,403	5.3	6.7
Seattle, WA	516,262	563,374	608,660	724,305	40.3	19.0
Sioux Falls, SD	102,262	123,975	153,888	177,117	73.2	15.1
Springfield, IL	108,997	111,454	116,250	115,888	6.3	-0.3
Tallahassee, FL	128,014	150,624	181,376	191,279	49.4	5.5
Tampa, FL	279,960	303,447	335,709	387,916	38.6	15.6
Tucson, AZ	417,942	486,699	520,116	541,482	29.6	4.1
Tulsa, OK	367,241	393,049	391,906	402,324	9.6	2.7
Tuscaloosa, AL	81,075	77,906	90,468	99,390	22.6	9.9
Virginia Beach, VA	393,069	425,257	437,994	450,201	14.5	2.8
Washington, DC	606,900	572,059	601,723	692,683	14.1	15.1
Wichita, KS	313,693	344,284	382,368	389,877	24.3	2.0
Winston-Salem, NC	168,139	185,776	229,617	244,115	45.2	6.3
U.S.	248,709,873	281,421,906	308,745,538	324,697,795	30.6	5.2

Note: (*) 2014-2019 5-year estimated population
Source: U.S. Census Bureau, 1990 Census, Census 2000, Census 2010, 2015-2019 American Community Survey 5-Year Estimates

Appendix A: Comparative Statistics

Population Growth: Metro Area

Area	1990 Census	2000 Census	2010 Census	2019* Estimate	Population Growth (%) 1990-2019	Population Growth (%) 2010-2019
Albuquerque, NM	599,416	729,649	887,077	912,108	52.2	2.8
Allentown, PA	686,666	740,395	821,173	837,610	22.0	2.0
Anchorage, AK	266,021	319,605	380,821	398,900	50.0	4.7
Ann Arbor, MI	282,937	322,895	344,791	367,000	29.7	6.4
Athens, GA	136,025	166,079	192,541	208,457	53.2	8.3
Atlanta, GA	3,069,411	4,247,981	5,268,860	5,862,424	91.0	11.3
Austin, TX	846,217	1,249,763	1,716,289	2,114,441	149.9	23.2
Baton Rouge, LA	623,853	705,973	802,484	854,318	36.9	6.5
Boise City, ID	319,596	464,840	616,561	710,743	122.4	15.3
Boston, MA	4,133,895	4,391,344	4,552,402	4,832,346	16.9	6.1
Boulder, CO	208,898	269,758	294,567	322,510	54.4	9.5
Cape Coral, FL	335,113	440,888	618,754	737,468	120.1	19.2
Cedar Rapids, IA	210,640	237,230	257,940	270,056	28.2	4.7
Charleston, SC	506,875	549,033	664,607	774,508	52.8	16.5
Charlotte, NC	1,024,331	1,330,448	1,758,038	2,545,560	148.5	44.8
Chicago, IL	8,182,076	9,098,316	9,461,105	9,508,605	16.2	0.5
Cincinnati, OH	1,844,917	2,009,632	2,130,151	2,201,741	19.3	3.4
Clarksville, TN	189,277	232,000	273,949	299,470	58.2	9.3
Cleveland, OH	2,102,219	2,148,143	2,077,240	2,056,898	-2.2	-1.0
College Station, TX	150,998	184,885	228,660	258,029	70.9	12.8
Colorado Springs, CO	409,482	537,484	645,613	723,498	76.7	12.1
Columbia, MO	122,010	145,666	172,786	205,369	68.3	18.9
Columbia, SC	548,325	647,158	767,598	824,278	50.3	7.4
Columbus, OH	1,405,176	1,612,694	1,836,536	2,077,761	47.9	13.1
Dallas, TX	3,989,294	5,161,544	6,371,773	7,320,663	83.5	14.9
Davenport, IA	368,151	376,019	379,690	381,175	3.5	0.4
Denver, CO	1,666,935	2,179,296	2,543,482	2,892,066	73.5	13.7
Des Moines, IA	416,346	481,394	569,633	680,439	63.4	19.5
Durham, NC	344,646	426,493	504,357	626,695	81.8	24.3
Edison, NJ	16,845,992	18,323,002	18,897,109	19,294,236	14.5	2.1
El Paso, TX	591,610	679,622	800,647	840,477	42.1	5.0
Fargo, ND	153,296	174,367	208,777	240,421	56.8	15.2
Fayetteville, NC	297,422	336,609	366,383	519,101	74.5	41.7
Fort Collins, CO	186,136	251,494	299,630	344,786	85.2	15.1
Fort Wayne, IN	354,435	390,156	416,257	406,305	14.6	-2.4
Fort Worth, TX	3,989,294	5,161,544	6,371,773	7,320,663*	83.5	14.9
Grand Rapids, MI	645,914	740,482	774,160	1,062,392	64.5	37.2
Greeley, CO	131,816	180,926	252,825	305,345	131.6	20.8
Green Bay, WI	243,698	282,599	306,241	319,401	31.1	4.3
Greensboro, NC	540,257	643,430	723,801	762,063	41.1	5.3
Honolulu, HI	836,231	876,156	953,207	984,821	17.8	3.3
Houston, TX	3,767,335	4,715,407	5,946,800	6,884,138	82.7	15.8
Huntsville, AL	293,047	342,376	417,593	457,003	55.9	9.4
Indianapolis, IN	1,294,217	1,525,104	1,756,241	2,029,472	56.8	15.6
Jacksonville, FL	925,213	1,122,750	1,345,596	1,503,574	62.5	11.7
Kansas City, MO	1,636,528	1,836,038	2,035,334	2,124,518	29.8	4.4
Lafayette, LA	208,740	239,086	273,738	489,914	134.7	79.0
Lakeland, FL	405,382	483,924	602,095	686,218	69.3	14.0
Las Vegas, NV	741,459	1,375,765	1,951,269	2,182,004	194.3	11.8
Lexington, KY	348,428	408,326	472,099	510,647	46.6	8.2
Lincoln, NE	229,091	266,787	302,157	330,329	44.2	9.3
Little Rock, AR	535,034	610,518	699,757	737,015	37.8	5.3
Los Angeles, CA	11,273,720	12,365,627	12,828,837	13,249,614	17.5	3.3
Louisville, KY	1,055,973	1,161,975	1,283,566	1,257,088	19.0	-2.1
Madison, WI	432,323	501,774	568,593	653,725	51.2	15.0

Table continued on following page.

Area	1990 Census	2000 Census	2010 Census	2019* Estimate	Population Growth (%) 1990-2019	Population Growth (%) 2010-2019
Manchester, NH	336,073	380,841	400,721	413,035	22.9	3.1
Memphis, TN	1,067,263	1,205,204	1,316,100	1,339,623	25.5	1.8
Miami, FL	4,056,100	5,007,564	5,564,635	6,090,660	50.2	9.5
Midland, TX	106,611	116,009	136,872	173,816	63.0	27.0
Milwaukee, WI	1,432,149	1,500,741	1,555,908	1,575,223	10.0	1.2
Minneapolis, MN	2,538,834	2,968,806	3,279,833	3,573,609	40.8	9.0
Nashville, TN	1,048,218	1,311,789	1,589,934	1,871,903	78.6	17.7
New Haven, CT	804,219	824,008	862,477	857,513	6.6	-0.6
New Orleans, LA	1,264,391	1,316,510	1,167,764	1,267,777	0.3	8.6
New York, NY	16,845,992	18,323,002	18,897,109	19,294,236	14.5	2.1
Oklahoma City, OK	971,042	1,095,421	1,252,987	1,382,841	42.4	10.4
Omaha, NE	685,797	767,041	865,350	931,779	35.9	7.7
Orlando, FL	1,224,852	1,644,561	2,134,411	2,508,970	104.8	17.5
Peoria, IL	358,552	366,899	379,186	406,883	13.5	7.3
Philadelphia, PA	5,435,470	5,687,147	5,965,343	6,079,130	11.8	1.9
Phoenix, AZ	2,238,480	3,251,876	4,192,887	4,761,603	112.7	13.6
Pittsburgh, PA	2,468,289	2,431,087	2,356,285	2,331,447	-5.5	-1.1
Portland, OR	1,523,741	1,927,881	2,226,009	2,445,761	60.5	9.9
Providence, RI	1,509,789	1,582,997	1,600,852	1,618,268	7.2	1.1
Provo, UT	269,407	376,774	526,810	616,791	128.9	17.1
Raleigh, NC	541,081	797,071	1,130,490	1,332,311	146.2	17.9
Reno, NV	257,193	342,885	425,417	460,924	79.2	8.3
Richmond, VA	949,244	1,096,957	1,258,251	1,269,530	33.7	0.9
Riverside, CA	2,588,793	3,254,821	4,224,851	4,560,470	76.2	7.9
Rochester, MN	141,945	163,618	186,011	217,964	53.6	17.2
Sacramento, CA	1,481,126	1,796,857	2,149,127	2,315,980	56.4	7.8
Salt Lake City, UT	768,075	968,858	1,124,197	1,201,043	56.4	6.8
San Antonio, TX	1,407,745	1,711,703	2,142,508	2,468,193	75.3	15.2
San Diego, CA	2,498,016	2,813,833	3,095,313	3,316,073	32.7	7.1
San Francisco, CA	3,686,592	4,123,740	4,335,391	4,701,332	27.5	8.4
San Jose, CA	1,534,280	1,735,819	1,836,911	1,987,846	29.6	8.2
Santa Rosa, CA	388,222	458,614	483,878	499,772	28.7	3.3
Savannah, GA	258,060	293,000	347,611	386,036	49.6	11.1
Seattle, WA	2,559,164	3,043,878	3,439,809	3,871,323	51.3	12.5
Sioux Falls, SD	153,500	187,093	228,261	259,348	69.0	13.6
Springfield, IL	189,550	201,437	210,170	209,167	10.3	-0.5
Tallahassee, FL	259,096	320,304	367,413	382,197	47.5	4.0
Tampa, FL	2,067,959	2,395,997	2,783,243	3,097,859	49.8	11.3
Tucson, AZ	666,880	843,746	980,263	1,027,207	54.0	4.8
Tulsa, OK	761,019	859,532	937,478	990,544	30.2	5.7
Tuscaloosa, AL	176,123	192,034	219,461	250,681	42.3	14.2
Virginia Beach, VA	1,449,389	1,576,370	1,671,683	1,761,729	21.5	5.4
Washington, DC	4,122,914	4,796,183	5,582,170	6,196,585	50.3	11.0
Wichita, KS	511,111	571,166	623,061	637,690	24.8	2.3
Winston-Salem, NC	361,091	421,961	477,717	666,216	84.5	39.5
U.S.	248,709,873	281,421,906	308,745,538	324,697,795	30.6	5.2

Note: (*) 2014-2019 5-year estimated population; Figures cover the Metropolitan Statistical Area (MSA)—see Appendix B for areas included
Source: U.S. Census Bureau, 1990 Census, Census 2000, Census 2010, 2015-2019 American Community Survey 5-Year Estimates

Appendix A: Comparative Statistics

Household Size: City

City	One	Two	Three	Four	Five	Six	Seven or More	Average Household Size
Albuquerque, NM	34.6	33.7	13.8	10.7	4.5	1.5	0.8	2.47
Allentown, PA	27.6	28.9	15.4	13.8	8.0	3.6	2.3	2.73
Anchorage, AK	26.3	33.0	16.9	12.5	6.6	2.4	2.0	2.69
Ann Arbor, MI	34.6	37.8	11.7	10.4	3.0	1.5	0.8	2.26
Athens, GA	33.4	35.2	14.5	11.2	3.6	1.4	0.4	2.35
Atlanta, GA	46.7	30.7	10.6	7.2	2.9	1.0	0.6	2.19
Austin, TX	34.5	32.7	14.3	11.3	4.4	1.5	0.9	2.44
Baton Rouge, LA	36.1	32.4	15.6	9.0	4.1	1.7	0.9	2.58
Boise City, ID	34.1	34.1	14.3	10.3	4.6	1.4	0.8	2.43
Boston, MA	36.2	32.4	15.4	9.4	3.9	1.6	0.8	2.36
Boulder, CO	33.8	36.8	14.5	10.9	2.7	0.7	0.3	2.27
Cape Coral, FL	23.7	43.0	14.2	12.3	4.4	1.6	0.5	2.81
Cedar Rapids, IA	34.1	33.9	14.0	10.5	4.4	2.2	0.6	2.33
Charleston, SC	35.4	37.8	14.2	9.0	2.4	0.6	0.1	2.31
Charlotte, NC	32.9	32.2	15.5	11.9	4.8	1.5	0.8	2.56
Chicago, IL	37.1	29.7	13.8	10.2	5.1	2.2	1.5	2.48
Cincinnati, OH	44.3	30.1	12.0	7.5	3.5	1.3	0.8	2.10
Clarksville, TN	24.7	30.7	19.6	15.1	5.8	2.3	1.3	2.66
Cleveland, OH	44.4	27.5	13.1	8.0	4.2	1.6	0.9	2.18
College Station, TX	29.7	33.8	16.5	14.1	3.5	1.8	0.4	2.53
Colorado Springs, CO	28.6	35.1	14.6	12.2	5.8	2.2	1.0	2.52
Columbia, MO	32.7	32.8	15.0	12.9	4.7	1.1	0.4	2.33
Columbia, SC	40.6	33.0	12.3	8.9	3.6	0.8	0.5	2.21
Columbus, OH	35.5	32.4	13.9	10.1	4.8	1.8	1.2	2.39
Dallas, TX	35.3	29.1	13.7	11.2	6.2	2.5	1.7	2.56
Davenport, IA	35.3	33.5	13.1	9.7	5.2	1.8	1.0	2.46
Denver, CO	38.2	32.9	12.0	9.5	4.3	1.6	1.2	2.29
Des Moines, IA	34.1	30.5	14.7	11.4	5.3	2.2	1.5	2.45
Durham, NC	33.9	33.5	15.4	10.1	4.4	1.6	0.8	2.36
Edison, NJ	18.9	29.0	21.1	20.3	6.4	2.5	1.5	2.86
El Paso, TX	25.5	28.5	17.7	15.9	7.5	3.2	1.3	2.97
Fargo, ND	36.4	34.0	14.4	8.9	4.2	1.3	0.5	2.14
Fayetteville, NC	35.6	31.3	15.3	10.7	4.2	1.8	0.8	2.42
Fort Collins, CO	24.7	37.9	17.8	13.8	4.3	0.9	0.4	2.44
Fort Wayne, IN	32.1	33.0	14.3	11.2	5.9	2.2	1.0	2.45
Fort Worth, TX	26.1	28.8	16.5	15.1	7.8	3.3	2.1	2.89
Grand Rapids, MI	33.1	31.4	13.8	11.1	5.9	2.5	1.9	2.53
Greeley, CO	26.0	31.4	16.1	13.3	8.2	3.2	1.3	2.72
Green Bay, WI	34.1	32.1	12.7	11.3	6.5	1.5	1.5	2.39
Greensboro, NC	34.2	33.1	15.4	10.2	4.6	1.4	0.7	2.37
Honolulu, HI	33.4	31.3	14.3	10.6	5.1	2.3	2.6	2.60
Houston, TX	32.3	28.9	15.2	12.3	6.6	2.8	1.7	2.65
Huntsville, AL	35.7	34.3	14.5	9.4	4.1	1.2	0.4	2.21
Indianapolis, IN	37.8	31.3	13.2	9.6	4.9	1.9	1.0	2.51
Jacksonville, FL	30.4	33.7	16.6	11.4	5.0	1.7	0.9	2.57
Kansas City, MO	37.0	31.9	12.9	10.0	4.9	1.8	1.1	2.35
Lafayette, LA	35.1	34.5	13.9	9.5	3.9	1.7	1.0	2.40
Lakeland, FL	33.1	37.5	14.3	8.9	3.6	1.6	0.7	2.50
Las Vegas, NV	30.6	31.6	15.3	11.5	6.2	2.7	1.7	2.70
Lexington, KY	31.5	35.0	15.1	11.2	4.6	1.6	0.6	2.37
Lincoln, NE	31.5	34.8	13.9	11.5	5.2	2.0	0.9	2.38
Little Rock, AR	36.6	32.0	14.0	10.1	4.6	1.8	0.7	2.37
Los Angeles, CA	30.2	28.8	15.3	13.0	6.8	2.9	2.5	2.80
Louisville, KY	33.3	32.9	15.3	10.5	4.8	1.8	1.0	2.43

Table continued on following page.

Appendix A: Comparative Statistics

City	One	Two	Three	Four	Five	Six	Seven or More	Average Household Size
Madison, WI	35.3	36.2	13.2	9.8	3.7	1.1	0.4	2.21
Manchester, NH	31.4	34.1	16.5	10.7	4.4	1.6	1.0	2.37
Memphis, TN	37.1	30.3	14.8	9.8	4.2	2.2	1.3	2.53
Miami, FL	37.3	31.0	16.1	8.8	3.9	1.5	0.9	2.51
Midland, TX	26.1	31.2	16.4	14.4	7.3	3.0	1.3	2.90
Milwaukee, WI	36.3	29.3	14.0	10.4	5.7	2.4	1.6	2.51
Minneapolis, MN	40.4	31.2	11.9	9.5	3.5	1.7	1.5	2.28
Nashville, TN	33.9	33.9	15.2	9.6	4.5	1.6	1.0	2.36
New Haven, CT	38.4	27.3	15.4	9.9	5.3	2.3	1.0	2.46
New Orleans, LA	45.9	29.2	12.6	7.8	2.6	1.0	0.6	2.45
New York, NY	32.2	28.4	16.2	12.5	5.9	2.5	2.0	2.60
Oklahoma City, OK	31.1	32.1	14.5	12.2	6.2	2.5	1.1	2.60
Omaha, NE	32.6	32.0	13.5	11.2	6.0	2.7	1.6	2.48
Orlando, FL	33.6	33.1	16.7	9.8	4.0	1.8	0.6	2.48
Peoria, IL	38.2	31.4	13.3	9.1	5.2	1.7	0.9	2.37
Philadelphia, PA	37.5	29.2	14.7	10.4	4.8	1.9	1.3	2.55
Phoenix, AZ	27.9	30.0	15.2	12.9	7.3	3.7	2.7	2.85
Pittsburgh, PA	43.6	32.4	12.8	6.7	2.5	1.1	0.6	2.02
Portland, OR	34.0	34.8	14.1	10.8	3.8	1.4	0.8	2.34
Providence, RI	33.2	29.0	15.6	11.7	7.0	1.7	1.5	2.67
Provo, UT	13.2	33.1	18.8	16.1	7.9	7.1	3.4	3.17
Raleigh, NC	33.0	32.4	15.2	12.4	4.7	1.3	0.6	2.42
Reno, NV	33.0	33.4	14.6	10.5	5.1	1.8	1.4	2.36
Richmond, VA	43.4	32.8	12.0	6.8	2.9	1.2	0.6	2.39
Riverside, CA	20.4	27.5	17.7	15.5	10.1	4.7	3.8	3.43
Rochester, MN	31.0	33.2	14.4	13.0	4.7	1.8	1.5	2.40
Sacramento, CA	30.9	30.7	14.7	12.1	6.0	2.9	2.3	2.66
Salt Lake City, UT	36.1	32.2	13.5	9.9	4.2	2.0	1.7	2.42
San Antonio, TX	29.9	29.5	16.2	12.9	6.7	2.8	1.7	2.96
San Diego, CA	27.5	33.4	16.1	13.1	5.7	2.3	1.5	2.70
San Francisco, CA	35.6	33.6	14.3	9.7	3.7	1.4	1.3	2.36
San Jose, CA	19.4	28.8	18.6	17.9	8.1	3.5	3.4	3.12
Santa Rosa, CA	28.2	32.6	15.3	13.2	6.2	2.3	2.0	2.66
Savannah, GA	33.5	34.0	15.6	9.8	4.3	1.4	1.0	2.55
Seattle, WA	38.5	35.6	12.5	8.8	2.9	0.8	0.6	2.11
Sioux Falls, SD	32.0	34.0	13.0	12.2	5.3	2.0	1.1	2.37
Springfield, IL	38.0	34.0	13.3	8.7	3.1	1.4	1.0	2.20
Tallahassee, FL	35.0	33.0	16.8	10.2	3.6	0.9	0.1	2.33
Tampa, FL	35.7	31.5	15.3	10.8	4.2	1.5	0.6	2.47
Tucson, AZ	34.6	31.2	14.7	10.8	5.1	2.0	1.3	2.42
Tulsa, OK	35.1	32.5	13.6	10.2	5.1	2.1	1.1	2.41
Tuscaloosa, AL	35.4	33.7	15.9	9.9	3.4	1.0	0.4	2.55
Virginia Beach, VA	24.4	34.4	17.5	14.8	5.8	1.9	0.8	2.58
Washington, DC	44.0	31.0	11.7	7.8	3.1	1.2	0.8	2.30
Wichita, KS	33.3	31.3	13.4	11.3	6.5	2.7	1.2	2.51
Winston-Salem, NC	35.7	31.5	15.0	9.4	5.2	1.8	1.1	2.46
U.S.	27.8	33.9	15.5	12.9	5.9	2.2	1.4	2.62

U.S. Census Bureau, 2015-2019 American Community Survey 5-Year Estimates

Appendix A: Comparative Statistics

Household Size: Metro Area

Metro Area	One	Two	Three	Four	Five	Six	Seven or More	Average Household Size
Albuquerque, NM	31.4	35.2	14.4	10.8	5.0	1.9	1.1	2.56
Allentown, PA	26.1	35.4	15.7	13.4	6.0	2.1	1.0	2.54
Anchorage, AK	25.5	33.6	16.4	12.7	6.8	2.6	2.1	2.83
Ann Arbor, MI	29.6	36.9	13.7	12.3	4.5	1.8	1.0	2.45
Athens, GA	28.9	35.3	15.2	13.1	4.8	1.6	0.8	2.50
Atlanta, GA	26.7	31.6	16.9	14.3	6.3	2.4	1.4	2.74
Austin, TX	27.9	33.1	15.5	13.9	6.0	2.1	1.2	2.71
Baton Rouge, LA	28.6	33.8	16.7	12.3	5.6	1.8	0.9	2.69
Boise City, ID	27.8	34.4	14.3	12.0	7.0	2.7	1.6	2.68
Boston, MA	27.7	33.0	16.6	14.3	5.4	1.7	0.9	2.55
Boulder, CO	28.7	36.3	15.5	12.9	4.6	1.2	0.4	2.44
Cape Coral, FL	28.0	44.7	11.5	9.0	4.1	1.6	0.8	2.64
Cedar Rapids, IA	29.6	36.5	13.8	11.9	5.0	2.0	0.8	2.41
Charleston, SC	29.1	35.6	16.5	11.7	4.6	1.5	0.6	2.60
Charlotte, NC	27.1	34.0	16.3	14.0	5.5	1.8	0.9	2.63
Chicago, IL	28.9	31.1	15.6	13.7	6.6	2.4	1.4	2.66
Cincinnati, OH	28.8	34.3	15.1	12.7	5.7	1.9	1.0	2.50
Clarksville, TN	24.9	32.2	18.3	14.2	6.2	2.5	1.2	2.64
Cleveland, OH	34.0	33.8	14.2	10.7	4.5	1.5	0.8	2.34
College Station, TX	28.1	33.9	15.7	13.2	5.1	2.6	1.2	2.61
Colorado Springs, CO	25.0	35.4	15.6	13.4	6.5	2.4	1.3	2.64
Columbia, MO	30.1	34.4	15.1	13.2	4.8	1.3	0.7	2.41
Columbia, SC	29.8	34.3	15.6	12.1	5.2	1.7	0.9	2.53
Columbus, OH	28.5	33.9	15.6	12.9	5.9	1.9	1.0	2.55
Dallas, TX	25.0	30.6	16.8	15.2	7.5	2.9	1.7	2.83
Davenport, IA	31.1	35.7	13.2	11.9	5.3	1.7	0.8	2.42
Denver, CO	28.2	34.3	14.9	13.2	5.7	2.1	1.3	2.57
Des Moines, IA	27.9	34.2	14.6	13.8	6.2	2.1	0.8	2.50
Durham, NC	30.5	35.7	15.4	11.2	4.8	1.3	0.7	2.42
Edison, NJ	28.0	29.4	16.9	14.5	6.5	2.4	1.9	2.70
El Paso, TX	23.8	28.1	17.8	16.5	8.3	3.5	1.6	3.06
Fargo, ND	31.1	35.0	14.5	11.6	5.0	1.5	0.8	2.31
Fayetteville, NC	30.7	31.5	16.0	12.4	5.8	2.2	1.0	2.64
Fort Collins, CO	24.2	40.2	15.7	12.3	5.1	1.5	0.5	2.45
Fort Wayne, IN	28.9	34.3	14.4	12.2	6.3	2.4	1.2	2.52
Fort Worth, TX	25.0	30.6	16.8	15.2	7.5	2.9	1.7	2.83
Grand Rapids, MI	24.8	34.6	14.9	14.3	6.9	2.7	1.4	2.65
Greeley, CO	20.5	33.4	16.7	15.7	8.3	3.2	1.8	2.85
Green Bay, WI	28.3	36.9	14.1	12.2	5.8	1.5	0.9	2.40
Greensboro, NC	29.4	35.0	16.1	11.4	5.0	1.8	1.0	2.48
Honolulu, HI	24.0	30.5	16.7	13.5	7.3	3.5	4.1	3.03
Houston, TX	24.1	29.7	17.1	15.6	8.1	3.1	1.9	2.89
Huntsville, AL	29.4	35.1	15.5	12.2	5.1	1.7	0.6	2.47
Indianapolis, IN	30.1	33.5	14.8	12.8	5.7	1.9	0.9	2.56
Jacksonville, FL	27.1	35.6	16.6	12.4	5.3	1.8	0.8	2.62
Kansas City, MO	29.0	34.1	14.8	12.9	5.8	2.0	1.1	2.52
Lafayette, LA	26.9	34.0	16.7	12.9	6.1	2.1	1.0	2.65
Lakeland, FL	25.2	37.9	15.1	11.6	5.9	2.5	1.4	2.86
Las Vegas, NV	28.5	32.8	15.3	12.3	6.5	2.6	1.7	2.76
Lexington, KY	28.4	35.6	15.9	12.3	5.0	1.7	0.7	2.44
Lincoln, NE	30.1	35.7	13.7	11.9	5.3	2.0	1.0	2.41
Little Rock, AR	29.8	34.2	15.9	11.8	5.2	1.8	0.8	2.55
Los Angeles, CA	24.5	28.6	17.0	15.4	7.9	3.4	2.8	2.99
Louisville, KY	30.3	34.1	15.7	11.7	5.1	1.8	0.9	2.51

Table continued on following page.

Metro Area	One	Two	Three	Four	Five	Six	Seven or More	Average Household Size
Madison, WI	30.1	36.8	14.0	12.1	4.6	1.4	0.7	2.35
Manchester, NH	25.5	36.2	16.4	13.5	5.2	1.9	1.0	2.51
Memphis, TN	29.8	32.5	16.2	12.3	5.3	2.2	1.3	2.64
Miami, FL	28.2	32.6	16.8	13.2	5.8	2.1	1.1	2.82
Midland, TX	26.3	30.8	15.9	14.4	7.8	2.9	1.6	2.93
Milwaukee, WI	31.5	34.3	14.0	11.9	5.2	1.8	0.9	2.45
Minneapolis, MN	27.9	34.1	14.8	13.6	5.8	2.1	1.3	2.56
Nashville, TN	26.0	34.8	16.7	13.3	5.8	2.0	1.0	2.59
New Haven, CT	31.2	33.0	16.1	12.3	4.8	1.7	0.7	2.51
New Orleans, LA	33.4	32.2	15.4	11.5	4.6	1.6	0.9	2.58
New York, NY	28.0	29.4	16.9	14.5	6.5	2.4	1.9	2.70
Oklahoma City, OK	28.2	34.1	15.4	12.6	6.0	2.3	1.1	2.62
Omaha, NE	28.4	33.9	14.3	12.6	6.4	2.7	1.5	2.54
Orlando, FL	24.8	34.2	17.4	13.9	5.9	2.3	1.1	2.83
Peoria, IL	31.3	35.3	14.0	11.0	5.2	2.0	0.8	2.42
Philadelphia, PA	29.1	32.3	16.2	13.5	5.7	1.9	1.0	2.60
Phoenix, AZ	26.4	34.4	14.4	12.6	6.7	3.0	2.2	2.76
Pittsburgh, PA	33.2	35.5	14.3	10.8	4.0	1.3	0.5	2.25
Portland, OR	26.8	35.4	15.3	13.4	5.3	2.2	1.2	2.56
Providence, RI	29.8	33.3	16.6	12.8	5.0	1.5	0.7	2.48
Provo, UT	11.9	28.6	15.6	15.6	12.4	9.0	6.5	3.55
Raleigh, NC	25.0	33.1	17.6	15.3	6.1	1.8	0.8	2.64
Reno, NV	28.2	35.0	15.5	11.4	5.7	2.3	1.5	2.47
Richmond, VA	29.4	34.2	16.0	12.3	5.3	1.8	0.7	2.57
Riverside, CA	20.4	28.3	16.3	16.0	10.1	4.9	3.7	3.28
Rochester, MN	27.2	36.2	14.1	13.5	5.3	2.2	1.2	2.45
Sacramento, CA	25.3	33.2	15.9	14.4	6.6	2.7	1.7	2.74
Salt Lake City, UT	22.4	30.5	15.8	14.3	8.6	4.9	3.2	3.00
San Antonio, TX	26.3	31.2	16.5	13.8	7.1	3.0	1.7	3.00
San Diego, CA	23.8	32.6	16.9	14.7	7.0	2.8	1.9	2.87
San Francisco, CA	26.2	31.9	16.9	14.8	6.1	2.2	1.6	2.71
San Jose, CA	20.1	30.6	18.8	17.7	7.2	2.9	2.4	2.96
Santa Rosa, CA	27.4	34.8	15.4	12.9	5.9	2.0	1.3	2.59
Savannah, GA	28.0	35.9	16.1	12.2	5.0	1.5	0.9	2.62
Seattle, WA	27.1	34.5	16.0	13.5	5.2	2.0	1.3	2.54
Sioux Falls, SD	28.6	35.0	13.6	13.1	6.2	2.1	1.1	2.46
Springfield, IL	32.9	35.7	14.0	10.6	4.2	1.6	0.7	2.30
Tallahassee, FL	30.5	35.2	17.0	11.0	4.2	1.2	0.5	2.43
Tampa, FL	30.8	36.7	14.7	10.8	4.4	1.5	0.8	2.51
Tucson, AZ	30.5	35.8	13.7	11.2	5.1	2.0	1.3	2.46
Tulsa, OK	28.2	34.5	15.2	12.1	5.9	2.4	1.2	2.56
Tuscaloosa, AL	29.4	35.0	16.4	11.5	5.3	1.3	0.8	2.69
Virginia Beach, VA	27.2	34.1	17.3	13.1	5.3	1.8	0.9	2.55
Washington, DC	27.2	30.8	16.5	14.6	6.5	2.6	1.6	2.75
Wichita, KS	29.9	32.8	14.0	11.6	7.0	2.8	1.4	2.56
Winston-Salem, NC	29.5	35.9	15.4	11.3	5.0	1.6	0.9	2.46
U.S.	27.8	33.9	15.5	12.9	5.9	2.2	1.4	2.62

Note: Figures cover the Metropolitan Statistical Area (MSA)—see Appendix B for areas included
Source: U.S. Census Bureau, 2015-2019 American Community Survey 5-Year Estimates

Race: City

City	White Alone[1] (%)	Black Alone[1] (%)	Asian Alone[1] (%)	AIAN[2] Alone[1] (%)	NHOPI[3] Alone[1] (%)	Other Race Alone[1] (%)	Two or More Races (%)
Albuquerque, NM	73.9	3.3	2.9	4.7	0.1	10.6	4.4
Allentown, PA	62.3	14.7	2.9	0.7	0.1	14.7	4.6
Anchorage, AK	62.6	5.6	9.6	7.9	2.4	2.4	9.5
Ann Arbor, MI	71.1	6.8	16.9	0.4	0.1	0.7	4.1
Athens, GA	63.2	28.0	3.9	0.1	0.1	2.1	2.6
Atlanta, GA	40.9	51.0	4.4	0.3	0.0	1.0	2.4
Austin, TX	72.6	7.8	7.6	0.7	0.1	7.8	3.5
Baton Rouge, LA	38.7	54.7	3.5	0.3	0.1	1.5	1.3
Boise City, ID	89.3	1.9	2.8	0.5	0.2	1.9	3.4
Boston, MA	52.8	25.2	9.7	0.3	0.1	6.7	5.3
Boulder, CO	87.4	1.2	5.8	0.2	0.1	1.5	3.8
Cape Coral, FL	89.5	5.2	1.8	0.2	0.0	1.8	1.6
Cedar Rapids, IA	83.9	7.8	2.9	0.3	0.2	1.1	3.8
Charleston, SC	74.1	21.7	1.9	0.1	0.1	0.6	1.5
Charlotte, NC	48.8	35.2	6.5	0.4	0.1	6.1	2.8
Chicago, IL	50.0	29.6	6.6	0.3	0.0	10.6	2.8
Cincinnati, OH	50.7	42.3	2.2	0.1	0.1	0.9	3.7
Clarksville, TN	65.1	24.3	2.5	0.7	0.5	1.8	5.2
Cleveland, OH	40.0	48.8	2.6	0.5	0.1	3.6	4.4
College Station, TX	77.8	7.6	10.1	0.3	0.0	1.5	2.7
Colorado Springs, CO	78.5	6.5	2.9	0.8	0.3	5.1	5.9
Columbia, MO	77.1	10.9	6.2	0.4	0.1	0.9	4.4
Columbia, SC	53.4	39.8	2.7	0.1	0.2	1.0	2.8
Columbus, OH	58.6	29.0	5.8	0.3	0.0	2.1	4.2
Dallas, TX	62.7	24.3	3.4	0.3	0.0	6.9	2.4
Davenport, IA	81.4	11.3	2.3	0.5	0.0	1.0	3.5
Denver, CO	76.1	9.2	3.7	0.9	0.2	6.1	3.8
Des Moines, IA	75.8	11.4	6.2	0.4	0.1	2.3	3.9
Durham, NC	49.2	38.7	5.4	0.3	0.0	3.4	3.2
Edison, NJ	35.3	8.2	48.7	0.3	0.1	4.0	3.5
El Paso, TX	80.1	3.6	1.4	0.6	0.2	11.4	2.7
Fargo, ND	84.6	7.0	3.5	1.2	0.0	0.5	3.1
Fayetteville, NC	44.6	42.1	2.9	1.1	0.4	2.9	6.1
Fort Collins, CO	88.3	1.6	3.5	1.0	0.1	1.5	4.0
Fort Wayne, IN	73.4	15.1	4.7	0.2	0.1	2.1	4.5
Fort Worth, TX	63.8	18.9	4.6	0.5	0.1	9.0	3.2
Grand Rapids, MI	67.2	18.6	2.4	0.4	0.0	5.7	5.6
Greeley, CO	88.3	2.4	1.4	1.2	0.2	3.7	2.8
Green Bay, WI	76.7	4.2	4.2	3.5	0.0	6.0	5.4
Greensboro, NC	47.3	41.4	5.0	0.5	0.1	2.7	3.0
Honolulu, HI	17.2	2.0	53.2	0.1	8.0	0.9	18.4
Houston, TX	57.0	22.6	6.8	0.3	0.1	11.1	2.2
Huntsville, AL	61.3	30.7	2.6	0.4	0.1	2.0	2.8
Indianapolis, IN	60.9	28.6	3.4	0.3	0.0	3.5	3.3
Jacksonville, FL	58.2	31.0	4.8	0.2	0.1	2.1	3.6
Kansas City, MO	60.9	28.2	2.7	0.4	0.2	4.0	3.6
Lafayette, LA	64.0	30.9	2.2	0.3	0.0	0.6	2.1
Lakeland, FL	72.3	20.5	2.2	0.4	0.1	2.8	1.8
Las Vegas, NV	61.9	12.2	6.9	0.9	0.8	12.1	5.2
Lexington, KY	74.9	14.6	3.8	0.2	0.0	2.8	3.8
Lincoln, NE	84.9	4.4	4.6	0.7	0.1	1.5	3.9
Little Rock, AR	50.3	42.0	3.3	0.3	0.1	1.8	2.3
Los Angeles, CA	52.1	8.9	11.6	0.7	0.2	22.8	3.8
Louisville, KY	69.9	23.6	2.7	0.2	0.1	1.0	2.6

Table continued on following page.

City	White Alone[1] (%)	Black Alone[1] (%)	Asian Alone[1] (%)	AIAN[2] Alone[1] (%)	NHOPI[3] Alone[1] (%)	Other Race Alone[1] (%)	Two or More Races (%)
Madison, WI	78.6	7.0	9.0	0.5	0.1	1.4	3.5
Manchester, NH	84.8	6.1	5.1	0.1	0.0	0.9	3.0
Memphis, TN	29.2	64.1	1.7	0.2	0.0	3.3	1.5
Miami, FL	76.1	16.8	1.1	0.2	0.0	4.0	1.7
Midland, TX	80.6	7.8	2.2	0.6	0.1	6.4	2.3
Milwaukee, WI	44.4	38.7	4.3	0.6	0.0	8.0	4.0
Minneapolis, MN	63.6	19.2	5.9	1.4	0.0	5.0	4.8
Nashville, TN	63.5	27.6	3.7	0.2	0.1	2.4	2.6
New Haven, CT	44.4	32.6	5.0	0.4	0.0	13.1	4.4
New Orleans, LA	33.9	59.5	2.9	0.2	0.0	1.5	1.9
New York, NY	42.7	24.3	14.1	0.4	0.1	14.7	3.6
Oklahoma City, OK	67.7	14.3	4.5	2.9	0.1	4.1	6.3
Omaha, NE	77.5	12.3	3.8	0.6	0.0	2.3	3.4
Orlando, FL	61.3	24.5	4.2	0.2	0.0	6.2	3.5
Peoria, IL	60.1	27.1	6.1	0.3	0.0	2.1	4.3
Philadelphia, PA	40.7	42.1	7.2	0.4	0.0	6.5	3.1
Phoenix, AZ	72.9	7.1	3.8	2.1	0.2	10.0	3.9
Pittsburgh, PA	66.8	23.0	5.8	0.2	0.0	0.6	3.5
Portland, OR	77.4	5.8	8.2	0.8	0.6	1.9	5.3
Providence, RI	55.1	16.8	6.0	1.0	0.1	16.3	4.7
Provo, UT	87.9	0.9	2.7	0.8	1.3	2.2	4.2
Raleigh, NC	58.3	29.0	4.6	0.4	0.0	4.8	2.9
Reno, NV	75.4	2.8	6.7	1.0	0.8	8.5	4.8
Richmond, VA	45.5	46.9	2.1	0.4	0.0	1.7	3.4
Riverside, CA	58.3	6.2	7.6	0.8	0.3	22.0	4.9
Rochester, MN	79.4	8.2	7.3	0.5	0.1	1.1	3.4
Sacramento, CA	46.3	13.2	18.9	0.7	1.7	11.7	7.4
Salt Lake City, UT	72.8	2.6	5.4	1.5	1.6	12.7	3.3
San Antonio, TX	80.3	7.0	2.8	0.8	0.1	6.0	3.0
San Diego, CA	65.1	6.4	16.7	0.5	0.4	5.6	5.3
San Francisco, CA	46.4	5.2	34.4	0.4	0.4	7.7	5.6
San Jose, CA	39.9	3.0	35.9	0.6	0.5	14.8	5.3
Santa Rosa, CA	66.8	2.6	5.5	1.3	0.6	17.1	6.0
Savannah, GA	38.9	53.9	2.6	0.3	0.1	1.4	2.8
Seattle, WA	67.3	7.3	15.4	0.5	0.3	2.3	6.9
Sioux Falls, SD	84.5	6.2	2.5	2.1	0.0	1.6	3.2
Springfield, IL	72.9	19.9	3.1	0.1	0.0	0.5	3.5
Tallahassee, FL	56.2	35.0	4.6	0.2	0.0	1.1	2.9
Tampa, FL	65.4	23.6	4.3	0.3	0.1	2.5	3.9
Tucson, AZ	72.1	5.2	3.2	3.7	0.2	10.2	5.4
Tulsa, OK	64.3	15.2	3.4	4.5	0.1	4.9	7.5
Tuscaloosa, AL	51.2	44.0	2.5	0.3	0.1	0.9	1.0
Virginia Beach, VA	66.3	19.0	6.7	0.3	0.1	2.1	5.6
Washington, DC	41.3	46.3	4.0	0.3	0.1	5.0	3.1
Wichita, KS	74.3	10.9	5.1	1.0	0.1	4.2	4.4
Winston-Salem, NC	56.6	34.9	2.5	0.3	0.1	2.8	2.8
U.S.	72.5	12.7	5.5	0.8	0.2	4.9	3.3

Note: (1) Alone is defined as not being in combination with one or more other races; (2) American Indian and Alaska Native; (3) Native Hawaiian and Other Pacific Islander
Source: U.S. Census Bureau, 2015-2019 American Community Survey 5-Year Estimates

Race: Metro Area

Metro Area	White Alone[1] (%)	Black Alone[1] (%)	Asian Alone[1] (%)	AIAN[2] Alone[1] (%)	NHOPI[3] Alone[1] (%)	Other Race Alone[1] (%)	Two or More Races (%)
Albuquerque, NM	74.9	2.7	2.3	6.0	0.1	10.0	4.0
Allentown, PA	84.0	6.0	2.9	0.2	0.0	3.7	3.1
Anchorage, AK	68.0	4.4	7.5	7.5	1.9	1.8	9.0
Ann Arbor, MI	73.6	11.9	9.1	0.4	0.0	0.8	4.2
Athens, GA	72.0	20.6	3.1	0.1	0.1	1.8	2.3
Atlanta, GA	53.4	34.2	5.9	0.4	0.0	3.4	2.7
Austin, TX	76.0	7.3	5.9	0.5	0.1	6.7	3.6
Baton Rouge, LA	59.2	35.3	1.9	0.2	0.0	1.4	1.9
Boise City, ID	88.0	1.0	1.9	0.7	0.2	4.6	3.5
Boston, MA	76.0	8.3	7.9	0.2	0.0	4.2	3.3
Boulder, CO	89.0	0.9	4.7	0.4	0.1	1.8	3.0
Cape Coral, FL	84.4	8.6	1.6	0.2	0.1	3.4	1.8
Cedar Rapids, IA	89.4	4.8	2.0	0.2	0.1	0.7	2.8
Charleston, SC	67.6	25.6	1.8	0.3	0.1	1.9	2.7
Charlotte, NC	66.9	22.8	3.7	0.4	0.1	3.6	2.5
Chicago, IL	65.7	16.6	6.6	0.3	0.0	8.0	2.7
Cincinnati, OH	81.8	12.0	2.6	0.1	0.0	0.9	2.6
Clarksville, TN	72.7	19.1	1.9	0.6	0.4	1.3	4.1
Cleveland, OH	73.4	19.9	2.3	0.2	0.0	1.3	2.9
College Station, TX	77.0	11.5	5.3	0.4	0.1	3.0	2.8
Colorado Springs, CO	80.1	6.2	2.7	0.8	0.4	4.0	5.9
Columbia, MO	82.3	8.6	3.9	0.4	0.1	0.9	3.8
Columbia, SC	59.6	33.4	2.1	0.2	0.1	1.8	2.7
Columbus, OH	75.3	15.5	4.2	0.2	0.0	1.3	3.4
Dallas, TX	68.3	15.8	6.9	0.5	0.1	5.4	3.0
Davenport, IA	85.1	7.6	2.3	0.3	0.0	1.7	3.0
Denver, CO	81.0	5.7	4.2	0.8	0.1	4.4	3.7
Des Moines, IA	86.9	5.2	3.9	0.3	0.1	1.1	2.5
Durham, NC	62.5	26.6	4.5	0.4	0.0	3.0	3.1
Edison, NJ	57.5	17.3	11.2	0.3	0.0	10.5	3.1
El Paso, TX	79.6	3.3	1.2	0.6	0.1	12.4	2.7
Fargo, ND	88.0	5.1	2.5	1.2	0.1	0.6	2.7
Fayetteville, NC	53.8	32.6	2.0	2.0	0.3	4.1	5.3
Fort Collins, CO	91.3	1.0	2.2	0.8	0.1	1.5	3.2
Fort Wayne, IN	80.4	10.6	3.5	0.2	0.0	1.7	3.6
Fort Worth, TX	68.3	15.8	6.9	0.5	0.1	5.4	3.0
Grand Rapids, MI	83.9	6.7	2.6	0.3	0.0	2.9	3.5
Greeley, CO	90.3	1.2	1.6	0.8	0.1	3.0	3.0
Green Bay, WI	87.1	2.1	2.7	2.2	0.0	2.9	3.0
Greensboro, NC	63.0	26.8	3.7	0.5	0.1	3.3	2.6
Honolulu, HI	20.9	2.4	42.7	0.2	9.5	1.0	23.2
Houston, TX	65.0	17.3	7.7	0.4	0.1	7.0	2.5
Huntsville, AL	70.5	22.1	2.4	0.6	0.1	1.5	2.8
Indianapolis, IN	76.6	15.2	3.2	0.2	0.0	2.0	2.7
Jacksonville, FL	69.3	21.5	3.8	0.3	0.1	1.8	3.4
Kansas City, MO	78.3	12.3	2.9	0.4	0.2	2.7	3.3
Lafayette, LA	70.6	24.6	1.7	0.3	0.0	0.8	2.0
Lakeland, FL	77.1	15.3	1.8	0.3	0.0	3.0	2.5
Las Vegas, NV	60.2	11.7	9.7	0.9	0.8	11.5	5.4
Lexington, KY	80.7	11.0	2.7	0.2	0.0	2.3	3.1
Lincoln, NE	86.6	3.8	4.0	0.7	0.1	1.3	3.5
Little Rock, AR	70.3	23.3	1.7	0.4	0.1	1.6	2.5
Los Angeles, CA	53.6	6.6	16.0	0.7	0.3	18.8	4.0
Louisville, KY	79.4	14.8	2.1	0.2	0.0	0.9	2.5

Table continued on following page.

Metro Area	White Alone[1] (%)	Black Alone[1] (%)	Asian Alone[1] (%)	AIAN[2] Alone[1] (%)	NHOPI[3] Alone[1] (%)	Other Race Alone[1] (%)	Two or More Races (%)
Madison, WI	86.0	4.4	5.0	0.3	0.0	1.4	2.8
Manchester, NH	89.4	2.9	4.0	0.1	0.1	0.9	2.5
Memphis, TN	46.3	47.1	2.1	0.2	0.0	2.3	1.9
Miami, FL	70.2	21.2	2.5	0.2	0.0	3.5	2.3
Midland, TX	82.1	6.5	1.9	0.6	0.1	6.4	2.4
Milwaukee, WI	72.5	16.5	3.7	0.4	0.0	3.8	2.9
Minneapolis, MN	78.7	8.5	6.6	0.6	0.0	2.2	3.4
Nashville, TN	77.6	15.3	2.8	0.2	0.0	1.6	2.5
New Haven, CT	73.3	13.5	4.0	0.2	0.0	5.7	3.3
New Orleans, LA	57.3	35.1	2.9	0.4	0.0	2.2	2.0
New York, NY	57.5	17.3	11.2	0.3	0.0	10.5	3.1
Oklahoma City, OK	73.7	10.2	3.2	3.6	0.1	2.8	6.5
Omaha, NE	84.0	7.7	2.9	0.5	0.1	1.9	2.9
Orlando, FL	69.7	16.6	4.3	0.3	0.1	5.7	3.3
Peoria, IL	85.4	8.8	2.3	0.2	0.0	0.8	2.4
Philadelphia, PA	66.6	21.0	5.9	0.2	0.0	3.4	2.8
Phoenix, AZ	77.8	5.5	4.0	2.3	0.2	6.5	3.7
Pittsburgh, PA	86.6	8.1	2.3	0.1	0.0	0.4	2.5
Portland, OR	81.1	2.8	6.7	0.8	0.5	3.0	5.0
Providence, RI	81.7	5.9	3.0	0.4	0.1	5.7	3.2
Provo, UT	91.7	0.6	1.5	0.5	0.9	1.8	3.1
Raleigh, NC	67.2	20.0	5.7	0.4	0.0	3.7	2.9
Reno, NV	77.6	2.3	5.3	1.6	0.6	8.1	4.4
Richmond, VA	61.1	29.7	3.8	0.3	0.1	1.8	3.1
Riverside, CA	60.5	7.4	6.8	0.8	0.3	19.5	4.7
Rochester, MN	87.4	4.5	4.3	0.3	0.1	1.1	2.4
Sacramento, CA	65.0	7.1	13.3	0.6	0.9	6.5	6.6
Salt Lake City, UT	79.7	1.8	3.9	0.8	1.4	9.0	3.4
San Antonio, TX	80.7	6.8	2.5	0.6	0.1	5.9	3.4
San Diego, CA	70.7	5.0	11.9	0.7	0.4	6.0	5.2
San Francisco, CA	49.0	7.3	26.1	0.5	0.7	10.2	6.2
San Jose, CA	45.6	2.4	35.4	0.5	0.4	10.4	5.2
Santa Rosa, CA	74.8	1.7	4.1	0.9	0.3	12.9	5.4
Savannah, GA	59.6	33.3	2.2	0.3	0.1	1.5	3.0
Seattle, WA	68.3	5.8	13.6	0.8	0.9	3.7	6.8
Sioux Falls, SD	88.3	4.5	1.8	1.6	0.0	1.1	2.7
Springfield, IL	82.8	12.1	1.9	0.1	0.1	0.4	2.6
Tallahassee, FL	60.6	32.7	2.7	0.2	0.0	1.3	2.4
Tampa, FL	77.8	12.2	3.4	0.3	0.1	2.9	3.3
Tucson, AZ	76.0	3.6	2.9	3.9	0.2	8.6	4.9
Tulsa, OK	71.2	8.0	2.5	7.3	0.1	2.7	8.2
Tuscaloosa, AL	60.6	35.8	1.4	0.2	0.0	0.8	1.1
Virginia Beach, VA	59.0	30.6	3.8	0.3	0.1	1.8	4.5
Washington, DC	53.5	25.3	10.1	0.3	0.1	6.5	4.2
Wichita, KS	80.9	7.5	3.7	0.9	0.1	2.9	4.0
Winston-Salem, NC	75.8	17.8	1.8	0.4	0.1	2.0	2.2
U.S.	72.5	12.7	5.5	0.8	0.2	4.9	3.3

Note: (1) Figures cover the Metropolitan Statistical Area (MSA)—see Appendix B for areas included; (1) Alone is defined as not being in combination with one or more other races; (2) American Indian and Alaska Native; (3) Native Hawaiian & Other Pacific Islander
Source: U.S. Census Bureau, 2015-2019 American Community Survey 5-Year Estimates

Hispanic Origin: City

City	Hispanic or Latino (%)	Mexican (%)	Puerto Rican (%)	Cuban (%)	Other Hispanic or Latino (%)
Albuquerque, NM	49.2	28.0	0.6	0.5	20.2
Allentown, PA	52.5	1.9	28.8	0.9	20.9
Anchorage, AK	9.2	4.8	1.4	0.1	2.8
Ann Arbor, MI	4.8	2.2	0.4	0.3	1.9
Athens, GA	10.9	6.7	0.7	0.4	3.1
Atlanta, GA	4.3	2.0	0.6	0.3	1.4
Austin, TX	33.9	27.2	0.9	0.7	5.2
Baton Rouge, LA	3.7	1.1	0.3	0.2	2.1
Boise City, ID	9.0	7.2	0.3	0.0	1.5
Boston, MA	19.8	1.2	5.3	0.5	12.9
Boulder, CO	9.7	6.0	0.4	0.4	2.9
Cape Coral, FL	20.9	2.0	5.0	7.8	6.1
Cedar Rapids, IA	4.0	2.8	0.2	0.0	1.0
Charleston, SC	3.2	1.3	0.5	0.2	1.2
Charlotte, NC	14.3	5.3	1.2	0.5	7.3
Chicago, IL	28.8	21.3	3.6	0.3	3.5
Cincinnati, OH	3.8	1.2	0.6	0.1	2.0
Clarksville, TN	11.5	5.2	3.7	0.3	2.3
Cleveland, OH	11.9	1.3	8.5	0.2	1.9
College Station, TX	15.8	11.2	0.3	0.4	3.9
Colorado Springs, CO	17.6	11.3	1.4	0.5	4.5
Columbia, MO	3.6	2.2	0.3	0.1	1.1
Columbia, SC	5.5	2.1	1.3	0.3	1.7
Columbus, OH	6.2	3.2	0.9	0.1	1.9
Dallas, TX	41.8	35.4	0.5	0.3	5.5
Davenport, IA	8.7	7.8	0.3	0.0	0.5
Denver, CO	29.9	23.7	0.6	0.2	5.4
Des Moines, IA	13.6	10.6	0.4	0.1	2.4
Durham, NC	13.8	6.1	1.1	0.2	6.4
Edison, NJ	9.9	1.8	2.5	0.8	4.8
El Paso, TX	81.4	76.9	1.1	0.1	3.2
Fargo, ND	3.0	1.9	0.4	0.0	0.6
Fayetteville, NC	12.4	4.2	4.1	0.4	3.7
Fort Collins, CO	11.6	8.2	0.4	0.1	3.0
Fort Wayne, IN	9.2	6.8	0.5	0.1	1.7
Fort Worth, TX	35.1	30.6	1.1	0.3	3.1
Grand Rapids, MI	16.1	9.5	1.5	0.2	4.8
Greeley, CO	38.6	31.0	0.6	0.3	6.7
Green Bay, WI	15.8	12.5	1.4	0.1	1.8
Greensboro, NC	7.9	4.7	0.7	0.2	2.2
Honolulu, HI	7.3	2.0	1.8	0.2	3.4
Houston, TX	45.0	31.8	0.6	0.8	11.7
Huntsville, AL	6.2	3.8	0.9	0.2	1.4
Indianapolis, IN	10.5	7.1	0.6	0.2	2.6
Jacksonville, FL	10.0	2.0	3.0	1.2	3.7
Kansas City, MO	10.6	8.0	0.4	0.3	1.9
Lafayette, LA	3.6	1.4	0.2	0.2	1.7
Lakeland, FL	16.4	3.5	6.3	2.5	4.0
Las Vegas, NV	33.1	24.7	1.2	1.3	5.9
Lexington, KY	7.2	4.8	0.7	0.2	1.5
Lincoln, NE	7.6	5.5	0.3	0.2	1.6
Little Rock, AR	7.4	4.8	0.3	0.3	2.1
Los Angeles, CA	48.5	32.2	0.4	0.4	15.4
Louisville, KY	5.6	2.0	0.5	1.9	1.2
Madison, WI	7.0	4.1	0.7	0.2	2.0

Table continued on following page.

City	Hispanic or Latino (%)	Mexican (%)	Puerto Rican (%)	Cuban (%)	Other Hispanic or Latino (%)
Manchester, NH	10.4	1.5	4.4	0.1	4.4
Memphis, TN	7.2	5.1	0.3	0.2	1.6
Miami, FL	72.7	1.9	3.4	35.0	32.4
Midland, TX	44.2	40.6	0.5	0.9	2.2
Milwaukee, WI	19.0	13.4	4.4	0.2	1.1
Minneapolis, MN	9.6	5.8	0.5	0.2	3.1
Nashville, TN	10.5	6.2	0.6	0.4	3.4
New Haven, CT	31.2	5.6	17.6	0.3	7.7
New Orleans, LA	5.5	1.3	0.3	0.4	3.5
New York, NY	29.1	4.0	8.1	0.5	16.5
Oklahoma City, OK	19.7	16.6	0.3	0.1	2.8
Omaha, NE	13.9	10.7	0.4	0.1	2.7
Orlando, FL	32.6	1.9	15.6	3.0	12.0
Peoria, IL	6.3	4.6	0.4	0.1	1.1
Philadelphia, PA	14.7	1.3	8.8	0.3	4.3
Phoenix, AZ	42.6	38.3	0.7	0.3	3.3
Pittsburgh, PA	3.2	1.0	0.7	0.2	1.3
Portland, OR	9.7	6.8	0.4	0.4	2.1
Providence, RI	43.3	1.8	9.3	0.3	31.9
Provo, UT	16.7	11.3	0.5	0.1	4.7
Raleigh, NC	11.2	5.1	1.2	0.4	4.5
Reno, NV	24.7	19.2	0.5	0.3	4.7
Richmond, VA	6.9	1.7	0.7	0.2	4.3
Riverside, CA	53.7	47.1	0.8	0.2	5.6
Rochester, MN	5.9	3.7	0.4	0.2	1.6
Sacramento, CA	28.9	24.6	0.7	0.2	3.3
Salt Lake City, UT	21.8	16.9	0.3	0.4	4.2
San Antonio, TX	64.2	56.9	1.3	0.3	5.7
San Diego, CA	30.3	26.6	0.7	0.2	2.8
San Francisco, CA	15.2	7.8	0.6	0.3	6.6
San Jose, CA	31.6	27.1	0.6	0.1	3.7
Santa Rosa, CA	32.8	28.8	0.4	0.1	3.5
Savannah, GA	5.8	2.3	1.5	0.2	1.8
Seattle, WA	6.7	3.9	0.4	0.2	2.1
Sioux Falls, SD	5.5	3.1	0.4	0.1	1.9
Springfield, IL	2.8	1.5	0.5	0.1	0.7
Tallahassee, FL	6.7	1.2	1.4	1.3	2.8
Tampa, FL	26.4	3.1	7.6	8.0	7.7
Tucson, AZ	43.6	39.5	0.8	0.2	3.1
Tulsa, OK	16.5	13.2	0.6	0.2	2.6
Tuscaloosa, AL	3.2	1.6	0.1	0.2	1.4
Virginia Beach, VA	8.2	2.5	2.4	0.3	3.0
Washington, DC	11.0	2.0	0.9	0.4	7.6
Wichita, KS	17.2	14.7	0.4	0.2	1.9
Winston-Salem, NC	15.0	9.9	1.4	0.2	3.5
U.S.	18.0	11.2	1.7	0.7	4.3

Note: Persons of Hispanic or Latino origin can be of any race
Source: U.S. Census Bureau, 2015-2019 American Community Survey 5-Year Estimates

Hispanic Origin: Metro Area

Metro Area	Hispanic or Latino (%)	Mexican (%)	Puerto Rican (%)	Cuban (%)	Other Hispanic or Latino (%)
Albuquerque, NM	49.0	27.7	0.5	0.4	20.4
Allentown, PA	17.0	1.2	9.2	0.3	6.2
Anchorage, AK	8.1	4.2	1.2	0.2	2.4
Ann Arbor, MI	4.7	2.6	0.3	0.2	1.6
Athens, GA	8.6	5.0	0.7	0.3	2.6
Atlanta, GA	10.7	5.6	1.0	0.4	3.6
Austin, TX	32.4	26.8	0.9	0.5	4.3
Baton Rouge, LA	4.0	1.5	0.3	0.2	2.0
Boise City, ID	13.7	11.6	0.3	0.1	1.6
Boston, MA	11.1	0.7	2.9	0.2	7.3
Boulder, CO	13.9	10.4	0.4	0.3	2.8
Cape Coral, FL	21.4	6.0	4.3	4.9	6.2
Cedar Rapids, IA	3.0	2.1	0.1	0.0	0.8
Charleston, SC	5.6	2.7	0.8	0.1	2.0
Charlotte, NC	10.1	4.7	1.0	0.4	4.1
Chicago, IL	22.1	17.3	2.2	0.2	2.4
Cincinnati, OH	3.2	1.5	0.4	0.1	1.2
Clarksville, TN	8.8	4.2	2.7	0.2	1.7
Cleveland, OH	5.8	1.3	3.4	0.1	1.0
College Station, TX	24.9	21.4	0.2	0.2	3.0
Colorado Springs, CO	16.7	10.3	1.7	0.4	4.4
Columbia, MO	3.2	2.1	0.2	0.1	0.8
Columbia, SC	5.5	2.8	1.1	0.2	1.4
Columbus, OH	4.2	2.1	0.7	0.1	1.3
Dallas, TX	28.9	23.9	0.7	0.3	4.0
Davenport, IA	8.7	7.7	0.4	0.1	0.6
Denver, CO	23.1	17.6	0.6	0.2	4.7
Des Moines, IA	7.1	5.4	0.2	0.1	1.4
Durham, NC	11.1	5.7	0.9	0.2	4.3
Edison, NJ	24.6	3.0	6.2	0.8	14.7
El Paso, TX	82.5	78.2	1.0	0.1	3.2
Fargo, ND	3.2	2.2	0.3	0.0	0.7
Fayetteville, NC	12.1	5.3	3.5	0.3	2.9
Fort Collins, CO	11.5	8.4	0.3	0.1	2.6
Fort Wayne, IN	7.0	5.2	0.4	0.1	1.3
Fort Worth, TX	28.9	23.9	0.7	0.3	4.0
Grand Rapids, MI	9.6	6.7	0.8	0.3	1.8
Greeley, CO	29.4	24.2	0.4	0.3	4.6
Green Bay, WI	7.4	5.8	0.7	0.0	0.9
Greensboro, NC	8.4	5.5	0.7	0.2	1.9
Honolulu, HI	9.8	2.9	3.1	0.1	3.7
Houston, TX	37.3	27.8	0.7	0.6	8.3
Huntsville, AL	5.2	3.2	0.7	0.2	1.0
Indianapolis, IN	6.7	4.4	0.5	0.1	1.7
Jacksonville, FL	8.9	1.8	2.8	1.2	3.1
Kansas City, MO	9.0	6.9	0.4	0.2	1.6
Lafayette, LA	4.0	2.1	0.2	0.2	1.5
Lakeland, FL	22.5	7.5	9.3	1.6	4.0
Las Vegas, NV	31.1	23.1	1.1	1.4	5.6
Lexington, KY	6.2	4.2	0.5	0.1	1.3
Lincoln, NE	6.8	4.9	0.3	0.2	1.5
Little Rock, AR	5.3	3.7	0.2	0.1	1.3
Los Angeles, CA	45.0	35.0	0.4	0.4	9.3
Louisville, KY	4.9	2.4	0.4	1.1	1.1
Madison, WI	5.7	3.6	0.5	0.1	1.5

Table continued on following page.

Metro Area	Hispanic or Latino (%)	Mexican (%)	Puerto Rican (%)	Cuban (%)	Other Hispanic or Latino (%)
Manchester, NH	6.8	1.0	2.5	0.2	3.0
Memphis, TN	5.6	4.0	0.2	0.1	1.2
Miami, FL	45.2	2.5	3.9	19.0	19.8
Midland, TX	44.7	41.6	0.5	0.7	1.9
Milwaukee, WI	10.7	7.4	2.3	0.1	0.9
Minneapolis, MN	5.9	3.8	0.3	0.1	1.6
Nashville, TN	7.3	4.4	0.5	0.2	2.2
New Haven, CT	18.1	1.9	10.6	0.4	5.3
New Orleans, LA	8.8	1.9	0.5	0.6	5.9
New York, NY	24.6	3.0	6.2	0.8	14.7
Oklahoma City, OK	13.3	10.9	0.3	0.1	2.0
Omaha, NE	10.4	7.9	0.4	0.1	2.0
Orlando, FL	30.7	2.9	15.2	2.4	10.1
Peoria, IL	3.5	2.5	0.3	0.0	0.6
Philadelphia, PA	9.4	1.9	4.6	0.3	2.7
Phoenix, AZ	30.9	27.1	0.7	0.3	2.8
Pittsburgh, PA	1.8	0.5	0.5	0.1	0.7
Portland, OR	12.0	9.2	0.4	0.2	2.2
Providence, RI	12.9	0.9	4.3	0.2	7.4
Provo, UT	11.7	7.7	0.3	0.1	3.7
Raleigh, NC	10.6	5.5	1.3	0.4	3.4
Reno, NV	24.3	18.9	0.6	0.3	4.4
Richmond, VA	6.3	1.6	1.0	0.2	3.5
Riverside, CA	51.0	44.4	0.8	0.3	5.5
Rochester, MN	4.4	2.9	0.2	0.1	1.2
Sacramento, CA	21.6	17.7	0.7	0.2	3.1
Salt Lake City, UT	18.0	13.3	0.5	0.1	4.1
San Antonio, TX	55.4	48.8	1.3	0.2	5.0
San Diego, CA	33.7	30.0	0.7	0.2	2.8
San Francisco, CA	21.8	14.2	0.7	0.2	6.7
San Jose, CA	26.5	22.1	0.5	0.1	3.7
Santa Rosa, CA	26.7	22.6	0.4	0.1	3.6
Savannah, GA	6.2	2.9	1.2	0.4	1.6
Seattle, WA	10.0	7.1	0.6	0.2	2.2
Sioux Falls, SD	4.3	2.5	0.3	0.1	1.5
Springfield, IL	2.3	1.3	0.4	0.1	0.5
Tallahassee, FL	6.6	1.9	1.3	1.0	2.4
Tampa, FL	19.6	3.8	6.2	4.0	5.6
Tucson, AZ	37.2	33.5	0.8	0.2	2.7
Tulsa, OK	9.9	7.8	0.4	0.1	1.6
Tuscaloosa, AL	3.5	2.2	0.2	0.1	1.0
Virginia Beach, VA	6.7	2.2	2.0	0.3	2.3
Washington, DC	15.8	2.3	1.1	0.3	12.1
Wichita, KS	13.1	11.0	0.4	0.1	1.5
Winston-Salem, NC	10.2	6.7	0.9	0.2	2.5
U.S.	18.0	11.2	1.7	0.7	4.3

Note: Persons of Hispanic or Latino origin can be of any race; Figures cover the Metropolitan Statistical Area (MSA)—see Appendix B for areas included
Source: U.S. Census Bureau, 2015-2019 American Community Survey 5-Year Estimates

Age: City

City	Under Age 5	Age 5–19	Age 20–34	Age 35–44	Age 45–54	Age 55–64	Age 65–74	Age 75–84	Age 85+	Median Age
Albuquerque, NM	5.9	19.0	22.6	13.0	12.0	12.2	8.8	4.4	1.8	36.6
Allentown, PA	7.6	22.8	24.6	11.9	11.3	10.0	6.5	3.3	2.0	31.6
Anchorage, AK	7.2	19.6	25.4	12.9	12.3	12.2	7.0	2.6	0.9	33.6
Ann Arbor, MI	3.7	18.5	40.1	9.5	8.3	8.2	6.8	3.4	1.5	27.5
Athens, GA	5.3	20.8	34.5	11.2	8.8	8.8	6.3	3.2	1.0	28.0
Atlanta, GA	5.4	16.9	30.7	13.8	11.8	9.8	6.8	3.4	1.4	33.3
Austin, TX	6.4	16.7	30.2	16.0	11.9	9.8	5.6	2.3	1.0	33.3
Baton Rouge, LA	6.7	19.6	28.3	10.5	10.1	11.1	8.0	3.9	1.9	31.5
Boise City, ID	5.7	18.9	23.1	14.0	12.3	12.0	8.4	3.7	1.8	36.6
Boston, MA	5.0	15.4	34.8	12.4	10.9	10.1	6.6	3.3	1.6	32.2
Boulder, CO	2.9	18.7	37.6	10.2	10.4	8.9	6.6	3.0	1.6	28.6
Cape Coral, FL	4.4	15.9	15.7	11.4	14.2	15.7	13.2	6.7	2.8	46.7
Cedar Rapids, IA	6.5	18.9	22.8	13.0	11.6	11.9	8.4	4.4	2.4	36.3
Charleston, SC	6.0	14.5	29.8	12.4	10.7	11.9	9.0	3.7	1.9	34.8
Charlotte, NC	6.8	19.4	25.1	14.8	13.1	10.7	6.4	2.8	1.1	34.2
Chicago, IL	6.3	17.0	27.3	14.0	11.9	10.9	7.2	3.7	1.5	34.6
Cincinnati, OH	7.1	19.0	28.3	11.3	10.5	11.6	7.0	3.3	1.9	32.2
Clarksville, TN	9.0	20.6	30.7	13.0	10.0	8.5	5.2	2.1	0.9	29.6
Cleveland, OH	6.3	18.3	23.7	11.5	12.4	13.8	8.0	4.2	1.8	36.3
College Station, TX	5.1	22.9	42.6	9.9	6.8	6.0	4.3	1.9	0.6	23.0
Colorado Springs, CO	6.5	19.3	24.6	12.6	11.9	11.6	8.1	3.8	1.5	34.7
Columbia, MO	5.9	19.0	34.6	11.0	9.5	9.4	6.0	3.2	1.3	28.5
Columbia, SC	5.1	23.2	31.9	10.1	10.1	9.4	6.2	2.8	1.2	28.5
Columbus, OH	7.3	18.2	29.4	12.9	11.3	10.6	6.2	2.7	1.3	32.2
Dallas, TX	7.5	19.9	26.4	13.7	11.8	10.4	6.1	2.9	1.2	32.7
Davenport, IA	6.4	19.2	21.8	12.3	12.3	12.7	8.6	4.1	2.5	36.7
Denver, CO	6.1	15.7	29.2	15.9	11.6	10.0	7.0	3.1	1.5	34.5
Des Moines, IA	6.9	19.7	24.5	13.0	12.0	11.8	7.1	3.3	1.6	34.2
Durham, NC	6.8	18.4	26.7	14.0	11.9	10.7	7.1	3.0	1.4	33.9
Edison, NJ	6.1	18.4	17.9	15.7	14.0	13.1	8.4	4.1	2.3	39.6
El Paso, TX	7.4	22.2	23.2	12.4	11.7	10.6	7.1	3.9	1.7	32.9
Fargo, ND	6.7	17.4	32.0	12.3	9.5	10.1	6.6	3.3	2.0	31.0
Fayetteville, NC	7.7	18.9	30.9	11.0	9.8	10.1	6.7	3.5	1.4	30.0
Fort Collins, CO	5.0	19.5	33.9	11.6	9.7	9.5	6.3	3.0	1.3	29.3
Fort Wayne, IN	7.1	20.6	22.2	12.1	11.7	12.1	8.3	3.8	1.8	35.0
Fort Worth, TX	8.0	22.5	23.3	14.0	12.4	10.1	5.9	2.6	1.2	32.6
Grand Rapids, MI	6.9	18.6	30.3	11.2	10.1	10.8	6.6	3.4	2.1	31.4
Greeley, CO	6.5	23.6	24.8	12.0	10.9	10.5	6.8	3.4	1.7	31.5
Green Bay, WI	7.6	20.3	22.8	12.4	12.3	11.8	7.2	3.7	1.9	34.5
Greensboro, NC	6.0	19.9	24.0	12.5	12.4	11.5	8.0	3.9	1.8	35.1
Honolulu, HI	5.2	14.1	22.0	13.0	12.8	12.9	10.5	5.5	3.9	41.5
Houston, TX	7.6	19.9	25.9	14.0	11.7	10.4	6.3	3.0	1.2	33.0
Huntsville, AL	6.1	17.6	23.8	11.6	12.1	12.7	8.9	5.2	2.1	36.9
Indianapolis, IN	7.3	19.8	24.1	12.8	11.9	11.9	7.2	3.4	1.5	34.2
Jacksonville, FL	6.9	18.3	23.3	12.7	12.8	12.5	8.2	3.8	1.5	35.9
Kansas City, MO	6.8	18.4	24.6	13.2	12.0	12.2	7.5	3.6	1.7	35.1
Lafayette, LA	5.7	18.5	24.4	11.5	11.5	13.5	8.9	4.2	1.7	35.8
Lakeland, FL	4.9	17.8	19.9	11.9	11.4	11.9	11.8	7.2	3.2	41.1
Las Vegas, NV	6.4	19.5	20.2	13.3	13.4	12.1	9.1	4.3	1.5	37.8
Lexington, KY	6.1	18.4	26.0	13.1	11.8	11.5	7.8	3.7	1.5	34.6
Lincoln, NE	6.5	19.9	26.7	12.4	10.5	10.9	7.7	3.6	1.7	32.7
Little Rock, AR	6.7	18.8	22.1	13.5	11.9	12.8	8.4	3.6	2.2	36.7
Los Angeles, CA	5.9	17.5	25.7	14.3	13.2	11.0	7.0	3.6	1.7	35.6
Louisville, KY	6.5	18.5	21.5	12.4	12.8	13.4	8.7	4.3	1.9	37.6

Table continued on following page.

Appendix A: Comparative Statistics

City	Under Age 5	Age 5–19	Age 20–34	Age 35–44	Age 45–54	Age 55–64	Age 65–74	Age 75–84	Age 85+	Median Age
Madison, WI	4.9	16.4	35.5	12.2	9.7	9.7	6.9	3.2	1.5	31.0
Manchester, NH	6.0	15.7	26.6	12.8	13.2	12.4	7.2	3.7	2.3	36.0
Memphis, TN	7.6	19.9	23.7	12.0	11.8	12.0	7.7	3.6	1.5	34.0
Miami, FL	5.9	13.4	23.0	14.6	14.5	11.8	8.5	5.8	2.6	40.1
Midland, TX	8.8	21.0	25.5	13.0	10.8	10.5	5.7	3.1	1.6	31.7
Milwaukee, WI	7.4	21.9	25.6	12.6	11.2	10.7	6.3	2.8	1.4	31.5
Minneapolis, MN	6.5	16.9	32.0	13.8	10.8	10.1	6.3	2.6	1.1	32.3
Nashville, TN	6.8	17.0	27.6	13.8	11.8	11.4	7.1	3.3	1.3	34.2
New Haven, CT	6.3	21.2	29.6	12.6	11.1	8.9	6.4	2.7	1.2	30.8
New Orleans, LA	5.9	16.6	24.6	13.4	12.1	13.3	8.7	3.7	1.7	36.8
New York, NY	6.5	16.5	24.3	13.7	12.7	11.8	8.1	4.4	2.0	36.7
Oklahoma City, OK	7.6	20.6	23.1	13.4	11.5	11.5	7.4	3.5	1.5	34.1
Omaha, NE	7.3	20.4	22.9	12.7	11.9	11.9	7.6	3.6	1.7	34.5
Orlando, FL	6.7	15.9	29.7	15.1	12.1	10.1	6.3	2.7	1.2	33.8
Peoria, IL	7.6	19.5	22.5	12.1	11.3	11.8	8.4	4.4	2.4	35.2
Philadelphia, PA	6.7	18.0	26.2	12.4	11.7	11.6	7.7	4.0	1.8	34.4
Phoenix, AZ	7.2	21.6	23.2	13.8	12.8	10.9	6.5	2.9	1.2	33.8
Pittsburgh, PA	4.7	15.4	33.3	10.6	9.5	11.8	8.1	4.3	2.3	32.9
Portland, OR	5.3	14.6	25.9	17.1	13.1	11.3	8.0	3.3	1.5	37.1
Providence, RI	6.3	21.9	28.3	12.3	10.9	9.4	5.9	3.2	1.7	30.6
Provo, UT	7.1	20.7	47.4	8.3	5.4	5.0	3.1	2.0	0.9	23.6
Raleigh, NC	5.9	18.9	27.5	14.5	12.7	9.9	6.4	2.9	1.3	33.6
Reno, NV	6.2	17.8	24.7	12.6	11.7	12.2	9.3	4.1	1.4	35.8
Richmond, VA	5.9	15.6	30.2	11.8	11.2	12.4	7.7	3.3	1.8	34.0
Riverside, CA	6.2	22.3	26.5	12.4	12.0	10.0	6.3	3.1	1.3	31.6
Rochester, MN	7.2	18.8	22.6	13.1	11.6	11.8	8.0	4.6	2.4	35.7
Sacramento, CA	6.6	18.8	25.4	13.5	11.6	11.1	7.8	3.5	1.8	34.5
Salt Lake City, UT	6.2	17.1	31.6	13.8	10.1	10.2	6.6	3.2	1.3	32.3
San Antonio, TX	6.9	21.0	24.2	13.2	12.0	10.7	7.1	3.5	1.5	33.6
San Diego, CA	5.9	16.8	27.4	13.9	12.3	11.0	7.3	3.7	1.6	34.9
San Francisco, CA	4.5	10.5	29.0	15.8	13.2	11.6	8.5	4.5	2.5	38.2
San Jose, CA	6.1	18.4	22.7	14.4	13.9	11.8	7.3	3.7	1.5	36.7
Santa Rosa, CA	5.9	17.8	21.2	12.8	12.6	12.9	9.6	4.8	2.3	38.8
Savannah, GA	6.4	18.2	29.1	11.6	10.4	11.2	7.7	3.7	1.7	32.6
Seattle, WA	4.8	12.8	31.8	15.3	12.3	10.7	7.4	3.3	1.8	35.3
Sioux Falls, SD	7.5	19.9	23.5	13.3	11.4	11.7	7.6	3.4	1.7	34.4
Springfield, IL	6.1	18.2	20.2	11.6	12.2	14.0	10.0	5.3	2.3	39.4
Tallahassee, FL	4.9	19.2	38.0	10.0	8.8	8.7	6.3	2.8	1.2	26.9
Tampa, FL	6.4	18.5	24.2	13.5	13.4	11.8	7.3	3.5	1.5	35.7
Tucson, AZ	6.0	19.1	26.5	11.9	10.9	11.2	8.3	4.2	1.9	33.7
Tulsa, OK	7.1	20.0	22.8	12.4	11.4	12.3	8.1	4.0	1.9	35.1
Tuscaloosa, AL	5.2	22.9	29.5	10.0	9.9	10.3	6.9	3.9	1.4	29.3
Virginia Beach, VA	6.3	18.2	23.7	13.0	12.7	12.1	8.1	4.0	1.6	36.2
Washington, DC	6.5	14.5	31.0	14.8	11.0	10.1	7.0	3.5	1.6	34.0
Wichita, KS	7.0	20.7	22.4	11.9	11.6	12.5	8.2	3.9	1.8	35.0
Winston-Salem, NC	6.5	20.9	21.8	12.4	12.1	12.0	8.1	4.3	1.7	35.5
U.S.	6.1	19.1	20.7	12.6	13.0	12.9	9.1	4.6	1.9	38.1

Source: U.S. Census Bureau, 2015-2019 American Community Survey 5-Year Estimates

Age: Metro Area

Metro Area	Under Age 5	Age 5–19	Age 20–34	Age 35–44	Age 45–54	Age 55–64	Age 65–74	Age 75–84	Age 85+	Median Age
Albuquerque, NM	5.7	19.2	20.7	12.6	12.4	13.2	9.8	4.7	1.8	38.2
Allentown, PA	5.3	18.7	18.6	11.9	13.8	14.1	9.9	5.2	2.6	41.4
Anchorage, AK	7.2	20.2	24.0	13.0	12.4	12.4	7.2	2.6	0.9	34.0
Ann Arbor, MI	4.9	19.5	27.4	11.5	11.8	11.5	8.2	3.7	1.6	33.6
Athens, GA	5.4	21.1	27.1	12.0	11.0	10.7	7.8	3.8	1.2	32.2
Atlanta, GA	6.4	21.0	20.6	14.0	14.3	11.8	7.5	3.2	1.1	36.4
Austin, TX	6.4	19.7	24.3	15.5	12.9	10.6	6.7	2.7	1.1	34.7
Baton Rouge, LA	6.5	20.1	22.7	12.7	12.2	12.2	8.4	3.9	1.4	35.6
Boise City, ID	6.3	21.7	20.0	13.4	12.5	11.8	8.7	4.0	1.4	36.3
Boston, MA	5.3	17.7	22.2	12.5	13.7	13.2	8.8	4.4	2.1	38.7
Boulder, CO	4.6	19.0	24.3	12.6	13.1	12.7	8.4	3.7	1.6	36.6
Cape Coral, FL	4.7	15.2	15.8	10.3	11.9	14.1	15.5	9.3	3.3	48.5
Cedar Rapids, IA	6.2	19.5	19.6	12.7	12.9	12.9	9.0	4.8	2.3	38.4
Charleston, SC	6.1	18.5	22.1	13.2	12.7	12.8	9.3	3.9	1.5	37.2
Charlotte, NC	6.2	20.2	20.1	13.9	14.2	12.1	8.2	3.8	1.4	37.5
Chicago, IL	6.1	19.4	21.0	13.3	13.3	12.7	8.2	4.1	1.8	37.5
Cincinnati, OH	6.3	20.1	19.9	12.4	13.2	13.4	8.7	4.2	1.9	37.9
Clarksville, TN	8.4	20.8	27.0	12.4	10.8	9.8	6.6	3.2	1.2	31.1
Cleveland, OH	5.6	18.1	18.9	11.6	13.3	14.5	10.1	5.4	2.5	41.3
College Station, TX	6.1	20.9	32.9	11.0	9.5	9.2	6.1	3.0	1.2	27.8
Colorado Springs, CO	6.6	20.2	23.6	12.5	12.1	12.1	7.9	3.5	1.3	34.6
Columbia, MO	5.8	19.4	28.5	11.6	10.7	11.3	7.5	3.7	1.4	32.1
Columbia, SC	5.8	20.2	21.6	12.5	12.7	12.7	8.9	4.1	1.5	36.6
Columbus, OH	6.7	19.8	22.2	13.4	13.0	12.1	7.8	3.6	1.5	36.0
Dallas, TX	7.0	21.8	21.5	14.2	13.4	11.2	6.8	3.1	1.1	34.8
Davenport, IA	6.2	19.3	18.3	12.3	12.5	13.8	10.0	5.3	2.4	39.7
Denver, CO	6.1	18.9	22.6	14.6	13.2	12.1	7.8	3.3	1.4	36.5
Des Moines, IA	7.0	20.5	20.7	13.7	12.8	11.9	7.9	3.9	1.6	36.2
Durham, NC	5.7	18.6	22.3	13.0	13.0	12.6	9.1	4.0	1.7	37.6
Edison, NJ	6.1	17.8	21.2	13.1	13.6	12.8	8.6	4.6	2.2	38.6
El Paso, TX	7.6	22.8	23.3	12.5	11.5	10.4	6.7	3.7	1.5	32.2
Fargo, ND	7.1	19.5	27.4	12.8	10.5	10.7	6.6	3.4	1.9	32.5
Fayetteville, NC	7.7	20.7	25.7	12.5	11.4	10.6	7.0	3.4	1.1	32.3
Fort Collins, CO	5.1	18.4	25.2	12.3	11.2	12.6	9.4	4.1	1.7	36.0
Fort Wayne, IN	7.0	21.1	20.1	12.3	12.4	12.6	8.6	4.1	1.8	36.4
Fort Worth, TX	7.0	21.8	21.5	14.2	13.4	11.2	6.8	3.1	1.1	34.8
Grand Rapids, MI	6.5	20.6	21.8	12.3	12.4	12.5	8.1	4.0	1.9	35.8
Greeley, CO	7.2	22.1	21.5	13.6	12.2	11.5	7.4	3.2	1.2	34.4
Green Bay, WI	6.2	19.7	19.2	12.4	13.4	13.7	9.0	4.6	1.8	38.8
Greensboro, NC	5.8	19.7	19.8	12.1	13.7	13.0	9.3	4.7	1.9	38.8
Honolulu, HI	6.4	17.0	22.6	12.7	12.1	11.9	9.4	5.0	2.9	37.9
Houston, TX	7.3	21.9	21.7	14.2	12.8	11.2	6.8	3.0	1.0	34.3
Huntsville, AL	5.8	19.0	20.3	12.4	14.1	13.5	8.6	4.5	1.6	38.7
Indianapolis, IN	6.7	20.5	20.7	13.2	13.1	12.3	8.0	3.8	1.6	36.5
Jacksonville, FL	6.2	18.5	20.7	12.7	13.3	13.2	9.5	4.3	1.6	38.3
Kansas City, MO	6.5	20.0	20.0	13.2	12.9	12.8	8.5	4.2	1.8	37.4
Lafayette, LA	6.9	20.2	21.3	12.6	12.4	12.9	8.1	4.0	1.6	36.0
Lakeland, FL	5.8	18.8	19.0	11.8	12.1	12.3	11.4	6.7	2.1	40.2
Las Vegas, NV	6.3	19.3	21.1	13.8	13.3	11.7	8.9	4.2	1.3	37.3
Lexington, KY	6.2	19.0	23.2	13.0	12.6	12.1	8.3	4.0	1.5	36.1
Lincoln, NE	6.4	20.4	25.0	12.3	10.9	11.4	8.1	3.8	1.8	33.7
Little Rock, AR	6.4	19.6	21.3	12.9	12.4	12.5	8.9	4.2	1.8	36.9
Los Angeles, CA	6.0	18.6	22.7	13.5	13.6	12.0	7.7	4.0	1.9	36.8
Louisville, KY	6.1	18.7	19.9	12.8	13.3	13.6	9.3	4.4	1.8	39.0

Table continued on following page.

Metro Area	Under Age 5	Age 5–19	Age 20–34	Age 35–44	Age 45–54	Age 55–64	Age 65–74	Age 75–84	Age 85+	Median Age
Madison, WI	5.6	18.2	24.4	13.0	12.3	12.5	8.5	3.8	1.7	36.2
Manchester, NH	5.2	17.8	19.8	12.3	14.9	14.7	9.0	4.3	1.9	40.7
Memphis, TN	6.8	20.7	20.8	12.7	12.9	12.5	8.3	3.8	1.4	36.3
Miami, FL	5.7	17.0	19.4	13.1	14.2	12.8	9.4	5.8	2.7	41.0
Midland, TX	8.8	22.1	24.4	13.1	10.6	10.8	5.8	3.1	1.5	31.7
Milwaukee, WI	6.2	19.6	20.4	12.5	12.8	13.3	8.7	4.3	2.2	37.8
Minneapolis, MN	6.5	19.7	20.7	13.3	13.3	13.0	8.0	3.8	1.7	37.1
Nashville, TN	6.4	19.4	22.1	13.7	13.3	12.3	8.0	3.6	1.3	36.4
New Haven, CT	5.2	18.2	20.2	11.8	13.7	13.8	9.5	4.9	2.6	40.3
New Orleans, LA	6.2	18.3	21.0	12.8	12.8	13.7	9.3	4.3	1.7	38.3
New York, NY	6.1	17.8	21.2	13.1	13.6	12.8	8.6	4.6	2.2	38.6
Oklahoma City, OK	6.8	20.6	22.2	13.0	11.8	12.0	8.1	3.9	1.6	35.2
Omaha, NE	7.2	21.0	20.8	13.2	12.3	12.2	8.0	3.8	1.6	35.7
Orlando, FL	5.9	18.7	22.2	13.7	13.3	11.7	8.5	4.3	1.7	37.2
Peoria, IL	6.3	19.1	18.5	12.3	12.6	13.5	9.9	5.3	2.6	39.9
Philadelphia, PA	5.9	18.6	20.7	12.3	13.4	13.5	8.9	4.6	2.1	38.8
Phoenix, AZ	6.4	20.3	21.0	13.1	12.5	11.4	8.9	4.6	1.7	36.7
Pittsburgh, PA	5.1	16.5	19.2	11.5	13.1	15.2	10.8	5.8	3.0	43.1
Portland, OR	5.7	18.1	21.3	14.7	13.3	12.5	9.0	3.8	1.7	38.1
Providence, RI	5.2	17.9	20.5	11.9	13.9	13.9	9.5	4.8	2.5	40.3
Provo, UT	9.6	28.3	26.8	12.6	8.4	6.7	4.5	2.3	0.8	24.8
Raleigh, NC	6.2	20.8	20.4	14.8	14.5	11.6	7.4	3.2	1.2	36.7
Reno, NV	6.0	18.1	21.5	12.2	12.8	13.2	10.2	4.4	1.4	38.5
Richmond, VA	5.8	18.7	20.7	12.8	13.6	13.5	9.2	4.1	1.8	38.8
Riverside, CA	6.8	22.1	21.8	12.8	12.5	11.2	7.5	3.8	1.4	34.5
Rochester, MN	6.7	19.8	18.9	12.6	12.4	13.4	8.8	5.0	2.3	38.4
Sacramento, CA	6.1	19.6	21.0	12.8	12.8	12.6	8.8	4.3	1.9	37.4
Salt Lake City, UT	7.6	22.6	23.3	14.6	11.2	10.1	6.4	3.0	1.1	32.7
San Antonio, TX	6.9	21.4	22.2	13.3	12.4	11.2	7.6	3.7	1.5	34.7
San Diego, CA	6.3	18.2	24.2	13.3	12.5	11.7	7.9	4.0	1.8	35.8
San Francisco, CA	5.5	16.5	22.0	14.5	13.8	12.6	8.7	4.4	2.1	39.0
San Jose, CA	6.1	18.6	22.3	14.5	13.8	11.7	7.4	4.0	1.8	37.1
Santa Rosa, CA	5.0	17.2	18.7	12.4	13.0	14.5	11.6	5.1	2.2	42.1
Savannah, GA	6.6	19.4	23.2	12.9	12.1	11.9	8.5	4.0	1.5	35.6
Seattle, WA	6.1	17.6	23.0	14.3	13.4	12.4	7.9	3.5	1.6	37.0
Sioux Falls, SD	7.6	20.7	21.4	13.5	11.8	12.0	7.8	3.4	1.8	35.2
Springfield, IL	5.8	19.0	18.4	12.2	13.1	14.2	10.1	5.1	2.1	40.4
Tallahassee, FL	5.2	18.9	27.4	11.5	11.2	11.8	8.7	3.8	1.5	33.8
Tampa, FL	5.4	16.8	18.9	12.4	13.5	13.6	10.9	6.0	2.5	42.1
Tucson, AZ	5.7	18.6	21.5	11.4	11.2	12.6	10.9	6.0	2.2	38.5
Tulsa, OK	6.7	20.5	20.1	12.6	12.4	12.7	8.9	4.5	1.7	37.0
Tuscaloosa, AL	6.0	20.5	24.3	11.8	11.5	12.0	8.4	4.1	1.5	34.4
Virginia Beach, VA	6.3	18.6	23.4	12.3	12.4	12.7	8.5	4.2	1.7	36.3
Washington, DC	6.5	19.0	21.3	14.3	14.0	12.1	7.7	3.6	1.4	37.0
Wichita, KS	6.9	21.3	20.4	12.1	11.8	12.7	8.3	4.3	1.9	36.0
Winston-Salem, NC	5.7	19.4	18.3	11.9	14.1	13.7	9.9	5.3	1.8	40.6
U.S.	6.1	19.1	20.7	12.6	13.0	12.9	9.1	4.6	1.9	38.1

Note: Figures cover the Metropolitan Statistical Area (MSA)—see Appendix B for areas included
Source: U.S. Census Bureau, 2015-2019 American Community Survey 5-Year Estimates

Religious Groups by Family

Area[1]	Catholic	Baptist	Non-Den.	Methodist[2]	Lutheran	LDS[3]	Pentecostal	Presbyterian[4]	Muslim[5]	Judaism
Albuquerque, NM	27.1	3.7	4.2	1.4	0.9	2.3	1.4	1.0	0.2	0.2
Allentown, PA	23.1	0.4	1.9	3.9	7.9	0.3	0.4	6.2	0.6	0.6
Anchorage, AK	6.9	5.0	6.4	1.3	1.9	5.1	1.8	0.6	0.2	0.1
Ann Arbor, MI	12.3	2.2	1.5	3.0	2.8	0.8	1.9	2.9	1.2	0.9
Athens, GA	4.4	16.2	2.2	8.3	0.3	0.8	2.8	2.0	0.3	0.2
Atlanta, GA	7.4	17.4	6.8	7.8	0.5	0.7	2.6	1.8	0.7	0.5
Austin, TX	16.0	10.3	4.5	3.6	1.9	1.1	0.8	1.0	1.2	0.2
Baton Rouge, LA	22.5	18.2	9.6	4.6	0.2	0.7	1.1	0.6	0.2	0.1
Boise City, ID	8.0	2.9	4.1	2.1	1.1	15.8	2.3	0.6	0.1	0.1
Boston, MA	44.3	1.1	1.0	0.9	0.3	0.4	0.6	1.6	0.4	1.4
Boulder, CO	20.1	2.3	4.7	1.7	3.0	2.9	0.4	2.0	0.1	0.7
Cape Coral, FL	16.2	4.9	3.0	2.5	1.1	0.5	4.3	1.4	0.9	0.2
Cedar Rapids, IA	18.8	2.3	3.0	7.3	11.3	0.8	1.8	3.2	0.5	0.1
Charleston, SC	6.1	12.4	7.0	10.0	1.1	0.9	2.0	2.3	0.1	0.3
Charlotte, NC	5.9	17.2	6.7	8.6	1.3	0.7	3.2	4.5	0.2	0.3
Chicago, IL	34.2	3.2	4.4	1.9	3.0	0.3	1.2	1.9	3.2	0.8
Cincinnati, OH	19.0	9.5	3.6	3.8	1.1	0.5	2.2	1.5	0.2	0.5
Clarksville, TN	4.0	30.9	2.2	6.1	0.5	1.5	1.8	1.0	0.1	<0.1
Cleveland, OH	28.8	4.3	3.3	2.8	2.5	0.3	1.1	2.0	0.1	1.4
College Station, TX	11.7	15.6	3.9	4.7	1.5	1.2	0.6	0.9	1.1	<0.1
Colorado Springs, CO	8.3	4.3	7.4	2.4	1.9	3.0	1.0	2.0	<0.1	0.1
Columbia, MO	6.6	14.6	5.4	4.3	1.7	1.3	1.0	2.3	0.3	0.2
Columbia, SC	3.1	18.0	5.2	9.3	3.4	1.0	2.6	3.3	0.1	0.2
Columbus, OH	11.7	5.3	3.5	4.7	2.4	0.7	1.9	2.0	0.8	0.5
Dallas, TX	13.3	18.7	7.7	5.2	0.7	1.1	2.1	0.9	2.4	0.3
Davenport, IA	14.9	4.9	2.7	5.3	8.6	0.8	1.4	2.9	0.9	0.1
Denver, CO	16.0	2.9	4.6	1.7	2.1	2.4	1.2	1.5	0.5	0.6
Des Moines, IA	13.6	4.7	3.3	6.9	8.2	0.9	2.3	2.9	0.3	0.3
Durham, NC	5.0	13.8	5.6	8.1	0.4	0.7	1.3	2.5	0.4	0.5
Edison, NJ	36.9	1.8	1.7	1.3	0.7	0.3	0.8	1.0	2.3	4.7
El Paso, TX	43.2	3.7	4.9	0.8	0.3	1.5	1.4	0.2	<0.1	0.2
Fargo, ND	17.4	0.4	0.4	3.3	32.5	0.6	1.5	1.8	0.1	<0.1
Fayetteville, NC	2.6	14.1	10.4	6.2	0.1	1.4	4.8	2.1	0.1	<0.1
Fort Collins, CO	11.8	2.2	6.3	4.3	3.4	2.9	4.7	1.9	0.1	<0.1
Fort Wayne, IN	14.2	6.0	6.8	5.1	8.5	0.4	1.4	1.6	0.2	0.1
Fort Worth, TX	13.3	18.7	7.7	5.2	0.7	1.1	2.1	0.9	2.4	0.3
Grand Rapids, MI	17.1	1.7	8.3	3.0	2.1	0.5	1.1	9.9	1.0	0.1
Greeley, CO	13.5	1.8	1.5	2.6	2.0	1.9	1.8	1.4	0.1	<0.1
Green Bay, WI	42.0	0.7	3.4	2.2	12.7	0.3	0.6	1.0	0.1	<0.1
Greensboro, NC	2.6	12.8	7.4	9.8	0.6	0.8	2.4	3.1	0.6	0.4
Honolulu, HI	18.2	1.9	2.2	0.8	0.3	5.1	4.1	1.4	<0.1	<0.1
Houston, TX	17.0	16.0	7.2	4.8	1.0	1.1	1.5	0.8	2.6	0.3
Huntsville, AL	3.9	27.6	3.1	7.5	0.7	1.1	1.2	1.7	0.2	0.1
Indianapolis, IN	10.5	10.2	7.1	4.9	1.6	0.7	1.6	1.6	0.2	0.3
Jacksonville, FL	9.8	18.5	7.7	4.5	0.6	1.1	1.9	1.6	0.6	0.4
Kansas City, MO	12.6	13.1	5.2	5.8	2.2	2.4	2.6	1.6	0.3	0.4
Lafayette, LA	47.0	14.7	3.9	2.5	0.2	0.4	2.9	0.1	0.1	<0.1
Lakeland, FL	7.5	13.6	5.0	3.9	0.9	0.7	4.0	1.6	0.4	<0.1
Las Vegas, NV	18.1	2.9	3.0	0.4	0.7	6.3	1.5	0.2	<0.1	0.3
Lexington, KY	6.7	24.9	2.3	5.9	0.4	1.0	2.1	1.3	0.1	0.3
Lincoln, NE	14.7	2.4	1.9	7.1	11.2	1.1	1.4	3.9	0.2	0.1
Little Rock, AR	4.5	25.9	6.0	7.3	0.5	0.9	2.8	0.8	0.1	0.1
Los Angeles, CA	33.8	2.7	3.6	1.0	0.6	1.7	1.7	0.9	0.7	0.9
Louisville, KY	13.6	25.0	1.7	3.7	0.6	0.8	0.9	1.1	0.5	0.4
Madison, WI	21.8	1.1	1.5	3.6	12.7	0.5	0.3	2.1	0.4	0.4

Table continued on following page.

Appendix A: Comparative Statistics   A-25

Area[1]	Catholic	Baptist	Non-Den.	Methodist[2]	Lutheran	LDS[3]	Pentecostal	Presbyterian[4]	Muslim[5]	Judaism
Manchester, NH	31.1	1.3	2.3	1.1	0.5	0.6	0.4	2.0	0.3	0.5
Memphis, TN	5.2	30.8	5.4	6.2	0.3	0.6	4.7	2.4	0.3	0.6
Miami, FL	18.5	5.3	4.1	1.2	0.4	0.5	1.7	0.6	0.9	1.5
Midland, TX	22.4	25.2	8.8	4.2	0.6	1.2	1.6	1.8	3.7	<0.1
Milwaukee, WI	24.6	3.1	3.8	1.5	10.7	0.4	1.9	1.5	0.5	0.5
Minneapolis, MN	21.7	2.4	2.9	2.7	14.4	0.6	1.7	1.8	0.4	0.7
Nashville, TN	4.1	25.2	5.8	6.1	0.3	0.7	2.1	2.1	0.3	0.1
New Haven, CT	35.3	1.4	1.9	1.5	0.6	0.3	1.0	2.2	0.5	1.2
New Orleans, LA	31.5	8.4	3.7	2.6	0.8	0.5	2.1	0.5	0.4	0.5
New York, NY	36.9	1.8	1.7	1.3	0.7	0.3	0.8	1.0	2.3	4.7
Oklahoma City, OK	6.3	25.3	7.0	10.6	0.7	1.2	3.1	0.9	0.2	0.1
Omaha, NE	21.6	4.5	1.8	3.9	7.8	1.7	1.2	2.2	0.5	0.4
Orlando, FL	13.2	6.9	5.6	2.9	0.9	0.9	3.2	1.3	1.3	0.2
Peoria, IL	11.4	5.5	5.2	4.9	6.1	0.5	1.5	2.8	5.2	0.1
Philadelphia, PA	33.4	3.9	2.8	2.9	1.8	0.3	0.8	2.1	1.2	1.3
Phoenix, AZ	13.3	3.4	5.1	1.0	1.6	6.1	2.9	0.6	0.1	0.3
Pittsburgh, PA	32.8	2.3	2.8	5.6	3.3	0.3	1.1	4.6	0.3	0.7
Portland, OR	10.5	2.3	4.5	1.0	1.6	3.7	2.0	0.9	0.1	0.3
Providence, RI	47.0	1.4	1.2	0.8	0.5	0.3	0.5	1.0	0.1	0.7
Provo, UT	1.3	<0.1	<0.1	0.1	<0.1	88.5	0.1	<0.1	<0.1	<0.1
Raleigh, NC	9.1	12.1	5.9	6.7	0.9	0.8	2.2	2.2	0.9	0.3
Reno, NV	14.3	1.5	3.1	0.9	0.7	4.6	1.9	0.4	<0.1	0.1
Richmond, VA	5.9	19.9	5.4	6.1	0.6	0.9	1.8	2.1	2.7	0.3
Riverside, CA	24.8	2.6	5.5	0.6	0.5	2.4	1.5	0.6	0.5	<0.1
Rochester, MN	23.3	1.6	4.6	4.8	21.0	1.1	1.2	2.9	0.2	0.2
Sacramento, CA	16.1	3.1	4.0	1.7	0.7	3.3	2.0	0.8	0.8	0.2
Salt Lake City, UT	8.9	0.8	0.5	0.5	0.5	58.9	0.6	0.3	0.4	0.1
San Antonio, TX	28.4	8.5	6.0	3.0	1.6	1.4	1.3	0.7	0.9	0.2
San Diego, CA	25.9	2.0	4.8	1.1	0.9	2.3	1.0	0.9	0.7	0.5
San Francisco, CA	20.7	2.5	2.4	1.9	0.5	1.5	1.2	1.1	1.2	0.8
San Jose, CA	26.0	1.3	4.2	1.0	0.5	1.4	1.1	0.7	1.0	0.6
Santa Rosa, CA	22.2	1.3	1.5	0.9	0.9	1.9	0.6	0.9	0.4	0.4
Savannah, GA	7.0	19.6	6.9	8.9	1.6	0.9	2.3	1.0	0.1	0.8
Seattle, WA	12.3	2.1	5.0	1.2	2.0	3.3	2.8	1.4	0.4	0.4
Sioux Falls, SD	14.9	3.0	1.5	3.8	21.4	0.7	1.0	6.2	0.3	<0.1
Springfield, IL	15.5	11.7	2.7	6.8	5.6	0.7	4.9	2.0	1.5	0.2
Tallahassee, FL	4.8	16.0	6.7	9.1	0.4	1.0	2.1	1.5	0.8	0.3
Tampa, FL	10.8	7.0	3.7	3.4	0.9	0.6	2.1	0.9	1.2	0.4
Tucson, AZ	20.7	3.3	3.7	1.3	1.5	2.9	1.5	1.0	<0.1	0.5
Tulsa, OK	5.8	22.9	7.6	9.2	0.7	1.1	3.3	1.2	0.3	0.2
Tuscaloosa, AL	1.7	32.2	4.5	8.3	<0.1	0.6	1.5	1.3	0.1	<0.1
Virginia Beach, VA	6.4	11.5	6.1	5.2	0.7	0.9	1.9	2.0	2.0	0.3
Washington, DC	14.5	7.3	4.8	4.5	1.2	1.1	1.0	1.3	2.3	1.1
Wichita, KS	14.5	13.4	3.1	7.1	1.7	1.4	1.9	1.6	0.1	<0.1
Winston-Salem, NC	3.5	17.4	9.3	12.4	0.7	0.6	2.5	2.2	0.3	0.1
U.S.	19.1	9.3	4.0	4.0	2.3	2.0	1.9	1.6	0.8	0.7

Note: Figures are the number of adherents as a percentage of the total population; (1) Figures cover the Metropolitan Statistical Area—see Appendix B for areas included; (2) Methodist/Pietist; (3) Latter Day Saints; (4) Reformed; (5) Figures are estimates
Source: Association of Statisticians of American Religious Bodies, 2010 U.S. Religion Census: Religious Congregations & Membership Study

Religious Groups by Tradition

Area	Catholic	Evangelical Protestant	Mainline Protestant	Other Tradition	Black Protestant	Orthodox
Albuquerque, NM	27.1	11.2	3.2	3.9	0.2	0.1
Allentown, PA	23.1	5.3	17.7	3.0	0.1	0.6
Anchorage, AK	6.9	15.6	3.5	6.8	0.3	0.6
Ann Arbor, MI	12.3	7.3	7.5	3.7	1.5	0.2
Athens, GA	4.4	21.1	9.7	1.7	2.4	0.1
Atlanta, GA	7.4	26.0	9.8	2.9	3.1	0.2
Austin, TX	16.0	16.1	6.3	3.9	1.3	0.1
Baton Rouge, LA	22.5	24.8	5.6	1.5	5.1	<0.1
Boise City, ID	8.0	12.9	4.3	16.7	<0.1	<0.1
Boston, MA	44.3	3.2	4.5	3.4	0.1	1.0
Boulder, CO	20.1	9.7	6.4	4.8	<0.1	0.2
Cape Coral, FL	16.2	14.3	4.6	2.0	0.3	0.1
Cedar Rapids, IA	18.8	13.7	17.5	1.9	0.1	0.2
Charleston, SC	6.1	19.6	11.1	1.8	7.3	0.1
Charlotte, NC	5.9	27.5	13.3	1.6	2.7	0.4
Chicago, IL	34.2	9.7	5.1	5.0	2.0	0.9
Cincinnati, OH	19.0	15.5	7.1	1.5	1.1	0.1
Clarksville, TN	4.0	35.3	7.2	1.6	2.4	<0.1
Cleveland, OH	28.8	9.0	7.5	2.6	2.1	0.8
College Station, TX	11.7	20.6	6.6	2.5	0.9	<0.1
Colorado Springs, CO	8.3	15.2	5.3	3.7	0.4	0.1
Columbia, MO	6.6	19.9	10.4	2.3	0.4	0.1
Columbia, SC	3.1	25.5	13.4	2.1	5.4	0.1
Columbus, OH	11.7	11.8	9.5	3.1	1.1	0.2
Dallas, TX	13.3	28.3	6.9	4.7	1.7	0.1
Davenport, IA	14.9	11.3	15.1	2.3	1.5	0.1
Denver, CO	16.0	11.0	4.5	4.6	0.3	0.3
Des Moines, IA	13.6	12.3	16.8	1.8	0.9	0.1
Durham, NC	5.0	19.3	11.7	2.9	3.1	<0.1
Edison, NJ	36.9	3.9	4.1	8.3	1.2	0.9
El Paso, TX	43.2	10.8	1.2	2.0	0.2	<0.1
Fargo, ND	17.4	10.7	30.8	0.8	<0.1	<0.1
Fayetteville, NC	2.6	26.7	7.8	1.7	4.3	0.1
Fort Collins, CO	11.8	18.8	5.9	3.9	<0.1	0.1
Fort Wayne, IN	14.2	24.6	9.1	0.9	2.4	0.2
Fort Worth, TX	13.3	28.3	6.9	4.7	1.7	0.1
Grand Rapids, MI	17.1	20.7	7.5	2.1	1.0	0.2
Greeley, CO	13.5	9.2	3.8	2.1	<0.1	<0.1
Green Bay, WI	42.0	14.1	8.1	0.6	<0.1	<0.1
Greensboro, NC	2.6	23.2	14.0	2.1	2.6	<0.1
Honolulu, HI	18.2	9.6	2.9	8.4	<0.1	<0.1
Houston, TX	17.0	24.9	6.6	4.9	1.3	0.2
Huntsville, AL	3.9	33.3	9.6	1.8	1.8	<0.1
Indianapolis, IN	10.5	18.2	9.6	1.6	1.8	0.2
Jacksonville, FL	9.8	27.1	5.6	2.9	4.2	0.2
Kansas City, MO	12.6	20.5	9.9	3.6	2.6	0.1
Lafayette, LA	47.0	12.7	3.2	0.7	9.2	<0.1
Lakeland, FL	7.5	24.6	5.2	1.4	1.7	<0.1
Las Vegas, NV	18.1	7.7	1.3	7.6	0.4	0.4
Lexington, KY	6.7	28.3	10.2	1.7	2.0	0.1
Lincoln, NE	14.7	14.8	16.2	2.0	0.1	<0.1
Little Rock, AR	4.5	33.9	8.1	1.7	3.4	<0.1
Los Angeles, CA	33.8	9.0	2.3	4.6	0.8	0.6
Louisville, KY	13.6	24.5	7.1	2.0	2.9	<0.1
Madison, WI	21.8	7.2	15.3	2.2	0.1	<0.1

Table continued on following page.

Area	Catholic	Evangelical Protestant	Mainline Protestant	Other Tradition	Black Protestant	Orthodox
Manchester, NH	31.1	5.1	4.4	1.8	<0.1	0.7
Memphis, TN	5.2	29.4	8.3	2.1	13.4	<0.1
Miami, FL	18.5	11.4	2.4	3.5	1.7	0.2
Midland, TX	22.4	35.4	7.2	5.3	1.0	<0.1
Milwaukee, WI	24.6	14.6	7.1	2.3	2.4	0.6
Minneapolis, MN	21.7	12.8	14.5	2.2	0.4	0.2
Nashville, TN	4.1	32.9	8.0	1.7	3.3	0.4
New Haven, CT	35.3	3.8	6.1	2.3	0.7	0.4
New Orleans, LA	31.5	12.7	4.0	2.1	2.9	0.1
New York, NY	36.9	3.9	4.1	8.3	1.2	0.9
Oklahoma City, OK	6.3	39.0	9.8	2.7	1.9	0.1
Omaha, NE	21.6	12.1	10.7	3.2	1.4	0.1
Orlando, FL	13.2	17.8	4.7	3.2	1.2	0.3
Peoria, IL	11.4	18.9	11.1	6.1	0.9	0.1
Philadelphia, PA	33.4	6.3	8.9	3.7	1.7	0.4
Phoenix, AZ	13.3	13.2	2.6	7.8	0.1	0.3
Pittsburgh, PA	32.8	7.3	13.8	2.0	0.8	0.6
Portland, OR	10.5	11.6	3.6	5.2	0.1	0.3
Providence, RI	47.0	2.8	4.7	1.6	<0.1	0.5
Provo, UT	1.3	0.4	<0.1	88.8	<0.1	<0.1
Raleigh, NC	9.1	19.9	10.1	3.2	1.7	0.2
Reno, NV	14.3	7.6	1.9	5.1	0.2	0.1
Richmond, VA	5.9	23.6	13.3	4.5	2.4	0.1
Riverside, CA	24.8	11.4	1.3	3.7	0.8	0.1
Rochester, MN	23.3	18.9	21.0	2.0	<0.1	0.1
Sacramento, CA	16.1	11.3	2.2	5.8	0.5	0.3
Salt Lake City, UT	8.9	2.6	1.2	60.0	0.1	0.4
San Antonio, TX	28.4	16.9	5.0	3.1	0.4	<0.1
San Diego, CA	25.9	9.7	2.4	5.2	0.3	0.2
San Francisco, CA	20.7	6.1	3.8	5.2	1.0	0.6
San Jose, CA	26.0	8.2	2.4	6.8	0.1	0.4
Santa Rosa, CA	22.2	5.3	2.3	4.8	<0.1	0.2
Savannah, GA	7.0	25.0	9.4	2.6	8.5	0.1
Seattle, WA	12.3	11.9	4.6	5.9	0.3	0.4
Sioux Falls, SD	14.9	12.9	28.0	1.2	0.1	0.1
Springfield, IL	15.5	21.4	11.6	3.1	2.1	0.1
Tallahassee, FL	4.8	21.9	6.3	2.9	9.1	0.1
Tampa, FL	10.8	13.6	5.1	3.1	1.1	0.8
Tucson, AZ	20.7	10.0	3.7	4.5	0.4	0.2
Tulsa, OK	5.8	34.6	11.2	2.1	1.5	<0.1
Tuscaloosa, AL	1.7	35.2	6.4	0.9	8.5	<0.1
Virginia Beach, VA	6.4	18.0	9.4	3.9	2.2	0.3
Washington, DC	14.5	12.4	8.7	5.9	2.3	0.6
Wichita, KS	14.5	20.7	11.0	2.4	1.8	0.2
Winston-Salem, NC	3.5	29.1	15.6	1.2	2.2	0.2
U.S.	19.1	16.2	7.3	4.3	1.6	0.3

Note: Figures are the number of adherents as a percentage of the total population; (1) Figures cover the Metropolitan Statistical Area—see Appendix B for areas included
Source: Association of Statisticians of American Religious Bodies, 2010 U.S. Religion Census: Religious Congregations & Membership Study

Ancestry: City

City	German	Irish	English	American	Italian	Polish	French[1]	Scottish	Dutch
Albuquerque, NM	9.0	7.0	6.4	3.8	2.9	1.4	1.7	1.6	0.7
Allentown, PA	10.3	4.9	1.7	2.1	4.4	1.7	0.9	0.5	1.1
Anchorage, AK	14.4	9.7	7.8	3.6	3.0	2.1	2.4	2.6	1.4
Ann Arbor, MI	17.1	9.9	9.5	3.8	4.9	6.0	3.0	2.7	2.3
Athens, GA	8.4	8.2	8.0	4.3	3.0	1.6	1.7	2.7	1.0
Atlanta, GA	6.1	5.6	7.2	5.4	2.6	1.4	1.7	1.8	0.6
Austin, TX	10.4	7.4	7.4	3.1	3.0	1.7	2.3	2.0	0.8
Baton Rouge, LA	5.2	5.0	4.5	5.5	3.3	0.4	6.9	1.3	0.3
Boise City, ID	16.7	11.8	18.5	4.5	3.7	1.7	2.4	3.9	1.7
Boston, MA	4.6	13.4	4.3	2.5	7.7	2.2	1.9	1.2	0.5
Boulder, CO	17.4	12.1	10.5	2.5	6.0	3.5	2.6	3.2	1.3
Cape Coral, FL	14.1	11.5	7.3	15.3	10.4	3.5	2.2	1.6	1.2
Cedar Rapids, IA	30.6	13.8	7.8	4.5	1.9	1.6	2.3	1.6	1.9
Charleston, SC	10.4	9.9	9.9	23.1	4.4	1.9	2.2	2.7	0.7
Charlotte, NC	8.7	7.0	6.6	4.7	3.4	1.6	1.4	1.9	0.7
Chicago, IL	7.3	7.5	2.4	2.0	4.0	5.6	1.0	0.6	0.5
Cincinnati, OH	17.7	10.0	5.3	3.9	3.5	1.7	1.6	1.2	0.8
Clarksville, TN	10.7	8.3	5.6	7.8	3.5	1.5	1.8	1.3	1.1
Cleveland, OH	9.0	8.3	2.6	2.1	4.8	3.8	0.9	0.6	0.5
College Station, TX	16.9	8.9	7.7	3.5	3.5	2.3	3.5	2.3	0.7
Colorado Springs, CO	18.6	11.0	9.7	4.3	4.8	2.3	2.9	2.6	1.5
Columbia, MO	23.9	12.3	8.8	5.6	3.7	2.4	2.5	1.9	1.5
Columbia, SC	9.9	6.9	8.3	5.3	2.9	1.3	2.0	2.2	0.8
Columbus, OH	16.4	10.1	6.1	4.3	4.9	2.2	1.7	1.7	0.9
Dallas, TX	5.1	4.0	4.5	3.8	1.5	0.8	1.2	1.1	0.4
Davenport, IA	28.8	15.3	6.3	4.0	2.3	2.1	1.5	1.5	1.8
Denver, CO	13.8	9.7	7.8	2.9	4.6	2.7	2.3	2.1	1.4
Des Moines, IA	20.3	11.6	6.6	3.6	3.9	1.0	1.8	1.3	2.6
Durham, NC	7.4	5.8	7.0	4.3	2.8	1.7	1.6	1.5	0.6
Edison, NJ	4.9	6.8	1.6	1.7	7.8	4.6	0.8	0.6	0.3
El Paso, TX	3.6	2.3	1.7	2.4	1.2	0.5	0.8	0.4	0.2
Fargo, ND	37.1	8.8	3.9	2.2	1.1	3.1	3.6	1.2	1.1
Fayetteville, NC	8.8	6.9	6.6	3.9	2.8	1.4	1.5	1.8	0.6
Fort Collins, CO	22.5	12.7	11.4	3.7	5.3	3.0	3.3	2.9	1.8
Fort Wayne, IN	24.3	9.5	6.9	5.7	2.4	2.1	3.0	1.5	1.3
Fort Worth, TX	7.4	6.0	5.6	5.0	1.9	0.9	1.5	1.4	0.7
Grand Rapids, MI	15.0	8.7	7.0	2.3	3.0	6.8	2.2	1.6	13.9
Greeley, CO	18.4	8.5	6.8	4.2	2.5	1.4	1.6	2.1	1.0
Green Bay, WI	29.5	9.3	3.8	3.4	2.3	7.9	4.2	0.6	3.0
Greensboro, NC	7.0	5.5	7.3	4.8	2.4	1.1	1.1	1.7	0.7
Honolulu, HI	4.1	3.3	2.8	1.2	1.8	0.7	0.8	0.6	0.3
Houston, TX	4.8	3.6	3.7	4.0	1.5	0.8	1.6	0.9	0.4
Huntsville, AL	8.6	8.8	8.7	11.4	2.4	0.9	1.8	2.0	0.9
Indianapolis, IN	13.5	8.6	5.9	5.9	2.2	1.6	1.5	1.5	1.0
Jacksonville, FL	7.9	7.8	6.0	5.4	3.8	1.5	1.4	1.5	0.8
Kansas City, MO	15.4	10.5	7.0	3.9	3.5	1.4	2.0	1.6	1.1
Lafayette, LA	7.4	5.5	5.7	6.4	3.8	0.4	17.8	1.1	0.5
Lakeland, FL	10.1	8.1	8.7	8.1	4.5	1.8	2.6	1.7	1.4
Las Vegas, NV	8.9	7.7	5.6	3.4	5.3	2.1	1.8	1.3	0.8
Lexington, KY	13.7	11.8	10.8	9.2	2.9	1.7	1.9	2.9	1.1
Lincoln, NE	33.2	11.3	8.0	3.6	2.3	2.5	2.1	1.5	2.0
Little Rock, AR	7.1	6.8	7.5	5.5	1.6	0.9	1.8	1.6	0.5
Los Angeles, CA	3.9	3.5	2.8	3.6	2.6	1.4	1.1	0.7	0.4
Louisville, KY	15.1	11.5	7.8	8.7	2.5	1.0	1.9	1.6	0.9
Madison, WI	31.4	12.4	8.1	2.0	4.1	5.7	2.9	1.5	1.8
Manchester, NH	6.6	19.3	9.0	2.9	8.2	3.9	13.5	3.2	0.5

Table continued on following page.

City	German	Irish	English	American	Italian	Polish	French[1]	Scottish	Dutch
Memphis, TN	3.4	4.2	3.9	3.9	1.6	0.7	1.0	1.0	0.3
Miami, FL	1.5	1.2	0.8	3.3	2.3	0.7	0.9	0.2	0.2
Midland, TX	6.8	6.0	6.7	4.4	1.4	0.6	1.6	1.6	0.7
Milwaukee, WI	16.3	5.6	2.1	1.2	2.7	6.6	1.3	0.5	0.7
Minneapolis, MN	20.9	10.1	5.6	1.8	2.7	4.0	2.5	1.4	1.4
Nashville, TN	8.4	7.9	7.3	8.2	2.4	1.3	1.7	1.9	0.8
New Haven, CT	4.1	6.5	3.2	1.1	7.7	2.1	1.3	0.6	0.5
New Orleans, LA	6.1	5.4	4.1	2.5	3.9	0.9	5.4	1.1	0.4
New York, NY	2.9	4.4	1.6	4.2	6.2	2.4	0.8	0.5	0.3
Oklahoma City, OK	10.6	8.1	6.2	5.9	1.9	0.8	1.5	1.5	0.9
Omaha, NE	25.2	13.1	6.9	3.0	4.1	3.6	2.0	1.3	1.4
Orlando, FL	6.3	5.3	4.5	5.6	4.3	1.6	1.7	1.3	0.5
Peoria, IL	18.3	11.3	6.7	4.7	3.1	1.9	2.1	1.2	1.0
Philadelphia, PA	6.4	10.4	2.6	2.3	7.4	3.3	0.7	0.5	0.3
Phoenix, AZ	9.9	7.1	5.5	3.0	3.8	2.0	1.7	1.3	0.9
Pittsburgh, PA	18.7	14.6	5.1	3.6	12.3	6.9	1.6	1.4	0.6
Portland, OR	15.9	11.1	10.5	4.6	4.3	2.3	3.0	2.9	1.9
Providence, RI	3.2	7.6	3.9	2.9	7.2	1.9	2.9	0.8	0.3
Provo, UT	10.1	4.1	23.0	3.0	2.0	0.8	1.6	4.8	1.4
Raleigh, NC	8.9	7.5	9.0	12.2	4.0	2.2	1.7	2.3	0.6
Reno, NV	12.8	10.8	9.1	3.9	6.1	1.7	2.6	2.2	1.1
Richmond, VA	6.9	6.3	7.4	4.2	3.5	1.3	1.4	2.1	0.5
Riverside, CA	5.9	4.6	4.1	3.1	2.9	0.9	1.6	1.0	0.8
Rochester, MN	29.1	11.3	6.1	3.0	2.0	3.6	2.1	1.3	1.7
Sacramento, CA	6.7	6.1	4.5	1.7	3.5	0.9	1.5	1.2	0.8
Salt Lake City, UT	10.4	6.7	14.9	3.3	3.3	1.5	2.0	3.3	1.9
San Antonio, TX	6.8	4.3	3.6	3.1	1.6	1.0	1.3	0.9	0.4
San Diego, CA	8.3	7.0	5.5	2.4	4.1	1.7	1.8	1.4	0.8
San Francisco, CA	7.1	7.7	5.1	2.8	4.5	1.8	2.3	1.4	0.8
San Jose, CA	5.0	4.0	3.5	1.8	3.3	0.9	1.2	0.8	0.5
Santa Rosa, CA	11.4	10.1	8.9	2.8	7.4	1.4	3.0	2.2	1.2
Savannah, GA	5.5	6.7	4.6	3.6	2.8	1.2	1.6	1.6	0.7
Seattle, WA	14.8	11.4	10.1	2.3	4.4	2.7	3.0	2.9	1.6
Sioux Falls, SD	35.1	11.2	5.3	3.2	1.5	1.7	2.2	1.2	5.6
Springfield, IL	20.1	12.8	9.0	4.8	4.7	2.1	2.3	1.7	1.2
Tallahassee, FL	8.5	8.1	7.8	3.8	3.7	1.8	1.9	2.1	0.7
Tampa, FL	8.7	8.0	6.0	6.2	6.0	2.0	2.0	1.5	0.8
Tucson, AZ	11.0	8.2	6.4	3.0	3.6	1.9	2.0	1.5	0.9
Tulsa, OK	11.0	9.1	7.5	6.2	2.0	0.9	1.9	2.0	1.0
Tuscaloosa, AL	5.8	6.6	5.6	7.3	2.3	0.9	1.2	2.2	0.6
Virginia Beach, VA	11.7	11.0	9.1	9.4	5.6	2.4	2.3	2.3	0.9
Washington, DC	6.9	6.7	5.2	2.3	3.9	2.2	1.5	1.4	0.7
Wichita, KS	19.3	9.5	7.8	5.0	1.7	1.0	2.2	1.6	1.5
Winston-Salem, NC	9.6	6.8	7.8	5.2	2.8	1.1	1.3	2.3	1.0
U.S.	13.3	9.7	7.2	6.2	5.1	2.8	2.3	1.7	1.2

Note: Figures are the percentage of the total population reporting a particular ancestry. The nine most commonly reported ancestries in the U.S. are shown. Figures include multiple ancestries (e.g. if a person reported being Irish and Italian, they were included in both columns); (1) Excludes Basque
Source: U.S. Census Bureau, 2015-2019 American Community Survey 5-Year Estimates

Ancestry: Metro Area

Metro Area	German	Irish	English	American	Italian	Polish	French[1]	Scottish	Dutch
Albuquerque, NM	8.7	6.8	6.4	4.3	2.8	1.3	1.7	1.6	0.7
Allentown, PA	24.3	13.5	5.8	4.5	12.8	5.2	1.6	1.1	2.3
Anchorage, AK	15.3	10.0	7.9	4.1	3.1	2.1	2.7	2.6	1.5
Ann Arbor, MI	19.0	10.7	9.9	6.6	4.7	6.4	3.1	2.6	2.1
Athens, GA	8.6	9.4	9.1	7.9	2.8	1.2	1.6	2.8	0.9
Atlanta, GA	6.6	6.6	7.2	9.2	2.5	1.2	1.4	1.7	0.6
Austin, TX	12.3	7.7	7.9	3.8	2.7	1.6	2.4	2.0	0.8
Baton Rouge, LA	6.8	6.6	5.0	7.8	4.7	0.5	12.3	1.1	0.3
Boise City, ID	16.1	9.6	17.1	5.1	3.4	1.2	2.4	3.2	2.1
Boston, MA	5.9	20.8	9.4	3.5	13.1	3.4	4.5	2.3	0.6
Boulder, CO	18.9	11.5	11.6	3.5	5.4	3.3	2.7	3.3	1.5
Cape Coral, FL	13.5	11.0	8.1	14.3	7.7	3.3	2.3	1.8	1.3
Cedar Rapids, IA	34.2	14.5	8.0	4.7	1.9	1.2	2.4	1.5	2.0
Charleston, SC	9.9	9.7	8.2	13.3	3.7	1.9	2.0	2.5	0.8
Charlotte, NC	11.0	8.4	7.8	9.1	3.9	1.7	1.6	2.3	0.9
Chicago, IL	14.3	10.8	4.2	2.6	6.6	8.8	1.4	0.9	1.2
Cincinnati, OH	27.2	13.8	8.3	7.1	4.2	1.6	1.9	1.8	1.2
Clarksville, TN	11.1	9.0	6.4	9.3	2.8	1.4	1.8	1.6	0.9
Cleveland, OH	18.8	13.4	7.0	3.8	9.8	7.7	1.5	1.5	0.9
College Station, TX	14.0	8.0	6.6	3.9	2.9	2.0	2.5	2.0	0.6
Colorado Springs, CO	18.8	10.9	9.4	4.4	4.9	2.4	2.8	2.7	1.5
Columbia, MO	25.0	11.9	9.0	6.8	3.0	1.7	2.4	2.0	1.5
Columbia, SC	10.0	7.4	7.3	8.5	2.3	1.1	1.7	2.0	0.7
Columbus, OH	21.8	12.6	8.5	6.3	5.4	2.4	1.9	2.1	1.3
Dallas, TX	8.6	6.5	6.7	6.3	2.1	1.1	1.7	1.6	0.7
Davenport, IA	27.7	14.7	7.6	4.2	2.4	2.1	1.8	1.5	2.0
Denver, CO	17.5	10.7	9.3	3.9	5.0	2.5	2.5	2.4	1.5
Des Moines, IA	27.1	13.0	8.4	4.3	3.2	1.3	1.9	1.7	3.8
Durham, NC	8.9	7.4	9.3	6.0	3.1	1.8	1.8	2.3	0.8
Edison, NJ	6.2	9.2	2.7	4.4	12.2	3.8	0.9	0.7	0.6
El Paso, TX	3.4	2.2	1.6	2.3	1.1	0.5	0.8	0.4	0.2
Fargo, ND	37.4	8.2	4.3	2.0	1.1	2.8	3.1	1.2	1.2
Fayetteville, NC	8.7	7.0	6.6	5.6	3.0	1.4	1.5	2.2	0.6
Fort Collins, CO	24.3	12.8	12.2	4.4	4.9	2.7	3.4	3.2	2.2
Fort Wayne, IN	27.0	9.3	7.2	6.9	2.6	2.1	3.3	1.6	1.4
Fort Worth, TX	8.6	6.5	6.7	6.3	2.1	1.1	1.7	1.6	0.7
Grand Rapids, MI	20.0	10.1	8.8	3.7	3.1	6.6	2.9	1.8	18.9
Greeley, CO	22.0	9.9	8.7	4.9	3.6	2.1	2.1	1.9	1.4
Green Bay, WI	36.3	9.7	4.1	3.6	2.2	9.8	4.3	0.7	4.4
Greensboro, NC	8.0	6.6	8.2	8.3	2.3	1.1	1.2	1.9	0.8
Honolulu, HI	5.1	3.8	3.3	1.3	2.0	0.9	1.1	0.9	0.4
Houston, TX	7.8	5.3	5.2	4.3	2.0	1.2	2.1	1.2	0.6
Huntsville, AL	8.9	9.5	9.3	12.2	2.2	1.1	1.8	2.1	1.0
Indianapolis, IN	17.3	10.0	8.0	9.3	2.7	1.9	1.8	1.8	1.4
Jacksonville, FL	10.0	9.6	7.9	7.9	4.6	1.9	1.9	2.0	0.9
Kansas City, MO	20.7	12.3	9.7	5.4	3.3	1.5	2.3	1.9	1.4
Lafayette, LA	6.3	4.2	3.8	9.0	2.4	0.4	18.4	0.7	0.3
Lakeland, FL	8.9	7.4	7.3	13.2	3.6	1.7	2.0	1.5	1.0
Las Vegas, NV	8.7	7.2	5.6	3.4	5.0	1.9	1.7	1.2	0.7
Lexington, KY	13.0	11.8	10.9	13.6	2.6	1.5	1.8	2.7	1.1
Lincoln, NE	34.6	11.1	8.0	3.7	2.2	2.5	2.1	1.4	2.2
Little Rock, AR	9.3	8.8	7.9	7.9	1.5	1.0	1.7	1.9	1.0
Los Angeles, CA	5.2	4.2	3.8	3.6	2.9	1.2	1.2	0.9	0.6
Louisville, KY	17.2	12.4	9.1	10.1	2.4	1.1	2.1	1.9	1.0
Madison, WI	37.1	13.1	8.5	2.8	3.8	5.4	2.8	1.5	1.9
Manchester, NH	8.4	20.8	13.0	3.5	10.0	4.4	12.4	3.4	0.8

Table continued on following page.

Metro Area	German	Irish	English	American	Italian	Polish	French[1]	Scottish	Dutch
Memphis, TN	5.2	6.3	6.0	7.1	2.1	0.7	1.2	1.4	0.5
Miami, FL	4.4	4.3	2.7	6.0	5.0	1.9	1.2	0.6	0.4
Midland, TX	6.9	6.1	6.4	4.5	1.4	0.6	1.6	1.5	0.6
Milwaukee, WI	33.0	9.8	4.3	2.0	4.3	10.8	2.5	0.9	1.3
Minneapolis, MN	29.1	10.9	5.6	3.1	2.6	4.4	3.3	1.3	1.5
Nashville, TN	10.0	9.6	9.2	10.8	2.7	1.4	1.8	2.2	1.0
New Haven, CT	7.9	14.9	6.8	2.7	20.6	6.2	3.5	1.2	0.6
New Orleans, LA	9.7	7.4	4.5	5.0	7.9	0.7	11.7	1.0	0.4
New York, NY	6.2	9.2	2.7	4.4	12.2	3.8	0.9	0.7	0.6
Oklahoma City, OK	12.0	9.1	7.2	7.6	2.0	0.9	1.7	1.7	1.2
Omaha, NE	29.2	13.6	7.9	3.6	3.9	3.7	2.1	1.4	1.7
Orlando, FL	8.2	7.3	6.1	7.6	5.1	1.9	1.9	1.4	0.7
Peoria, IL	27.2	12.4	9.1	6.7	3.9	2.0	2.4	1.8	1.6
Philadelphia, PA	14.6	18.0	7.0	3.2	13.0	5.0	1.4	1.3	0.8
Phoenix, AZ	12.5	8.3	7.7	3.9	4.4	2.4	2.1	1.6	1.1
Pittsburgh, PA	26.1	17.3	8.0	3.7	15.6	8.4	1.8	1.9	1.1
Portland, OR	17.2	10.4	10.4	4.7	3.9	1.8	2.9	2.9	1.9
Providence, RI	4.5	17.6	10.6	3.4	13.6	3.7	9.4	1.6	0.4
Provo, UT	10.5	4.8	26.7	4.7	2.4	0.6	1.9	4.9	1.6
Raleigh, NC	10.3	9.0	10.1	10.3	4.8	2.2	1.9	2.5	0.9
Reno, NV	13.6	10.9	9.4	3.9	6.5	1.8	2.8	2.2	1.2
Richmond, VA	9.2	7.9	10.7	6.7	3.7	1.6	1.6	2.1	0.7
Riverside, CA	7.1	5.6	4.5	2.9	3.0	0.9	1.6	1.0	0.9
Rochester, MN	35.4	11.7	6.2	3.2	1.7	3.3	2.2	1.3	2.0
Sacramento, CA	10.6	8.1	7.5	2.8	4.8	1.3	2.1	1.7	1.1
Salt Lake City, UT	10.0	5.6	20.0	4.3	2.9	0.9	1.8	3.9	2.0
San Antonio, TX	10.1	5.5	5.1	3.5	1.9	1.5	1.7	1.2	0.5
San Diego, CA	9.3	7.6	6.2	2.7	4.1	1.7	2.0	1.5	1.0
San Francisco, CA	7.6	7.2	5.7	2.4	4.7	1.5	1.9	1.5	0.8
San Jose, CA	6.1	4.8	4.5	1.9	3.7	1.2	1.5	1.1	0.7
Santa Rosa, CA	12.9	12.2	9.8	2.7	8.6	1.8	3.3	2.6	1.4
Savannah, GA	9.1	9.7	7.4	7.9	3.3	1.3	1.8	1.8	0.7
Seattle, WA	14.6	9.7	9.3	3.2	3.7	1.9	2.8	2.6	1.5
Sioux Falls, SD	37.2	10.8	5.2	3.8	1.4	1.6	2.1	1.0	6.4
Springfield, IL	23.5	13.6	10.0	5.6	5.0	2.0	2.4	1.9	1.4
Tallahassee, FL	8.4	8.2	8.0	5.2	3.3	1.6	1.9	2.3	0.9
Tampa, FL	12.3	10.8	7.8	8.6	7.5	3.0	2.6	1.8	1.1
Tucson, AZ	13.4	9.1	8.2	3.3	4.0	2.3	2.3	1.9	1.1
Tulsa, OK	12.9	10.5	8.0	6.7	1.9	1.0	2.1	2.0	1.2
Tuscaloosa, AL	5.1	6.5	5.3	11.4	1.6	0.6	1.0	1.8	0.5
Virginia Beach, VA	9.8	8.8	8.7	9.3	4.1	1.8	1.9	1.9	0.8
Washington, DC	9.3	8.3	6.9	4.1	4.3	2.3	1.6	1.6	0.7
Wichita, KS	21.8	9.9	8.1	6.7	1.7	1.0	2.3	1.9	1.6
Winston-Salem, NC	11.7	7.8	9.0	9.8	2.5	1.0	1.3	2.4	1.1
U.S.	13.3	9.7	7.2	6.2	5.1	2.8	2.3	1.7	1.2

Note: Figures are the percentage of the total population reporting a particular ancestry. The nine most commonly reported ancestries in the U.S. are shown. Figures include multiple ancestries (e.g. if a person reported being Irish and Italian, they were included in both columns); Figures cover the Metropolitan Statistical Area—see Appendix B for areas included; (1) Excludes Basque
Source: U.S. Census Bureau, 2015-2019 American Community Survey 5-Year Estimates

Foreign-Born Population: City

City	Any Foreign Country	Asia	Mexico	Europe	Caribbean	Central America[1]	South America	Africa	Canada
Albuquerque, NM	9.9	2.4	5.3	0.8	0.3	0.2	0.4	0.4	0.1
Allentown, PA	19.2	3.6	1.0	0.8	9.0	1.3	2.5	0.8	0.1
Anchorage, AK	10.9	6.2	0.9	1.1	0.5	0.1	0.5	0.6	0.4
Ann Arbor, MI	19.1	12.7	0.4	3.0	0.2	0.1	0.8	0.9	0.9
Athens, GA	10.1	2.9	3.0	0.9	0.4	1.0	1.0	0.7	0.2
Atlanta, GA	7.6	3.2	0.7	1.3	0.6	0.1	0.6	0.7	0.3
Austin, TX	18.8	6.0	7.4	1.3	0.6	1.7	0.6	0.8	0.3
Baton Rouge, LA	5.5	2.8	0.4	0.5	0.2	1.0	0.2	0.3	0.0
Boise City, ID	6.4	2.7	1.0	1.4	0.1	0.1	0.3	0.6	0.2
Boston, MA	28.3	7.6	0.4	3.4	8.2	2.6	2.4	3.1	0.4
Boulder, CO	11.0	4.4	1.2	2.8	0.2	0.3	1.0	0.3	0.4
Cape Coral, FL	15.2	1.4	0.7	2.1	6.8	0.7	2.8	0.1	0.6
Cedar Rapids, IA	6.1	2.7	0.7	0.5	0.1	0.1	0.2	1.5	0.1
Charleston, SC	4.8	1.7	0.6	1.3	0.4	0.1	0.3	0.2	0.2
Charlotte, NC	16.7	5.4	2.6	1.2	1.1	2.8	1.4	1.9	0.2
Chicago, IL	20.6	5.2	8.4	3.5	0.4	0.9	1.1	1.0	0.2
Cincinnati, OH	6.0	1.8	0.3	0.8	0.2	0.9	0.3	1.6	0.2
Clarksville, TN	5.3	1.7	1.1	0.9	0.4	0.4	0.4	0.3	0.1
Cleveland, OH	5.9	2.5	0.3	1.0	0.5	0.4	0.3	0.7	0.1
College Station, TX	13.4	7.9	1.6	1.0	0.1	0.5	1.2	0.9	0.2
Colorado Springs, CO	7.5	2.1	2.1	1.5	0.3	0.3	0.3	0.4	0.4
Columbia, MO	9.1	5.3	0.5	1.3	0.1	0.3	0.3	1.0	0.2
Columbia, SC	5.0	2.1	0.5	0.8	0.3	0.3	0.5	0.4	0.1
Columbus, OH	12.7	5.1	1.2	0.8	0.5	0.5	0.3	4.2	0.1
Dallas, TX	24.8	2.8	15.4	0.7	0.4	2.6	0.6	1.9	0.2
Davenport, IA	4.5	1.6	1.9	0.4	0.3	0.0	0.0	0.2	0.1
Denver, CO	15.0	3.0	7.3	1.4	0.3	0.8	0.5	1.4	0.3
Des Moines, IA	12.5	4.5	3.3	0.9	0.1	1.1	0.2	2.3	0.1
Durham, NC	15.0	4.6	2.8	1.1	0.6	3.2	0.7	1.5	0.4
Edison, NJ	46.9	37.6	1.0	2.8	1.5	0.3	1.7	1.8	0.2
El Paso, TX	23.1	1.1	20.7	0.5	0.1	0.3	0.2	0.2	0.0
Fargo, ND	9.0	3.5	0.1	1.0	0.2	0.1	0.2	3.7	0.2
Fayetteville, NC	7.1	2.3	0.6	1.0	0.9	0.8	0.6	0.6	0.1
Fort Collins, CO	6.8	3.0	1.2	1.4	0.1	0.2	0.4	0.3	0.2
Fort Wayne, IN	8.2	3.9	1.9	0.8	0.1	0.7	0.3	0.4	0.1
Fort Worth, TX	16.8	3.4	9.8	0.6	0.3	0.9	0.5	1.2	0.2
Grand Rapids, MI	10.9	2.3	3.3	1.2	0.6	1.8	0.2	1.3	0.3
Greeley, CO	11.5	1.0	7.4	0.4	0.2	1.2	0.2	1.1	0.1
Green Bay, WI	9.9	2.0	5.9	0.5	0.1	0.6	0.2	0.5	0.0
Greensboro, NC	11.0	3.9	2.0	1.2	0.6	0.6	0.5	2.0	0.2
Honolulu, HI	27.4	23.2	0.1	0.8	0.1	0.1	0.2	0.1	0.2
Houston, TX	29.3	6.0	11.4	1.1	1.1	6.3	1.3	1.9	0.2
Huntsville, AL	6.6	2.3	1.7	0.7	0.4	0.5	0.2	0.6	0.1
Indianapolis, IN	9.7	2.8	3.0	0.5	0.4	0.9	0.3	1.6	0.1
Jacksonville, FL	11.3	4.0	0.6	1.8	2.0	0.8	1.3	0.6	0.2
Kansas City, MO	8.2	2.5	2.3	0.6	0.5	0.6	0.3	1.2	0.1
Lafayette, LA	4.3	1.8	0.5	0.7	0.2	0.4	0.2	0.2	0.1
Lakeland, FL	10.9	1.8	1.3	0.8	4.0	0.5	1.4	0.2	0.9
Las Vegas, NV	21.0	5.3	9.2	1.6	1.1	2.3	0.8	0.4	0.4
Lexington, KY	9.7	3.7	2.4	1.0	0.2	0.5	0.3	1.2	0.2
Lincoln, NE	8.5	4.5	1.3	0.9	0.2	0.4	0.3	0.8	0.1
Little Rock, AR	7.7	2.7	2.3	0.7	0.1	1.0	0.3	0.5	0.1
Los Angeles, CA	36.9	11.0	12.5	2.4	0.3	8.4	1.1	0.7	0.4
Louisville, KY	7.7	2.5	0.7	0.9	1.6	0.4	0.3	1.2	0.1

Table continued on following page.

Appendix A: Comparative Statistics

City	Any Foreign Country	Asia	Mexico	Europe	Caribbean	Central America[1]	South America	Africa	Canada
Madison, WI	12.1	6.7	1.5	1.4	0.2	0.3	0.8	1.0	0.3
Manchester, NH	14.5	5.1	0.5	2.5	1.6	1.2	0.8	1.9	0.8
Memphis, TN	6.2	1.5	2.2	0.3	0.2	0.9	0.2	0.8	0.1
Miami, FL	58.3	1.1	0.9	2.0	32.5	11.9	9.6	0.3	0.2
Midland, TX	14.1	1.8	8.6	0.3	1.2	0.6	0.4	0.8	0.4
Milwaukee, WI	10.0	2.9	4.8	0.8	0.4	0.2	0.2	0.7	0.1
Minneapolis, MN	15.6	4.0	2.4	1.3	0.3	0.4	1.3	5.6	0.3
Nashville, TN	13.3	4.0	3.1	0.9	0.4	1.9	0.3	2.5	0.2
New Haven, CT	17.8	4.6	3.1	1.9	2.5	1.0	2.9	1.2	0.5
New Orleans, LA	5.5	2.0	0.3	0.8	0.3	1.5	0.3	0.2	0.1
New York, NY	36.8	10.9	2.0	5.3	10.2	1.4	4.8	1.7	0.3
Oklahoma City, OK	11.8	3.3	6.0	0.4	0.2	1.0	0.3	0.6	0.1
Omaha, NE	10.7	3.4	3.8	0.6	0.1	1.0	0.3	1.3	0.1
Orlando, FL	22.0	2.9	0.5	1.5	6.9	1.2	8.0	0.6	0.3
Peoria, IL	7.6	4.7	1.2	0.5	0.1	0.2	0.3	0.3	0.1
Philadelphia, PA	14.1	5.5	0.5	2.2	2.7	0.6	0.9	1.6	0.1
Phoenix, AZ	19.4	3.4	11.9	1.3	0.3	0.9	0.4	0.8	0.4
Pittsburgh, PA	9.0	4.8	0.3	1.9	0.3	0.1	0.5	0.8	0.2
Portland, OR	13.5	5.9	2.0	2.7	0.3	0.5	0.3	1.0	0.5
Providence, RI	28.7	4.2	0.6	2.2	12.3	5.0	1.4	2.7	0.2
Provo, UT	11.0	2.0	4.4	0.5	0.1	0.6	2.3	0.3	0.4
Raleigh, NC	13.4	3.9	2.7	1.4	0.9	1.4	0.7	2.1	0.3
Reno, NV	15.9	5.3	6.2	1.3	0.2	1.6	0.4	0.3	0.3
Richmond, VA	7.0	1.5	0.8	0.7	0.4	2.5	0.4	0.6	0.2
Riverside, CA	22.6	5.1	13.2	0.9	0.2	2.0	0.6	0.3	0.2
Rochester, MN	14.1	5.8	1.5	1.6	0.2	0.2	0.5	3.9	0.2
Sacramento, CA	22.2	10.7	6.9	1.5	0.1	0.8	0.2	0.6	0.2
Salt Lake City, UT	17.1	4.6	6.4	2.0	0.3	0.6	1.3	1.0	0.4
San Antonio, TX	14.3	2.6	9.1	0.6	0.2	0.8	0.4	0.3	0.1
San Diego, CA	26.1	11.9	9.1	2.3	0.2	0.5	0.8	0.9	0.4
San Francisco, CA	34.3	22.2	2.4	4.5	0.2	2.5	1.0	0.5	0.6
San Jose, CA	39.7	25.6	9.0	2.2	0.1	1.0	0.6	0.8	0.4
Santa Rosa, CA	20.1	4.0	11.6	1.7	0.0	0.9	0.3	0.8	0.3
Savannah, GA	6.2	2.7	0.7	0.9	0.4	0.4	0.5	0.3	0.1
Seattle, WA	18.8	10.6	1.2	2.5	0.1	0.5	0.5	2.1	1.0
Sioux Falls, SD	8.5	2.3	0.5	0.9	0.1	0.9	0.1	3.5	0.1
Springfield, IL	4.5	2.5	0.4	0.5	0.2	0.1	0.2	0.5	0.1
Tallahassee, FL	8.1	3.6	0.2	0.9	1.0	0.4	0.7	0.9	0.3
Tampa, FL	17.2	3.8	1.1	1.4	6.9	1.1	2.0	0.4	0.4
Tucson, AZ	15.3	2.7	9.5	1.0	0.1	0.4	0.3	0.9	0.3
Tulsa, OK	11.2	2.7	5.6	0.5	0.2	1.0	0.4	0.5	0.1
Tuscaloosa, AL	4.6	2.2	0.5	0.4	0.1	0.9	0.1	0.3	0.1
Virginia Beach, VA	9.4	4.9	0.5	1.6	0.7	0.6	0.5	0.4	0.1
Washington, DC	13.7	3.0	0.6	2.5	1.2	2.6	1.3	2.1	0.3
Wichita, KS	10.2	3.8	4.3	0.5	0.1	0.6	0.2	0.6	0.1
Winston-Salem, NC	9.9	2.1	4.3	0.7	0.4	1.1	0.5	0.6	0.1
U.S.	13.6	4.2	3.5	1.5	1.3	1.1	1.0	0.7	0.2

Note: (1) Excludes Mexico
Source: U.S. Census Bureau, 2015-2019 American Community Survey 5-Year Estimates

Foreign-Born Population: Metro Area

Metro Area	Any Foreign Country	Asia	Mexico	Europe	Caribbean	Central America[1]	South America	Africa	Canada
Albuquerque, NM	8.9	1.8	5.2	0.7	0.3	0.2	0.3	0.3	0.1
Allentown, PA	9.3	2.8	0.4	1.6	2.2	0.6	1.2	0.5	0.1
Anchorage, AK	8.9	4.9	0.7	1.1	0.4	0.1	0.4	0.5	0.3
Ann Arbor, MI	12.5	7.4	0.4	2.1	0.2	0.3	0.5	0.9	0.6
Athens, GA	7.8	2.3	2.1	0.8	0.3	0.9	0.7	0.5	0.1
Atlanta, GA	13.8	4.6	2.6	1.2	1.4	1.1	1.1	1.6	0.2
Austin, TX	15.2	4.5	6.4	1.1	0.4	1.2	0.6	0.7	0.3
Baton Rouge, LA	4.0	1.5	0.7	0.3	0.2	0.9	0.2	0.2	0.1
Boise City, ID	6.5	1.6	2.7	1.0	0.0	0.2	0.3	0.3	0.3
Boston, MA	18.9	6.1	0.2	3.3	3.4	1.6	2.1	1.6	0.5
Boulder, CO	10.7	3.5	2.8	2.3	0.1	0.3	0.7	0.3	0.5
Cape Coral, FL	16.7	1.3	2.5	2.0	5.9	1.8	2.0	0.1	1.1
Cedar Rapids, IA	3.8	1.8	0.5	0.4	0.1	0.1	0.1	0.8	0.1
Charleston, SC	5.4	1.5	1.1	1.0	0.3	0.5	0.5	0.2	0.2
Charlotte, NC	10.1	3.0	2.1	1.1	0.6	1.4	0.9	0.9	0.2
Chicago, IL	17.7	5.2	6.5	3.7	0.3	0.6	0.6	0.6	0.2
Cincinnati, OH	4.8	2.1	0.5	0.7	0.1	0.4	0.2	0.7	0.1
Clarksville, TN	4.1	1.3	0.7	0.7	0.3	0.3	0.3	0.3	0.1
Cleveland, OH	6.0	2.2	0.3	2.2	0.2	0.2	0.2	0.4	0.2
College Station, TX	12.5	4.2	5.5	0.7	0.1	0.5	0.7	0.7	0.1
Colorado Springs, CO	6.9	1.9	1.8	1.6	0.3	0.3	0.3	0.4	0.3
Columbia, MO	6.1	3.3	0.4	1.0	0.1	0.2	0.2	0.6	0.2
Columbia, SC	5.0	1.6	1.1	0.7	0.3	0.5	0.3	0.4	0.1
Columbus, OH	8.2	3.6	0.7	0.8	0.3	0.3	0.2	2.2	0.1
Dallas, TX	18.7	5.3	8.4	0.8	0.3	1.5	0.6	1.5	0.2
Davenport, IA	5.2	1.7	1.9	0.5	0.1	0.1	0.1	0.8	0.1
Denver, CO	12.1	3.3	4.9	1.4	0.2	0.5	0.5	1.0	0.3
Des Moines, IA	7.7	3.0	1.5	1.1	0.1	0.5	0.2	1.2	0.1
Durham, NC	11.7	3.6	2.6	1.4	0.4	2.0	0.5	0.9	0.4
Edison, NJ	29.5	8.7	1.5	4.4	6.9	2.0	4.4	1.4	0.2
El Paso, TX	24.2	1.0	22.0	0.4	0.1	0.3	0.2	0.2	0.0
Fargo, ND	6.7	2.7	0.2	0.8	0.1	0.1	0.2	2.4	0.3
Fayetteville, NC	6.2	1.6	1.4	0.9	0.7	0.8	0.4	0.3	0.1
Fort Collins, CO	5.6	1.9	1.3	1.3	0.1	0.2	0.4	0.2	0.2
Fort Wayne, IN	6.3	3.0	1.4	0.7	0.1	0.5	0.2	0.3	0.1
Fort Worth, TX	18.7	5.3	8.4	0.8	0.3	1.5	0.6	1.5	0.2
Grand Rapids, MI	6.8	2.1	1.8	1.0	0.4	0.6	0.1	0.5	0.2
Greeley, CO	8.7	0.9	5.9	0.4	0.2	0.6	0.2	0.5	0.1
Green Bay, WI	5.1	1.5	2.4	0.5	0.0	0.4	0.1	0.2	0.1
Greensboro, NC	8.8	2.9	2.5	0.8	0.4	0.6	0.4	1.0	0.2
Honolulu, HI	19.7	16.1	0.2	0.7	0.1	0.1	0.3	0.1	0.2
Houston, TX	23.4	6.0	8.9	1.0	0.8	3.6	1.3	1.4	0.3
Huntsville, AL	5.1	1.9	1.2	0.7	0.3	0.4	0.2	0.4	0.2
Indianapolis, IN	7.0	2.6	1.7	0.6	0.2	0.5	0.3	0.9	0.1
Jacksonville, FL	9.3	3.1	0.5	1.7	1.5	0.6	1.1	0.4	0.3
Kansas City, MO	6.9	2.3	2.0	0.6	0.2	0.6	0.3	0.7	0.1
Lafayette, LA	3.3	1.2	0.7	0.3	0.2	0.5	0.1	0.2	0.1
Lakeland, FL	10.0	1.3	2.3	0.9	2.8	0.6	1.4	0.2	0.5
Las Vegas, NV	22.2	7.2	8.2	1.6	1.1	2.0	0.9	0.8	0.4
Lexington, KY	7.5	2.6	2.1	0.9	0.2	0.5	0.2	0.8	0.1
Lincoln, NE	7.5	4.0	1.1	0.8	0.2	0.3	0.3	0.7	0.1
Little Rock, AR	4.3	1.4	1.3	0.5	0.1	0.6	0.2	0.2	0.1
Los Angeles, CA	33.1	12.8	12.1	1.7	0.3	4.3	0.9	0.6	0.3
Louisville, KY	5.9	1.9	0.9	0.7	0.9	0.3	0.2	0.7	0.1

Table continued on following page.

Percent of Population Born in

Metro Area	Any Foreign Country	Asia	Mexico	Europe	Caribbean	Central America[1]	South America	Africa	Canada
Madison, WI	7.6	3.6	1.2	1.0	0.1	0.2	0.6	0.6	0.2
Manchester, NH	9.7	3.6	0.4	1.8	1.0	0.5	0.8	0.9	0.8
Memphis, TN	5.3	1.7	1.6	0.4	0.2	0.5	0.2	0.6	0.1
Miami, FL	40.7	2.1	1.1	2.3	21.2	4.2	8.8	0.4	0.5
Midland, TX	13.4	1.6	8.8	0.3	1.0	0.5	0.3	0.6	0.3
Milwaukee, WI	7.4	2.8	2.3	1.3	0.2	0.2	0.2	0.4	0.1
Minneapolis, MN	10.7	4.2	1.3	1.1	0.2	0.4	0.5	2.8	0.2
Nashville, TN	8.3	2.6	2.0	0.7	0.2	1.0	0.3	1.1	0.2
New Haven, CT	12.7	3.3	1.0	2.8	1.9	0.5	1.9	0.9	0.3
New Orleans, LA	7.6	2.1	0.6	0.6	0.7	2.7	0.5	0.3	0.1
New York, NY	29.5	8.7	1.5	4.4	6.9	2.0	4.4	1.4	0.2
Oklahoma City, OK	7.9	2.4	3.5	0.4	0.1	0.6	0.3	0.4	0.1
Omaha, NE	7.4	2.4	2.5	0.6	0.1	0.7	0.2	0.9	0.1
Orlando, FL	18.5	3.0	1.1	1.5	5.7	1.1	5.2	0.6	0.3
Peoria, IL	3.3	1.7	0.6	0.4	0.0	0.1	0.1	0.1	0.1
Philadelphia, PA	11.0	4.5	0.9	1.9	1.3	0.4	0.6	1.1	0.2
Phoenix, AZ	14.3	3.4	7.2	1.3	0.3	0.6	0.3	0.5	0.6
Pittsburgh, PA	3.9	2.0	0.1	1.0	0.1	0.1	0.2	0.3	0.1
Portland, OR	12.6	5.0	3.1	2.3	0.1	0.5	0.3	0.6	0.4
Providence, RI	13.3	2.3	0.2	4.2	2.3	1.4	1.0	1.6	0.2
Provo, UT	7.3	1.1	2.8	0.5	0.1	0.5	1.6	0.2	0.3
Raleigh, NC	12.3	4.4	2.6	1.4	0.6	1.1	0.6	1.2	0.4
Reno, NV	14.0	3.9	6.1	1.1	0.2	1.5	0.4	0.3	0.3
Richmond, VA	7.9	3.2	0.6	1.0	0.4	1.4	0.5	0.6	0.1
Riverside, CA	21.3	4.9	12.3	0.8	0.2	1.7	0.6	0.4	0.3
Rochester, MN	8.5	3.4	1.0	1.1	0.1	0.3	0.3	2.1	0.2
Sacramento, CA	18.6	8.8	4.7	2.7	0.1	0.6	0.3	0.5	0.3
Salt Lake City, UT	12.4	3.1	4.6	1.2	0.1	0.6	1.4	0.6	0.3
San Antonio, TX	11.8	2.2	7.3	0.6	0.2	0.7	0.4	0.3	0.1
San Diego, CA	23.4	9.0	10.1	1.8	0.2	0.5	0.6	0.6	0.4
San Francisco, CA	30.7	17.5	4.9	2.9	0.2	2.5	1.0	0.7	0.5
San Jose, CA	38.6	25.4	7.0	3.1	0.1	0.9	0.7	0.7	0.5
Santa Rosa, CA	16.4	2.9	9.0	1.9	0.1	0.9	0.5	0.4	0.4
Savannah, GA	5.7	2.0	1.1	0.8	0.5	0.4	0.4	0.3	0.2
Seattle, WA	18.7	9.9	2.4	2.6	0.2	0.5	0.5	1.5	0.7
Sioux Falls, SD	6.2	1.6	0.4	0.7	0.1	0.7	0.1	2.4	0.1
Springfield, IL	3.1	1.6	0.3	0.4	0.1	0.1	0.1	0.3	0.1
Tallahassee, FL	6.1	2.2	0.5	0.8	0.9	0.5	0.5	0.6	0.2
Tampa, FL	13.9	2.8	1.3	2.2	3.7	0.8	1.9	0.5	0.6
Tucson, AZ	13.0	2.3	7.6	1.2	0.1	0.3	0.3	0.6	0.4
Tulsa, OK	6.6	1.9	2.9	0.5	0.1	0.5	0.3	0.3	0.1
Tuscaloosa, AL	3.4	1.1	0.9	0.4	0.1	0.6	0.1	0.2	0.1
Virginia Beach, VA	6.5	2.8	0.4	1.1	0.6	0.7	0.4	0.4	0.1
Washington, DC	22.8	8.2	0.8	1.8	1.1	4.9	2.2	3.5	0.2
Wichita, KS	7.4	2.7	3.0	0.4	0.1	0.4	0.2	0.4	0.1
Winston-Salem, NC	6.8	1.4	3.0	0.6	0.2	0.9	0.4	0.3	0.1
U.S.	13.6	4.2	3.5	1.5	1.3	1.1	1.0	0.7	0.2

Note: Figures cover the Metropolitan Statistical Area—see Appendix B for areas included; (1) Excludes Mexico
Source: U.S. Census Bureau, 2015-2019 American Community Survey 5-Year Estimates

Marital Status: City

City	Never Married	Now Married[1]	Separated	Widowed	Divorced
Albuquerque, NM	37.7	40.8	1.5	5.6	14.4
Allentown, PA	47.4	33.2	3.6	5.4	10.4
Anchorage, AK	34.5	48.4	1.8	3.6	11.7
Ann Arbor, MI	56.5	33.8	0.4	2.6	6.6
Athens, GA	54.4	32.2	1.6	3.5	8.2
Atlanta, GA	55.2	27.3	1.9	5.1	10.5
Austin, TX	43.2	40.9	1.7	3.1	11.0
Baton Rouge, LA	50.2	30.4	2.0	6.4	11.0
Boise City, ID	34.1	46.7	0.9	4.5	13.9
Boston, MA	56.0	30.3	2.6	3.9	7.2
Boulder, CO	55.6	32.4	0.8	2.6	8.6
Cape Coral, FL	25.5	52.0	1.5	7.3	13.7
Cedar Rapids, IA	35.2	45.7	1.0	6.0	12.1
Charleston, SC	41.9	41.6	1.5	5.2	9.7
Charlotte, NC	40.7	42.5	2.6	4.0	10.2
Chicago, IL	48.7	35.5	2.3	5.2	8.3
Cincinnati, OH	52.0	28.3	2.4	5.1	12.1
Clarksville, TN	30.2	50.9	2.2	4.0	12.6
Cleveland, OH	51.4	25.1	3.2	6.2	14.1
College Station, TX	59.7	32.4	0.8	2.1	5.0
Colorado Springs, CO	31.2	49.5	1.6	4.6	13.1
Columbia, MO	48.0	39.0	1.2	3.4	8.4
Columbia, SC	55.8	27.8	2.6	4.4	9.4
Columbus, OH	45.0	36.3	2.1	4.3	12.4
Dallas, TX	41.6	40.4	3.2	4.5	10.4
Davenport, IA	36.7	42.6	1.5	6.3	12.9
Denver, CO	42.5	39.5	1.8	4.0	12.2
Des Moines, IA	39.0	40.0	2.0	5.3	13.7
Durham, NC	43.1	39.9	2.5	4.3	10.2
Edison, NJ	25.7	61.0	1.0	6.1	6.2
El Paso, TX	35.3	44.5	3.5	5.8	10.8
Fargo, ND	42.8	42.9	1.1	4.5	8.7
Fayetteville, NC	38.4	40.7	3.6	5.5	11.8
Fort Collins, CO	46.6	40.6	0.8	3.3	8.7
Fort Wayne, IN	35.3	44.4	1.5	5.8	13.0
Fort Worth, TX	35.4	46.3	2.3	4.5	11.4
Grand Rapids, MI	46.2	36.9	1.3	5.1	10.4
Greeley, CO	35.8	46.0	1.7	5.1	11.3
Green Bay, WI	37.9	43.2	1.5	5.1	12.3
Greensboro, NC	42.2	38.4	2.6	5.7	11.0
Honolulu, HI	36.2	45.8	1.2	6.9	9.9
Houston, TX	41.0	41.3	3.2	4.6	9.9
Huntsville, AL	34.9	44.8	2.0	6.0	12.3
Indianapolis, IN	42.9	37.7	1.8	5.1	12.5
Jacksonville, FL	35.5	42.6	2.2	5.6	14.0
Kansas City, MO	39.7	39.9	2.1	5.4	12.9
Lafayette, LA	42.2	38.8	1.7	6.0	11.2
Lakeland, FL	34.9	41.7	2.1	8.2	13.1
Las Vegas, NV	34.9	43.3	2.3	5.5	14.1
Lexington, KY	38.8	43.1	1.7	4.6	11.8
Lincoln, NE	39.0	45.6	1.0	4.4	10.0
Little Rock, AR	37.7	39.9	2.5	6.2	13.7
Los Angeles, CA	45.8	38.8	2.6	4.6	8.2
Louisville, KY	36.3	42.1	2.1	6.1	13.4
Madison, WI	50.2	37.3	0.8	3.3	8.4
Manchester, NH	38.8	39.9	2.0	5.8	13.4

Table continued on following page.

City	Never Married	Now Married[1]	Separated	Widowed	Divorced
Memphis, TN	47.8	31.3	3.7	5.8	11.4
Miami, FL	40.2	36.0	3.7	6.6	13.5
Midland, TX	30.1	51.1	2.1	5.1	11.6
Milwaukee, WI	53.3	30.0	1.9	4.6	10.2
Minneapolis, MN	50.5	34.4	1.6	2.9	10.5
Nashville, TN	40.7	40.8	1.8	4.7	11.9
New Haven, CT	57.8	26.1	1.9	4.3	9.9
New Orleans, LA	49.2	29.4	2.7	5.9	12.8
New York, NY	43.4	40.4	3.0	5.4	7.8
Oklahoma City, OK	33.3	45.8	2.3	5.4	13.2
Omaha, NE	36.4	45.9	1.6	4.8	11.2
Orlando, FL	43.0	36.5	3.1	4.1	13.3
Peoria, IL	40.5	39.9	1.3	6.2	12.1
Philadelphia, PA	50.7	30.6	3.3	6.2	9.3
Phoenix, AZ	39.2	42.1	2.0	4.3	12.4
Pittsburgh, PA	52.4	30.7	1.9	5.8	9.3
Portland, OR	41.3	40.9	1.5	3.8	12.5
Providence, RI	54.4	30.6	2.3	4.2	8.5
Provo, UT	47.7	44.6	1.1	2.0	4.5
Raleigh, NC	42.7	40.3	2.5	3.7	10.8
Reno, NV	35.5	42.5	2.2	4.8	14.9
Richmond, VA	52.7	27.3	3.0	5.4	11.6
Riverside, CA	43.1	40.8	2.4	4.7	9.0
Rochester, MN	32.1	52.3	1.0	5.2	9.4
Sacramento, CA	40.2	41.0	2.4	5.1	11.4
Salt Lake City, UT	42.4	41.4	1.5	3.9	10.8
San Antonio, TX	39.0	40.6	3.1	5.2	12.1
San Diego, CA	40.0	44.3	1.7	4.1	9.8
San Francisco, CA	45.8	40.3	1.3	4.6	7.9
San Jose, CA	35.4	51.0	1.6	4.2	7.8
Santa Rosa, CA	34.6	44.5	1.9	5.5	13.5
Savannah, GA	47.5	31.2	3.0	5.9	12.4
Seattle, WA	44.5	41.1	1.2	3.4	9.9
Sioux Falls, SD	33.6	48.8	1.4	5.0	11.1
Springfield, IL	37.5	40.8	1.5	6.4	13.7
Tallahassee, FL	56.3	29.3	1.3	3.3	9.8
Tampa, FL	40.4	38.4	2.7	5.0	13.6
Tucson, AZ	42.5	36.0	2.2	5.4	14.0
Tulsa, OK	34.5	42.5	2.4	5.9	14.8
Tuscaloosa, AL	53.2	30.8	1.9	4.3	9.9
Virginia Beach, VA	30.4	51.1	2.4	5.0	11.1
Washington, DC	56.4	28.9	2.1	4.1	8.5
Wichita, KS	33.5	45.6	2.0	5.6	13.3
Winston-Salem, NC	40.4	39.9	2.8	5.9	11.1
U.S.	33.4	48.1	1.9	5.8	10.9

Note: Figures are percentages and cover the population 15 years of age and older; (1) Excludes separated
Source: U.S. Census Bureau, 2015-2019 American Community Survey 5-Year Estimates

Appendix A: Comparative Statistics

Marital Status: Metro Area

Metro Area	Never Married	Now Married[1]	Separated	Widowed	Divorced
Albuquerque, NM	34.9	43.9	1.5	5.8	13.9
Allentown, PA	32.3	49.3	2.1	6.4	9.9
Anchorage, AK	33.9	48.7	1.8	3.7	11.9
Ann Arbor, MI	43.0	44.1	0.8	3.7	8.4
Athens, GA	42.7	41.9	1.6	4.7	9.1
Atlanta, GA	35.3	47.4	1.9	4.6	10.8
Austin, TX	36.4	47.4	1.7	3.7	10.8
Baton Rouge, LA	37.2	43.2	2.1	6.1	11.4
Boise City, ID	29.6	52.2	1.1	4.5	12.6
Boston, MA	37.1	47.5	1.5	5.1	8.7
Boulder, CO	38.1	46.2	1.0	3.7	11.0
Cape Coral, FL	26.2	50.8	1.6	8.2	13.2
Cedar Rapids, IA	30.0	52.0	0.9	5.8	11.2
Charleston, SC	34.5	46.9	2.4	5.5	10.7
Charlotte, NC	32.6	49.4	2.4	5.2	10.3
Chicago, IL	37.0	46.9	1.6	5.5	8.9
Cincinnati, OH	32.3	49.0	1.6	5.7	11.3
Clarksville, TN	28.3	52.5	2.0	5.1	12.0
Cleveland, OH	34.9	45.0	1.6	6.6	11.8
College Station, TX	46.3	40.1	1.9	3.8	7.9
Colorado Springs, CO	29.5	53.1	1.5	4.2	11.8
Columbia, MO	40.0	44.6	1.2	4.4	9.7
Columbia, SC	36.6	44.2	2.8	5.7	10.7
Columbus, OH	34.7	47.0	1.7	4.9	11.6
Dallas, TX	32.8	50.3	2.1	4.4	10.5
Davenport, IA	29.9	50.2	1.3	6.6	12.0
Denver, CO	33.1	49.6	1.4	4.1	11.8
Des Moines, IA	29.9	52.1	1.3	5.0	11.8
Durham, NC	36.9	45.4	2.3	5.1	10.2
Edison, NJ	37.8	46.3	2.3	5.7	7.9
El Paso, TX	35.4	45.2	3.5	5.5	10.3
Fargo, ND	36.8	49.6	0.9	4.3	8.3
Fayetteville, NC	33.8	46.1	3.2	5.8	11.2
Fort Collins, CO	34.8	50.1	0.9	4.0	10.2
Fort Wayne, IN	31.5	49.6	1.3	5.7	11.9
Fort Worth, TX	32.8	50.3	2.1	4.4	10.5
Grand Rapids, MI	32.7	51.3	1.0	4.9	10.2
Greeley, CO	28.2	55.2	1.4	4.5	10.8
Green Bay, WI	30.2	53.2	0.9	5.2	10.5
Greensboro, NC	33.6	46.1	2.7	6.3	11.3
Honolulu, HI	33.9	50.1	1.2	6.3	8.6
Houston, TX	33.7	49.8	2.5	4.5	9.6
Huntsville, AL	30.1	50.8	1.7	5.6	11.8
Indianapolis, IN	33.5	47.9	1.4	5.3	11.9
Jacksonville, FL	31.4	47.8	1.9	5.8	13.2
Kansas City, MO	30.5	50.4	1.6	5.4	12.0
Lafayette, LA	34.7	46.2	1.9	6.0	11.3
Lakeland, FL	31.8	46.9	2.1	7.2	12.1
Las Vegas, NV	34.7	43.9	2.3	5.2	13.9
Lexington, KY	34.3	46.5	1.7	5.1	12.3
Lincoln, NE	36.7	48.2	0.9	4.4	9.7
Little Rock, AR	30.7	47.4	2.1	6.3	13.6
Los Angeles, CA	39.9	44.7	2.1	4.9	8.4
Louisville, KY	31.6	47.4	1.9	6.1	13.0
Madison, WI	36.5	48.8	0.8	4.2	9.6
Manchester, NH	30.4	51.3	1.4	5.3	11.6

Table continued on following page.

Metro Area	Never Married	Now Married[1]	Separated	Widowed	Divorced
Memphis, TN	38.4	42.0	2.9	5.7	11.0
Miami, FL	34.6	43.3	2.8	6.4	12.8
Midland, TX	29.2	51.8	2.0	5.0	11.9
Milwaukee, WI	37.0	46.4	1.1	5.5	10.1
Minneapolis, MN	33.2	51.4	1.0	4.3	10.1
Nashville, TN	32.0	50.3	1.6	5.0	11.2
New Haven, CT	37.9	43.6	1.3	6.2	10.9
New Orleans, LA	37.8	41.3	2.3	6.3	12.2
New York, NY	37.8	46.3	2.3	5.7	7.9
Oklahoma City, OK	31.4	48.3	2.0	5.6	12.7
Omaha, NE	31.4	51.6	1.3	4.9	10.7
Orlando, FL	34.8	46.0	2.2	5.2	11.8
Peoria, IL	29.9	50.3	1.1	7.0	11.8
Philadelphia, PA	37.2	45.5	2.1	6.0	9.2
Phoenix, AZ	34.0	47.2	1.6	5.1	12.1
Pittsburgh, PA	31.7	49.4	1.7	7.3	9.9
Portland, OR	32.1	50.0	1.4	4.5	12.0
Providence, RI	36.0	45.2	1.6	6.1	11.0
Provo, UT	32.3	58.4	1.0	2.7	5.6
Raleigh, NC	32.0	51.7	2.3	4.2	9.9
Reno, NV	30.9	48.6	1.9	4.9	13.7
Richmond, VA	34.9	46.0	2.5	5.8	10.9
Riverside, CA	36.0	47.0	2.3	5.1	9.6
Rochester, MN	27.8	56.9	0.8	5.1	9.4
Sacramento, CA	33.5	48.2	2.1	5.2	10.9
Salt Lake City, UT	32.1	52.1	1.7	3.8	10.3
San Antonio, TX	35.1	45.6	2.6	5.2	11.5
San Diego, CA	35.9	47.6	1.7	4.7	10.1
San Francisco, CA	36.3	48.7	1.5	4.7	8.8
San Jose, CA	33.6	53.2	1.4	4.2	7.5
Santa Rosa, CA	32.1	47.8	1.7	5.3	13.1
Savannah, GA	34.9	44.9	2.2	5.8	12.1
Seattle, WA	32.6	50.8	1.4	4.2	11.0
Sioux Falls, SD	30.2	53.1	1.2	5.0	10.5
Springfield, IL	32.1	47.5	1.3	6.1	13.0
Tallahassee, FL	43.9	39.0	1.6	4.6	10.9
Tampa, FL	31.2	45.9	2.1	7.0	13.9
Tucson, AZ	34.4	45.0	1.8	5.9	12.9
Tulsa, OK	28.4	50.3	1.9	6.2	13.2
Tuscaloosa, AL	40.8	41.1	2.1	5.6	10.3
Virginia Beach, VA	33.5	47.3	2.7	5.6	11.0
Washington, DC	36.1	48.9	1.9	4.4	8.8
Wichita, KS	30.0	50.3	1.6	5.9	12.2
Winston-Salem, NC	29.8	49.6	2.5	6.8	11.3
U.S.	33.4	48.1	1.9	5.8	10.9

Note: Figures are percentages and cover the population 15 years of age and older; Figures cover the Metropolitan Statistical Area—see Appendix B for areas included; (1) Excludes separated
Source: U.S. Census Bureau, 2015-2019 American Community Survey 5-Year Estimates

Appendix A: Comparative Statistics

Disability by Age: City

City	All Ages	Under 18 Years Old	18 to 64 Years Old	65 Years and Over
Albuquerque, NM	13.4	4.1	11.7	34.9
Allentown, PA	17.1	9.2	16.9	37.5
Anchorage, AK	11.4	3.6	10.3	36.3
Ann Arbor, MI	7.1	3.0	4.9	25.7
Athens, GA	11.5	6.6	9.4	35.1
Atlanta, GA	11.9	4.7	9.7	36.8
Austin, TX	8.4	3.9	6.9	30.7
Baton Rouge, LA	16.8	8.5	14.6	40.3
Boise City, ID	10.9	3.3	9.0	31.7
Boston, MA	11.9	5.3	8.9	41.0
Boulder, CO	6.3	2.8	4.5	23.5
Cape Coral, FL	12.9	3.4	9.3	29.9
Cedar Rapids, IA	10.6	3.5	8.5	29.7
Charleston, SC	9.9	2.8	7.2	30.6
Charlotte, NC	7.9	2.5	6.5	29.7
Chicago, IL	10.5	2.9	8.3	35.5
Cincinnati, OH	13.3	5.5	11.9	35.8
Clarksville, TN	14.9	4.7	16.1	41.1
Cleveland, OH	20.0	8.6	18.8	44.3
College Station, TX	6.3	3.8	4.9	28.7
Colorado Springs, CO	13.0	4.6	11.7	33.8
Columbia, MO	10.1	2.9	8.0	38.2
Columbia, SC	12.6	5.4	10.8	35.7
Columbus, OH	11.7	5.0	10.5	35.3
Dallas, TX	9.6	3.3	8.1	35.0
Davenport, IA	12.4	4.8	10.3	33.5
Denver, CO	9.6	3.5	7.4	33.5
Des Moines, IA	14.0	5.8	12.7	38.2
Durham, NC	9.1	2.9	7.3	31.9
Edison, NJ	8.2	3.3	5.3	29.0
El Paso, TX	13.7	5.0	11.3	43.4
Fargo, ND	10.0	2.8	7.7	36.5
Fayetteville, NC	17.5	6.7	16.6	44.5
Fort Collins, CO	7.9	2.8	6.0	30.0
Fort Wayne, IN	13.6	5.2	12.6	34.0
Fort Worth, TX	10.2	3.8	9.1	35.9
Grand Rapids, MI	13.2	5.4	12.0	35.8
Greeley, CO	11.2	2.3	10.2	36.2
Green Bay, WI	13.0	6.6	11.6	32.5
Greensboro, NC	10.7	4.3	8.7	30.9
Honolulu, HI	11.2	2.6	7.1	31.4
Houston, TX	9.5	3.2	7.7	35.6
Huntsville, AL	13.7	4.8	11.2	34.7
Indianapolis, IN	13.3	5.1	12.0	37.5
Jacksonville, FL	13.5	5.0	11.5	37.6
Kansas City, MO	12.7	3.9	11.2	36.2
Lafayette, LA	12.4	3.7	10.7	32.7
Lakeland, FL	15.8	4.3	11.8	37.1
Las Vegas, NV	12.9	3.7	10.8	36.3
Lexington, KY	12.4	4.5	10.7	34.3
Lincoln, NE	10.8	4.4	8.6	32.7
Little Rock, AR	13.4	5.8	11.5	35.4
Los Angeles, CA	10.1	3.1	7.3	37.3
Louisville, KY	14.8	4.6	13.4	36.4
Madison, WI	8.0	3.2	6.2	26.3

Table continued on following page.

City	All Ages	Under 18 Years Old	18 to 64 Years Old	65 Years and Over
Manchester, NH	14.1	6.0	11.7	39.8
Memphis, TN	13.5	5.1	12.0	37.8
Miami, FL	11.8	3.9	7.7	36.3
Midland, TX	9.7	2.4	8.2	38.5
Milwaukee, WI	13.0	5.7	11.8	38.8
Minneapolis, MN	11.2	4.7	10.1	32.9
Nashville, TN	11.5	4.0	9.8	35.4
New Haven, CT	10.2	5.2	8.6	31.9
New Orleans, LA	14.2	5.0	12.3	36.4
New York, NY	10.8	3.4	7.9	35.1
Oklahoma City, OK	13.2	4.2	12.0	38.6
Omaha, NE	10.9	3.3	9.7	32.3
Orlando, FL	10.1	5.4	8.2	32.5
Peoria, IL	12.4	3.2	11.0	33.2
Philadelphia, PA	16.7	6.0	15.0	43.2
Phoenix, AZ	10.7	3.9	9.5	34.7
Pittsburgh, PA	13.9	6.9	10.7	36.8
Portland, OR	12.1	4.1	10.0	35.4
Providence, RI	13.3	5.5	12.2	38.5
Provo, UT	8.2	4.2	6.8	38.3
Raleigh, NC	9.0	4.7	6.8	31.6
Reno, NV	12.2	5.2	10.3	30.7
Richmond, VA	15.2	6.7	13.2	38.0
Riverside, CA	11.2	3.9	9.1	40.7
Rochester, MN	10.5	4.7	8.2	30.1
Sacramento, CA	11.6	3.2	9.3	38.0
Salt Lake City, UT	10.8	3.2	9.1	35.7
San Antonio, TX	14.6	5.8	13.2	41.1
San Diego, CA	9.2	3.3	6.5	32.4
San Francisco, CA	10.2	2.3	6.3	35.2
San Jose, CA	8.6	2.6	6.1	33.1
Santa Rosa, CA	12.0	4.0	9.9	30.5
Savannah, GA	15.2	6.1	12.5	43.4
Seattle, WA	9.2	2.5	6.9	30.9
Sioux Falls, SD	10.2	3.3	9.0	30.1
Springfield, IL	14.9	5.8	12.9	33.6
Tallahassee, FL	9.9	4.7	8.2	30.5
Tampa, FL	12.2	3.7	9.9	39.4
Tucson, AZ	15.3	5.5	13.2	39.5
Tulsa, OK	14.5	4.7	13.5	36.2
Tuscaloosa, AL	11.1	2.8	9.5	32.4
Virginia Beach, VA	11.2	3.5	9.4	31.6
Washington, DC	11.7	4.1	9.6	35.3
Wichita, KS	13.7	4.6	12.4	36.3
Winston-Salem, NC	9.8	2.8	8.3	28.6
U.S.	12.6	4.2	10.3	34.5

Note: Figures show percent of the civilian noninstitutionalized population that reported having a disability. Disability status is determined from from six types of difficulty: vision, hearing, cognitive, ambulatory, self-care, and independent living. For children under 5 years old, hearing and vision difficulty are used to determine disability status. For children between the ages of 5 and 14, disability status is determined from hearing, vision, cognitive, ambulatory, and self-care difficulties. For people aged 15 years and older, they are considered to have a disability if they have difficulty with any one of the six difficulty types.
Source: U.S. Census Bureau, 2015-2019 American Community Survey 5-Year Estimates

Disability by Age: Metro Area

Metro Area	All Ages	Under 18 Years Old	18 to 64 Years Old	65 Years and Over
Albuquerque, NM	14.3	4.1	12.2	36.6
Allentown, PA	13.3	5.7	10.8	31.8
Anchorage, AK	11.9	3.7	11.0	36.5
Ann Arbor, MI	9.4	3.7	7.3	27.9
Athens, GA	12.5	6.0	10.1	35.8
Atlanta, GA	10.0	3.5	8.4	32.5
Austin, TX	9.2	3.7	7.6	31.4
Baton Rouge, LA	14.8	6.2	13.0	38.1
Boise City, ID	12.0	4.0	10.5	33.0
Boston, MA	10.6	4.0	7.8	31.3
Boulder, CO	8.1	3.0	6.1	25.6
Cape Coral, FL	13.9	3.8	9.9	28.2
Cedar Rapids, IA	10.4	3.6	8.1	29.8
Charleston, SC	12.2	4.0	10.0	33.9
Charlotte, NC	10.5	3.4	8.7	32.4
Chicago, IL	9.9	3.0	7.7	31.8
Cincinnati, OH	12.4	4.7	10.6	32.7
Clarksville, TN	16.5	5.7	16.6	43.2
Cleveland, OH	14.2	5.2	11.7	33.8
College Station, TX	9.5	4.1	7.3	35.2
Colorado Springs, CO	12.4	4.4	11.4	32.7
Columbia, MO	12.1	4.0	10.0	37.2
Columbia, SC	14.1	4.6	12.2	36.8
Columbus, OH	12.0	4.7	10.3	33.7
Dallas, TX	9.5	3.4	7.9	33.7
Davenport, IA	12.3	4.4	9.6	31.8
Denver, CO	9.3	3.2	7.4	30.8
Des Moines, IA	10.6	4.0	8.9	31.4
Durham, NC	11.4	3.9	9.1	32.3
Edison, NJ	10.0	3.2	7.2	31.6
El Paso, TX	13.8	5.5	11.5	44.6
Fargo, ND	9.5	3.1	7.4	33.9
Fayetteville, NC	16.4	6.0	15.7	43.7
Fort Collins, CO	9.7	3.1	7.4	28.1
Fort Wayne, IN	12.6	4.5	11.3	32.8
Fort Worth, TX	9.5	3.4	7.9	33.7
Grand Rapids, MI	11.4	4.0	9.8	31.7
Greeley, CO	10.3	3.0	8.9	34.6
Green Bay, WI	11.2	4.7	9.1	29.4
Greensboro, NC	12.7	4.5	10.7	32.5
Honolulu, HI	10.9	2.9	7.4	32.8
Houston, TX	9.4	3.3	7.8	34.0
Huntsville, AL	13.7	4.9	11.3	37.7
Indianapolis, IN	12.2	4.5	10.5	35.0
Jacksonville, FL	13.2	4.7	11.0	34.7
Kansas City, MO	12.1	3.9	10.2	34.2
Lafayette, LA	14.5	5.0	12.9	39.1
Lakeland, FL	15.4	5.7	12.4	34.7
Las Vegas, NV	12.1	3.8	9.9	34.8
Lexington, KY	13.5	5.1	11.8	35.5
Lincoln, NE	10.7	4.1	8.4	32.5
Little Rock, AR	15.7	5.9	13.8	39.5
Los Angeles, CA	9.6	3.0	6.8	33.9
Louisville, KY	14.1	4.2	12.4	35.5
Madison, WI	8.9	3.4	6.9	26.9

Table continued on following page.

Metro Area	All Ages	Under 18 Years Old	18 to 64 Years Old	65 Years and Over
Manchester, NH	11.8	4.7	9.5	31.8
Memphis, TN	12.9	4.5	11.2	36.4
Miami, FL	10.9	3.4	7.2	32.1
Midland, TX	9.8	2.3	8.3	39.5
Milwaukee, WI	11.4	4.2	9.1	31.6
Minneapolis, MN	9.9	3.7	8.0	30.0
Nashville, TN	12.0	4.0	10.2	35.2
New Haven, CT	11.6	4.0	8.8	31.5
New Orleans, LA	14.4	5.0	12.3	36.6
New York, NY	10.0	3.2	7.2	31.6
Oklahoma City, OK	13.9	4.3	12.2	39.4
Omaha, NE	11.0	3.5	9.6	32.2
Orlando, FL	12.2	5.1	9.6	34.5
Peoria, IL	12.0	3.4	9.5	32.2
Philadelphia, PA	12.7	4.6	10.5	33.4
Phoenix, AZ	11.5	3.7	9.3	32.6
Pittsburgh, PA	14.5	5.4	11.4	33.8
Portland, OR	11.9	3.9	9.7	34.1
Providence, RI	13.6	5.2	11.2	33.3
Provo, UT	7.8	3.3	7.1	32.8
Raleigh, NC	9.6	3.8	7.7	32.1
Reno, NV	12.1	4.7	9.9	30.7
Richmond, VA	12.6	5.0	10.4	32.6
Riverside, CA	11.3	3.6	9.1	37.5
Rochester, MN	10.2	4.0	7.7	29.4
Sacramento, CA	11.5	3.4	9.0	34.8
Salt Lake City, UT	9.4	3.5	8.3	32.4
San Antonio, TX	14.0	5.3	12.5	39.2
San Diego, CA	9.9	3.2	7.2	32.8
San Francisco, CA	9.7	2.9	6.8	31.5
San Jose, CA	8.1	2.4	5.4	31.2
Santa Rosa, CA	11.9	3.8	9.4	28.5
Savannah, GA	13.7	5.5	11.6	37.0
Seattle, WA	10.8	3.5	8.7	33.4
Sioux Falls, SD	9.9	3.1	8.8	29.7
Springfield, IL	13.7	5.4	11.4	32.9
Tallahassee, FL	12.7	5.9	10.2	33.9
Tampa, FL	14.0	4.4	10.8	34.3
Tucson, AZ	15.3	5.1	12.5	35.1
Tulsa, OK	14.5	4.6	12.9	37.9
Tuscaloosa, AL	14.4	4.0	12.4	40.2
Virginia Beach, VA	13.1	4.7	11.1	34.4
Washington, DC	8.7	3.0	6.7	29.1
Wichita, KS	13.4	4.9	11.7	36.1
Winston-Salem, NC	12.7	3.8	10.2	33.8
U.S.	12.6	4.2	10.3	34.5

Note: Figures show percent of the civilian noninstitutionalized population that reported having a disability. Disability status is determined from from six types of difficulty: vision, hearing, cognitive, ambulatory, self-care, and independent living. For children under 5 years old, hearing and vision difficulty are used to determine disability status. For children between the ages of 5 and 14, disability status is determined from hearing, vision, cognitive, ambulatory, and self-care difficulties. For people aged 15 years and older, they are considered to have a disability if they have difficulty with any one of the six difficulty types; Figures cover the Metropolitan Statistical Area—see Appendix B for areas included
Source: U.S. Census Bureau, 2015-2019 American Community Survey 5-Year Estimates

Male/Female Ratio: City

City	Males	Females	Males per 100 Females
Albuquerque, NM	272,468	286,906	95.0
Allentown, PA	59,101	61,814	95.6
Anchorage, AK	149,670	143,861	104.0
Ann Arbor, MI	60,089	60,646	99.1
Athens, GA	59,357	65,362	90.8
Atlanta, GA	237,192	251,608	94.3
Austin, TX	482,605	468,202	103.1
Baton Rouge, LA	107,345	116,804	91.9
Boise City, ID	112,637	113,478	99.3
Boston, MA	328,503	355,876	92.3
Boulder, CO	55,160	51,232	107.7
Cape Coral, FL	91,158	92,784	98.2
Cedar Rapids, IA	64,863	67,438	96.2
Charleston, SC	63,863	71,394	89.5
Charlotte, NC	412,035	445,390	92.5
Chicago, IL	1,317,791	1,391,743	94.7
Cincinnati, OH	145,900	155,494	93.8
Clarksville, TN	76,399	76,535	99.8
Cleveland, OH	185,274	200,008	92.6
College Station, TX	58,117	55,569	104.6
Colorado Springs, CO	232,440	232,431	100.0
Columbia, MO	58,250	62,980	92.5
Columbia, SC	67,638	65,635	103.1
Columbus, OH	429,868	448,685	95.8
Dallas, TX	657,714	672,898	97.7
Davenport, IA	50,216	51,953	96.7
Denver, CO	353,311	352,265	100.3
Des Moines, IA	106,316	109,320	97.3
Durham, NC	126,897	142,805	88.9
Edison, NJ	50,210	50,237	99.9
El Paso, TX	332,917	346,896	96.0
Fargo, ND	61,988	59,901	103.5
Fayetteville, NC	105,869	104,563	101.2
Fort Collins, CO	83,175	82,434	100.9
Fort Wayne, IN	128,483	137,269	93.6
Fort Worth, TX	428,238	446,163	96.0
Grand Rapids, MI	97,940	100,461	97.5
Greeley, CO	52,657	53,231	98.9
Green Bay, WI	51,929	52,848	98.3
Greensboro, NC	135,572	155,731	87.1
Honolulu, HI	173,837	175,148	99.3
Houston, TX	1,153,417	1,157,015	99.7
Huntsville, AL	94,803	101,416	93.5
Indianapolis, IN	416,893	447,554	93.1
Jacksonville, FL	431,133	459,334	93.9
Kansas City, MO	235,974	250,430	94.2
Lafayette, LA	61,742	64,924	95.1
Lakeland, FL	51,105	56,817	89.9
Las Vegas, NV	316,556	318,217	99.5
Lexington, KY	157,231	163,370	96.2
Lincoln, NE	142,589	141,250	100.9
Little Rock, AR	94,939	103,019	92.2
Los Angeles, CA	1,964,984	2,001,952	98.2
Louisville, KY	299,406	318,384	94.0
Madison, WI	126,190	128,787	98.0

Table continued on following page.

City	Males	Females	Males per 100 Females
Manchester, NH	56,510	55,599	101.6
Memphis, TN	308,460	343,472	89.8
Miami, FL	224,810	229,469	98.0
Midland, TX	70,558	67,991	103.8
Milwaukee, WI	286,081	308,467	92.7
Minneapolis, MN	212,823	207,501	102.6
Nashville, TN	319,844	343,906	93.0
New Haven, CT	61,926	68,405	90.5
New Orleans, LA	185,513	205,332	90.3
New York, NY	4,015,982	4,403,334	91.2
Oklahoma City, OK	316,500	327,192	96.7
Omaha, NE	234,719	241,143	97.3
Orlando, FL	134,785	146,047	92.3
Peoria, IL	54,542	58,990	92.5
Philadelphia, PA	747,479	831,596	89.9
Phoenix, AZ	813,775	819,242	99.3
Pittsburgh, PA	147,776	154,429	95.7
Portland, OR	319,869	325,422	98.3
Providence, RI	86,874	92,620	93.8
Provo, UT	57,489	58,914	97.6
Raleigh, NC	223,942	240,543	93.1
Reno, NV	124,568	121,932	102.2
Richmond, VA	107,430	119,192	90.1
Riverside, CA	162,664	163,750	99.3
Rochester, MN	56,262	59,295	94.9
Sacramento, CA	245,188	255,742	95.9
Salt Lake City, UT	100,748	97,008	103.9
San Antonio, TX	744,596	763,487	97.5
San Diego, CA	711,134	698,439	101.8
San Francisco, CA	446,286	428,675	104.1
San Jose, CA	518,708	508,982	101.9
Santa Rosa, CA	86,927	92,774	93.7
Savannah, GA	69,220	76,183	90.9
Seattle, WA	366,442	357,863	102.4
Sioux Falls, SD	88,410	88,707	99.7
Springfield, IL	54,935	60,953	90.1
Tallahassee, FL	90,053	101,226	89.0
Tampa, FL	188,134	199,782	94.2
Tucson, AZ	269,403	272,079	99.0
Tulsa, OK	195,534	206,790	94.6
Tuscaloosa, AL	47,718	51,672	92.3
Virginia Beach, VA	221,324	228,877	96.7
Washington, DC	328,644	364,039	90.3
Wichita, KS	191,730	198,147	96.8
Winston-Salem, NC	114,592	129,523	88.5
U.S.	159,886,919	164,810,876	97.0

Source: U.S. Census Bureau, 2015-2019 American Community Survey 5-Year Estimates

Male/Female Ratio: Metro Area

Metro Area	Males	Females	Males per 100 Females
Albuquerque, NM	448,642	463,466	96.8
Allentown, PA	411,125	426,485	96.4
Anchorage, AK	204,508	194,392	105.2
Ann Arbor, MI	181,923	185,077	98.3
Athens, GA	100,687	107,770	93.4
Atlanta, GA	2,834,134	3,028,290	93.6
Austin, TX	1,059,553	1,054,888	100.4
Baton Rouge, LA	417,717	436,601	95.7
Boise City, ID	354,905	355,838	99.7
Boston, MA	2,347,899	2,484,447	94.5
Boulder, CO	162,211	160,299	101.2
Cape Coral, FL	361,232	376,236	96.0
Cedar Rapids, IA	133,800	136,256	98.2
Charleston, SC	378,374	396,134	95.5
Charlotte, NC	1,235,495	1,310,065	94.3
Chicago, IL	4,654,160	4,854,445	95.9
Cincinnati, OH	1,079,705	1,122,036	96.2
Clarksville, TN	151,723	147,747	102.7
Cleveland, OH	993,227	1,063,671	93.4
College Station, TX	129,895	128,134	101.4
Colorado Springs, CO	365,383	358,115	102.0
Columbia, MO	100,711	104,658	96.2
Columbia, SC	399,998	424,280	94.3
Columbus, OH	1,022,627	1,055,134	96.9
Dallas, TX	3,601,569	3,719,094	96.8
Davenport, IA	187,831	193,344	97.1
Denver, CO	1,445,090	1,446,976	99.9
Des Moines, IA	336,082	344,357	97.6
Durham, NC	301,581	325,114	92.8
Edison, NJ	9,327,459	9,966,777	93.6
El Paso, TX	413,883	426,594	97.0
Fargo, ND	120,992	119,429	101.3
Fayetteville, NC	257,939	261,162	98.8
Fort Collins, CO	172,000	172,786	99.5
Fort Wayne, IN	198,843	207,462	95.8
Fort Worth, TX	3,601,569	3,719,094	96.8
Grand Rapids, MI	527,777	534,615	98.7
Greeley, CO	154,294	151,051	102.1
Green Bay, WI	159,123	160,278	99.3
Greensboro, NC	364,321	397,742	91.6
Honolulu, HI	496,066	488,755	101.5
Houston, TX	3,417,036	3,467,102	98.6
Huntsville, AL	224,226	232,777	96.3
Indianapolis, IN	991,392	1,038,080	95.5
Jacksonville, FL	733,355	770,219	95.2
Kansas City, MO	1,042,927	1,081,591	96.4
Lafayette, LA	238,957	250,957	95.2
Lakeland, FL	336,279	349,939	96.1
Las Vegas, NV	1,089,228	1,092,776	99.7
Lexington, KY	249,429	261,218	95.5
Lincoln, NE	165,977	164,352	101.0
Little Rock, AR	356,611	380,404	93.7
Los Angeles, CA	6,533,214	6,716,400	97.3
Louisville, KY	613,822	643,266	95.4
Madison, WI	325,952	327,773	99.4

Table continued on following page.

Metro Area	Males	Females	Males per 100 Females
Manchester, NH	205,394	207,641	98.9
Memphis, TN	640,257	699,366	91.5
Miami, FL	2,959,743	3,130,917	94.5
Midland, TX	87,984	85,832	102.5
Milwaukee, WI	767,950	807,273	95.1
Minneapolis, MN	1,771,443	1,802,166	98.3
Nashville, TN	913,820	958,083	95.4
New Haven, CT	413,519	443,994	93.1
New Orleans, LA	612,116	655,661	93.4
New York, NY	9,327,459	9,966,777	93.6
Oklahoma City, OK	682,133	700,708	97.3
Omaha, NE	461,556	470,223	98.2
Orlando, FL	1,226,241	1,282,729	95.6
Peoria, IL	200,311	206,572	97.0
Philadelphia, PA	2,939,397	3,139,733	93.6
Phoenix, AZ	2,366,181	2,395,422	98.8
Pittsburgh, PA	1,135,076	1,196,371	94.9
Portland, OR	1,210,509	1,235,252	98.0
Providence, RI	785,383	832,885	94.3
Provo, UT	311,659	305,132	102.1
Raleigh, NC	649,577	682,734	95.1
Reno, NV	232,199	228,725	101.5
Richmond, VA	613,475	656,055	93.5
Riverside, CA	2,270,726	2,289,744	99.2
Rochester, MN	107,432	110,532	97.2
Sacramento, CA	1,132,519	1,183,461	95.7
Salt Lake City, UT	603,034	598,009	100.8
San Antonio, TX	1,220,720	1,247,473	97.9
San Diego, CA	1,669,515	1,646,558	101.4
San Francisco, CA	2,325,587	2,375,745	97.9
San Jose, CA	1,004,573	983,273	102.2
Santa Rosa, CA	244,045	255,727	95.4
Savannah, GA	187,309	198,727	94.3
Seattle, WA	1,938,723	1,932,600	100.3
Sioux Falls, SD	130,188	129,160	100.8
Springfield, IL	100,527	108,640	92.5
Tallahassee, FL	184,249	197,948	93.1
Tampa, FL	1,502,972	1,594,887	94.2
Tucson, AZ	505,666	521,541	97.0
Tulsa, OK	486,355	504,189	96.5
Tuscaloosa, AL	120,524	130,157	92.6
Virginia Beach, VA	867,843	893,886	97.1
Washington, DC	3,028,975	3,167,610	95.6
Wichita, KS	316,050	321,640	98.3
Winston-Salem, NC	320,092	346,124	92.5
U.S.	159,886,919	164,810,876	97.0

Note: Figures cover the Metropolitan Statistical Area (MSA)—see Appendix B for areas included
Source: U.S. Census Bureau, 2015-2019 American Community Survey 5-Year Estimates

Gross Metropolitan Product

MSA[1]	2017	2018	2019	2020	Rank[2]
Albuquerque, NM	42.8	44.4	46.3	48.6	68
Allentown, PA	43.9	46.2	48.1	49.9	64
Anchorage, AK	27.4	28.3	29.3	30.6	102
Ann Arbor, MI	23.5	24.6	25.5	26.4	112
Athens, GA	10.1	10.5	10.8	11.2	205
Atlanta, GA	391.0	409.9	431.6	452.0	10
Austin, TX	145.1	156.6	164.6	174.0	25
Baton Rouge, LA	53.2	56.3	58.3	61.0	59
Boise City, ID	33.9	36.5	38.7	40.8	79
Boston, MA	449.5	472.7	493.6	515.0	8
Boulder, CO	25.6	27.2	28.7	29.9	107
Cape Coral, FL	28.3	30.0	31.8	33.4	93
Cedar Rapids, IA	17.8	18.4	18.8	19.4	141
Charleston, SC	42.5	44.6	46.7	49.0	67
Charlotte, NC	174.1	185.6	195.5	205.3	20
Chicago, IL	683.3	716.3	743.3	770.7	3
Cincinnati, OH	137.2	143.5	150.7	156.1	29
Clarksville, TN	11.0	11.6	12.2	12.6	194
Cleveland, OH	138.3	145.9	152.3	157.1	28
College Station, TX	9.9	10.6	11.2	11.7	204
Colorado Springs, CO	33.1	34.9	36.6	38.5	84
Columbia, MO	9.2	9.6	9.9	10.3	220
Columbia, SC	41.4	42.3	43.9	45.8	73
Columbus, OH	135.6	142.2	148.6	154.7	32
Dallas, TX	522.3	556.9	586.7	620.6	5
Davenport, IA	19.8	20.7	21.6	22.3	124
Denver, CO	211.6	225.3	235.8	246.9	18
Des Moines, IA	55.0	57.7	60.3	62.8	58
Durham, NC	43.4	45.5	48.0	50.7	65
Edison, NJ	1,765.5	1,851.9	1,932.1	2,007.4	1
El Paso, TX	28.3	29.4	30.5	31.5	97
Fargo, ND	15.3	16.1	16.8	17.5	156
Fayetteville, NC	17.2	17.6	18.1	18.8	149
Fort Collins, CO	17.4	18.4	19.7	20.7	139
Fort Wayne, IN	21.9	22.9	23.9	24.8	117
Fort Worth, TX	522.3	556.9	586.7	620.6	5
Grand Rapids, MI	60.6	63.6	66.2	68.3	54
Greeley, CO	12.8	13.8	14.7	15.6	178
Green Bay, WI	19.4	20.4	21.3	22.1	128
Greensboro, NC	41.5	43.0	44.3	45.7	71
Honolulu, HI	68.2	70.5	73.2	75.5	50
Houston, TX	478.1	513.9	546.1	583.7	7
Huntsville, AL	25.9	27.2	28.4	29.8	106
Indianapolis, IN	140.6	147.0	152.8	159.1	27
Jacksonville, FL	77.6	82.8	86.5	90.6	45
Kansas City, MO	131.8	138.2	144.1	149.7	33
Lafayette, LA	21.4	23.0	24.0	25.4	116
Lakeland, FL	21.4	22.6	23.6	24.6	119
Las Vegas, NV	112.8	119.1	124.1	130.3	36
Lexington, KY	29.7	30.8	31.9	33.0	90
Lincoln, NE	19.7	20.6	21.2	22.0	125
Little Rock, AR	38.5	39.8	41.1	42.7	76
Los Angeles, CA	1,067.7	1,125.5	1,164.2	1,207.3	2
Louisville, KY	75.3	78.1	81.3	83.9	48
Madison, WI	49.5	52.1	54.5	56.5	61
Manchester, NH	28.7	30.0	31.2	32.5	94

Table continued on following page.

MSA[1]	2017	2018	2019	2020	Rank[2]
Memphis, TN	72.9	76.2	79.4	82.2	49
Miami, FL	349.2	369.5	386.7	403.4	12
Midland, TX	27.1	35.0	38.1	44.4	83
Milwaukee, WI	104.6	109.2	112.8	116.2	37
Minneapolis, MN	260.9	273.1	284.6	296.0	14
Nashville, TN	134.3	142.5	149.8	156.5	30
New Haven, CT	46.1	47.8	49.7	51.2	62
New Orleans, LA	76.7	81.0	83.8	87.5	46
New York, NY	1,765.5	1,851.9	1,932.1	2,007.4	1
Oklahoma City, OK	74.2	79.6	83.2	88.3	47
Omaha, NE	63.3	65.9	68.5	71.0	52
Orlando, FL	134.1	142.4	150.7	158.6	31
Peoria, IL	19.2	20.1	20.9	21.6	133
Philadelphia, PA	445.1	465.5	485.8	504.6	9
Phoenix, AZ	248.0	264.9	280.3	294.0	16
Pittsburgh, PA	147.4	156.4	162.8	168.5	26
Portland, OR	165.9	175.7	183.8	191.1	21
Providence, RI	84.0	86.8	89.5	93.0	44
Provo, UT	25.7	27.9	29.5	31.2	104
Raleigh, NC	83.2	88.3	92.8	97.8	42
Reno, NV	26.8	28.8	30.8	32.3	99
Richmond, VA	83.0	87.2	91.0	94.7	43
Riverside, CA	161.6	171.0	178.3	186.9	22
Rochester, MN	12.6	13.2	13.9	14.4	182
Sacramento, CA	129.3	137.0	144.3	151.5	34
Salt Lake City, UT	87.9	93.6	97.8	102.5	41
San Antonio, TX	126.1	134.5	140.1	148.6	35
San Diego, CA	237.2	249.4	260.3	272.1	17
San Francisco, CA	512.2	547.3	578.7	605.5	6
San Jose, CA	281.6	303.1	321.2	334.7	13
Santa Rosa, CA	29.3	30.4	31.4	32.5	91
Savannah, GA	18.8	19.7	20.6	21.2	134
Seattle, WA	367.9	397.5	416.9	435.0	11
Sioux Falls, SD	19.6	20.5	21.5	22.4	127
Springfield, IL	10.3	10.7	11.0	11.4	202
Tallahassee, FL	16.4	17.1	17.9	18.7	152
Tampa, FL	148.2	156.6	164.0	172.0	24
Tucson, AZ	39.9	41.7	43.6	45.5	74
Tulsa, OK	57.2	60.9	63.7	67.4	55
Tuscaloosa, AL	11.8	12.4	13.0	13.4	190
Virginia Beach, VA	95.2	99.3	103.6	107.4	39
Washington, DC	539.6	562.6	585.8	612.1	4
Wichita, KS	34.3	35.7	37.0	38.0	81
Winston-Salem, NC	29.7	31.2	32.5	33.8	88

Note: Figures are in billions of dollars; (1) Metropolitan Statistical Area—see Appendix B for areas included; (2) Rank is based on 2018 data and ranges from 1 to 381.
Source: The U.S. Conference of Mayors, U.S. Metro Economies: GMP & Employment 2018-2020, September 2019

Economic Growth

MSA[1]	2015-17 (%)	2018 (%)	2019 (%)	2020 (%)	Rank[2]
Albuquerque, NM	0.7	1.4	2.6	2.5	252
Allentown, PA	1.2	2.6	2.3	1.6	210
Anchorage, AK	-1.5	-0.9	2.4	0.6	353
Ann Arbor, MI	2.1	2.5	1.9	1.3	123
Athens, GA	6.8	1.5	1.3	1.4	6
Atlanta, GA	3.7	2.8	3.6	2.6	47
Austin, TX	6.3	4.4	3.5	2.6	9
Baton Rouge, LA	1.6	0.8	1.2	2.4	170
Boise City, ID	3.7	5.5	4.1	3.2	45
Boston, MA	2.0	3.0	2.8	2.1	134
Boulder, CO	2.5	4.1	3.9	2.1	98
Cape Coral, FL	2.7	3.7	3.7	3.0	83
Cedar Rapids, IA	-1.6	0.9	0.8	1.0	354
Charleston, SC	5.0	2.4	2.9	2.6	16
Charlotte, NC	3.4	4.2	3.7	2.8	51
Chicago, IL	0.8	2.3	2.0	1.6	247
Cincinnati, OH	2.0	1.7	3.3	1.4	132
Clarksville, TN	-0.6	3.0	3.0	1.6	331
Cleveland, OH	1.7	1.9	2.8	0.9	160
College Station, TX	1.0	3.4	3.3	1.4	224
Colorado Springs, CO	2.9	3.1	3.0	2.8	73
Columbia, MO	0.9	1.6	1.5	1.8	242
Columbia, SC	0.8	-0.1	1.9	2.3	245
Columbus, OH	2.0	2.1	2.6	1.9	130
Dallas, TX	2.7	2.8	3.7	2.7	87
Davenport, IA	-0.2	2.4	2.4	1.2	311
Denver, CO	2.6	3.7	3.0	1.9	89
Des Moines, IA	2.8	1.8	2.7	1.9	78
Durham, NC	-2.0	2.9	3.7	3.5	363
Edison, NJ	1.3	2.6	2.6	1.6	196
El Paso, TX	0.9	1.5	1.6	1.4	244
Fargo, ND	0.4	2.1	2.6	2.0	283
Fayetteville, NC	-1.0	0.0	1.2	1.5	343
Fort Collins, CO	5.3	3.7	4.7	3.1	14
Fort Wayne, IN	1.9	2.5	2.5	1.3	149
Fort Worth, TX	2.7	2.8	3.7	2.7	87
Grand Rapids, MI	1.9	3.4	2.3	1.2	139
Greeley, CO	4.1	5.3	4.5	3.9	33
Green Bay, WI	1.2	3.2	2.6	1.2	203
Greensboro, NC	-0.2	1.5	1.2	1.2	312
Honolulu, HI	1.6	1.0	1.9	0.9	165
Houston, TX	-1.7	2.9	4.6	3.1	360
Huntsville, AL	1.8	3.0	2.5	2.7	155
Indianapolis, IN	2.5	1.9	2.1	2.0	101
Jacksonville, FL	4.1	4.3	2.6	2.5	34
Kansas City, MO	0.6	2.6	2.4	1.7	263
Lafayette, LA	-4.9	2.6	3.0	2.0	380
Lakeland, FL	2.7	3.2	2.5	2.4	82
Las Vegas, NV	1.5	3.1	2.3	2.7	182
Lexington, KY	1.6	1.3	2.0	1.1	167
Lincoln, NE	0.3	2.1	1.3	1.5	287
Little Rock, AR	0.4	0.9	1.6	1.5	286
Los Angeles, CA	2.3	3.5	1.8	1.6	110
Louisville, KY	0.7	1.4	2.3	1.2	254
Madison, WI	2.4	3.2	2.8	1.7	107
Manchester, NH	2.7	2.6	2.3	1.8	84

Table continued on following page.

MSA[1]	2015-17 (%)	2018 (%)	2019 (%)	2020 (%)	Rank[2]
Memphis, TN	0.1	2.3	2.3	1.4	299
Miami, FL	3.2	3.5	2.9	2.1	56
Midland, TX	1.0	13.0	9.2	3.6	231
Milwaukee, WI	0.9	2.1	1.5	0.9	243
Minneapolis, MN	1.9	2.3	2.5	1.9	144
Nashville, TN	4.0	3.9	3.3	2.3	39
New Haven, CT	1.2	1.7	2.1	0.9	204
New Orleans, LA	-0.6	1.2	1.3	2.0	329
New York, NY	1.3	2.6	2.6	1.6	196
Oklahoma City, OK	0.7	2.8	2.9	2.2	259
Omaha, NE	0.6	1.7	2.2	1.5	272
Orlando, FL	2.4	3.8	4.0	3.0	109
Peoria, IL	-4.0	2.5	2.0	1.3	376
Philadelphia, PA	1.4	1.9	2.7	1.7	188
Phoenix, AZ	3.3	4.5	4.0	2.7	54
Pittsburgh, PA	2.0	2.6	2.5	1.3	137
Portland, OR	3.9	3.5	2.6	1.6	42
Providence, RI	0.7	1.0	1.3	1.7	262
Provo, UT	6.6	6.5	4.0	3.7	7
Raleigh, NC	3.1	3.9	3.4	3.3	62
Reno, NV	4.3	5.3	4.9	2.5	27
Richmond, VA	1.5	3.0	2.6	1.8	179
Riverside, CA	3.0	3.4	2.3	2.6	65
Rochester, MN	3.6	2.9	3.1	1.1	48
Sacramento, CA	2.6	3.6	3.4	2.7	90
Salt Lake City, UT	2.3	3.7	2.6	2.7	114
San Antonio, TX	4.2	2.0	2.7	1.7	30
San Diego, CA	3.1	3.0	2.6	2.3	64
San Francisco, CA	4.8	5.1	4.3	2.5	18
San Jose, CA	7.0	6.0	4.6	2.2	5
Santa Rosa, CA	2.5	1.2	1.7	1.1	100
Savannah, GA	2.3	2.7	2.4	1.2	115
Seattle, WA	4.3	6.3	3.4	2.4	29
Sioux Falls, SD	1.2	1.6	3.2	2.2	206
Springfield, IL	-0.8	0.8	1.4	0.9	337
Tallahassee, FL	3.1	2.6	2.8	1.9	61
Tampa, FL	2.7	3.5	2.9	2.6	85
Tucson, AZ	2.0	2.7	2.8	2.0	133
Tulsa, OK	-3.3	1.3	3.1	1.7	373
Tuscaloosa, AL	1.0	2.8	3.4	1.5	227
Virginia Beach, VA	-0.4	2.2	2.5	1.4	323
Washington, DC	2.0	2.3	2.4	2.1	131
Wichita, KS	1.9	1.5	1.8	0.5	141
Winston-Salem, NC	-0.2	2.6	2.6	1.6	314
U.S.	1.9	2.9	2.3	2.1	—

Note: Figures are real gross metropolitan product (GMP) growth rates and represent annual average percent change;
(1) Metropolitan Statistical Area—see Appendix B for areas included; (2) Rank is based on 2017 2-year average annual percent change and ranges from 1 to 381
Source: The U.S. Conference of Mayors, U.S. Metro Economies: GMP & Employment 2018-2020, September 2019

Metropolitan Area Exports

Area	2014	2015	2016	2017	2018	2019	Rank[2]
Albuquerque, NM	1,564.0	1,761.2	999.7	624.2	771.5	1,629.7	114
Allentown, PA	3,152.5	3,439.9	3,657.2	3,639.4	3,423.2	3,796.3	66
Anchorage, AK	571.8	421.9	1,215.4	1,675.9	1,510.8	1,348.0	132
Ann Arbor, MI	1,213.6	1,053.0	1,207.9	1,447.4	1,538.7	1,432.7	128
Athens, GA	320.8	327.4	332.1	297.7	378.2	442.1	219
Atlanta, GA	19,870.3	19,163.9	20,480.1	21,748.0	24,091.6	25,800.8	14
Austin, TX	9,400.0	10,094.5	10,682.7	12,451.5	12,929.9	12,509.0	30
Baton Rouge, LA	7,528.3	6,505.4	6,580.5	8,830.3	10,506.1	8,981.2	40
Boise City, ID	3,143.4	2,668.0	3,021.7	2,483.3	2,771.7	2,062.8	101
Boston, MA	23,378.5	21,329.5	21,168.0	23,116.2	24,450.1	23,505.8	17
Boulder, CO	1,016.1	1,039.1	956.3	1,012.0	1,044.1	1,014.9	158
Cape Coral, FL	496.6	487.3	540.3	592.3	668.0	694.9	190
Cedar Rapids, IA	879.0	873.5	945.0	1,071.6	1,025.0	1,028.4	157
Charleston, SC	5,866.7	6,457.5	9,508.1	8,845.2	10,943.2	16,337.9	23
Charlotte, NC	12,885.3	13,985.8	11,944.1	13,122.5	14,083.2	13,892.4	27
Chicago, IL	47,340.1	44,820.9	43,932.7	46,140.2	47,287.8	42,438.8	4
Cincinnati, OH	22,280.7	24,127.0	26,326.2	28,581.8	27,396.3	28,778.3	11
Clarksville, TN	323.7	296.5	376.1	360.2	435.5	341.8	241
Cleveland, OH	10,706.5	9,629.7	8,752.9	8,944.9	9,382.9	8,829.9	41
College Station, TX	129.7	122.5	113.2	145.4	153.0	160.5	313
Colorado Springs, CO	856.6	832.4	786.9	819.7	850.6	864.2	172
Columbia, MO	237.7	214.0	213.7	224.0	238.6	291.4	260
Columbia, SC	2,007.9	2,011.8	2,007.7	2,123.9	2,083.8	2,184.6	97
Columbus, OH	6,245.6	6,201.6	5,675.4	5,962.2	7,529.5	7,296.6	47
Dallas, TX	28,669.4	27,372.9	27,187.8	30,269.1	36,260.9	39,474.0	7
Davenport, IA	6,563.2	5,711.8	4,497.6	5,442.7	6,761.9	6,066.3	51
Denver, CO	4,958.6	3,909.5	3,649.3	3,954.7	4,544.3	4,555.6	61
Des Moines, IA	1,361.8	1,047.8	1,052.2	1,141.2	1,293.7	1,437.8	126
Durham, NC	2,934.0	2,807.2	2,937.4	3,128.4	3,945.8	4,452.9	62
Edison, NJ	105,266.6	95,645.4	89,649.5	93,693.7	97,692.4	87,365.7	2
El Paso, TX	20,079.3	24,560.9	26,452.8	25,814.1	30,052.0	32,749.6	10
Fargo, ND	782.8	543.2	474.5	519.5	553.5	515.0	207
Fayetteville, NC	375.8	256.3	179.8	231.6	260.5	287.8	263
Fort Collins, CO	1,037.4	990.7	993.8	1,034.1	1,021.8	1,060.0	152
Fort Wayne, IN	1,581.1	1,529.0	1,322.2	1,422.8	1,593.3	1,438.5	125
Fort Worth, TX	28,669.4	27,372.9	27,187.8	30,269.1	36,260.9	39,474.0	7
Grand Rapids, MI	5,244.5	5,143.0	5,168.5	5,385.8	5,420.9	5,214.1	55
Greeley, CO	1,343.6	1,240.1	1,539.6	1,492.8	1,366.5	1,439.2	124
Green Bay, WI	988.7	968.1	1,044.0	1,054.8	1,044.3	928.2	167
Greensboro, NC	3,505.5	3,286.1	3,730.4	3,537.9	3,053.5	2,561.8	87
Honolulu, HI	765.5	446.4	330.3	393.6	438.9	308.6	250
Houston, TX	118,966.0	97,054.3	84,105.5	95,760.3	120,714.3	129,656.0	1
Huntsville, AL	1,440.4	1,344.7	1,827.3	1,889.2	1,608.7	1,534.2	122
Indianapolis, IN	9,539.4	9,809.4	9,655.4	10,544.2	11,069.9	11,148.7	33
Jacksonville, FL	2,473.7	2,564.4	2,159.0	2,141.7	2,406.7	2,975.5	79
Kansas City, MO	8,262.9	6,723.2	6,709.8	7,015.0	7,316.9	7,652.6	45
Lafayette, LA	1,532.7	1,165.2	1,335.2	954.8	1,001.7	1,086.2	148
Lakeland, FL	2,151.9	1,318.6	995.5	1,147.2	1,299.8	1,141.5	143
Las Vegas, NV	2,509.7	2,916.2	2,312.3	2,710.6	2,240.6	2,430.8	90
Lexington, KY	2,191.4	2,065.7	2,069.6	2,119.8	2,148.0	2,093.8	100
Lincoln, NE	1,173.9	1,189.3	796.9	860.9	885.6	807.0	177
Little Rock, AR	2,463.5	1,777.5	1,871.0	2,146.1	1,607.4	1,642.5	113
Los Angeles, CA	75,471.2	61,758.7	61,245.7	63,752.9	64,814.6	61,041.1	3
Louisville, KY	8,877.3	8,037.9	7,793.3	8,925.9	8,987.0	9,105.5	39
Madison, WI	2,369.5	2,280.4	2,204.8	2,187.7	2,460.2	2,337.6	93
Manchester, NH	1,575.4	1,556.6	1,465.2	1,714.7	1,651.4	1,587.1	118

Table continued on following page.

Area	2014	2015	2016	2017	2018	2019	Rank[2]
Memphis, TN	11,002.0	11,819.5	11,628.7	11,233.9	12,695.4	13,751.7	28
Miami, FL	37,969.5	33,258.5	32,734.5	34,780.5	35,650.2	35,498.9	8
Midland, TX	122.7	110.1	69.6	69.4	63.6	63.7	357
Milwaukee, WI	8,696.0	7,953.6	7,256.2	7,279.1	7,337.6	6,896.3	49
Minneapolis, MN	21,198.2	19,608.6	18,329.2	19,070.9	20,016.2	18,633.0	22
Nashville, TN	9,620.9	9,353.0	9,460.1	10,164.3	8,723.7	7,940.7	44
New Haven, CT	1,834.5	1,756.3	1,819.8	1,876.3	2,082.3	2,133.8	98
New Orleans, LA	34,881.5	27,023.3	29,518.8	31,648.5	36,570.4	34,109.6	9
New York, NY	105,266.6	95,645.4	89,649.5	93,693.7	97,692.4	87,365.7	2
Oklahoma City, OK	1,622.0	1,353.1	1,260.0	1,278.8	1,489.4	1,434.5	127
Omaha, NE	4,528.5	3,753.4	3,509.7	3,756.2	4,371.6	3,725.7	68
Orlando, FL	3,134.8	3,082.7	3,363.9	3,196.7	3,131.7	3,363.9	73
Peoria, IL	11,234.8	9,826.9	7,260.1	9,403.6	9,683.6	8,151.9	42
Philadelphia, PA	26,321.3	24,236.1	21,359.9	21,689.7	23,663.2	24,721.3	15
Phoenix, AZ	12,764.4	13,821.5	12,838.2	13,223.1	13,614.9	15,136.6	24
Pittsburgh, PA	10,015.8	9,137.1	7,971.0	9,322.7	9,824.2	9,672.9	38
Portland, OR	18,667.2	18,847.8	20,256.8	20,788.8	21,442.9	23,761.9	16
Providence, RI	6,595.1	5,048.8	6,595.7	7,125.4	6,236.6	7,424.8	46
Provo, UT	2,533.4	2,216.4	1,894.8	2,065.3	1,788.1	1,783.7	107
Raleigh, NC	2,713.1	2,553.4	2,620.4	2,865.8	3,193.2	3,546.8	70
Reno, NV	2,138.9	1,943.3	2,382.1	2,517.3	2,631.7	2,598.3	86
Richmond, VA	3,307.0	3,325.9	3,525.7	3,663.7	3,535.0	3,203.2	76
Riverside, CA	9,134.8	8,970.0	10,211.6	8,782.3	9,745.7	9,737.6	37
Rochester, MN	720.5	530.2	398.0	495.3	537.6	390.1	235
Sacramento, CA	7,143.9	8,101.2	7,032.1	6,552.6	6,222.8	5,449.2	53
Salt Lake City, UT	8,361.5	10,380.5	8,653.7	7,916.9	9,748.6	13,273.9	29
San Antonio, TX	25,781.8	15,919.2	5,621.2	9,184.1	11,678.1	11,668.0	32
San Diego, CA	18,585.7	17,439.7	18,086.6	18,637.1	20,156.8	19,774.1	20
San Francisco, CA	26,863.7	25,061.1	24,506.3	29,103.8	27,417.0	28,003.8	12
San Jose, CA	21,128.8	19,827.2	21,716.8	21,464.7	22,224.2	20,909.4	19
Santa Rosa, CA	1,103.7	1,119.8	1,194.3	1,168.2	1,231.7	1,234.5	135
Savannah, GA	5,093.4	5,447.5	4,263.4	4,472.0	5,407.8	4,925.5	58
Seattle, WA	61,938.4	67,226.4	61,881.0	59,007.0	59,742.9	41,249.0	5
Sioux Falls, SD	455.3	375.0	334.3	386.8	400.0	431.5	224
Springfield, IL	94.4	111.7	88.3	107.5	91.2	99.8	338
Tallahassee, FL	174.0	191.2	223.1	241.1	270.8	219.7	291
Tampa, FL	5,817.3	5,660.4	5,702.9	6,256.0	4,966.7	6,219.7	50
Tucson, AZ	2,277.4	2,485.9	2,563.9	2,683.9	2,824.8	2,943.7	81
Tulsa, OK	3,798.5	2,699.7	2,363.0	2,564.7	3,351.7	3,399.2	72
Tuscaloosa, AL	n/a	n/a	n/a	n/a	n/a	n/a	400
Virginia Beach, VA	3,573.2	3,556.4	3,291.1	3,307.2	3,950.6	3,642.4	69
Washington, DC	13,053.6	13,900.4	13,582.4	12,736.1	13,602.7	14,563.8	25
Wichita, KS	4,011.7	3,717.6	3,054.9	3,299.2	3,817.0	3,494.7	71
Winston-Salem, NC	1,441.9	1,267.4	1,234.6	1,131.7	1,107.5	1,209.1	137

Note: Figures are in millions of dollars; (1) Metropolitan Statistical Area—see Appendix B for areas included; (2) Rank is based on 2019 data and ranges from 1 to 386
Source: U.S. Department of Commerce, International Trade Administration, Office of Trade and Economic Analysis, Industry and Analysis, Exports by Metropolitan Area, extracted March 24, 2021

Building Permits: City

City	Single-Family 2018	2019	Pct. Chg.	Multi-Family 2018	2019	Pct. Chg.	Total 2018	2019	Pct. Chg.
Albuquerque, NM	1,115	906	-18.7	0	188	—	1,115	1,094	-1.9
Allentown, PA	0	0	0.0	0	0	0.0	0	0	0.0
Anchorage, AK	869	838	-3.6	214	221	3.3	1,083	1,059	-2.2
Ann Arbor, MI	126	96	-23.8	0	0	0.0	126	96	-23.8
Athens, GA	345	517	49.9	261	766	193.5	606	1,283	111.7
Atlanta, GA	1,184	728	-38.5	5,312	2,555	-51.9	6,496	3,283	-49.5
Austin, TX	4,433	4,568	3.0	8,850	10,141	14.6	13,283	14,709	10.7
Baton Rouge, LA	282	354	25.5	58	0	-100.0	340	354	4.1
Boise City, ID	844	698	-17.3	296	883	198.3	1,140	1,581	38.7
Boston, MA	49	37	-24.5	3,553	2,956	-16.8	3,602	2,993	-16.9
Boulder, CO	80	41	-48.8	667	286	-57.1	747	327	-56.2
Cape Coral, FL	2,245	1,878	-16.3	356	810	127.5	2,601	2,688	3.3
Cedar Rapids, IA	147	173	17.7	325	197	-39.4	472	370	-21.6
Charleston, SC	810	828	2.2	354	360	1.7	1,164	1,188	2.1
Charlotte, NC	n/a	n/a	n/a	n/a	n/a	n/a	n/a	n/a	n/a
Chicago, IL	439	410	-6.6	6,010	7,504	24.9	6,449	7,914	22.7
Cincinnati, OH	98	135	37.8	632	992	57.0	730	1,127	54.4
Clarksville, TN	669	1,428	113.5	269	160	-40.5	938	1,588	69.3
Cleveland, OH	114	78	-31.6	34	19	-44.1	148	97	-34.5
College Station, TX	459	398	-13.3	572	219	-61.7	1,031	617	-40.2
Colorado Springs, CO	n/a	n/a	n/a	n/a	n/a	n/a	n/a	n/a	n/a
Columbia, MO	261	338	29.5	2	166	8,200.0	263	504	91.6
Columbia, SC	449	464	3.3	28	10	-64.3	477	474	-0.6
Columbus, OH	555	512	-7.7	3,742	2,258	-39.7	4,297	2,770	-35.5
Dallas, TX	2,009	2,093	4.2	6,038	6,000	-0.6	8,047	8,093	0.6
Davenport, IA	68	122	79.4	0	196	—	68	318	367.6
Denver, CO	2,428	2,257	-7.0	5,450	5,073	-6.9	7,878	7,330	-7.0
Des Moines, IA	180	391	117.2	391	279	-28.6	571	670	17.3
Durham, NC	1,894	1,945	2.7	1,336	1,884	41.0	3,230	3,829	18.5
Edison, NJ	71	55	-22.5	100	175	75.0	171	230	34.5
El Paso, TX	1,588	1,873	17.9	621	413	-33.5	2,209	2,286	3.5
Fargo, ND	313	311	-0.6	897	172	-80.8	1,210	483	-60.1
Fayetteville, NC	241	240	-0.4	0	282	—	241	522	116.6
Fort Collins, CO	398	316	-20.6	673	632	-6.1	1,071	948	-11.5
Fort Wayne, IN	n/a	n/a	n/a	n/a	n/a	n/a	n/a	n/a	n/a
Fort Worth, TX	5,477	5,063	-7.6	3,833	6,276	63.7	9,310	11,339	21.8
Grand Rapids, MI	124	153	23.4	690	183	-73.5	814	336	-58.7
Greeley, CO	348	170	-51.1	190	697	266.8	538	867	61.2
Green Bay, WI	101	63	-37.6	0	0	0.0	101	63	-37.6
Greensboro, NC	597	548	-8.2	249	385	54.6	846	933	10.3
Honolulu, HI	n/a	n/a	n/a	n/a	n/a	n/a	n/a	n/a	n/a
Houston, TX	5,417	5,120	-5.5	7,820	10,343	32.3	13,237	15,463	16.8
Huntsville, AL	1,241	1,436	15.7	71	167	135.2	1,312	1,603	22.2
Indianapolis, IN	1,090	1,153	5.8	1,196	1,229	2.8	2,286	2,382	4.2
Jacksonville, FL	3,780	4,155	9.9	3,223	2,650	-17.8	7,003	6,805	-2.8
Kansas City, MO	813	619	-23.9	1,341	879	-34.5	2,154	1,498	-30.5
Lafayette, LA	n/a	n/a	n/a	n/a	n/a	n/a	n/a	n/a	n/a
Lakeland, FL	435	606	39.3	0	953	—	435	1,559	258.4
Las Vegas, NV	1,794	1,885	5.1	179	780	335.8	1,973	2,665	35.1
Lexington, KY	733	579	-21.0	1,056	804	-23.9	1,789	1,383	-22.7
Lincoln, NE	859	863	0.5	673	864	28.4	1,532	1,727	12.7
Little Rock, AR	325	480	47.7	145	539	271.7	470	1,019	116.8
Los Angeles, CA	2,636	2,647	0.4	13,663	11,740	-14.1	16,299	14,387	-11.7
Louisville, KY	1,183	1,207	2.0	2,080	2,204	6.0	3,263	3,411	4.5

Table continued on following page.

	Single-Family			Multi-Family			Total		
City	2018	2019	Pct. Chg.	2018	2019	Pct. Chg.	2018	2019	Pct. Chg.
Madison, WI	334	426	27.5	1,109	1,232	11.1	1,443	1,658	14.9
Manchester, NH	151	106	-29.8	59	26	-55.9	210	132	-37.1
Memphis, TN	n/a	n/a	n/a	n/a	n/a	n/a	n/a	n/a	n/a
Miami, FL	80	107	33.8	4,545	4,361	-4.0	4,625	4,468	-3.4
Midland, TX	1,222	1,290	5.6	0	0	0.0	1,222	1,290	5.6
Milwaukee, WI	39	15	-61.5	717	178	-75.2	756	193	-74.5
Minneapolis, MN	162	122	-24.7	3,463	4,691	35.5	3,625	4,813	32.8
Nashville, TN	3,560	3,830	7.6	3,268	5,935	81.6	6,828	9,765	43.0
New Haven, CT	4	4	0.0	456	695	52.4	460	699	52.0
New Orleans, LA	524	558	6.5	779	748	-4.0	1,303	1,306	0.2
New York, NY	417	332	-20.4	20,493	26,215	27.9	20,910	26,547	27.0
Oklahoma City, OK	2,955	3,243	9.7	142	128	-9.9	3,097	3,371	8.8
Omaha, NE	1,237	1,179	-4.7	1,650	965	-41.5	2,887	2,144	-25.7
Orlando, FL	790	747	-5.4	2,289	1,887	-17.6	3,079	2,634	-14.5
Peoria, IL	32	33	3.1	0	0	0.0	32	33	3.1
Philadelphia, PA	683	894	30.9	2,556	3,672	43.7	3,239	4,566	41.0
Phoenix, AZ	3,732	4,175	11.9	3,530	5,723	62.1	7,262	9,898	36.3
Pittsburgh, PA	90	78	-13.3	553	582	5.2	643	660	2.6
Portland, OR	775	703	-9.3	4,873	4,391	-9.9	5,648	5,094	-9.8
Providence, RI	1	14	1,300.0	0	183	–	1	197	19,600.0
Provo, UT	171	174	1.8	286	140	-51.0	457	314	-31.3
Raleigh, NC	1,304	380	-70.9	2,907	827	-71.6	4,211	1,207	-71.3
Reno, NV	1,351	1,176	-13.0	1,883	2,144	13.9	3,234	3,320	2.7
Richmond, VA	273	353	29.3	290	887	205.9	563	1,240	120.2
Riverside, CA	171	170	-0.6	503	509	1.2	674	679	0.7
Rochester, MN	347	296	-14.7	1,068	478	-55.2	1,415	774	-45.3
Sacramento, CA	1,610	1,538	-4.5	714	1,463	104.9	2,324	3,001	29.1
Salt Lake City, UT	109	127	16.5	793	3,359	323.6	902	3,486	286.5
San Antonio, TX	3,266	3,890	19.1	2,663	5,306	99.2	5,929	9,196	55.1
San Diego, CA	774	580	-25.1	3,678	3,361	-8.6	4,452	3,941	-11.5
San Francisco, CA	28	22	-21.4	5,150	3,178	-38.3	5,178	3,200	-38.2
San Jose, CA	238	514	116.0	2,598	1,831	-29.5	2,836	2,345	-17.3
Santa Rosa, CA	1,632	939	-42.5	69	251	263.8	1,701	1,190	-30.0
Savannah, GA	399	339	-15.0	0	0	0.0	399	339	-15.0
Seattle, WA	523	507	-3.1	7,395	10,277	39.0	7,918	10,784	36.2
Sioux Falls, SD	1,083	1,013	-6.5	898	643	-28.4	1,981	1,656	-16.4
Springfield, IL	74	57	-23.0	219	112	-48.9	293	169	-42.3
Tallahassee, FL	396	407	2.8	1,128	1,275	13.0	1,524	1,682	10.4
Tampa, FL	1,109	1,159	4.5	679	3,618	432.8	1,788	4,777	167.2
Tucson, AZ	680	999	46.9	860	817	-5.0	1,540	1,816	17.9
Tulsa, OK	471	629	33.5	343	580	69.1	814	1,209	48.5
Tuscaloosa, AL	353	321	-9.1	469	844	80.0	822	1,165	41.7
Virginia Beach, VA	534	667	24.9	245	683	178.8	779	1,350	73.3
Washington, DC	112	168	50.0	4,503	5,777	28.3	4,615	5,945	28.8
Wichita, KS	532	618	16.2	326	364	11.7	858	982	14.5
Winston-Salem, NC	1,251	1,185	-5.3	84	0	-100.0	1,335	1,185	-11.2
U.S.	855,300	862,100	0.7	473,500	523,900	10.6	1,328,800	1,386,000	4.3

Note: Figures represent new, privately-owned housing units authorized (unadjusted data); All permit data are based on estimates with imputation

Source: U.S. Census Bureau, Manufacturing, Mining, and Construction Statistics, Building Permits, 2018, 2019

Appendix A: Comparative Statistics

Building Permits: Metro Area

Metro Area	Single-Family 2018	Single-Family 2019	Pct. Chg.	Multi-Family 2018	Multi-Family 2019	Pct. Chg.	Total 2018	Total 2019	Pct. Chg.
Albuquerque, NM	2,086	1,872	-10.3	100	276	176.0	2,186	2,148	-1.7
Allentown, PA	1,082	1,078	-0.4	164	267	62.8	1,246	1,345	7.9
Anchorage, AK	938	878	-6.4	321	285	-11.2	1,259	1,163	-7.6
Ann Arbor, MI	652	608	-6.7	153	207	35.3	805	815	1.2
Athens, GA	729	821	12.6	340	770	126.5	1,069	1,591	48.8
Atlanta, GA	26,506	26,261	-0.9	12,935	6,575	-49.2	39,441	32,836	-16.7
Austin, TX	17,030	18,426	8.2	13,005	13,611	4.7	30,035	32,037	6.7
Baton Rouge, LA	3,509	3,612	2.9	413	10	-97.6	3,922	3,622	-7.6
Boise City, ID	6,923	7,570	9.3	1,994	3,062	53.6	8,917	10,632	19.2
Boston, MA	4,930	4,299	-12.8	9,253	10,789	16.6	14,183	15,088	6.4
Boulder, CO	899	742	-17.5	2,055	908	-55.8	2,954	1,650	-44.1
Cape Coral, FL	5,803	5,633	-2.9	3,918	3,472	-11.4	9,721	9,105	-6.3
Cedar Rapids, IA	490	509	3.9	469	305	-35.0	959	814	-15.1
Charleston, SC	4,787	4,758	-0.6	2,215	1,937	-12.6	7,002	6,695	-4.4
Charlotte, NC	16,407	16,253	-0.9	9,802	8,384	-14.5	26,209	24,637	-6.0
Chicago, IL	8,546	7,598	-11.1	9,135	10,487	14.8	17,681	18,085	2.3
Cincinnati, OH	4,282	4,488	4.8	1,794	1,535	-14.4	6,076	6,023	-0.9
Clarksville, TN	1,516	2,332	53.8	287	325	13.2	1,803	2,657	47.4
Cleveland, OH	2,733	2,584	-5.5	248	448	80.6	2,981	3,032	1.7
College Station, TX	1,023	1,091	6.6	833	389	-53.3	1,856	1,480	-20.3
Colorado Springs, CO	4,229	4,051	-4.2	1,505	1,457	-3.2	5,734	5,508	-3.9
Columbia, MO	555	633	14.1	2	166	8,200.0	557	799	43.4
Columbia, SC	4,478	4,209	-6.0	474	215	-54.6	4,952	4,424	-10.7
Columbus, OH	4,493	4,389	-2.3	4,947	3,701	-25.2	9,440	8,090	-14.3
Dallas, TX	36,832	34,939	-5.1	27,061	27,769	2.6	63,893	62,708	-1.9
Davenport, IA	490	533	8.8	69	268	288.4	559	801	43.3
Denver, CO	11,808	11,081	-6.2	9,921	8,227	-17.1	21,729	19,308	-11.1
Des Moines, IA	3,233	3,915	21.1	1,690	1,354	-19.9	4,923	5,269	7.0
Durham, NC	3,289	3,561	8.3	2,127	2,234	5.0	5,416	5,795	7.0
Edison, NJ	11,077	11,072	0.0	38,615	50,096	29.7	49,692	61,168	23.1
El Paso, TX	1,751	2,433	38.9	665	633	-4.8	2,416	3,066	26.9
Fargo, ND	1,080	939	-13.1	1,233	486	-60.6	2,313	1,425	-38.4
Fayetteville, NC	803	1,547	92.7	16	292	1,725.0	819	1,839	124.5
Fort Collins, CO	1,679	1,580	-5.9	1,265	910	-28.1	2,944	2,490	-15.4
Fort Wayne, IN	1,343	1,330	-1.0	541	626	15.7	1,884	1,956	3.8
Fort Worth, TX	36,832	34,939	-5.1	27,061	27,769	2.6	63,893	62,708	-1.9
Grand Rapids, MI	2,749	2,531	-7.9	1,105	1,624	47.0	3,854	4,155	7.8
Greeley, CO	3,194	3,335	4.4	913	1,052	15.2	4,107	4,387	6.8
Green Bay, WI	766	723	-5.6	435	407	-6.4	1,201	1,130	-5.9
Greensboro, NC	1,949	2,002	2.7	275	421	53.1	2,224	2,423	8.9
Honolulu, HI	983	912	-7.2	1,427	1,367	-4.2	2,410	2,279	-5.4
Houston, TX	40,321	39,507	-2.0	16,967	24,165	42.4	57,288	63,672	11.1
Huntsville, AL	2,870	3,399	18.4	71	167	135.2	2,941	3,566	21.3
Indianapolis, IN	7,291	7,120	-2.3	1,603	2,601	62.3	8,894	9,721	9.3
Jacksonville, FL	10,755	11,583	7.7	4,695	3,104	-33.9	15,450	14,687	-4.9
Kansas City, MO	5,608	4,811	-14.2	4,660	4,536	-2.7	10,268	9,347	-9.0
Lafayette, LA	1,657	1,632	-1.5	30	34	13.3	1,687	1,666	-1.2
Lakeland, FL	5,331	6,435	20.7	0	2,291	–	5,331	8,726	63.7
Las Vegas, NV	9,721	10,042	3.3	2,323	3,861	66.2	12,044	13,903	15.4
Lexington, KY	1,404	1,308	-6.8	1,368	938	-31.4	2,772	2,246	-19.0
Lincoln, NE	1,117	1,088	-2.6	687	1,010	47.0	1,804	2,098	16.3
Little Rock, AR	1,819	1,921	5.6	355	1,084	205.4	2,174	3,005	38.2
Los Angeles, CA	10,042	9,306	-7.3	19,482	21,248	9.1	29,524	30,554	3.5
Louisville, KY	3,104	3,122	0.6	2,409	2,644	9.8	5,513	5,766	4.6

Table continued on following page.

Metro Area	Single-Family 2018	Single-Family 2019	Pct. Chg.	Multi-Family 2018	Multi-Family 2019	Pct. Chg.	Total 2018	Total 2019	Pct. Chg.
Madison, WI	1,623	1,536	-5.4	2,029	1,807	-10.9	3,652	3,343	-8.5
Manchester, NH	709	691	-2.5	697	561	-19.5	1,406	1,252	-11.0
Memphis, TN	3,185	3,319	4.2	1,307	355	-72.8	4,492	3,674	-18.2
Miami, FL	7,022	7,241	3.1	12,531	13,447	7.3	19,553	20,688	5.8
Midland, TX	1,227	1,306	6.4	0	0	0.0	1,227	1,306	6.4
Milwaukee, WI	1,712	1,494	-12.7	2,057	925	-55.0	3,769	2,419	-35.8
Minneapolis, MN	8,985	9,610	7.0	9,221	12,804	38.9	18,206	22,414	23.1
Nashville, TN	13,470	14,460	7.3	5,689	8,242	44.9	19,159	22,702	18.5
New Haven, CT	406	399	-1.7	760	1,054	38.7	1,166	1,453	24.6
New Orleans, LA	3,046	3,241	6.4	818	785	-4.0	3,864	4,026	4.2
New York, NY	11,077	11,072	0.0	38,615	50,096	29.7	49,692	61,168	23.1
Oklahoma City, OK	5,430	5,924	9.1	300	633	111.0	5,730	6,557	14.4
Omaha, NE	2,791	2,633	-5.7	1,997	1,467	-26.5	4,788	4,100	-14.4
Orlando, FL	16,455	14,995	-8.9	12,427	9,475	-23.8	28,882	24,470	-15.3
Peoria, IL	228	218	-4.4	106	90	-15.1	334	308	-7.8
Philadelphia, PA	6,875	6,963	1.3	6,281	8,644	37.6	13,156	15,607	18.6
Phoenix, AZ	23,526	25,026	6.4	7,817	10,847	38.8	31,343	35,873	14.5
Pittsburgh, PA	2,977	2,830	-4.9	1,060	1,154	8.9	4,037	3,984	-1.3
Portland, OR	6,869	7,688	11.9	7,311	9,127	24.8	14,180	16,815	18.6
Providence, RI	1,553	1,592	2.5	410	456	11.2	1,963	2,048	4.3
Provo, UT	5,516	5,423	-1.7	1,325	1,524	15.0	6,841	6,947	1.5
Raleigh, NC	11,160	11,142	-0.2	4,790	2,178	-54.5	15,950	13,320	-16.5
Reno, NV	2,255	2,157	-4.3	2,195	3,106	41.5	4,450	5,263	18.3
Richmond, VA	4,498	4,481	-0.4	1,563	3,859	146.9	6,061	8,340	37.6
Riverside, CA	11,591	11,147	-3.8	3,218	3,452	7.3	14,809	14,599	-1.4
Rochester, MN	690	614	-11.0	1,126	497	-55.9	1,816	1,111	-38.8
Sacramento, CA	6,393	7,184	12.4	1,480	2,247	51.8	7,873	9,431	19.8
Salt Lake City, UT	5,391	4,760	-11.7	3,359	5,920	76.2	8,750	10,680	22.1
San Antonio, TX	8,013	9,103	13.6	3,484	6,792	94.9	11,497	15,895	38.3
San Diego, CA	3,489	3,019	-13.5	6,345	5,197	-18.1	9,834	8,216	-16.5
San Francisco, CA	4,048	4,076	0.7	13,373	9,805	-26.7	17,421	13,881	-20.3
San Jose, CA	2,466	2,603	5.6	6,278	3,627	-42.2	8,744	6,230	-28.8
Santa Rosa, CA	3,169	2,079	-34.4	110	350	218.2	3,279	2,429	-25.9
Savannah, GA	2,080	2,151	3.4	1,078	440	-59.2	3,158	2,591	-18.0
Seattle, WA	9,134	8,737	-4.3	19,052	17,862	-6.2	28,186	26,599	-5.6
Sioux Falls, SD	1,380	1,376	-0.3	1,008	743	-26.3	2,388	2,119	-11.3
Springfield, IL	193	149	-22.8	313	180	-42.5	506	329	-35.0
Tallahassee, FL	2,073	1,070	-48.4	1,128	1,275	13.0	3,201	2,345	-26.7
Tampa, FL	14,228	14,670	3.1	3,224	8,870	175.1	17,452	23,540	34.9
Tucson, AZ	3,240	3,490	7.7	1,164	823	-29.3	4,404	4,313	-2.1
Tulsa, OK	2,845	3,377	18.7	567	929	63.8	3,412	4,306	26.2
Tuscaloosa, AL	578	630	9.0	469	844	80.0	1,047	1,474	40.8
Virginia Beach, VA	4,168	4,345	4.2	1,436	1,563	8.8	5,604	5,908	5.4
Washington, DC	13,588	12,977	-4.5	12,169	13,827	13.6	25,757	26,804	4.1
Wichita, KS	1,223	1,389	13.6	735	737	0.3	1,958	2,126	8.6
Winston-Salem, NC	3,123	3,160	1.2	376	174	-53.7	3,499	3,334	-4.7
U.S.	855,300	862,100	0.7	473,500	523,900	10.6	1,328,800	1,386,000	4.3

Note: Figures cover the Metropolitan Statistical Area—see Appendix B for areas included; Figures represent new, privately-owned housing units authorized (unadjusted data); All permit data are based on estimates with imputation
Source: U.S. Census Bureau, Manufacturing, Mining, and Construction Statistics, Building Permits, 2018, 2019

Appendix A: Comparative Statistics

Housing Vacancy Rates

Metro Area[1]	Gross Vacancy Rate[2] (%) 2018	2019	2020	Year-Round Vacancy Rate[3] (%) 2018	2019	2020	Rental Vacancy Rate[4] (%) 2018	2019	2020	Homeowner Vacancy Rate[5] (%) 2018	2019	2020
Albuquerque, NM	8.3	7.9	5.1	7.9	7.4	4.9	7.8	6.5	5.4	1.8	1.9	1.4
Allentown, PA	9.3	7.7	4.9	7.1	5.8	4.8	5.7	4.0	3.9	0.9	1.4	0.7
Anchorage, AK	n/a	n/a	n/a	n/a	n/a	n/a	n/a	n/a	n/a	n/a	n/a	n/a
Ann Arbor, MI	n/a	n/a	n/a	n/a	n/a	n/a	n/a	n/a	n/a	n/a	n/a	n/a
Athens, GA	n/a	n/a	n/a	n/a	n/a	n/a	n/a	n/a	n/a	n/a	n/a	n/a
Atlanta, GA	7.8	7.6	5.8	7.4	7.3	5.4	6.6	7.0	6.4	1.1	1.3	0.8
Austin, TX	9.7	10.7	7.0	8.7	10.3	6.8	7.0	8.2	6.6	1.2	1.8	2.0
Baton Rouge, LA	13.0	13.9	12.6	11.8	13.0	11.8	7.6	10.2	7.4	1.4	1.9	1.7
Boise City, ID	n/a	n/a	n/a	n/a	n/a	n/a	n/a	n/a	n/a	n/a	n/a	n/a
Boston, MA	7.5	7.1	6.8	6.5	6.2	5.6	3.8	3.6	4.7	1.0	0.8	0.4
Boulder, CO	n/a	n/a	n/a	n/a	n/a	n/a	n/a	n/a	n/a	n/a	n/a	n/a
Cape Coral, FL	41.5	40.0	35.1	16.6	17.9	15.8	5.8	8.5	15.5	3.0	2.3	1.9
Cedar Rapids, IA	n/a	n/a	n/a	n/a	n/a	n/a	n/a	n/a	n/a	n/a	n/a	n/a
Charleston, SC	16.0	18.4	18.1	14.5	16.6	16.5	17.0	16.7	27.7	3.4	2.2	2.3
Charlotte, NC	8.5	9.3	6.6	8.1	9.0	6.3	5.6	7.6	5.6	1.7	1.8	1.0
Chicago, IL	7.5	7.6	7.4	7.4	7.6	7.2	7.0	5.7	7.4	1.6	1.5	1.2
Cincinnati, OH	6.8	8.6	6.6	6.7	8.4	6.2	4.4	10.7	7.9	1.5	1.1	0.7
Clarksville, TN	n/a	n/a	n/a	n/a	n/a	n/a	n/a	n/a	n/a	n/a	n/a	n/a
Cleveland, OH	10.4	10.1	9.3	10.3	9.9	8.8	6.9	3.8	5.5	0.9	1.1	0.7
College Station, TX	n/a	n/a	n/a	n/a	n/a	n/a	n/a	n/a	n/a	n/a	n/a	n/a
Colorado Springs, CO	n/a	n/a	n/a	n/a	n/a	n/a	n/a	n/a	n/a	n/a	n/a	n/a
Columbia, MO	n/a	n/a	n/a	n/a	n/a	n/a	n/a	n/a	n/a	n/a	n/a	n/a
Columbia, SC	8.9	10.6	7.2	8.8	10.4	7.1	9.4	9.3	4.5	1.9	1.5	0.7
Columbus, OH	7.4	4.5	4.7	7.4	4.2	4.5	8.6	4.3	5.9	1.5	0.8	0.3
Dallas, TX	7.8	7.6	6.4	7.6	7.3	6.4	7.4	6.9	7.2	1.4	1.5	0.7
Davenport, IA	n/a	n/a	n/a	n/a	n/a	n/a	n/a	n/a	n/a	n/a	n/a	n/a
Denver, CO	8.0	7.5	5.8	7.4	7.0	5.1	3.8	4.7	4.8	0.9	1.0	0.5
Des Moines, IA	n/a	n/a	n/a	n/a	n/a	n/a	n/a	n/a	n/a	n/a	n/a	n/a
Durham, NC	n/a	n/a	n/a	n/a	n/a	n/a	n/a	n/a	n/a	n/a	n/a	n/a
Edison, NJ	10.3	9.2	9.1	9.1	7.8	7.8	4.5	4.3	4.5	1.6	1.4	1.3
El Paso, TX	n/a	n/a	n/a	n/a	n/a	n/a	n/a	n/a	n/a	n/a	n/a	n/a
Fargo, ND	n/a	n/a	n/a	n/a	n/a	n/a	n/a	n/a	n/a	n/a	n/a	n/a
Fayetteville, NC	n/a	n/a	n/a	n/a	n/a	n/a	n/a	n/a	n/a	n/a	n/a	n/a
Fort Collins, CO	n/a	n/a	n/a	n/a	n/a	n/a	n/a	n/a	n/a	n/a	n/a	n/a
Fort Wayne, IN	n/a	n/a	n/a	n/a	n/a	n/a	n/a	n/a	n/a	n/a	n/a	n/a
Fort Worth, TX	7.8	7.6	6.4	7.6	7.3	6.4	7.4	6.9	7.2	1.4	1.5	0.7
Grand Rapids, MI	8.9	7.4	7.1	6.8	5.1	4.7	6.8	4.5	4.6	0.3	0.5	1.1
Greeley, CO	n/a	n/a	n/a	n/a	n/a	n/a	n/a	n/a	n/a	n/a	n/a	n/a
Green Bay, WI	n/a	n/a	n/a	n/a	n/a	n/a	n/a	n/a	n/a	n/a	n/a	n/a
Greensboro, NC	11.6	9.9	8.3	11.5	9.5	8.2	11.4	8.1	7.2	1.0	0.7	0.7
Honolulu, HI	14.0	11.7	10.0	12.9	10.9	9.6	6.5	5.7	5.5	1.4	1.8	1.0
Houston, TX	8.8	9.8	6.8	8.2	9.1	6.3	8.8	11.4	9.7	2.0	1.9	1.1
Huntsville, AL	n/a	n/a	n/a	n/a	n/a	n/a	n/a	n/a	n/a	n/a	n/a	n/a
Indianapolis, IN	8.7	7.2	7.3	8.6	6.7	7.0	9.9	7.0	10.4	1.5	1.5	0.8
Jacksonville, FL	10.1	10.1	9.5	9.3	9.8	9.3	5.6	5.2	7.5	1.3	1.0	1.5
Kansas City, MO	7.8	8.9	9.1	7.7	8.7	9.1	7.9	10.0	9.4	1.2	1.4	0.7
Lafayette, LA	n/a	n/a	n/a	n/a	n/a	n/a	n/a	n/a	n/a	n/a	n/a	n/a
Lakeland, FL	n/a	n/a	n/a	n/a	n/a	n/a	n/a	n/a	n/a	n/a	n/a	n/a
Las Vegas, NV	11.4	10.2	7.8	10.4	9.5	7.1	6.8	5.5	5.0	0.9	2.0	1.1
Lexington, KY	n/a	n/a	n/a	n/a	n/a	n/a	n/a	n/a	n/a	n/a	n/a	n/a
Lincoln, NE	n/a	n/a	n/a	n/a	n/a	n/a	n/a	n/a	n/a	n/a	n/a	n/a
Little Rock, AR	10.5	9.9	9.4	10.2	9.6	9.1	10.9	11.4	9.1	1.8	1.7	1.3
Los Angeles, CA	6.6	6.3	5.5	6.2	5.8	4.8	4.0	4.0	3.6	1.2	1.1	0.6
Louisville, KY	7.6	7.9	6.9	7.4	7.8	6.9	7.7	10.6	6.4	1.4	0.7	1.4

Table continued on following page.

Metro Area[1]	Gross Vacancy Rate[2] (%) 2018	2019	2020	Year-Round Vacancy Rate[3] (%) 2018	2019	2020	Rental Vacancy Rate[4] (%) 2018	2019	2020	Homeowner Vacancy Rate[5] (%) 2018	2019	2020
Madison, WI	n/a	n/a	n/a	n/a	n/a	n/a	n/a	n/a	n/a	n/a	n/a	n/a
Manchester, NH	n/a	n/a	n/a	n/a	n/a	n/a	n/a	n/a	n/a	n/a	n/a	n/a
Memphis, TN	12.6	9.9	7.3	12.5	9.9	7.0	11.7	10.6	6.6	1.6	1.4	1.0
Miami, FL	14.9	14.1	12.6	7.9	7.4	6.8	7.4	7.0	5.4	1.9	1.8	1.4
Midland, TX	n/a	n/a	n/a	n/a	n/a	n/a	n/a	n/a	n/a	n/a	n/a	n/a
Milwaukee, WI	8.1	8.0	6.6	7.8	7.8	6.3	5.9	6.6	4.6	1.4	0.6	0.6
Minneapolis, MN	3.9	4.4	4.7	3.3	3.8	3.7	4.1	4.1	4.0	0.4	0.5	0.5
Nashville, TN	5.9	7.8	6.5	5.8	7.5	6.1	7.5	8.6	7.3	0.8	1.2	0.7
New Haven, CT	10.9	11.9	9.4	10.0	11.1	8.4	5.6	8.3	7.8	1.4	1.5	0.2
New Orleans, LA	11.9	12.9	10.7	11.8	12.8	9.8	9.7	9.4	6.1	1.7	1.8	1.3
New York, NY	10.3	9.2	9.1	9.1	7.8	7.8	4.5	4.3	4.5	1.6	1.4	1.3
Oklahoma City, OK	11.5	10.8	7.5	11.2	10.4	7.3	11.8	8.6	6.4	2.7	2.7	0.9
Omaha, NE	7.1	5.6	5.6	6.1	4.8	5.3	7.1	6.3	6.5	0.7	0.6	0.5
Orlando, FL	19.4	16.0	12.9	16.2	12.7	9.8	5.8	8.3	8.6	2.6	2.5	1.2
Peoria, IL	n/a	n/a	n/a	n/a	n/a	n/a	n/a	n/a	n/a	n/a	n/a	n/a
Philadelphia, PA	9.0	8.3	6.0	8.9	8.1	5.8	6.4	7.1	5.4	1.2	1.3	0.7
Phoenix, AZ	12.6	10.3	8.9	7.8	6.2	5.3	6.2	5.0	4.9	1.4	1.0	0.7
Pittsburgh, PA	10.2	10.6	11.5	9.9	10.3	11.3	6.3	7.3	9.3	2.2	1.2	1.0
Portland, OR	6.8	6.6	5.5	6.0	5.6	4.9	3.8	4.4	4.3	1.4	0.9	0.8
Providence, RI	10.3	9.8	8.7	8.5	8.2	6.6	5.0	4.2	3.5	1.1	0.9	0.8
Provo, UT	n/a	n/a	n/a	n/a	n/a	n/a	n/a	n/a	n/a	n/a	n/a	n/a
Raleigh, NC	6.7	6.6	4.6	6.6	6.5	4.5	6.4	7.0	2.3	0.9	0.8	0.4
Reno, NV	n/a	n/a	n/a	n/a	n/a	n/a	n/a	n/a	n/a	n/a	n/a	n/a
Richmond, VA	8.0	8.5	6.0	8.0	8.5	6.0	5.4	9.5	2.7	2.1	1.3	0.9
Riverside, CA	15.1	14.9	11.8	9.1	9.6	7.5	5.1	4.5	4.4	1.6	1.7	0.8
Rochester, MN	n/a	n/a	n/a	n/a	n/a	n/a	n/a	n/a	n/a	n/a	n/a	n/a
Sacramento, CA	8.6	7.8	6.1	7.9	7.1	5.8	5.1	4.2	4.2	1.5	0.8	1.0
Salt Lake City, UT	5.0	4.8	5.7	4.7	4.8	5.6	6.1	5.0	6.2	0.5	0.8	0.3
San Antonio, TX	6.7	9.0	7.4	5.8	8.2	6.7	7.4	10.1	7.2	0.6	2.0	1.0
San Diego, CA	7.6	7.5	6.0	7.4	7.3	5.6	4.5	5.8	3.9	0.7	0.8	0.8
San Francisco, CA	7.5	7.1	6.4	7.4	6.9	6.2	5.4	3.8	5.3	0.9	0.9	0.5
San Jose, CA	5.8	5.6	4.7	5.8	5.6	4.7	4.6	3.7	4.4	0.5	0.5	n/a
Santa Rosa, CA	n/a	n/a	n/a	n/a	n/a	n/a	n/a	n/a	n/a	n/a	n/a	n/a
Savannah, GA	n/a	n/a	n/a	n/a	n/a	n/a	n/a	n/a	n/a	n/a	n/a	n/a
Seattle, WA	5.9	5.5	4.7	5.4	5.2	4.5	4.8	4.4	3.6	0.8	1.0	0.6
Sioux Falls, SD	n/a	n/a	n/a	n/a	n/a	n/a	n/a	n/a	n/a	n/a	n/a	n/a
Springfield, IL	n/a	n/a	n/a	n/a	n/a	n/a	n/a	n/a	n/a	n/a	n/a	n/a
Tallahassee, FL	n/a	n/a	n/a	n/a	n/a	n/a	n/a	n/a	n/a	n/a	n/a	n/a
Tampa, FL	16.1	16.2	13.0	11.9	12.7	10.1	9.9	10.7	8.9	2.1	1.6	1.5
Tucson, AZ	12.5	14.8	12.1	8.1	9.2	7.7	4.4	7.3	8.6	1.8	1.5	0.5
Tulsa, OK	11.7	8.4	9.4	11.6	8.0	8.8	10.1	8.5	8.6	2.6	1.6	0.8
Tuscaloosa, AL	n/a	n/a	n/a	n/a	n/a	n/a	n/a	n/a	n/a	n/a	n/a	n/a
Virginia Beach, VA	8.9	10.4	7.9	7.6	9.3	7.0	7.1	7.1	5.5	1.2	2.2	0.6
Washington, DC	7.0	7.1	6.5	6.7	6.7	6.2	6.2	5.6	5.5	1.1	1.1	0.7
Wichita, KS	n/a	n/a	n/a	n/a	n/a	n/a	n/a	n/a	n/a	n/a	n/a	n/a
Winston-Salem, NC	n/a	n/a	n/a	n/a	n/a	n/a	n/a	n/a	n/a	n/a	n/a	n/a
U.S.	12.3	12.0	10.6	9.7	9.5	8.2	6.9	6.7	6.3	1.5	1.4	1.0

Note: (1) Metropolitan Statistical Area—see Appendix B for areas included; (2) The percentage of the total housing inventory that is vacant; (3) The percentage of the housing inventory (excluding seasonal units) that is year-round vacant; (4) The percentage of rental inventory that is vacant for rent; (5) The percentage of homeowner inventory that is vacant for sale; n/a not available
Source: U.S. Census Bureau, Housing Vacancies and Homeownership Annual Statistics: 2018, 2019, 2020

Appendix A: Comparative Statistics

Bankruptcy Filings

City	Area Covered	Business Filings 2019	2020	% Chg.	Nonbusiness Filings 2019	2020	% Chg.
Albuquerque, NM	Bernalillo County	30	33	10.0	1,071	872	-18.6
Allentown, PA	Lehigh County	16	10	-37.5	599	433	-27.7
Anchorage, AK	Anchorage Borough	17	20	17.6	176	137	-22.2
Ann Arbor, MI	Washtenaw County	10	13	30.0	654	454	-30.6
Athens, GA	Clarke County	0	5	n/a	338	228	-32.5
Atlanta, GA	Fulton County	173	152	-12.1	4,013	2,591	-35.4
Austin, TX	Travis County	118	175	48.3	737	529	-28.2
Baton Rouge, LA	East Baton Rouge Parish	37	49	32.4	771	435	-43.6
Boise City, ID	Ada County	26	19	-26.9	878	589	-32.9
Boston, MA	Suffolk County	47	37	-21.3	530	279	-47.4
Boulder, CO	Boulder County	30	42	40.0	372	286	-23.1
Cape Coral, FL	Lee County	57	79	38.6	1,254	1,112	-11.3
Cedar Rapids, IA	Linn County	11	9	-18.2	365	285	-21.9
Charleston, SC	Charleston County	19	21	10.5	356	261	-26.7
Charlotte, NC	Mecklenburg County	64	45	-29.7	1,020	639	-37.4
Chicago, IL	Cook County	413	335	-18.9	27,789	16,384	-41.0
Cincinnati, OH	Hamilton County	48	25	-47.9	2,519	1,845	-26.8
Clarksville, TN	Montgomery County	11	6	-45.5	829	579	-30.2
Cleveland, OH	Cuyahoga County	69	96	39.1	6,013	4,189	-30.3
College Station, TX	Brazos County	7	6	-14.3	105	87	-17.1
Colorado Springs, CO	El Paso County	39	30	-23.1	1,525	1,154	-24.3
Columbia, MO	Boone County	6	8	33.3	375	263	-29.9
Columbia, SC	Richland County	11	12	9.1	837	520	-37.9
Columbus, OH	Franklin County	72	86	19.4	4,342	2,960	-31.8
Dallas, TX	Dallas County	355	568	60.0	3,572	2,452	-31.4
Davenport, IA	Scott County	10	7	-30.0	329	246	-25.2
Denver, CO	Denver County	68	91	33.8	1,338	1,029	-23.1
Des Moines, IA	Polk County	28	12	-57.1	962	782	-18.7
Durham, NC	Durham County	16	18	12.5	395	223	-43.5
Edison, NJ	Middlesex County	46	31	-32.6	1,718	1,097	-36.1
El Paso, TX	El Paso County	63	42	-33.3	2,079	1,290	-38.0
Fargo, ND	Cass County	4	5	25.0	198	183	-7.6
Fayetteville, NC	Cumberland County	8	8	0.0	795	506	-36.4
Fort Collins, CO	Larimer County	29	28	-3.4	558	404	-27.6
Fort Wayne, IN	Allen County	15	15	0.0	1,294	1,057	-18.3
Fort Worth, TX	Tarrant County	242	271	12.0	4,040	2,937	-27.3
Grand Rapids, MI	Kent County	35	47	34.3	935	613	-34.4
Greeley, CO	Weld County	20	21	5.0	691	509	-26.3
Green Bay, WI	Brown County	25	9	-64.0	599	418	-30.2
Greensboro, NC	Guilford County	25	21	-16.0	758	471	-37.9
Honolulu, HI	Honolulu County	35	46	31.4	1,225	1,106	-9.7
Houston, TX	Harris County	411	608	47.9	4,527	2,967	-34.5
Huntsville, AL	Madison County	20	42	110.0	1,463	1,024	-30.0
Indianapolis, IN	Marion County	100	39	-61.0	4,465	3,319	-25.7
Jacksonville, FL	Duval County	75	57	-24.0	2,349	1,604	-31.7
Kansas City, MO	Jackson County	36	26	-27.8	2,080	1,394	-33.0
Lafayette, LA	Lafayette Parish	44	22	-50.0	560	306	-45.4
Lakeland, FL	Polk County	31	53	71.0	1,466	1,168	-20.3
Las Vegas, NV	Clark County	228	204	-10.5	8,184	6,529	-20.2
Lexington, KY	Fayette County	56	54	-3.6	749	520	-30.6
Lincoln, NE	Lancaster County	16	11	-31.3	653	485	-25.7
Little Rock, AR	Pulaski County	233	30	-87.1	2,318	1,519	-34.5
Los Angeles, CA	Los Angeles County	882	857	-2.8	18,304	13,323	-27.2
Louisville, KY	Jefferson County	50	39	-22.0	2,893	2,174	-24.9
Madison, WI	Dane County	34	28	-17.6	773	527	-31.8

Table continued on following page.

City	Area Covered	Business Filings 2019	Business Filings 2020	% Chg.	Nonbusiness Filings 2019	Nonbusiness Filings 2020	% Chg.
Manchester, NH	Hillsborough County	25	27	8.0	519	339	-34.7
Memphis, TN	Shelby County	72	41	-43.1	9,622	5,523	-42.6
Miami, FL	Miami-Dade County	215	322	49.8	8,490	7,108	-16.3
Midland, TX	Midland County	32	11	-65.6	72	48	-33.3
Milwaukee, WI	Milwaukee County	43	48	11.6	6,315	4,019	-36.4
Minneapolis, MN	Hennepin County	62	92	48.4	2,032	1,552	-23.6
Nashville, TN	Davidson County	53	60	13.2	2,051	1,330	-35.2
New Haven, CT	New Haven County	47	33	-29.8	1,884	1,258	-33.2
New Orleans, LA	Orleans Parish	36	21	-41.7	683	391	-42.8
New York, NY	Bronx County	44	24	-45.5	2,486	1,498	-39.7
New York, NY	Kings County	327	182	-44.3	2,743	1,710	-37.7
New York, NY	New York County	244	480	96.7	1,210	854	-29.4
New York, NY	Queens County	206	127	-38.3	3,708	1,990	-46.3
New York, NY	Richmond County	22	19	-13.6	835	459	-45.0
Oklahoma City, OK	Oklahoma County	89	139	56.2	2,147	1,679	-21.8
Omaha, NE	Douglas County	39	16	-59.0	1,283	1,064	-17.1
Orlando, FL	Orange County	154	167	8.4	2,956	2,477	-16.2
Peoria, IL	Peoria County	16	6	-62.5	548	391	-28.6
Philadelphia, PA	Philadelphia County	88	116	31.8	2,222	1,162	-47.7
Phoenix, AZ	Maricopa County	344	261	-24.1	11,095	8,954	-19.3
Pittsburgh, PA	Allegheny County	140	116	-17.1	2,280	1,700	-25.4
Portland, OR	Multnomah County	62	59	-4.8	1,394	1,147	-17.7
Providence, RI	Providence County	38	29	-23.7	1,246	887	-28.8
Provo, UT	Utah County	37	31	-16.2	1,408	1,151	-18.3
Raleigh, NC	Wake County	91	75	-17.6	1,314	882	-32.9
Reno, NV	Washoe County	34	44	29.4	960	765	-20.3
Richmond, VA	Richmond city	18	21	16.7	897	695	-22.5
Riverside, CA	Riverside County	165	145	-12.1	6,195	4,455	-28.1
Rochester, MN	Olmsted County	9	4	-55.6	151	138	-8.6
Sacramento, CA	Sacramento County	95	124	30.5	3,208	2,300	-28.3
Salt Lake City, UT	Salt Lake County	56	60	7.1	4,109	3,232	-21.3
San Antonio, TX	Bexar County	191	128	-33.0	2,173	1,445	-33.5
San Diego, CA	San Diego County	308	269	-12.7	7,366	5,848	-20.6
San Francisco, CA	San Francisco County	58	67	15.5	564	384	-31.9
San Jose, CA	Santa Clara County	94	86	-8.5	1,446	1,018	-29.6
Santa Rosa, CA	Sonoma County	32	29	-9.4	531	388	-26.9
Savannah, GA	Chatham County	18	13	-27.8	1,220	729	-40.2
Seattle, WA	King County	115	96	-16.5	2,174	1,516	-30.3
Sioux Falls, SD	Minnehaha County	18	11	-38.9	349	268	-23.2
Springfield, IL	Sangamon County	8	8	0.0	436	311	-28.7
Tallahassee, FL	Leon County	35	17	-51.4	446	288	-35.4
Tampa, FL	Hillsborough County	155	110	-29.0	3,356	2,538	-24.4
Tucson, AZ	Pima County	50	32	-36.0	2,438	1,727	-29.2
Tulsa, OK	Tulsa County	44	45	2.3	1,555	1,163	-25.2
Tuscaloosa, AL	Tuscaloosa County	9	10	11.1	1,246	799	-35.9
Virginia Beach, VA	Virginia Beach city	18	14	-22.2	1,606	1,206	-24.9
Washington, DC	District of Columbia	50	50	0.0	789	449	-43.1
Wichita, KS	Sedgwick County	30	15	-50.0	1,381	941	-31.9
Winston-Salem, NC	Forsyth County	17	15	-11.8	537	363	-32.4
U.S.	U.S.	22,780	21,655	-4.9	752,160	522,808	-30.5

Note: Business filings include Chapter 7, Chapter 9, Chapter 11, Chapter 12, Chapter 13, Chapter 15, and Section 304; Nonbusiness filings include Chapter 7, Chapter 11, and Chapter 13

Source: Administrative Office of the U.S. Courts, Business and Nonbusiness Bankruptcy, County Cases Commenced by Chapter of the Bankruptcy Code, During the 12-Month Period Ending December 31, 2019 and Business and Nonbusiness Bankruptcy, County Cases Commenced by Chapter of the Bankruptcy Code, During the 12-Month Period Ending December 31, 2020

Income: City

City	Per Capita ($)	Median Household ($)	Average Household ($)
Albuquerque, NM	30,403	52,911	72,265
Allentown, PA	20,792	41,167	56,842
Anchorage, AK	41,415	84,928	109,988
Ann Arbor, MI	42,674	65,745	96,906
Athens, GA	23,726	38,311	59,118
Atlanta, GA	47,424	59,948	106,300
Austin, TX	43,043	71,576	102,876
Baton Rouge, LA	28,491	44,470	70,902
Boise City, ID	34,636	60,035	82,424
Boston, MA	44,690	71,115	107,608
Boulder, CO	44,942	69,520	109,410
Cape Coral, FL	29,970	61,599	76,925
Cedar Rapids, IA	32,290	58,511	75,289
Charleston, SC	42,872	68,438	98,288
Charlotte, NC	38,000	62,817	94,516
Chicago, IL	37,103	58,247	90,713
Cincinnati, OH	30,531	40,640	65,213
Clarksville, TN	25,239	53,604	65,458
Cleveland, OH	21,223	30,907	46,137
College Station, TX	27,541	45,820	73,853
Colorado Springs, CO	34,076	64,712	84,708
Columbia, MO	30,244	51,276	74,727
Columbia, SC	30,461	47,286	76,118
Columbus, OH	29,322	53,745	69,315
Dallas, TX	34,479	52,580	86,393
Davenport, IA	28,645	51,029	68,559
Denver, CO	43,770	68,592	99,151
Des Moines, IA	28,554	53,525	69,074
Durham, NC	34,329	58,905	82,573
Edison, NJ	44,667	103,076	127,171
El Paso, TX	22,734	47,568	64,025
Fargo, ND	35,205	55,551	78,237
Fayetteville, NC	24,823	45,024	58,752
Fort Collins, CO	34,482	65,866	87,406
Fort Wayne, IN	26,970	49,411	65,377
Fort Worth, TX	29,531	62,187	82,977
Grand Rapids, MI	26,120	50,103	65,615
Greeley, CO	26,222	57,586	72,302
Green Bay, WI	26,618	49,251	64,595
Greensboro, NC	29,628	48,964	71,453
Honolulu, HI	37,834	71,465	97,456
Houston, TX	32,521	52,338	84,179
Huntsville, AL	35,634	55,305	80,877
Indianapolis, IN	28,363	47,873	68,367
Jacksonville, FL	30,064	54,701	74,873
Kansas City, MO	32,348	54,194	75,137
Lafayette, LA	32,998	51,264	78,055
Lakeland, FL	28,042	47,511	67,899
Las Vegas, NV	30,761	56,354	79,657
Lexington, KY	34,442	57,291	83,111
Lincoln, NE	31,301	57,746	76,763
Little Rock, AR	35,966	51,485	83,730
Los Angeles, CA	35,261	62,142	96,416
Louisville, KY	30,943	53,436	74,580
Madison, WI	38,285	65,332	87,055
Manchester, NH	31,951	60,711	75,665

Table continued on following page.

City	Per Capita ($)	Median Household ($)	Average Household ($)
Memphis, TN	25,605	41,228	62,588
Miami, FL	28,804	39,049	68,105
Midland, TX	40,252	79,329	112,701
Milwaukee, WI	23,462	41,838	57,332
Minneapolis, MN	38,808	62,583	89,282
Nashville, TN	35,243	59,828	83,348
New Haven, CT	26,429	42,222	65,362
New Orleans, LA	31,385	41,604	71,938
New York, NY	39,828	63,998	102,946
Oklahoma City, OK	30,567	55,557	77,896
Omaha, NE	33,401	60,092	82,945
Orlando, FL	32,085	51,757	75,669
Peoria, IL	31,497	51,771	74,900
Philadelphia, PA	27,924	45,927	68,379
Phoenix, AZ	29,343	57,459	80,631
Pittsburgh, PA	34,083	48,711	72,981
Portland, OR	41,310	71,005	95,998
Providence, RI	26,560	45,610	71,136
Provo, UT	20,792	48,888	69,265
Raleigh, NC	38,494	67,266	94,359
Reno, NV	34,475	58,790	81,700
Richmond, VA	33,549	47,250	76,182
Riverside, CA	26,028	69,045	85,486
Rochester, MN	39,518	73,106	96,015
Sacramento, CA	31,956	62,335	83,189
Salt Lake City, UT	36,779	60,676	88,127
San Antonio, TX	25,894	52,455	70,778
San Diego, CA	41,112	79,673	108,864
San Francisco, CA	68,883	112,449	160,396
San Jose, CA	46,599	109,593	142,635
Santa Rosa, CA	36,935	75,630	96,786
Savannah, GA	25,664	43,307	63,984
Seattle, WA	59,835	92,263	128,184
Sioux Falls, SD	33,065	59,912	79,847
Springfield, IL	34,607	54,648	77,473
Tallahassee, FL	27,677	45,734	66,889
Tampa, FL	36,169	53,833	87,818
Tucson, AZ	23,655	43,425	58,057
Tulsa, OK	30,970	47,650	73,816
Tuscaloosa, AL	26,437	45,268	68,837
Virginia Beach, VA	37,776	76,610	96,936
Washington, DC	56,147	86,420	127,890
Wichita, KS	28,806	52,620	71,335
Winston-Salem, NC	28,821	45,750	71,423
U.S.	34,103	62,843	88,607

Source: U.S. Census Bureau, 2015-2019 American Community Survey 5-Year Estimates

Income: Metro Area

Metro Area	Per Capita ($)	Median Household ($)	Average Household ($)
Albuquerque, NM	29,747	54,072	73,512
Allentown, PA	34,637	67,652	88,415
Anchorage, AK	38,725	83,048	105,968
Ann Arbor, MI	41,399	72,586	101,787
Athens, GA	27,653	47,214	70,940
Atlanta, GA	35,296	68,316	94,723
Austin, TX	39,827	76,844	104,847
Baton Rouge, LA	31,082	58,912	81,614
Boise City, ID	30,508	60,568	80,438
Boston, MA	47,604	90,333	122,399
Boulder, CO	46,826	83,019	115,966
Cape Coral, FL	33,543	57,832	82,544
Cedar Rapids, IA	34,039	64,687	82,498
Charleston, SC	35,011	63,649	88,023
Charlotte, NC	34,558	63,217	89,212
Chicago, IL	38,157	71,770	100,233
Cincinnati, OH	34,575	63,987	86,633
Clarksville, TN	25,931	53,027	67,368
Cleveland, OH	33,785	56,008	79,168
College Station, TX	27,698	50,240	73,129
Colorado Springs, CO	33,795	68,687	88,185
Columbia, MO	29,534	54,808	74,042
Columbia, SC	29,894	55,971	75,154
Columbus, OH	34,441	65,150	87,472
Dallas, TX	35,278	70,281	97,589
Davenport, IA	31,571	58,531	76,075
Denver, CO	41,988	79,664	106,322
Des Moines, IA	36,310	70,126	90,791
Durham, NC	36,322	62,289	90,054
Edison, NJ	43,409	78,773	116,604
El Paso, TX	21,644	46,795	62,663
Fargo, ND	35,812	64,666	85,794
Fayetteville, NC	24,228	48,459	61,989
Fort Collins, CO	37,363	71,881	93,301
Fort Wayne, IN	29,383	55,341	73,578
Fort Worth, TX	35,278	70,281	97,589
Grand Rapids, MI	31,388	63,302	83,235
Greeley, CO	31,793	74,150	89,427
Green Bay, WI	32,520	62,405	79,316
Greensboro, NC	28,787	50,891	71,256
Honolulu, HI	36,816	85,857	109,304
Houston, TX	34,400	67,516	97,410
Huntsville, AL	34,918	64,483	86,328
Indianapolis, IN	33,699	61,552	85,193
Jacksonville, FL	33,304	61,723	84,690
Kansas City, MO	35,761	66,632	89,308
Lafayette, LA	27,955	51,955	72,041
Lakeland, FL	24,864	50,584	66,810
Las Vegas, NV	30,704	59,340	80,762
Lexington, KY	33,153	58,685	82,094
Lincoln, NE	32,360	61,031	80,274
Little Rock, AR	30,599	54,746	76,145
Los Angeles, CA	35,916	72,998	104,698
Louisville, KY	32,630	59,158	80,682
Madison, WI	39,484	72,374	93,923
Manchester, NH	40,955	81,460	103,090

Table continued on following page.

Metro Area	Per Capita ($)	Median Household ($)	Average Household ($)
Memphis, TN	29,453	53,209	76,187
Miami, FL	32,522	56,775	86,518
Midland, TX	38,966	79,140	109,861
Milwaukee, WI	35,491	62,389	86,290
Minneapolis, MN	41,204	80,421	104,946
Nashville, TN	35,479	66,347	91,202
New Haven, CT	38,009	69,905	94,740
New Orleans, LA	31,072	53,084	76,818
New York, NY	43,409	78,773	116,604
Oklahoma City, OK	31,301	59,084	80,805
Omaha, NE	34,825	67,885	88,578
Orlando, FL	29,875	58,368	80,864
Peoria, IL	32,575	59,397	79,057
Philadelphia, PA	39,091	72,343	100,889
Phoenix, AZ	32,522	63,883	87,543
Pittsburgh, PA	36,208	60,535	82,754
Portland, OR	38,544	74,792	97,930
Providence, RI	35,991	67,818	89,281
Provo, UT	26,153	74,387	93,213
Raleigh, NC	38,370	75,851	100,551
Reno, NV	36,087	64,801	89,057
Richmond, VA	36,413	68,529	92,171
Riverside, CA	27,003	65,121	85,373
Rochester, MN	38,754	73,697	95,925
Sacramento, CA	35,563	72,280	96,023
Salt Lake City, UT	32,829	74,842	96,196
San Antonio, TX	29,071	60,327	81,852
San Diego, CA	38,073	78,980	106,600
San Francisco, CA	55,252	106,025	147,703
San Jose, CA	55,547	122,478	163,355
Santa Rosa, CA	42,178	81,018	108,169
Savannah, GA	32,088	59,459	82,125
Seattle, WA	45,750	86,856	115,653
Sioux Falls, SD	33,453	65,621	83,463
Springfield, IL	35,603	62,533	82,720
Tallahassee, FL	28,766	51,874	72,487
Tampa, FL	32,276	55,285	78,248
Tucson, AZ	29,707	53,379	73,554
Tulsa, OK	30,633	55,739	77,341
Tuscaloosa, AL	25,759	50,408	67,811
Virginia Beach, VA	33,907	66,759	86,062
Washington, DC	49,881	103,751	134,513
Wichita, KS	29,414	57,379	74,900
Winston-Salem, NC	28,986	50,774	71,206
U.S.	34,103	62,843	88,607

Note: Figures cover the Metropolitan Statistical Area (MSA)—see Appendix B for areas included
Source: U.S. Census Bureau, 2015-2019 American Community Survey 5-Year Estimates

Household Income Distribution: City

City	\<$15,000	$15,000-$24,999	$25,000-$34,999	$35,000-$49,999	$50,000-$74,999	$75,000-$99,999	$100,000-$149,999	$150,000 and up
Albuquerque, NM	13.1	10.8	10.4	13.1	17.7	12.0	13.3	9.4
Allentown, PA	15.9	13.8	13.0	15.2	19.3	10.2	8.0	4.5
Anchorage, AK	5.3	5.1	6.3	9.9	17.4	13.8	20.5	21.6
Ann Arbor, MI	14.5	7.3	7.6	9.3	15.8	11.4	14.5	19.7
Athens, GA	21.0	14.6	11.3	13.3	14.1	8.7	9.9	7.2
Atlanta, GA	15.4	9.6	8.0	10.6	14.8	10.3	12.8	18.5
Austin, TX	8.6	6.5	7.9	11.6	17.5	12.3	16.6	19.0
Baton Rouge, LA	18.2	13.1	11.0	12.0	15.5	9.1	11.4	9.7
Boise City, ID	10.2	9.7	9.3	13.2	18.2	12.3	14.8	12.3
Boston, MA	16.1	8.1	6.3	8.4	13.0	10.3	15.7	22.2
Boulder, CO	13.6	7.5	7.3	10.0	14.3	10.1	13.9	23.4
Cape Coral, FL	8.7	7.8	9.1	13.7	20.5	15.8	15.3	9.1
Cedar Rapids, IA	9.0	8.8	10.0	13.9	20.9	13.4	15.1	8.9
Charleston, SC	11.2	7.7	7.0	10.7	17.0	12.8	17.4	16.1
Charlotte, NC	8.6	7.9	9.7	13.3	17.9	12.5	14.6	15.5
Chicago, IL	14.0	10.3	8.9	11.0	15.1	11.2	13.8	15.7
Cincinnati, OH	21.1	12.6	11.2	12.3	15.6	9.1	9.4	8.7
Clarksville, TN	10.4	8.7	11.3	16.2	20.8	14.2	12.7	5.6
Cleveland, OH	27.1	15.1	12.9	13.7	14.2	7.9	5.7	3.4
College Station, TX	21.3	11.1	9.2	11.2	12.4	10.9	12.5	11.4
Colorado Springs, CO	8.8	8.3	8.5	12.5	19.0	13.8	16.2	12.8
Columbia, MO	14.8	10.6	9.8	13.8	15.2	11.2	13.6	11.0
Columbia, SC	17.9	11.5	10.8	11.7	15.6	10.9	10.4	11.2
Columbus, OH	12.1	9.7	10.2	14.4	19.5	13.3	13.4	7.3
Dallas, TX	11.8	10.4	10.7	14.7	17.9	10.6	10.8	13.1
Davenport, IA	12.5	11.4	10.6	14.6	19.1	12.3	12.1	7.4
Denver, CO	10.0	7.3	7.9	11.3	17.3	12.5	15.7	18.1
Des Moines, IA	12.0	10.6	10.2	14.2	19.9	13.7	12.4	7.1
Durham, NC	10.3	8.4	10.0	13.5	17.4	12.7	14.5	13.2
Edison, NJ	4.9	4.3	4.1	8.9	12.6	13.7	21.3	30.1
El Paso, TX	14.3	12.2	11.1	14.3	19.1	10.8	11.5	6.7
Fargo, ND	11.1	10.1	9.7	13.8	18.2	14.0	12.6	10.4
Fayetteville, NC	14.5	12.0	12.4	16.4	19.2	11.1	9.3	5.2
Fort Collins, CO	9.7	8.7	8.0	12.2	17.1	12.9	15.8	15.5
Fort Wayne, IN	11.5	11.3	11.9	15.8	19.4	12.6	10.8	6.6
Fort Worth, TX	10.2	8.3	9.5	12.0	18.8	13.4	15.5	12.3
Grand Rapids, MI	13.0	11.8	10.0	15.2	19.4	12.7	11.7	6.4
Greeley, CO	11.9	9.8	8.3	13.5	18.9	13.7	15.7	8.1
Green Bay, WI	11.9	10.9	11.8	16.2	19.6	12.6	11.4	5.5
Greensboro, NC	13.5	10.9	11.5	15.1	18.0	11.2	11.3	8.4
Honolulu, HI	10.1	6.9	6.8	11.8	16.8	12.8	17.0	17.6
Houston, TX	12.6	11.1	10.8	13.5	16.7	10.6	11.3	13.5
Huntsville, AL	13.7	10.7	10.0	11.8	15.2	10.9	13.9	13.8
Indianapolis, IN	13.5	11.1	11.8	15.3	17.9	11.3	11.0	8.0
Jacksonville, FL	11.3	9.4	10.1	14.6	19.4	13.2	12.9	9.2
Kansas City, MO	12.1	10.1	10.4	14.0	17.6	12.2	13.5	10.1
Lafayette, LA	15.8	11.1	10.1	12.0	17.1	10.2	11.1	12.7
Lakeland, FL	12.5	11.9	12.5	15.3	19.2	11.7	9.9	7.1
Las Vegas, NV	11.8	9.5	9.7	13.8	17.5	13.0	14.0	10.7
Lexington, KY	11.5	9.6	9.9	13.0	17.6	12.2	14.2	12.1
Lincoln, NE	9.6	9.2	10.5	13.9	19.3	13.0	14.7	9.9
Little Rock, AR	12.7	11.0	10.4	14.7	16.5	10.4	11.2	13.0
Los Angeles, CA	12.4	9.3	8.7	11.5	15.4	11.4	14.4	16.9
Louisville, KY	12.4	10.3	10.2	13.9	17.8	12.5	12.7	10.1

Table continued on following page.

	Percent of Households Earning							
City	Under $15,000	$15,000 -$24,999	$25,000 -$34,999	$35,000 -$49,999	$50,000 -$74,999	$75,000 -$99,999	$100,000 -$149,999	$150,000 and up
Madison, WI	10.3	7.6	8.8	12.1	17.7	13.3	16.4	13.6
Manchester, NH	10.1	8.6	9.9	12.5	19.8	13.3	16.3	9.3
Memphis, TN	18.3	13.5	11.8	14.6	16.5	9.4	8.8	7.0
Miami, FL	20.8	14.1	11.6	12.3	14.5	8.8	8.6	9.4
Midland, TX	6.7	6.7	6.9	9.8	17.3	13.7	18.0	20.8
Milwaukee, WI	17.8	13.1	11.7	15.1	17.2	10.6	9.6	4.8
Minneapolis, MN	13.0	8.7	8.2	11.6	16.0	12.3	14.6	15.5
Nashville, TN	9.8	8.5	9.3	14.1	18.9	13.6	14.3	11.8
New Haven, CT	20.2	11.9	11.1	12.5	15.8	9.6	9.7	9.4
New Orleans, LA	22.1	12.2	10.3	11.5	14.2	8.8	9.9	10.9
New York, NY	14.3	9.0	7.9	10.2	14.3	11.1	14.3	18.9
Oklahoma City, OK	11.3	9.5	10.0	14.0	18.6	12.6	13.3	10.7
Omaha, NE	10.5	8.8	8.8	13.5	18.5	13.4	14.4	12.1
Orlando, FL	12.5	10.4	11.1	14.2	19.8	10.9	10.8	10.3
Peoria, IL	16.8	11.0	8.8	12.0	17.3	11.6	11.8	10.7
Philadelphia, PA	19.1	11.2	10.2	12.7	15.8	10.5	11.0	9.4
Phoenix, AZ	10.4	9.3	9.5	14.3	18.5	12.6	13.6	11.9
Pittsburgh, PA	17.5	11.6	10.0	11.8	15.9	11.3	11.2	10.6
Portland, OR	10.6	7.2	7.8	10.4	16.4	13.0	16.9	17.7
Providence, RI	20.2	12.0	9.0	11.4	16.7	11.1	10.0	9.7
Provo, UT	12.2	12.9	12.3	13.5	18.9	11.8	10.6	7.8
Raleigh, NC	7.3	7.3	8.9	13.2	18.4	13.5	15.8	15.6
Reno, NV	9.2	9.5	9.5	14.5	18.6	12.7	14.5	11.5
Richmond, VA	17.6	11.0	10.1	13.3	16.2	10.2	10.5	11.0
Riverside, CA	9.0	7.6	8.3	11.4	17.8	14.8	17.6	13.6
Rochester, MN	8.2	7.0	7.1	11.6	17.6	14.1	17.8	16.6
Sacramento, CA	11.3	9.0	8.7	11.7	17.3	13.1	15.6	13.3
Salt Lake City, UT	12.0	8.5	9.1	12.4	17.6	12.5	14.3	13.7
San Antonio, TX	12.7	10.4	10.6	14.0	19.0	12.1	12.5	8.7
San Diego, CA	8.1	6.6	6.8	10.0	15.9	12.9	17.8	21.8
San Francisco, CA	9.7	5.8	4.9	6.2	9.8	9.0	15.6	38.9
San Jose, CA	6.2	4.8	4.9	7.2	12.0	10.7	18.0	36.2
Santa Rosa, CA	7.0	5.9	7.1	11.0	18.4	14.8	18.5	17.3
Savannah, GA	17.5	13.1	10.9	14.8	16.5	10.9	9.7	6.7
Seattle, WA	8.8	5.3	5.6	8.7	13.5	11.4	18.3	28.4
Sioux Falls, SD	8.8	8.3	10.7	13.2	19.0	14.4	15.2	10.5
Springfield, IL	13.7	10.7	9.6	12.1	17.2	13.0	12.9	10.9
Tallahassee, FL	16.8	10.9	11.7	13.8	17.3	10.2	10.4	8.8
Tampa, FL	14.6	10.3	9.9	12.2	15.8	10.7	12.0	14.6
Tucson, AZ	15.8	13.2	11.7	15.6	17.9	10.8	9.7	5.3
Tulsa, OK	14.2	11.6	11.2	15.2	17.4	10.3	10.1	10.0
Tuscaloosa, AL	19.4	11.0	11.0	12.3	16.5	9.4	10.2	10.2
Virginia Beach, VA	5.3	5.4	7.4	11.7	19.1	15.8	19.9	15.4
Washington, DC	12.9	6.0	5.9	7.7	12.2	10.6	16.4	28.2
Wichita, KS	12.3	10.5	10.5	14.6	18.7	12.0	12.8	8.7
Winston-Salem, NC	15.4	11.8	11.9	14.3	16.9	11.2	9.8	8.7
U.S.	10.3	8.9	8.9	12.3	17.2	12.7	15.1	14.5

Source: U.S. Census Bureau, 2015-2019 American Community Survey 5-Year Estimates

Household Income Distribution: Metro Area

Metro Area	Under $15,000	$15,000 -$24,999	$25,000 -$34,999	$35,000 -$49,999	$50,000 -$74,999	$75,000 -$99,999	$100,000 -$149,999	$150,000 and up
Albuquerque, NM	12.4	10.7	10.0	13.3	18.0	12.5	13.1	9.8
Allentown, PA	7.9	8.4	8.7	12.2	17.9	13.9	16.9	14.2
Anchorage, AK	6.1	5.6	6.5	9.9	17.2	13.7	20.5	20.5
Ann Arbor, MI	10.6	7.1	7.1	10.5	16.0	12.5	16.7	19.6
Athens, GA	16.4	12.1	10.3	13.5	15.2	10.2	12.6	9.6
Atlanta, GA	8.4	7.6	8.3	12.1	17.8	13.3	16.2	16.1
Austin, TX	7.3	6.0	7.3	11.1	17.3	13.3	18.1	19.8
Baton Rouge, LA	12.6	9.8	9.4	11.5	16.4	11.9	15.5	12.9
Boise City, ID	9.5	8.6	9.4	13.5	19.8	13.6	15.2	10.5
Boston, MA	8.8	6.2	5.8	8.3	13.5	11.8	18.5	27.1
Boulder, CO	8.5	6.0	6.6	10.2	14.5	12.4	17.2	24.5
Cape Coral, FL	9.4	9.1	10.3	13.9	19.6	13.2	13.3	11.3
Cedar Rapids, IA	7.7	7.9	9.1	13.3	19.3	14.4	16.9	11.4
Charleston, SC	10.0	8.4	8.5	12.1	18.4	13.5	15.6	13.6
Charlotte, NC	8.9	8.6	9.2	12.7	18.1	13.0	15.1	14.4
Chicago, IL	9.3	7.9	7.8	10.8	16.0	12.8	17.0	18.4
Cincinnati, OH	10.2	8.7	8.6	11.8	17.6	13.2	16.0	13.8
Clarksville, TN	11.4	9.1	10.8	16.0	19.7	13.7	12.4	6.8
Cleveland, OH	12.6	9.7	9.8	13.0	17.4	12.4	13.9	11.2
College Station, TX	16.3	11.0	9.8	12.7	15.8	11.5	12.8	10.2
Colorado Springs, CO	7.8	7.4	8.1	12.0	19.0	14.3	17.4	13.9
Columbia, MO	12.0	10.0	10.1	13.9	17.4	12.8	14.2	9.5
Columbia, SC	12.2	9.1	10.1	13.4	18.4	13.4	13.6	9.8
Columbus, OH	9.2	8.1	8.6	12.4	18.2	13.5	16.5	13.5
Dallas, TX	7.7	7.1	8.3	12.0	17.8	13.2	16.7	17.2
Davenport, IA	10.2	9.4	9.5	13.4	19.0	13.8	15.4	9.3
Denver, CO	6.7	5.8	6.7	10.8	17.1	13.7	18.9	20.2
Des Moines, IA	7.2	7.5	8.1	12.0	18.8	14.4	17.6	14.3
Durham, NC	10.0	8.6	9.3	12.7	16.8	12.6	14.7	15.3
Edison, NJ	10.5	7.5	7.0	9.3	13.9	11.4	16.4	24.1
El Paso, TX	14.6	12.2	11.4	14.5	19.0	10.8	11.2	6.3
Fargo, ND	9.4	8.6	8.2	12.1	18.3	15.3	15.7	12.4
Fayetteville, NC	13.8	11.1	11.2	15.5	18.9	12.5	11.5	5.6
Fort Collins, CO	7.9	7.9	7.3	11.6	17.2	14.1	17.9	16.1
Fort Wayne, IN	9.4	9.8	10.9	14.8	19.8	13.7	13.3	8.3
Fort Worth, TX	7.7	7.1	8.3	12.0	17.8	13.2	16.7	17.2
Grand Rapids, MI	7.6	9.0	8.8	13.5	19.8	14.4	15.9	11.0
Greeley, CO	7.7	6.9	7.2	11.0	17.7	16.3	19.3	13.9
Green Bay, WI	8.2	8.5	9.5	13.5	19.2	14.6	16.4	10.0
Greensboro, NC	12.4	10.8	11.3	14.7	18.2	12.2	11.9	8.6
Honolulu, HI	7.1	5.1	5.9	9.6	15.8	13.9	20.2	22.5
Houston, TX	8.8	8.3	8.7	11.7	16.8	12.3	15.8	17.7
Huntsville, AL	10.4	9.2	8.8	11.5	16.1	12.5	16.4	15.0
Indianapolis, IN	9.6	8.7	9.4	13.2	17.9	13.3	15.1	12.8
Jacksonville, FL	9.5	8.3	9.2	13.4	18.8	13.6	14.7	12.4
Kansas City, MO	8.4	7.8	8.7	12.6	17.8	13.9	16.8	14.1
Lafayette, LA	14.4	11.5	10.3	12.4	16.1	12.4	13.4	9.6
Lakeland, FL	11.1	11.2	11.2	16.0	19.9	12.6	11.3	6.8
Las Vegas, NV	10.2	8.8	9.7	13.9	18.6	13.5	14.5	11.0
Lexington, KY	10.9	9.4	9.7	13.1	17.5	13.1	14.7	11.5
Lincoln, NE	8.9	8.8	9.9	13.4	19.0	13.3	15.9	10.8
Little Rock, AR	12.0	10.0	10.4	13.7	18.1	11.9	14.1	9.8
Los Angeles, CA	9.6	7.7	7.6	10.6	15.6	12.4	16.5	20.1
Louisville, KY	10.2	9.3	9.4	13.6	18.4	13.4	14.4	11.4

Table continued on following page.

Metro Area	Under $15,000	$15,000 -$24,999	$25,000 -$34,999	$35,000 -$49,999	$50,000 -$74,999	$75,000 -$99,999	$100,000 -$149,999	$150,000 and up
Madison, WI	7.3	6.8	7.9	11.9	17.8	14.4	18.5	15.5
Manchester, NH	6.3	6.3	7.3	9.8	16.1	13.8	19.9	20.5
Memphis, TN	13.2	10.6	10.2	13.4	17.4	11.8	13.0	10.4
Miami, FL	11.8	9.9	9.8	13.0	17.2	11.7	13.3	13.4
Midland, TX	6.9	6.9	7.1	9.9	17.1	13.5	18.1	20.6
Milwaukee, WI	10.4	9.1	8.7	12.7	17.1	12.9	15.8	13.2
Minneapolis, MN	6.7	6.1	6.7	10.6	16.4	14.2	19.4	19.7
Nashville, TN	8.0	7.5	8.6	13.0	18.6	14.1	16.2	14.0
New Haven, CT	10.0	8.2	7.6	11.1	16.2	12.5	16.5	17.9
New Orleans, LA	14.8	10.9	9.6	12.2	16.4	11.6	13.0	11.5
New York, NY	10.5	7.5	7.0	9.3	13.9	11.4	16.4	24.1
Oklahoma City, OK	10.1	9.2	9.6	13.6	18.8	13.3	14.1	11.2
Omaha, NE	8.4	7.7	8.0	12.3	18.1	14.4	17.5	13.5
Orlando, FL	9.5	9.2	10.1	14.0	18.9	13.1	13.7	11.5
Peoria, IL	10.4	9.1	9.0	13.2	19.5	13.5	14.8	10.5
Philadelphia, PA	10.0	7.8	7.7	10.4	15.6	12.6	16.6	19.3
Phoenix, AZ	8.9	8.0	8.8	13.0	18.5	13.4	15.7	13.7
Pittsburgh, PA	10.6	9.7	9.3	12.3	17.4	12.9	15.5	12.3
Portland, OR	7.7	6.7	7.4	11.1	17.3	14.0	18.3	17.6
Providence, RI	11.0	8.8	7.9	10.8	15.9	13.2	17.0	15.4
Provo, UT	6.1	6.2	7.5	11.8	18.9	16.1	19.5	14.0
Raleigh, NC	6.5	6.6	7.6	11.7	17.1	13.7	18.2	18.6
Reno, NV	7.9	8.4	8.5	13.2	18.9	13.8	16.3	13.1
Richmond, VA	9.0	7.4	8.0	12.4	17.2	13.4	17.3	15.3
Riverside, CA	9.4	8.5	8.8	11.9	17.6	13.5	16.5	13.8
Rochester, MN	7.1	7.0	7.4	11.6	18.0	14.2	18.8	16.0
Sacramento, CA	9.1	7.6	7.7	10.6	16.6	13.1	17.4	17.9
Salt Lake City, UT	6.5	5.9	7.2	11.4	19.1	15.2	19.2	15.5
San Antonio, TX	10.3	8.9	9.4	12.8	18.7	13.2	14.8	11.9
San Diego, CA	7.6	6.7	7.1	10.3	16.1	13.0	18.0	21.1
San Francisco, CA	7.2	5.2	5.2	7.2	11.7	11.0	17.5	35.0
San Jose, CA	5.5	4.3	4.5	6.6	10.8	10.0	17.5	40.9
Santa Rosa, CA	6.7	6.0	6.8	10.0	16.6	14.2	18.5	21.1
Savannah, GA	10.6	9.5	9.2	13.0	17.8	13.8	14.6	11.4
Seattle, WA	6.7	5.4	5.9	9.5	15.7	13.3	19.5	23.9
Sioux Falls, SD	7.6	7.5	9.7	12.5	19.2	15.6	16.9	11.0
Springfield, IL	10.5	9.0	8.9	11.9	17.4	14.1	16.1	12.0
Tallahassee, FL	13.5	10.2	10.8	13.9	17.5	12.1	12.2	9.7
Tampa, FL	10.9	10.0	10.3	14.0	18.0	12.4	13.2	11.1
Tucson, AZ	12.0	10.6	10.2	14.3	18.2	12.3	12.7	9.6
Tulsa, OK	10.9	10.0	10.1	14.0	18.4	12.6	13.4	10.4
Tuscaloosa, AL	16.4	10.6	10.2	12.4	17.8	11.5	12.7	8.4
Virginia Beach, VA	8.7	7.7	8.2	12.3	18.8	14.4	17.1	12.7
Washington, DC	5.8	4.1	4.8	7.5	13.3	12.6	19.9	31.9
Wichita, KS	10.5	9.5	9.7	14.2	19.2	13.1	14.5	9.4
Winston-Salem, NC	12.1	11.3	11.0	14.8	18.0	12.8	11.6	8.3
U.S.	10.3	8.9	8.9	12.3	17.2	12.7	15.1	14.5

Note: Figures cover the Metropolitan Statistical Area (MSA)—see Appendix B for areas included
Source: Source: U.S. Census Bureau, 2015-2019 American Community Survey 5-Year Estimates

Poverty Rate: City

City	All Ages	Under 18 Years Old	18 to 64 Years Old	65 Years and Over
Albuquerque, NM	16.9	24.0	16.1	9.5
Allentown, PA	25.7	37.4	22.4	15.8
Anchorage, AK	9.0	13.1	8.1	5.5
Ann Arbor, MI	22.3	9.8	27.3	7.7
Athens, GA	29.9	33.7	32.2	9.4
Atlanta, GA	20.8	33.5	18.1	16.1
Austin, TX	13.2	18.0	12.3	9.4
Baton Rouge, LA	24.8	35.7	23.9	11.5
Boise City, ID	13.7	16.2	13.6	10.7
Boston, MA	18.9	27.7	16.5	20.9
Boulder, CO	20.4	6.3	25.2	6.9
Cape Coral, FL	10.4	13.1	10.3	8.6
Cedar Rapids, IA	12.5	17.0	12.2	7.0
Charleston, SC	13.2	14.7	13.8	8.8
Charlotte, NC	12.8	18.6	11.4	8.6
Chicago, IL	18.4	26.8	16.2	15.5
Cincinnati, OH	26.3	39.0	24.2	13.9
Clarksville, TN	14.5	18.5	13.5	9.0
Cleveland, OH	32.7	48.2	29.8	20.5
College Station, TX	29.6	12.3	35.9	7.9
Colorado Springs, CO	11.7	15.8	11.1	7.0
Columbia, MO	21.8	15.1	26.2	5.0
Columbia, SC	21.8	26.8	21.9	13.2
Columbus, OH	19.5	29.3	17.4	11.6
Dallas, TX	18.9	29.3	15.6	14.4
Davenport, IA	16.6	24.3	15.5	9.0
Denver, CO	12.9	18.2	11.6	10.9
Des Moines, IA	16.1	23.2	14.7	9.3
Durham, NC	15.9	24.5	14.3	8.4
Edison, NJ	5.7	6.8	5.1	6.8
El Paso, TX	19.1	27.1	15.9	17.6
Fargo, ND	13.2	12.8	14.3	7.6
Fayetteville, NC	19.3	28.0	17.4	11.6
Fort Collins, CO	16.3	10.3	19.3	7.7
Fort Wayne, IN	16.0	24.1	14.5	7.5
Fort Worth, TX	14.5	20.0	12.5	11.4
Grand Rapids, MI	20.4	28.9	19.4	10.1
Greeley, CO	16.2	19.6	16.1	9.3
Green Bay, WI	14.9	19.7	13.9	9.7
Greensboro, NC	18.5	26.7	17.1	11.5
Honolulu, HI	10.6	12.2	10.1	10.9
Houston, TX	20.1	31.2	16.6	14.2
Huntsville, AL	16.8	25.5	16.2	7.9
Indianapolis, IN	18.0	26.8	16.1	10.2
Jacksonville, FL	14.9	21.9	13.0	11.3
Kansas City, MO	16.1	24.3	14.5	9.6
Lafayette, LA	19.7	27.7	18.9	11.4
Lakeland, FL	16.4	23.5	15.5	12.3
Las Vegas, NV	15.3	21.3	14.1	10.6
Lexington, KY	16.8	20.4	17.5	7.4
Lincoln, NE	13.5	14.2	14.8	6.4
Little Rock, AR	16.6	23.8	15.2	10.9
Los Angeles, CA	18.0	25.7	16.0	15.6
Louisville, KY	15.9	24.0	14.6	9.4
Madison, WI	16.9	11.8	19.9	5.9

Table continued on following page.

City	All Ages	Under 18 Years Old	18 to 64 Years Old	65 Years and Over
Manchester, NH	14.1	19.8	13.2	10.1
Memphis, TN	25.1	40.8	21.1	13.6
Miami, FL	23.4	31.8	19.0	31.6
Midland, TX	9.2	11.5	7.7	11.8
Milwaukee, WI	25.4	36.7	22.7	13.6
Minneapolis, MN	19.1	25.5	18.2	13.2
Nashville, TN	15.1	24.2	13.2	9.2
New Haven, CT	26.5	36.2	24.7	16.3
New Orleans, LA	23.7	34.2	21.6	18.1
New York, NY	17.9	25.1	15.6	18.2
Oklahoma City, OK	16.1	23.7	14.2	9.0
Omaha, NE	13.4	18.7	12.3	8.5
Orlando, FL	17.2	24.4	15.4	14.8
Peoria, IL	19.7	24.6	20.1	10.1
Philadelphia, PA	24.3	34.8	22.2	17.6
Phoenix, AZ	18.0	26.6	15.6	10.8
Pittsburgh, PA	20.5	27.2	20.7	12.8
Portland, OR	13.7	15.5	13.9	10.4
Providence, RI	25.5	34.7	23.0	20.6
Provo, UT	26.3	19.6	30.2	7.9
Raleigh, NC	12.6	17.8	11.9	6.7
Reno, NV	13.5	15.8	14.0	8.2
Richmond, VA	23.2	37.0	21.5	13.2
Riverside, CA	13.9	17.9	13.0	10.5
Rochester, MN	10.1	12.8	10.0	5.7
Sacramento, CA	16.6	21.9	15.5	12.3
Salt Lake City, UT	16.6	20.4	16.4	10.9
San Antonio, TX	17.8	26.1	15.4	12.8
San Diego, CA	12.8	15.7	12.6	9.4
San Francisco, CA	10.3	10.0	9.7	13.6
San Jose, CA	8.7	9.3	8.4	9.5
Santa Rosa, CA	10.3	13.7	9.8	7.7
Savannah, GA	21.9	30.9	20.8	12.4
Seattle, WA	11.0	10.9	10.9	11.2
Sioux Falls, SD	10.4	12.9	9.9	8.0
Springfield, IL	18.6	29.8	17.5	8.4
Tallahassee, FL	26.4	24.3	29.3	9.9
Tampa, FL	18.6	26.5	16.2	17.6
Tucson, AZ	22.5	30.5	21.9	13.0
Tulsa, OK	19.4	29.7	17.7	8.8
Tuscaloosa, AL	24.0	24.2	26.6	10.3
Virginia Beach, VA	7.3	10.2	6.9	4.5
Washington, DC	16.2	24.0	14.5	14.5
Wichita, KS	15.9	22.0	15.0	8.8
Winston-Salem, NC	20.7	32.0	18.6	10.4
U.S.	13.4	18.5	12.6	9.3

Note: Figures are percentage of people whose income during the past 12 months was below the poverty level;
Source: U.S. Census Bureau, 2015-2019 American Community Survey 5-Year Estimates

Appendix A: Comparative Statistics

Poverty Rate: Metro Area

Metro Area	All Ages	Under 18 Years Old	18 to 64 Years Old	65 Years and Over
Albuquerque, NM	16.2	22.6	15.5	10.1
Allentown, PA	10.4	16.3	9.3	6.8
Anchorage, AK	9.4	12.8	8.6	6.0
Ann Arbor, MI	14.0	12.0	16.1	6.7
Athens, GA	22.0	25.1	23.8	8.1
Atlanta, GA	12.1	17.4	10.7	8.6
Austin, TX	10.8	13.3	10.5	7.2
Baton Rouge, LA	15.9	21.8	14.9	10.0
Boise City, ID	11.9	13.5	11.8	9.1
Boston, MA	9.3	11.3	8.8	9.1
Boulder, CO	11.7	8.5	13.8	6.3
Cape Coral, FL	13.1	22.1	12.8	7.9
Cedar Rapids, IA	10.0	12.8	9.8	6.6
Charleston, SC	12.9	18.9	11.7	8.7
Charlotte, NC	11.7	16.5	10.7	8.2
Chicago, IL	11.8	16.5	10.7	9.1
Cincinnati, OH	12.2	16.8	11.5	7.8
Clarksville, TN	14.7	19.0	13.7	9.7
Cleveland, OH	14.3	20.7	13.6	9.0
College Station, TX	22.7	20.1	25.8	9.1
Colorado Springs, CO	10.0	13.1	9.6	6.3
Columbia, MO	17.2	15.0	20.1	6.5
Columbia, SC	15.0	20.2	14.3	9.5
Columbus, OH	13.2	18.5	12.2	7.9
Dallas, TX	11.7	16.6	10.1	8.5
Davenport, IA	12.5	18.8	11.5	7.5
Denver, CO	8.8	11.4	8.3	6.9
Des Moines, IA	9.3	11.6	9.0	6.3
Durham, NC	14.2	20.6	13.6	7.8
Edison, NJ	12.8	17.7	11.4	12.0
El Paso, TX	20.2	28.6	16.7	18.6
Fargo, ND	11.1	11.1	11.9	6.3
Fayetteville, NC	17.9	24.8	16.3	11.4
Fort Collins, CO	11.6	9.4	13.5	6.4
Fort Wayne, IN	13.0	19.4	11.7	6.5
Fort Worth, TX	11.7	16.6	10.1	8.5
Grand Rapids, MI	11.0	13.7	10.9	6.9
Greeley, CO	10.0	12.0	9.5	8.4
Green Bay, WI	9.6	12.5	9.0	7.3
Greensboro, NC	16.0	23.2	14.9	10.0
Honolulu, HI	8.3	10.1	7.8	7.8
Houston, TX	13.7	19.8	11.7	10.0
Huntsville, AL	12.7	18.5	11.8	7.7
Indianapolis, IN	12.4	17.5	11.4	7.4
Jacksonville, FL	12.6	17.7	11.6	8.9
Kansas City, MO	10.5	15.0	9.6	6.8
Lafayette, LA	19.1	26.4	17.4	13.7
Lakeland, FL	15.8	24.7	14.5	9.9
Las Vegas, NV	13.7	19.3	12.6	9.2
Lexington, KY	15.8	20.9	15.9	7.6
Lincoln, NE	12.2	12.5	13.5	5.8
Little Rock, AR	15.1	20.5	14.2	9.7
Los Angeles, CA	13.9	19.2	12.5	12.2
Louisville, KY	12.5	18.2	11.6	7.9
Madison, WI	10.3	8.7	11.8	5.6

Table continued on following page.

Metro Area	All Ages	Under 18 Years Old	18 to 64 Years Old	65 Years and Over
Manchester, NH	7.8	9.4	7.6	6.1
Memphis, TN	17.6	27.8	15.0	10.1
Miami, FL	14.6	20.2	12.6	15.1
Midland, TX	9.5	13.2	7.5	11.1
Milwaukee, WI	13.3	19.3	12.3	8.4
Minneapolis, MN	8.6	11.0	8.1	6.6
Nashville, TN	11.4	15.7	10.6	7.6
New Haven, CT	11.7	17.3	11.0	7.6
New Orleans, LA	17.3	25.2	15.7	12.5
New York, NY	12.8	17.7	11.4	12.0
Oklahoma City, OK	13.9	19.0	13.2	7.5
Omaha, NE	10.3	13.5	9.6	7.2
Orlando, FL	13.7	19.6	12.5	9.9
Peoria, IL	12.2	15.5	12.4	6.9
Philadelphia, PA	12.4	16.9	11.7	8.6
Phoenix, AZ	13.7	19.6	12.8	8.2
Pittsburgh, PA	11.2	14.9	11.0	8.0
Portland, OR	10.6	13.1	10.5	7.7
Providence, RI	12.0	16.9	11.1	9.6
Provo, UT	10.7	9.5	12.0	5.5
Raleigh, NC	9.8	13.4	9.1	6.3
Reno, NV	11.2	14.0	11.2	7.7
Richmond, VA	11.2	15.8	10.5	7.6
Riverside, CA	14.8	20.5	13.2	10.7
Rochester, MN	8.3	10.4	8.1	5.6
Sacramento, CA	13.4	16.8	13.2	8.9
Salt Lake City, UT	9.0	10.7	8.6	6.7
San Antonio, TX	14.4	20.6	12.7	10.4
San Diego, CA	11.6	14.7	11.1	8.9
San Francisco, CA	9.0	10.2	8.7	8.7
San Jose, CA	7.5	7.9	7.3	8.0
Santa Rosa, CA	9.2	10.7	9.4	7.0
Savannah, GA	13.7	18.4	13.1	8.7
Seattle, WA	9.0	10.8	8.6	7.8
Sioux Falls, SD	8.7	10.4	8.3	7.2
Springfield, IL	14.2	22.8	13.2	6.9
Tallahassee, FL	20.0	22.1	21.9	8.4
Tampa, FL	13.5	18.6	12.8	10.3
Tucson, AZ	16.8	23.9	16.9	8.8
Tulsa, OK	14.3	20.9	13.3	7.7
Tuscaloosa, AL	19.2	24.7	19.2	10.6
Virginia Beach, VA	11.3	17.1	10.2	6.9
Washington, DC	7.8	9.9	7.2	7.2
Wichita, KS	13.0	17.4	12.3	8.2
Winston-Salem, NC	16.0	24.8	14.6	9.0
U.S.	13.4	18.5	12.6	9.3

Note: Figures are percentage of people whose income during the past 12 months was below the poverty level; Figures cover the Metropolitan Statistical Area—see Appendix B for areas included
Source: U.S. Census Bureau, 2015-2019 American Community Survey 5-Year Estimates

Employment by Industry

Metro Area[1]	(A)	(B)	(C)	(D)	(E)	(F)	(G)	(H)	(I)	(J)	(K)	(L)	(M)	(N)
Albuquerque, NM	6.8	n/a	17.3	4.9	20.9	1.3	8.7	3.8	n/a	2.8	16.5	10.9	2.8	2.9
Allentown, PA	3.5	n/a	20.8	3.6	10.5	1.2	7.7	10.5	n/a	3.4	12.8	10.8	10.9	3.8
Anchorage, AK	7.4	6.0	19.2	4.6	20.8	2.1	8.0	1.1	1.3	3.4	10.9	12.1	6.9	2.9
Ann Arbor, MI	2.2	n/a	13.3	3.0	38.3	2.8	4.6	6.3	n/a	2.5	14.0	7.3	2.2	3.0
Athens, GA	n/a	n/a	n/a	n/a	29.7	n/a	10.2	n/a	n/a	n/a	9.1	11.3	n/a	n/a
Atlanta, GA	4.7	4.6	13.1	6.6	12.0	3.5	8.8	6.0	<0.1	3.3	19.5	10.5	6.1	5.3
Austin, TX	6.4	n/a	11.2	6.2	16.9	3.6	9.5	5.8	n/a	3.8	18.6	10.0	2.6	4.9
Baton Rouge, LA	10.7	10.5	13.5	4.2	20.0	1.1	8.8	7.5	0.1	3.8	12.3	10.5	3.9	3.3
Boise City, ID	8.2	n/a	14.3	6.0	13.6	1.0	9.2	8.1	n/a	3.4	15.2	11.9	3.8	4.7
Boston, MA[4]	4.1	n/a	22.8	8.6	11.0	3.4	6.3	4.2	n/a	3.1	22.3	8.0	2.4	3.2
Boulder, CO	3.0	n/a	13.3	3.8	18.9	4.5	6.5	11.3	n/a	3.1	21.2	9.5	1.1	3.5
Cape Coral, FL	12.6	n/a	11.4	4.9	15.8	0.9	13.5	2.4	n/a	4.0	14.0	14.9	2.4	2.8
Cedar Rapids, IA	6.0	n/a	14.8	8.2	11.3	2.1	6.8	14.0	n/a	3.4	10.2	11.0	7.7	4.1
Charleston, SC	5.7	n/a	11.9	4.4	18.2	1.5	11.5	7.6	n/a	3.8	15.5	12.3	4.2	2.9
Charlotte, NC	5.6	n/a	10.1	9.1	12.8	1.9	9.4	8.5	n/a	3.5	17.4	10.6	6.1	4.6
Chicago, IL[2]	3.5	3.4	16.5	7.8	11.4	1.8	6.5	7.6	<0.1	4.1	19.1	9.6	6.4	5.1
Cincinnati, OH	4.2	n/a	15.8	6.9	11.8	1.2	8.9	10.5	n/a	3.4	15.7	10.1	5.7	5.2
Clarksville, TN	3.8	n/a	12.9	3.3	20.6	1.0	12.1	11.7	n/a	3.4	10.6	13.9	2.9	n/a
Cleveland, OH	3.7	n/a	19.4	6.5	12.8	1.2	8.3	11.2	n/a	3.3	15.0	9.7	3.6	4.8
College Station, TX	5.7	n/a	10.1	3.1	37.9	1.1	11.3	4.4	n/a	2.5	9.0	10.4	1.7	2.2
Colorado Springs, CO	6.3	n/a	14.7	6.5	18.4	1.8	9.5	4.0	n/a	5.9	16.6	11.6	2.2	2.0
Columbia, MO	n/a	n/a	n/a	n/a	29.2	n/a	n/a	n/a	n/a	n/a	n/a	10.9	n/a	n/a
Columbia, SC	4.4	n/a	12.2	8.1	21.7	1.2	8.9	7.9	n/a	3.8	12.4	10.8	4.4	3.6
Columbus, OH	4.1	n/a	14.5	8.0	16.4	1.3	7.6	6.7	n/a	3.6	16.4	9.3	7.9	3.7
Dallas, TX[2]	5.4	n/a	11.7	9.7	11.9	2.5	8.5	6.7	n/a	2.8	19.5	9.5	5.6	5.6
Davenport, IA	n/a	n/a	n/a	n/a	n/a	n/a	n/a	n/a	n/a	n/a	n/a	n/a	n/a	n/a
Denver, CO	7.5	n/a	12.8	7.7	13.5	3.4	7.3	4.7	n/a	3.7	18.8	9.7	5.5	5.0
Des Moines, IA	5.8	n/a	13.9	15.8	12.6	1.6	7.8	5.6	n/a	3.5	13.7	10.9	3.4	4.9
Durham, NC	2.9	n/a	22.1	5.1	19.9	1.7	6.2	10.4	n/a	3.3	15.3	7.4	2.5	2.6
Edison, NJ[2]	3.8	n/a	22.7	9.4	14.1	3.8	6.0	2.7	n/a	3.8	16.4	8.9	4.2	3.7
El Paso, TX	5.5	n/a	14.8	4.1	22.2	1.4	10.5	5.1	n/a	2.5	11.8	12.3	5.5	3.7
Fargo, ND	6.4	n/a	19.3	8.3	13.3	2.1	8.1	7.1	n/a	3.4	9.5	10.9	4.6	6.4
Fayetteville, NC	3.7	n/a	11.5	2.9	31.8	0.7	11.5	6.2	n/a	3.3	8.6	13.6	3.9	1.5
Fort Collins, CO	7.0	n/a	11.2	4.1	25.0	1.8	8.8	8.4	n/a	3.8	12.2	11.7	2.3	3.1
Fort Wayne, IN	5.3	n/a	19.1	5.5	8.8	0.9	8.4	16.5	n/a	4.7	9.9	11.3	4.6	4.6
Fort Worth, TX[2]	6.8	n/a	12.8	6.3	12.8	0.8	10.1	9.2	n/a	3.5	11.5	11.8	9.0	4.9
Grand Rapids, MI	4.7	n/a	17.6	5.0	9.0	1.0	5.8	20.4	n/a	3.7	13.6	9.2	3.5	5.9
Greeley, CO	14.9	n/a	9.8	4.2	15.9	0.4	8.1	13.1	n/a	3.4	10.7	10.5	4.6	4.0
Green Bay, WI	4.8	n/a	15.5	6.8	11.1	0.8	7.5	17.9	n/a	4.7	11.1	9.6	5.1	4.7
Greensboro, NC	4.5	n/a	14.3	5.2	12.1	1.2	8.5	14.5	n/a	3.3	13.0	11.1	6.4	5.3
Honolulu, HI	6.5	n/a	15.2	5.3	22.5	1.3	12.0	2.1	n/a	4.1	12.8	9.7	4.8	3.2
Houston, TX	8.9	6.7	13.2	5.4	14.0	0.9	9.5	6.9	2.2	3.5	16.1	10.1	5.7	5.2
Huntsville, AL	4.0	n/a	8.7	2.9	21.2	0.8	8.0	10.6	n/a	3.2	25.5	10.4	1.6	2.5
Indianapolis, IN	5.5	5.4	15.1	6.7	12.7	1.0	8.5	8.4	<0.1	3.5	15.9	9.8	7.9	4.4
Jacksonville, FL	6.6	6.5	15.4	9.6	10.8	1.2	10.4	4.4	<0.1	3.4	15.6	11.3	7.1	3.6
Kansas City, MO	4.9	n/a	14.6	7.4	13.7	1.3	8.1	7.4	n/a	3.8	17.7	10.3	5.7	4.6
Lafayette, LA	10.1	4.9	16.8	5.2	13.4	1.0	10.1	7.0	5.2	3.4	11.1	14.0	3.2	4.2
Lakeland, FL	6.3	n/a	14.6	5.8	11.7	0.7	8.7	7.2	n/a	2.5	13.9	13.5	10.0	4.5
Las Vegas, NV	7.0	6.9	11.4	5.8	11.2	1.0	21.4	2.6	<0.1	2.9	14.3	12.4	7.0	2.5
Lexington, KY	5.0	n/a	13.0	3.7	19.4	0.9	8.8	10.5	n/a	3.6	14.8	11.2	4.7	3.9
Lincoln, NE	5.1	n/a	16.6	6.8	21.9	1.7	7.6	7.0	n/a	3.6	11.4	9.8	5.9	2.3
Little Rock, AR	4.9	n/a	16.7	6.3	19.3	1.4	8.0	5.3	n/a	5.0	12.5	11.2	4.6	4.2
Los Angeles, CA[2]	3.5	3.5	20.1	5.1	13.4	4.3	8.5	7.4	<0.1	2.8	14.4	9.7	5.4	4.8
Louisville, KY	4.3	n/a	14.3	7.3	10.8	1.2	7.8	12.6	n/a	3.5	13.1	10.0	10.2	4.4
Madison, WI	4.6	n/a	12.6	5.9	21.5	4.5	6.4	9.1	n/a	5.2	13.5	10.3	2.4	3.6
Manchester, NH[3]	5.0	n/a	22.6	7.2	10.6	2.8	6.7	7.0	n/a	3.7	15.2	11.5	3.2	4.0

Table continued on following page.

Appendix A: Comparative Statistics A-75

Metro Area[1]	(A)	(B)	(C)	(D)	(E)	(F)	(G)	(H)	(I)	(J)	(K)	(L)	(M)	(N)
Memphis, TN	3.6	n/a	14.6	4.5	12.9	0.7	8.9	6.8	n/a	4.2	15.4	10.0	12.6	5.3
Miami, FL[2]	4.5	4.4	16.5	7.2	12.1	1.6	9.2	3.7	<0.1	3.9	15.9	12.0	7.1	6.0
Midland, TX	28.0	n/a	7.3	4.8	11.2	0.7	10.1	3.3	n/a	3.7	9.4	10.5	5.2	5.2
Milwaukee, WI	3.6	3.6	20.5	6.0	9.6	1.5	7.1	13.9	<0.1	5.4	14.3	9.4	3.6	4.5
Minneapolis, MN	4.3	n/a	17.7	8.7	12.9	1.6	5.3	10.2	n/a	3.6	16.6	9.8	4.0	4.7
Nashville, TN	4.8	n/a	14.8	6.9	11.8	2.4	9.2	7.9	n/a	3.8	17.3	10.0	6.5	4.0
New Haven, CT[3]	3.5	n/a	28.4	4.0	12.7	1.3	6.5	8.2	n/a	3.5	10.9	9.6	7.1	3.8
New Orleans, LA	5.6	4.9	19.1	5.2	13.5	1.0	11.9	5.6	0.7	4.0	13.2	11.5	5.2	3.8
New York, NY[2]	3.8	n/a	22.7	9.4	14.1	3.8	6.0	2.7	n/a	3.8	16.4	8.9	4.2	3.7
Oklahoma City, OK	6.0	4.8	15.4	5.4	20.2	0.9	10.4	5.2	1.2	4.3	12.8	10.7	4.8	3.4
Omaha, NE	6.2	n/a	16.0	9.2	13.2	1.9	8.5	6.8	n/a	3.5	14.3	10.9	5.5	3.4
Orlando, FL	7.0	7.0	13.1	6.5	10.6	2.0	15.1	4.0	<0.1	3.3	18.2	12.2	3.7	3.8
Peoria, IL	4.7	n/a	19.8	4.4	11.9	0.9	7.3	13.0	n/a	4.7	13.0	11.5	4.4	3.8
Philadelphia, PA[2]	2.6	n/a	32.1	6.3	14.4	1.9	6.0	3.5	n/a	3.7	14.7	7.7	4.1	2.4
Phoenix, AZ	6.2	6.1	15.9	9.4	11.1	1.6	8.9	6.1	0.1	3.0	16.8	11.3	5.3	3.7
Pittsburgh, PA	5.8	5.1	22.8	6.8	10.2	1.6	7.5	7.2	0.6	3.7	15.5	10.6	4.4	3.4
Portland, OR	6.4	6.3	15.8	6.2	12.4	2.1	6.3	10.6	0.1	3.2	16.4	10.4	4.8	4.8
Providence, RI[3]	4.5	4.5	21.4	6.6	13.2	1.0	8.6	8.7	<0.1	4.0	13.1	11.6	3.4	3.2
Provo, UT	9.5	n/a	18.7	4.3	11.9	4.7	8.2	7.3	n/a	2.1	15.2	13.2	1.7	2.6
Raleigh, NC	6.5	n/a	12.4	5.1	14.9	3.4	9.0	4.6	n/a	3.9	20.5	11.6	3.4	4.0
Reno, NV	7.4	7.2	11.5	4.5	12.4	1.2	12.3	10.3	0.2	2.3	14.4	9.9	9.3	3.9
Richmond, VA	6.1	n/a	14.7	8.0	16.4	0.9	7.9	4.6	n/a	4.2	17.2	10.3	5.3	3.8
Riverside, CA	7.3	7.2	16.6	2.8	16.2	0.5	8.3	6.0	<0.1	2.4	10.4	11.8	12.9	4.2
Rochester, MN	4.0	n/a	44.7	2.3	10.5	1.1	5.8	8.3	n/a	2.9	4.7	10.6	2.2	2.3
Sacramento, CA	7.5	7.5	16.4	5.3	24.0	1.0	8.0	3.6	<0.1	2.8	13.8	10.5	4.0	2.7
Salt Lake City, UT	6.6	n/a	11.6	8.3	14.1	2.7	7.5	7.8	n/a	2.7	17.5	10.4	5.9	4.4
San Antonio, TX	5.8	5.2	15.1	8.9	16.6	1.7	10.8	4.8	0.5	3.2	14.7	10.6	3.8	3.4
San Diego, CA	6.3	6.3	15.2	5.3	16.9	1.5	9.3	8.1	<0.1	2.9	18.2	10.4	2.6	2.8
San Francisco, CA[2]	3.9	3.9	13.5	7.9	11.9	10.3	6.5	3.4	<0.1	2.9	26.8	6.6	3.9	1.9
San Jose, CA	4.8	4.7	15.9	3.5	8.7	10.0	5.4	15.7	<0.1	1.9	22.3	7.2	1.6	2.6
Santa Rosa, CA	8.7	8.6	17.4	3.9	14.2	1.1	8.2	11.8	0.1	3.0	11.9	12.9	2.3	4.0
Savannah, GA	4.6	n/a	14.0	3.2	13.0	0.8	12.2	9.3	n/a	3.7	14.3	11.8	9.1	3.4
Seattle, WA[2]	6.3	6.2	13.1	5.2	12.2	8.1	6.2	8.6	<0.1	3.4	16.4	12.8	3.4	3.9
Sioux Falls, SD	5.5	n/a	22.2	9.9	9.4	1.5	7.8	9.0	n/a	3.7	9.4	12.0	3.6	5.4
Springfield, IL	3.3	n/a	20.4	6.0	25.9	1.7	6.6	2.8	n/a	5.7	10.5	11.7	2.0	2.7
Tallahassee, FL	4.5	n/a	13.7	4.2	32.8	1.7	9.4	1.9	n/a	5.0	12.8	10.0	1.3	2.0
Tampa, FL	6.2	6.1	15.5	9.2	11.2	1.7	9.9	4.9	<0.1	3.3	18.7	11.7	3.2	3.9
Tucson, AZ	5.3	4.8	18.1	4.6	19.8	1.3	9.3	7.1	0.5	3.3	12.2	11.3	5.4	1.8
Tulsa, OK	6.7	5.6	16.1	5.1	12.7	1.3	9.5	11.1	1.0	4.4	13.0	11.1	4.9	3.6
Tuscaloosa, AL	6.4	n/a	8.3	3.8	26.4	0.8	9.2	16.5	n/a	3.8	9.2	10.3	2.8	1.9
Virginia Beach, VA	5.2	n/a	14.2	5.0	20.5	1.2	10.0	7.4	n/a	4.1	14.8	11.2	3.6	2.3
Washington, DC[2]	5.0	n/a	12.8	4.5	22.8	2.3	7.3	1.4	n/a	6.4	24.5	8.0	2.6	1.8
Wichita, KS	5.8	n/a	16.3	4.1	14.3	1.2	10.3	15.5	n/a	3.5	11.8	10.6	3.3	2.8
Winston-Salem, NC	4.5	n/a	20.8	4.9	11.4	0.6	9.2	12.6	n/a	3.0	13.4	11.8	4.4	2.9
U.S.	5.5	5.1	16.3	6.1	15.2	1.9	9.0	8.5	0.4	3.8	14.4	10.9	4.6	3.9

Note: All figures are percentages covering non-farm employment as of December 2020 and are not seasonally adjusted; (1) Figures cover the Metropolitan Statistical Area (MSA) except where noted. See Appendix B for areas included; (2) Metropolitan Division; (3) New England City and Town Area; (4) New England City and Town Area Division; (A) Construction, Mining, and Logging (some areas report Construction separate from Mining and Logging); (B) Construction; (C) Education and Health Services; (D) Financial Activities; (E) Government; (F) Information; (G) Leisure and Hospitality; (H) Manufacturing; (I) Mining and Logging; (J) Other Services; (K) Professional and Business Services; (L) Retail Trade; (M) Transportation and Utilities; (N) Wholesale Trade; n/a not available
Source: Bureau of Labor Statistics, Current Employment Statistics, Employment, Hours, and Earnings, December 2020

Appendix A: Comparative Statistics

Labor Force, Employment and Job Growth: City

City	Civilian Labor Force Dec. 2019	Dec. 2020	% Chg.	Workers Employed Dec. 2019	Dec. 2020	% Chg.
Albuquerque, NM	284,609	280,764	-1.3	273,259	260,057	-4.8
Allentown, PA	56,275	55,559	-1.2	52,716	50,085	-4.9
Anchorage, AK	147,801	150,509	1.8	140,718	142,180	1.0
Ann Arbor, MI	66,802	63,917	-4.3	65,636	62,017	-5.5
Athens, GA	59,225	58,747	-0.8	57,596	55,706	-3.2
Atlanta, GA	264,779	266,767	0.7	256,964	248,040	-3.4
Austin, TX	601,055	606,519	0.9	587,607	576,501	-1.8
Baton Rouge, LA	111,969	112,989	0.9	106,514	104,304	-2.0
Boise City, ID	134,753	133,502	-0.9	131,600	127,739	-2.9
Boston, MA	399,841	382,754	-4.2	391,993	354,899	-9.4
Boulder, CO	66,229	64,864	-2.0	65,025	60,677	-6.6
Cape Coral, FL	93,172	90,468	-2.9	90,578	86,083	-4.9
Cedar Rapids, IA	73,629	67,681	-8.0	71,125	64,790	-8.9
Charleston, SC	75,308	72,571	-3.6	73,919	69,583	-5.8
Charlotte, NC	499,499	492,206	-1.4	483,932	461,278	-4.6
Chicago, IL	1,322,199	1,308,831	-1.0	1,281,869	1,177,846	-8.1
Cincinnati, OH	147,410	148,764	0.9	142,030	139,857	-1.5
Clarksville, TN	63,787	65,851	3.2	61,432	60,949	-0.7
Cleveland, OH	156,471	151,177	-3.3	149,465	137,384	-8.0
College Station, TX	62,425	62,445	0.0	60,916	59,698	-2.0
Colorado Springs, CO	238,705	245,635	2.9	232,124	223,547	-3.7
Columbia, MO	68,108	67,049	-1.5	66,459	64,199	-3.4
Columbia, SC	58,665	58,030	-1.0	57,222	55,091	-3.7
Columbus, OH	478,751	473,342	-1.1	463,416	448,688	-3.1
Dallas, TX	703,081	714,931	1.6	681,628	663,820	-2.6
Davenport, IA	51,918	47,841	-7.8	49,753	45,379	-8.7
Denver, CO	423,917	436,113	2.8	414,090	395,349	-4.5
Des Moines, IA	115,631	106,451	-7.9	111,652	101,736	-8.8
Durham, NC	150,280	147,613	-1.7	145,981	139,307	-4.5
Edison, NJ	55,345	54,084	-2.2	54,066	51,214	-5.2
El Paso, TX	305,478	303,471	-0.6	295,039	280,221	-5.0
Fargo, ND	69,702	73,397	5.3	68,423	71,067	3.8
Fayetteville, NC	76,883	75,832	-1.3	73,263	69,057	-5.7
Fort Collins, CO	103,931	102,364	-1.5	101,963	94,647	-7.1
Fort Wayne, IN	128,470	131,139	2.0	124,594	125,226	0.5
Fort Worth, TX	444,954	448,335	0.7	431,424	417,064	-3.3
Grand Rapids, MI	103,987	101,472	-2.4	100,701	95,669	-5.0
Greeley, CO	55,458	56,828	2.4	54,063	51,159	-5.3
Green Bay, WI	53,859	54,419	1.0	52,110	51,623	-0.9
Greensboro, NC	147,165	143,483	-2.5	141,957	132,895	-6.3
Honolulu, HI	452,859	447,861	-1.1	443,191	411,864	-7.0
Houston, TX	1,168,794	1,162,957	-0.5	1,128,145	1,071,532	-5.0
Huntsville, AL	99,396	97,639	-1.7	97,185	94,305	-2.9
Indianapolis, IN	446,151	467,925	4.8	433,373	443,878	2.4
Jacksonville, FL	469,934	463,646	-1.3	457,089	438,293	-4.1
Kansas City, MO	262,205	262,873	0.2	252,990	245,170	-3.0
Lafayette, LA	59,376	59,649	0.4	56,669	56,144	-0.9
Lakeland, FL	47,582	47,525	-0.1	46,092	44,428	-3.6
Las Vegas, NV	316,225	301,287	-4.7	305,003	270,332	-11.3
Lexington, KY	175,216	173,151	-1.1	170,118	164,394	-3.3
Lincoln, NE	160,552	162,129	0.9	156,783	157,418	0.4
Little Rock, AR	96,600	95,461	-1.1	93,594	90,677	-3.1
Los Angeles, CA	2,095,690	1,987,043	-5.1	2,011,531	1,777,290	-11.6
Louisville, KY	402,027	394,489	-1.8	388,284	371,824	-4.2
Madison, WI	157,534	157,457	0.0	154,347	151,326	-1.9

Table continued on following page.

City	Civilian Labor Force Dec. 2019	Civilian Labor Force Dec. 2020	% Chg.	Workers Employed Dec. 2019	Workers Employed Dec. 2020	% Chg.
Manchester, NH	66,041	64,338	-2.5	64,553	61,492	-4.7
Memphis, TN	299,167	316,351	5.7	287,040	285,384	-0.5
Miami, FL	234,913	222,511	-5.2	231,476	205,346	-11.2
Midland, TX	88,858	84,069	-5.3	87,068	77,687	-10.7
Milwaukee, WI	271,222	276,192	1.8	260,380	253,283	-2.7
Minneapolis, MN	245,206	236,236	-3.6	238,869	224,977	-5.8
Nashville, TN	413,927	420,401	1.5	404,589	396,582	-1.9
New Haven, CT	65,459	65,774	0.4	63,121	59,553	-5.6
New Orleans, LA	179,138	182,736	2.0	170,426	162,218	-4.8
New York, NY	4,055,234	3,856,031	-4.9	3,932,458	3,408,146	-13.3
Oklahoma City, OK	322,420	325,821	1.0	313,116	308,959	-1.3
Omaha, NE	243,405	245,582	0.8	236,406	237,000	0.2
Orlando, FL	170,544	162,722	-4.5	166,541	149,954	-9.9
Peoria, IL	50,615	47,156	-6.8	47,924	43,020	-10.2
Philadelphia, PA	729,738	699,455	-4.1	690,247	634,633	-8.0
Phoenix, AZ	885,177	887,360	0.2	853,111	820,050	-3.8
Pittsburgh, PA	157,702	150,397	-4.6	151,169	140,388	-7.1
Portland, OR	376,061	380,047	1.0	366,666	355,132	-3.1
Providence, RI	86,891	84,686	-2.5	83,544	77,341	-7.4
Provo, UT	68,223	69,278	1.5	66,963	67,577	0.9
Raleigh, NC	260,153	256,088	-1.5	252,404	241,439	-4.3
Reno, NV	139,960	134,597	-3.8	136,175	127,830	-6.1
Richmond, VA	119,856	116,571	-2.7	116,483	108,936	-6.4
Riverside, CA	156,209	155,456	-0.4	151,257	142,354	-5.8
Rochester, MN	65,938	64,249	-2.5	64,352	61,741	-4.0
Sacramento, CA	237,846	239,336	0.6	230,186	217,425	-5.5
Salt Lake City, UT	117,922	119,415	1.2	115,531	115,159	-0.3
San Antonio, TX	740,486	738,883	-0.2	720,097	690,895	-4.0
San Diego, CA	724,077	722,739	-0.1	704,952	665,731	-5.5
San Francisco, CA	589,286	566,193	-3.9	578,146	529,919	-8.3
San Jose, CA	558,215	552,450	-1.0	545,337	515,386	-5.4
Santa Rosa, CA	90,456	87,703	-3.0	88,298	81,635	-7.5
Savannah, GA	66,855	68,668	2.7	64,804	63,654	-1.7
Seattle, WA	475,147	468,970	-1.3	464,721	440,258	-5.2
Sioux Falls, SD	106,508	105,414	-1.0	103,166	102,274	-0.8
Springfield, IL	56,539	55,105	-2.5	54,362	51,115	-5.9
Tallahassee, FL	102,369	97,422	-4.8	99,536	91,619	-7.9
Tampa, FL	205,639	203,778	-0.9	200,162	191,493	-4.3
Tucson, AZ	271,283	268,958	-0.8	259,611	246,980	-4.8
Tulsa, OK	196,335	194,348	-1.0	190,196	182,480	-4.0
Tuscaloosa, AL	48,708	47,374	-2.7	47,449	45,126	-4.9
Virginia Beach, VA	234,164	226,000	-3.4	228,643	216,261	-5.4
Washington, DC	416,329	413,158	-0.7	397,389	376,699	-5.2
Wichita, KS	189,743	189,451	-0.1	183,423	180,980	-1.3
Winston-Salem, NC	118,986	117,479	-1.2	114,945	109,601	-4.6
U.S.	164,007,000	160,017,000	-2.4	158,504,000	149,613,000	-5.6

Note: Data is not seasonally adjusted and covers workers 16 years of age and older
Source: Bureau of Labor Statistics, Local Area Unemployment Statistics

Labor Force, Employment and Job Growth: Metro Area

Metro Area[1]	Civilian Labor Force Dec. 2019	Dec. 2020	% Chg.	Workers Employed Dec. 2019	Dec. 2020	% Chg.
Albuquerque, NM	442,230	434,669	-1.7	423,884	402,897	-4.9
Allentown, PA	448,501	434,989	-3.0	428,188	408,208	-4.6
Anchorage, AK	195,036	197,957	1.5	184,796	186,758	1.0
Ann Arbor, MI	200,349	192,221	-4.0	196,082	185,271	-5.5
Athens, GA	99,032	97,723	-1.3	96,483	93,287	-3.3
Atlanta, GA	3,128,881	3,107,968	-0.6	3,045,413	2,939,513	-3.4
Austin, TX	1,255,200	1,267,150	0.9	1,224,993	1,202,103	-1.8
Baton Rouge, LA	417,880	416,461	-0.3	399,191	391,186	-2.0
Boise City, ID	381,230	377,479	-0.9	371,231	360,351	-2.9
Boston, MA[4]	1,694,809	1,609,639	-5.0	1,662,542	1,505,214	-9.4
Boulder, CO	197,746	194,238	-1.7	193,839	180,878	-6.6
Cape Coral, FL	353,248	344,421	-2.5	344,074	327,001	-4.9
Cedar Rapids, IA	148,694	136,358	-8.3	143,975	131,243	-8.8
Charleston, SC	395,683	381,666	-3.5	387,938	365,144	-5.8
Charlotte, NC	1,373,470	1,344,434	-2.1	1,331,441	1,267,112	-4.8
Chicago, IL[2]	3,687,479	3,541,085	-3.9	3,574,836	3,232,803	-9.5
Cincinnati, OH	1,128,063	1,122,791	-0.4	1,090,733	1,069,559	-1.9
Clarksville, TN	118,102	120,516	2.0	113,647	112,488	-1.0
Cleveland, OH	1,049,216	997,566	-4.9	1,009,725	921,287	-8.7
College Station, TX	137,059	137,930	0.6	133,696	130,968	-2.0
Colorado Springs, CO	356,603	365,426	2.4	346,681	333,941	-3.6
Columbia, MO	99,481	97,891	-1.6	97,069	93,768	-3.4
Columbia, SC	403,325	396,126	-1.7	394,519	379,089	-3.9
Columbus, OH	1,105,853	1,087,829	-1.6	1,070,103	1,037,232	-3.0
Dallas, TX[2]	2,719,675	2,742,810	0.8	2,640,356	2,571,653	-2.6
Davenport, IA	194,473	181,630	-6.6	185,909	172,320	-7.3
Denver, CO	1,688,220	1,720,681	1.9	1,650,053	1,575,283	-4.5
Des Moines, IA	366,728	336,296	-8.3	356,630	324,997	-8.8
Durham, NC	305,270	298,535	-2.2	296,522	283,058	-4.5
Edison, NJ[2]	7,008,087	6,694,644	-4.4	6,780,009	6,077,482	-10.3
El Paso, TX	367,648	366,204	-0.3	354,536	336,718	-5.0
Fargo, ND	138,402	143,685	3.8	135,435	139,201	2.7
Fayetteville, NC	148,437	145,648	-1.8	141,883	133,739	-5.7
Fort Collins, CO	209,156	205,612	-1.6	205,003	190,294	-7.1
Fort Wayne, IN	216,998	220,641	1.6	210,942	212,055	0.5
Fort Worth, TX[2]	1,311,941	1,316,316	0.3	1,273,454	1,230,725	-3.3
Grand Rapids, MI	575,885	557,316	-3.2	561,939	534,032	-4.9
Greeley, CO	172,545	174,099	0.9	168,655	159,598	-5.3
Green Bay, WI	172,794	173,847	0.6	167,575	165,813	-1.0
Greensboro, NC	371,920	360,292	-3.1	359,136	336,201	-6.3
Honolulu, HI	452,859	447,861	-1.1	443,191	411,864	-7.0
Houston, TX	3,462,635	3,445,575	-0.4	3,336,616	3,169,170	-5.0
Huntsville, AL	229,898	224,806	-2.2	225,028	218,441	-2.9
Indianapolis, IN	1,060,176	1,101,669	3.9	1,032,445	1,057,751	2.4
Jacksonville, FL	794,684	779,448	-1.9	774,172	742,219	-4.1
Kansas City, MO	1,145,405	1,145,812	0.0	1,109,920	1,089,310	-1.8
Lafayette, LA	210,923	212,283	0.6	200,667	199,150	-0.7
Lakeland, FL	308,057	308,560	0.1	298,597	287,817	-3.6
Las Vegas, NV	1,136,500	1,084,944	-4.5	1,096,609	971,954	-11.3
Lexington, KY	273,326	269,822	-1.2	265,044	256,418	-3.2
Lincoln, NE	186,998	188,745	0.9	182,613	183,294	0.3
Little Rock, AR	354,854	348,009	-1.9	343,794	333,024	-3.1
Los Angeles, CA[2]	5,171,306	4,867,991	-5.8	4,946,895	4,270,635	-13.6
Louisville, KY	674,729	662,325	-1.8	652,752	628,916	-3.6
Madison, WI	390,192	389,396	-0.2	381,370	373,552	-2.0

Table continued on following page.

Appendix A: Comparative Statistics A-79

Metro Area[1]	Civilian Labor Force Dec. 2019	Civilian Labor Force Dec. 2020	% Chg.	Workers Employed Dec. 2019	Workers Employed Dec. 2020	% Chg.
Manchester, NH[3]	123,691	119,789	-3.1	121,082	115,342	-4.7
Memphis, TN	647,507	668,382	3.2	622,648	618,793	-0.6
Miami, FL[2]	1,377,214	1,301,119	-5.5	1,353,568	1,197,859	-11.5
Midland, TX	110,792	105,257	-5.0	108,522	96,833	-10.7
Milwaukee, WI	811,069	812,442	0.1	785,335	763,907	-2.7
Minneapolis, MN	2,037,880	1,953,111	-4.1	1,976,964	1,864,309	-5.7
Nashville, TN	1,102,127	1,112,635	0.9	1,076,372	1,054,820	-2.0
New Haven, CT[3]	331,537	326,637	-1.4	321,457	303,291	-5.6
New Orleans, LA	596,687	591,186	-0.9	570,042	542,565	-4.8
New York, NY[2]	7,008,087	6,694,644	-4.4	6,780,009	6,077,482	-10.3
Oklahoma City, OK	687,962	693,472	0.8	668,536	660,099	-1.2
Omaha, NE	496,578	495,217	-0.2	483,022	480,259	-0.5
Orlando, FL	1,372,173	1,294,626	-5.6	1,337,648	1,204,999	-9.9
Peoria, IL	173,154	158,961	-8.2	165,096	148,160	-10.2
Philadelphia, PA[2]	1,031,591	989,425	-4.0	980,295	906,853	-7.4
Phoenix, AZ	2,548,680	2,536,430	-0.4	2,456,125	2,361,237	-3.8
Pittsburgh, PA	1,217,975	1,157,008	-5.0	1,162,800	1,080,640	-7.0
Portland, OR	1,332,520	1,316,280	-1.2	1,294,803	1,235,940	-4.5
Providence, RI[3]	695,900	674,373	-3.0	673,941	622,895	-7.5
Provo, UT	319,576	325,243	1.7	313,261	316,139	0.9
Raleigh, NC	731,065	715,982	-2.0	709,901	678,982	-4.3
Reno, NV	261,692	251,522	-3.8	254,486	238,896	-6.1
Richmond, VA	692,884	665,116	-4.0	675,329	631,884	-6.4
Riverside, CA	2,087,383	2,086,402	0.0	2,014,602	1,896,009	-5.8
Rochester, MN	125,263	121,785	-2.7	121,567	117,057	-3.7
Sacramento, CA	1,104,616	1,096,884	-0.7	1,069,620	1,010,465	-5.5
Salt Lake City, UT	679,607	687,168	1.1	665,544	663,455	-0.3
San Antonio, TX	1,218,568	1,213,928	-0.3	1,184,374	1,136,070	-4.0
San Diego, CA	1,597,099	1,593,875	-0.2	1,552,857	1,466,461	-5.5
San Francisco, CA[2]	1,054,065	1,010,523	-4.1	1,034,791	948,543	-8.3
San Jose, CA	1,090,183	1,071,686	-1.7	1,065,627	1,007,069	-5.5
Santa Rosa, CA	259,689	250,632	-3.4	253,575	234,440	-7.5
Savannah, GA	187,692	190,082	1.2	182,609	179,365	-1.7
Seattle, WA[2]	1,724,567	1,722,800	-0.1	1,683,121	1,619,303	-3.7
Sioux Falls, SD	155,466	153,813	-1.0	150,743	149,521	-0.8
Springfield, IL	106,114	102,509	-3.4	102,129	96,019	-5.9
Tallahassee, FL	195,372	185,262	-5.1	190,212	175,456	-7.7
Tampa, FL	1,566,692	1,540,183	-1.6	1,525,133	1,459,839	-4.2
Tucson, AZ	504,172	497,081	-1.4	483,909	460,365	-4.8
Tulsa, OK	481,673	474,408	-1.5	466,612	447,916	-4.0
Tuscaloosa, AL	120,183	116,579	-3.0	117,420	111,848	-4.7
Virginia Beach, VA	858,173	834,317	-2.7	834,872	790,145	-5.3
Washington, DC[2]	2,779,621	2,686,651	-3.3	2,705,388	2,537,166	-6.2
Wichita, KS	315,547	315,051	-0.1	305,590	301,566	-1.3
Winston-Salem, NC	329,944	323,658	-1.9	319,404	304,539	-4.6
U.S.	164,007,000	160,017,000	-2.4	158,504,000	149,613,000	-5.6

Note: Data is not seasonally adjusted and covers workers 16 years of age and older; (1) Figures cover the Metropolitan Statistical Area (MSA) except where noted. See Appendix B for areas included; (2) Metropolitan Division; (3) New England City and Town Area; (4) New England City and Town Area Division
Source: Bureau of Labor Statistics, Local Area Unemployment Statistics

Appendix A: Comparative Statistics

Unemployment Rate: City

City	Jan.	Feb.	Mar.	Apr.	May	Jun.	Jul.	Aug.	Sep.	Oct.	Nov.	Dec.
Albuquerque, NM	4.4	4.4	5.5	12.8	9.4	9.1	13.2	11.2	9.5	7.5	6.3	7.4
Allentown, PA	6.6	6.6	8.2	20.1	18.3	19.8	19.0	16.9	12.9	12.1	10.7	9.9
Anchorage, AK	5.1	4.5	4.7	13.9	12.3	12.0	10.8	6.5	6.4	5.3	6.0	5.5
Ann Arbor, MI	2.0	1.8	1.9	12.4	11.6	8.9	6.6	5.7	5.0	3.3	2.8	3.0
Athens, GA	3.5	3.5	4.7	12.2	9.0	7.7	7.9	5.8	5.9	4.3	5.1	5.2
Atlanta, GA	3.6	3.7	5.4	13.4	11.9	11.0	10.6	8.6	8.4	6.1	7.4	7.0
Austin, TX	2.6	2.5	3.6	12.5	11.6	7.4	6.9	5.6	6.4	4.9	5.7	4.9
Baton Rouge, LA	5.7	4.1	6.2	14.7	15.0	11.6	11.3	9.1	8.8	10.1	9.2	7.7
Boise City, ID	2.8	2.4	2.3	12.6	9.6	5.9	5.2	4.0	5.8	5.3	4.8	4.3
Boston, MA	2.7	2.6	2.4	14.6	16.6	19.3	18.2	12.9	11.1	7.7	6.6	7.3
Boulder, CO	2.1	2.4	4.2	9.4	8.1	9.6	6.5	5.4	4.9	4.9	4.7	6.5
Cape Coral, FL	3.2	3.0	4.4	16.2	14.0	10.0	11.0	7.2	6.0	5.2	5.2	4.8
Cedar Rapids, IA	4.0	3.5	4.1	14.2	12.9	11.3	9.3	10.1	6.8	4.7	4.9	4.3
Charleston, SC	2.2	2.3	2.5	14.6	14.0	9.9	9.7	7.1	5.0	3.9	3.9	4.1
Charlotte, NC	3.8	3.5	4.0	13.0	13.9	8.8	10.2	8.0	8.1	6.8	6.7	6.3
Chicago, IL	3.7	3.5	5.0	18.7	17.2	18.6	15.2	15.5	14.4	10.5	8.6	10.0
Cincinnati, OH	4.7	4.3	4.7	15.1	13.7	12.7	11.1	11.2	10.0	7.5	6.4	6.0
Clarksville, TN	4.4	4.3	3.8	17.2	11.3	11.2	11.4	9.9	7.3	8.4	5.8	7.4
Cleveland, OH	5.9	6.4	9.0	26.1	21.9	19.4	17.3	15.9	15.3	10.3	9.0	9.1
College Station, TX	2.8	2.6	3.7	8.2	8.1	5.9	5.3	4.2	4.7	3.9	4.9	4.4
Colorado Springs, CO	3.3	3.4	6.1	13.0	10.0	10.7	7.1	6.4	6.1	6.1	6.2	9.0
Columbia, MO	3.1	2.4	2.5	6.6	6.7	5.8	5.2	5.2	3.0	2.7	2.9	4.3
Columbia, SC	3.1	3.1	3.1	8.9	10.2	9.1	9.1	6.9	5.1	4.4	4.6	5.1
Columbus, OH	4.1	3.7	4.1	14.6	12.4	11.3	9.8	9.8	8.8	6.5	5.7	5.2
Dallas, TX	3.4	3.3	4.8	13.0	12.8	8.9	8.4	7.1	8.4	6.9	8.0	7.1
Davenport, IA	4.9	4.2	4.7	15.4	15.0	12.1	10.3	9.6	7.0	5.2	5.3	5.1
Denver, CO	2.8	2.8	5.3	13.4	11.5	12.0	8.8	7.9	7.3	7.3	7.2	9.3
Des Moines, IA	4.6	4.0	4.4	14.6	14.0	12.2	9.5	9.1	6.6	4.6	4.5	4.4
Durham, NC	3.4	3.1	3.7	10.1	11.4	7.6	8.8	6.7	6.8	5.7	5.7	5.6
Edison, NJ	2.8	2.7	2.4	11.7	11.3	12.7	11.0	8.4	4.9	5.8	7.4	5.3
El Paso, TX	3.8	3.6	5.1	14.5	14.0	9.1	8.4	6.9	8.1	6.7	8.9	7.7
Fargo, ND	2.5	2.3	2.3	9.6	8.5	7.0	5.5	4.0	3.0	3.1	3.1	3.2
Fayetteville, NC	5.8	5.2	6.0	15.7	16.8	10.8	12.9	10.1	10.4	9.0	9.0	8.9
Fort Collins, CO	2.4	2.5	4.4	11.5	8.7	9.3	6.2	5.5	5.1	5.0	5.0	7.5
Fort Wayne, IN	3.6	3.5	3.2	20.6	14.9	12.9	9.6	7.7	6.8	6.0	5.6	4.5
Fort Worth, TX	3.5	3.3	5.0	13.5	13.1	8.9	8.3	7.1	8.1	6.7	7.9	7.0
Grand Rapids, MI	3.8	3.2	3.3	26.7	22.0	16.0	11.5	10.0	8.7	5.9	5.2	5.7
Greeley, CO	3.1	3.2	5.6	10.3	9.3	11.2	8.4	7.9	7.5	7.3	7.7	10.0
Green Bay, WI	4.2	3.8	3.2	14.6	14.4	10.2	8.1	7.0	5.1	5.7	4.9	5.1
Greensboro, NC	4.4	4.0	4.6	15.3	15.8	10.0	11.6	9.1	9.0	7.7	7.7	7.4
Honolulu, HI	2.8	2.5	2.1	20.5	20.8	12.2	11.5	11.0	13.6	12.4	9.1	8.0
Houston, TX	3.9	3.7	5.4	14.4	14.1	10.0	9.8	8.4	9.8	7.7	8.8	7.9
Huntsville, AL	2.8	2.4	2.6	11.8	8.6	7.5	7.8	5.6	6.4	5.3	3.8	3.4
Indianapolis, IN	3.4	3.2	3.1	14.0	11.3	12.6	9.9	8.4	7.7	7.0	6.4	5.1
Jacksonville, FL	3.3	3.1	4.6	11.5	11.0	8.4	9.7	6.4	5.5	5.6	5.7	5.5
Kansas City, MO	4.1	3.7	4.1	11.7	12.3	9.2	9.0	9.0	5.7	4.9	5.0	6.7
Lafayette, LA	5.4	4.0	6.1	13.5	12.8	9.3	9.1	7.2	7.0	7.9	7.0	5.9
Lakeland, FL	3.8	3.5	4.9	11.4	12.0	9.4	10.7	7.3	6.4	6.5	6.9	6.5
Las Vegas, NV	4.0	3.9	7.3	32.1	27.1	16.7	15.8	14.9	13.9	13.5	11.7	10.3
Lexington, KY	3.5	3.1	4.1	14.1	9.0	4.5	4.6	6.7	4.8	6.2	4.5	5.1
Lincoln, NE	2.8	2.7	3.7	9.6	5.3	5.9	5.2	3.9	3.3	2.7	2.7	2.9
Little Rock, AR	3.7	3.6	4.6	12.0	11.7	10.4	10.1	10.4	9.8	7.9	7.7	5.0
Los Angeles, CA	4.5	4.6	6.6	20.7	21.0	20.0	18.8	17.1	15.5	11.8	10.6	10.6
Louisville, KY	4.1	3.7	4.7	16.5	11.7	5.3	5.3	7.7	5.6	7.4	5.4	5.7
Madison, WI	2.7	2.3	1.9	10.4	9.7	7.8	6.2	5.4	3.9	4.3	3.7	3.9

Table continued on following page.

City	\multicolumn{12}{c}{2020}
	Jan.	Feb.	Mar.	Apr.	May	Jun.	Jul.	Aug.	Sep.	Oct.	Nov.	Dec.
Manchester, NH	3.0	3.0	2.7	20.0	18.4	10.5	9.2	7.8	6.7	4.5	4.3	4.4
Memphis, TN	4.9	4.9	4.2	14.5	12.9	15.3	17.4	16.3	12.5	13.1	8.7	9.8
Miami, FL	1.4	1.4	3.7	12.4	12.8	12.5	15.4	8.6	13.6	9.3	8.4	7.7
Midland, TX	2.3	2.3	3.3	9.9	12.3	9.2	9.1	7.8	9.2	7.7	8.8	7.6
Milwaukee, WI	4.9	4.7	4.1	15.8	15.7	13.1	11.4	10.1	8.2	9.2	7.9	8.3
Minneapolis, MN	2.5	2.6	2.8	10.0	11.6	11.4	10.5	10.3	7.8	5.2	4.6	4.8
Nashville, TN	2.7	2.7	2.4	16.1	12.3	12.0	12.3	10.6	7.7	6.9	4.7	5.7
New Haven, CT	4.9	4.8	4.0	7.0	8.8	10.6	11.8	9.7	9.1	7.5	10.0	9.5
New Orleans, LA	5.5	4.2	6.3	22.2	20.7	15.9	15.1	12.6	12.4	15.1	13.6	11.2
New York, NY	3.8	3.8	4.2	15.5	20.2	18.7	18.8	14.9	14.7	11.7	11.7	11.6
Oklahoma City, OK	2.9	2.7	2.7	15.8	13.7	7.2	7.6	5.9	5.5	6.3	6.0	5.2
Omaha, NE	3.5	3.3	4.8	10.8	6.6	7.5	6.8	5.2	4.5	3.5	3.3	3.5
Orlando, FL	2.8	2.7	4.0	18.2	21.7	16.9	17.0	12.0	10.4	9.0	8.6	7.8
Peoria, IL	5.2	4.3	4.0	19.2	18.0	16.5	13.8	13.2	11.8	8.5	8.6	8.8
Philadelphia, PA	6.0	5.9	7.0	17.0	16.4	18.2	18.1	15.8	12.0	10.8	9.7	9.3
Phoenix, AZ	4.0	3.9	5.5	12.9	8.8	10.5	11.3	6.5	6.9	8.4	8.2	7.6
Pittsburgh, PA	4.7	4.6	5.6	15.2	13.6	13.8	14.6	12.2	8.9	7.7	6.9	6.7
Portland, OR	3.2	3.2	3.4	16.2	15.9	14.3	13.1	10.7	9.0	7.5	6.4	6.6
Providence, RI	4.7	4.7	5.9	19.5	18.7	15.2	14.9	16.7	13.3	8.5	8.5	8.7
Provo, UT	2.3	2.3	3.2	6.4	5.3	4.0	3.2	3.0	3.3	2.6	2.8	2.5
Raleigh, NC	3.6	3.3	3.9	12.4	13.2	8.2	9.1	6.9	6.9	5.9	5.9	5.7
Reno, NV	3.4	3.2	5.5	20.9	16.9	9.1	8.5	7.6	7.0	6.5	5.7	5.0
Richmond, VA	3.5	3.2	3.8	14.1	12.1	11.8	12.1	9.5	9.3	7.6	6.5	6.5
Riverside, CA	3.9	3.8	4.8	13.5	13.6	13.4	12.6	9.7	9.4	8.2	7.4	8.4
Rochester, MN	2.3	2.5	2.5	7.2	10.4	9.1	7.5	6.7	4.9	4.0	3.6	3.9
Sacramento, CA	4.0	3.8	4.9	14.5	14.5	14.0	13.1	10.4	10.2	8.7	8.0	9.2
Salt Lake City, UT	2.6	2.6	4.1	12.8	10.9	7.4	6.1	5.3	5.4	4.2	4.2	3.6
San Antonio, TX	3.2	3.1	4.5	13.8	13.0	8.5	8.3	6.9	7.9	6.3	7.4	6.5
San Diego, CA	3.2	3.1	4.0	14.7	14.9	13.7	12.2	9.3	8.7	7.1	6.3	7.9
San Francisco, CA	2.3	2.3	3.1	12.6	12.7	12.5	11.1	8.5	8.3	6.7	5.7	6.4
San Jose, CA	2.8	2.7	3.6	13.8	13.1	12.4	10.9	8.4	8.1	6.5	5.7	6.7
Santa Rosa, CA	3.0	2.9	3.8	14.9	13.6	12.2	10.4	8.0	7.7	6.7	6.1	6.9
Savannah, GA	3.7	3.7	5.1	18.5	13.7	11.3	11.0	8.8	8.8	6.3	7.5	7.3
Seattle, WA	2.4	2.2	5.3	13.7	13.2	9.0	7.9	6.8	6.5	4.2	3.9	6.1
Sioux Falls, SD	3.5	3.3	3.1	11.6	10.4	7.3	6.0	4.6	3.7	3.2	3.2	3.0
Springfield, IL	3.8	3.2	2.9	14.9	14.2	13.2	10.5	10.0	9.2	6.5	6.9	7.2
Tallahassee, FL	3.4	3.0	4.4	9.2	9.1	7.8	9.5	6.2	5.3	5.7	6.0	6.0
Tampa, FL	3.1	3.0	4.3	12.6	12.2	9.7	11.6	7.8	6.6	6.4	6.4	6.0
Tucson, AZ	4.7	4.4	6.3	13.8	9.2	10.9	11.7	6.6	7.1	8.7	8.6	8.2
Tulsa, OK	3.2	3.1	3.0	16.2	14.2	7.9	8.6	6.8	6.4	7.4	7.1	6.1
Tuscaloosa, AL	3.2	2.7	3.0	17.9	11.9	10.4	10.6	7.6	8.6	7.0	5.0	4.7
Virginia Beach, VA	2.9	2.6	3.1	12.2	9.4	8.2	7.7	6.0	5.9	4.6	4.2	4.3
Washington, DC	5.0	4.9	5.5	10.6	9.0	9.2	9.5	8.9	8.8	8.2	8.4	8.8
Wichita, KS	4.0	4.1	3.5	19.2	15.6	12.1	12.3	11.6	9.1	7.4	7.0	4.5
Winston-Salem, NC	4.2	3.7	4.3	12.9	13.9	8.8	10.3	8.0	8.2	6.9	6.8	6.7
U.S.	4.0	3.8	4.5	14.4	13.0	11.2	10.5	8.5	7.7	6.6	6.4	6.5

Note: Data is not seasonally adjusted and covers workers 16 years of age and older; All figures are percentages
Source: Bureau of Labor Statistics, Local Area Unemployment Statistics

Appendix A: Comparative Statistics

Unemployment Rate: Metro Area

Metro Area[1]	Jan.	Feb.	Mar.	Apr.	May	Jun.	Jul.	Aug.	Sep.	Oct.	Nov.	Dec.
Albuquerque, NM	4.6	4.6	5.7	12.3	9.1	9.0	13.1	11.1	9.5	7.5	6.4	7.3
Allentown, PA	5.0	5.0	5.7	16.2	13.8	14.1	12.8	10.6	7.5	6.9	6.5	6.2
Anchorage, AK	5.7	5.0	5.2	14.3	12.5	12.2	11.0	6.6	6.5	5.3	6.1	5.7
Ann Arbor, MI	2.5	2.2	2.3	14.8	13.9	10.7	8.0	6.9	6.1	4.0	3.4	3.6
Athens, GA	3.2	3.3	4.3	11.1	8.0	6.7	6.7	4.9	4.9	3.7	4.4	4.5
Atlanta, GA	3.2	3.3	4.4	12.7	9.9	8.6	8.6	6.4	6.6	4.6	5.6	5.4
Austin, TX	2.8	2.6	3.8	12.2	11.4	7.3	6.8	5.5	6.3	5.0	5.9	5.1
Baton Rouge, LA	5.1	3.8	5.6	13.0	12.6	9.6	9.2	7.2	7.0	8.0	7.2	6.1
Boise City, ID	3.2	2.7	2.6	12.3	9.2	5.8	5.2	4.1	6.0	5.4	4.9	4.5
Boston, MA[4]	2.7	2.6	2.4	14.2	15.3	16.9	15.5	10.7	9.3	6.7	5.9	6.5
Boulder, CO	2.4	2.4	4.4	9.7	8.3	9.6	6.7	5.8	5.3	5.2	5.1	6.9
Cape Coral, FL	3.1	3.0	4.3	14.6	13.0	9.6	10.7	7.1	5.9	5.4	5.4	5.1
Cedar Rapids, IA	3.8	3.4	3.9	12.5	11.1	9.6	7.9	8.3	5.6	3.8	4.1	3.8
Charleston, SC	2.4	2.5	2.6	12.1	12.2	9.0	9.2	6.9	5.0	4.0	4.0	4.3
Charlotte, NC	3.7	3.4	3.9	12.7	13.2	8.3	9.3	7.1	7.0	5.9	5.9	5.8
Chicago, IL[2]	3.8	3.7	3.9	16.4	15.8	15.7	13.3	13.0	12.2	8.8	8.9	8.7
Cincinnati, OH	4.3	4.0	4.4	14.1	11.2	9.0	7.6	7.9	6.8	5.6	4.8	4.7
Clarksville, TN	4.6	4.4	4.3	16.1	10.5	8.8	9.0	8.5	6.2	7.5	5.4	6.7
Cleveland, OH	5.0	5.4	6.2	21.8	17.3	12.7	9.2	8.1	8.8	7.2	7.1	7.6
College Station, TX	2.9	2.7	3.9	8.7	8.7	6.3	5.8	4.7	5.5	4.5	5.5	5.0
Colorado Springs, CO	3.3	3.4	6.2	12.6	9.7	10.5	6.9	6.2	5.9	6.0	6.0	8.6
Columbia, MO	3.2	2.5	2.6	6.5	6.5	5.7	5.1	5.1	2.9	2.6	2.8	4.2
Columbia, SC	2.7	2.8	2.8	8.5	9.3	7.8	7.8	6.0	4.4	3.7	3.8	4.3
Columbus, OH	4.2	3.8	4.2	13.7	11.0	9.9	8.3	8.3	7.4	5.5	4.9	4.7
Dallas, TX[2]	3.3	3.2	4.6	12.6	12.1	8.1	7.5	6.2	7.3	5.9	7.1	6.2
Davenport, IA	4.7	4.0	4.0	15.3	14.4	11.5	9.4	8.5	7.1	5.0	5.0	5.1
Denver, CO	2.7	2.8	5.2	12.3	10.5	11.1	7.9	7.0	6.5	6.5	6.4	8.5
Des Moines, IA	3.5	3.0	3.4	11.8	10.9	9.2	7.2	6.7	4.8	3.3	3.5	3.4
Durham, NC	3.5	3.1	3.7	9.6	10.6	6.9	7.9	5.9	6.0	5.2	5.2	5.2
Edison, NJ[2]	3.8	3.6	3.8	15.1	16.3	18.3	17.6	14.0	10.7	10.5	10.4	9.2
El Paso, TX	4.0	3.8	5.4	14.9	14.6	9.5	8.8	7.3	8.6	7.1	9.4	8.1
Fargo, ND	2.8	2.6	2.5	7.7	7.2	6.4	5.1	3.9	3.0	2.9	3.0	3.1
Fayetteville, NC	5.4	4.9	5.6	14.6	15.4	9.8	11.6	9.1	9.3	8.2	8.3	8.2
Fort Collins, CO	2.5	2.6	4.7	11.1	8.6	9.2	6.2	5.6	5.2	5.1	5.2	7.4
Fort Wayne, IN	3.4	3.3	3.0	19.4	13.5	11.2	8.2	6.5	5.7	5.1	4.8	3.9
Fort Worth, TX[2]	3.3	3.2	4.7	13.1	12.6	8.3	7.7	6.5	7.5	6.1	7.3	6.5
Grand Rapids, MI	2.9	2.5	2.6	21.5	17.1	12.0	8.4	7.2	6.3	4.2	3.7	4.2
Greeley, CO	2.7	2.9	5.1	9.9	8.6	10.1	7.3	6.6	6.3	6.2	6.4	8.3
Green Bay, WI	4.0	3.7	3.1	12.9	12.1	8.6	6.7	5.6	4.1	4.8	4.2	4.6
Greensboro, NC	4.3	3.9	4.5	14.8	14.5	9.0	10.2	7.8	7.9	6.9	6.9	6.7
Honolulu, HI	2.8	2.5	2.1	20.5	20.8	12.2	11.5	11.0	13.6	12.4	9.1	8.0
Houston, TX	4.1	3.9	5.5	14.3	13.9	9.7	9.5	8.1	9.6	7.7	8.9	8.0
Huntsville, AL	2.7	2.3	2.5	10.7	7.4	6.4	6.4	4.5	5.1	4.2	3.1	2.8
Indianapolis, IN	3.2	2.9	2.8	13.3	10.2	10.6	7.8	6.6	6.0	5.4	5.0	4.0
Jacksonville, FL	3.1	3.0	4.3	11.2	10.4	7.8	8.8	5.7	4.8	4.8	5.0	4.8
Kansas City, MO	3.7	3.4	3.5	11.3	10.8	7.8	7.6	7.3	5.0	4.4	4.4	4.9
Lafayette, LA	5.7	4.3	6.4	13.0	12.4	9.2	9.1	7.4	7.3	8.2	7.3	6.2
Lakeland, FL	3.7	3.5	4.9	14.0	17.6	13.6	13.2	9.2	7.9	7.1	7.0	6.7
Las Vegas, NV	3.9	3.9	7.2	34.0	28.8	17.8	16.6	15.6	14.6	13.7	11.8	10.4
Lexington, KY	3.7	3.3	4.2	15.2	9.1	4.4	4.5	6.5	4.7	6.1	4.4	5.0
Lincoln, NE	2.7	2.6	3.7	9.3	5.2	5.7	5.0	3.8	3.2	2.7	2.7	2.9
Little Rock, AR	3.7	3.6	4.6	10.9	10.2	9.0	8.3	8.4	7.8	6.4	6.4	4.3
Los Angeles, CA[2]	4.9	4.7	5.6	18.2	18.8	17.9	18.2	17.5	13.2	12.0	11.9	12.3
Louisville, KY	3.9	3.5	4.3	16.8	11.8	6.5	5.6	7.0	5.3	6.5	4.9	5.0
Madison, WI	3.1	2.8	2.3	11.1	9.7	7.5	6.0	5.1	3.7	4.2	3.7	4.1

Table continued on following page.

Metro Area[1]	2020 Jan.	Feb.	Mar.	Apr.	May	Jun.	Jul.	Aug.	Sep.	Oct.	Nov.	Dec.
Manchester, NH[3]	2.8	2.8	2.5	17.4	15.8	9.0	7.9	6.5	5.6	3.8	3.7	3.7
Memphis, TN	4.4	4.4	3.8	12.8	10.7	11.9	13.1	11.9	9.2	9.6	6.7	7.4
Miami, FL[2]	1.8	1.6	2.2	10.3	10.3	10.1	15.2	9.1	12.6	8.5	8.2	7.9
Midland, TX	2.4	2.3	3.4	10.1	12.6	9.5	9.5	8.1	9.5	8.0	9.3	8.0
Milwaukee, WI	4.0	3.8	3.2	13.6	12.9	10.2	8.6	7.5	5.9	6.6	5.7	6.0
Minneapolis, MN	3.1	3.1	3.1	9.2	10.1	9.2	8.2	7.8	5.9	4.2	4.0	4.5
Nashville, TN	2.8	2.8	2.5	15.2	11.1	10.2	10.0	8.4	6.1	6.1	4.2	5.2
New Haven, CT[3]	4.2	4.1	3.4	7.2	8.5	9.3	9.7	7.7	7.1	5.5	7.4	7.1
New Orleans, LA	5.2	3.9	5.9	19.0	17.4	12.8	11.9	9.7	9.4	11.2	10.0	8.2
New York, NY[2]	3.8	3.6	3.8	15.1	16.3	18.3	17.6	14.0	10.7	10.5	10.4	9.2
Oklahoma City, OK	2.9	2.7	2.7	14.8	12.9	6.9	7.1	5.6	5.1	5.9	5.6	4.8
Omaha, NE	3.2	3.1	4.3	10.0	6.4	6.9	6.0	4.6	3.9	3.0	2.9	3.0
Orlando, FL	3.0	2.9	4.2	16.8	21.1	16.1	15.4	10.8	9.2	7.8	7.4	6.9
Peoria, IL	5.0	4.2	3.8	17.7	15.4	13.5	10.8	9.8	8.6	6.1	6.3	6.8
Philadelphia, PA[2]	5.5	5.4	6.4	16.3	15.5	17.0	16.7	14.5	10.9	9.8	8.8	8.3
Phoenix, AZ	4.0	3.8	5.4	12.5	8.3	9.8	10.4	5.9	6.2	7.4	7.4	6.9
Pittsburgh, PA	5.2	5.2	6.1	16.4	13.6	12.9	13.1	10.9	7.9	6.9	6.3	6.6
Portland, OR	3.4	3.5	3.6	14.2	14.0	11.8	11.2	9.1	7.9	6.6	5.8	6.1
Providence, RI[3]	4.1	4.1	4.7	18.2	16.7	13.7	12.7	12.7	10.1	6.5	6.8	7.6
Provo, UT	2.5	2.5	3.6	7.9	6.2	4.4	3.6	3.4	3.8	3.1	3.3	2.8
Raleigh, NC	3.5	3.2	3.7	11.0	11.5	7.0	7.9	6.0	6.1	5.2	5.2	5.2
Reno, NV	3.4	3.2	5.6	20.4	16.0	8.7	8.2	7.3	6.7	6.3	5.6	5.0
Richmond, VA	3.1	2.8	3.4	11.2	9.4	8.9	8.8	6.9	6.8	5.5	4.9	5.0
Riverside, CA	4.1	4.0	5.2	14.7	15.1	14.3	13.4	10.5	10.2	8.7	7.9	9.1
Rochester, MN	3.1	3.1	3.1	6.9	9.3	8.1	6.6	5.8	4.2	3.5	3.4	3.9
Sacramento, CA	3.9	3.8	4.8	14.0	13.7	12.8	11.6	9.0	8.7	7.3	6.7	7.9
Salt Lake City, UT	2.6	2.7	4.0	11.2	9.4	6.4	5.3	4.7	5.2	4.1	4.2	3.5
San Antonio, TX	3.2	3.1	4.5	13.3	12.7	8.3	8.0	6.6	7.7	6.2	7.3	6.4
San Diego, CA	3.3	3.2	4.2	15.0	15.2	13.8	12.4	9.5	8.9	7.5	6.6	8.0
San Francisco, CA[2]	2.2	2.2	3.0	12.1	12.0	11.8	10.3	7.9	7.7	6.3	5.4	6.1
San Jose, CA	2.7	2.7	3.5	12.0	11.3	10.8	9.5	7.3	7.0	5.8	5.2	6.0
Santa Rosa, CA	2.9	2.8	3.7	14.5	13.0	11.6	10.0	7.5	7.2	6.0	5.5	6.5
Savannah, GA	3.3	3.3	4.4	15.3	10.8	8.6	8.5	6.5	6.7	4.7	5.6	5.6
Seattle, WA[2]	2.7	2.6	5.3	16.2	12.6	10.7	9.5	7.9	7.4	6.5	6.1	6.0
Sioux Falls, SD	3.4	3.2	3.0	10.5	9.4	6.7	5.6	4.3	3.4	3.0	3.0	2.8
Springfield, IL	3.9	3.2	2.9	14.2	13.1	11.7	9.2	8.7	7.8	5.5	5.9	6.3
Tallahassee, FL	3.2	2.9	4.2	8.3	8.1	7.0	8.4	5.5	4.7	5.0	5.4	5.3
Tampa, FL	3.1	3.0	4.3	13.2	12.2	9.0	10.2	6.7	5.7	5.4	5.5	5.2
Tucson, AZ	4.5	4.2	6.0	12.8	8.4	9.9	10.6	5.9	6.3	7.8	7.7	7.4
Tulsa, OK	3.2	3.0	3.0	15.1	12.9	7.1	7.6	6.1	5.7	6.6	6.4	5.6
Tuscaloosa, AL	2.9	2.5	2.8	16.6	10.8	9.0	9.1	6.3	7.1	6.0	4.4	4.1
Virginia Beach, VA	3.3	3.0	3.6	12.1	10.0	9.2	9.2	7.4	7.2	5.8	5.1	5.3
Washington, DC[2]	3.1	3.0	3.4	10.0	8.9	8.4	8.1	6.9	6.9	6.4	5.7	5.6
Wichita, KS	3.8	3.8	3.3	17.7	14.1	10.8	11.0	10.3	8.0	6.6	6.5	4.3
Winston-Salem, NC	3.9	3.5	4.1	12.7	12.7	7.7	8.8	6.6	6.8	5.9	6.0	5.9
U.S.	4.0	3.8	4.5	14.4	13.0	11.2	10.5	8.5	7.7	6.6	6.4	6.5

Note: Data is not seasonally adjusted and covers workers 16 years of age and older; All figures are percentages; (1) Figures cover the Metropolitan Statistical Area (MSA) except where noted. See Appendix B for areas included; (2) Metropolitan Division; (3) New England City and Town Area; (4) New England City and Town Area Division
Source: Bureau of Labor Statistics, Local Area Unemployment Statistics

Appendix A: Comparative Statistics

Average Hourly Wages: Occupations A – C

Metro Area[1]	Accountants/ Auditors	Automotive Mechanics	Book- keepers	Carpenters	Cashiers	Computer Programmers	Computer Systems Analysts
Albuquerque, NM	33.46	21.98	20.06	20.67	11.88	38.33	39.87
Allentown, PA	36.61	21.48	20.16	23.11	11.53	40.11	42.51
Anchorage, AK	39.02	22.66	23.63	33.12	14.55	44.08	41.47
Ann Arbor, MI	36.68	30.73	21.60	27.75	12.05	38.47	40.58
Athens, GA	31.72	20.47	17.40	19.07	10.70	32.83	43.69
Atlanta, GA	42.18	23.13	21.75	20.56	11.10	44.52	45.29
Austin, TX	37.28	26.39	20.95	19.33	12.25	42.42	41.18
Baton Rouge, LA	31.10	22.33	19.99	24.74	10.14	40.35	39.72
Boise City, ID	36.48	21.60	20.17	18.39	12.59	32.61	45.73
Boston, MA[2]	43.60	24.14	25.10	31.31	14.22	49.27	50.79
Boulder, CO	40.09	24.42	22.25	25.30	14.13	39.10	48.44
Cape Coral, FL	31.26	21.32	20.50	19.97	11.99	42.99	37.54
Cedar Rapids, IA	35.32	22.27	19.62	24.33	11.59	39.02	40.35
Charleston, SC	32.87	23.69	18.26	28.28	11.63	39.15	41.06
Charlotte, NC	42.38	23.40	20.71	19.73	10.98	48.79	48.01
Chicago, IL	37.81	24.87	22.39	34.74	12.61	49.84	45.00
Cincinnati, OH	36.81	22.26	20.71	24.06	11.71	44.99	47.80
Clarksville, TN	30.21	18.81	18.23	18.80	11.06	n/a	36.97
Cleveland, OH	36.64	22.16	20.46	25.76	12.11	39.60	40.53
College Station, TX	29.37	25.23	17.40	20.32	11.70	48.32	38.11
Colorado Springs, CO	36.33	25.52	19.93	24.48	13.94	34.84	49.76
Columbia, MO	29.02	20.93	17.87	24.13	11.10	30.68	38.55
Columbia, SC	29.39	21.06	17.97	23.15	10.58	43.48	37.52
Columbus, OH	36.98	21.18	21.79	24.76	11.99	44.57	44.18
Dallas, TX	40.31	23.53	21.33	19.85	11.39	53.87	49.58
Davenport, IA	32.27	20.88	19.51	25.19	11.12	42.62	44.10
Denver, CO	42.62	24.69	22.73	25.92	14.48	43.53	51.32
Des Moines, IA	37.04	24.11	21.99	22.21	11.87	35.53	42.70
Durham, NC	39.14	22.27	21.86	19.68	10.92	47.50	45.42
Edison, NJ	50.83	24.31	24.50	34.16	14.25	46.28	55.05
El Paso, TX	31.64	16.30	16.08	16.69	10.53	40.15	37.37
Fargo, ND	32.72	24.61	20.00	23.07	12.34	36.01	42.32
Fayetteville, NC	35.70	17.98	17.77	19.91	10.55	30.98	38.38
Fort Collins, CO	35.94	24.03	21.32	23.09	14.29	35.42	42.76
Fort Wayne, IN	34.36	18.77	19.67	20.21	11.30	25.61	37.13
Fort Worth, TX	40.31	23.53	21.33	19.85	11.39	53.87	49.58
Grand Rapids, MI	33.78	21.17	19.56	23.43	11.96	34.14	37.61
Greeley, CO	39.19	25.37	20.19	22.97	13.76	n/a	58.55
Green Bay, WI	33.64	20.09	20.68	26.03	11.26	37.56	39.08
Greensboro, NC	38.57	22.14	19.86	17.69	10.55	40.70	45.51
Honolulu, HI	31.74	25.73	21.44	39.88	13.68	39.65	38.51
Houston, TX	40.30	22.98	21.66	21.53	11.62	49.83	59.65
Huntsville, AL	35.97	23.40	20.47	20.55	10.97	41.94	49.70
Indianapolis, IN	37.22	21.50	20.88	24.11	11.33	45.99	40.06
Jacksonville, FL	32.52	20.49	20.33	19.12	11.34	38.38	37.87
Kansas City, MO	35.61	23.49	20.58	28.51	12.02	42.04	36.99
Lafayette, LA	31.83	18.68	18.14	19.37	9.98	35.29	39.77
Lakeland, FL	36.15	22.44	18.64	18.81	11.96	31.46	37.47
Las Vegas, NV	33.27	21.01	20.44	29.29	12.02	41.98	43.58
Lexington, KY	34.06	20.09	19.10	22.60	11.15	37.18	39.27
Lincoln, NE	33.35	22.34	19.37	19.78	11.87	36.02	36.79
Little Rock, AR	32.28	20.29	18.68	20.70	11.78	37.05	35.10
Los Angeles, CA	40.22	25.83	24.20	32.37	14.82	47.38	53.54
Louisville, KY	36.49	20.16	19.65	25.97	11.25	36.56	41.09
Madison, WI	35.56	23.85	21.38	27.06	12.20	51.95	44.21

Table continued on following page.

Metro Area[1]	Accountants/Auditors	Automotive Mechanics	Book-keepers	Carpenters	Cashiers	Computer Programmers	Computer Systems Analysts
Manchester, NH[2]	36.21	23.60	20.53	22.51	11.60	33.07	45.34
Memphis, TN	34.52	25.99	21.21	21.37	10.80	41.07	39.88
Miami, FL	38.52	21.77	21.28	20.93	11.76	41.74	44.55
Midland, TX	49.58	30.42	23.19	20.45	13.31	57.40	n/a
Milwaukee, WI	36.97	21.67	21.43	27.70	11.60	40.27	40.47
Minneapolis, MN	37.42	23.75	22.79	27.95	13.27	43.22	49.04
Nashville, TN	34.65	21.80	21.53	22.23	11.54	45.25	40.00
New Haven, CT[2]	40.03	23.80	23.77	29.32	12.79	47.26	46.09
New Orleans, LA	33.52	19.89	18.98	22.06	10.47	49.80	46.68
New York, NY	50.83	24.31	24.50	34.16	14.25	46.28	55.05
Oklahoma City, OK	38.02	23.73	19.72	20.80	11.03	38.30	38.44
Omaha, NE	35.78	22.47	20.56	19.96	12.22	38.65	41.38
Orlando, FL	35.16	19.62	20.04	21.12	11.70	41.55	44.36
Peoria, IL	38.38	20.73	18.98	31.69	11.40	39.55	45.55
Philadelphia, PA	41.21	22.53	22.28	30.86	11.77	48.82	50.50
Phoenix, AZ	36.29	22.21	21.58	23.50	13.39	44.18	44.56
Pittsburgh, PA	35.65	20.59	19.36	28.43	11.02	41.89	41.16
Portland, OR	38.49	24.48	22.58	29.13	14.68	45.18	48.24
Providence, RI[2]	41.50	21.85	22.70	25.77	13.17	51.83	47.51
Provo, UT	30.23	23.85	19.47	21.85	12.14	42.53	40.09
Raleigh, NC	36.22	23.93	20.23	20.64	11.17	47.69	47.56
Reno, NV	31.29	25.37	21.43	25.23	12.11	44.10	43.87
Richmond, VA	39.89	24.49	21.27	22.33	11.07	45.10	47.11
Riverside, CA	36.22	24.02	22.43	26.58	14.92	43.59	43.34
Rochester, MN	33.90	21.22	20.99	26.07	12.84	29.59	41.46
Sacramento, CA	40.32	26.48	22.61	28.08	15.49	39.13	50.27
Salt Lake City, UT	33.91	21.58	20.00	22.62	12.06	41.48	37.30
San Antonio, TX	35.76	20.68	20.96	20.42	11.81	46.43	47.72
San Diego, CA	43.00	25.61	23.56	28.60	14.50	48.42	45.56
San Francisco, CA	48.60	31.07	26.61	36.44	16.58	60.30	60.27
San Jose, CA	49.48	30.53	27.26	31.80	17.29	54.58	64.41
Santa Rosa, CA	44.34	28.46	26.79	35.33	15.89	44.87	43.31
Savannah, GA	33.08	25.13	20.20	22.91	10.51	38.06	49.67
Seattle, WA	42.21	26.17	24.43	33.25	16.50	n/a	54.00
Sioux Falls, SD	34.97	20.87	17.77	18.73	12.24	28.31	37.94
Springfield, IL	34.50	21.31	20.55	29.86	11.24	47.45	45.09
Tallahassee, FL	27.29	21.76	19.47	20.05	11.07	31.03	29.13
Tampa, FL	37.28	21.62	20.88	19.31	11.46	38.78	42.77
Tucson, AZ	34.29	21.59	18.88	20.44	13.57	42.88	41.83
Tulsa, OK	36.62	19.11	21.11	24.67	11.12	40.37	45.55
Tuscaloosa, AL	34.36	20.19	17.36	19.72	10.43	30.43	43.48
Virginia Beach, VA	36.21	25.63	20.21	20.84	11.14	n/a	47.27
Washington, DC	47.13	27.27	24.81	24.98	13.22	50.51	56.09
Wichita, KS	33.82	18.41	17.96	18.76	11.17	39.71	36.62
Winston-Salem, NC	35.91	20.17	19.63	19.79	10.16	42.82	44.65

Notes: (1) Figures cover the Metropolitan Statistical Area (MSA) except where noted. See Appendix B for areas included; (2) New England City and Town Area; n/a not available
Source: Bureau of Labor Statistics, May 2020 Metro Area Occupational Employment and Wage Estimates

Average Hourly Wages: Occupations C – E

Metro Area	Comp. User Support Specialists	Construction Laborers	Cooks, Restaurant	Customer Service Reps.	Dentists	Electricians	Engineers, Electrical
Albuquerque, NM	21.74	16.94	12.77	16.16	77.97	23.25	58.20
Allentown, PA	27.07	21.92	13.74	17.59	66.64	27.36	50.31
Anchorage, AK	29.69	26.02	14.62	19.54	101.03	33.57	54.83
Ann Arbor, MI	23.79	22.53	15.59	18.78	71.19	33.74	42.05
Athens, GA	21.34	14.82	12.71	15.83	n/a	26.34	51.49
Atlanta, GA	28.15	16.51	13.35	17.73	77.08	27.77	47.62
Austin, TX	25.88	15.85	13.15	17.26	77.48	25.85	52.09
Baton Rouge, LA	24.19	17.93	12.04	16.40	91.40	26.16	53.11
Boise City, ID	24.03	16.83	12.67	16.30	105.24	24.69	48.27
Boston, MA[2]	33.22	28.35	16.99	22.68	100.75	34.07	55.65
Boulder, CO	30.99	18.47	15.58	20.26	107.71	26.35	52.75
Cape Coral, FL	23.30	16.84	15.40	16.51	83.47	21.88	53.83
Cedar Rapids, IA	20.83	19.76	11.87	19.74	55.16	29.19	51.76
Charleston, SC	26.66	16.83	13.15	18.77	70.75	22.35	47.79
Charlotte, NC	25.75	15.96	13.03	18.80	83.93	22.29	48.47
Chicago, IL	26.71	32.05	14.66	20.08	92.31	40.50	46.52
Cincinnati, OH	24.74	22.97	12.99	17.97	103.00	23.55	43.84
Clarksville, TN	20.86	15.26	10.88	16.79	n/a	23.71	42.56
Cleveland, OH	24.39	23.80	13.11	19.37	101.12	29.21	41.38
College Station, TX	21.68	15.89	11.24	14.68	n/a	24.78	19.71
Colorado Springs, CO	26.65	17.48	14.36	17.16	59.66	24.26	52.77
Columbia, MO	21.99	19.97	12.27	15.32	95.89	22.23	n/a
Columbia, SC	24.58	16.93	11.80	16.92	63.01	25.77	44.63
Columbus, OH	26.89	24.18	13.34	18.35	92.26	22.93	42.67
Dallas, TX	24.78	17.39	13.00	18.59	110.94	23.96	51.08
Davenport, IA	23.82	20.58	11.98	17.03	77.64	28.51	47.09
Denver, CO	30.27	19.27	15.39	19.75	99.20	26.85	47.84
Des Moines, IA	26.48	18.81	14.39	21.09	90.74	24.79	40.35
Durham, NC	30.19	15.67	14.28	19.11	109.88	24.99	48.84
Edison, NJ	31.34	29.45	17.33	21.93	81.29	40.48	54.54
El Paso, TX	20.29	13.74	11.29	12.83	92.58	18.18	41.46
Fargo, ND	22.59	21.54	15.48	18.69	83.78	28.94	47.67
Fayetteville, NC	23.78	15.30	11.83	16.47	92.25	21.06	41.81
Fort Collins, CO	28.31	18.20	14.74	17.04	84.69	30.01	52.44
Fort Wayne, IN	23.05	19.96	13.24	18.84	80.13	26.13	48.46
Fort Worth, TX	24.78	17.39	13.00	18.59	110.94	23.96	51.08
Grand Rapids, MI	25.00	17.99	13.49	18.78	115.44	23.51	39.99
Greeley, CO	28.57	18.27	15.14	16.42	80.53	27.27	51.35
Green Bay, WI	25.96	20.76	13.61	18.77	105.02	27.59	40.42
Greensboro, NC	24.49	15.45	12.56	18.30	72.13	23.33	49.13
Honolulu, HI	25.51	30.70	16.72	19.16	103.97	38.38	43.60
Houston, TX	24.90	17.92	12.03	17.51	69.53	25.57	54.61
Huntsville, AL	24.21	15.88	12.69	17.48	78.91	23.75	51.86
Indianapolis, IN	24.33	19.53	13.36	18.96	69.38	28.17	44.98
Jacksonville, FL	24.83	16.85	12.99	17.90	72.89	21.37	45.99
Kansas City, MO	26.35	22.20	13.89	18.68	82.22	29.28	43.98
Lafayette, LA	26.20	17.63	13.15	16.07	n/a	23.40	43.43
Lakeland, FL	26.15	16.45	12.88	15.53	97.38	19.94	43.16
Las Vegas, NV	24.94	17.98	15.83	17.00	98.54	33.90	40.75
Lexington, KY	25.92	18.55	13.47	16.56	n/a	23.98	41.54
Lincoln, NE	22.54	17.18	14.40	16.32	60.36	24.62	47.42
Little Rock, AR	23.55	14.24	11.97	17.45	95.92	19.85	44.73
Los Angeles, CA	29.62	23.18	15.95	20.32	65.87	37.25	58.88
Louisville, KY	24.98	18.87	13.45	17.72	61.30	28.14	42.60
Madison, WI	28.38	20.82	13.02	20.69	117.88	28.07	46.09

Table continued on following page.

Appendix A: Comparative Statistics   A-87

Metro Area	Comp. User Support Specialists	Construction Laborers	Cooks, Restaurant	Customer Service Reps.	Dentists	Electricians	Engineers, Electrical
Manchester, NH[2]	27.45	19.30	15.58	20.34	111.95	26.41	52.51
Memphis, TN	23.06	15.86	12.46	18.07	71.03	24.89	46.46
Miami, FL	26.17	16.41	14.96	17.41	100.72	22.68	46.88
Midland, TX	24.74	17.43	13.11	17.41	n/a	28.94	52.80
Milwaukee, WI	25.85	23.25	13.14	20.22	98.32	33.98	44.41
Minneapolis, MN	28.26	28.53	16.38	21.32	105.18	35.78	50.53
Nashville, TN	24.09	17.16	13.19	18.01	75.33	25.45	45.40
New Haven, CT[2]	28.52	22.06	15.54	20.29	120.40	34.67	50.33
New Orleans, LA	24.41	16.66	12.31	16.48	74.68	27.52	54.15
New York, NY	31.34	29.45	17.33	21.93	81.29	40.48	54.54
Oklahoma City, OK	24.90	16.58	13.18	16.47	80.68	24.21	47.52
Omaha, NE	25.85	18.60	13.66	18.15	113.83	27.78	44.63
Orlando, FL	24.93	16.61	14.06	17.02	81.37	22.29	50.42
Peoria, IL	27.32	20.86	13.39	15.80	118.44	33.87	n/a
Philadelphia, PA	29.11	24.78	14.84	20.23	81.37	36.95	53.04
Phoenix, AZ	25.78	19.60	14.46	18.18	97.79	23.86	48.56
Pittsburgh, PA	24.98	21.30	13.04	18.03	71.78	31.54	47.12
Portland, OR	29.15	23.09	16.02	20.20	107.31	37.04	46.08
Providence, RI[2]	29.98	26.78	15.08	19.39	120.18	28.88	52.32
Provo, UT	26.06	16.78	13.93	16.82	n/a	22.38	35.78
Raleigh, NC	27.29	16.83	15.74	18.53	95.72	21.78	48.22
Reno, NV	24.94	20.58	14.82	17.38	99.87	26.92	43.83
Richmond, VA	26.74	15.20	12.97	17.99	79.04	26.98	47.93
Riverside, CA	29.70	24.28	15.12	19.74	84.77	26.51	48.20
Rochester, MN	27.37	23.17	14.87	17.51	93.21	30.42	48.07
Sacramento, CA	41.51	24.49	15.22	21.08	93.37	30.07	52.08
Salt Lake City, UT	26.07	18.26	13.09	18.57	60.05	26.94	47.95
San Antonio, TX	23.60	16.05	12.33	16.77	72.46	25.37	45.10
San Diego, CA	29.34	23.87	15.90	20.38	53.63	30.22	50.09
San Francisco, CA	37.82	28.43	19.21	24.01	85.30	51.29	58.99
San Jose, CA	34.93	27.64	17.22	22.94	94.63	41.61	72.35
Santa Rosa, CA	28.84	25.31	17.33	20.34	98.37	35.19	50.52
Savannah, GA	24.02	16.07	12.17	14.71	84.25	25.83	59.47
Seattle, WA	30.88	27.11	17.85	22.61	81.64	39.81	57.72
Sioux Falls, SD	20.11	16.27	13.58	17.26	78.71	24.23	46.65
Springfield, IL	29.20	26.62	11.66	17.52	86.11	34.16	45.48
Tallahassee, FL	21.83	14.26	13.54	16.05	78.74	21.70	44.42
Tampa, FL	24.82	15.90	13.00	17.32	71.77	22.08	46.52
Tucson, AZ	24.98	17.41	13.83	16.79	102.12	25.23	44.68
Tulsa, OK	24.46	16.60	12.51	16.05	n/a	23.73	49.81
Tuscaloosa, AL	29.04	15.01	10.38	16.06	73.08	25.65	43.67
Virginia Beach, VA	26.72	16.64	13.23	15.33	88.32	23.97	46.70
Washington, DC	32.03	18.44	15.40	21.22	105.63	31.72	62.57
Wichita, KS	22.03	16.12	12.82	16.56	77.90	25.06	43.33
Winston-Salem, NC	24.73	15.83	10.93	17.29	72.88	22.44	43.40

Notes: (1) Figures cover the Metropolitan Statistical Area (MSA) except where noted. See Appendix B for areas included; (2) New England City and Town Area; n/a not available
Source: Bureau of Labor Statistics, May 2020 Metro Area Occupational Employment and Wage Estimates

Average Hourly Wages: Occupations F – H

Metro Area	Fast Food and Counter Workers	Financial Managers	First-Line Supervisors/ of Office Workers	General and Operations Managers	Hair-dressers/ Cosme-tologists	Home Health and Personal Care Aides	Janitors/ Cleaners
Albuquerque, NM	10.64	55.09	27.54	56.14	10.84	11.86	12.36
Allentown, PA	11.10	75.32	28.94	57.29	15.22	12.94	15.88
Anchorage, AK	12.54	54.93	32.38	58.03	14.27	16.10	16.48
Ann Arbor, MI	11.86	65.04	29.64	68.81	13.02	12.34	16.01
Athens, GA	9.77	52.35	24.64	45.41	10.25	12.00	12.46
Atlanta, GA	9.99	72.80	28.87	59.99	18.33	12.85	12.66
Austin, TX	11.34	72.96	31.36	57.34	15.92	11.06	14.50
Baton Rouge, LA	9.49	53.55	24.60	56.42	14.04	9.70	10.97
Boise City, ID	9.99	52.76	27.07	43.73	14.95	14.05	13.26
Boston, MA[2]	14.13	79.09	34.34	73.18	21.89	16.31	18.88
Boulder, CO	13.56	90.36	31.98	76.38	20.61	16.10	17.25
Cape Coral, FL	10.94	54.85	27.05	47.49	15.61	12.65	14.35
Cedar Rapids, IA	11.05	59.04	28.10	53.31	14.88	14.05	15.15
Charleston, SC	10.81	69.92	27.74	59.94	15.78	12.19	11.86
Charlotte, NC	10.65	83.71	28.74	64.43	15.60	11.20	12.26
Chicago, IL	11.94	75.24	32.97	66.06	15.60	13.73	15.85
Cincinnati, OH	11.06	67.69	29.76	59.57	14.55	12.32	15.23
Clarksville, TN	9.43	50.27	22.51	45.76	11.69	11.14	13.50
Cleveland, OH	11.12	73.35	29.66	63.12	15.00	11.54	14.61
College Station, TX	10.09	63.69	26.16	45.76	13.83	10.56	13.33
Colorado Springs, CO	12.80	71.91	28.53	62.51	19.89	14.62	14.95
Columbia, MO	12.41	57.39	26.61	41.33	15.87	12.15	14.70
Columbia, SC	9.32	58.42	27.64	54.33	17.75	11.20	12.24
Columbus, OH	10.98	68.77	29.82	58.25	17.11	12.26	14.37
Dallas, TX	10.98	77.10	30.67	62.23	12.81	10.68	14.25
Davenport, IA	10.58	53.76	26.30	48.05	13.57	13.27	14.93
Denver, CO	13.34	85.61	32.53	74.73	20.09	14.62	14.92
Des Moines, IA	11.04	66.80	31.26	53.18	15.31	14.13	13.43
Durham, NC	11.19	79.52	30.27	68.80	15.35	11.60	14.70
Edison, NJ	14.03	103.21	36.45	82.87	18.53	15.37	18.58
El Paso, TX	9.41	51.61	24.23	45.01	11.55	9.04	10.97
Fargo, ND	12.69	70.22	27.09	55.50	16.88	15.07	14.65
Fayetteville, NC	10.16	61.97	24.74	57.51	12.44	10.47	12.75
Fort Collins, CO	13.48	72.34	28.34	58.87	16.06	15.01	15.54
Fort Wayne, IN	10.87	57.58	28.51	55.31	13.03	12.24	11.86
Fort Worth, TX	10.98	77.10	30.67	62.23	12.81	10.68	14.25
Grand Rapids, MI	11.69	58.03	27.84	58.14	16.59	12.98	14.15
Greeley, CO	13.23	81.29	30.36	63.01	16.59	15.20	15.03
Green Bay, WI	10.40	60.24	30.04	66.79	14.46	12.75	14.61
Greensboro, NC	9.88	69.84	27.42	63.64	12.88	11.02	12.65
Honolulu, HI	13.15	60.38	29.59	58.24	18.80	14.07	16.41
Houston, TX	10.42	74.03	29.80	61.00	11.85	10.15	12.52
Huntsville, AL	9.32	65.66	26.99	71.84	11.25	9.93	12.52
Indianapolis, IN	10.96	68.18	30.65	59.89	15.32	12.21	13.87
Jacksonville, FL	10.31	63.49	28.46	52.07	16.47	12.37	12.06
Kansas City, MO	11.82	72.08	30.56	53.57	15.00	12.06	14.78
Lafayette, LA	9.61	49.98	24.38	59.04	11.41	9.98	11.01
Lakeland, FL	10.43	52.81	26.80	46.19	12.89	11.86	12.29
Las Vegas, NV	10.95	57.63	25.95	62.09	10.29	12.47	15.19
Lexington, KY	9.92	57.27	28.00	48.43	11.98	12.60	13.88
Lincoln, NE	11.43	58.67	26.69	50.22	13.35	13.55	13.37
Little Rock, AR	10.81	54.43	25.88	49.18	12.59	11.53	12.24
Los Angeles, CA	14.39	76.00	30.99	67.85	18.20	14.88	17.45
Louisville, KY	10.27	58.62	27.96	50.02	15.10	14.08	13.55

Table continued on following page.

Appendix A: Comparative Statistics   A-89

Metro Area	Fast Food and Counter Workers	Financial Managers	First-Line Supervisors/ of Office Workers	General and Operations Managers	Hair-dressers/ Cosme-tologists	Home Health and Personal Care Aides	Janitors/ Cleaners
Madison, WI	11.02	71.61	31.88	65.89	13.94	13.95	15.37
Manchester, NH[2]	11.88	67.78	32.11	65.40	13.19	14.37	14.07
Memphis, TN	9.95	56.29	27.64	55.82	14.51	10.93	12.43
Miami, FL	10.90	72.93	30.04	55.19	13.80	12.10	12.75
Midland, TX	11.26	68.87	32.21	66.38	12.71	11.08	12.72
Milwaukee, WI	10.56	72.24	32.60	73.76	15.73	12.15	14.55
Minneapolis, MN	12.90	71.92	31.32	62.40	16.45	14.26	16.97
Nashville, TN	10.76	59.60	28.46	59.95	15.12	11.82	14.02
New Haven, CT[2]	13.15	67.42	33.60	71.07	15.79	14.00	17.93
New Orleans, LA	10.17	61.27	24.86	60.79	9.97	9.90	11.80
New York, NY	14.03	103.21	36.45	82.87	18.53	15.37	18.58
Oklahoma City, OK	10.46	56.40	26.50	53.95	13.21	11.30	12.31
Omaha, NE	11.57	60.81	27.79	51.20	17.22	12.78	14.62
Orlando, FL	10.44	67.64	27.02	50.37	14.70	12.02	12.97
Peoria, IL	10.98	60.22	28.72	50.68	14.84	12.88	12.80
Philadelphia, PA	11.82	82.22	33.44	74.57	16.17	12.96	15.31
Phoenix, AZ	13.06	64.55	29.32	58.07	16.74	13.34	14.73
Pittsburgh, PA	10.89	70.81	29.25	62.42	13.16	12.79	14.91
Portland, OR	13.97	65.29	30.19	61.17	16.58	15.31	16.47
Providence, RI[2]	13.21	78.87	33.57	71.70	16.31	15.37	15.75
Provo, UT	10.47	59.60	25.62	41.04	16.12	13.22	12.21
Raleigh, NC	10.01	68.49	28.13	70.88	14.20	11.45	12.29
Reno, NV	10.29	63.61	28.05	58.60	14.28	11.98	14.42
Richmond, VA	10.56	75.79	29.92	63.13	17.54	10.69	11.90
Riverside, CA	14.71	62.41	29.71	57.31	15.64	14.69	18.37
Rochester, MN	12.92	53.96	27.84	50.55	14.11	14.58	15.51
Sacramento, CA	14.18	65.80	31.37	59.57	16.75	14.17	17.86
Salt Lake City, UT	10.14	56.64	27.69	44.41	16.35	14.68	12.49
San Antonio, TX	11.01	67.11	26.77	61.53	12.89	10.91	12.76
San Diego, CA	14.44	74.59	31.30	69.74	18.23	14.88	17.57
San Francisco, CA	16.35	92.01	36.43	78.04	18.55	16.57	20.31
San Jose, CA	16.36	92.45	34.48	84.61	18.18	15.80	19.37
Santa Rosa, CA	14.43	69.07	31.18	61.63	17.02	16.21	17.54
Savannah, GA	10.40	49.27	26.00	50.31	11.68	11.70	12.39
Seattle, WA	16.04	76.28	37.04	73.17	22.82	16.24	21.21
Sioux Falls, SD	11.13	74.37	26.26	71.01	14.81	13.74	13.97
Springfield, IL	10.42	56.43	28.36	47.01	22.21	12.19	14.82
Tallahassee, FL	10.45	47.46	29.66	45.46	13.94	12.80	12.76
Tampa, FL	10.81	67.64	29.24	54.46	14.14	11.61	16.79
Tucson, AZ	12.90	53.26	25.41	46.52	16.70	13.18	14.72
Tulsa, OK	9.55	71.06	28.40	51.58	13.46	10.71	12.05
Tuscaloosa, AL	9.61	66.99	25.70	56.16	13.19	9.91	13.78
Virginia Beach, VA	10.94	66.75	28.75	53.58	12.55	10.52	12.31
Washington, DC	13.58	85.16	34.55	74.88	19.24	14.06	16.30
Wichita, KS	9.74	62.41	27.44	50.93	12.99	11.16	13.86
Winston-Salem, NC	10.40	73.56	26.29	59.21	12.93	11.42	11.67

Notes: (1) Figures cover the Metropolitan Statistical Area (MSA) except where noted. See Appendix B for areas included;
(2) New England City and Town Area; n/a not available
Source: Bureau of Labor Statistics, May 2020 Metro Area Occupational Employment and Wage Estimates

Appendix A: Comparative Statistics

Average Hourly Wages: Occupations L – N

Metro Area	Landscapers	Lawyers	Maids/House-keepers	Maintenance/Repairers	Marketing Managers	Network Admin.	Nurses, Licensed Practical
Albuquerque, NM	14.47	55.30	10.78	19.40	47.06	39.32	24.25
Allentown, PA	16.36	68.66	12.98	22.76	63.74	37.86	24.54
Anchorage, AK	17.23	55.18	15.11	24.45	49.02	39.64	33.65
Ann Arbor, MI	16.81	55.39	13.25	22.11	61.92	39.05	25.79
Athens, GA	16.07	37.80	10.10	17.26	61.63	32.23	21.52
Atlanta, GA	15.33	71.75	10.69	20.23	70.03	43.84	23.16
Austin, TX	15.64	69.36	11.26	18.11	74.00	41.06	23.83
Baton Rouge, LA	15.13	54.49	10.56	21.06	50.44	37.90	20.42
Boise City, ID	15.86	54.48	11.86	19.32	63.98	39.11	23.88
Boston, MA[2]	20.13	84.41	16.40	25.61	74.50	48.82	29.40
Boulder, CO	19.74	n/a	14.29	23.36	85.29	44.95	26.24
Cape Coral, FL	14.77	n/a	11.54	19.02	54.42	35.40	21.43
Cedar Rapids, IA	16.24	55.33	12.33	22.65	68.01	40.48	21.30
Charleston, SC	15.16	52.10	11.57	19.55	60.30	41.69	23.22
Charlotte, NC	15.09	69.55	11.69	21.36	72.17	40.33	22.77
Chicago, IL	16.89	76.45	14.09	23.38	68.69	43.67	28.45
Cincinnati, OH	14.62	67.43	12.24	21.32	66.12	38.88	23.84
Clarksville, TN	14.10	38.91	11.38	21.41	n/a	33.32	20.91
Cleveland, OH	17.07	71.56	12.07	21.06	66.16	42.80	23.78
College Station, TX	14.63	61.53	11.96	17.32	77.65	33.45	23.37
Colorado Springs, CO	15.28	57.73	13.68	20.63	80.71	39.94	27.45
Columbia, MO	14.70	43.61	11.43	15.89	54.36	34.22	21.46
Columbia, SC	13.75	57.84	11.26	19.16	57.61	38.25	21.20
Columbus, OH	15.69	54.42	12.55	21.51	73.13	41.93	22.50
Dallas, TX	16.49	72.23	12.05	21.14	74.99	43.23	25.11
Davenport, IA	16.09	70.60	11.68	20.79	61.19	37.00	21.77
Denver, CO	18.07	73.11	13.60	21.58	83.15	46.05	27.16
Des Moines, IA	17.08	63.08	12.53	21.27	64.28	41.04	23.35
Durham, NC	15.20	59.34	13.46	22.26	74.28	46.08	24.21
Edison, NJ	18.58	86.62	18.17	24.50	93.77	50.99	27.54
El Paso, TX	11.21	60.78	9.75	15.17	54.66	32.96	23.69
Fargo, ND	18.32	54.07	13.61	21.03	61.56	36.75	22.24
Fayetteville, NC	12.88	59.59	10.39	19.76	54.51	41.86	22.65
Fort Collins, CO	16.84	69.74	14.18	21.34	88.50	36.89	25.42
Fort Wayne, IN	14.26	59.12	11.29	21.47	60.08	32.57	22.79
Fort Worth, TX	16.49	72.23	12.05	21.14	74.99	43.23	25.11
Grand Rapids, MI	16.69	57.05	13.11	19.48	60.07	34.56	23.52
Greeley, CO	18.15	51.46	13.31	22.36	72.61	35.49	28.99
Green Bay, WI	16.03	51.55	12.13	22.68	60.63	33.41	20.81
Greensboro, NC	13.66	59.43	10.64	20.20	69.84	41.07	22.20
Honolulu, HI	19.34	56.12	19.89	24.13	52.09	40.41	26.08
Houston, TX	14.69	70.00	11.44	20.96	78.48	46.20	23.54
Huntsville, AL	15.69	56.43	10.54	17.99	72.22	40.01	19.99
Indianapolis, IN	16.30	60.41	12.05	20.39	61.76	40.98	23.39
Jacksonville, FL	14.63	61.24	12.55	19.96	68.66	37.71	22.65
Kansas City, MO	19.56	62.18	12.00	21.06	69.34	41.35	23.04
Lafayette, LA	15.41	45.40	9.86	17.55	43.77	34.54	19.08
Lakeland, FL	14.43	44.81	11.52	20.58	62.00	36.25	20.98
Las Vegas, NV	15.39	63.43	15.89	22.82	65.55	42.05	28.50
Lexington, KY	15.36	51.94	11.20	20.46	50.14	30.83	21.39
Lincoln, NE	14.29	56.03	13.51	21.24	43.46	35.90	22.16
Little Rock, AR	13.87	42.89	11.04	16.67	55.06	35.22	21.72
Los Angeles, CA	19.04	86.64	16.19	22.77	77.25	46.74	29.91
Louisville, KY	15.83	57.01	12.16	22.04	68.47	37.55	21.89
Madison, WI	17.69	57.68	14.08	21.18	64.29	37.64	23.27

Table continued on following page.

Metro Area	Landscapers	Lawyers	Maids/House-keepers	Maintenance/Repairers	Marketing Managers	Network Admin.	Nurses, Licensed Practical
Manchester, NH[2]	16.72	66.91	12.82	23.16	75.31	41.64	27.45
Memphis, TN	13.86	51.22	11.39	19.63	47.56	36.25	21.46
Miami, FL	14.82	81.48	11.96	18.62	65.38	41.99	23.34
Midland, TX	16.68	79.48	12.97	19.94	81.11	44.09	25.03
Milwaukee, WI	17.16	67.17	13.05	22.36	65.22	36.67	25.10
Minneapolis, MN	18.17	65.42	15.37	24.86	74.13	42.76	25.10
Nashville, TN	14.16	62.16	12.20	20.31	59.03	37.49	21.95
New Haven, CT[2]	21.07	72.97	14.36	24.76	62.79	46.03	27.76
New Orleans, LA	13.11	59.17	11.03	19.02	48.62	34.09	21.91
New York, NY	18.58	86.62	18.17	24.50	93.77	50.99	27.54
Oklahoma City, OK	14.58	60.36	11.38	18.60	66.70	37.72	21.30
Omaha, NE	16.84	60.84	12.85	21.39	53.21	40.66	22.70
Orlando, FL	14.06	58.70	11.93	18.05	58.36	40.84	22.30
Peoria, IL	14.85	63.40	12.71	20.89	71.93	35.66	22.80
Philadelphia, PA	16.87	73.14	14.54	22.62	75.68	41.45	27.69
Phoenix, AZ	14.91	68.90	13.30	20.64	64.49	42.05	27.24
Pittsburgh, PA	15.16	60.20	12.74	21.02	67.26	38.22	21.99
Portland, OR	18.52	68.32	15.17	22.37	65.90	43.03	27.81
Providence, RI[2]	17.76	61.76	15.61	24.03	78.17	44.50	28.42
Provo, UT	16.13	73.52	12.41	20.26	54.83	39.72	22.86
Raleigh, NC	15.42	66.00	12.05	21.71	71.46	43.77	23.23
Reno, NV	15.83	59.64	13.96	23.28	55.19	41.53	30.36
Richmond, VA	15.83	67.92	12.10	21.90	74.21	43.79	23.80
Riverside, CA	16.79	79.37	15.65	22.90	62.78	43.26	29.90
Rochester, MN	17.47	56.23	13.55	20.95	55.51	38.82	24.74
Sacramento, CA	19.87	73.57	18.56	22.64	73.63	45.57	31.24
Salt Lake City, UT	16.86	72.69	12.37	20.90	62.53	39.60	25.62
San Antonio, TX	14.36	61.79	11.83	18.51	71.37	38.99	22.64
San Diego, CA	16.37	70.82	15.49	22.57	71.15	47.47	31.68
San Francisco, CA	21.71	97.08	21.46	27.95	94.36	51.30	35.83
San Jose, CA	22.59	111.35	19.47	26.36	101.54	64.55	36.51
Santa Rosa, CA	19.15	84.04	16.93	25.05	77.45	43.90	35.97
Savannah, GA	14.12	60.11	10.61	17.68	53.92	36.94	21.45
Seattle, WA	20.08	66.70	16.36	24.21	81.40	48.50	29.46
Sioux Falls, SD	16.01	62.19	11.67	19.64	66.03	32.40	19.44
Springfield, IL	16.70	50.23	12.27	21.57	51.93	37.76	21.99
Tallahassee, FL	13.54	48.96	10.81	17.35	47.03	31.12	20.87
Tampa, FL	14.01	57.69	11.21	18.38	70.07	40.32	22.60
Tucson, AZ	14.30	70.81	14.77	18.16	54.39	37.56	26.53
Tulsa, OK	14.93	68.67	11.08	18.93	66.79	35.66	21.60
Tuscaloosa, AL	14.92	54.99	10.48	16.55	46.18	36.95	19.30
Virginia Beach, VA	14.23	62.89	12.23	19.55	70.12	36.79	21.44
Washington, DC	17.19	89.46	15.44	24.33	84.55	49.25	26.79
Wichita, KS	13.64	47.07	11.59	18.91	59.34	35.01	21.14
Winston-Salem, NC	14.43	60.44	11.31	19.93	64.53	39.48	22.11

Notes: (1) Figures cover the Metropolitan Statistical Area (MSA) except where noted. See Appendix B for areas included; (2) New England City and Town Area; n/a not available
Source: Bureau of Labor Statistics, May 2020 Metro Area Occupational Employment and Wage Estimates

Average Hourly Wages: Occupations N – P

Metro Area	Nurses, Registered	Nursing Assistants	Office Clerks	Physical Therapists	Physicians	Plumbers	Police Officers
Albuquerque, NM	36.89	14.68	13.26	42.37	93.46	22.34	27.77
Allentown, PA	34.19	16.29	18.15	42.47	n/a	33.01	34.49
Anchorage, AK	45.34	19.45	21.95	50.03	131.18	42.17	46.36
Ann Arbor, MI	39.09	17.55	16.78	42.90	92.84	35.65	33.41
Athens, GA	34.14	13.24	15.96	38.70	95.71	n/a	21.06
Atlanta, GA	36.53	16.57	17.83	42.77	127.01	26.53	24.70
Austin, TX	35.23	14.69	19.62	41.53	107.02	25.23	36.91
Baton Rouge, LA	31.33	12.25	13.85	43.09	104.38	29.38	21.21
Boise City, ID	35.63	14.84	17.45	39.54	115.74	24.22	30.14
Boston, MA[2]	47.79	18.34	21.18	41.62	86.54	40.46	37.76
Boulder, CO	39.80	17.23	22.67	44.97	132.80	25.79	40.27
Cape Coral, FL	34.06	15.25	17.14	41.34	125.98	21.62	26.01
Cedar Rapids, IA	29.59	14.88	18.09	37.39	120.60	29.06	31.16
Charleston, SC	33.46	14.93	15.18	37.56	134.84	26.03	24.33
Charlotte, NC	33.86	14.08	17.52	41.50	100.25	21.86	25.91
Chicago, IL	37.48	15.55	19.15	47.77	108.91	44.20	39.61
Cincinnati, OH	34.60	15.17	18.74	43.02	116.48	26.11	33.14
Clarksville, TN	31.25	13.32	15.39	43.19	113.83	24.00	22.17
Cleveland, OH	35.16	14.82	19.54	42.93	n/a	32.16	31.03
College Station, TX	33.67	12.92	15.42	40.64	n/a	20.44	31.50
Colorado Springs, CO	36.85	15.90	20.41	41.34	106.98	24.78	35.01
Columbia, MO	31.38	14.29	16.36	37.16	123.11	31.70	24.57
Columbia, SC	31.88	13.61	13.78	42.64	92.46	20.01	21.56
Columbus, OH	33.37	13.95	19.08	42.28	108.46	28.16	39.05
Dallas, TX	37.50	14.89	18.25	46.10	98.81	24.37	35.24
Davenport, IA	28.77	14.33	15.96	38.74	125.45	28.20	29.69
Denver, CO	38.12	17.19	22.26	42.29	119.46	29.30	41.15
Des Moines, IA	30.83	15.70	19.88	41.96	118.88	25.94	33.62
Durham, NC	34.04	14.98	18.39	37.70	60.22	23.42	25.52
Edison, NJ	45.63	19.48	19.03	47.81	99.88	35.78	41.48
El Paso, TX	35.14	13.03	15.07	46.19	113.76	18.19	30.62
Fargo, ND	35.67	16.56	20.46	39.52	n/a	26.34	32.53
Fayetteville, NC	36.31	12.73	15.84	41.85	125.79	21.51	22.19
Fort Collins, CO	37.00	16.20	20.49	38.37	114.80	26.03	40.60
Fort Wayne, IN	30.07	14.32	16.90	42.52	122.85	27.79	29.01
Fort Worth, TX	37.50	14.89	18.25	46.10	98.81	24.37	35.24
Grand Rapids, MI	33.54	14.54	18.46	40.21	103.72	25.17	30.97
Greeley, CO	34.49	15.51	21.15	43.71	117.71	25.41	36.09
Green Bay, WI	33.10	15.41	17.63	43.41	134.65	32.94	34.68
Greensboro, NC	33.75	13.32	16.51	43.44	133.51	24.87	24.42
Honolulu, HI	51.33	18.53	18.01	46.01	129.46	32.64	39.30
Houston, TX	40.85	14.11	20.18	40.55	97.14	26.71	32.55
Huntsville, AL	28.17	13.37	12.64	41.60	126.02	26.09	25.95
Indianapolis, IN	33.96	14.71	18.04	42.89	125.04	25.96	31.19
Jacksonville, FL	32.50	13.39	16.95	39.98	120.42	22.43	28.73
Kansas City, MO	33.77	14.40	17.65	42.64	77.69	32.53	27.86
Lafayette, LA	n/a	10.90	13.13	41.06	97.24	26.72	20.08
Lakeland, FL	31.77	13.41	16.98	45.93	111.82	21.29	28.08
Las Vegas, NV	44.58	16.81	18.26	54.41	112.43	29.48	38.04
Lexington, KY	30.92	14.26	16.76	41.60	117.61	30.48	23.72
Lincoln, NE	32.83	14.76	15.31	41.91	114.19	26.77	31.80
Little Rock, AR	33.20	13.43	17.00	37.99	90.23	22.80	24.32
Los Angeles, CA	54.38	18.28	19.87	50.77	111.66	29.04	53.23
Louisville, KY	31.94	14.54	17.26	41.20	119.15	28.33	25.33
Madison, WI	39.58	17.70	19.30	41.01	123.11	32.30	31.59

Table continued on following page.

Metro Area	Nurses, Registered	Nursing Assistants	Office Clerks	Physical Therapists	Physicians	Plumbers	Police Officers
Manchester, NH[2]	36.90	16.63	19.87	40.56	145.31	27.62	30.42
Memphis, TN	32.84	13.99	16.64	44.13	60.99	25.56	24.96
Miami, FL	34.76	13.66	17.51	39.20	103.07	22.66	35.19
Midland, TX	32.87	15.50	19.18	51.29	n/a	22.43	32.02
Milwaukee, WI	36.90	15.65	18.75	43.06	118.39	34.14	36.14
Minneapolis, MN	41.41	18.64	20.45	41.29	113.38	39.45	38.98
Nashville, TN	32.75	13.98	17.06	37.77	98.61	27.20	25.18
New Haven, CT[2]	41.58	17.50	19.49	48.99	109.62	37.97	36.22
New Orleans, LA	34.10	12.28	13.40	43.01	105.80	27.86	24.02
New York, NY	45.63	19.48	19.03	47.81	99.88	35.78	41.48
Oklahoma City, OK	32.94	13.44	15.49	43.27	98.08	27.58	27.64
Omaha, NE	33.90	15.61	17.67	40.54	113.21	33.69	32.51
Orlando, FL	32.37	13.57	17.28	41.78	87.69	21.20	28.75
Peoria, IL	32.97	14.10	18.03	42.48	108.82	38.03	26.30
Philadelphia, PA	38.45	15.82	19.59	45.60	110.75	33.19	36.66
Phoenix, AZ	39.13	16.56	20.25	44.20	117.44	25.87	34.93
Pittsburgh, PA	33.74	15.25	17.82	41.00	61.88	31.40	32.43
Portland, OR	47.45	18.03	19.73	44.08	84.07	37.75	39.52
Providence, RI[2]	39.75	16.41	19.47	41.73	101.63	29.94	31.88
Provo, UT	32.54	14.31	17.04	43.98	101.67	26.23	26.67
Raleigh, NC	33.71	14.25	17.60	40.47	131.23	21.78	25.39
Reno, NV	38.61	15.69	19.47	43.31	n/a	32.93	n/a
Richmond, VA	38.19	14.34	17.47	48.16	100.13	24.50	28.11
Riverside, CA	52.80	17.66	18.80	49.86	101.93	28.90	50.52
Rochester, MN	34.67	17.06	18.54	41.15	120.62	35.99	33.04
Sacramento, CA	64.59	20.17	19.88	53.64	125.17	30.79	48.23
Salt Lake City, UT	34.93	15.33	17.52	39.40	120.03	26.94	30.14
San Antonio, TX	36.11	13.97	17.09	41.28	104.54	21.49	29.60
San Diego, CA	53.66	19.08	19.89	47.32	115.36	30.73	44.39
San Francisco, CA	71.73	23.28	23.83	49.69	90.09	51.01	58.93
San Jose, CA	70.61	20.18	21.97	51.92	106.37	40.79	63.02
Santa Rosa, CA	60.02	18.91	21.01	52.11	110.94	36.11	55.62
Savannah, GA	31.19	12.86	17.14	42.25	79.65	25.97	22.03
Seattle, WA	45.73	18.20	21.98	44.19	121.55	39.45	41.70
Sioux Falls, SD	29.70	13.76	13.70	35.64	136.24	21.69	30.58
Springfield, IL	34.64	14.66	18.74	44.92	131.59	36.97	33.66
Tallahassee, FL	31.79	12.60	14.97	40.99	100.02	21.64	27.13
Tampa, FL	34.28	14.08	17.66	39.93	104.01	22.02	30.94
Tucson, AZ	36.86	15.70	19.72	42.86	96.12	24.44	31.18
Tulsa, OK	32.44	13.14	16.37	41.95	101.73	26.45	27.25
Tuscaloosa, AL	28.76	12.79	12.79	47.83	104.43	22.88	26.12
Virginia Beach, VA	35.27	14.43	15.93	43.59	103.50	23.91	27.28
Washington, DC	40.14	16.19	20.88	46.02	98.67	27.93	37.03
Wichita, KS	28.59	13.31	14.06	43.59	72.44	23.76	23.57
Winston-Salem, NC	33.96	13.84	16.40	47.63	59.26	21.42	21.49

Notes: (1) Figures cover the Metropolitan Statistical Area (MSA) except where noted. See Appendix B for areas included; (2) New England City and Town Area; n/a not available
Source: Bureau of Labor Statistics, May 2020 Metro Area Occupational Employment and Wage Estimates

Average Hourly Wages: Occupations P – S

Metro Area	Postal Mail Carriers	R.E. Sales Agents	Retail Salespersons	Sales Reps., Technical/ Scientific	Secretaries, Exc. Leg./ Med./Exec.	Security Guards	Surgeons
Albuquerque, NM	25.35	27.94	13.71	53.85	17.98	14.03	117.34
Allentown, PA	25.45	20.93	13.51	35.66	18.99	14.13	n/a
Anchorage, AK	25.19	35.74	16.71	41.68	21.33	21.46	n/a
Ann Arbor, MI	25.59	23.92	15.17	50.25	21.85	18.21	n/a
Athens, GA	24.88	27.22	12.23	22.13	15.66	15.56	121.05
Atlanta, GA	25.44	35.07	13.86	41.84	17.67	13.91	120.75
Austin, TX	25.90	32.45	13.91	51.09	18.80	16.12	123.62
Baton Rouge, LA	25.30	20.08	12.82	38.42	17.00	15.22	140.15
Boise City, ID	25.46	19.41	14.97	29.05	17.35	13.31	97.30
Boston, MA[2]	26.35	43.81	16.09	51.61	23.99	18.44	130.15
Boulder, CO	25.69	29.36	16.67	52.42	20.24	16.82	138.32
Cape Coral, FL	25.50	25.90	13.39	35.11	18.26	13.12	117.59
Cedar Rapids, IA	25.60	20.45	13.27	55.20	19.13	17.64	n/a
Charleston, SC	25.11	24.16	14.34	31.33	17.96	15.38	n/a
Charlotte, NC	25.80	26.82	14.40	45.84	19.39	15.19	n/a
Chicago, IL	25.88	21.35	14.74	43.30	20.83	16.67	126.47
Cincinnati, OH	26.01	22.97	14.27	54.66	18.99	17.36	136.71
Clarksville, TN	25.31	13.84	13.05	28.37	16.54	17.01	n/a
Cleveland, OH	25.57	25.39	13.80	44.45	18.72	15.88	n/a
College Station, TX	25.72	26.12	12.40	38.39	16.65	12.99	n/a
Colorado Springs, CO	25.33	36.06	15.75	51.66	17.72	16.33	138.49
Columbia, MO	24.78	15.74	16.35	37.54	17.90	15.12	n/a
Columbia, SC	25.03	21.37	13.33	35.54	19.69	15.89	n/a
Columbus, OH	25.57	24.24	14.13	43.53	19.06	17.50	130.76
Dallas, TX	25.84	32.44	14.22	42.11	19.17	15.96	96.15
Davenport, IA	25.05	35.10	16.04	41.15	17.40	16.63	n/a
Denver, CO	25.33	43.38	16.33	53.97	20.86	17.65	122.99
Des Moines, IA	25.38	24.89	13.93	48.46	21.68	16.81	n/a
Durham, NC	26.10	23.48	12.83	64.20	20.51	24.93	n/a
Edison, NJ	25.82	47.39	17.06	53.94	21.58	18.33	103.27
El Paso, TX	25.52	28.82	11.77	n/a	15.48	12.85	n/a
Fargo, ND	25.35	30.08	15.57	41.70	19.41	14.99	n/a
Fayetteville, NC	25.38	31.75	12.89	n/a	17.36	19.85	n/a
Fort Collins, CO	25.02	28.43	15.06	44.49	18.64	14.53	n/a
Fort Wayne, IN	25.01	23.92	13.59	39.15	18.02	17.34	102.77
Fort Worth, TX	25.84	32.44	14.22	42.11	19.17	15.96	96.15
Grand Rapids, MI	25.56	26.79	14.74	36.78	18.94	14.23	n/a
Greeley, CO	24.67	n/a	17.48	42.69	18.73	16.81	n/a
Green Bay, WI	25.05	27.21	15.84	45.73	18.17	14.03	n/a
Greensboro, NC	26.02	21.07	13.99	47.50	18.17	14.07	n/a
Honolulu, HI	26.27	34.78	16.86	41.95	22.13	16.81	125.38
Houston, TX	25.54	30.11	13.06	45.56	19.08	14.70	109.57
Huntsville, AL	25.08	n/a	14.19	40.45	17.89	15.08	n/a
Indianapolis, IN	25.51	24.10	15.14	58.59	18.14	15.06	83.72
Jacksonville, FL	26.36	32.81	12.90	55.76	18.29	12.98	n/a
Kansas City, MO	25.56	25.16	14.32	42.28	18.80	19.75	134.82
Lafayette, LA	25.61	20.02	13.19	41.34	15.02	11.63	n/a
Lakeland, FL	25.73	24.66	13.99	50.71	16.80	13.69	125.71
Las Vegas, NV	25.67	33.49	14.32	55.81	19.28	15.70	n/a
Lexington, KY	25.61	21.40	13.53	40.76	18.81	13.31	n/a
Lincoln, NE	25.26	26.16	13.66	39.84	18.52	17.86	142.38
Little Rock, AR	25.59	n/a	13.77	31.84	16.05	14.70	n/a
Los Angeles, CA	26.77	29.45	17.09	49.22	22.28	16.50	89.22
Louisville, KY	25.74	31.08	13.26	42.65	18.47	13.24	134.53
Madison, WI	24.45	22.36	15.01	38.52	20.01	18.11	n/a

Table continued on following page.

Metro Area	Postal Mail Carriers	R.E. Sales Agents	Retail Salespersons	Sales Reps., Technical/Scientific	Secretaries, Exc. Leg./Med./Exec.	Security Guards	Surgeons
Manchester, NH[2]	25.30	23.78	14.27	48.55	18.80	17.13	n/a
Memphis, TN	25.90	28.54	14.05	42.81	18.28	13.18	n/a
Miami, FL	25.74	33.05	14.10	43.52	17.95	14.33	102.70
Midland, TX	24.14	43.87	15.66	47.47	18.67	17.54	n/a
Milwaukee, WI	25.52	24.22	15.05	42.81	19.69	15.28	n/a
Minneapolis, MN	25.48	22.43	15.67	43.88	21.10	18.83	n/a
Nashville, TN	25.66	22.88	14.62	38.86	20.08	14.59	87.98
New Haven, CT[2]	25.57	n/a	15.78	51.87	23.42	16.82	n/a
New Orleans, LA	25.18	n/a	12.85	32.30	17.67	14.16	n/a
New York, NY	25.82	47.39	17.06	53.94	21.58	18.33	103.27
Oklahoma City, OK	25.83	27.06	14.42	47.84	16.56	17.63	n/a
Omaha, NE	25.62	26.55	14.47	27.54	18.29	18.67	97.62
Orlando, FL	25.63	21.86	13.90	45.86	17.38	13.36	107.64
Peoria, IL	25.20	22.91	13.31	41.09	16.53	18.73	n/a
Philadelphia, PA	25.80	23.80	15.36	39.35	20.84	15.80	127.73
Phoenix, AZ	26.14	25.87	15.31	45.74	18.93	15.32	n/a
Pittsburgh, PA	25.28	35.64	14.07	41.12	18.26	14.45	n/a
Portland, OR	25.16	27.75	16.66	51.50	22.16	16.55	137.03
Providence, RI[2]	25.36	34.42	16.55	43.31	22.02	15.82	135.97
Provo, UT	25.17	19.82	14.08	35.28	17.09	18.95	n/a
Raleigh, NC	25.99	25.85	13.72	53.76	18.82	16.13	n/a
Reno, NV	25.58	18.91	16.30	50.40	20.94	18.12	n/a
Richmond, VA	25.32	31.14	14.11	52.19	19.17	13.71	129.69
Riverside, CA	26.10	n/a	16.16	47.48	21.05	16.42	116.37
Rochester, MN	24.97	25.68	15.36	44.55	18.15	15.79	n/a
Sacramento, CA	26.14	40.54	16.20	49.21	21.10	17.05	n/a
Salt Lake City, UT	25.55	n/a	15.78	45.08	19.50	17.37	120.78
San Antonio, TX	25.93	30.87	13.97	43.36	17.05	16.35	n/a
San Diego, CA	26.30	n/a	16.36	49.07	21.27	16.24	n/a
San Francisco, CA	26.61	35.07	18.15	57.04	25.23	20.24	120.47
San Jose, CA	26.28	48.70	20.75	69.16	24.97	21.24	124.63
Santa Rosa, CA	25.08	n/a	18.83	58.81	22.47	17.86	n/a
Savannah, GA	25.33	26.46	13.07	42.67	16.91	15.61	135.03
Seattle, WA	25.94	34.15	18.51	53.25	23.36	19.56	110.96
Sioux Falls, SD	25.69	n/a	16.24	59.28	14.98	14.66	135.63
Springfield, IL	25.77	19.54	14.55	41.97	17.85	23.01	137.30
Tallahassee, FL	25.24	26.87	14.02	38.03	17.26	13.85	n/a
Tampa, FL	25.84	27.84	14.16	38.88	17.85	16.60	99.80
Tucson, AZ	26.13	28.26	14.92	41.86	17.67	14.50	n/a
Tulsa, OK	25.76	43.74	13.54	39.78	16.99	15.16	n/a
Tuscaloosa, AL	24.94	29.55	14.23	n/a	17.36	13.60	n/a
Virginia Beach, VA	25.12	31.60	12.74	47.42	19.12	16.77	n/a
Washington, DC	25.68	32.62	15.08	60.70	23.83	22.34	128.61
Wichita, KS	25.19	34.94	16.50	48.42	17.11	15.40	n/a
Winston-Salem, NC	26.12	29.77	12.78	46.13	18.63	19.14	n/a

Notes: (1) Figures cover the Metropolitan Statistical Area (MSA) except where noted. See Appendix B for areas included; (2) New England City and Town Area; n/a not available
Source: Bureau of Labor Statistics, May 2020 Metro Area Occupational Employment and Wage Estimates

Appendix A: Comparative Statistics

Average Hourly Wages: Occupations T – W

Metro Area	Teacher Assistants[3]	Teachers, Secondary School[3]	Telemarketers	Truck Drivers, Heavy	Truck Drivers, Light	Waiters/ Waitresses
Albuquerque, NM	10.86	25.68	n/a	20.15	18.42	10.00
Allentown, PA	14.41	34.29	13.77	23.61	17.65	13.50
Anchorage, AK	19.53	40.19	n/a	28.67	24.80	12.41
Ann Arbor, MI	14.25	30.94	n/a	23.07	20.97	12.42
Athens, GA	9.86	28.26	n/a	24.12	22.33	11.05
Atlanta, GA	11.99	30.58	13.88	24.03	19.17	11.09
Austin, TX	12.63	28.51	16.75	21.42	23.43	11.41
Baton Rouge, LA	10.61	25.88	13.65	20.24	16.72	9.75
Boise City, ID	13.33	24.81	13.26	22.95	18.28	12.34
Boston, MA[2]	18.17	39.93	18.30	25.04	22.25	16.02
Boulder, CO	16.60	33.44	n/a	21.44	21.14	15.29
Cape Coral, FL	14.99	31.83	13.57	21.06	18.21	12.55
Cedar Rapids, IA	12.78	25.85	12.92	18.16	16.81	10.61
Charleston, SC	12.41	28.34	9.27	20.05	17.41	9.82
Charlotte, NC	12.78	25.96	16.80	23.25	17.99	11.80
Chicago, IL	14.87	39.72	15.22	26.10	23.89	11.30
Cincinnati, OH	14.28	30.87	15.21	24.06	19.05	11.05
Clarksville, TN	13.56	33.45	n/a	19.83	19.57	10.91
Cleveland, OH	14.60	34.51	11.42	23.90	19.82	10.71
College Station, TX	9.90	23.45	n/a	18.16	17.70	9.94
Colorado Springs, CO	14.25	25.06	16.71	23.30	19.39	15.23
Columbia, MO	13.47	25.88	n/a	21.47	19.86	11.41
Columbia, SC	12.27	28.01	16.21	21.90	17.53	9.40
Columbus, OH	14.60	33.80	14.44	22.67	19.28	11.77
Dallas, TX	11.50	28.25	17.10	24.27	20.71	9.50
Davenport, IA	13.57	27.87	14.32	23.94	17.03	11.62
Denver, CO	15.53	29.76	18.67	26.50	20.37	15.26
Des Moines, IA	13.66	29.67	14.89	24.12	16.86	10.63
Durham, NC	12.80	26.34	12.24	19.82	20.75	12.65
Edison, NJ	17.07	43.94	18.00	27.38	21.27	18.12
El Paso, TX	13.05	30.31	10.36	23.37	17.27	9.93
Fargo, ND	16.34	31.20	n/a	24.48	20.00	12.90
Fayetteville, NC	11.91	22.89	n/a	17.95	17.42	9.29
Fort Collins, CO	14.31	n/a	n/a	22.10	18.76	16.23
Fort Wayne, IN	12.40	26.62	n/a	21.76	19.38	13.50
Fort Worth, TX	11.50	28.25	17.10	24.27	20.71	9.50
Grand Rapids, MI	14.25	29.14	12.06	22.41	20.39	14.47
Greeley, CO	14.61	25.80	n/a	25.81	20.06	12.56
Green Bay, WI	16.03	28.94	n/a	22.82	19.81	9.89
Greensboro, NC	12.38	24.19	n/a	24.63	17.87	10.40
Honolulu, HI	15.68	n/a	12.79	25.82	18.43	30.11
Houston, TX	10.92	29.18	14.80	23.21	20.42	11.44
Huntsville, AL	10.13	26.12	n/a	19.59	17.60	9.19
Indianapolis, IN	13.05	27.37	16.60	23.26	20.81	12.55
Jacksonville, FL	12.80	30.73	12.86	21.69	18.78	12.21
Kansas City, MO	13.33	26.10	15.91	24.16	18.51	11.20
Lafayette, LA	11.30	25.17	n/a	20.88	14.72	9.79
Lakeland, FL	11.20	24.22	12.40	22.02	22.47	11.43
Las Vegas, NV	15.75	28.05	12.82	23.35	17.59	13.15
Lexington, KY	15.32	28.71	n/a	25.24	22.54	10.77
Lincoln, NE	14.87	30.70	11.05	26.01	19.74	10.59
Little Rock, AR	11.35	26.77	12.43	24.40	14.91	10.92
Los Angeles, CA	18.25	41.94	15.89	24.13	21.40	16.07
Louisville, KY	15.06	27.29	n/a	25.60	20.42	11.01
Madison, WI	15.69	27.83	12.02	25.51	18.09	12.03

Table continued on following page.

Metro Area	Teacher Assistants[3]	Teachers, Secondary School[3]	Telemarketers	Truck Drivers, Heavy	Truck Drivers, Light	Waiters/ Waitresses
Manchester, NH[2]	15.12	28.80	n/a	24.56	18.27	13.46
Memphis, TN	12.21	26.97	15.50	22.93	19.09	9.84
Miami, FL	13.47	31.76	14.05	19.63	17.20	12.57
Midland, TX	10.43	28.63	n/a	24.50	21.89	9.28
Milwaukee, WI	16.15	29.89	16.04	24.97	17.36	11.33
Minneapolis, MN	16.69	31.99	18.31	25.51	21.47	15.04
Nashville, TN	13.09	25.02	18.69	25.40	17.83	9.89
New Haven, CT[2]	15.38	37.68	17.96	24.73	19.11	13.86
New Orleans, LA	12.38	26.55	17.07	22.70	18.90	9.90
New York, NY	17.07	43.94	18.00	27.38	21.27	18.12
Oklahoma City, OK	10.86	23.79	14.03	24.44	18.01	11.61
Omaha, NE	14.35	30.82	12.49	21.91	18.84	10.79
Orlando, FL	13.12	27.96	12.95	22.29	19.05	12.53
Peoria, IL	12.78	28.02	16.30	23.04	19.39	10.60
Philadelphia, PA	14.25	34.95	17.40	25.10	20.12	13.00
Phoenix, AZ	13.68	27.18	16.21	23.93	19.25	19.03
Pittsburgh, PA	14.11	34.46	12.75	26.03	17.58	13.55
Portland, OR	17.44	39.42	18.26	25.23	20.13	15.65
Providence, RI[2]	17.30	37.01	16.66	24.14	20.19	14.06
Provo, UT	13.67	38.46	14.13	20.44	18.31	12.13
Raleigh, NC	11.87	27.24	n/a	22.00	16.96	11.79
Reno, NV	10.42	25.59	14.61	25.19	21.37	11.35
Richmond, VA	12.74	n/a	14.96	23.73	21.33	12.03
Riverside, CA	17.96	41.62	15.27	25.57	22.32	14.16
Rochester, MN	15.75	30.87	n/a	23.53	16.41	15.44
Sacramento, CA	17.41	39.16	15.61	25.88	19.96	16.21
Salt Lake City, UT	13.35	29.93	12.47	24.57	20.04	10.55
San Antonio, TX	11.97	28.34	19.63	20.54	21.17	10.02
San Diego, CA	16.96	41.03	15.07	24.67	23.99	15.63
San Francisco, CA	19.29	44.41	n/a	27.78	25.20	19.64
San Jose, CA	19.75	44.47	16.69	27.47	24.95	17.28
Santa Rosa, CA	17.76	42.66	n/a	26.90	23.21	17.56
Savannah, GA	12.45	26.54	n/a	22.16	17.24	9.30
Seattle, WA	19.79	38.01	21.37	26.88	22.88	20.75
Sioux Falls, SD	12.32	23.01	n/a	22.48	18.48	10.59
Springfield, IL	12.03	27.07	n/a	24.22	18.96	10.05
Tallahassee, FL	13.00	24.52	14.79	20.09	17.87	12.10
Tampa, FL	14.49	30.07	13.79	20.31	17.75	14.24
Tucson, AZ	13.63	21.17	14.70	23.53	18.79	17.12
Tulsa, OK	11.41	26.46	12.45	27.46	18.88	9.11
Tuscaloosa, AL	9.49	24.81	n/a	20.28	18.27	9.02
Virginia Beach, VA	13.86	32.96	13.91	19.71	19.40	11.59
Washington, DC	17.52	41.57	14.54	24.43	22.49	15.99
Wichita, KS	13.20	27.00	12.02	22.85	17.72	9.40
Winston-Salem, NC	11.38	24.47	n/a	23.68	17.90	10.37

Notes: (1) Figures cover the Metropolitan Statistical Area (MSA) except where noted. See Appendix B for areas included; (2) New England City and Town Area; (3) Hourly wages were calculated from annual wage data assuming a 40 hour work week; n/a not available
Source: Bureau of Labor Statistics, May 2020 Metro Area Occupational Employment and Wage Estimates

Means of Transportation to Work: City

City	Car/Truck/Van Drove Alone	Car/Truck/Van Car-pooled	Public Transportation Bus	Public Transportation Subway	Public Transportation Railroad	Bicycle	Walked	Other Means	Worked at Home
Albuquerque, NM	80.6	9.0	1.8	0.0	0.1	1.1	1.9	1.0	4.4
Allentown, PA	67.4	17.2	4.9	0.0	0.0	0.1	5.4	1.2	3.9
Anchorage, AK	76.3	11.8	1.5	0.0	0.0	1.3	2.9	2.3	4.0
Ann Arbor, MI	54.0	6.4	10.3	0.2	0.0	3.9	16.5	0.7	8.0
Athens, GA	72.5	10.0	4.6	0.0	0.0	1.4	4.4	1.5	5.6
Atlanta, GA	67.1	6.3	6.6	3.4	0.2	1.1	5.0	2.2	8.1
Austin, TX	73.7	9.1	3.2	0.1	0.1	1.3	2.4	1.3	8.7
Baton Rouge, LA	80.3	9.8	2.4	0.0	0.0	0.6	3.4	0.6	2.9
Boise City, ID	79.6	7.3	0.6	0.0	0.0	2.8	2.5	1.1	6.0
Boston, MA	38.3	5.9	13.5	17.8	1.1	2.3	15.1	2.6	3.4
Boulder, CO	50.8	5.5	7.3	0.0	0.0	9.9	11.1	1.1	14.5
Cape Coral, FL	81.7	9.0	0.1	0.0	0.0	0.2	0.8	1.2	7.0
Cedar Rapids, IA	84.0	8.2	0.8	0.0	0.0	0.5	1.7	1.1	3.6
Charleston, SC	76.4	7.0	0.8	0.0	0.0	2.4	5.0	1.7	6.8
Charlotte, NC	76.3	9.3	2.4	0.4	0.2	0.1	2.1	1.5	7.7
Chicago, IL	48.8	7.7	13.3	13.0	1.8	1.7	6.5	2.0	5.2
Cincinnati, OH	72.3	8.8	7.0	0.0	0.0	0.4	5.7	1.1	4.7
Clarksville, TN	85.9	7.8	0.9	0.0	0.0	0.0	1.3	1.3	2.7
Cleveland, OH	69.3	10.8	8.9	0.5	0.1	0.6	5.1	1.5	3.2
College Station, TX	78.2	9.3	2.8	0.0	0.0	2.1	2.7	1.0	3.8
Colorado Springs, CO	77.8	10.9	0.9	0.0	0.0	0.6	1.9	0.9	6.9
Columbia, MO	77.1	10.5	1.3	0.0	0.0	1.3	4.8	0.9	4.2
Columbia, SC	64.1	6.1	1.8	0.0	0.0	0.5	21.9	2.2	3.4
Columbus, OH	79.4	8.3	3.1	0.0	0.0	0.6	3.1	1.1	4.4
Dallas, TX	76.7	11.0	2.9	0.4	0.3	0.2	2.1	1.5	4.9
Davenport, IA	85.6	6.6	0.9	0.0	0.0	0.4	2.3	0.5	3.7
Denver, CO	69.1	7.7	4.4	0.9	0.5	2.2	4.7	1.9	8.5
Des Moines, IA	80.1	9.7	2.2	0.1	0.0	0.4	2.9	1.2	3.5
Durham, NC	76.9	9.3	3.6	0.0	0.0	0.6	2.4	1.3	5.8
Edison, NJ	69.4	9.0	0.5	0.5	12.6	0.3	1.7	1.2	4.8
El Paso, TX	81.1	10.6	1.6	0.0	0.0	0.2	1.4	1.9	3.2
Fargo, ND	82.8	8.3	0.9	0.0	0.0	0.6	3.7	0.8	2.9
Fayetteville, NC	77.2	9.4	0.6	0.0	0.0	0.2	7.8	1.7	3.1
Fort Collins, CO	71.9	7.2	2.2	0.0	0.0	5.4	4.2	1.0	8.0
Fort Wayne, IN	83.4	9.6	0.8	0.0	0.0	0.3	1.6	0.7	3.7
Fort Worth, TX	81.5	11.4	0.6	0.0	0.2	0.2	1.2	0.8	4.1
Grand Rapids, MI	75.3	11.1	3.6	0.1	0.0	1.1	4.1	1.0	3.8
Greeley, CO	79.5	11.3	0.6	0.0	0.0	0.7	2.8	1.2	3.9
Green Bay, WI	79.7	10.2	1.4	0.0	0.0	0.5	2.3	1.9	3.9
Greensboro, NC	81.9	7.6	1.9	0.0	0.0	0.2	1.9	0.9	5.6
Honolulu, HI	57.2	13.0	11.6	0.0	0.0	1.6	8.5	4.0	3.9
Houston, TX	77.7	10.4	3.5	0.1	0.0	0.4	2.0	2.0	4.0
Huntsville, AL	86.1	7.0	0.4	0.0	0.0	0.2	1.3	1.1	4.0
Indianapolis, IN	82.0	9.2	1.8	0.0	0.0	0.5	1.9	1.1	3.5
Jacksonville, FL	80.3	9.2	1.8	0.0	0.0	0.5	1.7	1.6	4.8
Kansas City, MO	81.5	7.8	2.5	0.0	0.0	0.2	2.0	1.2	4.9
Lafayette, LA	84.3	6.7	1.2	0.0	0.0	1.2	2.3	0.9	3.5
Lakeland, FL	80.5	10.5	0.8	0.0	0.0	0.3	1.6	1.8	4.6
Las Vegas, NV	78.0	9.8	3.4	0.0	0.0	0.2	1.5	2.8	4.2
Lexington, KY	78.5	9.3	1.9	0.0	0.0	0.6	3.7	1.5	4.4
Lincoln, NE	81.0	9.0	1.3	0.0	0.0	1.2	3.4	0.6	3.4
Little Rock, AR	81.6	9.8	0.9	0.0	0.0	0.1	1.8	1.5	4.2
Los Angeles, CA	69.6	8.8	7.8	0.9	0.2	1.0	3.4	2.0	6.3
Louisville, KY	79.6	8.9	3.1	0.0	0.0	0.4	2.0	1.8	4.3

Table continued on following page.

Appendix A: Comparative Statistics

City	Car/Truck/Van Drove Alone	Car-pooled	Bus	Subway	Railroad	Bicycle	Walked	Other Means	Worked at Home
Madison, WI	64.3	7.0	9.1	0.0	0.1	4.5	9.1	1.3	4.7
Manchester, NH	79.1	11.0	0.7	0.0	0.1	0.3	3.2	1.3	4.2
Memphis, TN	82.0	10.5	1.4	0.0	0.0	0.2	1.6	1.3	2.9
Miami, FL	69.4	8.3	7.9	1.0	0.2	0.9	4.0	3.2	5.2
Midland, TX	85.1	10.1	0.2	0.0	0.0	0.1	0.6	1.0	2.8
Milwaukee, WI	72.8	10.2	7.2	0.0	0.1	0.8	4.6	0.8	3.5
Minneapolis, MN	60.5	7.4	11.2	1.1	0.2	4.0	7.4	2.3	5.8
Nashville, TN	77.7	10.0	2.0	0.0	0.1	0.2	2.4	1.2	6.4
New Haven, CT	58.7	9.1	10.5	0.1	1.1	3.1	11.4	1.2	4.7
New Orleans, LA	68.0	9.1	5.9	0.0	0.0	3.1	5.4	2.7	5.7
New York, NY	22.3	4.5	10.1	43.9	1.5	1.3	10.0	2.2	4.3
Oklahoma City, OK	82.6	10.5	0.5	0.0	0.0	0.1	1.5	1.1	3.6
Omaha, NE	81.7	9.1	1.4	0.0	0.0	0.3	2.3	1.3	4.0
Orlando, FL	79.0	8.0	3.4	0.1	0.0	0.6	1.8	1.9	5.3
Peoria, IL	80.1	9.5	2.4	0.0	0.0	0.3	2.7	1.1	3.7
Philadelphia, PA	50.3	8.2	16.0	5.6	2.8	2.1	8.5	2.3	4.2
Phoenix, AZ	74.6	12.6	2.7	0.1	0.1	0.6	1.6	1.9	5.9
Pittsburgh, PA	55.3	8.1	16.9	0.4	0.0	1.8	10.7	1.2	5.6
Portland, OR	57.3	8.3	9.9	0.9	0.3	6.0	5.8	3.0	8.5
Providence, RI	64.5	12.0	5.2	0.1	1.2	0.7	9.5	1.3	5.5
Provo, UT	62.0	11.8	2.6	0.2	1.1	2.4	13.0	1.6	5.3
Raleigh, NC	78.2	8.0	1.9	0.1	0.0	0.4	1.6	1.3	8.5
Reno, NV	75.2	12.6	2.3	0.0	0.0	0.8	3.6	1.1	4.4
Richmond, VA	71.1	9.5	5.5	0.1	0.1	2.1	5.2	1.8	4.6
Riverside, CA	76.4	12.6	1.7	0.0	0.7	0.7	2.6	1.1	4.2
Rochester, MN	70.6	12.5	6.2	0.0	0.0	1.0	4.3	0.9	4.4
Sacramento, CA	74.4	10.4	2.0	0.2	0.4	1.9	2.8	2.2	5.6
Salt Lake City, UT	67.8	10.5	4.8	0.4	0.8	2.5	5.1	2.7	5.5
San Antonio, TX	78.7	11.3	2.9	0.0	0.0	0.2	1.7	1.5	3.8
San Diego, CA	74.7	8.6	3.6	0.0	0.1	0.8	3.1	1.8	7.2
San Francisco, CA	32.1	6.9	22.0	8.8	1.7	4.0	11.8	6.1	6.6
San Jose, CA	75.8	11.7	2.6	0.3	1.2	0.8	1.8	1.6	4.2
Santa Rosa, CA	77.9	11.5	1.6	0.0	0.1	1.2	1.7	1.1	4.8
Savannah, GA	72.0	11.0	4.4	0.1	0.0	1.7	4.7	1.9	4.2
Seattle, WA	46.5	7.2	20.1	1.3	0.1	3.5	11.3	2.5	7.4
Sioux Falls, SD	84.3	8.5	0.8	0.0	0.0	0.5	2.0	0.6	3.4
Springfield, IL	81.8	7.9	2.2	0.1	0.0	0.7	2.1	1.3	3.9
Tallahassee, FL	78.5	8.7	2.4	0.0	0.0	0.8	3.3	1.5	4.8
Tampa, FL	77.1	8.8	2.1	0.0	0.0	1.0	2.4	1.5	6.9
Tucson, AZ	74.5	10.6	3.3	0.0	0.0	2.4	3.1	1.7	4.5
Tulsa, OK	80.2	10.7	0.9	0.0	0.0	0.3	1.8	2.1	4.0
Tuscaloosa, AL	84.2	8.1	0.8	0.1	0.0	0.5	1.8	0.6	3.9
Virginia Beach, VA	82.1	8.6	0.7	0.0	0.0	0.5	2.4	1.6	3.9
Washington, DC	33.5	5.2	13.2	21.1	0.3	4.5	13.4	2.3	6.6
Wichita, KS	83.5	9.5	0.7	0.0	0.0	0.3	1.5	1.3	3.2
Winston-Salem, NC	81.9	8.3	1.7	0.0	0.0	0.2	2.1	1.1	4.7
U.S.	76.3	9.0	2.4	1.9	0.6	0.5	2.7	1.4	5.2

Note: Figures are percentages and cover workers 16 years of age and older
Source: U.S. Census Bureau, 2015-2019 American Community Survey 5-Year Estimates

Means of Transportation to Work: Metro Area

Metro Area	Drove Alone	Car-pooled	Bus	Subway	Railroad	Bicycle	Walked	Other Means	Worked at Home
Albuquerque, NM	80.6	9.6	1.3	0.0	0.2	0.8	1.7	1.1	4.8
Allentown, PA	81.7	8.4	1.5	0.1	0.1	0.2	2.4	1.1	4.6
Anchorage, AK	75.7	11.5	1.3	0.0	0.0	1.0	2.7	3.2	4.5
Ann Arbor, MI	71.8	7.9	5.1	0.1	0.0	1.6	7.0	0.6	5.9
Athens, GA	76.3	10.3	2.8	0.0	0.0	0.9	2.9	1.2	5.6
Atlanta, GA	77.3	9.2	2.0	0.8	0.1	0.2	1.3	1.6	7.4
Austin, TX	76.3	9.2	1.8	0.1	0.1	0.8	1.8	1.2	8.8
Baton Rouge, LA	84.8	8.7	0.8	0.0	0.0	0.3	1.5	0.9	3.1
Boise City, ID	79.9	8.9	0.3	0.0	0.0	1.2	1.7	1.1	6.8
Boston, MA	66.4	7.2	4.1	6.7	2.2	1.1	5.4	1.7	5.3
Boulder, CO	65.0	7.2	4.7	0.0	0.0	4.2	5.0	1.0	12.8
Cape Coral, FL	79.0	10.2	0.6	0.0	0.0	0.6	1.2	2.0	6.3
Cedar Rapids, IA	84.7	7.5	0.5	0.0	0.0	0.3	2.0	0.7	4.2
Charleston, SC	81.1	8.2	0.7	0.0	0.0	0.7	2.3	1.2	5.8
Charlotte, NC	80.4	8.9	1.1	0.2	0.1	0.1	1.4	1.2	6.6
Chicago, IL	70.0	7.7	4.4	4.4	3.3	0.7	3.0	1.4	5.2
Cincinnati, OH	82.3	8.0	1.7	0.0	0.0	0.2	2.0	0.8	5.0
Clarksville, TN	84.0	8.1	0.7	0.0	0.0	0.1	3.1	1.3	2.7
Cleveland, OH	81.4	7.7	2.7	0.2	0.1	0.3	2.2	1.1	4.4
College Station, TX	79.8	10.7	1.7	0.0	0.0	1.3	1.9	1.1	3.5
Colorado Springs, CO	77.0	10.4	0.6	0.0	0.0	0.4	3.4	1.0	7.0
Columbia, MO	78.9	10.7	0.8	0.0	0.0	0.8	3.3	0.9	4.5
Columbia, SC	80.7	8.6	0.6	0.0	0.0	0.1	4.4	1.9	3.6
Columbus, OH	82.2	7.6	1.6	0.0	0.0	0.4	2.2	1.0	5.0
Dallas, TX	80.6	9.7	0.9	0.2	0.2	0.1	1.2	1.2	5.8
Davenport, IA	85.6	6.8	0.9	0.0	0.0	0.2	2.0	0.9	3.6
Denver, CO	75.3	8.1	2.8	0.6	0.3	0.8	2.2	1.5	8.4
Des Moines, IA	83.6	7.8	1.1	0.0	0.0	0.2	1.8	0.8	4.6
Durham, NC	76.5	8.7	3.4	0.0	0.0	0.7	2.8	1.3	6.7
Edison, NJ	49.2	6.3	7.5	20.0	3.9	0.7	5.9	2.0	4.5
El Paso, TX	80.7	10.6	1.3	0.0	0.0	0.1	1.6	2.1	3.5
Fargo, ND	82.2	8.6	0.7	0.0	0.0	0.5	2.8	0.8	4.4
Fayetteville, NC	81.3	9.2	0.3	0.0	0.0	0.1	4.2	1.4	3.4
Fort Collins, CO	74.9	8.0	1.5	0.0	0.0	3.1	2.7	1.2	8.6
Fort Wayne, IN	83.9	9.0	0.6	0.0	0.0	0.3	1.4	0.7	4.2
Fort Worth, TX	80.6	9.7	0.9	0.2	0.2	0.1	1.2	1.2	5.8
Grand Rapids, MI	81.9	9.1	1.4	0.0	0.0	0.5	2.2	0.8	4.2
Greeley, CO	80.4	9.6	0.5	0.0	0.0	0.3	1.9	1.0	6.2
Green Bay, WI	83.8	7.9	0.7	0.0	0.0	0.2	1.8	0.9	4.7
Greensboro, NC	82.7	9.0	0.9	0.0	0.0	0.1	1.4	0.9	4.9
Honolulu, HI	64.7	14.2	8.0	0.0	0.0	0.9	5.5	2.7	4.0
Houston, TX	80.8	9.8	1.9	0.0	0.0	0.2	1.3	1.4	4.5
Huntsville, AL	88.0	6.2	0.2	0.0	0.0	0.1	0.8	1.0	3.7
Indianapolis, IN	83.2	8.3	0.8	0.0	0.0	0.3	1.5	0.9	4.9
Jacksonville, FL	80.9	8.2	1.2	0.0	0.0	0.5	1.5	1.7	6.0
Kansas City, MO	83.7	7.8	0.8	0.0	0.0	0.1	1.2	0.9	5.4
Lafayette, LA	84.8	8.2	0.5	0.0	0.0	0.4	1.9	1.1	3.0
Lakeland, FL	83.4	9.4	0.5	0.0	0.0	0.4	1.0	1.4	4.0
Las Vegas, NV	78.8	9.8	3.3	0.0	0.0	0.3	1.5	2.2	4.2
Lexington, KY	79.9	9.3	1.3	0.0	0.0	0.4	3.1	1.3	4.6
Lincoln, NE	81.3	8.9	1.1	0.0	0.0	1.1	3.3	0.6	3.7
Little Rock, AR	83.9	9.5	0.5	0.0	0.0	0.2	1.3	1.1	3.5
Los Angeles, CA	75.1	9.5	4.1	0.4	0.3	0.7	2.5	1.6	5.8
Louisville, KY	82.0	8.5	1.8	0.0	0.0	0.2	1.6	1.3	4.6

Table continued on following page.

Metro Area	Car/Truck/Van Drove Alone	Car-pooled	Public Transportation Bus	Subway	Railroad	Bicycle	Walked	Other Means	Worked at Home
Madison, WI	75.0	7.5	4.2	0.0	0.0	2.2	5.0	0.9	5.1
Manchester, NH	81.4	8.1	0.8	0.0	0.1	0.1	2.1	0.9	6.4
Memphis, TN	84.6	9.2	0.7	0.0	0.0	0.1	1.0	1.1	3.3
Miami, FL	77.9	9.1	2.8	0.3	0.2	0.6	1.6	1.8	5.7
Midland, TX	84.8	9.7	0.2	0.0	0.0	0.1	1.1	0.8	3.3
Milwaukee, WI	80.9	7.8	3.1	0.0	0.1	0.5	2.6	0.7	4.3
Minneapolis, MN	77.5	8.1	4.1	0.2	0.2	0.8	2.3	1.1	5.8
Nashville, TN	80.8	9.4	0.9	0.0	0.1	0.1	1.3	1.1	6.3
New Haven, CT	78.3	8.4	2.8	0.1	0.9	0.5	3.3	1.0	4.7
New Orleans, LA	78.1	9.8	2.3	0.0	0.0	1.1	2.5	1.7	4.5
New York, NY	49.2	6.3	7.5	20.0	3.9	0.7	5.9	2.0	4.5
Oklahoma City, OK	83.2	9.4	0.4	0.0	0.0	0.3	1.6	1.0	4.1
Omaha, NE	83.8	8.2	0.8	0.0	0.0	0.2	1.7	1.0	4.2
Orlando, FL	79.7	9.8	1.5	0.0	0.1	0.4	1.1	1.6	5.9
Peoria, IL	84.9	7.3	1.1	0.0	0.0	0.3	2.1	0.9	3.6
Philadelphia, PA	72.5	7.6	5.0	1.9	2.3	0.6	3.6	1.3	5.2
Phoenix, AZ	76.1	11.1	1.7	0.1	0.0	0.8	1.5	1.8	7.0
Pittsburgh, PA	76.6	8.3	5.1	0.2	0.0	0.3	3.4	1.1	5.0
Portland, OR	70.3	9.1	4.8	0.7	0.2	2.2	3.4	2.0	7.4
Providence, RI	80.7	8.6	1.5	0.2	1.0	0.2	3.1	0.8	3.9
Provo, UT	73.1	11.4	1.1	0.2	0.9	0.9	4.1	1.2	7.2
Raleigh, NC	79.7	8.3	0.8	0.0	0.0	0.2	1.1	0.9	8.9
Reno, NV	77.2	12.0	1.8	0.0	0.0	0.6	2.6	1.1	4.7
Richmond, VA	81.1	8.6	1.4	0.0	0.1	0.5	1.7	1.3	5.3
Riverside, CA	78.9	11.5	0.9	0.1	0.4	0.3	1.5	1.3	5.3
Rochester, MN	74.1	11.5	4.0	0.0	0.0	0.6	3.6	0.8	5.3
Sacramento, CA	76.8	9.4	1.6	0.2	0.2	1.4	1.8	1.5	7.1
Salt Lake City, UT	75.4	11.1	2.1	0.3	0.5	0.8	2.1	1.5	6.2
San Antonio, TX	79.5	10.7	1.9	0.0	0.0	0.2	1.7	1.3	4.7
San Diego, CA	76.2	8.6	2.5	0.0	0.2	0.6	2.9	1.9	7.0
San Francisco, CA	57.6	9.5	7.6	7.6	1.5	1.9	4.7	3.0	6.6
San Jose, CA	74.9	10.6	2.4	0.3	1.5	1.7	2.1	1.6	5.0
Santa Rosa, CA	74.6	11.3	1.6	0.0	0.2	1.0	2.7	1.3	7.4
Savannah, GA	79.5	9.7	1.8	0.1	0.0	0.8	2.4	1.6	4.2
Seattle, WA	67.5	10.0	8.7	0.4	0.5	1.1	4.0	1.5	6.2
Sioux Falls, SD	84.3	8.1	0.5	0.0	0.0	0.4	2.1	0.6	4.1
Springfield, IL	83.3	8.0	1.3	0.1	0.0	0.5	1.7	1.0	4.3
Tallahassee, FL	81.1	9.2	1.4	0.0	0.0	0.6	2.0	1.3	4.3
Tampa, FL	78.9	8.8	1.3	0.0	0.0	0.6	1.4	1.6	7.4
Tucson, AZ	76.8	10.0	2.2	0.0	0.0	1.5	2.3	1.8	5.4
Tulsa, OK	82.8	9.6	0.4	0.0	0.0	0.2	1.2	1.5	4.2
Tuscaloosa, AL	85.3	9.0	0.5	0.0	0.0	0.2	1.1	0.5	3.4
Virginia Beach, VA	81.3	8.3	1.4	0.0	0.0	0.4	3.3	1.4	3.8
Washington, DC	65.8	9.3	4.8	7.8	0.8	0.9	3.3	1.5	5.9
Wichita, KS	84.0	8.7	0.4	0.0	0.0	0.4	1.7	1.2	3.5
Winston-Salem, NC	83.6	8.9	0.7	0.0	0.0	0.1	1.3	0.9	4.5
U.S.	76.3	9.0	2.4	1.9	0.6	0.5	2.7	1.4	5.2

Note: Figures are percentages and cover workers 16 years of age and older; (1) Figures cover the Metropolitan Statistical Area—see Appendix B for areas included
Source: U.S. Census Bureau, 2015-2019 American Community Survey 5-Year Estimates

Travel Time to Work: City

City	Less Than 10 Minutes	10 to 19 Minutes	20 to 29 Minutes	30 to 44 Minutes	45 to 59 Minutes	60 to 89 Minutes	90 Minutes or More
Albuquerque, NM	11.1	35.8	28.1	17.7	3.1	2.8	1.4
Allentown, PA	11.5	34.8	28.6	14.6	4.2	4.1	2.2
Anchorage, AK	16.3	44.7	23.7	10.4	2.3	1.1	1.5
Ann Arbor, MI	12.9	45.5	19.9	13.3	5.3	2.4	0.7
Athens, GA	17.4	48.3	16.9	8.8	3.6	3.0	2.0
Atlanta, GA	6.8	28.7	26.4	22.2	7.6	5.2	3.1
Austin, TX	9.5	31.8	24.3	22.1	7.1	3.8	1.4
Baton Rouge, LA	11.9	39.3	25.5	15.1	3.6	2.8	1.9
Boise City, ID	13.7	46.2	25.8	10.4	1.5	1.3	1.1
Boston, MA	7.1	19.1	19.6	30.3	12.1	9.6	2.2
Boulder, CO	17.6	45.9	16.3	10.3	5.6	3.3	1.0
Cape Coral, FL	7.9	23.9	23.5	26.5	10.4	5.8	2.0
Cedar Rapids, IA	18.0	49.5	18.0	9.7	2.2	1.5	1.1
Charleston, SC	11.4	31.9	26.3	21.1	6.5	1.5	1.3
Charlotte, NC	8.2	28.3	26.6	24.4	7.1	3.5	2.0
Chicago, IL	4.5	16.0	17.4	30.6	15.3	12.8	3.5
Cincinnati, OH	11.0	33.2	27.0	19.2	4.5	3.2	1.9
Clarksville, TN	10.8	34.3	24.5	15.6	5.7	7.4	1.7
Cleveland, OH	9.4	33.3	27.0	19.5	5.0	3.7	2.0
College Station, TX	16.5	56.7	17.6	5.9	0.5	1.8	1.2
Colorado Springs, CO	11.6	35.9	28.5	15.2	3.5	3.0	2.3
Columbia, MO	20.2	55.0	11.8	8.2	2.8	0.8	1.2
Columbia, SC	31.3	36.6	17.6	9.7	1.8	1.8	1.2
Columbus, OH	10.0	34.5	29.8	18.8	3.7	2.1	1.1
Dallas, TX	7.9	26.6	23.0	26.5	8.0	5.9	2.0
Davenport, IA	17.0	47.8	20.8	9.0	3.1	1.2	1.0
Denver, CO	7.5	28.5	24.6	26.0	8.0	3.9	1.5
Des Moines, IA	13.0	43.8	27.2	11.9	1.9	1.1	1.0
Durham, NC	9.4	37.4	26.3	18.0	4.5	3.0	1.6
Edison, NJ	6.4	23.1	17.4	18.1	11.2	14.0	9.7
El Paso, TX	9.8	34.4	27.7	19.6	4.4	2.2	1.9
Fargo, ND	20.9	54.9	17.6	3.3	1.0	1.4	0.8
Fayetteville, NC	20.6	37.5	22.3	12.5	3.3	2.1	1.6
Fort Collins, CO	16.5	42.6	19.9	11.0	5.1	3.5	1.4
Fort Wayne, IN	12.2	40.5	27.4	12.5	3.1	2.4	1.9
Fort Worth, TX	8.4	28.3	22.5	23.9	8.7	6.2	2.0
Grand Rapids, MI	15.0	42.9	24.4	11.6	3.3	2.0	0.9
Greeley, CO	16.1	37.4	16.2	14.7	5.9	7.4	2.3
Green Bay, WI	18.1	48.8	19.4	7.7	3.1	1.8	1.1
Greensboro, NC	12.1	41.4	24.1	14.7	3.5	2.6	1.6
Honolulu, HI	7.9	35.3	23.7	22.0	5.5	4.3	1.4
Houston, TX	7.3	25.5	22.2	27.8	8.9	6.4	1.9
Huntsville, AL	12.8	41.7	26.3	15.2	2.3	0.7	0.9
Indianapolis, IN	9.7	30.0	29.9	22.1	4.3	2.5	1.5
Jacksonville, FL	8.3	27.7	27.5	25.6	6.5	2.9	1.6
Kansas City, MO	11.4	33.4	28.1	20.0	4.5	1.6	1.1
Lafayette, LA	16.4	42.1	20.4	12.5	2.5	2.8	3.3
Lakeland, FL	10.8	43.4	20.1	14.4	5.8	3.5	2.0
Las Vegas, NV	6.9	23.9	29.3	28.7	6.4	2.7	2.0
Lexington, KY	12.4	38.0	27.6	14.9	3.2	2.5	1.4
Lincoln, NE	17.2	44.8	23.1	9.3	2.5	2.1	1.1
Little Rock, AR	14.0	44.4	26.5	10.8	2.0	1.3	1.1
Los Angeles, CA	5.9	21.8	19.0	28.3	10.8	10.5	3.8
Louisville, KY	9.3	32.4	30.1	20.3	4.4	2.2	1.4
Madison, WI	14.4	40.7	24.1	15.3	2.9	1.9	0.8

Table continued on following page.

City	Less Than 10 Minutes	10 to 19 Minutes	20 to 29 Minutes	30 to 44 Minutes	45 to 59 Minutes	60 to 89 Minutes	90 Minutes or More
Manchester, NH	14.1	38.3	19.2	14.5	5.9	4.8	3.2
Memphis, TN	10.2	32.9	30.2	20.5	3.6	1.6	1.0
Miami, FL	4.9	21.3	22.7	31.7	10.2	7.4	1.8
Midland, TX	16.1	49.1	17.2	11.1	2.6	2.0	1.9
Milwaukee, WI	10.1	36.6	25.8	19.3	4.0	2.7	1.5
Minneapolis, MN	8.1	32.0	30.9	20.9	4.2	2.8	1.2
Nashville, TN	8.7	29.1	26.2	23.8	7.2	3.5	1.5
New Haven, CT	13.6	40.4	20.1	13.1	4.7	4.7	3.4
New Orleans, LA	9.9	33.9	25.4	19.7	4.5	4.2	2.3
New York, NY	3.8	12.1	13.4	27.1	16.4	19.5	7.7
Oklahoma City, OK	11.2	35.5	29.5	17.7	3.3	1.5	1.3
Omaha, NE	14.0	41.0	27.8	12.4	2.3	1.5	0.9
Orlando, FL	7.8	27.2	25.9	26.7	6.8	3.4	2.2
Peoria, IL	18.6	49.5	19.8	7.6	1.9	1.8	0.8
Philadelphia, PA	6.1	18.7	19.7	28.0	12.6	10.6	4.4
Phoenix, AZ	8.8	26.7	25.5	24.9	7.5	4.7	1.9
Pittsburgh, PA	9.4	31.5	25.8	22.9	5.1	3.7	1.6
Portland, OR	7.8	26.3	27.0	24.5	7.7	4.9	1.8
Providence, RI	12.2	39.9	20.8	14.3	5.6	4.1	3.1
Provo, UT	21.3	45.3	17.3	9.0	2.7	2.9	1.4
Raleigh, NC	9.8	33.0	25.8	21.0	5.7	3.1	1.7
Reno, NV	14.4	43.5	22.1	12.1	3.7	2.7	1.5
Richmond, VA	9.8	37.9	28.5	16.4	3.2	2.6	1.5
Riverside, CA	8.9	26.2	19.9	21.7	7.6	9.4	6.4
Rochester, MN	19.3	55.7	13.6	6.3	2.2	1.7	1.2
Sacramento, CA	8.0	31.2	25.1	22.5	5.9	4.0	3.3
Salt Lake City, UT	12.3	45.3	22.8	13.0	3.6	1.9	1.0
San Antonio, TX	8.5	30.8	27.2	22.1	6.1	3.3	2.0
San Diego, CA	7.6	32.1	27.6	21.7	5.7	3.4	1.8
San Francisco, CA	3.8	18.0	20.5	30.3	12.3	11.2	3.9
San Jose, CA	5.1	22.4	22.1	27.7	10.8	8.7	3.1
Santa Rosa, CA	13.8	39.2	21.7	13.6	3.9	4.6	3.2
Savannah, GA	16.0	40.0	22.3	12.8	4.4	3.2	1.4
Seattle, WA	6.7	23.4	24.4	28.6	10.5	5.0	1.5
Sioux Falls, SD	16.1	52.3	22.4	5.4	1.4	1.3	1.1
Springfield, IL	18.2	51.5	18.5	6.1	1.8	2.3	1.6
Tallahassee, FL	14.6	44.7	23.9	12.3	2.1	1.3	1.0
Tampa, FL	11.1	30.5	23.6	21.8	6.7	4.3	1.9
Tucson, AZ	11.9	34.4	25.0	19.7	4.8	2.5	1.6
Tulsa, OK	14.6	44.5	25.7	10.5	2.0	1.5	1.2
Tuscaloosa, AL	14.6	44.8	25.9	7.4	3.5	2.8	1.0
Virginia Beach, VA	10.7	29.8	28.1	22.3	5.1	2.7	1.4
Washington, DC	4.9	18.5	22.5	32.4	12.6	7.1	2.0
Wichita, KS	14.2	44.9	27.2	9.7	1.7	1.2	1.2
Winston-Salem, NC	13.6	40.8	23.8	13.7	4.2	2.1	1.8
U.S.	12.2	28.4	20.8	20.8	8.3	6.4	2.9

Note: Figures are percentages and include workers 16 years old and over
Source: U.S. Census Bureau, 2015-2019 American Community Survey 5-Year Estimates

Travel Time to Work: Metro Area

Metro Area	Less Than 10 Minutes	10 to 19 Minutes	20 to 29 Minutes	30 to 44 Minutes	45 to 59 Minutes	60 to 89 Minutes	90 Minutes or More
Albuquerque, NM	10.8	31.6	26.2	20.5	5.7	3.6	1.6
Allentown, PA	12.4	27.6	23.1	18.1	7.4	7.3	4.1
Anchorage, AK	15.7	41.0	21.8	10.8	4.3	4.0	2.5
Ann Arbor, MI	10.6	32.7	24.5	19.3	7.6	4.1	1.3
Athens, GA	14.1	41.1	21.4	12.9	4.7	3.5	2.2
Atlanta, GA	7.0	22.1	19.6	24.9	12.3	10.4	3.8
Austin, TX	9.6	27.1	22.3	23.1	10.0	6.1	1.8
Baton Rouge, LA	9.8	27.7	22.0	22.5	9.2	6.5	2.3
Boise City, ID	12.7	34.6	25.6	18.4	5.1	2.2	1.3
Boston, MA	9.0	22.0	17.9	24.4	12.1	11.0	3.7
Boulder, CO	13.7	34.4	21.4	17.6	7.0	4.6	1.3
Cape Coral, FL	8.7	25.3	23.1	25.6	10.2	5.1	2.0
Cedar Rapids, IA	17.4	40.6	21.6	13.1	3.9	2.0	1.3
Charleston, SC	8.7	25.6	24.3	26.0	9.3	4.4	1.7
Charlotte, NC	9.3	27.1	22.7	24.0	9.6	5.2	2.1
Chicago, IL	8.2	21.5	18.4	25.2	12.4	10.8	3.5
Cincinnati, OH	10.9	27.5	25.3	23.4	7.8	3.6	1.5
Clarksville, TN	15.2	32.1	21.1	17.4	6.1	6.0	2.1
Cleveland, OH	11.2	28.3	25.5	23.1	7.3	3.3	1.4
College Station, TX	15.6	49.4	19.1	10.1	2.3	2.1	1.5
Colorado Springs, CO	11.6	32.8	27.2	17.4	5.0	3.7	2.3
Columbia, MO	17.5	45.5	17.3	12.4	4.3	1.5	1.4
Columbia, SC	12.5	29.6	23.5	22.3	6.8	3.4	1.9
Columbus, OH	11.0	29.7	26.3	21.8	6.6	3.2	1.4
Dallas, TX	8.6	25.0	21.3	25.6	10.5	7.0	2.1
Davenport, IA	17.9	37.4	24.3	13.6	3.7	1.9	1.3
Denver, CO	8.0	24.9	23.0	26.3	10.2	5.8	1.8
Des Moines, IA	15.2	35.2	27.3	16.3	3.4	1.5	1.1
Durham, NC	9.8	31.6	24.8	21.2	6.8	4.2	1.5
Edison, NJ	6.7	18.2	16.1	23.9	12.7	15.3	7.1
El Paso, TX	10.7	32.6	26.8	20.6	4.9	2.4	2.0
Fargo, ND	18.5	50.6	19.3	7.0	2.0	1.6	1.1
Fayetteville, NC	14.4	29.4	23.3	20.1	6.6	4.1	2.1
Fort Collins, CO	14.5	34.6	22.0	15.6	6.4	5.1	1.9
Fort Wayne, IN	12.7	36.5	28.2	15.0	3.5	2.3	1.8
Fort Worth, TX	8.6	25.0	21.3	25.6	10.5	7.0	2.1
Grand Rapids, MI	14.8	35.3	24.9	16.1	5.0	2.5	1.5
Greeley, CO	11.9	27.1	19.2	22.3	9.5	7.5	2.5
Green Bay, WI	18.1	40.0	21.7	12.9	3.8	2.0	1.5
Greensboro, NC	12.2	34.8	25.3	18.4	5.0	2.6	1.7
Honolulu, HI	9.0	24.9	19.6	25.3	9.8	8.5	3.0
Houston, TX	7.7	23.3	19.4	26.5	11.8	8.9	2.5
Huntsville, AL	10.3	32.1	27.8	21.7	5.6	1.6	1.0
Indianapolis, IN	11.4	27.5	24.4	24.1	7.6	3.5	1.5
Jacksonville, FL	8.8	25.4	24.4	26.0	9.0	4.5	1.8
Kansas City, MO	12.2	30.7	25.2	21.7	6.6	2.6	1.1
Lafayette, LA	15.1	32.4	21.0	18.4	5.2	3.7	4.3
Lakeland, FL	8.4	30.0	21.7	21.0	9.9	6.3	2.7
Las Vegas, NV	7.4	27.5	29.0	26.1	5.4	2.7	1.9
Lexington, KY	14.3	34.6	25.1	17.7	4.5	2.5	1.3
Lincoln, NE	17.1	41.8	23.8	11.2	2.9	2.0	1.2
Little Rock, AR	12.6	33.0	23.4	19.9	7.0	2.8	1.3
Los Angeles, CA	6.9	24.4	19.5	25.4	10.2	9.8	3.7
Louisville, KY	9.7	29.9	27.3	22.6	6.4	2.6	1.5
Madison, WI	15.6	32.6	24.3	18.6	5.2	2.5	1.1

Table continued on following page.

Metro Area	Less Than 10 Minutes	10 to 19 Minutes	20 to 29 Minutes	30 to 44 Minutes	45 to 59 Minutes	60 to 89 Minutes	90 Minutes or More
Manchester, NH	11.1	29.7	19.7	19.8	8.6	7.2	3.9
Memphis, TN	10.2	28.3	26.7	24.1	6.8	2.7	1.2
Miami, FL	6.4	22.6	22.0	27.9	10.3	8.1	2.7
Midland, TX	15.8	46.2	17.9	12.5	3.1	2.6	1.8
Milwaukee, WI	11.9	31.6	25.8	21.3	5.5	2.5	1.4
Minneapolis, MN	10.2	27.3	25.1	23.7	8.1	4.3	1.4
Nashville, TN	9.2	26.5	21.7	23.4	10.6	6.6	2.0
New Haven, CT	11.5	31.8	22.9	19.5	6.6	4.8	2.9
New Orleans, LA	10.5	30.6	22.2	20.9	7.6	5.6	2.5
New York, NY	6.7	18.2	16.1	23.9	12.7	15.3	7.1
Oklahoma City, OK	12.3	32.0	25.7	20.3	5.7	2.4	1.5
Omaha, NE	13.9	36.4	27.5	15.8	3.7	1.7	1.0
Orlando, FL	7.1	22.9	22.9	28.1	11.1	5.6	2.3
Peoria, IL	18.6	34.8	23.6	15.1	4.4	2.1	1.4
Philadelphia, PA	9.2	23.6	20.3	24.0	11.1	8.5	3.3
Phoenix, AZ	9.9	26.2	23.7	23.7	9.0	5.7	1.9
Pittsburgh, PA	11.8	26.6	21.0	22.8	9.5	6.2	2.1
Portland, OR	10.2	26.9	22.6	23.1	9.3	5.8	2.1
Providence, RI	11.9	29.9	21.9	19.6	7.6	5.9	3.2
Provo, UT	18.0	35.3	20.1	15.5	5.6	3.9	1.6
Raleigh, NC	8.9	27.5	24.4	23.9	8.7	4.8	1.9
Reno, NV	12.1	37.7	25.0	16.6	4.2	2.7	1.7
Richmond, VA	8.7	29.1	27.4	23.2	6.3	3.1	2.0
Riverside, CA	9.4	26.2	18.6	19.7	8.5	10.4	7.2
Rochester, MN	18.9	41.6	18.4	12.8	3.9	2.7	1.7
Sacramento, CA	9.9	28.2	22.3	23.0	8.1	4.9	3.5
Salt Lake City, UT	10.5	33.4	27.0	19.6	5.6	2.8	1.1
San Antonio, TX	9.0	28.1	24.3	23.2	8.5	4.7	2.2
San Diego, CA	8.2	28.9	24.3	23.5	7.7	5.1	2.2
San Francisco, CA	6.4	22.0	17.4	23.7	12.5	12.9	5.1
San Jose, CA	6.6	25.0	22.6	25.1	9.6	7.8	3.2
Santa Rosa, CA	15.1	32.2	20.4	16.8	5.8	5.9	3.9
Savannah, GA	11.0	30.6	24.1	21.2	7.7	4.1	1.3
Seattle, WA	7.7	22.2	20.8	25.5	11.4	9.0	3.4
Sioux Falls, SD	16.5	44.0	24.6	10.0	2.4	1.4	1.2
Springfield, IL	15.6	42.6	23.6	11.5	2.7	2.3	1.7
Tallahassee, FL	11.0	34.3	24.8	20.4	5.6	2.4	1.5
Tampa, FL	9.6	26.9	21.6	23.0	10.1	6.5	2.3
Tucson, AZ	10.7	28.9	24.6	23.6	7.4	3.0	1.9
Tulsa, OK	13.3	33.9	26.5	18.1	4.5	2.2	1.4
Tuscaloosa, AL	11.3	32.4	26.5	16.5	6.6	5.0	1.7
Virginia Beach, VA	11.3	30.6	23.9	21.4	7.1	4.0	1.7
Washington, DC	5.9	18.9	17.7	25.7	14.2	13.1	4.6
Wichita, KS	16.3	37.5	26.5	14.3	2.8	1.4	1.3
Winston-Salem, NC	12.0	33.3	24.5	19.1	6.1	2.8	2.1
U.S.	12.2	28.4	20.8	20.8	8.3	6.4	2.9

Note: Figures are percentages and include workers 16 years old and over; Figures cover the Metropolitan Statistical Area—see Appendix B for areas included
Source: U.S. Census Bureau, 2015-2019 American Community Survey 5-Year Estimates

2020 Presidential Election Results

City	Area Covered	Biden	Trump	Jorgensen	Hawkins	Other
Albuquerque, NM	Bernalillo County	61.0	36.6	1.5	0.5	0.4
Allentown, PA	Lehigh County	53.1	45.5	1.2	0.1	0.2
Anchorage, AK	State of Alaska	42.8	52.8	2.5	0.0	1.9
Ann Arbor, MI	Washtenaw County	72.4	25.9	0.9	0.3	0.4
Athens, GA	Clarke County	70.1	28.1	1.6	0.1	0.1
Atlanta, GA	Fulton County	72.6	26.2	1.2	0.0	0.0
Austin, TX	Travis County	71.4	26.4	1.5	0.3	0.4
Baton Rouge, LA	East Baton Rouge Parish	55.5	42.5	1.2	0.0	0.8
Boise City, ID	Ada County	46.1	50.0	2.0	0.1	1.8
Boston, MA	Suffolk County	80.6	17.5	0.9	0.5	0.5
Boulder, CO	Boulder County	77.2	20.6	1.2	0.3	0.6
Cape Coral, FL	Lee County	39.9	59.1	0.5	0.1	0.3
Cedar Rapids, IA	Linn County	55.6	41.9	1.6	0.3	0.7
Charleston, SC	Charleston County	55.5	42.6	1.5	0.3	0.1
Charlotte, NC	Mecklenburg County	66.7	31.6	1.0	0.3	0.5
Chicago, IL	Cook County	74.2	24.0	0.8	0.5	0.5
Cincinnati, OH	Hamilton County	57.1	41.3	1.2	0.3	0.0
Clarksville, TN	Montgomery County	42.3	55.0	1.9	0.2	0.7
Cleveland, OH	Cuyahoga County	66.4	32.3	0.7	0.3	0.3
College Station, TX	Brazos County	41.6	55.9	2.1	0.3	0.1
Colorado Springs, CO	El Paso County	42.7	53.5	2.4	0.3	1.0
Columbia, MO	Boone County	54.8	42.3	2.2	0.3	0.4
Columbia, SC	Richland County	68.4	30.1	1.0	0.4	0.1
Columbus, OH	Franklin County	64.7	33.4	1.2	0.3	0.4
Dallas, TX	Dallas County	64.9	33.3	1.0	0.4	0.4
Davenport, IA	Scott County	50.7	47.2	1.2	0.2	0.7
Denver, CO	Denver County	79.6	18.2	1.2	0.3	0.7
Des Moines, IA	Polk County	56.5	41.3	1.3	0.2	0.7
Durham, NC	Durham County	80.4	18.0	0.8	0.3	0.4
Edison, NJ	Middlesex County	60.2	38.2	0.7	0.3	0.6
El Paso, TX	El Paso County	66.7	31.6	1.0	0.5	0.2
Fargo, ND	Cass County	46.8	49.5	2.9	0.0	0.7
Fayetteville, NC	Cumberland County	57.4	40.8	1.1	0.3	0.4
Fort Collins, CO	Larimer County	56.2	40.8	1.8	0.3	0.9
Fort Wayne, IN	Allen County	43.2	54.3	2.2	0.0	0.3
Fort Worth, TX	Tarrant County	49.3	49.1	1.2	0.3	0.0
Grand Rapids, MI	Kent County	51.9	45.8	1.5	0.3	0.5
Greeley, CO	Weld County	39.6	57.6	1.7	0.2	0.9
Green Bay, WI	Brown County	45.5	52.7	1.3	0.0	0.5
Greensboro, NC	Guilford County	60.8	37.7	0.8	0.2	0.4
Honolulu, HI	Honolulu County	62.5	35.7	0.9	0.6	0.4
Houston, TX	Harris County	56.0	42.7	1.0	0.3	0.0
Huntsville, AL	Madison County	44.8	52.8	1.9	0.0	0.5
Indianapolis, IN	Marion County	63.3	34.3	1.8	0.1	0.4
Jacksonville, FL	Duval County	51.1	47.3	1.0	0.2	0.5
Kansas City, MO	Jackson County	59.8	37.9	1.4	0.4	0.5
Lafayette, LA	Lafayette Parish	34.7	63.3	1.3	0.0	0.7
Lakeland, FL	Polk County	42.2	56.6	0.8	0.1	0.4
Las Vegas, NV	Clark County	53.7	44.3	0.9	0.0	1.1
Lexington, KY	Fayette County	59.2	38.5	1.6	0.1	0.6
Lincoln, NE	Lancaster County	52.3	44.6	2.4	0.0	0.7
Little Rock, AR	Pulaski County	60.0	37.5	1.0	0.3	1.3
Los Angeles, CA	Los Angeles County	71.0	26.9	0.8	0.5	0.8
Louisville, KY	Jefferson County	59.1	39.0	1.2	0.1	0.7
Madison, WI	Dane County	75.5	22.9	1.1	0.1	0.6
Manchester, NH	Hillsborough County	52.8	45.2	1.7	0.0	0.3

Table continued on following page.

City	Area Covered	Biden	Trump	Jorgensen	Hawkins	Other
Memphis, TN	Shelby County	64.4	34.0	0.6	0.2	0.8
Miami, FL	Miami-Dade County	53.3	46.0	0.3	0.1	0.3
Midland, TX	Midland County	20.9	77.3	1.3	0.2	0.2
Milwaukee, WI	Milwaukee County	69.1	29.3	0.9	0.0	0.7
Minneapolis, MN	Hennepin County	70.5	27.2	1.0	0.3	1.0
Nashville, TN	Davidson County	64.5	32.4	1.1	0.2	1.8
New Haven, CT	New Haven County	58.0	40.6	0.9	0.4	0.0
New Orleans, LA	Orleans Parish	83.1	15.0	0.9	0.0	1.0
New York, NY	Bronx County	83.3	15.9	0.2	0.3	0.3
New York, NY	Kings County	76.8	22.1	0.3	0.4	0.4
New York, NY	New York County	86.4	12.2	0.5	0.4	0.5
New York, NY	Queens County	72.0	26.9	0.3	0.4	0.4
New York, NY	Richmond County	42.0	56.9	0.4	0.3	0.4
Oklahoma City, OK	Oklahoma County	48.1	49.2	1.8	0.0	0.9
Omaha, NE	Douglas County	54.4	43.1	2.0	0.0	0.6
Orlando, FL	Orange County	60.9	37.8	0.7	0.2	0.4
Peoria, IL	Peoria County	51.9	45.6	1.6	0.6	0.4
Philadelphia, PA	Philadelphia County	81.2	17.9	0.7	0.1	0.2
Phoenix, AZ	Maricopa County	50.1	48.0	1.5	0.0	0.3
Pittsburgh, PA	Allegheny County	59.4	39.0	1.2	0.0	0.4
Portland, OR	Multnomah County	79.2	17.9	1.2	0.6	1.0
Providence, RI	Providence County	60.5	37.6	0.8	0.0	1.0
Provo, UT	Utah County	26.3	66.7	3.6	0.3	3.1
Raleigh, NC	Wake County	62.3	35.8	1.2	0.3	0.5
Reno, NV	Washoe County	50.8	46.3	1.4	0.0	1.5
Richmond, VA	Richmond City	82.9	14.9	1.5	0.0	0.6
Riverside, CA	Riverside County	53.0	45.0	1.0	0.3	0.6
Rochester, MN	Olmsted County	54.2	43.4	1.2	0.3	0.9
Sacramento, CA	Sacramento County	61.4	36.1	1.4	0.5	0.7
Salt Lake City, UT	Salt Lake County	53.0	42.1	2.2	0.4	2.2
San Antonio, TX	Bexar County	58.2	40.1	1.1	0.4	0.2
San Diego, CA	San Diego County	60.2	37.5	1.3	0.5	0.5
San Francisco, CA	San Francisco County	85.3	12.7	0.7	0.6	0.7
San Jose, CA	Santa Clara County	72.6	25.2	1.1	0.5	0.6
Santa Rosa, CA	Sonoma County	74.5	23.0	1.3	0.6	0.6
Savannah, GA	Chatham County	58.6	39.9	1.4	0.0	0.0
Seattle, WA	King County	75.0	22.2	1.5	0.5	0.8
Sioux Falls, SD	Minnehaha County	43.8	53.3	2.8	0.0	0.0
Springfield, IL	Sangamon County	46.7	51.1	1.4	0.6	0.3
Tallahassee, FL	Leon County	63.3	35.1	0.8	0.2	0.5
Tampa, FL	Hillsborough County	52.7	45.8	0.8	0.2	0.5
Tucson, AZ	Pima County	58.4	39.8	1.5	0.0	0.3
Tulsa, OK	Tulsa County	40.9	56.5	1.8	0.0	0.8
Tuscaloosa, AL	Tuscaloosa County	41.9	56.7	1.0	0.0	0.4
Virginia Beach, VA	Virginia Beach City	51.6	46.2	1.8	0.0	0.4
Washington, DC	District of Columbia	92.1	5.4	0.6	0.5	1.4
Wichita, KS	Sedgwick County	42.6	54.4	2.4	0.0	0.5
Winston-Salem, NC	Forsyth County	56.2	42.3	0.9	0.2	0.4
U.S.	U.S.	51.3	46.8	1.2	0.3	0.5

Note: Results are percentages and may not add to 100% due to rounding
Source: Dave Leip's Atlas of U.S. Presidential Elections

House Price Index (HPI)

Metro Area[1]	National Ranking[3]	Quarterly Change (%)	One-Year Change (%)	Five-Year Change (%)	Since 1991Q1 (%)
Albuquerque, NM	42	2.20	7.86	27.05	163.46
Allentown, PA	59	2.10	7.47	23.78	102.86
Anchorage, AK	205	1.39	4.88	9.73	184.56
Ann Arbor, MI	224	0.98	3.78	29.65	164.45
Athens, GA	66	1.41	7.40	43.79	181.78
Atlanta, GA	110	1.95	6.57	40.75	164.55
Austin, TX	30	3.27	8.26	41.08	401.86
Baton Rouge, LA	230	1.37	3.54	17.61	188.52
Boise City, ID	1	4.90	13.83	78.91	350.41
Boston, MA[2]	167	1.93	5.51	29.37	228.40
Boulder, CO	227	1.79	3.59	36.23	436.16
Cape Coral, FL	84	3.11	7.07	33.53	188.18
Cedar Rapids, IA	218	1.99	4.00	17.00	130.16
Charleston, SC	130	1.32	6.11	36.39	284.93
Charlotte, NC	60	2.55	7.46	41.48	183.15
Chicago, IL[2]	239	1.11	2.98	16.74	122.65
Cincinnati, OH	98	1.97	6.79	31.23	131.06
Clarksville, TN	n/a	n/a	n/a	n/a	n/a
Cleveland, OH	50	2.24	7.63	30.38	104.70
College Station, TX	n/a	n/a	n/a	n/a	n/a
Colorado Springs, CO	19	3.08	8.89	51.30	301.84
Columbia, MO	212	1.63	4.42	20.40	150.92
Columbia, SC	181	1.37	5.23	24.67	125.47
Columbus, OH	65	2.05	7.40	37.73	163.06
Dallas, TX[2]	206	2.07	4.81	38.75	203.48
Davenport, IA	225	0.97	3.73	15.46	153.27
Denver, CO	164	1.71	5.57	42.32	404.42
Des Moines, IA	237	1.39	3.15	20.11	154.39
Durham, NC	161	1.51	5.61	34.97	182.89
Edison, NJ[2]	220	1.50	3.91	23.15	199.59
El Paso, TX	158	1.05	5.68	18.03	118.41
Fargo, ND	240	0.70	2.82	16.07	201.82
Fayetteville, NC	n/a	n/a	n/a	n/a	n/a
Fort Collins, CO	217	1.38	4.19	38.15	365.72
Fort Wayne, IN	53	1.29	7.55	35.84	111.44
Fort Worth, TX[2]	191	2.39	5.13	42.54	191.04
Grand Rapids, MI	71	2.11	7.32	44.57	175.35
Greeley, CO	177	1.80	5.33	46.65	333.63
Green Bay, WI	169	2.46	5.48	28.92	157.42
Greensboro, NC	128	1.99	6.14	27.91	106.32
Honolulu, HI	250	1.23	0.53	16.08	154.83
Houston, TX	211	1.45	4.53	23.50	211.24
Huntsville, AL	9	3.60	9.98	30.56	124.28
Indianapolis, IN	46	2.17	7.74	36.43	135.15
Jacksonville, FL	136	2.34	6.06	43.85	224.14
Kansas City, MO	75	2.00	7.29	37.81	175.77
Lafayette, LA	221	0.62	3.89	8.70	180.99
Lakeland, FL	8	4.29	10.11	53.44	194.73
Las Vegas, NV	171	1.70	5.46	50.47	163.25
Lexington, KY	200	1.46	5.04	28.47	155.18
Lincoln, NE	198	2.22	5.09	30.00	177.71
Little Rock, AR	196	1.79	5.10	16.24	131.58
Los Angeles, CA[2]	193	1.98	5.13	31.04	214.04
Louisville, KY	111	2.46	6.56	29.08	178.89
Madison, WI	202	1.80	4.96	27.32	218.96

Table continued on following page.

Metro Area[1]	National Ranking[3]	Quarterly Change (%)	One-Year Change (%)	Five-Year Change (%)	Since 1991Q1 (%)
Manchester, NH	17	3.48	9.02	33.95	167.53
Memphis, TN	90	1.82	6.94	33.17	120.34
Miami, FL[2]	124	1.83	6.32	38.91	334.89
Midland, TX	n/a	n/a	n/a	n/a	n/a
Milwaukee, WI	172	1.59	5.45	26.53	171.34
Minneapolis, MN	157	1.56	5.70	30.96	210.96
Nashville, TN	88	1.88	6.96	45.40	266.19
New Haven, CT	99	2.80	6.78	15.33	80.58
New Orleans, LA	174	2.09	5.37	22.52	226.15
New York, NY[2]	220	1.50	3.91	23.15	199.59
Oklahoma City, OK	182	1.07	5.23	21.46	179.09
Omaha, NE	154	1.72	5.74	31.76	176.42
Orlando, FL	119	1.83	6.36	44.80	198.33
Peoria, IL	238	0.87	3.00	6.40	120.92
Philadelphia, PA[2]	145	1.50	5.90	33.20	191.57
Phoenix, AZ	7	3.44	10.26	47.39	283.82
Pittsburgh, PA	123	1.67	6.33	26.47	167.39
Portland, OR	127	2.22	6.27	37.96	381.42
Providence, RI	89	2.66	6.95	31.83	154.93
Provo, UT	23	3.08	8.61	46.91	339.23
Raleigh, NC	159	1.84	5.67	34.46	180.65
Reno, NV	96	2.61	6.81	48.07	229.64
Richmond, VA	134	2.05	6.10	28.56	172.25
Riverside, CA	86	2.74	7.03	34.65	169.25
Rochester, MN	116	1.70	6.45	32.58	175.69
Sacramento, CA	93	2.73	6.92	37.42	166.72
Salt Lake City, UT	15	3.24	9.07	50.25	408.84
San Antonio, TX	149	2.10	5.83	34.99	224.63
San Diego, CA	141	1.97	6.01	30.38	235.91
San Francisco, CA[2]	253	-3.20	-6.72	10.12	283.50
San Jose, CA	251	0.55	0.10	18.04	296.60
Santa Rosa, CA	246	1.59	2.15	26.52	225.13
Savannah, GA	214	0.50	4.40	33.56	221.18
Seattle, WA[2]	97	2.16	6.81	48.46	324.48
Sioux Falls, SD	139	2.09	6.03	29.70	212.39
Springfield, IL	248	0.83	1.79	8.16	85.25
Tallahassee, FL	186	1.55	5.20	30.45	154.52
Tampa, FL	33	2.36	8.17	52.43	254.29
Tucson, AZ	29	2.33	8.30	39.73	202.45
Tulsa, OK	179	1.98	5.26	22.61	153.16
Tuscaloosa, AL	n/a	n/a	n/a	n/a	n/a
Virginia Beach, VA	144	1.54	5.90	17.40	170.16
Washington, DC[2]	189	1.67	5.16	21.40	197.71
Wichita, KS	49	1.50	7.67	27.26	136.03
Winston-Salem, NC	94	2.58	6.92	28.40	118.04
U.S.[4]	—	3.81	10.77	38.99	205.12

Note: The HPI is a weighted repeat sales index. It measures average price changes in repeat sales or refinancings on the same properties. This information is obtained by reviewing repeat mortgage transactions on single-family properties whose mortgages have been purchased or securitized by Fannie Mae or Freddie Mac since January 1975; (1) figures cover the Metropolitan Statistical Area (MSA) unless noted otherwise—see Appendix B for areas included; (2) Metropolitan Division—see Appendix B for areas included; (3) Rankings are based on annual percentage change, for all MSAs containing at least 15,000 transactions over the last 10 years and ranges from 1 to 253; (4) figures based on a weighted division average; all figures are for the period ended December 31, 2020; n/a not available
Source: Federal Housing Finance Agency, Change in Metropolitan Area House Price Indexes, April 7, 2021

Home Value Distribution: City

Area	Under $50,000	$50,000 -$99,999	$100,000 -$149,999	$150,000 -$199,999	$200,000 -$299,999	$300,000 -$499,999	$500,000 -$999,999	$1,000,000 or more
Albuquerque, NM	4.5	4.4	16.9	25.1	29.5	15.9	3.3	0.5
Allentown, PA	4.5	22.0	35.2	24.0	8.7	4.1	1.1	0.4
Anchorage, AK	5.3	1.9	4.8	7.0	26.9	40.9	12.2	1.0
Ann Arbor, MI	1.3	3.6	6.0	8.2	25.2	37.6	15.7	2.4
Athens, GA	6.3	12.9	19.9	21.9	20.3	12.7	5.4	0.7
Atlanta, GA	4.5	10.1	9.6	10.6	16.6	19.7	20.2	8.8
Austin, TX	2.2	2.2	4.8	9.1	24.3	33.0	20.1	4.3
Baton Rouge, LA	5.6	17.7	15.6	19.4	21.4	12.9	5.8	1.6
Boise City, ID	3.9	1.9	8.6	17.4	31.6	26.6	9.0	1.0
Boston, MA	1.6	0.3	0.4	1.4	8.2	34.1	40.4	13.5
Boulder, CO	3.8	1.7	1.8	3.3	4.1	13.3	48.9	23.1
Cape Coral, FL	1.6	3.1	11.1	22.6	34.1	20.2	6.5	0.9
Cedar Rapids, IA	5.5	16.3	34.2	20.9	16.3	5.1	1.4	0.2
Charleston, SC	1.5	2.6	4.6	8.2	26.4	31.1	19.0	6.6
Charlotte, NC	2.1	8.2	17.3	17.6	21.0	19.5	10.9	3.4
Chicago, IL	2.7	7.0	11.1	15.0	23.8	24.1	12.5	3.9
Cincinnati, OH	6.9	25.4	22.2	11.9	14.7	11.5	6.2	1.3
Clarksville, TN	4.3	14.1	28.9	26.6	19.0	5.6	0.9	0.5
Cleveland, OH	28.8	44.0	14.0	5.9	3.6	2.1	1.2	0.4
College Station, TX	2.1	1.3	7.4	21.9	35.6	24.9	6.1	0.9
Colorado Springs, CO	3.0	2.1	6.5	14.5	33.6	30.4	8.6	1.2
Columbia, MO	3.4	7.4	19.0	22.8	25.7	17.2	4.2	0.3
Columbia, SC	4.5	15.3	19.7	16.0	15.6	16.5	10.9	1.6
Columbus, OH	5.9	19.5	23.8	20.7	19.8	7.9	2.0	0.3
Dallas, TX	6.7	19.2	15.4	10.7	12.6	17.6	13.2	4.6
Davenport, IA	6.3	24.6	28.4	16.1	15.6	7.4	1.1	0.4
Denver, CO	1.3	1.6	3.3	6.8	19.5	34.6	27.3	5.6
Des Moines, IA	5.9	21.6	33.1	20.5	12.1	4.8	1.8	0.2
Durham, NC	1.8	5.3	14.5	20.5	30.8	20.3	5.9	1.0
Edison, NJ	2.1	1.8	1.9	2.7	17.0	47.4	25.4	1.6
El Paso, TX	5.1	25.0	32.7	18.5	12.5	4.8	1.2	0.3
Fargo, ND	4.0	4.3	12.6	25.0	30.8	18.6	4.0	0.6
Fayetteville, NC	5.0	26.2	28.2	19.3	13.7	5.5	1.7	0.3
Fort Collins, CO	3.2	1.1	1.5	3.6	19.8	52.8	16.7	1.3
Fort Wayne, IN	10.6	30.1	28.9	16.1	9.6	3.7	0.9	0.1
Fort Worth, TX	6.2	17.3	17.6	19.3	22.9	11.9	4.0	0.8
Grand Rapids, MI	4.7	19.6	30.0	24.3	15.0	5.0	1.3	0.2
Greeley, CO	7.1	2.5	7.2	15.2	36.3	27.2	4.3	0.2
Green Bay, WI	3.3	20.8	35.3	20.4	12.8	5.7	1.5	0.3
Greensboro, NC	3.5	19.2	24.5	18.3	18.2	11.4	3.7	1.2
Honolulu, HI	0.8	0.8	0.8	1.4	7.2	22.6	42.5	24.0
Houston, TX	5.4	19.6	18.1	13.0	14.5	15.8	10.0	3.6
Huntsville, AL	5.3	17.9	15.0	16.6	22.8	16.6	4.6	1.1
Indianapolis, IN	7.1	22.9	27.0	18.8	12.5	8.0	3.1	0.7
Jacksonville, FL	7.4	15.2	17.4	19.0	24.0	11.9	3.9	1.2
Kansas City, MO	11.2	17.4	19.4	18.4	18.5	10.8	3.6	0.7
Lafayette, LA	5.5	8.2	14.9	23.2	23.8	16.0	6.5	1.9
Lakeland, FL	18.2	15.4	16.7	19.4	18.7	8.6	2.6	0.5
Las Vegas, NV	2.4	4.3	8.7	15.4	31.4	27.3	8.6	1.9
Lexington, KY	2.6	8.8	21.0	21.1	22.4	16.6	6.0	1.4
Lincoln, NE	3.5	9.8	25.5	23.9	23.3	11.2	2.4	0.5
Little Rock, AR	6.5	19.3	16.8	17.5	15.9	15.4	7.0	1.6
Los Angeles, CA	1.2	0.8	0.7	0.8	4.8	25.2	44.5	22.1
Louisville, KY	5.5	15.7	24.8	18.2	17.6	13.0	4.4	0.8
Madison, WI	1.6	2.6	8.5	18.5	35.6	25.7	6.7	0.8

Table continued on following page.

Area	Under $50,000	$50,000-$99,999	$100,000-$149,999	$150,000-$199,999	$200,000-$299,999	$300,000-$499,999	$500,000-$999,999	$1,000,000 or more
Manchester, NH	1.9	3.0	8.3	21.6	47.9	15.7	1.4	0.2
Memphis, TN	14.5	34.7	17.4	12.4	9.9	6.8	3.3	1.0
Miami, FL	2.2	4.6	6.0	9.8	24.1	29.6	16.1	7.5
Midland, TX	4.9	9.0	12.7	17.4	28.4	18.3	7.8	1.4
Milwaukee, WI	9.1	27.3	29.6	17.9	10.6	3.6	1.5	0.4
Minneapolis, MN	1.4	4.0	10.7	16.1	31.3	24.7	10.0	1.9
Nashville, TN	2.1	5.0	13.5	17.4	27.0	23.1	10.0	1.9
New Haven, CT	2.7	7.9	14.1	25.8	28.0	14.9	6.0	0.7
New Orleans, LA	2.8	7.9	13.8	18.6	19.9	20.5	13.0	3.7
New York, NY	2.9	1.3	1.9	2.4	6.6	23.7	41.4	19.9
Oklahoma City, OK	7.9	18.0	19.9	20.8	18.9	10.2	3.4	0.8
Omaha, NE	4.2	14.8	25.8	21.8	19.0	10.5	3.2	0.7
Orlando, FL	2.9	10.7	13.4	13.0	24.6	24.6	8.8	2.1
Peoria, IL	12.6	25.4	21.8	15.6	13.8	8.1	2.4	0.4
Philadelphia, PA	6.7	19.4	18.6	18.0	19.6	11.3	5.1	1.3
Phoenix, AZ	4.3	6.3	11.0	17.7	26.4	23.0	9.6	1.7
Pittsburgh, PA	11.8	27.6	18.0	12.8	12.4	10.6	5.7	1.0
Portland, OR	1.9	0.8	1.5	3.8	16.7	41.6	30.5	3.2
Providence, RI	2.1	5.3	16.9	25.7	23.9	15.6	8.6	1.9
Provo, UT	3.5	1.2	6.4	13.5	34.5	29.0	9.8	2.2
Raleigh, NC	2.0	2.7	11.4	19.4	27.1	24.8	10.8	1.8
Reno, NV	4.1	2.9	3.7	7.5	22.3	43.2	13.7	2.5
Richmond, VA	2.0	11.4	13.9	15.4	20.8	21.7	11.5	3.3
Riverside, CA	2.9	1.6	1.7	3.4	17.5	55.6	15.4	1.9
Rochester, MN	2.9	4.5	16.5	26.0	27.6	17.9	4.2	0.4
Sacramento, CA	2.5	2.0	3.5	7.2	26.0	39.6	17.2	2.0
Salt Lake City, UT	2.9	1.4	6.7	13.0	23.6	29.7	19.5	3.3
San Antonio, TX	6.8	24.5	20.0	18.4	17.9	9.4	2.5	0.6
San Diego, CA	1.6	1.0	0.8	1.1	5.3	27.4	47.6	15.3
San Francisco, CA	1.1	0.5	0.4	0.3	1.2	3.9	34.9	57.8
San Jose, CA	1.5	1.4	1.4	0.9	1.9	7.2	50.0	35.6
Santa Rosa, CA	2.7	2.0	1.7	1.5	5.2	30.6	50.0	6.2
Savannah, GA	6.1	20.2	20.4	19.5	18.7	9.4	4.6	1.1
Seattle, WA	0.6	0.4	0.4	1.0	5.0	22.3	52.5	17.8
Sioux Falls, SD	5.5	6.6	17.7	24.4	27.0	14.4	3.8	0.7
Springfield, IL	10.0	24.9	23.4	15.7	15.7	7.9	2.3	0.2
Tallahassee, FL	2.9	9.9	16.8	19.3	26.8	19.3	4.0	1.0
Tampa, FL	3.8	10.8	11.7	14.7	20.7	20.1	13.6	4.5
Tucson, AZ	10.6	13.5	22.6	24.6	19.6	6.8	1.9	0.3
Tulsa, OK	9.0	22.8	22.3	15.7	13.8	10.4	4.9	1.2
Tuscaloosa, AL	4.4	11.2	21.2	19.0	19.4	15.1	8.2	1.4
Virginia Beach, VA	2.2	1.5	6.1	12.6	33.7	30.5	11.1	2.3
Washington, DC	1.2	0.8	1.1	1.9	9.5	25.7	41.0	18.8
Wichita, KS	8.4	26.6	22.6	18.2	14.6	7.0	2.3	0.3
Winston-Salem, NC	6.6	19.7	24.8	20.8	13.4	8.8	5.2	0.8
U.S.	6.9	12.0	13.3	14.0	19.6	19.3	11.4	3.4

Note: Figures are percentages and cover owner-occupied housing units.
Source: U.S. Census Bureau, 2015-2019 American Community Survey 5-Year Estimates

Home Value Distribution: Metro Area

MSA[1]	Under $50,000	$50,000 -$99,999	$100,000 -$149,999	$150,000 -$199,999	$200,000 -$299,999	$300,000 -$499,999	$500,000 -$999,999	$1,000,000 or more
Albuquerque, NM	5.8	7.6	16.8	22.7	25.8	15.5	4.8	1.0
Allentown, PA	3.8	7.3	14.4	20.0	28.2	21.4	4.3	0.6
Anchorage, AK	4.9	2.6	5.2	9.3	29.6	37.3	10.3	0.9
Ann Arbor, MI	5.5	6.1	8.0	13.7	24.9	28.8	11.3	1.7
Athens, GA	8.8	12.2	17.4	17.3	21.0	16.1	6.2	1.0
Atlanta, GA	3.7	9.2	14.8	18.0	22.5	20.7	9.3	1.8
Austin, TX	3.3	3.9	6.9	12.7	27.8	28.3	13.9	3.2
Baton Rouge, LA	8.7	12.3	15.0	20.4	24.0	14.3	4.3	1.0
Boise City, ID	4.4	4.2	11.1	17.9	28.9	25.3	7.3	1.0
Boston, MA	1.6	1.0	1.6	3.6	14.5	38.5	31.8	7.4
Boulder, CO	2.9	1.1	1.3	2.9	10.6	31.6	38.3	11.3
Cape Coral, FL	6.2	8.9	11.8	16.4	24.5	20.2	9.2	2.8
Cedar Rapids, IA	6.5	13.7	27.1	19.7	20.8	9.2	2.4	0.6
Charleston, SC	6.0	7.5	11.6	15.3	23.1	21.1	11.7	3.7
Charlotte, NC	4.8	11.4	16.7	17.1	21.5	18.7	7.8	1.9
Chicago, IL	3.2	7.2	12.4	16.4	25.5	23.1	9.9	2.4
Cincinnati, OH	4.8	15.3	21.4	18.8	21.0	13.6	4.3	0.7
Clarksville, TN	6.6	17.3	23.7	21.4	19.5	9.0	1.8	0.7
Cleveland, OH	7.6	20.0	21.6	17.9	18.4	10.7	3.0	0.7
College Station, TX	10.0	13.0	13.2	18.1	23.3	16.1	5.3	1.0
Colorado Springs, CO	3.1	2.0	6.1	14.3	31.7	31.1	10.4	1.2
Columbia, MO	5.4	11.2	19.9	20.9	22.9	14.8	4.3	0.7
Columbia, SC	8.6	16.9	22.6	18.7	17.1	11.2	4.2	0.8
Columbus, OH	4.8	13.1	18.2	18.8	23.1	16.5	4.9	0.7
Dallas, TX	4.5	11.1	14.5	15.9	23.1	20.9	7.9	1.9
Davenport, IA	7.3	23.5	24.9	17.5	15.3	9.1	2.0	0.4
Denver, CO	2.2	1.3	2.3	5.3	19.2	42.7	23.3	3.5
Des Moines, IA	4.5	11.9	19.7	19.9	24.4	14.9	4.2	0.5
Durham, NC	5.0	7.8	14.2	16.4	23.6	22.0	9.7	1.4
Edison, NJ	2.0	1.4	2.4	3.9	13.2	35.1	32.1	9.9
El Paso, TX	7.7	26.8	31.4	17.2	11.2	4.3	1.1	0.2
Fargo, ND	3.7	5.3	13.1	23.0	30.1	19.4	4.8	0.7
Fayetteville, NC	8.8	21.8	23.2	20.1	18.1	6.2	1.5	0.4
Fort Collins, CO	3.9	1.4	1.6	4.7	20.7	46.4	19.1	2.2
Fort Wayne, IN	8.4	24.8	26.3	17.2	13.7	7.2	2.0	0.4
Fort Worth, TX	4.5	11.1	14.5	15.9	23.1	20.9	7.9	1.9
Grand Rapids, MI	6.7	11.6	20.2	21.8	22.4	13.0	3.6	0.7
Greeley, CO	4.6	2.7	4.6	9.7	28.6	36.6	12.0	1.1
Green Bay, WI	4.0	11.9	22.8	22.2	24.5	11.3	2.6	0.6
Greensboro, NC	7.0	19.7	23.7	17.7	17.2	10.7	3.4	0.7
Honolulu, HI	0.7	0.6	0.8	1.0	5.0	19.6	54.6	17.7
Houston, TX	5.3	12.1	16.7	17.8	22.0	16.9	6.9	2.3
Huntsville, AL	6.4	13.8	17.3	19.0	23.7	15.1	3.9	0.8
Indianapolis, IN	5.6	16.1	22.3	19.0	18.5	13.4	4.4	0.8
Jacksonville, FL	5.8	12.0	14.1	16.8	24.6	18.1	6.7	1.8
Kansas City, MO	6.2	12.8	17.6	18.7	22.7	16.1	5.0	0.9
Lafayette, LA	14.7	16.0	16.1	19.5	19.3	10.1	3.5	0.8
Lakeland, FL	14.7	18.2	16.8	18.6	20.6	8.3	2.2	0.6
Las Vegas, NV	3.5	4.3	8.0	14.1	31.6	28.6	8.2	1.7
Lexington, KY	3.5	9.9	22.0	20.7	21.4	15.4	5.9	1.3
Lincoln, NE	3.2	9.4	23.4	22.6	23.4	13.8	3.7	0.5
Little Rock, AR	7.9	17.6	22.4	19.5	18.4	10.1	3.2	0.9
Los Angeles, CA	1.9	1.4	0.9	1.2	4.9	25.2	47.5	17.0
Louisville, KY	4.8	13.7	22.6	18.9	20.8	13.6	4.5	0.9
Madison, WI	2.1	3.9	9.7	16.6	32.4	26.6	7.5	1.2

Table continued on following page.

Appendix A: Comparative Statistics

MSA[1]	Under $50,000	$50,000 -$99,999	$100,000 -$149,999	$150,000 -$199,999	$200,000 -$299,999	$300,000 -$499,999	$500,000 -$999,999	$1,000,000 or more
Manchester, NH	1.9	2.5	5.9	12.0	37.5	32.8	6.7	0.7
Memphis, TN	9.1	21.8	18.2	16.5	18.6	11.2	3.6	0.9
Miami, FL	4.0	7.1	8.7	11.9	22.9	28.5	12.5	4.5
Midland, TX	8.7	10.4	11.9	15.9	26.2	17.9	7.5	1.3
Milwaukee, WI	3.7	8.8	15.1	18.2	27.1	20.0	6.0	1.1
Minneapolis, MN	2.7	2.7	7.9	16.7	32.8	27.1	8.8	1.4
Nashville, TN	2.9	6.1	13.1	16.5	25.6	23.0	10.5	2.3
New Haven, CT	2.0	4.9	10.6	17.0	29.8	26.8	7.6	1.2
New Orleans, LA	4.2	9.0	16.8	20.8	24.8	16.4	6.4	1.6
New York, NY	2.0	1.4	2.4	3.9	13.2	35.1	32.1	9.9
Oklahoma City, OK	7.5	17.7	21.3	19.6	18.4	10.9	3.7	1.0
Omaha, NE	3.9	12.1	23.4	21.0	22.0	13.5	3.4	0.7
Orlando, FL	6.1	8.5	11.7	17.0	28.6	20.3	6.2	1.7
Peoria, IL	8.6	25.9	23.0	17.4	15.3	7.6	1.9	0.4
Philadelphia, PA	3.4	7.3	10.2	14.8	26.3	26.2	10.1	1.7
Phoenix, AZ	5.5	5.2	8.7	15.2	28.2	25.2	9.8	2.2
Pittsburgh, PA	8.8	20.3	19.2	17.8	17.5	12.0	3.6	0.7
Portland, OR	3.2	1.3	2.1	4.9	21.0	42.8	22.1	2.6
Providence, RI	2.1	2.0	5.7	14.1	33.3	31.2	10.0	1.7
Provo, UT	2.4	0.9	3.6	10.1	32.2	37.0	12.1	1.7
Raleigh, NC	3.5	5.0	11.9	15.5	25.7	27.6	9.6	1.3
Reno, NV	4.0	2.8	4.2	7.5	23.6	38.4	15.4	4.1
Richmond, VA	2.4	5.3	11.7	18.2	29.4	23.7	8.2	1.2
Riverside, CA	4.9	3.4	4.1	6.8	21.0	40.8	17.0	2.0
Rochester, MN	4.6	6.8	16.1	22.2	24.5	19.3	5.5	1.0
Sacramento, CA	2.8	1.7	2.2	4.5	17.7	42.3	25.8	3.0
Salt Lake City, UT	2.9	1.2	5.2	11.5	29.6	34.2	13.7	1.7
San Antonio, TX	6.8	18.2	16.6	17.7	20.5	14.2	4.9	1.2
San Diego, CA	2.5	1.9	1.4	1.4	5.2	29.3	46.1	12.2
San Francisco, CA	1.2	0.9	0.8	0.8	2.8	13.2	43.9	36.2
San Jose, CA	1.3	1.0	1.2	0.9	1.8	6.4	40.1	47.3
Santa Rosa, CA	2.6	2.6	1.6	1.2	4.2	22.2	51.9	13.7
Savannah, GA	5.7	11.2	17.1	19.2	23.1	14.9	7.1	1.6
Seattle, WA	2.5	1.2	2.0	4.2	15.3	34.2	32.0	8.5
Sioux Falls, SD	5.6	7.7	16.6	22.7	26.5	15.7	4.4	0.8
Springfield, IL	8.2	23.3	22.4	17.8	18.2	8.0	1.9	0.2
Tallahassee, FL	8.3	15.3	16.5	16.9	22.4	15.2	4.6	0.8
Tampa, FL	8.8	13.0	13.5	16.7	23.7	16.4	6.4	1.6
Tucson, AZ	8.4	10.7	16.2	19.9	22.5	15.4	5.8	1.0
Tulsa, OK	9.4	18.7	21.7	19.4	17.3	9.4	3.4	0.8
Tuscaloosa, AL	13.0	14.9	17.5	20.5	19.7	9.8	3.9	0.7
Virginia Beach, VA	3.3	3.8	10.2	17.0	31.5	25.1	7.7	1.2
Washington, DC	1.5	1.0	2.1	4.7	17.1	35.8	31.2	6.7
Wichita, KS	8.3	24.2	22.6	19.1	15.6	7.8	2.0	0.4
Winston-Salem, NC	7.4	16.9	24.5	20.0	17.2	9.9	3.5	0.6
U.S.	6.9	12.0	13.3	14.0	19.6	19.3	11.4	3.4

Note: (1) Figures cover the Metropolitan Statistical Area (MSA)—see Appendix B for areas included; Figures are percentages and cover owner-occupied housing units.
Source: U.S. Census Bureau, 2015-2019 American Community Survey 5-Year Estimates

Homeownership Rate

Metro Area	2012	2013	2014	2015	2016	2017	2018	2019	2020
Albuquerque, NM	62.8	65.9	64.4	64.3	66.9	67.0	67.9	70.0	69.5
Allentown, PA	75.5	71.5	68.2	69.2	68.9	73.1	72.1	67.8	68.8
Anchorage, AK	n/a	n/a	n/a	n/a	n/a	n/a	n/a	n/a	n/a
Ann Arbor, MI	n/a	n/a	n/a	n/a	n/a	n/a	n/a	n/a	n/a
Athens, GA	n/a	n/a	n/a	n/a	n/a	n/a	n/a	n/a	n/a
Atlanta, GA	62.1	61.6	61.6	61.7	61.5	62.4	64.0	64.2	66.4
Austin, TX	60.1	59.6	61.1	57.5	56.5	55.6	56.1	59.0	65.4
Baton Rouge, LA	71.4	66.6	64.8	64.2	64.8	66.9	66.6	66.2	72.1
Boise City, ID	n/a	n/a	n/a	n/a	n/a	n/a	n/a	n/a	n/a
Boston, MA	66.0	66.3	62.8	59.3	58.9	58.8	61.0	60.9	61.2
Boulder, CO	n/a	n/a	n/a	n/a	n/a	n/a	n/a	n/a	n/a
Cape Coral, FL	n/a	n/a	n/a	62.9	66.5	65.5	75.1	72.0	77.4
Cedar Rapids, IA	n/a	n/a	n/a	n/a	n/a	n/a	n/a	n/a	n/a
Charleston, SC	n/a	n/a	n/a	65.8	62.1	67.7	68.8	70.7	75.5
Charlotte, NC	58.3	58.9	58.1	62.3	66.2	64.6	67.9	72.3	73.3
Chicago, IL	67.1	68.2	66.3	64.3	64.5	64.1	64.6	63.4	66.0
Cincinnati, OH	63.4	63.3	65.5	65.9	64.9	65.7	67.3	67.4	71.1
Clarksville, TN	n/a	n/a	n/a	n/a	n/a	n/a	n/a	n/a	n/a
Cleveland, OH	64.2	65.8	69.2	68.4	64.8	66.6	66.7	64.4	66.3
College Station, TX	n/a	n/a	n/a	n/a	n/a	n/a	n/a	n/a	n/a
Colorado Springs, CO	n/a	n/a	n/a	n/a	n/a	n/a	n/a	n/a	n/a
Columbia, MO	n/a	n/a	n/a	n/a	n/a	n/a	n/a	n/a	n/a
Columbia, SC	65.6	68.9	69.5	66.1	63.9	70.7	69.3	65.9	69.7
Columbus, OH	60.7	60.5	60.0	59.0	57.5	57.9	64.8	65.7	65.6
Dallas, TX	61.8	59.9	57.7	57.8	59.7	61.8	62.0	60.6	64.7
Davenport, IA	n/a	n/a	n/a	n/a	n/a	n/a	n/a	n/a	n/a
Denver, CO	61.8	61.0	61.9	61.6	61.6	59.3	60.1	63.5	62.9
Des Moines, IA	n/a	n/a	n/a	n/a	n/a	n/a	n/a	n/a	n/a
Durham, NC	n/a	n/a	n/a	n/a	n/a	n/a	n/a	n/a	n/a
Edison, NJ	51.5	50.6	50.7	49.9	50.4	49.9	49.7	50.4	50.9
El Paso, TX	n/a	n/a	n/a	n/a	n/a	n/a	n/a	n/a	n/a
Fargo, ND	n/a	n/a	n/a	n/a	n/a	n/a	n/a	n/a	n/a
Fayetteville, NC	n/a	n/a	n/a	n/a	n/a	n/a	n/a	n/a	n/a
Fort Collins, CO	n/a	n/a	n/a	n/a	n/a	n/a	n/a	n/a	n/a
Fort Wayne, IN	n/a	n/a	n/a	n/a	n/a	n/a	n/a	n/a	n/a
Fort Worth, TX	61.8	59.9	57.7	57.8	59.7	61.8	62.0	60.6	64.7
Grand Rapids, MI	76.9	73.7	71.6	75.8	76.2	71.7	73.0	75.2	71.8
Greeley, CO	n/a	n/a	n/a	n/a	n/a	n/a	n/a	n/a	n/a
Green Bay, WI	n/a	n/a	n/a	n/a	n/a	n/a	n/a	n/a	n/a
Greensboro, NC	64.9	67.9	68.1	65.4	62.9	61.9	63.2	61.7	65.8
Honolulu, HI	56.1	57.9	58.2	59.6	57.9	53.8	57.7	59.0	56.9
Houston, TX	62.1	60.5	60.4	60.3	59.0	58.9	60.1	61.3	65.3
Huntsville, AL	n/a	n/a	n/a	n/a	n/a	n/a	n/a	n/a	n/a
Indianapolis, IN	67.1	67.5	66.9	64.6	63.9	63.9	64.3	66.2	70.0
Jacksonville, FL	66.6	69.9	65.3	62.5	61.8	65.2	61.4	63.1	64.8
Kansas City, MO	65.1	65.6	66.1	65.0	62.4	62.4	64.3	65.0	66.7
Lafayette, LA	n/a	n/a	n/a	n/a	n/a	n/a	n/a	n/a	n/a
Lakeland, FL	n/a	n/a	n/a	n/a	n/a	n/a	n/a	n/a	n/a
Las Vegas, NV	52.6	52.8	53.2	52.1	51.3	54.4	58.1	56.0	57.3
Lexington, KY	n/a	n/a	n/a	n/a	n/a	n/a	n/a	n/a	n/a
Lincoln, NE	n/a	n/a	n/a	n/a	n/a	n/a	n/a	n/a	n/a
Little Rock, AR	n/a	n/a	n/a	65.8	64.9	61.0	62.2	65.0	67.7
Los Angeles, CA	49.9	48.7	49.0	49.1	47.1	49.1	49.5	48.2	48.5
Louisville, KY	63.3	64.5	68.9	67.7	67.6	71.7	67.9	64.9	69.3
Madison, WI	n/a	n/a	n/a	n/a	n/a	n/a	n/a	n/a	n/a
Manchester, NH	n/a	n/a	n/a	n/a	n/a	n/a	n/a	n/a	n/a

Table continued on following page.

Metro Area	2012	2013	2014	2015	2016	2017	2018	2019	2020
Memphis, TN	60.5	56.2	57.2	59.6	61.8	62.4	63.5	63.7	62.5
Miami, FL	61.8	60.1	58.8	58.6	58.4	57.9	59.9	60.4	60.6
Midland, TX	n/a	n/a	n/a	n/a	n/a	n/a	n/a	n/a	n/a
Milwaukee, WI	61.9	60.0	55.9	57.0	60.4	63.9	62.3	56.9	58.5
Minneapolis, MN	70.8	71.7	69.7	67.9	69.1	70.1	67.8	70.2	73.0
Nashville, TN	64.9	63.9	67.1	67.4	65.0	69.4	68.3	69.8	69.8
New Haven, CT	62.2	62.0	62.4	64.6	59.4	58.7	65.0	65.1	63.4
New Orleans, LA	62.4	61.4	60.6	62.8	59.3	61.7	62.6	61.1	66.3
New York, NY	51.5	50.6	50.7	49.9	50.4	49.9	49.7	50.4	50.9
Oklahoma City, OK	67.3	67.6	65.7	61.4	63.1	64.7	64.6	64.3	68.3
Omaha, NE	72.4	70.6	68.7	69.6	69.2	65.5	67.8	66.9	68.6
Orlando, FL	68.0	65.5	62.3	58.4	58.5	59.5	58.5	56.1	64.2
Peoria, IL	n/a	n/a	n/a	n/a	n/a	n/a	n/a	n/a	n/a
Philadelphia, PA	69.5	69.1	67.0	67.0	64.7	65.6	67.4	67.4	69.2
Phoenix, AZ	63.1	62.2	61.9	61.0	62.6	64.0	65.3	65.9	67.9
Pittsburgh, PA	67.9	68.3	69.1	71.0	72.2	72.7	71.7	71.5	69.8
Portland, OR	63.9	60.9	59.8	58.9	61.8	61.1	59.2	60.0	62.5
Providence, RI	61.7	60.1	61.6	60.0	57.5	58.6	61.3	63.5	64.8
Provo, UT	n/a	n/a	n/a	n/a	n/a	n/a	n/a	n/a	n/a
Raleigh, NC	67.7	65.5	65.5	67.4	65.9	68.2	64.9	63.0	68.2
Reno, NV	n/a	n/a	n/a	n/a	n/a	n/a	n/a	n/a	n/a
Richmond, VA	67.0	65.4	72.6	67.4	61.7	63.1	62.9	66.4	66.5
Riverside, CA	58.2	56.3	56.8	61.1	62.9	59.9	62.3	64.4	65.8
Rochester, MN	n/a	n/a	n/a	n/a	n/a	n/a	n/a	n/a	n/a
Sacramento, CA	58.6	60.4	60.1	60.8	60.5	60.1	64.1	61.6	63.4
Salt Lake City, UT	66.9	66.8	68.2	69.1	69.2	68.1	69.5	69.2	68.0
San Antonio, TX	67.5	70.1	70.2	66.0	61.6	62.5	64.4	62.6	64.2
San Diego, CA	55.4	55.0	57.4	51.8	53.3	56.0	56.1	56.7	57.8
San Francisco, CA	53.2	55.2	54.6	56.3	55.8	55.7	55.6	52.8	53.0
San Jose, CA	58.6	56.4	56.4	50.7	49.9	50.4	50.4	52.4	52.6
Santa Rosa, CA	n/a	n/a	n/a	n/a	n/a	n/a	n/a	n/a	n/a
Savannah, GA	n/a	n/a	n/a	n/a	n/a	n/a	n/a	n/a	n/a
Seattle, WA	60.4	61.0	61.3	59.5	57.7	59.5	62.5	61.5	59.4
Sioux Falls, SD	n/a	n/a	n/a	n/a	n/a	n/a	n/a	n/a	n/a
Springfield, IL	n/a	n/a	n/a	n/a	n/a	n/a	n/a	n/a	n/a
Tallahassee, FL	n/a	n/a	n/a	n/a	n/a	n/a	n/a	n/a	n/a
Tampa, FL	67.0	65.3	64.9	64.9	62.9	60.4	64.9	68.0	72.2
Tucson, AZ	64.9	66.1	66.7	61.4	56.0	60.1	63.8	60.1	67.1
Tulsa, OK	66.5	64.1	65.3	65.2	65.4	66.8	68.3	70.5	70.1
Tuscaloosa, AL	n/a	n/a	n/a	n/a	n/a	n/a	n/a	n/a	n/a
Virginia Beach, VA	62.0	63.3	64.1	59.4	59.6	65.3	62.8	63.0	65.8
Washington, DC	66.9	66.0	65.0	64.6	63.1	63.3	62.9	64.7	67.9
Wichita, KS	n/a	n/a	n/a	n/a	n/a	n/a	n/a	n/a	n/a
Winston-Salem, NC	n/a	n/a	n/a	n/a	n/a	n/a	n/a	n/a	n/a
U.S.	65.4	65.1	64.5	63.7	63.4	63.9	64.4	64.6	66.6

Note: Figures are percentages and cover the Metropolitan Statistical Area—see Appendix B for areas included; n/a not available
Source: U.S. Census Bureau, Housing Vacancies and Homeownership Annual Statistics: 2012-2020

Year Housing Structure Built: City

City	2010 or Later	2000 -2009	1990 -1999	1980 -1989	1970 -1979	1960 -1969	1950 -1959	1940 -1949	Before 1940	Median Year
Albuquerque, NM	4.3	16.3	15.3	15.5	19.6	10.3	11.5	4.4	2.8	1981
Allentown, PA	2.1	5.0	3.8	5.5	10.6	12.1	16.1	7.2	37.6	1953
Anchorage, AK	3.5	12.2	11.6	26.4	28.2	10.8	6.0	1.0	0.3	1981
Ann Arbor, MI	3.7	6.3	10.8	10.8	17.2	18.2	12.6	5.0	15.6	1969
Athens, GA	3.8	17.7	20.3	15.6	16.5	12.2	6.6	2.4	4.8	1985
Atlanta, GA	8.1	22.3	10.6	7.9	8.4	12.6	11.7	6.1	12.3	1979
Austin, TX	12.8	18.1	15.7	19.6	15.9	7.6	4.9	2.6	2.8	1988
Baton Rouge, LA	5.9	9.9	8.7	12.9	22.4	17.3	11.7	5.9	5.3	1974
Boise City, ID	6.5	11.9	22.5	15.0	19.2	7.1	7.1	4.4	6.2	1984
Boston, MA	5.0	6.5	4.2	5.9	7.9	7.8	7.3	5.8	49.6	1941
Boulder, CO	6.2	7.7	11.2	17.3	21.5	18.3	8.1	2.0	7.6	1976
Cape Coral, FL	3.8	37.8	17.8	22.9	11.9	4.7	0.8	0.2	0.1	1995
Cedar Rapids, IA	6.9	11.1	13.0	8.2	14.4	13.9	12.3	4.2	16.0	1972
Charleston, SC	12.3	20.3	12.8	13.8	10.2	8.3	6.1	4.1	12.2	1987
Charlotte, NC	8.9	23.1	19.4	15.1	12.0	9.5	6.6	2.6	2.8	1991
Chicago, IL	2.6	8.0	4.9	4.3	7.5	9.7	11.9	9.3	41.8	1949
Cincinnati, OH	2.3	3.7	4.2	5.3	9.9	13.0	12.2	8.1	41.2	1951
Clarksville, TN	13.0	22.8	20.9	13.2	12.4	8.6	4.7	2.5	2.0	1993
Cleveland, OH	1.7	3.8	3.2	2.4	5.4	7.1	12.5	11.3	52.6	<1940
College Station, TX	16.2	24.0	19.8	16.0	16.5	4.0	2.2	0.7	0.6	1995
Colorado Springs, CO	6.5	15.7	15.9	18.6	18.3	10.2	7.1	1.9	5.8	1984
Columbia, MO	12.6	21.5	17.9	12.0	12.5	10.7	5.1	2.2	5.5	1991
Columbia, SC	6.1	15.8	11.6	8.9	10.1	11.9	13.6	11.2	10.8	1972
Columbus, OH	5.9	11.4	15.4	13.0	15.0	12.0	10.8	5.0	11.6	1977
Dallas, TX	7.1	10.6	10.3	17.2	17.3	13.4	13.7	5.2	5.2	1977
Davenport, IA	3.4	8.6	7.9	5.9	15.7	13.3	11.2	5.6	28.5	1964
Denver, CO	9.0	11.3	6.6	7.4	14.2	10.9	15.0	6.6	18.9	1969
Des Moines, IA	3.2	7.3	6.5	6.4	13.4	10.5	15.2	8.2	29.3	1958
Durham, NC	11.6	21.0	16.3	15.4	10.5	8.8	6.6	3.8	6.1	1989
Edison, NJ	1.7	4.7	9.3	23.3	13.6	20.3	17.4	4.5	5.1	1972
El Paso, TX	9.8	15.2	13.4	14.0	16.5	10.8	11.5	4.1	4.6	1982
Fargo, ND	16.1	15.8	16.5	13.8	14.0	6.0	6.9	2.6	8.2	1989
Fayetteville, NC	6.9	11.9	18.1	16.9	21.6	13.2	6.6	2.9	1.8	1982
Fort Collins, CO	10.2	17.5	21.3	15.2	18.8	7.1	3.2	1.6	5.2	1989
Fort Wayne, IN	1.5	6.6	14.3	11.7	16.7	15.0	12.2	6.6	15.3	1970
Fort Worth, TX	9.9	24.5	11.5	13.2	9.8	8.2	11.3	5.3	6.3	1987
Grand Rapids, MI	2.5	4.2	6.1	7.0	8.5	10.3	15.7	8.9	36.8	1953
Greeley, CO	6.3	19.3	15.7	10.1	21.2	10.3	6.7	2.6	7.8	1982
Green Bay, WI	1.6	7.6	10.3	12.9	17.8	13.1	15.0	5.7	16.0	1970
Greensboro, NC	5.2	15.0	17.9	16.6	14.4	11.2	10.2	3.8	5.5	1983
Honolulu, HI	4.2	6.9	7.9	9.5	25.3	22.8	12.8	5.5	5.1	1971
Houston, TX	8.6	13.4	9.9	14.6	21.1	13.4	10.3	4.5	4.3	1978
Huntsville, AL	11.8	12.9	10.8	15.6	13.2	21.0	9.5	2.4	2.8	1981
Indianapolis, IN	3.4	9.2	13.2	12.1	13.5	13.1	12.7	6.1	16.8	1971
Jacksonville, FL	6.2	19.3	15.3	15.5	12.7	10.0	11.1	4.8	5.1	1984
Kansas City, MO	4.6	9.9	9.3	8.6	12.0	12.7	14.3	6.3	22.1	1966
Lafayette, LA	7.2	13.3	10.4	18.0	21.7	13.4	9.0	3.9	3.1	1979
Lakeland, FL	3.4	15.1	13.2	19.6	20.2	10.4	8.8	3.3	6.0	1981
Las Vegas, NV	5.2	23.0	32.0	16.6	9.9	7.4	4.2	1.3	0.5	1993
Lexington, KY	6.1	15.5	15.8	14.0	15.0	13.5	9.7	3.1	7.3	1981
Lincoln, NE	7.3	13.7	15.0	10.4	15.3	10.0	11.2	3.0	14.0	1978
Little Rock, AR	6.2	11.2	11.2	14.3	19.6	15.2	9.9	5.2	7.1	1976
Los Angeles, CA	3.2	5.6	5.7	10.2	13.7	14.1	17.4	9.8	20.3	1962
Louisville, KY	4.3	11.0	11.7	6.9	12.7	13.8	14.8	7.4	17.4	1968
Madison, WI	7.1	14.4	13.1	10.9	13.9	11.5	10.4	4.8	14.0	1977

Table continued on following page.

City	2010 or Later	2000-2009	1990-1999	1980-1989	1970-1979	1960-1969	1950-1959	1940-1949	Before 1940	Median Year
Manchester, NH	1.9	6.7	8.1	15.9	10.4	7.9	10.3	6.1	32.6	1961
Memphis, TN	2.0	7.0	10.0	12.4	18.2	14.9	19.1	8.7	7.7	1970
Miami, FL	7.6	19.0	6.4	8.3	13.3	9.8	14.7	11.7	9.2	1973
Midland, TX	12.9	8.5	13.8	18.4	11.7	11.6	18.5	3.0	1.5	1982
Milwaukee, WI	1.5	3.3	2.9	3.9	8.7	11.1	20.2	9.8	38.6	1951
Minneapolis, MN	5.8	6.7	3.6	6.8	9.0	7.5	9.5	6.8	44.3	1948
Nashville, TN	9.3	14.6	12.4	15.3	14.8	12.2	10.6	4.5	6.2	1981
New Haven, CT	3.1	4.8	2.6	7.1	8.0	9.7	9.4	7.5	47.7	1943
New Orleans, LA	3.4	7.1	3.5	7.3	13.7	11.1	12.1	7.7	34.0	1957
New York, NY	2.8	5.6	3.7	4.8	7.1	12.5	13.0	9.9	40.6	1949
Oklahoma City, OK	9.4	13.1	9.5	14.9	16.1	12.6	10.6	5.5	8.4	1978
Omaha, NE	3.4	7.4	13.0	11.0	15.6	14.6	11.1	4.2	19.7	1970
Orlando, FL	9.6	21.6	16.3	16.9	13.9	7.2	8.6	2.9	3.0	1989
Peoria, IL	3.3	8.7	7.4	6.8	15.2	12.5	14.0	7.9	24.3	1963
Philadelphia, PA	2.7	3.0	3.2	3.7	7.1	10.7	16.3	11.6	41.7	1947
Phoenix, AZ	4.3	16.7	16.3	17.1	19.6	11.7	10.1	2.5	1.8	1983
Pittsburgh, PA	2.3	3.0	3.5	4.4	6.7	8.7	12.6	8.9	49.8	1940
Portland, OR	5.8	10.5	8.8	6.4	10.7	9.2	12.0	8.2	28.3	1962
Providence, RI	0.6	4.5	3.7	5.5	9.2	5.9	7.6	6.8	56.2	<1940
Provo, UT	4.6	11.8	21.1	14.3	17.7	10.4	7.6	5.1	7.3	1981
Raleigh, NC	10.7	25.0	19.0	17.3	10.6	7.7	4.5	2.1	3.1	1992
Reno, NV	6.2	19.7	19.2	13.9	18.3	9.5	7.2	3.0	3.0	1987
Richmond, VA	4.0	5.4	4.9	6.3	11.3	12.4	15.0	9.1	31.7	1956
Riverside, CA	2.8	11.5	10.6	16.4	18.4	12.1	16.0	5.0	7.2	1975
Rochester, MN	8.9	18.3	14.3	14.6	13.0	10.1	9.6	3.3	7.9	1984
Sacramento, CA	2.3	15.7	8.9	15.7	14.6	11.7	12.4	7.9	10.9	1975
Salt Lake City, UT	5.3	6.6	7.4	7.7	12.1	10.0	13.2	8.7	29.1	1959
San Antonio, TX	7.3	15.9	13.7	16.6	15.0	10.2	10.1	5.7	5.6	1982
San Diego, CA	3.9	10.3	11.4	17.7	21.2	12.5	12.1	4.3	6.7	1977
San Francisco, CA	3.7	6.6	4.3	5.3	7.6	8.2	8.4	9.1	46.8	1944
San Jose, CA	5.2	9.3	10.6	12.9	24.2	18.6	11.0	3.0	5.2	1975
Santa Rosa, CA	2.9	12.4	13.0	19.4	21.8	11.8	8.2	4.9	5.6	1979
Savannah, GA	6.3	11.3	7.4	9.8	12.7	12.6	15.0	8.1	16.7	1968
Seattle, WA	10.4	13.2	8.3	7.9	8.2	8.7	9.8	8.3	25.2	1968
Sioux Falls, SD	13.3	18.3	15.1	10.5	13.8	7.3	9.1	3.8	8.6	1987
Springfield, IL	2.3	8.8	12.6	9.6	16.5	12.7	11.3	7.0	19.2	1970
Tallahassee, FL	3.9	18.2	20.8	17.7	18.0	9.2	7.5	3.2	1.5	1986
Tampa, FL	7.8	17.9	12.4	11.8	11.9	10.0	14.4	5.2	8.7	1980
Tucson, AZ	2.6	12.6	13.4	16.2	21.4	11.5	14.8	3.9	3.7	1978
Tulsa, OK	3.6	6.1	9.5	13.3	21.0	14.4	16.8	6.4	9.0	1972
Tuscaloosa, AL	12.9	17.6	15.5	11.5	13.7	10.4	8.8	5.2	4.3	1987
Virginia Beach, VA	4.9	10.8	13.7	27.9	21.4	12.8	6.1	1.3	1.1	1983
Washington, DC	7.3	8.1	3.3	4.4	7.1	11.4	12.6	11.7	34.1	1953
Wichita, KS	4.2	10.2	12.9	12.5	12.8	9.3	20.0	7.4	10.7	1972
Winston-Salem, NC	4.7	14.0	12.1	14.3	16.7	13.6	11.8	5.4	7.4	1977
U.S.	5.2	14.0	13.9	13.4	15.2	10.6	10.3	4.9	12.6	1978

Note: Figures are percentages except for Median Year
Source: U.S. Census Bureau, 2015-2019 American Community Survey 5-Year Estimates

Year Housing Structure Built: Metro Area

Metro Area	2010 or Later	2000-2009	1990-1999	1980-1989	1970-1979	1960-1969	1950-1959	1940-1949	Before 1940	Median Year
Albuquerque, NM	4.2	17.6	18.2	17.0	18.0	9.2	9.1	3.7	3.0	1984
Allentown, PA	3.0	11.5	10.6	11.1	12.0	9.7	11.2	5.3	25.5	1968
Anchorage, AK	4.5	17.2	13.0	25.7	24.4	9.0	5.0	0.9	0.4	1984
Ann Arbor, MI	3.7	13.2	17.0	11.5	16.1	12.6	10.1	4.2	11.8	1977
Athens, GA	5.0	18.1	21.7	17.4	15.3	10.1	5.5	2.0	5.0	1987
Atlanta, GA	6.2	24.3	21.5	17.7	13.0	7.6	4.8	1.9	2.9	1991
Austin, TX	16.4	25.1	18.1	16.4	11.6	4.9	3.3	1.8	2.3	1995
Baton Rouge, LA	9.4	19.8	14.6	15.0	17.4	10.2	6.9	2.9	3.9	1986
Boise City, ID	10.5	24.6	21.4	10.3	16.2	4.7	4.4	3.0	4.9	1993
Boston, MA	4.0	7.6	7.4	10.4	11.2	10.2	10.8	5.3	33.2	1961
Boulder, CO	6.5	12.1	19.3	17.2	20.8	11.6	4.6	1.5	6.4	1983
Cape Coral, FL	5.6	31.3	17.7	21.4	14.8	5.5	2.5	0.5	0.7	1993
Cedar Rapids, IA	6.8	14.2	14.6	7.5	13.4	12.3	9.9	3.6	17.7	1975
Charleston, SC	11.9	21.4	16.6	16.4	14.2	8.2	5.2	2.4	3.6	1990
Charlotte, NC	9.2	24.1	19.5	13.5	11.5	8.4	6.5	3.1	4.2	1991
Chicago, IL	2.4	11.5	11.1	9.0	14.2	11.6	13.0	6.1	21.0	1968
Cincinnati, OH	3.7	12.4	14.4	10.7	13.8	10.7	11.9	4.9	17.6	1974
Clarksville, TN	10.7	20.0	20.9	12.1	15.2	9.2	6.2	2.5	3.1	1991
Cleveland, OH	2.3	7.1	8.7	6.8	12.4	13.4	18.1	7.6	23.7	1960
College Station, TX	12.7	21.0	17.7	17.0	15.8	6.1	5.2	2.0	2.4	1991
Colorado Springs, CO	7.6	18.8	16.9	17.5	17.0	8.9	6.5	1.6	5.2	1986
Columbia, MO	9.5	19.4	18.0	12.8	15.4	10.1	5.3	2.5	7.2	1988
Columbia, SC	8.0	19.5	18.5	14.3	15.9	9.7	7.0	3.3	3.8	1987
Columbus, OH	5.8	14.2	16.5	11.7	14.4	11.1	10.2	4.1	12.2	1979
Dallas, TX	10.0	20.0	16.1	18.1	14.2	8.7	7.5	2.7	2.7	1988
Davenport, IA	3.6	7.5	8.3	6.4	16.6	13.4	11.9	7.1	25.2	1964
Denver, CO	7.4	16.4	15.2	14.2	18.6	9.3	9.2	2.8	6.8	1982
Des Moines, IA	10.4	16.7	12.6	8.7	13.6	8.6	9.1	4.2	16.1	1979
Durham, NC	9.3	19.7	18.7	15.8	12.4	9.2	6.4	3.0	5.6	1989
Edison, NJ	2.8	6.7	6.1	7.7	9.8	13.7	15.9	8.8	28.6	1958
El Paso, TX	11.0	16.5	14.6	14.5	15.7	9.7	10.1	3.6	4.2	1985
Fargo, ND	15.1	18.4	14.2	11.2	14.9	6.9	7.4	2.7	9.1	1988
Fayetteville, NC	9.3	17.9	21.7	14.5	16.4	9.6	5.6	2.4	2.5	1989
Fort Collins, CO	10.3	18.8	20.1	13.5	19.1	7.1	3.6	1.7	5.8	1989
Fort Wayne, IN	3.8	11.0	15.2	10.9	15.2	13.0	10.8	5.4	14.7	1974
Fort Worth, TX	10.0	20.0	16.1	18.1	14.2	8.7	7.5	2.7	2.7	1988
Grand Rapids, MI	4.7	12.4	16.3	12.1	14.0	9.5	10.4	5.0	15.7	1977
Greeley, CO	10.9	28.6	16.3	7.4	15.2	6.2	4.4	2.4	8.6	1994
Green Bay, WI	5.2	15.0	16.4	12.4	15.4	9.6	9.3	4.2	12.4	1979
Greensboro, NC	5.0	15.9	18.9	14.5	14.7	10.9	9.5	4.5	6.1	1983
Honolulu, HI	5.1	10.2	11.5	12.2	24.1	18.9	10.7	4.0	3.3	1975
Houston, TX	11.9	21.5	14.4	15.5	16.9	8.4	6.2	2.6	2.4	1989
Huntsville, AL	10.8	19.7	17.8	16.1	11.3	13.7	6.4	1.9	2.2	1989
Indianapolis, IN	6.5	15.5	16.7	10.6	12.5	10.6	10.3	4.4	12.8	1979
Jacksonville, FL	8.6	22.7	16.6	16.6	12.4	8.0	8.0	3.4	3.9	1989
Kansas City, MO	4.8	13.7	14.5	12.3	15.4	11.6	11.4	4.4	11.8	1977
Lafayette, LA	9.5	16.6	12.9	15.5	16.4	10.4	9.3	4.1	5.2	1983
Lakeland, FL	5.8	23.8	17.7	18.2	15.1	7.7	6.5	2.1	3.2	1989
Las Vegas, NV	7.2	30.1	29.1	14.6	10.6	5.1	2.2	0.7	0.4	1996
Lexington, KY	6.4	17.2	17.0	13.9	14.8	11.5	8.0	3.3	7.9	1983
Lincoln, NE	7.3	14.1	15.1	10.1	15.6	10.0	10.3	2.8	14.7	1978
Little Rock, AR	9.3	18.2	16.7	13.7	17.0	10.8	7.1	3.4	3.7	1986
Los Angeles, CA	2.9	6.1	7.6	12.3	16.1	15.9	18.7	8.4	11.9	1967
Louisville, KY	4.4	13.1	14.2	9.2	15.2	12.4	12.6	6.2	12.8	1974
Madison, WI	6.5	16.2	15.6	11.1	15.0	9.6	7.8	3.5	14.6	1980

Table continued on following page.

Metro Area	2010 or Later	2000-2009	1990-1999	1980-1989	1970-1979	1960-1969	1950-1959	1940-1949	Before 1940	Median Year
Manchester, NH	3.0	10.1	10.3	20.9	15.3	9.6	7.1	3.7	19.9	1976
Memphis, TN	4.2	15.7	17.1	13.7	16.2	10.8	11.9	5.3	5.1	1980
Miami, FL	4.1	13.0	15.1	19.4	21.4	12.3	9.8	2.8	2.1	1981
Midland, TX	14.0	11.4	14.5	18.0	11.2	10.5	15.9	2.8	1.7	1984
Milwaukee, WI	2.7	8.2	10.8	8.0	13.0	11.5	16.3	6.8	22.9	1964
Minneapolis, MN	5.1	14.3	14.4	14.5	14.7	9.8	9.7	3.7	13.9	1979
Nashville, TN	10.7	19.7	17.8	14.3	13.6	9.2	6.9	3.1	4.7	1989
New Haven, CT	1.8	5.6	7.1	12.3	13.3	12.3	15.2	7.1	25.2	1962
New Orleans, LA	3.8	11.9	9.8	13.3	19.3	13.6	10.1	4.8	13.5	1974
New York, NY	2.8	6.7	6.1	7.7	9.8	13.7	15.9	8.8	28.6	1958
Oklahoma City, OK	9.3	15.0	11.1	14.8	17.2	12.0	9.6	4.8	6.2	1980
Omaha, NE	6.8	14.3	13.0	9.9	14.6	12.0	8.7	3.4	17.2	1976
Orlando, FL	8.8	23.8	20.6	20.2	12.8	5.9	5.2	1.2	1.5	1992
Peoria, IL	3.1	9.0	8.6	6.0	17.3	12.3	14.3	8.0	21.4	1965
Philadelphia, PA	3.1	7.8	9.6	10.0	12.1	11.9	15.7	7.5	22.2	1964
Phoenix, AZ	6.6	25.4	20.3	17.2	16.1	7.3	5.1	1.2	0.9	1991
Pittsburgh, PA	2.8	6.5	7.7	7.5	11.9	11.5	16.7	8.9	26.4	1959
Portland, OR	6.3	14.5	18.6	11.3	17.2	8.4	7.1	4.6	11.9	1981
Providence, RI	1.9	6.3	8.1	11.1	12.2	11.0	11.6	6.6	31.4	1960
Provo, UT	14.0	25.9	19.2	9.3	13.6	5.0	5.4	3.1	4.6	1995
Raleigh, NC	12.7	25.9	23.0	15.2	9.3	5.9	3.7	1.6	2.8	1995
Reno, NV	5.5	21.1	20.6	15.2	18.9	8.9	5.3	2.2	2.3	1988
Richmond, VA	5.9	14.9	15.3	16.1	15.1	9.7	9.4	4.3	9.2	1981
Riverside, CA	4.2	20.5	14.6	21.9	15.7	8.9	8.5	2.8	2.8	1985
Rochester, MN	7.0	18.0	14.3	12.1	13.5	9.0	8.0	3.4	14.6	1981
Sacramento, CA	3.5	17.6	15.1	16.6	18.3	10.9	10.0	3.7	4.2	1982
Salt Lake City, UT	8.9	15.5	15.5	12.6	18.4	8.8	8.7	3.6	8.0	1982
San Antonio, TX	11.4	20.2	14.5	15.4	13.5	8.4	7.7	4.2	4.6	1988
San Diego, CA	3.7	12.0	12.5	18.6	22.6	12.2	10.7	3.5	4.2	1979
San Francisco, CA	3.2	7.7	8.2	11.1	14.9	13.4	13.7	7.8	19.9	1966
San Jose, CA	5.6	9.0	10.6	12.6	21.6	18.0	13.9	3.6	5.1	1974
Santa Rosa, CA	2.5	10.6	13.6	18.6	21.0	11.6	8.5	5.0	8.4	1978
Savannah, GA	9.0	20.7	16.3	13.8	12.0	7.8	8.1	4.3	8.0	1987
Seattle, WA	7.7	15.2	15.5	14.4	14.2	11.0	7.4	4.4	10.1	1982
Sioux Falls, SD	11.9	18.7	15.3	9.5	14.0	6.8	8.1	3.7	12.1	1986
Springfield, IL	3.1	9.9	13.2	9.1	16.9	11.9	11.6	6.7	17.5	1971
Tallahassee, FL	4.0	18.7	22.6	19.2	16.2	8.3	6.6	2.6	1.7	1988
Tampa, FL	5.6	16.4	14.1	20.1	21.0	9.5	8.5	2.0	2.7	1983
Tucson, AZ	4.5	18.6	17.5	17.8	19.6	8.5	8.9	2.5	2.2	1985
Tulsa, OK	6.7	14.4	12.7	14.3	19.3	10.5	10.6	4.5	7.0	1979
Tuscaloosa, AL	9.2	18.7	18.7	14.2	14.6	9.7	7.1	4.0	3.9	1988
Virginia Beach, VA	6.0	12.7	15.2	18.9	15.8	11.8	9.7	4.2	5.7	1981
Washington, DC	6.7	14.5	14.4	15.8	14.0	12.0	9.4	4.9	8.3	1981
Wichita, KS	4.7	11.9	14.1	12.2	13.3	8.5	17.9	6.0	11.3	1975
Winston-Salem, NC	4.5	15.6	17.2	15.7	16.7	10.9	8.9	4.3	6.3	1982
U.S.	5.2	14.0	13.9	13.4	15.2	10.6	10.3	4.9	12.6	1978

Note: Figures are percentages except for Median Year; Figures cover the Metropolitan Statistical Area—see Appendix B for areas included
Source: U.S. Census Bureau, 2015-2019 American Community Survey 5-Year Estimates

Gross Monthly Rent: City

City	Under $500	$500-$999	$1,000-$1,499	$1,500-$1,999	$2,000-$2,499	$2,500-$2,999	$3,000 and up	Median ($)
Albuquerque, NM	8.1	54.4	29.1	6.5	1.1	0.3	0.4	873
Allentown, PA	10.0	39.6	38.7	10.0	1.4	0.3	0.0	1,004
Anchorage, AK	4.0	21.8	36.9	19.9	11.7	4.1	1.4	1,320
Ann Arbor, MI	4.6	23.6	39.5	19.8	7.3	2.4	2.8	1,237
Athens, GA	7.9	59.5	24.2	6.6	1.4	0.2	0.1	856
Atlanta, GA	11.3	27.5	33.6	18.8	5.6	1.7	1.5	1,153
Austin, TX	3.1	18.1	45.2	22.4	7.1	2.3	1.8	1,280
Baton Rouge, LA	10.1	54.4	25.7	5.9	3.2	0.5	0.3	879
Boise City, ID	5.6	50.5	34.7	6.9	1.4	0.3	0.7	957
Boston, MA	16.5	11.4	16.6	22.7	15.3	8.2	9.3	1,620
Boulder, CO	2.8	9.4	35.1	25.4	14.8	5.5	6.9	1,554
Cape Coral, FL	0.9	22.4	46.8	22.5	5.0	1.0	1.4	1,244
Cedar Rapids, IA	15.8	61.0	20.2	1.5	0.6	0.3	0.7	767
Charleston, SC	6.4	20.8	40.8	22.1	5.9	1.8	2.2	1,257
Charlotte, NC	3.8	30.9	46.3	14.5	2.9	0.8	0.7	1,135
Chicago, IL	9.6	31.9	31.5	15.2	6.7	3.0	2.1	1,112
Cincinnati, OH	19.1	56.0	18.0	4.5	1.3	0.4	0.7	738
Clarksville, TN	5.8	48.7	35.6	7.8	1.8	0.1	0.1	961
Cleveland, OH	21.9	58.1	15.8	2.7	0.9	0.3	0.2	719
College Station, TX	3.2	48.7	27.6	14.1	5.0	1.0	0.5	983
Colorado Springs, CO	3.9	34.3	38.3	17.5	3.5	1.8	0.7	1,131
Columbia, MO	6.1	58.0	26.4	5.7	3.3	0.3	0.2	887
Columbia, SC	10.1	48.2	31.9	7.6	1.6	0.1	0.5	933
Columbus, OH	6.4	48.7	35.7	7.1	1.5	0.4	0.3	961
Dallas, TX	4.3	41.0	36.7	11.7	3.6	1.4	1.1	1,052
Davenport, IA	9.2	68.6	16.4	3.2	0.8	0.7	1.1	771
Denver, CO	8.2	18.4	35.8	23.2	9.6	3.2	1.6	1,311
Des Moines, IA	8.6	61.1	25.1	4.1	0.9	0.2	0.1	855
Durham, NC	7.4	36.4	42.6	10.3	2.0	0.5	0.8	1,058
Edison, NJ	2.8	5.8	39.4	35.3	13.2	2.6	0.9	1,528
El Paso, TX	15.2	53.4	25.4	4.9	0.5	0.3	0.2	837
Fargo, ND	7.0	65.6	20.7	5.3	1.1	0.2	0.1	823
Fayetteville, NC	5.6	51.7	36.6	5.2	0.7	0.2	0.1	947
Fort Collins, CO	2.9	20.0	39.7	26.3	9.1	1.4	0.7	1,346
Fort Wayne, IN	11.5	71.0	15.0	1.5	0.7	0.2	0.1	764
Fort Worth, TX	4.9	39.7	35.0	15.5	3.1	0.9	0.9	1,060
Grand Rapids, MI	10.2	48.9	31.0	6.5	2.8	0.5	0.1	925
Greeley, CO	9.2	40.3	32.2	14.0	3.2	0.6	0.5	1,007
Green Bay, WI	12.0	71.3	15.4	1.0	0.1	0.1	0.2	730
Greensboro, NC	6.8	61.7	26.0	3.4	1.2	0.4	0.5	877
Honolulu, HI	6.9	13.3	30.4	22.3	11.3	6.7	9.2	1,491
Houston, TX	3.8	42.7	34.6	12.8	3.3	1.4	1.4	1,041
Huntsville, AL	11.3	59.9	24.2	3.2	0.5	0.6	0.4	827
Indianapolis, IN	6.2	58.7	28.2	5.3	1.0	0.2	0.3	892
Jacksonville, FL	6.6	36.6	42.2	11.8	2.2	0.3	0.4	1,065
Kansas City, MO	8.7	48.0	33.8	7.2	1.5	0.5	0.4	941
Lafayette, LA	9.9	54.6	27.8	6.1	1.3	0.3	0.1	890
Lakeland, FL	5.6	44.6	39.6	7.9	1.4	0.6	0.3	999
Las Vegas, NV	4.7	35.4	41.8	13.8	2.9	0.8	0.6	1,102
Lexington, KY	8.1	52.5	30.6	5.8	2.2	0.4	0.3	896
Lincoln, NE	9.5	58.4	25.0	4.9	0.8	0.3	1.0	852
Little Rock, AR	9.9	54.3	29.0	4.8	0.8	0.6	0.6	872
Los Angeles, CA	5.3	15.7	32.0	22.6	12.4	6.1	5.9	1,450
Louisville, KY	13.7	54.1	25.9	4.9	0.7	0.4	0.3	846
Madison, WI	3.4	34.3	42.0	13.9	4.1	1.3	1.0	1,118

Table continued on following page.

City	Under $500	$500 -$999	$1,000 -$1,499	$1,500 -$1,999	$2,000 -$2,499	$2,500 -$2,999	$3,000 and up	Median ($)
Manchester, NH	7.4	28.2	45.1	15.4	2.5	0.7	0.6	1,135
Memphis, TN	8.1	54.6	31.2	4.7	0.9	0.2	0.2	901
Miami, FL	10.7	26.3	30.0	17.0	9.3	3.8	2.9	1,183
Midland, TX	1.7	26.0	41.3	19.5	7.5	2.9	1.2	1,262
Milwaukee, WI	9.1	60.2	24.2	4.7	1.2	0.4	0.2	858
Minneapolis, MN	12.8	35.3	30.2	14.4	4.7	1.4	1.1	1,027
Nashville, TN	8.7	31.5	39.8	14.1	4.0	1.1	0.8	1,100
New Haven, CT	13.3	18.7	41.2	19.5	5.1	1.5	0.8	1,196
New Orleans, LA	12.8	37.4	33.7	11.5	3.0	0.9	0.6	998
New York, NY	10.6	14.6	28.1	22.1	11.0	5.6	8.0	1,443
Oklahoma City, OK	8.1	57.1	27.0	6.0	1.2	0.4	0.4	871
Omaha, NE	7.7	51.6	31.4	7.0	1.3	0.3	0.7	923
Orlando, FL	3.7	24.7	48.8	17.6	4.0	0.8	0.4	1,196
Peoria, IL	15.6	58.0	20.6	3.7	1.0	0.3	0.9	806
Philadelphia, PA	11.0	35.4	34.7	11.6	4.4	1.5	1.3	1,042
Phoenix, AZ	4.5	40.2	40.2	11.5	2.4	0.6	0.5	1,053
Pittsburgh, PA	13.6	40.7	28.8	11.2	4.0	1.0	0.7	958
Portland, OR	6.5	22.1	38.1	20.9	8.1	2.7	1.6	1,248
Providence, RI	19.5	31.1	35.2	9.8	2.6	0.7	1.1	994
Provo, UT	12.8	49.7	24.3	10.2	2.3	0.5	0.2	877
Raleigh, NC	3.9	31.6	47.0	13.2	3.0	0.5	0.8	1,121
Reno, NV	5.6	42.2	33.7	14.3	3.2	0.5	0.6	1,029
Richmond, VA	12.6	35.0	37.0	11.7	2.7	0.3	0.6	1,025
Riverside, CA	3.4	16.0	39.3	28.9	9.9	1.8	0.7	1,378
Rochester, MN	9.1	43.7	30.2	13.0	1.7	0.9	1.3	974
Sacramento, CA	5.9	24.1	38.5	23.4	6.1	1.4	0.6	1,263
Salt Lake City, UT	8.9	42.8	31.8	12.5	3.1	0.6	0.4	985
San Antonio, TX	7.6	43.3	36.4	10.0	1.7	0.4	0.6	992
San Diego, CA	3.4	10.2	25.9	26.9	18.7	8.9	6.0	1,695
San Francisco, CA	9.3	13.0	15.6	15.3	13.6	11.7	21.4	1,895
San Jose, CA	4.5	6.9	13.6	20.9	19.2	16.2	18.7	2,107
Santa Rosa, CA	5.4	8.4	30.1	27.8	18.2	6.9	3.2	1,609
Savannah, GA	10.0	38.1	39.8	8.9	1.8	0.5	1.0	1,019
Seattle, WA	6.5	10.0	27.1	28.0	14.9	7.0	6.4	1,614
Sioux Falls, SD	8.5	65.9	19.8	4.0	0.6	0.5	0.8	827
Springfield, IL	12.4	62.3	19.5	3.4	1.1	1.1	0.2	805
Tallahassee, FL	5.3	42.2	39.8	8.5	3.2	0.6	0.3	1,023
Tampa, FL	8.1	30.2	37.6	16.0	4.8	1.9	1.5	1,131
Tucson, AZ	7.9	57.2	27.6	5.4	1.1	0.4	0.5	846
Tulsa, OK	10.9	59.4	24.1	3.6	1.0	0.5	0.6	829
Tuscaloosa, AL	13.1	57.0	22.2	4.6	1.9	0.3	1.0	844
Virginia Beach, VA	3.2	12.0	47.9	26.8	6.9	1.7	1.6	1,367
Washington, DC	10.4	13.2	24.7	21.1	13.6	8.2	8.9	1,541
Wichita, KS	11.6	61.3	22.4	3.3	0.6	0.2	0.7	809
Winston-Salem, NC	10.9	62.6	21.5	3.5	0.9	0.2	0.4	806
U.S.	9.4	36.2	30.0	14.0	5.6	2.4	2.4	1,062

Note: Figures are percentages except for Median; Gross rent is the contract rent plus the estimated average monthly cost of utilities (electricity, gas, and water and sewer) and fuels (oil, coal, kerosene, wood, etc.) if these are paid by the renter (or paid for the renter by someone else).
Source: U.S. Census Bureau, 2015-2019 American Community Survey 5-Year Estimates

Gross Monthly Rent: Metro Area

MSA[1]	Under $500	$500 -$999	$1,000 -$1,499	$1,500 -$1,999	$2,000 -$2,499	$2,500 -2,999	$3,000 and up	Median ($)
Albuquerque, NM	8.0	52.5	30.1	7.5	1.1	0.3	0.4	892
Allentown, PA	9.5	34.3	38.5	13.6	2.6	0.7	0.8	1,066
Anchorage, AK	4.2	23.2	37.1	19.7	10.8	3.7	1.3	1,288
Ann Arbor, MI	5.5	33.9	37.6	14.7	4.5	1.6	2.2	1,114
Athens, GA	8.4	59.5	23.6	6.2	1.5	0.5	0.2	853
Atlanta, GA	4.8	28.9	45.0	16.1	3.4	0.9	0.8	1,156
Austin, TX	3.1	19.4	44.5	22.7	6.7	2.1	1.6	1,273
Baton Rouge, LA	8.9	50.9	29.0	7.6	2.9	0.4	0.3	922
Boise City, ID	8.2	47.3	34.8	7.4	1.6	0.4	0.5	958
Boston, MA	12.4	13.4	25.6	23.5	13.2	6.1	5.8	1,475
Boulder, CO	4.0	11.7	34.6	27.2	13.3	5.0	4.2	1,495
Cape Coral, FL	4.2	29.8	43.3	14.3	4.8	1.6	2.0	1,154
Cedar Rapids, IA	16.9	60.9	18.9	1.9	0.5	0.3	0.7	753
Charleston, SC	6.1	29.6	40.2	17.0	4.2	1.5	1.4	1,156
Charlotte, NC	6.1	41.0	37.9	11.2	2.4	0.8	0.6	1,030
Chicago, IL	7.7	32.0	34.9	15.8	5.8	2.2	1.7	1,122
Cincinnati, OH	12.3	54.7	24.8	5.7	1.5	0.4	0.7	842
Clarksville, TN	8.7	49.9	32.7	7.3	1.3	0.2	0.0	919
Cleveland, OH	13.0	57.6	23.2	4.3	1.1	0.3	0.5	817
College Station, TX	6.3	51.7	26.5	10.6	3.6	0.8	0.5	935
Colorado Springs, CO	3.8	31.8	36.9	21.1	4.0	1.8	0.6	1,173
Columbia, MO	7.9	59.1	25.3	4.5	2.8	0.3	0.2	862
Columbia, SC	7.6	50.4	32.4	7.2	1.5	0.5	0.4	933
Columbus, OH	7.6	48.3	34.3	7.3	1.6	0.5	0.4	953
Dallas, TX	3.4	33.2	40.0	16.3	4.7	1.4	1.0	1,139
Davenport, IA	15.1	61.8	17.1	3.9	0.9	0.4	0.8	765
Denver, CO	5.1	16.7	37.2	26.2	10.2	2.9	1.7	1,380
Des Moines, IA	7.3	54.0	30.1	6.2	1.3	0.2	0.7	904
Durham, NC	7.9	38.7	39.1	10.0	2.5	0.6	1.1	1,033
Edison, NJ	9.4	13.9	30.7	23.1	11.0	5.3	6.7	1,439
El Paso, TX	15.0	53.4	25.4	5.2	0.5	0.3	0.2	837
Fargo, ND	8.0	62.0	21.3	6.7	1.4	0.4	0.3	837
Fayetteville, NC	7.3	50.9	33.4	7.2	1.1	0.1	0.1	932
Fort Collins, CO	4.1	23.2	37.4	25.2	7.7	1.7	0.7	1,297
Fort Wayne, IN	11.5	69.3	16.1	2.0	0.8	0.2	0.1	771
Fort Worth, TX	3.4	33.2	40.0	16.3	4.7	1.4	1.0	1,139
Grand Rapids, MI	8.8	56.1	26.7	5.7	1.9	0.3	0.3	884
Greeley, CO	7.7	36.4	33.4	16.3	4.0	1.0	1.2	1,085
Green Bay, WI	9.9	69.3	18.6	1.4	0.3	0.2	0.3	784
Greensboro, NC	9.6	63.4	22.4	2.9	1.0	0.3	0.5	834
Honolulu, HI	5.6	10.4	24.1	20.3	14.1	10.0	15.5	1,745
Houston, TX	3.8	37.0	37.0	15.6	4.0	1.4	1.2	1,101
Huntsville, AL	10.9	59.8	24.0	3.9	0.6	0.5	0.3	836
Indianapolis, IN	6.3	54.7	30.5	6.4	1.4	0.3	0.5	916
Jacksonville, FL	5.9	34.8	41.3	13.6	3.2	0.7	0.6	1,093
Kansas City, MO	8.2	46.4	34.4	8.0	2.0	0.5	0.6	961
Lafayette, LA	15.3	57.0	21.5	4.8	1.2	0.1	0.1	811
Lakeland, FL	6.7	45.8	33.6	11.3	1.8	0.5	0.3	978
Las Vegas, NV	2.8	34.4	42.1	15.9	3.5	0.8	0.6	1,132
Lexington, KY	9.6	55.1	28.1	4.9	1.7	0.3	0.3	867
Lincoln, NE	9.9	58.2	24.9	4.8	0.8	0.4	1.0	848
Little Rock, AR	10.1	58.9	25.0	4.7	0.6	0.4	0.3	845
Los Angeles, CA	4.2	12.7	30.8	25.7	14.0	6.7	5.9	1,545
Louisville, KY	13.1	54.3	26.6	4.6	0.8	0.4	0.3	854
Madison, WI	5.0	40.5	38.5	11.6	2.9	0.9	0.6	1,046

Table continued on following page.

MSA[1]	Under $500	$500-$999	$1,000-$1,499	$1,500-$1,999	$2,000-$2,499	$2,500-2,999	$3,000 and up	Median ($)
Manchester, NH	6.9	24.7	42.8	19.9	4.2	0.9	0.5	1,191
Memphis, TN	7.8	50.9	32.8	6.4	1.5	0.3	0.3	930
Miami, FL	5.2	17.0	37.9	24.5	9.5	3.4	2.4	1,363
Midland, TX	2.0	25.1	41.0	20.1	7.5	3.2	1.1	1,269
Milwaukee, WI	7.7	54.1	28.9	6.7	1.6	0.5	0.3	903
Minneapolis, MN	9.2	32.4	35.9	16.1	4.2	1.2	1.1	1,102
Nashville, TN	8.0	35.2	38.0	13.3	3.6	1.1	0.8	1,073
New Haven, CT	10.4	24.6	41.3	17.0	4.6	1.2	1.0	1,153
New Orleans, LA	9.3	41.9	35.6	10.0	2.2	0.6	0.5	991
New York, NY	9.4	13.9	30.7	23.1	11.0	5.3	6.7	1,439
Oklahoma City, OK	8.2	56.4	27.3	6.2	1.3	0.3	0.4	876
Omaha, NE	8.2	50.7	31.0	7.5	1.4	0.4	0.7	927
Orlando, FL	2.9	25.1	46.3	19.7	4.2	1.1	0.7	1,210
Peoria, IL	16.6	60.9	17.6	2.6	1.0	0.4	1.0	764
Philadelphia, PA	8.1	29.1	38.4	15.9	5.4	1.7	1.4	1,143
Phoenix, AZ	3.6	34.4	40.9	15.4	3.6	1.1	1.1	1,124
Pittsburgh, PA	15.6	51.9	23.2	6.0	1.9	0.6	0.8	831
Portland, OR	4.8	20.9	42.1	21.8	7.1	1.8	1.4	1,271
Providence, RI	16.0	37.6	31.8	10.3	2.8	0.6	0.7	968
Provo, UT	6.6	39.1	33.3	15.8	3.7	0.9	0.6	1,054
Raleigh, NC	4.9	32.8	43.7	13.4	3.4	0.8	1.0	1,113
Reno, NV	4.9	39.3	34.7	15.9	3.7	0.8	0.8	1,074
Richmond, VA	7.3	30.2	44.1	13.9	2.9	0.8	0.8	1,117
Riverside, CA	4.2	22.6	34.7	23.5	9.9	3.7	1.5	1,326
Rochester, MN	11.5	47.5	27.7	10.0	1.5	0.7	0.9	908
Sacramento, CA	4.6	22.7	37.5	23.2	8.1	2.4	1.4	1,290
Salt Lake City, UT	5.4	33.3	41.2	15.4	3.3	0.8	0.7	1,114
San Antonio, TX	7.0	40.8	36.6	11.8	2.3	0.7	0.8	1,024
San Diego, CA	3.5	9.9	28.1	27.2	17.0	8.2	6.2	1,658
San Francisco, CA	6.0	9.4	17.2	21.4	18.2	11.9	15.8	1,905
San Jose, CA	3.5	5.8	11.6	18.8	20.7	17.2	22.4	2,249
Santa Rosa, CA	5.2	10.6	27.7	27.0	17.3	7.6	4.5	1,621
Savannah, GA	7.3	33.4	43.3	12.0	2.8	0.4	0.8	1,086
Seattle, WA	5.1	14.0	31.4	27.7	12.8	5.0	4.0	1,492
Sioux Falls, SD	9.4	64.4	20.0	4.4	0.7	0.4	0.8	829
Springfield, IL	11.4	63.1	19.9	3.6	0.9	0.9	0.2	818
Tallahassee, FL	6.9	44.2	36.9	8.4	2.9	0.5	0.2	991
Tampa, FL	4.9	33.9	40.4	14.9	3.6	1.4	1.0	1,115
Tucson, AZ	7.2	51.4	30.9	7.5	1.6	0.7	0.8	907
Tulsa, OK	10.7	56.8	26.1	4.4	1.0	0.5	0.5	852
Tuscaloosa, AL	17.1	54.6	21.8	4.2	1.5	0.2	0.6	819
Virginia Beach, VA	7.0	26.2	41.2	18.4	4.9	1.3	1.0	1,180
Washington, DC	4.6	7.8	25.4	32.2	16.6	7.3	6.1	1,690
Wichita, KS	11.4	60.3	22.5	4.0	0.9	0.3	0.7	818
Winston-Salem, NC	12.9	63.9	18.9	3.1	0.7	0.2	0.2	773
U.S.	9.4	36.2	30.0	14.0	5.6	2.4	2.4	1,062

Note: (1) Figures cover the Metropolitan Statistical Area (MSA)—see Appendix B for areas included; Figures are percentages except for Median; Gross rent is the contract rent plus the estimated average monthly cost of utilities (electricity, gas, and water and sewer) and fuels (oil, coal, kerosene, wood, etc.) if these are paid by the renter (or paid for the renter by someone else).
Source: U.S. Census Bureau, 2015-2019 American Community Survey 5-Year Estimates

Highest Level of Education: City

City	Less than H.S.	H.S. Diploma	Some College, No Deg.	Associate Degree	Bachelors Degree	Masters Degree	Profess. School Degree	Doctorate Degree
Albuquerque, NM	10.3	22.5	23.4	8.5	19.4	10.6	2.7	2.5
Allentown, PA	21.0	38.0	18.3	7.4	9.6	3.9	1.0	0.8
Anchorage, AK	6.1	23.4	25.4	9.0	22.2	9.5	3.1	1.3
Ann Arbor, MI	2.7	7.1	10.0	4.2	30.2	26.9	7.1	11.7
Athens, GA	12.1	19.8	17.1	6.9	22.1	13.4	3.0	5.6
Atlanta, GA	9.1	18.9	15.3	4.9	28.9	15.1	5.3	2.5
Austin, TX	10.6	15.6	16.7	5.4	32.3	13.6	3.3	2.5
Baton Rouge, LA	12.0	27.8	22.5	4.5	19.3	8.8	2.6	2.5
Boise City, ID	4.9	21.4	23.1	9.1	26.8	10.1	2.7	1.9
Boston, MA	12.8	19.7	13.1	4.6	27.0	14.5	4.8	3.4
Boulder, CO	3.1	6.2	11.1	3.6	36.2	24.7	6.4	8.7
Cape Coral, FL	8.2	37.3	21.0	10.1	15.8	5.3	1.3	0.9
Cedar Rapids, IA	6.7	26.6	22.2	12.4	22.9	6.6	1.5	1.0
Charleston, SC	5.1	17.6	16.3	7.9	33.8	12.6	4.5	2.2
Charlotte, NC	10.9	17.1	20.0	7.7	28.9	11.7	2.6	1.1
Chicago, IL	14.9	22.5	17.3	5.8	23.3	11.3	3.3	1.6
Cincinnati, OH	11.9	24.4	19.1	7.4	21.4	10.4	3.1	2.1
Clarksville, TN	7.1	27.9	26.9	10.5	18.7	6.9	0.8	1.2
Cleveland, OH	19.2	32.7	23.2	7.4	10.9	4.5	1.4	0.7
College Station, TX	5.6	11.4	17.0	7.4	29.3	15.7	3.3	10.3
Colorado Springs, CO	6.1	20.0	23.4	10.6	24.3	12.0	2.0	1.5
Columbia, MO	4.8	18.1	18.7	6.2	27.4	14.9	4.6	5.3
Columbia, SC	10.6	20.1	18.6	6.9	24.4	12.8	3.9	2.7
Columbus, OH	10.2	25.5	20.6	7.2	23.8	9.4	1.9	1.5
Dallas, TX	22.5	21.7	17.8	4.6	21.0	8.3	2.9	1.1
Davenport, IA	9.5	32.5	21.8	10.7	17.0	6.3	1.5	0.8
Denver, CO	12.0	16.8	16.5	5.3	30.2	13.1	4.2	2.0
Des Moines, IA	13.7	29.5	21.2	8.9	18.6	5.5	1.7	0.9
Durham, NC	11.9	16.4	15.5	6.5	25.8	14.7	4.2	4.8
Edison, NJ	7.9	19.5	11.7	5.4	30.0	20.3	2.8	2.5
El Paso, TX	19.7	23.0	24.0	8.2	16.7	6.4	1.2	0.8
Fargo, ND	5.7	20.9	19.6	13.8	28.0	8.0	2.1	1.8
Fayetteville, NC	8.3	24.4	29.4	10.6	18.0	6.7	1.5	1.0
Fort Collins, CO	3.5	15.1	17.7	8.3	32.3	16.8	2.4	4.0
Fort Wayne, IN	11.5	28.2	22.1	10.3	18.3	7.1	1.4	1.0
Fort Worth, TX	17.8	24.9	20.8	6.9	20.0	7.1	1.5	1.1
Grand Rapids, MI	13.3	21.9	20.5	7.9	24.4	8.7	2.0	1.4
Greeley, CO	15.5	27.2	23.4	9.1	15.4	7.2	1.2	1.0
Green Bay, WI	12.5	31.4	20.1	11.2	17.9	5.1	1.1	0.7
Greensboro, NC	10.2	21.5	21.7	8.4	24.1	10.0	2.3	1.8
Honolulu, HI	11.0	23.5	18.3	10.1	23.7	8.3	3.2	2.0
Houston, TX	21.1	22.8	17.8	5.5	20.0	8.6	2.6	1.6
Huntsville, AL	9.0	18.7	20.3	7.9	26.4	13.8	1.8	2.2
Indianapolis, IN	14.2	27.9	19.4	7.6	20.0	7.6	2.1	1.1
Jacksonville, FL	10.5	28.4	22.3	10.1	19.1	7.0	1.7	0.8
Kansas City, MO	10.0	25.3	22.0	7.4	22.2	9.3	2.5	1.2
Lafayette, LA	10.5	27.0	20.0	4.3	25.6	8.5	2.7	1.4
Lakeland, FL	12.0	33.0	19.5	9.6	16.8	6.7	1.6	0.9
Las Vegas, NV	15.2	27.6	24.6	8.0	16.0	5.9	1.9	0.8
Lexington, KY	8.8	19.6	20.5	7.5	24.4	12.0	4.1	3.2
Lincoln, NE	6.7	21.3	21.2	11.2	24.8	9.8	2.2	2.8
Little Rock, AR	8.7	22.2	21.1	6.2	23.7	11.0	4.3	2.8
Los Angeles, CA	22.5	19.2	17.6	6.2	22.6	7.6	2.8	1.4
Louisville, KY	10.4	28.6	22.9	8.1	17.9	8.5	2.3	1.2
Madison, WI	4.5	14.2	15.3	8.0	32.1	16.2	4.2	5.3

Table continued on following page.

City	Less than H.S.	H.S. Diploma	Some College, No Deg.	Associate Degree	Bachelors Degree	Masters Degree	Profess. School Degree	Doctorate Degree
Manchester, NH	12.7	29.1	18.9	9.3	20.3	7.3	1.7	0.9
Memphis, TN	14.3	30.6	23.3	5.6	15.7	7.1	2.0	1.3
Miami, FL	22.0	28.4	12.5	7.4	17.9	7.1	3.6	1.1
Midland, TX	14.9	25.2	23.2	7.7	20.7	5.9	1.7	0.7
Milwaukee, WI	16.0	30.2	21.9	7.2	15.9	6.5	1.3	0.9
Minneapolis, MN	10.0	15.1	17.1	7.3	30.4	13.6	4.0	2.5
Nashville, TN	11.2	22.3	18.9	6.4	25.8	10.3	2.9	2.1
New Haven, CT	14.4	32.2	14.0	4.5	15.7	10.7	4.2	4.3
New Orleans, LA	13.5	22.8	21.5	4.7	21.2	9.9	4.4	2.0
New York, NY	17.8	24.0	13.7	6.3	22.2	11.2	3.2	1.5
Oklahoma City, OK	13.6	25.4	22.9	7.3	19.7	7.5	2.4	1.1
Omaha, NE	10.5	22.3	21.9	7.7	24.3	8.9	2.9	1.5
Orlando, FL	9.6	23.2	18.4	10.8	25.4	8.3	3.0	1.3
Peoria, IL	10.6	24.3	21.5	8.6	20.7	10.2	2.7	1.3
Philadelphia, PA	15.3	32.6	16.7	5.7	17.3	8.1	2.6	1.6
Phoenix, AZ	18.1	23.6	22.0	7.7	18.3	7.3	2.0	1.0
Pittsburgh, PA	7.1	25.5	15.1	7.9	23.2	13.1	4.3	3.9
Portland, OR	7.6	15.1	20.3	6.6	30.1	13.8	4.1	2.4
Providence, RI	18.4	31.4	15.2	5.0	16.1	8.6	2.9	2.5
Provo, UT	7.1	14.3	26.5	8.9	29.7	8.9	1.6	2.8
Raleigh, NC	8.2	15.6	17.8	7.5	32.4	13.1	3.1	2.3
Reno, NV	11.0	22.2	25.0	8.2	20.6	8.4	2.3	2.3
Richmond, VA	14.6	21.8	18.4	5.6	23.5	11.0	3.1	2.0
Riverside, CA	19.4	26.3	23.7	7.7	13.5	6.4	1.4	1.7
Rochester, MN	6.0	18.7	17.2	11.4	25.7	12.1	5.2	3.7
Sacramento, CA	14.7	21.3	22.4	8.5	21.2	7.7	2.9	1.3
Salt Lake City, UT	11.2	17.5	17.7	7.0	25.7	12.5	4.6	3.7
San Antonio, TX	17.6	26.3	22.4	7.7	16.6	6.7	1.7	1.0
San Diego, CA	11.9	15.1	19.7	7.4	27.0	12.2	3.7	3.0
San Francisco, CA	11.5	12.1	13.3	5.0	34.8	15.4	5.0	2.8
San Jose, CA	15.4	16.6	16.8	7.5	25.7	13.6	2.0	2.5
Santa Rosa, CA	13.8	19.3	24.5	9.8	20.1	8.0	2.9	1.5
Savannah, GA	12.4	26.8	25.9	6.7	17.8	7.6	1.6	1.2
Seattle, WA	5.2	9.6	15.0	6.2	36.7	18.1	5.3	3.9
Sioux Falls, SD	7.7	24.8	20.8	11.5	23.8	8.1	2.2	1.1
Springfield, IL	8.7	25.9	22.1	7.6	21.5	9.8	3.3	1.2
Tallahassee, FL	6.5	17.0	19.0	9.3	26.2	13.8	3.9	4.3
Tampa, FL	12.1	25.6	16.0	7.7	23.3	9.6	3.9	1.7
Tucson, AZ	15.0	23.6	25.6	8.4	16.5	7.8	1.4	1.6
Tulsa, OK	12.7	25.3	22.6	7.9	20.7	7.2	2.5	1.1
Tuscaloosa, AL	10.9	27.3	19.9	5.0	21.0	10.3	2.5	3.1
Virginia Beach, VA	6.5	21.0	25.7	10.9	22.6	10.2	2.1	1.1
Washington, DC	9.1	16.8	12.6	3.0	24.8	21.2	8.4	4.2
Wichita, KS	11.7	26.4	24.0	7.9	19.1	8.1	1.8	1.1
Winston-Salem, NC	11.8	24.9	21.5	7.4	20.8	8.9	3.0	1.9
U.S.	12.0	27.0	20.4	8.5	19.8	8.8	2.1	1.4

Note: Figures cover persons age 25 and over
Source: U.S. Census Bureau, 2015-2019 American Community Survey 5-Year Estimates

Highest Level of Education: Metro Area

Metro Area	Less than H.S.	H.S. Diploma	Some College, No Deg.	Associate Degree	Bachelors Degree	Masters Degree	Profess. School Degree	Doctorate Degree
Albuquerque, NM	11.4	24.6	23.3	8.5	17.9	9.8	2.3	2.2
Allentown, PA	10.0	34.2	17.1	9.3	18.3	8.4	1.6	1.2
Anchorage, AK	6.3	26.0	26.2	9.1	20.1	8.5	2.6	1.2
Ann Arbor, MI	4.7	14.6	17.6	7.1	26.3	18.8	4.7	6.0
Athens, GA	12.2	24.5	16.8	7.1	19.9	11.8	3.1	4.5
Atlanta, GA	10.4	23.9	19.5	7.6	24.0	10.6	2.5	1.5
Austin, TX	10.1	19.1	19.6	6.5	28.8	11.6	2.5	1.9
Baton Rouge, LA	12.6	32.2	21.4	6.2	18.0	6.6	1.7	1.3
Boise City, ID	8.2	25.8	24.8	9.4	21.3	7.4	1.7	1.3
Boston, MA	8.3	22.1	14.5	7.0	26.0	15.2	3.5	3.3
Boulder, CO	5.0	11.7	15.1	6.1	34.0	18.8	4.1	5.2
Cape Coral, FL	11.6	31.0	20.3	8.9	17.6	7.2	2.2	1.2
Cedar Rapids, IA	5.7	29.0	21.5	12.8	21.9	6.9	1.4	0.8
Charleston, SC	9.3	25.4	20.1	9.5	23.0	8.9	2.4	1.2
Charlotte, NC	11.0	23.5	21.1	9.2	23.5	9.0	1.8	0.9
Chicago, IL	11.3	23.9	19.5	7.2	23.0	10.9	2.6	1.4
Cincinnati, OH	9.0	29.7	19.2	8.4	21.0	9.3	2.0	1.4
Clarksville, TN	9.3	30.2	25.4	10.3	16.1	6.8	1.1	0.9
Cleveland, OH	9.4	28.9	21.8	8.7	18.9	8.7	2.4	1.2
College Station, TX	13.4	22.2	20.4	6.5	20.6	9.6	2.2	5.1
Colorado Springs, CO	5.6	20.5	24.0	11.3	23.5	11.8	1.8	1.4
Columbia, MO	6.4	23.7	19.8	7.4	24.5	11.3	3.2	3.7
Columbia, SC	10.1	26.9	21.2	9.0	20.1	9.2	1.8	1.5
Columbus, OH	8.5	27.7	19.6	7.5	23.4	9.7	2.2	1.4
Dallas, TX	14.4	22.3	21.1	7.0	23.0	9.2	1.9	1.1
Davenport, IA	9.0	30.5	23.0	10.5	17.2	7.3	1.5	0.8
Denver, CO	8.8	19.9	19.8	7.7	27.7	11.8	2.7	1.6
Des Moines, IA	7.5	25.6	20.2	10.3	25.4	7.7	2.2	1.1
Durham, NC	11.2	19.8	16.1	7.6	23.2	13.2	4.0	4.9
Edison, NJ	13.5	24.7	14.8	6.7	23.4	12.1	3.3	1.6
El Paso, TX	21.7	23.7	23.1	8.2	15.7	5.7	1.1	0.7
Fargo, ND	5.2	21.0	21.0	14.2	27.4	7.9	1.8	1.5
Fayetteville, NC	10.4	27.3	27.5	11.1	15.7	6.2	1.0	0.8
Fort Collins, CO	4.1	19.0	20.4	9.2	28.0	13.9	2.1	3.2
Fort Wayne, IN	10.4	29.2	21.7	10.9	18.4	6.9	1.5	0.9
Fort Worth, TX	14.4	22.3	21.1	7.0	23.0	9.2	1.9	1.1
Grand Rapids, MI	8.8	27.2	22.0	9.3	21.8	8.1	1.7	1.1
Greeley, CO	11.9	27.3	24.1	9.1	18.6	7.0	1.1	0.9
Green Bay, WI	8.0	32.1	19.7	12.4	19.6	6.0	1.5	0.7
Greensboro, NC	13.2	26.7	21.7	8.9	19.2	7.5	1.5	1.3
Honolulu, HI	8.1	25.9	20.3	10.7	22.9	8.1	2.5	1.5
Houston, TX	16.3	23.2	20.6	7.1	21.0	8.4	2.0	1.5
Huntsville, AL	9.8	22.7	20.2	8.1	24.2	11.9	1.4	1.7
Indianapolis, IN	10.3	27.9	19.3	7.9	22.4	8.8	2.2	1.3
Jacksonville, FL	9.1	27.7	21.8	10.0	20.6	7.9	1.9	1.1
Kansas City, MO	8.0	25.5	21.6	7.7	23.5	10.2	2.3	1.2
Lafayette, LA	15.9	36.4	18.6	5.7	16.4	5.0	1.3	0.7
Lakeland, FL	15.0	34.7	20.9	9.2	13.2	5.2	1.1	0.7
Las Vegas, NV	13.9	28.5	25.1	8.1	16.2	5.8	1.6	0.8
Lexington, KY	9.9	24.2	20.8	7.9	21.3	10.3	3.2	2.4
Lincoln, NE	6.3	21.9	21.2	11.7	24.5	9.7	2.2	2.6
Little Rock, AR	9.6	29.3	23.0	7.8	18.9	8.0	2.1	1.5
Los Angeles, CA	19.3	19.8	19.2	7.2	22.4	8.2	2.5	1.4
Louisville, KY	9.9	29.6	22.3	8.6	17.9	8.4	2.2	1.1
Madison, WI	4.7	21.0	17.9	10.3	27.7	12.1	3.0	3.2

Table continued on following page.

Metro Area	Less than H.S.	H.S. Diploma	Some College, No Deg.	Associate Degree	Bachelors Degree	Masters Degree	Profess. School Degree	Doctorate Degree
Manchester, NH	7.9	25.8	18.2	10.0	24.3	10.9	1.6	1.3
Memphis, TN	12.0	29.2	23.5	7.1	17.4	7.9	1.9	1.2
Miami, FL	14.5	26.5	17.4	9.3	20.2	7.9	2.9	1.2
Midland, TX	15.7	25.9	23.5	7.8	19.3	5.8	1.4	0.6
Milwaukee, WI	8.5	26.5	20.6	8.7	23.0	9.0	2.3	1.3
Minneapolis, MN	6.4	21.2	20.0	10.4	27.4	10.4	2.6	1.6
Nashville, TN	10.0	26.4	20.2	7.3	23.5	9.0	2.2	1.6
New Haven, CT	9.9	30.7	17.1	7.3	18.6	11.2	3.1	2.1
New Orleans, LA	13.1	28.2	22.5	5.8	19.0	7.3	2.8	1.2
New York, NY	13.5	24.7	14.8	6.7	23.4	12.1	3.3	1.6
Oklahoma City, OK	11.0	27.3	23.6	7.5	19.6	7.6	2.0	1.3
Omaha, NE	8.3	23.8	22.5	9.1	23.8	9.0	2.3	1.3
Orlando, FL	10.5	25.8	19.9	11.5	21.3	7.8	2.0	1.0
Peoria, IL	8.3	30.5	23.2	10.4	18.1	7.2	1.5	0.9
Philadelphia, PA	9.3	29.0	16.7	7.1	22.4	10.8	2.7	1.9
Phoenix, AZ	12.5	23.0	24.4	8.6	20.0	8.3	1.9	1.2
Pittsburgh, PA	6.1	32.4	16.4	10.2	21.3	9.8	2.3	1.7
Portland, OR	7.9	19.9	23.6	8.8	24.7	10.5	2.6	1.9
Providence, RI	12.3	28.8	18.0	8.6	19.6	9.2	1.9	1.5
Provo, UT	5.5	16.8	26.7	10.7	27.7	9.2	1.6	1.7
Raleigh, NC	8.3	17.7	18.2	9.0	29.6	12.6	2.4	2.2
Reno, NV	11.3	23.6	25.7	8.6	19.2	7.8	2.1	1.8
Richmond, VA	10.1	25.1	20.0	7.4	23.1	10.5	2.3	1.6
Riverside, CA	18.9	26.6	24.6	8.2	13.9	5.6	1.3	0.9
Rochester, MN	5.9	23.9	19.1	12.4	22.7	9.7	3.8	2.5
Sacramento, CA	10.7	21.2	24.7	9.9	21.8	7.8	2.6	1.4
Salt Lake City, UT	9.2	23.0	23.9	9.0	22.5	8.7	2.3	1.5
San Antonio, TX	14.9	26.3	22.6	8.0	18.0	7.5	1.7	1.0
San Diego, CA	12.6	18.2	22.3	8.1	23.8	10.0	2.9	2.1
San Francisco, CA	10.9	15.5	17.3	6.6	29.3	13.7	3.8	2.9
San Jose, CA	11.9	14.4	15.4	6.9	27.3	17.5	2.7	3.9
Santa Rosa, CA	11.2	18.7	25.0	9.6	22.2	8.6	3.1	1.6
Savannah, GA	10.2	26.3	24.2	7.9	19.5	8.4	2.2	1.3
Seattle, WA	7.4	19.4	21.0	9.3	26.6	11.7	2.7	2.0
Sioux Falls, SD	7.1	26.1	20.6	12.7	23.2	7.3	2.0	1.0
Springfield, IL	7.4	27.7	22.7	8.3	21.2	9.0	2.6	1.0
Tallahassee, FL	9.4	23.7	19.8	8.7	22.0	10.4	2.9	3.1
Tampa, FL	10.4	28.9	20.5	9.8	19.6	7.6	2.0	1.2
Tucson, AZ	11.6	22.2	25.1	8.7	18.7	9.4	2.3	2.0
Tulsa, OK	10.6	29.1	23.7	8.9	18.9	6.3	1.7	0.9
Tuscaloosa, AL	12.9	31.7	21.1	6.9	16.6	7.5	1.4	1.9
Virginia Beach, VA	8.6	24.9	24.7	9.9	19.5	9.3	1.8	1.2
Washington, DC	9.1	18.2	16.0	5.9	25.8	17.6	4.3	3.2
Wichita, KS	9.9	26.5	24.4	8.6	19.6	8.3	1.7	1.0
Winston-Salem, NC	13.0	29.4	21.6	9.3	17.4	6.5	1.6	1.2
U.S.	12.0	27.0	20.4	8.5	19.8	8.8	2.1	1.4

Note: Figures cover persons age 25 and over; Figures cover the Metropolitan Statistical Area—see Appendix B for areas included
Source: U.S. Census Bureau, 2015-2019 American Community Survey 5-Year Estimates

School Enrollment by Grade and Control: City

City	Preschool (%) Public	Preschool (%) Private	Kindergarten (%) Public	Kindergarten (%) Private	Grades 1 - 4 (%) Public	Grades 1 - 4 (%) Private	Grades 5 - 8 (%) Public	Grades 5 - 8 (%) Private	Grades 9 - 12 (%) Public	Grades 9 - 12 (%) Private
Albuquerque, NM	59.3	40.7	87.2	12.8	91.8	8.2	90.0	10.0	92.0	8.0
Allentown, PA	73.8	26.2	82.8	17.2	87.8	12.2	88.3	11.7	89.0	11.0
Anchorage, AK	56.6	43.4	94.0	6.0	92.3	7.7	92.5	7.5	95.1	4.9
Ann Arbor, MI	25.7	74.3	94.1	5.9	91.8	8.2	87.6	12.4	94.2	5.8
Athens, GA	67.9	32.1	92.6	7.4	91.9	8.1	88.8	11.2	88.5	11.5
Atlanta, GA	54.3	45.7	84.5	15.5	87.8	12.2	79.5	20.5	80.1	19.9
Austin, TX	51.0	49.0	86.9	13.1	89.3	10.7	88.9	11.1	91.0	9.0
Baton Rouge, LA	66.8	33.2	75.3	24.7	80.3	19.7	79.5	20.5	80.8	19.2
Boise City, ID	30.6	69.4	84.8	15.2	90.0	10.0	91.7	8.3	89.1	10.9
Boston, MA	50.7	49.3	84.9	15.1	85.7	14.3	86.8	13.2	87.8	12.2
Boulder, CO	44.0	56.0	84.5	15.5	92.5	7.5	93.4	6.6	92.2	7.8
Cape Coral, FL	84.8	15.2	94.8	5.2	92.0	8.0	93.0	7.0	91.8	8.2
Cedar Rapids, IA	67.5	32.5	86.4	13.6	88.9	11.1	93.0	7.0	90.0	10.0
Charleston, SC	41.2	58.9	78.8	21.2	83.4	16.6	78.9	21.1	78.9	21.1
Charlotte, NC	47.5	52.5	90.5	9.5	90.7	9.3	87.6	12.4	89.8	10.2
Chicago, IL	58.4	41.6	79.9	20.1	85.9	14.1	85.4	14.6	87.4	12.6
Cincinnati, OH	64.7	35.3	73.1	26.9	77.6	22.4	80.1	19.9	80.8	19.2
Clarksville, TN	57.3	42.7	90.6	9.4	93.7	6.3	92.5	7.5	92.4	7.6
Cleveland, OH	74.3	25.7	79.3	20.7	79.6	20.4	77.9	22.1	79.8	20.2
College Station, TX	46.9	53.1	85.1	14.9	86.5	13.5	93.5	6.5	92.7	7.3
Colorado Springs, CO	57.1	42.9	89.3	10.7	92.5	7.5	92.5	7.5	92.0	8.0
Columbia, MO	36.1	63.9	76.7	23.3	87.5	12.5	88.1	11.9	88.8	11.2
Columbia, SC	57.2	42.8	74.3	25.7	88.1	11.9	87.7	12.3	86.7	13.3
Columbus, OH	60.3	39.7	85.3	14.7	87.7	12.3	87.2	12.8	87.3	12.7
Dallas, TX	69.2	30.8	91.0	9.0	92.0	8.0	91.7	8.3	91.6	8.4
Davenport, IA	57.0	43.0	86.1	13.9	89.3	10.7	84.3	15.7	92.8	7.2
Denver, CO	64.4	35.6	86.3	13.7	91.4	8.6	91.0	9.0	91.4	8.6
Des Moines, IA	73.0	27.0	90.0	10.0	89.0	11.0	91.7	8.3	92.3	7.7
Durham, NC	52.1	47.9	91.9	8.1	88.8	11.2	87.3	12.7	89.7	10.3
Edison, NJ	30.2	69.8	67.7	32.3	90.1	9.9	90.0	10.0	91.6	8.4
El Paso, TX	78.5	21.5	93.3	6.7	95.0	5.0	94.6	5.4	96.2	3.8
Fargo, ND	53.4	46.6	94.7	5.3	90.4	9.6	89.3	10.7	93.7	6.3
Fayetteville, NC	63.5	36.5	88.7	11.3	87.2	12.8	87.4	12.6	89.7	10.3
Fort Collins, CO	41.9	58.1	91.7	8.3	94.5	5.5	95.1	4.9	94.6	5.4
Fort Wayne, IN	45.5	54.5	83.5	16.5	79.5	20.5	82.2	17.8	81.3	18.7
Fort Worth, TX	62.0	38.0	87.1	12.9	92.6	7.4	90.7	9.3	92.8	7.2
Grand Rapids, MI	60.4	39.6	74.5	25.5	83.4	16.6	83.4	16.6	84.9	15.1
Greeley, CO	69.6	30.4	83.6	16.4	91.5	8.5	92.6	7.4	95.3	4.7
Green Bay, WI	71.8	28.2	85.7	14.3	90.6	9.4	84.6	15.4	91.1	8.9
Greensboro, NC	53.2	46.8	89.5	10.5	93.4	6.6	90.2	9.8	91.6	8.4
Honolulu, HI	34.7	65.3	79.6	20.4	83.3	16.7	73.0	27.0	74.8	25.2
Houston, TX	66.9	33.1	90.8	9.2	94.2	5.8	92.7	7.3	93.5	6.5
Huntsville, AL	59.4	40.6	87.2	12.8	80.1	19.9	82.9	17.1	84.8	15.2
Indianapolis, IN	61.8	38.2	85.6	14.4	88.5	11.5	87.1	12.9	89.2	10.8
Jacksonville, FL	57.5	42.5	84.3	15.7	84.3	15.7	81.7	18.3	83.5	16.5
Kansas City, MO	57.7	42.3	85.3	14.7	90.1	9.9	88.3	11.7	85.4	14.6
Lafayette, LA	60.7	39.3	64.2	35.8	74.4	25.6	73.3	26.7	80.6	19.4
Lakeland, FL	61.7	38.3	85.0	15.0	83.6	16.4	83.7	16.3	88.0	12.0
Las Vegas, NV	65.7	34.3	88.6	11.4	91.3	8.7	91.7	8.3	93.0	7.0
Lexington, KY	44.2	55.8	86.4	13.6	87.2	12.8	86.6	13.4	86.1	13.9
Lincoln, NE	44.8	55.2	73.8	26.2	84.9	15.1	86.5	13.5	86.4	13.6
Little Rock, AR	60.3	39.7	82.3	17.7	82.7	17.3	82.0	18.0	79.8	20.2
Los Angeles, CA	60.2	39.8	88.1	11.9	89.0	11.0	88.6	11.4	88.8	11.2
Louisville, KY	51.1	48.9	80.2	19.8	83.4	16.6	79.9	20.1	79.3	20.7
Madison, WI	53.6	46.4	85.3	14.7	88.4	11.6	87.0	13.0	91.0	9.0

Table continued on following page.

City	Preschool (%) Public	Preschool (%) Private	Kindergarten (%) Public	Kindergarten (%) Private	Grades 1 - 4 (%) Public	Grades 1 - 4 (%) Private	Grades 5 - 8 (%) Public	Grades 5 - 8 (%) Private	Grades 9 - 12 (%) Public	Grades 9 - 12 (%) Private
Manchester, NH	52.6	47.4	86.1	13.9	89.9	10.1	93.1	6.9	89.5	10.5
Memphis, TN	67.2	32.8	87.3	12.7	87.9	12.1	87.2	12.8	85.5	14.5
Miami, FL	56.0	44.0	86.7	13.3	88.1	11.9	85.6	14.4	90.8	9.2
Midland, TX	64.4	35.6	89.1	10.9	86.0	14.0	88.3	11.7	89.9	10.1
Milwaukee, WI	73.5	26.5	79.4	20.6	77.1	22.9	75.8	24.2	81.4	18.6
Minneapolis, MN	53.4	46.6	85.1	14.9	88.2	11.8	88.9	11.1	87.7	12.3
Nashville, TN	50.7	49.3	87.4	12.6	85.6	14.4	83.4	16.6	82.0	18.0
New Haven, CT	83.6	16.4	94.0	6.0	94.8	5.2	93.8	6.2	92.2	7.8
New Orleans, LA	50.3	49.7	77.0	23.0	80.1	19.9	80.0	20.0	78.9	21.1
New York, NY	60.9	39.1	79.2	20.8	82.7	17.3	82.2	17.8	82.3	17.7
Oklahoma City, OK	73.4	26.6	91.7	8.3	91.8	8.2	91.0	9.0	90.2	9.8
Omaha, NE	53.5	46.5	82.0	18.0	83.5	16.5	85.3	14.7	83.2	16.8
Orlando, FL	62.2	37.8	86.4	13.6	91.2	8.8	85.0	15.0	93.3	6.7
Peoria, IL	60.1	39.9	70.0	30.0	83.9	16.1	83.4	16.6	88.7	11.3
Philadelphia, PA	56.8	43.2	79.1	20.9	79.1	20.9	80.6	19.4	80.1	19.9
Phoenix, AZ	62.7	37.3	90.0	10.0	92.9	7.1	92.4	7.6	93.1	6.9
Pittsburgh, PA	48.0	52.0	77.1	22.9	73.1	26.9	75.8	24.2	81.5	18.5
Portland, OR	39.4	60.6	84.8	15.2	88.0	12.0	87.1	12.9	85.1	14.9
Providence, RI	51.6	48.4	87.8	12.2	86.0	14.0	85.4	14.6	88.6	11.4
Provo, UT	53.8	46.2	95.7	4.3	93.9	6.1	95.8	4.2	88.5	11.5
Raleigh, NC	43.5	56.5	89.3	10.7	90.6	9.4	89.2	10.8	90.6	9.4
Reno, NV	60.7	39.3	86.1	13.9	94.1	5.9	93.2	6.8	94.0	6.0
Richmond, VA	58.6	41.4	91.1	8.9	87.8	12.2	80.8	19.2	87.1	12.9
Riverside, CA	66.0	34.0	90.5	9.5	94.0	6.0	93.6	6.4	95.0	5.0
Rochester, MN	50.9	49.1	80.4	19.6	86.9	13.1	87.1	12.9	91.4	8.6
Sacramento, CA	68.9	31.1	92.8	7.2	93.2	6.8	92.9	7.1	92.6	7.4
Salt Lake City, UT	47.7	52.3	88.2	11.8	91.2	8.8	91.0	9.0	92.8	7.2
San Antonio, TX	70.1	29.9	90.3	9.7	93.1	6.9	92.9	7.1	92.6	7.4
San Diego, CA	52.5	47.5	92.9	7.1	90.9	9.1	91.2	8.8	91.5	8.5
San Francisco, CA	37.5	62.5	73.1	26.9	72.2	27.8	68.1	31.9	75.0	25.0
San Jose, CA	41.9	58.1	81.2	18.8	87.0	13.0	87.0	13.0	86.8	13.2
Santa Rosa, CA	53.6	46.4	94.6	5.4	95.9	4.1	92.5	7.5	92.0	8.0
Savannah, GA	67.6	32.4	93.0	7.0	90.1	9.9	91.0	9.0	89.6	10.4
Seattle, WA	32.6	67.4	79.7	20.3	81.6	18.4	75.9	24.1	79.8	20.2
Sioux Falls, SD	51.1	48.9	87.3	12.7	88.2	11.8	87.5	12.5	84.2	15.8
Springfield, IL	65.7	34.3	80.4	19.6	81.9	18.1	83.9	16.1	85.6	14.4
Tallahassee, FL	48.6	51.4	86.3	13.7	85.9	14.1	83.3	16.7	87.4	12.6
Tampa, FL	49.9	50.1	83.4	16.6	89.5	10.5	85.7	14.3	84.5	15.5
Tucson, AZ	74.0	26.0	85.8	14.2	89.6	10.4	91.3	8.7	92.8	7.2
Tulsa, OK	67.6	32.4	87.1	12.9	88.3	11.7	85.8	14.2	85.2	14.8
Tuscaloosa, AL	62.5	37.5	91.8	8.2	86.2	13.8	92.2	7.8	85.1	14.9
Virginia Beach, VA	37.7	62.3	77.3	22.7	90.2	9.8	88.7	11.3	92.7	7.3
Washington, DC	77.1	22.9	92.3	7.7	87.6	12.4	82.7	17.3	82.6	17.4
Wichita, KS	62.5	37.5	83.7	16.3	85.4	14.6	84.7	15.3	84.2	15.8
Winston-Salem, NC	55.3	44.7	94.1	5.9	93.3	6.7	90.8	9.2	93.2	6.8
U.S.	59.1	40.9	87.6	12.4	89.5	10.5	89.4	10.6	90.1	9.9

Note: Figures shown cover persons 3 years old and over
Source: U.S. Census Bureau, 2015-2019 American Community Survey 5-Year Estimates

Appendix A: Comparative Statistics

School Enrollment by Grade and Control: Metro Area

Metro Area	Preschool (%) Public	Preschool (%) Private	Kindergarten (%) Public	Kindergarten (%) Private	Grades 1-4 (%) Public	Grades 1-4 (%) Private	Grades 5-8 (%) Public	Grades 5-8 (%) Private	Grades 9-12 (%) Public	Grades 9-12 (%) Private
Albuquerque, NM	64.5	35.5	85.6	14.4	90.1	9.9	89.4	10.6	91.7	8.3
Allentown, PA	49.0	51.0	85.5	14.5	89.4	10.6	90.5	9.5	91.0	9.0
Anchorage, AK	58.3	41.7	92.4	7.6	90.7	9.3	90.5	9.5	92.8	7.2
Ann Arbor, MI	49.6	50.4	89.6	10.4	87.3	12.7	87.7	12.3	91.8	8.2
Athens, GA	67.9	32.1	90.9	9.1	90.1	9.9	86.0	14.0	86.7	13.3
Atlanta, GA	56.0	44.0	86.9	13.1	91.0	9.0	89.2	10.8	89.9	10.1
Austin, TX	51.5	48.5	88.1	11.9	90.7	9.3	90.7	9.3	92.4	7.6
Baton Rouge, LA	57.1	42.9	76.9	23.1	81.4	18.6	81.7	18.3	81.4	18.6
Boise City, ID	37.7	62.3	86.1	13.9	91.1	8.9	92.8	7.2	90.5	9.5
Boston, MA	45.7	54.3	87.7	12.3	91.2	8.8	89.8	10.2	86.9	13.1
Boulder, CO	50.7	49.3	84.7	15.3	90.8	9.2	90.8	9.2	93.9	6.1
Cape Coral, FL	65.5	34.5	89.7	10.3	92.6	7.4	91.5	8.5	90.8	9.2
Cedar Rapids, IA	69.1	30.9	87.8	12.2	89.0	11.0	92.3	7.7	92.3	7.7
Charleston, SC	51.2	48.8	86.2	13.8	89.8	10.2	89.3	10.7	90.4	9.6
Charlotte, NC	50.2	49.8	90.0	10.0	90.5	9.5	88.9	11.1	90.4	9.6
Chicago, IL	58.0	42.0	84.8	15.2	89.3	10.7	89.0	11.0	90.6	9.4
Cincinnati, OH	53.4	46.6	78.8	21.2	83.1	16.9	83.9	16.1	82.5	17.5
Clarksville, TN	62.9	37.1	92.1	7.9	88.8	11.2	89.5	10.5	89.0	11.0
Cleveland, OH	54.9	45.1	81.2	18.8	81.4	18.6	82.0	18.0	84.1	15.9
College Station, TX	60.1	39.9	86.1	13.9	88.9	11.1	92.4	7.6	93.3	6.7
Colorado Springs, CO	62.1	37.9	89.5	10.5	92.5	7.5	92.6	7.4	92.2	7.8
Columbia, MO	47.1	52.9	84.2	15.8	88.0	12.0	89.0	11.0	90.3	9.7
Columbia, SC	57.9	42.1	88.4	11.6	91.0	9.0	92.1	7.9	92.9	7.1
Columbus, OH	55.0	45.0	85.2	14.8	88.8	11.2	88.9	11.1	89.3	10.7
Dallas, TX	58.9	41.1	90.2	9.8	92.6	7.4	92.3	7.7	92.4	7.6
Davenport, IA	69.0	31.0	89.9	10.1	91.6	8.4	91.6	8.4	93.2	6.8
Denver, CO	59.6	40.4	90.1	9.9	92.5	7.5	92.0	8.0	91.9	8.1
Des Moines, IA	65.6	34.4	87.6	12.4	91.6	8.4	91.3	8.7	92.1	7.9
Durham, NC	49.5	50.5	88.6	11.4	89.6	10.4	88.8	11.2	90.8	9.2
Edison, NJ	54.8	45.2	82.3	17.7	85.6	14.4	85.7	14.3	85.1	14.9
El Paso, TX	81.0	19.0	93.9	6.1	95.1	4.9	94.8	5.2	96.4	3.6
Fargo, ND	58.8	41.2	93.6	6.4	89.5	10.5	89.3	10.7	93.8	6.2
Fayetteville, NC	63.5	36.5	88.7	11.3	87.7	12.3	88.9	11.1	89.4	10.6
Fort Collins, CO	52.2	47.8	91.0	9.0	92.3	7.7	91.9	8.1	91.4	8.6
Fort Wayne, IN	42.6	57.4	78.5	21.5	77.9	22.1	79.3	20.7	81.7	18.3
Fort Worth, TX	58.9	41.1	90.2	9.8	92.6	7.4	92.3	7.7	92.4	7.6
Grand Rapids, MI	62.5	37.5	82.2	17.8	84.8	15.2	86.2	13.8	86.1	13.9
Greeley, CO	69.7	30.3	89.1	10.9	91.9	8.1	94.0	6.0	93.9	6.1
Green Bay, WI	69.2	30.8	85.4	14.6	88.9	11.1	88.4	11.6	93.2	6.8
Greensboro, NC	50.5	49.5	89.4	10.6	90.3	9.7	89.1	10.9	90.3	9.7
Honolulu, HI	36.3	63.7	80.0	20.0	85.3	14.7	78.3	21.7	76.8	23.2
Houston, TX	58.1	41.9	90.2	9.8	93.1	6.9	93.0	7.0	93.3	6.7
Huntsville, AL	54.3	45.7	85.8	14.2	82.9	17.1	82.7	17.3	86.0	14.0
Indianapolis, IN	53.8	46.2	87.2	12.8	89.5	10.5	89.2	10.8	89.2	10.8
Jacksonville, FL	55.1	44.9	86.2	13.8	86.3	13.7	84.3	15.7	86.7	13.3
Kansas City, MO	58.1	41.9	88.5	11.5	89.6	10.4	89.2	10.8	89.4	10.6
Lafayette, LA	66.9	33.1	79.2	20.8	81.0	19.0	79.8	20.2	81.3	18.7
Lakeland, FL	69.5	30.5	85.9	14.1	89.0	11.0	86.1	13.9	90.5	9.5
Las Vegas, NV	61.7	38.3	89.8	10.2	92.5	7.5	92.9	7.1	93.4	6.6
Lexington, KY	47.1	52.9	83.9	16.1	88.1	11.9	86.9	13.1	86.8	13.2
Lincoln, NE	44.3	55.7	75.3	24.7	84.3	15.7	86.7	13.3	86.9	13.1
Little Rock, AR	63.2	36.8	87.1	12.9	88.9	11.1	88.9	11.1	87.4	12.6
Los Angeles, CA	58.5	41.5	88.4	11.6	90.8	9.2	91.0	9.0	91.4	8.6
Louisville, KY	49.2	50.8	82.9	17.1	84.2	15.8	81.4	18.6	81.3	18.7
Madison, WI	66.3	33.7	88.6	11.4	90.0	10.0	90.0	10.0	94.2	5.8

Table continued on following page.

Metro Area	Preschool (%) Public	Preschool (%) Private	Kindergarten (%) Public	Kindergarten (%) Private	Grades 1-4 (%) Public	Grades 1-4 (%) Private	Grades 5-8 (%) Public	Grades 5-8 (%) Private	Grades 9-12 (%) Public	Grades 9-12 (%) Private
Manchester, NH	42.4	57.6	83.7	16.3	87.1	12.9	89.9	10.1	88.9	11.1
Memphis, TN	61.4	38.6	86.2	13.8	86.6	13.4	86.3	13.7	84.7	15.3
Miami, FL	50.3	49.7	83.3	16.7	86.2	13.8	86.7	13.3	87.2	12.8
Midland, TX	64.3	35.7	89.1	10.9	86.9	13.1	90.0	10.0	90.3	9.7
Milwaukee, WI	56.6	43.4	80.0	20.0	80.5	19.5	79.7	20.3	85.2	14.8
Minneapolis, MN	59.4	40.6	88.5	11.5	89.4	10.6	90.1	9.9	91.6	8.4
Nashville, TN	47.3	52.7	86.2	13.8	87.1	12.9	86.3	13.7	84.4	15.6
New Haven, CT	65.1	34.9	90.7	9.3	92.2	7.8	90.5	9.5	89.3	10.7
New Orleans, LA	53.6	46.4	77.3	22.7	78.1	21.9	77.7	22.3	76.0	24.0
New York, NY	54.8	45.2	82.3	17.7	85.6	14.4	85.7	14.3	85.1	14.9
Oklahoma City, OK	72.1	27.9	90.7	9.3	91.2	8.8	90.8	9.2	90.7	9.3
Omaha, NE	57.3	42.7	85.4	14.6	85.7	14.3	87.2	12.8	85.9	14.1
Orlando, FL	55.2	44.8	81.0	19.0	86.3	13.7	85.6	14.4	89.6	10.4
Peoria, IL	61.4	38.6	82.9	17.1	89.1	10.9	89.1	10.9	91.0	9.0
Philadelphia, PA	46.0	54.0	81.8	18.2	84.9	15.1	84.9	15.1	83.3	16.7
Phoenix, AZ	60.3	39.7	89.4	10.6	92.0	8.0	92.5	7.5	92.9	7.1
Pittsburgh, PA	49.3	50.7	85.0	15.0	88.0	12.0	88.3	11.7	89.8	10.2
Portland, OR	42.8	57.2	86.2	13.8	89.0	11.0	89.5	10.5	90.3	9.7
Providence, RI	53.8	46.2	89.9	10.1	90.4	9.6	89.6	10.4	88.5	11.5
Provo, UT	53.3	46.7	91.6	8.4	92.9	7.1	94.4	5.6	94.4	5.6
Raleigh, NC	38.9	61.1	88.2	11.8	89.0	11.0	87.8	12.2	89.9	10.1
Reno, NV	58.2	41.8	85.6	14.4	92.7	7.3	92.9	7.1	93.2	6.8
Richmond, VA	41.9	58.1	89.0	11.0	89.8	10.2	88.6	11.4	90.3	9.7
Riverside, CA	68.6	31.4	91.8	8.2	94.4	5.6	94.2	5.8	94.9	5.1
Rochester, MN	62.6	37.4	85.5	14.5	87.3	12.7	89.1	10.9	92.1	7.9
Sacramento, CA	62.3	37.7	90.7	9.3	92.4	7.6	92.5	7.5	93.1	6.9
Salt Lake City, UT	54.5	45.5	88.8	11.2	92.6	7.4	93.4	6.6	93.7	6.3
San Antonio, TX	65.9	34.1	90.4	9.6	92.9	7.1	92.1	7.9	92.5	7.5
San Diego, CA	54.0	46.0	90.5	9.5	92.1	7.9	92.1	7.9	92.4	7.6
San Francisco, CA	41.3	58.7	84.2	15.8	86.3	13.7	85.8	14.2	87.2	12.8
San Jose, CA	36.2	63.8	81.2	18.8	85.7	14.3	85.4	14.6	86.2	13.8
Santa Rosa, CA	48.6	51.4	93.0	7.0	92.8	7.2	90.3	9.7	90.9	9.1
Savannah, GA	58.3	41.7	92.2	7.8	86.1	13.9	87.8	12.2	85.9	14.1
Seattle, WA	41.4	58.6	83.9	16.1	88.3	11.7	88.3	11.7	90.5	9.5
Sioux Falls, SD	53.6	46.4	88.3	11.7	88.4	11.6	89.2	10.8	86.8	13.2
Springfield, IL	66.2	33.8	86.4	13.6	87.2	12.8	88.6	11.4	90.1	9.9
Tallahassee, FL	49.6	50.4	86.3	13.7	86.0	14.0	81.7	18.3	86.2	13.8
Tampa, FL	57.1	42.9	84.8	15.2	86.9	13.1	87.1	12.9	88.3	11.7
Tucson, AZ	65.7	34.3	87.8	12.2	90.4	9.6	90.1	9.9	92.1	7.9
Tulsa, OK	69.4	30.6	88.7	11.3	88.9	11.1	88.2	11.8	87.7	12.3
Tuscaloosa, AL	66.5	33.5	89.8	10.2	87.4	12.6	90.3	9.7	86.1	13.9
Virginia Beach, VA	53.4	46.6	83.0	17.0	89.4	10.6	89.3	10.7	91.4	8.6
Washington, DC	44.9	55.1	86.1	13.9	88.7	11.3	87.9	12.1	88.3	11.7
Wichita, KS	63.1	36.9	83.3	16.7	86.3	13.7	87.3	12.7	86.6	13.4
Winston-Salem, NC	56.2	43.8	91.8	8.2	93.0	7.0	90.3	9.7	90.8	9.2
U.S.	59.1	40.9	87.6	12.4	89.5	10.5	89.4	10.6	90.1	9.9

Note: Figures shown cover persons 3 years old and over; Figures cover the Metropolitan Statistical Area—see Appendix B for areas included
Source: U.S. Census Bureau, 2015-2019 American Community Survey 5-Year Estimates

Educational Attainment by Race: City

City	High School Graduate or Higher (%)					Bachelor's Degree or Higher (%)				
	Total	White	Black	Asian	Hisp.[1]	Total	White	Black	Asian	Hisp.[1]
Albuquerque, NM	89.7	91.1	92.0	85.5	82.5	35.2	38.1	31.2	48.3	21.5
Allentown, PA	79.0	81.5	83.0	81.3	68.2	15.3	17.9	7.3	37.1	6.0
Anchorage, AK	93.9	96.5	93.6	84.0	85.3	36.1	43.2	19.6	25.2	22.3
Ann Arbor, MI	97.3	98.1	90.6	97.8	92.0	76.0	78.4	38.2	86.4	68.6
Athens, GA	87.9	90.9	81.5	94.5	57.0	44.0	54.8	18.6	73.2	19.8
Atlanta, GA	90.9	97.7	84.4	96.1	82.5	51.8	78.0	25.7	84.6	46.0
Austin, TX	89.4	91.2	89.6	93.9	72.3	51.7	55.1	28.8	77.0	25.8
Baton Rouge, LA	88.0	96.2	82.2	84.1	73.9	33.2	53.4	15.9	54.7	21.7
Boise City, ID	95.1	95.7	86.2	89.1	84.2	41.6	41.8	29.9	51.2	22.0
Boston, MA	87.2	93.0	83.8	78.9	70.0	49.7	65.7	21.8	53.2	23.7
Boulder, CO	96.9	97.5	92.2	96.1	76.4	76.0	76.9	39.9	80.4	42.1
Cape Coral, FL	91.8	92.3	89.3	88.5	86.9	23.3	23.7	19.8	24.7	18.7
Cedar Rapids, IA	93.3	94.7	83.4	83.8	75.8	32.1	32.7	15.0	51.2	21.0
Charleston, SC	94.9	97.4	86.9	93.5	91.4	53.1	61.0	22.3	67.3	45.6
Charlotte, NC	89.1	92.7	90.4	81.4	60.0	44.3	55.4	29.4	58.3	17.0
Chicago, IL	85.1	88.7	85.2	87.1	68.4	39.5	50.9	21.4	60.5	16.5
Cincinnati, OH	88.1	92.1	83.0	93.1	73.2	37.1	52.6	14.5	80.7	31.0
Clarksville, TN	92.9	93.5	92.6	85.2	87.2	27.6	28.1	24.7	41.9	18.2
Cleveland, OH	80.8	83.3	80.0	71.5	67.4	17.5	24.9	9.7	39.5	9.0
College Station, TX	94.4	95.1	87.8	95.2	85.6	58.6	58.8	29.4	80.9	45.8
Colorado Springs, CO	93.9	95.3	94.2	86.3	80.6	39.9	42.7	25.7	48.4	20.9
Columbia, MO	95.2	96.3	90.0	94.6	91.4	52.2	54.8	21.2	73.9	36.0
Columbia, SC	89.4	95.4	81.8	96.8	86.4	43.8	62.6	19.6	78.1	35.2
Columbus, OH	89.8	92.0	86.8	85.3	75.6	36.6	42.3	19.7	57.7	23.2
Dallas, TX	77.5	75.2	86.8	85.5	51.1	33.4	38.9	19.4	65.8	11.0
Davenport, IA	90.5	92.2	83.6	69.2	72.8	25.6	27.4	10.5	28.0	15.5
Denver, CO	88.0	90.3	86.9	83.4	64.7	49.4	54.5	24.7	53.9	15.9
Des Moines, IA	86.3	89.7	81.3	60.8	57.2	26.7	29.2	13.6	20.3	9.0
Durham, NC	88.1	90.1	87.6	90.5	49.4	49.6	60.1	34.2	73.9	13.6
Edison, NJ	92.1	92.8	94.7	93.0	82.0	55.5	37.2	35.0	77.0	24.1
El Paso, TX	80.3	81.1	95.7	90.1	76.4	25.1	25.7	30.5	54.0	20.7
Fargo, ND	94.3	96.1	81.9	71.8	92.0	40.0	41.7	20.2	46.6	21.2
Fayetteville, NC	91.7	93.7	90.6	86.3	88.5	27.2	31.3	22.9	43.0	21.7
Fort Collins, CO	96.5	96.9	97.0	93.4	84.3	55.5	55.8	40.2	72.3	34.2
Fort Wayne, IN	88.5	91.9	84.4	52.6	61.8	27.8	30.7	15.6	28.3	9.8
Fort Worth, TX	82.2	84.4	88.6	80.8	59.2	29.7	33.8	21.5	42.8	12.2
Grand Rapids, MI	86.7	90.8	83.2	72.3	50.3	36.4	43.1	17.4	43.9	11.9
Greeley, CO	84.5	86.2	79.2	80.0	65.6	24.8	25.9	16.6	43.4	8.4
Green Bay, WI	87.5	90.4	83.1	74.3	53.5	24.8	27.0	15.3	20.0	6.5
Greensboro, NC	89.8	93.4	88.5	75.2	64.2	38.2	49.1	24.5	41.9	18.2
Honolulu, HI	89.0	97.6	97.5	85.5	91.9	37.2	53.0	24.5	36.6	27.9
Houston, TX	78.9	78.0	88.8	86.9	58.5	32.9	37.4	22.6	58.9	13.6
Huntsville, AL	91.0	94.0	85.4	91.1	63.8	44.1	50.3	28.4	59.3	22.8
Indianapolis, IN	85.8	88.0	84.6	76.2	57.3	30.9	36.0	18.2	47.1	12.5
Jacksonville, FL	89.5	91.0	86.7	88.7	82.3	28.6	31.5	19.1	49.5	24.6
Kansas City, MO	90.0	93.2	86.5	80.3	70.2	35.2	43.5	16.6	47.2	18.6
Lafayette, LA	89.5	93.6	79.4	94.8	57.4	38.2	47.0	15.1	56.8	21.2
Lakeland, FL	88.0	89.3	83.3	81.6	78.8	25.9	27.5	15.7	51.0	19.5
Las Vegas, NV	84.8	87.5	89.2	91.1	63.5	24.6	26.9	18.2	40.7	9.9
Lexington, KY	91.2	93.4	85.4	91.1	61.0	43.6	47.7	19.5	68.5	19.2
Lincoln, NE	93.3	95.0	86.1	79.2	70.1	39.6	40.7	23.8	46.7	19.3
Little Rock, AR	91.3	93.8	88.2	95.3	61.3	41.8	54.6	22.6	70.2	10.2
Los Angeles, CA	77.5	80.9	88.7	90.3	56.3	34.4	39.8	26.5	54.9	12.3
Louisville, KY	89.6	90.7	86.9	81.4	80.2	29.9	32.9	17.8	49.0	25.8
Madison, WI	95.5	96.8	87.6	92.5	77.3	57.9	59.7	22.7	71.7	34.2

Table continued on following page.

Appendix A: Comparative Statistics

City	High School Graduate or Higher (%) Total	White	Black	Asian	Hisp.[1]	Bachelor's Degree or Higher (%) Total	White	Black	Asian	Hisp.[1]
Manchester, NH	87.3	88.4	79.2	76.4	67.0	30.1	29.7	22.1	44.6	14.9
Memphis, TN	85.7	91.7	84.1	87.0	49.5	26.2	44.5	15.9	57.0	11.2
Miami, FL	78.0	78.7	74.2	90.4	75.3	29.6	32.2	14.8	63.5	25.9
Midland, TX	85.1	85.8	85.6	81.7	71.3	28.9	30.3	18.1	51.7	11.9
Milwaukee, WI	84.0	89.1	83.0	68.8	62.2	24.6	35.3	12.6	27.1	9.3
Minneapolis, MN	90.0	96.2	74.6	82.6	59.9	50.4	61.2	14.3	54.8	21.0
Nashville, TN	88.8	90.4	88.2	77.9	57.0	41.1	46.5	27.6	49.2	15.4
New Haven, CT	85.6	87.5	87.2	96.8	70.9	34.9	46.6	19.9	78.7	13.6
New Orleans, LA	86.5	95.7	81.0	75.8	80.9	37.6	63.9	19.7	40.4	35.9
New York, NY	82.2	88.7	83.5	76.1	68.9	38.1	51.0	24.4	42.4	18.6
Oklahoma City, OK	86.4	87.5	89.0	81.2	54.5	30.7	33.2	20.3	41.4	10.4
Omaha, NE	89.5	91.5	86.9	70.4	54.3	37.7	40.7	18.9	49.4	12.0
Orlando, FL	90.4	92.8	84.6	92.6	86.8	38.1	43.3	21.8	60.3	28.8
Peoria, IL	89.4	92.4	81.4	94.7	71.6	34.9	39.6	13.4	75.4	21.9
Philadelphia, PA	84.7	89.2	84.6	73.0	67.2	29.7	41.6	17.3	40.3	14.6
Phoenix, AZ	81.9	84.0	87.5	84.9	62.1	28.6	30.2	21.8	57.4	10.3
Pittsburgh, PA	92.9	94.5	88.6	90.9	87.1	44.6	50.2	18.4	78.3	48.4
Portland, OR	92.4	94.8	85.9	76.9	76.1	50.4	54.3	23.9	41.2	31.0
Providence, RI	81.6	86.4	84.4	79.3	71.9	30.1	38.0	19.1	48.1	10.4
Provo, UT	92.9	93.1	98.0	93.2	75.2	43.1	43.4	27.2	52.9	18.6
Raleigh, NC	91.8	95.9	89.7	86.8	61.2	50.9	61.8	31.0	60.0	21.9
Reno, NV	89.0	91.4	91.3	91.6	64.6	33.5	35.3	21.2	48.1	12.5
Richmond, VA	85.4	92.3	78.8	81.7	50.8	39.6	61.8	15.5	62.5	14.3
Riverside, CA	80.6	83.5	92.0	87.2	68.5	23.0	23.8	26.5	47.8	11.8
Rochester, MN	94.0	96.3	77.2	83.8	74.1	46.7	47.8	18.0	59.9	26.2
Sacramento, CA	85.3	89.2	90.1	79.7	73.0	33.1	39.6	21.0	37.4	17.7
Salt Lake City, UT	88.8	94.2	82.2	83.8	62.2	46.5	51.8	26.7	61.5	16.5
San Antonio, TX	82.4	82.4	91.1	87.2	74.8	26.0	26.0	23.9	53.1	16.4
San Diego, CA	88.1	89.2	91.3	88.7	69.1	45.9	48.1	25.8	53.8	20.4
San Francisco, CA	88.5	96.7	88.4	79.3	78.9	58.1	73.8	30.5	46.7	34.2
San Jose, CA	84.6	88.6	91.8	87.0	67.5	43.7	44.2	35.5	55.9	15.9
Santa Rosa, CA	86.2	91.3	87.6	87.1	62.8	32.6	37.4	30.2	40.2	12.1
Savannah, GA	87.6	93.0	83.3	85.8	79.4	28.2	42.9	15.5	46.7	27.1
Seattle, WA	94.8	97.8	86.8	88.4	83.5	64.0	69.8	29.5	61.5	43.0
Sioux Falls, SD	92.3	94.7	74.7	70.8	65.3	35.2	37.6	14.3	36.4	14.3
Springfield, IL	91.3	93.4	81.2	91.7	87.8	35.8	38.6	17.8	64.9	33.6
Tallahassee, FL	93.5	96.4	88.2	96.0	88.5	48.2	56.9	28.1	80.7	39.6
Tampa, FL	87.9	90.1	82.9	86.7	78.3	38.6	44.4	16.8	63.0	23.5
Tucson, AZ	85.0	88.0	84.3	86.7	72.7	27.4	30.1	21.3	48.0	14.0
Tulsa, OK	87.3	89.9	88.8	74.8	57.6	31.5	36.5	17.6	37.8	10.7
Tuscaloosa, AL	89.1	94.4	84.1	84.5	73.8	36.9	54.1	17.6	53.0	11.5
Virginia Beach, VA	93.5	95.3	91.1	88.2	84.5	36.0	38.8	26.4	40.6	25.5
Washington, DC	90.9	98.1	86.3	94.9	73.1	58.5	89.5	27.3	81.9	47.3
Wichita, KS	88.3	90.4	87.4	81.3	62.8	30.1	32.9	15.2	36.3	13.0
Winston-Salem, NC	88.2	89.9	87.8	87.7	58.1	34.5	41.8	21.0	65.7	13.5
U.S.	88.0	89.9	86.0	87.1	68.7	32.1	33.5	21.6	54.3	16.4

Note: Figures shown cover persons 25 years old and over; (1) People of Hispanic origin can be of any race
Source: U.S. Census Bureau, 2015-2019 American Community Survey 5-Year Estimates

Educational Attainment by Race: Metro Area

Metro Area	High School Graduate or Higher (%)					Bachelor's Degree or Higher (%)				
	Total	White	Black	Asian	Hisp.[1]	Total	White	Black	Asian	Hisp.[1]
Albuquerque, NM	88.6	90.4	91.0	87.3	81.1	32.2	35.0	30.4	47.8	19.1
Allentown, PA	90.0	91.1	88.0	87.5	74.9	29.5	30.1	19.5	54.6	13.2
Anchorage, AK	93.7	95.6	93.5	83.9	86.3	32.3	37.0	19.5	25.0	21.3
Ann Arbor, MI	95.3	96.3	89.2	96.6	85.5	55.9	57.7	27.4	83.0	42.9
Athens, GA	87.8	90.1	80.3	91.0	60.0	39.4	44.5	17.6	69.9	22.2
Atlanta, GA	89.6	91.0	90.5	87.5	64.9	38.6	42.6	30.2	58.1	20.6
Austin, TX	89.9	91.4	91.0	92.5	74.0	44.8	46.7	29.1	71.8	23.0
Baton Rouge, LA	87.4	90.5	82.8	86.1	67.5	27.6	31.9	18.5	53.2	16.4
Boise City, ID	91.8	93.4	88.7	86.6	67.8	31.7	32.5	27.9	46.7	11.4
Boston, MA	91.7	94.3	85.2	86.0	72.0	48.1	50.6	26.3	62.3	22.8
Boulder, CO	95.0	95.8	87.8	93.8	71.6	62.1	62.8	30.5	72.5	26.5
Cape Coral, FL	88.4	90.0	79.5	88.6	71.0	28.2	29.4	15.9	45.3	14.8
Cedar Rapids, IA	94.3	95.2	84.0	81.4	77.6	31.0	31.3	15.4	51.7	22.0
Charleston, SC	90.7	93.7	84.4	86.3	71.1	35.6	42.6	16.5	49.0	20.5
Charlotte, NC	89.0	90.8	88.4	84.9	63.1	35.1	37.7	25.9	58.1	17.7
Chicago, IL	88.7	91.4	87.8	90.7	68.0	38.0	41.6	22.7	64.7	14.8
Cincinnati, OH	91.0	91.9	86.6	88.9	74.1	33.6	34.8	19.2	65.9	24.6
Clarksville, TN	90.7	91.2	89.6	85.6	86.2	24.8	24.9	22.2	43.3	19.1
Cleveland, OH	90.6	92.3	85.2	86.8	74.6	31.2	34.5	15.1	61.5	15.8
College Station, TX	86.6	87.3	85.3	94.0	63.3	37.5	39.3	16.5	78.4	15.9
Colorado Springs, CO	94.4	95.5	94.5	87.4	82.7	38.5	40.5	27.2	44.8	20.9
Columbia, MO	93.6	94.3	89.3	93.9	86.8	42.7	43.8	18.8	71.2	34.4
Columbia, SC	89.9	91.7	87.9	90.5	65.1	32.7	37.3	23.2	58.9	20.0
Columbus, OH	91.5	92.7	87.4	88.5	76.6	36.7	38.3	21.5	63.7	25.6
Dallas, TX	85.6	85.9	91.0	88.8	60.3	35.2	35.8	27.4	62.0	14.0
Davenport, IA	91.0	92.6	79.5	80.4	72.9	26.9	27.6	13.8	46.8	15.6
Denver, CO	91.2	92.8	89.8	86.0	71.0	43.8	46.2	27.0	52.1	16.7
Des Moines, IA	92.5	94.2	84.6	74.1	62.8	36.5	37.6	19.8	38.7	13.6
Durham, NC	88.8	91.0	86.3	91.3	52.7	45.3	51.4	28.8	72.3	16.9
Edison, NJ	86.5	90.8	85.4	83.5	71.4	40.4	46.0	25.6	54.5	19.6
El Paso, TX	78.3	79.5	95.3	90.1	74.4	23.2	24.0	29.9	52.6	19.2
Fargo, ND	94.8	96.1	81.7	78.4	83.4	38.6	39.8	22.2	46.8	19.5
Fayetteville, NC	89.6	91.5	89.7	84.8	80.2	23.7	25.6	21.5	39.3	19.3
Fort Collins, CO	95.9	96.2	95.7	92.2	83.8	47.3	47.5	37.8	62.7	25.1
Fort Wayne, IN	89.6	91.9	85.2	57.5	63.5	27.8	29.4	15.8	33.7	10.4
Fort Worth, TX	85.6	85.9	91.0	88.8	60.3	35.2	35.8	27.4	62.0	14.0
Grand Rapids, MI	91.2	93.1	85.7	75.2	63.7	32.7	34.3	18.3	37.3	14.2
Greeley, CO	88.1	89.1	84.2	87.9	66.6	27.5	28.0	27.2	42.4	9.1
Green Bay, WI	92.0	93.5	83.2	83.1	57.0	27.8	28.5	17.3	44.2	9.2
Greensboro, NC	86.8	88.9	86.1	76.4	57.6	29.5	32.0	23.0	42.6	13.7
Honolulu, HI	91.9	97.3	97.0	88.8	93.4	35.0	48.3	29.9	36.1	25.2
Houston, TX	83.7	83.6	91.0	87.8	64.1	32.8	33.3	27.5	56.6	15.0
Huntsville, AL	90.2	91.6	86.8	92.7	66.6	39.2	40.9	31.4	61.9	24.3
Indianapolis, IN	89.7	91.3	85.9	82.6	63.7	34.7	36.7	20.7	56.2	17.6
Jacksonville, FL	90.9	92.2	87.2	89.4	84.3	31.4	33.8	19.7	49.7	27.0
Kansas City, MO	92.0	93.6	88.5	85.5	69.0	37.1	39.7	20.7	54.8	17.8
Lafayette, LA	84.1	87.0	76.3	73.1	63.9	23.4	26.4	13.0	34.9	12.3
Lakeland, FL	85.0	86.1	82.2	80.4	73.1	20.2	20.6	15.0	41.5	14.6
Las Vegas, NV	86.1	88.3	89.7	90.4	66.8	24.5	25.9	17.8	38.8	10.5
Lexington, KY	90.1	91.6	85.1	91.1	60.8	37.3	39.2	19.0	64.5	16.9
Lincoln, NE	93.7	95.2	86.1	78.9	70.4	39.0	39.8	23.9	46.3	19.7
Little Rock, AR	90.4	91.8	87.4	90.5	67.5	30.4	32.7	21.8	54.3	13.8
Los Angeles, CA	80.7	83.2	89.9	88.2	62.2	34.5	36.6	27.3	53.4	13.3
Louisville, KY	90.1	90.9	87.2	86.3	74.0	29.6	31.0	18.3	54.2	22.7
Madison, WI	95.3	96.2	88.8	90.9	76.4	46.1	46.2	23.9	68.0	26.7

Table continued on following page.

Metro Area	High School Graduate or Higher (%)					Bachelor's Degree or Higher (%)				
	Total	White	Black	Asian	Hisp.[1]	Total	White	Black	Asian	Hisp.[1]
Manchester, NH	92.1	92.6	83.7	88.3	71.7	38.1	37.4	24.0	64.8	19.4
Memphis, TN	88.0	91.9	85.2	87.9	57.7	28.3	35.7	19.1	58.2	14.8
Miami, FL	85.5	86.9	81.4	87.5	80.0	32.3	35.4	19.8	51.6	27.7
Midland, TX	84.3	84.9	85.7	83.4	69.6	27.1	28.3	18.3	54.5	10.6
Milwaukee, WI	91.5	94.4	83.8	83.5	68.7	35.6	39.9	14.3	51.0	14.5
Minneapolis, MN	93.6	96.3	82.6	81.2	68.5	42.0	44.3	22.0	45.3	20.1
Nashville, TN	90.0	90.9	88.5	84.0	62.9	36.2	37.5	28.2	51.5	17.3
New Haven, CT	90.1	91.8	87.6	90.1	74.4	35.0	37.4	20.2	65.3	15.6
New Orleans, LA	86.9	90.6	82.0	77.4	75.1	30.3	36.8	18.7	38.7	19.2
New York, NY	86.5	90.8	85.4	83.5	71.4	40.4	46.0	25.6	54.5	19.6
Oklahoma City, OK	89.0	89.9	90.0	84.3	60.6	30.5	32.0	21.3	46.0	13.2
Omaha, NE	91.7	93.1	88.0	76.7	61.2	36.3	37.7	21.5	49.7	14.8
Orlando, FL	89.5	91.1	85.8	88.8	83.6	32.2	33.9	22.8	52.3	23.2
Peoria, IL	91.7	92.9	80.3	92.4	75.4	27.7	28.1	12.8	69.8	20.9
Philadelphia, PA	90.7	93.2	87.5	84.6	70.1	37.9	42.1	21.4	57.1	17.8
Phoenix, AZ	87.5	89.1	90.1	88.6	68.5	31.5	32.3	25.7	58.9	13.1
Pittsburgh, PA	93.9	94.4	89.7	88.2	88.0	34.9	35.3	20.2	70.7	36.8
Portland, OR	92.1	93.5	88.2	86.7	68.7	39.8	40.3	28.0	52.1	19.5
Providence, RI	87.7	89.2	85.5	85.5	73.3	32.3	33.7	22.3	51.6	14.0
Provo, UT	94.5	94.9	97.4	94.6	75.3	40.3	40.6	35.4	58.9	20.2
Raleigh, NC	91.7	94.1	89.0	92.4	62.5	46.8	50.5	30.8	73.2	20.1
Reno, NV	88.7	91.0	90.3	91.8	63.3	30.8	32.5	21.7	45.4	11.0
Richmond, VA	89.9	92.8	85.0	88.8	67.3	37.4	43.4	21.8	64.0	21.3
Riverside, CA	81.1	83.7	89.6	90.4	67.4	21.7	22.0	23.8	48.6	10.7
Rochester, MN	94.1	95.5	78.3	84.4	71.3	38.7	38.7	18.1	58.0	23.1
Sacramento, CA	89.3	92.0	90.4	84.3	74.1	33.5	34.8	23.0	44.1	17.9
Salt Lake City, UT	90.8	94.0	85.4	86.8	69.0	35.0	37.2	25.1	51.4	14.3
San Antonio, TX	85.1	85.3	92.2	87.5	76.1	28.2	28.4	28.8	51.7	17.2
San Diego, CA	87.4	88.2	91.8	89.2	69.8	38.8	39.5	25.9	51.3	17.8
San Francisco, CA	89.1	93.6	90.7	87.3	71.5	49.7	56.1	28.8	55.4	21.7
San Jose, CA	88.1	90.4	92.0	90.8	69.3	51.5	49.4	38.2	65.5	17.6
Santa Rosa, CA	88.8	92.9	89.3	88.9	64.6	35.5	39.3	29.8	44.4	14.1
Savannah, GA	89.8	92.0	86.2	84.2	81.2	31.5	36.7	19.8	45.2	26.2
Seattle, WA	92.6	95.0	89.6	88.8	73.3	43.0	43.8	25.8	56.1	22.4
Sioux Falls, SD	92.9	94.5	75.5	72.1	66.9	33.5	35.0	14.4	37.1	15.6
Springfield, IL	92.6	93.9	81.6	92.7	87.0	33.9	35.2	17.4	64.0	31.5
Tallahassee, FL	90.6	93.9	83.5	96.3	82.1	38.4	44.1	23.0	79.3	30.2
Tampa, FL	89.6	90.8	87.0	85.4	80.2	30.4	30.9	22.4	51.7	22.6
Tucson, AZ	88.4	90.9	87.6	88.0	75.8	32.4	35.1	25.6	53.1	16.3
Tulsa, OK	89.4	90.9	89.5	77.7	63.4	27.7	29.8	19.2	37.0	12.4
Tuscaloosa, AL	87.1	89.9	82.8	81.1	70.1	27.4	33.4	16.2	51.8	11.5
Virginia Beach, VA	91.4	93.9	87.2	87.3	84.0	31.9	36.2	22.1	43.3	24.8
Washington, DC	90.9	94.1	91.5	91.1	68.0	50.9	59.2	34.8	65.1	25.7
Wichita, KS	90.1	91.7	87.1	81.9	65.8	30.6	32.3	17.2	36.9	15.3
Winston-Salem, NC	87.0	87.9	86.9	87.2	56.7	26.6	27.7	20.6	54.6	12.2
U.S.	88.0	89.9	86.0	87.1	68.7	32.1	33.5	21.6	54.3	16.4

Note: Figures shown cover persons 25 years old and over; Figures cover the Metropolitan Statistical Area—see Appendix B for areas included; (1) People of Hispanic origin can be of any race
Source: U.S. Census Bureau, 2015-2019 American Community Survey 5-Year Estimates

Cost of Living Index

Urban Area	Composite	Groceries	Housing	Utilities	Transp.	Health	Misc.
Albuquerque, NM	93.8	104.8	84.5	87.7	97.2	99.8	96.6
Allentown, PA	104.4	98.4	114.0	103.4	104.8	94.6	100.6
Anchorage, AK	124.5	132.6	140.0	124.0	114.8	144.2	109.7
Ann Arbor, MI	n/a	n/a	n/a	n/a	n/a	n/a	n/a
Athens, GA	n/a	n/a	n/a	n/a	n/a	n/a	n/a
Atlanta, GA	102.8	103.4	103.5	85.1	103.6	107.1	106.0
Austin, TX	99.7	91.2	105.5	95.2	90.7	105.8	101.4
Baton Rouge	99.4	102.6	92.3	85.4	100.5	104.5	106.5
Boise City, ID	98.7	94.5	97.5	81.9	108.5	103.0	102.8
Boston, MA	151.0	109.3	228.6	120.5	112.0	118.3	129.3
Boulder, CO	n/a	n/a	n/a	n/a	n/a	n/a	n/a
Cape Coral, FL	100.6	107.8	89.6	98.8	98.7	108.5	106.3
Cedar Rapids, IA	96.2	94.8	83.0	102.1	96.6	107.0	103.9
Charleston, SC	97.2	99.7	93.2	120.4	86.6	97.5	95.9
Charlotte, NC	98.2	101.7	88.8	95.6	90.7	105.1	106.0
Chicago, IL	120.6	101.9	155.7	92.4	125.9	100.0	109.4
Cincinnati, OH	99.7	91.2	105.5	95.2	90.7	105.8	101.4
Clarksville, TN	n/a	n/a	n/a	n/a	n/a	n/a	n/a
Cleveland, OH	96.9	106.0	83.3	96.1	99.4	104.4	102.6
College Station, TX	n/a	n/a	n/a	n/a	n/a	n/a	n/a
Colorado Springs, CO	101.1	95.9	101.3	97.2	97.7	108.6	104.1
Columbia, MO	91.8	95.5	75.0	100.0	92.0	102.6	99.8
Columbia, SC	93.5	103.1	72.7	126.2	87.1	79.9	100.5
Columbus, OH	92.6	98.6	81.2	89.1	95.5	88.5	99.7
Dallas, TX	108.2	100.2	118.8	106.8	96.7	105.4	106.7
Davenport, IA	92.0	99.7	76.9	98.9	105.8	105.3	93.7
Denver, CO	111.3	98.3	139.3	80.5	100.9	103.6	106.6
Des Moines, IA	89.9	95.2	80.2	90.1	99.1	95.4	92.3
Durham, NC	n/a	n/a	n/a	n/a	n/a	n/a	n/a
Edison, NJ[1]	120.6	108.7	149.3	105.8	107.8	102.5	112.4
El Paso, TX	87.7	102.3	73.7	85.7	99.0	99.3	89.0
Fargo, ND	98.6	111.5	77.6	90.5	100.4	120.1	108.9
Fayetteville, NC	n/a	n/a	n/a	n/a	n/a	n/a	n/a
Fort Collins, CO	n/a	n/a	n/a	n/a	n/a	n/a	n/a
Fort Wayne, IN	86.9	86.7	62.3	95.7	99.5	101.5	98.6
Fort Worth, TX	94.9	92.4	88.4	107.2	96.9	101.5	96.2
Grand Rapids, MI	94.1	92.8	87.4	98.5	104.1	92.3	96.3
Greeley, CO	n/a	n/a	n/a	n/a	n/a	n/a	n/a
Green Bay, WI	91.1	91.0	77.9	97.4	97.7	101.8	96.6
Greensboro, NC[2]	90.8	101.4	66.7	94.6	92.0	119.5	100.5
Honolulu, HI	192.9	165.0	332.6	172.3	138.2	118.8	124.2
Houston, TX	95.8	88.4	91.2	105.8	95.2	92.0	100.3
Huntsville, AL	91.3	95.1	66.6	99.0	97.3	96.4	104.7
Indianapolis, IN	92.4	94.1	78.4	105.4	97.9	90.6	98.0
Jacksonville, FL	91.7	98.4	88.0	97.7	86.0	83.7	92.7
Kansas City, MO	95.8	102.4	82.6	100.6	92.6	105.9	101.7
Lafayette, LA	88.9	101.8	72.0	88.0	104.7	88.0	93.3
Lakeland, FL	n/a	n/a	n/a	n/a	n/a	n/a	n/a
Las Vegas, NV	103.6	95.8	118.3	98.6	114.0	100.2	94.2
Lexington, KY	92.7	89.9	83.7	95.6	96.7	78.9	100.7
Lincoln, NE	93.0	95.6	78.7	90.2	93.4	105.8	102.2
Little Rock, AR	96.0	95.1	88.1	97.4	94.7	89.6	103.2
Los Angeles, CA	146.7	116.3	230.6	106.2	134.8	110.8	112.0
Louisville, KY	94.1	91.8	79.8	94.6	98.1	105.2	103.7
Madison, WI	107.0	107.6	108.6	99.8	104.4	124.0	106.0
Manchester, NH	108.9	102.2	109.6	117.9	104.1	116.0	108.9

Table continued on following page.

Urban Area	Composite	Groceries	Housing	Utilities	Transp.	Health	Misc.
Memphis, TN	99.7	91.2	105.5	95.2	90.7	105.8	101.4
Miami, FL	115.0	110.5	144.3	102.0	101.5	100.6	102.7
Midland, TX	102.1	93.6	91.5	106.6	104.1	96.5	112.6
Milwaukee, WI	96.7	93.4	100.5	94.8	99.8	115.9	92.4
Minneapolis, MN	106.6	103.6	102.9	97.5	104.4	105.6	113.9
Nashville, TN	98.9	99.5	98.5	97.0	97.9	92.4	100.4
New Haven, CT	122.3	111.0	128.5	136.7	110.6	115.8	121.9
New Orleans, LA	105.0	102.6	125.5	81.5	101.3	115.1	96.1
New York, NY[3]	181.6	128.4	339.0	121.4	113.7	107.1	123.1
Oklahoma City, OK	86.0	93.3	69.6	95.3	86.2	95.0	92.1
Omaha, NE	92.3	96.8	83.6	99.4	98.3	96.4	93.3
Orlando, FL	92.1	100.7	85.1	97.2	89.3	88.3	94.1
Peoria, IL	92.9	89.7	76.5	93.7	106.3	96.8	102.7
Philadelphia, PA	110.9	118.7	116.5	105.6	116.1	101.8	104.8
Phoenix, AZ	99.3	99.7	103.8	109.5	107.2	90.1	91.9
Pittsburgh, PA	103.1	111.9	105.7	116.1	114.0	93.1	92.6
Portland, OR	134.7	112.4	186.4	87.1	131.0	115.6	119.4
Providence, RI	119.2	106.7	132.8	126.4	112.1	109.3	114.6
Provo, UT	98.2	93.0	96.1	84.7	100.7	94.5	105.4
Raleigh, NC	95.4	92.7	89.0	98.3	90.9	103.8	100.9
Reno, NV	114.1	118.7	125.8	85.9	126.3	113.9	107.6
Richmond, VA	94.2	89.0	86.0	97.6	86.9	106.7	102.1
Riverside, CA	99.7	91.2	105.5	95.2	90.7	105.8	101.4
Rochester, MN	n/a	n/a	n/a	n/a	n/a	n/a	n/a
Sacramento, CA	118.4	120.2	134.2	102.9	139.0	113.6	104.8
Salt Lake City, UT	103.6	108.0	106.7	87.8	103.6	105.7	103.6
San Antonio, TX	89.5	88.0	82.2	87.6	89.1	87.2	96.5
San Diego, CA	142.1	116.1	216.3	123.2	129.2	107.3	107.3
San Francisco, CA	197.9	131.3	368.9	123.0	145.3	129.6	133.4
San Jose, CA	n/a	n/a	n/a	n/a	n/a	n/a	n/a
Santa Rosa, CA	n/a	n/a	n/a	n/a	n/a	n/a	n/a
Savannah, GA	89.5	95.7	66.2	96.0	94.9	106.1	100.0
Seattle, WA	157.5	129.1	227.6	108.0	137.8	128.6	136.2
Sioux Falls, SD	92.5	96.3	86.3	84.7	91.9	107.7	96.3
Springfield, IL	n/a	n/a	n/a	n/a	n/a	n/a	n/a
Tallahassee, FL	97.5	107.4	93.3	86.5	96.2	99.6	99.9
Tampa, FL	91.2	104.8	79.2	85.9	99.4	98.3	93.7
Tucson, AZ	97.5	100.5	87.9	99.9	101.1	98.7	102.0
Tulsa, OK	86.0	96.2	62.7	99.5	84.4	91.6	96.1
Tuscaloosa, AL	n/a	n/a	n/a	n/a	n/a	n/a	n/a
Virginia Beach, VA[4]	94.1	92.7	89.1	97.4	92.2	90.4	98.7
Washington, DC	159.9	116.0	277.1	117.9	110.6	95.8	118.1
Wichita, KS	91.1	94.3	69.6	99.3	95.3	96.1	102.5
Winston-Salem, NC	90.8	101.4	66.7	94.6	92.0	119.5	100.5
U.S.	100.0	100.0	100.0	100.0	100.0	100.0	100.0

Note: The Cost of Living Index measures regional differences in the cost of consumer goods and services, excluding taxes and non-consumer expenditures, for professional and managerial households in the top income quintile. It is based on more than 50,000 prices covering almost 60 different items for which prices are collected three times a year by chambers of commerce, economic development organizations or university applied economic centers in each participating urban area. The numbers shown should be read as a percentage above or below the national average of 100. For example, a value of 115.4 in the groceries column indicates that grocery prices are 15.4% higher than the national average. Small differences in the index numbers should not be interpreted as significant. In cases where data is not available for the city, data for the metro area or for a neighboring city has been provided and noted as follows: (1) Middlesex-Monmouth NJ; (2) Winston-Salem, NC; (3) Brooklyn, NY; (4) Hampton Roads-SE Virginia
Source: The Council for Community and Economic Research (formerly ACCRA), Cost of Living Index, 2020

Grocery Prices

Urban Area	T-Bone Steak ($/pound)	Frying Chicken ($/pound)	Whole Milk ($/half gal.)	Eggs ($/dozen)	Orange Juice ($/64 oz.)	Coffee ($/11.5 oz.)
Albuquerque, NM	11.18	1.16	2.10	1.41	3.96	4.63
Allentown, PA	13.52	1.36	2.09	1.36	3.47	3.73
Anchorage, AK	13.95	1.71	2.73	2.19	4.39	5.84
Ann Arbor, MI	n/a	n/a	n/a	n/a	n/a	n/a
Athens, GA	n/a	n/a	n/a	n/a	n/a	n/a
Atlanta, GA	14.32	1.30	1.99	1.25	3.76	4.92
Austin, TX	9.67	1.02	1.84	1.39	3.22	4.23
Baton Rouge	11.70	1.42	2.65	1.53	3.69	4.26
Boise City, ID	11.77	1.13	1.37	1.18	3.69	4.46
Boston, MA	13.53	1.64	2.27	2.00	3.73	4.41
Boulder, CO	n/a	n/a	n/a	n/a	n/a	n/a
Cape Coral, FL	11.21	1.92	2.40	1.51	3.36	3.34
Cedar Rapids, IA	10.99	1.68	2.49	1.24	3.31	4.86
Charleston, SC	12.80	1.27	2.25	1.26	3.53	4.42
Charlotte, NC	12.19	1.46	1.69	1.34	3.54	4.02
Chicago, IL	12.67	1.99	2.42	1.47	3.96	4.48
Cincinnati, OH	13.16	1.25	1.42	1.09	3.61	4.28
Clarksville, TN	n/a	n/a	n/a	n/a	n/a	n/a
Cleveland, OH	14.49	1.83	1.55	1.32	3.72	4.57
College Station, TX	n/a	n/a	n/a	n/a	n/a	n/a
Colorado Springs, CO	13.95	1.39	1.76	1.27	3.39	4.55
Columbia, MO	11.89	1.53	2.18	1.08	3.56	4.44
Columbia, SC	12.24	1.40	2.19	1.31	3.54	4.28
Columbus, OH	12.68	1.16	1.58	1.17	3.53	7.19
Dallas, TX	10.44	1.48	1.97	1.15	3.45	4.51
Davenport, IA	11.56	1.53	2.60	1.32	3.44	4.60
Denver, CO	12.57	1.48	1.76	1.46	3.36	4.17
Des Moines, IA	12.05	1.51	2.18	1.34	3.05	4.24
Durham, NC	n/a	n/a	n/a	n/a	n/a	n/a
Edison, NJ[1]	13.96	1.67	2.41	1.60	3.51	4.06
El Paso, TX	10.83	2.02	2.67	1.85	3.93	5.38
Fargo, ND	n/a	n/a	n/a	n/a	n/a	n/a
Fayetteville, NC	n/a	n/a	n/a	n/a	n/a	n/a
Fort Collins, CO	n/a	n/a	n/a	n/a	n/a	n/a
Fort Wayne, IN	11.87	1.07	1.31	0.74	3.13	3.47
Fort Worth, TX	9.35	1.87	1.92	1.26	3.55	4.49
Grand Rapids, MI	12.68	1.12	1.59	1.25	3.34	3.25
Greeley, CO	n/a	n/a	n/a	n/a	n/a	n/a
Green Bay, WI	11.37	1.10	1.93	1.51	3.64	4.47
Greensboro, NC[2]	11.86	1.27	1.55	1.45	3.94	4.03
Honolulu, HI	13.84	2.45	4.31	3.77	5.44	8.69
Houston, TX	11.29	1.13	1.58	1.42	3.50	3.84
Huntsville, AL	13.10	1.45	1.62	0.95	3.75	4.36
Indianapolis, IN	11.98	1.37	1.68	1.13	3.34	4.17
Jacksonville, FL	12.36	1.49	2.21	1.46	3.30	3.86
Kansas City, MO	11.83	1.92	1.87	1.17	3.22	3.44
Lafayette, LA	11.14	1.16	2.19	1.69	3.82	4.26
Lakeland, FL	n/a	n/a	n/a	n/a	n/a	n/a
Las Vegas, NV	10.89	1.35	2.46	2.07	3.99	4.69
Lexington, KY	10.82	1.11	1.64	1.16	3.18	3.69
Lincoln, NE	11.88	1.46	2.21	1.42	3.03	4.13
Little Rock, AR	10.99	1.16	1.78	1.43	3.23	3.89
Los Angeles, CA	12.32	1.72	2.19	2.88	4.09	4.90
Louisville, KY	12.70	1.09	1.15	1.02	3.13	4.01
Madison, WI	14.10	1.61	2.26	1.17	3.46	4.65

Table continued on following page.

Appendix A: Comparative Statistics   A-139

Urban Area	T-Bone Steak ($/pound)	Frying Chicken ($/pound)	Whole Milk ($/half gal.)	Eggs ($/dozen)	Orange Juice ($/64 oz.)	Coffee ($/11.5 oz.)
Manchester, NH	13.66	1.19	2.79	1.52	3.41	3.66
Memphis, TN	9.64	0.98	1.79	1.27	3.09	4.05
Miami, FL	12.55	1.73	3.16	1.71	3.67	4.00
Midland, TX	10.05	1.16	1.51	1.47	3.37	4.14
Milwaukee, WI	12.91	1.22	1.98	1.11	3.38	4.14
Minneapolis, MN	13.63	2.10	2.60	1.81	3.71	4.67
Nashville, TN	13.20	1.42	1.96	1.05	3.65	4.37
New Haven, CT	10.42	1.51	2.52	1.73	3.32	4.03
New Orleans, LA	10.51	1.21	2.30	1.63	3.63	3.83
New York, NY[3]	15.20	2.36	2.82	2.78	4.36	4.74
Oklahoma City, OK	11.70	1.34	1.87	1.23	3.23	4.07
Omaha, NE	11.27	1.24	2.00	1.87	3.47	4.87
Orlando, FL	11.14	1.27	2.39	1.31	3.60	3.91
Peoria, IL	10.98	1.03	1.32	0.93	3.45	5.99
Philadelphia, PA	13.82	1.60	2.18	1.99	4.08	4.54
Phoenix, AZ	13.58	1.68	1.63	1.80	3.71	4.84
Pittsburgh, PA	13.64	1.61	2.03	1.35	3.36	4.62
Portland, OR	11.98	1.58	2.12	2.36	4.10	5.30
Providence, RI	12.73	1.75	2.52	2.17	3.57	4.42
Provo, UT	11.04	1.66	1.50	1.46	3.65	4.66
Raleigh, NC	10.15	0.97	1.61	1.19	3.79	3.83
Reno, NV	12.84	1.58	2.93	2.07	3.36	5.86
Richmond, VA	11.36	1.05	1.58	0.86	3.20	3.78
Riverside, CA	n/a	n/a	n/a	n/a	n/a	n/a
Rochester, MN	n/a	n/a	n/a	n/a	n/a	n/a
Sacramento, CA	10.84	1.31	2.66	2.50	4.16	5.46
Salt Lake City, UT	11.44	1.81	1.73	1.32	3.44	4.51
San Antonio, TX	9.89	1.01	1.63	1.66	3.14	3.93
San Diego, CA	12.27	1.72	2.19	2.88	4.09	5.21
San Francisco, CA	14.94	1.80	2.83	3.16	4.26	6.63
San Jose, CA	n/a	n/a	n/a	n/a	n/a	n/a
Santa Rosa, CA	n/a	n/a	n/a	n/a	n/a	n/a
Savannah, GA	11.65	1.51	1.76	1.50	3.22	3.92
Seattle, WA	12.88	2.15	2.50	2.13	4.05	6.00
Sioux Falls, SD	n/a	n/a	n/a	n/a	n/a	n/a
Springfield, IL	n/a	n/a	n/a	n/a	n/a	n/a
Tallahassee, FL	11.54	1.56	2.71	1.70	3.95	3.85
Tampa, FL	11.11	1.74	2.66	1.68	3.43	4.28
Tucson, AZ	13.61	1.65	1.59	1.89	3.70	5.03
Tulsa, OK	11.20	1.30	2.00	1.38	3.44	3.89
Tuscaloosa, AL	n/a	n/a	n/a	n/a	n/a	n/a
Virginia Beach, VA[4]	11.03	1.20	1.75	1.35	3.88	3.85
Washington, DC	13.57	1.80	2.46	1.80	3.91	4.77
Wichita, KS	11.94	1.23	1.75	0.94	3.70	4.17
Winston-Salem, NC	11.86	1.27	1.55	1.45	3.94	4.03
Average*	11.78	1.39	2.05	1.47	3.57	4.34
Minimum*	8.03	0.94	1.03	0.74	2.94	3.02
Maximum*	15.86	2.65	4.31	3.77	5.44	8.69

Note: *T-Bone Steak* (price per pound); *Frying Chicken* (price per pound, whole fryer); *Whole Milk* (half gallon carton); *Eggs* (price per dozen, Grade A, large); *Orange Juice* (64 oz. Tropicana or Florida Natural); *Coffee* (11.5 oz. can, vacuum-packed, Maxwell House, Hills Bros, or Folgers); (*) Average, minimum, and maximum values for all 284 areas in the Cost of Living Index report; n/a not available; In cases where data is not available for the city, data for the metro area or for a neighboring city has been provided and noted as follows: (1) Middlesex-Monmouth NJ; (2) Winston-Salem, NC; (3) Brooklyn, NY; (4) Hampton Roads-SE Virginia
Source: The Council for Community and Economic Research (formerly ACCRA), Cost of Living Index, 2020

Housing and Utility Costs

Urban Area	New Home Price ($)	Apartment Rent ($/month)	All Electric ($/month)	Part Electric ($/month)	Other Energy ($/month)	Telephone ($/month)
Albuquerque, NM	329,645	874	-	114.55	40.75	183.90
Allentown, PA	397,306	1,488	-	100.14	86.52	189.10
Anchorage, AK	535,483	1,257	-	111.07	136.23	184.30
Ann Arbor, MI	n/a	n/a	n/a	n/a	n/a	n/a
Athens, GA	n/a	n/a	n/a	n/a	n/a	n/a
Atlanta, GA	380,418	1,245	-	87.42	33.41	185.10
Austin, TX	370,234	1,530	-	105.65	45.12	185.50
Baton Rouge	333,881	1,144	101.95	-	-	179.00
Boise City, ID	366,858	1,252	-	63.83	62.43	170.20
Boston, MA	744,522	3,157	-	72.47	161.39	181.10
Boulder, CO	n/a	n/a	n/a	n/a	n/a	n/a
Cape Coral, FL	328,513	1,061	158.56	-	-	187.80
Cedar Rapids, IA	322,911	831	-	139.90	48.93	180.80
Charleston, SC	325,960	1,372	228.13	-	-	187.30
Charlotte, NC	269,325	1,257	158.05	-	-	179.90
Chicago, IL	537,912	2,334	-	80.80	51.09	203.20
Cincinnati, OH	293,448	944	-	76.98	57.83	179.10
Clarksville, TN	n/a	n/a	n/a	n/a	n/a	n/a
Cleveland, OH	291,327	1,120	-	84.52	69.85	180.60
College Station, TX	n/a	n/a	n/a	n/a	n/a	n/a
Colorado Springs, CO	377,643	1,386	-	89.03	76.10	182.20
Columbia, MO	313,945	808	-	96.59	60.50	190.50
Columbia, SC	258,420	885	-	116.56	131.89	185.80
Columbus, OH	281,476	1,136	-	68.54	59.10	179.90
Dallas, TX	371,745	1,705	-	133.58	55.19	185.50
Davenport, IA	248,085	880	-	85.19	52.80	191.30
Denver, CO	530,852	1,545	-	59.31	46.19	186.50
Des Moines, IA	300,464	712	-	79.70	55.44	180.80
Durham, NC	n/a	n/a	n/a	n/a	n/a	n/a
Edison, NJ[1]	532,983	1,597	-	102.88	71.38	179.90
El Paso, TX	242,558	908	-	93.81	45.21	185.50
Fargo, ND	n/a	n/a	n/a	n/a	n/a	n/a
Fayetteville, NC	n/a	n/a	n/a	n/a	n/a	n/a
Fort Collins, CO	n/a	n/a	n/a	n/a	n/a	n/a
Fort Wayne, IN	204,729	859	-	93.81	50.38	184.30
Fort Worth, TX	258,331	1,164	-	133.52	54.42	184.70
Grand Rapids, MI	299,711	1,144	-	102.23	68.00	181.00
Greeley, CO	n/a	n/a	n/a	n/a	n/a	n/a
Green Bay, WI	304,129	813	-	82.41	78.05	179.40
Greensboro, NC[2]	248,204	1,242	158.18	-	-	169.60
Honolulu, HI	1,386,483	3,315	470.38	-	-	178.30
Houston, TX	297,296	1,119	-	161.68	38.31	184.00
Huntsville, AL	256,311	792	156.41	-	-	181.80
Indianapolis, IN	278,798	1,039	-	104.81	67.00	184.30
Jacksonville, FL	275,940	1,277	158.65	-	-	188.30
Kansas City, MO	299,164	1,207	-	96.98	60.15	189.70
Lafayette, LA	244,456	952	-	88.34	52.94	180.20
Lakeland, FL	n/a	n/a	n/a	n/a	n/a	n/a
Las Vegas, NV	412,949	1,205	-	120.44	50.07	175.30
Lexington, KY	309,955	976	-	79.97	77.60	206.50
Lincoln, NE	296,778	867	-	70.14	53.85	194.40
Little Rock, AR	371,333	740	-	85.47	57.54	197.30
Los Angeles, CA	841,834	2,775	-	122.73	62.94	189.50
Louisville, KY	273,187	1,038	-	80.02	77.60	180.80
Madison, WI	433,233	1,119	-	103.73	65.58	179.40

Table continued on following page.

Urban Area	New Home Price ($)	Apartment Rent ($/month)	All Electric ($/month)	Part Electric ($/month)	Other Energy ($/month)	Telephone ($/month)
Manchester, NH	362,551	1,625	-	117.62	88.11	180.00
Memphis, TN	273,404	903	-	90.75	43.22	185.00
Miami, FL	447,771	2,208	162.18	-	-	188.20
Midland, TX	301,432	1,078	-	125.29	39.71	184.40
Milwaukee, WI	358,549	1,315	-	102.30	56.96	178.70
Minneapolis, MN	386,294	1,204	-	95.03	65.60	181.00
Nashville, TN	339,380	1,130	-	88.87	55.47	185.00
New Haven, CT	393,588	1,995	-	170.80	131.69	178.60
New Orleans, LA	520,536	1,618	-	58.74	38.53	180.20
New York, NY[3]	1,278,996	3,486	-	95.03	78.96	189.50
Oklahoma City, OK	258,612	873	-	92.78	58.17	188.40
Omaha, NE	305,521	1,100	-	89.62	56.82	194.40
Orlando, FL	294,196	1,148	164.06	-	-	187.90
Peoria, IL	306,592	771	-	80.23	81.73	191.30
Philadelphia, PA	426,075	1,517	-	100.69	93.28	192.10
Phoenix, AZ	362,970	1,639	189.67	-	-	178.50
Pittsburgh, PA	378,703	1,232	-	108.94	101.72	190.60
Portland, OR	623,494	2,459	-	81.22	62.64	170.50
Providence, RI	430,197	1,800	-	125.74	114.83	189.00
Provo, UT	382,813	1,129	-	68.02	58.46	187.20
Raleigh, NC	308,897	1,309	-	103.82	58.98	179.90
Reno, NV	489,573	1,330	-	82.05	42.67	177.90
Richmond, VA	318,880	1,135	-	94.98	81.43	178.00
Riverside, CA	n/a	n/a	n/a	n/a	n/a	n/a
Rochester, MN	n/a	n/a	n/a	n/a	n/a	n/a
Sacramento, CA	484,470	1,948	-	145.58	46.79	186.50
Salt Lake City, UT	401,866	1,164	-	74.91	60.06	187.80
San Antonio, TX	271,143	1,396	-	96.33	37.17	184.30
San Diego, CA	797,634	2,351	-	183.35	64.21	176.00
San Francisco, CA	1,362,163	4,098	-	183.22	84.62	198.20
San Jose, CA	n/a	n/a	n/a	n/a	n/a	n/a
Santa Rosa, CA	n/a	n/a	n/a	n/a	n/a	n/a
Savannah, GA	218,111	905	155.12	-	-	182.20
Seattle, WA	854,748	2,680	186.95	-	-	194.20
Sioux Falls, SD	n/a	n/a	n/a	n/a	n/a	n/a
Springfield, IL	n/a	n/a	n/a	n/a	n/a	n/a
Tallahassee, FL	344,867	1,132	124.57	-	-	189.90
Tampa, FL	278,508	1,296	165.98	-	-	189.50
Tucson, AZ	372,120	955	-	121.08	48.38	185.50
Tulsa, OK	239,022	680	-	87.50	59.74	188.20
Tuscaloosa, AL	n/a	n/a	n/a	n/a	n/a	n/a
Virginia Beach, VA[4]	317,054	1,200	-	97.52	76.48	185.90
Washington, DC	1,020,885	3,033	-	135.39	69.36	184.50
Wichita, KS	254,831	771	-	100.11	56.39	188.70
Winston-Salem, NC	248,204	1,242	158.18	-	-	169.60
Average*	368,594	1,168	170.86	100.47	65.28	184.30
Minimum*	190,567	502	91.58	31.42	26.08	169.60
Maximum*	2,227,806	4,738	470.38	280.31	280.06	206.50

Note: **New Home Price** (2,400 sf living area, 8,000 sf lot, in urban area with full utilities); **Apartment Rent** (950 sf 2 bedroom/1.5 or 2 bath, unfurnished, excluding all utilities except water); **All Electric** (average monthly cost for an all-electric home); **Part Electric** (average monthly cost for a part-electric home); **Other Energy** (average monthly cost for natural gas, fuel oil, coal, wood, and any other forms of energy except electricity); **Telephone** (price includes the base monthly rate plus taxes and fees for three lines of mobile phone service); (*) Average, minimum, and maximum values for all 284 areas in the Cost of Living Index report; n/a not available; In cases where data is not available for the city, data for the metro area or for a neighboring city has been provided and noted as follows: (1) Middlesex-Monmouth NJ; (2) Winston-Salem, NC; (3) Brooklyn, NY; (4) Hampton Roads-SE Virginia
Source: The Council for Community and Economic Research (formerly ACCRA), Cost of Living Index, 2020

Appendix A: Comparative Statistics

Health Care, Transportation, and Other Costs

Urban Area	Doctor ($/visit)	Dentist ($/visit)	Optometrist ($/visit)	Gasoline ($/gallon)	Beauty Salon ($/visit)	Men's Shirt ($)
Albuquerque, NM	106.93	98.97	108.12	1.85	39.81	30.50
Allentown, PA	75.54	110.86	106.13	2.54	43.55	25.80
Anchorage, AK	206.08	147.12	219.89	2.59	54.87	16.85
Ann Arbor, MI	n/a	n/a	n/a	n/a	n/a	n/a
Athens, GA	n/a	n/a	n/a	n/a	n/a	n/a
Atlanta, GA	119.80	105.78	110.27	2.23	47.13	27.27
Austin, TX	117.55	121.27	114.00	2.00	50.41	32.54
Baton Rouge	114.78	104.33	127.76	1.89	50.62	40.67
Boise City, ID	124.87	83.97	133.84	2.37	36.81	42.44
Boston, MA	194.00	108.27	102.75	2.19	64.17	44.46
Boulder, CO	n/a	n/a	n/a	n/a	n/a	n/a
Cape Coral, FL	123.46	110.14	85.53	2.45	33.41	25.30
Cedar Rapids, IA	122.25	115.00	102.58	2.15	37.59	28.78
Charleston, SC	131.23	102.76	81.87	2.06	57.83	27.44
Charlotte, NC	121.12	112.88	119.06	2.35	39.10	31.86
Chicago, IL	104.96	101.82	96.76	2.51	65.57	32.92
Cincinnati, OH	109.23	105.08	96.61	2.29	34.80	33.72
Clarksville, TN	n/a	n/a	n/a	n/a	n/a	n/a
Cleveland, OH	121.47	119.67	86.00	2.25	31.40	37.72
College Station, TX	n/a	n/a	n/a	n/a	n/a	n/a
Colorado Springs, CO	126.71	105.77	114.08	2.41	42.90	28.17
Columbia, MO	126.58	89.08	104.24	1.99	39.17	33.37
Columbia, SC	102.00	59.00	51.67	2.00	41.63	20.62
Columbus, OH	130.99	84.54	59.28	2.38	39.83	34.09
Dallas, TX	121.08	133.84	97.86	1.92	44.45	38.73
Davenport, IA	142.33	96.83	93.08	2.16	34.50	43.03
Denver, CO	111.77	105.51	104.86	2.49	44.29	30.30
Des Moines, IA	110.85	82.19	108.45	2.17	32.13	15.16
Durham, NC	n/a	n/a	n/a	n/a	n/a	n/a
Edison, NJ[1]	94.50	113.15	101.33	2.26	36.40	41.77
El Paso, TX	133.61	82.94	87.16	2.15	30.42	28.66
Fargo, ND	n/a	n/a	n/a	n/a	n/a	n/a
Fayetteville, NC	n/a	n/a	n/a	n/a	n/a	n/a
Fort Collins, CO	n/a	n/a	n/a	n/a	n/a	n/a
Fort Wayne, IN	129.50	94.17	89.56	2.30	33.00	33.48
Fort Worth, TX	91.05	108.33	92.25	1.83	53.57	39.58
Grand Rapids, MI	98.00	94.78	105.11	2.23	32.55	17.24
Greeley, CO	n/a	n/a	n/a	n/a	n/a	n/a
Green Bay, WI	176.50	81.33	74.00	1.71	22.70	30.51
Greensboro, NC[2]	124.74	139.81	109.70	2.12	35.48	39.18
Honolulu, HI	145.88	86.68	195.37	3.30	70.00	58.06
Houston, TX	88.11	111.03	119.84	1.92	61.37	33.46
Huntsville, AL	112.22	100.06	109.44	2.06	33.33	31.87
Indianapolis, IN	88.25	92.92	65.90	2.12	37.63	42.14
Jacksonville, FL	77.42	94.87	70.67	2.20	56.67	23.45
Kansas City, MO	108.18	107.03	106.75	2.02	38.27	33.28
Lafayette, LA	113.42	79.60	103.22	1.92	40.73	32.66
Lakeland, FL	n/a	n/a	n/a	n/a	n/a	n/a
Las Vegas, NV	106.13	96.98	105.92	2.36	46.67	29.07
Lexington, KY	82.39	76.80	74.07	2.08	37.90	38.67
Lincoln, NE	148.06	94.73	104.48	2.20	40.62	43.69
Little Rock, AR	125.22	69.23	101.50	1.89	42.83	35.86
Los Angeles, CA	125.00	110.78	125.58	3.31	76.50	32.87
Louisville, KY	133.98	82.89	71.56	2.28	49.58	32.27
Madison, WI	201.33	113.22	57.00	2.18	48.44	33.55

Table continued on following page.

Appendix A: Comparative Statistics   A-143

Urban Area	Doctor ($/visit)	Dentist ($/visit)	Optometrist ($/visit)	Gasoline ($/gallon)	Beauty Salon ($/visit)	Men's Shirt ($)
Manchester, NH	152.49	121.64	101.89	2.00	41.18	34.23
Memphis, TN	84.25	77.68	74.47	1.94	36.63	25.89
Miami, FL	111.06	107.78	105.63	2.24	70.00	23.08
Midland, TX	98.67	109.17	103.22	2.03	33.61	25.58
Milwaukee, WI	175.40	101.10	60.00	2.01	41.93	22.41
Minneapolis, MN	147.85	86.94	89.59	2.06	34.39	34.39
Nashville, TN	94.18	107.94	91.08	2.05	35.67	32.97
New Haven, CT	130.27	107.76	112.13	2.30	47.72	35.60
New Orleans, LA	156.11	111.89	94.77	2.02	48.89	27.54
New York, NY[3]	116.89	116.47	100.16	2.32	70.14	49.22
Oklahoma City, OK	112.21	93.98	102.53	1.90	40.17	18.12
Omaha, NE	119.00	78.66	114.83	2.07	34.01	23.77
Orlando, FL	83.46	97.71	100.39	2.10	54.17	17.78
Peoria, IL	114.08	79.00	141.52	2.36	30.00	29.99
Philadelphia, PA	133.89	96.86	108.61	2.43	60.55	31.89
Phoenix, AZ	96.33	89.83	96.17	2.49	41.67	27.57
Pittsburgh, PA	93.55	102.37	90.39	2.55	34.18	22.73
Portland, OR	168.67	101.75	146.25	2.78	56.44	41.23
Providence, RI	157.87	92.75	131.39	2.15	48.53	38.26
Provo, UT	99.81	84.76	97.49	2.39	36.53	24.62
Raleigh, NC	145.22	99.00	98.89	2.27	48.42	30.33
Reno, NV	155.00	114.56	117.17	2.98	40.13	21.17
Richmond, VA	139.74	99.40	116.20	2.01	44.43	29.26
Riverside, CA	n/a	n/a	n/a	n/a	n/a	n/a
Rochester, MN	n/a	n/a	n/a	n/a	n/a	n/a
Sacramento, CA	194.75	94.80	148.50	3.24	62.28	24.56
Salt Lake City, UT	107.49	101.65	89.78	2.44	34.97	23.53
San Antonio, TX	86.07	87.61	97.83	1.90	45.96	31.37
San Diego, CA	125.00	107.18	117.65	3.24	64.57	32.48
San Francisco, CA	149.63	132.68	144.57	3.46	82.05	42.08
San Jose, CA	n/a	n/a	n/a	n/a	n/a	n/a
Santa Rosa, CA	n/a	n/a	n/a	n/a	n/a	n/a
Savannah, GA	109.21	127.37	93.79	2.10	35.80	25.61
Seattle, WA	136.39	143.77	158.73	3.19	50.33	36.89
Sioux Falls, SD	n/a	n/a	n/a	n/a	n/a	n/a
Springfield, IL	n/a	n/a	n/a	n/a	n/a	n/a
Tallahassee, FL	126.07	111.09	69.75	2.25	36.64	33.99
Tampa, FL	99.22	105.57	99.12	2.11	37.26	23.11
Tucson, AZ	138.05	91.20	96.00	2.14	51.51	49.50
Tulsa, OK	109.61	90.61	99.06	1.77	35.56	23.57
Tuscaloosa, AL	n/a	n/a	n/a	n/a	n/a	n/a
Virginia Beach, VA[4]	83.17	103.67	98.57	2.00	38.97	36.02
Washington, DC	109.41	94.31	79.25	2.31	66.76	37.74
Wichita, KS	100.20	86.82	148.22	2.03	39.58	43.51
Winston-Salem, NC	124.74	139.81	109.70	2.12	35.48	39.18
Average*	115.44	99.32	108.10	2.21	39.27	31.37
Minimum*	36.68	59.00	51.36	1.71	19.00	11.00
Maximum*	219.00	153.10	250.97	3.46	82.05	58.33

Note: **Doctor** (general practitioners routine exam of an established patient); **Dentist** (adult teeth cleaning and periodic oral examination); **Optometrist** (full vision eye exam for established adult patient); **Gasoline** (one gallon regular unleaded, national brand, including all taxes, cash price at self-service pump if available); **Beauty Salon** (woman's shampoo, trim, and blow-dry); **Men's Shirt** (cotton/polyester dress shirt, pinpoint weave, long sleeves); (*) Average, minimum, and maximum values for all 284 areas in the Cost of Living Index report; n/a not available; In cases where data is not available for the city, data for the metro area or for a neighboring city has been provided and noted as follows: (1) Middlesex-Monmouth NJ; (2) Winston-Salem, NC; (3) Brooklyn, NY; (4) Hampton Roads-SE Virginia
Source: The Council for Community and Economic Research (formerly ACCRA), Cost of Living Index, 2020

Number of Medical Professionals

City	Area Covered	MDs[1]	DOs[1,2]	Dentists	Podiatrists	Chiropractors	Optometrists
Albuquerque, NM	Bernalillo County	457.1	20.1	87.2	9.9	24.4	16.9
Allentown, PA	Lehigh County	347.8	83.3	88.3	12.2	29.5	20.0
Anchorage, AK	Anchorage Borough	360.0	46.1	128.5	4.9	63.2	31.3
Ann Arbor, MI	Washtenaw County	1,272.3	41.4	183.4	7.3	26.7	17.1
Athens, GA	Clarke County	313.5	14.9	53.8	4.7	21.0	16.4
Atlanta, GA	Fulton County	510.9	12.8	71.1	5.3	55.1	17.2
Austin, TX	Travis County	320.3	19.2	72.2	4.2	34.0	16.3
Baton Rouge, LA	East Baton Rouge Parish	388.4	7.2	75.9	4.5	12.5	13.9
Boise City, ID	Ada County	290.3	33.1	81.0	3.5	55.4	19.5
Boston, MA	Suffolk County	1,479.8	15.2	222.3	10.0	14.1	34.1
Boulder, CO	Boulder County	351.8	32.7	106.1	6.1	80.9	26.4
Cape Coral, FL	Lee County	190.7	29.8	49.8	8.3	27.4	12.6
Cedar Rapids, IA	Linn County	185.1	22.1	73.7	8.4	59.5	18.1
Charleston, SC	Charleston County	796.9	31.0	109.6	4.9	50.8	21.9
Charlotte, NC	Mecklenburg County	329.6	14.2	69.9	3.4	32.8	14.0
Chicago, IL	Cook County	432.8	23.4	94.5	12.4	28.7	20.8
Cincinnati, OH	Hamilton County	612.8	25.1	75.7	10.0	20.3	21.8
Clarksville, TN	Montgomery County	95.5	14.6	46.9	2.4	13.4	12.9
Cleveland, OH	Cuyahoga County	714.3	51.5	109.6	18.1	18.4	17.2
College Station, TX	Brazos County	258.7	19.0	52.4	3.1	17.5	15.7
Colorado Springs, CO	El Paso County	196.9	31.0	104.5	4.4	43.6	24.6
Columbia, MO	Boone County	815.9	59.8	69.8	5.5	35.5	27.2
Columbia, SC	Richland County	356.3	15.9	91.6	7.2	23.8	19.7
Columbus, OH	Franklin County	424.6	61.9	93.1	7.1	24.8	27.1
Dallas, TX	Dallas County	335.5	20.5	86.8	4.0	36.5	13.5
Davenport, IA	Scott County	233.2	52.1	79.2	4.6	182.7	16.8
Denver, CO	Denver County	595.6	32.7	76.3	6.6	36.2	16.9
Des Moines, IA	Polk County	213.2	96.7	73.9	10.8	55.3	21.0
Durham, NC	Durham County	1,131.3	15.8	75.0	4.0	19.3	14.6
Edison, NJ	Middlesex County	375.0	19.5	90.9	9.9	25.5	20.0
El Paso, TX	El Paso County	195.0	12.9	46.5	3.9	8.7	10.1
Fargo, ND	Cass County	392.7	19.4	79.7	4.4	73.1	31.3
Fayetteville, NC	Cumberland County	200.3	23.1	104.9	6.0	9.8	18.2
Fort Collins, CO	Larimer County	239.5	29.9	79.6	5.9	55.5	21.0
Fort Wayne, IN	Allen County	264.5	27.5	66.4	5.5	21.9	25.8
Fort Worth, TX	Tarrant County	183.1	34.4	60.4	4.4	27.0	15.9
Grand Rapids, MI	Kent County	343.8	69.5	74.6	4.7	37.0	25.1
Greeley, CO	Weld County	129.9	16.5	45.9	2.8	22.8	12.3
Green Bay, WI	Brown County	244.7	24.3	80.5	3.4	46.9	18.1
Greensboro, NC	Guilford County	252.9	14.1	57.0	5.0	14.1	10.2
Honolulu, HI	Honolulu County	351.0	17.3	101.1	3.4	19.6	24.3
Houston, TX	Harris County	333.5	11.5	70.7	4.7	22.3	20.4
Huntsville, AL	Madison County	275.5	12.0	56.6	3.8	23.3	19.0
Indianapolis, IN	Marion County	438.4	21.4	90.3	6.1	15.8	19.8
Jacksonville, FL	Duval County	351.1	22.9	83.3	8.4	25.0	16.2
Kansas City, MO	Jackson County	307.2	59.9	90.2	6.4	45.2	20.2
Lafayette, LA	Lafayette Parish	367.7	9.9	68.7	3.7	32.7	13.1
Lakeland, FL	Polk County	124.5	10.0	34.1	4.3	18.1	9.7
Las Vegas, NV	Clark County	177.4	34.8	63.7	4.3	19.6	13.1
Lexington, KY	Fayette County	728.8	36.6	148.5	7.4	22.6	23.2
Lincoln, NE	Lancaster County	218.3	12.6	101.5	5.3	45.1	21.6
Little Rock, AR	Pulaski County	737.4	14.3	77.6	4.6	22.5	21.4
Los Angeles, CA	Los Angeles County	302.4	13.5	89.6	6.4	30.1	18.7
Louisville, KY	Jefferson County	476.6	13.3	109.6	7.8	28.8	15.5
Madison, WI	Dane County	610.2	21.2	73.9	4.6	44.1	22.3
Manchester, NH	Hillsborough County	237.8	25.3	82.7	5.5	25.9	20.1

Table continued on following page.

City	Area Covered	MDs[1]	DOs[1,2]	Dentists	Podiatrists	Chiropractors	Optometrists
Memphis, TN	Shelby County	403.7	10.3	73.6	3.6	13.2	31.6
Miami, FL	Miami-Dade County	344.1	16.5	69.8	10.3	18.3	14.4
Midland, TX	Midland County	150.1	9.3	54.9	2.3	13.6	11.9
Milwaukee, WI	Milwaukee County	374.6	21.6	83.9	7.7	20.4	10.9
Minneapolis, MN	Hennepin County	524.3	22.3	99.8	5.2	73.2	21.5
Nashville, TN	Davidson County	647.2	12.2	81.1	4.3	25.6	16.9
New Haven, CT	New Haven County	556.7	10.7	79.9	10.1	26.9	17.3
New Orleans, LA	Orleans Parish	808.2	18.2	74.3	3.8	9.5	6.2
New York, NY	New York City	483.9	16.6	91.0	13.6	16.5	17.6
Oklahoma City, OK	Oklahoma County	410.1	41.7	105.6	5.3	27.3	18.3
Omaha, NE	Douglas County	540.6	27.5	97.0	5.3	41.1	20.5
Orlando, FL	Orange County	311.3	22.1	50.7	3.7	26.6	12.8
Peoria, IL	Peoria County	558.6	41.5	86.5	8.4	50.8	20.6
Philadelphia, PA	Philadelphia County	571.9	44.8	81.1	17.2	15.6	17.7
Phoenix, AZ	Maricopa County	245.6	31.3	68.2	6.6	33.2	15.5
Pittsburgh, PA	Allegheny County	642.7	43.9	98.1	10.9	44.7	20.9
Portland, OR	Multnomah County	634.2	31.0	99.8	5.3	74.7	22.4
Providence, RI	Providence County	496.3	18.1	60.6	9.9	20.3	20.7
Provo, UT	Utah County	116.3	19.0	61.0	4.6	25.5	11.0
Raleigh, NC	Wake County	276.9	11.4	71.6	3.5	26.5	16.6
Reno, NV	Washoe County	294.4	20.9	70.0	4.0	28.0	24.0
Richmond, VA	Richmond City	740.3	28.4	143.2	10.8	7.4	16.5
Riverside, CA	Riverside County	127.8	15.3	52.4	2.6	16.3	12.8
Rochester, MN	Olmsted County	2,492.4	48.6	126.3	6.3	41.1	24.0
Sacramento, CA	Sacramento County	315.5	15.7	78.3	4.6	22.0	18.1
Salt Lake City, UT	Salt Lake County	376.7	17.1	78.4	6.5	27.1	13.5
San Antonio, TX	Bexar County	324.7	18.6	89.2	5.3	16.3	18.1
San Diego, CA	San Diego County	325.9	18.3	90.9	4.3	34.4	19.1
San Francisco, CA	San Francisco County	814.1	13.6	156.7	10.4	39.6	29.4
San Jose, CA	Santa Clara County	421.9	10.9	118.4	6.8	42.7	27.5
Santa Rosa, CA	Sonoma County	279.6	18.2	93.7	6.7	40.9	18.2
Savannah, GA	Chatham County	352.0	18.0	69.8	6.9	19.0	13.5
Seattle, WA	King County	489.5	15.6	109.7	6.4	46.7	21.8
Sioux Falls, SD	Minnehaha County	362.3	25.7	55.4	6.2	58.0	19.2
Springfield, IL	Sangamon County	631.8	26.1	85.3	5.7	40.1	21.1
Tallahassee, FL	Leon County	304.5	14.1	49.0	3.4	23.8	18.7
Tampa, FL	Hillsborough County	344.9	26.1	58.9	5.6	26.4	14.2
Tucson, AZ	Pima County	361.9	24.6	65.1	5.4	19.1	15.9
Tulsa, OK	Tulsa County	269.3	122.0	69.7	4.0	38.8	23.5
Tuscaloosa, AL	Tuscaloosa County	228.0	9.1	49.7	5.3	20.5	15.8
Virginia Beach, VA	Virginia Beach City	252.3	13.3	77.3	7.6	27.3	16.9
Washington, DC	District of Columbia	779.6	16.7	123.0	8.9	9.4	14.5
Wichita, KS	Sedgwick County	258.0	35.2	65.9	2.5	42.6	28.1
Winston-Salem, NC	Forsyth County	660.3	29.3	62.3	5.8	16.5	17.8
U.S.	U.S.	282.9	22.7	71.2	6.2	28.1	16.9

Note: All figures are rates per 100,000 population; Data as of 2019 unless noted; (1) Data as of 2018 and includes all active, non-federal physicians; (2) Doctor of Osteopathic Medicine
Source: U.S. Department of Health and Human Services, Health Resources and Services Administration, Bureau of Health Professions, Area Resource File (ARF) 2019-2020

Health Insurance Coverage: City

City	With Health Insurance	With Private Health Insurance	With Public Health Insurance	Without Health Insurance	Population Under Age 19 Without Health Insurance
Albuquerque, NM	92.1	60.9	43.0	7.9	3.4
Allentown, PA	88.8	47.3	49.7	11.2	5.0
Anchorage, AK	88.8	70.3	30.4	11.2	8.2
Ann Arbor, MI	97.3	87.7	19.7	2.7	1.1
Athens, GA	86.5	68.5	26.9	13.5	7.3
Atlanta, GA	89.7	69.2	28.3	10.3	4.9
Austin, TX	86.4	73.3	20.2	13.6	8.9
Baton Rouge, LA	90.3	59.2	41.1	9.7	3.5
Boise City, ID	91.1	75.8	26.8	8.9	4.4
Boston, MA	96.5	67.2	36.7	3.5	1.3
Boulder, CO	95.9	84.0	20.1	4.1	1.2
Cape Coral, FL	87.4	65.9	36.8	12.6	8.6
Cedar Rapids, IA	95.5	74.3	34.3	4.5	2.7
Charleston, SC	91.9	78.0	25.5	8.1	3.3
Charlotte, NC	87.5	68.5	26.3	12.5	6.4
Chicago, IL	90.4	60.3	36.9	9.6	3.4
Cincinnati, OH	92.7	59.1	41.6	7.3	4.5
Clarksville, TN	91.6	71.5	33.7	8.4	3.4
Cleveland, OH	92.3	44.0	57.3	7.7	3.1
College Station, TX	92.0	85.0	13.7	8.0	4.9
Colorado Springs, CO	92.2	68.7	36.6	7.8	4.2
Columbia, MO	93.2	81.9	20.6	6.8	3.6
Columbia, SC	91.2	72.0	29.7	8.8	2.7
Columbus, OH	91.0	64.0	34.8	9.0	5.4
Dallas, TX	76.4	51.8	30.3	23.6	14.8
Davenport, IA	94.4	66.2	40.2	5.6	3.3
Denver, CO	90.7	65.5	33.0	9.3	4.2
Des Moines, IA	93.1	64.7	41.0	6.9	3.5
Durham, NC	87.5	68.8	28.3	12.5	7.3
Edison, NJ	94.6	81.1	22.8	5.4	1.3
El Paso, TX	80.9	54.7	33.8	19.1	9.1
Fargo, ND	93.5	80.6	24.3	6.5	4.1
Fayetteville, NC	90.0	65.3	40.4	10.0	3.3
Fort Collins, CO	94.0	78.7	24.3	6.0	5.0
Fort Wayne, IN	91.0	65.0	36.5	9.0	5.6
Fort Worth, TX	81.7	60.6	27.5	18.3	11.7
Grand Rapids, MI	91.4	62.1	39.6	8.6	3.9
Greeley, CO	91.5	63.7	38.4	8.5	4.3
Green Bay, WI	92.1	66.1	35.9	7.9	3.7
Greensboro, NC	89.7	65.9	34.1	10.3	4.5
Honolulu, HI	96.1	77.7	34.5	3.9	2.4
Houston, TX	76.9	51.9	30.8	23.1	13.1
Huntsville, AL	90.2	72.8	32.9	9.8	4.2
Indianapolis, IN	89.5	62.3	36.7	10.5	6.0
Jacksonville, FL	88.0	64.7	33.9	12.0	6.8
Kansas City, MO	88.2	68.6	29.1	11.8	6.6
Lafayette, LA	91.3	67.0	35.3	8.7	3.1
Lakeland, FL	90.0	62.2	41.4	10.0	5.2
Las Vegas, NV	87.7	61.6	36.0	12.3	7.2
Lexington, KY	93.2	71.6	32.5	6.8	4.3
Lincoln, NE	92.3	78.5	25.2	7.7	5.2
Little Rock, AR	91.6	65.6	37.6	8.4	4.8
Los Angeles, CA	88.6	54.4	40.5	11.4	4.2
Louisville, KY	94.6	67.1	40.3	5.4	2.7
Madison, WI	96.0	83.8	22.2	4.0	2.2

Table continued on following page.

City	With Health Insurance	With Private Health Insurance	With Public Health Insurance	Without Health Insurance	Population Under Age 19 Without Health Insurance
Manchester, NH	90.1	64.0	36.3	9.9	3.7
Memphis, TN	86.3	55.7	41.0	13.7	6.3
Miami, FL	80.2	46.7	36.7	19.8	8.6
Midland, TX	83.3	71.1	19.7	16.7	14.7
Milwaukee, WI	90.7	54.1	44.9	9.3	3.3
Minneapolis, MN	93.4	66.8	34.5	6.6	3.4
Nashville, TN	87.9	67.1	29.8	12.1	6.9
New Haven, CT	91.1	50.8	46.7	8.9	2.8
New Orleans, LA	90.8	56.3	42.9	9.2	3.4
New York, NY	92.5	58.3	43.0	7.5	2.4
Oklahoma City, OK	85.4	64.0	32.1	14.6	7.1
Omaha, NE	89.8	71.3	27.7	10.2	5.8
Orlando, FL	84.8	62.3	29.4	15.2	7.5
Peoria, IL	94.2	65.7	41.1	5.8	3.0
Philadelphia, PA	91.9	56.9	45.2	8.1	3.5
Phoenix, AZ	85.9	57.2	36.0	14.1	9.5
Pittsburgh, PA	94.7	73.5	33.4	5.3	3.3
Portland, OR	93.6	71.5	32.0	6.4	2.8
Providence, RI	92.5	53.2	46.4	7.5	3.1
Provo, UT	88.8	77.8	17.3	11.2	10.7
Raleigh, NC	89.8	74.2	24.5	10.2	5.4
Reno, NV	90.2	68.4	32.1	9.8	8.1
Richmond, VA	88.0	62.6	34.9	12.0	6.5
Riverside, CA	90.6	58.9	38.2	9.4	3.6
Rochester, MN	95.7	79.4	30.4	4.3	2.4
Sacramento, CA	94.2	62.2	42.1	5.8	2.2
Salt Lake City, UT	87.4	72.5	22.1	12.6	11.7
San Antonio, TX	83.3	60.1	32.7	16.7	8.6
San Diego, CA	92.2	69.7	31.6	7.8	3.6
San Francisco, CA	96.3	75.7	29.4	3.7	1.5
San Jose, CA	94.8	72.3	30.4	5.2	2.1
Santa Rosa, CA	92.4	67.6	37.9	7.6	4.9
Savannah, GA	83.0	57.3	34.5	17.0	7.7
Seattle, WA	95.8	80.6	24.0	4.2	1.4
Sioux Falls, SD	92.2	77.2	26.5	7.8	4.9
Springfield, IL	95.7	69.1	42.2	4.3	1.7
Tallahassee, FL	91.6	76.3	25.1	8.4	4.2
Tampa, FL	88.3	62.5	32.9	11.7	5.4
Tucson, AZ	88.5	56.5	42.8	11.5	8.1
Tulsa, OK	83.4	58.9	35.1	16.6	8.2
Tuscaloosa, AL	92.6	72.0	31.2	7.4	2.5
Virginia Beach, VA	92.4	80.7	25.8	7.6	3.8
Washington, DC	96.3	70.4	35.6	3.7	2.0
Wichita, KS	87.9	67.3	32.3	12.1	6.6
Winston-Salem, NC	87.6	62.4	36.3	12.4	4.9
U.S.	91.2	67.9	35.1	8.8	5.1

Note: Figures are percentages that cover the civilian noninstitutionalized population
Source: U.S. Census Bureau, 2015-2019 American Community Survey 5-Year Estimates

Health Insurance Coverage: Metro Area

Metro Area	With Health Insurance	With Private Health Insurance	With Public Health Insurance	Without Health Insurance	Population Under Age 19 Without Health Insurance
Albuquerque, NM	91.7	60.2	44.2	8.3	4.1
Allentown, PA	94.5	73.3	35.4	5.5	3.0
Anchorage, AK	87.8	68.3	31.3	12.2	9.4
Ann Arbor, MI	96.5	83.3	25.9	3.5	1.8
Athens, GA	87.6	69.5	28.5	12.4	6.7
Atlanta, GA	87.2	69.3	26.8	12.8	7.5
Austin, TX	87.5	74.5	21.7	12.5	8.1
Baton Rouge, LA	91.7	66.4	35.5	8.3	3.3
Boise City, ID	89.6	71.7	30.2	10.4	4.8
Boston, MA	97.1	76.7	32.7	2.9	1.3
Boulder, CO	95.4	79.5	25.6	4.6	2.1
Cape Coral, FL	86.7	62.4	43.6	13.3	9.3
Cedar Rapids, IA	96.5	77.1	33.1	3.5	2.0
Charleston, SC	89.5	71.1	31.4	10.5	5.7
Charlotte, NC	89.8	70.7	29.3	10.2	4.8
Chicago, IL	92.4	70.2	31.7	7.6	3.2
Cincinnati, OH	94.8	73.1	32.8	5.2	3.1
Clarksville, TN	91.8	69.1	37.2	8.2	5.3
Cleveland, OH	94.7	69.2	38.4	5.3	3.4
College Station, TX	87.4	73.5	23.1	12.6	8.4
Colorado Springs, CO	92.8	71.1	35.3	7.2	4.1
Columbia, MO	92.8	79.5	24.1	7.2	4.6
Columbia, SC	90.5	70.4	33.6	9.5	3.7
Columbus, OH	93.3	71.2	32.1	6.7	4.2
Dallas, TX	83.6	66.0	24.9	16.4	11.0
Davenport, IA	95.3	72.9	37.3	4.7	2.7
Denver, CO	92.6	72.6	29.2	7.4	4.0
Des Moines, IA	95.6	77.4	31.2	4.4	2.2
Durham, NC	89.7	71.7	29.7	10.3	6.1
Edison, NJ	92.8	67.2	36.0	7.2	2.9
El Paso, TX	79.7	52.6	33.9	20.3	9.8
Fargo, ND	94.6	82.1	24.4	5.4	4.2
Fayetteville, NC	89.3	64.6	38.7	10.7	3.6
Fort Collins, CO	94.1	76.0	29.1	5.9	4.7
Fort Wayne, IN	91.5	69.2	33.1	8.5	6.4
Fort Worth, TX	83.6	66.0	24.9	16.4	11.0
Grand Rapids, MI	94.6	75.5	31.5	5.4	3.1
Greeley, CO	92.1	70.1	32.2	7.9	4.6
Green Bay, WI	94.8	75.7	30.4	5.2	3.6
Greensboro, NC	89.6	65.5	35.2	10.4	4.7
Honolulu, HI	96.7	80.4	32.2	3.3	2.0
Houston, TX	81.9	62.1	26.6	18.1	11.1
Huntsville, AL	91.4	76.2	29.9	8.6	3.3
Indianapolis, IN	91.9	71.6	31.0	8.1	5.3
Jacksonville, FL	89.1	68.7	32.7	10.9	6.6
Kansas City, MO	91.1	75.3	27.2	8.9	5.2
Lafayette, LA	90.1	62.1	38.5	9.9	3.6
Lakeland, FL	87.3	59.0	41.4	12.7	7.2
Las Vegas, NV	88.3	64.2	33.7	11.7	7.4
Lexington, KY	93.7	70.8	34.5	6.3	4.0
Lincoln, NE	92.9	79.5	24.9	7.1	4.8
Little Rock, AR	92.4	67.0	38.9	7.6	4.4
Los Angeles, CA	90.9	60.6	37.4	9.1	3.8
Louisville, KY	94.6	71.4	36.4	5.4	3.3
Madison, WI	96.1	83.5	24.7	3.9	2.1

Table continued on following page.

Metro Area	With Health Insurance	With Private Health Insurance	With Public Health Insurance	Without Health Insurance	Population Under Age 19 Without Health Insurance
Manchester, NH	93.8	76.9	28.9	6.2	2.6
Memphis, TN	89.2	64.7	35.4	10.8	5.0
Miami, FL	84.9	58.9	33.6	15.1	7.8
Midland, TX	83.6	71.1	20.2	16.4	14.0
Milwaukee, WI	94.4	71.8	34.1	5.6	2.4
Minneapolis, MN	95.7	78.0	29.6	4.3	3.0
Nashville, TN	90.7	72.1	28.7	9.3	5.1
New Haven, CT	95.0	68.2	38.7	5.0	2.2
New Orleans, LA	90.3	60.4	40.1	9.7	3.7
New York, NY	92.8	67.2	36.0	7.2	2.9
Oklahoma City, OK	87.5	68.6	30.8	12.5	6.2
Omaha, NE	92.3	75.9	27.0	7.7	4.3
Orlando, FL	87.6	65.5	31.5	12.4	6.9
Peoria, IL	95.2	73.5	37.2	4.8	2.9
Philadelphia, PA	94.4	73.2	34.0	5.6	2.9
Phoenix, AZ	89.5	65.4	34.9	10.5	8.2
Pittsburgh, PA	96.2	77.0	35.8	3.8	1.7
Portland, OR	94.0	73.3	32.6	6.0	2.8
Providence, RI	96.1	70.9	38.8	3.9	2.1
Provo, UT	91.9	81.7	17.4	8.1	6.0
Raleigh, NC	91.0	75.9	24.8	9.0	4.6
Reno, NV	90.6	69.8	32.2	9.4	7.7
Richmond, VA	91.8	75.2	29.4	8.2	4.6
Riverside, CA	91.4	57.5	42.0	8.6	3.9
Rochester, MN	95.5	79.9	30.3	4.5	3.7
Sacramento, CA	94.9	69.3	38.2	5.1	2.5
Salt Lake City, UT	89.7	77.5	20.1	10.3	8.2
San Antonio, TX	85.3	65.1	31.0	14.7	8.1
San Diego, CA	92.2	68.4	33.8	7.8	3.8
San Francisco, CA	95.7	75.5	30.5	4.3	2.1
San Jose, CA	95.6	76.7	27.4	4.4	1.9
Santa Rosa, CA	93.9	71.6	36.7	6.1	3.2
Savannah, GA	87.0	67.6	30.1	13.0	6.2
Seattle, WA	94.4	75.9	29.2	5.6	2.5
Sioux Falls, SD	92.8	78.9	25.1	7.2	4.5
Springfield, IL	96.2	74.3	37.4	3.8	1.6
Tallahassee, FL	91.2	73.4	30.0	8.8	4.6
Tampa, FL	88.1	63.3	36.8	11.9	6.3
Tucson, AZ	90.8	62.2	42.6	9.2	7.1
Tulsa, OK	86.6	65.8	32.6	13.4	7.6
Tuscaloosa, AL	92.3	70.5	33.7	7.7	2.5
Virginia Beach, VA	91.6	75.2	30.5	8.4	4.6
Washington, DC	92.4	78.2	25.2	7.6	4.5
Wichita, KS	89.8	71.6	30.3	10.2	5.8
Winston-Salem, NC	89.1	66.0	35.7	10.9	4.9
U.S.	91.2	67.9	35.1	8.8	5.1

Note: Figures are percentages that cover the civilian noninstitutionalized population; Figures cover the Metropolitan Statistical Area (MSA)—see Appendix B for areas included
Source: U.S. Census Bureau, 2015-2019 American Community Survey 5-Year Estimates

Appendix A: Comparative Statistics

Crime Rate: City

City	All Crimes	Murder	Rape	Robbery	Aggrav. Assault	Burglary	Larceny-Theft	Motor Vehicle Theft
Albuquerque, NM	n/a	14.9	86.5	302.4	948.0	n/a	3,672.1	965.4
Allentown, PA	2,669.6	5.7	52.5	139.5	188.7	427.6	1,656.1	199.4
Anchorage, AK	5,505.8	11.1	187.7	215.8	829.9	588.0	3,141.1	532.1
Ann Arbor, MI	1,979.8	1.6	62.7	37.4	149.7	160.3	1,455.7	112.3
Athens, GA[2]	3,562.0	4.8	45.6	98.5	266.6	546.8	2,415.5	184.1
Atlanta, GA[1]	5,423.2	17.7	49.4	221.5	480.1	621.2	3,366.4	666.8
Austin, TX	4,111.4	3.2	54.2	98.5	245.0	440.5	2,962.9	307.1
Baton Rouge, LA	6,226.7	31.7	23.6	292.3	588.7	1,023.3	3,904.9	362.1
Boise City, ID	1,859.8	1.7	70.9	19.0	188.9	203.2	1,276.2	99.9
Boston, MA	n/a	6.0	33.1	148.7	419.5	243.7	1,515.1	n/a
Boulder, CO	3,282.4	0.9	37.8	34.1	183.4	373.2	2,421.7	231.3
Cape Coral, FL	1,237.0	2.6	8.2	18.5	87.0	141.1	895.5	83.9
Cedar Rapids, IA	3,593.1	1.5	20.1	61.9	173.9	624.6	2,438.7	272.4
Charleston, SC	2,632.8	5.8	36.9	68.7	261.8	211.2	1,688.9	359.5
Charlotte, NC	4,665.2	10.9	33.6	209.2	485.8	574.6	2,997.5	353.7
Chicago, IL	3,925.8	18.2	65.1	294.9	565.0	353.8	2,293.4	335.5
Cincinnati, OH	5,147.1	21.1	92.3	287.5	443.7	911.5	2,945.6	445.4
Clarksville, TN	3,370.7	8.8	64.4	72.5	433.1	339.4	2,160.7	291.9
Cleveland, OH	5,983.8	24.1	125.4	496.3	870.8	1,129.0	2,610.6	727.6
College Station, TX	1,948.1	0.8	40.3	36.1	111.5	327.9	1,282.2	149.3
Colorado Springs, CO	4,251.7	4.8	89.9	101.1	389.2	500.4	2,521.6	644.6
Columbia, MO	2,914.8	8.8	55.2	59.2	197.6	399.1	1,944.5	250.4
Columbia, SC	6,027.4	21.7	65.8	164.4	523.2	684.7	3,898.6	669.0
Columbus, OH	3,811.3	8.9	97.3	199.8	197.3	641.1	2,274.1	392.8
Dallas, TX	4,184.2	14.5	58.5	322.7	467.2	675.6	1,893.4	752.4
Davenport, IA	4,421.2	2.0	82.0	121.1	389.7	727.6	2,763.9	335.0
Denver, CO	4,492.4	9.2	97.8	165.3	476.6	544.2	2,473.0	726.3
Des Moines, IA	4,802.5	6.4	53.6	129.6	522.5	1,045.9	2,443.4	601.2
Durham, NC	4,537.6	13.2	43.2	223.3	450.3	703.6	2,833.6	270.4
Edison, NJ	1,450.9	1.0	9.0	18.9	54.8	137.6	1,139.8	89.7
El Paso, TX	1,863.7	5.8	45.1	49.2	252.5	152.6	1,234.6	123.9
Fargo, ND	3,572.4	3.9	87.1	61.2	298.2	651.4	2,163.7	306.9
Fayetteville, NC	4,401.4	11.4	55.8	134.1	674.1	651.2	2,691.1	183.7
Fort Collins, CO	2,389.9	0.6	24.0	21.1	171.5	204.8	1,834.5	133.4
Fort Wayne, IN	3,122.5	9.7	53.8	132.5	165.6	367.5	2,182.5	210.9
Fort Worth, TX	3,132.8	7.5	51.4	106.2	279.4	433.7	1,890.3	364.4
Grand Rapids, MI	2,545.1	4.0	71.4	135.8	426.2	294.8	1,364.7	248.3
Greeley, CO	2,680.0	1.8	65.0	61.3	225.2	309.4	1,737.2	280.1
Green Bay, WI	2,145.9	2.9	74.3	46.7	380.0	233.4	1,290.6	118.1
Greensboro, NC	4,507.7	14.4	37.9	208.4	558.0	743.2	2,614.5	331.2
Honolulu, HI	n/a	n/a	n/a	n/a	n/a	n/a	n/a	n/a
Houston, TX	5,391.7	11.7	53.0	388.3	619.2	723.3	3,040.2	556.0
Huntsville, AL[2]	5,635.0	11.3	88.1	184.5	621.0	731.7	3,462.6	535.9
Indianapolis, IN[1]	5,402.0	18.5	77.1	351.1	826.1	893.6	2,671.9	563.7
Jacksonville, FL	3,956.9	14.2	60.9	142.3	430.0	539.6	2,460.9	309.0
Kansas City, MO	5,287.3	30.2	70.0	290.9	1,040.2	619.0	2,470.5	766.4
Lafayette, LA	4,829.0	11.1	12.6	116.8	383.6	814.6	3,236.9	253.4
Lakeland, FL	3,189.7	6.2	56.1	86.4	163.0	390.2	2,306.7	180.9
Las Vegas, NV	3,302.8	5.0	86.3	127.1	312.8	638.7	1,694.3	438.6
Lexington, KY	3,294.7	8.0	53.7	111.0	123.9	471.4	2,248.9	277.9
Lincoln, NE	3,133.7	1.7	110.9	57.0	213.3	339.4	2,255.4	155.9
Little Rock, AR	7,638.8	19.2	105.4	197.1	1,195.2	887.2	4,696.0	538.9
Los Angeles, CA	3,115.5	6.4	56.6	240.4	428.7	343.9	1,649.9	389.5
Louisville, KY	4,578.4	13.9	29.8	149.2	494.0	638.9	2,670.2	582.4

Table continued on following page.

| | All Crimes | Violent Crimes |||| Property Crimes |||
City		Murder	Rape	Robbery	Aggrav. Assault	Burglary	Larceny -Theft	Motor Vehicle Theft
Madison, WI	2,833.9	1.5	41.0	83.1	234.2	400.4	1,865.1	208.6
Manchester, NH	2,972.7	5.3	54.9	117.8	422.5	264.8	1,970.9	136.4
Memphis, TN	8,029.9	29.2	72.0	373.9	1,426.3	1,204.3	4,302.1	622.1
Miami, FL	4,260.9	8.9	31.6	160.0	392.5	368.6	2,959.2	340.1
Midland, TX[1]	2,261.0	3.6	42.8	42.1	199.2	269.9	1,504.9	198.5
Milwaukee, WI	3,887.3	16.4	72.3	323.4	920.4	608.2	1,362.8	583.8
Minneapolis, MN	5,442.7	10.7	106.5	299.1	509.5	788.1	3,056.0	672.8
Nashville, TN	5,114.2	12.1	63.7	287.8	709.5	490.9	3,150.5	399.8
New Haven, CT	4,694.5	10.0	34.5	246.0	604.6	505.0	2,743.4	551.0
New Orleans, LA	6,437.3	30.7	196.2	256.8	661.1	543.2	4,001.3	748.0
New York, NY	2,030.3	3.8	33.1	159.9	374.0	117.5	1,276.2	65.9
Oklahoma City, OK	4,813.7	11.4	81.9	135.0	493.9	943.3	2,572.2	576.1
Omaha, NE	4,256.7	4.9	80.6	110.3	417.0	357.9	2,615.8	670.2
Orlando, FL	5,565.2	8.6	69.8	183.5	476.5	501.2	3,889.5	436.1
Peoria, IL	4,792.9	22.5	58.6	241.5	721.0	683.2	2,666.8	399.3
Philadelphia, PA[1]	4,005.6	22.1	69.0	331.6	486.0	409.4	2,329.5	357.9
Phoenix, AZ	4,013.5	7.8	67.4	189.3	434.4	560.8	2,334.7	419.0
Pittsburgh, PA[1]	3,594.8	18.8	40.0	230.0	289.9	443.2	2,331.9	241.0
Portland, OR	5,748.0	4.4	55.6	147.9	336.8	634.3	3,597.6	971.4
Providence, RI	3,507.4	7.2	59.0	134.1	295.9	397.7	2,349.8	263.7
Provo, UT	1,623.0	0.9	37.5	11.1	65.7	139.1	1,259.5	109.2
Raleigh, NC	2,038.8	1.0	34.3	67.4	153.0	251.1	1,375.4	156.5
Reno, NV	2,658.9	4.7	70.0	121.1	362.1	323.2	1,314.3	463.5
Richmond, VA	3,962.4	23.8	19.5	166.9	252.7	427.4	2,702.0	370.1
Riverside, CA	3,443.6	5.1	41.7	142.8	316.3	390.7	2,099.6	447.4
Rochester, MN	2,096.1	0.8	52.4	28.7	132.8	238.4	1,535.5	107.4
Sacramento, CA	3,809.2	6.6	24.7	202.2	393.6	582.4	2,071.1	528.7
Salt Lake City, UT	6,369.7	6.4	115.6	199.1	391.3	637.3	4,397.7	622.4
San Antonio, TX	5,032.7	6.7	104.5	126.0	471.1	524.1	3,301.1	499.0
San Diego, CA	2,244.2	3.5	38.9	93.4	226.0	245.7	1,278.0	358.7
San Francisco, CA	6,175.2	4.5	36.6	344.8	283.7	524.1	4,501.9	479.6
San Jose, CA	2,858.0	3.1	64.5	128.7	242.0	395.6	1,435.0	589.0
Santa Rosa, CA	2,097.4	1.7	82.1	70.8	327.2	273.2	1,167.6	174.8
Savannah, GA[1]	2,865.5	11.6	35.1	110.2	248.5	364.9	1,824.4	270.8
Seattle, WA	5,081.0	3.7	46.9	175.3	359.6	944.1	3,074.2	477.3
Sioux Falls, SD	3,528.6	2.2	62.5	36.6	381.9	374.4	2,316.5	354.5
Springfield, IL	5,218.0	7.9	94.4	181.8	493.0	908.3	3,300.9	231.7
Tallahassee, FL	4,675.5	10.3	101.0	129.2	456.2	608.4	3,022.5	348.0
Tampa, FL	2,033.7	7.7	30.0	71.2	296.1	255.2	1,242.9	130.6
Tucson, AZ	3,960.4	7.3	96.1	201.5	383.5	455.3	2,406.4	410.3
Tulsa, OK	6,298.2	13.7	84.9	178.7	709.5	1,206.4	3,350.0	755.0
Tuscaloosa, AL[1]	4,843.6	4.9	46.2	137.6	316.4	739.9	3,289.0	309.5
Virginia Beach, VA	1,890.0	6.7	17.6	43.6	61.5	118.0	1,513.7	128.9
Washington, DC	5,223.0	23.5	48.5	334.3	570.9	260.7	3,659.5	325.6
Wichita, KS	6,462.8	9.0	94.1	118.2	919.8	686.3	4,044.6	590.9
Winston-Salem, NC	n/a	n/a	n/a	n/a	n/a	n/a	n/a	n/a
U.S.	2,489.3	5.0	42.6	81.6	250.2	340.5	1,549.5	219.9

Note: Figures are crimes per 100,000 population in 2019 except where noted; n/a not available; (1) 2018 data; (2) 2017 data
Source: FBI Uniform Crime Reports, 2017, 2018, 2019

Crime Rate: Suburbs

Suburbs[1]	All Crimes	Murder	Rape	Robbery	Aggrav. Assault	Burglary	Larceny-Theft	Motor Vehicle Theft
Albuquerque, NM	n/a	2.5	28.6	23.0	502.8	n/a	995.5	214.2
Allentown, PA	n/a	n/a	n/a	n/a	n/a	n/a	n/a	n/a
Anchorage, AK	5,634.3	10.9	32.6	92.4	277.1	787.8	3,955.4	478.1
Ann Arbor, MI	2,017.9	2.4	69.1	38.7	296.3	218.0	1,258.3	135.0
Athens, GA[3]	1,855.9	1.2	18.1	14.5	111.2	289.0	1,349.3	72.5
Atlanta, GA[2]	2,666.3	4.6	24.0	82.5	168.8	373.2	1,770.4	242.7
Austin, TX	1,564.4	1.9	43.6	23.6	126.5	212.3	1,059.4	97.1
Baton Rouge, LA	3,048.0	7.9	29.9	42.8	339.8	380.5	2,107.7	139.3
Boise City, ID	1,329.9	1.2	52.7	7.5	176.3	201.4	798.8	92.1
Boston, MA	n/a	1.4	30.1	41.9	212.4	126.0	804.5	n/a
Boulder, CO	2,439.7	0.9	83.1	20.9	175.3	269.8	1,686.5	203.0
Cape Coral, FL	1,476.1	3.1	40.1	61.0	201.4	186.4	880.9	103.2
Cedar Rapids, IA	911.9	0.0	21.6	5.0	95.2	183.1	523.4	83.6
Charleston, SC	3,168.8	9.6	42.3	61.1	290.1	419.0	2,025.9	320.8
Charlotte, NC	n/a	n/a	n/a	n/a	n/a	n/a	n/a	n/a
Chicago, IL	n/a	n/a	n/a	n/a	n/a	n/a	n/a	n/a
Cincinnati, OH	1,749.6	1.5	34.0	32.1	73.6	224.7	1,269.6	114.0
Clarksville, TN	1,876.6	4.7	31.4	23.3	124.1	401.6	1,146.8	144.8
Cleveland, OH	1,401.7	1.8	21.7	34.6	90.5	189.4	985.7	77.9
College Station, TX	2,466.8	2.7	79.5	46.6	193.9	419.9	1,565.3	158.9
Colorado Springs, CO	1,634.0	3.7	56.3	25.7	166.4	213.4	951.5	216.8
Columbia, MO	1,774.1	3.5	37.8	13.0	145.2	253.8	1,150.8	170.0
Columbia, SC	3,564.0	5.9	45.8	67.3	428.2	503.6	2,152.4	360.8
Columbus, OH	1,836.3	2.6	36.4	25.9	60.9	251.9	1,366.9	91.7
Dallas, TX	n/a	n/a	n/a	n/a	n/a	n/a	n/a	n/a
Davenport, IA	1,880.3	2.2	46.1	31.4	202.5	306.7	1,169.0	122.5
Denver, CO	n/a	n/a	n/a	n/a	n/a	n/a	n/a	n/a
Des Moines, IA	n/a	n/a	n/a	n/a	n/a	n/a	n/a	n/a
Durham, NC	1,853.6	2.7	22.5	32.4	157.6	332.5	1,221.8	84.0
Edison, NJ	n/a	n/a	n/a	n/a	n/a	n/a	n/a	n/a
El Paso, TX	1,251.9	0.6	37.2	15.8	195.1	156.6	746.2	100.4
Fargo, ND	1,642.9	0.0	34.9	22.4	76.5	277.5	1,087.8	143.8
Fayetteville, NC	n/a	n/a	n/a	n/a	n/a	n/a	n/a	n/a
Fort Collins, CO	1,855.9	1.1	44.9	14.6	189.3	184.4	1,296.7	124.9
Fort Wayne, IN	1,097.2	2.8	35.5	32.1	128.3	146.4	649.7	102.5
Fort Worth, TX	n/a	n/a	n/a	n/a	n/a	n/a	n/a	n/a
Grand Rapids, MI	n/a	1.8	81.2	19.6	146.3	n/a	933.5	85.2
Greeley, CO	1,419.9	1.4	41.0	12.3	90.5	171.1	940.9	162.6
Green Bay, WI	928.9	0.9	26.1	3.2	61.9	81.6	725.8	29.3
Greensboro, NC	2,421.7	6.7	29.9	53.7	258.8	475.5	1,421.1	175.9
Honolulu, HI	n/a	n/a	n/a	n/a	n/a	n/a	n/a	n/a
Houston, TX	n/a	n/a	n/a	n/a	n/a	n/a	n/a	n/a
Huntsville, AL[3]	2,220.1	4.2	32.4	31.2	227.3	432.2	1,337.1	155.6
Indianapolis, IN[2]	1,699.1	2.5	23.1	28.7	114.1	199.2	1,200.7	130.7
Jacksonville, FL	1,592.3	2.2	35.2	25.3	166.6	235.0	1,031.9	96.1
Kansas City, MO	n/a	n/a	n/a	n/a	n/a	n/a	n/a	n/a
Lafayette, LA	2,832.6	6.6	29.8	51.6	358.4	551.2	1,694.4	140.6
Lakeland, FL	1,687.2	2.6	17.0	33.6	217.9	249.4	1,045.5	121.2
Las Vegas, NV	2,501.4	4.6	36.8	114.4	354.9	390.7	1,310.3	289.7
Lexington, KY	2,369.2	0.5	30.9	28.3	60.2	318.5	1,748.7	182.1
Lincoln, NE	1,017.1	0.0	77.9	0.0	41.1	119.0	705.4	73.6
Little Rock, AR	n/a	6.8	60.7	54.6	393.0	n/a	n/a	278.3
Los Angeles, CA	2,574.0	4.1	31.4	148.3	263.3	400.2	1,366.0	360.7
Louisville, KY	1,847.8	1.9	21.7	30.8	98.0	230.7	1,263.0	201.7

Table continued on following page.

Appendix A: Comparative Statistics

Suburbs[1]	All Crimes	Violent Crimes - Murder	Violent Crimes - Rape	Violent Crimes - Robbery	Violent Crimes - Aggrav. Assault	Property Crimes - Burglary	Property Crimes - Larceny-Theft	Property Crimes - Motor Vehicle Theft
Madison, WI	1,351.6	1.0	24.7	18.3	82.4	169.4	971.3	84.6
Manchester, NH	1,000.0	1.6	42.2	12.2	35.9	81.4	789.2	37.5
Memphis, TN	2,498.8	6.8	34.3	50.8	297.1	361.2	1,515.0	233.6
Miami, FL	3,417.0	6.9	35.0	125.5	289.7	268.7	2,428.8	262.4
Midland, TX[2]	2,400.0	11.5	25.9	31.7	368.8	299.6	1,293.6	368.8
Milwaukee, WI	1,671.2	1.4	20.7	24.3	79.0	124.4	1,348.6	72.7
Minneapolis, MN	2,224.5	1.6	36.4	48.6	98.2	238.6	1,611.4	189.7
Nashville, TN	1,872.5	2.8	29.2	26.7	236.4	201.0	1,238.9	137.5
New Haven, CT	1,934.6	2.2	24.3	47.9	77.5	206.4	1,361.4	214.9
New Orleans, LA	2,472.9	9.3	22.9	43.8	209.1	290.9	1,767.8	129.1
New York, NY	n/a	n/a	n/a	n/a	n/a	n/a	n/a	n/a
Oklahoma City, OK	2,410.6	4.4	46.1	32.5	150.0	447.5	1,495.7	234.3
Omaha, NE	1,880.3	2.3	43.8	23.0	147.2	232.1	1,212.2	219.7
Orlando, FL	2,485.9	4.1	42.0	75.9	269.2	341.2	1,573.1	180.5
Peoria, IL	1,462.2	1.7	46.0	15.2	161.7	265.2	890.0	82.4
Philadelphia, PA[2]	1,935.5	7.6	16.3	96.8	235.8	202.8	1,235.3	140.9
Phoenix, AZ	n/a	2.9	40.6	49.3	192.6	n/a	1,530.6	165.3
Pittsburgh, PA[2]	1,402.7	3.5	23.7	33.2	168.7	159.1	958.5	55.9
Portland, OR	2,077.6	1.6	48.3	37.5	128.0	233.0	1,381.8	247.4
Providence, RI	1,466.1	1.7	43.0	37.4	173.7	203.4	912.5	94.2
Provo, UT	1,312.0	1.1	30.2	7.2	46.1	131.5	1,018.1	77.8
Raleigh, NC	1,325.7	2.1	14.8	21.7	90.6	209.5	912.4	74.6
Reno, NV	1,965.3	1.4	55.1	47.4	262.9	331.5	1,041.2	225.8
Richmond, VA	2,045.4	4.9	28.3	37.0	106.2	170.5	1,580.8	117.6
Riverside, CA	2,643.4	5.8	29.0	111.1	273.8	441.1	1,367.7	414.9
Rochester, MN	653.1	1.0	9.7	2.9	67.2	122.6	407.8	41.9
Sacramento, CA	2,195.0	3.4	28.3	73.9	172.0	335.6	1,366.4	215.3
Salt Lake City, UT	3,178.0	2.3	62.6	48.1	186.0	349.3	2,211.9	317.8
San Antonio, TX	1,855.5	2.5	37.7	25.0	148.4	294.5	1,199.2	148.3
San Diego, CA	1,801.2	1.9	28.6	81.2	214.0	218.1	1,020.7	236.8
San Francisco, CA	2,534.2	1.3	42.6	87.1	128.4	294.1	1,778.4	202.3
San Jose, CA	2,582.6	1.5	27.9	54.6	118.4	291.8	1,875.3	213.0
Santa Rosa, CA	1,577.8	1.9	41.0	36.6	283.0	232.0	903.5	79.7
Savannah, GA[2]	3,497.3	5.3	37.2	67.1	245.2	497.1	2,366.1	279.1
Seattle, WA	n/a	n/a	n/a	n/a	n/a	n/a	n/a	n/a
Sioux Falls, SD	1,221.6	1.2	42.1	3.6	128.8	358.7	568.1	119.2
Springfield, IL	1,395.2	1.1	40.2	32.6	269.7	340.4	605.7	105.5
Tallahassee, FL	2,203.5	2.6	40.1	31.7	278.9	510.7	1,198.9	140.5
Tampa, FL	1,969.7	3.4	37.9	46.7	187.8	210.4	1,356.1	127.3
Tucson, AZ	2,634.2	3.2	25.3	38.5	115.5	349.9	1,905.9	195.9
Tulsa, OK	2,046.1	4.5	38.9	18.4	159.8	420.8	1,190.3	213.3
Tuscaloosa, AL[2]	2,503.0	3.3	28.5	41.7	249.6	518.3	1,449.1	212.5
Virginia Beach, VA	3,057.1	8.5	39.5	83.1	293.8	282.1	2,149.5	200.6
Washington, DC	n/a	n/a	26.7	61.2	96.5	98.4	1,055.9	126.4
Wichita, KS	n/a	1.6	42.3	14.5	156.8	271.8	n/a	129.8
Winston-Salem, NC	n/a	n/a	n/a	n/a	n/a	n/a	n/a	n/a
U.S.	2,489.3	5.0	42.6	81.6	250.2	340.5	1,549.5	219.9

Note: Figures are crimes per 100,000 population in 2019 except where noted; n/a not available; (1) All areas within the metro area that are located outside the city limits; (2) 2018 data; (3) 2017 data
Source: FBI Uniform Crime Reports, 2017, 2018, 2019

Appendix A: Comparative Statistics

Crime Rate: Metro Area

Metro Area[1]	All Crimes	Murder	Rape	Robbery	Aggrav. Assault	Burglary	Larceny -Theft	Motor Vehicle Theft
Albuquerque, NM	n/a	10.1	64.0	194.0	775.3	n/a	2,633.7	674.0
Allentown, PA	n/a	n/a	n/a	n/a	n/a	n/a	n/a	n/a
Anchorage, AK	5,513.6	11.1	178.4	208.4	796.7	600.1	3,190.1	528.8
Ann Arbor, MI	2,005.3	2.1	67.0	38.3	248.1	199.0	1,323.3	127.5
Athens, GA[4]	2,882.3	3.4	34.7	65.0	204.7	444.1	1,990.8	139.7
Atlanta, GA[3]	2,895.7	5.7	26.1	94.1	194.7	393.9	1,903.2	278.0
Austin, TX	2,697.1	2.5	48.3	56.9	179.2	313.8	1,905.9	190.5
Baton Rouge, LA	3,871.0	14.1	28.3	107.4	404.3	547.0	2,573.0	197.0
Boise City, ID	1,493.5	1.3	58.3	11.1	180.2	201.9	946.2	94.5
Boston, MA[2]	n/a	3.0	31.1	78.6	283.6	166.5	1,048.9	n/a
Boulder, CO	2,717.9	0.9	68.2	25.3	178.0	303.9	1,929.3	212.4
Cape Coral, FL	1,415.7	3.0	32.0	50.3	172.4	174.9	884.6	98.3
Cedar Rapids, IA	2,229.3	0.7	20.9	33.0	133.8	400.0	1,464.5	176.4
Charleston, SC	3,076.7	8.9	41.4	62.4	285.2	383.3	1,968.0	327.5
Charlotte, NC	n/a	n/a	n/a	n/a	n/a	n/a	n/a	n/a
Chicago, IL[2]	n/a	n/a	n/a	n/a	n/a	n/a	n/a	n/a
Cincinnati, OH	2,214.3	4.1	42.0	67.0	124.2	318.7	1,498.9	159.4
Clarksville, TN	2,648.0	6.8	48.4	48.7	283.6	369.5	1,670.2	220.7
Cleveland, OH	2,254.7	5.9	41.0	120.5	235.8	364.4	1,288.2	198.9
College Station, TX	2,233.6	1.9	61.8	41.9	156.8	378.5	1,438.0	154.6
Colorado Springs, CO	3,313.4	4.4	77.8	74.1	309.4	397.5	1,958.8	491.3
Columbia, MO	2,454.0	6.7	48.2	40.5	176.4	340.4	1,623.9	217.9
Columbia, SC	3,955.7	8.4	49.0	82.7	443.3	532.4	2,430.1	409.8
Columbus, OH	2,676.7	5.3	62.3	99.9	119.0	417.5	1,752.9	219.8
Dallas, TX[2]	n/a	n/a	n/a	n/a	n/a	n/a	n/a	n/a
Davenport, IA	2,565.2	2.1	55.8	55.5	253.0	420.1	1,598.8	179.8
Denver, CO	n/a	n/a	n/a	n/a	n/a	n/a	n/a	n/a
Des Moines, IA	n/a	n/a	n/a	n/a	n/a	n/a	n/a	n/a
Durham, NC	3,020.8	7.3	31.5	115.4	284.9	493.9	1,922.7	165.1
Edison, NJ[2]	n/a	n/a	n/a	n/a	n/a	n/a	n/a	n/a
El Paso, TX	1,749.1	4.9	43.7	42.9	241.7	153.3	1,143.1	119.5
Fargo, ND	2,635.2	2.0	61.8	42.4	190.5	469.8	1,641.1	227.6
Fayetteville, NC	n/a	n/a	n/a	n/a	n/a	n/a	n/a	n/a
Fort Collins, CO	2,112.3	0.8	34.8	17.7	180.7	194.2	1,555.0	129.0
Fort Wayne, IN	2,418.7	7.3	47.5	97.6	152.6	290.7	1,649.8	173.2
Fort Worth, TX[2]	n/a	n/a	n/a	n/a	n/a	n/a	n/a	n/a
Grand Rapids, MI	n/a	2.2	79.4	41.3	198.6	n/a	1,014.1	115.7
Greeley, CO	1,848.3	1.6	49.2	28.9	136.3	218.1	1,211.6	202.6
Green Bay, WI	1,324.3	1.5	41.8	17.3	165.3	130.9	909.3	58.2
Greensboro, NC	3,226.1	9.7	33.0	113.3	374.2	578.8	1,881.3	235.7
Honolulu, HI	n/a	n/a	n/a	n/a	n/a	n/a	n/a	n/a
Houston, TX	n/a	n/a	n/a	n/a	n/a	n/a	n/a	n/a
Huntsville, AL[4]	3,685.7	7.3	56.3	97.0	396.3	560.7	2,249.3	318.9
Indianapolis, IN[3]	3,285.3	9.3	46.3	166.8	419.1	496.7	1,830.9	316.2
Jacksonville, FL	2,980.1	9.2	50.3	94.0	321.2	413.8	1,870.6	221.0
Kansas City, MO	n/a	n/a	n/a	n/a	n/a	n/a	n/a	n/a
Lafayette, LA	3,349.4	7.8	25.3	68.5	365.0	619.4	2,093.7	169.8
Lakeland, FL	1,922.4	3.2	23.1	41.8	209.3	271.5	1,242.9	130.5
Las Vegas, NV	3,089.8	4.9	73.2	123.7	324.0	572.8	1,592.2	399.1
Lexington, KY	2,949.0	5.2	45.2	80.1	100.1	414.3	2,062.1	242.1
Lincoln, NE	2,843.7	1.5	106.4	49.2	189.7	309.2	2,043.0	144.7
Little Rock, AR	n/a	10.1	72.6	92.6	607.0	n/a	n/a	347.8
Los Angeles, CA[2]	2,790.2	5.1	41.5	185.0	329.4	377.7	1,479.4	372.2
Louisville, KY	3,300.8	8.3	26.0	93.8	308.7	447.9	2,011.8	404.3

Table continued on following page.

Appendix A: Comparative Statistics   A-155

Metro Area[1]	All Crimes	Violent Crimes				Property Crimes		
		Murder	Rape	Robbery	Aggrav. Assault	Burglary	Larceny-Theft	Motor Vehicle Theft
Madison, WI	1,932.4	1.2	31.0	43.6	141.9	259.9	1,321.5	133.2
Manchester, NH	1,534.7	2.6	45.6	40.8	140.7	131.1	1,109.5	64.3
Memphis, TN	5,173.9	17.6	52.5	207.1	843.3	769.0	2,863.0	421.5
Miami, FL[2]	3,563.1	7.3	34.4	131.5	307.5	286.0	2,520.6	275.9
Midland, TX[3]	2,288.6	5.1	39.5	40.1	232.9	275.8	1,463.0	232.3
Milwaukee, WI	2,501.8	7.0	40.0	136.4	394.4	305.7	1,353.9	264.3
Minneapolis, MN	2,605.3	2.7	44.7	78.3	146.9	303.6	1,782.3	246.9
Nashville, TN	3,020.0	6.1	41.4	119.1	403.9	303.6	1,915.5	230.4
New Haven, CT	2,383.4	3.5	25.9	80.1	163.2	255.0	1,586.2	269.5
New Orleans, LA	3,701.4	15.9	76.6	109.8	349.1	369.1	2,459.9	320.9
New York, NY[2]	n/a	n/a	n/a	n/a	n/a	n/a	n/a	n/a
Oklahoma City, OK	3,530.9	7.7	62.8	80.3	310.3	678.7	1,997.6	393.6
Omaha, NE	3,059.7	3.6	62.0	66.4	281.1	294.5	1,908.8	443.3
Orlando, FL	2,829.9	4.6	45.1	87.9	292.4	359.1	1,831.9	209.0
Peoria, IL	2,386.5	7.5	49.5	78.0	316.9	381.2	1,383.1	170.3
Philadelphia, PA[2,3]	3,462.1	18.3	55.2	270.0	420.3	355.2	2,042.3	300.9
Phoenix, AZ	n/a	4.6	49.8	97.1	275.1	n/a	1,804.9	251.9
Pittsburgh, PA[3]	1,687.7	5.5	25.8	58.8	184.5	196.1	1,137.0	80.0
Portland, OR	3,049.5	2.4	50.2	66.7	183.3	339.3	1,968.5	439.1
Providence, RI	1,692.5	2.3	44.8	48.1	187.3	225.0	1,071.9	113.0
Provo, UT	1,368.4	1.1	31.6	7.9	49.6	132.9	1,061.8	83.5
Raleigh, NC	1,570.3	1.7	21.5	37.4	112.0	223.8	1,071.2	102.7
Reno, NV	2,336.2	3.2	63.1	86.8	315.9	327.1	1,187.2	352.9
Richmond, VA	2,388.9	8.3	26.7	60.3	132.4	216.6	1,781.7	162.9
Riverside, CA	2,700.9	5.7	29.9	113.4	276.9	437.5	1,420.4	417.2
Rochester, MN	1,425.3	0.9	32.6	16.7	102.3	184.6	1,011.3	76.9
Sacramento, CA	2,548.0	4.1	27.5	102.0	220.5	389.6	1,520.5	283.8
Salt Lake City, UT	3,700.3	3.0	71.3	72.8	219.5	396.4	2,569.6	367.6
San Antonio, TX	3,796.6	5.1	78.5	86.7	345.6	434.8	2,483.3	362.6
San Diego, CA	1,992.1	2.6	33.1	86.4	219.1	230.0	1,131.6	289.3
San Francisco, CA[2]	4,482.9	3.0	39.4	225.0	211.5	417.2	3,236.0	350.7
San Jose, CA	2,725.6	2.3	46.9	93.1	182.6	345.7	1,646.7	408.3
Santa Rosa, CA	1,763.5	1.8	55.7	48.8	298.8	246.8	997.9	113.7
Savannah, GA[3]	3,107.5	9.2	35.9	93.7	247.2	415.6	2,032.0	274.0
Seattle, WA[2]	n/a	n/a	n/a	n/a	n/a	n/a	n/a	n/a
Sioux Falls, SD	2,815.3	1.9	56.2	26.4	303.7	369.5	1,775.9	281.7
Springfield, IL	3,514.4	4.8	70.3	115.3	393.5	655.2	2,099.8	175.4
Tallahassee, FL	3,458.0	6.5	71.0	81.2	368.9	560.3	2,124.4	245.8
Tampa, FL	1,977.8	4.0	36.9	49.8	201.5	216.1	1,341.8	127.7
Tucson, AZ	3,328.8	5.3	62.4	123.9	255.9	405.1	2,168.0	308.2
Tulsa, OK	3,757.4	8.2	57.4	83.0	381.0	737.0	2,059.5	431.3
Tuscaloosa, AL[3]	3,445.1	4.0	35.6	80.3	276.5	607.5	2,189.7	251.6
Virginia Beach, VA	2,759.6	8.0	33.9	73.0	234.6	240.3	1,987.4	182.3
Washington, DC[2]	n/a	n/a	29.8	99.9	163.6	121.4	1,424.4	154.6
Wichita, KS	n/a	6.1	74.0	77.9	623.3	525.2	n/a	411.7
Winston-Salem, NC[3]	n/a	n/a	n/a	n/a	n/a	n/a	n/a	n/a
U.S.	2,489.3	5.0	42.6	81.6	250.2	340.5	1,549.5	219.9

Note: Figures are crimes per 100,000 population in 2019 except where noted; n/a not available; (1) Figures cover the Metropolitan Statistical Area except where noted; (2) Metropolitan Division (MD); (3) 2018 data; (4) 2017 data
Source: FBI Uniform Crime Reports, 2017, 2018, 2019

Temperature & Precipitation: Yearly Averages and Extremes

City	Extreme Low (°F)	Average Low (°F)	Average Temp. (°F)	Average High (°F)	Extreme High (°F)	Average Precip. (in.)	Average Snow (in.)
Albuquerque, NM	-17	43	57	70	105	8.5	11
Allentown, PA	-12	42	52	61	105	44.2	32
Anchorage, AK	-34	29	36	43	85	15.7	71
Ann Arbor, MI	-21	39	49	58	104	32.4	41
Athens, GA	-8	52	62	72	105	49.8	2
Atlanta, GA	-8	52	62	72	105	49.8	2
Austin, TX	-2	58	69	79	109	31.1	1
Baton Rouge, LA	8	57	68	78	103	58.5	Trace
Boise City, ID	-25	39	51	63	111	11.8	22
Boston, MA	-12	44	52	59	102	42.9	41
Boulder, CO	-25	37	51	64	103	15.5	63
Cape Coral, FL	26	65	75	84	103	53.9	0
Cedar Rapids, IA	-34	36	47	57	105	34.4	33
Charleston, SC	6	55	66	76	104	52.1	1
Charlotte, NC	-5	50	61	71	104	42.8	6
Chicago, IL	-27	40	49	59	104	35.4	39
Cincinnati, OH	-25	44	54	64	103	40.9	23
Clarksville, TN	-17	49	60	70	107	47.4	11
Cleveland, OH	-19	41	50	59	104	37.1	55
College Station, TX	-2	58	69	79	109	31.1	1
Colorado Springs, CO	-24	36	49	62	99	17.0	48
Columbia, MO	-20	44	54	64	111	40.6	25
Columbia, SC	-1	51	64	75	107	48.3	2
Columbus, OH	-19	42	52	62	104	37.9	28
Dallas, TX	-2	56	67	77	112	33.9	3
Davenport, IA	-24	40	50	60	108	31.8	33
Denver, CO	-25	37	51	64	103	15.5	63
Des Moines, IA	-24	40	50	60	108	31.8	33
Durham, NC	-9	48	60	71	105	42.0	8
Edison, NJ	-8	46	55	63	105	43.5	27
El Paso, TX	-8	50	64	78	114	8.6	6
Fargo, ND	-36	31	41	52	106	19.6	40
Fayetteville, NC	-9	48	60	71	105	42.0	8
Fort Collins, CO	-25	37	51	64	103	15.5	63
Fort Wayne, IN	-22	40	50	60	106	35.9	33
Fort Worth, TX	-1	55	66	76	113	32.3	3
Grand Rapids, MI	-22	38	48	57	102	34.7	73
Greeley, CO	-25	37	51	64	103	15.5	63
Green Bay, WI	-31	34	44	54	99	28.3	46
Greensboro, NC	-8	47	58	69	103	42.5	10
Honolulu, HI	52	70	77	84	94	22.4	0
Houston, TX	7	58	69	79	107	46.9	Trace
Huntsville, AL	-11	50	61	71	104	56.8	4
Indianapolis, IN	-23	42	53	62	104	40.2	25
Jacksonville, FL	7	58	69	79	103	52.0	0
Kansas City, MO	-23	44	54	64	109	38.1	21
Lafayette, LA	8	57	68	78	103	58.5	Trace
Lakeland, FL	18	63	73	82	99	46.7	Trace
Las Vegas, NV	8	53	67	80	116	4.0	1
Lexington, KY	-21	45	55	65	103	45.1	17
Lincoln, NE	-33	39	51	62	108	29.1	27
Little Rock, AR	-5	51	62	73	112	50.7	5
Los Angeles, CA	27	55	63	70	110	11.3	Trace
Louisville, KY	-20	46	57	67	105	43.9	17
Madison, WI	-37	35	46	57	104	31.1	42

Table continued on following page.

City	Extreme Low (°F)	Average Low (°F)	Average Temp. (°F)	Average High (°F)	Extreme High (°F)	Average Precip. (in.)	Average Snow (in.)
Manchester, NH	-33	34	46	57	102	36.9	63
Memphis, TN	0	52	65	77	107	54.8	1
Miami, FL	30	69	76	83	98	57.1	0
Midland, TX	-11	50	64	77	116	14.6	4
Milwaukee, WI	-26	38	47	55	103	32.0	49
Minneapolis, MN	-34	35	45	54	105	27.1	52
Nashville, TN	-17	49	60	70	107	47.4	11
New Haven, CT	-7	44	52	60	103	41.4	25
New Orleans, LA	11	59	69	78	102	60.6	Trace
New York, NY	-2	47	55	62	104	47.0	23
Oklahoma City, OK	-8	49	60	71	110	32.8	10
Omaha, NE	-23	40	51	62	110	30.1	29
Orlando, FL	19	62	72	82	100	47.7	Trace
Peoria, IL	-26	41	51	61	113	35.4	23
Philadelphia, PA	-7	45	55	64	104	41.4	22
Phoenix, AZ	17	59	72	86	122	7.3	Trace
Pittsburgh, PA	-18	41	51	60	103	37.1	43
Portland, OR	-3	45	54	62	107	37.5	7
Providence, RI	-13	42	51	60	104	45.3	35
Provo, UT	-22	40	52	64	107	15.6	63
Raleigh, NC	-9	48	60	71	105	42.0	8
Reno, NV	-16	33	50	67	105	7.2	24
Richmond, VA	-8	48	58	69	105	43.0	13
Riverside, CA	24	53	66	78	114	n/a	n/a
Rochester, MN	-40	34	44	54	102	29.4	47
Sacramento, CA	18	48	61	73	115	17.3	Trace
Salt Lake City, UT	-22	40	52	64	107	15.6	63
San Antonio, TX	0	58	69	80	108	29.6	1
San Diego, CA	29	57	64	71	111	9.5	Trace
San Francisco, CA	24	49	57	65	106	19.3	Trace
San Jose, CA	21	50	59	68	105	13.5	Trace
Santa Rosa, CA	23	42	57	71	109	29.0	n/a
Savannah, GA	3	56	67	77	105	50.3	Trace
Seattle, WA	0	44	52	59	99	38.4	13
Sioux Falls, SD	-36	35	46	57	110	24.6	38
Springfield, IL	-24	44	54	63	112	34.9	21
Tallahassee, FL	6	56	68	79	103	63.3	Trace
Tampa, FL	18	63	73	82	99	46.7	Trace
Tucson, AZ	16	55	69	82	117	11.6	2
Tulsa, OK	-8	50	61	71	112	38.9	10
Tuscaloosa, AL	-6	51	63	74	106	53.5	2
Virginia Beach, VA	-3	51	60	69	104	44.8	8
Washington, DC	-5	49	58	67	104	39.5	18
Wichita, KS	-21	45	57	68	113	29.3	17
Winston-Salem, NC	-8	47	58	69	103	42.5	10

Source: National Climatic Data Center, International Station Meteorological Climate Summary, 9/96

Appendix A: Comparative Statistics

Weather Conditions

City	Temperature 10°F & below	Temperature 32°F & below	Temperature 90°F & above	Daytime Sky Clear	Daytime Sky Partly cloudy	Daytime Sky Cloudy	Precipitation 0.01 inch or more precip.	Precipitation 1.0 inch or more snow/ice	Thunder-storms
Albuquerque, NM	4	114	65	140	161	64	60	9	38
Allentown, PA	n/a	123	15	77	148	140	123	20	31
Anchorage, AK	n/a	194	n/a	50	115	200	113	49	2
Ann Arbor, MI	n/a	136	12	74	134	157	135	38	32
Athens, GA	1	49	38	98	147	120	116	3	48
Atlanta, GA	1	49	38	98	147	120	116	3	48
Austin, TX	<1	20	111	105	148	112	83	1	41
Baton Rouge, LA	<1	21	86	99	150	116	113	<1	73
Boise City, ID	n/a	124	45	106	133	126	91	22	14
Boston, MA	n/a	97	12	88	127	150	253	48	18
Boulder, CO	24	155	33	99	177	89	90	38	39
Cape Coral, FL	n/a	n/a	115	93	220	52	110	0	92
Cedar Rapids, IA	n/a	156	16	89	132	144	109	28	42
Charleston, SC	<1	33	53	89	162	114	114	1	59
Charlotte, NC	1	65	44	98	142	125	113	3	41
Chicago, IL	n/a	132	17	83	136	146	125	31	38
Cincinnati, OH	14	107	23	80	126	159	127	25	39
Clarksville, TN	5	76	51	98	135	132	119	8	54
Cleveland, OH	n/a	123	12	63	127	175	157	48	34
College Station, TX	<1	20	111	105	148	112	83	1	41
Colorado Springs, CO	21	161	18	108	157	100	98	33	49
Columbia, MO	17	108	36	99	127	139	110	17	52
Columbia, SC	<1	58	77	97	149	119	110	1	53
Columbus, OH	n/a	118	19	72	137	156	136	29	40
Dallas, TX	1	34	102	108	160	97	78	2	49
Davenport, IA	n/a	137	26	99	129	137	106	25	46
Denver, CO	24	155	33	99	177	89	90	38	39
Des Moines, IA	n/a	137	26	99	129	137	106	25	46
Durham, NC	n/a	n/a	39	98	143	124	110	3	42
Edison, NJ	n/a	90	24	80	146	139	122	16	46
El Paso, TX	1	59	106	147	164	54	49	3	35
Fargo, ND	n/a	180	15	81	145	139	100	38	31
Fayetteville, NC	n/a	n/a	39	98	143	124	110	3	42
Fort Collins, CO	24	155	33	99	177	89	90	38	39
Fort Wayne, IN	n/a	131	16	75	140	150	131	31	39
Fort Worth, TX	1	40	100	123	136	106	79	3	47
Grand Rapids, MI	n/a	146	11	67	119	179	142	57	34
Greeley, CO	24	155	33	99	177	89	90	38	39
Green Bay, WI	n/a	163	7	86	125	154	120	40	33
Greensboro, NC	3	85	32	94	143	128	113	5	43
Honolulu, HI	n/a	n/a	23	25	286	54	98	0	7
Houston, TX	n/a	n/a	96	83	168	114	101	1	62
Huntsville, AL	2	66	49	70	118	177	116	2	54
Indianapolis, IN	19	119	19	83	128	154	127	24	43
Jacksonville, FL	<1	16	83	86	181	98	114	1	65
Kansas City, MO	22	110	39	112	134	119	103	17	51
Lafayette, LA	<1	21	86	99	150	116	113	<1	73
Lakeland, FL	n/a	n/a	85	81	204	80	107	<1	87
Las Vegas, NV	<1	37	134	185	132	48	27	2	13
Lexington, KY	11	96	22	86	136	143	129	17	44
Lincoln, NE	n/a	145	40	108	135	122	94	19	46
Little Rock, AR	1	57	73	110	142	113	104	4	57
Los Angeles, CA	0	<1	5	131	125	109	34	0	1
Louisville, KY	8	90	35	82	143	140	125	15	45

Table continued on following page.

| | Temperature ||| Daytime Sky ||| Precipitation |||
City	10°F & below	32°F & below	90°F & above	Clear	Partly cloudy	Cloudy	0.01 inch or more precip.	1.0 inch or more snow/ice	Thunderstorms
Madison, WI	n/a	161	14	88	119	158	118	38	40
Manchester, NH	n/a	171	12	87	131	147	125	32	19
Memphis, TN	1	53	86	101	152	112	104	2	59
Miami, FL	n/a	n/a	55	48	263	54	128	0	74
Midland, TX	1	62	102	144	138	83	52	3	38
Milwaukee, WI	n/a	141	10	90	118	157	126	38	35
Minneapolis, MN	n/a	156	16	93	125	147	113	41	37
Nashville, TN	5	76	51	98	135	132	119	8	54
New Haven, CT	n/a	n/a	7	80	146	139	118	17	22
New Orleans, LA	0	13	70	90	169	106	114	1	69
New York, NY	n/a	n/a	18	85	166	114	120	11	20
Oklahoma City, OK	5	79	70	124	131	110	80	8	50
Omaha, NE	n/a	139	35	100	142	123	97	20	46
Orlando, FL	n/a	n/a	90	76	208	81	115	0	80
Peoria, IL	n/a	127	27	89	127	149	115	22	49
Philadelphia, PA	5	94	23	81	146	138	117	14	27
Phoenix, AZ	0	10	167	186	125	54	37	<1	23
Pittsburgh, PA	n/a	121	8	62	137	166	154	42	35
Portland, OR	n/a	37	11	67	116	182	152	4	7
Providence, RI	n/a	117	9	85	134	146	123	21	21
Provo, UT	n/a	128	56	94	152	119	92	38	38
Raleigh, NC	n/a	n/a	39	98	143	124	110	3	42
Reno, NV	14	178	50	143	139	83	50	17	14
Richmond, VA	3	79	41	90	147	128	115	7	43
Riverside, CA	0	4	82	124	178	63	n/a	n/a	5
Rochester, MN	n/a	165	9	87	126	152	114	40	41
Sacramento, CA	0	21	73	175	111	79	58	<1	2
Salt Lake City, UT	n/a	128	56	94	152	119	92	38	38
San Antonio, TX	n/a	n/a	112	97	153	115	81	1	36
San Diego, CA	0	<1	4	115	126	124	40	0	5
San Francisco, CA	0	6	4	136	130	99	63	<1	5
San Jose, CA	0	5	5	106	180	79	57	<1	6
Santa Rosa, CA	n/a	43	30	n/a	365	n/a	n/a	n/a	2
Savannah, GA	<1	29	70	97	155	113	111	<1	63
Seattle, WA	n/a	38	3	57	121	187	157	8	8
Sioux Falls, SD	n/a	n/a	n/a	95	136	134	n/a	n/a	n/a
Springfield, IL	19	111	34	96	126	143	111	18	49
Tallahassee, FL	<1	31	86	93	175	97	114	1	83
Tampa, FL	n/a	n/a	85	81	204	80	107	<1	87
Tucson, AZ	0	18	140	177	119	69	54	2	42
Tulsa, OK	6	78	74	117	141	107	88	8	50
Tuscaloosa, AL	1	57	59	91	161	113	119	1	57
Virginia Beach, VA	<1	53	33	89	149	127	115	5	38
Washington, DC	2	71	34	84	144	137	112	9	30
Wichita, KS	13	110	63	117	132	116	87	13	54
Winston-Salem, NC	3	85	32	94	143	128	113	5	43

Note: Figures are average number of days per year
Source: National Climatic Data Center, International Station Meteorological Climate Summary, 9/96

Appendix A: Comparative Statistics

Air Quality Index

MSA[1] (Days[2])	Good	Moderate	Unhealthy for Sensitive Groups	Unhealthy	Very Unhealthy	Maximum	Median
Albuquerque, NM (365)	44.1	54.8	1.1	0.0	0.0	108	53
Allentown, PA (365)	75.3	23.6	1.1	0.0	0.0	119	42
Anchorage, AK (365)	71.8	24.9	2.2	1.1	0.0	160	31
Ann Arbor, MI (365)	80.5	19.5	0.0	0.0	0.0	88	39
Athens, GA (365)	67.1	32.9	0.0	0.0	0.0	87	44
Atlanta, GA (365)	44.4	50.4	4.9	0.3	0.0	172	52
Austin, TX (365)	68.2	31.2	0.5	0.0	0.0	115	44
Baton Rouge, LA (365)	61.4	36.2	2.5	0.0	0.0	119	45
Boise City, ID (365)	67.9	31.2	0.5	0.3	0.0	165	44
Boston, MA (365)	79.7	20.0	0.3	0.0	0.0	122	43
Boulder, CO (365)	62.2	36.4	1.4	0.0	0.0	119	47
Cape Coral, FL (365)	89.9	9.9	0.3	0.0	0.0	108	36
Cedar Rapids, IA (365)	78.6	21.4	0.0	0.0	0.0	84	39
Charleston, SC (357)	84.3	15.4	0.3	0.0	0.0	140	38
Charlotte, NC (365)	54.8	40.3	4.9	0.0	0.0	136	49
Chicago, IL (365)	33.2	62.2	4.4	0.3	0.0	174	55
Cincinnati, OH (365)	38.1	56.4	5.5	0.0	0.0	147	54
Clarksville, TN (365)	84.1	15.9	0.0	0.0	0.0	87	40
Cleveland, OH (365)	50.7	47.4	1.9	0.0	0.0	119	50
College Station, TX (352)	100.0	0.0	0.0	0.0	0.0	17	0
Colorado Springs, CO (365)	71.0	29.0	0.0	0.0	0.0	100	45
Columbia, MO (245)	97.6	2.4	0.0	0.0	0.0	71	38
Columbia, SC (365)	72.3	27.1	0.5	0.0	0.0	136	43
Columbus, OH (365)	64.9	34.8	0.3	0.0	0.0	101	46
Dallas, TX (365)	49.6	42.5	7.7	0.3	0.0	156	51
Davenport, IA (365)	59.5	39.7	0.8	0.0	0.0	115	46
Denver, CO (365)	24.9	69.0	5.5	0.5	0.0	154	58
Des Moines, IA (365)	83.8	16.2	0.0	0.0	0.0	100	39
Durham, NC (365)	75.3	24.7	0.0	0.0	0.0	92	44
Edison, NJ (365)	46.3	49.3	4.4	0.0	0.0	150	51
El Paso, TX (365)	40.3	56.2	3.0	0.5	0.0	157	53
Fargo, ND (363)	90.1	9.4	0.3	0.3	0.0	156	33
Fayetteville, NC (363)	77.7	22.3	0.0	0.0	0.0	84	41
Fort Collins, CO (365)	57.0	41.4	1.6	0.0	0.0	129	48
Fort Wayne, IN (365)	64.7	35.1	0.3	0.0	0.0	101	45
Fort Worth, TX (365)	49.6	42.5	7.7	0.3	0.0	156	51
Grand Rapids, MI (365)	81.6	18.4	0.0	0.0	0.0	100	38
Greeley, CO (365)	69.0	30.1	0.8	0.0	0.0	125	45
Green Bay, WI (365)	85.2	14.8	0.0	0.0	0.0	97	36
Greensboro, NC (365)	79.7	20.3	0.0	0.0	0.0	90	43
Honolulu, HI (365)	92.9	7.1	0.0	0.0	0.0	94	29
Houston, TX (365)	46.8	44.7	7.1	1.1	0.3	202	52
Huntsville, AL (361)	70.6	29.4	0.0	0.0	0.0	93	44
Indianapolis, IN (365)	40.5	58.1	1.4	0.0	0.0	119	54
Jacksonville, FL (365)	67.1	32.6	0.3	0.0	0.0	114	43
Kansas City, MO (365)	57.5	42.2	0.3	0.0	0.0	137	47
Lafayette, LA (365)	76.7	23.3	0.0	0.0	0.0	84	41
Lakeland, FL (365)	86.0	14.0	0.0	0.0	0.0	100	36
Las Vegas, NV (365)	42.2	56.4	1.4	0.0	0.0	122	54
Lexington, KY (365)	83.0	17.0	0.0	0.0	0.0	80	42
Lincoln, NE (360)	93.9	6.1	0.0	0.0	0.0	66	31
Little Rock, AR (365)	64.4	35.6	0.0	0.0	0.0	79	45
Los Angeles, CA (365)	18.1	57.0	17.0	7.7	0.3	201	72
Louisville, KY (365)	53.4	45.5	1.1	0.0	0.0	136	49

Table continued on following page.

MSA[1] (Days[2])	Percent of Days when Air Quality was...					AQI Statistics	
	Good	Moderate	Unhealthy for Sensitive Groups	Unhealthy	Very Unhealthy	Maximum	Median
Madison, WI (365)	78.1	21.9	0.0	0.0	0.0	93	39
Manchester, NH (365)	96.7	3.3	0.0	0.0	0.0	80	37
Memphis, TN (365)	60.5	38.1	1.4	0.0	0.0	148	45
Miami, FL (364)	78.3	21.2	0.5	0.0	0.0	146	41
Midland, TX (n/a)	n/a	n/a	n/a	n/a	n/a	n/a	n/a
Milwaukee, WI (365)	69.6	29.6	0.8	0.0	0.0	115	44
Minneapolis, MN (365)	58.6	40.5	0.5	0.3	0.0	200	46
Nashville, TN (365)	62.7	37.0	0.3	0.0	0.0	101	45
New Haven, CT (365)	76.7	19.5	3.3	0.5	0.0	159	41
New Orleans, LA (365)	62.7	36.7	0.5	0.0	0.0	112	45
New York, NY (365)	46.3	49.3	4.4	0.0	0.0	150	51
Oklahoma City, OK (365)	55.9	43.6	0.5	0.0	0.0	119	48
Omaha, NE (365)	77.5	22.5	0.0	0.0	0.0	97	40
Orlando, FL (365)	81.1	17.3	1.6	0.0	0.0	122	39
Peoria, IL (365)	78.1	21.4	0.5	0.0	0.0	101	41
Philadelphia, PA (365)	49.3	46.3	4.4	0.0	0.0	150	51
Phoenix, AZ (365)	13.7	71.5	11.5	0.5	0.8	886	74
Pittsburgh, PA (365)	35.3	60.3	3.3	1.1	0.0	161	56
Portland, OR (365)	78.1	21.1	0.8	0.0	0.0	128	38
Providence, RI (365)	79.2	20.3	0.5	0.0	0.0	126	44
Provo, UT (365)	69.3	30.4	0.3	0.0	0.0	107	46
Raleigh, NC (365)	65.5	34.5	0.0	0.0	0.0	93	46
Reno, NV (365)	66.8	33.2	0.0	0.0	0.0	97	46
Richmond, VA (365)	74.5	25.5	0.0	0.0	0.0	100	44
Riverside, CA (365)	11.5	48.8	21.6	15.9	2.2	213	89
Rochester, MN (364)	86.0	14.0	0.0	0.0	0.0	84	36
Sacramento, CA (365)	47.1	47.1	5.8	0.0	0.0	140	52
Salt Lake City, UT (365)	46.3	49.0	4.7	0.0	0.0	136	51
San Antonio, TX (365)	53.7	44.7	1.4	0.3	0.0	169	49
San Diego, CA (365)	23.8	69.3	6.3	0.5	0.0	169	64
San Francisco, CA (365)	69.6	27.9	2.5	0.0	0.0	150	43
San Jose, CA (365)	72.1	26.8	1.1	0.0	0.0	136	43
Santa Rosa, CA (365)	95.3	4.7	0.0	0.0	0.0	87	33
Savannah, GA (365)	80.8	19.2	0.0	0.0	0.0	87	39
Seattle, WA (365)	64.7	34.8	0.5	0.0	0.0	142	45
Sioux Falls, SD (365)	87.9	11.8	0.3	0.0	0.0	105	36
Springfield, IL (360)	79.7	20.3	0.0	0.0	0.0	87	40
Tallahassee, FL (365)	74.5	25.2	0.3	0.0	0.0	119	40
Tampa, FL (365)	73.2	25.2	1.6	0.0	0.0	132	43
Tucson, AZ (365)	61.6	37.8	0.5	0.0	0.0	103	47
Tulsa, OK (365)	68.2	31.2	0.5	0.0	0.0	105	45
Tuscaloosa, AL (264)	90.9	9.1	0.0	0.0	0.0	87	35
Virginia Beach, VA (365)	86.8	13.2	0.0	0.0	0.0	97	40
Washington, DC (365)	57.3	39.7	2.7	0.3	0.0	157	47
Wichita, KS (365)	82.5	17.5	0.0	0.0	0.0	97	40
Winston-Salem, NC (365)	61.6	38.4	0.0	0.0	0.0	97	45

Note: The Air Quality Index (AQI) is an index for reporting daily air quality. EPA calculates the AQI for five major air pollutants regulated by the Clean Air Act: ground-level ozone, particle pollution (also known as particulate matter), carbon monoxide, sulfur dioxide, and nitrogen dioxide. The AQI runs from 0 to 500. The higher the AQI value, the greater the level of air pollution and the greater the health concern. There are six AQI categories: "Good" The AQI is between 0 and 50. Air quality is considered satisfactory; "Moderate" The AQI is between 51 and 100. Air quality is acceptable; "Unhealthy for Sensitive Groups" When AQI values are between 101 and 150, members of sensitive groups may experience health effects; "Unhealthy" When AQI values are between 151 and 200 everyone may begin to experience health effects; "Very Unhealthy" AQI values between 201 and 300 trigger a health alert; "Hazardous" AQI values over 300 trigger health warnings of emergency conditions; Data covers the entire county unless noted otherwise; (1) Data covers the Metropolitan Statistical Area—see Appendix B for areas included; (2) Number of days with AQI data in 2019
Source: U.S. Environmental Protection Agency, Air Quality Index Report, 2019

Appendix A: Comparative Statistics

Air Quality Index Pollutants

MSA[1] (Days[2])	Carbon Monoxide	Nitrogen Dioxide	Ozone	Sulfur Dioxide	Particulate Matter 2.5	Particulate Matter 10
Albuquerque, NM (365)	0.0	0.0	69.0	0.0	18.1	12.9
Allentown, PA (365)	0.0	3.6	61.4	0.0	35.1	0.0
Anchorage, AK (365)	1.4	0.0	0.0	0.0	69.9	28.8
Ann Arbor, MI (365)	0.0	0.0	66.6	0.0	33.4	0.0
Athens, GA (365)	0.0	0.0	37.3	0.0	62.7	0.0
Atlanta, GA (365)	0.0	2.5	46.8	0.0	50.7	0.0
Austin, TX (365)	0.0	1.9	48.8	0.0	49.3	0.0
Baton Rouge, LA (365)	0.0	1.6	47.9	0.3	50.1	0.0
Boise City, ID (365)	0.0	1.1	44.4	0.0	51.0	3.6
Boston, MA (365)	0.0	4.1	57.5	0.0	38.4	0.0
Boulder, CO (365)	0.0	0.0	73.7	0.0	26.3	0.0
Cape Coral, FL (365)	0.0	0.0	68.8	0.0	30.1	1.1
Cedar Rapids, IA (365)	0.0	0.0	47.9	1.1	51.0	0.0
Charleston, SC (357)	0.0	0.0	67.2	0.0	32.5	0.3
Charlotte, NC (365)	0.0	0.0	66.6	0.0	33.4	0.0
Chicago, IL (365)	0.0	5.5	24.1	4.9	62.5	3.0
Cincinnati, OH (365)	0.0	1.6	41.4	6.0	50.1	0.8
Clarksville, TN (365)	0.0	0.0	72.9	0.0	27.1	0.0
Cleveland, OH (365)	0.0	0.3	40.5	0.5	55.1	3.6
College Station, TX (352)	0.0	0.0	0.0	100.0	0.0	0.0
Colorado Springs, CO (365)	0.0	0.0	94.5	0.0	4.9	0.5
Columbia, MO (245)	0.0	0.0	100.0	0.0	0.0	0.0
Columbia, SC (365)	0.0	0.0	71.8	0.0	28.2	0.0
Columbus, OH (365)	0.0	1.4	49.0	0.0	49.3	0.3
Dallas, TX (365)	0.0	3.0	56.2	0.0	40.8	0.0
Davenport, IA (365)	0.0	0.0	37.8	0.0	41.9	20.3
Denver, CO (365)	0.0	16.4	57.8	0.3	17.3	8.2
Des Moines, IA (365)	0.0	0.8	67.4	0.0	31.8	0.0
Durham, NC (365)	0.0	0.0	56.7	1.6	41.6	0.0
Edison, NJ (365)	0.0	17.5	39.2	0.0	43.3	0.0
El Paso, TX (365)	0.0	5.8	55.9	0.0	37.5	0.8
Fargo, ND (363)	0.0	2.5	72.7	0.0	24.2	0.6
Fayetteville, NC (363)	0.0	0.0	56.7	0.0	42.1	1.1
Fort Collins, CO (365)	0.0	0.0	92.3	0.0	7.7	0.0
Fort Wayne, IN (365)	0.0	0.0	48.5	0.0	51.5	0.0
Fort Worth, TX (365)	0.0	3.0	56.2	0.0	40.8	0.0
Grand Rapids, MI (365)	0.0	2.5	69.9	0.0	26.3	1.4
Greeley, CO (365)	0.0	0.0	64.7	0.0	35.3	0.0
Green Bay, WI (365)	0.0	0.0	51.0	1.1	47.9	0.0
Greensboro, NC (365)	0.0	0.0	63.6	0.0	29.3	7.1
Honolulu, HI (365)	0.3	0.8	71.8	17.8	9.0	0.3
Houston, TX (365)	0.0	4.4	47.1	0.5	47.1	0.8
Huntsville, AL (361)	0.0	0.0	42.9	0.0	55.1	1.9
Indianapolis, IN (365)	0.0	0.0	34.2	1.1	64.7	0.0
Jacksonville, FL (365)	0.0	0.0	48.2	2.7	49.0	0.0
Kansas City, MO (365)	0.0	2.5	48.2	0.0	45.5	3.8
Lafayette, LA (365)	0.0	0.0	58.4	0.0	41.6	0.0
Lakeland, FL (365)	0.0	0.0	67.9	0.5	31.5	0.0
Las Vegas, NV (365)	0.3	5.5	69.0	0.0	23.0	2.2
Lexington, KY (365)	0.0	2.7	52.9	0.0	44.4	0.0
Lincoln, NE (360)	0.0	0.0	63.6	21.1	15.3	0.0
Little Rock, AR (365)	0.0	0.5	40.0	0.0	59.5	0.0
Los Angeles, CA (365)	0.0	9.0	56.2	0.0	32.3	2.5
Louisville, KY (365)	0.0	2.7	45.8	0.0	51.5	0.0

Table continued on following page.

Appendix A: Comparative Statistics

MSA[1] (Days[2])	Carbon Monoxide	Nitrogen Dioxide	Ozone	Sulfur Dioxide	Particulate Matter 2.5	Particulate Matter 10
Madison, WI (365)	0.0	0.0	45.5	0.0	54.5	0.0
Manchester, NH (365)	0.0	0.0	97.5	0.0	2.5	0.0
Memphis, TN (365)	0.0	2.5	51.0	0.0	46.6	0.0
Miami, FL (364)	0.3	3.6	37.4	0.0	58.5	0.3
Midland, TX (n/a)	n/a	n/a	n/a	n/a	n/a	n/a
Milwaukee, WI (365)	0.0	2.7	51.8	0.0	43.3	2.2
Minneapolis, MN (365)	0.0	1.4	31.2	1.1	43.0	23.3
Nashville, TN (365)	0.0	6.8	40.5	0.0	52.6	0.0
New Haven, CT (365)	0.0	4.1	67.7	0.0	27.1	1.1
New Orleans, LA (365)	0.0	0.8	45.8	8.8	44.4	0.3
New York, NY (365)	0.0	17.5	39.2	0.0	43.3	0.0
Oklahoma City, OK (365)	0.0	1.1	52.9	0.0	45.8	0.3
Omaha, NE (365)	0.0	0.0	52.3	3.3	40.8	3.6
Orlando, FL (365)	0.0	0.0	80.5	0.0	19.5	0.0
Peoria, IL (365)	0.0	0.0	55.6	0.5	43.8	0.0
Philadelphia, PA (365)	0.0	3.6	50.1	0.0	46.3	0.0
Phoenix, AZ (365)	0.0	0.8	46.3	0.0	19.7	33.2
Pittsburgh, PA (365)	0.0	0.0	29.3	6.3	64.4	0.0
Portland, OR (365)	0.0	2.2	56.4	0.0	41.4	0.0
Providence, RI (365)	0.0	2.2	70.7	0.0	26.8	0.3
Provo, UT (365)	0.0	1.9	81.4	0.0	16.2	0.5
Raleigh, NC (365)	0.3	0.3	46.8	0.0	52.6	0.0
Reno, NV (365)	0.0	1.1	80.5	0.0	17.0	1.4
Richmond, VA (365)	0.0	4.4	67.4	0.0	28.2	0.0
Riverside, CA (365)	0.0	3.0	62.5	0.0	24.4	10.1
Rochester, MN (364)	0.0	0.0	53.6	0.0	46.4	0.0
Sacramento, CA (365)	0.0	0.3	71.0	0.0	27.1	1.6
Salt Lake City, UT (365)	0.0	8.8	67.1	0.0	22.7	1.4
San Antonio, TX (365)	0.0	0.8	44.1	0.0	54.8	0.3
San Diego, CA (365)	0.0	0.5	48.2	0.0	50.4	0.8
San Francisco, CA (365)	0.0	6.3	52.1	0.0	41.6	0.0
San Jose, CA (365)	0.0	0.5	64.7	0.0	33.7	1.1
Santa Rosa, CA (365)	0.0	0.8	70.7	0.0	25.8	2.7
Savannah, GA (365)	0.0	0.0	40.0	15.9	44.1	0.0
Seattle, WA (365)	0.0	8.5	43.3	0.0	48.2	0.0
Sioux Falls, SD (365)	0.0	2.5	84.1	0.0	12.9	0.5
Springfield, IL (360)	0.0	0.0	50.8	0.0	49.2	0.0
Tallahassee, FL (365)	0.0	0.0	47.7	0.0	52.3	0.0
Tampa, FL (365)	0.0	0.0	58.4	1.1	39.5	1.1
Tucson, AZ (365)	0.0	0.3	71.5	0.0	5.5	22.7
Tulsa, OK (365)	0.0	0.0	65.2	0.0	34.8	0.0
Tuscaloosa, AL (264)	0.0	0.0	71.2	0.0	28.8	0.0
Virginia Beach, VA (365)	0.0	12.1	61.9	0.0	26.0	0.0
Washington, DC (365)	0.0	6.8	61.9	0.0	31.2	0.0
Wichita, KS (365)	0.0	1.4	72.6	0.0	23.6	2.5
Winston-Salem, NC (365)	0.0	2.7	47.1	0.0	50.1	0.0

Note: The Air Quality Index (AQI) is an index for reporting daily air quality. EPA calculates the AQI for five major air pollutants regulated by the Clean Air Act: ground-level ozone, particle pollution (also known as particulate matter), carbon monoxide, sulfur dioxide, and nitrogen dioxide. The AQI runs from 0 to 500. The higher the AQI value, the greater the level of air pollution and the greater the health concern; (1) Data covers the Metropolitan Statistical Area—see Appendix B for areas included; (2) Number of days with AQI data in 2019
Source: U.S. Environmental Protection Agency, Air Quality Index Report, 2019

Air Quality Trends: Ozone

MSA[1]	1990	1995	2000	2005	2010	2015	2016	2017	2018	2019
Albuquerque, NM	0.072	0.070	0.072	0.073	0.066	0.066	0.065	0.069	0.074	0.067
Allentown, PA	0.093	0.091	0.091	0.086	0.080	0.070	0.073	0.067	0.067	0.064
Anchorage, AK	n/a	n/a	n/a	n/a	n/a	n/a	n/a	n/a	n/a	n/a
Ann Arbor, MI	n/a	n/a	n/a	n/a	n/a	n/a	n/a	n/a	n/a	n/a
Athens, GA	n/a	n/a	n/a	n/a	n/a	n/a	n/a	n/a	n/a	n/a
Atlanta, GA	0.104	0.103	0.101	0.087	0.076	0.070	0.073	0.068	0.068	0.071
Austin, TX	0.088	0.089	0.088	0.082	0.074	0.073	0.064	0.070	0.072	0.065
Baton Rouge, LA	0.105	0.091	0.090	0.090	0.075	0.069	0.066	0.069	0.069	0.066
Boise City, ID	n/a	n/a	n/a	n/a	n/a	n/a	n/a	n/a	n/a	n/a
Boston, MA	n/a	n/a	n/a	n/a	n/a	n/a	n/a	n/a	n/a	n/a
Boulder, CO	n/a	n/a	n/a	n/a	n/a	n/a	n/a	n/a	n/a	n/a
Cape Coral, FL	n/a	n/a	n/a	n/a	n/a	n/a	n/a	n/a	n/a	n/a
Cedar Rapids, IA	n/a	n/a	n/a	n/a	n/a	n/a	n/a	n/a	n/a	n/a
Charleston, SC	0.068	0.071	0.078	0.073	0.067	0.054	0.059	0.062	0.058	0.064
Charlotte, NC	n/a	n/a	n/a	n/a	n/a	n/a	n/a	n/a	n/a	n/a
Chicago, IL	0.074	0.094	0.073	0.084	0.070	0.066	0.074	0.071	0.073	0.069
Cincinnati, OH	0.091	0.091	0.081	0.085	0.075	0.068	0.071	0.067	0.074	0.067
Clarksville, TN	n/a	n/a	n/a	n/a	n/a	n/a	n/a	n/a	n/a	n/a
Cleveland, OH	0.085	0.092	0.076	0.083	0.077	0.071	0.072	0.070	0.074	0.070
College Station, TX	n/a	n/a	n/a	n/a	n/a	n/a	n/a	n/a	n/a	n/a
Colorado Springs, CO	n/a	n/a	n/a	n/a	n/a	n/a	n/a	n/a	n/a	n/a
Columbia, MO	n/a	n/a	n/a	n/a	n/a	n/a	n/a	n/a	n/a	n/a
Columbia, SC	0.093	0.079	0.096	0.082	0.070	0.056	0.065	0.059	0.060	0.066
Columbus, OH	0.090	0.091	0.085	0.084	0.073	0.066	0.069	0.065	0.062	0.060
Dallas, TX	0.095	0.105	0.096	0.097	0.080	0.077	0.070	0.073	0.078	0.071
Davenport, IA	n/a	n/a	n/a	n/a	n/a	n/a	n/a	n/a	n/a	n/a
Denver, CO	0.077	0.070	0.069	0.072	0.070	0.073	0.071	0.072	0.071	0.068
Des Moines, IA	n/a	n/a	n/a	n/a	n/a	n/a	n/a	n/a	n/a	n/a
Durham, NC	n/a	n/a	n/a	n/a	n/a	n/a	n/a	n/a	n/a	n/a
Edison, NJ	0.101	0.106	0.090	0.091	0.081	0.075	0.073	0.070	0.073	0.067
El Paso, TX	0.080	0.078	0.082	0.074	0.072	0.071	0.068	0.073	0.077	0.074
Fargo, ND	n/a	n/a	n/a	n/a	n/a	n/a	n/a	n/a	n/a	n/a
Fayetteville, NC	0.087	0.081	0.086	0.084	0.071	0.060	0.064	0.063	0.064	0.061
Fort Collins, CO	0.066	0.072	0.074	0.076	0.072	0.069	0.070	0.067	0.073	0.065
Fort Wayne, IN	0.086	0.094	0.086	0.081	0.067	0.061	0.068	0.063	0.071	0.063
Fort Worth, TX	0.095	0.105	0.096	0.097	0.080	0.077	0.070	0.073	0.078	0.071
Grand Rapids, MI	0.102	0.089	0.073	0.085	0.071	0.066	0.075	0.065	0.072	0.065
Greeley, CO	n/a	n/a	n/a	n/a	n/a	n/a	n/a	n/a	n/a	n/a
Green Bay, WI	n/a	n/a	n/a	n/a	n/a	n/a	n/a	n/a	n/a	n/a
Greensboro, NC	n/a	n/a	n/a	n/a	n/a	n/a	n/a	n/a	n/a	n/a
Honolulu, HI	0.034	0.049	0.044	0.042	0.046	0.048	0.047	0.046	0.046	0.053
Houston, TX	0.119	0.114	0.102	0.087	0.079	0.083	0.066	0.070	0.073	0.074
Huntsville, AL	0.079	0.080	0.088	0.075	0.071	0.063	0.066	0.063	0.065	0.063
Indianapolis, IN	0.084	0.094	0.081	0.080	0.069	0.064	0.070	0.067	0.073	0.067
Jacksonville, FL	0.080	0.068	0.072	0.076	0.068	0.060	0.057	0.059	0.060	0.062
Kansas City, MO	0.075	0.098	0.088	0.084	0.072	0.063	0.066	0.069	0.073	0.063
Lafayette, LA	n/a	n/a	n/a	n/a	n/a	n/a	n/a	n/a	n/a	n/a
Lakeland, FL	0.066	0.071	0.079	0.074	0.064	0.062	0.064	0.072	0.065	0.066
Las Vegas, NV	n/a	n/a	n/a	n/a	n/a	n/a	n/a	n/a	n/a	n/a
Lexington, KY	0.078	0.088	0.077	0.078	0.070	0.069	0.066	0.063	0.063	0.059
Lincoln, NE	0.057	0.060	0.057	0.056	0.050	0.061	0.058	0.062	0.062	0.056
Little Rock, AR	0.080	0.086	0.090	0.083	0.072	0.063	0.064	0.060	0.066	0.059
Los Angeles, CA	0.134	0.114	0.091	0.085	0.076	0.083	0.083	0.093	0.084	0.080
Louisville, KY	0.075	0.087	0.088	0.083	0.076	0.070	0.070	0.064	0.067	0.064
Madison, WI	0.077	0.084	0.072	0.079	0.062	0.064	0.068	0.064	0.066	0.059
Manchester, NH	n/a	n/a	n/a	n/a	n/a	n/a	n/a	n/a	n/a	n/a

Table continued on following page.

MSA[1]	1990	1995	2000	2005	2010	2015	2016	2017	2018	2019
Memphis, TN	0.088	0.095	0.092	0.086	0.076	0.065	0.069	0.063	0.069	0.065
Miami, FL	0.068	0.072	0.075	0.065	0.064	0.061	0.061	0.064	0.064	0.058
Midland, TX	n/a	n/a	n/a	n/a	n/a	n/a	n/a	n/a	n/a	n/a
Milwaukee, WI	0.095	0.106	0.082	0.092	0.079	0.069	0.074	0.072	0.073	0.066
Minneapolis, MN	0.068	0.084	0.065	0.074	0.066	0.061	0.061	0.062	0.065	0.059
Nashville, TN	0.089	0.092	0.084	0.078	0.073	0.065	0.067	0.063	0.068	0.064
New Haven, CT	n/a	n/a	n/a	n/a	n/a	n/a	n/a	n/a	n/a	n/a
New Orleans, LA	0.082	0.088	0.091	0.079	0.074	0.067	0.065	0.063	0.065	0.062
New York, NY	0.101	0.106	0.090	0.091	0.081	0.075	0.073	0.070	0.073	0.067
Oklahoma City, OK	0.078	0.086	0.082	0.077	0.071	0.067	0.066	0.070	0.072	0.067
Omaha, NE	0.054	0.075	0.063	0.069	0.058	0.055	0.063	0.061	0.063	0.050
Orlando, FL	0.081	0.075	0.080	0.083	0.069	0.060	0.064	0.067	0.062	0.062
Peoria, IL	0.071	0.082	0.072	0.075	0.064	0.062	0.067	0.066	0.070	0.063
Philadelphia, PA	0.102	0.109	0.099	0.091	0.083	0.074	0.075	0.073	0.075	0.067
Phoenix, AZ	0.080	0.087	0.082	0.077	0.076	0.072	0.071	0.075	0.074	0.071
Pittsburgh, PA	0.080	0.095	0.082	0.082	0.075	0.069	0.068	0.066	0.068	0.062
Portland, OR	0.081	0.065	0.059	0.059	0.056	0.064	0.057	0.073	0.062	0.058
Providence, RI	0.106	0.107	0.087	0.090	0.072	0.070	0.075	0.076	0.074	0.064
Provo, UT	0.070	0.068	0.083	0.078	0.070	0.073	0.072	0.073	0.073	0.073
Raleigh, NC	0.093	0.081	0.087	0.082	0.071	0.065	0.069	0.066	0.063	0.064
Reno, NV	0.074	0.069	0.067	0.069	0.068	0.071	0.070	0.068	0.077	0.063
Richmond, VA	0.083	0.089	0.080	0.082	0.079	0.062	0.065	0.063	0.062	0.061
Riverside, CA	0.146	0.129	0.104	0.102	0.093	0.094	0.096	0.099	0.097	0.091
Rochester, MN	n/a	n/a	n/a	n/a	n/a	n/a	n/a	n/a	n/a	n/a
Sacramento, CA	0.088	0.093	0.087	0.087	0.074	0.074	0.077	0.073	0.079	0.068
Salt Lake City, UT	n/a	n/a	n/a	n/a	n/a	n/a	n/a	n/a	n/a	n/a
San Antonio, TX	0.090	0.095	0.078	0.084	0.072	0.079	0.071	0.073	0.072	0.075
San Diego, CA	0.112	0.093	0.084	0.079	0.075	0.070	0.073	0.077	0.069	0.071
San Francisco, CA	0.058	0.074	0.057	0.057	0.061	0.062	0.059	0.060	0.053	0.060
San Jose, CA	0.079	0.085	0.070	0.065	0.073	0.067	0.063	0.065	0.061	0.062
Santa Rosa, CA	0.063	0.071	0.061	0.050	0.053	0.059	0.055	0.062	0.055	0.056
Savannah, GA	n/a	n/a	n/a	n/a	n/a	n/a	n/a	n/a	n/a	n/a
Seattle, WA	0.082	0.062	0.056	0.053	0.053	0.059	0.054	0.076	0.067	0.052
Sioux Falls, SD	n/a	n/a	n/a	n/a	n/a	n/a	n/a	n/a	n/a	n/a
Springfield, IL	n/a	n/a	n/a	n/a	n/a	n/a	n/a	n/a	n/a	n/a
Tallahassee, FL	n/a	n/a	n/a	n/a	n/a	n/a	n/a	n/a	n/a	n/a
Tampa, FL	0.080	0.075	0.081	0.075	0.067	0.062	0.064	0.064	0.065	0.065
Tucson, AZ	0.073	0.078	0.074	0.075	0.068	0.065	0.065	0.070	0.069	0.065
Tulsa, OK	0.086	0.091	0.081	0.072	0.069	0.061	0.064	0.065	0.067	0.062
Tuscaloosa, AL	n/a	n/a	n/a	n/a	n/a	n/a	n/a	n/a	n/a	n/a
Virginia Beach, VA	0.085	0.084	0.083	0.078	0.074	0.061	0.062	0.059	0.061	0.059
Washington, DC	0.088	0.093	0.082	0.081	0.077	0.067	0.069	0.065	0.066	0.061
Wichita, KS	0.077	0.069	0.080	0.074	0.075	0.064	0.062	0.063	0.064	0.062
Winston-Salem, NC	0.084	0.086	0.089	0.080	0.078	0.065	0.069	0.066	0.064	0.062
U.S.	0.088	0.089	0.082	0.080	0.073	0.068	0.069	0.068	0.069	0.065

Note: (1) Data covers the Metropolitan Statistical Area—see Appendix B for areas included; n/a not available. The values shown are the composite ozone concentration averages among trend sites based on the highest fourth daily maximum 8-hour concentration in parts per million. These trends are based on sites having an adequate record of monitoring data during the trend period. Data from exceptional events are included.
Source: U.S. Environmental Protection Agency, Air Quality Monitoring Information, "Air Quality Trends by City, 1990-2019"

Maximum Air Pollutant Concentrations: Particulate Matter, Ozone, CO and Lead

Metro Aea	PM 10 (ug/m³)	PM 2.5 Wtd AM (ug/m³)	PM 2.5 24-Hr (ug/m³)	Ozone (ppm)	Carbon Monoxide (ppm)	Lead (ug/m³)
Albuquerque, NM	141	7.7	20	0.069	1	n/a
Allentown, PA	31	8.5	26	0.065	n/a	0.04
Anchorage, AK	148	8.2	42	n/a	2	n/a
Ann Arbor, MI	n/a	8.5	22	0.060	n/a	n/a
Athens, GA	n/a	9.8	21	0.063	n/a	n/a
Atlanta, GA	40	10.8	24	0.075	2	n/a
Austin, TX	38	9.5	21	0.065	2	n/a
Baton Rouge, LA	51	9.2	23	0.070	1	0
Boise City, ID	83	6.9	25	0.057	1	n/a
Boston, MA	34	7.5	17	0.065	1	n/a
Boulder, CO	52	7.4	36	0.069	n/a	n/a
Cape Coral, FL	51	7.4	14	0.062	n/a	n/a
Cedar Rapids, IA	38	7.9	20	0.060	n/a	n/a
Charleston, SC	54	6.9	14	0.064	n/a	n/a
Charlotte, NC	36	9.5	18	0.074	1	n/a
Chicago, IL	73	10.8	26	0.071	2	0.19
Cincinnati, OH	108	11.9	26	0.072	2	n/a
Clarksville, TN	n/a	n/a	n/a	0.061	n/a	n/a
Cleveland, OH	79	10.8	26	0.071	2	0.01
College Station, TX	n/a	n/a	n/a	n/a	n/a	n/a
Colorado Springs, CO	32	5.0	13	0.065	2	n/a
Columbia, MO	n/a	n/a	n/a	0.058	n/a	n/a
Columbia, SC	35	7.2	15	0.067	1	n/a
Columbus, OH	39	9.7	22	0.068	1	n/a
Dallas, TX	40	9.0	19	0.076	1	0.23
Davenport, IA	129	8.6	22	0.066	1	n/a
Denver, CO	111	10.0	29	0.078	2	n/a
Des Moines, IA	39	7.0	19	0.064	1	n/a
Durham, NC	27	7.7	15	0.063	n/a	n/a
Edison, NJ	34	11.0	24	0.073	2	n/a
El Paso, TX	79	8.5	25	0.075	2	0.01
Fargo, ND	78	6.5	18	0.062	n/a	n/a
Fayetteville, NC	30	7.4	16	0.061	n/a	n/a
Fort Collins, CO	n/a	6.0	20	0.071	1	n/a
Fort Wayne, IN	n/a	9.0	22	0.063	n/a	n/a
Fort Worth, TX	40	9.0	19	0.076	1	0.23
Grand Rapids, MI	104	8.3	24	0.065	1	0.01
Greeley, CO	n/a	9.0	26	0.065	1	n/a
Green Bay, WI	n/a	7.3	19	0.061	n/a	n/a
Greensboro, NC	33	6.8	15	0.064	n/a	n/a
Honolulu, HI	32	3.9	8	0.053	1	n/a
Houston, TX	63	10.7	27	0.081	2	n/a
Huntsville, AL	34	7.4	14	0.063	n/a	n/a
Indianapolis, IN	57	12.6	27	0.067	2	n/a
Jacksonville, FL	57	8.6	20	0.065	1	n/a
Kansas City, MO	71	7.6	17	0.064	1	n/a
Lafayette, LA	52	7.9	17	0.063	n/a	n/a
Lakeland, FL	57	7.7	19	0.067	n/a	n/a
Las Vegas, NV	104	8.0	26	0.070	2	n/a
Lexington, KY	28	8.0	17	0.059	n/a	n/a
Lincoln, NE	n/a	6.5	17	0.056	n/a	n/a
Little Rock, AR	38	10.3	23	0.060	1	n/a
Los Angeles, CA	159	11.0	28	0.101	3	0.02
Louisville, KY	40	10.5	23	0.068	2	n/a
Madison, WI	35	8.0	21	0.059	n/a	n/a

Table continued on following page.

Appendix A: Comparative Statistics   A-167

Metro Area	PM 10 (ug/m³)	PM 2.5 Wtd AM (ug/m³)	PM 2.5 24-Hr (ug/m³)	Ozone (ppm)	Carbon Monoxide (ppm)	Lead (ug/m³)
Manchester, NH	n/a	3.0	10	0.057	0	n/a
Memphis, TN	54	8.8	19	0.070	1	n/a
Miami, FL	54	8.9	19	0.060	2	n/a
Midland, TX	n/a	n/a	n/a	n/a	n/a	n/a
Milwaukee, WI	58	9.3	24	0.068	1	n/a
Minneapolis, MN	98	8.0	23	0.062	1	0.07
Nashville, TN	32	9.2	18	0.066	1	n/a
New Haven, CT	67	7.7	18	0.084	1	n/a
New Orleans, LA	79	7.8	17	0.063	2	0.09
New York, NY	34	11.0	24	0.073	2	n/a
Oklahoma City, OK	63	10.0	21	0.066	1	n/a
Omaha, NE	50	7.8	22	0.062	2	0.06
Orlando, FL	49	6.9	16	0.072	1	n/a
Peoria, IL	n/a	8.0	19	0.064	n/a	n/a
Philadelphia, PA	49	9.8	26	0.072	2	0
Phoenix, AZ	990	10.9	30	0.076	2	0.05
Pittsburgh, PA	86	12.2	39	0.064	3	0
Portland, OR	32	7.0	25	0.065	1	n/a
Providence, RI	37	8.3	18	0.066	2	n/a
Provo, UT	53	6.1	21	0.066	1	n/a
Raleigh, NC	30	8.9	17	0.064	1	n/a
Reno, NV	78	6.0	16	0.066	2	n/a
Richmond, VA	27	8.4	20	0.064	1	n/a
Riverside, CA	243	12.8	36	0.106	1	0.01
Rochester, MN	n/a	n/a	n/a	0.054	n/a	n/a
Sacramento, CA	90	8.4	30	0.079	1	n/a
Salt Lake City, UT	67	9.0	31	0.073	1	n/a
San Antonio, TX	42	8.9	21	0.075	1	n/a
San Diego, CA	153	13.7	27	0.076	2	0.02
San Francisco, CA	34	9.4	19	0.072	2	n/a
San Jose, CA	75	9.1	21	0.064	2	0.07
Santa Rosa, CA	73	5.7	14	0.056	1	n/a
Savannah, GA	n/a	n/a	n/a	0.060	n/a	n/a
Seattle, WA	22	8.5	28	0.056	1	n/a
Sioux Falls, SD	37	3.9	16	0.065	1	n/a
Springfield, IL	n/a	8.2	18	0.062	n/a	n/a
Tallahassee, FL	n/a	7.7	20	0.063	1	n/a
Tampa, FL	64	7.7	17	0.070	1	0.09
Tucson, AZ	139	3.8	9	0.065	1	n/a
Tulsa, OK	36	8.7	22	0.066	1	0.01
Tuscaloosa, AL	n/a	7.9	15	0.060	n/a	n/a
Virginia Beach, VA	20	7.1	18	0.061	1	n/a
Washington, DC	46	9.1	25	0.075	2	n/a
Wichita, KS	64	7.5	18	0.062	n/a	n/a
Winston-Salem, NC	33	9.5	24	0.065	n/a	n/a
NAAQS[1]	150	15.0	35	0.075	9	0.15

Note: Data from exceptional events are included; Data covers the Metropolitan Statistical Area—see Appendix B for areas included; (1) National Ambient Air Quality Standards; ppm = parts per million; ug/m³ = micrograms per cubic meter; n/a not available
Concentrations: Particulate Matter 10 (coarse particulate)—highest second maximum 24-hour concentration; Particulate Matter 2.5 Wtd AM (fine particulate)—highest weighted annual mean concentration; Particulate Matter 2.5 24-Hour (fine particulate)—highest 98th percentile 24-hour concentration; Ozone—highest fourth daily maximum 8-hour concentration; Carbon Monoxide—highest second maximum non-overlapping 8-hour concentration; Lead—maximum running 3-month average
Source: U.S. Environmental Protection Agency, Air Quality Monitoring Information, "Air Quality Statistics by City, 2019"

Maximum Air Pollutant Concentrations: Nitrogen Dioxide and Sulfur Dioxide

Metro Area	Nitrogen Dioxide AM (ppb)	Nitrogen Dioxide 1-Hr (ppb)	Sulfur Dioxide AM (ppb)	Sulfur Dioxide 1-Hr (ppb)	Sulfur Dioxide 24-Hr (ppb)
Albuquerque, NM	9	44	n/a	4	n/a
Allentown, PA	11	43	n/a	6	n/a
Anchorage, AK	n/a	n/a	n/a	n/a	n/a
Ann Arbor, MI	n/a	n/a	n/a	n/a	n/a
Athens, GA	n/a	n/a	n/a	n/a	n/a
Atlanta, GA	16	50	n/a	5	n/a
Austin, TX	12	32	n/a	2	n/a
Baton Rouge, LA	10	45	n/a	16	n/a
Boise City, ID	n/a	n/a	n/a	3	n/a
Boston, MA	14	49	n/a	10	n/a
Boulder, CO	n/a	n/a	n/a	n/a	n/a
Cape Coral, FL	n/a	n/a	n/a	n/a	n/a
Cedar Rapids, IA	n/a	n/a	n/a	25	n/a
Charleston, SC	n/a	n/a	n/a	14	n/a
Charlotte, NC	11	37	n/a	3	n/a
Chicago, IL	17	56	n/a	79	n/a
Cincinnati, OH	18	49	n/a	134	n/a
Clarksville, TN	n/a	n/a	n/a	n/a	n/a
Cleveland, OH	10	45	n/a	23	n/a
College Station, TX	n/a	n/a	n/a	8	n/a
Colorado Springs, CO	n/a	n/a	n/a	10	n/a
Columbia, MO	n/a	n/a	n/a	n/a	n/a
Columbia, SC	3	31	n/a	3	n/a
Columbus, OH	10	42	n/a	n/a	n/a
Dallas, TX	12	46	n/a	7	n/a
Davenport, IA	n/a	n/a	n/a	5	n/a
Denver, CO	27	69	n/a	7	n/a
Des Moines, IA	6	37	n/a	n/a	n/a
Durham, NC	n/a	n/a	n/a	41	n/a
Edison, NJ	21	66	n/a	11	n/a
El Paso, TX	14	n/a	n/a	n/a	n/a
Fargo, ND	4	39	n/a	3	n/a
Fayetteville, NC	n/a	n/a	n/a	n/a	n/a
Fort Collins, CO	n/a	n/a	n/a	n/a	n/a
Fort Wayne, IN	n/a	n/a	n/a	n/a	n/a
Fort Worth, TX	12	46	n/a	7	n/a
Grand Rapids, MI	6	36	n/a	14	n/a
Greeley, CO	n/a	n/a	n/a	n/a	n/a
Green Bay, WI	n/a	n/a	n/a	5	n/a
Greensboro, NC	n/a	n/a	n/a	n/a	n/a
Honolulu, HI	4	28	n/a	62	n/a
Houston, TX	17	56	n/a	14	n/a
Huntsville, AL	n/a	n/a	n/a	n/a	n/a
Indianapolis, IN	9	37	n/a	n/a	n/a
Jacksonville, FL	11	39	n/a	41	n/a
Kansas City, MO	11	47	n/a	7	n/a
Lafayette, LA	n/a	n/a	n/a	n/a	n/a
Lakeland, FL	n/a	n/a	n/a	26	n/a
Las Vegas, NV	24	58	n/a	5	n/a
Lexington, KY	6	42	n/a	4	n/a
Lincoln, NE	n/a	n/a	n/a	33	n/a
Little Rock, AR	8	38	n/a	13	n/a
Los Angeles, CA	23	78	n/a	8	n/a
Louisville, KY	15	49	n/a	15	n/a
Madison, WI	n/a	n/a	n/a	2	n/a

Table continued on following page.

Metro Area	Nitrogen Dioxide AM (ppb)	Nitrogen Dioxide 1-Hr (ppb)	Sulfur Dioxide AM (ppb)	Sulfur Dioxide 1-Hr (ppb)	Sulfur Dioxide 24-Hr (ppb)
Manchester, NH	n/a	n/a	n/a	1	n/a
Memphis, TN	10	40	n/a	2	n/a
Miami, FL	15	48	n/a	1	n/a
Midland, TX	n/a	n/a	n/a	n/a	n/a
Milwaukee, WI	13	47	n/a	4	n/a
Minneapolis, MN	8	41	n/a	10	n/a
Nashville, TN	14	51	n/a	n/a	n/a
New Haven, CT	12	46	n/a	2	n/a
New Orleans, LA	10	43	n/a	53	n/a
New York, NY	21	66	n/a	11	n/a
Oklahoma City, OK	12	n/a	n/a	1	n/a
Omaha, NE	n/a	n/a	n/a	38	n/a
Orlando, FL	4	30	n/a	3	n/a
Peoria, IL	n/a	n/a	n/a	17	n/a
Philadelphia, PA	13	52	n/a	17	n/a
Phoenix, AZ	25	52	n/a	5	n/a
Pittsburgh, PA	10	37	n/a	80	n/a
Portland, OR	11	33	n/a	3	n/a
Providence, RI	17	52	n/a	2	n/a
Provo, UT	9	42	n/a	n/a	n/a
Raleigh, NC	9	34	n/a	2	n/a
Reno, NV	11	46	n/a	3	n/a
Richmond, VA	12	43	n/a	14	n/a
Riverside, CA	29	74	n/a	7	n/a
Rochester, MN	n/a	n/a	n/a	n/a	n/a
Sacramento, CA	12	55	n/a	3	n/a
Salt Lake City, UT	18	55	n/a	13	n/a
San Antonio, TX	7	40	n/a	4	n/a
San Diego, CA	14	47	n/a	1	n/a
San Francisco, CA	15	48	n/a	15	n/a
San Jose, CA	14	52	n/a	2	n/a
Santa Rosa, CA	4	28	n/a	n/a	n/a
Savannah, GA	n/a	n/a	n/a	50	n/a
Seattle, WA	18	57	n/a	6	n/a
Sioux Falls, SD	5	31	n/a	2	n/a
Springfield, IL	n/a	n/a	n/a	n/a	n/a
Tallahassee, FL	n/a	n/a	n/a	n/a	n/a
Tampa, FL	10	37	n/a	11	n/a
Tucson, AZ	7	30	n/a	1	n/a
Tulsa, OK	7	n/a	n/a	6	n/a
Tuscaloosa, AL	n/a	n/a	n/a	n/a	n/a
Virginia Beach, VA	8	40	n/a	3	n/a
Washington, DC	16	49	n/a	5	n/a
Wichita, KS	6	21	n/a	3	n/a
Winston-Salem, NC	7	34	n/a	5	n/a
NAAQS[1]	53	100	30	75	140

Note: Data from exceptional events are included; Data covers the Metropolitan Statistical Area—see Appendix B for areas included; (1) National Ambient Air Quality Standards; ppb = parts per billion; n/a not available
Concentrations: Nitrogen Dioxide AM—highest arithmetic mean concentration; Nitrogen Dioxide 1-Hr—highest 98th percentile 1-hour daily maximum concentration; Sulfur Dioxide AM—highest annual mean concentration; Sulfur Dioxide 1-Hr—highest 99th percentile 1-hour daily maximum concentration; Sulfur Dioxide 24-Hr—highest second maximum 24-hour concentration
Source: U.S. Environmental Protection Agency, Air Quality Monitoring Information, "Air Quality Statistics by City, 2019"

Appendix B: Metropolitan Area Definitions

Metropolitan Statistical Areas (MSA), Metropolitan Divisions (MD), New England City and Town Areas (NECTA), and New England City and Town Area Divisions (NECTAD)

Note: In March 2020, the Office of Management and Budget (OMB) announced changes to metropolitan and micropolitan statistical area definitions. Both current and historical definitions (December 2009) are shown below. If the change only affected the name of the metro area, the counties included were not repeated.

Albuquerque, NM MSA
Bernalillo, Sandoval, Torrance, and Valencia Counties

Allentown-Bethlehem-Easton, PA-NJ MSA
Carbon, Lehigh, and Northampton Counties, PA; Warren County, NJ

Anchorage, AK MSA
Anchorage Municipality and Matanuska-Susitna Borough

Ann Arbor, MI MSA
Washtenaw County

Athens-Clarke County, GA MSA
Clarke, Madison, Oconee, and Oglethorpe Counties

Atlanta-Sandy Springs-Roswell, GA MSA
Barrow, Bartow, Butts, Carroll, Cherokee, Clayton, Cobb, Coweta, Dawson, DeKalb, Douglas, Fayette, Forsyth, Fulton, Gwinnett, Haralson, Heard, Henry, Jasper, Lamar, Meriwether, Morgan, Newton, Paulding, Pickens, Pike, Rockdale, Spalding, and Walton Counties
Previously Atlanta-Sandy Springs-Marietta, GA MSA
Barrow, Bartow, Butts, Carroll, Cherokee, Clayton, Cobb, Coweta, Dawson, DeKalb, Douglas, Fayette, Forsyth, Fulton, Gwinnett, Haralson, Heard, Henry, Jasper, Lamar, Meriwether, Newton, Paulding, Pickens, Pike, Rockdale, Spalding, and Walton Counties

Austin-Round Rock, TX MSA
Previously Austin-Round Rock-San Marcos, TX MSA
Bastrop, Caldwell, Hays, Travis, and Williamson Counties

Baton Rouge, LA MSA
Ascension, East Baton Rouge, East Feliciana, Iberville, Livingston, Pointe Coupee, St. Helena, West Baton Rouge, and West Feliciana Parishes
Previously Baton Rouge, LA MSA
Ascension, East Baton Rouge, Livingston, and West Baton Rouge Parishes

Boise City, ID MSA
Previously Boise City-Nampa, ID MSA
Ada, Boise, Canyon, Gem, and Owyhee Counties

Boston, MA

Boston-Cambridge-Newton, MA-NH MSA
Previously Boston-Cambridge-Quincy, MA-NH MSA
Essex, Middlesex, Norfolk, Plymouth, and Suffolk Counties, MA; Rockingham and Strafford Counties, NH

Boston, MA MD
Previously Boston-Quincy, MA MD
Norfolk, Plymouth, and Suffolk Counties

Boston-Cambridge-Nashua, MA-NH NECTA
Includes 157 cities and towns in Massachusetts and 34 cities and towns in New Hampshire
Previously Boston-Cambridge-Quincy, MA-NH NECTA
Includes 155 cities and towns in Massachusetts and 38 cities and towns in New Hampshire

Boston-Cambridge-Newton, MA NECTA Division
Includes 92 cities and towns in Massachusetts
Previously Boston-Cambridge-Quincy, MA NECTA Division
Includes 97 cities and towns in Massachusetts

Boulder, CO MSA
Boulder County

Cape Coral-Fort Myers, FL MSA
Lee County

Cedar Rapids, IA, MSA
Benton, Jones, and Linn Counties

Charleston-North Charleston, SC MSA
Previously Charleston-North Charleston- Summerville, SC MSA
Berkeley, Charleston, and Dorchester Counties

Charlotte-Concord-Gastonia, NC-SC MSA
Cabarrus, Gaston, Iredell, Lincoln, Mecklenburg, Rowan, and Union Counties, NC; Chester, Lancaster, and York Counties, SC
Previously Charlotte-Gastonia-Rock Hill, NC-SC MSA
Anson, Cabarrus, Gaston, Mecklenburg, and Union Counties, NC; York County, SC

Chicago, IL

Chicago-Naperville-Elgin, IL-IN-WI MSA
Previous name: Chicago-Joliet-Naperville, IL-IN-WI MSA
Cook, DeKalb, DuPage, Grundy, Kane, Kendall, Lake, McHenry, and Will Counties, IL; Jasper, Lake, Newton, and Porter Counties, IN; Kenosha County, WI

Chicago-Naperville-Arlington Heights, IL MD
Cook, DuPage, Grundy, Kendall, McHenry, and Will Counties
Previous name: Chicago-Joliet-Naperville, IL MD
Cook, DeKalb, DuPage, Grundy, Kane, Kendall, McHenry, and Will Counties

Elgin, IL MD
DeKalb and Kane Counties
Previously part of the Chicago-Joliet-Naperville, IL MD

Gary, IN MD
Jasper, Lake, Newton, and Porter Counties

Lake County-Kenosha County, IL-WI MD
Lake County, IL; Kenosha County, WI

Cincinnati, OH-KY-IN MSA
Brown, Butler, Clermont, Hamilton, and Warren Counties, OH; Boone, Bracken, Campbell, Gallatin, Grant, Kenton, and Pendleton County, KY; Dearborn, Franklin, Ohio, and Union Counties, IN
Previously Cincinnati-Middletown, OH-KY-IN MSA
Brown, Butler, Clermont, Hamilton, and Warren Counties, OH; Boone, Bracken, Campbell, Gallatin, Grant, Kenton, and Pendleton County, KY; Dearborn, Franklin, and Ohio Counties, IN

Clarksville, TN-KY MSA
Montgomery and Stewart Counties, TN; Christian and Trigg Counties, KY

Cleveland-Elyria-Mentor, OH MSA
Cuyahoga, Geauga, Lake, Lorain, and Medina Counties

College Station-Bryan, TX MSA
Brazos, Burleson and Robertson Counties

Colorado Springs, CO MSA
El Paso and Teller Counties

Columbia, MO MSA
Boone and Howard Counties

Columbia, SC MSA
Calhoun, Fairfield, Kershaw, Lexington, Richland and Saluda Counties

Columbus, OH MSA
Delaware, Fairfield, Franklin, Licking, Madison, Morrow, Pickaway, and Union Counties

Dallas, TX

Dallas-Fort Worth-Arlington, TX MSA
Collin, Dallas, Denton, Ellis, Hunt, Johnson, Kaufman, Parker, Rockwall, Tarrant, and Wise Counties

Dallas-Plano-Irving, TX MD
Collin, Dallas, Denton, Ellis, Hunt, Kaufman, and Rockwall Counties

Davenport-Moline-Rock Island, IA-IL MSA
Henry, Mercer, and Rock Island Counties, IA; Scott County

Denver-Aurora-Lakewood, CO MSA
Previously Denver-Aurora-Broomfield, CO MSA
Adams, Arapahoe, Broomfield, Clear Creek, Denver, Douglas, Elbert, Gilpin, Jefferson, and Park Counties

Des Moines-West Des Moines, IA MSA
Dallas, Guthrie, Madison, Polk, and Warren Counties

Durham-Chapel Hill, NC MSA
Chatham, Durham, Orange, and Person Counties

Edison, NJ
See New York, NY (New York-Jersey City-White Plains, NY-NJ MD)

El Paso, TX MSA
El Paso County

Fargo, ND-MN MSA
Cass County, ND; Clay County, MN

Fayetteville, NC MSA
Cumberland, and Hoke Counties

Fort Collins, CO MSA
Previously Fort Collins-Loveland, CO MSA
Larimer County

Fort Wayne, IN MSA
Allen, Wells, and Whitley Counties

Fort Worth, TX

Dallas-Fort Worth-Arlington, TX MSA
Collin, Dallas, Denton, Ellis, Hunt, Johnson, Kaufman, Parker, Rockwall, Tarrant, and Wise Counties

Fort Worth-Arlington, TX MD
Hood, Johnson, Parker, Somervell, Tarrant, and Wise Counties

Grand Rapids-Wyoming, MI MSA
Barry, Kent, Montcalm, and Ottawa Counties
Previously Grand Rapids-Wyoming, MI MSA
Barry, Ionia, Kent, and Newaygo Counties

Greeley, CO MSA
Weld County

Green Bay, WI MSA
Brown, Kewaunee, and Oconto Counties

Greensboro-High Point, NC MSA
Guilford, Randolph, and Rockingham Counties

Honolulu, HI MSA
Honolulu County

Houston-The Woodlands-Sugar Land-Baytown, TX MSA
Austin, Brazoria, Chambers, Fort Bend, Galveston, Harris, Liberty, Montgomery, and Waller Counties
Previously Houston-Sugar Land-Baytown, TX MSA
Austin, Brazoria, Chambers, Fort Bend, Galveston, Harris, Liberty, Montgomery, San Jacinto, and Waller Counties

Huntsville, AL MSA
Limestone and Madison Counties

Indianapolis-Carmel, IN MSA
Boone, Brown, Hamilton, Hancock, Hendricks, Johnson, Marion, Morgan, Putnam, and Shelby Counties

Jacksonville, FL MSA
Baker, Clay, Duval, Nassau, and St. Johns Counties

Kansas City, MO-KS MSA
Franklin, Johnson, Leavenworth, Linn, Miami, and Wyandotte Counties, KS; Bates, Caldwell, Cass, Clay, Clinton, Jackson, Lafayette, Platte, and Ray Counties, MO

Lafayette, LA MSA
Acadia, Iberia, Lafayette, St. Martin, and Vermilion Parishes

Lakeland-Winter Haven, FL MSA
Polk County

Las Vegas-Henderson-Paradise, NV MSA
Previously Las Vegas-Paradise, NV MSA
Clark County

Lexington-Fayette, KY MSA
Bourbon, Clark, Fayette, Jessamine, Scott, and Woodford Counties

Lincoln, NE MSA
Lancaster and Seward Counties

Little Rock-North Little Rock-Conway, AR MSA
Faulkner, Grant, Lonoke, Perry, Pulaski, and Saline Counties

Los Angeles, CA

Los Angeles-Long Beach-Anaheim, CA MSA
Previously Los Angeles-Long Beach-Santa Ana, CA MSA
Los Angeles and Orange Counties

Los Angeles-Long Beach-Glendale, CA MD
Los Angeles County

Anaheim-Santa Ana-Irvine, CA MD
Previously Santa Ana-Anaheim-Irvine, CA MD
Orange County

Appendix B: Metropolitan Area Definitions   A-173

Louisville/Jefferson, KY-IN MSA
Clark, Floyd, Harrison, Scott, and Washington Counties, IN; Bullitt, Henry, Jefferson, Oldham, Shelby, Spencer, and Trimble Counties, KY

Madison, WI MSA
Columbia, Dane, and Iowa Counties

Manchester, NH

Manchester-Nashua, NH MSA
Hillsborough County

Manchester, NH NECTA
Includes 11 cities and towns in New Hampshire
Previously Manchester, NH NECTA
Includes 9 cities and towns in New Hampshire

Memphis, TN-AR-MS MSA
Fayette, Shelby and Tipton Counties, TN; Crittenden County, AR; DeSoto, Marshall, Tate and Tunica Counties, MS

Miami, FL

Miami-Fort Lauderdale-West Palm Beach, FL MSA
Previously Miami-Fort Lauderdale-Pompano Beach, FL MSA
Broward, Miami-Dade, and Palm Beach Counties

Miami-Miami Beach-Kendall, FL MD
Miami-Dade County

Midland, TX MSA
Martin, and Midland Counties

Milwaukee-Waukesha-West Allis, WI MSA
Milwaukee, Ozaukee, Washington, and Waukesha Counties

Minneapolis-St. Paul-Bloomington, MN-WI MSA
Anoka, Carver, Chisago, Dakota, Hennepin, Isanti, Le Sueur, Mille Lacs, Ramsey, Scott, Sherburne, Sibley, Washington, and Wright Counties, MN; Pierce and St. Croix Counties, WI

Nashville-Davidson-Murfreesboro-Franklin, TN MSA
Cannon, Cheatham, Davidson, Dickson, Hickman, Macon, Robertson, Rutherford, Smith, Sumner, Trousdale, Williamson, and Wilson Counties

New Haven-Milford, CT MSA
New Haven County

New Orleans-Metarie-Kenner, LA MSA
Jefferson, Orleans, Plaquemines, St. Bernard, St. Charles, St. James, St. John the Baptist, and St. Tammany Parish
Previously New Orleans-Metarie-Kenner, LA MSA
Jefferson, Orleans, Plaquemines, St. Bernard, St. Charles, St. John the Baptist, and St. Tammany Parish

New York, NY

New York-Newark-Jersey City, NY-NJ-PA MSA
Bergen, Essex, Hudson, Hunterdon, Middlesex, Monmouth, Morris, Ocean, Passaic, Somerset, Sussex, and Union Counties, NJ; Bronx, Dutchess, Kings, Nassau, New York, Orange, Putnam, Queens, Richmond, Rockland, Suffolk, and Westchester Counties, NY; Pike County, PA
Previous name: New York-Northern New Jersey-Long Island, NY-NJ-PA MSA
Bergen, Essex, Hudson, Hunterdon, Middlesex, Monmouth, Morris, Ocean, Passaic, Somerset, Sussex, and Union Counties, NJ; Bronx, Kings, Nassau, New York, Putnam, Queens, Richmond, Rockland, Suffolk, and Westchester Counties, NY; Pike County, PA

Dutchess County-Putnam County, NY MD
Dutchess and Putnam Counties
Dutchess County was previously part of the Poughkeepsie-Newburgh-Middletown, NY MSA. Putnam County was previously part of the New York-Wayne-White Plains, NY-NJ MD

Nassau-Suffolk, NY MD
Nassau and Suffolk Counties

New York-Jersey City-White Plains, NY-NJ MD
Bergen, Hudson, Middlesex, Monmouth, Ocean, and Passaic Counties, NJ; Bronx, Kings, New York, Orange, Queens, Richmond, Rockland, and Westchester Counties, NY
Previous name: New York-Wayne-White Plains, NY-NJ MD
Bergen, Hudson, and Passaic Counties, NJ; Bronx, Kings, New York, Putnam, Queens, Richmond, Rockland, and Westchester Counties, NY

Newark, NJ-PA MD
Essex, Hunterdon, Morris, Somerset, Sussex, and Union Counties, NJ; Pike County, PA
Previous name: Newark-Union, NJ-PA MD
Essex, Hunterdon, Morris, Sussex, and Union Counties, NJ; Pike County, PA

Oklahoma City, OK MSA
Canadian, Cleveland, Grady, Lincoln, Logan, McClain, and Oklahoma Counties

Omaha-Council Bluffs, NE-IA MSA
Harrison, Mills, and Pottawattamie Counties, IA; Cass, Douglas, Sarpy, Saunders, and Washington Counties, NE

Orlando-Kissimmee-Sanford, FL MSA
Lake, Orange, Osceola, and Seminole Counties

Peoria, IL MSA
Marshall, Peoria, Stark, Tazewell, and Woodford Counties

Philadelphia, PA

Philadelphia-Camden-Wilmington, PA-NJ-DE-MD MSA
New Castle County, DE; Cecil County, MD; Burlington, Camden, Gloucester, and Salem Counties, NJ; Bucks, Chester, Delaware, Montgomery, and Philadelphia Counties, PA

Camden, NJ MD
Burlington, Camden, and Gloucester Counties

Montgomery County-Bucks County-Chester County, PA MD
Bucks, Chester, and Montgomery Counties
Previously part of the Philadelphia, PA MD

Philadelphia, PA MD
Delaware and Philadelphia Counties
Previous name: Philadelphia, PA MD
Bucks, Chester, Delaware, Montgomery, and Philadelphia Counties

Wilmington, DE-MD-NJ MD
New Castle County, DE; Cecil County, MD; Salem County, NJ

Phoenix-Mesa-Scottsdale, AZ MSA
Previously Phoenix-Mesa-Glendale, AZ MSA
Maricopa and Pinal Counties

Pittsburgh, PA MSA
Allegheny, Armstrong, Beaver, Butler, Fayette, Washington, and Westmoreland Counties

Portland-Vancouver-Hillsboro, OR-WA MSA
Clackamas, Columbia, Multnomah, Washington, and Yamhill Counties, OR; Clark and Skamania Counties, WA

Providence, RI
Providence-New Bedford-Fall River, RI-MA MSA
Previously Providence-New Bedford-Fall River, RI-MA MSA
Bristol County, MA; Bristol, Kent, Newport, Providence, and Washington Counties, RI
Providence-Warwick, RI-MA NECTA
Includes 12 cities and towns in Massachusetts and 36 cities and towns in Rhode Island
Previously Providence-Fall River-Warwick, RI-MA NECTA
Includes 12 cities and towns in Massachusetts and 37 cities and towns in Rhode Island

Provo-Orem, UT MSA
Juab and Utah Counties

Raleigh, NC MSA
Previously Raleigh-Cary, NC MSA
Franklin, Johnston, and Wake Counties

Reno, NV MSA
Previously Reno-Sparks, NV MSA
Storey and Washoe Counties

Richmond, VA MSA
Amelia, Caroline, Charles City, Chesterfield, Dinwiddie, Goochland, Hanover, Henrico, King William, New Kent, Powhatan, Prince George, and Sussex Counties; Colonial Heights, Hopewell, Petersburg, and Richmond Cities

Riverside-San Bernardino-Ontario, CA MSA
Riverside and San Bernardino Counties

Rochester, MN MSA
Dodge, Fillmore, Olmsted, and Wabasha Counties

Sacramento—Roseville—Arden-Arcade, CA MSA
El Dorado, Placer, Sacramento, and Yolo Counties

Salt Lake City, UT MSA
Salt Lake and Tooele Counties

San Antonio-New Braunfels, TX MSA
Atascosa, Bandera, Bexar, Comal, Guadalupe, Kendall, Medina, and Wilson Counties

San Diego-Carlsbad, CA MSA
Previously San Diego-Carlsbad-San Marcos, CA MSA
San Diego County

San Francisco, CA
San Francisco-Oakland-Hayward, CA MSA
Previously San Francisco-Oakland- Fremont, CA MSA
Alameda, Contra Costa, Marin, San Francisco, and San Mateo Counties
San Francisco-Redwood City-South San Francisco, CA MD
San Francisco and San Mateo Counties
Previously San Francisco-San Mateo-Redwood City, CA MD
Marin, San Francisco, and San Mateo Counties

San Jose-Sunnyvale-Santa Clara, CA MSA
San Benito and Santa Clara Counties

Santa Rosa, CA MSA
Previously Santa Rosa-Petaluma, CA MSA
Sonoma County

Savannah, GA MSA
Bryan, Chatham, and Effingham Counties

Seattle, WA
Seattle-Tacoma-Bellevue, WA MSA
King, Pierce, and Snohomish Counties
Seattle-Bellevue-Everett, WA MD
King and Snohomish Counties

Sioux Falls, SD MSA
Lincoln, McCook, Minnehaha, and Turner Counties

Springfield, IL MSA
Menard and Sangamon Counties

Tallahassee, FL MSA
Gadsden, Jefferson, Leon, and Wakulla Counties

Tampa-St. Petersburg-Clearwater, FL MSA
Hernando, Hillsborough, Pasco, and Pinellas Counties

Tucson, AZ MSA
Pima County

Tulsa, OK MSA
Creek, Okmulgee, Osage, Pawnee, Rogers, Tulsa, and Wagoner Counties

Tuscaloosa, AL MSA
Hale, Pickens, and Tuscaloosa Counties

Virginia Beach-Norfolk-Newport News, VA-NC MSA
Currituck County, NC; Chesapeake, Hampton, Newport News, Norfolk, Poquoson, Portsmouth, Suffolk, Virginia Beach and Williamsburg cities, VA; Gloucester, Isle of Wight, James City, Mathews, Surry, and York Counties, VA

Washington, DC
Washington-Arlington-Alexandria, DC-VA-MD-WV MSA
District of Columbia; Calvert, Charles, Frederick, Montgomery, and Prince George's Counties, MD; Alexandria, Fairfax, Falls Church, Fredericksburg, Manassas Park, and Manassas cities, VA; Arlington, Clarke, Culpepper, Fairfax, Fauquier, Loudoun, Prince William, Rappahannock, Spotsylvania, Stafford, and Warren Counties, VA; Jefferson County, WV
Previously Washington-Arlington-Alexandria, DC-VA-MD-WV MSA
District of Columbia; Calvert, Charles, Frederick, Montgomery, and Prince George's Counties, MD; Alexandria, Fairfax, Falls Church, Fredericksburg, Manassas Park, and Manassas cities, VA; Arlington, Clarke, Fairfax, Fauquier, Loudoun, Prince William, Spotsylvania, Stafford, and Warren Counties, VA; Jefferson County, WV
Washington-Arlington-Alexandria, DC-VA-MD-WV MD
District of Columbia; Calvert, Charles, and Prince George's Counties, MD; Alexandria, Fairfax, Falls Church, Fredericksburg, Manassas Park, and Manassas cities, VA; Arlington, Clarke, Culpepper, Fairfax, Fauquier, Loudoun, Prince William, Rappahannock, Spotsylvania, Stafford, and Warren Counties, VA; Jefferson County, WV
Previously Washington-Arlington-Alexandria, DC-VA-MD-WV MD
District of Columbia; Calvert, Charles, and Prince George's Counties, MD; Alexandria, Fairfax, Falls Church, Fredericksburg, Manassas Park, and Manassas cities, VA; Arlington, Clarke, Fairfax, Fauquier, Loudoun, Prince William, Spotsylvania, Stafford, and Warren Counties, VA; Jefferson County, WV

Wichita, KS MSA
Butler, Harvey, Kingman, Sedgwick, and Sumner Counties

Winston-Salem, NC MSA
Davidson, Davie, Forsyth, Stokes, and Yadkin Counties

Appendix C: Government Type and Primary County

This appendix includes the government structure of each place included in this book. It also includes the county or county equivalent in which each place is located. If a place spans more than one county, the county in which the majority of the population resides is shown.

Albuquerque, NM
Government Type: City
County: Bernalillo

Allentown, PA
Government Type: City
County: Lehigh

Anchorage, AK
Government Type: Municipality
Borough: Anchorage

Ann Arbor, MI
Government Type: City
County: Washtenaw

Athens, GA
Government Type: Consolidated city-county
County: Clarke

Atlanta, GA
Government Type: City
County: Fulton

Austin, TX
Government Type: City
County: Travis

Baton Rouge, LA
Government Type: Consolidated city-parish
Parish: East Baton Rouge

Boise City, ID
Government Type: City
County: Ada

Boston, MA
Government Type: City
County: Suffolk

Boulder, CO
Government Type: City
County: Boulder

Cape Coral, FL
Government Type: City
County: Lee

Cedar Rapids, IA
Government Type: City
County: Linn

Charleston, SC
Government Type: City
County: Charleston

Charlotte, NC
Government Type: City
County: Mecklenburg

Chicago, IL
Government Type: City
County: Cook

Cincinnati, OH
Government Type: City
County: Hamilton

Clarksville, TN
Government Type: City
County: Montgomery

Cleveland, OH
Government Type: City
County: Cuyahoga

College Station, TX
Government Type: City
County: Brazos

Colorado Springs, CO
Government Type: City
County: El Paso

Columbia, MO
Government Type: City
County: Boone

Columbia, SC
Government Type: City
County: Richland

Columbus, OH
Government Type: City
County: Franklin

Dallas, TX
Government Type: City
County: Dallas

Davenport, IA
Government Type: City
County: Scott

Denver, CO
Government Type: City
County: Denver

Des Moines, IA
Government Type: City
County: Polk

Durham, NC
Government Type: City
County: Durham

Edison, NJ
Government Type: Township
County: Middlesex

El Paso, TX
Government Type: City
County: El Paso

Fargo, ND
Government Type: City
County: Cass

Fayetteville, NC
Government Type: City
County: Cumberland

Fort Collins, CO
Government Type: City
County: Larimer

Fort Wayne, IN
Government Type: City
County: Allen

Fort Worth, TX
Government Type: City
County: Tarrant

Grand Rapids, MI
Government Type: City
County: Kent

Greeley, CO
Government Type: City
County: Weld

Green Bay, WI
Government Type: City
County: Brown

Greensboro, NC
Government Type: City
County: Guilford

Honolulu, HI
Government Type: Census Designated Place (CDP)
County: Honolulu

Houston, TX
Government Type: City
County: Harris

Huntsville, AL
Government Type: City
County: Madison

Indianapolis, IN
Government Type: City
County: Marion

Jacksonville, FL
Government Type: City
County: Duval

Kansas City, MO
Government Type: City
County: Jackson

Lafayette, LA
Government Type: City
Parish: Lafayette

Lakeland, FL
Government Type: City
County: Polk

Las Vegas, NV
Government Type: City
County: Clark

Lexington, KY
Government Type: Consolidated city-county
County: Fayette

Lincoln, NE
Government Type: City
County: Lancaster

Little Rock, AR
Government Type: City
County: Pulaski

Los Angeles, CA
Government Type: City
County: Los Angeles

Louisville, KY
Government Type: Consolidated city-county
County: Jefferson

Madison, WI
Government Type: City
County: Dane

Manchester, NH
Government Type: City
County: Hillsborough

Memphis, TN
Government Type: City
County: Shelby

Miami, FL
Government Type: City
County: Miami-Dade

Midland, TX
Government Type: City
County: Midland

Milwaukee, WI
Government Type: City
County: Milwaukee

Minneapolis, MN
Government Type: City
County: Hennepin

Nashville, TN
Government Type: Consolidated city-county
County: Davidson

New Haven, CT
Government Type: City
County: New Haven

New Orleans, LA
Government Type: City
Parish: Orleans

New York, NY
Government Type: City
Counties: Bronx; Kings; New York; Queens; Staten Island

Oklahoma City, OK
Government Type: City
County: Oklahoma

Omaha, NE
Government Type: City
County: Douglas

Orlando, FL
Government Type: City
County: Orange

Peoria, IL
Government Type: City
County: Peoria

Philadelphia, PA
Government Type: City
County: Philadelphia

Phoenix, AZ
Government Type: City
County: Maricopa

Pittsburgh, PA
Government Type: City
County: Allegheny

Portland, OR
Government Type: City
County: Multnomah

Providence, RI
Government Type: City
County: Providence

Provo, UT
Government Type: City
County: Utah

Raleigh, NC
Government Type: City
County: Wake

Reno, NV
Government Type: City
County: Washoe

Richmond, VA
Government Type: Independent city
County: Richmond city

Riverside, CA
Government Type: City
County: Riverside

Rochester, MN
Government Type: City
County: Olmsted

Sacramento, CA
Government Type: City
County: Sacramento

Salt Lake City, UT
Government Type: City
County: Salt Lake

San Antonio, TX
Government Type: City
County: Bexar

San Diego, CA
Government Type: City
County: San Diego

San Francisco, CA
Government Type: City
County: San Francisco

San Jose, CA
Government Type: City
County: Santa Clara

Santa Rosa, CA
Government Type: City
County: Sonoma

Savannah, GA
Government Type: City
County: Chatham

Seattle, WA
Government Type: City
County: King

Sioux Falls, SD
Government Type: City
County: Minnehaha

Springfield, IL
Government Type: City
County: Sangamon

Tallahassee, FL
Government Type: City
County: Leon

Tampa, FL
Government Type: City
County: Hillsborough

Tucson, AZ
Government Type: City
County: Pima

Tulsa, OK
Government Type: City
County: Tulsa

Tuscaloosa, AL
Government Type: City
County: Tuscaloosa

Virginia Beach, VA
Government Type: Independent city
County: Virginia Beach city

Washington, DC
Government Type: City
County: District of Columbia

Wichita, KS
Government Type: City
County: Sedgwick

Winston-Salem, NC
Government Type: City
County: Forsyth

Appendix D: Chambers of Commerce

Albuquerque, NM
Albuquerque Chamber of Commerce
P.O. Box 25100
Albuquerque, NM 87125
Phone: (505) 764-3700
Fax: (505) 764-3714
http://www.abqchamber.com

Albuquerque Economic Development Dept
851 University Blvd SE, Suite 203
Albuquerque, NM 87106
Phone: (505) 246-6200
Fax: (505) 246-6219
http://www.cabq.gov/econdev

Allentown, PA
Greater Lehigh Valley Chamber of Commerce
Allentown Office
840 Hamilton Street, Suite 205
Allentown, PA 18101
Phone: (610) 751-4929
Fax: (610) 437-4907
http://www.lehighvalleychamber.org

Anchorage, AK
Anchorage Chamber of Commerce
1016 W Sixth Avenue
Suite 303
Anchorage, AK 99501
Phone: (907) 272-2401
Fax: (907) 272-4117
http://www.anchoragechamber.org

Anchorage Economic Development Department
900 W 5th Avenue
Suite 300
Anchorage, AK 99501
Phone: (907) 258-3700
Fax: (907) 258-6646
http://aedcweb.com

Ann Arbor, MI
Ann Arbor Area Chamber of Commerce
115 West Huron
3rd Floor
Ann Arbor, MI 48104
Phone: (734) 665-4433
Fax: (734) 665-4191
http://www.annarborchamber.org

Ann Arbor Economic Development Department
201 S Division
Suite 430
Ann Arbor, MI 48104
Phone: (734) 761-9317
http://www.annarborspark.org

Athens, GA
Athens Area Chamber of Commerce
246 W Hancock Avenue
Athens, GA 30601
Phone: (706) 549-6800
Fax: (706) 549-5636
http://www.aacoc.org

Athens-Clarke County Economic Development Department
246 W. Hancock Avenue
Athens, GA 30601
Phone: (706) 613-3233
Fax: (706) 613-3812
http://www.athensbusiness.org

Atlanta, GA
Metro Atlanta Chamber of Commerce
235 Andrew Young International Blvd NW
Atlanta, GA 30303
Phone: (404) 880-9000
Fax: (404) 586-8464
http://www.metroatlantachamber.com

Austin, TX
Greater Austin Chamber of Commerce
210 Barton Springs Road
Suite 400
Austin, TX 78704
Phone: (512) 478-9383
Fax: (512) 478-6389
http://www.austin-chamber.org

Baton Rouge, LA
Baton Rouge Area Chamber
451 Florida Street
Suite 1050
Baton Rouge, LA 70801
Phone: (225) 381-7125
http://www.brac.org

Boise City, ID
Boise Metro Chamber of Commerce
250 S 5th Street
Suite 800
Boise City, ID 83701
Phone: (208) 472-5200
Fax: (208) 472-5201
http://www.boisechamber.org

Boston, MA
Greater Boston Chamber of Commerce
265 Franklin Street
12th Floor
Boston, MA 02110
Phone: (617) 227-4500
Fax: (617) 227-7505
http://www.bostonchamber.com

Boulder, CO
Boulder Chamber of Commerce
2440 Pearl Street
Boulder, CO 80302
Phone: (303) 442-1044
Fax: (303) 938-8837
http://www.boulderchamber.com

City of Boulder Economic Vitality Program
P.O. Box 791
Boulder, CO 80306
Phone: (303) 441-3090
http://www.bouldercolorado.gov

Cape Coral, FL
Chamber of Commerce of Cape Coral
2051 Cape Coral Parkway East
Cape Coral, FL 33904
Phone: (239) 549-6900
Fax: (239) 549-9609
http://www.capecoralchamber.com

Cedar Rapids, IA
Cedar Rapids Chamber of Commerce
424 First Avenue NE
Cedar Rapids, IA 52401
Phone: (319) 398-5317
Fax: (319) 398-5228
http://www.cedarrapids.org

Cedar Rapids Economic Development
50 Second Avenue Bridge
Sixth Floor
Cedar Rapids, IA 52401-1256
Phone: (319) 286-5041
Fax: (319) 286-5141
http://www.cedar-rapids.org

Charleston, SC
Charleston Metro Chamber of Commerce
P.O. Box 975
Charleston, SC 29402
Phone: (843) 577-2510
http://www.charlestonchamber.net

Charlotte, NC
Charlotte Chamber of Commerce
330 S Tryon Street
P.O. Box 32785
Charlotte, NC 28232
Phone: (704) 378-1300
Fax: (704) 374-1903
http://www.charlottechamber.com

Charlotte Regional Partnership
1001 Morehead Square Drive
Suite 200
Charlotte, NC 28203
Phone: (704) 347-8942
Fax: (704) 347-8981
http://www.charlotteusa.com

Chicago, IL
Chicagoland Chamber of Commerce
200 E Randolph Street
Suite 2200
Chicago, IL 60601-6436
Phone: (312) 494-6700
Fax: (312) 861-0660
http://www.chicagolandchamber.org

City of Chicago Department of Planning and Development
City Hall, Room 1000
121 North La Salle Street
Chicago, IL 60602
Phone: (312) 744-4190
Fax: (312) 744-2271
https://www.cityofchicago.org/city/en/depts/dcd.html

Cincinnati, OH
Cincinnati USA Regional Chamber
3 East 4th Street
Suite 200
Cincinnati, Ohio 45202
Phone: (513) 579-3111
https://www.cincinnatichamber.com

Clarksville, TN
Clarksville Area Chamber of Commerce
25 Jefferson Street
Suite 300
Clarksville, TN 37040
Phone: (931) 647-2331
http://www.clarksvillechamber.com

Cleveland, OH
Greater Cleveland Partnership
1240 Huron Rd. E
Suite 300
Cleveland, OH 44115
Phone: (216) 621-3300
https://www.gcpartnership.com

College Station, TX
Bryan-College Station Chamber of Commerce
4001 East 29th St, Suite 175
Bryan, TX 77802
Phone: (979) 260-5200
http://www.bcschamber.org

Colorado Springs, CO
Colorado Springs Chamber and EDC
102 South Tejon Street
Suite 430
Colorado Springs, CO 80903
Phone: (719) 471-8183
https://coloradospringschamberedc.com

Columbia, MO
Columbia Chamber of Commerce
300 South Providence Rd.
P.O. Box 1016
Columbia, MO 65205-1016
Phone: (573) 874-1132
Fax: (573) 443-3986
http://www.columbiamochamber.com

Columbia, SC
The Columbia Chamber
930 Richland Street
Columbia, SC 29201
Phone: (803) 733-1110
Fax: (803) 733-1113
http://www.columbiachamber.com

Columbus, OH
Greater Columbus Chamber
37 North High Street
Columbus, OH 43215
Phone: (614) 221-1321
Fax: (614) 221-1408
http://www.columbus.org

Dallas, TX
City of Dallas Economic Development Department
1500 Marilla Street
5C South
Dallas, TX 75201
Phone: (214) 670-1685
Fax: (214) 670-0158
http://www.dallas-edd.org

Greater Dallas Chamber of Commerce
700 North Pearl Street
Suite1200
Dallas, TX 75201
Phone: (214) 746-6600
Fax: (214) 746-6799
http://www.dallaschamber.org

Davenport, IA
Quad Cities Chamber
331 W. 3rd Street
Suite 100
Davenport, IA 52801
Phone: (563) 322-1706
https://quadcitieschamber.com

Denver, CO
Denver Metro Chamber of Commerce
1445 Market Street
Denver, CO 80202
Phone: (303) 534-8500
Fax: (303) 534-3200
http://www.denverchamber.org

Downtown Denver Partnership
511 16th Street
Suite 200
Denver, CO 80202
Phone: (303) 534-6161
Fax: (303) 534-2803
http://www.downtowndenver.com

Des Moines, IA
Des Moines Downtown Chamber
301 Grand Ave
Des Moines, IA 50309
Phone: (515) 309-3229
http://desmoinesdowntownchamber.com

Greater Des Moines Partnership
700 Locust Street
Suite 100
Des Moines, IA 50309
Phone: (515) 286-4950
Fax: (515) 286-4974
http://www.desmoinesmetro.com

Durham, NC
Durham Chamber of Commerce
P.O. Box 3829
Durham, NC 27702
Phone: (919) 682-2133
Fax: (919) 688-8351
http://www.durhamchamber.org

North Carolina Institute of Minority Economic Development
114 W Parish Street
Durham, NC 27701
Phone: (919) 956-8889
Fax: (919) 688-7668
http://www.ncimed.com

Edison, NJ
Edison Chamber of Commerce
939 Amboy Avenue
Edison, NJ 08837
Phone: (732) 738-9482
http://www.edisonchamber.com

El Paso, TX
City of El Paso Department of Economic Development
2 Civic Center Plaza
El Paso, TX 79901
Phone: (915) 541-4000
Fax: (915) 541-1316
http://www.elpasotexas.gov

Greater El Paso Chamber of Commerce
10 Civic Center Plaza
El Paso, TX 79901
Phone: (915) 534-0500
Fax: (915) 534-0510
http://www.elpaso.org

Southwest Indiana Chamber
318 Main Street
Suite 401
Evansville, IN 47708
Phone: (812) 425-8147
Fax: (812) 421-5883
https://swinchamber.com

Fargo, ND
Chamber of Commerce of Fargo Moorhead
202 First Avenue North
Fargo, ND 56560
Phone: (218) 233-1100
Fax: (218) 233-1200
http://www.fmchamber.com

Greater Fargo-Moorhead Economic Development Corporation
51 Broadway, Suite 500
Fargo, ND 58102
Phone: (701) 364-1900
Fax: (701) 293-7819
http://www.gfmedc.com

Fayetteville, NC
Fayetteville Regional Chamber
1019 Hay Street
Fayetteville, NC 28305
Phone: (910) 483-8133
Fax: (910) 483-0263
http://www.fayettevillencchamber.org

Fort Collins, CO
Fort Collins Chamber of Commerce
225 South Meldrum
Fort Collins, CO 80521
Phone: (970) 482-3746
Fax: (970) 482-3774
https://fortcollinschamber.com

Fort Wayne, IN
City of Fort Wayne Economic Development
1 Main St
1 Main Street
Fort Wayne, IN 46802
Phone: (260) 427-1111
Fax: (260) 427-1375
http://www.cityoffortwayne.org

Greater Fort Wayne Chamber of Commerce
826 Ewing Street
Fort Wayne, IN 46802
Phone: (260) 424-1435
Fax: (260) 426-7232
http://www.fwchamber.org

Fort Worth, TX
City of Fort Worth Economic Development
City Hall
900 Monroe Street
Suite 301
Fort Worth, TX 76102
Phone: (817) 392-6103
Fax: (817) 392-2431
http://www.fortworthgov.org

Fort Worth Chamber of Commerce
777 Taylor Street
Suite 900
Fort Worth, TX 76102-4997
Phone: (817) 336-2491
Fax: (817) 877-4034
http://www.fortworthchamber.com

Grand Rapids, MI
Grands Rapids Area Chamber of Commerce
111 Pearl Street N.W.
Grand Rapids, MI 49503
Phone: (616) 771-0300
Fax: (616) 771-0318
http://www.grandrapids.org

Greeley, CO
Greeley Chamber of Commerce
902 7th Avenue
Greeley, CO 80631
Phone: (970) 352-3566
https://greeleychamber.com

Green Bay, WI
Economic Development
100 N Jefferson St
Room 202
Green Bay, WI 54301
Phone: (920) 448-3397
Fax: (920) 448-3063
http://www.ci.green-bay.wi.us

Green Bay Area Chamber of Commerce
300 N. Broadway
Suite 3A
Green Bay, WI 54305-1660
Phone: (920) 437-8704
Fax: (920) 593-3468
http://www.titletown.org

Greensboro, NC
Greensboro Area Chamber of Commerce
342 N. Elm Street
Greensboro, NC 27401
Phone: (336) 387-8301
Fax: (336) 275-9299
http://www.greensboro.org

Honolulu, HI
The Chamber of Commerce of Hawaii
1132 Bishop Street
Suite 402
Honolulu, HI 96813
Phone: (808) 545-4300
Fax: (808) 545-4369
http://www.cochawaii.com

Houston, TX
Greater Houston Partnership
1200 Smith Street
Suite 700
Houston, TX 77002-4400
Phone: (713) 844-3600
Fax: (713) 844-0200
http://www.houston.org

Huntsville, AL
Chamber of Commerce of
Huntsville/Madison County
225 Church Street
Huntsville, AL 35801
Phone: (256) 535-2000
Fax: (256) 535-2015
http://www.huntsvillealabamausa.com

Indianapolis, IN
Greater Indianapolis Chamber of Commerce
111 Monument Circle
Suite 1950
Indianapolis, IN 46204
Phone: (317) 464-2222
Fax: (317) 464-2217
http://www.indychamber.com

The Indy Partnership
111 Monument Circle
Suite 1800
Indianapolis, IN 46204
Phone: (317) 236-6262
Fax: (317) 236-6275
http://indypartnership.com

Jacksonville, FL
Jacksonville Chamber of Commerce
3 Independent Drive
Jacksonville, FL 32202
Phone: (904) 366-6600
Fax: (904) 632-0617
http://www.myjaxchamber.com

Kansas City, MO
Greater Kansas City Chamber of Commerce
2600 Commerce Tower
911 Main Street
Kansas City, MO 64105
Phone: (816) 221-2424
Fax: (816) 221-7440
http://www.kcchamber.com

Kansas City Area Development Council
2600 Commerce Tower
911 Main Street
Kansas City, MO 64105
Phone: (816) 221-2121
Fax: (816) 842-2865
http://www.thinkkc.com

Lafayette, LA
Greater Lafayette Chamber of Commerce
804 East Saint Mary Blvd.
Lafayette, LA 70503
Phone: (337) 233-2705
Fax: (337) 234-8671
http://www.lafchamber.org

Lakeland, FL
Lakeland Chamber of Commerce
35 Lake Morton Dr.
Lakeland, FL 33801
Phone: (863) 688-8551
https://www.lakelandchamber.com

Las Vegas, NV
Las Vegas Chamber of Commerce
6671 Las Vegas Blvd South
Suite 300
Las Vegas, NV 89119
Phone: (702) 735-1616
Fax: (702) 735-0406
http://www.lvchamber.org

Las Vegas Office of Business Development
400 Stewart Avenue
City Hall
Las Vegas, NV 89101
Phone: (702) 229-6011
Fax: (702) 385-3128
http://www.lasvegasnevada.gov

Lexington, KY
Greater Lexington Chamber of Commerce
330 East Main Street
Suite 100
Lexington, KY 40507
Phone: (859) 254-4447
Fax: (859) 233-3304
http://www.commercelexington.com

Lexington Downtown Development
Authority
101 East Vine Street
Suite 500
Lexington, KY 40507
Phone: (859) 425-2296
Fax: (859) 425-2292
http://www.lexingtondda.com

Lincoln, NE
Lincoln Chamber of Commerce
1135 M Street
Suite 200
Lincoln, NE 68508
Phone: (402) 436-2350
Fax: (402) 436-2360
http://www.lcoc.com

Little Rock, AR
Little Rock Regional Chamber
One Chamber Plaza
Little Rock, AR 72201
Phone: (501) 374-2001
Fax: (501) 374-6018
http://www.littlerockchamber.com

Appendix D: Chambers of Commerce

Los Angeles, CA
Los Angeles Area Chamber of Commerce
350 South Bixel Street
Los Angeles, CA 90017
Phone: (213) 580-7500
Fax: (213) 580-7511
http://www.lachamber.org

Los Angeles County Economic
Development Corporation
444 South Flower Street
34th Floor
Los Angeles, CA 90071
Phone: (213) 622-4300
Fax: (213) 622-7100
http://www.laedc.org

Louisville, KY
The Greater Louisville Chamber of
Commerce
614 West Main Street
Suite 6000
Louisville, KY 40202
Phone: (502) 625-0000
Fax: (502) 625-0010
http://www.greaterlouisville.com

Madison, WI
Greater Madison Chamber of Commerce
615 East Washington Avenue
P.O. Box 71
Madison, WI 53701-0071
Phone: (608) 256-8348
Fax: (608) 256-0333
http://www.greatermadisonchamber.com

Manchester, NH
Greater Manchester Chamber of Commerce
889 Elm Street
Manchester, NH 03101
Phone: (603) 666-6600
Fax: (603) 626-0910
http://www.manchester-chamber.org

Manchester Economic Development Office
One City Hall Plaza
Manchester, NH 03101
Phone: (603) 624-6505
Fax: (603) 624-6308
http://www.yourmanchesternh.com

Memphis, TN
Greater Memphis Chamber
22 North Front Street, Suite 200
Memphis, TN 38103-2100
Phone: (901) 543-3500
https://memphischamber.com

Miami, FL
Greater Miami Chamber of Commerce
1601 Biscayne Boulevard
Ballroom Level
Miami, FL 33132-1260
Phone: (305) 350-7700
Fax: (305) 374-6902
http://www.miamichamber.com

The Beacon Council
80 Southwest 8th Street
Suite 2400
Miami, FL 33130
Phone: (305) 579-1300
Fax: (305) 375-0271
http://www.beaconcouncil.com

Midland, TX
Midland Chamber of Commerce
109 N. Main
Midland, TX 79701
Phone: (432) 683-3381
Fax: (432) 686-3556
http://www.midlandtxchamber.com

Milwaukee, WI
Greater Milwaukee Chamber of Commerce
6815 W. Capitol Drive
Suite 300
Milwaukee, WI 53216
Phone: (414) 465-2422
http://www.gmcofc.org

Metropolitan Milwaukee Association of
Commerce
756 N. Milwaukee Street
Suite 400
Milwaukee, WI 53202
Phone: (414) 287-4100
Fax: (414) 271-7753
https://www.mmac.org

Minneapolis, MN
Minneapolis Community Development
Agency
Crown Roller Mill
105 5th Avenue South
Suite 200
Minneapolis, MN 55401
Phone: (612) 673-5095
Fax: (612) 673-5100
http://www.ci.minneapolis.mn.us

Minneapolis Regional Chamber
81 South Ninth Street
Suite 200
Minneapolis, MN 55402
Phone: (612) 370-9100
Fax: (612) 370-9195
http://www.minneapolischamber.org

Nashville, TN
Nashville Area Chamber of Commerce
211 Commerce Street
Suite 100
Nashville, TN 37201
Phone: (615) 743-3000
Fax: (615) 256-3074
http://www.nashvillechamber.com

Tennessee Valley Authority Economic
Development
400 West Summit Hill Drive
Knoxville TN 37902
Phone: (865) 632-2101
http://www.tvaed.com

New Haven, CT
Greater New Haven Chamber of Commerce
900 Chapel Street
10th Floor
New Haven, CT 06510
Phone: (203) 787-6735
https://www.gnhcc.com

New Orleans, LA
New Orleans Chamber of Commerce
1515 Poydras Street
Suite 1010
New Orleans, LA 70112
Phone: (504) 799-4260
Fax: (504) 799-4259
http://www.neworleanschamber.org

New York, NY
New York City Economic Development
Corporation
110 William Street
New York, NY 10038
Phone: (212) 619-5000
http://www.nycedc.com

The Partnership for New York City
One Battery Park Plaza
5th Floor
New York, NY 10004
Phone: (212) 493-7400
Fax: (212) 344-3344
http://www.pfnyc.org

Oklahoma City, OK
Greater Oklahoma City Chamber of
Commerce
123 Park Avenue
Oklahoma City, OK 73102
Phone: (405) 297-8900
Fax: (405) 297-8916
http://www.okcchamber.com

Omaha, NE
Omaha Chamber of Commerce
1301 Harney Street
Omaha, NE 68102
Phone: (402) 346-5000
Fax: (402) 346-7050
http://www.omahachamber.org

Orlando, FL
Metro Orlando Economic Development
Commission of Mid-Florida
301 East Pine Street
Suite 900
Orlando, FL 32801
Phone: (407) 422-7159
Fax: (407) 425.6428
http://www.orlandoedc.com

Orlando Regional Chamber of Commerce
75 South Ivanhoe Boulevard
P.O. Box 1234
Orlando, FL 32802
Phone: (407) 425-1234
Fax: (407) 839-5020
http://www.orlando.org

Peoria, IL
Peoria Area Chamber
100 SW Water Street
Peoria, IL 61602
Phone: (309) 495-5900
http://www.peoriachamber.org

Philadelphia, PA
Greater Philadelphia Chamber of Commerce
200 South Broad Street
Suite 700
Philadelphia, PA 19102
Phone: (215) 545-1234
Fax: (215) 790-3600
http://www.greaterphilachamber.com

Phoenix, AZ
Greater Phoenix Chamber of Commerce
201 North Central Avenue
27th Floor
Phoenix, AZ 85073
Phone: (602) 495-2195
Fax: (602) 495-8913
http://www.phoenixchamber.com

Greater Phoenix Economic Council
2 North Central Avenue
Suite 2500
Phoenix, AZ 85004
Phone: (602) 256-7700
Fax: (602) 256-7744
http://www.gpec.org

Pittsburgh, PA
Allegheny County Industrial Development Authority
425 6th Avenue
Suite 800
Pittsburgh, PA 15219
Phone: (412) 350-1067
Fax: (412) 642-2217
http://www.alleghenycounty.us

Greater Pittsburgh Chamber of Commerce
425 6th Avenue
12th Floor
Pittsburgh, PA 15219
Phone: (412) 392-4500
Fax: (412) 392-4520
http://www.alleghenyconference.org

Portland, OR
Portland Business Alliance
200 SW Market Street
Suite 1770
Portland, OR 97201
Phone: (503) 224-8684
Fax: (503) 323-9186
http://www.portlandalliance.com

Providence, RI
Greater Providence Chamber of Commerce
30 Exchange Terrace
Fourth Floor
Providence, RI 02903
Phone: (401) 521-5000
Fax: (401) 351-2090
http://www.provchamber.com

Rhode Island Economic Development Corporation
Providence City Hall
25 Dorrance Street
Providence, RI 02903
Phone: (401) 421-7740
Fax: (401) 751-0203
http://www.providenceri.com

Provo, UT
Provo-Orem Chamber of Commerce
51 South University Avenue
Suite 215
Provo, UT 84601
Phone: (801) 851-2555
Fax: (801) 851-2557
http://www.thechamber.org

Raleigh, NC
Greater Raleigh Chamber of Commerce
800 South Salisbury Street
Raleigh, NC 27601-2978
Phone: (919) 664-7000
Fax: (919) 664-7099
http://www.raleighchamber.org

Reno, NV
Greater Reno-Sparks Chamber of Commerce
1 East First Street
16th Floor
Reno, NV 89505
Phone: (775) 337-3030
Fax: (775) 337-3038
http://www.reno-sparkschamber.org

The Chamber Reno-Sparks-Northern Nevada
449 S. Virginia St.
2nd Floor
Reno, NV 89501
Phone: (775) 636-9550
http://www.thechambernv.org

Richmond, VA
Greater Richmond Chamber
600 East Main Street
Suite 700
Richmond, VA 23219
Phone: (804) 648-1234
http://www.grcc.com

Greater Richmond Partnership
901 East Byrd Street
Suite 801
Richmond, VA 23219-4070
Phone: (804) 643-3227
Fax: (804) 343-7167
http://www.grpva.com

Riverside, CA
Greater Riverside Chambers of Commerce
3985 University Avenue
Riverside, CA 92501
Phone: (951) 683-7100
https://www.riverside-chamber.com

Rochester, MN
Rochester Area Chamber of Commerce
220 South Broadway
Suite 100
Rochester, MN 55904
Phone: (507) 288-1122
Fax: (507) 282-8960
http://www.rochestermnchamber.com

Sacramento, CA
Sacramento Metro Chamber
One Capitol Mall
Suite 700
Sacramento, CA 95814
Phone: (916) 552-6800
https://metrochamber.org

Salt Lake City, UT
Department of Economic Development
451 South State Street
Room 425
Salt Lake City, UT 84111
Phone: (801) 535-7240
Fax: (801) 535-6331
http://www.slcgov.com/economic-development

Salt Lake Chamber
175 E. University Blvd. (400 S)
Suite 600
Salt Lake City, UT 84111
Phone: (801) 364-3631
http://www.slchamber.com

San Antonio, TX
The Greater San Antonio Chamber of Commerce
602 E. Commerce Street
San Antonio, TX 78205
Phone: (210) 229-2100
Fax: (210) 229-1600
http://www.sachamber.org

San Antonio Economic Development Department
P.O. Box 839966
San Antonio, TX 78283-3966
Phone: (210) 207-8080
Fax: (210) 207-8151
http://www.sanantonio.gov/edd

San Diego, CA
San Diego Economic Development Corp.
401 B Street
Suite 1100
San Diego, CA 92101
Phone: (619) 234-8484
Fax: (619) 234-1935
http://www.sandiegobusiness.org

San Diego Regional Chamber of Commerce
402 West Broadway
Suite 1000
San Diego, CA 92101-3585
Phone: (619) 544-1300
Fax: (619) 744-7481
http://www.sdchamber.org

Appendix D: Chambers of Commerce

San Francisco, CA
San Francisco Chamber of Commerce
235 Montgomery Street
12th Floor
San Francisco, CA 94104
Phone: (415) 392-4520
Fax: (415) 392-0485
http://www.sfchamber.com

San Jose, CA
Office of Economic Development
60 South Market Street
Suite 470
San Jose, CA 95113
Phone: (408) 277-5880
Fax: (408) 277-3615
http://www.sba.gov

The Silicon Valley Organization
101 W Santa Clara Street
San Jose, CA 95113
Phone: (408) 291-5250
https://www.thesvo.com

Santa Rosa, CA
Santa Rosa Chamber of Commerce
1260 North Dutton Avenue
Suite 272
Santa Rosa, CA 95401
Phone: (707) 545-1414
http://www.santarosachamber.com

Savannah, GA
Economic Development Authority
131 Hutchinson Island Road
4th Floor
Savannah, GA 31421
Phone: (912) 447-8450
Fax: (912) 447-8455
http://www.seda.org

Savannah Chamber of Commerce
101 E. Bay Street
Savannah, GA 31402
Phone: (912) 644-6400
Fax: (912) 644-6499
http://www.savannahchamber.com

Seattle, WA
Greater Seattle Chamber of Commerce
1301 Fifth Avenue
Suite 2500
Seattle, WA 98101
Phone: (206) 389-7200
Fax: (206) 389-7288
http://www.seattlechamber.com

Sioux Falls, SD
Sioux Falls Area Chamber of Commerce
200 N. Phillips Avenue
Suite 102
Sioux Falls, SD 57104
Phone: (605) 336-1620
Fax: (605) 336-6499
http://www.siouxfallschamber.com

Springfield, IL
The Greater Springfield Chamber of Commerce
1011 S. Second Street
Springfield, IL 62704
Phone: (217) 525-1173
Fax: (217) 525-8768
http://www.gscc.org

Tallahassee, FL
Greater Tallahassee Chamber of Commerce
300 E. Park Avenue
P.O. Box 1638
Tallahassee, FL 32301
Phone: (850) 224-8116
Fax: (850) 561-3860
http://www.talchamber.com

Tampa, FL
Greater Tampa Chamber of Commerce
P.O. Box 420
Tampa, FL 33601-0420
Phone: (813) 276-9401
Fax: (813) 229-7855
http://www.tampachamber.com

Tucson, AZ
Tucson Metro Chamber
212 E. Broadway Blvd
Tucson, AZ 85701
Phone: (520) 792-1212
https://tucsonchamber.org

Tulsa, OK
Tulsa Regional Chamber
One West Third Street
Suite 100
Tulsa, OK 74103
Phone: (918) 585-1201
https://www.tulsachamber.com

Tuscaloosa, AL
The Chamber of Commerce of West Alabama
2201 Jack Warner Parkway
Building C
Tuscaloosa, AL 35401
Phone: (205) 758-7588
https://tuscaloosachamber.com

Virginia Beach, VA
Hampton Roads Chamber of Commerce
500 East Main Street
Suite 700
Virginia Beach, VA 23510
Phone: (757) 664-2531
http://www.hamptonroadschamber.com

Washington, DC
District of Columbia Chamber of Commerce
1213 K Street NW
Washington, DC 20005
Phone: (202) 347-7201
Fax: (202) 638-6762
http://www.dcchamber.org

District of Columbia Office of Planning and Economic Development
J.A. Wilson Building
1350 Pennsylvania Ave NW
Suite 317
Washington, DC 20004
Phone: (202) 727-6365
Fax: (202) 727-6703
http://www.dcbiz.dc.gov

Wichita, KS
Wichita Regional Chamber of Commerce
350 W Douglas Avennue
Wichita, KS 67202
Phone: (316) 265-7771
https://www.wichitachamber.org

Winston-Salem, NC
Winston-Salem Chamber of Commerce
411 West Fourth Street
Suite 211
Winston-Salem, NC 27101
Phone: (336) 728-9200
http://www.winstonsalem.com

Appendix E: State Departments of Labor

Alabama
Alabama Department of Labor
P.O. Box 303500
Montgomery, AL 36130-3500
Phone: (334) 242-3072
https://www.labor.alabama.gov

Alaska
Dept of Labor and Workforce Devel.
P.O. Box 11149
Juneau, AK 99822-2249
Phone: (907) 465-2700
http://www.labor.state.ak.us

Arizona
Industrial Commission or Arizona
800 West Washington Street
Phoenix, AZ 85007
Phone: (602) 542-4411
https://www.azica.gov

Arkansas
Department of Labor
10421 West Markham
Little Rock, AR 72205
Phone: (501) 682-4500
http://www.labor.ar.gov

California
Labor and Workforce Development
445 Golden Gate Ave., 10th Floor
San Francisco, CA 94102
Phone: (916) 263-1811
http://www.labor.ca.gov

Colorado
Dept of Labor and Employment
633 17th St., 2nd Floor
Denver, CO 80202-3660
Phone: (888) 390-7936
https://www.colorado.gov/CDLE

Connecticut
Department of Labor
200 Folly Brook Blvd.
Wethersfield, CT 06109-1114
Phone: (860) 263-6000
http://www.ctdol.state.ct.us

Delaware
Department of Labor
4425 N. Market St., 4th Floor
Wilmington, DE 19802
Phone: (302) 451-3423
http://dol.delaware.gov

District of Columbia
Department of Employment Services
614 New York Ave., NE, Suite 300
Washington, DC 20002
Phone: (202) 671-1900
http://does.dc.gov

Florida
Florida Department of Economic Opportunity
The Caldwell Building
107 East Madison St. Suite 100
Tallahassee, FL 32399-4120
Phone: (800) 342-3450
http://www.floridajobs.org

Georgia
Department of Labor
Sussex Place, Room 600
148 Andrew Young Intl Blvd., NE
Atlanta, GA 30303
Phone: (404) 656-3011
http://dol.georgia.gov

Hawaii
Dept of Labor & Industrial Relations
830 Punchbowl Street
Honolulu, HI 96813
Phone: (808) 586-8842
http://labor.hawaii.gov

Idaho
Department of Labor
317 W. Main St.
Boise, ID 83735-0001
Phone: (208) 332-3579
http://www.labor.idaho.gov

Illinois
Department of Labor
160 N. LaSalle Street, 13th Floor
Suite C-1300
Chicago, IL 60601
Phone: (312) 793-2800
https://www.illinois.gov/idol

Indiana
Indiana Department of Labor
402 West Washington Street, Room W195
Indianapolis, IN 46204
Phone: (317) 232-2655
http://www.in.gov/dol

Iowa
Iowa Workforce Development
1000 East Grand Avenue
Des Moines, IA 50319-0209
Phone: (515) 242-5870
http://www.iowadivisionoflabor.gov

Kansas
Department of Labor
401 S.W. Topeka Blvd.
Topeka, KS 66603-3182
Phone: (785) 296-5000
http://www.dol.ks.gov

Kentucky
Department of Labor
1047 U.S. Hwy 127 South, Suite 4
Frankfort, KY 40601-4381
Phone: (502) 564-3070
http://www.labor.ky.gov

Louisiana
Louisiana Workforce Commission
1001 N. 23rd Street
Baton Rouge, LA 70804-9094
Phone: (225) 342-3111
http://www.laworks.net

Maine
Department of Labor
45 Commerce Street
Augusta, ME 04330
Phone: (207) 623-7900
http://www.state.me.us/labor

Maryland
Department of Labor, Licensing & Regulation
500 N. Calvert Street
Suite 401
Baltimore, MD 21202
Phone: (410) 767-2357
http://www.dllr.state.md.us

Massachusetts
Dept of Labor & Workforce Development
One Ashburton Place
Room 2112
Boston, MA 02108
Phone: (617) 626-7100
http://www.mass.gov/lwd

Michigan
Department of Licensing and Regulatory Affairs
611 W. Ottawa
P.O. Box 30004
Lansing, MI 48909
Phone: (517) 373-1820
http://www.michigan.gov/lara

Minnesota
Dept of Labor and Industry
443 Lafayette Road North
Saint Paul, MN 55155
Phone: (651) 284-5070
http://www.doli.state.mn.us

Mississippi
Dept of Employment Security
P.O. Box 1699
Jackson, MS 39215-1699
Phone: (601) 321-6000
http://www.mdes.ms.gov

Missouri
Labor and Industrial Relations
P.O. Box 599
3315 W. Truman Boulevard
Jefferson City, MO 65102-0599
Phone: (573) 751-7500
https://labor.mo.gov

Appendix E: State Departments of Labor

Montana
Dept of Labor and Industry
P.O. Box 1728
Helena, MT 59624-1728
Phone: (406) 444-9091
http://www.dli.mt.gov

Nebraska
Department of Labor
550 S 16th Street
Lincoln, NE 68508
Phone: (402) 471-9000
https://dol.nebraska.gov

Nevada
Dept of Business and Industry
3300 W. Sahara Ave
Suite 425
Las Vegas, NV 89102
Phone: (702) 486-2750
http://business.nv.gov

New Hampshire
Department of Labor
State Office Park South
95 Pleasant Street
Concord, NH 03301
Phone: (603) 271-3176
https://www.nh.gov/labor

New Jersey
Department of Labor & Workforce Development
John Fitch Plaza, 13th Floor
Suite D
Trenton, NJ 08625-0110
Phone: (609) 777-3200
http://lwd.dol.state.nj.us/labor

New Mexico
Department of Workforce Solutions
401 Broadway, NE
Albuquerque, NM 87103-1928
Phone: (505) 841-8450
https://www.dws.state.nm.us

New York
Department of Labor
State Office Bldg. # 12
W.A. Harriman Campus
Albany, NY 12240
Phone: (518) 457-9000
https://www.labor.ny.gov

North Carolina
Department of Labor
4 West Edenton Street
Raleigh, NC 27601-1092
Phone: (919) 733-7166
https://www.labor.nc.gov

North Dakota
North Dakota Department of Labor and Human Rights
State Capitol Building
600 East Boulevard, Dept 406
Bismark, ND 58505-0340
Phone: (701) 328-2660
http://www.nd.gov/labor

Ohio
Department of Commerce
77 South High Street, 22nd Floor
Columbus, OH 43215
Phone: (614) 644-2239
http://www.com.state.oh.us

Oklahoma
Department of Labor
4001 N. Lincoln Blvd.
Oklahoma City, OK 73105-5212
Phone: (405) 528-1500
https://www.ok.gov/odol

Oregon
Bureau of Labor and Industries
800 NE Oregon St., #32
Portland, OR 97232
Phone: (971) 673-0761
http://www.oregon.gov/boli

Pennsylvania
Dept of Labor and Industry
1700 Labor and Industry Bldg
7th and Forster Streets
Harrisburg, PA 17120
Phone: (717) 787-5279
http://www.dli.pa.gov

Rhode Island
Department of Labor and Training
1511 Pontiac Avenue
Cranston, RI 02920
Phone: (401) 462-8000
http://www.dlt.state.ri.us

South Carolina
Dept of Labor, Licensing & Regulations
P.O. Box 11329
Columbia, SC 29211-1329
Phone: (803) 896-4300
http://www.llr.state.sc.us

South Dakota
Department of Labor & Regulation
700 Governors Drive
Pierre, SD 57501-2291
Phone: (605) 773-3682
http://dlr.sd.gov

Tennessee
Dept of Labor & Workforce Development
Andrew Johnson Tower
710 James Robertson Pkwy
Nashville, TN 37243-0655
Phone: (615) 741-6642
http://www.tn.gov/workforce

Texas
Texas Workforce Commission
101 East 15th St.
Austin, TX 78778
Phone: (512) 475-2670
http://www.twc.state.tx.us

Utah
Utah Labor Commission
160 East 300 South, 3rd Floor
Salt Lake City, UT 84114-6600
Phone: (801) 530-6800
https://laborcommission.utah.gov

Vermont
Department of Labor
5 Green Mountain Drive
P.O. Box 488
Montpelier, VT 05601-0488
Phone: (802) 828-4000
http://labor.vermont.gov

Virginia
Dept of Labor and Industry
Powers-Taylor Building
13 S. 13th Street
Richmond, VA 23219
Phone: (804) 371-2327
http://www.doli.virginia.gov

Washington
Dept of Labor and Industries
P.O. Box 44001
Olympia, WA 98504-4001
Phone: (360) 902-4200
http://www.lni.wa.gov

West Virginia
Division of Labor
749 B Building 6
Capitol Complex
Charleston, WV 25305
Phone: (304) 558-7890
https://labor.wv.gov

Wisconsin
Dept of Workforce Development
201 E. Washington Ave., #A400
P.O. Box 7946
Madison, WI 53707-7946
Phone: (608) 266-6861
http://dwd.wisconsin.gov

Wyoming
Department of Workforce Services
1510 East Pershing Blvd.
Cheyenne, WY 82002
Phone: (307) 777-7261
http://www.wyomingworkforce.org

2021 Title List

Visit www.GreyHouse.com for Product Information, Table of Contents, and Sample Pages.

Opinions Throughout History
Opinions Throughout History: The Death Penalty
Opinions Throughout History: Diseases & Epidemics
Opinions Throughout History: Drug Use & Abuse
Opinions Throughout History: The Environment
Opinions Throughout History: Gender: Roles & Rights
Opinions Throughout History: Globalization
Opinions Throughout History: Guns in America
Opinions Throughout History: Immigration
Opinions Throughout History: Law Enforcement in America
Opinions Throughout History: National Security vs. Civil & Privacy Rights
Opinions Throughout History: Presidential Authority
Opinions Throughout History: Robotics & Artificial Intelligence
Opinions Throughout History: Social Media Issues
Opinions Throughout History: Sports & Games
Opinions Throughout History: Voters' Rights

This is Who We Were
This is Who We Were: Colonial America (1492-1775)
This is Who We Were: 1880-1899
This is Who We Were: In the 1900s
This is Who We Were: In the 1910s
This is Who We Were: In the 1920s
This is Who We Were: A Companion to the 1940 Census
This is Who We Were: In the 1940s (1940-1949)
This is Who We Were: In the 1950s
This is Who We Were: In the 1960s
This is Who We Were: In the 1970s
This is Who We Were: In the 1980s
This is Who We Were: In the 1990s
This is Who We Were: In the 2000s
This is Who We Were: In the 2010s

Working Americans
Working Americans—Vol. 1: The Working Class
Working Americans—Vol. 2: The Middle Class
Working Americans—Vol. 3: The Upper Class
Working Americans—Vol. 4: Children
Working Americans—Vol. 5: At War
Working Americans—Vol. 6: Working Women
Working Americans—Vol. 7: Social Movements
Working Americans—Vol. 8: Immigrants
Working Americans—Vol. 9: Revolutionary War to the Civil War
Working Americans—Vol. 10: Sports & Recreation
Working Americans—Vol. 11: Inventors & Entrepreneurs
Working Americans—Vol. 12: Our History through Music
Working Americans—Vol. 13: Education & Educators
Working Americans—Vol. 14: African Americans
Working Americans—Vol. 15: Politics & Politicians
Working Americans—Vol. 16: Farming & Ranching
Working Americans—Vol. 17: Teens in America

Education
Complete Learning Disabilities Resource Guide
Educators Resource Guide
The Comparative Guide to Elem. & Secondary Schools
Charter School Movement
Special Education: A Reference Book for Policy & Curriculum Development

Grey House Health & Wellness Guides
Autoimmune Disorders Handbook & Resource Guide
Cancer Handbook & Resource Guide
Cardiovascular Disease Handbook & Resource Guide
Dementia Handbook & Resource Guide

Consumer Health
Autoimmune Disorders Handbook & Resource Guide
Cancer Handbook & Resource Guide
Cardiovascular Disease Handbook & Resource Guide
Comparative Guide to American Hospitals
Complete Mental Health Resource Guide
Complete Resource Guide for Pediatric Disorders
Complete Resource Guide for People with Chronic Illness
Complete Resource Guide for People with Disabilities
Older Americans Information Resource

General Reference
African Biographical Dictionary
American Environmental Leaders
America's College Museums
Constitutional Amendments
Encyclopedia of African American Writing
Encyclopedia of Invasions & Conquests
Encyclopedia of Prisoners of War & Internment
Encyclopedia of Rural America
Encyclopedia of the Continental Congresses
Encyclopedia of the United States Cabinet
Encyclopedia of War Journalism
The Environmental Debate
The Evolution Wars: A Guide to the Debates
Financial Literacy Starter Kit
From Suffrage to the Senate
The Gun Debate: Gun Rights & Gun Control in the U.S.
History of Canada
Historical Warrior Peoples & Modern Fighting Groups
Human Rights and the United States
Political Corruption in America
Privacy Rights in the Digital Age
The Religious Right and American Politics
Speakers of the House of Representatives, 1789-2021
US Land & Natural Resources Policy
The Value of a Dollar 1600-1865 Colonial to Civil War
The Value of a Dollar 1860-2019
World Cultural Leaders of the 20th Century

Business Information
Business Information Resources
The Complete Broadcasting Industry Guide: Television, Radio, Cable & Streaming
Directory of Mail Order Catalogs
Environmental Resource Handbook
Food & Beverage Market Place
The Grey House Guide to Homeland Security Resources
The Grey House Performing Arts Industry Guide
Guide to Healthcare Group Purchasing Organizations
Guide to U.S. HMOs and PPOs
Guide to Venture Capital & Private Equity Firms
Hudson's Washington News Media Contacts Guide
New York State Directory
Sports Market Place

Grey House Publishing | Salem Press | H.W. Wilson | 4919 Route, 22 PO Box 56, Amenia NY 12501-0056

2021 Title List

Visit www.GreyHouse.com for Product Information, Table of Contents, and Sample Pages.

Statistics & Demographics
America's Top-Rated Cities
America's Top-Rated Smaller Cities
The Comparative Guide to American Suburbs
Profiles of America
Profiles of California
Profiles of Florida
Profiles of Illinois
Profiles of Indiana
Profiles of Massachusetts
Profiles of Michigan
Profiles of New Jersey
Profiles of New York
Profiles of North Carolina & South Carolina
Profiles of Ohio
Profiles of Pennsylvania
Profiles of Texas
Profiles of Virginia
Profiles of Wisconsin

Canadian Resources
Associations Canada
Canadian Almanac & Directory
Canadian Environmental Resource Guide
Canadian Parliamentary Guide
Canadian Venture Capital & Private Equity Firms
Canadian Who's Who
Cannabis Canada
Careers & Employment Canada
Financial Post: Directory of Directors
Financial Services Canada
FP Bonds: Corporate
FP Bonds: Government
FP Equities: Preferreds & Derivatives
FP Survey: Industrials
FP Survey: Mines & Energy
FP Survey: Predecessor & Defunct
Health Guide Canada
Libraries Canada
Major Canadian Cities: Compared & Ranked, First Edition

Weiss Financial Ratings
Financial Literacy Basics
Financial Literacy: How to Become an Investor
Financial Literacy: Planning for the Future
Weiss Ratings Consumer Guides
Weiss Ratings Guide to Banks
Weiss Ratings Guide to Credit Unions
Weiss Ratings Guide to Health Insurers
Weiss Ratings Guide to Life & Annuity Insurers
Weiss Ratings Guide to Property & Casualty Insurers
Weiss Ratings Investment Research Guide to Bond & Money Market Mutual Funds
Weiss Ratings Investment Research Guide to Exchange-Traded Funds
Weiss Ratings Investment Research Guide to Stock Mutual Funds
Weiss Ratings Investment Research Guide to Stocks

Books in Print Series
American Book Publishing Record® Annual
American Book Publishing Record® Monthly
Books In Print®
Books In Print® Supplement
Books Out Loud™
Bowker's Complete Video Directory™
Children's Books In Print®
El-Hi Textbooks & Serials In Print®
Forthcoming Books®
Law Books & Serials In Print™
Medical & Health Care Books In Print™
Publishers, Distributors & Wholesalers of the US™
Subject Guide to Books In Print®
Subject Guide to Children's Books In Print®

Grey House Publishing | Salem Press | H.W. Wilson | 4919 Route, 22 PO Box 56, Amenia NY 12501-0056

SALEM PRESS

2021 Title List

Visit www.SalemPress.com for Product Information, Table of Contents, and Sample Pages.

LITERATURE

Critical Insights: Authors
Louisa May Alcott
Sherman Alexie
Isabel Allende
Maya Angelou
Isaac Asimov
Margaret Atwood
Jane Austen
James Baldwin
Saul Bellow
Roberto Bolano
Ray Bradbury
Gwendolyn Brooks
Albert Camus
Raymond Carver
Willa Cather
Geoffrey Chaucer
John Cheever
Joseph Conrad
Charles Dickens
Emily Dickinson
Frederick Douglass
T. S. Eliot
George Eliot
Harlan Ellison
Louise Erdrich
William Faulkner
F. Scott Fitzgerald
Gustave Flaubert
Horton Foote
Benjamin Franklin
Robert Frost
Neil Gaiman
Gabriel Garcia Marquez
Thomas Hardy
Nathaniel Hawthorne
Robert A. Heinlein
Lillian Hellman
Ernest Hemingway
Langston Hughes
Zora Neale Hurston
Henry James
Thomas Jefferson
James Joyce
Jamaica Kincaid
Stephen King
Martin Luther King, Jr.
Barbara Kingsolver
Abraham Lincoln
Mario Vargas Llosa
Jack London
James McBride
Cormac McCarthy
Herman Melville
Arthur Miller
Toni Morrison
Alice Munro
Tim O'Brien
Flannery O'Connor
Eugene O'Neill
George Orwell
Sylvia Plath
Philip Roth
Salman Rushdie
Mary Shelley
John Steinbeck
Amy Tan
Leo Tolstoy
Mark Twain
John Updike
Kurt Vonnegut
Alice Walker
David Foster Wallace
Edith Wharton
Walt Whitman
Oscar Wilde
Tennessee Williams
Richard Wright
Malcolm X

Critical Insights: Works
Absalom, Absalom!
Adventures of Huckleberry Finn
Aeneid
All Quiet on the Western Front
Animal Farm
Anna Karenina
The Awakening
The Bell Jar
Beloved
Billy Budd, Sailor
The Book Thief
Brave New World
The Canterbury Tales
Catch-22
The Catcher in the Rye
The Crucible
Death of a Salesman
The Diary of a Young Girl
Dracula
Fahrenheit 451
The Grapes of Wrath
Great Expectations
The Great Gatsby
Hamlet
The Handmaid's Tale
Harry Potter Series
Heart of Darkness
The Hobbit
The House on Mango Street
How the Garcia Girls Lost Their Accents
The Hunger Games Trilogy
I Know Why the Caged Bird Sings
In Cold Blood
The Inferno
Invisible Man
Jane Eyre
The Joy Luck Club
King Lear
The Kite Runner
Life of Pi
Little Women
Lolita
Lord of the Flies
Macbeth
The Metamorphosis
Midnight's Children
A Midsummer Night's Dream
Moby-Dick
Mrs. Dalloway
Nineteen Eighty-Four
The Odyssey
Of Mice and Men
One Flew Over the Cuckoo's Nest
One Hundred Years of Solitude
Othello
The Outsiders
Paradise Lost
The Pearl
The Poetry of Baudelaire
The Poetry of Edgar Allan Poe
A Portrait of the Artist as a Young Man
Pride and Prejudice
The Red Badge of Courage
Romeo and Juliet
The Scarlet Letter
Short Fiction of Flannery O'Connor
Slaughterhouse-Five
The Sound and the Fury
A Streetcar Named Desire
The Sun Also Rises
A Tale of Two Cities
The Tales of Edgar Allan Poe
Their Eyes Were Watching God
Things Fall Apart
To Kill a Mockingbird
War and Peace
The Woman Warrior

Critical Insights: Themes
The American Comic Book
American Creative Non-Fiction
The American Dream
American Multicultural Identity
American Road Literature
American Short Story
American Sports Fiction
The American Thriller
American Writers in Exile
Censored & Banned Literature
Civil Rights Literature, Past & Present
Coming of Age
Conspiracies
Contemporary Canadian Fiction
Contemporary Immigrant Short Fiction
Contemporary Latin American Fiction
Contemporary Speculative Fiction
Crime and Detective Fiction
Crisis of Faith
Cultural Encounters
Dystopia
Family
The Fantastic
Feminism

Grey House Publishing | Salem Press | H.W. Wilson | 4919 Route, 22 PO Box 56, Amenia NY 12501-0056

SALEM PRESS

2021 Title List

Visit www.SalemPress.com for Product Information, Table of Contents, and Sample Pages.

Flash Fiction
Gender, Sex and Sexuality
Good & Evil
The Graphic Novel
Greed
Harlem Renaissance
The Hero's Quest
Historical Fiction
Holocaust Literature
The Immigrant Experience
Inequality
LGBTQ Literature
Literature in Times of Crisis
Literature of Protest
Magical Realism
Midwestern Literature
Modern Japanese Literature
Nature & the Environment
Paranoia, Fear & Alienation
Patriotism
Political Fiction
Postcolonial Literature
Pulp Fiction of the '20s and '30s
Rebellion
Russia's Golden Age
Satire
The Slave Narrative
Social Justice and American Literature
Southern Gothic Literature
Southwestern Literature
Survival
Technology & Humanity
Violence in Literature
Virginia Woolf & 20th Century Women Writers
War

Critical Insights: Film
Bonnie & Clyde
Casablanca
Alfred Hitchcock
Stanley Kubrick

Critical Approaches to Literature
Critical Approaches to Literature: Feminist
Critical Approaches to Literature: Moral
Critical Approaches to Literature: Multicultural
Critical Approaches to Literature: Psychological

Critical Surveys of Literature
Critical Survey of American Literature
Critical Survey of Drama
Critical Survey of Graphic Novels: Heroes & Superheroes
Critical Survey of Graphic Novels: History, Theme, and Technique
Critical Survey of Graphic Novels: Independents and Underground Classics
Critical Survey of Graphic Novels: Manga
Critical Survey of Long Fiction
Critical Survey of Mystery and Detective Fiction
Critical Survey of Mythology & Folklore: Gods & Goddesses
Critical Survey of Mythology & Folklore: Heroes and Heroines
Critical Survey of Mythology & Folklore: Love, Sexuality, and Desire
Critical Survey of Mythology & Folklore: World Mythology
Critical Survey of Poetry
Critical Survey of Poetry: Contemporary Poets
Critical Survey of Science Fiction & Fantasy Literature
Critical Survey of Shakespeare's Plays
Critical Survey of Shakespeare's Sonnets
Critical Survey of Short Fiction
Critical Survey of World Literature
Critical Survey of Young Adult Literature

Cyclopedia of Literary Characters & Places
Cyclopedia of Literary Characters
Cyclopedia of Literary Places

Introduction to Literary Context
American Poetry of the 20th Century
American Post-Modernist Novels
American Short Fiction
English Literature
Plays
World Literature

Magill's Literary Annual
Magill's Literary Annual, 2021
Magill's Literary Annual, 2020
Magill's Literary Annual, 2019

Masterplots
Masterplots, Fourth Edition
Masterplots, 2010-2018 Supplement

Notable Writers
Notable African American Writers
Notable American Women Writers
Notable Mystery & Detective Fiction Writers
Notable Native American Writers & Writers of the American West
Novels into Film: Adaptations & Interpretation
Recommended Reading: 600 Classics Reviewed

Grey House Publishing | Salem Press | H.W. Wilson | 4919 Route, 22 PO Box 56, Amenia NY 12501-0056

SALEM PRESS

2021 Title List

Visit www.SalemPress.com for Product Information, Table of Contents, and Sample Pages.

HISTORY

The Decades
The 1910s in America
The Twenties in America
The Thirties in America
The Forties in America
The Fifties in America
The Sixties in America
The Seventies in America
The Eighties in America
The Nineties in America
The 2000s in America
The 2010s in America

Defining Documents in American History
Defining Documents: The 1900s
Defining Documents: The 1910s
Defining Documents: The 1920s
Defining Documents: The 1930s
Defining Documents: The 1950s
Defining Documents: The 1960s
Defining Documents: The 1970s
Defining Documents: American Citizenship
Defining Documents: The American Economy
Defining Documents: The American Revolution
Defining Documents: The American West
Defining Documents: Business Ethics
Defining Documents: Capital Punishment
Defining Documents: Civil Rights
Defining Documents: Civil War
Defining Documents: The Cold War
Defining Documents: Dissent & Protest
Defining Documents: Drug Policy
Defining Documents: The Emergence of Modern America
Defining Documents: Environment & Conservation
Defining Documents: Espionage & Intrigue
Defining Documents: Exploration and Colonial America
Defining Documents: The Formation of the States
Defining Documents: The Free Press
Defining Documents: The Gun Debate
Defining Documents: Immigration & Immigrant Communities
Defining Documents: The Legacy of 9/11
Defining Documents: LGBTQ+
Defining Documents: Manifest Destiny and the New Nation
Defining Documents: Native Americans
Defining Documents: Political Campaigns, Candidates & Discourse
Defining Documents: Postwar 1940s
Defining Documents: Prison Reform
Defining Documents: Secrets, Leaks & Scandals
Defining Documents: Slavery
Defining Documents: Supreme Court Decisions
Defining Documents: Reconstruction Era
Defining Documents: The Vietnam War
Defining Documents: U.S. Involvement in the Middle East
Defining Documents: World War I
Defining Documents: World War II

Defining Documents in World History
Defining Documents: The 17th Century
Defining Documents: The 18th Century
Defining Documents: The 19th Century
Defining Documents: The 20th Century (1900-1950)
Defining Documents: The Ancient World
Defining Documents: Asia
Defining Documents: Genocide & the Holocaust
Defining Documents: Nationalism & Populism
Defining Documents: Pandemics, Plagues & Public Health
Defining Documents: Renaissance & Early Modern Era
Defining Documents: The Middle Ages
Defining Documents: The Middle East
Defining Documents: Women's Rights

Great Events from History
Great Events from History: The Ancient World
Great Events from History: The Middle Ages
Great Events from History: The Renaissance & Early Modern Era
Great Events from History: The 17th Century
Great Events from History: The 18th Century
Great Events from History: The 19th Century
Great Events from History: The 20th Century, 1901-1940
Great Events from History: The 20th Century, 1941-1970
Great Events from History: The 20th Century, 1971-2000
Great Events from History: Modern Scandals
Great Events from History: African American History
Great Events from History: The 21st Century, 2000-2016
Great Events from History: LGBTQ Events
Great Events from History: Human Rights

Great Lives from History
Computer Technology Innovators
Fashion Innovators
Great Athletes
Great Athletes of the Twenty-First Century
Great Lives from History: African Americans
Great Lives from History: American Heroes
Great Lives from History: American Women
Great Lives from History: Asian and Pacific Islander Americans
Great Lives from History: Inventors & Inventions
Great Lives from History: Jewish Americans
Great Lives from History: Latinos
Great Lives from History: Scientists and Science
Great Lives from History: The 17th Century
Great Lives from History: The 18th Century
Great Lives from History: The 19th Century
Great Lives from History: The 20th Century
Great Lives from History: The 21st Century, 2000-2017
Great Lives from History: The Ancient World
Great Lives from History: The Incredibly Wealthy
Great Lives from History: The Middle Ages
Great Lives from History: The Renaissance & Early Modern Era
Human Rights Innovators
Internet Innovators
Music Innovators
Musicians and Composers of the 20th Century
World Political Innovators

Grey House Publishing | Salem Press | H.W. Wilson | 4919 Route, 22 PO Box 56, Amenia NY 12501-0056

2021 Title List

Visit www.SalemPress.com for Product Information, Table of Contents, and Sample Pages.

History & Government
American First Ladies
American Presidents
The 50 States
The Ancient World: Extraordinary People in Extraordinary Societies
The Bill of Rights
The Criminal Justice System
The U.S. Supreme Court

SOCIAL SCIENCES
Civil Rights Movements: Past & Present
Countries, Peoples and Cultures
Countries: Their Wars & Conflicts: A World Survey
Education Today: Issues, Policies & Practices
Encyclopedia of American Immigration
Ethics: Questions & Morality of Human Actions
Issues in U.S. Immigration
Principles of Sociology: Group Relationships & Behavior
Principles of Sociology: Personal Relationships & Behavior
Principles of Sociology: Societal Issues & Behavior
Racial & Ethnic Relations in America
World Geography

SCIENCE
Ancient Creatures
Applied Science
Applied Science: Engineering & Mathematics
Applied Science: Science & Medicine
Applied Science: Technology
Biomes and Ecosystems
Earth Science: Earth Materials and Resources
Earth Science: Earth's Surface and History
Earth Science: Earth's Weather, Water and Atmosphere
Earth Science: Physics and Chemistry of the Earth
Encyclopedia of Climate Change
Encyclopedia of Energy
Encyclopedia of Environmental Issues
Encyclopedia of Global Resources
Encyclopedia of Mathematics and Society
Forensic Science
Notable Natural Disasters
The Solar System
USA in Space

Principles of Science
Principles of Anatomy
Principles of Astronomy
Principles of Behavioral Science
Principles of Biology
Principles of Biotechnology
Principles of Botany
Principles of Chemistry
Principles of Climatology
Principles of Information Technology
Principles of Computer Science
Principles of Ecology
Principles of Energy
Principles of Geology
Principles of Marine Science
Principles of Mathematics
Principles of Modern Agriculture
Principles of Pharmacology
Principles of Physical Science
Principles of Physics
Principles of Programming & Coding
Principles of Robotics & Artificial Intelligence
Principles of Scientific Research
Principles of Sustainability
Principles of Zoology

HEALTH
Addictions, Substance Abuse & Alcoholism
Adolescent Health & Wellness
Aging
Cancer
Community & Family Health Issues
Integrative, Alternative & Complementary Medicine
Genetics and Inherited Conditions
Infectious Diseases and Conditions
Magill's Medical Guide
Nutrition
Psychology & Behavioral Health
Women's Health

Principles of Health
Principles of Health: Allergies & Immune Disorders
Principles of Health: Anxiety & Stress
Principles of Health: Depression
Principles of Health: Diabetes
Principles of Health: Nursing
Principles of Health: Obesity
Principles of Health: Pain Management
Principles of Health: Prescription Drug Abuse

Grey House Publishing | Salem Press | H.W. Wilson | 4919 Route, 22 PO Box 56, Amenia NY 12501-0056

SALEM PRESS

2021 Title List

Visit www.SalemPress.com for Product Information, Table of Contents, and Sample Pages.

CAREERS

Careers: Paths to Entrepreneurship
Careers in the Arts: Fine, Performing & Visual
Careers in Building Construction
Careers in Business
Careers in Chemistry
Careers in Communications & Media
Careers in Education & Training
Careers in Environment & Conservation
Careers in Financial Services
Careers in Forensic Science
Careers in Gaming
Careers in Green Energy
Careers in Healthcare
Careers in Hospitality & Tourism
Careers in Human Services
Careers in Information Technology
Careers in Law, Criminal Justice & Emergency Services
Careers in the Music Industry
Careers in Manufacturing & Production
Careers in Nursing
Careers in Physics
Careers in Protective Services
Careers in Psychology & Behavioral Health
Careers in Public Administration
Careers in Sales, Insurance & Real Estate
Careers in Science & Engineering
Careers in Social Media
Careers in Sports & Fitness
Careers in Sports Medicine & Training
Careers in Technical Services & Equipment Repair
Careers in Transportation
Careers in Writing & Editing
Careers Outdoors
Careers Overseas
Careers Working with Infants & Children
Careers Working with Animals

BUSINESS

Principles of Business: Accounting
Principles of Business: Economics
Principles of Business: Entrepreneurship
Principles of Business: Finance
Principles of Business: Globalization
Principles of Business: Leadership
Principles of Business: Management
Principles of Business: Marketing

Grey House Publishing | Salem Press | H.W. Wilson | 4919 Route, 22 PO Box 56, Amenia NY 12501-0056

2021 Title List

Visit www.HWWilsonInPrint.com for Product Information, Table of Contents, and Sample Pages.

The Reference Shelf
Affordable Housing
Aging in America
Alternative Facts, Post-Truth and the Information War
The American Dream
American Military Presence Overseas
Arab Spring
Artificial Intelligence
The Business of Food
Campaign Trends & Election Law
College Sports
Conspiracy Theories
Democracy Evolving
The Digital Age
Dinosaurs
Embracing New Paradigms in Education
Faith & Science
Families - Traditional & New Structures
Food Insecurity & Hunger in the United States
Future of U.S. Economic Relations: Mexico, Cuba, & Venezuela
Global Climate Change
Graphic Novels and Comic Books
Guns in America
Hate Crimes
Immigration
Internet Abuses & Privacy Rights
Internet Law
LGBTQ in the 21st Century
Marijuana Reform
National Debate Topic 2014/2015: The Ocean
National Debate Topic 2015/2016: Surveillance
National Debate Topic 2016/2017: US/China Relations
National Debate Topic 2017/2018: Education Reform
National Debate Topic 2018/2019: Immigration
National Debate Topic 2019/2021: Arms Sales
National Debate Topic 2020/2021: Criminal Justice Reform
National Debate Topic 2021/2022
New Frontiers in Space
The News and its Future
Policing in 2020
Politics of the Oceans
Pollution
Prescription Drug Abuse
Propaganda and Misinformation
Racial Tension in a Postracial Age
Reality Television
Representative American Speeches, Annual Edition
Rethinking Work
Revisiting Gender
Robotics
Russia
Social Networking
The South China Sea Conflict
Space Exploration and Development
Sports in America
The Supreme Court
The Transformation of American Cities
The Two Koreas
U.S. Infrastructure
Vaccinations
Whistleblowers

Core Collections
Children's Core Collection
Fiction Core Collection
Graphic Novels Core Collection
Middle & Junior High School Core
Public Library Core Collection: Nonfiction
Senior High Core Collection
Young Adult Fiction Core Collection

Current Biography
Current Biography Cumulative Index 1946-2021
Current Biography Monthly Magazine
Current Biography Yearbook

Readers' Guide to Periodical Literature
Abridged Readers' Guide to Periodical Literature
Readers' Guide to Periodical Literature

Indexes
Index to Legal Periodicals & Books
Short Story Index
Book Review Digest

Sears List
Sears List of Subject Headings
Sears: Lista de Encabezamientos de Materia

History
American Game Changers: Invention, Innovation & Transformation
American Reformers
Speeches of the American Presidents

Facts About Series
Facts About the 20th Century
Facts About American Immigration
Facts About China
Facts About the Presidents
Facts About the World's Languages

Nobel Prize Winners
Nobel Prize Winners: 1901-1986
Nobel Prize Winners: 1987-1991
Nobel Prize Winners: 1992-1996
Nobel Prize Winners: 1997-2001
Nobel Prize Winners: 2002-2018

Famous First Facts
Famous First Facts
Famous First Facts About American Politics
Famous First Facts About Sports
Famous First Facts About the Environment
Famous First Facts: International Edition

American Book of Days
The American Book of Days
The International Book of Days

Grey House Publishing | Salem Press | H.W. Wilson | 4919 Route, 22 PO Box 56, Amenia NY 12501-0056